ENCYCLOPEDIA OF AMERICAN POLITICAL PARTIES AND ELECTIONS

Larry J. Sabato

Howard R. Ernst

Facts On File
An imprint of Infobase Publishing

Encyclopedia of American Political Parties and Elections

Copyright © 2006 by Larry J. Sabato and Howard R. Ernst

Facts On File, Inc.
An imprint of Infobase Publishing
132 West 31st Street
New York NY 10001

Library of Congress Cataloging-in-Publication Data

Sabato, Larry.
Encyclopedia of American political parties and elections /
Larry J. Sabato, Howard R. Ernst.
p. cm.
Includes bibliographical references and index.
ISBN 0-8160-5875-X (hardcover : alk. paper) 1. Political parties—United States—
Encyclopedias. 2. Elections—United States—Encyclopedias. 3. United States—Politics
and government—Encyclopedias. I. Ernst, Howard R., 1970- II. Title.
JK2261.S218 2006
324.273'03—dc22   2005013377

Facts On File books are available at special discounts when purchased in bulk
quantities for businesses, associations, institutions, or sales promotions. Please call
our Special Sales Department in New York at (212) 967-8800 or (800) 322-8755.

You can find Facts On File on the World Wide Web at http://www.factsonfile.com

Text design by Joan M. McEvoy

Cover design by Cathy Rincon

Printed in the United States of America

VB DS 10 9 8 7 6 5 4 3 2 1

This book is printed on acid-free paper.

Contents

List of Entries

Contributor List

William Adler, City University of New York
J. Mark Alcorn, Fond du Lac Community and Tribal College
Brad L. Alexander, Emory University
Lawrence M. Anderson, University of Wisconsin–Whitewater
Brook B. Andrews, Arlington, Virginia
Brian K. Arbour, University of Texas–Austin
Gayle R. Avant, Baylor University
Julia R. Azari, Yale University

Daniel Ballard, American University
Richard P. Barberio, State University of New York–Oneonta
William L. Barnes, Miami University
Andrew W. Barrett, Marquette University
Jody Baumgartner, East Carolina University
Neil J. Beck, Harvard University
Marija Bekafigo, University of Florida
Michael Billok, Georgetown University Law Center
J. Michael Bitzer, Catawba College
Robert G. Boatright, Clark University
Janet K. Boles, Marquette University
Julio Borquez, University of Michigan–Dearborn
Shannon L. Bow, University of Florida
Matthew Bowman, University of Utah
Kevin M. Brady, Texas Christian University
F. Erik Brooks, Georgia Southern University
Steven P. Brown, Auburn University
Peter Brownfeld, political reporter based in Washington, D.C.
Brian J. Brox, University of Texas–Austin
Claudia Bryant, Western Carolina University
Jill M. Budny, Marquette University
Gary Bugh, Nelson A. Rockefeller College
    of Public Affairs and Policy
Robert Butts, Texas Christian University

John Cadigan, American University
Damon M. Cann, Stony Brook University

Celia M. Carroll, Washington and Lee University
John W. Carter, United States Naval Academy
Odul Celep, State University of New York–Binghamton
Jamie Patrick Chandler, Hunter College
Molly Clancy, University of Virginia Center for Politics
Cal Clark, Auburn University
Janet Clark, State University of West Georgia
Justin P. Coffey, DePaul University
Zachary Courser, University of Virginia

Derrek M. Davis, Austin Community College
Matthew DeSantis, University of Florida
Robert E. Dewhirst, Northwest Missouri State University
Brian DiSarro, University of Iowa
Scott Dittloff, University of the Incarnate Word
Brendan J. Doherty, University of California–Berkeley

Michael B. Ernst, University of North Carolina–Greensboro
Suzanne E. Evans, University of California–Berkeley

Mary L. Fehler, Texas Christian University
Terri Susan Fine, University of Central Florida
Ole J. Forsberg, University of Tennessee
Stephen E. Frantzich, United States Naval Academy
Luis Fuentes-Rohwer, Indiana University–Bloomington

Jason Gainous, University of Florida
Sherry Walker Gainous, University of Florida
Jessica Gerrity, Indiana University–Bloomington
Edward. G. Carmines, Indiana University–Bloomington
Mark Givens, American University
Marcia L. Godwin, University of La Verne

Michael W. Hail, Morehead State University
Mary Hallock Morris, University of Southern Indiana
William Hardy, University of Tennessee

Gordon E. Harvey, University of Louisiana–Monroe
Andrea C. Hatcher, Vanderbilt University
Danny Hayes, University of Texas–Austin
Tony L. Hill, Massachusetts Institute of Technology
John Paul Hill, University of Georgia

Peter Jackson, University of Virginia Center for Politics
Bonnie J. Johnson, University of Kansas
Mary Lynn F. Jones, online editor of *The Hill*
Ryan Jordan, Princeton University

Kate Kenski, Annenberg Public Policy Center
Lisa Kimbrough, Raleigh, North Carolina
Daniel T. Kirsch, Brandeis University
Jeffrey Kraus, Wagner College

Christopher Larimer, University of Nebraska–Lincoln
Bruce A. Larson, Fairleigh Dickinson University
Jeremy B. Lupoli, American University

Christopher J. Mandernach, United States Naval Academy
Jeff A. Martineau, Claremont McKenna College
Seth C. McKee, University of Texas–Austin
Mark J. McKenzie, University of Texas–Austin
Roger M. Michalski, University of Michigan–Ann Arbor
Samuel Millar, Harvard University
Sarah Miller, Lourdes College
Alan L. Morrell, University of Utah

Francis Neely, San Francisco State University
Garrison Nelson, University of Vermont
Stephen Nemeth, University of Iowa
Paul J. Nuti, Harvard University

Allison Clark Odachowski, University of Florida
Laura R. Olson, Clemson University

Costas Panagopoulos, New York University
Joel Parker, University of Texas–Austin
J. Christopher Paskewich, University of Connecticut
Jamie Pimlott, University of Florida
R. Matthew Poteat, North Carolina State University

Kenneth Quinnell, Florida State University

Chapman Rackaway, Fort Hays State University
Ryan Rakness, University of Virginia
Mitzi Ramos, University of Illinois–Chicago
Kirk A. Randazzo, University of Kentucky
Gautham Rao, University of Chicago
Joel A. Rayan, University of Arizona

Wim Roefs, University of South Carolina
John Rouse, Ball State University

Maya Sabatello, University of Southern California
Ronald C. Schurin, University of Connecticut
Joshua J. Scott, University of Virginia Center for Politics
Reynolds J. Scott-Childress, Catholic University
John L. S. Simpkins, Furman University
Daniel A. Smith, University of Florida
David A. Smith, Baylor University
Gregory A. Smith, University of Virginia
Matt Smyth, University of Virginia Center for Politics
Jae-Jae Spoon, University of Michigan
Jack St. Croix, Harvard University
Meredith Staples, Rutgers University
Glenn L. Starks, Virginia Commonwealth University
Mark Stencel, *Congressional Quarterly*
Bruce E. Stewart, University of Georgia
Jacob R. Straus, University of Florida
Tim Sultan, Harvard University
Dari E. Sylvester, Stony Brook University

Ryan Teten, Northern Kentucky University
Alex Theodoridis, University of California–Berkeley
Antonio Thompson, University of Kentucky
Mary C. Thornberry, Davidson College
Clayton Thyne, University of Iowa
John P. Todsen, University of New Mexico
James B. Tuttle, Shepherd College

Brian Urlacher, University of Connecticut

Justin S. Vaughn, Texas A&M University
Richard L. Vining, Jr., Emory University

Michael W. Wagner, Indiana University
Adam L. Warber, Clemson University
Bret A. Weber, University of Utah
Marc D. Weiner, Rutgers University
William Bland Whitley, University of Florida
Peter W. Wielhouwer, Regent University
Charles H. Wilson, III, Gainesville College
Jonathan Winburn, Indiana University
David W. Winder, Valdosta State University
Thomas Phillip Wolf, Indiana University Southeast
J. David Woodard, Clemson University

John Todd Young, Ball State University

Donald A. Zinman, University of Texas–Austin
Nathan Zook, University of Tennessee

Introduction

Electoral politics in the United States enters the early 21st century with a tarnished reputation. In a post-Watergate, post–dangling chad, post–campaign finance reform world, many have persuasively argued the reputation is well deserved. Critics make their case with a battery of information, pointing to the declining rate of voter participation, increased rate of incumbency reelection, weakening of responsible political parties, dearth of electoral choices, and the pernicious influence of money in the electoral process. They remind us that the seemingly endless parade of abuses, and alleged abuses, reported in the 24-hour news cycle, has left much of the public alienated from a political system that they neither trust nor understand.

This encyclopedia, however, offers the reader a chance to pause and reflect, and to begin to fill in the all-important context that is too often missing from the current political dialogue. Benefiting from a comprehensive and historical review of the subject, the work offers an alternative to the historically devoid, often cynical view of politics that permeates the popular culture. Like a vast mosaic viewed from an appropriate distance, this work offers a valuable glimpse into the promise and direction of electoral politics in the United States.

The promise of democracy is revealed as a process by which society attempts to peacefully address its often irreconcilable differences. It is the means by which society pursues its common goals and the chief mechanism by which the nation allocates its collective rewards and responsibilities. Electoral politics in the United States has enabled its citizens to achieve collectively what they could not achieve individually, and, equally important, it has done so while securing the sanctity of individual rights.

Taken as a whole, this encyclopedia also reveals the general direction of electoral politics in the United States. Like an indomitable river, democracy in the United States has tended to flow toward its sources—the sovereign people. As suffrage rights and electoral options have grown, democracy has strengthened in size and scope, altering the landscape that guides its general direction. The river metaphor, however, is not intended to suggest that democratization in the United States was inevitable, easy, or achieved by following the course of least resistance. Quite the contrary, the entries that make up this encyclopedia reveal a monumental struggle for political rights—one in which individuals worked against tremendous obstacles, often at great personal cost, and more often than not failed to achieve their immediate goals. The entries also reveal the raw face of resistance and the motivations and deeds of those Americans who opposed change.

Pursuing these and other themes was not the intent of the authors or editors of this work, nor will they be obvious to the casual user of this reference work. Our desire was to achieve comprehensive coverage of the key concepts related to electoral politics, with the hope that the work would be of use to journalists, government officials, teachers, and students of politics. In the process, we learned a great deal from our colleagues, rekindled our appreciation for electoral politics, and discovered several undeniable themes. We are grateful to Facts On File for this opportunity.

This was a substantial project. The encyclopedia represents the work of more than 150 authors, mostly from the fields of history and political science, though we were pleased to accept contributions from qualified political practitioners and journalists. There are more than 450 entries, covering a wide range of electoral terms. While there are not separate entries for individual political figures, as space limitations prohibited such entries, important political leaders are discussed in detail throughout the text and can be identified in the index.

We thank all of the dedicated individuals who made contributions to this project. We also thank the professional staff at the University of Virginia Center for Politics for their diligent commitment to this project. Ken Stroupe, Joshua Scott, Molly Clancy, Peter Jackson, Matt Smyth, and Alex Theodoridis offered both substantive and administrative support. Interns at the Center for Politics, Crystal Howard, Samantha Silverberg, and especially Andrew Butler and Katie Grote, also made substantial contributions to the project. Support from the United States Naval Academy Political Science Department and Research Council also assisted this project.

Larry Sabato would like to dedicate his work to all his University of Virginia students who have participated in politics and to the staff and interns at the University of Virginia Center for Politics. Howard Ernst would like to make a special thank you to Tracey Ernst for her patience and support, and he would like to dedicate his work to his parents and to Simon, Emily, and Oliver.

Larry J. Sabato
Howard R. Ernst

absentee voting

Absentee voting generally refers to the process of casting a BALLOT at a location other than a voting station on ELECTION DAY. As each state has its own election procedures, absentee voting policies vary from state to state. According to the Committee for the Study of the American ELECTORATE, there are two general types of absentee voting policies: (1) "restrictive" absentee voting, whereby an applicant must state one of a number of listed reasons in order to vote by absentee ballot, and (2) "liberal" absentee voting, also known as "no fault" or "no excuse" absentee voting, whereby an applicant need not state any reason in order to vote by absentee ballot. In restrictive absentee states, the accepted reasons for receiving an absentee ballot vary, but they may include the following: age, illness, physical disability or handicap, service as an election officer or volunteer, out-of-town travel, religious holiday conflict, military service, and/or being a college or university student temporarily living away from home.

Under the UNIFORMED AND OVERSEAS CITIZENS ABSENTEE VOTING ACT of 1986 (UOCAVA), all states must "permit absent uniformed services voters and overseas voters to use absentee registration procedures and to vote by absentee ballot in GENERAL, SPECIAL, PRIMARY, and RUNOFF ELECTIONS for Federal office." Absentee ballots are obtained by contacting one's local county or city election official. Depending on the state, election officials may be the county clerk, county auditor, county registrar or supervisor of elections, or the board of elections.

While voting traditionally is thought of as the act of expressing a preference in a legally authorized or sanctioned venue on a specific day, many states have changed their voting procedures by allowing citizens to vote before election day in order to make the act of voting easier and thus potentially increase voter participation. Forms of voting alternative to traditional voting at a polling station on election day include absentee voting, EARLY VOTING, INTERNET VOTING, and MAIL VOTING. While absentee voting often, but not always, is conducted using the mail, it differs from voting-only-by-mail policies, which refer to elections in which mail balloting is the only way that a citizen may cast a ballot. Currently, Oregon is the only state that conducts all of its elections by mail.

The earliest absentee voting laws provided absentee voting to voters in the armed forces. A few states enacted absentee voting policies during the Civil War. It was not until 1896 in Vermont that absentee laws were extended to civilians.

California was the first state to pass unrestricted absentee voting legislation. Unrestricted absentee voting was first used in California's 1978 elections. Since its passage, increasing percentages of voters have voted by mail. In 1962, 2.6 percent of California voters voted by absentee ballot in the general election. In 1978, 4.8 percent of those individuals who voted in the primary election cast their votes through absentee ballots, and 4.4 percent voted by absentee ballot in the general election. Two years later in California's first presidential election that gave voters the option to vote absentee, 5.1 percent of voters in the primary election and 6.3 percent of voters in the general election used absentee ballots. By 2000, these percentages increased to 22.8 percent of ballots cast absentee in the primary election and 24.5 percent in the general election.

In recent years, laws governing absentee voting have been changed in many states to allow voters to cast ballots by mail without a qualifying excuse, such as work, illness, or religious holiday conflict. Data from the National Annenberg Election Survey suggest that 15 percent of those who voted in the 2000 general election cast their ballots before election day. In those states with no excuse absentee balloting, early voting, and/or vote-only-by-mail policies, 23.5 percent of the voters cast their votes before election day.

According to the Committee for the Study of the American Electorate (CSAE), there were 23 states that had liberal or no excuse absentee voting laws in 2004. These states were Alaska, Arizona, California, Colorado, Florida,

Hawaii, Idaho, Iowa, Kansas, Maine, Montana, Nebraska, Nevada, New Mexico, North Carolina, North Dakota, Oklahoma, South Dakota, Utah, Vermont, Washington, Wisconsin, and Wyoming. Of these no excuse absentee states, nine were also early voting states and 12 provided "in person absentee" voting.

While election day is thought to be the time when people cast their ballots, in many states, elections no longer take place on a single day. Through absentee and early voting, elections now take place over a longer period of time. Data from the National Annenberg Election Survey show that in the 2000 general election, approximately 5 percent of the voting electorate had already cast their ballots 15 days before election day. Nine days before election day, about 10 percent of the voters had already cast their ballots. The data also suggest that those voters who cast their ballots before election day were 7.2 percent more likely to report having cast their ballots for George W. Bush for president than those who voted on election day. When adopted, absentee and early voting policies have the capacity to change how and where people vote, thus changing how campaigns are conducted. Given the increased adoption of no-fault absentee voting in recent years, campaigns will be more inclined to use campaign funds to mobilize voters by getting them to cast their votes as soon as voting is permitted.

Further reading: Dubin, Jeffrey A., and Gretchen A. Kalsow. "Comparing Absentee and Precinct Voters: A View Over Time." *Political Behavior* 18, no. 4 (1996): 369–392; Karp, Jeffrey A., and Susan A. Banducci. "Absentee Voting, Mobilization and Participation." *American Politics Research* 29, no. 2 (2001): 183–195; Kenski, Kate. "The National Annenberg Election Survey 2000." *The Polling Report* 19, no. 15 (2003): 1, 7–8.

—Kate Kenski

advertisements (political), all types

Political advertisements are PAID MEDIA exposures that aim to influence public opinion on an issue, legislation, or most frequently, a candidate running for election. These ads are classified by degree of negativity, sponsor, ad buy, and medium. Often referred to as "paid media," these attempts to affect political attitudes have been a part of the American political system since its inception. In the 1920s and 1930s, radio advertisements became the preferred medium, as they reached a larger audience than printed handbills. Following the end of World War II, television ads became the primary venue for paid media.

As television penetration rates increased after the late 1940s, candidates realized that television was a powerful medium for mass communication. Initially, candidates purchased long blocks of television time to broadcast speeches, much like they had previously used radio. Campaign commercials became popular after they were first featured in the 1952 contest between Dwight Eisenhower and Adlai Stevenson. Republicans spent nearly $1.5 million in that campaign to broadcast a group of 20-second ads called "Eisenhower Answers America." The ads featured the nominee answering questions from "average citizens." In the years that followed, developments enhanced the role commercials play in political campaigns. More recent studies have also examined the tone, content, and sponsorship of campaign commercials as well as the impact of exposure to political ads on television.

Advertisements are the lifeblood of the modern political campaign, claiming well more than half of a candidate's WAR CHEST in recent presidential campaigns. In the 2004 elections, candidates, political parties, and INTEREST GROUPS spent more than $1.6 billion on television ads alone. Advertisements for the election or defeat of a particular candidate or party are the most prevalent political ads, with pure issue ads accounting for less than 10 percent of the ads aired in recent campaigns. Issue ads designed to influence legislative action account for an even smaller share. The campaign and media consultants who produce these ads on behalf of candidates spend considerable time preparing even the minute details in what usually amounts to 30 seconds of exposure. Part of this process is polling and researching the ad's overall message and specific images, text, sound, and editing techniques before finally testing the advertisement before one or many FOCUS GROUPS.

Critics claim negative ads exaggerate claims, distort facts, and heighten public disenchantment with POLITICS and the democratic process. Scholars disagree, however, about the effect of negative ads on political participation. Early experimental studies conducted by Stephen Ansolabehere and Shanto Iyengar indicated that negative ads decrease turnout and polarize the ELECTORATE. Subsequent research has questioned this relationship, however, and some results show that negative ads may actually increase turnout in elections.

One complication scholars encounter when studying the impact of negative campaign commercials is consensus about what constitutes a negative ad. Negativity is a subjective concept and can vary from one researcher to another. While some scholars categorize ads as either promotional (positive) or attack (negative), others differentiate between these two extremes and a third possibility, contrast ads. Contrast ads criticize the opposition but they also present the candidate's own position. Some analysis of campaign commercials in recent elections suggest that a substantial portion of ads contrast candidates' positions rather than attack or promote a candidate.

The tone of a campaign commercial is wholly separate from the content. Some scholars believe the primary focus of commercials has shifted away from policy-oriented messages to more personality-driven appeals. Scholarly analysis, however, reveal few solid trends. Commercials focused primarily on candidates' personal qualities until 1984 (except in 1968), but emphasis appears to have shifted to issues in the 1980s (except in 1996). In 2000, most ads (43 percent) featured policy-specific appeals, while only 33 percent stressed personal qualities.

An ad's message is part of an overall communications strategy to influence public opinion, and an ad's content is responsible for conveying a particular theme or idea. The visuals of a campaign ad are the most remembered by viewers. Video or still images are used to associate a candidate or issue with an already known person, place, or event that will evoke a positive or negative impression. In 1996, Democrats effectively used images of House Speaker Newt Gingrich with Republican presidential candidate Bob Dole and his congressional RUNNING MATES. The effect was to tie the growing unpopularity of Gingrich with Republicans campaigning for election. Visuals have also been used to positively portray a candidate, such as when President Bill Clinton used footage of himself standing with police officers in the same campaign to counter the perception that he was "soft on crime." Visual text—words appearing in big, bold letters—is used in political ads to grab the viewer's attention, focus the message, and leave a lasting impression on the viewer.

While visuals are the most effective means for communicating a message or theme, the more subtle characteristics contribute to the tone of the ad. Color advertisements often portend positive ads, while black-and-white visuals are used with great success to increase the unfavorable impressions left from watching a negative ad. The use of audio—music, sound, and voice-overs—is also important in evaluating political advertisements, particularly in assessing their tone. Somber and baleful music is associated with negative advertisements, as is the use of male announcers. Elated and upbeat musical scores are frequently used in positive ads in concert with imagery that casts a propitious light on the candidate or issue.

Analyzing the content, overall message, and the above criteria, political ads are classified by tone and even further subcategories. Positive ads highlight the accomplishments and qualities of a candidate or issue and often contain no reference to the opposing candidate or viewpoint. The early campaign stages feature positive ads designed to introduce the candidate: glittering generalities, such as "He'll continue to be the best fighter we can have for jobs and the economy"; testimonials, such as an ENDORSEMENT from a well-known figure; and "plain folks" ads that portray the candidate as an average person who engages in everyday activities.

Contrast ads compare the candidates or issues, helping the audience to justify why their vote for a particular candidate or support of a particular issue is better than the opposition. Card-stacking ads present an impressive array of statistics, legislative or executive accomplishments, or quotes. Bandwagon ads portray the sense that the candidate or issue has the most support and the popular American sentiment that "everybody is doing it."

Negative ads are attacks on the opposition. Purely negative ads make no mention of a candidate or issue to support, although some advertisements that may seem to be contrast ads are simply a veiled attempt at mudslinging. There is, however, no agreed-upon standard for where a contrast ad stops and a negative one begins.

Just as politicians have been advertising since the founding of the republic, so, too, have politicians been "going negative." The 1828 presidential campaign saw handbills claiming Andrew Jackson had massacred Indians and stabbed a man in the back.

The first political ads to air on television in the 1952 presidential campaign were no exception. The most famous of all negative ads, President Lyndon Johnson's 1964 "Daisy" advertisement, featured a young girl plucking petals from a flower as a mushroom cloud erupted in the background. The roots of the "Daisy" ad lay in the labeling by the Democrats, throughout the 1964 campaign, of Barry Goldwater as an extremist both in terms of his ideological attachments and his view of the use of nuclear weapons. The ad was part of a larger campaign to turn Goldwater's CAMPAIGN SLOGAN, "In your heart you know he is right," into the unspoken mantra, "In your guts you know he is nuts." This particular issue had stemmed from Goldwater's advocacy to permit greater leeway to battlefield commanders to use tactical nuclear weapons. While relaxing rules that govern the tactical use of nuclear weapons had been considered for some time by the military establishment and Washington insiders, the issue failed to resonate with the voters, who held few distinctions between defensive, strategic, and tactical nuclear weapons. Instead, it became an issue around which Democrats could rally against Goldwater. As a result, the issue was used by Democrats and the Johnson campaign to characterize Goldwater as having little reluctance to engage in nuclear war. Despite being aired only once, the "Daisy" ad has had a profound impact and is still the standard by which subsequent advertisements have been judged. The ad demonstrated, even while political advertising was still in its infancy, the powerful impact of images and the potential role television could and would later play in the campaign process.

Ronald Reagan's 1984 spot "Bear in the Woods" was the most frequently remembered ad from his reelection campaign against Democrat Walter Mondale. This spot is still distinctive for its subtlety and its use of parable as a device for conveying a complex policy message. The ad was intended to illustrate Reagan's position that peaceful relations with the Soviet Union were best attained through military preparedness—peace through strength. The ad tried to deliver that message without any mention of the Soviet

Union, military spending, diplomacy, or any other aspect of U.S.-Soviet relations.

The spot features a large bear (representing the Soviet Union) lumbering across the landscape, walking through trees and across a river. The sound of a heartbeat can be heard in the background, along with the following voiceover: "There's a bear in the woods. For some people, the bear is easy to see; others don't see it at all. Some people say the bear is tame; others say it's vicious and dangerous. Since no one can be sure who is right, isn't it smart to be as strong as the bear . . . if there is a bear." As the narrative ends, the bear comes upon an unarmed man standing alone in the woods. The bear then takes a step back. The spot closes with a still shot of Ronald Reagan standing next to an American flag, along with the tag "President Reagan: Prepared for Peace."

The "Bear" ad was strategically important to the Reagan campaign in that it underscored a theme the president had articulated earlier in the year, most notably in a speech delivered at Normandy, but there is disagreement about viewer reaction to the "Bear" ad. Reagan campaign strategists say that when they tested the spot in 1984, test subjects clearly understood the peace-through-strength message of the ad. At the same time, survey-based studies suggested that the spot did little to raise the salience of U.S.–Soviet relations in the minds of voters.

Republican efforts to go negative four years later proved much more effective. The "Willie Horton" political advertisement was used by the Bush National Security POLITICAL ACTION COMMITTEE in the 1988 PRESIDENTIAL ELECTION against the Democratic nominee, Massachusetts governor Michael Dukakis. This advertisement used powerful symbols to play on race-based fears in the American public. In response to sagging poll numbers, George H. W. Bush's backers aired the infamous "Willie Horton" advertisement. Horton, a black man serving a murder sentence of life without parole for first-degree murder, was the central image of the advertisement. The advertisement, using grainy black-and-white images, tells the story of Horton raping a woman and assaulting her companion while on an unguarded 48-hour weekend furlough.

The advertisement was officially called "Revolving Doors," and it attacked the Massachusetts prison furlough program by showing prisoners entering and exiting a prison. While Republicans argued the advertisement was a legitimate statement regarding Dukakis's record on crime, Democrats screamed "racism." After the advertisement aired on television, Bush continued to publicly criticize Dukakis and weekend furlough programs. For example, during a campaign speech in Kingsburg, California, Bush remarked "You have a choice this fall. . . . Between one who puts criminals behind bars, and a liberal governor who let murderers not eligible for parole out on furlough." While it is impossible to say whether this particular advertisement

helped Bush in his victory that year, his tough-on-crime stance became a central theme of the campaign, one that resonated with voters during the late 1980s.

Not all political ads are meant to influence elections, as the 1993 "Harry and Louise" ad aired by an insurance interest group to help defeat the Clinton health care plan demonstrated. "This plan forces us to buy our insurance through those new mandatory government health alliances," claims fictional Louise, to which Harry responds "Run by tens of thousands of new bureaucrats." Ultimately, the ad and the campaign to defeat the Clinton plan was successful, playing on fears of bureaucracy, even while the news media and White House debunked the claims of Harry and Louise.

Similarly, the REPUBLICAN NATIONAL COMMITTEE issued an ad in favor of George W. Bush's presidential bid citing his prescription drug plan for Medicare. Playing on fears of government control of health care, the announcer reads and visual text shows "The Gore Prescription Plan: [Let] Bureaucrats Decide." For a split second, the phrase "RATS" flashes on screen. While Bush denied it, Gore levied charges of using subliminal messages to influence voters.

Perhaps the most contentious negative advertising campaign was waged during the 2004 presidential election. Following John Kerry's acceptance speech at the DEMO-CRATIC NATIONAL CONVENTION in Boston, Swift Boat Veterans for Truth began airing ads claiming Kerry had misled voters about his record in Vietnam. The advertising campaign proved even more effective because, among other reasons, during his acceptance speech Kerry made many overt references to his military service, using it to bolster his credibility on the campaign's preeminent issue: national security.

In a study of 433 prominent political ads from 1952 to 2000, 56 percent of the ads were coded as negative. Until the 1964 presidential contest, however, most were still positive. While the 1972 and 1976 campaigns were not nearly as negative as the two preceding ones—due to increased media skepticism and moral outrage associated with the Watergate SCANDAL—that trend faded, with every campaign since then airing more negative than positive political advertisements.

Political campaigns air negative ads because they are frequently more effective than their positive counterparts. Because they usually focus on policy issues, viewers tend to recall them better than positive ads extolling generic platitudes, and, generally, they have been found to be more informative. More important is the news media coverage of paid advertisements. Following reforms to the nominating process in 1968 that created more primaries and fewer candidates chosen in smoke-filled rooms—coupled with a new atmosphere of investigative journalism fueled by the Watergate scandal—media coverage of campaigns has shifted from stories about speeches and travel schedules to more analysis of campaign tactics. Part of this shift has included an increase in the coverage of political advertising. Many news outlets have "ad tracker" features on their Web sites allowing visitors to view ads that never air in their media market. In the thick of the campaign season, network and cable newscasts frequently devote airtime to the latest, and often the most controversial, political advertisements.

The best example of this phenomenon comes from the effectiveness of the aforementioned Swift Boat Veterans for Truth advertising campaign during the 2004 presidential election. Despite a modest ad buy of $550,000 in a few media markets, within two weeks of the initial airing one-third of survey respondents had seen the ad, and almost one in four had heard about it. While only those in the selected media markets had the opportunity to view the spot, titled "Any Questions?" the text, audio, and video of the ad was played and replayed on cable and network news and talk radio, and printed in newspapers around the country. While many of the ad's charges were debunked in the media and eventually by John Kerry personally, almost half the ad's viewers found the claims believable.

Political scientists are also turning their attention to the Internet as a medium for political advertising. Recent elections have featured banner or pop-up ads urging the election or defeat of a particular candidate. In 2004, www.washingtonpost.com, home to the *Washington Post*, featured all types of ads for John Kerry, while nationaljournal.com, home to *National Journal* magazine, often featured ads to defeat Tom Dashle's reelection to his Senate seat and position as Democratic minority leader. Much as television transformed the way politicians campaigned in the 1950s, so, too, might Internet advertisements usher in a new era of political advertising.

Further reading: Goldstein, Ken, and Paul Freedman. "Lessons Learned: Campaign Advertising in the 2000 Elections." *Political Communication* 19 (2002): 5–28; Krasno, J., and D. Seltz. *Buying Time.* New York: Brennan Center for Justice, 2000; West, Darrell M. *Air Wars: Television Advertising in Election Campaigns.* 3rd ed. Washington, D.C.: Congressional Quarterly Press, 2001.

—Peter Jackson, Costas Panagopoulos, Julio Borquez, F. Erick Brooks, Stephen Nemeth

advertisements (political), negative

Negative advertisements are a campaign tactic whereby a candidate or those who support a candidate seek to define an electoral opponent in negative terms. These ads take many forms and appear in all forms of media (television, radio, newspaper, DIRECT MAIL, Internet, and other types of media). Negative ads focus on a variety of things, but most concentrate on the candidate's character and personality, his or her public record (particularly a voting record, if available), the candidate's fitness for the job, or the potential negative consequences to the voter if this person wins the election.

Candidates and their campaign staffs often conduct "deep research" into the backgrounds of their opponents to discover potentially embarrassing and politically harmful information that can be exploited in negative advertisements. Research is conducted into an opponent's voting record, past speeches or writings, personal lives, and any other available information (including arrest records and even divorce proceedings). Any votes a candidate cast that are unpopular with the general public or specific subgroups within the ELECTORATE may be exploited. Anything a candidate ever said that can be construed as negative is fair game in negative advertising. Other potential exploitable material includes mistakes a candidate has made in life or negative events that occurred during previously held political offices. Information that is so explosive that it might taint both candidates is often leaked to the press, distancing the campaign from the issues.

As long as politicians have run for office in the United States, candidates have tried to paint their opponents in negative terms. With the rise of the mass media, in particular television, the concept of negative advertising has expanded and become one of the primary expenditures in any campaign for public office. The first significant negative ad in television history was the so-called Daisy advertisement aired by the Lyndon B. Johnson campaign against his Republican opponent, Barry Goldwater. The ad showed an innocent young girl picking daisies in a field when a countdown began. As the countdown reached zero, a nuclear explosion was shown, first reflected in the little girl's eyes, then encompassing the whole screen. A voiceover told viewers "These are the stakes" before the screen showed "Vote for President Johnson." The clear implication of the commercial was that a vote for Goldwater was a vote for a dangerous world in which nuclear annihilation was a real possibility.

A more recent example was the "Willie Horton" ad that attacked Democrat Michael Dukakis in the 1988 PRESIDENTIAL ELECTION. Paid for by an organization independent of Republican candidate George H. W. Bush, the commercial showed the menacing face of the convicted Massachusetts murderer Willie Horton, who had committed a rape and murder while released from prison through a weekend pass program supported by Dukakis. The advertisement openly stated that the Democrat was weak on crime and implied that such incidents would increase if Dukakis were voted into the White House.

The effectiveness of negative advertising is unclear. There is little evidence to suggest that negative advertisements are any more effective in helping candidates win elections than are positive ads. The strongest effect they have is in driving up the "negatives," or negative ratings, of the targeted candidate without increasing anyone's positive ratings. This may lead voters to cast their BALLOTs against the negatively defined candidate rather than voting in favor of the candidate doing the attacking. An unintended effect of negative campaigning may be an increase in voter cynicism, which may drive voters away from elections altogether as they abandon a political system defined by its negativity. The evidence is mixed as to whether negative advertising depresses VOTER TURNOUT, but it is clear that there has been a decline in American voter turnout during the period when the use of negative advertising increased.

Proponents of negative advertising argue that negative ads, especially ads that focus on an incumbent's voting record, can actually serve as useful educational tools for voters. The information, if factual and not taken out of context, can help the electorate hold elected officials accountable and might be used to reduce the considerable advantages of incumbency. Likewise, information about a candidate's personal indiscretions, which is often more controversial than policy-based negative ads, can provide voters information about a candidate's character and professional judgment. Even the strongest supporters of negative advertisements do not support ads that are factually incorrect or blatantly misleading. In fact, most negative advertisements are based in truth, even if they are exaggerated or twisted so that they portray the candidate as negatively as possible.

Regardless of one's view of negative advertisements, there is little that can be done from an official standpoint to limit negative advertising. Regulation or limitation of negative campaigning, at least negative campaigning based in truth, is considered to be a violation of the free speech clause of the First Amendment of the Constitution. As long as politicians believe that negative advertisements are effective and as long as the electorate allows the negative ads to influence their votes, they will continue to be aired.

Further reading: American Museum of the Moving Image. "Presidential Political Advertisements." Available online. URL: http://livingroomcandidate.movingimage.us. Accessed August 10, 2005; Ansolabehere, Stephen, et al. "Does Attack Advertising Demobilize the Electorate?" *American Political Science Review* 88 (1994): 829–838; Jamieson, Kathleen Hall. *Dirty Politics: Deception, Distraction and Democracy.* New York: Oxford University Press, 1992; Kahn, Kim Fridkin, and Patrick J. Kenney. "Do Negative Campaigns Mobilize or Suppress Turnout?" *American Political Science Review* 93 (1999): 877–889.

—Kenneth Quinnell

Alien and Sedition Acts

The Alien and Sedition Acts are four controversial laws passed in 1798 by the Federalists, who had controlled both Congress and the White House since the ratification of the Constitution. This legislation was introduced in response to the threat of war with France and was designed to undermine support for Thomas Jefferson's newly formed DEMOCRATIC-REPUBLICAN PARTY. This fledgling organization was sympathetic to the French and was also highly critical of Federalist policies. The Alien and Sedition Acts are significant because the controversy surrounding them contributed to the defeat of the Federalists in the critical election of 1800. In addition, the Sedition Act, in particular, presented one of the earliest challenges to the First Amendment and helped to reinforce Americans' opinions concerning the importance of freedom of speech.

The Alien and Sedition Acts were passed after American relations with France had deteriorated due to the signing of the Jay Treaty with Great Britain in 1795, which resulted in French attacks on American ships in 1797, and the XYZ Affair. As a result of these circumstances, the Federalists grew suspicious of French immigrants living in the United States. They also became wary of Jefferson's new party because it embraced the democratic ideals of the French Revolution and counted a number of French immigrants among its supporters. In order to weaken the political influence of these groups, Congress passed the Naturalization Act, which denied CITIZENSHIP to aliens from enemy nations during time of war and also extended the residency requirement for all aliens seeking American citizenship. Next, it approved the Alien Act and the Alien Enemies Act, which allowed the president to restrain or deport any aliens judged to be a threat to the safety of the country, particularly those from enemy nations. Finally, in order to silence the dissenting voices of Jefferson's supporters, the Federalists passed the Sedition Act, which made it illegal for anyone to utter or publish "false, scandalous and malicious" speech with the intention of defaming the government and its representatives or arousing contempt for its laws. Those found guilty of violating this law, which included a number of newspaper editors who favored the Democratic-Republicans, faced a fine and incarceration.

In response, Jefferson and James Madison drafted the Kentucky and Virginia Resolutions, which criticized the passage of the Alien and Sedition Acts as an illegitimate expansion of federal power and for violating the freedoms of speech and press protected by the First Amendment. They also declared the right of the states to nullify acts of the national government that they deemed unconstitutional. The Federalists maintained that the three acts dealing with aliens were authorized by the Necessary and Proper Clause and argued the Sedition Act was consistent with British common law tradition because it did not allow "prior restraint"—prohibition of speech before the fact. Despite this defense, the public's negative reaction to this legislation sapped the strength of the Federalists and contributed to the success of the Democratic-Republicans in the election of 1800. The Alien and Sedition Acts helped bring about the first peaceful transfer of power from one party to another in the nation's history. Furthermore, the controversy also taught Americans the importance of interpreting the First Amendment broadly in order to protect the free exchange of ideas that is essential to the success of the TWO-PARTY SYSTEM and a democratic form of government.

Further reading: Curtis, Michael Kent. *Free Speech, "The People's Darling Privilege:" Struggles for Freedom of Expression in American History.* Durham, N.C.: Duke University Press, 2000; Magee, James. *Freedom of Expression.* Westport, Conn.: Greenwood Press, 2002; Watkins, William. *Reclaiming the American Revolution: The Kentucky and Virginia Resolutions and Their Legacy.* New York: Palgrave Macmillan, 2004.

—Jill M. Budny

American Association of Retired Persons (AARP)

AARP, formally known as the American Association of Retired Persons, is the leading nonprofit, nonpartisan political advocacy organization for older Americans. Founded in 1958 by retired California schoolteacher Dr. Ethel Percy Andrus, AARP's membership currently numbers more than 35 million people aged 50 and over. In its early days, AARP was largely focused on DIRECT MAIL marketing of financial products to individuals over the age of 50. These services remain a significant part of AARP's operations. Now, through its approximately 3,500 local chapters, AARP provides a much broader array of services for its members such as work-training programs, tax-counseling services, community outreach and education programs, as well as travel services.

After its merger with the National Retired Teachers Association in 1982, AARP established itself as the primary group in the United States dedicated to promoting the interests of Americans age 50 and over. It has identified its main goals as securing economic and physical well-being and improving the quality of life for its members as they near retirement or transition to a reduced role in the workforce. AARP pursues these goals through a policy institute that serves as a think tank on issues that affect those near retirement and the elderly.

In FY 2003, AARP spent more than $57 million on legislative activities, such as lobbying members of Congress and informing its members about pertinent legislative developments. A large portion of this expenditure was devoted to securing passage of the Medicare prescription drug benefit. AARP's role in the passage of the legislation caused the group to come under intense attack, largely because the group aligned itself with the Republican majorities in the House and Senate to ensure that the bill reached the president, who then signed it into law. Opponents of the bill charged that AARP was acting in its economic interests, not in the interests of its members, as the group stood to realize a substantial profit from its insurance activities.

Through its advocacy efforts, AARP has assembled a group of individuals from a variety of racial, economic, cultural, and regional backgrounds, all of whom are concerned about issues affecting older Americans. AARP maintains offices in each of the 50 states as well as in the District of Columbia, Puerto Rico, and the U.S. Virgin Islands. Its headquarters are located in Washington, D.C.

Further reading: American Association of Retired Persons. Available online. URL: http://www.aarp.org. Accessed August 10, 2005; Blahous, Charles P., III. *Reforming Social Security for Ourselves and Our Posterity.* Westport, Conn.: Praeger, 2000, published in cooperation with the Center for Strategic and International Studies. Cohen, Lee M. *Justice Across Generations: What Does It Mean?* Washington, D.C.: Public Policy Institute, American Association of Retired Persons, 1993; Van Atta, Dale. *Trust Betrayed: Inside the AARP.* Washington, D.C.: Regnery Publication, 1998.

—John L. S. Simpkins

American Independent Party

The American Independent Party (AIP) is a conservative California-based third party. The party currently has BALLOT ACCESS in California, where it plays an active role in state POLITICS. The AIP also serves as the California affiliate of the national Constitution Party.

The party's stances on most domestic issues are more conservative than the REPUBLICAN PARTY's. For example, the AIP supports abolition of the personal income tax, disbanding the Internal Revenue Service, and generating tax revenue through tariffs and excise taxes. The AIP also calls for major restrictions on legal immigration into the United States and more aggressive efforts to control illegal immigration. On issues such as trade and foreign policy, the AIP takes mostly protectionist and isolationist positions. The party opposes free trade agreements such as the North American Free Trade Agreement (NAFTA) and the General Agreement on Tariffs and Trade (GATT). The AIP also calls for the United States to withdraw from the World Trade Organization, to participate less in the United Nations, and to end foreign aid. The party takes traditional conservative stances on abortion, criminal justice, gun control, affirmative action, and education.

The AIP was founded on July 8, 1967, at a convention of activists in Bakersfield, California. The new party was dedicated to limited government, states' rights, local control of education, and less interventionist foreign policy. Ballot access rules for THIRD PARTIES in California were very stringent at the time, and the AIP struggled at first to gain the necessary signatures for ballot access in the 1968 PRESIDENTIAL ELECTION. In the fall of 1967, the CAMPAIGN ORGANIZATION of former Alabama governor George Wallace worked with the AIP to gather the signatures and party registrations necessary to qualify the AIP for ballot access.

For several weeks during the fall of 1967, Wallace toured California making speeches to rally support for his candidacy and the AIP. The AIP's impressive signature and registration drive in California provided the Wallace campaign with considerable political momentum, ultimately resulting in ballot access for his candidacy in all 50 states. Wallace, who was formally nominated as the AIP presidential candidate for 1968, won more than 13 percent of the POPULAR VOTE and 46 electoral votes, one of the best third party performances in American PRESIDENTIAL ELECTION history.

After the 1968 presidential election, the national AIP split into competing FACTIONS and smaller splinter parties, frequently nominating candidates for office at many levels. Today, the California-based AIP remains an active force in state politics, though with little electoral success.

Further reading: American Independent Party. Available online. URL: http://www.aipca.org. Accessed August 10, 2005; Carlson, Jody. *George C. Wallace and the Politics of Powerlessness: The Wallace Campaigns for the Presidency, 1964–1976.* New Brunswick, N.J.: Transaction Books, 1981.
—Donald A. Zinman

American Labor Party

The American Labor Party (ALP) was assembled in 1936 by a COALITION of labor leaders and liberal activists in New York who wished to support President Franklin Roosevelt's bid for a second term independent of supporting the DEMOCRATIC PARTY itself. The party garnered 270,000 votes for Roosevelt in the 1936 election and again endorsed his candidacy in 1940. It was led primarily by labor activists David Dubinsky of the International Ladies Garment Workers Union (ILGWU), a moderate liberal, and Sidney Hillman, a socialist and head of the Amalgamated Clothing Workers Union (ACWA), which had ties to American communism. The party was the prime mover behind the election of two Harlem congressmen in the late 1930s, Vito Marcantonio and Leo Isacson, and was also behind the victorious 1937 FUSION TICKET candidacy of the Republican mayor of New York, Fiorello LaGuardia.

By 1944, a FACTION within the party led by Hillman's allies, and with ties to the Communist Party, attempted to take over the ALP by withholding support from Roosevelt in the election of that year. They were successful in wrestling control from and expelling Dubinsky's faction, which called itself a "Liberal-Labor" coalition, but the ALP endorsed Roosevelt after the split. The conflict precipitated the formation of the LIBERAL PARTY by the Dubinsky-led faction, which subsequently endorsed Roosevelt for reelection to a fourth term. Breaking with its normal support of the Democrats' nominee, the party supported former vice president Henry A. Wallace for president in 1948, the nominee of the National Progressive Party. Wallace's program was supportive of increased spending on education and

health care, conciliation with the Soviet Union, and public works. Wallace gained 500,000 votes, 8 percent of the total vote in New York in 1948 on the Labor line, marking the party's high-water mark.

Shortly after the 1948 campaign, the two ALP-supported congressmen lost their Harlem seats. In 1952, its endorsed candidate for president, Vincent Hallinan, gained only 64,000 votes in New York State, less than 1 percent of the statewide vote. Its gubernatorial nominee did not poll the minimum 50,000 votes needed in 1954 to retain BALLOT status in New York for the next four years, and thus the party voted itself out of existence in 1956, after it had lost credibility with voters and any ability to influence elections in New York State.

Further reading: Dubinsky, David. *David Dubinsky: A Life with Labor.* New York: Simon & Schuster, 1977; Danish, Max D. *The World of David Dubinsky.* Cleveland, Ohio: World Publishing Company, 1957.
—Daniel T. Kirsch

Anti-Federalists

The Anti-Federalists existed as an inchoate POLITICAL PARTY that was as remarkable for its lack of party structure as for its brief, though profound, effect on American POLITICS. The Anti-Federalists were "states' rights" advocates who favored revision of the ARTICLES OF CONFEDERATION rather than a new constitution. They distrusted unchecked government power and viewed centralization of authority as despotic. As such, they strongly opposed the new Constitution both because they held the entire process under which it was developed and ratified to be fundamentally flawed and because they viewed its alterations in the national union as establishing too powerful a government.

The Anti-Federalists were concerned that the constitutional foundation of government and the rule of law were undermined by the illegitimate process proposed by the PHILADELPHIA CONVENTION of 1787. The Articles of Confederation allowed for an amendment process, but the Philadelphia Convention and the new Federalists had completely set aside constitutional principles and procedures in proposing a unique state-by-state REFERENDUM on the matter. The nationalist designs of the Federalists were guised in terms of "mixed" government, neither wholly national nor confederal, but federal. And in making the case for the new constitution, Federalists presented a rhetorical confusion not only by use of the term *federalist,* which, as Martin Diamond has noted, meant confederal in the lexicon of the day, but also by emphasizing the limitations on national power and the reserved powers of the states. David Walker notes, "Because the authors of The Federalist Papers had to convince antifederalists that the system was sufficiently federal (confederal, in the eighteenth-century sense), they tended to overemphasize these features."

The debates were fierce, and the fate of the proposed constitution remained uncertain from 1787 through the summer of 1788. In the Anti-Federalist paper "The Dissent of the Pennsylvania Minority," the Anti-Federalist state legislators who were subjected to intimidation and deception in the Pennsylvania legislature by the majority Federalists provided an account of the events surrounding that state's ratification process and the reasons for their objections. They remarked on the proposed constitution: "The powers vested in Congress by this constitution, must necessarily annihilate and absorb the legislative, executive, and judicial powers of the several states, and produce from their ruins one consolidated government, which from the nature of things will be an iron-handed despotism . . . the new government will not be a confederacy of states as it ought, but one consolidated government, founded upon the destruction of the several governments of the states."

The Anti-Federalists vigorously objected in state after state as ratification was debated and voted upon. Though victorious in achieving a rejection vote in Rhode Island in March 1788, the Anti-Federalists witnessed the ratification of Virginia and New York in the summer of 1788, which brought to nine the number of states needed to establish the new constitution. Though it should be noted that the ratifications in New York and Virginia were mitigated by the Anti-Federalist influenced "conditional" approvals, 20 in Virginia and 31 in New York, these conditions represented significant contributions of the Anti-Federalists to the ultimate design and interpretation of the Constitution. These contributions were part of the immediate amendments proposed and passed by the first Congress under the new Constitution that became known as the Bill of Rights. Because of these contributions, the Anti-Federalists significantly influenced the Constitution, and as Herbert Storing has noted, were "junior partners" in the American constitutional founding.

The Anti-Federalist political legacy is reflected by the incorporation of the core elements of the Anti-Federalist agenda in both the Bill of Rights and in the bipartisan consensus that the concerns of the Anti-Federalists about government power and their populist paradigm that they enjoy today. The core philosophies and constitutional thought of the Anti-Federalists formed the core of the beliefs upon which the DEMOCRATIC-REPUBLICAN PARTY was ultimately founded. Certainly major elements of Anti-Federalist thought have been articulated by presidents from Jefferson to Reagan. The Anti-Federalist influence endures in both its effect on the establishment of the Constitution and its effect on states' rights as variously articulated by advocates in both major parties for devolutionary policies.

Further reading: Allen, W. B., and Gordon Lloyd, eds. *The Essential Anti-Federalist.* Lanham, Md.: Rowman & Littlefield, 2002; Bloom, Allan, ed. *Confronting the Consti-* *tution.* Washington, D.C.: AEI Press, 1990; Storing, Herbert J., ed. *The Complete Anti-Federalist.* Chicago: University of Chicago Press, 1981; Walker, David B. *The Rebirth of American Federalism.* Chatham, N.J.: Chatham House, 1995.

—Michael W. Hail

Anti-Masonic Party

The Anti-Masonic Party was a 19th-century third party formed in opposition to Masonic societies. Although its signature issue was opposition to secret societies, the party also took stands on many major political issues, such as support for temperance, Sunday closing laws, and public education. While the party's political life was short-lived, it made a number of important contributions to the development of the American party system.

In 1826, a former member of the Freemason society, William Morgan, disappeared in New York State and was rumored to have been murdered. Morgan had previously written a book revealing many secrets of the Masonic order. Public hysteria in opposition to Masonry spread throughout the nation, especially in the Northeast. With little evidence, New Yorkers who opposed Martin van Buren's wing of the state's ruling DEMOCRATIC PARTY, the Albany Regency, spread rumors that the Masons were responsible for Morgan's murder. They had hoped to cut into the Albany Regency's political support from evangelical Christians, who regarded membership in secret societies as inconsistent with the Bible.

Local anti-Mason organizations formed throughout the Northeast to work for the electoral defeat of known members of Masonic societies. The Anti-Masonic Party was formally established in New York City in 1828. A purely northern party that appealed to the poorer classes and evangelicals, the Anti-Masons won the governorships of Vermont in 1831 and Pennsylvania in 1835. At their peak, the Anti-Masons won 25 seats in the House of Representatives in the 1832 election. In the 1832 PRESIDENTIAL ELECTION, the Anti-Masons nominated former attorney general William Wirt as their candidate, although he was a former Mason himself. Wirt won almost 8 percent of the POPULAR VOTE and seven electoral votes. He carried the state of Vermont and polled strongly throughout Pennsylvania and New England.

The Anti-Masons rapidly declined in popularity after the 1836 PRESIDENTIAL ELECTION, with most of their members joining the new WHIG PARTY. In large part, this was because the party lost its signature issue, which frequently happens to many third political parties. Membership in Masonic organizations declined in the 1830s, existing Masonic organizations became less active, and public hysteria against secret societies waned.

The Anti-Masonic Party made one lasting contribution to the development of political parties. In 1831, the Anti-

The "Antimasonic Apron," produced in 1831. The apron was a symbol for the contrasts between the Masons and the Anti-Masons. *(HarpWeek, LLC)*

Masons held the first-ever national nominating convention in Baltimore to both nominate a presidential candidate and issue a party platform. Soon afterward, the major parties adopted these practices as well.

Further reading: Ratner, Lorman. *Antimasonry: The Crusade and the Party.* Englewood Cliffs, N.J.: Prentice Hall, 1969; Vaughn, William Preston. *The Antimasonic Party in the United States, 1826–1843.* Lexington: University Press of Kentucky, 1983.

—Donald A. Zinman

approval rating

A political figure's approval rate represents the percentage of people who approve of the way the elected official is handling the job. It is a truism in American POLITICS that politicians must maintain popular support in order to retain their political power. While the truism concerning the politician's standing with his or her public applies to all who seek political power, it is especially applicable to the American president. Indeed, a vast majority of the effort to measure public approval in an empirical fashion has concentrated on measuring the public's sentiment toward the president. While the president receives the vast amount of attention given to approval ratings, many polling organizations also poll the approval ratings of members of Congress, governors, Supreme Court justices, and governmental institutions more broadly.

It was the Gallup organization that led the way to systematically capturing approval ratings. Beginning in the early 1930s, George Gallup began conducting polls that posed questions to respondents about presidential approval. From 1935 to 1937, there was considerable fluctuation in the wording of the questions, as Gallup and his colleagues were concerned with finding an appropriate way of asking people about their approval of the president's job performance without conflating their results with issues such as the relative likability of the president. Beginning in 1937, Gallup began to ask respondents whether they were "for or against Roosevelt today." The following year, Gallup introduced a new dichotomy, that of approval-disapproval, to the question. In late fall of 1938, faced with evidence that his wording of the question was confusing, Gallup began to specifically ask about the respondents' approval of the way the president was handling his job.

In 1945, the Gallup survey team adopted a question wording format that has been consistently applied ever since. Today, when respondents are surveyed by Gallup (and the numerous other polling organizations that have adopted the Gallup way of wording the question), the question posed is "Do you approve or disapprove of the way [president's name] is handling his job as president?" In addition, the polling organization has consistently asked this question toward the beginning of its surveys, in order to avoid contaminating the response with effects from other questions.

The Gallup organization also asks its respondents numerous types of identifying questions, so as to isolate the effects of certain demographic characteristics on variations in the approval rating. These demographic groups include obvious and traditional classifications such as race, gender, region, and age, but also politically and socially relevant attributes such as PARTY IDENTIFICATION and religious affiliation. Respondents are also questioned about whether they live in a union household, level of education attained, occupation, income, and the size of the community in which they live. In order to arrive at measures of a president's approval rating that are statistically reliable and mirror the feelings of the general public as closely as possible, Gallup makes use of a random sampling technique that includes approximately 1,000 cases. Following questionnaire collection, the organization weights the sample so that the demographic characteristics of the respondents match the current demographic makeup of the nation.

A great deal of scholarship has attempted to determine the variables that shape approval rating, as well as to determine the impact the approval rating has on political success. Indeed, the relationship has often been assumed to be reciprocal. That is, presidents and other politicians who are popular are more likely to be successful, and those that are successful are more likely to be rewarded with high approval ratings.

More so than any other factor, party identification shapes predispositions toward presidential approval ratings. Simply put, the president's fellow partisans are more predisposed to approve of the president, while respondents identifying with the OPPOSITION PARTY are predisposed against the president. As the nation has grown increasingly polarized—beginning with the Reagan administration, continuing through the tumultuous Clinton administration, and certainly evident in the current Bush administration—the gap between the ratings of each party has grown markedly.

Another source of approval rating predisposition is found in the persistence of approval. That is, while the public generally accords a president higher approval ratings following the election, these generally positive feelings tend to wane as presidents begin to make tough decisions and alienate blocs of citizens and voters. Often referred to as "honeymoons," these periods of generally positive evaluation last varying lengths, but rarely more than the first year or two of a president's first term in office.

Long-term decline is another source of approval disposition among the ELECTORATE. Generally speaking, the disposition of the American electorate to positively evaluate a president has been declining over the last several decades. Indeed, there seemed to be a shift in the equilibrium of presidential approval around the late 1960s and early 1970s, often referred to as the Nixon era. This trend appears to be explainable, as this period of time was marked by the Vietnam War, the CIVIL RIGHTS MOVEMENT, Watergate, and a host of other difficult moments for the American polity.

Another important source of approval predisposition is the dichotomy between a president's personality and his policy. The American electorate has often been accused of evaluating its president more on personal characteristics than policy preferences, a charge that would seem to stick given the public's relative inattention to policy debates and details. In reality, however, this does not seem to be the case, as presidents often suffer sharp swings in approval even as public views of their personality remain stable. In addition, Americans seem quite able to separate their views of personality and policy. The cases of Ronald Reagan and Bill Clinton are examples of this trend. Reagan, now considered one of the most polarizing figures in American political history, was much beloved for his personal attributes, even as his policy positions were disdained by a large portion of Americans. Bill Clinton, conversely, left office with nearly two-thirds of Americans viewing him as a good president, but the same amount disapproving of his character.

As there are a number of influences on the public's general predispositions toward the president, so are there several factors that influence variation in an individual's approval of the president, and, thus, the aggregate nature of the approval rating. These external factors include shock events, salience issues, and responsibility issues. Historical occasions can shock the level of presidential approval ratings. These times are often referred to as rally events, and though they often lead to meaningful policy and political change, their effects are often not durable. Perhaps the quintessential example of a rally event was the American public's response after September 11, 2001. Immediately following the terrorist attacks on New York, Washington, D.C., and Pennsylvania, President George W. Bush's approval rating skyrocketed. With time, Bush's approval began to drop and continued to do so at a remarkably constant rate over the next four years, with slight pauses during the MIDTERM ELECTIONS of 2002 and at the start of the war with Iraq.

Salience refers to whatever is on the minds of the respondents when they evaluate the president. This assumes that a president's approval rating is shaped by the public's opinion of other things that matter to them, even if the president has little influence over those factors. How salient an issue is varies over time and across people and has been found to be tied closely with economic issues. For example, when the economy is the top popular concern (which is quite often, but almost always during economic downturns), presidents tend to be evaluated on the state of the economy.

A second factor that shapes approval change concerns responsibility, and particularly the degree to which the public holds a president "responsible" for a particular area of performance. Among other things, this, too, relates directly to the public's evaluation of the economy, as some view the president as primarily responsible for economic conditions, while others have a more complex view of economic determinants. While a president's approval rating can be shaped by the public's impression of the president's performance on those issues that they care about and for which they hold him responsible, recent studies have shown that the public is not narrowly self-interested in such appraisals, but rather that people often form their opinions based on how they feel the president's performance has affected the broader national interests, as opposed to their own pocketbooks.

While presidents possess very little control over these influencing factors, this does not stop them from believing that public support is the key to presidential success, or from going to great lengths to elicit public support. Recent scholarship, however, has found that presidents are rarely successful in their appeals to the public, due in part to increasing difficulty in getting their message out to the public, and due also in part to decreasing receptivity on the part of the public to listen to messages. Moreover, scholars have continually demonstrated that approval maintains a marginal, at best, influence on presidential success. Nonetheless, presidents still insist that such appeals are the lynchpin of their success, and if they are not successful it is because they have not "gone public" enough. Despite recent admonitions concerning the virtue of "staying private," given the inordinate value approval ratings are believed to possess, presidents are not likely to heed the advice.

Further reading: Edwards, George C., III. *At the Margins: Presidential Leadership of Congress.* New Haven, Conn.: Yale University Press, 1989; Edwards, George C., III. *On Deaf Ears: The Failure of the Bully Pulpit.* New Haven, Conn.: Yale University Press, 2003; Edwards, George C., III, with Alec M. Gallup. *Presidential Approval: A Sourcebook.* Baltimore: Johns Hopkins University Press, 1990; Edwards, George C., III, and Stephen J. Wayne. *Presidential Leadership: Politics and Policy Making.* 6th ed. Belmont, Calif.: Wadsworth, 2003; Kernell, Samuel. *Going Public: New Strategies of Presidential Leadership.* 3rd ed. Washington, D.C.: Congressional Quarterly Press, 1997; Roper Center for Public Opinion Research. Available online. URL: http://roperweb.ropercenter.uconn.edu. Accessed August 10, 2005.

—Justin S. Vaughn

Article I, U.S. Constitution

Article I is the first and longest of the Constitution's seven articles. The 10 sections that make up Article I establish the contours of the legislative branch and introduce important constitutional principles such as the separation of powers and federalism.

The very short first section establishes that the legislative powers granted in the Constitution shall be vested in a Congress that has two bodies, a Senate and House of Representatives. Section two (the House of Representatives) and section three (the Senate) outline the basic nature of representation, structure, and requirements of the two houses of Congress. Article I explicitly states that a bill cannot become a law until a majority in both the House and the Senate passes it. Sections four, five, and six take up matters such as the frequency of assembly, compensation, and the need for an accurate and complete record of proceedings. Section seven establishes and outlines the procedures by which the president may veto legislation and Congress may then override the president's veto. Section eight enumerates 17 distinct legislative powers such as the authority to tax and spend and to declare war. Section eight also begins and ends with broad grants of power such as "to provide for the general Defence and general Welfare of the United States" and "to make all Laws necessary and proper for carrying into Execution the foregoing Powers." Section nine places explicit limits on the types of laws that can be passed. Finally, section 10 places limits on the legislative authority of the states so as to limit the potential for conflict between Congress and the states.

The bicameral legislature of the United States is a unique product of the ideas and concerns of the DELE-GATES of the Constitutional Convention. The framers of the Constitution had to find a way to invest enough power in the legislature to overcome the division and avoid the ineffectiveness of the ARTICLES OF CONFEDERATION, while being sensitive to the concerns of the various states. At the Constitutional Convention the delegates from the larger states generally favored a legislative body in which representation was based on population, while the delegates from the smaller states wanted to protect the principle of federalism. The creation of the bicameral legislature, an idea that had been looked on favorably even before the conflict over representation, was a compromise solution by which representation in the House was based on population and representation in the Senate on the equality of the states. Because of its short terms (two years) and smaller constituencies, the House of Representatives was intended to be the branch closest to the people and to popular feeling. The Senate, on the other hand, was intended to be the more deliberate and stable body serving longer six-year terms and selected by the state legislatures.

Article I also differentiated between the two bodies of the legislature in assigning particular areas of responsibility. For instance, the House, being the body closer to the people, was given exclusive authority to originate revenue bills (taxes) in Article I, section seven, while the Senate, thought to be the more stable body, was given special responsibility in the areas of foreign affairs (the ratification of treaties) and the confirmation of appointments to high executive offices.

The present Congress looks somewhat different than the early Congress. This is partly because of the expansion and growth of the United States of America. The most striking change might be the tremendous increase in the number of representatives and the represented. The number of senators has increased from 26 to 100 (a union of 13 states has grown to 50 states). The House has also grown from 65 to 435 members, and the average size of a CONGRESSIONAL DISTRICT has increased from roughly 40,000 to about 650,000 citizens.

The character and scope of Congress has also changed, especially in the 20th century. Contrary to the expectations of the framers, the present House of Representatives has a very low turnover rate and is largely made up of career legislators. Incumbents are hard to beat on ELECTION DAY and slow to retire. Also, the development of political parties has led to important innovations to the practical operation of the legislative branch. While still responsible for representing their constituents and passing good legislation, Congress has also taken on the responsibility for initiating investigations into matters of public concern. This was justified by a broad interpretation of the "Necessary and Proper" clause in Article I, section eight. During the last century, Congress was increasingly both burdened and empowered by its responsibility to oversee a greatly enlarged federal bureaucracy. Congress has also had to deal with an invigorated executive branch that has increasingly sought to dominate policy development. Though these challenges are significant, there is no reason to believe that the institution created by Article I will not adapt to these challenges.

The Constitution is also subject to change by amendment. The contours of the legislative branch as described by Article I have been considerably altered by amendments. The individual rights protected by the Bill of Rights (which extend the limits described in section nine) placed significant limits on the powers of the legislative branch. The individual rights and limits of congressional power in the Bill of Rights and Article I, section nine, distinguish Congress from the British Parliament, which in theory can pass any law it wishes. The Thirteenth, FOURTEENTH, and FIFTEENTH AMENDMENTs have conferred important additional powers. The SEVENTEENTH AMENDMENT removed the selection of senators from the state legislatures as specified in Article I, section three, and placed it with the citizens of each state. The passage of the Sixteenth Amendment, which authorized the federal government to tax income, also significantly altered and increased the power of Congress from its original powers under Article I.

Article I must be understood and interpreted in relation to the whole Constitution. In American political history, the weight of constitutional interpretation rests heavily on the decisions of the Supreme Court. The decision in *McCulloch v. Maryland* (1819) is widely believed to be the most important moment in the interpretation of Article I. This decision rejected the opinion that the "Necessary and Proper" clause should be interpreted as limiting congressional power. The unanimous decision in *McCulloch v. Maryland* recognized Congress's power to charter the Bank of the United States and in so doing recognized a broad congressional power implied in the "Necessary and Proper" clause. The Congress of the United States cannot pass any law it might wish, but it has certainly avoided the weakness of the legislative branch under the Articles of Confederation.

Further reading: Greenberg, Ellen. *The House and Senate Explained: The People's Guide to Congress.* New York: Norton, 1996; Kurland, Philip, and Ralph Lerner. *The Founders' Constitution: Preamble through Article 1, Section 8, Clause 4.* Indianapolis: The Liberty Fund, 2000.
—Ryan Rakness

Article II, U.S. Constitution

Article II of the U.S. Constitution outlines the organization, powers, and responsibilities of the American executive. Article II attempts to balance the founders' distaste of a strong executive with the need for greater executive power as recognized from the weaknesses of the ARTICLES OF CONFEDERATION. The founders achieved such balance

through ambiguity, providing broad parameters for the executive but few details. Some argue the ambiguity stems from irreconcilable differences among the founders, while others argue the intentional ambiguity allows for flexibility and growth in response to unforeseen future demands. That presidents have exploited the ambiguity over time is unquestionable. Nowhere does Article II include provisions for a presidential cabinet, for example, nor does the article mention the president's ability to issue executive orders. These two now indispensable facets of the office demonstrate the executive branch's growth beyond at least the literal detail of the founders' plan for the presidency in Article II.

The framers divided Article II into four sections. Section one details the administration of the executive. The section begins by "vesting" executive power in a president with a four-year term, serving together with a single vice president. The clause represents the culmination of the protracted debate over what form of executive leadership the new nation required—a single executive, multiple executives, an executive council, or some combination thereof—and the office's length of term.

To select the president, Article II creates a middle body of "electors" to stand between the people—or the state legislatures, as written—and the president. The electors, whose numbers would match each state's total number of senators and representatives, cast a single BALLOT for the executive. The candidate receiving an absolute majority becomes president; the second-place finisher becomes the vice president. Absent a clear majority, the election moves to the U.S. House of Representatives, where each state garners one vote. A simple majority in this second House of Representatives vote determines the president. Though the TWELFTH AMENDMENT changed some of these procedures—removing the second-place selection system for vice president, for example—and electors' votes today nearly mirror the general public's votes, the framers' intent of a buffer between the people and the president remains.

Section one follows with the formal requirements for the presidency. An eligible individual must be a natural-born citizen or a citizen of the United States at the time of adoption of the Constitution, must have "attained to the age of thirty-five years," and "been fourteen years a resident within the United States." Section one also clearly establishes the vice president as successor to presidential "powers and duties," though it leaves unclear whether the vice president actually *ascends* to the presidency, an issue not clearly resolved until the Twenty-Fifth Amendment in 1967. Section one concludes with the presidential oath of office.

Section two details the president's specific powers, some of which provide the president with only limited oversight by the other branches, allowing executive flexibility and, therefore, avenues for substantive expansion of executive powers. For example, section two identifies the president as commander in chief of the nation's army, navy, and the state militias when federalized. Though the legislative branch retains the power to declare war, presidents have acted as commander in chief to deploy troops and conduct military actions that appear warlike in all but name. The president may also fill vacancies that happen at times when the Senate is in recess, a power that, when skillfully applied, allows presidents to circumvent the formal legislative check on executive appointments. Section two also provides the president with the near-unchecked power to grant pardons and reprieves in cases excluding impeachment.

Other powers in section two are provided with explicit counterweights by other branches. Only with the "advice and consent" of the Senate does the president maintain the power to make treaties and to appoint ambassadors, Supreme Court justices, "public ministers and consuls," and all other "officers . . . whose appointments are not herein otherwise provided for."

Finally, section two grants the president the power to require the executive departments to provide their "opinion, in writing," on any subject relating to "the duties of their respective offices." The power is a significant departure from the earlier Articles of Confederation, which demanded that executive departments report directly to the legislative branch. To some, this single power provides the substantive constitutional basis for presidential management of the executive branch.

Whereas section two details powers, section three outlines some powers but also executive responsibilities. Specific powers include the ability to convene Congress and to commission officers of the United States. Also, the president may propose legislation to Congress on "such measures as he shall judge necessary and expedient." This power further expands the president's role in the legislative process as outlined in ARTICLE I.

Section three also details a number of presidential responsibilities. The president shall "from time to time" provide Congress information on the state of the union. The obligation is fulfilled today by the president's annual State of the Union speech to a joint session of Congress, though as written the obligation need not be either annual or a formal speech. The president also must receive foreign ambassadors and other public ministers.

In addition to the reporting power outlined in section two, section three contains the other formal responsibility from which most executive power derives: The president shall "take care that the laws be faithfully executed." Given the executive branch's responsibility to execute legislative decisions, this statement clearly and succinctly places control of the executive branch and executive activity with the president.

Finally, section four, the shortest of the four sections, covers a president's removal from office. Though Article I touches on the procedures for impeachment, section four clearly identifies the standard for impeachment. Namely, the president, as well as the vice president and other "civil Officers," shall be impeached and removed from office for "treason, bribery, or other high crimes or misdemeanors."

Further reading: Cornell Law School, Legal Information Center. Available online. URL: http://www.law.cornell.edu. Accessed August 10, 2005; Kurian, George T., ed. *A Historical Guide to the U.S. Government.* New York: Oxford University Press, 1998; Nelson, Michael, ed. *Guide to the Presidency.* 3rd ed. Washington, D.C.: CQ Press, 2002.

—Chris Mandernach

Article III, U.S. Constitution

That the judiciary should be the third subject of the framer's attention, attended to only after careful delineation of the powers of the legislature and executive branches, seemed natural. As Hamilton famously predicted in Federalist No. 78, the judiciary appeared likely to be the "least dangerous branch" in terms of oppressing the citizenry. Three short sections deal with judges and court structure, judicial power, and the definition of treason. Brevity has not meant simplicity, however; these few sentences have yielded a multitude of politically controversial cases.

The first section grants the judicial power to a court system separate from the other two branches. Specifics of structure and procedure are left vague. Only a Supreme Court is specifically required. Other "inferior" courts are possible as Congress might choose "to ordain and establish." Lack of specificity as to the number of judges prompted Franklin Roosevelt to consider his famous Court packing scheme in the 1930s, a plan defeated in Congress but with enough political drive to produce a change in perspective in crucial decisions about the New Deal (*National Labor Relations Board v. Jones and Laughlin Steel*, 301 U.S. 1 [1937]). The framers established lifetime appointment "during good Behavior" for these judges, though the actual appointment process and the possibility of impeachment are dealt with in ARTICLES II and I, respectively. (Judges in specialized federal courts such as the tax court draw their authority from Article I but do not enjoy lifetime tenure.)

The Judiciary Act of 1789 provided for a federally appointed judge in each state and also established a system of circuit courts to be composed of district court judges and a member of the Supreme Court, who would "ride circuit" around the states to handle the first level of appeals. In *Stuart v. Baird*, the Court upheld a politically motivated congressional reshuffling of judicial duties, including the cancellation of a term of the Supreme Court. Although judicial review is not specifically mentioned, it became a major source of tension between executive and judicial branches in *Marbury v. Madison* (1803). A three-tier system of federal courts emerged: 94 U.S. district courts (at least one per state); 13 U.S. circuit courts of appeal (appellate jurisdiction only); and the Supreme Court, with a narrow original jurisdiction and appeals from both lower federal courts and from the highest state courts.

Section two spells out the jurisdiction of the federal court system in deceptively simple terms, defining judicial power as cases in law and equity and controversies between certain groups of claimants. Putting these two phrases together, the Supreme Court has fashioned a rule that limits the judicial scope of "cases and controversies" (*Muskrat v. U.S.*). The Court has adopted additional self-imposed rules that limit its willingness to hear cases not felt to be genuine controversies. Advisory opinions and other quasi-judicial duties are specifically excluded. Individual judges have at times accepted additional assignments (Justice Jackson's service on the Nuremberg tribunal being the most famous). The Court will not rule on issues that are unripe (*Renne v. Geary*) or moot (*DeFunis v. Odegard*). Congress has persuaded judges to become involved in helping to draft technical matters relating to courts (the federal sentencing act).

The issue of original versus appellate jurisdiction gained national attention when Chief Justice John Marshall found a section of the Judiciary Act of 1789 unconstitutional in its application to a case involving judicial commissions (*Marbury v. Madison*). Earlier, the Supreme Court had upheld a federal tax on carriages (*Hylton v. U.S.*), despite the lack of a genuinely adversarial relationship between the parties. *Marbury* illustrated the tendency of politically partisan cases to generate partisan heat since it pitted the Federalist judges against Jeffersonian Democrats.

Perhaps the most difficult limitation on the Court's willingness to hear cases centers on the concept of standing. Because the common law is based on an adversarial system of justice that assumes two mutually antagonistic parties, each with a concrete stake in the outcome of the case, the Court has ruled that any party to a case must have an immediate personal injury that can be relieved by the Court's decision. As Justice O'Connor conceded in *Allen v. Wright*, "[S]tanding doctrine incorporates concepts concededly not susceptible of precise definition." Individuals generally do not have standing to bring suits involving government spending (*Valley Forge Christian College v. American United*) or to challenge specific governmental acts unless the injury is both personal and immediate (*City of L.A. v. Lyons*).

Another major limitation derives from the concept of political questions. The Court defers to Congress and the president (though not to state governments) in issues in which power seems to have been granted them or when the judiciary seems to have no expertise in the matter at hand. Challenges to executive power may succeed (*Youngstown Sheet and Tube v. Sawyer*), especially when the tug of war is between the other two branches or when the judiciary itself has an immediate stake (*United States v. Nixon*). The best single statement of all these issues can be found in *BAKER V. CARR*, the REAPPORTIONMENT case in which the Court found that refusal to reapportion state legislatures involved an equal protection claim that it could legitimately decide. The issue was deemed justiciable, that is, suitable for judicial resolution. The Court has bent the rules at times, most notably in abortion cases (*Roe v. Wade*) in which the plaintiff had clearly resolved a pregnancy long before the Court decided the case. Despite the tenuous link to specific constitutional language, the Court does at times use these rules to avoid an otherwise potentially embarrassing case (*Goldwater v. Carter*).

Section three provides a detailed description of treason. Made leery of royal prerogative in discovering enemies and confiscating property, the framers made standards of treason very difficult to meet. In an early test of this section, Chief Justice Marshall found that Aaron Burr had not committed treason (*United States v. Burr*), a ruling that produced a great partisan outcry from Jeffersonians. Thus, all three sections have produced controversial rulings, many of which enhanced the power of the judiciary itself.

Further reading: Abraham, Henry J. *The Judiciary.* 8th ed. Dubuque, Iowa: Wm. C. Brown, 1987; Carp, Robert A. *Judicial Process in America.* Washington, D.C.: CQ Press, 2004; Hall, Kermit L., ed. *The Oxford Companion to the Supreme Court of the United States.* New York: Oxford University Press, 2002; Kurland, Philip, and Ralph Lerner. *The Founders' Constitution.* Vol. 4. Chicago: University of Chicago Press, 1987.

—Mary C. Thornberry

Articles of Confederation

The Articles of Confederation were the nation's original constitutional system following independence from England. The United States developed and adopted the Articles of Confederation during the Revolutionary War with Great Britain. In 1776, independently selected representatives of the thirteen colonies met as a Continental Congress to adopt the Declaration of Independence. This congress initiated and organized the Revolutionary War, while a committee led by John Dickinson of Delaware drafted the original compact known as the Articles of Confederation.

Until the articles, the thirteen original states were normally called the American Colonies, but the new country in Article I was given the name the United States of America, which is just one of numerous legacies of the original constitution. The first principle of government was stated as follows in Article II: "Each state retains its sovereignty, freedom, and independence, and every power, jurisdiction, and right, which is not by this Confederation expressly delegated to the United States, in Congress assembled." The articles were overwhelmingly a "states' rights" document, because the thirteen colonies fighting for independence were distinct polities with separate governments, each a sovereign state.

Under the Articles of Confederation, Congress consisted of DELEGATES from each of the states selected by the state legislatures of the thirteen states, and these delegates voted as states, not as individuals (thus, there were 13 votes). Measures passed by Congress required nine of 13 votes, but any fundamental alterations in national policy or changes to the articles required unanimity of all 13 states. Congress was a single branch of government, and it had the power to conduct foreign affairs, make treaties, declare war, maintain the military, coin money, and establish post offices. But the articles were a constitution of limited powers under which the national government was constrained by limited fiscal capacity and insufficient administrative structures. Congress could not raise money by collecting taxes, had no control over foreign exchange, and could not force the states to comply with federal laws. Thus, the national government was essentially dependent on the willingness of the states to comply with its measures, and often the states refused to cooperate. This lack of cooperation had the unanimity required to change the articles at their core.

The articles frequently required a specific number of states to vote in favor of any significant legislation in order to pass. Nine, mentioned in several places, was a minimum required to agree to things such as a declaration of war or the admission of new states. As soon as one new state was added, that "nine" would no longer be the two-thirds it was theoretically intended to be, and to comprehensively correct each instance of "nine" would require the assent of all states (as 13 were required to change the articles). Several attempts to change the articles prior to the adoption of the Federalist Constitution had been held up by a single state's refusal to cooperate.

The articles were ratified July 9, 1778, by 10 states (Massachusetts, New York, Pennsylvania, Virginia, North Carolina, South Carolina, Georgia, Connecticut, Rhode Island, and New Hampshire), followed by New Jersey on November 26, 1778, and by Delaware on February 23, 1779. Maryland held off two years more, acceding to them on March 1, 1781. Maryland sought concessions from several large states, most notably the relinquishment of western land claims to the national government. The Revolutionary War ended two years later, in April 1783, and as postwar issues, both economic and political, brought increased pressures on the new governmental system, calls for reform mounted.

The articles contained several flaws in need of reform. The United States had no independent power of taxation, relying on the good faith of the states to pay the national government as requested. In several instances, such requests for funds were ignored by states, and since the national government had no power of enforcement, there was little that could be done. National solvency was in question, which created domestic and foreign economic and political effects.

The articles did not provide sufficient authority for dealing with nonpayment of state debts, resulting in encroachments by the British on the borders set by the Treaty of Paris, as well as by the Spanish on the southern borders of the United States. The United States also had no power to regulate commerce among the states, leading to bitter tariff wars among the states. Combined with inflation and the economic depression that set in after the war ended, an economic crisis paralleled the political crisis as efforts to reform the articles were continually frustrated.

In January 1786, Virginia called for a meeting of the states at Annapolis to discuss modification of the articles, but this was attended only by five state delegates. Afterward, a popular uprising began in Massachusetts led by the bankrupt farmer Daniel Shays. For six months, Shays and his rebels terrorized the Massachusetts countryside and met with ineffective national response. The inability of U.S. forces to deal effectively with Shays's Rebellion combined with the mounting economic and political pressures to change the articles. In May, Congress called a convention in Philadelphia for the purpose of proposing amendments to the articles, which was attended by 12 states. The result was a protracted struggle between Federalists and ANTI-FEDERALISTS that resulted in eventual ratification of the present U.S. Constitution, which displaced the articles as the supreme national constitution in 1789.

Further reading: Adams, Willi Paul. *The First American Constitutions.* Lanham, Md.: Rowman & Littlefield, 2001; Bradford, M. E. *Original Intentions: On the Making and Ratification of the United States Constitution.* Athens: University of Georgia Press, 1993; Jensen, Merrill. *The Articles of Confederation: An Interpretation of the Social-Constitutional History of the American Revolution.* Madison: University of Wisconsin Press, 1970.

—Michael W. Hail

at-large elections

At-large elections are those in which the entire body of voters votes as one electoral district. Today, in states with small populations, such as Alaska and Wyoming, the House seat is voted upon at-large, as those states have only one representative. Until 1843, when Congress passed the Congressional Redistricting Act, most states used at-large districts to choose their members of the House of Representatives. From 1787 to 1843, all but five states elected members of Congress based on at-large districts. In some larger cities in America city council elections are currently held on an at-large basis.

During the Progressive Era of the early 20th century, structural reformers emphasized at-large elections as a way to reduce the corruption of cities. To reduce the electoral hold over certain ward seats and to ensure that city councillors had support throughout an entire city, many cities instituted at-large elections. To support their arguments and to give the movement a greater acceptability among the ELECTORATE, the Progressives noted the similarity between city officials elected at-large and U.S. senators, who are better able to guide the entire nation instead of focusing on the often petty, parochial goals of the House.

The move to at-large elections succeeded in reducing the power of neighborhood political organizations. Unfortunately, at-large elections also reduced the power of minorities. As minorities tended to congregate in neighborhoods, they were simply out-voted by the majority in city-wide races. Thus, minorities who were able to elect someone from their neighborhood were often unable to attain the necessary electoral numbers to elect one of their neighbors in a citywide election.

The U.S. Supreme Court decided that election plans that might dilute minority voting strength could be successfully challenged (e.g., *Thornberg v. Gingles* 1986; *Gomez v. Watsonville* 1988). Because of these decisions, at-large districts are coming under increasing legal pressure to solve the problem of minority underrepresentation. Solutions used by cities include returning to SINGLE-MEMBER DISTRICTS, eliminating at-large districts, and creating a hybrid of the two systems.

The voting system in Seattle illustrates this point. The city councilors are elected at-large. Responding to charges that this system inhibits minority representation, Seattle placed a measure before the voters in the election of 2003 to decide if the city should retain its at-large districts or should return to the neighborhood-based ward districts. The citizens narrowly voted to retain the current at-large elections even though they kept Seattle in an ever-shrinking minority of cities that use at-large elections.

Further reading: Brockington, David, Todd Donovan, Shaun Bowler, and Robert Brischetto. "Minority Representation under Cumulative and Limited Voting." *Journal of Politics* 60 (1998): 1,108–1,125; Davidson, Chandler, and George Korbel. "At-Large Elections and Minority-Group Representation: A Re-Examination of Historical and Contemporary Evidence." *Journal of Politics* 43 (1981): 982–1,005; Welch, Susan. "The Impact of At-Large Elections on the Representation of Blacks and Hispanics." *Journal of Politics* 52 (1990): 1,050–1,076.

—Ole J. Forsberg

Australian ballot

The Australian ballot is a BALLOT that assures the privacy of voters; it is created and distributed by the government for the election of public officials and is a staple of modern American VOTING SYSTEMS. The Australian ballot is unique in its requirement that the government print the ballot, since parties in America before the 20th century often printed ballots themselves. These ballots were often color coded or unique in size or shape so that interested parties could easily tell which candidate individuals supported.

First introduced in 1856 in Victoria and South Australia, the secret ballot quickly spread throughout Australia, and by the turn of the 20th century it was used throughout the country. Its inception in America came in 1892, when all states adopted the Australian ballot in lieu of ballots distributed by private parties and individuals. The original experiment, which in the United States was designed as a Progressive reform to wrest control away from partisan political machines, was not without its problems, as citizens found the system overly cumbersome. Instead of picking up ballots from a local candidate or party, or simply writing up their own ballots at home, voters had to wait in line at designated polling places in order to cast their votes.

Today, the voting booth, a secret balloting system paid for by the government, is the modern extension of the Australian ballot. The fact that government entities now maintain voting systems, however, has brought about new controversy as varied types of voting systems, including punch cards and BUTTERFLY BALLOTS, have fallen under scrutiny in recent elections. These controversies have prompted extensive lawsuits primarily at the expense of state governments.

Further reading: Fredman, Lionel E. *The Australian Ballot: The Story of an American Reform.* East Lansing: Michigan State Press, 1968; Rusk, Jerrold G. "The Effect of the Australian Ballot Reform on Split Ticket Voting: 1876–1908." *American Political Science Review* 64 (1970): 1,220–1,238; Senior, E. D. *Australian Systems of Voting; The Ballot and the Scrutiny.* Sydney: Current Book Distributors, 1946.

—Jeremy B. Lupoli

B

Baker v. Carr **369 U.S. 186** (1962)

Under the directives of its state constitution, the Tennessee legislature is required to reapportion its state house and senate every 10 years, following the national CENSUS. Yet, after its REAPPORTIONMENT of 1901, the legislature refused to reapportion any longer. This decision had grave repercussions. As time passed, the great migrations from rural areas to urban centers within the state gradually rendered the 1901 lines obsolete.

Reformers sought to prod the legislators into action with help from the state supreme court. The court, however, refused to intervene, as did the U.S. Supreme Court. The argument against intervention was that this was a classic "political thicket," explained Supreme Court Justice Frankfurter in *Colegrove v. Green* (1946). Dissatisfied citizens were encouraged to take their complaints to their state legislature or to invoke the "ample powers of Congress." Federal courts at the time were not willing to partake in the campaign against malapportioned districts.

The climate changed by the late 1950s, as a federal district court in Minnesota held, in *Magraw v. Donovan,* that the federal courts had jurisdiction "because of the federal constitutional issue asserted." The impetus of this opinion offered a glimmer of hope to the Tennessee reformers, who then brought a second challenge to the Tennessee REDISTRICTING plan. A three-judge federal district court disagreed once again with this challenge, citing the strong precedent against judicial intervention. Ultimately, it would be up to the Supreme Court to decide the matter.

The choices facing the Supreme Court were made more difficult in light of the clear unfairness reflected by the existing districting plan. On the side of nonintervention stood Justice Frankfurter and, at the conference after the first oral argument, Justices Clark and Harlan. On the side of intervention stood Justices Douglas and Black, who had dissented in *Colegrove v. Green,* as well as Justice Brennan and Chief Justice Warren. Justice Whittaker sided with the latter group, yet refused to join a five-member majority. The

remaining justice, Potter Stewart, pushed for a reargument, and the Court so ordered a week later.

After the second oral argument, Justice Stewart joined a fragile Court majority in favor of Court intervention. Justice Clark sided with the Frankfurter camp, since the plaintiffs could still "invoke the ample powers of Congress" for relief. He also noted that the plaintiffs had not made MALAPPORTIONMENT a campaign issue. These two facts led him to the view that the plaintiffs had not exhausted all possible avenues of relief. Yet, while in the process of writing a separate dissent, Justice Clark changed his mind. He came to understand the case as one presenting a classic lock-up scenario, whereby the people of Tennessee could do nothing in the face of a recalcitrant legislature.

As soon as Justice Clark changed his mind, the rest of the pieces quickly fell into place. Up to seven justices (assuming Justice Goldberg followed through on his earlier stance and Justice Stewart stayed on board) would side with the plaintiffs and open the federal courts to voting rights claimants. The opinion itself was uninspiring, and it ultimately remanded the case to the lower court for further proceedings consistent with the decision. This approach immediately raised the question at the heart of the academic and juridical debate post-*Baker*. What is the standard for lower courts to examine redistricting plans under the Equal Protection Clause?

The Court's words on this score are widely quoted: "Judicial standards under the Equal Protection Clause are well-developed and familiar, and it has been open to courts since the enactment of the FOURTEENTH AMENDMENT to determine, if on the particular facts they must, that a discrimination reflects no policy, but simply arbitrary and capricious action." This sentence may be understood in at least two ways. The leading understanding of the Baker standard contends that this "murky" sentence offered redistricters and lower courts very little guidance in carrying out the promise of *Baker*. This reading is bolstered by the Court's subsequent decision in REYNOLDS V. SIMS (1964), when it pronounced the "one person, one vote" standard.

A second understanding looks instead to the facts at issue in *Baker*, as well as Justice Clark's change of heart. The districts under scrutiny in *Baker* had been last drawn decades ago, and the population disparities thus made very little sense. During the second oral argument, in fact, the Court asked the lawyer for the state whether he could defend and justify the lines as they then existed, and he confessed that perhaps the legislature could do it, but he could not. The disparities reflected what Justice Clark labeled a "crazy quilt." In general, the Court may have simply demanded from the state a legitimate interest in support of the plan. Further, it must also be reasonably understood as carrying out the interest asserted. This was clearly something that Tennessee could not do. Notably, the lower courts that heard challenges to state redistricting plans soon after *Baker* understood the *Baker* standard precisely along these lines.

The legacy of *Baker v. Carr* cannot be overstated. This case opened the doors of the federal courts to redistricting claims, but it accomplished much more. Thanks to *Baker*, the Court is now an active player in controversies over the law of democracy, from BALLOT ACCESS to campaign finance, racial and political GERRYMANDERing, and the associational rights of political parties, to name only a few. In its most extreme rendition, *BUSH V. GORE* (2000) owes its existence, if indirectly, to *Baker v. Carr*. The case has also had a lasting effect in political culture as reflected by the major political parties. In removing the "political questions" obstacle, *Baker* ensured that the political parties may involve the federal courts when dissatisfied by political outcomes. This is seen often in redistricting controversies, though not only there.

All the same, *Baker* must be hailed as a great moment in the history of the Court. In intervening as it did, the Court offered the judiciary as an option when recalcitrant political actors behave in self-interested ways, to the detriment of the public. In light of the grave and extreme conditions witnessed by the middle of the century and the degree of inactivity seen across the country, *Baker v. Carr* was a case whose time had come.

Further reading: Katzenbach, Nicholas B. "Some Reflections on Baker v. Carr." *Vanderbilt Law Review* 15 (1962): 829, 832–833; Lewis, Anthony. "Legislative Apportionment and the Federal Courts." *Harvard Law Review* 71 (1958): 1,057; Supreme Court Historical Society. Available online. URL: http://www.supremecourthistory.org. Accessed August 10, 2005.

—Luis Fuentes-Rohwer

ballot

Ballots are lists of all of the official candidates and ballot measures under consideration in a given election. Ballots can have many formats. Traditional paper ballots are organized by party or by office. Voters mark a box next to the name of the candidates for whom they want to vote and, when finished, put the ballot in a locked ballot box. When the polls are closed, the ballot boxes are unlocked, the ballots are removed, and all the votes are tallied. Paper ballots are the most inexpensive type of ballot but also require the most labor to tally. The tallying of the votes is also more prone to counting errors than other types of ballot because of the likelihood of human error. However, there is a physical record of how each voter voted, so RECOUNTS, if necessary, can easily occur.

To improve the accuracy of the vote counting procedure, machine readable ballots are often used. Machine readable ballots can use optical character recognition (OCR) technology whereby a computer reads a pencil mark in a box next to candidate names or use punch card technology whereby voters punch out preperforated holes next to candidate names. Machines read the holes in the ballots and tally votes based on the holes.

Machine readable ballots come in many forms, including the so-called BUTTERFLY BALLOT. A butterfly ballot is a ballot that looks like a book with the names of candidates and offices printed in the book with holes next to each candidate's name. The individual voter's ballot is a separate piece of paper with preperforated holes that line up with the holes in the butterfly ballot "book." This ballot is slid into the butterfly "book," and voters then use a small tool to punch out the perforation next to the name of each candidate for whom they want to vote. The ballot is removed and the votes are counted by a machine that registers all the holes in the ballot as votes for individual candidates.

The butterfly ballot was at the center of the controversy in the 2000 PRESIDENTIAL ELECTION in Florida because of claims that the holes were not lined up properly, causing people to cast votes for a candidate other than the one they intended to vote for. An additional problem was that the tool used to punch out the perforations did not function properly, meaning that the hole was not completely punched out in some instances. This caused the machines to erroneously not count votes because of "hanging" (three sides of the perforated hole detached but not the fourth), "dimpled" (the perforations are still largely intact, but there is a small indentation in the perforated hole), or "pregnant" (the perforations are still largely intact, but there is a pronounced indentation in the perforated hole) CHADs. The ballots were then individually inspected to try to determine the "intent" of the voter.

To further increase the speed and accuracy of the vote counting process, alternative ballot forms are used. While there is no physical ballot with alternative ballot forms, the layout of the candidates for office mimics the paper ballot. Voters simply flip a switch next to their choices or use touch screens to select the candidates. When they complete the selection process they pull a lever or confirm their selections, and the votes are cast. There is some concern that the computerized ballots do not have a physical record with which to conduct recounts.

Ballots are generally arranged following one of two formats: the party column ballot or the office block ballot. The party column ballot lists all candidates for office from a party in the same column. Party column ballots make it easier for voters to vote a straight ticket. Voters can simply run down the column and check off all the candidates for a particular party. Party column ballots also often have a "straight party vote" option whereby voters can mark one box that casts a vote for every candidate from the party of their choice.

The office block ballot arranges candidates not by party but by office. Candidates for a particular office are arranged in blocks together with their party affiliation indicated next to their names. This makes it harder to cast a vote for all the candidates of a single party. If a voter wishes to vote a straight ticket, he or she needs to go through the ballot and search for the candidates of a particular party and then check each candidate individually. Many office block ballots now also include a straight ticket option at the top of the ballot.

NONPARTISAN ELECTION ballots look much like office block ballots except they do not have any party designation next to the candidates' names. Nonpartisan ballots are primarily used in local elections and judicial elections to depoliticize the selection process.

The ballots used today in the United States replaced the "ticket" system used in the 18th and 19th centuries. With the ticket system, parties printed what were often color-coded ballots or tickets, which they distributed to party members. Party members would take their ticket to a polling place and deposit their ticket (or often tickets) into a box in plain view of anyone who wanted to monitor how people voted. Party organizers could easily see how people voted because the tickets of one party were distinct from those of other parties. It also provided easy opportunities for multiple voting and other fraudulent electoral activities. The AUSTRALIAN BALLOT is a ballot printed and controlled by the state. When voters arrive at the polling place, they are given one ballot by an election official. They then fill out the ballot in secret.

Further reading: Amy, Douglas James. *Behind the Ballot Box: A Citizen's Guide to Voting Systems.* Westport, Conn.: Greenwood Press, 2000; Federal Election Commission. Available online. URL: http://www.fec.gov. Accessed August 10, 2005.

—Scott Dittloff

ballot access

Ballot access is the legal standing given to candidates or political parties to appear on voters' BALLOTs in each jurisdiction of the United States. Typically, access to ballots is restricted to candidates who meet signature requirements or pay a filing fee, or both. Ballot access laws vary across states and jurisdictions and differ by level of office and by party status.

Ballot access laws can affect the electoral process in meaningful ways, and scholars have demonstrated systematic effects. For example, by tightening access established parties can discourage new parties or independent challengers, thereby giving a distinct advantage to incumbents and major parties. This may have a chilling effect on policy by favoring the status quo over new parties and candidates with bold new ideas. Alternatively, easy access may encourage unqualified candidates and could potentially confuse voters with frivolous choices. During the 2003 California gubernatorial RECALL election, for example, more than 135 candidates appeared on the ballot (not including write-ins), many of them poorly qualified.

From 1888 to 1931, states realized that the major parties could stifle competition by limiting access to ballots. As the two major political parties we know today became institutionalized, ballot access became increasingly restrictive. In 1924, a candidate could appear on the presidential ballot in all 48 states by obtaining roughly 50,000 signatures (or 0.25 percent of the total number of votes cast in the last election). By 1980, a prospective candidate needed more than 680,000 signatures (adjusted to 48 states) (or 0.75 percent of the total number of previous votes). Essentially, it had become three times as difficult to appear on the ballot in those same 48 states. This trend toward more restrictive access continued until the early 1970s, when several significant U.S. Supreme Court decisions signaled a shift toward more open access.

Lawsuits over ballot access generally involve two basic constitutional rights: free speech and equal protection. Proponents claim that the right to appear on a ballot and the right to solicit votes is protected by the First Amendment as free speech. They claim that citizens are entitled to vote for candidates of their choice. Further, the FOURTEENTH AMENDMENT's equal protection clause guarantees that those seeking access to the ballot have the same rights as those already on the ballot. It was this argument that played a central role in *BULLOCK V. CARTER* (1972), a Supreme Court case that significantly expanded candidates' rights. The Court's holding established the principle that states could not use excessive filing fees (or filing fees alone) as a means of distinguishing "serious" candidates from the others. This was a significant step for minor parties and independent candidates because it promised relief from excessive filing fees and sent the message to the states that access had become too restrictive.

Two years later in *Lubin v. Parish*, the Supreme Court again increased protections by extending to primaries the state laws that applied to general ELECTIONS. Years after states had steadily tightened ballot access, the courts began to exert influence. The Supreme Court also ruled that filing fees are unconstitutional unless states that impose such fees provide low-income candidates who cannot afford to pay ("paupers") with alternative ways to gain access to the ballot. Since 1974, however, courts have been reluctant to enforce or define "excessive" filing fees.

In addition to filing fees, there are sometimes additional requirements prospective candidates and minor parties must satisfy. Many states require that a certain number of signatures be collected by the prospective candidate or party from registered voters in that state. The number of signatures required can range from 275 in Tennessee to more than 167,000 in Florida. (There are differences in how many signatures an independent candidate needs to be included on a ballot versus a POLITICAL PARTY on that same ballot.) Some states restrict who can sign a petition. In Texas, for example, petitions for new parties cannot include signatures from anyone who voted in either major party PRIMARY that year. In Virginia, a petitioner can seek signatures only in his or her own CONGRESSIONAL DISTRICT. In Oklahoma, candidates can appear on the ballot for a small fee unless those candidates are Libertarian or REFORM PARTY contenders, in which case they must obtain 51,781 signatures.

Some states may also require candidates to pay to have signatures on their petitions verified, creating additional obstacles and tightening ballot access. Florida has charged candidates $.10 per name to verify signatures. With 167,000 required signatures for minor party registration, a $16,700 fee can be a significant hurdle for a fledgling party.

Proponents claim that it is in the best interest and spirit of democracy for ballot access to be as open as possible. They argue that open access expands options for voters and permits candidate choices to be narrowed by natural—not artificial—selection. On the opposite end of the spectrum, defenders of stricter ballot access insist that restrictive laws produce more serious, committed candidates with broader appeal.

Scholars have demonstrated that ballot access limitations affect electoral competition. Recent studies provide evidence that restrictive ballot access laws (both signature requirements and filing fees) erect substantial barriers to entry and hamper both major and minor party participation in electoral contests.

Further reading: Lawson, Kaye. "How State Laws Undermine Parties." In A. James Reichley, ed., *Elections American Style*. Washington, D.C.: The Brookings Institution, 1987; Stratmann, Thomas. "Ballot Access Restrictions and Candidate Entry in Elections." *European Journal of Political Economy* 18 (2004): 1–15.
—Costas Panagopoulos

ballot initiative

Ballot initiatives are proposals for statutes, resolutions, or constitutional amendments that are *initiated* by citizens and placed on the BALLOT in an election for the people to adopt or reject. The ballot initiative is one of several forms

of direct democracy and the only form that allows citizens to both create and approve laws, largely supplanting the roles of the legislative and the executive branches of government in the process of creating public policy.

There is great variation in the use of ballot initiatives within the United States. State-level ballot initiatives are authorized in 24 states: Alaska, Arizona, Arkansas, California, Colorado, Florida, Idaho, Illinois, Maine, Massachusetts, Michigan, Mississippi, Missouri, Montana, Nebraska, Nevada, North Dakota, Ohio, Oklahoma, Oregon, South Dakota, Utah, Washington, and Wyoming. However, the highest use states have been Arizona, California, Colorado, Oregon, and Washington. California consistently ranks as the top initiative state, with several initiatives at each statewide PRIMARY and GENERAL ELECTION, and Oregon usually ranks second. According to a 2001–02 survey by the International City/County Management Association, about 58 percent of cities have provisions for initiatives. There is no federal provision for a national ballot initiative. In states that do allow ballot initiatives, there are many differences as to the type of initiative, the requirements for ballot qualification, and even the issues that ballot initiatives are allowed to address.

There are several types of ballot initiatives, distinguished primarily by whether the process allows for statutory initiatives or constitutional initiatives. Statutory initiatives create or change laws or resolutions, while constitutional initiatives amend the state's constitution. A distinction can also be made regarding whether the initiative is direct or indirect. Direct initiatives allow the proposals to go directly on the ballot, while indirect initiatives require that the proposal be submitted to the legislature prior to the appearance on the ballot. Initiative states can allow any combination of the above four categories, but most specify both direct statutory and constitutional initiatives.

The requirements for ballot qualification (getting an initiative proposal on the ballot) vary by state, but typically include a signature threshold and time limits. A number of signatures of registered voters must be gathered within a certain period of time. The number of signatures for statewide ballot initiatives is most commonly 10-20 percent of the number of voters in the most recent gubernatorial election, and the time period ranges from as long as four years to as short as two months. Some states require that a certain number of signatures be gathered in a percentage of counties or election districts, while others require no geographical distribution of signatures. In addition, each state has different technical qualifications in place, such as proper titling and formatting, whether or not the initiative can cover more than one issue, or if certain issues, such as revenues and budgeting, are off limits to the initiative process.

Union, populist, progressive, and agrarian reform movements began advocating for the initiative in the 1880s, using

Swiss direct democracy procedures as models. Nebraska allowed the initiative in city charters beginning in 1897. The initiative was first adopted into a state constitution in 1898 in South Dakota, and most of the adopting states added the initiative to their state constitutions during the Progressive Era. Florida and Illinois adopted the initiative in the 1970s. Mississippi was the last state to adopt the initiative, in 1992. Although there were U.S. Senate hearings in the 1970s on proposals for a national initiative and the REFORM PARTY included the national initiative in its 2000 platform, there has not been major support for a constitutional amendment to establish the initiative on the federal level.

Use of the ballot initiative has varied over the years. In the early 20th century, initiative states used ballot initiatives with regularity, but in the post–World War II era use tapered off significantly. In the 1970s, the frequency of initiative use climbed, exceeding the level of use early in the century, and has remained consistent. Some states use the initiative sparingly, while others use initiatives frequently. For example, South Dakotans placed just one initiative on ballots between the years 1950 and 1969. By contrast, California and Oregon often experience more than 10 ballot initiatives per election period. However, fewer than half of the initiatives that appear on ballots gain approval by voters. This varies by state as well, but few states exceed 50 percent approval rates, and those tend to be states that are among the lowest in usage.

A number of vocal critics argue that the initiative process has become corrupted by special interests. There are established signature gathering firms and prominent initiative activists in the high-use initiative states. Entertainment figures such as the actor-director Rob Reiner and the actor Arnold Schwarzenegger, before he ran for governor, successfully sponsored initiatives in California. According to the political scientist Richard Ellis, about a third of California initiatives in recent decades have been sponsored by elected officials or candidates. Well-funded proponents can generally qualify their measures for the ballot, and campaign spending on ballot measures, unlike candidate elections, is not subject to CAMPAIGN CONTRIBUTION LIMITS, creating at least the perception that money is having a significant influence on the process.

Critics also point to issue elections as low-turnout and low-information elections that do not necessarily reflect the preferences of the public in the spirit of direct democracy. It has been argued that citizens lack the knowledge and the expertise that the legislatures have in regard to creating laws and will potentially create bad or unconstitutional law. To further complicate matters, many statutes passed by initiative require funding and enabling legislation, which is the responsibility of the legislature and the executive branch, limiting the impact of citizen-led legislation.

There are additional criticisms about policy outcomes. Unlike legislatures that must pass balanced budgets, voters can simultaneously restrict taxes and revenues while approving new programs and bonds. California and Oregon have most obviously suffered from resulting structural budget problems. Voters in several states passed initiatives sponsored by gaming interests that do not appear to provide reasonable tax revenues or safeguards against corruption. There are also concerns about the differences between state legislature constituencies, based on CENSUS populations, and statewide electorates, based on the number of participating voters. For example, California governor Pete Wilson successfully used the initiative process in the early 1990s to pass several ballot measures that would not have been supported by the state legislature. Finally, controversial but successful initiatives are often subject to expensive and time-consuming litigation, undermining the legitimacy of the initiative process and voter trust in political institutions.

Despite the fear regarding ballot initiatives, most studies suggest that the influence of money over initiative elections has been overstated. In fact, many prominent issues have been decided by states using ballot initiatives. Contemporary issues involved include gun control, affirmative action programs, medicinal use of marijuana, a variety of tax issues, and, most recently, issues surrounding same-sex marriage. Historically, these measures granted women the vote in initiative states, fought child labor, and have been used for and against prohibition. Moreover, ballot initiatives are allowed in thousands of municipal, county, and special use governments and are used commonly to resolve policy issues such as transportation planning, land use and conservation, parks and recreation facilities, and public safety. The continued use of the ballot initiative to resolve issues of public significance will undoubtedly shape future public policy in the states.

Further reading: Bowler, Shaun, Todd Donovan, and Caroline J. Tolbert, eds. *Citizens as Legislators: Direct Democracy in the United States.* Columbus: Ohio State University Press, 1998; Magleby, David B. *Direct Legislation: Voting on Ballot Propositions in the United States.* Baltimore: Johns Hopkins University Press, 1984; Sabato, Larry J., Bruce A. Larson, and Howard R. Ernst, eds. *Dangerous Democracy? The Battle over Ballot Initiatives in America.* Lanham, Md.: Rowman & Littlefield, 2001; Schmidt, David D. *Citizen Lawmakers: The Ballot Initiative Revolution.* Philadelphia: Temple University Press, 1989.

—Marcia L. Godwin and Joel A. Rayan

ballot initiatives, affirmative action

Affirmative action BALLOT INITIATIVES use the mechanisms of direct democracy (i.e., statewide ballot initiatives) to eliminate or severely curtail the use of affirmative action policies in a particular state. Affirmative action is a collection of policies that give preferential treatment to people based on their membership in a particular group, such as those defined by sex, ethnicity, or race. Affirmative action has been instituted by universities, businesses, and governments to help overcome the effects of past discrimination, by favoring certain groups of people in college admissions, hiring, and promotion, and the awarding of government contracts.

Since its inception in the 1960s, affirmative action has been widely controversial. Critics view it as a form of "reverse discrimination" that violates the principle that all individuals are equal under the law and that actually perpetuates the racial distinctions it intends to overcome. Supporters of the policy argue that it takes time to overcome the momentum of history, and the policy is a necessary step so long as discrimination continues to exist in the country and the remnants of discrimination persist (i.e., vast inequalities exist among the various groups).

The battle for and against affirmative action has led to contentious battles between those who support the policy and those seeking to end race-based preferences. In 1996, California voters approved Proposition 209 (California Civil Rights Initiative), a ballot initiative that intended to end affirmative action throughout the state. Its wording specifically prohibited governments from "discriminat[ing] against, or grant[ing] preferential treatment to, any individual or group on the basis of race, sex, color, ethnicity or national origin in the operation of public employment, public education or public contracting." It went into effect on August 28 despite challenges by minority groups. On September 4, the U.S. Supreme Court refused an emergency request for a stay of enforcement of the new law. Two months later the Supreme Court again refused to hear a challenge to Proposition 209, upholding the federal court ruling that the ban was not unconstitutional. While the University of California system no longer considers race as an admission criterion, administrators still take into account extenuating circumstances, such as poverty and upbringing, in selecting prospective students.

The second successful anti–affirmative action ballot initiative was Proposition 200. The goal of this state of Washington initiative was similar to Proposition 209. It aimed to ban the state from giving preferential treatment to specific groups of individuals. Before this initiative took form, Washington's 86 percent white population had elected African Americans as mayor of Seattle and as King County executive; in 1996, voters made Gary Locke the first Chinese-American governor of a mainland state. Given the state's history, both sponsors and opponents of Proposition 200 believed that the passing of this initiative would result in clones being offered in other states and increase the chances of similar national legislation being passed.

This initiative received a large contribution from Ward Connerly, a Sacramento businessman and conservative activist, who was also the chief sponsor for the previous California initiative. He gave $170,000 through his American Civil Rights Institute to hire a professional signature-gathering organization in Tacoma. Soon afterward, Americans for Hope, Growth and Opportunity also donated in-kind support valued at $35,000. Meanwhile, there was fierce opposition against Proposition 200. Opponents included Governor Locke, who benefited from affirmative action in gaining admission to Yale Law School, Senator Patty Murray, and most other Democratic elected officials in the state. Moreover, most of the state's major newspapers opposed the measure, as did business giants including Microsoft Corp., Boeing Co., Starbucks Coffee Co., U.S. Bank, and Eddie Bauer, Inc. Nevertheless, Connerly gained an edge when state officials approved the use of the California initiative language on the Washington BALLOT, which avoided mentioning the phrase *affirmative action*, and in spite of the difficult tussle Washington state voters passed Proposition 200 in 1998.

The ballot initiatives against affirmative action have not all been successful. In 2000, the Florida Supreme Court forced Connerly to abandon a similar plan for a statewide measure in Florida. In June 2003, the Supreme Court struck down the University of Michigan's undergraduate admissions policy, which awarded 20 points for underrepresented minorities. The high court, however, upheld the law school's admissions policies, which use race as an admissions factor. The Court's decision failed to resolve the long-standing debate over affirmative action. Immediately after the ruling, affirmative action supporters in California and Washington began exploring ways they might use ballot initiatives to lift the bans on racial preference in admissions. Also, officials at the University of Georgia and University of Texas, whose court-ordered bans were lifted by the ruling, announced plans to reintroduce preference programs.

Ballot initiatives are attractive now because supporters on both sides believe that the Michigan decision may resonate in areas outside higher education. Employers, for instance, may have a higher comfort level in their private affirmative action programs. The ballot campaign, on the other hand, could cause a headache for conservative candidates, because such initiatives are polarizing and tend to increase VOTER TURNOUT among racial minorities and other Democratic-leaning constituencies. The situation would become even more difficult if the measure were on several ballots at the same time, thereby increasing the regional and national attention given to the issue.

Further reading: Sowell, Thomas. *Affirmative Action around the World: An Empirical Study.* New Haven, Conn.: Yale University Press, 2004; Curry, George, and Cornel West. *The Affirmative Action Debate.* Reading, Mass.: Addison-Wesley, 1996.

—Taiyu Chen

ballot initiatives, campaign reform

Campaign reform is a term that refers to alterations to the processes surrounding elections and campaigns for public office or publicly decided issues. Many significant aspects of campaign reform have originally found support and strength at the ballot box, at both the state and local levels. Suffragettes and prohibitionists worked, often in tandem, to secure the vote for women in state and local elections and to abolish the production and sale of alcohol in the late 19th and early 20th centuries, years before such policies were enacted nationally. More recently, two prominent campaign issues have been reformed by way of the ballot initiative: TERM LIMITS for state legislators and publicly funded election campaigns, otherwise known as clean elections.

Achieving political reform through the popular initiative process is a well used tactic for those seeking to circumvent the status quo maintained by existing power structures. Most notable, perhaps, is California's Proposition 13, the 1978 state constitutional amendment limiting property tax increases in the state and requiring public approval of any future tax increases. Proposition 13 received nearly two-thirds approval in the state and garnered national attention, with many initiative-wielding states following the example over the next several years. Although Proposition 13 is an example of political reform that is unrelated to campaign reform, the underlying premise of the action remains relevant to efforts to achieve reform of an aspect of campaigns: the lack of responsiveness by lawmakers to public concern for reform.

Imposing term limits on state lawmakers represents a prime example of elected officials resisting a public desire to make changes to the electoral system. Term limits restrict the number of terms for which any individual can hold a single publicly elected office. While nearly two-thirds of the states have term limits for governors and other popularly elected members of the executive branch, limiting the length of service for state legislators was not implemented until 1990, when voters in California and Colorado approved constitutional amendment ballot measures to restrict the tenure of legislators. Between 1990 and 2000, 15 other states imposed such restrictions, 13 by ballot measure.

Resistance to legislative term limits by state legislatures is understandable; many lawmakers would naturally oppose such efforts in order to preserve any effectiveness or legislative acumen developed through years of experience. Proponents of term limits have argued that lawmakers are loathe to relinquish the power they may have accumulated through those years of service. Advocates for term limits have primarily taken the route of the popular initiative to enact the restrictions, arguing that the lawmakers are unlikely to impose such restrictions on themselves. However, not all term limit measures were enacted through the ballot box. The Oklahoma state legislature approved term limits in 1990, effective in 2004, and the Utah state legis-lature did so in 1994 but repealed the constitutional amendment in 2003 before it could take effect. (Utah does not allow for constitutional amendments by way of popular initiative.)

Another significant recent campaign reform waged through the initiative process has been campaign financing. The movement for public financing of campaigns has been in existence for many years, and, in fact, presidential candidates benefit from public MATCHING FUNDS in each PRESIDENTIAL ELECTION. On the state level, however, public funding for electoral campaigns has been thrust into the forefront, with five states approving "clean elections" by ballot initiative or REFERENDUM since 1998. The North Carolina legislature passed statewide campaign reform legislation in 2002 (the only state legislature to do so), and similar efforts are underway in 36 other states, by both popular initiative and referendum and by legislative action.

Arizona and Maine were the first states to pass publicly financed campaign legislation, both by popular initiative. The system requires candidates to gather a large number of minimal donations from their CONSTITUENCY to be eligible for public financing. Once eligible, candidates accepting public financing must adhere to strict spending guidelines and accounting and disclosure procedures. The system is available to any statewide or legislative candidate, yet is voluntary, and no candidate is compelled to participate. Proponents of this legislation suggest that public financing will limit the amount of money spent by campaigns, reduce the influence of economically prominent special interests, and provide a level "playing field" for a wider range of candidates, especially from THIRD PARTIES.

Opponents claim that limitations to campaign funding constitute a restriction on political expression, a violation of the First Amendment right to free speech. Public campaign finance, opponents suggest, is equivalent to forcing individuals in the public to support political views and candidates that they may not agree with. Further, adversaries of public financing suggest that it will do little, if anything, to alter the relationship between special interests and the behavior of individual legislators. Many candidates who decline to participate say they are able to more effectively raise funds privately.

Clean elections in both Maine and Arizona faced many obstacles to their implementation. Opponents have challenged public financing in the courts, attempted to weaken its provisions in the legislatures, and attempted to nullify the programs with countermeasures in subsequent elections, yet no public financing program has been eliminated or seriously diminished. While campaign finance reform efforts are not exclusive to states wielding the initiative process, it is in those states and by the method of citizen-led legislation that these and other efforts at fundamental reform to the system of electoral campaigns have often found their best and most successful staging grounds.

Further reading: Carey, John M., Richard G. Niemi, and Lynda W. Powell. *Term Limits in State Legislatures.* Chicago: University of Chicago Press, 2000; Sabato, Larry J., Howard R. Ernst, and Bruce A. Larson, eds. *Dangerous Democracy? The Battle over Ballot Initiatives in America.* Lanham, Md.: Rowman & Littlefield, 2001.

—Joel A. Rayan

ballot initiatives, environmental issues

Ballot initiatives on environmental issues are considered to be an indicator of the constituents' readiness to support and pay for environmental reforms. Using a BALLOT initiative, the voters in a state or locality can propose that an environmental issue be considered either (1) by the legislature or (2) by the people in a REFERENDUM, or direct vote, on a law or amendment. The procedures involved in an environmental ballot initiative vary from state to state and locality to locality. In addition, statewide ballot initiatives are mostly a western phenomenon, and not all states and localities offer their citizens the chance to vote on environmental policy issues.

During the 1990s, the environmentally related ballot initiatives included efforts to minimize air pollution, limit timber harvesting and eliminate clear-cutting practices, ban certain types of commercial fishing nets and curtail fishery harvests, and improve water quality in rivers and streams by prohibiting certain mining and agricultural practices. Other topics that were under consideration included bans on certain types of hunting and trapping practices, efforts to close nuclear power plants and prevent the importation of hazardous waste, and the prohibition of new billboards. Some of the most popular initiatives at both the state and local levels dealt with urban sprawl and open space issues, such as developing growth management plans, establishing land trust programs, and funding the maintenance and/or acquisition of parks and other open spaces.

According to the Initiative and Referendum Institute at the University of Southern California, 16 states introduced some form of ballot initiative pertaining to environmental reforms, nuclear policies, or animal welfare from 1990 to 2000. Oregon (14 initiatives), California (nine initiatives), Colorado (seven initiatives), and Arizona (six initiatives) had the most statewide votes on environmental ballot initiatives during this period. Other states that had direct ballot initiatives during the 1990s included Florida, Idaho, Missouri, Montana, North Dakota, South Dakota, and Washington. Five other states, Alaska, Maine, Massachusetts, Michigan, and Ohio, had indirect ballot initiatives whereby the state legislature deliberated on a proposed amendment or statute before placing it on the ballot for voter consideration. These statewide environmental initiatives had a mixed success rate; of the 68 initiatives that were voted on during the 1990s, only 28 (approximately 41 percent) were passed.

Ballot measures have been used since the early 1900s to influence environmental policy. In 1924, for example, Californians voted to ban all dams on the Klamath River. Prior to this date, only 10 other environmental initiatives had been on a ballot, six of which were in Arizona and four in Oregon. Environmental ballot initiatives were proposed at low levels through the early 1960s, but the concept was given new life in the 1970s.

Between 1970 and the early 1990s, the use of ballot initiatives grew as environmentalists worked to preserve open spaces, protect wild and scenic rivers, and stall the growth of the nuclear industry in the West. The campaigns behind these initiatives were low-budget affairs that were used when state legislatures appeared to be "captured" by a special interest. During the 1970s and 1980s, 76 statewide environmental initiatives were placed on the ballot in 16 different states. Not all of these efforts were successful; for example, an initiative that would have dedicated portions of the Stanislaus River as part of the California Wild and Scenic Rivers System failed in 1974.

In 1990, environmentalists won 61 percent of their ballot propositions. However, they lost the fight for one of their largest, most publicized campaigns. The "Big Green" initiative in California would have imposed restrictions on offshore drilling, pesticide use, and air pollution while also dealing with ozone protections, logging, and recycling. Various industries in the state formed a COALITION that waged a $10 million campaign against the initiative; subsequently, the proposition was defeated. Industries had since developed two successful strategies for defeating environmental ballot initiatives: outspending the competition and placing counterinitiatives on the ballot. These counterinitiatives serve to confuse voters over which initiative would help the environment.

Environmental interests have also altered their approach in campaigning for ballot initiatives. Campaigns are limited to a narrow environmental topic and have well-developed messages that come from the use of polling and FOCUS GROUPS. The environmental groups work to build broad coalitions while drawing upon their national networks for FUNDRAISING. They also prepare in advance for lawsuits that may challenge their petitions.

Initiatives are still used today at the state and local levels. In June 2004, the Pala Band of Mission Indians successfully collected the signatures needed to challenge the development of the Gregory Canyon Landfill in California. Earlier that year, the residents of Inglewood, California, defeated a ballot initiative that would have allowed Wal-Mart to build a store without going through public hearings or developing an environmental impact statement.

Further reading: Guber, Deborah. "Environmental Voting in the American States: A Tale of Two Initiatives." *State and Local Government Review* 33, no. 2 (2001): 120–132; The

Initiative and Referendum Institute. Available online. URL: http://www.iandrinstitute.org/ballotwatch.htm. Accessed on August 10, 2005.

—Mary Hallock Morris

ballot initiatives, tax issues

Voters in several of the 24 mostly western states that permit ballot initiatives have come to expect that at least one tax-related initiative will appear on their statewide ballots each election. The initiative, whereby citizens collect a specified number of valid signatures in order to place either a statutory or a constitutional amendment measure on the BALLOT for fellow voters to adopt or reject, is the most participatory form of DIRECT DEMOCRACY. The adoption of the initiative process in the American states, which mostly took place during the Progressive Era, has had the pronounced effect of institutionalizing and intensifying citizen-led protests over the issue of taxes in the American states.

Tax issues are the most common type of measure to appear on statewide ballots for voters to consider. There are several kinds of initiated tax issues, including tax and expenditure limitations (TELs), tax increases, and bond measures. According to the Initiative and Referendum Institute's database, there have been 359 citizen-initiated statewide tax issues on the ballots of 21 states between 1904 and 2000. Voters have adopted 124 of the initiatives, rejecting the remaining 235. Since the Progressive Era, ballot campaigns dealing with taxes have tended to be cyclical in nature, episodically flaring up and dying back down in the states every few years or so.

Initiative campaigns dealing with tax issues, it should be noted, are not solely concerned with fiscal or economic issues. Since the first tax-related ballot initiatives were placed on a statewide ballot and passed by the voters (in Oregon in 1906), ballot campaigns dealing with taxes have been infused with symbolism. Popular protests for and against taxes have an inherent populist appeal, as tax-related issues on the ballot are as much about POLITICS and power as they are about economics.

Perhaps more than any other subject matter on the ballot, antitax ballot initiatives have embodied this populist spirit. By far the most celebrated tax limitation issue to appear on a statewide ballot was the 1978 property tax limitation measure, Proposition 13. In 1978, tax crusader Howard Jarvis mobilized Californians with his crass rallying cry, "I'm mad as hell, and I'm not going to take it any more." In June 1978, Jarvis's 389-word ballot measure won 65 percent of the POPULAR VOTE; more citizens voted for and against the measure than for the candidates who ran in the Democratic and Republican parties' gubernatorial primaries. The measure, which went into effect in July 1978, immediately required local governments to limit any ad valorem tax on real property to 1 percent of assessed valuation while scaling back assessed values of properties to 1975–76 levels. It also prohibited any new state or local taxes without the approval of two-thirds of the ELECTORATE. After its implementation, Proposition 13 cut California's property tax revenue by an estimated 57 percent in fiscal year 1978–79, reducing the annual revenue of local governments by $6 billion.

During the campaign, Jarvis claimed he was leading "a people's movement" that went far beyond merely reducing property taxes. The underriding goal of the measure was to curb the power of local (and by extension, state) governments by forcing them to reduce property taxes. "Tonight," the indefatigable Jarvis blared at his triumphal election night party, "was a victory against money, the politicians, the government." Once the populist rhetoric of tax crusaders is peeled away, though, tax-related ballot measures such as Proposition 13 are far less GRASSROOTS-driven than is generally assumed. Many tax limitation ballot initiatives, Proposition 13 included, are underwritten, both financially and organizationally, by vested special interests.

Notwithstanding its less-than-grassroots provenance, Proposition 13 forever altered the political landscape of California as well as other states that allow the initiative. Jarvis's initiative sparked a series of copycat tax-related measures around the country. Similar measures were immediately implemented in Massachusetts and Michigan, and within two years, 43 states had adopted comparable TELs and income tax reductions. In all, voters in states permitting the initiative considered 100 statewide antitax measures between 1978 and 2002 that aimed to abolish, cut, or limit taxes; citizens approved 45 of the measures. The flow of antitax measures appearing on the ballot has remained fairly constant over the years, with voters passing 21 of the 52 antitax initiatives between 1990 and 2002.

Beyond Proposition 13, scholars have devoted considerable attention to the impact of tax-related ballot initiatives, most notably TELs, on public policy. Several states have adopted legislation modeled after a 1992 Colorado ballot initiative, the Taxpayers Bill of Rights, known as TABOR. Narrowly adopted by voters (after having rejected similar measures in 1988 and 1990), TABOR was conceived by Douglas Bruce, a Colorado Springs lawyer and rental property investor. TABOR stipulated that state and local legislative bodies could not increase taxes without a popular vote, and also that government spending would be limited to spending in the previous year, plus an index of inflation and population growth. Governments must refund to taxpayers any surplus revenues or ask citizens, via a REFERENDUM, to retain the surplus revenue. In lean years, when government revenues fall short of previous revenues, a ratchet mechanism goes into effect, limiting future government spending. In Colorado, where the economy has been in a recession since 2001, the TABOR ratchet—in combination with a 2000 citizen-initiated measure, Amendment 23, which mandates K-12 education funding—has indeed cut government spending and has forced state and local governments to rein in an array of social services and education programs.

According to some scholars, there are clear tax-related policy differences between states that have the initiative and those that do not. Per capita spending, for example, is generally lower in states that permit the initiative than in noninitiative states. In addition, governmental spending decisions tend to be more decentralized and less redistributional in states with the initiative compared to those that do not allow the process. It is, of course, in the eye of the beholder as to whether these tax and spending patterns are good or bad in both a policy and a normative sense. Whatever one's position on the substantive outcomes of tax-related ballot issues, there is little question that tax issues will continue to appear on statewide ballots in the foreseeable future.

Further reading: Initiative and Referendum Institute. Available online. URL: http://www.iandrinstitute.org. Accessed on August 10, 2005; Sabato, Larry J., Howard R. Ernst, and Bruce A. Larson. *Dangerous Democracy? The Battle over Ballot Initiatives in America.* Lanham, Md.: Rowman & Littlefield, 2001; Schwadron, Terry, and Paul Richter, eds. *California and the American Tax Revolt.* Berkeley: University of California Press, 1984; Sears, David, and Jack Citrin. *Tax Revolt.* Cambridge, Mass.: Harvard University Press, 1982; Smith, Daniel A. *Tax Crusaders and the Politics of Direct Democracy.* New York: Routledge, 1998.

—Daniel A. Smith

ballot initiatives, term limits

The TERM LIMITS movement, which advocated limiting the number of terms a state or federal legislator could serve in office, began receiving national attention in 1990. Proponents of term limits decried the stagnant professional political culture of American legislatures such as the Congress, where incumbency rates had reached more than 95 percent. Advocates claimed that legislators were concentrating their efforts on reelection and the maintenance of their own political careers rather than the welfare of the voters.

Figuring that legislatures would be highly unlikely to approve limits on their own abilities to seek political office, organizations such as U.S. Term Limits began working to have term-limit ballot initiatives placed on state BALLOTS across the country. By 1994, the term-limit movement had won tremendous political victories in several states: of 24 states that had an initiative process, 22 had approved legislative term limits.

The freshmen members of the newly elected Republican Congress, many of whom strongly supported term limits in their own campaigns, pledged their support for a proposed constitutional amendment. Many had also pledged to serve only three terms if elected that year. However, less than 10 years later, many courts and state legislatures have overturned term limits, support in Congress for a constitutional amendment has disappeared, and many representatives who had pledged to limit their own terms in 1994 have since reneged without consequences. While many states still retain limits on their state legislators, the frenzy among voters and activists for term limits has all but vanished.

The idea of constitutionally limiting the terms of office a legislator could serve is a very old one in American POLITICS. The ARTICLES OF CONFEDERATION, ratified in 1781, included a provision to limit DELEGATEs, appointed annually by state legislatures, to three years in office over a six-year period. At the Constitutional Convention of 1787, the Virginia Plan included a provision for term limits, but it was removed without significant debate. During the 19th century, turnover in Congress was extremely high, with the majority of incumbents choosing to serve only one or two terms in office. Serving in Congress was unappealing to many: Washington, D.C., was extremely remote and unsettled, and the size and power of the federal government was limited. With the growth of federal power in the early 20th century and improved conditions in Washington, rates of incumbency began to rise, and career politicians became more commonplace. Beginning in 1947, after the passage of the TWENTY-SECOND AMENDMENT that limited presidential terms of office, proposals for congressional term limits were made sporadically but rarely received much interest or attention from voters or politicians.

The first significant political movement in support of term limits had its roots in Republican political circles starting around 1988. Supporters within the REPUBLICAN PARTY managed to place an ENDORSEMENT of term limits in their 1988 party platform, but the move received little attention. Over the next two years, bolstered by strong public sentiment in favor of term limits, groups such as Americans to Limit Congressional Terms (ALCT) and Citizens for Congressional Reform (CCR) began to form and helped focus attention on the problems of incumbency and the proposals for reform. In 1990, voters in Oklahoma, Colorado, and California all approved term-limit initiatives. A year later, Washington state narrowly rejected a term-limit initiative, largely due to a strong campaign against it by Thomas Foley, a representative from the Spokane area since 1964, and then SPEAKER OF THE HOUSE. Undaunted by this reversal, advocates for term limits continued their campaigns, and public sentiment was strongly behind them. Polls during 1991 showed up to 70 percent of the ELECTORATE in favor of term-limits. In 1992, voters in 14 states approved term-limit initiatives, and two years later initiatives in an additional six states passed by large majorities.

The Republican Party especially benefited from the term-limit movement. Until 1994, Democrats had held power in the House of Representatives since 1956, and during the same period, Republicans had made only brief

Franklin D. Roosevelt with Phyllis Fay Firebagh, daughter of a veteran, while campaigning in 1944 for his fourth term in office. Since the passage of the Twenty-second Amendment in 1947, all presidents have been limited to two terms. *(Franklin D. Roosevelt Presidential Library and Museum)*

inroads into the Senate. During the 1994 congressional campaign, many powerful Democratic legislators, such as Dan Rostenkowski, the chair of the House Ways and Means Committee, and Speaker Tom Foley, were attacked as career politicians, more interested in maintaining their personal power and prestige than in the needs of the voters. Rostenkowski, an 18-term incumbent, was under indictment for abusing the power of his office, and Foley had made himself a lightning rod for discontent thanks to his campaign against term limits four years previously. Both were defeated, Foley being the first sitting Speaker to lose office since 1862, and Rostenkowski left Congress to eventually serve a prison term for his abuses in office. Republicans took both houses of Congress that year, gaining 52 seats in the House and nine in the Senate.

Most state term-limit initiatives affected both state and federal candidates for office. Critics had suggested that states placing additional requirements on federal candidates was unconstitutional, but the question would not reach the U.S. Supreme Court until *U.S. TERM LIMITS V.* *THORNTON*, 514 U.S. 779 (1995). The Court, in striking down an Arkansas initiative, declared states not to have the power to add additional qualifications or requirements for federal office. In 1997 and 1998, the Massachusetts and Washington state supreme courts struck down term limits in their own states, declaring a state constitutional amendment would be required. The Supreme Court of Oregon followed suit in 2002. The Idaho and Utah state legislatures recently managed to overturn their states' term-limit initiatives. In 2004, with the Wyoming Supreme Court invalidating its state's term-limit law, only 15 states continued to have legislative term limits.

The effects of term limits in improving the quality of legislative representation are uncertain. A 1998 study suggests term limits have had no effect on the demographic composition of legislatures and have shifted power away from party leaders toward governors and legislative staff. However, the study also found members of legislatures with term limits to spend less time securing pork barrel projects and more time on the political problems of their states.

While the term-limit movement seems to have stalled, and the future of some states' term-limit laws is uncertain, the political battle over legislative incumbency forced many politicians out of office and significantly changed the political landscape in America.

Further reading: Carey, John, Richard Niemi, and Lynda Powell. *Term Limits in State Legislatures.* Ann Arbor: University of Michigan Press, 2000; Initiative and Referendum Institute. Available online. URL: http://www.iandrinstitute. org. Accessed August 10, 2005; Pilon, Roger. *The Politics and Law of Term Limits.* Washington, D.C.: Cato Institution, 1994; Sabato, Larry J., Howard R. Ernst, and Bruce A. Larson, eds. *Dangerous Democracy? The Battle over Ballot Initiatives in America.* Lanham, Md.: Rowman & Littlefield, 2001; Sarbaugh-Thompson, Marjorie. *The Political and Institutional Effects of Term Limits.* New York: Palgrave Macmillan, 2004.

—Zachary Courser

bandwagon effect

The bandwagon effect is the tendency of a political candidate to gain in popularity not because of merit, but because of the perception that other people support the candidate. The term dates to the mid-19th century, when circus showmen such as P. T. Barnum brought their colorful bandwagons with musicians through the streets of towns. At the turn of the 20th century, political candidates such as William Jennings Bryan used bandwagons and musicians as stages from which to generate noise and the enthusiasm of crowds. As the wagons rolled through town, people leaped onto the bandwagon, attracting both supporters of the candidate and people who were simply caught up in the excitement of the commotion.

The bandwagon effect is also the tendency of popular candidates to develop a kind of inertia, remaining relatively popular because the public accepts them uncritically. Opposing information, often based in fact and important to the contest, may be rejected by the public because it relates to a popular candidate. Competing ideas or candidates often must overcome the bandwagon effect before they can, in turn, be accepted and become popular. For example, incumbent candidates tend to profit from the bandwagon effect when seeking reelection, since people already recognize the successful candidate, leading them to stick with a proven winner.

Today the bandwagon effect has produced a "phenomenon business" in which political engineers attempt to generate and maintain support for the candidate they represent. Managers and strategic planners attempt to create and time momentum so that the candidate goes into the final stages of a campaign appearing confident in victory. The political managers work through media, both paid and earned, to convey an image that their candidate enjoys widespread and growing support. They prod voters to support their candidate or risk "throwing away their vote."

Further reading: Basu, Kaushik. *Prelude to Political Economy: A Study of the Social and Political Foundations of Economics.* Oxford: Oxford University Press, 2000; Minogue, Kenneth R. *Politics: A Very Short Introduction.* Oxford: Oxford University Press, 1995.

—James B. Tuttle

barnstorm

Barnstorming refers to an intense period of focused political campaigning over a relatively short period of time. The term came into inception during the latter half of the 19th century, when the invention of the locomotive first allowed national candidates to crisscross the country campaigning in a manner that has now become the norm. Barnstorming's meaning was derived from the campaign practice of using barns as settings for spirited campaign speeches meant to invigorate political supporters. The strategy was to deliver a large number of such speeches in a blitzkrieg-like style to maximize the effect on potential voters.

An early example of barnstorming occurred during the 1900 PRESIDENTIAL ELECTION. William Jennings Bryan made use of his charismatic and explosive speaking style as he traveled by locomotive across the country in a vain attempt to defeat the incumbent, William McKinley. In fact, the whistles blown as trains pulled into stations gave rise to the related term *whistlestopping*. The two terms *barnstorming* and *whistlestopping* are often used interchangeably, though whistlestopping originally denoted a more spontaneous form of campaigning. Unlike the strategically planned barnstorming tours, whistlestopping referred to short ad-lib speeches that politicians gave in small towns in which their train briefly stopped. Both barnstorming and whistlestopping have gained more of a negative connotation over the years as the public came to see them more as forms of pure political pandering. This fact has in no way rendered barnstorming obsolete as a campaign tool. Barnstorming has remained a campaign staple throughout the 20th century. President Harry Truman's legendary upset victory over Thomas Dewey in 1948 was in part a result of the momentum created by a late barnstorming tour that made Dewey seem complacent by comparison.

Different campaigns can use barnstorming in different ways depending on their needs. For example, in September of 1952 Dwight Eisenhower and Adlai Stevenson each barnstormed the nation in support of their presidential campaigns. Stevenson visited traditional Democratic strongholds in an attempt to shore up the same electoral votes his predecessor, President Truman, had won. However, it was Eisenhower's more aggressive attempts to convert those outside the Republican faithful that secured him the election. Increasingly, barnstorming has been used in closely contested elections in which the outcome is in doubt. In the 2002 midterm congressional elections, President George W. Bush's barnstorming of several key states, such as Colorado, Florida, and Minnesota, helped the REPUBLICAN PARTY to electoral victories.

Barnstorming has certainly evolved from its original 19th-century meaning, shedding the associated whistle-blowing trains and farmyard pulpits. However, the idea of mass political campaigning has not only survived into modern times, it has also flourished in the wake of numerous innovations in technology, transportation, and campaign strategies. Politicians continue to tour the nation in support of their candidacy, party, or favored policy initiative. However, today the concept of barnstorming is just as likely to be used in vast media campaigns designed to inundate voters more effectively than any 19th-century politician could ever have envisioned.

Further reading: Karabell, Zachary. *The Last Campaign: How Harry Truman Won the 1948 Election.* New York: Knopf, 2000; Morris, Dick. *Power Plays: Win or Lose. How History's Great Leaders Play the Game.* New York: Reagan Books, 2002.

—Mark Givens

bellwether

A bellwether is a leader or leading indicator of a trend. Historically, the term dates to the 15th century, when shepherds tied a bell around the neck of a castrated ram (wether). This sheep then acted as a leader, followed by the rest of the flock. When first applied to humans, the term had a negative connotation. It implied that such a person was followed not because of any intrinsic merit, but because he was wearing a bell, which could be transferred to any other sheep. It also disparaged those who followed the bellwether, comparing them to the mindless sheep.

Since that time, the connotations of the term have broadened, and it is most often used in a positive or neutral sense. In the 16th century, Queen Elizabeth used the term to describe Lord Chancellor Sir Christopher Hatton, whom she referred to as her bellwether. What she prized was not his ability to lead, but his uncanny knowledge of the sentiment of her court on matters of state. The modern meaning of the term has less to do with leadership than it does with the ability to forecast general trends from isolated events.

Today, the term *bellwether* is applied to a person, place, or idea seen as a leading indicator of trends in POLITICS, business, and public sentiment. Paris, for example, has long been considered the bellwether of the fashion industry. Certain stocks are also considered bellwethers, leading indicators of trends in the market. In political campaigns, particular districts, counties, or states are often considered bellwethers of larger voting trends. Among states, New Mexico is often considered a bellwether state for presiden-

tial races, voting for the winning candidate in almost every presidential race since 1912, when New Mexico became a state. At the county level, Cook County, Oregon, is often referred to by election forecasters as a bellwether county for its ability to regularly choose presidential winners.

Further reading: Fair, Ray C. *Predicting Presidential Elections and Other Things.* Stanford, Calif.: Stanford University Press, 2002; Lavrakas, Paul J. *Election Polls, the News Media, and Democracy.* New York: Chatham House, 2000.

—James B. Tuttle

benchmark poll

A benchmark poll is a relatively long survey usually conducted early in a campaign. It is designed to provide in-depth analysis of the political environment surrounding a particular campaign. A benchmark poll is conducted either immediately before or after a candidate decides to seek office. Indeed, most pollsters argue that candidates should conduct a benchmark poll before they enter a race, as most campaign decisions are made in light of the poll's findings, and it provides a baseline by which campaign progress can be charted.

A benchmark poll provides a campaign with a great deal of information. The poll tests the name identification of the candidate as well as that of all possible opponents. It also assesses the electoral strength of the candidate in various head-to-head match-ups. If the candidate is not the incumbent, the benchmark poll will be used to measure citizens' assessments of the incumbent. It will also be used to gather information on the demographics of the ELECTORATE as well as their issue preferences and their responses to the issue positions of the candidate and his or her possible opponents.

A benchmark poll is usually the first step in a campaign's PUBLIC OPINION POLLING operation, followed by trial heat surveys (also known as brushfire polls), FOCUS GROUPS, and TRACKING POLLS nearer to ELECTION DAY. However, the fact that benchmark polls are conducted early in the campaign gives rise to a concern over the accuracy of the results. If the poll is conducted too early in the campaign, respondents may not yet be paying attention either to the candidates in the race or the issues that will define the race. As a result, the poll may report on attitudes that are likely to change over the course of the campaign. On the other hand, the campaign cannot wait too long to conduct the benchmark poll, as its results help the campaign devise its message, theme, and strategy.

A benchmark poll typically requires 300 to 400 respondents in a congressional race and anywhere from 500 to 1,200 respondents in a statewide race. The poll generally involves a 15- to 20-minute interview per respondent during which perhaps 90 to 100 questions will be asked. A benchmark poll will cost from $12,000 to $16,000 or more if the campaign requests a larger sample size or a longer questionnaire. Often groups of candidates will combine resources to fund a benchmark poll (particularly if they represent overlapping constituencies), or parties will fund the poll and offer it to candidates as an in-kind donation.

Further reading: Asher, Herbert. *Polling and the Public: What Every Citizen Should Know.* 5th ed. Washington, D.C.: Congressional Quarterly Press, 2001.

—Brian J. Brox

Bipartisan Campaign Reform Act of 2002   *See* McCain-Feingold Campaign Finance Reform.

Blue Dog Democrats

A group of conservative House Democrats, the Blue Dog Democrats represent a COALITION of Democrats, mostly southern, who share conservative economic views. The Blue Dogs officially formed during the 104th Congress (1995–96) following the 1994 REPUBLICAN REVOLUTION as a way to solidify their advantage as a strategic voting bloc. By the 108th Congress (2003–04) the Blue Dogs had grown to 36 members from across the country, becoming more of a policy-oriented group than a regional coalition. It now meets as an official congressional caucus. Its primary goal is to offer a moderate to conservative Democratic viewpoint that works to form bipartisan coalitions with moderate Republicans in the hope of forming a middle-of-the-road congressional agenda.

While they began as a predominately southern group, the Blue Dogs should not be confused with YELLOW DOG DEMOCRATS, though they derive their name from that expression. Yellow Dog Democrats were a loyal and strongly partisan group of southern voters who, the saying went, would vote for a yellow dog before voting for a Republican. The name *Blue Dog* comes from the idea that the group's moderate to conservative agenda had been "choked blue" by the DEMOCRATIC PARTY leading up to the 1994 elections. One of the founding principles of the Blue Dogs was less partisan loyalty and more independence from the Democratic Party leadership. The Blue Dogs are comparable to the "Boll Weevils," a group of southern House members from the early 1980s who as a group defected from the Democrats to vote with the Republicans on economic and budgetary issues.

The primary significance of the Blue Dogs in congressional POLITICS is their ability to serve as the SWING VOTE between the Republican majority and the Democratic minority. Due to the small Republican majority in Congress during the late 1990s and into the 2000s, these conservative Democrats can use their votes in a strategic manner that often results in the difference between legislation passing or failing.

Further reading: Blue Dog Democrats. Available online. URL: http://www.bluedogdemocrats.com. Accessed August 10, 2005; Hammond, Susan Webb. *Congressional Caucuses in National Policy Making.* Baltimore: Johns Hopkins University Press, 1998; Iton, Richard. *Solidarity Blues: Race, Culture and the American Left.* Chapel Hill: University of North Carolina Press, 2000; Schneider, Jerrold E. *Campaign Finance Reform and the Future of the Democratic Party.* New York: Routledge, 2002.

—Jonathan Winburn

blue states

A term derived from the graphics used by the television and cable news networks during their coverage of the 2000 PRESIDENTIAL ELECTION. The blue states voted for Al Gore, the Democratic candidate, while RED STATES supported Republican George W. Bush. These electoral maps illustrated a sharply divided ELECTORATE. The blue states tend to be in the Northeast, upper Midwest and Pacific Coast, with the Great Plains, South, and the rest of the Midwest being red states. This political divide has also been described as reflecting a cultural divide in American society.

While describing states generally, the blue-red dichotomy obscures some other political differences. Urban areas were more likely to be Democratic (blue), whether or not they were in blue or red states, while rural areas were likely to be red. African Americans tended to vote Democratic, regardless of their geographic location. Some states are sharply divided. Pennsylvania is liberal in the Philadelphia and Pittsburgh metropolitan areas at each end of the state, while central Pennsylvania is quite conservative.

Blue states have a number of demographic differences from red states. As a result, the terms have taken on cultural implications implying that the blue states are more liberal while the red states are more conservative. Blue states are more urban, are home to more college graduates, have higher per capita government expenditures, and are more ethnically and racially diverse than red states.

Economically, while in many red states agriculture is an important part of the state economy, the economies of blue states are dominated by information and service industries. Average household incomes in the blue states tend to be higher than those of red states.

There are some who suggest that this red state–blue state divide reflects a "culture war" in American society. It has been argued that the red states are traditional, religious, self-disciplined, and patriotic. The blue states are characterized as modern, secular, self-expressive, and uncomfortable with displays of patriotism. In their 2003 survey, the Pew Research Center for People and the Press found that one of the most significant differences between Democratic and Republican identifiers was church attendance, with Republicans being more likely to attend church services than Democrats.

Following the 2004 PRESIDENTIAL ELECTION, the blue state–red state divide was clearer than ever. A Zogby International poll conducted in December 2003 found sharp differences between respondents in blue and red states over issues such as the right to abortion, same-sex unions, and gun control, with voters in blue states more likely to be in favor than those in red states. The poll also found that 52 percent of red state voters attended church services on a weekly basis, while 34 percent of the respondents in blue states did, continuing what some suggest is a religious-cultural-political divide in contemporary American POLITICS. Moreover, the electoral map, with few exceptions, was colored nearly the same in 2004 as it had been in the 2000 election.

Further reading: Brooks, David. "One Nation, Slightly Divisible." *Atlantic Monthly* 288, no. 5 (2001): 53–65; Frank, Thomas. *What's The Matter with Kansas? How Conservatives Won the Heart of America.* New York: Metropolitan Books, 2004; Greenberg, Stanley B. *The Two Americas: Our Current Political Deadlock and How to Break It.* New York: Thomas Dunne Books, 2004; Himmelfarb, Gertrude. *One Nation, Two Cultures: A Searching Examination of American Society in the Aftermath of Our Cultural Revolution.* New York: Alfred A. Knopf, 1999; Zogby International. *America: Blue vs. Red States, Republicans vs. Democrats; Two Separate Nations in a Race for the White House.* Utica, N.Y.: Zogby International, 2003.

—Jeffrey Kraus

Buckley v. Valeo 424 U.S. 1 (1976)

Buckley v. Valeo was the landmark 1976 U.S, Supreme Court campaign finance decision that upheld limitations on political contributions while overturning other restrictions on campaign spending as violative of the First Amendment.

In 1974, Congress amended the FEDERAL ELECTION CAMPAIGN ACT of 1971 in response to the concern that unregulated money could have a corrupting effect on federal elections. Among other things, the 1974 amendments limited the amount of money that individuals and groups could contribute to a single candidate, imposed ceilings on CAMPAIGN EXPENDITURES, and restricted the amount of a candidate's own money that could be spent. It also imposed several reporting and disclosure requirements and mandated the formation of the Federal Elections Commission to oversee the entire regulatory process. On January 2, 1975, New York senator James L. Buckley, Democratic presidential candidate and former senator from Minnesota Eugene McCarthy, and several other politicians and political organizations filed suit in federal court arguing that the new campaign reforms violated their First Amendment rights to freedom of speech and association. When the Court of Appeals for the District of Columbia Circuit rejected most of Buckley's arguments, he appealed to the Supreme Court, which scheduled the case for oral arguments in November 1975.

On January 30, 1976, the Supreme Court handed down an unsigned per curiam decision. Throughout its long, complicated ruling, the Court struggled with the conflict between the free speech rights of both contributors and candidates and Congress's desire to lessen the influence of money in federal campaigns. The fragmentation on the bench over these issues was clearly evident in the five separate dissents that accompanied the ruling.

The Court began its analysis by considering the limitations set by the legislation on campaign contributions. Individuals were prohibited from contributing more than $1,000 to any single candidate, while organized "political committees" could contribute up to $5,000 per candidate. No contributor, however, could give more than $25,000 in total contributions annually. Critics of the legislation argued that these limitations infringed upon the free speech rights of those who wished to express themselves politically by donating money. The Court, however, upheld the restrictions, noting that one's ability to communicate one's political views about a particular candidate was only marginally restricted by limits on financial contributions because there were many other ways for a person to convey his or her political opinions than through monetary donations. Thus, according to the Court, while a contribution may serve "as a general expression of support for the candidate and his views, [it] does not communicate the underlying basis of support. The quantity of communication by the contributor does not increase perceptibly with the size of his contribution."

Although the Court acknowledged that there were valid First Amendment arguments against the contribution limits, these were outweighed by the law's stated purpose to "limit the actuality and appearance of corruption resulting from large individual financial contributions," which the Court found to be constitutionally sound. In practical terms, the Court saw its decision as simply requiring candidates and political groups to appeal to a wider range of people for financial support.

The Court then went on to consider the First Amendment challenges to the spending restrictions put into place by the law. The law restricted the amount of money that outside groups could spend on candidates to $1,000. It also limited the amount of personal funds that candidates could devote to their own campaigns. Overall campaign expenditures were also capped at varying dollar amounts depending on the office being sought. The Court was much more sympathetic to the First Amendment arguments against these regulations, noting that the law's spending limits "impose significantly more severe restrictions on protected freedoms of political expression and association than do its limitations on financial contributions."

In declaring the expenditure limits unconstitutional, the Court ruled that such restrictions reduce the "quantity of expression by restricting the number of issues discussed, the depth of their exploration, and the size of the audience reached." Modern political campaigns not only expended funds on such traditional activities as printing handbills, renting facilities for various campaign uses, and transporting the candidate, but also, the Court acknowledged, relied increasingly on expensive mass media. Laws regulating the amount of money that could be spent in an election thus placed "substantial and direct restrictions on the ability of candidates, citizens, and associations to engage in protected political expression."

Specifically, the Court held that the restriction on expenditures on behalf of candidates by individuals and groups constituted a serious infringement of free speech. Were the law to be upheld, contributors who wished to advertise their views relative to a particular candidate would face criminal charges if they exceeded the permissible dollar amount. Such restrictions simply could not be tolerated. Similarly, the Court ruled that limiting the amount that a candidate could spend out of his or her own pocket was unconstitutional. "The candidate," the decision stated, "no less than any other person, has a First Amendment right to engage in the discussion of public issues and vigorously and tirelessly to advocate his own election." The overall spending caps mandated by the law were also held to be constitutionally invalid. While the government may regulate campaign finance to a degree, the "First Amendment denies [it] the power to determine that spending to promote one's political views is wasteful, excessive, or unwise."

Much of the harshest criticism of the Court's opinion in this case was directed at the ruling's selective embrace of the Free Speech Clause. The five justices who dissented from parts of the per curiam ruling questioned whether there was any substantive difference between money donated and money spent when it came to campaigns and free speech. Nonetheless, the Court's decision would serve as the fundamental basis for all campaign finance reform proposals for the next quarter century.

Further reading: Banks, Christopher P., and John C. Green, eds. *Superintending Democracy: The Courts and the Political Process.* Akron, Ohio: University of Akron Press, 2001; Parker, Richard A., ed. *Free Speech on Trial: Communication Perspectives on Landmark Supreme Court Decisions.* Tuscaloosa: University of Alabama Press, 2003; Supreme Court Historical Society. Available online. URL: http://www.supremecourthistory.org. Accessed August 10, 2005.

—Steven P. Brown

bullet voting
Bullet voting occurs when voters cast BALLOTS for fewer candidates than there are elective positions on the ballot. In multiseat districts or AT-LARGE ELECTIONS, all candidates compete against all others. Voters may "single-shot" for one candidate. Voters strategically cast fewer votes than they are permitted. This strategy promotes the election of their most favored candidate and reduces the chance of electing their second or third choice.

This type of voting is common among minority groups or when gender is an issue in an election. Voters, faced with a choice among several candidates or their preferred party, but only one candidate from their preferred demographic group/ethnic group, might choose to cast a vote for one candidate rather than the entire party SLATE. If a sufficient number of voters adopt this strategy, it can help assure that the specific candidate is most likely to represent the party.

Choice voting, or the "single transferable vote," is a reform of bullet voting. It enables voters to maximize their votes' effectiveness through ranking candidates. Like-minded voters win an equitable number of seats no matter how many candidates seek their support. Voters rank candidates by indicating the order of their preference. Voters rank as many or as few candidates as they prefer.

Bullet voting and its reforms are a sharp contrast to SINGLE-MEMBER DISTRICTS, where sum-zero results emerge. It is a rational strategy employed by a relatively small number of savvy voters in multiseat districts and at-large elections.

Further reading: Hill, Steven. *Fixing Elections: The Failure of America's Winner-Take-All Politics.* New York: Routledge, 2003; Patterson, Thomas E. *The Vanishing Voter: Public Involvement in an Age of Uncertainty.* New York: Alfred A. Knopf, 2002.

—John Rouse

Bull Moose Party
The Bull Moose Party refers to the popular name given to the National PROGRESSIVE PARTY, an unsuccessful attempt by Theodore Roosevelt to return to the presidency after the incumbent, William Howard Taft, had been named the Republican nominee in 1912. The roots of the Bull Moose Party lie in the gradually escalating conflict between progressives and conservatives within each party. In the case of the Republicans, Theodore Roosevelt had been able to bridge those divides with political compromises and through personal friendships with conservatives such as Elihu Root and progressives such as Wisconsin senator Robert LaFollette.

Roosevelt's handpicked successor, Taft was less successful in preventing the differences between the progressives and conservatives from becoming a public battle. Originally elected to continue Roosevelt's policies, Taft became alienated from progressive Republicans by gradually allying himself with the conservative FACTION of the party. Taft's support of tariff revision, his dismissal of cabinet members supported by Roosevelt, his alliance with

A 1912 cartoon satirizing Theodore Roosevelt's Bull Moose Party *(Cartoon by Charles Jay Budd; HarpWeek, LLC)*

the fear of tyrannical government that guided the founding fathers to create the Bill of Rights. These rights, while necessary to ensure personal freedoms, were responsible for creating trusts and large corporations that threatened personal freedom in the same way as tyrannical governments once did. As a result, government had to abandon its passive role and play a part in the regulation of businesses, political organizations, and labor unions.

Roosevelt's campaign energized the masses and tapped into the growing spirit of progressivism that was building in a variety of cities and states throughout the country. In the Republican primaries, Roosevelt garnered victories over the incumbent in all six contests, yet those achievements rang hollow in Chicago as the conservative power base within the REPUBLICAN PARTY allowed Taft to win the NOMINATION at the REPUBLICAN NATIONAL CONVENTION in June.

Taft's victory for the nomination infuriated Roosevelt and brought the conflict that had been brewing within the Republican Party between conservatives and progressives to the forefront. Roosevelt supporters condemned the actions of the conservatives and left the convention, deciding instead to hold their own impromptu convention in Chicago. It was immediately after this "rump" convention that the National Progressive Party became official. The "Bull Moose" nickname was attached to the party by the newspapers because Roosevelt commented that he felt as fit as a bull moose.

At the Bull Moose convention, also in Chicago, LaFollette continued to hold hopes that despite Roosevelt's popularity, he would win the nomination. It quickly became apparent that while the idea of the party was progressive ideals, the appeal of the party was Theodore Roosevelt. Not surprisingly, Roosevelt won the nomination on the first BALLOT by acclamation. LaFollette, stung by the loss, refused to support the party or its ticket of Roosevelt and Governor Hiram Johnson of California. LaFollette instead threw his support to the Democratic nominee, Woodrow Wilson.

Roosevelt advocated revolutionary ideals for the Bull Moose Party, ones that mirrored some of the calls of the earlier POPULIST PARTY. The platform of the party was along the lines of the new nationalism under which Roosevelt had earlier campaigned. The party called for WOMEN SUFFRAGE, the creation of a labor department, increased conservation, a graduated income tax, and the institution of initiative, REFERENDUM, and RECALL measures.

The Bull Moose Party achieved one goal by defeating Taft but failed in its other by losing to Wilson. It won 27 percent of the vote cast, captured second place, and garnered 88 electoral votes to mark the best finish of any third party in American history. The Bull Moose did not fare well in other races, as they failed to win any gubernatorial posts or senatorial positions. The loss was demoralizing as many

Speaker of the House Joe Cannon against a progressive Republican and Democratic "uprising," and the firing of chief forester Gifford Pinchot, in what later became known as the Ballinger-Pinchot controversy, did not endear him to many of his former allies within the progressive wing.

LaFollette led the opposition when he created the National Progressive Republican League. The unstated goal of this new organization, one that would provide the foundations for the Bull Moose, was the defeat of Taft in 1912. While LaFollette did create the organization and was the driving force behind the progressive upheaval, he did not prove to be the center around which the opposition to Taft coalesced. Only Roosevelt had the political clout to provide that center and did so when he announced his candidacy early in 1912.

Roosevelt's campaign centered on a program he called New Nationalism. The program was based on the philosophy from Herbert Croly's book *The Promise of American Life.* In it, Croly discussed the spirit of individualism and

went back to the Republican Party, but others, including Roosevelt, stayed on.

The elections in 1914 proved worse for the Bull Moose, as nearly all its candidates were defeated, and Republicans gained in strength. Roosevelt began to drift out of favor with the progressives as he became involved in the issue of military readiness and the looming threat posed by the Germans. Many in the party saw Roosevelt's advocacy of the issue as incompatible with the earlier positions he had championed.

By 1916, the party was a shell of its former self, and its platform reflected more conservative issues. To the party they had once vilified, the Bull Moose extended an olive branch by expressing their approval, if the Republicans nominated the Bull Moose candidate, namely, Roosevelt. Instead, the Republicans nominated Charles Evans Hughes, and the Bull Moose once again nominated Roosevelt. Roosevelt declined the nomination, endorsed Hughes, and returned to the Republican Party. With Roosevelt gone, the Bull Moose Party was finished.

The Bull Moose Party, although ultimately an ephemeral organization, succeeded in bringing greater attention to a variety of issues through its platform of social legislation. Many of the issues championed by the Bull Moose would become law, most notably the passage of the NINETEENTH AMENDMENT, which gave women the right to vote. The Bull Moose legacy continued to Franklin Roosevelt's administration, with many supporters of the New Deal having once been included in the colorful although unsuccessful third party attempt to capture the presidency.

Further reading: Gable, John A. *The Bull Moose Years: Theodore Roosevelt and the Progressive Party.* Port Washington, N.Y.: Kennikat Press, 1978; Mowry, George E. *Theodore Roosevelt and the Progressive Movement.* Madison: University of Wisconsin Press, 1946.

—Stephen Nemeth

Bullock v. Carter 405 U.S. 134 (1972)

This was one of many cases during the 1960s and 1970s that dealt with voting and the FOURTEENTH AMENDMENT and its application to the states. In 1970, a number of potential candidates for local offices were denied placement on the DEMOCRATIC PARTY primary ballot in Texas. Under Texas statute, persons wanting to run for local political offices (primaries) were required to pay filing fees to the local party committees to help defray the costs of conducting the elections and to regulate the primary ballot. The costs were estimated and apportioned among the candidates "in light of the importance, emolument, and term of office." Writing for a unanimous Supreme Court, Chief Justice Warren Burger held that the filing fee system was in violation of the equal protection clause of the Fourteenth Amendment. Arguing that the state was not denying the vote nor diluting votes cast, but rather regulating the ability to be put on

the ballot, Burger maintained that the "rational basis" test should be applied rather than a more scrutinizing standard.

Principle to applying this standard was the distinction between candidates for office and voters themselves. Citing *McDonald v. Board of Education* (1969), Burger argued that denying a place on the ballot is not considered a fundamental right, whereas, per REYNOLDS V. SIMS (1964), voting is "a fundamental political right." Burger denied that the statute furthered the goals that the state claimed. The effect of the statute was that persons lacking either adequate funds or financial backing were denied a place on the ballot, thus giving the "affluent" a leg up. Conceding that the state has an interest in regulating the number of candidates on the ballot, Burger contended that "a State cannot achieve its objectives by totally arbitrary means." Burger went further in arguing that there are other ways to ensure that only "serious" contenders are placed on the ballot. While again conceding that the costs of an election are a legitimate state concern, Burger contended that the democratic process outstrips the burden put on the taxpayer by the costs of running elections.

Bullock is significant because it does not assume that all restrictions on voting and elections are a suspect class and because it looks at the impact on the democratic process. Ironically, later the Court would use this in a vigorous way to attempt to curb the reach of the U.S Congress in its attempt to enforce the Fourteenth Amendment in *Seminole Tribe of Florida v. Florida* (1996) and its progeny.

—Jeff A. Martineau

bundling

Bundling is a campaign finance practice wherein an individual or organization, such as a POLITICAL ACTION COMMITTEE (PAC), collects a number of contributions from separate donors and bundles them together for delivery to a political campaign for the implicit purpose of influencing the campaign. Contributions by individuals are limited by federal law to $2,000 per candidate, thereby reducing the impact of any single contributor. Larger donations, combined through bundling, are more likely to make candidates take notice of the bundler and his or her agenda. For example, an individual who collects 100 contributions and bundles them together can deliver $200,000 to the campaign and gain the political influence that is believed to come with such contributions.

Bundles usually are gathered together from like-minded citizens who support a particular agenda or favor a particular issue stance. Corporations, which are banned from making direct contributions to political campaigns under federal laws, have been known to solicit contributions from employees and their families, bundle them together, and thus circumvent CAMPAIGN FINANCE LAWS.

The practice of bundling arose as a reaction to the campaign finance reform laws passed in the 1970s, beginning with the Federal Election Campaign Act of 1971. Reformers sought to limit the corrupting influence of large campaign contributions on politicians and passed a series of laws, banning direct corporate and union donations and limiting the amounts that individuals and PACs could contribute. As old avenues of raising funds were closed, new avenues were opened. Moneyed interests soon learned to exploit loopholes in the system and took advantage of so-called SOFT MONEY contributions, self-financed campaigns, and bundling.

Bundling is an important concept because it is a way for donors to work around the campaign finance reform laws in order to maximize their political influence. This process allows LOBBYISTS, PACs, and others to effectively make large contributions that would be illegal under normal circumstances. Several attempts have been made over the years to outlaw the practice of bundling, but none have been successful to date.

Further reading: Wilcox, Clyde, and Joe Wesley. "Dead Law: The Federal Election Finance Regulations, 1974–1996." *PS: Political Science and Politics* 31 (1998): 14–17.

—Kenneth Quinnell

Bush v. Gore 531 U.S. 98 (2000)

Bush v. Gore was the U.S. Supreme Court decision that ended a Florida Supreme Court order requiring a RECOUNT of BALLOTS cast in the 2000 PRESIDENTIAL ELECTION. As a result, George W. Bush won Florida's electoral votes and became the 43rd president of the United States.

On November 26, 2000, after extended legal maneuvering by attorneys for both Vice President Al Gore and Texas governor George W. Bush and nearly three weeks after voters went to the polls to choose the next president, Florida finally certified its election results, declaring Bush the winner. The following day, as permitted by Florida law, Gore filed a complaint contesting the results. His attorneys claimed that because a number of illegal votes were counted, while other legal votes were not, Bush's razor-thin margin of victory might well hinge on recounting the ballots in several Florida counties.

The state circuit court that received the initial complaint rejected Gore's challenge, stating that he had not demonstrated how the outcome of the election would be altered by recounting the votes. However, on appeal, the Florida Supreme Court ruled that in some instances Gore had satisfied the standard of proof necessary to initiate a recount, particularly in Miami-Dade County, where as many as 9,000 ballots lay uncounted. These ballots, in which there was no apparent choice for president (known as undervotes) or in which more than one candidate was selected (overvotes), were automatically rejected because the tabulating machines could not detect in them a vote for president.

The Florida Supreme Court ordered a hand recount of these ballots, instructing those who would oversee the process to count as legal any vote where "a clear indication of the intent of the voter" was detected. It ruled further that manual recounts were permissible in any Florida county that had not yet conducted its own review of the undervotes cast within its jurisdiction. The court also ordered that the votes that had been identified in earlier recounts in Palm Beach and Miami-Dade counties be added to the final voting tally even though the election results had already been certified.

Bush's legal team appealed the Florida court's sweeping decision to the United States Supreme Court, arguing, among other things, that the lower court had violated the equal protection clause of the FOURTEENTH AMENDMENT by ordering the recount without providing a uniform standard by which the ballots in question should be retabulated. On December 9, 2000, the Supreme Court ordered the recount to stop until it could conduct a hearing on the matter. Oral arguments were held two days later, and on December 12, the Court issued its opinion.

The Court's ruling, an unsigned per curiam decision, held that the equal protection clause of the Fourteenth Amendment had been violated. The Court did not fault the lower court's efforts to protect the fundamental right to vote by providing for a manual recount. However, it was critical of the vague instructions that accompanied the Florida court's ruling. In ordering the manual recount, the state supreme court had stipulated that the only ballots that could be counted were those where voter intent could be clearly discerned. Yet, in failing to provide uniform standards by which such intent could be determined, the Florida Supreme Court basically ensured that the ballot inspection process would be arbitrary and unequal. As the U.S. Supreme Court's opinion noted, "[T]he question is not whether to believe a witness but how to interpret the marks or holes or scratches on an inanimate object, a piece of cardboard or paper . . . The fact-finder confronts a thing, not a person."

As evidence of the erratic possibilities that might ensue in the absence of uniform standards, the Court referenced Palm Beach County, which had already recounted some of its ballots by hand. Voting officials there commenced the manual recount under 1990 guidelines that did not permit the inclusion of those ballots that still had a paper CHAD completely attached to the marked hole. The county subsequently changed its recount procedures to permit the counting of any ballot through which light could be seen, even if the chad was still attached. It then reverted to the 1990 standard and finally, under a court order, began to count ballots with "dimpled chads," or light indentations in the paper. That such a variety of procedures would be used to recount the ballots in just one county led the Court to question what assortment of recounting methods might be observed statewide. As the Court noted, this simply was "not a process with sufficient guarantees of equal treatment."

In addition to the standardless review, the U.S. Supreme Court found unequal treatment inherent in the very ballots that would be recounted. Under the Florida Supreme Court's order, the votes subject to the manual recount included those that had been discarded because they were unreadable by the voting machines. A hand recount would still discard overvotes because more than one presidential candidate had been selected. Undervotes, however, would be scrutinized for any marking that might indicate the voter's choice and be tallied accordingly. The U.S. Supreme Court found this problematic because, although all improperly filled out ballots had been rejected by the machines, only undervotes could potentially be added back into the vote total.

The implementation of the Florida court's ruling was also accompanied by practical difficulties, according to the Supreme Court. No direction was given as to who would actually recount the ballots, what type of training would be provided for those individuals, or what process would govern disputes that might arise in determining whether voter intent was evident on a particular ballot. In short, the U.S. Supreme Court held that the lower court's recount order did not even begin to approach "the rudimentary requirements of equal treatment and fundamental fairness."

Having determined that the recount as mandated by the Florida court violated the equal protection clause of the Fourteenth Amendment, the Supreme Court turned its attention to what should follow. The Court noted that in order to properly address the equal protection problems created by the recount order, a tremendous amount of work needed to be done. For example, uniform standards would have to be crafted, adopted, and implemented. Additionally, any modification of existing voting machines or purchasing of new equipment necessary to satisfy the equal protection concerns of the Court could proceed only with the approval of the Florida secretary of state and then only after an appropriate period of testing and evaluation. The Supreme Court concluded that these and other changes simply could not be put into place quickly enough to remedy the equal protection problems immediately at hand.

That fact, coupled with the statutory requirement that contested PRESIDENTIAL ELECTIONS in Florida be settled by the 12th day of December so that electors could be selected, led the Court to conclude: "That date is upon us, and there is no recount procedure in place under the State Supreme Court's order that comports with minimal constitutional standards. Because it is evident that any recount seeking to meet the December 12 date will be unconstitutional for the reasons we have discussed, we reverse the judgment of the Supreme Court of Florida." With that dec-

laration, both the contested vote in Florida and the 2000 presidential election were over.

Although only five justices joined the per curiam opinion, Justices David Souter and Stephen Breyer also agreed that there were serious equal protection problems with the lower court's recount order. However, in separate dissenting opinions, they questioned why the recount could not go forward under a stricter standard. Both were equally critical of the majority's decision to intervene in the case in the first place, arguing that state law and state courts should govern state elections. Indeed, although they acknowledged that the equal protection clause of the Fourteenth Amendment had been violated by the Florida court's vague recount order, both justices questioned why the majority opinion could not simply remand the case back to the Florida Supreme Court with instructions to correct the constitutional deficiencies rather than halting the recount process altogether.

The other two dissenting justices, John Paul Stevens and Ruth Bader Ginsburg, found no problems with the lower court's opinion and would have upheld the recount order. Justice Stevens predicted that the greatest injury inflicted by the Supreme Court's decision might well be upon itself. "Although we may never know with complete certainty the identity of the winner of this year's Presidential election, the identity of the loser is perfectly clear. It is the Nation's confidence in the judge as an impartial guardian of the law."

Further reading: Ceaser, James W., and Andrew Busch. *The Perfect Tie.* Lanham, Md.: Rowman & Littlefield, 2001; Greene, Abner. *Understanding the 2000 Election: A Guide to the Legal Battles That Decided the Presidency.* New York: New York University Press, 2001; Posner, Richard. *Breaking the Deadlock: The 2000 Election, the Constitution, and the Courts.* Princeton, N.J.: Princeton University Press, 2001; Supreme Court Historical Society. Available online. URL: http://www.supremecourthistory.org. Accessed August 10, 2005.

—Steven P. Brown

butterfly ballot

The butterfly ballot is a two-page BALLOT used with punch-card VOTING SYSTEMS. The key feature of the butterfly ballot is that it is spread across two facing pages, like a butterfly with its wings open. Voters indicate their choices by punching a hole between the two pages.

The butterfly ballot is believed to have caused a spoiling of votes in the 2000 PRESIDENTIAL ELECTION in Palm Beach County, Florida. Though this was undoubtedly not the first time the butterfly design had caused problems, the butterfly ballot became infamous as a result of its use in this election. It happened that the top hole, referenced by the top line on the left page, was to vote for Republican

George W. Bush. The second line on the left page was to vote for Democrat Al Gore. But the second *hole*, referenced by the top line on the *right* page, was to vote for Reform candidate Patrick M. Buchanan.

It is believed that many people had trouble understanding the butterfly design and unintentionally voted for Buchanan instead of Gore. This is evidenced by the large number of voters who punched the hole for Buchanan for president and then voted for Democrats in other races on the ballot. Another group of voters punched two holes, apparently thinking they had to vote for both president and vice president. By voting for two candidates, they spoiled their presidential vote. The "overvotes," as these ballots are known, were disproportionately cast by people who voted Democratic on the rest of the ballot.

The problem was not only the butterfly ballot in Palm Beach County but also other problems with computer punch-card voting throughout Florida. This is an antiquated voting system developed in the 1960s and replaced in most of the United States by more sophisticated voting machines, notably optical scanners, which are highly sensitive to even the slightest marking on a ballot. The punch-card system, as indicated, involves the voter making a hole in a card by punching through a small perforation called a CHAD.

Not every hole is fully punched, owing to a light touch on the part of the voter. If the chad is not completely punched, the tabulating machines will not read the vote. The remedy proposed by the Gore campaign was to manually RECOUNT every undervoted ballot in the presidential race and look for evidence that the voter tried to punch out the chad and count that as a vote. The operative idea was that very few people vote in an election and skip the presidential race (usually 1 percent or less).

The process was complicated by the undervoted ballots having various types of chads. Some were adhering to the ballot by only one corner and were called "hanging" chads. Others were holding on by two corners and were called "swinging" chads. Others were separated only at one corner and were called "tri-tip" chads. Yet others remained connected at all corners but had an indentation, suggesting the voter inserted his or her stylus for a particular candidate but did not punch. These were called "dimpled" or "pregnant" chads. There was no agreement as to what constituted a vote, other than that a fully punched chad was a vote. As a result of the 2000 debacle in Florida, the demise of the computer punch-card voting system in general and the butterfly ballot in particular was expedited.

Further reading: Dover, E. D. *The Disputed Presidential Election of 2000: A History and Reference Guide.* Westport, Conn.: Greenwood Press, 2003; Kaplan, David A. *The Accidental President: How 413 Lawyers, 9 Supreme Court Justices, and 5,963,110 (Give or Take a Few) Floridians Landed George W. Bush in the White House.* New York: William Morrow, 2001; Toobin, Jeffrey. *Too Close to Call: The Thirty-six Day Battle to Decide the 2000 Election.* New York: Random House, 2001; Saltman, Roy G. *Accuracy, Integrity, and Security in Computerized Vote-Tallying.* Gaithersburg, Md.: National Bureau of Standards, 1988.

—Tony L. Hill

C

campaign, general election

General election campaigns are electoral contests among party nominees and other INDEPENDENT candidates to determine who will hold office for the next term. GENERAL ELECTIONS are usually held on the Tuesday following the first Monday in November. Every race for elective office culminates in a general election campaign, regardless of level, from city council to the president of the United States. A general election is the voter's opportunity to express his or her preferences about the effectiveness of the government and have a say in its future direction.

In the republic's early days, the general election campaign was the only publicly contested BALLOT election. Primaries were nonexistent, as the political PARTY ORGANIZATIONS controlled the power of NOMINATION. Election campaigns were raucous affairs, conducted partly by speeches on tree stumps at public events and partly through a partisan newspaper press. With party loyalty and VOTER TURNOUT both high throughout the 1800s, general election campaigns were little more than elaborate GET-OUT-THE-VOTE drives.

CAMPAIGN SLOGANS were a common electioneering practice. William Henry Harrison, who as a general had won the Battle of Tippecanoe in Indiana, used "Tippecanoe and Tyler too" as his 1840 slogan, and the adage remains an identifiable campaign slogan a century and a half later. Mudslinging, or negative attack campaigns, has also been part of general elections from the early days. Thomas Jefferson and John Adams attacked each other in 1800, while Grover Cleveland was accused of fathering an illegitimate child during his campaigns for the nation's highest office in the late 1800s.

As the 20th century dawned, general election campaigns were preceded by PRIMARY elections within the political parties. An independent press also focused attention on the general election campaign and turned the thrust of those campaigns from a party-centered model to a candidate-centered one. To reduce fraud, voters were required to register before they could vote in an election. General election campaigns became progressively more dependent on broadcast media such as radio and television, and the divorce of power from political parties meant that candidates had to organize, fund, and publicize their campaigns. The predominance of the candidate's role in the general election campaign led to a greater emphasis on FUNDRAISING and professional assistance in the form of hired political consultants to perform the technical tasks of the election campaign such as producing and purchasing media advertising, managing the day-to-day activities of the campaign, polling, and campaign strategy.

Most general election campaigns are decided on election night with a decisive victory for one candidate or another. However, in 2000, one of the most contentious and difficult general election campaigns for president ended in an effective tie. While Gore began with a strong lead in opinion polls, Bush eroded Gore's lead over time. It took more than a month and a Supreme Court decision to ultimately determine the winner in this closely fought PRESIDENTIAL ELECTION.

Candidates continue to contest general election campaigns, only now their attention is usually divided between the general and the prerequisite election campaign, the primary. In some dominant one-party areas, in fact, the primary election is more important than the general. In Kansas, for instance, the REPUBLICAN PARTY is the dominant political force. Republican support is so strong that in many cases the candidate who wins the Republican primary is virtually guaranteed to win the general election campaign. In other states, a contentious primary election can expend vital resources, giving the eventual nominee a difficult fundraising path to general election campaign competitiveness.

Independent candidates generally do not have primary competition, though they must usually undergo a lengthy and difficult petition process merely to be listed on the ballot. Once on the ballot, those candidates without a party generally lose due to the widespread support for the two dominant American parties.

Modern political campaigns are more expensive than ever: U.S. senator Jon Corzine (D, New Jersey) spent $63 million of his own assets in his 2000 campaign for the Senate. U.S. House races typically spend more than $1 million on their contests, and estimates of the 2004 PRESIDENTIAL ELECTION cost suggest that more than a billion dollars was spent by candidates, parties, and other interested actors.

Despite the increased cost and constant media attention, voter participation in general election campaigns has declined since World War II, reaching an all-time low for presidential elections at 49.1 percent of eligible voters in 1996. Since 1996, there has been an up-tick in participation. Moreover, registered voter turnout in presidential elections remains high, with more than 70 percent of eligible registered voters casting a ballot in 2000 and 2004.

Further reading: Flanigan, William H., and Nancy Zingale. *Political Behavior of the American Electorate.* Washington, D.C.: Congressional Quarterly Press, 2003; Kavanagh, Dennis. *Election Campaigning.* Oxford: Blackwell, 1995; Patterson, Thomas E. *The Vanishing Voter.* New York: Vintage Books, 2004; Popkin, Samuel L. *The Reasoning Voter.* Chicago: University of Chicago Press, 1993.

—Chapman Rackaway

campaign, Internet

An Internet campaign is the use of Internet technologies, such as electronic mail (e-mail) and the World Wide Web (WWW, or Web), to communicate campaign messages directly to voters. The Internet's interactive communication nature makes it relatively easy for candidates or INTEREST GROUPS to organize mass groups for political rallies, GET-OUT-THE-VOTE (GOTV) drives, and other political events. Candidates use the Internet for voter outreach, volunteer recruitment, FUNDRAISING, and feedback from the citizens who visit their sites.

In the 1990s, the Internet, a nebulous network of computers interconnected over data transmission lines, provided candidates with a new opportunity to spread their message, this time directly to the voters. Unlike radio and television, the Internet allows two-way communication. Not only can the campaigns distribute their messages to the voters, but voters can provide feedback, contribute to campaigns, and organize themselves using the electronic communications tools available online. Candidates can use e-mail messages to reach large numbers of voters with the same message, or establish World Wide Web pages to have a presence where voters can find a message completely controlled by the campaign and its strategists.

While DIRECT MAIL and television provide more exposure than e-mails and Web sites, campaigns can control costs better with Web sites. Direct mailings require printing and mailing, both of which are cost-intensive. A Web site, once online, need only be updated regularly by staffers

or consultants. The cost for posting material on a Web site is incurred only once, and there is no additional cost per person viewing the material, unlike a mail piece.

Regarding broadcast communication, Web sites provide three advantages over television: First, Web sites are much more cost effective than buying television time. Second, television paid spots run from 15 to 60 seconds. A Web site can provide as much information as the candidates wish to post, and voters can spend as much time paying attention to the site as they want. Third, candidate attempts to "earn" media time can produce added exposure but also the risk of analysis detrimental to the candidate that undermines the EARNED MEDIA, while with a Web site the campaign can control all of the message that a visitor receives.

The Web's capability to track who views the site and its specific content pages can provide the campaign valuable data about potential voters. By 1996, both the major party presidential nominees had Web sites, and the innovative campaign technique was already trickling down to House, Senate, and statewide races.

In the short time since Bob Dole haltingly spelled out the Web address of his campaign site in a 1996 PRESIDENTIAL DEBATE, candidates have aggressively embraced the Internet as a campaign medium. In 2000, a voter looking for information on the two major party nominees for president needed to go no further than George W. Bush or Al Gore's Web sites. The two campaign Web sites included press releases, texts of speeches, live video, and critiques of the opposing candidate's stands. The sites contained additional information for those wishing to receive e-mail newsletters, to volunteer for placing yard signs, and to make donations. Congressional campaigns followed suit, with numerous consulting firms specializing in campaign Web site design.

In 2002, 88 percent of all incumbent members of Congress, 92 percent of CHALLENGERS, and 99 percent of all open seat candidates had campaign Web sites, and 41 percent of all candidates used a specialized Web consultant to construct their sites, according to the Congressional Campaign Study from the University of Maryland's Center for American Politics and Citizenship. While not as widespread as congressional sites, many state representatives (particularly in areas of high-technology development, such as Silicon Valley in California) have put simple pages online with contact information, schedules of appearances, and campaign information for voters to digest.

In 2004, campaigns continue to develop Internet resources. One of the innovators in Internet campaigning was former Vermont governor Howard Dean, a Democratic hopeful for president. Dean used the Web site Meetup.com to organize gatherings of his scattered supporters to expand his campaign's presence. The Dean campaign attracted 138,000 volunteers to meet at 820 locations to work for the candidate in November 2003. Dean was also the first candidate to introduce a "blog," or daily Web log of campaign appearances and news analysis to provide constant new content and encourage regular viewings of his site. Finally, Dean became the first candidate to raise a majority of his funds through contributions given from visitors to his Web site. According to the Federal Elections Commission, Dean's INTERNET FUNDRAISING accounted for $7.9 million of the $14.8 million Dean earned from supporters in the final quarter of 2003.

The Internet as a technology and communication medium is still in the early stages of development. As broadband Internet connections expand throughout America and the world, the opportunities to use the more technical aspects of the Internet will continue to expand. The pace of POLITICS has quickened as the instantaneous nature of the Internet has been used to some of its potential by campaigns. Candidates can place press releases online immediately following an issue, and campaign news is available close to real time. Political campaigns, as a result, have had to become much more attentive and fast-moving to respond to the quicker pace of the Internet campaign.

For the Internet campaign to be an integral part of politicking in the future, inequalities in the diffusion of Internet access must be minimized. For example, white families, particularly those with higher incomes, are much more likely to have access to the Internet than are African Americans. Unlike direct mail, for which almost all voters have a mailing address to which candidates can send correspondences, if voters do not have a computer with Internet access available to them, the Internet campaign cannot reach these voters. As technology continues to advance and access to the Internet becomes nearly universal, its importance as a political tool is likely to increase dramatically.

Further reading: Bimber, Bruce, and Richard Davis. *Campaigning Online: The Internet in U.S. Elections.* New York: Oxford University Press, 2003; Herrnson, Paul S. *Congressional Elections.* 4th ed. Washington, D.C.: CQ Press, 2002; History of Campaign Websites. Available online. URL: http://iml.jou.ufl.edu/projects/fall01%5CDu-Bose. Accessed August 10, 2005; Trippi, Joe. *The Revolution Will Not Be Televised: Democracy, the Internet, and the Overthrow of Everything.* New York: Regan Books, 2004.

—Chapman Rackaway

campaign, media

The media are central actors in modern political campaigns, and attempts to influence the public through thoughtful media campaigns have become an important part of American electoral POLITICS. Candidates employ election strategies that aim to use the media to focus public attention on the issues that help them and hurt their opponents. These strategies, crafted either by professional consultants or the candidate, constitute the modern media campaign. The principal tools of media campaigns attempt to influence media coverage by trying to "earn media" and by using campaign funds to pay for advertisements ("PAID MEDIA").

EARNED MEDIA is the coverage that is provided as "news" by the media to the public. Candidates have only limited control over earned media, but it is often seen as more credible than the candidates' own advertisements. Politicians use several strategies such as news releases, press conferences, media events, and photo opportunities to try to generate news coverage. Of course, journalists ultimately decide what makes news. This means that a candidate's mistakes, controversial statements, and SCANDALS are as likely to make the nightly news as coverage that favors the candidate's campaign themes.

In modern campaigns, alternative forms of earned media coverage have become an essential part of the process. Today presidential candidates make their appointed rounds on late-night television, *Larry King Live, Saturday Night Live,* the *Oprah Winfrey Show,* and the *Daily Show.* Candidates are often more comfortable on programs such as these than the more combative cable news programs, since they foster a more supportive atmosphere and help the candidates look more like regular Americans. Additionally, debates and national conventions are also venues in which candidates receive free coverage under fairly controlled environments.

Not all candidates are equally capable of attracting earned media coverage. Candidates for the House of Representatives typically have a difficult time attracting news coverage. This is especially true for unknown CHALLENGERs who have little appeal to news programmers. Incumbents also have a FUNDRAISING advantage over challengers, making it easier for reelection seekers to buy ad time on television, adding to the incumbent's media advantage.

Paid media, or advertising, is a powerful weapon in a candidate's campaign arsenal because it enables a candidate to control the message brought to the public. Advertising can affect political learning in the public, set voters' issue agendas, answer opponents' claims, and influence the criteria voters use to make political decisions. The bulk of spending in American campaigns, at all levels of the political process, is directed at paid media. It can take the shape of expensive television or radio advertisements or might consist of things as simple and time-tested as bumper stickers, yard signs, and buttons. What these campaign tactics have in common is that they are designed to influence how people vote by delivering a carefully crafted message that costs money.

The 2004 PRESIDENTIAL ELECTION season dramatically highlighted how the use of the Internet can also be a valuable media tool. The Democratic PRIMARY candidate Howard Dean used the Web to raise unprecedented amounts of money in the form of small, individual donations. His Web site's Web log, or "blog," described life on the campaign trail and instantly required all other serious candidates to add a blog to their own Web site.

Since the point of media campaigns is not to educate voters but to influence the way people vote, they come with several important consequences. Media campaigns are often associated with low levels of voter knowledge in the United States. For example, when voters were polled to see if they could identify issue positions with the right presidential candidate in 2000, the most common answer was "I don't know." Voters correctly matched a candidate to an issue position 34 percent of the time and were wrong in another 19 percent of their answers. To combat this, many media critics have called on the mass media to decrease its penchant for horserace coverage (stories focusing on who is winning) and increase the amount of stories about candidates' issue positions, past records, and differences from other candidates.

Many political scientists, however, have found evidence that voters are able to use minimal amounts of information to make "rational" decisions. For instance, a voter who can match the candidate's party label to his or her own party preference is likely to vote for the person who most closely matches the voter's own issue preferences. The media are especially helpful to UNDECIDED VOTERS, who often use the information provided to them by the media to help them make their final decisions.

Beyond the important issue of voter knowledge, research points to several additional consequences of media politics. Some scholars argue that the pervasiveness of the media has resulted in a decline in the importance of political parties (though other scholars vehemently contest this notion). Others argue that journalists and PUNDITs have grown too powerful, especially in their ability to identify FRONTRUNNERS in PRESIDENTIAL PRIMARIES. Others argue that the traits that make a candidate good on television do not necessarily translate into leadership traits once in office. And finally, the importance of paid media, which grows in expense with each ELECTION CYCLE, is believed to have transformed American electoral politics into a race to raise money.

Further reading: American Museum of the Moving Image. Available online. URL: http://livingroomcandidate. movingimage.us. Accessed August 10, 2005; Graber, Doris A. *Mass Media and American Politics*. Washington, D.C.: CQ Press, 1997; Iyengar, Shanto, and Richard Reeves. *Do the Media Govern?: Politicians, Voters, and Reporters in America*. Thousand Oaks, Calif.: Sage Publications, 1997; Paletz, David L. *The Media in American Politics: Contents and Consequences*. 2nd ed. New York: Longman, 2002.

—Michael W. Wagner

campaign, nomination

Since the election of 1796, there has been a preliminary contest for the selection of presidential candidates for the national political parties. What began as an arcane, haphazard, and informal congressional caucus and state legislature–dominated process overtly controlled by elites in the Federalist and Jeffersonian eras, evolved gradually into a more formalized, national convention-based process. With the introduction of the nominating party PRIMARY in the Progressive Era, the conventions themselves became more and more formalized, objectively more democratic, and ultimately less consequential.

At the end of President Washington's second term, two competing national parties had clearly emerged—the Democratic-Republicans (not associated with either the modern Democratic or Republican Parties), led by Jefferson, and the Federalists, led by Alexander Hamilton. Democratic-Republicans universally agreed on Jefferson for president, and thus no meeting for NOMINATION was required. The Federalists, however, had to call a gathering of sorts to nominate John Adams. After Adams's first term, both parties called a formal congressional caucus to meet in secret to nominate their candidates for the presidency, again choosing Jefferson and Adams.

From the election of 1800 through the election of 1820, relatively secret caucuses of the two major parties' members of Congress, with a modicum of variance (e.g., the Federalists holding a caucus of state party leaders in 1808), were the mechanisms for choosing their presidential and vice presidential candidates. The Federalists never again won an election after Adams's first term and after 1812 were nearly extinct. Thus, in the two elections following 1812, the Democratic-Republican congressional caucus's choice for president, in both instances James Monroe, was met with no opposition. In 1824, however, only five states sent their congressional delegations to meet for a nominating caucus, and its candidate, William H. Crawford, was met with three-pronged opposition from Henry Clay, Andrew Jackson, and John Quincy Adams, all of whom disavowed the caucus as corrupt and whose home states were guaranteeing them places on the BALLOT regardless of any organization's nomination. In the 1828 election, President Adams and Senator Jackson were nominated by various state legislatures and state nominating conventions.

Beginning with the 1832 ELECTION CYCLE, the ANTI-MASONIC PARTY called a national convention to nominate William Wirt for president and to proclaim its principles of Anti-Masonry. The Jacksonian Democrats did likewise, assembling a convention of DELEGATEs from each state, nominating Andrew Jackson, and providing a platform of principles on which the president was running for reelection. The short-lived National Republicans did the same, assembling a convention of state delegates in Baltimore, nominating Henry Clay for president, and issuing a statement of principle, yet not a platform.

Thereafter, every major POLITICAL PARTY that nominated a candidate for president followed the format laid out in that election of 1832 of a national nominating convention that chose a presidential and vice presidential candidate and issued a party platform, or statement of principle. Both parties, the Democratic in particular, however, institutionalized various convention rules that were meant to resolve quadrennial regional conflicts within the party, such as the "two-thirds rule" or the "UNIT RULE."

For most of the period from 1832 until the Progressive Era of the early 1900s, the chief requirement for nomination was to amass the required number of delegates in one of the major parties' national conventions, be it a simple majority or a two-thirds majority needed to nominate a candidate, and a candidate was virtually assured a spot on the ballot of every state in the Union. If a candidate hoped to win, he often would have a substantial regional or state base of support (in the South, for instance, or in a large state such as New York or Virginia) that was enough to preclude another candidate's realistic chance of attaining a majority of delegates and winning the nomination. If there was no national consensus about the overwhelming choice of the party, if the party did not have an incumbent running for reelection, or if there was sufficient majority opposition to a candidate with substantial support (e.g., the "Stop Grant" forces of the Republican convention in 1880), it might take dozens of ballots and several days to winnow the field down to a manageable number of candidates and ultimately choose a nominee.

Beginning in 1900, the statewide public nominating primary was introduced in Florida's delegate selection process, the purpose of which was to "pledge"—in a binding way, commit—that state's convention delegates to vote for a particular candidate on the first ballot of the convention. By 1912, 13 states were holding primaries to choose the REPUBLICAN PARTY's nominee. Though more than 50 percent of the votes cast in those 13 primaries were for former president Theodore Roosevelt, a slight majority of delegates at the national convention voted for and thus nominated Taft on the first ballot of the 1912 Republican convention. Taft had allied with the leaders of the party in all the other states that had not yet held primaries, the traditional method of building support as opposed to popular appeal.

Since 1912, primaries have become an increasingly vital part of the nominating process, and a majority of states now hold PRESIDENTIAL PRIMARIES to choose their pledged delegates to the national conventions, to the point that the convention itself has become largely a formality, and the parties' nominees are chosen months before the convention. There was an effort in the Progressive Era to move toward a national day of primaries, but, almost a century after that effort began, the quadrennial process is still largely a product of uncoordinated state primaries scheduled in no particular order. Many states hold presidential primaries a significantly long time after a majority of delegates have been won, guaranteeing the nomination to a particular candidate, through both popular election and through the votes of party leaders who still hold sway in both major parties' nomination processes. Many states also do not hold presidential primaries, deferring to the other, perhaps larger, states to choose the party's nominee.

Since the 1950s, two small, rural states, Iowa and New Hampshire, have held the first primaries in the election cycle, as early as January of an election year that ends in November. A large number of states with large populations, such as California, New York, and Massachusetts, have grouped their presidential primaries into an event called SUPER TUESDAY in which a large enough number of delegates are chosen to de facto decide the party's nominee as early as March, while the de jure, pro forma nominating convention is not held until July or August.

In order to sustain enough popular interest in a campaign to last from January, when the first primary is held, until July or August, a candidate must, as of 2004, spend upwards of $200,000,000 in campaign costs of advertising and overhead maintenance, most of it raised from the financial services industry in both major parties, even if that candidate is an incumbent without major opposition within his or her own party. After the nominating conventions, each candidate receives approximately $75 million (in 2004, subject to change, usually increase, during every election) in federal funds to carry out the GENERAL ELECTION. In order to be a viable candidate in Iowa and New Hampshire, as well as on Super Tuesday, candidates needed to raise at least $50 million in the year preceding the general election. While several candidates may appear in party-sponsored candidate debates, there are typically only two or three who are able to present themselves as viable party candidates capable of raising enough money in financial contributions for his or her campaign by the time Iowa and New Hampshire hold their primaries.

The process has changed and evolved much over the last two centuries, but fundamentally, in order to attain the nomination of one of the two major parties, one must still have a significant base of support within or independent of the party proper well before the general election in order to run for the presidency. In 1800, Congress's favor had to be curried in order to win the nomination from the party's congressional caucus, but in 2004, the favor of significant financial interests and party leaders, as well as voters, must be gained in order to become a party's choice for the presidency.

Further reading: Benson, Lee. *The Concept of Jacksonian Democracy.* Princeton, N.J.: Princeton University

Press, 1961; Brown, Clifford Waters, Lynda W. Powell, and Clyde Wilcox. *Serious Money: Fundraising and Contributing in Presidential Nomination Campaigns*. Cambridge: Cambridge University Press, 1995.

—Daniel T. Kirsch

campaign, political

In the political context, the term *campaign* is used to describe an effort to advance a candidate or platform via electoral, legislative, GRASSROOTS, or communications strategies. The word has its origins in describing a series of military maneuvers designed to pursue a strategic goal. This original application explains the etymological origins of campaign. It is a slight distortion of a term, originating from Latin, referring to a large open space or field. The military employment arises from the traditional physical locus of armed combat. It recalls a time when armies clashed on battlefields as opposed to in cities and towns. The usage of the word *campaign* has extended itself to many activities resembling a military effort, from a corporate marketing strategy to an athletic team's season. POLITICS is one realm in which the metaphor has become embedded.

In its broadest sense, the notion of a campaign has always been central to all complex political interaction and certainly has consistently figured in American politics. Political actors, from individuals to INTEREST GROUPS, have always been defined in terms of certain aspirations, and their efforts have often been strategically intended to seek desired outcomes.

As noted earlier, political campaigns can be identified in legislative settings. LOBBYISTs certainly mount campaigns. Often their tactics are limited to those employed behind closed doors or person to person. Sometimes, though, an effort to affect legislation, either in Congress or at a state house, involves a broader mobilization of public support. One prominent such example was the television advertisement series launched by insurance providers to bolster their opposition to the Clinton health care proposal. Campaigns have even featured prominently in nondemocratic systems, in which public outpourings can force action on the part of those holding political power.

The term *campaign* is most persistently used in politics to discuss the pursuit of electoral objectives, such as electing or defeating a candidate or passing or rejecting a BALLOT INITIATIVE. In this context, *campaign* is used as both a noun and a verb. As a noun, the word is applied to describe either the entirety of a contest (encompassing all vying candidates or platforms), or to identify one particular side of the contest. One can either talk about America's quadrennial presidential campaign or specifically reference candidate X's campaign. More specifically, the latter noun usage can refer either to the strategies employed by one political side or the actual team of individuals employing those strategies. The verb form of the word denotes activities

undertaken as part of a campaign. For example, one can note that a candidate made a stop to campaign in a local eatery or at a factory.

The objectives of an electoral campaign can vary widely. The focus is often not so simple as placing a candidate in an office. The increased incidence of ballot initiatives and referenda in America means that many campaigns seek to directly impact the law.

When political office is the object of a campaign, goals can still be quite nuanced. In most elections in the United States, the winner is the highest vote getter. In such cases, the simplest goal might be to receive at least one more vote than any other candidate. Some U.S. election laws, however, alter this dynamic. Laws providing for runoffs, for instance, might create a situation in which a campaign's goal in the GENERAL ELECTION may be to get a particular candidate past that initial contest and strategically keep other candidates from advancing to a runoff ballot.

Even in the absence of such complications, objectives may differ. A favored incumbent might consider a campaign unsuccessful if he or she fails to win by a sufficient landslide. Lyndon Johnson, for example, was proven vulnerable in a 1968 NEW HAMPSHIRE PRIMARY, despite the fact that he soundly defeated CHALLENGER Eugene McCarthy in the Granite State. Johnson eventually opted not to seek an additional term. Conversely, a little-known challenger may be pleased with a relatively modest showing if her goal was to gain credibility for a future political pursuit. A variant of this is repeatedly played out during the nominating portion of America's presidential campaign season when candidates seek to build momentum by exceeding expectations, though not necessarily winning, in primaries or caucuses.

If the goal of a campaign is simply to win an election, by whatever margin, the approach may still vary substantively. A campaign might focus on increasing its candidate's vote total. On the other hand, a campaign might plot to suppress an opponent's numbers. Often, campaigns pursue a combination of these two strategies. The structure of an electoral system can greatly influence tactical behavior as well. America's ELECTORAL COLLEGE system, for instance, dictates that candidates are not ultimately seeking the highest vote total nationally, so campaign strategies are based on maximizing a candidate's allotment of electors.

Some campaigns never hold out serious hopes of victory. This has especially been true of "third-party" ventures. Ralph Nader's 2000 run for president was said to have aspired to 5 percent of the POPULAR VOTE, a goal not reached, but one that would have allowed his GREEN PARTY to receive federal funding during the next ELECTION CYCLE. Goals short of ballot tally victory, for both major and third-party campaigns, can include raising issue salience, establishing a PARTY ORGANIZATION, forcing a favored candidate or party to spend funds, increasing or decreasing

VOTER TURNOUT to influence another contest, and even gaining publicity to boost a nonpolitical business venture.

Much about campaigning in America has changed since the political system was established. For instance, it was not always considered appropriate to openly pursue personal political advancement, especially publicly. Particularly at the level of presidential politics, early candidates did not seek office in the modern sense. The first contest characterized by a mass vote mobilization effort fitting today's paradigm was Andrew Jackson's 1828 campaign against John Quincy Adams.

Since that time, presidential campaigns have grown to gargantuan proportions, involving thousands of campaign staffers and hundreds of millions of dollars. Certainly, many campaigns below the presidential level still operate with little or no staff and on limited budgets. However, at almost every level, from municipal elections on up, competitive races demand massive expenditures and sophisticated CAMPAIGN ORGANIZATIONS. Many attribute the skyrocketing cost of campaigns to the greater role of television advertising in message delivery. The increased complexity of campaigning has promoted a proliferation of campaign professionals. Campaigns for higher-level offices typically feature paid campaign staffs as well as teams of consultants ranging in specialization from PAID MEDIA and polling to FUNDRAISING and GET-OUT-THE-VOTE mobilization.

Despite the growth of the campaign industry and the rising cost of campaigns, some disagreement still exists in academic circles as to the actual affect of campaigns on electoral outcomes. Some argue that the conditions surrounding an election and the personality traits of the candidates are far more impactful upon the result. Others see the role of campaigns and the events they generate, such as debates and stump speeches, as instrumental in electoral politics.

Further reading: Faucheux, Ronald A., ed. *Winning Elections: Political Campaign Management, Strategy, and Tactics.* New York: M. Evans & Company, 2001; Shea, Daniel M. *Campaign Craft: The Strategies, Tactics, and Art of Political Campaign Management.* Westport, Conn.: Praeger Publishers, 1996; Thurber, James A., and Candice J. Nelson, eds. *Campaigns and Elections American Style (Transforming American Politics).* Boulder, Colo.: Westview Press, 1995.

—Alex Theodoridis

campaign buttons

While their role in message delivery has become more limited than it once was, campaign buttons remain one of the most popular political collectibles. Buttons have figured prominently in American political history, and they are still considered a staple of electoral campaigning.

American politicians as early as George Washington were reported to have worn political buttons. These early

Campaign button from 1900 with the McKinley-Roosevelt slogan, "Four Years More of the Full Dinner Pail" *(David J. & Janice L. Frent Collection/Corbis)*

versions, however, share more of a resemblance with today's broaches than with our modern image of a button. They were essentially pieces of metal modestly bearing a slogan or name.

Campaign buttons took a step forward in the 1830s, when advances in photographic technology allowed shots of candidates to be attached to pins. This offered many citizens their first opportunity to glimpse a candidate's image.

A major technological advancement came in the 1890s, when Whitehead and Hoag, a company in New Jersey, patented a procedure for constructing the modern button. This process used a relatively new material, called celluloid, layered over a piece of paper with an image imprinted on it, then over a metal backing and a pin. All of these components were then pressed together, resulting in what remains the most common form of button.

Political campaigns were quick to use the new technology, which made button production far more cost-effective. The 1896 race between William McKinley and William Jennings Bryan saw the first mass use of modern-style political buttons.

That usage has continued to this day. At times, campaign buttons have been a significant feature of a campaign effort. The most notable and perhaps most successful example was the placement of Dwight D. Eisenhower's slogan, "I Like Ike," on political buttons. This motto was ideally suited for the medium. Its brevity meant that it fit perfectly and readably on the face of a button, and the direct, first-person phrasing meant that the individual donning the pin was making a bold statement about both

Eisenhower and herself. "I Like Ike" continues to be regarded as one of the most effective slogans in American campaign history, and political buttons played an instrumental role in its dissemination.

The campaign button is ideally suited for the demonstration of political opinions by one individual to another in a setting characterized by high rates of interpersonal contact. The current social structure, for a variety of reasons, increasingly favors such demonstrations via other vehicles, such as automobile bumper stickers and yard signs. Even in those settings in which buttons would excel, modern campaigns often opt for more inexpensive disposable lapel stickers.

The decreased practical value of political buttons is also probably linked to the increased extent to which campaigns are waged over the television airwaves. Whereas citizens were once convinced that their friends and neighbors supported certain candidates or causes by the display of political buttons, the modern campaign seeks to create that bandwagon, or opinion-leader, effect through careful scripting and casting of campaign advertisements.

Further reading: Hake, Ted. *Encyclopedia of Political Buttons: United States 1896–1972.* York, Pa.: Hake's Americana & Collectibles, 1985; Thurber, James A., and Candice J. Nelson, eds. *Campaigns and Elections American Style (Transforming American Politics).* Boulder, Colo.: Westview Press, 1995.

—Alex Theodoridis

campaign consultant

A paid professional charged with the strategic or administrative development of a political campaign. Campaign consultants may assist a candidate in managing the campaign, developing campaign strategy, conducting opinion polls, raising money for the race, producing or buying broadcast and print advertisements, and creating DIRECT MAIL appeals. Additionally, consultants may provide direction for a POLITICAL PARTY's electioneering efforts, as well as public relations assistance and lobbying support to INTEREST GROUPS. Consultants usually operate in firms, often associated with one political party or the other. Many consultants begin their careers by working for a political party in an official capacity before leaving for a career in consultancy. Unlike CAMPAIGN MANAGERS, political consultants are not employees of the campaign but are instead privately contracted consultants. In most cases, political consultants do not work exclusively for one campaign, as they often have multiple clients in different localities. They also differ from campaign managers in that they are not responsible for the day-to-day administrative matters of a campaign.

Throughout the first century of American elections, political parties managed the administration, FUNDRAISING, and strategy of political campaigns because candidates relied on the party for direction. The parties may have assigned a particular individual to aid specific campaigns, particularly persons with abundant personal contacts or flexible work schedules. As political parties progressively weakened throughout the 20th century, candidates looked to other sources to guide them in the operation of their campaigns. Radio and television created methods for candidates to appeal to voters directly, bypassing the party apparatus and requiring approaches to those new media. Since political campaigns are analogous to public relations campaigns, consultants in the modern mold evolved from public relations professionals. Party loyalists lacked that expertise, but professionals with broadcast training could help candidates formulate a media-friendly image.

In *The Rise of Political Consultants*, Larry Sabato points to the state of California and Pacific Gas and Electric (PG&E) Company's fight over the state's Central Valley Project in 1933 as the first example of a public information campaign using political paid professionals. The state legislature passed the Central Valley Project, which created a flood control and irrigation program for the northern part of the state. PG&E immediately began a BALLOT INITIATIVE campaign to overturn the project. The Central Valley Project proponents hired a press agent and public relations specialist to defeat the initiative, and they succeeded. Ironically, PG&E later hired the two consultants who defeated their initiative. One of those consultants, Clem Whitaker, would play a vital role in the birth of campaign consulting as a profession.

The very first political consulting firm, Campaigns, Inc., was founded in California in the 1930s by Clem Whitaker and Leone Baxter. That California was the birthplace of political consulting is not surprising, since the party apparatus in the state had been weakened due to Progressive Era reforms that had been adopted by the state between 1910 and 1930. These reforms left political consultants to provide services to California candidates that parties were providing in other states. California continued to remain at the forefront of the industry as consultants rose in power and influence in the 1970s and 1980s.

Across the United States, the use of consultants continued to grow into the 1950s, and by the 1970s their participation in the development of campaigns was a regular occurrence. Continual party decline and advancing technologies made campaigns much more specialized and in need of expertise that professionals could provide. Specialists consulting in computers and databases, media production and buying, polling, research, and voter outreach emerged from the original public relations model of consulting. By the 1990s, the field was large enough to yield its own magazine, *Campaigns and Elections,* and a network of professionals who provided services to any campaign.

Consultants are especially important today for candidates without extensive experience in campaigning. Candidates hire consultants throughout the course of a campaign to execute plans that will satisfy their overall goals. Early in a campaign, a candidate may hire a pollster, fundraiser, and strategic consultant to plan the message and approach the campaign will take. Later, the candidate may hire a technology consultant for voter databases, a media producer and buyer, and a World Wide Web consultant to craft other forms of campaign communication. Media, technology, and strategy have developed to such a degree that "learning on the job" will result in candidates losing by wide margins. Television is one area where consultants are important. Image-making, purchasing television time in ways to maximize exposure among likely and UNDECIDED VOTERS, and effective dialogue in ads are skills that most people lack. A paid professional allows the candidate to create a television presence that synchronizes well with the campaign's strategy. Computer technology is an emergent area in campaign consultancy. Firms build World Wide Web pages, develop and use lists of voters in the campaign's district to target LIKELY VOTERS and potential fundraising sources, and develop or use software for campaign finance compliance accounting and scheduling.

As the profession of political consulting has risen in prominence in American campaigns, so has the celebrity of individual political consultants. Perhaps the most famous political consultant is James Carville, whose Cajun accent and outsized personality, as well as his noteworthy romantic relationship with Republican consultant Mary Matalin, made Carville a press favorite during his 1992 work for Bill Clinton's first presidential campaign. After helping Clinton to victory that year and marrying Matalin the next, Carville has remained in the limelight, writing several best-selling books and appearing not only on political programs but also in situation comedies and movies. More recently in the George W. Bush administration, political consultant Karl Rove has achieved star status. Rove has been a focus of Democratic criticism of the Bush administration, as he is seen as a key figure not only in Bush's political decisions but also in his policy decisions. Republicans, on the other hand, have lauded Rove's involvement in the Bush administration.

It is important to note that consultants make strategic choices when deciding whether to work with a campaign, and campaigns also think strategically when hiring a consulting firm. A series of losses can cause consultants to lose professional prestige and can hurt a consultant financially in this highly competitive business. Thus, consultants seek out candidates who have a high chance of success, so as to pad the firm's win-lose rate. Likewise, competitive campaigns seek out prestigious consultants not just for their advice, but also as a public symbol of the campaign's seriousness and competitiveness. Early in a political contest, political insiders often note which campaigns have hired prominent consultants, which in turn can lead to increased monetary donations and press coverage.

Consultant use is widespread in elections today. Presidential and senatorial elections are uniform in their employment of professionals to manage, strategize, and reach out to voters in their campaigns. Congressional races are not uniform in their use, but consultants are still widely relied upon as campaigning's "hired guns." In the 2002 CONGRESSIONAL ELECTIONS, according to a survey by Paul Herrnson, consultant use was widespread particularly among those in competitive races. For competitive CHALLENGERS of incumbent House members, 81 percent used a consultant for polling and 69 percent hired out their media advertising. Strong open seat candidates, the other category of strong competition in House races, showed large percentages of consultant use: 43 percent used consultants for issue and OPPOSITION RESEARCH, 60 percent for direct mail outreach, and 46 percent for mass phone banking. *Campaigns and Elections* magazine estimates that campaign consultancy is now nearly a billion-dollar business. Despite negative public attitudes toward political professionals, consultants now appear to be a relatively permanent part of the American political campaign. Furthermore, reliance on consultants underscores the general weakness of American political parties.

Further reading: Bailey, Michael A., Ronald A. Faucheux, Paul S. Herrnson, and Clyde Wilcox. *Campaigns and Elections: Contemporary Case Studies.* Washington, D.C.: CQ Press, 2000; Burton, Michael John, and Daniel M. Shea. *Campaign Mode: Strategic Vision in Congressional Elections.* Lanham, Md.: Rowman & Littlefield, 2003; Johnson, Dennis W. *No Place for Amateurs: How Political Consultants Are Reshaping American Democracy.* New York: Routledge, 2001; Sabato, Larry J. *The Rise of Political Consultants.* New York: Basic Books, 1981; Simpson, Dick. *Winning Elections.* New York: Longman, 1996; Thurber, James A., and Candice J. Nelson. *Campaign Warriors.* Washington, D.C.: Brookings Institution, 2000; Trent, Judith S., and Robert V. Friedenburg. *Political Campaign Communication.* Westwood, Conn.: Praeger Publishers, 2000.

—Brian Arbour and Chapman Rackaway

campaign consultant, media

A media campaign consultant is a paid, outside adviser to a campaign who suggests how, when, and where a candidate should deliver his or her campaign message and what that message should be. Due to the importance of television in campaigning, most major presidential, gubernatorial, Senate, and House candidates hire a media consultant. Media consultants are key members of a candidate's inner circle, in part because candidates are unlikely to succeed unless they can articulate their message. Media consultants determine the campaign's media strategy by shaping the candidate's message, deciding how to respond to attacks from the opponent, producing ads for the candidate, selecting markets in which to purchase ads, choosing when to run ads, talking to the press about the candidate's message, and acting as a sounding board for the candidate.

Media consultants work with other top advisers, such as pollsters, to determine how best to reach specific demographic groups. They are responsible for introducing a candidate to voters; distilling his or her message into brief spots, usually 30 seconds long; and determining which parts of a candidate's agenda are most important to convey to voters. Similarly, they highlight which parts of an opponent's record or views are most disturbing.

Consultants use advertising techniques to sell their candidates, such as Robert Squier's strategy of having Florida Democrat Bob Graham perform different jobs on "work days" as part of his successful 1978 gubernatorial campaign. Campaign commercials often rely on many of the same themes, such as fear or humor, as do corporate commercials. Media consultants may also coin catchy slogans to help voters remember the candidate. FOCUS GROUPS test most ads before they air publicly.

The rise of media consultants is a relatively recent phenomenon. Presidential candidates did not buy television ads before 1948, when less than 3 percent of American households had a television set. Even in 1952, when 45 percent of households owned a television, most media consultants were not important players but rather "technicians who purchased the air time, checked the lighting, supervised the make-up, arranged the set, and timed the speech," according to Kathleen Hall Jamieson. Still, Dwight Eisenhower's campaign saw the value in television, especially as advisers sought to manipulate his image from bumbling speaker to one who looked in command of issues when he talked. Media consultants became more influential in campaigns in the 1960s and 1970s, as more households purchased televisions and as candidates turned to outside advisers to fill the roles traditionally handled by political parties. By 1972, 85 percent of major Senate candidates and more than half of such House candidates ran television ads.

Media consultants enjoy a prominent role in campaigns because they influence the image voters have of the candidates. Accordingly, they oversee a large part of the campaign's budget. In March of 2004, for instance, President George W. Bush's reelection campaign spent $50 million; almost $41 million of it went to Maverick Media, a firm run by Bush media adviser Mark McKinnon. Mass-media advertising generally consumes about 45 percent of a congressional campaign's budget. Consultants make money on the ads, whether or not they are successful, because they charge a fee to place ads on stations.

In recent years, consultants have looked beyond purchasing ads on network television and radio as part of their paid-media strategy. Determining which markets will help influence votes is a key part of a media consultant's job. Many candidates now buy ads on cable television, which reaches fewer households than network television but is less expensive and can target specific audiences. Bush relied largely on cable to attack Senator John Kerry (D, Mass.) in the spring of 2004; his commercials aired on networks such as the Fox News Channel and ESPN, channels likely to reach his base.

Campaigns also used Web ads, both on their own sites and outside sites, as well as blogs to get out their message. Their free-media strategy included scheduling appearances on friendly outlets such as *The Daily Show* with Jon Stewart, which attracts young voters, and *Dr. Phil*, whose audience is largely women. CAMPAIGN LITERATURE, such as brochures, is another aspect of media strategy.

Many media consultants run their own companies and are well-known political figures in their own right. After Jimmy Carter won the White House in 1976, he sent media consultant Gerald Rafshoon a note that read, "I'll always be grateful that I was able to contribute in a small way to the victory of Rafshoon agency." Most media consultants have a large number of clients, in part to protect their win-lose record in the event a prominent candidate loses.

Media consultants often are personally close to candidates. Carter Eskew, who was a media consultant to Vice President Al Gore's 2000 presidential campaign, had worked on virtually all of Gore's previous campaigns. Robert Shrum, who held the same role for Kerry 2004, is close to Senator Edward Kennedy (D, Mass.), who provided many of Kerry's top advisers. Shrum was highly sought-after among Democratic presidential candidates, leading to what some observers dubbed the "Shrum primary" before the actual primaries.

Shrum suggested that Kerry wage a positive campaign, one emphasizing his service in the Vietnam War, rather than attack his Democratic PRIMARY opponents and Bush. A former journalist and speechwriter, he also helped Kerry prepare for the PRESIDENTIAL DEBATES. But Shrum's strategy was criticized by some Democrats, who thought Kerry should respond more forcefully to attacks by Bush and 527 groups such as the Swift Boat Veterans for Truth. During the last months of the campaign, Kerry brought in Democratic advisers Mike McCurry and Joe Lockhart to help him adopt a more aggressive tone.

A onetime songwriter and a Democrat, McKinnon's strategy was to attack Kerry throughout the campaign for changing his mind frequently on issues. He also came up with the circular podium from which Bush delivered his address at the 2004 convention, meant to portray Bush as in touch with voters. In addition, McKinnon developed ads that fell outside of certain campaign finance laws, thus freeing up money to purchase additional ads. Other media consultants well known within the political community include Democrat Mandy Grunwald, who worked on Bill Clinton's

1992 campaign, and Republicans Alex Castellanos and Stuart Stevens, both of whom worked on Bush's 2004 campaign.

Further reading: Jacobson, Gary C. *The Politics of Congressional Elections.* 6th ed. New York: Pearson Education, 2004; Jamieson, Kathleen Hall. *Packaging the Presidency: A History and Criticism of Presidential Campaign Advertising.* New York: Oxford University Press, 1992; Sabato, Larry J. *The Rise of Political Consultants: New Ways of Winning Elections.* New York: Basic Books, 1981.

—Mary Lynn F. Jones

campaign contribution limits

Campaign contribution limits are legal barriers placed on the type and maximum amount that individuals, political parties, or other interested groups may contribute to candidates for office, electioneering INTEREST GROUPS, or political parties. Limits may also be placed on the total amount of their own money candidates can spend on races, the maximum amount spent on a campaign, and the amount of money that interests and individuals can spend independently on behalf of candidates. The constant intent of campaign contribution limits is to reduce the potentially corrupting influence of money on the political process.

Former California assembly speaker Jesse Unruh is credited with stating that "money is the mother's milk of politics." However, politicians occasionally attempt to wean themselves from the pull of campaign contributions by limiting the amounts they can accept from donors. Originally, individuals and businesses could give unlimited sums to the parties and their candidates, leading to the widespread belief among the population that politicians were for sale.

In 1907, as a response to public dissatisfaction with the perceived corruption in politics, Congress passed the TILLMAN ACT, the first modern form of campaign contribution limitation. According to Tillman, registered corporations could not directly contribute to political campaigns. In 1910, the Publicity Act mandated reporting any contribution more than $100 in value. However, the laws were riddled with loopholes and suffered from rampant noncompliance.

In 1971, the most comprehensive effort to limit federal campaign contributions came in the form of the FEDERAL ELECTION CAMPAIGN ACT (FECA). Along with amendments in 1974, the FECA made all donations more than $25 subject to reporting, limited the amount candidates could spend on their own campaigns, and set limits on the amount individuals and groups could spend in campaigns. Individuals were limited to contributing $1,000 to candidates per election, $5,000 to interest groups, and $10,000 to parties. Groups could contribute no more than $5,000 to a candidate, and the parties were limited to contributions of $20,000 or less.

Despite a long history of campaign contribution limits at the federal level, the American states have been much slower to respond in kind. Now, according to the Campaign Disclosure Project, 49 of 50 states require the reporting of campaign contributions, 47 post data about those contributions on their state Web sites, and 48 have some form of campaign contribution limit in place. The state limits range from maximums of $250 contributions in five states to $2,000 in two. Currently, only two states do not place some form of ceiling on the amount of money an individual can contribute to a campaign, either in the form of a donation from a citizen or for the candidate's contribution to his or her own election.

Perhaps the most visible and significant violation of campaign contribution limits was the case of James Buckley, U.S. senator from New York. Buckley spent significant amounts of his personal fortune in running for the Senate, violating the limits placed on candidates in the FECA's 1974 amendments. Valeo, the Senate clerk who refused to seat Buckley after he won the seat, became the defendant in *BUCKLEY V. VALEO* (1976). In that case, the Supreme Court decided that Buckley's ability to spend his own money on a campaign could not be limited by the FECA and struck down the self-financing portion of the FECA as unconstitutional. In 2002, the Buckley ruling allowed a wealthy investment banker, John Corzine, to successfully run for the U.S. Senate from New Jersey. Fully self-financed, Corzine spent more than $60 million of his own money to win the seat.

Loopholes remained in the 1974 law, particularly one that allowed contributors to donate money to political parties (especially businesses, directly from their treasuries) for "party building activities," which were intended to include office space for the parties and GET-OUT-THE-VOTE (GOTV) drives. These contributions were known as SOFT MONEY. However, in 1996 the Supreme Court decided in *Colorado Republican Federal Campaign Committee v. FEC* that soft money could be used by the parties to pay for advertisements that did not expressly call for the election or defeat of a candidate. As a result, the parties began to run "issue" advertisements with negative statements about candidates of the other party and admonitions for voters to voice their displeasure to the candidates.

Despite the presence and expansion of limits, money continues to flow into politics in greater amounts than ever. The FECA did not, as originally intended, clean up corruption in politics or remove the stigma of influence peddling from campaign contributions. However, public support for increased limitations on campaign contributions remains very high. In 2002, President George W. Bush signed the Bipartisan Campaign Reform Act (BCRA, commonly known by its two Senate sponsors, John McCain of Arizona and Russ Feingold of Wisconsin, as MCCAIN-FEINGOLD), which doubled the individual contribution limits to campaigns and also banned soft money. The U.S. Supreme Court in 2003 upheld all of the McCain-Feingold provisions. As campaigners look to find new ways to circumvent these recent limits, undoubtedly future efforts will emerge to place new limits on campaign money, particularly in the states as they lag behind the national government's reform programs.

Further reading: Federal Election Commission. Available online. URL: http://www.fec.gov. Accessed August 10, 2005; Institute for Money in State Politics. Available online. URL: http://www.followthemoney.org. Accessed August 10, 2005; Herrnson, Paul S. *Congressional Elections.* 4th ed. Washington, D.C.: Congressional Quarterly Press, 2003; Morris, Dwight, and Murielle Gamache. *Gold Plated Politics: The 1992 Congressional Races.* Washington, D.C.: Congressional Quarterly Press, 1994; Magleby, David. *The Other Campaign: Soft Money and Issue Advocacy in the 2000 Congressional Elections.* Lanham, Md.: Rowman & Littlefield, 2003; Center for Responsive Politics. Available online. URL: http://www.opensecrets.org; Accessed August 10, 2005; Sorauf, Frank J. *Inside Campaign Finance: Myths and Realities.* New Haven, Conn.: Yale University Press, 1992.

—Chapman Rackaway

campaign contributions

Campaign contributions are donations by individuals or organizations to candidates, political parties, or other political organizations. There are two types of contributions, conventionally known as HARD MONEY and SOFT MONEY. Hard money contributions can be used by candidates, parties, or political organizations for any purpose, while soft money contributions are donations to parties or INTEREST GROUPS that cannot be used in coordination with a candidate's campaign and may not be used for communications that directly advocate the election or defeat of a candidate.

Hard money contribution limits for individuals were increased as part of the Bipartisan Campaign Reform Act (BCRA) of 2002. Currently, individuals may give no more than $2,000 per ELECTION CYCLE to any candidate, up to a total of $37,500. Both of these amounts are indexed to inflation. Prior to BCRA, individuals could give $1,000 to a candidate per election cycle, up to a total of $25,000. Individuals may also make contributions to POLITICAL ACTION COMMITTEES (PACs) of as much as $5,000, and as much as $20,000 to political parties, up to a total of $57,500 for PACs and parties combined. PACs may give up to $5,000 to any candidate per election cycle; this amount is not indexed to inflation. There is no limit on the total amount of money PACs can contribute to candidates. Political parties may give up to $5,000 to a House candidate and $35,000 to a Senate candidate; again, these limits are not indexed to inflation and there is no limit on total contributions from parties. Corporations and labor unions are prohibited from donating money to candidates, although corporations and

labor unions can form PACs. Candidates may make unlimited personal contributions to their own campaigns, although the "Millionaire's Amendment" to BCRA raised the contribution limits for candidates who are running against an opponent who has spent more than $250,000 of his or her own money. Contribution limits in such cases are raised according to a sliding scale; they can be raised as much as sixfold (that is, up to $12,000). Such contributions do not count against the total limits for donors, and when the millionaire provisions are triggered, parties may give unlimited amounts to candidates. Candidates who loan themselves money are prohibited from repaying more than $250,000 of their loans.

Prior to BCRA, individuals, corporations, or labor unions could make unlimited soft money contributions to political parties. In the 2000 election cycle, the political parties raised approximately $500 million in soft money and $741 million in hard money. BCRA prohibits soft money contributions to the national party organizations, although it does permit soft money contributions to state parties, subject to limitations on use and to state laws. It was expected that this change would dramatically decrease the influence of the political PARTY ORGANIZATIONS on the 2004 elections and increase the influence of so-called 527 organizations (named for the section of the tax code they file under), which could continue to accept donations in unlimited amounts and use these donations for political purposes—as long as they did not coordinate with a candidate or expressly advocate the election or defeat of a candidate.

Candidates, PACs, and parties are required by law to publicly disclose the name, address, amount given, and occupation of anyone who contributes more than $200 to them. The FEDERAL ELECTION COMMISSION maintains a database of all contributors. It is thus possible to know the total number of individuals who have made large contributions, but it is not possible to know the total number of citizens who contribute to federal candidates.

In 2000, approximately 51 percent of the campaign contributions received by House candidates came from individuals, 31 percent came from PACs, 2 percent came from the parties, and 11 percent was from the candidates themselves. In the Senate, 53 percent of campaign contributions in 2000 came from individuals, 13 percent came from PACs, 4 percent came from parties, and 24 percent came from the candidates. Incumbent members of both chambers of Congress tend to be more successful at garnering contributions from PACs than are CHALLENGERS or open seat candidates. Approximately 40 percent of incumbents' contributions in the House are from PACs, while slightly over 20 percent of incumbents' contributions in the Senate are from PACs. For challengers and open seat candidates in both chambers, approximately 10 percent of contributions come from PACs. Candidates in PRESIDENTIAL

PRIMARIES are much more dependent on individual contributions; in 2000, Al Gore and Bill Bradley did not accept PAC contributions in the primaries, while George W. Bush received less than 3 percent of his money from PACs, and John McCain received approximately 10 percent of his money from PACs.

Public opinion surveys such as the NATIONAL ELECTION STUDY have estimated that on average, slightly less than 10 percent of voting-age citizens contribute to political candidates each year. These individuals tend to be wealthier, better educated, and older than the average citizen. Contributors are also more likely to describe themselves as conservative and to belong to the REPUBLICAN PARTY than the average citizen. Among the various forms of political participation, however, the act of making a campaign contribution is unique in that making a contribution is not highly correlated with other types of participation—that is, if one makes a contribution this does not mean one is also likely to actively campaign for a candidate, to try to persuade others to vote for a candidate, or to engage in other types of political activity. This has led some political scientists to refer to contributions to political candidates or political causes as "checkbook participation"—that is, as a surrogate for spending time helping a campaign.

Studies of individuals who make large contributions (contributions of $200 or more) indicate that these individuals tend to give to multiple candidates and to be habitual givers. More than half of those who contribute to candidates for the House of Representatives say that they give in most elections, and slightly less than half of those who give to Senate candidates give in most elections. Overall, 72 percent of those who contributed $200 or more to any political organization said that they made a contribution in most elections.

There have been several controversies regarding campaign contributions. First, one of the major causes of the BCRA was the soft money spending of the political parties, particularly in the 1996 and 2000 PRESIDENTIAL ELECTIONS, and public criticism of the FUNDRAISING practices of the presidential candidates. President Clinton, for instance, was criticized for providing special access to the White House for those who contributed large amounts of soft money to the DEMOCRATIC PARTY. Because soft money contributions are unregulated, it has been argued, it is much more likely that individuals who make large contributions will receive political favors, such as audiences with political leaders on issues of personal concern. It has been argued that these large donors tend to have narrow economic interests at stake in elections, interests that most citizens do not share.

Similar arguments have been made regarding PAC contributions. There are approximately 4,000 PACs that are able to donate money to candidates, although fewer than 3,000 PACs make donations in each cycle. PACs contributed $245 million to congressional candidates in 2000. A long-running debate among political scientists revolves around whether PAC contributions influence electoral or legislative outcomes, or whether PAC contributions are designed to secure access to legislators. Despite the large amounts of money contributed by PACs to legislators, most research has failed to find a link between PAC contributions and policy outcomes. Despite the size and resources of many of the largest PACs, the fact that the maximum PAC contribution is only 2.5 times larger than the largest possible individual contribution may reduce the ability of an individual PAC to affect legislative outcomes due to its direct contributions alone.

With the prohibition on soft money contributions, many individuals and organizations have taken to BUNDLING contributions—that is, soliciting hard money contributions for a candidate from a number of individuals and presenting them to the candidate together, so that the candidate knows the individual or organization who asked these individuals to write the checks. This has been a practice of interest groups for several years. The liberal organization EMILY's LIST has bundled contributions for women candidates and raised $9.7 million for candidates in 2002. The conservative, antitax Club for Growth has pursued a similar strategy, bundling money for Republican candidates, often in PRIMARY elections; the group bundled a total of approximately $2 million for candidates in 2002. And MOVEON.ORG, an organization that bundles smaller contributions, bundled a total of $4.1 million in 2002.

Candidates, as well, have worked to encourage bundled contributions. Both George W. Bush and John Kerry had special programs for individuals who could bundle particular amounts of contributions. The 2004 Bush campaign assigned tracking numbers to individuals and instructed them to have those who bundled contributions at their request write the tracking number on their checks. Individuals who bundled at least $100,000 were dubbed "Pioneers," and individuals who bundled at least $200,000 were dubbed "Rangers." These programs have raised concerns similar to those raised over soft money—that individuals who bundled large amounts of money for candidates would receive preferential treatment.

More broadly, some have bemoaned the declining amounts of money raised by candidates in small contributions. Editorials on the 2002 and 2004 elections frequently noted that candidates tend to solicit money from those who have a history of making large contributions. Much of the publicity surrounding Howard Dean's primary campaign concerned his campaign's ability to use the Internet to raise money from first-time donors and small donors.

Many states have experimented with reforms designed to encourage more citizens to contribute and to reward small contributions. Laws regarding political contributions vary across states; some states provide public financing contingent on limiting the amount of money a candidate accepts in contributions, while others allow fairly large contributions to candidates. Since 1992, Minnesota has had a political contribution refund program, in which Minnesota residents who make a contribution to a state candidate or party can receive a refund of up to $50 within six weeks of making the contribution. Arizona provides tax credits of up to $500 to individuals who contribute to the state's Clean Elections program, a fund that distributes money to candidates who agree to abide by contribution and spending limits. And four states, Arkansas, Ohio, Oregon, and Virginia, provide tax credits of $25 to $50 to individuals who contribute to state candidates. Evidence on the effectiveness of these programs is mixed. Each of these programs is designed to encourage citizens with lower incomes to give, or to encourage candidates to solicit contributions from individuals whom they might otherwise ignore.

Further reading: *Campaigns & Elections Magazine*. Available online. URL: http://www.campaignline.com. Accessed August 10, 2005; Federal Elections Commission. Available online. URL: http://www.fec.gov. Accessed August 10, 2005; Francia, Peter L., John C. Green, Paul S. Herrnson, Lynda W. Powell, and Clyde Wilcox. *The Financiers of Congressional Elections*. New York: Columbia University Press, 2003; Malbin, Michael J., and Thomas L. Gais. *The Day after Reform: Sobering Campaign Finance Lessons from the American States*. New York: Rockefeller Institute Press, 1998; Ornstein, Norman J., Thomas E. Mann, and Michael J. Malbin. *Vital Statistics on Congress, 2001–2002*. Washington, D.C.: American Enterprise Institute, 2002; Rosenstone, Steven J., and John Mark Hansen. *Mobilization, Participation, and Democracy*. New York: Macmillan, 1993; Verba, Sidney, Kay Lehman Schlozman, and Henry E. Brady. *Voice and Equality: Civic Voluntarism in American Politics*. Cambridge, Mass.: Harvard University Press, 1995; Wright, John R. *Interest Groups and Congress: Lobbying, Contributions, and Influence*. New York: Longman, 2003.
—Robert G. Boatright

campaign ethics

Campaign ethics concerns the application of theories of moral behavior to the campaign-related behavior of individuals and groups. Ethics may be viewed as an extension of morality, encompassing efforts to understand the moral obligations of individuals and groups to other individuals, groups, and the community. Morality entails one's understanding of "right" and "wrong," and ethics are the principles by which that understanding guides one's behavior. Ethics may also be related to group membership or to a person's role and responsibilities in society.

Applied, or practical, ethics involves the effort to comprehend behavior as right or wrong (moral) and to apply the pertinent (ethical) behavioral standards to practical problems. Campaign ethics is how to apply normative theories of morality to the campaign-related behavior of individuals (such as candidates, political consultants, and campaign staff) and groups (such as political parties, INTEREST GROUPS, the media, and voters) in the context of the effort to win elections.

Ethical challenges in POLITICS have long been recognized, both for persons holding political office ("Power tends to corrupt and absolute power corrupts absolutely"—Lord Acton) and for those seeking office ("Whenever a man has cast a longing eye on offices, a rottenness begins in his conduct"—Thomas Jefferson). Efforts to apply ethical standards to political campaigns are nothing new, either. The PROGRESSIVE MOVEMENT of the late 19th century introduced AT-LARGE ELECTIONS in order to ameliorate voter bribery and violations of BALLOT secrecy.

Modern efforts to regulate, formally or informally, campaign conduct have been traced by some analysts to the Watergate SCANDAL of the early 1970s. This scandal led to campaign finance reform through the FEDERAL ELECTION CAMPAIGN ACT (1974, and revisions) and later to the Bipartisan Campaign Reform Act (2002). Media scrutiny of politicians and their campaigns increased, too. The press is now more willing to examine the behavior and truthfulness of candidates and their advertising than in the years before Watergate.

Political scientists and practitioners have considered what governing theories are applicable to campaigns, and Stephen Medvic's book on campaign ethics suggests two approaches to evaluating whether campaign activity is ethical. The civic responsibility model posits that campaigns serve the democratic system primarily because they are the mechanisms for selecting persons to positions of great public trust. Therefore, the actions of the campaign must be evaluated according to their effects on the democratic political process and its citizens. The self-interest approach suggests that campaigners can simply be permitted to pursue actions that serve their own financial and political interests. The actions are evaluated, in large measure, according to their successful attainment of goals such as winning elections. In this laissez-faire perspective, a kind of invisible hand (as envisioned by Adam Smith in a free market economy) reveals through election outcomes the "rightness" or "wrongness" of behavior.

Ethical concerns pertain to many kinds of campaign activities. Some are heavily regulated, while others are not regulated at all. Where legal standards do not exist, some other ethical gauge applies, or perhaps, as some assert, no standard exists. The challenge for practitioners and observers alike is in agreeing on the applicable ethical standards. For example, there is a body of law designed to protect the integrity of the democratic process. SUFFRAGE is established by statute or constitutional amendment, citizens must register in order to vote, and they may vote only one time in a single election. Efforts to intimidate prospective voters and to commit voting fraud are proscribed.

Concerns with the influence of monied interests in politics led national and state governments to regulate campaign contributions and spending. Legal boundaries are thus established, ostensibly in the public interest, but concerns exist about the effects of such legislation on the scope and quality of political participation. Nonlegal ethical issues related to campaign finance may involve principles of stewardship. For example, if a candidate is the recipient of a donation, what responsibility is there to the donor for the way in which that money is spent?

The truthfulness of campaign messages is often considered an ethical matter, though the U.S. Constitution's First Amendment limits regulation of these communications. Because holding political office is a matter of public trust, candidates (and their agents—political consultants and the like) are expected to tell the truth about themselves and their opponents. If candidates lie, then the quality of their representation may be called into question, with ramifications for the public's perception of the legitimacy of representative government.

What constitutes telling the truth in politics is often a matter of debate. For example, a candidate's specific votes may be taken out of context and mischaracterize his or her actual policy position on an issue. An ad may technically tell the truth about a candidate, but may also lead viewers to draw a false inference about the candidate. Damaging or embarrassing information about a candidate's family members, distant past, or personal life are often, though not always, considered ethically "off-limits," depending on its perceived relevance to the office being sought.

The civility of campaigns may be an ethical issue. Concerns about "attack" advertisements are based on the argument that they may increase citizen cynicism about and alienation from the political system, though evidence on this point is ambiguous. Campaign communications that play on racial tensions or attack on the basis of a candidate's gender or sexual orientation are considered uncivil nowadays.

Citizens may, in the civic responsibility model, have ethical obligations to participate as fully as possible in the political process. There is, however, a well-established notion that many people do not vote because they do not see it in their own interest to do so.

The media have obligations to the community and political system as a function of their role in informing a democratic polity about election-related issues. They are often criticized, however, for not paying enough attention to substantive policy issues.

Finally, political consultants, like other professionals, probably have some level of ethical accountability for their roles in the democratic process. The major organization of campaigners (the American Association of Political Consultants, or AAPC), for example, has established a code of ethics for its members. Critics of the code point out, however, that it has no real enforcement mechanism, does not apply to the majority of political consultants (who are not AAPC members), and may not fully articulate the obligations of consultants to the political system.

The variety of ethical conflicts reveals that applied campaign ethics is unevenly developed: There is no consensus on what constitutes an ethical campaign. The tension between what is good for the democratic process and what is good for a political actor informs ethical expectations, while legal boundaries apply to only a limited set of campaign activities. Campaign ethics clearly appears to entail something more, and also something less, than mere law.

Further reading: Carter, Stephen. *Integrity.* New York: HarperCollins, 1996; Jamieson, Kathleen Hall. *Dirty Politics: Deception, Distraction, and Democracy.* Oxford: Oxford University Press, 1992; Nelson, Candice J., David A. Dulio, and Stephen K. Medvic. *Shades of Gray: Perspectives on Campaign Ethics.* Washington, D.C.: Brookings Institution, 2002; Sabato, Larry J., and Glen R. Simpson. *Dirty Little Secrets: The Persistence of Corruption in American Politics.* New York: Random House, 1996.

—Peter W. Wielhouwer

campaign expenditures

Campaigns have become more and more expensive. Overall spending for congressional races nationwide has increased nearly eightfold over the past three decades, from approximately $42 million in 1976 to more than $328 million in 2000. Spending has increased for incumbents, CHALLENGERS, and candidates in open seat races. For challengers, the cost of mounting a successful campaign has increased most steeply. In 1974, the average challenger who defeated an incumbent spent $341,032; by 2000, the average successful challenger spent nearly $2 million.

Scholars trace the escalating costs of campaigns to a number of factors. Explanations include the growth in voting age population (up 39 percent since 1974), resulting in the candidates' need to communicate with more voters, and the changing means and conditions of effective campaigning. Candidates must increasingly rely on expensive campaign communications mechanisms, broadcast television and radio advertisements, and DIRECT MAIL. Furthermore, as the number of broadcast media channels has increased, voters' attention to POLITICS has decreased, the impact of persuasive media has dwindled, and campaigns have been required to consistently augment their overall investments in advertising over time. Others argue that candidates rely less on the political parties for campaign services than they did in the past. Campaigns must increasingly purchase these costly services (polling, get-out-the-vote, research, media production) on their own. Beyond that, lower levels of campaign and party volunteers and increasing campaign professionalism mean that campaigns must hire costly professionals to perform work previously done by volunteers.

Not only have campaigns become more costly, but also challengers' access to funds has become increasingly limited. Researchers report that incumbents are systematically advantaged when it comes to financing campaigns. Challengers are consistently outspent by incumbents. One plausible explanation for incumbents' campaign funding advantage is the role played by POLITICAL ACTION COMMITTEES (PAC). These groups have become key players in financing congressional campaigns over the past 30 years, and their resources have been directed primarily toward incumbents. Consider that the number of PACs currently registered with the FEDERAL ELECTION COMMISSION exceeds 4,000 and that, on average, more than half of the total PAC resources are distributed to incumbents seeking reelection. The percentage of total PAC money that has been directed toward House incumbents has steadily increased with each ELECTION CYCLE, reaching a peak of 60 percent in 1998. Challengers in U.S. House elections, on the other hand, consistently receive less than 15 percent of all PAC contributions during each election cycle. The average incumbent receives nearly 40 cents of every dollar raised from PACs, while the average House challenger receives only 14 cents of every dollar from these groups.

All of this amounts to a situation in which challengers find it more difficult to launch competitive campaigns. On average, fewer than 10 percent of challengers raise enough funds in each election cycle to be competitive against their incumbent opponents. (A challenger is defined as competitive when his or her expenditure level equals or exceeds the incumbent opponent's.) In no election cycle since 1972 have more than three out of 10 challengers matched or exceeded the expenditure levels of incumbents in the same cycle. In the five most recent elections, only 5 percent of challengers have waged financially competitive campaigns against incumbents on average. In fact, since 1972, the percentage of challengers who were able to match or exceed the expenditure levels of their opponents has systematically declined in each election cycle.

Candidates and their agents raise substantial amounts of money in order to wage effective campaigns by mobilizing voters. Studies conducted by Paul Herrnson at the University of Maryland reveal that despite differences in the overall amount of money raised by categories of candidates, campaigns budget similarly. The lion's share of expenditures is reserved for communications. House candidates typically spend more than half of their funds on communicating with voters, primarily via television. The average candidate for the U.S. House of Representatives allocates 17 percent of the total budget to television advertising. An analysis of campaign commercials broadcast in the nation's top 75 media markets during the 2000 election cycle reveals that a total of $672 million was spent to broadcast more than 3,300 unique television ads a total of 940,000 times across America on behalf of candidates for federal office. Other communications media are not entirely neglected, however. In an average budget, 10 percent is devoted to direct mail communications, 7 percent to radio, and 4 percent to purchase newspaper ads. CAMPAIGN LITERATURE accounts for 10 percent of the total campaign budget, and 3 percent is typically allocated to GET-OUT-THE-VOTE efforts. A total of 40 percent of funds is spent on overhead, including FUNDRAISING, staff salaries, and travel. Less than one-tenth of a campaign's budget is reserved for research. The average campaign spends 4 percent of its budget on polling and 3 percent on issue and OPPOSITION RESEARCH.

The degree to which campaign spending affects electoral outcomes has been a heavily researched area. Scholars disagree about the impact of spending, however, and the literature provides few conclusive results. Research in this area faces a significant challenge in specifying the accurate causal mechanism that congressional spending takes. That is to say, analysts have difficulty determining whether incumbent spending affects chances of winning or if expectations of the outcome influence fund-raising and spending. In technical terms, it is plausible that spending is an endogenous variable, thereby making estimates of its effect on vote shares unreliable. Scholars recognize that expectations about victory may influence spending, rendering measures of association that either exaggerate the effect of challenger spending on votes or underestimate the effects of incumbent spending. The problem is that it is difficult to determine with confidence the degree to which analysis either overestimate or underestimate the impact. As a result, the debate over how to interpret campaign spending continues in the current literature.

While incumbents are more proficient at fund-raising, much of the early literature on campaign spending asserts that challenger spending is much more effective than incumbent expenditures. Scholars assert that campaign spending has different effects for incumbents and nonincumbents because expenditures are subject to diminishing returns. Because incumbents have the ability to use their official resources, such as their personal staff and their franking privileges, the addition of information about their attributes purported during the campaign adds relatively little value to what constituents already know about them. Thus, money spent by incumbents does them comparatively little good. Empirical studies have suggested that votes for incumbents are unrelated to how much money is spent on the campaign; instead, factors such as NAME RECOGNITION, credit claiming, and advertising drive incumbent support.

Challengers, on the other hand, are typically unknown to the district, and their ability to expose themselves to voters is directly related to their campaign efforts. Additional expenditures thus directly affect the level of support for the challenger. Put differently, challengers simply appear to get more bang for their buck.

The results of early studies, then, show that the more incumbents spend, the more likely they are to lose. This is because incumbents are likely to spend large amounts of money on an election only if they are faced with a legitimate challenger. Gary Jacobson has noted that, at the very least, incumbent spending does not appear to correlate with electoral outcomes in the same way that challenger spending correlates with vote share. Conversely, the more challengers spend, regardless of how much the incumbent spends in the race, the better are the prospects for victory.

These results, along with other conclusions provided by initial studies, have been contested and reexamined by subsequent research. Other scholars have found that both incumbent and challenger spending can affect vote shares and contend that campaign spending can benefit both challengers and incumbents, particularly if incumbents use resources to define challengers for the voters in a way that is beneficial to the incumbent. Despite more than two decades of scholarship in this area, the exact relationship between campaign spending and electoral results remains elusive.

Further reading: Center for Responsive Politics. Available online. URL: http://www.opensecrets.org. Accessed August 10, 2005; Federal Election Commission. Available online. URL: http://www.fec.gov. Accessed August 10, 2005; Jacobson, Gary. *The Politics of Congressional Elections.* 4th ed. New York: Longman, 1997; Herrnson, Paul. *Congressional Elections: Campaigning at Home and in Washington.* 3rd ed. Washington, D.C.: CQ Press, 2000.
—Costas Panagopoulos

campaign finance laws

Campaign finance laws are the rules that regulate the amount of money political candidates, parties, and organizations can receive, the sources from which they can receive money, and the permissible uses of that money. In the past half-century, there have been three major periods of campaign finance regulation in the United States—the era before the Federal Elections and Campaigns Act (FECA) of 1971 and its subsequent amendments, the era from 1974 to 2002, when FECA regulated political campaigns, and the current era, following the enactment of the Bipartisan Campaign Reform Act (BCRA) of 2002.

Prior to FECA, there had been several laws regulating various aspects of campaign finance. Most of these laws were addressed to particular types of contributors rather than to the larger circumstances of politicians' campaigns. For instance, the Civil Service Reform Act of 1883 prohibited contributions from federal employees, the TILLMAN ACT of 1907 prohibited contributions from corporations, and the Taft-Hartley Act of 1947 prohibited contributions

from labor unions. The FEDERAL CORRUPT PRACTICES ACT of 1925 required disclosure of contributions. Several laws, including the Federal Corrupt Practices Act and the HATCH ACT of 1940, limited the amounts an individual could contribute to an individual campaign committee, but because candidates could establish multiple campaign committees, these laws had little effect.

The original FECA and its 1974 amendments established limits on candidate spending; on the contributions of individuals and POLITICAL ACTION COMMITTEES (PACs) to candidates, parties, or political committees; and on the amount of money a candidate could spend on his or her own campaign. FECA, along with the REVENUE ACT of 1971, also established a public funding system for presidential campaigns, financed through a voluntary income tax check-off. Disclosure requirements were strengthened, and the FEDERAL ELECTION COMMISSION (FEC) was established to enforce and clarify campaign finance laws. Finally, FECA limited the amount of money individuals or organizations could spend in coordination with a political campaign.

In *BUCKLEY V. VALEO* (1976), the Supreme Court struck down several provisions of FECA. It ruled that it was a violation of the First Amendment to limit the amount of money an individual could raise and spend in a campaign, and that it was a similar violation to limit the amount of money an individual could contribute to his or her own campaign. The Court did allow the limits on spending in presidential campaigns to stand because these limits were contingent on receipt of public funds. And the Court did uphold the limits on contributions from individuals and PACs. Thus, from the passage of FECA until 2002, individuals were limited to contributing no more than $1,000 per candidate, up to a total of $25,000, and PACs were limited to contributing no more than $5,000 to a candidate.

At the congressional level, many have contended that FECA abetted the development of PACs and increased the reliance of congressional candidates—and particularly congressional incumbents—on PACs. The number of registered PACs grew from 608 to 4,009 between 1974 and 1984, and by this time PACs were the source of more than one-third of the contributions to House candidates and approximately one-fifth of the contributions to Senate candidates. Despite this, FECA has been said to have reduced the reliance of candidates on individual donors and organizations during this time period. That is, because of the contribution limits, it is unlikely that any one donor or organization will contribute enough to a candidate to have an influence on that candidate's campaign. At the presidential level, FECA also restrained spending. All major party nominees abided by FECA's spending limits in their PRIMARY campaigns from 1976 through 1996, and the public funding of GENERAL ELECTION campaigns ensured that candidates could not outspend one another.

During the 1990s, however, two major developments took place that, according to many politicians, undermined FECA's restrictions. First, recall that FECA limited the ability of individuals and organizations to spend money in a coordinated fashion with a campaign. The FEC has interpreted this as a prohibition on advocacy that explicitly encourages voters to vote for or against a candidate. Yet during the 1990s, several advocacy organizations began to advertise heavily on television, describing candidates in a manner virtually indistinguishable from a candidate's campaign advertisement but without using "magic words" such as "vote for," "vote against," "support," or "oppose." Second, although corporations and labor unions cannot make direct contributions to candidates, FECA did not prohibit them from contributing to political parties as long as this money was used for "party-building" activities. During the 1990s, political parties began to solicit so-called SOFT MONEY donations from corporations, labor unions, and wealthy individuals. Because these funds were not distributed by the parties to candidates or used to advocate the election or defeat of a candidate, they were not subject to contribution limits.

BCRA was a response to both of these developments. The two major components of BCRA are a ban on soft money contributions to the national parties and severe restrictions on so-called electioneering advertisements by advocacy groups. These restrictions prohibit organizations that receive corporate or labor funding from broadcasting advertisements that refer to a candidate for election within 30 days of that candidate's primary election or 60 days of the general election. BCRA also raised individual contribution limits from $1,000 to $2,000 per candidate, to a total of $37,500, and indexed these limits to inflation. Finally, BCRA included a "millionaire's amendment" that increases the contribution limits to a candidate whose opponent has spent significant amounts of his or her own money in a campaign. BCRA took effect the day after the 2002 election. Several individuals and organizations, including members of Congress, labor unions, and other advocacy groups, immediately filed suit against BCRA. In *McConnell v. FEC*, the Supreme Court upheld all of the major provisions of BCRA.

Although each of these pieces of legislation undeniably addressed long-standing problems in the financing of federal elections, each of them also was catalyzed by a particular event. The Civil Service Reform Act, for instance, was passed on the heels of the assassination of President Garfield by a disgruntled seeker of a civil service position. Although the original FECA grew out of recommendations that had been circulating since the Kennedy administration, and although the original bill was passed in 1971, the comprehensive 1974 amendments were passed following FUNDRAISING abuses of the 1972 election and the Watergate SCANDAL. In the case of BCRA, the bill's Senate cosponsors, Republican John McCain and Democrat Russell Feingold, had circulated similar bills in each Congress since 1995, and earlier versions of what became BCRA had passed the House and been filibustered in the Senate. The 2000 elections, in which Democrats gained seats in the Senate, helped to ensure enough votes for passage of the bill, but controversies over Enron and other corporations linked to the Bush administration were frequently invoked as justification for tighter campaign finance regulation by supporters. It has been argued that incumbent members of Congress tend to be reluctant to alter campaign finance laws because they would therefore be altering the system under which they were elected, and that sudden events or scandals provide the necessary impetus for Congress to alter campaign finance laws.

Both supporters and opponents of campaign finance reforms have referred to the "hydraulic theory," the notion that campaign finance laws are destined to be ineffective in the long run because money, like water seeking the lowest level, will inevitably find its way into the political process. Just as the provisions of FECA unraveled during the 1990s, so, many have argued, the provisions of BCRA will gradually unravel over the coming ELECTION CYCLES. Although FECA did abet the formation of PACs, the major changes in campaign financing that led to BCRA took place two decades after the passage of FECA. Several developments since the passage of BCRA have prompted criticism from Senator McCain and other proponents of BCRA. Most notably, the soft money prohibition has severely limited the ability of political parties to raise money for electoral activities, and as a result, several new "527" organizations have been formed as a conduit for large individual contributions, labor contributions, and corporate contributions. These organizations, so named because of their tax status, are able to engage in advertising, VOTER REGISTRATION, and voter mobilization activities that were once the province of the parties. Two large 527 organizations, America Coming Together and the Media Fund, were formed in 2003 and raised more than $100 million for activities in the 2004 election cycle that supported Democratic candidates. Two of the largest contributors to 527 groups, George Soros and Peter Lewis, funneled more than $45 million to 527s in 2004. Despite calls for restraint by reform organizations and by the REPUBLICAN PARTY, the FEC chose in May of 2004 not to rule on the legality of these activities until after the 2004 election.

Another major development in campaign financing, although it is not a direct consequence of BCRA, has been the erosion of the presidential public financing system established in FECA. As noted above, PRESIDENTIAL PRIMARIES candidates receive MATCHING FUNDS for individual contributions if they agree to restrict their aggregate spending and their spending in each state. In 1996, Republican primary candidate Steve Forbes declined matching funds, and in 2000, Forbes and George W. Bush declined matching funds. This enabled Bush to substantially outspend his opponents in the primary. In 2004, Democrats Howard Dean and John Kerry, as well as Bush, declined matching funds, and both Kerry and Bush raised money for their campaigns well into the summer. Together, the two probably raised more than three times the primary limit. During this same period, the amount of money in the matching fund declined, as fewer citizens checked off the box on their income tax return. This raises the possibility that even if future candidates do accept matching funds, there may not be matching fund money available for them. It is likely that Congress will consider legislation to alter the presidential financing system within the next decade.

The FEC is a critical player in contemporary debates about campaign finance laws. As noted above, the FEC was created as part of the FECA to enforce and clarify campaign finance laws. Because the FEC must include three Democrats and three Republicans, critics have charged that the FEC is unable to move quickly to prosecute violations of campaign finance laws or to clarify rules in cases in which one party or the other will be penalized. Measures to abolish or dramatically reorganize the FEC have been introduced in Congress since the passage of BCRA.

With the passage of BCRA, it is likely that those who would still seek to reform campaign finance laws at the federal level will turn to the state level in order to evaluate the effects of state campaign finance laws. State laws vary dramatically; some states have no limits on individual contributions, while others have implemented strict limits on contributions and expenditures. Five states currently have at least partial public funding of legislative elections. The effects of the public funding systems introduced in Maine and Arizona in 2000 are likely to be studied by reformers for their effects on competitiveness in these states.

Further reading: Alexander, Herbert. *Financing Politics: Money, Elections, and Political Reform.* Washington, D.C.: Congressional Quarterly Press, 1984; Campaign Finance Institute. *Participation, Competition, and Engagement: How to Revive and Improve Public Funding for Presidential Nomination Politics.* Washington, D.C.: Campaign Finance Institute; 2004; Center for Responsive Politics. Available online. URL: http://www.opensecrets.org. Accessed August 10, 2005; Federal Elections Commission. Available online. URL: http://www.fec.gov. Accessed August 10, 2005; Sorauf, Frank. *Inside Campaign Finance: Myths and Realities.* New Haven, Conn.: Yale University Press, 1992.
—Robert G. Boatright

campaign literature

Campaign literature is printed material to promote a candidate or ballot measure in an election. From the very first elections in the United States, there has been the need to publicize the candidates, parties, and issues involved in

A flyer from the Nixon campaign of 1960 *(Duke University Special Collections Library)*

campaigns. Campaign literature was therefore essential in the days before broadcast media. The first forms of campaign literature were handbills posted publicly by parties and candidates in the Colonial and post-Revolutionary eras.

Perhaps the most famous campaign literature was the juxtaposed Federalist and Anti-Federalist papers, posted in public places and reprinted in newspapers supporting and opposing constitutional ratification. Until the mid-20th century, there was no change in the format or substance of campaign literature. Parties would publicly distribute parts of their platforms with daguerreotypes of presidential nominees or symbols of party unity. After World War II, however, campaign literature evolved. Color printing, die-cutting for alternate sizes, and photography all combined to give campaign literature a more professional and distinctive look. Instead of posting handbills, candidates were placing the pieces directly in voters' hands in postcard or brochure formats.

Today directly mailed campaign literature is a staple of the political electioneering process. Candidates for office, volunteers, and motivated citizens for ballot measures regularly distribute literature on door-to-door canvassing days, at campaign events, and anywhere that voters may be found. A recent innovation that has proved very useful to political actors is the marriage of campaign literature with a quality voter database including policy preferences and perhaps VOTER REGISTRATION information. By TARGETING different pieces to different constituencies based on their data, campaigners can speak directly to voters on issues that matter to them.

A candidate who wishes to specifically target older voters on the issue of Social Security can do so while not wasting the message on younger voters who would not be as interested and may in fact be repelled by the message. In ballot issues such as referenda, the same practice can apply. A local bond issue to pay for school improvements can be sent exclusively to families with school-age children to deliver a message with the most impact to the people most likely to be affected by the policy. While DIRECT MAIL gets less attention from scholars and PUNDITS than television ads, the specificity of message and control capabilities makes directly delivered campaign literature a vital part of the modern campaign.

Further reading: Grey, Lawrence. *How to Win a Local Election.* New York: Evans, 1994; Shaw, Catherine. *The Campaign Manager.* Denver: Westview Press, 2004; Shea, Daniel, and Michael Burton. *Campaign Craft.* New York: Praeger, 2002; Trent, Judith, and Robert Friedenberg. *Political Campaign Communication.* Lanham, Md.: Rowman & Littlefield, 2004; UCLA Online Campaign Literature Archive. Available online. URL: http://digital.library.ucla.edu/campaign. Accessed August 10, 2005.

—Chapman Rackaway

campaign manager

Modern political campaigns typically have numerous paid staff working full time, as well as consultants working on a part-time basis. Additionally, there are large numbers of volunteers and supporters involved in a campaign at any given point in time. The person who has overall responsibility for managing and coordinating the activities of these individuals on a daily basis is almost always the campaign manager.

Although nearly all campaigns have them, the actual role of a campaign manager tends to vary widely depending on the size of the campaign and the preferences of the candidate. In some situations, a campaign manager will focus primarily on tactical decisions and "making the trains run on time," with one or more consultants establishing strategic directions for the campaign.

In other cases, the campaign manager will make strategy decisions, leaving execution and tactics to lower-level staff. More often than not, campaign managers serve as public voices for their candidates, speaking to the news media and at public events the candidate cannot attend.

Most campaign managers learn their skills on the job, typically by working on smaller races and in other roles and then moving into a management capacity. However, some institutions of higher education, such as the Campaign Management Institute at American University in Washington, D.C., now offer formal training in campaign management, and many individuals seeking jobs as campaign managers obtain such credentials. Additionally, political parties and partisan organizations offer training in running campaigns for both candidates and staff.

Candidates running for public office typically hire their campaign managers before anyone else, although some candidates put their FUND-RAISING staff in place first and then hire their campaign manager and other political staff as funds become available. In addition to working for political candidates, campaign managers may also work for INTEREST GROUPS or political parties advocating the enactment or defeat of a particular public policy. The same skills used to elect candidates are then applied to building public support for a policy issue.

Further reading: Dulio, David A. *For Better or Worse?: How Political Consultants Are Changing Elections in the United States.* Albany: State University of New York Press, 2004; Johnson, Dennis W. *No Place for Amateurs: How Political Consultants Are Reshaping American Democracy.* New York: Routledge, 2001; Sabato, Larry. *The Rise of Political Consultants: New Ways of Winning Elections.* New York: Basic, 1981; Shaw, Catherine M. *The Campaign Manager: Running and Winning Local Elections.* Boulder, Colo.: Westview, 2000; Shea, Daniel M. *Campaign Craft: The Strategies, Tactics, and Art of Political Campaign Management.* Rev. ed. Westport, Conn.: Praeger, 1996; Thurber, James A., and Candice J. Nelson, eds. *Campaign Warriors: The Role of Political Consultants in American Elections.* Washington, D.C.: Brookings Institution Press, 2000.

—Brad Alexander

campaign organization

Campaign organization refers to an important and evolving development in modern elections. Since the 1950s, political campaigns have shifted from being controlled by PARTY BOSSES to control by highly efficient organizations of political consultants and business professionals who manage and execute all aspects of increasingly complex campaigns. During the mass party period, from the 1830s to the 1950s, political campaigns relied on the "spoils system": PATRONAGE that went to party workers of the winning party at the expense of workers from the losing party. Today, however, with the weakening role of political parties in elections and the rise of celebrity candidates, the spoils system has evolved into the employment of individuals with specialized knowledge in campaign management, marketing, image making, debating, and policy research in exchange for a salary. The average campaign organization now has a brief existence; consultants dispense their expertise and then move on to the next campaign once the election ends. The modern campaign organization is now a business enterprise.

The presidential campaign of Andrew Jackson in 1828 saw the first significant expressions of the party machine's involvement in elections. During his two administrations, Jackson replaced federal office holders with a cadre of

DEMOCRATIC PARTY volunteers and supporters. The new president's hiring decisions had more to do with political fitness of job candidates than civil service skill. Jacksonian Democrats relied on local, autonomous party units to see to the business of elections. This strategy complemented the sociopolitical culture of 19th-century America. As individual states removed the property requirement for voting between 1815 and 1830, newly enfranchised white male voters hungered for political involvement. Local party units often mobilized voters with parades, catchy slogans, and speeches by military heroes, and the potential for monetary employment and social rewards. Supporters who demonstrated an ability to deliver large numbers of votes earned the friendship of party leaders and politicians.

The Tammany Society of New York City and its hegemonic grip on New York POLITICS in the mid-19th century reveals the highest expression of the party machine's involvement in campaigns and elections. Between the 1830s and the 1870s, Tammany deepened its association with the Democratic Party, controlling all aspects of the political process, including selecting appropriate party loyalists as political candidates, cultivating a strong voter base by earning the loyalty of the city's ever-expanding immigrant community, and stacking government jobs with party supporters. Backroom, smoke-filled meetings and subterfuge by Tammany leaders invariably determined the political life or death of ambitious office seekers. At the same time, the parties' increasing involvement in elections fueled an explosion of graft and corruption: BALLOT stuffing, violence, and bribery were common electoral tactics in Tammany Hall. Progressive era reforms ranging from the Civil Service Reform Act of 1883, introduction of the secret ballot at the turn of the 20th century, and the drastic social and cultural changes of the Great Depression and World War II gradually diminished the influence of the party machine in electoral politics.

Since 1950, the rise of advanced technology in the campaign process, the dominance of mass-marketing techniques, and the need for expensive, broad-based political advertising and mobilization efforts to entice a disinterested ELECTORATE to the polls has sidelined the role of volunteers, family, and party leaders in favor of professionals who have technical expertise in law, accounting, media production, media buying, and advertising. Much like the modern corporation, campaign professionals with solid reputations have become sought-after wizards by ambitious office seekers.

The modern campaign organization typically consists of two formal divisions headed by a professional CAMPAIGN MANAGER. On the one hand, paid staff, consultants, close advisers known as the "kitchen cabinet," and a campaign and finance committee oversee the day-to-day operations of the campaign. On the other hand, a group of policy advisers drafts the campaign's long-term policy goals and identi-

fies the most appropriate issues (i.e., messages) for the candidate to discuss on the campaign trail.

Unlike the party machine of the past, today's political candidates often court reputable campaign professionals to join their campaign. Top consulting firms are often inundated with offers. Richard Viguerie, a dominant force in DIRECT MAIL campaigns in the 1970s, claimed that he refused 98 percent of requests for his services during the midterm elections of 1978. Candidates who are able to demonstrate strong abilities to muster financial contributions, gain credible media coverage, and exert popularity in polls usually have a pick of the most successful political consulting firms. Less-qualified candidates are often left fighting for attention from the lower-tier professionals late in the political race.

Another unique feature of the modern campaign organization is its streamlined staff. Execution of most of the complex, highly technical campaign tactics and strategies is subcontracted out to media buyers, advertising and public relations firms, mobilization organizations, and pollsters. Some candidates often rely on the "one-stop" shopping campaign consulting firms where expertise ranging from market research to direct mail marketing is available to the candidate in-house.

The impact of the campaign professional within the campaign organization tends to vary across campaigns. The candidate makes the ultimate decision on the direction and overall strategy of the campaign, and a candidate's ability to win at the polls is highly dependent on how effective the candidate is at building and managing the campaign organization. However, survey research conducted by the American Association of Political Consultants reveals that 44 percent of political consultants agree that most candidates tend to take a broader role in their campaigns, relying on the campaign organization to make the decisions regarding the execution of the day-to-day tactics of the race.

The most significant question regarding the modern campaign organization's impact on electoral politics is whether campaign professionals change the conduct of the campaign and the nature of agenda setting. On one hand, some political scientists argue that the rise of political consultants decreases the ideological nature of the campaign organization. The nature of the business of campaign consultancy tends to minimize partisanship in favor of consultants' long-term financial prospects on future campaigns. On the other hand, other political scientists find that the increasing sophistication of the campaign organization and its focus on mass-marketing techniques, polls, and sophisticated computer technology has helped further alienate voters and dramatically increased the costs of elections. In 2004 alone, the cost of the presidential race between George W. Bush and John Kerry exceeded $1 billion, with much of the expenses paying for political advertising, polling, market research, and voter mobilization efforts.

Further reading: Hrebenar, Ronald J., Matthew J. Burbank, and Robert C. Benedict. *Political Parties, Interest Groups, and Political Campaigns.* Boulder, Colo.: Westview Press, 1999; Polsby, Nelson W., and Aaron Wildavsky. *Presidential Elections: Strategies and Structures of American Politics.* 11th ed. New York: Rowman & Littlefield, 2004; Thurber, James A., and Candice J. Nelson, eds. *Campaigns and Elections American Style.* Boulder, Colo.: Westview Press, 1995.

—Jamie Patrick Chandler

campaign pollster

A campaign pollster is a paid consultant who designs and analyzes public opinion polls for a candidate's campaign. Almost all candidates for federal office and many politicians seeking local and statewide offices rely on campaign pollsters. Campaign pollsters craft questions to investigate what voters view as the candidate's strengths and weaknesses, what demographic groups support the candidate, what voters think of the candidate's policy positions, and how the candidate compares to his or her opponent. They then analyze the results, giving candidates advice on how to shape and communicate their message to voters, which voters to target, and where and when to direct their campaign resources (namely money, advertisements, and staff). Campaign pollsters differ from academic pollsters and media pollsters, who are not affiliated with a specific candidate and use their results to forecast elections or study general trends rather than to plan election strategy.

The first campaign pollster in the United States to successfully use scientific polling practices was George Gallup, who helped his mother-in-law win election as Iowa's secretary of state in 1932 and accurately predicted the 1936 presidential race. Gallup confirmed the power of his sampling methods in the 1936 race when he accurately predicted not only the election but also that the *Literary Digest* poll, a rival group that used an unscientific STRAW POLL, would inaccurately predict the presidential race. By the mid-1960s, campaign polling based on many of the techniques pioneered by Gallup was adopted by presidential, senatorial, and gubernatorial candidates. About half of House candidates used pollsters at that time.

Most pollsters are key members of a candidate's inner circle. They review results from previous elections to derive a general sense of the ELECTORATE and track a candidate's numbers throughout the campaign, with polls conducted more frequently as ELECTION DAY nears. They may also design questions for FOCUS GROUPS to seek more in-depth answers to how the candidate is faring and which messages to stress. The work of campaign pollsters is often supplemented by polling done for political parties. For example, the National Republican Congressional Committee directed $5 million for polling in 65 House races in 2002.

Many pollsters have well-known affiliations with candidates, such as Lou Harris, who polled for John F. Kennedy; Patrick Caddell, who worked for Jimmy Carter; Richard Wirthlin, who gauged voter reaction for Ronald Reagan; and Stanley Greenberg, who conducted surveys for Bill Clinton. Candidates who win, especially presidential candidates, continue to poll while in office to gauge what voters think of their policies and to prepare for their next election. President George W. Bush spent $1.7 million on polling during the first two years of his administration, while President Bill Clinton spent $4.8 million during the same period.

While many campaigns prefer to keep their results private, pollsters working for candidates struggling in other polls may release findings that show the candidate doing better than expected.

Further reading: Herrnson, Paul S. *Congressional Elections: Campaigning at Home and in Washington.* Washington, D.C.: CQ Press, 2004; Sabato, Larry. *The Rise of Political Consultants: New Ways of Winning Elections.* New York: Basic Books, 1981; Tenpas, Kathryn Dunn. "Words vs. Deeds: President George W. Bush and Polling." *Brookings Review* 21 (2003): 32–35.

—Mary Lynn F. Jones

campaign slogans

Campaign slogans are phrases or words used by political candidates seeking public office in order to inspire voters to cast their BALLOTs on behalf of that candidate. The slogans seek to distill the platform, philosophy, record, and/or qualifications of the candidate in a few simple-to-understand and simple-to-remember words that provide a cue for voters come ELECTION DAY. The more successful the campaign slogan, the more likely the average voter is to remember the slogan positively and the more likely to vote for that candidate.

Most slogans shy away from issue content and instead focus more on image. Most slogans are remarkably similar, regardless of party affiliation. They tend to emphasize a few key themes such as the candidate's "honesty" and "experience," how "tough on crime" the candidate is, how the candidate "stands up to special interests," how he or she "fights higher taxes," or how much of a "regular person" he or she is. The hope is that these simple messages will resonate with voters and influence the way they cast their ballots.

Campaign slogans in the United States have existed as long as have elections. A promotional coin from the reelection campaign of George Washington called for "Success to the United States." During the 1812 presidential campaign, James Madison's supporters celebrated the War of 1812 with the slogan "On to Canada," while the supporters of his opponent, DeWitt Clinton, countered with "Too Much Virginia," an attack on the dominance of national POLITICS by Virginians. The practice of employing campaign slogans to influence electoral success was brought to new heights in the 1840 PRESIDENTIAL ELECTION campaign of William Henry Harrison, whose slogan was "Tippecanoe and Tyler, Too." The slogan celebrated Harrison, a hero at the Battle of Tippecanoe, and Tyler, his RUNNING MATE.

Several themes are commonly repeated in campaign slogans. These tried-and-true themes have been used by many candidates, both winners and losers. Many politicians try to paint themselves as the most "American" candidate in the race (Woodrow Wilson, "An American for America") or as the candidate most connected to the public (Harry Truman, "Friend of the People"; William McKinley, "Our Choice").

Candidates often stress time-related themes. Some candidates focus on the future (Franklin Roosevelt, "Drive Ahead with Roosevelt"; Richard Nixon, "For the Future"), while others stress the need for change (Ronald Reagan in 1980, "Are You Better Off Than You Were Four Years Ago?" Walter Mondale, "America Needs a Change"). Incumbents stress the importance of staying the course, noting how change will make things worse (Abraham Lincoln, "Don't Swap Horses in the Middle of the Stream").

Other slogans stress candidates' outsider status, suggesting that they have not been corrupted by the system. Third party candidates often condemn the overall system and the two major parties (Ross Perot, "Perot to the Rescue"). Some slogans focus on the image of candidates (Zachary Taylor, "General Taylor Never Surrenders") or their careers before running for office (Jimmy Carter, "Not Just Peanuts").

Word play has a long tradition in political slogans. Some candidates use rhymes (Dwight Eisenhower, "I Like Ike"; Adlai Stevenson, "All the Way with Adlai"), while others make use of puns (Calvin Coolidge, "Keep Cool with COOLidge"). Some candidates offer vague generalities designed to soothe the public (Gerald Ford, "He's Making Us Proud Again"; Ronald Reagan, "It's Morning Again in America"), while others focus on specific issues (Bill Clinton, "It's the Economy, Stupid!").

Some campaigns get downright negative, such as the 1884 presidential campaign in which the James Blaine campaign made an issue of Grover Cleveland's illegitimate child with the slogan "Ma, Ma, Where's My Pa, Gone to the White House, Ha, Ha, Ha." Cleveland countered with "Blaine, Blaine, James G. Blaine, the Continental Liar from the State of Maine." Some politicians refuse to settle for one slogan and use multiple choices (George W. Bush, "Compassionate Conservatism," "Leave No Child Behind," "Real Plans for Real People," and "Reformer with Results").

Campaign slogans have been placed on a variety of products, including buttons, bumper stickers, posters, pens, t-shirts, calendars, toys, bubblegum cigars, and even fortune cookies. At conventions and rallies, supporters of the candidates often chant the slogans as a show of support. It is difficult to know whether slogans have a real impact on electoral chances, but it is certain that candidates put some effort into choosing the right slogans, and the media often give much airplay and serious debate to the topic of campaign slogans.

Further reading: Boller, Paul F. *Presidential Campaigns.* New York: Oxford University Press, 1996; Jamieson, Kathleen Hall. *Packaging the Presidency: A History and Criticism of Presidential Campaign Advertising.* New York: Oxford University Press, 1996; Roberts, Robert N., and Scott J. Hammond. *Encyclopedia of Presidential Campaigns, Slogans, Issues, and Platforms.* Westport, Conn.: Greenwood Press, 2004.

—Kenneth Quinnell

candidate

A candidate is a person who seeks election to public office. Candidates must meet certain eligibility requirements to run. Generally, candidates must be eligible to vote for and hold the office they are seeking and reside in the area they seek to represent. Some states require that candidates live in the area for a set period of time before the election.

Candidates must file paperwork submitting their candidacies to local, state, or federal election offices by a date determined by the applicable election office. Requirements vary depending on the office being sought, but in many cases, candidates must collect a set number of signatures from residents, file a statement of organization, and pay a filing fee. Many candidates are also required to file regular campaign finance reports and disclose personal financial information. Depending on election laws, some candidates are limited in how much money their campaigns can spend in PRIMARY and GENERAL ELECTIONS.

In addition, candidates for federal office must meet age requirements. Candidates for the House must be age 25 by the time they take office, age 30 for the Senate, and age 35 for the White House. Only citizens born in the United States are eligible to run for president.

Candidates have a network of support to help them. Paid advisers such as a CAMPAIGN MANAGER, fundraiser, and pollster often run the campaign's day-to-day aspects, allowing the candidate to focus on activities such as meeting voters and FUND-RAISING. Candidates may be recruited by party leaders or decide to run on their own.

Support from the party and party donors usually depends on how strong a candidate is, how weak an opponent is, the partisan make-up of the area, and the general mood of the ELECTORATE. Candidates running in open seat races—in which the incumbent has retired, was defeated in the primary, or has died—generally have a better chance of winning than a candidate challenging the incumbent. Write-in candidates, whose names are not printed on the BALLOT but are written in by voters, are rarely elected.

There is no limit to the number of candidates who can seek an office. In 2003, 135 candidates ran for governor of

California as voters RECALLed Governor Gray Davis (D, Calif.). In rare cases, candidates can appear on the ballot for two offices at the same time. In 2000, Senator Joe Lieberman (D, Conn.) ran for reelection and was the DEMOCRATIC PARTY's vice-presidential nominee. In 2004, 10 Democrats sought to be their party's presidential candidate. Senator John Kerry (D, Mass.) emerged as the nominee, challenging President George W. Bush, the sole Republican candidate, in November.

Further reading: Jacobson, Gary C. *The Politics of Congressional Elections.* 6th ed. New York: Pearson Education, 2004; Federal Election Commission. Available online. URL: http://www.fec.gov. Accessed August 10, 2005.

—Mary Lynn F. Jones

candidate-centered elections

Candidate-centered elections are an artifact of the late 20th and early 21st century. They are the result of historical trends that began to manifest in the national elections of the 1980s and 1990s. They represent a change in the focal points of campaigns and elections in America, the passing of the mantle from parties to candidates. That is, the concept of candidate-centered elections refers to the increasing prominence of candidate characteristics, attributes, and qualities in the decision making schemes of American voters.

Scholars of American voting behavior have long saluted PARTY IDENTIFICATION as the dominant predictor of candidate selection. From seminal studies in the mid-20th century, such as *The American Voter,* to sophisticated statistical analysis in the very recent past, party identification has long been the key independent variable of interest when explaining voter behavior. However, as the salience of partisan attachment in the American ELECTORATE began to decline, beginning in the 1950s and spanning the remainder of the century, voters increasingly evaluated candidates on social and economic factors. With the decline of partisanship as a mediating factor in candidate selection, American voters began to look to the personal attributes of candidates when determining for whom they would cast their BALLOT.

Candidate-centered POLITICS has come to characterize both presidential and CONGRESSIONAL ELECTIONS. In elections for both types of office, candidates are responsible for their own campaigns, with most of the attention on them rather than on the parties of which they may be members. This is due in large part to the self-selection of most candidates, rather than their recruitment by parties. Indeed, candidates must campaign even for the right to represent their party, which is largely done in PRIMARY elections. Because of this, they must assemble their own CAMPAIGN ORGANIZATIONS and staffs, which often remain in place after they secure the right to appear as the party's nominee in the GENERAL ELECTION.

Technological advances have also greatly contributed to the rise of the candidate-centered election. First through radio, then television and mail, and now the Internet, candidates can communicate directly with voters, developing a "personal" relationship with the electorate. Modern technology enables candidates to fill the role once played by PATRONAGE and PARTY BOSSES, gaining control of their own political destiny.

The effects of the trend toward candidate-centered elections can be most readily observed in the changing nature of contemporary national campaigns. Since political elites drive the dissemination of political information as well as frame issues and candidate choices for the masses, campaigns have become the lenses through which voters view elections and the individuals running in them. Candidates and campaigns have become increasingly focused on defining themselves in a positive manner for the electorate and have also become increasingly concerned with negatively defining their opponents.

Most scholars suggest the election of 1980, when Ronald Reagan defeated a struggling incumbent Jimmy Carter, was the first explicitly candidate-centered PRESIDENTIAL ELECTION. However, a similar case can be made for 1976, when Carter campaigned as a Georgia farmer and Sunday school teacher on a platform of morality and outsider status to both national politics and the DEMOCRATIC PARTY. Reagan also defeated Carter using a personality-based campaign, both with respect to identifying himself in personal terms and by identifying Carter personally as an unsuccessful chief administrator, indeed as a presidential failure.

This trend continued through the Reagan administration and into the Bush administration, following George H. W. Bush's defeat of Massachusetts governor Michael Dukakis. The 1988 campaign was also highlighted by candidate-centered politics—not only with Bush attaching his presidential persona to the continuation of Reagan's, but also with the portrayal of Dukakis as a "Massachusetts liberal" and friend of Willie Horton—rather than a battle between Republican and Democratic platforms and positions.

Bush continued the candidate-centered phenomenon into the 1990s, eschewing the "vision thing" and instead campaigning on his personal strength in foreign policy and his "points of light," along with a negative campaigning strategy focused on the character flaws of his CHALLENGER, Arkansas governor Bill Clinton. "The Man from Hope," however, retorted with his own candidate-centered appeals, including his common-man experience and outsider status as well as a highly touted appeal to the state of the economy. Clinton won reelection with relative ease in 1996 over the Republican "war hero and quarterback" ticket of Robert Dole and Jack Kemp.

The 2000 election marked the crystallization of candidate-centered politics in America, when Clinton's vice president, Al Gore, squared off against Texas governor George W. Bush. Bush, the victor, campaigned as a "compassionate conservative" against Gore, who was portrayed as the scion of Clintonian values. This election also brought into the mainstream the political tactic of saddling one's opponent with an unsavory identification, a political tradition by no means new to American politics, although it had never before been a legitimate centerpiece of campaign strategy.

Candidate-centered politics has taken hold in the United States to such an extent that party affiliation is rarely mentioned and certainly not actively embraced in contemporary campaigning. Indeed, George W. Bush's self-identification as a "uniter, not a divider" reflects far broader historical developments than mere sound bite stratagems. Bush was saying to the electorate that he did not want to be characterized as "just" a Republican, but rather as an individual leader who could bring people together. Candidate-centered presidential elections have also led to an increasing frequency of INDEPENDENT candidates, with every presidential election since 1992 featuring a significant third party challenger, namely in the form of Ross Perot or Ralph Nader. Perot and Nader represent different types of responses to the candidate-centered dynamic inherent in contemporary presidential elections. Perot himself followed the candidate-centered mold, offering little more than "reform" to his supporters, while Nader represented the progressive policy interests of leftist-oriented voters who felt abandoned by the recent image-dominated presidential candidates of the Democratic Party.

The rise of candidate-centered politics and elections in America has had more effect than merely changing the nature of contemporary campaigning. Indeed, both public policy and media coverage have changed dramatically. As presidential candidates campaign on their résumés and character more and more and on policy platforms less and less, both presidents and the public are affected. Presidents are less able to claim policy mandates, and the public is less able to anticipate policy behavior on the part of the officials they have selected. Moreover, the media is less and less concerned with the policy positions of political elites and more focused on the personal side of politics. This serves to foster an increasingly unaware electorate, governed by individuals less beholden to policy commitments than to image maintenance.

Further reading: American Museum of the Moving Image. Available online. URL: http://livingroomcandidate. movingimage.us. Accessed August 10, 2005; Wattenberg, Martin P. "The Decline of Political Partisanship in the United States: Negativity or Neutrality?" *American Political Science Review* 75 (1981): 941–950; Wattenberg, Martin P. "From Parties to Candidates: Examining the Role of the Media." *Public Opinion Quarterly* 46 (1982): 216–227;

Wattenberg, Martin P. *The Decline of American Political Parties, 1952–1988.* Cambridge, Mass.: Harvard University Press, 1990; Wattenberg, Martin P. *The Rise of Candidate-Centered Politics: Presidential Elections of the 1980s.* Cambridge, Mass.: Harvard University Press, 1991.

—Justin S. Vaughn

casework

Casework, or "constituent service," is the term given to the activity that elected officials perform to address the individual problems of constituents. In the U.S. House of Representatives and the Senate, elected officials are often called on to help constituents locate a missing Social Security check, give passes to sessions of Congress for those visiting Washington, D.C., and provide answers to constituents' questions about federal programs. In state legislatures, representatives provide assistance to constituents on more localized concerns.

Prior to the Legislative Reorganization Act of 1946, congressional lawmakers often personally wrote letters to federal agencies on behalf of their constituents' concerns. Today, most casework in Congress and the nation's statehouses is done by staff. Though the amount of casework requests varies greatly by district, most members take their casework seriously, usually instructing their staffs to respond to a request for help from a constituent within a week or less. Many legislators deal with some casework directly by e-mail, at town hall meetings, and during the local "office hours" some representatives hold when they are in their home district.

When constituents are satisfied with the help they receive, research has shown they are more likely to support the elected official at the ballot box. Thus, many members try to generate casework by contacting their constituents directly. One way to do this is through the franking privilege, which allows elected officials to send mail to constituents free of charge as long as the information in the mailing does not actively try to influence a constituent's vote. Franking is designed to help representatives keep citizens informed about their lawmakers' actions in Washington. However, the messages are almost uniformly positive, painting the representative in a very appealing light, which, in essence, amounts to free advertising for the representative, adding to the advantage incumbents enjoy in their bids for reelection.

While some have argued that casework inflates the chances a representative will be reelected, the actual amount of electoral assistance provided by casework is uncertain. The electoral influence of casework is limited by the amount of staff resources an elected official can assign to casework and by the fact that a legislator's POLITICAL PARTY and policy positions also influence electoral decisions. Nevertheless, citizens who have benefited from casework, even when they are in the opposite party of their representative, have been found to be more likely to vote for their representative than are citizens who have not had casework done for them.

Further reading: Campbell, Andrea Louise. *How Policies Make Citizens: Senior Political Activism and the American Welfare State.* Princeton, N.J.: Princeton University Press, 2003; Price, David Eugene. *The Congressional Experience.* Boulder, Colo.: Westview Press, 2000; U.S. House of Representatives. Available online. URL: http://www.house.gov. Accessed August 10, 2005; U.S. Senate. Available online. URL: http://www.senate.gov. Accessed August 10, 2005.
—Michael W. Wagner

caucus

The word *caucus* is probably of Native American origin. Its earliest recorded use was as a reference to a political meeting in the 1763 diary of John Adams. As a noun, *caucus* refers to a meeting of legislators or POLITICAL PARTY members, whether the entire party or a smaller group organized around a shared interest. The purpose of a caucus is either to shape policy direction or choose a party's candidates for a GENERAL ELECTION. As a verb, *caucus* means the act of meeting with other party or group members for any of the above purposes. Two distinct forms of caucuses have developed over the years, the legislative caucus and the nominating caucus. Although historically similar, they are examined separately here.

A legislative caucus is a group of legislators; a partisan legislative caucus is the organization of all political party members in a legislative chamber. In the U.S. Congress, these partisan groups are called either caucus or conference: the House Republican Conference, the House Democratic Caucus, the Senate Republican Conference, and the Senate Democratic Conference. Partisan caucuses are the most fundamental organizational unit of Congress. Although somewhat less important in the Senate, in both chambers they fill leadership posts, make committee assignments, provide members with various services, serve as a policy forum, promote partisan unity, and help members in their reelection campaigns.

In addition to partisan groupings, other caucuses are organized to advocate particular interests. One of the first interest caucuses of any import was the Democratic Study Group (DSG). Formed in 1959, it was established by northern liberals to counter the intraparty influence of southern conservatives, who held the chairmanships of most congressional committees. There were few interest-based caucuses in Congress until the early 1970s, when they began to proliferate, a growth concurrent with and probably related to the increase in the number of INTEREST GROUPS at about the same time.

Interest caucuses can have partisan or bipartisan membership; they can also bridge the gap between the House and the Senate. For example, the CONGRESSIONAL BLACK CAUCUS, established in 1976, is a bipartisan group of African-American members of both the House and Senate that works to further the interests of African Americans. Other examples of interest caucuses include the Coastal Caucus, the Freshman Caucus, and the Women's Caucus. Interest caucuses may be large, with hundreds of members and staff, or small, with a handful of members. Some are permanent, while some dissolve at the end of a given Congress. Typically, about 200 exist at any given time, but because many are not permanent it is difficult to know exactly how many there are at any given time. The summer 2003 edition of the *Congressional Staff Directory* listed contact information for 166 House and 20 Senate caucuses.

Legislative caucuses exist and are organized similarly in all state legislatures. Moreover, use of the term is not peculiar to American POLITICS. For example, it has been used in British politics since the 1870s. The Australian Labor Party is commonly referred to as the Labor Caucus. In New Zealand and Canada, the term *caucus* is used by virtually all parties to refer to their parliamentary group (and in Canada, provincial legislatures as well).

Subsequent to the ratification of the U.S. Constitution, legislative caucuses began to emerge at local and state levels of government, mainly to nominate candidates for executive offices (mayors, governors, presidents). Rhode Island has the distinction of being the first state to hold a state nominating caucus, when in 1790 the legislature met to nominate candidates for governor and lieutenant governor. By 1796, every state in the Union had adopted the practice, and in many states legislative caucuses soon began nominating SLATES of presidential electors as well. At the national level, two informal congressional caucuses emerged in 1796 to nominate and solidify support for their respective presidential candidates. "King Caucus," as it became known, was used until 1824 but by 1832 was replaced by the party national convention system for nominating presidential tickets. Henceforth, congressional caucuses would be used only to discuss policy concerns and shape strategy. Nominating caucuses continue to be used at state and local levels.

Caucuses are also used in some states to select DELEGATES to party national conventions for the purpose of nominating presidential and vice presidential candidates. The number of states holding presidential nominating caucuses varies from one ELECTION CYCLE to the next, because states have the responsibility for regulating and administering elections. In addition, state parties for the most part manage their own affairs. In 2004, the DEMOCRATIC PARTY held presidential nominating caucuses in 13 states and the District of Columbia; in recent years the number has hovered at around 10.

There are three main types of presidential nominating caucuses, differentiated according to who may participate.

In a closed caucus, participation is limited to voters who are registered with the respective party; for example, only registered Republicans can participate in closed Republican caucuses. In an open caucus, any registered voter may participate. The rules governing semiopen caucuses vary from state to state. Generally, any voter registered with the party can participate in that party's caucus, and in most there are provisions allowing independents and people registered with other parties to participate provided they change their registration to the party holding the caucus.

Party leaders generally prefer closed caucuses, in large part out of fear of CROSSOVER VOTING, also known as raiding, whereby, for example, Democratic party regulars might participate in a Republican caucus to support a weaker Republican candidate whom they believe their Democratic candidate will have an easier time beating in November. However, research provides scant evidence that crossover voting occurs to the point that it affects election results.

A presidential nominating caucus is actually many different caucuses, held at local schools, public buildings, and even in private homes. It is also a multistaged process: A series of caucuses is actually held before delegates to the national convention are selected. In each round, individuals are selected to serve as delegates to the next round. For example, in Iowa, caucuses occur at the PRECINCT, county, CONGRESSIONAL DISTRICT, and finally state level, where delegates to the national convention are chosen. Different STATE PARTY COMMITTEES use different models with respect to the levels at which geographic caucuses are held. Some, for example, hold caucuses only at county and state levels. In addition, if an incumbent president is running for reelection, his party will typically forgo some of the earlier caucuses. For example, in 2004, several Republican state party organizations did not hold precinct-level caucuses, since George W. Bush was the only candidate on the BALLOT.

There are significant differences in how Democrats and Republicans conduct nominating caucuses, based principally on how delegates are apportioned among candidates and selected. Republicans usually conduct a STRAW POLL of those attending the caucus. The candidate who receives the most votes gets all of the delegates. In Republican caucuses, those who wish to serve as a delegate volunteer and are generally appointed. Democrats follow a completely different set of procedures. Party rules award delegates proportional to the votes the candidate receives, with a 15 percent threshold to receive any delegates. During the caucus, supporters of various candidates congregate in different areas of the room and at the designated time express support by a show of hands. If a candidate does not meet the 15 percent threshold, supporters may lend their support to another candidate or remain uncommitted. Those who wish to serve as delegates in subsequent caucuses are selected from within the candidate grouping to which they belong. Although delegates are not formally bound to the decision of the caucus, they generally follow the wishes expressed by caucus-goers.

In comparison to states that use a PRIMARY system, participation in caucuses is low. For example, in 2004, approximately 120,000 citizens participated in the Iowa Democratic caucuses, a number thought to be a record. In 2000, roughly 60,000 participated; in other years it has been estimated at half that amount. Turnout in other states varies as well but is generally quite low. Low participation is a function of the fact that caucus participation demands a high level of commitment. Participants typically spend a good deal of time acquainting themselves with candidates and issues (particularly in Iowa), and the event itself can take up to several hours. Thus, those who do participate in presidential nominating caucuses are not representative of the general ELECTORATE. They tend to be better educated, more politically aware, come from higher income brackets, and are slightly older compared with other citizens. They also tend to be more ideologically extreme (more liberal or more conservative) than average party identifiers or voters.

The IOWA CAUCUS is the most visible of all presidential nominating caucuses because since 1972 it has been the first delegate selection event of the year, a place secured for it in the rules of the DEMOCRATIC NATIONAL COMMITTEE. The 1972 Iowa caucus set the stage for the rise in prominence of the event and provides insight into how Iowa affects the dynamics of the primary-caucus season. In the Democratic caucus that year, the DARK-HORSE CANDIDATE, George McGovern, finished a strong second to Edmund Muskie, previously considered the front-runner. This immediately boosted McGovern's media visibility and viability, and he eventually secured the Democratic NOMINATION. The post-Iowa boost was singled out as being at least partially responsible for his success.

Leaders of both state parties in Iowa took note of the attention paid to the 1972 event and scheduled their caucuses to be the first of the 1976 season. Learning from the lesson of 1972, Jimmy Carter spent a considerable amount of his campaign's resources campaigning in Iowa throughout the summer and fall of 1975. The strategy paid off. By fall, the largely unknown Carter was being mentioned with some frequency in the media as a viable contender for the Democratic nomination, which he eventually secured.

Thus, the notion that success in Iowa could be parlayed into national success grew. Since 1976, the Iowa caucus has attracted a disproportionate amount of attention from the media relative to Iowa's importance in the ELECTORAL COLLEGE. For example, one study showed that 14 percent of all coverage of the 1980 nomination by United Press International and CBS News was devoted to Iowa. In 1987, the *New York Times* ran almost 70 stories on the Iowa caucus and in 1988, almost 50. As a consequence of this media attention, presidential candidates spend a great deal of time and money campaigning in Iowa. For example, the Democratic nominee in 2004, John Kerry, spent 73 days in Iowa in 2003. The Democrat Howard Dean spent almost $3 million in television advertising in Iowa in 2003 and early 2004.

The winner of Iowa does not always become the eventual nominee. In fact, from 1972 to 2004, the winner of the 12 Iowa caucuses has won the nomination only eight times. The effects of the Iowa caucus on the dynamics of the nomination season center around expected and actual success. Doing better than expected in Iowa seems to help increase the prominence, and thus the chances, of future primary success of lesser-known candidates. This was certainly the case, for example, for John Edwards in 2004, who placed second behind John Kerry (himself a surprise winner) and ahead of previous frontrunner Howard Dean. This immediately placed Edwards on the national stage and paved the way for what became a two-man race between Edwards and Kerry. Conversely, placing lower than expected can doom a candidacy. Kerry's win in 2004 sent Dean's candidacy into a downward spiral.

Further reading: Mayer, William G. "Caucuses: How They Work, What Difference They Make." In William G. Mayer, ed., *In Pursuit of the White House: How We Choose Our Presidential Nominees.* Chatham, N.J.: Chatham House, 1996; Cook, Rhodes. *The Presidential Nominating Process: A Place for Us?* Lanham, Md.: Rowman & Littlefield, 2004.

—Jody Baumgartner

census

The census is the mechanism for counting population in the United States as prescribed by the Constitution in Article 1, Section 2. While the primary purpose of the census is to provide an accurate population count for the division of congressional seats among the states, the population figures are also used for many other important purposes. Federal and state governments base many funding decisions on the census figures, including social services, farm subsidies, and highway funding. The Census Bureau, a part of the Department of Commerce, conducts the decennial count. The 2000 census used more than 860,000 temporary employees and cost more than $6 billion, making it the largest peacetime mobilization of resources and personnel in government history.

The first census was conducted in 1790 and reported a U.S. population of just fewer than 4 million people. The 2000 census put the population at more than 280 million people, an increase of nearly 32 million from the 1990 count. According to the 2000 census, Hispanics and African Americans make up the two largest ethnic minority groups in the United States, with each group constituting approximately 12.5 percent of the population, or 35 million people.

Census estimates from 2002 identified Hispanics as the nation's largest minority, surpassing African Americans for the first time in American history.

While seemingly straightforward and nonpolitical, the 2000 census created controversy over the method of counting the population. It is believed that the census has historically undercounted members of specific disadvantaged groups. These groups include the homeless and ethnic minorities, such as migrant Hispanics and inner-city African Americans. Advocates for these groups proposed the use of statistical sampling, which would allow statistical estimations to account for undercounting associated with traditional census procedures. The issue became a political hotbed, with Democrats generally supporting the use of sampling and Republicans in favor of the traditional head count. The Democrats hoped that larger numbers from traditionally undercounted groups would gain them seats in key areas, and the Republicans favored the individual head count since it tends to count more of their primary supporters. While the Census Bureau implemented a sampling component to its methods in 2000, a federal court struck down the plan and ruled that sampling could not be used for apportioning seats for the House of Representatives but that it could be used for demographic purposes.

Further reading: Anderson, Margo J. *The American Census: A Social History.* New Haven, Conn.: Yale University Press, 1988; Brewer, Cynthia A. *Mapping Census 2000: The Geography of U.S. Diversity.* Washington, D.C.: U.S. Dept. of Commerce, Economics and Statistics Administration, U.S. Census Bureau, 2001; Hinckley, Kathleen. *Your Guide to the Federal Census.* Cincinnati, Ohio: Betterway Books, 2002; U.S. Census Bureau. Available online. URL: http://www.census.gov. Accessed August 10, 2005.

—Jonathan Winburn

chad

Chad refers to a small, perforated card stock tab that is the by-product of punch card balloting. The term gained national attention during the 2000 PRESIDENTIAL ELECTION between Democrat Albert Gore and Republican George W. Bush. During this close election, the final decision came down to the controversial results from the state of Florida, in particular the outcome in the three counties making up south Florida—Dade, Broward, and Palm Beach.

Part of the controversy stemmed from the results of Palm Beach County's BUTTERFLY BALLOT, which was believed to have confused some of the county's voters. The election became even more heated when it became apparent that not all votes had been counted due to flaws in the punch card machines. BALLOTS had been disqualified when the punch styluses failed to adequately remove the chads, making it difficult for the election machines to read the ballots.

The chad debate became even more complicated after the hand RECOUNTs began. The question of what constituted a vote became a key issue in lawsuits that quickly reached the Florida and U.S. Supreme Courts. While these cases were being argued in the highest courts, both parties sent representatives to oversee the unfolding hand recounts. (Warren Christopher represented the Democrats and James Baker represented the Republicans.) One representative from each party examined each ballot in an attempt to prevent foul play. Issues regarding "hanging" or "swinging" chads (i.e., chads punched clean through but remaining connected on one side) and "dimpled" or "pregnant" chads (i.e., chads that were not perforated but marked by an indentation presumably caused by the punch stylus) became key issues as the vote counters attempted to interpret the intent of voters. In the end, the chad debate became a moot point when the U.S. Supreme Court made the decision that the machine recounts would stand, securing Florida's electoral votes and the presidency for George W. Bush.

Further reading: Nakashima, Ellen, et al. *Deadlock: The Inside Story of America's Closest Election.* New York: Public Affairs, 2001; Rakove, Jack N., ed. *The Unfinished Election of 2000.* New York: Basic Books, 2001; Wayne, Stephen J. *The Road to The White House, 2000: The Politics of Presidential Elections.* Boston: Bedford/St. Martin, 2000.

—Michael B. Ernst

challenger

A challenger is a candidate for political office who opposes an incumbent. A challenger can either run against a member of a different party in the GENERAL ELECTION or can challenge a member of his or her own party in a PRIMARY contest. In either case, challengers in the United States face long odds. Incumbents usually enjoy advantages in NAME RECOGNITION, FUND-RAISING, media attention, and the benefits of office, such as communicating with voters by franked (i.e., free) mail. In 2002, just 4 percent of challengers (16 total) defeated House members, while 14 percent (four total) defeated senators.

Challengers, though rarely successful, are a staple of American POLITICS; every president since George Washington has had at least one challenger. They run for office because they believe the incumbent is vulnerable and think they would do a better job of governing than the incumbent, and they receive support from party officials and other backers.

Given the narrow margin that currently exists between the two parties in Congress, party leaders have opted not to invest heavily in challengers. Likewise, the historically low success rate of challengers makes it difficult for them to attract campaign funds from other sources. In 2000, the mean for spending by House challengers was $369,823,

while for incumbents it was $814,507. REDISTRICTING has also been used to create SAFE SEATs for many incumbents, further stacking the cards against challengers.

Several factors can help a challenger's chances of winning. The first is when discontented voters punish the party in power, such as in 1994, when Republicans regained control of the House and Senate. Another occurs in the election immediately following redistricting, when the lines of lawmakers' districts change, and they no longer enjoy INCUMBENCY ADVANTAGES in all parts of the new area. A third is when the incumbent is tainted by SCANDAL but still seeks reelection, as happened in 2002 with Representative Gary Condit (D, Calif.), who had been involved with the missing intern Chandra Levy. Finally, challengers can ride the COATTAILS of another popular candidate, especially in PRESIDENTIAL ELECTION years.

Not all challengers are political novices. Some politicians are repeat challengers, running against the same incumbent or for the same office in consecutive elections. Former representative John Thune (R, S.Dak.) challenged Senator Tim Johnson (D, S.Dak.) in 2002, lost, and then ran against Senator Tom Daschle (D, S.Dak.) in 2004. An incumbent running against the current occupant of another office is also a challenger but brings experience and name recognition that improves his or her chance of victory.

Further reading: Herrnson, Paul S. *Congressional Elections: Campaigning at Home and in Washington.* Washington, D.C.: CQ Press, 2004; Sidlow, Edward I. *Challenging the Incumbent: An Underdog's Undertaking.* Washington, D.C.: CQ Press, 2004.

—Mary Lynn F. Jones

Christian Coalition

Pat Robertson, an ordained Southern Baptist minister and host of the Christian Broadcasting Network's flagship program, *The 700 Club,* was defeated in his 1988 run for the presidency, coming in third behind Bob Dole and George Bush in the Republican primaries. Rather than face the prospect of the people who had rallied behind his campaign withdrawing from the political arena, Robertson invited campaign staffers and supporters to Atlanta in September 1989 for a meeting to discuss the future of religious conservatism in the United States. One proposal at the meeting was to stage an immense rally called the American Congress of Christian Citizens as a show of political influence. A second proposal was to develop a GRASSROOTS movement that would engage in state-by-state recruitment and training in accordance with suggestions by a Republican political operative, Ralph Reed.

In 1990, the idea for a large Christian rally faded, while the proposal for the Christian Coalition grassroots movement was adopted. Robertson became the first president of the Christian Coalition, while Reed became its executive director. The purpose of the organization was to represent Christians before governmental bodies, train Christian leaders to be effective in their social and political activities, defend the legal rights of Christians, protest biases against Christians, speak out for Christians, and monitor issues and legislation in order to provide information to Christians.

During the 1990s, the Christian Coalition expanded into one of the largest conservative grassroots movements in the country, with more than 2 million members. It became active in taking what it considered to be profamily and prolife stances. When it began, it was considered a small wing on the fringes of the REPUBLICAN PARTY. With its increase in numbers it was gradually embraced by the mainstream Republican Party, providing the party much needed grassroots support. Some members, however, began to feel the Christian Coalition was compromising or even sacrificing its emphasis on faith and spirituality for increased political power. The most recent president of the Christian Coalition, Roberta Combs, has emphasized the slogan "Faith with Action" in order to remind members that the coalition is a faith-based organization that seeks spiritual renewal and the aspirations of Christians in government.

Further reading: Reed, Ralph. *Active Faith: How Christians Are Changing the Soul of American Politics.* New York: Free Press, 1996; Watson, Justin. *The Christian Coalition: Dreams of Restoration, Demands for Recognition.* New York: St. Martin's Press, 1996; Christian Coalition. Available online. URL: http://www.cc.org. Accessed August 10, 2005.

—Nathan Zook

citizenship

Citizenship refers to one's membership in a particular state. Under a liberal theory of the state, influenced by John Locke's theory of social contract, citizenship has been traditionally defined as a status of having to participate in, to be present in, and to enjoy particular privileges that are bestowed only to members of the state, including SUFFRAGE rights, property rights, and the right to enjoy the rule of law. Acquisition of citizenship grants equal membership and equal treatment in all public institutions of the state. In exchange, citizens presumably have a special sense of loyalty to the state and an obligation to obey its laws.

The concept of citizenship has developed via a series of struggles. The French Revolution in the 18th century marked a turning point. Processes of commercialization, capitalism, and industrialization during the 18th and 19th centuries, especially in Europe, catalyzed the evolution of the modern concept of the nation-state and a strong sense of national consciousness, presuming to replace and cut across preexisting social, ethnic, and cultural statuses and identities. In practice, however, various minority groups, including women, the poor, and other minority groups such as African Americans in the United States, were consistently denied political and legal rights. Although in developed societies the formal barriers have largely been removed, to this day other groups, such as persons with disabilities, are still denied citizenship rights in various countries around the world.

Further development of the concept of citizenship to include social welfare rights occurred in the early 20th century. Acknowledging that economic, social, and political inequalities place informal barriers on citizens' abilities to fully enjoy citizenship privileges led states, including the United States, to provide various public services to citizens, including education, health care, and so on as a means to accommodate the struggle for social justice and for a more inclusive political community. While the United States and other Western states increasingly recognize the necessity of ensuring access to all institutions of civil society, including those held by private entities, as a condition for equal citizenship, it is still not fully endorsed or implemented.

Acquiring citizenship is contingent on the domestic laws of each state. Most commonly, including in the United States, citizenship is a birthright of being born to parents who are already the state's citizens or were born in territories administered by it. Admission can also be on the basis of residency (as was the case with Native Americans) and through immigration policies. Some states, including the United States, grant citizenship also in special humanitarian and political circumstances, such as political asylum. Although citizenship assumes a special commitment of a citizen to a state, one may hold dual and multiple citizenships if allowed under domestic law.

The concept of citizenship currently faces two key challenges. Globalization has led some scholars to suggest "world citizenship" rather than "national," and ethnic fragmentation and multiculturalism has led to suggestions of "fragmented citizenship," consisting of overlapping loyalties and various individual commitments and memberships rather than exclusivity to a nation-state.

Further reading: Gilbert, Paul. *Peoples, Cultures and Nations in Political Philosophy.* Washington, D.C.: Georgetown University Press, 2000; Spinner, Jeff. *The Boundaries of Citizenship: Race, Ethnicity and Nationality in the Liberal State.* Baltimore: Johns Hopkins University Press, 1996.

—Maya Sabatello

Citizens Party

The Citizens Party was one of many unsuccessful, short-lived third party movements in American history. Concerned with pollution, the widening gap between rich and poor, and the concentration of political and economic power, a COALITION of populists and dissident liberals organized the Citizens Party in 1979. The party's platform advocated for public control of multinational corporations, the nationalization of private oil companies, decreased military spending, limited price controls, the end of nuclear power, increased spending for social services, and enhanced economic democracy.

In 1980, the Citizens Party, opting to organize at the national rather than local level, nominated Barry Commoner for president. Commoner was a biologist and environmental activist who embraced environmental issues during the 1960s and advocated for the end of fossil fuels. Like other supporters of the Citizens Party, Commoner critiqued capitalism, arguing that the desire to make a profit had made Americans disregard what was in their long-term interest. He also claimed that government officials were making decisions that did not benefit average citizens, but big business. La Donna Harris, a Native American activist and the wife of then U.S. senator Fred Harris (D, Okla.), ran as the Citizens Party's vice presidential nominee.

Commoner campaigned heavily in Pennsylvania, New York, Illinois, California, and Michigan. These states, Commoner and his supporters believed, would be more receptive to the Citizens Party's platform, largely due to the fact that they had supported antinuclear and environmental legislation. In addition to the Commoner-Harris ticket, the Citizens Party fielded two candidates for the U.S. Senate, seven for the House, and 13 for lesser offices. Commoner won just 0.3 percent of the vote, or 234,294 votes, in 1980.

In 1984, the Citizens Party nominated Sonia Johnson as its presidential nominee and Richard Walton of Rhode Island for vice president. Johnson had gained notoriety when the Mormon Church excommunicated her in 1979 for supporting the Equal Rights Amendment. The Johnson-Walton ticket did poorly during the 1984 election, winning only 0.08 percent of the POPULAR VOTE, or 72,200 votes. At the local level, however, the Citizens Party prevailed in Burlington, Vermont, and other environmentalist strongholds. The party disbanded shortly after the 1984 election but did leave a legacy, as many of its members became loyal supporters of the GREEN PARTY.

Further reading: Commoner, Barry. *The Politics of Energy.* New York: Knopf, 1979; Koch, Jeffrey W. "Political Cynicism and Third Party Support in American Presidential Elections." *American Politics Research* 31 (2003): 48–65.

—Bruce E. Stewart

civil rights legislation

Civil rights legislation consists of statutes that are enacted to prevent discrimination based on race, sex, religion, age, previous condition of servitude, physical limitation, national origin, and other distinctions. As a result of the mass struggle for equal rights, two landmark pieces of legislation have become the cornerstone of civil rights legislation in the United States—the Civil Rights Act of 1964 and the VOTING RIGHTS ACT of 1965.

Civil rights legislation has a long and storied history in the United States. The Civil Rights Act of 1866 passed despite a failed veto attempt by Andrew Johnson. The legislation was passed, during RECONSTRUCTION and aimed to destroy Black Codes, which the southern states had enacted to suppress the rights of newly freed slaves. Another important early piece of civil rights legislation was the Civil Rights Act of 1875. This legislation declared that all individuals had equal access to accommodations, public conveyances, and places of amusement such as theaters. The legislation was declared unconstitutional by the Supreme Court in 1883 and thus left an opening for southern states to enact Jim Crow laws. It was almost 75 years until another civil rights bill was passed. The Civil Rights Act of 1957 created the United States Commission on Civil Rights and strengthened the civil rights division of the Department of Justice, which was to be directed by the attorney general. President Dwight Eisenhower and his administration, Attorney General Herbert Brownwell, House Speaker Sam Rayburn, and Senate Majority Leader Lyndon B. Johnson were all advocates for the bill.

Although the Civil Rights Act of 1957 was significant because it gave teeth to the civil rights division of the Justice Department, the Civil Rights Act of 1964 was by far the most significant and comprehensive civil rights legislation in U.S. history. The act was passed in response to the assassination of President John F. Kennedy during the beginning of the Johnson presidency. The bill had been developed by the Kennedy administration, in part as a response to the problems encountered by civil rights protesters in Birmingham, Alabama, in the spring of 1963. The legislation was submitted to Congress on June 19, 1963. Johnson maneuvered the omnibus bill through Congress despite a southern filibuster. Johnson signed the bill on July 2, 1964. The Civil Rights Act of 1964 and subsequent legislation also declared strong legislative policy against discrimination in public schools and colleges, which assisted in eliminating de jure segregation and desegregating southern institutions.

Title I of the Civil Rights Act of 1964 prohibited a number of southern practices to limit black voting, including the use of overly strict LITERACY TESTS. Title II was the most controversial part of the bill, guaranteeing blacks equal access to public accommodations such as hotels, motels, restaurants, and places of amusement. Title III gave the attorney general the authority to file suits for the desegregation of public facilities other than public schools. Title IV gave funds for technical assistance to schools facing issues associated with desegregation. Title VI of the Civil Rights Act prohibited discrimination in federally funded programs. Title VII prohibited employment discrimination when the employer was engaged in interstate commerce.

Also in 1964, the Twenty-fourth Amendment outlawed the poll tax in federal elections, and in 1966, the Supreme Court struck down the use of poll taxes in state elections as a violation of the Fourteenth Amendment's equal protection clause.

In 1965, Congress enacted the Voting Rights Act, giving blacks access to the ballot box. Federal observers were placed at southern polls to ensure equal voting rights. The act outlawed literacy tests as a condition of voting in seven southern states where black voting was much lower than by whites. Also, the act assisted black voting by sending federal registrars to states in which 50 percent of the voting age population had not been registered to vote in the 1964 presidential election. The Voting Rights Act of 1965 has had tremendous positive effects on black voting in the South, where voter registration and voting rates have dramatically increased. By the mid-1970s, blacks were voting in numbers comparable to whites, and there was a growing number of black elected officials. The Voting Rights Act was amended in 1982, outlawing discriminatory effects in elections and districting, regardless of the intent. The benchmark of judging the discriminatory effects of a given system would be the degree to which black voting power was diluted.

Further reading: Behr, Joshua. *Race, Ethnicity, and the Politics of City Redistricting: Minority Opportunity Districts and the Election of Hispanics and Blacks to City Councils.* New York: State University of New York Press, 2004; Davidson, Chandler, and Bernard Grofman. *Quiet Revolution in the South: The Impact of the Voting Rights Act, 1965–1990.* Princeton, N.J.: Princeton University, 1994; Morris, Roy. *Fraud of the Century: Rutherford B. Hayes and Samuel Tilden, and the Stolen Election of 1876.* New York: Simon & Schuster, 2003.

—F. Erik Brooks

Civil Rights movement

While civil rights movements in this country have deep roots and concern the struggles of all groups that have experienced legal discrimination, the modern Civil Rights movement is generally associated with the struggle for the legal rights of African Americans during the mid- to late 20th century. The political movement spurred the enactment of national civil rights legislation and contributed to a transformation in the political landscape of the United States. Though it is difficult to date the beginning of this movement meaningfully, two key events point to an early period of the modern civil rights movement: the National Association for the Advancement of Colored People's (NAACP) victory in *Brown v. Board of Education* (1954) and the Montgomery, Alabama, bus boycott in 1955.

Some of the groups at the forefront in the struggle for civil rights were the National Association for the Advancement of Colored People, the Congress of Racial Equality, the Urban League, the Student Nonviolent Committee, and the Southern Christian Leadership Conference. From the 1930s through the 1960s, many of the groups became targets of state and federal government investigations. The Federal Bureau of Investigation investigated many of these groups and attempted to link them to communism, while southern state governments attempted to outlaw the groups outright. Also during this time, domestic terrorist groups such as the Ku Klux Klan and the White Citizens Council cast a cloud of terror on blacks attempting to vote in the South.

The foundation of the Civil Rights movement was anchored in the NAACP's legal campaign against state-sanctioned segregation. On May 17, 1954, the Supreme Court unanimously ruled in *Brown v. Board of Education* (1954) that the notion of separate but equal was inherently unequal and therefore unconstitutional. In *Brown* the Court overturned its earlier ruling in *Plessy v. Ferguson* (1896), in which the Supreme Court had legitimized the "separate but equal" doctrine. The Court issued an additional ruling one year after the initial *Brown* decision, which is often called *Brown II.* The second *Brown* decision dealt with the implementation of the 1954 decision and included the now famous phrase "with all deliberate speed." These words left a loophole that allowed public groups, politicians, and policy makers to systematically subvert and delay the *Brown* decision for many years. With white southern resistance in full force, the Court allowed for a gradual implementation, which usually turned into inactivity by southern state governments.

After the *Brown* decision, voter registration and education accelerated for blacks. In the mid-1950s, NAACP chapters began a push to increase the number of blacks on southern state voter rolls. In 1954 in Mississippi, just 4 percent of the state's eligible black voters were registered. Those attempting to exercise their right to vote were often targets of reprisals from white southerners entrenched in the tradition of segregation and disenfranchisement. Those leading voter registration movements were also beaten and gunned down for their political activity.

In December 1955, Rosa Parks refused to give up her seat on a Montgomery city bus to a white man. Rosa Parks's refusal was the impetus of the Montgomery bus boycott. The boycott lasted for 381 days, and it catapulted a young Baptist minister, Martin Luther King, Jr., to the leadership of the boycott and the movement for black civil rights. Through the efforts of King and the Montgomery Improvement Association, the boycott brought national and international attention to the plight of blacks in the South and to the civil rights struggle.

In 1958, the Civil Rights Commission, a newly formed arm of the Justice Department, sent investigators to Alabama to investigate claims of voter discrimination. In Macon County, Alabama, a black organization that had been organized during the 1940s shared its records documenting patterns of discrimination against blacks in voting. In turn,

A Kennedy-Johnson campaign flyer from 1960 focusing on Kennedy's commitment to human and civil rights *(Duke University Special Collections Library)*

the commission held nationally televised hearings in Montgomery, Alabama. During the hearings, mounds of evidence were presented that showed a deceptive and calculated system used by registrars in Macon County, Alabama, to stop blacks from registering to vote and from voting.

Early in 1963, civil rights leaders and the Southern Christian Leadership Conference launched Project Confrontation in Birmingham, Alabama. Headed by Fred Shuttlesworth and Martin Luther King, Jr., Project Confrontation began with a boycott of downtown stores that refused to hire blacks. Demonstrations were also held in protest of the city's segregation laws. King, who was arrested for his part in the demonstrations, wrote from his jail cell his now famous "Letter from a Birmingham Jail." The letter was in response to a group of white ministers who criticized the civil rights leaders for allegedly striking chords of disharmony between the races.

In May 1963, Birmingham children and youths marched downtown. The police arrested more than 900 people and placed them in jail cells. The next day, more than 1,000 people returned for another march. This time, Eugene "Bull" Connor, the police chief of Birmingham, turned police dogs and fire hoses on the young demonstrators. Once again, these events were captured on television. The television footage of children being brutalized outraged many and fueled a public outcry.

During this period in Selma, Alabama, the Student Nonviolent Coordinating Committee and the Southern Christian Leadership Conference worked with the Dallas County Voters League to remove impediments to black voting. In 1965, Martin Luther King, Jr., began a series of marches geared toward bringing attention to the violence and discrimination that kept blacks from voting. After several attacks on blacks by police, King decided to plan a march from Selma to Montgomery, the state's capital, to deliver a personal petition to Governor George C. Wallace. On March 7, 1965, as marchers attempted to cross the Edmund Pettus Bridge, they were beaten back across the bridge. Alabama state troopers used tear gas and billy clubs to thwart the march; this horrendous event became known as "Bloody Sunday." As a result, President Johnson addressed the nation and introduced a comprehensive civil rights bill to Congress. On August 6, 1965, after years of resistance from SOUTHERN DEMOCRATS who controlled key positions in Congress, President Johnson signed the Voting Rights Act into law, which provided federal supervision of voter registration practices and opened the polls for blacks. The Civil Rights movement had a tremendous effect on the political and social consciousness of the United States. Essentially, it marked the fruition of the FOURTEENTH and FIFTEENTH AMENDMENTS, opening the democratic process for blacks in the United States.

Further reading: Branch, Taylor. *Parting the Waters: America in the King Years 1954–63.* New York: Simon & Schuster, 1988; Branch, Taylor. *Pillar of Fire: America in the King Years, 1963–65.* New York: Simon & Schuster, 1998; Kluger, Richard. *Simple Justice: The History of Brown v. Board of Education . . . and of Black America's Century-Long Struggle for Equality under Law.* New York: Knopf, 1975; Morris, Aldon D. *The Origins of the Civil Rights Movement.* New York: Free Press, 1984; Sitkoff, Harvard. *The Struggle for Black Equality: 1954–1992.* New York: Hill & Wang, 1993.

—F. Erik Brooks

coalition

In its formal usage, *coalition* refers to the arrangement by which two or more political parties agree to support each other. Coalitions are most commonly found in parliamentary governmental systems. In those systems, the effective head of state, who has a title such as prime minister, premier, or chancellor, is required to have the support of the legislative branch of government. That usually means this official must be backed by a majority of the lower house of parliament, the chamber that is most directly responsible to the ELECTORATE. Most parliamentary systems use PROPORTIONAL REPRESENTATION for elected members of parliament. These proportional electoral systems usually result in a proliferation of parties that have representation in parliament, with the result that no party has a majority. In order to create a legislative majority, two or more parties form a coalition. The cabinet is then selected from the members of that coalition, with the leader of the largest party serving as effective head of state.

Informal systems of cooperation have also been called coalitions. Two examples were notable in Congress during

the 20th century: the 1911 coalition of Democrats, Progressives, and Republicans that shared the powers of the autocratic SPEAKER OF THE HOUSE OF REPRESENTATIVES, Joseph Cannon, and the congressional coalition of conservative Republicans and SOUTHERN DEMOCRATS that emerged in the late 1930s. They agreed on fiscal policy and a limited role for the national government. This coalition was exceptionally successful since its members included southern Democrats who chaired key committees in both houses of Congress. In the 1980s and early 1990s, YELLOW DOG and BLUE DOG DEMOCRATS represented FACTIONS within the congressional party that might temporarily oppose the party leadership and cooperate with the Republican caucus.

INTEREST GROUPS may form coalitions as those groups lobby to support or oppose a governmental policy. These are customarily short-term arrangements and may include factions within Congress as well as support from the White House. Once the unifying issue is resolved, the coalition disappears.

Coalition has also been employed in the analysis of voting. The sectors of society that persistently support a POLITICAL PARTY have been characterized as coalitions. For example, the DEMOCRATIC PARTY, at times, has been said to have a coalition of voters composed of union members, Catholics, African Americans, and Jewish Americans. Voting coalitions tend to be unstable since there is no organizational structure to hold them together.

Further reading: Patterson, James T. *Congressional Conservatism and the New Deal; The Growth of the Conservative Coalition in Congress, 1933–1939.* Lexington: University of Kentucky Press, 1967; Wright, John R. *Interest Groups and Congress: Lobbying, Contributions, and Influence.* Boston: Allyn & Bacon, 1996.

—Thomas Phillip Wolf

coattails

The concept of coattails conjures up an image of a winning presidential candidate pulling his partisans into Congress, governors' mansions, and statehouses along with him, as they hitch a metaphorical ride on his coattails of popularity. In reality, the concept refers to an electoral victory for a fellow member of the president's party whereby the effect of the president's campaign provides the additional increment of votes that allows the down-ticket candidate to win. Thus, there are two assumptions implicit in this concept. To posit the presence of coattails is to assume that voters cast their BALLOTS for senators, representatives, and other subpresidential candidates to at least some extent on the basis of their affection or positive evaluation of the presidential candidate, and that the lower candidate would not have received these votes otherwise.

Recent scholarship has put forward a theory of surge and decline that suggests that VOTER TURNOUT surges in PRESIDENTIAL ELECTION years and declines in MIDTERM ELECTIONS. The additional voters in presidential election years are more sensitive to the effects of presidential coattails than are their counterparts who also participate in CONGRESSIONAL ELECTIONS. This suggests a different kind of presidential coattail, attributable not to the characteristics or popularity of individual presidential candidates, but rather to the presence of a presidential election itself.

Much like the past 50 years of scholarship, the historical record of coattail effects has been largely mixed. Indeed, some of the nation's strongest presidents have been ushered into office with relatively minute, if not nonexistent, coattails. Recent history has shown a relative dearth of presidential coattails. George H. W. Bush came into office in 1988 as the Republicans lost seats in both the House of Representatives and the Senate. Bill Clinton won in 1992 as the Democrats saw losses in the House of Representatives and no gain in the Senate. When Clinton secured reelection, he did so with only small gains in the House and a net loss of two seats in the Senate. In the recent 2000 election, George W. Bush's Republican colleagues in both the House and Senate saw their numbers decline.

This is not to say that coattail effects have been absent from the political scene in the 20th century. In fact, some of the most momentous policy programs in modern history have been enacted following presidential elections that featured considerable coattail effects. For example, Franklin Delano Roosevelt's successful passage of much of the legislation that became known as the New Deal was thanks in part to a major shift in party seats following the 1932 election. Similarly, Lyndon Johnson's Great Society and Ronald Reagan's early budget and tax victories were due in large part to increased legislative support by partisans swept in on their coattails in the elections of 1964 and 1980, respectively.

Recent scholarship has examined the presence of coattails in American elections and has generally found that while the effect does exist, it is generally small, highly conditional, and on the wane. Congressional elections are determined to a great extent by incumbency and party, with relatively few seats seen as competitive in a given year. In a study of coattail effects between 1952 and 1980, only one of more than 70 congressional races characterized by coattail effects featured an incumbent. It is only when predominant factors such as party and incumbency are not present that coattails, along with other external factors, matter.

Even in such cases, coattails have often been "wasted." Scholars have put forward the argument that presidential coattails have been available in certain cases, but there was a lack of congressional candidates to ride them. This was particularly true in the 1970s and 1980s, when conditions favorable to Republicans were presented in the South, but a great many Democratic candidates went unchallenged. This was especially the case in 1972, as Richard Nixon pursued his SOUTHERN STRATEGY to great success. Although Nixon ran tremendously well all across the South, the REPUBLICAN PARTY had failed to nurture and recruit strong congressional candidates, thus wasting the potential pulling effect that the Nixon campaign possessed.

As the POLITICS of REDISTRICTING has increasingly resulted in SAFE SEATS for incumbents, and as competition for open seats increasingly occurs not in the GENERAL ELECTION between Republicans and Democrats, but rather within a single dominant party during the primaries, the conditions for presidential coattail effects have diminished. Thus, as the absence of predominant factors such as party and incumbency has become an ever-increasing rarity, the declining evidence of presidential coattails in congressional elections is easily understood.

Further reading: Campbell, James E. *The Presidential Pulse of Congressional Elections.* 2nd ed. Lexington: University Press of Kentucky, 1997; Edwards, George C., III. *Presidential Influence in Congress.* San Francisco: W. H. Freeman, 1980; Edwards, George C., III. *The Public Presidency.* New York: St. Martin's Press, 1983; Ferejohn, John A., and Randall L. Calvert. "Presidential Coattails in Historical Perspective." *American Journal of Political Science* 28 (1984): 127–146; Jacobson, Gary C. *The Politics of Congressional Elections.* 3rd ed. New York: HarperCollins, 1992; Miller, Warren E. "Presidential Coattails: A Study in Political Myth and Methodology." *Public Opinion Quarterly* 19 (1955): 353–368; Moos, Malcolm. *Politics, Presidents, and Coattails.* Baltimore: Johns Hopkins University Press, 1952.

—Justin S. Vaughn

Commission on Presidential Debates

The Republican and Democratic Parties created the Commission on Presidential Debates in 1987 to facilitate debates between the leading presidential and vice presidential candidates. The commission hosted its first debate in the 1988 PRESIDENTIAL ELECTION between George H. W. Bush and Michael Dukakis, and has held debates for each succeeding election.

Before the Commission on Presidential Debates emerged on the national scene, debates in presidential POLITICS were scarce. PRESIDENTIAL DEBATES were seldom held in the 20th century (only one prior to 1976), and there were no face-to-face presidential debates prior to the 20th century. While many people believe the famous LINCOLN-DOUGLAS DEBATES (between Abraham Lincoln and Stephen Douglas) in Illinois in 1858 were examples of early presidential debates, they were, in fact, debates for a U.S. Senate election. This series of debates is often held as one of the most significant points of Lincoln's career, and even though he lost the election, it proved that someone who had humble beginnings could rise up and share the stage with one of the day's great orators. In addition, both Lincoln and Douglas brought political issues directly to the people by traveling throughout Illinois to hold the debate series.

The first face-to-face presidential debate, and also the first televised presidential debate, took place in 1960 between John F. Kennedy and Richard Nixon. This debate pitted a rising star (Kennedy) against a sitting vice president (Nixon). While the substance of the debate was essential in differentiating the two candidates, its historical significance centers on the television broadcast. Kennedy's advisers used television to portray his youth to the nation, while Nixon came across as tired and ill to the television viewers. Perhaps the most interesting dichotomy of this debate is that for people who watched on television, Kennedy was the clear winner, while those who listened on the radio believed that Nixon was the victor. The 1960 debate is believed to have been a key factor for Kennedy, who many people had not seen previously, in one of the closest elections in American history.

Even after the success of the Kennedy and Nixon debate, presidential debates did not become firmly entrenched on the national scene until the creation of the Commission on Presidential Debates in 1987. Since those initial debates, the commission has helped both parties negotiate the number of debates for each ELECTION CYCLE, their location, the format of the debates, and the participants. This has allowed each election since 1988 to have at least two debates (a presidential and a vice presidential) and often more. The commission's success has brought political discussion into the living rooms of millions of Americans and helped to distinguish between the candidates for the nation's most important election. Nevertheless, the commission has been criticized by third-party candidates, who are often not invited to participate in the debates, for restricting access to this important forum of communication.

Further reading: Commission on Presidential Debates. Available online. URL: http://www.debates.org. Accessed August 10, 2005; Schroeder, Alan. *Presidential Debates: 40 Years of High-Risk TV.* New York: Columbia University Press, 2000.

—Jacob R. Straus

Committee on Political Education (COPE)

The Committee on Political Education (COPE) serves as the political arm of the AFL-CIO. The American Federation of Labor (AFL) and the Congress of Industrial Organizations (CIO) merged in 1955 to represent a variety of national and international labor unions. At that time, the

AFL and CIO joined their POLITICAL ACTION COMMITTEES (AFL's League for Political Education and CIO's Political Action Committee) to create COPE. The national organization of the AFL-CIO includes a national COPE staffing unit that coordinates political activities with COPE organizations housed within state and local AFL-CIO chapters. The national AFL-CIO renamed its COPE unit the "Political Department" following the election of John J. Sweeney as AFL-CIO president in 1995. However, the name COPE continues to be used to refer to AFL-CIO's federal political action committee, and numerous state and local AFL-CIO chapters retain the term COPE to refer to departments that undertake political activities at the GRASS-ROOTS level.

The main function of COPE has been to ensure the election of political candidates at the federal, state, and local levels who support the core philosophy and policy agenda of the AFL-CIO. In order to influence the electoral process, COPE undertakes a variety of political activities including sponsoring VOTER REGISTRATION drives in local communities; disseminating brochures, political posters, and other materials to educate union members about the candidates and policy issues in upcoming elections; collecting campaign contributions from union members and local AFL-CIO chapters; and providing financial assistance to candidates. In addition, COPE is responsible for managing the AFL-CIO's national political action committee. Although it mainly provides financial assistance and political support to Democratic candidates, COPE occasionally assists in the election of Republican candidates who sympathize with the core policy concerns of organized labor.

In order to assist in their election strategies, COPE maintains an extensive computerized database of political information on political incumbents and CHALLENGERS. In addition, COPE staff members collect both national and state voting and public opinion statistics during PRIMARY and GENERAL ELECTIONS. They subsequently share this wealth of information with those candidates that are endorsed by the AFL-CIO.

Another major responsibility of COPE has been to monitor the legislative activities of the U.S. Congress. COPE develops AFL-CIO voting scorecards for each congressional session based on individual roll call votes cast by each member of both the House of Representatives and the Senate. COPE rates each congressional member in terms of whether the AFL-CIO judges that member's vote to have been "right" or "wrong" in relation to the policy views of organized labor. The total number of "right" votes is then converted to a percentage. The AFL-CIO rates members of Congress who have percentages close to 100.0 percent as strong supporters of labor issues, while scores close to 0.0 percent represent opponents. COPE also includes in each scorecard the lifetime percentage of "right" and "wrong" votes cast by each member during his or her congressional career.

Further reading: Biersack, Robert, Paul S. Herrnson, and Clyde Wilcox. *After the Revolution: PACs, Lobbies, and the Republican Congress.* Boston: Allyn & Bacon, 1999; Dark, Taylor E. *The Unions and the Democrats: An Enduring Alliance.* Ithaca, N.Y.: Cornell University Press, 1999; Smith, Judith G. *Political Brokers: Money, Organizations, Power and People.* New York: Liveright, 1972.

—Adam L. Warber

Common Cause

A POLITICAL ACTION COMMITTEE (PAC) founded in 1970 by John Gardner, and established as a nonpartisan citizens' lobby, the main goal of the organization is to make government more effective and representative of citizens' interests. Given its original focus on national POLITICS, the organization's agenda reflects the issues of that era: the Vietnam War, civil rights, and campaign finance. The organization's issue agenda has not changed much since the 1970s; civil rights and campaign finance reform are still very high priorities for Common Cause. However, because the organization is nonpartisan, it does not take a particular position on these issues and focuses instead on the process by which decisions are made or the structure of decision making, that is, the rules and procedures used by politicians and bureaucrats.

Common Cause typically does not get involved with presidential appointments because of its desire to remain nonpartisan. However, many of the issues important to members have ideological overtones. For example, during the 1980s, President Reagan nominated Robert Bork to the Supreme Court. The governing board of Common Cause, which is the policy-making body of the organization, found Bork's record on civil rights to be too egregious to ignore. It publicly declared him unfit to be a Supreme Court justice. Due to the pressure exerted by organized interests, including Common Cause, Bork did not pass the Senate confirmation hearings and did not become a Supreme Court justice.

In the case of Bork, Common Cause opposed his NOMINATION because of the substance of his record on civil rights. More commonly the organization focuses on the ethics of government officials. This is especially true of the local chapters, which exist in all 50 states. With 200,000 dues-paying members, Common Cause is a relatively robust citizen-based PAC. It receives 73 percent of its income from member dues and small contributions; 10 percent of its income comes from donations of more than $1,000. The organization does not accept federal grants or contributions from labor unions or corporations in excess of $1,000.

Benefits of membership are many. The organization provides members with information about members of Congress—biographical sketches, committee membership, roll-call votes—as well as data on local, state, and federal elections. It also provides updates on legislation, committee meetings, and agency activities that relate to the main issues and missions of the organization.

Further reading: Common Cause. Available online. URL: http://www.commoncause.org. Accessed August 10, 2005.

—Jamie Pimlott

Communications Act of 1934

The Communications Act of 1934 enacted the regulatory broadcast statute that has served as the basis for more than 70 years of U.S. communications policy and created the FEDERAL COMMUNICATIONS COMMISSION (FCC), a single government agency empowered to issue licenses, classify stations, inspect radio equipment, prohibit censorship, curb radio monopolies, and increase public control over the airwaves. The act also established the EQUAL TIME RULE, a provision requiring radio, television, and cable stations to treat candidates for political office equally when distributing airtime.

Little regulation existed prior to Westinghouse's first broadcast from KDKA Radio in Pittsburgh, Pennsylvania, on October 27, 1920, and Congress took seven years to create the Radio Act of 1927. Between 1920 and 1927, the federal government regulated the radio industry under the Radio Act of 1912, legislation that established Commerce Department control over the assignment of radio frequencies for radio telephone and radio telegraphy. Although the broadcast band was not mentioned in the act, the Commerce secretary interpreted it as assigning the Commerce Department with the responsibility to issue new broadcast radio licenses. A federal court nullified this interpretation, however, when it ruled for the defense in the case of *U.S. v. Zenith Corporation* in 1926. The Commerce Department sued Zenith for abusing its license. Zenith aired content during times not permitted and expanded its signal strength beyond its assigned frequency.

Congress responded with the Radio Act of 1927, which established the Federal Radio Commission (FRC), an agency empowered to assign broadcast frequencies, classify radio stations, and regulate competitive interference. Congress gave the agency only temporary, experimental status and appropriated no money for its operation. From 1928 to 1934 the FRC functioned as a licensing authority on a year-to-year basis but did little to advance regulatory policy for fear that if it were too assertive Congress would cancel its charter.

During the same period, reformers called for the creation of a single government agency responsible for the regulation of all broadcast communications. Legislators made an attempt to combine the radio division of the Commerce Department with the FRC during the 72nd congressional session, but Herbert Hoover's pocket veto ended the effort. President Franklin Delano Roosevelt renewed reformers' hopes in early 1934 when he formed an interdepartmental committee charged with lobbying Congress for the creation of the FCC. Despite strong resistance by AT&T and other telephone and telegraph companies, FDR's support for reform ensured the act's passage. Roosevelt signed the bill into law on June 18, 1934.

The printed version ran to 45 pages and was divided into six parts, or titles, and several dozen smaller sections. In 1967, Congress added a provision for the operation and funding of the Corporation for Public Broadcasting, and in 1984 a seventh title was added concerning the regulation of cable television. Additional sections on cable regulations were added under the Cable Act of 1992.

Several attempts to rewrite or eliminate the act have arisen, most notably in the mid-1970s and the mid-1990s, and recent events may stimulate further calls for reform. In the summer of 2003, the Bush administration sparked a standoff with Congress after it relaxed FCC media ownership rules. The new rules would have permitted networks such as Fox and NBC to buy more television stations, enabling them to reach 45 percent of the national audience, up from the current national cap of 35 percent. The Senate voted 55 to 44 to block the president's changes, but the House compromised. Congress agreed to cap the increase at 39 percent. In 2004, the FCC succeeded in raising its indecency fines after Janet Jackson's breast was bared during a live, televised Super Bowl performance on CBS, and Howard Stern made several profanity laced statements during his radio talk show on Clear Channel. The FCC fined CBS $550,000 and Clear Channel $1.75 million, a dramatic increase over its usual maximum fine of $32,500.

Further reading: McChesney, Robert W. *Telecommunications, Mass Media, and Democracy: The Battle for the Control of U.S. Broadcasting, 1928–1935.* New York: Oxford University Press, 1993; Paglin, Max D. *A Legislative History of the Communications Act of 1934.* New York: Oxford University Press, 1989; Rosen, Philip. *The Modern Stentors: Radio Broadcasters and the Federal Government, 1920–1934.* London: Greenwood Press, 1980.

—Jamie Patrick Chandler

Communist Party of the United States

The Communist Party of the United States (CPUSA) is one of the most prominent Marxist-Leninist political movements in the United States. The historical roots of the CPUSA go back to 1919, when a group split from the left-wing SOCIALIST PARTY due to disagreement over the Bolshevik Revolution in Russia. Left-wing activists and pro-Soviet socialists jointly established two rival parties: the Communist Party of America and the Communist Labor Party. These two parties united to form the Communist Party of the United States in Chicago in 1919.

After its foundation, the Federal Bureau of Investigation (FBI) and Attorney General A. Mitchell Palmer consistently attacked the CPUSA. During the McCarthy era of the late 1940s and 1950s (named after Joseph McCarthy, a Republican senator from Wisconsin), several leaders and members of the CPUSA were prosecuted and incarcerated following convictions for "conspiring to teach and advocate the overthrow of the U.S. government." Even though the party has gone underground and changed its name to avoid confrontation with the U.S. government several times, it has never completely dissolved.

The massive upsurge of left-wing and libertarian movements during the 1960s and 1970s and especially the growing opposition to the U.S. involvement in the Vietnam War helped the CPUSA experience a rising level of acceptance by intellectual groups in the United States. Well-known members of the CPUSA were invited to provide speeches on college and university campuses, and party membership grew to around 25,000 people during the 1970s. The CPUSA ran candidates for president and vice president in four elections between 1972 and 1984. The party decided to end its nationwide electoral campaigns and did not run a candidate in any PRESIDENTIAL ELECTION after 1984 due to a significant decline in membership. The CPUSA still runs candidates for local offices.

The case of the CPUSA exemplifies the variety of political movements and ideologies in contemporary American POLITICS. Even though the political agenda of the CPUSA has changed over time, major themes of the organization have remained the same. Members of the CPUSA advocated unemployment insurance, organization and unionization rights, and social security for the working classes during the 1930s. Today they describe their three most important aims as defeating the current Bush administration, achieving reforms that "put the well-being of the people before private profits," and replacing the influence of private business with labor organizations in order to assure that economic security and people's needs become primary concerns of society.

Further reading: Communist Party of the United States. Available online. URL: http://www.cpusa.org. Accessed August 10, 2005; Gerassi, John. "The Comintern, the Fronts, and the CPUSA." In Michael E. Brown, Randy Martin, Frank Rosengarten, and George Snedeker, eds., *New Studies in the Politics and Culture of U.S. Communism.* New York: Monthly Review Press, 1993; Ottanelli, Fraser M. *The Communist Party of the United States: From the Depression to World War II.* New Brunswick, N.J.: Rutgers University Press, 1991.

—Odul Celep

competitive election

A competitive election is one in which each candidate has a legitimate chance of winning. In measuring competitiveness, some political scientists define an election as competitive if the margin of victory is 10 percent or less of the total vote. Others use 5 percent or less as a cutoff point. In general, those studying Congress usually use the 10 percent cutoff, and those studying the presidency use the 5 percent figure.

Free, fair, and competitive elections are hallmarks of representative government. Competition is a spur to democracy. Competitive elections give voters clear choices and provide them with the necessary information to hold elected officials accountable at the ballot box. Also important to representation and responsiveness is participation. There is a strong positive correlation between competition and VOTER TURNOUT. When elections are competitive, individual voters feel their votes matter. Also, in competitive elections, parties work harder to mobilize voters.

In U.S. history, the late 1800s was a time of highly competitive elections at the local, state, and national levels. The Gilded Age was a time of high voter participation, partisan stability, and THIRD PARTIES. One factor that stimulated so much activity was that elected officials could use PATRONAGE to reward voters. This dynamic began to change in the first half of the 20th century, typified by Democratic, one-party control in the South and significant Republican dominance in the North. Much research has focused on the consequences of the lack of competition in the South during this time. Based on his research of southern POLITICS, V. O. Key, Jr., hypothesized that competitive elections produce policies more favorable to lower socioeconomic classes because elected officials try to appeal to the greater number of voters in moderate- and low-income groups. From the late 1800s to the mid-1900s, one-party dominance of the South was a main contributor to the systematic disenfranchisement of black voters.

Competitive elections have different implications at different levels of government. Local elections for offices such as county clerk and city council are sometimes prone to a shortage of opponents and even candidates. Seats in state legislatures and in the U.S. House of Representatives have become less competitive due to the practice of partisan REDISTRICTING, which ensures seats for one or the other party. In the U.S. House, the number of competitive seats has gone down since the late 1960s. Incumbents in the House of Representatives are thought to be advantaged due to their constituency services, legislative staff, the franking privilege, and campaign funding. Some strong incumbents continue to raise large amounts of campaign funds simply to ward off CHALLENGERS. The biggest threat to an incumbent is an experienced challenger. At the presidential level, the ELECTORAL COLLEGE focuses the candidates' attention on whichever states are competitive. In order to make the best use of resources, presidential candidates do not waste their time on safe states or lost causes. The 2004 presidential campaigns focused on battleground states such as Florida, Ohio, West Virginia, Pennsylvania, Iowa, Missouri, Washington, Oregon, and Wisconsin, where the two candidates concentrated their commercials and campaign visits. Showing just how important these states were, the candidates took the opportunity to specifically mention them in their debates.

Further reading: Barrilleaux, Charles, Thomas Holbrook, and Laura Langer. "Electoral Competition, Legislative Balance, and American State Welfare Policy." *American Journal of Political Science* 46 (2002): 415–427; Franklin, Mark N. *Voter Turnout and the Dynamics of Electoral Competition in Established Democracies since 1945.* Cambridge: Cambridge University Press, 2004; Kornbluh, Mark Lawrence. *Why America Stopped Voting: The Decline of Participatory Democracy and the Emergence of Modern American Politics.* New York: New York University Press, 2000; Key, V. O., Jr. *Southern Politics in State and Nation.* New York: Knopf, 1949; Mayer, Kenneth R., and John M. Wood. "The Impact of Public Financing on Electoral Competitiveness: Evidence from Wisconsin, 1964–1990." *Legislative Studies Quarterly* 20 (1995): 69–88.

—Bonnie J. Johnson

Congressional Black Caucus

The Congressional Black Caucus (CBC) is a group of black members of Congress who represent issues facing minorities and the poor. At its genesis, 13 black members of the House of Representatives formed an alliance to give political power and legitimate representation to blacks in CONGRESSIONAL DISTRICTS. The alliance was first known as the Democratic Select Committee. At the suggestion of Charles Rangel of New York, a founding member of the group, the Democratic Select Committee changed its name to the Congressional Black Caucus in 1971. The CBC became one of the most important voices in confronting issues that face poor and minority people. The goals of the CBC are to positively influence the course of events pertinent to blacks and to advance agendas aimed at protecting human rights and civil rights for all people.

In 1969, there were just nine blacks that held seats in Congress, which hampered them from passing legislation that assisted blacks and other minorities. On January 2, 1969, Charles Diggs, a black Democrat from Michigan, formed the Democratic Select Committee with the vision that if the collective power of blacks in Congress could be harnessed, then black issues could legitimately get on the public's agenda.

In its infancy, the Democratic Select Committee investigated the murders of Black Panther Party members and played a large role in defeating the confirmation of a conservative Supreme Court nominee. On June 18, 1971, the committee was reorganized as the CBC, with Charles Diggs as its first chairperson. Other members included Ralph Metcalf (Illinois), Charles Rangel (New York), Shirley Chisholm (New York), Ronald Dellums (California), Augustus Hawkins (California), Louis Stokes (Ohio), William Clay, Sr. (Missouri), John Conyers (Michigan), Parren Mitchell (Maryland), Walter Fauntroy (District of Columbia), George Collins (Illinois), and Robert Nix (Pennsylvania). More recently, Kwesi Mfume, Maxine Waters, Donald Payne, James Clyburn, Eddie Bernice Johnson, and Elijah Cummings have led the CBC.

At the formation of the CBC, there was opposition from blacks and whites. Black conservatives charged that the CBC was attempting to be the mouthpiece for all blacks, while white liberals did not believe the CBC had enough political strength to make a difference. White conservatives have labeled the group as outside the mainstream and have attempted to isolate its members. Despite opposition, the CBC gained national attention with an aggressive agenda and a lofty list of goals. A defining moment in the CBC was when its members presented President Richard Nixon with a list of recommendations on foreign and domestic issues. The CBC launched a series of hearings and seminars conducted around the nation to build COALITIONs with other minority officials and national leaders who shared deep concerns for blacks and the poor. In the recent past, the group has tackled such issues as affirmative action, health care, and the U.S. budget deficit and remains one of the most tightly knit groups on Capitol Hill.

Further reading: Barker, Lucius Jefferson, Mack Jones, and Katherine Tate. *African Americans and the American Political System.* Upper Saddle River, N.J.: Prentice Hall, 1998; Bisitis, David. *The Congressional Black Caucus in the 103rd Congress.* Lanham, Md.: Rowman & Littlefield, 1994; Congressional Black Caucus. Available online. URL: http://www.house.gov/cummings/cbc/cbchome.htm. Accessed August 10, 2005; Sighn, Robert. *The Congressional Black Caucus: Racial Politics in the U.S. Congress.* Thousand Oaks, Calif.: Sage Publications, 1998.

—F. Erik Brooks

congressional campaign committees

Congressional campaign committees are NATIONAL PARTY COMMITTEES made up of members of Congress whose goal is to elect additional members of their own party to national office. There are four major congressional campaign committees that represent the interests of both major parties in both the House and the Senate. In the House of Representatives, Democratic campaign efforts are channeled through the Democratic Congressional Campaign Committee, while the Republicans rely on the National Republi-

can Congressional Committee. On the Senate side, the Democrats have the DEMOCRATIC SENATORIAL CAMPAIGN COMMITTEE (DSCC), and the Republicans have the NATIONAL REPUBLICAN SENATORIAL COMMITTEE (NRSC).

Formed in the mid-1970s in the wake of Watergate and the FEDERAL ELECTION CAMPAIGN ACT, these committees raise funds for congressional and Senate elections and distribute those funds to current members facing reelection as well as to promising CHALLENGERs of their own party. It is through this collection and distribution of campaign funds that the various campaign committees make their most significant impact on the outcome of CONGRESSIONAL ELECTIONS. The committees give vulnerable incumbents access to needed resources, and promising challengers—or challengers facing weak incumbents of the other party—can gain the resources they need for the daunting task of winning an open-seat election (in which there is no incumbent) or defeating an opposing party incumbent.

Funding campaigns is not the only function that congressional campaign committees perform. For example, the Democratic Congressional Campaign Committee (DCCC) is charged with recruiting, assisting, and electing Democrats to the U.S. House of Representatives. Recruiting is particularly important in order to regain control of a chamber of Congress when a party is in the minority. An excellent example of this would be the recent victory of Stephanie Herseth to an open House seat in South Dakota. South Dakota is a traditionally Republican state, especially in PRESIDENTIAL ELECTION years. However, the DCCC was able to recruit Herseth (a member of a prominent political family in South Dakota) to run for the open seat and eventually win a narrow election.

Congressional campaign committees also provide assistance ranging from designing and executing field operations to polling, creating radio and television commercials, FUNDRAISING, communications, and management consulting. For example, the National Republican Congressional Committee (NRCC) boasts that it supports the election of Republicans to the House through direct financial contributions to candidates and REPUBLICAN PARTY organizations; technical and research assistance to Republican candidates and PARTY ORGANIZATIONS; VOTER REGISTRATION, education, and turnout programs; and other party-building activities. Also, the Democratic Senatorial Campaign Committee is known for helping its candidates with everything from polling and media advice to issuing research and the latest techniques for campaigning on the Internet.

This support has been especially important in recent years due to the extremely narrow divisions of power in both chambers following the 2000 and 2002 elections. Just prior to the 2004 elections, Republicans held a razor-thin 11-seat majority in the House of Representatives, and in the U.S. Senate the power differential was even narrower. In this environment, the power of congressional campaign committees to win even a few close elections can have a profound impact on national public policy. For example, Democratic senator Jean Carnahan lost her Missouri senate seat by only 1 percent of the vote. Republican challenger Norm Coleman was able to win a Democratic open seat by only 2.19 percent of the vote in Minnesota. Had these two close elections gone the other way, the Republican Party would have lost control of the Senate.

For these reasons, congressional campaign committees such as the DSCC and NRSC tend to focus their resources carefully on those select races where their support could tip the balance in favor of their party's candidate. As a result, this dictates heavy involvement in open seat races (races with no incumbent on the BALLOT), and those select cases of weak opposition incumbents or strong party challengers. Such contests have historically provided the greatest chance of turnover in party control.

Further reading: Democratic Congressional Campaign Committee. Available online. URL: http://www.democratic action.org. Accessed August 10, 2005; Democratic Senatorial Campaign Committee. Available online. URL: http://www.dscc.org. Accessed August 10, 2005; Herrnson, Paul S. *Congressional Elections: Campaigning at Home and in Washington.* Washington, D.C.: CQ Press, 2003; Jacobson, Gary C. *The Politics of Congressional Elections.* 5th ed. New York: Addison-Wesley, 2000; Kloodny, Robin. *Pursuing Majorities: Congressional Campaign Committees in American Politics.* Norman: University of Oklahoma Press, 1998; National Republican Congressional Committee. Available online. URL: http://nrcc.org. Accessed August 10, 2005; National Republican Senatorial Committee. Available online. URL: http://www.nrsc.org. Accessed August 10, 2005.

—Brian DiSarro

congressional district

A congressional district refers to one of 435 geographically based electoral districts for the House of Representatives. A single member is elected from each district to serve a two-year term. The districts are reapportioned and redrawn every 10 years in accordance with the population figures provided by the decennial CENSUS. Congressional districts refer only to the House of Representatives, as Senate elections are for statewide offices.

The Constitution established congressional districts apportioned according to population following each decennial census. The initial census in 1790 produced 105 districts with a population of 33,000 per district. By 1830, with the nation's population rapidly increasing, district populations rose to 47,700, and the number of districts increased from 105 to 242. From 1840 to 1900, the number of seats rose from 232 to 390. By 1910, the number of districts reached 435, and many members felt any further growth would limit efficiency and harm representation by potentially having an unruly body.

Capping the number of districts, however, meant that some states would lose districts in the future to the faster growing states, and the plan was initially met with resistance. The completion of the 1920 census further complicated matters, as it showed that for the first time the majority of Americans lived in urban and not rural areas. This was a major obstacle to limiting the number of districts and reallocating them based on equal population given the country's traditional rural stronghold in legislative POLITICS. These facts coupled with large population shifts as transportation improved resulted in a bitter political stalemate over the issue. The issue was not resolved until 1929, when Congress passed a law for a permanent REAPPORTIONMENT system that set the number of seats at 435.

The Constitution established that districts are to be divided based on equal population. However, this has not always been the case. As late as the 1960 census, congressional districts were still malapportioned (i.e., unequal in population). In extreme cases, some districts contained as much as three times the population as did other districts, meaning one-third the representation. In most cases, these disparities favored rural interests, as states were reluctant to create urban districts to balance the growth of cities. The Supreme Court changed this practice in the early 1960s in what is now known as the Reapportionment Revolution. Beginning with *BAKER V. CARR* (1962), the Court established through a series of rulings the one-person-one-vote principle as the leading criterion for establishing congressional districts. It ruled that no population disparity was too small, and that all congressional districts were to adhere to strict population standards.

Following the 2000 census, the ideal population for a congressional district is 646,952. This is an increase of nearly 75,000 from the 1990 ideal size of 572,466. While district populations are similar, the geographic sizes have a large variation. The smallest districts are 10 densely populated square miles in New York City, and the largest covers 586,000 square miles in Alaska. The range of sizes is often quite striking within states as well. For example, the 23rd district in Texas spans more than 55,000 square miles across the sparsely populated western part of the state, an area larger than 19 other states. A few urban districts in the state, in both Dallas and Houston, consist of less than 50 square miles total.

After the 2000 census, seven states (Alaska, Delaware, Montana, North Dakota, South Dakota, Vermont, and Wyoming) were apportioned only one seat. In cases in which a state's population is not large enough for two seats under the reapportionment formula, the states have only one at-large district. In states with particularly small populations, such as Wyoming and Vermont, the state population does not reach the 646,952 ideal, resulting in slight overrepresentation in these states. The four largest states currently hold slightly more than 30 percent of all congressional districts. California is the largest, with 53 districts, followed by Texas (32), New York (29), and Florida (25).

While the geographic components of districts are important, most members of Congress think about their districts primarily in terms of the constituents that make up their district. Political scientist Richard Fenno found that members have a home style they project to their district depending on the makeup and character of their district in hopes of gaining the trust of their constituents. Members try to show constituents they are accessible to the district and are available to meet their needs. Most members of Congress relate directly to their districts through CASEWORK and allocative representation. Casework refers to the individual constituency services the members provide to the district, while allocative representation relates to the projects and grants members are able to bring back to the district.

Congressional districts are also described in terms of their electoral competitiveness. Safe districts, also known as SAFE SEATS, are ones that one party predictably wins. Swing districts refer to the shrinking number of competitive seats in which either party can win on ELECTION DAY.

Further reading: Hawkings, David, et al. *Politics in America 2004: The 108th Congress.* Washington, D.C.: CQ Press, 2003; Herrnson, Paul S. *Congressional Elections.* 4th ed. Washington, D.C.: CQ Press, 2002; Jacobson, Gary. *The Politics of Congressional Elections.* 5th ed. New York: Longman, 2001.

—Jonathan Winburn

congressional elections

Congressional elections are held every two years. There are elections for one-third of the U.S. Senate and for all of the House of Representatives. Some of these elections are held concurrently with the PRESIDENTIAL ELECTIONS, while others are midterm elections (i.e., held midway through a president's term in office).

Each House seat represents a geographic CONSTITUENCY, and every member is elected from a unique, or "single-member," district by plurality rule (the candidate with the most votes wins the election even if the candidate fails to win an outright majority of the total vote). Each of the 50 states is assured at least one seat in the House, with the rest allocated to the states by population. Alaska, for example, has only one seat in the House, while California currently has 53 seats. The total number of seats in the House of Representatives is 435, with the seats reapportioned among the states every 10 years following the decennial CENSUS.

The Senate was originally designed to represent the interests of states, and up until 1913 senators were selected by state legislatures and not elected by the people. Only

since the passage of the SEVENTEENTH AMENDMENT to the Constitution, during the Progressive Era of the early 20th century, have senators been directly elected by the voters. Every state has two senators elected for six-year terms, and one-third of senate seats are up for reelection every two years. Since there are 50 states, there are 100 senators, and every two years there are either 33 or 34 senators facing reelection.

Several political observers have noted that throughout most of this century, congressional elections were "party-centered." Because most voters had long-term loyalties toward one POLITICAL PARTY or the other, they tended to cast their votes along party lines. Members of Congress were often reelected, sometimes holding their position for decades, because a majority of their constituents supported their party. Their efforts as individual candidates often only marginally affected their support.

In the 1960s, however, national elections became increasingly "candidate-centered." The ability to campaign over television, to raise huge amounts of money, to conduct polls, and to wage other aspects of modern campaigning made voters more aware of the candidate as an individual. As a result, voters began to consider the strengths and weaknesses of the candidates in addition to their party loyalties. In recent elections, this process has further intensified with the rise of the Internet. Barely a factor in 1996, by 2004 the Internet became a major tool of both political organizing and FUND-RAISING. Candidates with strong messages were able to organize meet-ups and raise millions of dollars online, dramatically changing the nature of POLITICS and political campaigning.

The power of political parties in congressional elections should not be discounted. Party influence is still stronger here than it is at the presidential level. This is chiefly due to the power and influence of CONGRESSIONAL CAMPAIGN COMMITTEES. Congressional Campaign Committees are NATIONAL PARTY COMMITTEES, made up of members of Congress, whose goal is to elect additional members of their own party to national office. There are four major congressional campaign committees that represent the interests of both major parties in both the House and the Senate. In the House of Representatives, Democratic campaign efforts are channeled through the Democratic Congressional Campaign Committee, while the Republicans rely on the National Republican Congressional Committee. On the Senate side, the Democrats have the DEMOCRATIC SENATORIAL CAMPAIGN COMMITTEE, and the Republicans have the NATIONAL REPUBLICAN SENATORIAL COMMITTEE.

Formed in the mid-1970s in the wake of Watergate and the FEDERAL ELECTION CAMPAIGN ACT, these committees were an attempt to raise funds for congressional and Senate elections and distribute those funds to current members facing reelection as well as to promising CHAL-

LENGERS of their own party. It is through this collection and distribution of campaign funds that the various campaign committees make their most significant impact on the outcome of congressional elections.

Allocating campaign funds is not the only function of congressional campaign committees. Congressional campaign committees can provide assistance ranging from designing and executing field operations to polling, creating radio and television commercials, fund-raising, communications, and management consulting. For example, the National Republican Congressional Committee (NRCC) boasts that it supports the election of Republicans to the House through direct financial contributions to candidates and REPUBLICAN PARTY organizations; technical and research assistance to Republican candidates and PARTY ORGANIZATIONS; VOTER REGISTRATION, education, and turnout programs; and other party-building activities. Also, the Democratic Senatorial Campaign Committee is known for helping its candidates with everything from polling and media advice to issues research and the latest techniques for campaigning on the Internet.

This support, both financial and otherwise, can prove crucial to determining both individual races as well as the overall composition and control of Congress itself. For these reasons, congressional campaign committees tend to focus their resources carefully on those select races where their support could tip the balance in favor of their party's candidate. As a result, this dictates heavy involvement in open-seat races and those select cases of weak opposition incumbents or strong party challengers. Such contests have historically provided the greatest chance of turnover of party control. Hence, both parties focus their resources there in order to either regain the majority, or build on their majority in the chamber.

OPEN SEAT ELECTIONS are elections in which no incumbent is running for office. These elections are important because they are often the most competitive and the most susceptible to party change. It has been well documented that there is a substantial INCUMBENCY ADVANTAGE that politicians running for reelection enjoy. In the U.S. Congress specifically, this advantage usually results in a biennial incumbency reelection rate of around 90 to 95 percent. This is due mainly to the power of the office, the ready-made campaign staff, the amount of press coverage that an incumbent can generate, high NAME RECOGNITION, and the large amounts of money that an incumbent is able to raise and spend. Therefore, in elections in which no incumbent is on the BALLOT, the OPPOSITION PARTY usually stands a much greater chance of winning the election than would otherwise be the case.

Mid-term elections are congressional elections that fall in the middle of a president's term. They have traditionally been used as an indicator of the president's performance. It has long been a common assumption that the president's party usually loses House and Senate seats in midterm elections. However, in recent mid-terms (1998 and 2002), the party of the president has bucked historical trends to win seats.

Researchers debate the power of presidential COATTAILS in congressional elections (i.e., the link between support for a president in the GENERAL ELECTION and support for other members of the president's party in the same election). For example, in 1952, the Republican Eisenhower won 56 percent of the votes in the general election. He was overwhelmingly popular, and in 1952 the Republicans also won both the Senate and House elections, giving them full control of the federal government. In 1954, however, the Democrats won a majority in the midterm elections and control of Congress. In the 1956 general election, Eisenhower was reelected with 58 percent of the vote. Nevertheless, Congress remained dominated by the Democrats.

From the existing research, it is unclear whether presidential contests directly affect congressional elections. Some researchers contend that coattails are a powerful part of the political environment. Others suggest that a popular president may influence the turnout of voters but has little effect on the way people vote in congressional elections. Other researchers contend that local factors are more important for congressional elections than the status of the president or national issues. The issue remains unresolved.

Further reading: Dodd, Lawrence C., and Bruce I. Oppenheimer. *Congress Reconsidered.* Washington, D.C.: CQ Press, 2000; Fenno, Richard F. *Home Style: House Members in Their Districts.* New York: Longman, 2002; Herrnson, Paul S. *Congressional Elections: Campaigning at Home and in Washington.* Washington, D.C.: CQ Press, 2003; Jacobson, Gary C. *The Politics of Congressional Elections.* 5th ed. New York: Addison-Wesley, 2001; Mayhew, David. *Congress: The Electoral Connection.* New Haven, Conn.: Yale University Press, 1975; University of Virginia Center for Politics Crystal Ball. Available online. URL: http://www.centerforpolitics.org/crystalball. Accessed August 10, 2005.

—Brian DiSarro

Connecticut Plan

The Connecticut Plan, also known as the Connecticut Compromise, addressed representation in the congress for the proposed federal constitution of 1787. It was perhaps the most important compromise during the course of the Constitutional Convention, coming as it did at a time when the DELEGATES were deadlocked and nearing dissolution of the meeting.

During the summer, the delegates were split over the form that the new federal government should take. Some favored the Virginia Plan (also known as the larger state plan), under which the new government would resemble the British government. Others favored the NEW JERSEY PLAN (also known as the smaller state plan), which represented a revision of the ARTICLES OF CONFEDERATION, but not a radical break with the spirit of that document.

Much of the debate in the early weeks of the convention centered around the Virginia Plan, which, by virtue of its early preparation and presentation to the delegates, had managed to steal the stage. The main thrust of this plan was to correct the inequality that the large states saw embodied in the one-state, one-vote principle that was in effect in the congress of the Articles of Confederation. However, the small states did not feel that the equal SUFFRAGE principle was flawed. They instead felt that it was essential to protect their influence in the government and made it clear that they would not agree to the Virginia Plan's bicameral format, with both chambers based on population. Some of the small state delegates, including Delaware's entire delegation, had been instructed in their commissions to leave the convention if equal suffrage was eliminated. On the other hand, the delegates from the large states felt that the idea of equal suffrage was unfair by its very nature, and they planned to fight to keep it out of the new system of government.

On June 9, 1787, the subject of suffrage in the legislature under the new congress finally came to the floor of the convention for debate. The discussion was quite heated, and threats to dissolve the convention and the entire union flew back and forth between the various delegations. However, the simple coincidence that the subject had been raised on a Saturday may have saved the convention. The next day, the traditional break in the week, gave the inflamed passions of the various delegations time to cool before taking up the question again at the next session. It also allowed for private and informal meetings to occur at which alternate plans and compromises might be worked out. The following Monday, Roger Sherman of Connecticut proposed that "the proportion of suffrage in the first branch should be according to the respective numbers of free inhabitants; and that in the second branch or Senate, each State should have one vote and no more."

Sherman was well known and respected by the other delegates to the convention. Most scholars agree that his voice was second only to Madison's in influence. He was the leader of his state's delegation, and even his political foes respected him. Sherman's plan was not altogether new; he had proposed this idea as far back as 1776 as a method for representation in the Continental Congress, but it had been rejected then as a plan that was too radical to be workable.

For a little more than two weeks, the convention debated the Virginia Plan and the New Jersey Plan, the latter of which proposed purely equal suffrage for the states in a unicameral legislature. Finally, however, the compromise was returned to in the last days of June and, while PROPORTIONAL REPRESENTATION for the lower house was passed on June 29, the convention deadlocked over the question of equal representation on July 2. At the end of the day, the matter was referred to a committee made up of one member from each state: Elbridge Gerry (Massachusetts), Oliver Ellsworth (Connecticut), Robert Yates (New York), William Patterson (New Jersey), Ben Franklin (Pennsylvania), Gunning Bedford (Delaware), Luther Martin (Maryland), George Mason (Virginia), William Davy (North Carolina), John Rutledge (South Carolina), and Abraham Baldwin (Georgia).

The committee came back from the Independence Day break with a proposal that for all intents and purposes mirrored Roger Sherman's proposal, with the addition that all bills that dealt with money from the public treasury would originate from the lower house. This was a concession on the part of the smaller states that they hoped would help them gain the equal representation in the upper house that they so desired. After much debate, the proposal was finally agreed to on July 16 by a vote of five (Connecticut, New Jersey, Delaware, Maryland, North Carolina) to four (Pennsylvania, Virginia, South Carolina, Georgia), with Massachusetts divided evenly.

Interstate disputes normally now occur on the basis of region rather than size, so it may seem a little strange to modern readers to see the states divided in this way. However, the Connecticut Plan came at a fortuitous point in the convention's work. The structure that was agreed on stayed essentially the same into the final document; the only changes were the move from one senator to two for each state and the removal of the restriction on the Senate with regards to amending bills dealing with money from the public treasury.

The THREE-FIFTHS COMPROMISE, in which slaves were to be counted as three-fifths of the population for representation and taxation, is typically appended to the Connecticut Compromise to form the Great Compromise. This is a little misleading, however, in that Roger Sherman had little, if anything, to do with that proposal. While a major compromise in and of itself, it in fact passed separately on July 12.

Further reading: Collier, Christopher. *Decision at Philadelphia: The Constitutional Convention of 1787*. New York: Ballantine Books, 1987; Madison, James. *Notes of the Debates in the Federal Convention of 1787*. New York: Norton, 1987.

—John P. Todsen

constituency

A constituency is the ELECTORATE of a particular district or state or, in the case of the president, the entire country. Candidates seek to satisfy enough of a particular constituency in order to win office.

Candidates running for office spend large sums of time and money to understand the needs and preferences of their constituency. This process does not stop once a candidate is elected, as officials interested in staying in office must always keep an eye toward the next election. Politicians use polls, FOCUS GROUPS, and other methods to discover what their constituents prefer and use various other tactics to keep their constituents happy.

Congressional staffs spend much of their time engaged in CASEWORK, which is helping constituents on a personal level. This can involve anything from helping a retiree track down a lost Social Security check, to helping a small business owner deal with federal regulations, to writing letters of reference for applicants to military academies. Another tactic commonly used is the bringing of so-called "pork barrel" projects to the home constituency. These are funds taken from the federal treasury that benefit only one particular state or district. Officials also visit their home districts often to make public appearances in order to make sure that the voters remember who they are and know that the official is interested in local matters.

There are three primary theories of how an official represents his or her constituency, the instructed delegate theory, the trustee theory, and the politico theory. An instructed delegate is one who votes exactly as the constituency wants him or her to, basing his or her votes on polls and focus groups. A trustee is someone who, once having won an election, is given free reign to vote his or her own conscience. The idea is that once the official wins election, he or she has the trust of the people, who have shown their confidence in the official's wisdom by his or her election. The politico votes with the electorate on most issues, but on key issues of conscience, follows his or her own judgment.

In reality, most officials behave as politicos, never as constrained as true instructed delegates or as free to exercise their judgment as trustees. Issues that voters have intense feelings about and are knowledgeable about are more likely to be issues for which officials defer to the desires of the constituency and act as an instructed delegate. Issues that the voters lack knowledge of or do not have intense feelings about are likely to be the issues whereby the trustee theory is applied. Most officials do not stray very far from the values and beliefs of their constituency, however, because they are usually a product of the community from which they were elected. This means that they were raised with the same values that their constituency was raised with, and therefore they tend to have similar beliefs and opinions.

Constituencies in the United States vary widely from state to state and between urban and rural areas. There are wide variations in constituencies within states as well. Florida, for example, has a southern population that is multiethnic and has a large Hispanic-Latino population, a central area that is more racially homogenous and that includes a significant retiree population, and a northern region that is significantly more rural and lower in average income. Candidates in each of these areas vary widely in party, IDE-OLOGY, and background, and statewide officials, such as senators and governors, must learn how to appeal to these disparate groups to win elections.

The overall constituency of the country has also changed substantially over the years. When the Constitution was first ratified, the only voters that candidates needed to appeal to were the white male property owners who were eligible to vote in most states. Since then, SUFFRAGE has been expanded to include non–property owners, blacks, women, citizens aged 18 to 21, and citizens from the District of Columbia. Over the years, immigration has substantially altered American constituencies as well, from the early influx of Jewish and European immigrants to the more recent waves of new citizens from Central and South America. It is projected that whites will no longer be a majority of the U.S. population by 2050, as the Hispanic-Latino and African-American populations continue to grow rapidly and white population growth slows.

Further reading: Arnold, R. Douglas. *The Logic of Congressional Action.* New Haven, Conn.: Yale University Press, 1992; Fenno, Richard F., Jr. *Home Style: House Members in Their Districts.* Boston: Little, Brown, 1978; Jacobson, Gary C. *The Politics of Congressional Elections.* 5th ed. New York: Longman, 2001.

—Kenneth Quinnell

Contract with America

The Contract with America was a campaign initiative proposed by House Minority Whip Newt Gingrich in the 1994 election. Gingrich, who was the presumptive person to lead the House Republicans in the new Congress due to the retirement of Minority Leader Robert Michel, rallied 367 Republican incumbents and CHALLENGERs to sign the contract on the steps of the Capitol on September 27, 1994. The contract was a pledge to bring 10 key issues, all of which had widespread support in the general public, to floor votes within 100 days of the party taking control of Congress. The Republicans won control of both houses of Congress in 1994, and Gingrich became SPEAKER OF THE HOUSE. The House voted on all contract items in the specified time period, finishing on April 5, 1995. In a series of 15 votes, the House passed every part of the contract except a constitutional amendment fixing TERM LIMITS for senators and members of Congress.

- On January 4, the House unanimously passed the Congressional Accountability Act of 1995, a measure to make Congress responsible for a group of laws that those in the private sector must follow, such as the Family and Medical Leave Act, the Fair Labor Standards Act, and the Occupational Safety and Health Act.
- On January 25, the House obtained the needed two-

thirds vote to propose a constitutional amendment requiring a balanced federal budget. On March 2, the Senate failed by one vote to pass the amendment.

- On February 1, the House passed the Unfunded Mandates Reform Act of 1995. Unfunded mandates are federal laws that require states to perform certain acts but without providing the states the necessary funds to perform them. The Senate passed its own version of the bill, which was adopted by the House. President Clinton signed it into law on March 22.

- On February 6, the House passed legislation giving the president a line-item veto over appropriations bills and targeted tax credits.

- On February 8, the House passed a bill to relax the exclusionary rule. The exclusionary rule says that if evidence in a criminal case is obtained in violation of the defendant's rights (such as a search without a warrant), it cannot be used as evidence. The bill provided that such evidence can be used if the officers believed their search was in conformity with the Fourth Amendment (which provides for no unreasonable searches or seizures). The Senate did not act on the bill.

- On February 14, the House passed legislation appropriating funds for block grants for law enforcement purposes. The Senate did not act on the bill.

- On February 16, the House passed legislation seeking expansion of the North Atlantic Treaty Organization, reform of the United Nations, limiting the control of U.S. forces by the United Nations, and a revitalization of missile defense.

- On February 24, the House passed a bill declaring a moratorium on new federal regulations. On February 28, the House passed legislation requiring risk assessment to determine priorities in federal regulations. On March 3, the House passed a bill requiring the government to compensate private property owners whose property had been devalued due to government regulations. The Senate did not act on the bills.

- On March 7, the House passed legislation making the loser in federal civil litigation pay the legal expenses of other parties. This act was designed to reform tort proceedings in court, whereby plaintiffs risk only their own legal expenses if they lose. The Senate did not act on the bill.

- On March 10, the House passed legislation making it more difficult for people to sue manufacturers over defective products. The Senate passed the bill with amendments, and the conference committee report was passed on March 29, 1996. President Clinton vetoed the bill, and the veto was sustained in the House.

- On March 24, the House passed a bill containing a sweeping series of measures to reduce welfare dependence, restrict food stamp eligibility, and require the teaching of abstinence as a part of sexual education. This

bill passed the Senate, and the conference committee report was passed on December 22. President Clinton vetoed the bill, and the House took no action to override the veto.

- On March 29, the House failed to reach the two-thirds majority needed to propose a constitutional amendment limiting terms for senators and members of Congress.

- On April 5, completing the Contract with America, the House passed tax legislation "to strengthen the American family and create jobs." The centerpiece of the bill was a $500 tax credit for each child under 18. The Senate took no action on the bill.

Although few of the legislative initiatives were successful, due to the inability of Gingrich and his partisans to bring the Senate into the movement, they highlight the agenda the House Republicans were pressing in the 1990s and provide insights into Gingrich's legislative priorities.

Further reading: Gimpel, James. *Fulfilling the Contract: The First 100 Days*, Boston: Allyn & Bacon, 1995; Gingrich, Newt, et al. *Contract with America: The Bold Plan by Rep. Newt Gingrich, Rep. Dick Armey and the House Republicans to Change the Nation.* New York: Times Books, 1994.
—Tony L. Hill

convention bounce

A convention bounce is the boost a presidential nominee enjoys in the polls immediately following his party's nominating convention. The boost is directly related to the intense media attention that the candidate and the candidate's party receive during the convention. While all recent candidates have experienced convention bounces, they vary in size and staying power.

President Jimmy Carter's spokesman used the term in 1980 to describe Carter's improvement in the polls after the Democratic convention. He noted that Carter received the "post-convention bounce we hoped for." Presidential candidates since 1964 have typically enjoyed a 5 percent convention bounce, according to the Gallup Poll. Most bounces range from 4 to 8 percentage points, although the amount of the bounce often varies depending on which poll is cited.

The bounce comes as the candidate receives a week of widespread and generally positive media attention with little news from the opponent's campaign. A bounce can be especially helpful for a candidate who is unknown or viewed negatively going into the convention. Speeches by party leaders and the nominee, which are often covered live by commercial and cable networks, provide a way to rally supporters and attract undecided voters. Announcing the vice presidential nominee shortly before the convention can enhance the candidate's bump in the polls. An anticipated convention bounce was one of the reasons John Kerry remained secretive about his choice of RUNNING

MATE during the summer of 2004 and opted to formally accept his party's NOMINATION at the Democratic convention in Boston rather than delay acceptance to take advantage of a loophole in the existing CAMPAIGN FINANCE LAWS.

In 2000, George W. Bush received a four-point bounce after his party's convention in Philadelphia, while Al Gore had an eight-point bounce after the Democratic convention in Los Angeles, according to the CNN/USA Today/Gallup Poll. But there is no guarantee how long a convention bounce will last or that the candidate with the bigger bounce will win the election. In a close campaign, such as 2000, convention bounces tend to cancel each other out before ELECTION DAY.

More important than the bounce is how a candidate polls shortly before the election, a measure of preelection momentum. In 1984, Walter Mondale's bounce had him barely trailing President Ronald Reagan in the polls after the Democratic convention in San Francisco, although Mondale lost in a landslide in November, but in 1992, although Bill Clinton trailed President George H. W. Bush heading into the Democrats' New York convention, his convention bounce lasted through the fall and helped lead him to the White House.

Further reading: Goldstein, Michael L. *Guide to the 2004 Presidential Election.* Washington, D.C.: CQ Press, 2003; Hrebenar, Ronald J. *Political Parties, Interest Groups and Political Campaigns.* Boulder, Colo.: Westview Press, 1999; Wayne, Stephen J. *The Road to the White House 2000: The Politics of Presidential Elections.* New York: Bedford/St. Martin's, 2000.

—Mary Lynn F. Jones

coordinated expenditures

Coordinated expenditures take place when a POLITICAL PARTY spends money on behalf of a candidate for federal office and does so in coordination with the candidate or members of his or her campaign. More specifically, the FEDERAL ELECTION COMMISSION defines them as disbursements that are "made in cooperation, consultation or concert with, or at the request or suggestion of, a candidate, a candidate's authorized committee, or their agents, or a political party committee or its agents." Generally speaking, when somebody spends money on behalf of a candidate, that spending is considered a CAMPAIGN CONTRIBUTION and is subject to limits as outlined in the Bipartisan Campaign Reform Act. However, in addition to direct contributions to a candidate to federal office (currently limited to $5,000 per election for party committees), parties can also spend money to pay for polling, advertisements, or other campaign activities and do so in coordination with the candidate or campaign.

While coordinated expenditures do not count against the contribution limit for that candidate, they are subject to

their own special limit rules that vary with committee type, location, and year. The coordinated expenditure limits were set in 1974 at 2 cents times the voting age population of the country or state for presidential and Senate candidates, respectively, and $10,000 for House candidates, plus a cost-of-living adjustment. In 2004 the party committee coordinated expenditure limits were roughly $16.25 million for presidential candidates, between $75,000 and $1.6 million for Senate candidates, and $37,000 for House candidates. In addition, parties that make coordinated expenditures are prohibited from making INDEPENDENT EXPENDITURES on behalf of that candidate once formally nominated (and parties making independent expenditures are prohibited from making coordinated expenditures). All committees established and maintained by the national and state political parties of the candidate who is the beneficiary of the coordinated spending are bound by this prohibition.

Coordinated expenditures continue to play an important role in American campaigns, though their source is changing. Between 1996 and 2000, the NATIONAL PARTY COMMITTEES decreased their coordinated expenditures by between 20 and 30 percent, while state and local party committees increased their coordinated expenditures by between 140 and 270 percent. Despite this change in source, the overall amount of coordinated spending declined for both parties during the period. While some argue that this decrease in coordinated expenditures (funded with HARD MONEY) is due to a shift by parties toward SOFT MONEY spending, the ban on soft money that took effect following the 2002 elections means that coordinated expenditures are likely to return as an important source of party assistance to candidates.

Further reading: Dwyre, Diana, and Robin Kolodny. "Throwing out the Rule Book: Party Financing of the 2000 Elections." In David B. Magleby, ed., *Financing the 2000 Election.* Washington, D.C.: Brookings Institution Press, 2002.

—Brian J. Brox

county chairperson

The county chairperson is the person who runs a POLITICAL PARTY in a particular county. Local parties work at the GRASSROOTS level to offer criticism of their political opponents, run campaigns, recruit candidates, and allow people to meet and discuss issues such as unemployment, pollution, and crime. Local parties encourage people to participate in the political process. Successful parties need to be well organized, and it is the county chairperson's job to make this possible.

Party members often elect the county chairperson. However, governors or committees sometimes appoint a chairperson to head the party in a county. Governor Jeb Bush, for instance, appointed Richard T. Crotty to chair the REPUBLICAN PARTY in Orange County, Florida. The chairperson's chief responsibility is to ensure that his political party is able to plug people into the political process at the county level.

The chairperson organizes rallies, plans strategy, and selects people to go into the community and raise public awareness of local issues. This can often be a daunting task. In *Not All Politics Is Local*, former chairman for the DEMO-CRATIC PARTY in Allen County, Ohio, William D. Angel, Jr., complained that internal divisions plague local parties, thereby creating disorder.

The state and national party structure also makes it difficult for county chairpersons to recruit at the grassroots level. According to Angel, "state and national campaigns operate with minimal activity among grassroots loyalists, for the new politics holds that mass-marketing candidates is a more efficient way to reach the voters than mobilizing armies of volunteers to campaign door to door." Nonetheless, the county chairperson remains an important position, ensuring that a political party has the leadership and organization to gain support at the local level.

Further reading: Angel, William D., Jr. *Not All Politics Is Local: Reflections of a Former County Chairman.* Kent, Ohio: Kent State University Press, 2002; Frendreis, John P., James L. Gibson, and Laura L. Vertz. "The Electoral Relevance of Local Party Organizations." *American Political Science Review* 84, no. 1 (1990): 225–235.

—Bruce E. Stewart

credentials committee

The credentials committee is one of the standard committees of a POLITICAL PARTY's convention. The function of this committee is to certify that the DELEGATEs that represent a state at a national convention are the duly authorized persons to represent that state at the convention. State conventions have credentials committees to perform this function for counties, CONGRESSIONAL DISTRICTS, or other substate PARTY ORGANIZATIONS.

The first credentials committee was that of Democratic-Republicans from three New England states that met in 1814 at Hartford, Connecticut, to express dissatisfaction with the conduct of the War of 1812. In the 1830s, when the national political parties began to use conventions to nominate presidential candidates, a credentials committee became part of the convention structure.

At times, a national party's credentials committee has played a crucial role in determining who would be the party's presidential nominee. In the 1912 Republican nominating process, the June 18 convention began with former president Theodore Roosevelt having won 278 delegates in the 12 PRESIDENTIAL PRIMARIES. Totals for President William Howard Taft and Wisconsin's U.S. senator Robert M. LaFollette, Sr., were 48 and 36, respectively, in those primaries. The majority of the 1,078 delegates were

selected in caucus states, particularly in the South, where the REPUBLICAN PARTY consisted largely of presidential appointments, such as postmasters. Taft controlled those and the national committee. For state after state, the credentials committee seated Taft delegates. The consequence was that Taft received 502 votes, Roosevelt 107, LaFollette 41, and two other hopefuls a total of 19. A total of 349 delegates refrained from voting. Claiming fraud, the Roosevelt forces left the convention to hold their own convention in August, nominating Roosevelt on the Progressive ticket. That party was generally known as the Bull Moose, echoing a statement by the party's nominee.

The 1952 Republican Party NOMINATION was also settled by decisions of the party's credentials committee. Both Senator Robert Taft of Ohio and General Dwight Eisenhower came to the convention with large numbers of delegates committed to their nomination. Eisenhower had more, but not a majority. Those states with both Taft and Eisenhower delegations were not permitted to take their seats until the credentials committee designated which was the valid delegation. Eisenhower's forces won credentials committee ENDORSEMENT in key states, including the large Texas delegation, which gave the general a narrow majority on the first BALLOT.

The 1964 DEMOCRATIC PARTY's credentials committee confronted a situation that did not threaten the nomination of President Lyndon Johnson but reflected the civil rights controversy of that era. In addition to the regular Democratic delegation from Mississippi, a "Freedom" Democratic delegation lead by Fanny Lou Hamer insisted that its membership, which was integrated, should be recognized as the state's delegation. The credentials committee proposed seating those members of the regular delegation that agreed to sign a pledge asserting their support of the party in the GENERAL ELECTION and providing two at-large seats for the "Freedom" delegates. Both forces declined the compromise. Only 14 of Alabama's delegation signed a similar pledge, as required. The changes in the presidential nominating processes, enacted in the 1970s, by which delegates are overwhelmingly selected in primaries, makes it unlikely that credentials committees will play prominent roles in the future.

Further reading: Pomper, Gerald. *Nominating the President: The Politics of Convention Choice.* New York: Norton, 1996; Roseboom, Eugene H. *A Short History of Presidential Elections.* 3rd ed. New York: Collier Books, 1967.

—Thomas Phillip Wolf

critical elections

Critical elections are those rare occurrences when a single trip to the polls by the ELECTORATE results in quick, durable, and meaningful political change. In order for an election to enter this special class of electoral contests, it must be characterized by a swift and decisive reorganization of partisan loyalties and have high VOTER TURNOUT and organizational staying power for elections to come. The changes that follow an election of this kind are spurred by the introduction of a new set of national issues that do not fit within the existing alignment, or scope of debate, between the major political parties. In a critical election, voters make their electoral choices based on their views of the new issue, and that issue informs subsequent partisan debate. Developed by the political scientist V. O. Key in 1955, the critical elections perspective developed into the standard way that political scientists view REALIGNMENT, the term used to describe changes in majority partisan loyalty in the electorate and the MAJORITY PARTY in Congress and the White House.

Using data from several New England townships, Key called the elections of 1896 and 1928 critical elections. Many students of realignment have amended that claim, arguing that there have been at least three cases of critical elections in the nation's history: 1860, 1896, and 1928/32. Some scholars also consider 1964 and 1994 to be critical elections, but these claims are widely disputed, especially since the 1964 election did not result in a new congressional majority and the 1994 election did not fall in a PRESIDENTIAL ELECTION year. The 1860 election came on the eve of the Civil War, the 1896 election featured a bitter debate about whether the nation should adopt the gold standard, and the 1932 election was steeped in arguments about how to address the Great Depression. Thus, critical elections were argued to occur at times of national catastrophe.

Central to the appeal of the critical elections perspective is its focus on the importance of political parties. Rather than entering into a constitutional crisis every time there is a national upheaval, students of critical realignment argue that voters use parties to spur major national policy changes. Thus, political scientists, who have long argued for the importance of political parties, have much invested in realignment theory's success. The political scientist David Brady argues that during realignments, political parties gather and articulate interests, translate those interests into policy demands, and provide a stable electoral base for policy directions that match the new issue agenda that engineered the critical election. Thus, the three levels of political parties—the party-in-electorate, the party-in-organization, and the party-in-government—are relatively united during realigning periods. The shifts in the popular distribution of public support for the major parties (and thus, the vote) results in a new majority party that has unified control of the executive and legislative branches of government.

Key's idea of a critical election was developed into a general theory of realignment in 1970 by Walter Dean Burnham. He outlined what he believed to be the five major conditions of a typical realignment: 1) quick and sharp changes in the majority party voter COALITIONs,

which take place every 30 to 38 years; 2) the introduction of a third party, which highlights how the current alignment is not able to manage public debate on a new issue; 3) uncharacteristic stress in the socioeconomic system; 4) an especially large distance in the ideological gap between the major parties; and 5) a durability that affects public policy for years to come. Burnham cited the three commonly named critical elections and Andrew Jackson's 1828 rise to power as examples of critical realignment.

Interestingly, one of the first to offer an alternate perspective to the critical elections perspective was V. O. Key himself. Just four years after his 1955 article naming critical elections, he developed the idea of a "secular realignment," or the movement of members of a particular population from one party to another and taking several presidential elections to occur. This gradual type of realignment could take decades to fully be realized. Other alternate explanations for meaningful partisan change abound as well. Some scholars suggest that the critical realignment perspective is of little use in the modern era as the electorate has undergone a DEALIGNMENT, or the process by which voters move away from identifying themselves with either major POLITICAL PARTY. Dealignment proponents argue that parties became less important during the 1960s, 1970s, and 1980s, forcing those expecting critical elections in the 1960s and 1990s to keep waiting.

Another perspective, called "issue evolution," argues, much like Key's notion of secular realignment, that meaningful partisan change is slow. The model of issue evolution suggests that elected officials and other political elites polarize over a new issue or set of related issues that cut across the existing alignment. Over time, the public becomes aware of these changes and decides to make their partisan choices based on where the two parties stand on the issue(s). One example of such an evolutionary issue is that of race. From the 1960s through the 1980s, elite, and then mass, opinions about race gradually came to guide partisan choices at the ballot box. More recent work has demonstrated that the abortion issue engineered a long-term partisan transformation that is consistent with the issue evolution perspective.

The appeal of perspectives such as the one proffered by proponents of issue evolution is that realignment is not treated as an either/or situation, thus making it able to account for more subtle, and perhaps more meaningful, political change. Still, the critical election perspective has endured, both in political science and in the mass media, as a way to predict and interpret election results.

Further reading: Key, V. O., Jr. "A Theory of Critical Elections." *Journal of Politics* 17 (1955): 3–18; Brady, David W. *Critical Elections and Congressional Policy Making.* Stanford, Calif.: Stanford University Press, 1988.

—Michael W. Wagner

cross-filing

This is a practice that permits a candidate to be listed on the PRIMARY ballot of more than one POLITICAL PARTY. Cross-filing was a product of the Progressive reform movement in California during the early 20th century. It was among the substantial package of electoral reforms that included the REFERENDUM, the RECALL, the initiative, and nonpartisan local elections. These electoral innovations were designed to weaken political parties and INTEREST GROUPS. Cross-filing was used in California from 1914 through 1958. This provision was closely associated with Hiram Johnson, who was governor of California, Theodore Roosevelt's RUNNING MATE in 1912, and subsequently longtime U.S. senator.

A cross-filing candidate had to win the NOMINATION of his own party. Thus, in 1918, when Republican James Rolph, Jr., won the DEMOCRATIC PARTY primary but trailed on the Republican ballot, he was disqualified from the GENERAL ELECTION, and the winner of the Republican primary was promptly declared elected. The law was amended so that a party, in this instance, the Democrats, could appoint a general election nominee.

The REPUBLICAN PARTY was far more successful with cross-filing. Since California and the nation were generally Republican until the early 1930s, this was not remarkable. Yet, after a brief decline in the early 1930s, that party again came to dominate local and state elections, although Democrats were a substantial majority of registered voters. Republican success was abetted by the emergence of the California Republican Assembly (CRA) in the 1930s. Units of the CRA organized in each county and endorsed candidates in the primaries. At CRA state conventions, statewide and congressional candidates were endorsed. Most were victorious.

Inspired by the 1952 presidential candidacy of Adlai Stevenson, Democrats created California Democratic Councils (CDC) in each county, which endorsed Democratic candidates following the example of the CRA. The CDC, along with a 1952 law that required the party registration of cross-filed candidates to be shown on the ballot, began to diminish Republican achievements with cross-filing, which was repealed in 1958.

—Thomas Phillip Wolf

crossover voting

Crossover voting occurs when voters who are affiliated with one party cross partisan lines in order to vote for a candidate running under the banner of an opposing party. Crossover voting is commonly discussed as it relates to voting behavior in PRIMARY elections, whereby voters attempt to influence the nominating process of an opposing party (i.e., strategic crossover voting), but it may also refer to voters in GENERAL ELECTIONS who vote for a candidate of a party other than the one with which they are most closely aligned (sincere crossover voting).

Sincere crossover voting occurs when a voter who traditionally supports one party is lured to vote for one or more candidates of the opposing party by the appeal of a particular candidate or set of issues. It is generally thought that this kind of crossover voting appears far more often in practice than strategic crossover.

Strategic crossover voting, on the other hand, takes place when members of a party vote in a primary other than their own in order to nominate an undesirable candidate, thereby increasing their party's chance of victory in the general election. Such behavior is also referred to as "raiding," since members of one party essentially raid the other party's primary.

In the United States, the ability of voters to cross partisan lines is often constrained by state-level partisan registration laws. This occurs because individual states are allowed to set their own requirements for determining whether a person must be a registered party member in order to vote.

In states with closed primaries, only party members are allowed to vote in each party's primary. Conversely, in states with open primaries, anyone may vote in a primary, regardless of whether they registered a particular partisan affiliation. These laws do not stop voters from crossing over in the general election, but they may limit the ability of voters to move across partisan lines in primaries. This remains a developing area of election law, with court decisions and legal changes shifting the requirements within particular states on an ongoing basis. Understanding the exact level of crossover voting in the United States is often difficult because, unlike in many other Western democracies, party registration requirements and customs in the United States are relatively weak and vary greatly from state to state.

Further reading: Cain, Bruce E., and Elisabeth Gerber. *Voting at the Political Fault Line: California's Experiment with the Blanket Primary.* Berkeley: University Press of California, 2002.

—Brad Alexander

cumulative voting

Under cumulative voting systems, voters are allotted a set number of votes equal to the number of seats to be filled. This approach gives voters the flexibility to cast their allotted votes in whatever manner they choose. They may cast multiple votes for a single candidate or may distribute their votes to as many candidates as they wish. Cumulative voting systems are especially beneficial to minorities because at-large and multimember district systems do not allow for single-member districts that might be drawn in a manner that incorporates a majority of minorities in a particular district.

Cumulative voting arrangements first appeared in colonial South Africa in the 1850s in an effort to prevent one party from monopolizing legislative councils. Illinois used a cumulative voting scheme for the election of general state assembly members from 1870 until 1980. Under the Illinois system, three representatives were elected in each district, and voters were allowed to cast one vote for each of three candidates, one and a half votes for each of two candidates, or all three votes for a single candidate.

More recently, local jurisdictions in Illinois, New Mexico, South Dakota, and Alabama have adopted cumulative voting systems in their efforts to curb minority vote dilution. Public response to cumulative voting has been generally positive. These systems allow voters to concentrate their support on their preferred candidate or candidates. This approach is especially helpful in local elections in which information levels are low. Voters may feel compelled to vote for as many candidates as they are allowed even if they do not know the names, backgrounds, or other relevant information about the candidates.

Cumulative voting is often seen as a response to election-related problems as well as a way to increase VOTER TURNOUT in local elections. Minority groups are given the opportunity to back their favored candidate, thereby increasing the chances for m ore diversity at the local level. At-large and multimember district systems are a means to offset GERRYMANDERing of single-member districts as well as the requirement that one must receive a plurality of votes in single-member district systems. This confronts concerns about vote dilution as well as enhances political empowerment for minority voters, candidates, and office holders.

Further reading: Kaplan, Dave. "Alternative Election Methods: A Fix for a Besieged System?" *Congressional Quarterly Weekly Report* 52, no. 13 (1994): 812.

—Terri Fine

D

dark-horse candidate

A dark-horse candidate historically refers to a candidate who wins a party's NOMINATION after multiple BALLOTs at the party's convention. But in recent years, as the importance of nominating conventions has waned, the meaning of the term has broadened to refer to a long shot candidate seen as having little chance of winning either the party's nomination or the GENERAL ELECTION.

Benjamin Disraeli used the term to describe horse racing in 1831 in *The Young Duke*, writing, "A dark horse, which had never been thought of and which the careless St. James had never even observed in the list, rushed past the grand stand in sweeping triumph." The term now fits in neatly with the media's trend toward horse race journalism and penchant for using sports analogies to describe presidential POLITICS.

The appeal of a dark-horse is that he or she is generally unknown and may provide a compromise choice to party leaders who have trouble choosing among other candidates. An early example of a successful dark-horse candidate was Democrat James Polk in 1844. The presidential nominating process at the time required candidates to receive the support of two-thirds of convention DELEGATEs to win the nomination. Former president Martin Van Buren, who lost his 1840 reelection race, won the first ballot but failed to win sufficient votes to take the nomination. Polk, an ex-Tennessee governor who was considered a possible vice presidential pick, was entered on the eighth ballot and won the two-thirds vote on the ninth ballot. WHIG PARTY members tried to use Polk's obscurity against him, asking, "Who is James K. Polk?" Even so, Polk defeated his better-known opponent, Henry Clay, in the general election.

Eight years later, Democrat Franklin Pierce, a former New Hampshire senator, became a candidate on the 35th ballot after delegates failed to award the two-thirds vote necessary to Lewis Cass, James Buchanan, William Marcy, or Stephen Douglas. Pierce was chosen as the party's nominee on the 49th ballot and went on to the White House. Democrats made a slogan of their dark horse presidential candidates, declaring, "We Polked You in 1844, We'll Pierce You in 1852."

Other presidents who were dark-horse candidates included Republicans Rutherford B. Hayes, who won his party's nomination on the seventh ballot in 1876; James Garfield, who triumphed on the 36th ballot in 1880; and Warren G. Harding, who took the nomination on the 10th ballot in 1920. The longest ballot contest in American history occurred in 1924, when John W. Davis won the Democratic nomination on the 103rd ballot, although he did not go on to the White House. In 1936, Democrats changed their convention rules and required a candidate to win a simple majority, rather than the two-thirds of votes previously necessary to gain the nomination. Since that time, a candidate has been selected on the first ballot in every convention except 1952, when Adlai Stevenson was chosen on the third ballot.

As the nomination process has changed, the parties' nominating conventions no longer hold the element of surprise. Thanks to a frontloaded PRIMARY calendar, voters in 2004 knew that President George W. Bush and John Kerry would be the Republican and Democratic nominees, respectively, by March, months before the party conventions. Bush won his party's nomination without opposition.

Howard Dean, the former governor of Vermont, was dismissed as a dark-horse candidate early in 2003 in a field that included several well-known senators and representatives. Dean used this period of relative obscurity to build a powerful Internet GRASSROOTS and FUND-RAISING network. Based on his initial success in the polls and having raised a large sum of money, the press dubbed him the FRONTRUNNER a few months prior to the IOWA CAUCUSes. Dean lost there, however, and never regained his momentum.

Another dark-horse candidate in the 2004 presidential race was Wesley Clark, a retired general from Arkansas that supporters thought had the best chance of challenging Bush on national security issues. By the time Clark entered the race in mid-September 2003, however, other candidates had already signed up top campaign strategists, raised

President James K. Polk *(Library of Congress)*

much of the Democratic establishment, quickly assumed the frontrunner title. His victory in Iowa propelled him to win most of the other primary contests.

Several dark-horse candidates have won congressional or gubernatorial races in recent years. In 1990, Carleton College professor Paul Wellstone, a Democrat, relied on grassroots support to unseat a better-funded incumbent, Senator Rudy Boschwitz (R, Minn.). Eight years later, wrestler Jesse Ventura, an INDEPENDENT, appealed to young voters and took advantage of Minnesota's same-day VOTER REGISTRATION to defeat his major party CHALLENGERS in a three-way split.

Further reading: Beschloss, Michael. *American Heritage Illustrated History of the Presidents.* New York: Crown Publishers, 2000; DeGregorio, William. *The Complete Book of U.S. Presidents.* New York: Dembner Books, 1989.
—Mary Lynn F. Jones

dealignment

Dealignment refers to a general erosion in the partisan attachments of voters. In contrast to REALIGNMENT, which signifies long-term shifts in electoral support from one party to another, dealignment portrays an overall decline in party support. Many scholars contend that dealignment was a defining feature of the American ELECTORATE from the late 1960s until the early 1980s. Dealignment was thought to portend increased volatility and instability in voter preferences.

Several important trends pointed to electoral dealignment during this time. Most notably, voters expressed weaker allegiances to the major parties, and a growing percentage of people considered themselves INDEPENDENTS. By the late 1970s, nearly 40 percent of Americans were self-described independents. In addition, there was an increase in interelection "floating," or switching of presidential party preference, increased SPLIT-TICKET VOTING, and a weakening of the link between PARTY IDENTIFICATION and vote choice.

Events such as Vietnam, antiwar protest, urban unrest, and Watergate are often listed as important contributors to dealignment. Just as these events led to an overall decline in trust in government, so, too, did they feed a disaffection with parties and party POLITICS. Changes in the PRESIDENTIAL NOMINATING PROCESS, such as the increased use of PRIMARY elections and the increasingly candidate-centered nature of campaigning, have also been cited as factors making parties less salient to voters. Other factors include the end of the PATRONAGE system, the weakening of party machines, population shifts to suburban areas that are beyond the reach of MACHINE POLITICS, and the creation of modern welfare programs that are free from the influence of partisan favor.

The strongest dealigning effects have been seen among young Americans just entering the electorate in the 1960s

money from key donors, and had many months of experience running a national campaign. Clark, a first-time candidate, made several gaffes that hurt his campaign and failed to win a state before dropping his bid.

In the modern context, the shortened primary calendar, the importance of money in politics, and the strength of the party establishments in choosing nominees make it tough for dark-horse candidates to succeed. In crowded presidential fields, dark-horse candidates are often dismissed by the press, which devotes most of its limited resources to covering the frontrunner and other top-tier candidates. Unlike Carter in the 1976 presidential race, who crept up on his opponents by focusing most of his attention on Iowa and New Hampshire, candidates now must run a national campaign and visit numerous states before the Iowa caucuses are held. They must also raise enough money to hire staff and air television commercials in multiple states.

While dark horses in the past may have acted as a safety net if the frontrunner stumbled, there is no such protection today. After Dean placed third in Iowa, Kerry, the choice of

and 1970s. Studies found that young people at that time held weaker party attachments than earlier generations of young voters, and unlike earlier generations, their partisanship did not solidify over time.

There is some evidence that the trend toward increased dealignment in the American electorate subsided during the 1980s. The number of independent voters has leveled off, as has the incidence of ticket-splitting. Moreover, party identification appears to have a stronger impact on presidential vote choice now than before the dealignment era.

Further reading: Beck, Paul Allen. "The Dealignment Era in America." In Russell J. Dalton, Scott C. Flanagan, and Paul Allen Beck, eds., *Electoral Change in Advanced Industrial Democracies: Realignment or Dealignment?* Princeton, N.J.: Princeton University Press, 1984; Wattenberg, Martin P. *The Decline of American Political Parties, 1952–1996.* Cambridge, Mass.: Harvard University Press, 1998.

—Julio Borquez

delegate

Delegates are the individuals who actually nominate their party's presidential and vice presidential candidates at the quadrennial national party conventions. Delegates may be selected as pledged to a specific presidential candidate or as unpledged (or uncommitted) to a candidate.

The first major party national nominating convention was held by the DEMOCRATIC PARTY in 1832. Prior to that time, presidential candidates had been selected by each party's caucus in Congress. This meant that areas that did not elect members of Congress from a party would not be represented at the caucus. Later, delegates from unrepresented areas would be added, creating a "mixed caucus" of members of Congress and party leaders. For Andrew Jackson, the convention demonstrated his belief in mass democracy. Jackson instituted a number of rules, including apportionment of delegates on the basis of electoral votes, the practice of state delegations casting BALLOTs, and requiring that the nominee receive two-thirds of the delegate votes cast (in 1936 the Democrats changed to a majority rule).

Originally, delegates were selected through state conventions. Later, many states adopted the party caucus as the method for selecting delegates. These early methods meant that delegates were chosen by state party leaders who controlled the loyalties of the delegates. Party leaders were often accused of trading convention floor votes (in "smoke-filled rooms") for power, PATRONAGE, and bribes. Today, most delegates are selected through PRESIDENTIAL PRIMARIES (which were held for the first time in 10 states in 1912).

The most significant changes in the delegate selection process occurred after the 1968 Democratic National Convention, when a special Committee on Party Structure and Delegate Selection (chaired by South Dakota senator George S. McGovern and often referred to as the McGovern Commission) made a number of recommendations requiring representation of women, youth, and minorities in state delegations, that delegates be selected in the calendar year of the election, and that all state parties adopt formal rules for delegate selection. The party also prohibited the UNIT RULE, a practice that had permitted the casting of all of a state delegation's votes for the candidate favored by a majority of the delegation.

Apportionment of Delegates

The system of delegate apportionment is similar to the ELECTORAL COLLEGE system, in which each state is assigned a number of electoral votes equal to its total representation in Congress. However, instead of basing the apportionment on congressional seats, each party allocates delegates based on formulas that take into account the state's electoral votes and the strength of support for the party's presidential candidates in previous GENERAL ELECTIONS. In addition, a number of overseas territories, which do not have votes in the Electoral College, send delegates to the conventions.

Delegate Selection

The Democrats and Republicans use different methods to select delegates. In 2004, the Democrats assigned about half of the delegates through a proportional allotment that was based on the vote in presidential primaries and caucuses held in each state. Based on the results at the CONGRESSIONAL DISTRICT level, delegates were split among the candidates. The actual delegates are selected from lists submitted by each campaign to the state Democratic committee. Candidates who gain 15 percent of the vote in a PRIMARY or caucus will win delegates in that state. The largest bloc of delegates is chosen through presidential primaries. Some states conduct caucuses, a process that usually starts with local meetings and culminates with the selection of the state's national convention delegates at a state party convention.

In addition to the proportionately selected delegates, the Democrats provide for pledged and unpledged at-large delegates and party leaders and elected officials (known as PLEOs, or "SUPERDELEGATES"). The pledged PLEOs must be approved by the campaign that they wish to support. Also known as "add-on delegates," they can be used to help meet the Democratic Party's "affirmative action goals" with respect to women and minorities. The Democratic Party requires that each state delegation be equally divided between men and women. In contrast, the Republicans encourage their state parties to have an equal division but do not require it.

Unpledged PLEOs are not required to commit to any presidential candidate. Typically, these "superdelegates" will

include all members of the DEMOCRATIC NATIONAL COM-
MITTEE, Democratic governors of states and territories,
Democratic members of Congress, the mayor of Washington, D.C., and 21 "distinguished party leaders." The
unpledged delegates give state delegations some flexibility
on the convention floor. In 2004, the Democrats had 795
unpledged "superdelegates." In contrast, the Republicans
favor "winner-take-all" elections, in which all the state's delegates are required to support the winner of the state's presidential primary or caucus.

The Democratic Party's rules establish a period when
delegates can be selected. With the exceptions of the IOWA
CAUCUSES and the New Hampshire presidential primary, all
delegates are to be selected no earlier than the first Tuesday
in February and no later than the second week in June.
While the REPUBLICAN PARTY does not have a similar
requirement, most of its delegates are elected during the
same period since most are selected through state-run presidential primaries and no state will open the polls on separate dates for each party.

One of the more significant changes in the delegate
selection process has been the FRONT-LOADING of the process. Historically, the primary season began in the late win-
ter with the New Hampshire presidential primary and
continued throughout the spring with primaries and caucuses scattered throughout the season, concluding with
June primaries in California, New Jersey, and New York.
However, as the early primaries became more significant,
states with later primaries found that the NOMINATION had
been determined prior to their event. As a result, many
states have moved up their primaries so that candidates will
campaign in their states.

In 2004, 36 states had selected 75 percent of the
Democratic Party's national convention delegates by March
9 (known as SUPER TUESDAY due to the large number of
primaries and caucuses held that day, 50 days after the process had begun with the Iowa caucuses). This front-loading
has led to the presumptive nominees being in place months
before the national conventions (which are held between
July and September), making those events anticlimactic. It
also has accelerated the pace of presidential campaigns,
with candidates raising money and campaigning more than
two years before the PRESIDENTIAL ELECTION.

Each delegate casts one vote, and the first candidate
to receive a majority of the delegate votes (2,162 votes at
the 2004 Democratic convention; 1,255 at the REPUBLI-
CAN NATIONAL CONVENTION) becomes the party's presidential nominee. Delegates also vote to nominate the
party's vice presidential candidate (who is selected by the
presidential candidate; the last time a presidential nominee did not select a RUNNING MATE was in 1956, when
Democrat Adlai Stevenson allowed the convention to
select his running mate, Estes Kefauver) and adopt the
party platform (the declaration of the party's principles,

policies, and goals). In addition to delegates, alternate delegates are also selected. The alternates may replace delegates who do not attend the convention.

Further reading: Davis, James W. *National Conventions
in an Age of Reform.* Westport, Conn.: Greenwood Press,
1983; Rapoport, Ronald B. *The Life of the Parties: Activists
in Presidential Politics.* Lexington: University Press of Kentucky, 1986; Shafer, Byron. *Bifurcated Politics: Evolution
and Reform in the National Party Convention.* Cambridge,
Mass.: Harvard University Press, 1988.

—Jeffrey Kraus

demagoguery

The concept of demagoguery has been understood in two
distinct ways. The first understanding of the concept,
derived from the ancient Greeks, was an unbiased reference
to a leader of the people. The more common and recent
usage of the term is far more value laden and refers to political leaders who seek and wield political power by appealing
to the emotions, fears, and prejudices of a particular group.
While demagogues in ancient Greece would also be
referred to as mass leaders and DELEGATES of the people,
demagogues of the 20th century would be labeled as fire-
brands, troublemakers, fomenters, or incendiary instigators.

Much of why contemporary American POLITICS
eschews demagoguery can be tied to the founding of the
American republic, when key leaders such as Madison and
Hamilton felt that the effect of public sentiment on government and politics, rather than being solicited, should be
mediated. To better understand the pejorative nature of
demagoguery in America, it is instructive to examine both
the classic roots of the concept and the contemporary
implications.

In ancient Greece, demagoguery went part and parcel
with democracy. To be a demagogue was to be nothing more
than a popular leader. This is not to say that all Greek
thinkers looked fondly upon such leadership. Euripides
referred to demagogues as intemperate men of loose tongues
who lead the populace to mischief with empty words, while
Aristophanes asserted that in order to qualify as a demagogue, one need only be foul-mouthed, base-born, and possess an otherwise low, mean disposition. These sordid views
of popular leadership shared the common assumption that if
a politician were to follow the opinions of the public, rather
than attempt to shape them, he must be doing it for selfish
and manipulative designs. M. I. Finley has noted that the
demagogue, in such a perspective, is driven to achieve power
and wealth, and in doing so he surrenders his principles and
panders to the people in every way. Thus, it was not the
appeals to the interests of the *demos,* or lower classes, that
troubled these ancient critics. Rather, it was their skepticism
that such appeals were genuine. Demagoguery could be
good or bad; Aristophanes and Euripides simply assumed

that those who would pander did so only out of greed, although the possibility for sincerity was still available.

In the American case, this distinction between "good" and "bad" demagoguery is no longer made, as the concept has become conflated with dishonesty and manipulation. While indeed there are more than a few examples of American demagogues who used race-baiting, religious bigotry, and class warfare as the keys to their own political kingdoms, there are at least a few examples of leaders who were sincere in their advocacy for the powerless and voiceless. The key difference between Greek and American conceptions of demagoguery is that while in Greece both the manipulative and the sincere were considered demagogues, in the United States it is only the dishonest man or woman who is labeled a demagogue. Perceived sincerity brings with it different labels, such as social movement organizer or mass leader. Moreover, this value-laden label ignores the shared situation from which both demagogues and mass leaders arise. As Allan Nevins noted in the introduction to Reinhard Luthin's seminal text on this topic, demagoguery often springs from some wrong, neglect, or falsehood for which society bears a responsibility. As groups of people or regions continue to suffer from conditions that naturally breed dissent, dissent eventually arrives, and along with it comes the call for, or at least susceptibility to, leaders who promise to change the oppression of the existing order.

The 20th century is full of examples to support Nevins's assertion, perhaps none better than the nation's demagogue par excellence, the legendary Louisiana politician Huey P. Long. Long grew up around the turn of the 20th century in Winn Parish, a hotbed of populism that was feeling increasingly estranged from the power centers of Louisiana politics, New Orleans and Baton Rouge. Much like his counterpart, California's Father Coughlin, Long represented a meaningful portion of Louisiana society that was somehow marginal to the larger society. Long was an outsider, representing fellow outsiders to a political society that was turning away from rural agrarianism and toward an industrialized and educated middle class. As wealth and power began to disproportionately find themselves in communities other than those such as Winn Parish, Long began to suggest grandiose redistribution schemes and massive development programs with a rhetorical flourish that appealed to his fellow outsiders. Long himself embraced, albeit perhaps not consistently, the label of demagogue, arguing that he was indeed a demagogue since he had promised and delivered school books, roads, and bridges to those who did not have them. He also, however, presided over a political career that featured graft, bribery, and occasional political violence. Long was certainly a demagogue in both the Greek and American senses, although those who label him with the pejorative should also recognize the conditions that he and other politicians like him arose from, and that Long often did keep the pandering promises he made.

Demagoguery in America has declined considerably in contemporary politics. This is in part due to the continuing decline of the conditions that breed demagogues. It is also partially due to the increasing connectedness of the nation through education, a robust middle class, technology, and infrastructure, as well as the numerous political access points the average citizen possesses. Because of these developments, demagogues no longer have as frequent an opportunity to incite the passions of the American *demos*.

Further reading: Finley, M. I. "Athenian Demagogues." *Past and Present* 21 (1962): 3–24; Luthin, Reinhard H. *American Demagogues: Twentieth Century.* Boston: Beacon Press, 1954; Williams, T. Harry. *Huey Long.* New York: Vintage Books, 1969.

—Justin S. Vaughn

democracy, direct

Direct democracy is a form of government whereby citizens directly participate in decision-making processes. In its purest form, direct democracy would have all citizens developing, debating, and deciding all issues of public importance. In the modern sense, direct citizen participation in the United States and other modern democracies is limited to only a few of the issues and questions facing society at a given time; most governmental activity is conducted by the representatives elected by the citizens. Contemporary direct democracy consists of three separate mechanisms by which people can directly participate in the political process: the BALLOT INITIATIVE, the REFERENDUM, and the RECALL.

Although direct democracy can be traced to the classical democracies of ancient Greece, there are virtually no current examples of government operated entirely by direct citizen participation. Rather, modern democracies operate in the form of a republic in which citizens choose individuals to represent them in government, referred to as indirect, or representative, democracy. The United States, all 50 state governments, and almost all local governments are representative democracies. The town hall systems used in New England townships are the closest examples of classic direct democracy in action, but even in these systems, representatives are chosen to conduct business for a large portion of governmental activity.

While classical direct democracy is not employed in modern democracies, direct citizen participation in political processes has not been abandoned. Contemporary direct democracy provides citizens the ability to create and then approve or reject laws or constitutional amendments (initiatives), to approve or reject laws and amendments created by the legislature (referenda), and to remove elected officials (recalls). Although the movement to provide direct democracy was at its peak during the Progressive Era of the late 19th and early 20th centuries, contemporary direct democracy has its historical roots in the town meetings of the colonial United States, dating to the 17th century. In the mid-19th century, the U.S. Congress required that all new state constitutions be referred to citizens for approval, and in 1897, South Dakota became the first state to allow its citizens the power of the initiative. By 1926 (1957 including Alaska and Hawaii) every state in the Union provided some form of direct democracy, although the types available vary from state to state. Although direct democracy has been embraced by the states in some form or another, there is no method of direct democracy that is used on the national level in the United States.

There are three types of direct democracy (referendum, initiative, and recall), and each type has different forms that vary by state. The referendum has two basic forms: popular referenda, whereby voters petition to approve or reject passed legislation before it is enacted, and legislative referenda, whereby the legislature (or sometimes other public officials) places items on the BALLOT for voters to approve or reject. Legislative referenda propose laws or statutes, and legislative amendments are constitutional amendments proposed by the legislature. All states (except Delaware) require that constitutional amendments proposed and/or passed by the legislature be subject to voter approval. A total of 23 states give their lawmakers the option to use the legislative referendum for statutes, while 24 allow the popular referendum.

The initiative is how proposals for statutes or amendments are created by voters and placed on the ballot for approval. Statutory initiatives propose laws, and constitutional initiatives propose amendments to the state constitution. Some states require indirect initiative, whereby proposals must be first given to the legislature for consideration before the proposal can advance to the ballot. Direct initiative states allow qualified proposals to proceed directly to the ballot. Proposals qualify for the ballot primarily by gathering signatures of a certain percentage of eligible voters within a specified amount of time. A total of 24 states have initiative provisions, 21 of them for statutory initiatives, and 18 states allow for constitutional initiatives.

Using the recall, voters can remove an elected official outside the normal process of elections. While the process varies in the 18 states that allow the statewide recall, the recall requires petitioning of eligible voters' signatures, followed by an election to determine the fate of the official. Some states allow for all elected officials to be recalled, while others exempt some officials, typically judges. A total of 36 states allow for recall of various local officials. The recall gained national attention in 2003, when Gray Davis of California became only the second governor in U.S. history to be removed by recall, with voters selecting film star Arnold Schwarzenegger as his replacement. Recall of high-profile offices such as governor, mayor, or state judge get the most attention, but most recall efforts target lower-level officers such as city council and school board members.

While the legislative referendum and amendments are used with regularity, popular referenda appear on ballots infrequently. Some states require that certain issues, such as tax increases and legislative salary increases, must automatically go before voters. Issues that have recently been considered via referenda include land use proposals, easing restrictions on TERM LIMITS, and constitutional amendments prohibiting same-sex marriage. The initiative is the second most frequently used form of direct democracy, although fewer than half gain voter approval. By contrast, about three in every five legislative referenda are approved. This may be explained by the different subjects involved in referenda and initiatives. Many referenda deal with questions of taxation or allocation of funds toward programs such as education, whereas the field of issues considered by initiatives tends to be far broader. Recent initiatives placed on state ballots include questions regarding assisted suicide, medical marijuana, campaign finance reform, animal rights, and gaming. The recall is used less frequently than either the referendum or the initiative, primarily because of the high signature thresholds (typically about 25 percent) required.

Advocates argue that the central concepts behind direct democracy are the return of political power and responsibility to citizens, prevention of corruption and concentration of political power among the economic and political elite, and encouragement of greater governmental responsiveness to citizen preferences. Skeptics claim that while direct democracy provides citizens with the potential for greater control over government, it is the economically powerful who use the tools of direct democracy most successfully. Opponents further argue that direct democracy is contradictory to the principles of representative government, undermining the system of popular elections. Supporters have pressed for national direct democracy, arguing that representative government regularly fails to respond to public sentiment and to resolve many important issues.

Further reading: Cronin, Thomas E. *Direct Democracy: The Politics of Initiative, Referendum and Recall.* Cambridge, Mass.: Harvard University Press, 1989; Initiative & Referendum Institute. Available online. URL: http://www. iandrinstitute.org. Accessed August 10, 2005; Magleby, David B. *Direct Legislation: Voting on Ballot Propositions in the United States.* Baltimore: Johns Hopkins University Press, 1984; Sabato, Larry J., Howard R. Ernst, and Bruce A. Larson, eds. *Dangerous Democracy? The Battle over Ballot Initiatives in America.* Lanham, Md.: Rowman & Littlefield, 2001.

—Joel A. Rayan

democracy, representative

Representative democracies rely on an individual, or a body of individuals, to make political decisions on behalf of the citizenry. In a representative system, popular sovereignty is maintained, as these representatives are accountable to an ELECTORATE, called the representatives' CONSTITUENCY. Citizens do not retain the right to craft and enact the laws that govern them (as is the case in DIRECT DEMOCRACY) but instead select people to make political decisions on their behalf.

In a representative system, citizens give representatives authority to act as their agents or proxies and make decisions in their name. The interests of this group constrain the initiative of representatives. Periodic elections serve to keep representatives accountable to the electorate. Historically, representative democracies have been defended on the grounds that they allow the most virtuous, competent, or professional individuals in a community to make decisions. This is opposed to direct democracies, in which all citizens share directly in sovereign power. Representatives, the argument continues, bring expertise to the task of managing a government and are better suited to govern than the average person.

Representative democracies thus combine popular control and input into the workings of government through exceptional leadership, yet without burdening common citizens with sustained and substantial political duties. Rather than participating in POLITICS directly, citizens choose representatives who conduct the business of the government. The role of citizens consequently becomes one of periodically choosing suitable agents to do their bidding so that the citizens can pursue their own private interests, rather than having to engage as constantly in politics as a direct democracy presupposes.

The historical roots of the concept of representative democracy are closely tied to fluctuating appraisals of the practicability and desirability of direct democracies. Ancient Greece had no term for *representative* or an articulated theory of representation, even though it had some institutions that could be called representative. Similarly, even though the English language inherited the word-family surrounding *representation* from the Romans, their use of the term did not apply to people representing other people. The explicit historical roots of the concept of representative democracy are instead founded on a mistrust of direct democracy and the search for a regime form that could rival monarchies and be practicable in modern nation-states.

Early understandings of representative democracy emerged in the late 17th century and became articulated and institutionalized during the 18th century. The *FEDERALIST PAPERS*, written to advocate the ratification of the U.S. Constitution, mark one of the key moments of transforming the concept of democracy along representative lines.

Direct democracies were thought of as either simply unattainable or impracticable (due to the presumed ignorance of average citizens), too limited due to constraints on size, or too inefficient, burdensome, and time-consuming for a community to adjudicate political questions. The concept of representative democracy was seen as a way to combat the deficiencies of direct democracy and adapt democracy to the modern world while retaining its key positive features. In a world of large nation-states, it was believed that direct democracies would be logistically unrealistic. Even if all people could physically come together to make political decisions, their choices would still be constrained by the intellectual limitations of the common citizen.

A representative democracy allows for the transformation of democratic institutions and the conceptual self-understanding of its citizenry. Rather than being constrained to small city-states, this model democracy can realistically encompass large nations and select from among its population the most able to make decisions in the name of the constituency that elected them. Self-determination, in the sense of being the author and subject of the laws that govern oneself, is still present but removed by one layer from the citizens.

Articulations of the concept of representative democracy in the 19th century highlighted the elements most closely aligned with liberalism, particularly fear of a too powerful, uncontrollable central state. Benjamin Constant in particular emphasized the liberal conception of liberty that underlies representative models of democracy, while J. S. Mill focused more on the utilitarian virtues of the representative system, elaborating on the efficiency of representative democracies (in finding good solutions for given ends) as well as their function of helping to educate the masses.

During the 20th century, in response to critics such as Vladimir Lenin and Carl Schmitt (who prophesied the decline of representative forms of democracy), political theorists such as Joseph Schumpeter and Anthony Downs reinvigorated the notion of representative democracy as a well-suited method for solving political questions in an apt manner. Representative democracy was now seen as pure method, devoid of substantive content. This feature sharply distinguished representative democracies from fascism and the more insidious manifestations of communism. Following this conceptual trend, an increasing number of nations organized themselves in representative forms of democracy during the same time span, and already existing representative institutions became more directly accountable to the citizenry (e.g., the SEVENTEENTH AMENDMENT to the U.S. Constitution).

Questions surrounding notions of adequate representation as well as limits on the authority of representatives have been, and still are, part of a spirited debate. Should a representative be understood as a mere tool, doing what the constituency tells him or her to do? Or should a representative rely on her own experience and sometimes act against the express wishes of the constituency? Should the representative consider only the interests of his home district or decide based on what is best for the country as a whole? Or is perhaps the focus on interests misguided, and is it more important that representatives descriptively represent their constituencies? Should the representative's race and ethnicity mirror the dominant group of her district? Should gender equality be a goal of representation?

The number of representative democracies has expanded tremendously since its conceptual birth. Currently a large number of representative democracies exist throughout the globe. Few people believe in the practical viability of a direct democracy, and consequently, assuming the desirability of democracy generally, representative democracies remain the main alternative. In fact, the prevalence of representative government has become so hegemonic that the majority of people in the world live under a regime that claims to be a representative form of democracy. In the United States, representative institutions exist at all levels of the federal hierarchy. Through them the people choose their political leaders and periodically hold them accountable.

Further reading: Downs, Anthony. *An Economic Theory of Democracy.* New York: Harper & Row, 1957; Pitkin, Hanna. *The Concept of Representation.* Berkeley: University of California Press, 1967; Schumpeter, Joseph. *Capitalism, Socialism, and Democracy.* New York: Harper, 1942.

—Roger M. Michalski

Democratic Leadership Council

Founded in 1985 by DEMOCRATIC PARTY activist Al From, the Democratic Leadership Council (DLC) is a nonprofit corporation with numerous ties to, but no formal connections with, the national Democratic Party organization. The DLC had its birth in the desire of socially and fiscally moderate Democrats to redirect their party toward a more centrist IDEOLOGY and strategy for campaigning and governing. This aspiration on the part of the DLC's founding members was in response to what they perceived as a weakening of the Democratic Party's fortunes in electoral POLITICS. While describing itself as a movement within the party, the DLC provides a number of party-type services and functions, such as candidate recruitment and policy formulation, in an effort to shape the future of the national party. It maintains a think tank, the Progressive Policy Institute, and produces a number of publications, including *Blueprint,* the DLC's policy journal.

The DLC describes its approach to politics and governing as emanating from a "third way" political philosophy that is not replicated by the conservatism of the REPUBLICAN PARTY or the liberalism of the Democratic Party. According to the DLC, its reliance on the third way—an explicit rejection of previous ideological and policy motifs—allows it to call members "New Democrats" as opposed to the past incarnation of the dominant FACTION within the party.

The impact of the DLC on American politics has been and continues to be sizable. In terms of the electoral success of DLC adherents, in the 108th Congress, nearly half the members of the Democratic caucus in the U.S. House of Representatives and U.S. Senate are formally affiliated with the DLC. Moreover, DLC members firmly populate elected positions at the state and local levels. Since its birth, DLC members have dominated Democratic presidential politics with Bill Clinton, Al Gore, Joe Lieberman, and John Kerry being the most notable examples. However, the dominance of DLC-affiliated presidential candidates was directly challenged by the insurgent candidacy of Howard Dean, who was openly hostile toward the DLC.

The policy implications of the DLC and its third way philosophy are hard to gauge. Critics fault DLC policy initiatives for what they perceive as incremental answers to comprehensive problems, or more pointedly, for the DLC's supposed willingness to offer solutions tailored to garner support from conservatives and Republicans. Supporters argue that third way policy prescriptions of moderation appeal to the median voter and have a higher likelihood of adoption in an increasingly polarized and competitive partisan environment.

Further reading: Democratic Leadership Council. Available online. URL: http://www.dlc.org. Accessed August 10, 2005; Kenneth S. Baer. *Reinventing Democrats: The Politics of Liberalism from Reagan to Clinton.* Lawrence: University of Kansas Press, 2000; Hale, Jon F. "Making of the New Democrats." *Political Science Quarterly* 110, no. 2 (1995): 207–232.

—Richard P. Barberio

Democratic National Committee (DNC)

The Democratic National Committee (DNC) was formed in 1848, although the DEMOCRATIC PARTY claims ties that go back as far as Thomas Jefferson in 1792. The national committee was created to manage the affairs of the Democratic Party between the national conventions.

The DNC has 440 members. These members are selected based on PROPORTIONAL REPRESENTATION and gender. States with larger populations receive more committee members, and each state's delegation must be divided equally between men and women.

The national committee's responsibilities include issuing the call to the national convention; conducting the party's presidential campaign; filling vacancies in the NOMINATIONS for the office of president and vice president; formulating and disseminating party policy; and electing a chairperson, five vice chairpersons, a treasurer, a secretary, a national finance chair, and other officers of the national committee.

The national chairperson presides over meetings of the Democratic National Committee and its executive committee. The executive committee is responsible for conducting the affairs of the Democratic Party between the meetings of the full Democratic National Committee. It is made up of the chairpersons of the four regional caucuses of the Democratic National Committee plus other members from a specific list of Democratic organizations and caucuses. These include organizations and caucuses based on gender, race, national origin, and sexual orientation. The national chairperson serves full time and is specifically directed to maintain impartiality during the Democratic Party presidential nominating process.

The national finance chair and the treasurer are the financial advisers to the national chairperson and the executive committee of the Democratic National Committee. The national finance organizations established by the Democratic National Committee have the additional responsibilities of advising and assisting the state Democratic Parties and individual Democratic candidates in securing funds for their purposes. It should be noted that a major change in the way funds are raised occurred during the 2004 ELECTION CYCLE. The Internet has now become an important means for raising funds, allowing Americans to contribute funds to the party and candidate of their choice in a convenient and direct manner.

The Democratic National Committee has three standing committees. They are the credentials committee, resolutions committee, and the rules and bylaws committee. The credentials committee is charged with resolving all challenges to the credentials of the Democratic National Committee members. Any Democrat may challenge the credentials of any member of the Democratic National Committee from his or her state. The credentials committee will conduct a hearing on the matter following established procedures and then present a written report to the national committee that makes a determination on the challenge.

The resolutions committee studies all resolutions by members of the Democratic National Committee that are proposed for adoption by the national committee. The resolutions committee documents its work, provides the national committee with copies of the resolutions it recommends, and discusses resolutions that it does not recommend for adoption.

The rules and bylaws committee considers all recommendations for amendments to the rules and bylaws of the Democratic National Committee and to the charter of the Democratic Party of the United States. The recommendations for amendments must be made by a member of the Democratic National Committee and must be submitted and processed in accordance with established procedures. The reporting requirements are similar to those of the resolutions committee.

In summary, the Democratic National Committee endeavors to achieve the stated goals of the national Democratic Party in a manner that is impartial, nondiscriminatory, and that follows established rules and procedures.

Further reading: Bone, Hugh A. *Party Committees and National Politics*. Seattle: University of Washington Press, 1958; Cotter, Cornelius P., and Bernard C. Hennessy. *Politics without Power: The National Party Committees*. New York: Atherton Press, 1964; Goldman, Ralph M. *The National Party Chairmen and Committees: Factionalism at the Top*. Armonk, N.Y.: M.E. Sharpe, 1990; Klinkner, Philip A. *The Losing Parties: Out-Party National Committees*. New Haven, Conn.: Yale University Press, 1994; Shafer, Byron E. *The Quiet Revolution: The Struggle for the Democratic Party and the Shaping of Post-Reform Politics*. New York: Russell Sage, 1983.

—Tim Sultan

Democratic National Committee chair

Andrew Jackson's transformation of American POLITICS from the 1820s through 1840 shifted the balance of power from the Capitol and its top-down congressional caucus presidential nominating system to a decentralized system dominated by mid-level political organizers. Often characterized as the second American party system, Jackson and his Democratic allies used the extension of white male SUFFRAGE to restructure presidential politics.

Institutional party arrangements that grew out of this era included the national nominating conventions, national committees, and national chairs. Jackson's Democrats were not the inventors of the nominating convention. That honor belongs to the ANTI-MASONIC PARTY, which used a national nominating convention in 1831 to select former attorney general William Wirt of Maryland as its presidential nominee. The Anti-Masonic Party disappeared quickly but its legacy—the national nominating convention—continues today.

Jackson used the initial Democratic Convention to jettison troublesome vice president John C. Calhoun of South Carolina, whose commitment to the states' rights doctrine of nullification challenged Jackson. Calhoun's replacement, Secretary of State Martin Van Buren of New York, was also a key party builder. The Democrats adopted the two-thirds rule for NOMINATION first used by the Anti-Masons. Van Buren was not a slaveholder so the rule for the presidential and vice presidential selections gave the South a veto over nominations and protected the "peculiar institution" of slavery. Nominated twice, in 1835 and 1840, Van Buren was thwarted by the two-thirds rule in 1844 despite holding a DELEGATE majority. The 1844 nomination went to former Speaker of the House James K. Polk of Tennessee, a Jacksonian known as "Young Hickory," who ended Henry Clay's third and final bid for the presidency.

Polk's declining health opened the nomination in 1848, and, as Democrats battled for the nomination, the party created the post of national chair and named Benjamin Hallett of Massachusetts. The 1848 defeat of Democratic nominee Lewis Cass of Michigan by Whig Zachary Taylor led to a 49-BALLOT contest in 1852. Winning nomination was a former general and U.S. senator, Franklin Pierce of New Hampshire. New England party leaders such as Hallett of Massachusetts and David Smalley of Vermont and Democratic nominees and New Hampshire natives Cass and Pierce, as well as 1860's nominee Vermont native Stephen A. Douglas of Illinois, were known pejoratively as "doughfaces"—northern apologists of slavery—a direct consequence of the South-protecting two-thirds rule.

Democrats met three times in 1860 to select nominees. The deadlocked Charleston, South Carolina, convention caused Democrats to split into northern and southern wings. Northern Democrats chose Senator Douglas as their nominee while SOUTHERN DEMOCRATS chose Vice President John C. Breckinridge of Kentucky. Douglas's ally, Smalley, was replaced as national chair by financier August Belmont of New York, head of the New York office of the Rothschild family. A prowar Democrat, Belmont served as chair from 1860 to 1872 and was responsible for financing the DEMOCRATIC PARTY during the Civil War and RECONSTRUCTION. Belmont and well-heeled fellow New York national chairs Augustus Schell (1872–76) and Abram S. Hewitt (1876–77) solidified the prominent role of New York State in the post–Civil War Democratic Party. From 1868 to 1892, six of seven Democratic presidential nominees were New York residents: George McClellan (1864), Horatio Seymour (1868), Horace Greeley (1872), Samuel J. Tilden (1876), and Grover Cleveland (1884, 1888, and 1892). Another corporate leader, Senator William H. Barnum of Connecticut, a distant cousin of circus impresario Phineas T. Barnum, maintained the Northeast's dominance of the post from 1877 until his death in 1889. With 12 years each in the post, Belmont and Barnum were the longest-serving Democratic national chairs.

Barnum's linkage of corporate power and elective office holding was continued by Senator Calvin Brice of Ohio (1889–92). Brice's ties to New York's money men earned him the post, but his difficulties with ex-president Cleveland led him to be replaced by William Harrity of Pennsylvania, a lifelong politician (1892–96). The Populist eruption over the free coinage of silver led in 1896 to the first presidential nomination of ex-representative William Jennings Bryan of Nebraska and the first southern chair of the DEMOCRATIC NATIONAL COMMITTEE (DNC), ex-Confederate soldier and pro-silverite, Senator James K. Jones of Arkansas (1896–1904). Bryan's strength in the South, the agricultural Midwest, and the mountain West diminished the Democratic Party in the Northeast, and as Bryan's influence grew, the chair echoed these changes. Jones was followed by Thomas Taggart, the Irish-born mayor of Indianapolis (1904–08).

Bryan's third unsuccessful run in 1908 led the national chair to return to the Northeast with the naming of publisher and later New York State chair Norman E. Mack (1908–12); William F. McCombs of New York (1912–16); Vance McCormick of Pennsylvania (1916–19); and Homer S. Cummings of Connecticut (1919–20). This was also the time when, in 1916, Virginia-born New Jersey governor Woodrow Wilson became the first Democrat since Andrew Jackson in 1832 to win two consecutive presidential terms.

By the 1920s, Democratic presidential nominees openly chose their own national chairs, with the 1920 nominee, Governor James Cox of Ohio, selecting fellow Ohioan George White (1920–21); 1924 nominee ex-ambassador John W. Davis of West Virginia choosing fellow West Virginian Clem Shaver (1924–28); and 1928 nominee, Governor Al Smith of New York, selecting the fiscally conservative John J. Raskob of Maryland (1928–32). Representative Cordell Hull of Tennessee was national chair in the years between White's departure in 1921 and Shaver's appointment in 1924.

The bitter 1932 nomination battle between former allies Al Smith and Franklin Roosevelt led to Raskob's replacement as national chair and his eventual departure from the Democratic Party. Raskob's replacement, James A. Farley, a Tammany Hall Democrat, served for FDR's first two terms (1933–41). FDR's election led to three national chairs serving in his cabinet: Cordell Hull as secretary of state, Homer S. Cummings as attorney general, and Farley as postmaster general. FDR's goal of remaking the Democratic Party in his own image accounted for this unusual confluence of organizational party leaders as prominent members of the administration. It was on Jim Farley's watch in 1936 that the Democrats finally rid themselves of the two-thirds rule and the southern veto. The loss of that veto and FDR's 1937 effort to pack the Supreme Court led many southern congressional Democrats to ally themselves with Republicans in 1938 to form the Conservative Coalition. With FDR facing resistance from the congressional party, he needed to maintain tighter control over the organizational one.

Jim Farley sought the 1940 nomination for himself but was steamrollered by FDR's third term candidacy. Farley's successor was another New York City ward leader and one-time New York secretary of state, Edward J. Flynn (1940–43). Following Flynn's departure, each of the next three national chairs held cabinet posts, with Farley's replacement as postmaster general, Frank C. Walker of Pennsylvania, serving as national chair (1943–44). Next was Robert C. Hannegan of Missouri, who first succeeded Walker as national chair (1944–47) and then as postmaster general. Hannegan's active role as chair led to Vice President Henry A. Wallace being replaced by a very reluctant junior U.S. senator, Harry S. Truman from Missouri. Hannegan served as Truman's postmaster general and national chair until ill health intervened, and he was replaced in 1947 by Senator J. Howard McGrath of Rhode Island (1947–49). McGrath left the chair when he was named attorney general. The integration of the chair into the cabinet during the Roosevelt and Truman administrations represented a fusion of the organizational and the presidential parties.

Although Harry Truman retained the presidency in the 1948 election, southern Democratic control of Congress greatly limited any liberal initiatives. The next chairs, William M. Boyle, Jr., of Missouri (1949–51) and Frank E. McKinney of Indiana (1951–52), were figureheads. Governor Adlai Stevenson of Illinois, the 1952 and 1956 nominee, attempted to give the DNC more direction with his selections of Stephen A. Mitchell of Illinois (1952–54) and Paul M. Butler of Indiana (1955–60). Butler tried to create an advisory council uniting congressional and organizational Democrats into an ideological steering committee. However, congressional Democrats led by two Texans, Speaker of the House Sam Rayburn and Senate Majority Leader Lyndon Johnson, nixed the plan. Butler did not survive the 1960 Democratic convention.

Senator Henry M. Jackson of Washington state was Senator John F. Kennedy's choice to chair the DNC in his campaign (1960–61). Kennedy's election led to the appointment of Connecticut party chair and political mastermind John M. Bailey, who served from 1961 until his death in 1968. While Kennedy respected Bailey, he and President Johnson micromanaged the DNC from the White House, virtually ignoring the national chair. Bailey was succeeded for a short time (1968–69) by Postmaster General Lawrence F. O'Brien, an original member of John Kennedy's "Irish Mafia" who had the misfortune of having to deal with the bitter fallout of the horrendous 1968 Chicago convention.

Senator Fred Harris of Oklahoma (1969–70) served briefly and surrendered the post of national chair to seek the 1972 nomination. Larry O'Brien returned as chair, and it was his office in Washington's Watergate Hotel that was the target of burglars working for the REPUBLICAN NATIONAL COMMITTEE (RNC). Their capture and subsequent trial led to the collapse of Richard Nixon's presidency in 1974.

South Dakota's Senator George S. McGovern named Jean Westwood of Colorado, the first female chair, to lead the national committee during his ill-fated 1972 campaign that lost 49 states. She was replaced by Texas lawyer and fundraiser Robert Strauss, who held the post from 1972 until his appointment as special trade representative by President Jimmy Carter in 1977. Strauss was succeeded by former Maine governor Kenneth Curtis (1977–78) until Curtis was named ambassador to Canada. Another Texas lawyer, John C. White, was named by Carter for the remainder of the term (1978–81).

Charles Manatt of California (1981–85) followed White and had to preside over another 49-state loss by former vice president Walter Mondale to President Ronald Reagan. Manatt's replacement, Paul Kirk of Massachusetts, was a longtime ally of the Kennedy family, and his tenure (1985–88) coincided with the 1988 nomination of Governor Michael S. Dukakis of Massachusetts.

The growing influence of the moderate DEMOCRATIC LEADERSHIP COUNCIL appeared in the choice of African-American lawyer Ronald H. Brown of Washington, D.C., as national chair in 1989. Governor Bill Clinton of Arkansas won the White House and named Brown to be secretary of commerce (in the FDR tradition), a post Brown held until his 1996 death in a plane crash in Croatia. Under Clinton, the DNC borrowed a concept pioneered by the RNC in 1983 of naming two chairs—a general chair who would be a public spokesman for the party and a national chair who would run the DNC. Senator Christopher Dodd of Connecticut served as general chair until 1997, when he was replaced by Colorado governor Roy Romer. Romer held the post until 1999, when a longtime romantic entanglement surfaced while he was simultaneously defending President Clinton from similar charges. He was succeeded as general chair by Philadelphia mayor Ed Rendell (1999–2001). Clinton's choices for national chair were David Wilhelm of Illinois (1993–96), Donald Fowler of South Carolina (1996–97), businessman Steven Grossman of Massachusetts (1997–99), and Joe Andrew of Indiana (1999–2001). It was these men who oversaw the record-setting financial contributions for the Clinton administration in the 1990s. The last Clinton-affiliated DNC chair, Terry McAuliffe (2001–04), was the former finance chair who was responsible for designing the heavily front-loaded PRIMARY calendar of 2004 that led to the early confirmation of Senator John F. Kerry of Massachusetts as the party's presidential nominee.

In a major break from Democratic precedent, former Vermont governor and presidential contender, Howard B. Dean III, was named chair of the National Committee in 2005. Dean is the first former presidential candidate in either party to be selected for the national chairmanship. The enthusiasm of Dean's opposition to the Iraq War and his commitment to move DNC funds from Washington-based lobbying activities to state party organizations provided him with the votes needed to win the chairmanship. However, Dean's penchant for well-publicized and ill-timed remarks that contributed to sinking his 2004 candidacy have persisted into his chairmanship, leading to tensions with the Democratic leaders of Congress.

Further reading: Bone, Hugh A. *Party Committees and National Politics.* Seattle: University of Washington Press, 1958; Cotter, Cornelius P., and Bernard C. Hennessy. *Politics without Power: The National Party Committees.* New York: Atherton Press, 1964; Goldman, Ralph M. *The National Party Chairmen and Committees: Factionalism at the Top.* Armonk, N.Y.: M.E. Sharpe, 1990; Klinkner, Philip A. *The Losing Parties: Out-Party National Committees.*

New Haven, Conn.: Yale University Press, 1994; Shafer, Byron E. *The Quiet Revolution: The Struggle for the Democratic Party and the Shaping of Post-Reform Politics.* New York: Russell Sage, 1983.

—Garrison Nelson

Democratic National Convention

Beginning in 1832, the DEMOCRATIC PARTY has held national nominating conventions in order to accomplish four goals, the first three of which have become subordinated to the fourth: 1) to show its presence and strength in every state in the Union in which its party operates, 2) to nominate candidates for president and vice president, 3) to draft a platform detailing the principles the party stands for and policies it will implement if its presidential nominee is victorious in the next election, and 4) to rally the party faithful and use the news media to expose the party in a positive way to the national ELECTORATE.

To participate, each state party (e.g., the California State Democratic Party or the New York State Democratic Party) must send a certain number of DELEGATEs to the convention. It has become more formalized in order to apportion delegates among the state parties fairly. They are chosen according to various criteria having to do at many times in its history with the state's share of the ELECTORAL COLLEGE vote and the success of the party's presidential candidate in the last election, and the amount of national party leaders who live in or serve in office in that state. Delegates are selected according to both national party rules and the selection process rules of each state individually.

Since its first convention, the Democrats have touted themselves as the PEOPLE'S PARTY and, at least in their platform language, have tended to use rhetoric that scorns "moneyed interest" and associates the other major party with that interest as much as possible. Perhaps one of the most consequential examples of this was the "Cross of Gold" speech made by William Jennings Bryan at the 1896 convention, which supported the coinage of "free silver" over the gold standard, the latter seen by midwestern and southern farmers as a source of enrichment for the already wealthy eastern establishment. Bryan, an unknown Nebraska congressman, won the presidential NOMINATION by comparing the maintenance of the gold standard to the crucifixion, to the delight of convention delegates.

There had existed a system for nominating candidates for president by the political parties that preceded the Democratic Party, but never a formal convention. The movement toward a convention was spearheaded chiefly by Martin Van Buren of New York and his southern allies. The party existed chiefly as a vehicle to run Andrew Jackson for president and elect his allies to office. It later became a source of continuity in maintaining the image of the "Jacksonian" party even after the "General of New Orleans" had left the political scene. Because the party's convention was

seen as such a concrete representation of the party itself, it is only natural that some of the most important political maneuvering of election years occurred during the convention. Since the onset of the PRIMARY, however, the conventions have become less acrimonious, chiefly because the main decision-making functions of presidential nomination and platform crafting have been supplanted by electoral processes that occur before the convention.

From 1832, its first convention, until 1936, the convention operated under what was called the "two-thirds rule." According to the two-thirds rule, no candidate could be nominated without the consent of at least two-thirds of the delegates to the national convention. Only twice during that time did a candidate garner a majority without being able to gather the two-thirds majority. This happened when Martin Van Buren attempted to gain the party's nomination for a third straight election in 1844, despite having lost a bid for a second term in 1840. He eventually lost the 1844 nod to James K. Polk, who won the election and was the favorite candidate of the elder statesman Jackson, a fellow Tennesseean. The other occurrence was in 1912, when Champ Clark won a majority, but only Woodrow Wilson was able to attain the two-thirds majority needed to win.

President Franklin D. Roosevelt, as part of his effort to assert his control over the party, ordered his lieutenants to strike down the two-thirds rule by overturning it during the 1936 nominating convention. The rule was seen as a boon to the South, since the southern delegates, who voted as a bloc, had a virtual veto over any presidential candidate despite holding only a minority of delegates. As an olive branch to the southern states, the Democrats began in 1944 to allot delegates in part according to how many votes were received by the Democratic nominee in the previous PRESIDENTIAL ELECTION, the so-called bonus rule.

Roosevelt broke many taboos with the Democratic Party structure, including the method of accepting the party's nomination itself. As a symbol of independence from and support within the party, nominees had, since the start of conventions, not attended the proceedings and offered a letter of acceptance several weeks after the end of the convention. Roosevelt felt it important to shock the delegates and the nation by offering a speech in person to the convened delegates.

A particularly contentious issue in the history of Democratic Party conventions has been the platform battles involving the party's stance on racial issues. In two elections these issues caused the party to split because of a walkout staged by disaffected members, both times southerners. In 1860, when the party nominated Stephen Douglas and took no stand on the legality of slavery in the western territories, SOUTHERN DEMOCRATS walked out, staging a separate convention that nominated John C. Breckinridge. The 1924 convention refused to condemn the actions of the KU KLUX KLAN, an organization dedicated to terrorizing racial minority groups in an attempt to keep minority voters from the polls and from gaining political influence. In 1948, President Harry Truman pushed through a plank that took a strong pro–civil rights stance for African Americans, prompting several southern delegations to walk out and hold a separate convention that nominated J. Strom Thurmond for president.

In an attempt to modernize the party structure for conventions, the DEMOCRATIC NATIONAL COMMITTEE in 1968 charged a commission, the McGovern-Fraser commission, with proposing a uniform set of rules for the party that had not hitherto existed. Their recommendations were implemented, and they fixed the number of "pledged" (committed to vote for a candidate on the first ballot of the convention because of a state's primary or caucus) delegates at around 3,000, and approximated the number of party leaders ("super-delegates," i.e., members of Congress, governors, former presidents, etc.) in the state who were free to vote for any candidate on the first ballot at about 1,500. The number of delegates allocated to each state was to be calculated using a formula that incorporated Electoral College votes of the state and the success of the Democratic candidates in the last three presidential elections.

The McGovern-Fraser rules did not mandate that state parties conduct primaries, and thus largely left the method for choosing delegates to the state parties. As of 2004, almost every state (as well as the District of Columbia and the territories that send party delegations to the national conventions, such as Guam and Puerto Rico) conducts Democratic PRESIDENTIAL PRIMARIES. A majority of total delegates are pledged to vote for the eventual nominee on the first ballot after SUPER TUESDAY, when 13 states cast their primary ballots, bringing the total to approximately 30 states that have had the opportunity to vote in the primaries. Thus, the 2004 convention was, more so than ever, largely a media event designed to garner support for the candidates for president and vice president, who had already effectively been nominated.

Further reading: Benson, Lee. *The Concept of Jacksonian Democracy.* Princeton, N.J.: Princeton University Press, 1961; DeGregorio, William A. *The Complete Book of U.S. Presidents: From George Washington to George W. Bush.* New York: Barnes & Noble Books, 2004; Milkis, Sidney M. *The President and the Parties: The Transformation of the American Party System since the New Deal.* Oxford: Oxford University Press, 1993.

—Daniel T. Kirsch

Democratic Party

During its history, the Democratic Party has espoused policies and housed constituent groups ranging widely over the spectrum of American political IDEOLOGY. It has been the party of states' rights and the party of a strong, centralized federal government. It has been the party of the rugged individual and the party of the intellectual elite. It has been the party of farmers and the party of urban immigrants. It has been the party of southern segregationists and the party of the CIVIL RIGHTS MOVEMENT.

The Democratic Party traces its roots to a group assembled in the 1790s by Thomas Jefferson and James Madison in opposition to Alexander Hamilton and the Federalists. Members of this early COALITION, which was more a congressional caucus than a POLITICAL PARTY, were referred to as Republicans or Democratic-Republicans (which has no relation to the modern REPUBLICAN PARTY). This early installment of today's Democratic Party was founded on the belief that the power of the federal government must be strictly limited. It advocated states' rights, reflecting the distrust of centralized regimes shared by many in America, especially small landowners, and promoted the protection of liberty above all.

In 1800, Jefferson became the first among these Democratic-Republicans to be elected president. The group's dominance continued through 1825 with the administrations of James Madison and James Monroe. Monroe led the nation during the "Era of Good Feeling" and was not challenged for his second term in office. Division among the Democratic-Republicans forced the 1824 PRESIDENTIAL ELECTION to be decided eventually in favor of John Quincy Adams, by the House of Representatives. This highly contested and questioned outcome would set into motion the establishment of the modern Democratic Party.

Andrew Jackson, whose 1824 totals in both the POPULAR VOTE and ELECTORAL COLLEGE had exceeded those of John Quincy Adams, organized his supporters into what would gradually became known as the Democratic Party. Jackson's GRASSROOTS organization would win him the presidency in 1828, making him the Democratic Party's first president.

The period from Jackson's ascent until 1856 was characterized by the competition between the Whigs and the Democrats, with the Democrats as the MAJORITY PARTY. It was during this period that modern party competition and organization took shape. Nominating conventions emerged, and party organizational structures were formed, from the local level to national committees. The DEMOCRATIC NATIONAL COMMITTEE (DNC), for instance, which is charged with organizing the party and developing the party platform, has been in operation since 1848.

Jackson won two terms, in 1828 and 1832. His vice president, Martin Van Buren, was elected president in 1836. Democratic nominee James K. Polk won the presidency in 1844 on a platform of national expansion. Democratic candidates Franklin Pierce and James Buchanan were elected in 1852 and 1856, respectively.

The election of 1860 marked the beginning of a long era of minority status for the Democratic Party. The party split in two, with northern and southern wings. SOUTHERN DEMOCRATS preferred to allow new states to decide for themselves on the issue of slavery, and Democrats from the North believed that decision should rest with the U.S. Supreme Court. This schism produced two separate Democratic candidates for president in 1860. Stephen Douglas was the nominee of the northern branch of the party, and the southerners put forward John Breckinridge. This division facilitated the election to the presidency of Abraham Lincoln from the relatively new Republican Party. From this point through the present, the two major political parties in the United States have been the Democratic Party and the Republican Party.

During the Civil War and RECONSTRUCTION, the Democratic Party was largely discredited in all but the South. A series of Democratic presidential nominees fell to defeat. Democrat Samuel Tilden won the popular vote in 1876, but Congress decided the contested election in favor of Republican Rutherford B. Hayes. Grover Cleveland broke the Democrats' drought in presidential POLITICS by winning two nonconsecutive terms in the White House in 1884 and 1892. An economic crisis during Cleveland's second term further weakened the party's position and prompted the Democrats to choose William Jennings Bryan as their 1896 nominee. Bryan, who also received the NOMINATION of the POPULIST PARTY, was the dominant figure in the highly divided Democratic Party of the late 19th and early 20th centuries. He was the party's nominee in three elections (1896, 1900, and 1908). In the first election, he primarily advocated silver coinage. In the next two, his focus was on an anti-imperialist foreign policy.

The Democrats nearly nominated Bryan for a fourth time in 1912, but instead chose Woodrow Wilson. In that year, Republican votes were divided, with incumbent president William Howard Taft taking the party nomination and former president Theodore Roosevelt running as a Bull Moose Republican. This split allowed Wilson, who ran on a New Freedom platform, to take the presidency. During his first term, Wilson pushed forward ambitious legislation. He lowered tariffs, created a graduated federal income tax, and established the Federal Reserve and Federal Trade Commission. He was reelected in 1916, boasting that he had kept the United States out of World War I. After his election, however, Wilson led the nation into the war.

The 1920s saw another lull for Democrats. Three consecutive nominees lost. The last of these, Alfred E. Smith, was the first Catholic to run for president of the United States with a major party nomination.

The stock market crash of 1929 that began the Great Depression set the stage for the election in 1932 of Democratic nominee Franklin D. Roosevelt. He offered a beleaguered America a New Deal, a package of policies that included the creation of the Tennessee Valley Authority, a departure from the gold standard, deficit spending, and higher taxes for the wealthy. His agenda for recovery marked the first time a president from the party of Thomas Jefferson and Andrew Jackson advocated and achieved such a massive expansion in the role of the federal government. Among the many lasting products of this era was the Social Security system. His success in leading the nation during this tumultuous time allowed Roosevelt to be reelected three times, in 1936, 1940 and 1944. Beginning with the Japanese attack at Pearl Harbor in 1941, Roosevelt led the nation into World War II. Roosevelt died shortly after being elected president for the fourth time.

His long tenure as president allowed the Democratic Party to finally rise from its post–Civil War nadir. On the political front, Roosevelt transformed the makeup of the Democratic Party. He and his policies brought black, Jewish, and Catholic voters as well as southern whites and industrial workers together under the Democratic Party umbrella. This powerful combination came to be known as the NEW DEAL COALITION. The unstable mixture proved a difficult balance for the party. The southern whites were often located on the conservative end of the American ideology spectrum, while Democrats from the Northeast were often far more liberal. This dichotomy often demanded that party leaders perform a balancing act in their efforts to placate the party's various FACTIONS.

The battle in the 1940s, 1950s, and 1960s over segregation and civil rights eventually took its toll on the New Deal Coalition. In 1948, that tension came to a head. Harry S. Truman, who had succeeded Roosevelt, pledged during his nominating convention acceptance speech to support the cause of civil rights for blacks. A group of southern Democrats, led by Strom Thurmond of South Carolina, walked out of the convention and formed the States' Rights Democratic Party, better known as the Dixiecrats. This group offered Thurmond as its presidential nominee, almost causing Truman to lose the GENERAL ELECTION to Republican Thomas Dewey. Since 1948, the South has gradually gone from the Democratic "Solid South" to a Republican stronghold, breaking up the New Deal Coalition.

Despite the Dixiecrat split, Truman was reelected in 1948. His administration saw the end of World War II and the implementation of the Marshall Plan as the cold war in Europe began in earnest. After Truman, the era of Democratic leadership in the White House that began with Roosevelt was interrupted when the Republican Party tapped popular World War II hero, General Dwight D. Eisenhower, as its nominee in 1952 and 1956.

In 1960, Democrat John F. Kennedy became the first Catholic elected president of the United States. While an assassin's bullet limited Kennedy's tenure as president to slightly more than 1,000 days, he left an unmistakable mark on his nation and his party. Kennedy voiced a call for America to claim a place as the moral leader of the free world, pushing the nation to strive for greatness, be it in pursuit of international human rights or in the quest for victory in the space race. It was perhaps only after his death that Kennedy's legacy took full shape. After 1963, Kennedy's vice president and successor in the Oval Office, Lyndon Johnson, was able to push forward an ambitious agenda, known as the Great Society, designed to fulfill Kennedy's vision for the nation. A key component of the Great Society was the passage of the 1964 Civil Rights Act, which further solidified support of the Democratic Party among the black community. Johnson was able to pass significant legislation increasing the federal government's role in combating poverty and disease, including the creation of Medicare. On the foreign policy front, the most notable product of Johnson's administration was an escalation of U.S. involvement in Vietnam. Opposition to this war would eventually divide the Democrats. Amid this division, Johnson decided not to seek the Democratic nomination in 1968, even though, having served less than half of Kennedy's initial term, he was constitutionally eligible to run again.

The 1968 Democratic National Convention, which nominated Hubert H. Humphrey, was marked by antiwar protest and street violence. That year had seen the assassination of John F. Kennedy's brother, Robert Kennedy, as he campaigned for the Democratic nomination. Humphrey, whose most notable CHALLENGER for the nomination was Eugene McCarthy, would go on to lose the general election to Richard M. Nixon.

The aftermath of the Watergate SCANDAL, which forced Nixon to resign from the presidency, allowed Jimmy Carter to defeat Gerald Ford, who had succeeded (and pardoned) Nixon, in the 1976 election. Carter's administration was continually challenged by a sluggish economy and perceptions of ineffectual leadership, which led to his defeat in 1980 by Republican Ronald Reagan. Reagan led a successful conservative movement that continues to provide the driving force behind the Republican Party. The success of Reagan's movement limited success for Democratic presidential hopefuls through three ELECTION CYCLES. This can be attributed, in part, to the appeal of Reagan's brand of conservatism to some Democrats, who were numerous enough to earn the title REAGAN DEMOCRATS.

A recent push within the Democratic Party, organizationally based in the DEMOCRATIC LEADERSHIP COUNCIL, has advocated a more centrist platform and the selection of more moderate candidates. In 1992, William Jefferson Clinton, a product of this centrist movement, defeated incumbent Republican president George Herbert Walker Bush. While Clinton's election helped reinvigorate the Democratic Party, his 1994 midterm elections saw the Republicans take the House and Senate, ending nearly 60 years of almost continuous Democratic dominance in Congress. Clinton was reelected in 1996 but spent most of his second term mired in a scandal surrounding an adulterous sexual relationship with White House intern Monica Lewinsky. This scandal led to Clinton's impeachment by the House, but not to conviction in the Senate.

In 2000, Clinton's vice president, Al Gore, won the popular vote but lost in a controversial Electoral College tally to Republican nominee George W. Bush. Gore's defeat came despite the unprecedented economic boom experienced by Americans during the Clinton years. The 2000 election results seem to describe a country nearly evenly divided between "blue" and "red"—Democratic and Republican—states. The Northeast and West provide the bases of electoral support for the Democratic Party, while Republicans appear to dominate in the middle of the country and in the South. The Democratic Party's 2004 presidential nominee, Senator John F. Kerry, hailed from Massachusetts, in the heart of the Democrats' northeast stronghold.

The Democratic National Committee continues to serve as the center of the Democratic Party's organization, running the nominating convention, coordinating the development of the platform, and serving as a channel for national campaign FUND-RAISING. Beneath the surface of the DNC is a structure of party members, chairpersons, and committees that link the local organizations with the national party. The Democratic Congressional Campaign Committee (DCCC) and the DEMOCRATIC SENATORIAL CAMPAIGN COMMITTEE (DSCC) are charged with the election of Democrats to the two houses of Congress.

The use of a donkey as the Democratic Party symbol can be traced to a pejorative use of the term "jackass" to describe Andrew Jackson. He and his supporters eventually embraced this attack, placing the image of a donkey on CAMPAIGN LITERATURE. In the 1870s, cartoonist Thomas Nast, perhaps unknowingly, resurrected the symbol, and it has been used ever since. While the Republican Party has formally identified the elephant as its symbol, the donkey remains an unofficial mascot for the Democrats.

Further reading: Maisel, L. Sandy. *Parties and Elections in America: The Electoral Process.* 3rd ed. Lanham, Md.: Rowman & Littlefield, 2002; Sabato, Larry J., and Bruce Larson. *The Party's Just Begun: Shaping Political Parties for America's Future.* 2nd ed. New York: Longman, 2002; Witcover, Jules. *Party of the People: A History of the Democrats.* New York: Random House, 2003.

—Alex Theodoridis

Democratic Party platforms

Democratic Party platforms are generally created by committees that meet at the party's nominating convention, in the months preceding a PRESIDENTIAL ELECTION. They present a unified view of the party's position on issues likely to be important in the election. The process by which the platforms are developed requires balancing between potentially conflicting electoral concerns by appealing to the broader ELECTORATE in order to win the election while also meeting the expectations of the party's core CON-STITUENCY. The platform sets the political agenda by identifying the issues that are important as well as the party's position on these issues. A platform is composed of "planks," specific statements about certain issues. The platform does not play a very prominent role in national elections, as elections have become increasingly candidate-centered, and candidates increasingly strive to prove that they are capable of making decisions separately from established party authorities.

Issue positions are couched within broader themes. The themes of the 2000 DEMOCRATIC PARTY were "peace, prosperity, and progress." Under the umbrella of these three themes, other issues, such as education, were addressed. Parts of the platform also responded directly to the Republicans' proposed policies. The aim of the platform was clearly not just to share the Democrats' message, but to contrast it with the stated goals of the Republicans, particularly presidential candidate George W. Bush.

The Democrats published their first platform in 1840, which was the first American party platform. Both the content and form of the Democratic Party platform have changed considerably over 160 years. In the 19th century platforms did not have overarching themes but rather addressed issues individually. Several factors influenced the tone of Democratic Party platforms, such as incumbency. Different types of issues also became salient at different times. During wartime, international issues took precedence in the platform. At other times, economic issues got more space in the platform. Platforms also became much longer over time.

The following is a breakdown of the important issues in Democratic Party platforms by decade. After platforms were introduced in the Democratic Party in 1840, they often reflected general commitments to certain principles, such as states' rights or a straightforward pro or con position on particular issues, such as the creation of a national bank. Platforms in this decade also took on a decidedly populist tone, praising the idea of the popular will of the American people. Platforms in the 1850s were similar. They included ENDORSEMENTS of past actions, such as the "war in Mexico," and resolutions not to agitate the conflict over slavery.

Not surprisingly, platforms in the 1860s and into the 1870s reflected great concern over Civil War issues such as slavery, sectional conflict, and states' rights. The changing content of the Democratic Party platforms reflected not only the shifts over time in the salience of particular issues, but also fundamental shifts in the ideas espoused by the party. The 1860 platform, for instance, included a condemnation of states' efforts to avoid upholding the Fugitive Slave Law. The 1860 platform (which diverged into two different platforms put forth by two different FACTIONS within the party, the Breckinridge faction and the Douglas faction, although the two platforms were very similar) also expressed uncontroversial messages such as that it was the duty of the government to protect the security and property of its citizens. On the eve of the defeat of the Confederacy, the 1864 Democratic Party platform explicitly defended southern interests and states' rights and, unsurprisingly, focused much more on potential solutions to the war and resolutions to the problems at stake than did the 1860 platform, written before the war began. After the South was defeated, the Democratic platform in 1868 was rife with defensiveness against the defeated ideas of the Confederacy. As in the 1864 platform, it defended states' rights. In response to RECONSTRUCTION-era developments, the platform called for the abolition of the Freedmen's Bureau as well as other "political instrumentalities designed to secure Negro supremacy." Democratic party platforms of the 1860s generally featured fewer than 10 planks, or points of resolution, and emphasized the concerns of the Confederacy in the Civil War, such as states' rights and racial defensiveness, as well as uncontroversial claims about improving security and the economy.

In the 1870s, platforms began to expand in terms of the range of issues covered. Concerns about taxation and economics emerged, as well as demands for civil service reform and an end to the PATRONAGE and corruption that plagued government employment. The 1872 platform stipulated that a condition necessary for true civil service reform was "that no president shall be a candidate for reelection." The 1876 platform emphasized corruption and the need for civil service reform, as well as dissatisfaction with taxation and tariffs. In particular in the 1876 platform, the Democrats' status as the nonincumbent party in the White House was apparent in the language used to condemn the policies of the administration and portray the status quo as detrimental to ordinary people, particularly those in the South. Like the platforms in the 1860s, the superiority of local and state-level government was emphasized. Platforms in this decade were slightly longer, but still not more than 10 to 12 planks.

Party platforms in the 1880s took on a distinctly more partisan and competitive tone than in previous decades. The 1884 platform, which was considerably longer than previous platforms as well, did not divide issues into planks but rather began by condemning the REPUBLICAN PARTY generally and then went into more specific criticisms of particular policies, such as the failure of Congress to significantly reduce tariffs. Platforms in this era also had a decidedly nativist tone, calling for an end to Chinese immigration and denouncing policies that had allegedly allocated resources to nonresident aliens instead of Americans.

In the 1890s, money and economic issues dominated platforms, which denounced "monometallism" as bad for the American people. Platforms also took specific positions such as favoring strengthening the Interstate Commerce Commission in order to limit railroad trusts. Nativist themes continued, as the immigration plank in the 1896 platform called for limited immigration in order to ensure jobs for Americans.

Continuing many of the themes articulated in the 1890 platforms, the 1900 platform continued to be a reaction to the policies of a Republican administration, finding fault with the American military presence in the Philippines. Major themes were similar to previous decades: opposition to trusts, calls for civil service reform and limitation of government expenditure, antiimperialism, and opposition to protective tariffs.

Economic and other domestic concerns continued to prevail in the 1910s. Tariffs, antitrust issues, and economics remained important. The 1912 platform also endorsed the recently passed constitutional amendments creating a federal income tax and calling for the direct popular election of senators. It also contained a plank requesting that the national committee consider PRESIDENTIAL PRIMARIES. Old themes of labor rights, single-term limits for presidents, and civil service reform were still present.

At the outset of the "roaring" 1920s, platforms were self-congratulatory and sang the praises of the achievements of the Wilson administration with regard to economic policy and the winning of World War I. In later platforms, the themes returned to condemnation of Republican policies. Platforms also became considerably longer in the decades following the turn of the century.

Not surprisingly, platforms in the 1930s reacted to the Great Depression. The focus of platforms largely shifted to economic issues such as labor, unemployment, and agricultural policy.

International events of the 1940s influenced platforms in the years leading up to and during U.S. involvement in World War II. The 1940 platform underscored the party's commitment to the Monroe Doctrine and asserted that it opposed U.S. involvement in the war. Economic issues remained largely the same as in previous decades, but the 1940 platform included a section expressing the party's support for "legitimate business." Like the platforms from the 1920s, the 1944 platform touted the achievements of the Democratic administration, particularly in the realm of economic policy, but without specifically mentioning the New Deal. The platform also contained endorsement of the Democratic administration's handling of the war. Policy prescriptions also appeared, such as the endorsement of Jewish immigrants to the Palestinian territory and the endorsement of agricultural policies as postwar programs.

In the aftermath of World War II, platforms in the 1950s contained a great deal of specific information about the party's positions on international issues, such as the United Nations and the state of Israel. The party's stance on immigration was relaxed somewhat from previous decades, with mention of the party's sympathy for refugees from communist countries. The atomic bomb also featured prominently in the 1952 platform. The 1956 platform focused on the failures of President Eisenhower, particularly in the realm of foreign policy.

In the 1960s, as the cold war unfolded, the Democratic Party platforms became increasingly dominated by foreign policy issues such as arms control and America's image in the world. The 1964 platform also contained references to peace and to the assassination of President Kennedy. The 1968 platform defended U.S. involvement in the Vietnam War and praised the Civil Rights Act of 1964.

Once again out of the White House at the beginning of the 1970s, the Democrats focused on condemning the policies of President Nixon in the 1972 platform and explicitly endorsing U.S. withdrawal from the Vietnam conflict. Economic issues took precedence in the 1976 platform, focusing on antiinflation and unemployment solutions, as well as highlighting the failings of the previous Republican administrations. This platform also introduced lengthy sections on education and health care, and underscored social issues such as equal opportunity employment and civil rights. Defense was mentioned relatively late in the platform but was treated extensively, advocating strategic arms limitation and new approaches that placed less emphasis on the size of the defense budget.

The 1980 platform made an attempt to defend the record of the incumbent Democratic administration, acknowledging that in four years the Democrats had not been able to solve all of the country's problems, many of which it "inherited" from periods of Republican leadership. Economic issues featured prominently in the platform, both pointing out achievements of the Carter administration and laying out plans to solve existing problems. Trade, tariffs, and labor concerns were still important issues, reflecting continuing ties to labor constituencies. The platform also expressed the party's commitment to economic opportunity for women and minorities.

By the 1984 election, the Republicans were once again in control of the presidency. The 1984 platform launched a more polemical attack on the Reagan administration, with statements such as, "the President who destroyed the Environmental Protection Agency will decide whether toxic dumps get cleaned up." The 1988 platform reverted to statements focusing on the beliefs of the Democratic Party and emphasized mainly domestic issues. International issues did not appear until relatively near the end of the document, and included human rights promotion, endorsement of arms control, and condemnation of apartheid in South Africa.

The 1992 platform more closely resembled the 1984 platform, in that it focused on the failures of the incumbent administration. Domestic issues were most important, particularly economic issues, though the platform touched on a wide variety of specific domestic issues. The foreign policy sections were mostly dedicated to human rights and democratization issues, and plans to make America more economically competitive with countries such as Germany and Japan.

The 1996 platform represented a dramatic departure from those of the 1970s, 1980s, and 1992 because the incumbent president was a Democrat and the country was experiencing positive developments economically in a time of relative peace. Therefore, the platform was neither defensive nor apologetic, but rather full of plans for improvement and statements of belief about the way the country should be.

The 2000 platform emphasized the accomplishments of the Clinton administration. The platform was divided into three themes: peace, prosperity, and progress, and included plans for innovations in domestic policy such as education and Social Security reform. Perhaps as a reflection of the economic prosperity of the time, or perhaps as an indicator of the attempt to change the party's image, labor issues did not figure as prominently in the platform as in previous decades. The three themed sections of the platform allowed for coverage of both international and domestic issues, making the platform quite extensive.

Since platforms were first introduced by the Democratic Party in 1840, they have changed a great deal in both content and form. Platforms have become much longer and more comprehensive, addressing specific issues at length and eschewing broader statements of principle, at least those that could be controversial. In terms of content, the party's positions on race and equality have clearly shifted since before the Civil War. In later decades, a greater commitment to progressive social issues can be seen in the platform, while the commitment to labor issues is downplayed.

Further reading: Gerring, John. *Party Ideologies in America, 1828–1996.* Cambridge: Cambridge University Press, 1998; Schlesinger, Arthur M., Jr., ed. *History of U.S. Political Parties.* New York: Chelsea House, 1973.

—Julia R. Azari

Democratic Party symbol

Though first used as a means to insult the DEMOCRATIC PARTY, the donkey mascot has been used in conjunction with the Democratic Party since 1828, even though it has never been officially adopted by the party. The connection between the donkey and the Democratic Party originated with Andrew Jackson's 1828 presidential campaign. Jackson's opponents used a "play on words" with his name by labeling him a "jackass." Rather than being offended by the moniker, Jackson took advantage of the association and began using a donkey in his campaign posters. The donkey continued to be associated with Jackson into his presidency as a symbol of Jackson's stubbornness.

Because Jackson was a Democrat, an association grew among Jackson, the Democratic Party, and the donkey. Political cartoonists further popularized the use of the don-

Carter supporter dressed in donkey head *(CORBIS)*

key as the Democratic Party symbol in an 1837 cartoon titled "A Modern Baalim and His Ass." The cartoon depicted Jackson leading a donkey that refused to follow. Here, the donkey represented the Democratic Party that refused to be led by the former president even though Jackson was considered the Democratic leader.

Famed political cartoonist Thomas Nast regularly portrayed the Democratic Party as a donkey and helped cement the donkey as the Democratic Party's symbol. Beginning in 1870, Nast published cartoons in *Harper's Weekly* that used the donkey to represent individual party members, Democratic editors, and newspapers owned by the Democratic Party. The first of Nast's cartoons that associated the Democratic Party with the donkey showed a donkey kicking a dead lion. The dead lion represented Lincoln's secretary of war, Edwin M. Stanton, who had recently died. Nast's intent was to show the sentiment of the Democrats' antiwar FACTION. Other newspapers and political cartoonists reinforced the association. In 1880, the *New*

York Daily Graphic portrayed Democratic presidential candidate Winfield S. Hancock leading a team of party crusaders into battle while riding a donkey. Because Hancock was expected to lose that election, the portrayal suggested a weak, misdirected party.

The Democratic Party sees the donkey as an appropriate symbol because it is loveable, humble, homely, intelligent, and courageous. The REPUBLICAN PARTY sees the donkey as an appropriate Democratic Party symbol because it is stubborn, silly, and ridiculous. In any case, the donkey has become the undisputed symbol of the nation's oldest POLITICAL PARTY, the Democratic Party.

Further reading: Democratic Party. Available online. URL: http://www.democrats.org. Accessed August 10, 2005; Witcover, Jules. *Party of the People: A History of the Democrats.* New York: Random House, 2003.

—Terri Fine

Democratic-Republican Party

The Democratic-Republican Party, also referred to as the Madisonians or the Jeffersonians, began as a loosely aligned group that shared their opposition to the Federalist programs introduced in the 1790s. Many of these programs, proposed by Alexander Hamilton, favored merchants, speculators, and the rich. Opposition was led by James Madison in the House of Representatives and Thomas Jefferson as secretary of state.

Although the term *party* was avoided in the early 1790s, events of that decade developed a definite split in American IDEOLOGY. When Hamilton, as secretary of the Treasury, proposed his financial plan to Congress, opposition expanded. The Federalist plan advocated funding the national debt, the power to tax, and the establishment of a national bank. The national debt would incorporate foreign and domestic debt as well as state debts. Opposition to this funding came from states that had already paid off much of their debt. Also, the outstanding debt had been trading at a discount and was purchased by speculators. Hamilton's plan called for funding at par, which rewarded the speculators without benefiting those who provided goods and services during the Revolution.

The power to tax upset farmers in the West. They feared that a lack of hard currency would prevent them from paying taxes and result in foreclosure. They feared that eastern interests would then purchase their land for virtually nothing.

The constitutionality of the bank pitted Hamilton and Jefferson against one another. Jefferson believed in a narrow interpretation of the Constitution, which meant only those powers specifically mentioned in the document were permissible. Hamilton's broad interpretation saw the "necessary and proper clause" as the method of chartering a national bank since it would benefit the government by collecting taxes. George Washington agreed with Hamilton's interpretation and signed the national bank into existence.

The major break between the two FACTIONS occurred over the ratification of Jay's Treaty. John Jay, former chief justice of the Supreme Court, was sent by Washington to negotiate with Great Britain about neutral rights for American ships. The English and the French were engaged in a war, and the Democratic-Republicans felt a stronger connection to France than to Great Britain, viewing the French as an ally in democracy. When Jay's Treaty revealed an alliance with the British, the Democratic-Republicans were outraged. In hindsight, Jay's Treaty might have been the best relationship possible between the fledgling United States and the powerful British, but it did not comply with all the hopes of Americans. The treaty was ratified in the Senate in a partisan vote. The Democratic-Republicans in the House of Representatives attempted to derail the treaty by not appropriating the needed funding. The House eventually passed the appropriation bill, and the two factions were cemented as political parties.

The Democratic-Republicans won the election of 1800, putting Thomas Jefferson into the presidency. The FEDERALIST PARTY lost national power but remained in existence until after the War of 1812. Jefferson, Madison, and James Monroe were all elected to the highest office as Democratic-Republicans. By the election of 1824, however, the Democratic-Republican Party had developed factions. Four candidates, all claiming to be part of the party, ran for the presidency. John Quincy Adams, Henry Clay, William Crawford, and Andrew Jackson split the electoral vote, causing the House of Representatives to make a decision. Adams, with the support of Clay, won the presidency under the banner of National Republicans. By the election of 1828, Jackson ran as a Democrat and defeated Adams. The Democratic-Republicans had divided and would never again have a national CONSTITUENCY.

The Democratic-Republican Party was the first political organization to truly function as a party. The Federalists never really accepted opposition as legitimate. The Democratic-Republicans organized and elected three two-term presidents, Jefferson, Madison, and Monroe. They gained control of both the House of Representatives and the Senate. Although the ideology of the party seemed to shift between 1800 and 1824, the Democratic-Republicans represented the majority of Americans and acknowledged their positions. The party founded by Madison and Jefferson developed a baseline for future political parties and the peaceful transition of government from one party to another.

Further reading: Elkins, Stanley, and Eric McKitrick. *The Age of Federalism.* New York: Oxford University Press, 1993; Smelser, Marshall. *The Democratic Republic 1801–1815.* Prospect Heights, Ill.: Waveland Press, 1968.

—Sarah Miller

Democratic Senatorial Campaign Committee

The Democratic Senatorial Campaign Committee (DSCC) is a NATIONAL PARTY COMMITTEE made up of Democratic senators, whose goal is to elect greater numbers of Democrats to the U.S. Senate. Its rival is the NATIONAL REPUBLICAN SENATORIAL COMMITTEE, which tries to elect Republicans to those same Senate seats.

Formed in the mid-1970s in the wake of Watergate and the FEDERAL ELECTION CAMPAIGN ACT, these committees were created to raise funds for Senate elections and distribute those funds to current senators facing reelection as well as to promising CHALLENGERS of their own party. It is through this collection and distribution of campaign funds that the DSCC makes its most significant impact on the biennial Senate elections. Prominent Democratic senators can amass large enough campaign warchests to ward off potential challengers, vulnerable Democratic incumbents have access to the money they need to launch effective campaigns, and promising Democratic challengers—or Democratic challengers facing weak Republican incumbents—can gain the resources they need for the daunting task of winning an open-seat election or defeating an incumbent senator. In addition, over the years the DSCC has adapted to provide even greater support to Democratic senatorial candidates, providing everything from polling and media advice to issue research and techniques for campaigning on the Internet.

This support, both financial and otherwise, can prove crucial to determining both individual Senate races and the overall control of the Senate itself. This is especially true due to the extremely narrow divisions of power in the Senate following the 2000 and 2002 elections. For example, in 2002, Democratic senator Tim Johnson won reelection to his South Dakota Senate seat by a mere 0.15 percent of the vote. Similarly, in 2002, Democratic senator Jean Carnahan lost her Missouri Senate seat by only 1 percent of the vote. For these reasons, the DSCC tends to focus its resources very carefully on those select races in which its support could tip the balance in favor of the Democratic candidate. This mostly involves heavy investment in open-seat races (races with no incumbent on the ballot), and those select cases of weak Democratic incumbents or strong Democratic challengers.

Further reading: Democratic Senatorial Campaign Committee. Available online. URL: http://www.dscc.org. Accessed August 10, 2005; Herrnson, Paul S. *Congressional Elections: Campaigning at Home and in Washington.* Washington, D.C.: CQ Press, 2003; Jacobson, Gary C. *The Politics of Congressional* Elections. 5th ed. New York: Addison-Wesley, 2000; Kloodny, Robin. *Pursuing Majorities: Congressional Campaign Committees in American Politics.* Norman: University of Oklahoma Press, 1998.

—Brian DiSarro

direct mail

Direct mail is persuasive political mail sent directly to voters in an attempt to influence their voting decision. The most common form of direct mail is the multiple fold, full-color flyer printed on high-quality, glossy paper. Direct mail pieces also exist as letters contained in envelopes, stand-alone postcards, and electronic mail. While television, radio, and print forms of voter outreach dominate modern campaigns, direct mail has three distinct advantages over these forms of communication: cost, TARGETING, and flexibility.

Campaigns employ direct mail because the costs are often substantially less than the costs associated with other popular forms of voter outreach. The cost of conventional direct mail includes printing and postage, while electronic mail is virtually free to deliver. In addition to these expenses, campaigns typically purchase postal addresses or e-mail addresses (i.e., mail lists) from direct mail firms that specialize in collecting such information. Direct mail campaigns are particularly common in populous media markets such as New York and Los Angeles, in which CONGRESSIONAL DISTRICTS of more than 600,000 people make up only about 10 percent of the media market, driving television advertising costs out of reach for many candidates. Cost is also a reason why direct mail is the most common form of campaign communication for smaller campaigns, such as for state legislature, city council, and school board.

The second advantage of direct mail is targeting. Since direct mail pieces are sent to specific voters or households, campaigns can purchase or create their own mailing lists that target particular voters with specific information that is relevant to them. By knowing which party a person belong to, if they give money to certain types of candidates, if they subscribe to a specific magazine or newspaper, and other relevant information, the campaign can craft specific letters for specific types of voters. Campaigns can use direct mail to transmit more partisan and ideological messages to their partisan base voters, while using less partisan messages to attract SWING VOTERs. The power of targeting helps explain why campaigns that can afford large purchases of televised advertising continue to use direct mail.

The third advantage of direct mail is flexibility. Direct mail offers campaigns flexibility in at least two ways. First, improvements in word processing and database programs allow campaigns to include personal information in a direct mail piece, including a voter's name and polling place. Second, direct mail provides campaigns the flexibility to more easily respond to attacks by opponents, particularly in the last few days of a campaign. Direct mail, especially letters signed by the candidate, can be turned around in 24 to 48 hours. Combined, these advantages assure direct mail a prominent place in American electoral POLITICS.

Further reading: Green, Donald P. *Get out the Vote!: How to Increase Voter Turnout.* Washington, D.C.: Brookings

Institution Press, 2004; Newman, Bruce I. *The Marketing of the President: Political Marketing as Campaign Strategy.* Thousand Oaks, Calif.: Sage Publications, 1994; Trent, Judith S. *Political Campaign Communication: Principles and Practices.* Lanham, Md.: Rowman & Littlefield, 2004.

—Brian Arbour

direct primary

A direct primary is an election in which citizens select nominees from the various political parties to run for elective offices. Unlike GENERAL ELECTIONs, in which the candidates are from different parties and the winner of the contest will take the office, PRIMARY elections are intraparty contests, that is, elections in which individuals within the same party vie for the party's NOMINATION for a particular office and the ability to square off with the nominees from other parties.

It is important to note that political parties are not mentioned in the U.S. Constitution, and the notion of primary elections was not considered by the nation's founders. Direct citizen participation was a concern, however. There were many safeguards against the "tyranny of the majority" built into the document to limit direct citizen involvement, such as the ELECTORAL COLLEGE and appointment of senators. As political parties developed, the process of selecting nominees to run for both state and federal offices became the domain of the parties, with little or no input from citizens in the selection process.

The movement for direct citizen participation in this process began largely at the state and local levels, and like many political reforms in America, made great progress during the Progressive Era of the late 19th and early 20th centuries. True to Progressive ideals, the effort to incorporate citizens into political processes was seen as a way to combat corruption and limit the concentration of political power. By allowing citizens rather than the party elite to decide who the party nominees would be, the direct primary would reduce the power of PARTY BOSSES and encourage greater citizen participation. Wisconsin became the first state to enact direct primary laws for statewide offices in 1903, the effort led by the Progressive icon Robert LaFollette, and nearly all states had adopted the direct primary for federal and state offices by the mid-1920s.

The typical methods for determining party nominees prior to primary elections were either conventions or caucuses. DELEGATES representing the PARTY ORGANIZATIONS would meet formally in a nomination convention, while caucuses consisted of many smaller, less-formal gatherings of partisans whose cumulative decisions would produce a nominee. Both methods were susceptible to the domination of the process by established forces within the party. In conventions, delegates represented special interests and the party leadership and organization rather than the rank and file party members. Caucuses were vulnerable to "packing" by those representing the established interests.

The logic for the introduction of the direct primary for choosing party nominees was straightforward: If the party controlled the processes of nomination, then those who controlled the party would control the process and ultimately control the political activity of government. Relieving the party of such control would serve as way to return power to the public and ensure the integrity of democratic principles in the process.

While most states had incorporated the direct primary into the electoral process via statute or constitutional provision by the 1920s, this requirement applies only to offices that represent the individual states or political subdivisions within the state. Statewide elected offices such as governor or secretary of state, state legislative posts, and offices in the United States Congress all fall under these restrictions because these positions represent citizens within a state. State jurisdiction for the direct primary does not extend to party nominations for the president of the United States, however, because the president represents all citizens of the nation. The use of the direct primary for presidential nominees was not a significant factor in the presidential nominating process until reforms were adopted by the major parties in the early 1970s.

Because primary elections are intraparty contests to decide the party nomination for an office, there exists debate on how these elections should operate and who should be able to participate. While separate primary elections for different political parties typically do not occur for statewide offices, states differ in how these contests are waged. In states with closed primaries, only registered members of a POLITICAL PARTY are allowed to participate in the selection of that party's nominee. This method is said to ensure that party nominees will represent the preferences of the party membership but is criticized for excluding citizens who are not officially affiliated with any political party or are members of minor parties that may not field candidates in all elections. Alternatively, some states use an open primary system in which any registered voter can vote for any candidate, regardless of voter or candidate political party affiliation. While this method includes INDEPENDENT and nonaffiliated voters, it also provides the possibility of strategic CROSSOVER VOTING, whereby voters cast BALLOTs for the candidate from an opposing party considered to be the weakest CHALLENGER to their party's presumptive nominee. Still other states employ a mixed primary system whereby voters who are registered members of political parties can vote only for their party's candidates, yet independent and nonaffiliated voters are able to participate as well.

The effects of the direct primary on elections, candidates, participation, and parties are the subject of considerable debate. Conventional wisdom suggests that direct primaries weakened the hold of special interests and political party machines on the processes of candidate selection, thus weakening the role of political parties in general. Consequently, public preferences dictate party nominee selection, and a wider range of participants seeking elective office has emerged, marking a fundamental shift in American POLITICS from party-centered politics to candidate-centered politics. Further, the shift of power away from the parties has required the parties to become more responsive to the public, and there has been a loss of party strength and discipline, particularly in the U.S. Congress.

Others, however, challenge such claims on many counts. Primary voters are argued to be more like members of the party elite than the general voting public, and therefore the claim of public preference as a guide for nominee selection is questionable. While the selection of party nominees is decided by votes, the interests and FACTIONS within parties still have a great deal of influence over the field of candidates. Additionally, some argue that the direct primary has not fundamentally shifted power away from parties, but from monolithic power centers within the parties, forcing party organizations to become more competitive in search of public support and allowing individual candidates to compete for support within the party organization. While the direct primary enables citizens to assert a greater voice in the process of nominee selection, places greater emphasis on candidates, and may have played a role in diminishing strict adherence to party positions by its members, the effects of the direct primary seem neither as far-reaching or dramatic as many early accounts predicted.

Further reading: Merriam, Charles E., and Louise Overacker. *Primary Elections*. Chicago: University of Chicago Press, 1928; Ranney, Austin. *Curing the Mischiefs of Faction: Party Reform in America*. Berkeley: University of California Press, 1975; Ware, Alan. *The American Direct Primary*. Cambridge: Cambridge University Press, 2002.
—Joel A. Rayan

dirty campaign tricks

This term refers to underhanded, often illegal, activities to undermine electoral support for a political opponent. The trick may be blatant lies or distortions of the position or behavior of an opponent. Perhaps the most mundane type of dirty trick is the defacement or stealing of an opponent's campaign signs and posters. On occasion, a candidate or his or her backers remove their own candidate's signs and publicly blame the opposing campaign for that act.

Accounts of early election campaigns in the United States and Britain confirm that such tactics are not new, although the specific phrase *dirty tricks* is primarily associated with the Watergate SCANDAL of the early 1970s. While several members of President Nixon's administration committed dirty tricks, the term came to be linked with Daniel Segretti, whose name in Italian means "secret." He was the principal facilitator of activities to impair first the 1972 campaigns of what the White House deemed the more

formidable aspirants for the Democratic presidential NOMINATION, and second the GENERAL ELECTION campaign of the nominee, South Dakota's senator George McGovern.

Segretti's dirty tricks were considered inconsequential but were significant because they had a destabilizing effect. Tricks included offering bogus free lunches and false bulk orders of pizza and liquor to those attending FUND-RAISING events for Maine's senator Edmund Muskie. The result was animosity among Democrats who thought other Democrats were performing these deceptions. Segretti was active in 16 states that held Democratic primaries and contacted at least 80 people to set up an organization. His work in the first two primaries, Florida and New Hampshire, was notably effective. In Florida, he distributed 300 Day-Glo posters that said "Help Muskie in Bussing More Children Now." At a George Wallace rally there, printed cards were handed out that read "If You Liked Hitler You'll Love Wallace." On the reverse was printed "Vote Muskie." Segretti also sent out letters on which he forged the signatures of Senators Hubert Humphrey of Minnesota and Henry Jackson of Washington, who were also Democratic presidential aspirants.

Segretti, who operated largely on his own as to the specific actions to be taken, reported to White House appointments secretary Dwight Chapin, who took orders from H. R. "Bob" Haldeman, one of President Nixon's two principal aides. None of the three had substantial political experience, which may have contributed to their misbehavior. All were eventually convicted for their parts in the larger Watergate scandal and served prison time.

Efforts to dissuade candidates and their advocates from the use of dirty tricks have usually been unsuccessful, each side in an election believing that the other would not abstain from underhanded tactics despite what she or he might say—or sign. Just prior to the 1954 CONGRESSIONAL ELECTIONS, a group of distinguished Republicans and Democrats created the Fair Campaign Practices Committee (FCPC), which adopted a code that was mailed to every congressional candidate to sign and return to the committee. It dissolved after the election. In early 1958, the committee was revived on a permanent basis, with Charles P. Taft, son of the former president and brother of a leading U.S. senator, as chairman and Bruce Felknor as executive director.

Felknor continued in that post until the FCPC was disbanded in 1978. The FCPC never had any punitive powers but used disclosure of shady campaign tactics to enlighten voters about candidates' ethical conduct. Understandably, candidates exposed by the committee were critical of the FCPC. Its demise was attributed to two primary factors: It never had a financial angel to fund it and was persistently in need of money. Moreover, while the Internal Revenue Service initially granted the FCPC an exemption from taxes, throughout its two-decade existence the FCPC was persistently harassed by that taxation agency. Felknor's books on his FCPC tenure probably have the largest inventory of dirty campaign tricks of any source. No comparable non-partisan entity has emerged to succeed the FCPC and monitor campaign practices.

Often unofficial surrogates of a candidate conduct dirty tricks. An example is the infamous 1988 "Willie Horton" television ad, which condemned the Massachusetts prison furlough policy that resulted in Horton committing murder in another state. This implied that Massachusetts governor Michael Dukakis, the Democratic presidential candidate, was responsible for Horton's furlough. This television spot, which was not run by his opponent, was misleading since Dukakis had no role in enacting the furlough law, signed years before by a Republican governor.

In 2004, television ads from a group of Vietnam veterans condemned the Vietnam record of Democratic presidential nominee, Massachusetts senator John Kerry. There were clear contradictions by some spokesmen in the ad with what they had previously said about Kerry. Officials of the campaign committee of President George W. Bush denied any connection with the anti-Kerry veterans group, but several Bush supporters, including those who contributed large sums or other assistance to Bush campaigns, also provided funding for the ads or gave other aid to the anti-Kerry group.

Response to this ad illustrates a frequent consequence of surrogate ploys: In reporting and covering surrogate operations, the national media unintentionally provide far more extensive dissemination of the surrogate message than the original broadcast of the ad. This was also true of the 1964 Democratic television clip of a small girl plucking petals from a daisy, followed by a photograph of a nuclear explosion, implying that Arizona's senator Barry Goldwater, the Republican presidential candidate, would use nuclear weapons if elected. President Lyndon Johnson immediately ordered that broadcast of the clip be stopped. It was, but it has persistently been rebroadcast as an example of a dirty campaign trick.

Richard Nixon often complained that the Democratic prankster Dick Tuck, who tormented Nixon in many campaigns, mistreated him. At a 1962 Nixon rally, Tuck distributed signs and fortune cookies printed with "Welcome Nixon" and a phrase in Chinese below, which said "What about the Hughes Loan?" That referred to a $250,000 loan to Nixon from Howard Hughes, which had not been repaid according to press reports at the time.

On occasion, it is difficult to determine whether a campaign tactic is a dirty trick. In 1950, when Florida senator Claude Pepper sought renomination, his PRIMARY election opponent, George Smathers, mentioned that Pepper's wife, who was active in theatrical circles, was a "thespian," a term apparently unfamiliar to Florida voters. Observers thought this label was significant in Smathers's victory in the primary, which led to his succeeding Pepper in the Senate.

With constitutional protection of free speech and free press and disagreement on what constitutes proper campaign tactics, it is likely that dirty campaign tricks will endure in American electoral POLITICS.

Further reading: Emery, Fred. *Watergate: The Corruption of American Politics and the Fall of Richard Nixon.* New York: Times Books, 1994; Felknor, Bruce L. *Dirty Politics.* New York: Norton, 1966; Felknor, Bruce L. *Political Mischief: Smear, Sabotage, and Reform in U.S. Elections.* New York: Praeger, 1992; Kutler, Stanley I. *The Wars of Watergate.* New York: Knopf, 1990.

—Thomas Phillip Wolf

disenfranchisement

Throughout most of the history of the United States there have been groups of citizens who have been denied the vote for one reason or another. At the time the United States achieved independence, most people in this country could not vote. After the Revolutionary War, the franchise was predominantly limited to white, property-owning males and, in some cases, further restricted to those who acknowledged the existence of a god or swore an allegiance to Christianity.

Many restrictions were initiated to be certain that only those with a "stake in society" voted. It was generally considered undesirable for people who were dependent upon others to vote. Women, for example, were considered to be dependent on adult men and consequently were denied the vote. Other groups of people who have at one time or another experienced disenfranchisement in this country include African Americans, Roman Catholics, Jewish Americans, non-landowners, immigrants, Native Americans, residents of the District of Columbia, and convicted felons.

The prerequisites to vote have varied from state to state, with ownership of property being one of the most common stipulations in the early republic. Of the original 13 states, 10 stipulated a landowning requirement, while states admitted after 1790 did not have property-owning qualifications. Support for landowning qualifications began to disappear following the Revolution and continued to decline through the mid-19th century. Virginia was the last state to retain a real property requirement in all elections held in the state, and North Carolina finally eliminated its landowning requirement for Senate elections in the mid-1850s. On the eve of the Civil War, only two property requirements remained in existence in the United States, one applying to foreign-born residents in Rhode Island and the other a New York provision applying to African Americans.

African Americans were legally guaranteed the right to vote in 1870 with the ratification of the FIFTEENTH AMENDMENT, though it took another hundred years of struggle to overcome legal and illegal voting restrictions faced by African Americans. The year the amendment was ratified, hundreds of freedmen were killed by violence precisely aimed at preventing them from voting or holding office. Beginning in 1890, there was a systematic effort by southern states to legally disenfranchise African-American voters. Democrats attempted to strengthen their hold on the South by modifying voting laws in ways that would not overtly violate the Fifteenth Amendment, though they would suppress the black vote. In addition to physical violence against African Americans, they were subject to racial GERRYMANDERing, GRANDFATHER CLAUSES, LITERACY TESTS, POLL TAXes with procedures making payment difficult, restrictive registration laws, and white primaries.

Many of these devices of discrimination were used in the South well into the 20th century. The WHITE PRIMARY excluded African Americans from voting in Democratic primaries in the South. Because the outcome of GENERAL ELECTIONS in the one-party-dominated South was for all intents and purposes determined in the Democratic primaries, the white primaries effectively disfranchised African Americans. This highly effective method of denying African Americans the right to vote was declared unconstitutional by the Supreme Court in *SMITH V. ALLWRIGHT*, 321 U.S. 649 (1944).

It was not until 1964, with the ratification of the TWENTY-FOURTH AMENDMENT, that the poll tax, which many southern states had made cumulative for even greater effect, was struck down. The literacy test was another means to disenfranchise African Americans as well as immigrants. In the 1840s the idea of literacy tests surfaced in discussions in northern states as a technique to prevent immigrants from voting. While the idea never made it past the discussion stage in the North, it reappeared in the South as another way to disenfranchise African Americans. Support for these tests became widespread in the 1870s. As late as 1959, by *Lassiter v. Northhampton County Bd. of Elections*, 360 U.S. 45 (1959), the Supreme Court upheld some form of the literacy test. It was not until *Oregon v Mitchell*, 400 U.S. 112 (1970) that the Court held Congress did have the power, via the Fifteenth Amendment, to ban literacy tests or other means of disenfranchising blacks in both federal and state elections.

As early as 1838 women were allowed to vote in Kentucky in school elections if they were widows or unmarried and owned property subject to taxation for schools. Throughout the 19th century more states and territories gave women the right to vote in one type of election or another. All states or territories where women had achieved full enfranchisement in the 19th century were west of the Mississippi River. A total of 20 states or territories had fully enfranchised women prior to the ratification of the NINETEENTH AMENDMENT in 1920. The mobilization for World War I gave new energy to the SUFFRAGE fight for women in the early 20th century. President Woodrow Wilson was so impressed with the work of women for the war effort that he renewed earlier calls he had made for their full enfranchisement.

The most important modern milestone in the struggle for universal voting rights occurred when Congress passed the 1965 Voting Rights Act. The legislation addressed discriminatory voting practices by attempting to curb disenfranchisement, particularly in states and counties where fewer than 50 percent of adults had gone to the polls in 1964. This act stated that not only were poll taxes racially discriminatory, but also they kept economically deprived people from voting. This act was consistent with section two of the Twenty-Fourth Amendment, which gave Congress the power to pass legislation to prevent poll taxes.

By the early 1980s through Supreme Court decisions, actions by the executive branch, and legislation passed by Congress, the United States had achieved near universal suffrage. Economic discrimination, literacy tests, unreasonable residency requirements, and other means to prevent citizens of this country from voting had been eliminated and, with the ratification of the TWENTY-SIXTH AMENDMENT in 1971 (lowering the voting age to 18) suffrage rights have never been greater in the United States.

Further reading: Hine, Diane Clark. *Black Victory: The Rise and Fall of the White Primary in Texas*. Columbia: University of Missouri Press, 2003; Key, V. O. *Southern Politics in State and Nation*. New York: Knopf, 1949; Keyssar, Alexander. *The Right to Vote: The Contested History of Democracy in the United States*. New York: Basic Books, 2000.

—J. Mark Alcorn

Dixiecrats

The Dixiecrats, also known as the States' Rights Democratic Party, was a minor POLITICAL PARTY that splintered from the national DEMOCRATIC PARTY in 1948. The Dixiecrats sought to preserve the economic and social hierarchy of the South, which included the subordination of African Americans and the perpetuation of segregation. The States' Rights Party also opposed the centralization of power in the hands of the federal government and the development of the public welfare state under the New Deal. The Dixiecrats feared that increasing interference by the federal government, with its liberal stance toward civil rights and the empowerment of the laboring class, would disrupt the status quo in the South. Although the States' Rights Party was short-lived, its formation was significant for marking the initial dissolution of the NEW DEAL COALITION in the South and for signaling the beginning of the end of Democratic Party dominance in that region of the country.

Although conservative SOUTHERN DEMOCRATS were already disgruntled by the economic and social changes

Governor Strom Thurmond of South Carolina, the States' Rights presidential candidate (Dixiecrat) in 1948 *(New York World-Telegram and* Sun *Newspaper Photograph Collection, Library of Congress)*

they witnessed as a result of their party's New Deal liberalism and World War II, it was ultimately the national party's acceptance of a new civil rights plank in its platform that galvanized the Dixiecrats to bolt and form a new party. In February 1948, President Truman addressed Congress on the topic of civil rights and presented a 10-point program aimed at improving the status of African Americans. This plan included provisions for creating a permanent Commission on Civil Rights, protecting blacks' voting rights, offering federal protection against lynching, and establishing a Fair Employment Practice Commission to eliminate discrimination in the workplace. Many southerners were enraged by these proposals and condemned Truman for creating a rift within the Democratic Party. Responding to Truman's speech, Representative William M. Colmer of Mississippi declared to Congress: "Not only did that message provoke serious racial controversies, but it raised anew the issue of the rights of the sovereign states as against a strong centralized government and drove a devastating wedge into the unity of the Democratic Party." Conservative southern Democrats pledged themselves to oppose Truman's NOMINATION for the upcoming PRESIDENTIAL ELECTION at their party's convention later that year.

When the Democratic convention met in July, southerners were unable to achieve this goal. Truman was chosen as the presidential nominee by an overwhelming majority. Furthermore, the Democrats adopted a new pro–civil rights platform. In the eyes of most civil rights leaders, this platform was quite moderate and rather disappointing, but to conservative southerners it was a devastating blow. It was the catalyst that triggered 13 DELEGATEs from Alabama and Mississippi to leave the convention in protest.

Responding to Truman's renomination and the civil rights plank, disaffected southerners gathered in Birmingham to develop a strategy to deny both major parties enough electoral votes to win the election outright. States' Rights Democrats believed that they could replace Truman on southern BALLOTs with their own candidates, or at least gain a spot on ballots for States' Rights Democratic nominees. Dixiecrats succeeded in replacing the national Democratic candidates and electors in South Carolina, Alabama, Mississippi, and Louisiana. In the other old Confederacy states, along with North Dakota and Kentucky, States' Rights Democrats were listed as a third party. Following the Birmingham convention, Dixiecrats met in Houston to nominate then governors Strom Thurmond of South Carolina and Fielding Wright of Mississippi as their presidential and vice presidential candidates, respectively.

Although only Alabama and Mississippi pledged their electors for the Dixiecrat ticket at the convention, the new party's leadership developed an election strategy that anticipated the support of the rest of the southern bloc in the November election. According to this strategy, if the Dixiecrats could secure 127 ELECTORAL COLLEGE votes in the South, they could prevent either of the two national parties from gaining the 266 votes needed to win the election outright. As a result, the House of Representatives would be required to decide the election, and the Dixiecrats believed they could exercise considerable influence over this decision.

However, when the votes were tallied in November, the States' Rights Party fell far short of its goal. It won only four states: Alabama, Mississippi, South Carolina, and Louisiana, plus one vote from Tennessee for a total of 39 votes. Rather than sweeping the entire South, the Dixiecrats were able to carry only those states where they had manipulated state election laws to list Thurmond and Wright as the official Democratic candidates, and kept the names of Truman and his running mate, Alben W. Barkley, off the ballot. Shortly after this defeat, Thurmond began to distance himself from the Dixiecrats. He hoped to broaden his appeal in order to win a seat in the Senate in the 1950 election and would eventually leave the Democrats altogether in 1964 when he joined the REPUBLICAN PARTY. Those Dixiecrats who served in Congress were never expelled from the national legislature despite their rebellion against the national party. In fact, they subsequently pulled off a major victory against Truman by successfully thwarting all the CIVIL RIGHTS LEGISLATION he proposed to Congress. Not a single measure from his 10-point plan was passed.

Following the 1948 election, most Dixiecrats returned begrudgingly to the Democratic Party. However, with the increased presence of liberal voices for civil rights in the national party, southern Democrats began to defect to the Republican Party, particularly after the 1964, 1968, and 1980 PRESIDENTIAL ELECTIONS. Most notably, the 1948 Dixiecrat presidential nominee, Strom Thurmond, left the Democratic Party to join the Republicans in 1964. Many scholars believe that the 1948 States' Rights Democratic Party was the first sign of fission within the Democratic New Deal Coalition and the modern Republican Party's success in the South.

Although the Dixiecrats were not successful in establishing a permanent third party, their defection from the Democrats proved to be an important first step in cracking the "solid South." In Thurmond's words, the Dixiecrats proved they could "pull four states away from the national Democratic Party and show the sky wouldn't fall. Ever since then the South was independent." In addition to moving the South closer to a TWO-PARTY SYSTEM, today the Dixiecrats are remembered for their opposition to civil rights and their support for segregation. This legacy remains quite powerful, even 50 years later, as evidenced by the country's reaction to comments made by former Senate Majority Leader Trent Lott at the 100th birthday party of Strom Thurmond in December 2002. After Lott proudly recalled that his state of Mississippi had voted for Thurmond as the Dixiecrat candidate in 1948, Lott remarked that if the rest of the country had supported the Dixiecrats and Thurmond, the nation "wouldn't have had all these problems over all these years." Lott was severely criticized for this expression of support for the ideals of the Dixiecrats. He apologized for his remarks, but still received pressure from the members of both major parties to step down as Majority Leader. On December 20, 2002, Lott resigned his leadership post but kept his seat in the Senate.

Further reading: Ader, Emile B. "Why the Dixiecrats Failed." *Journal of Politics* 5, no. 3 (1953): 356–369; Frederickson, Kari. *The Dixiecrat Revolt and the End of the Solid South, 1932–1968.* Chapel Hill: University of North Carolina Press, 2001; Key, V. O. *Southern Politics in State and Nation.* New York: Knopf, 1949.

—Jill M. Budny and J. Michael Bitzer

doctrine of responsible parties

The doctrine of responsible parties, also known as the doctrine (or theory) of party government, holds three basic tenets: First, that a POLITICAL PARTY should have a well-defined IDEOLOGY that translates into a clear set of policy positions; second, that candidates running for office under that party label should adhere to that ideology and advance those policy positions in their campaigns; and third, that once members of that party are elected to office they should carry out those policy positions, that is, they should keep their campaign promises. Proponents of the doctrine argue that it is the best party system because under it voters can choose between candidates with clearly identified competing policy agendas and can easily hold the winning candidates accountable if they fail, once in office, to act on their campaign promises.

In the American context, the doctrine is most closely associated with the 1950 report of the Committee on Political Parties, a group of leading political scientists and public administration specialists formed by the American Political Science Association in the late 1940s to study the condition of the American political party system and make recommendations to improve it. That report, entitled "Toward a More Responsible Two Party System," comprised a set of normative goals designed to move the American party system, as the title states, toward greater political responsibility. The centerpiece of the report was its recommendation that each party conduct its own business in a coherent and disciplined manner. While the normative goals speak to the character of the parties, the committee also contemplated a party system comprised of two strong parties, rather than just one dominant party. Indeed, perhaps the most critical aspect of the doctrine is that there be meaningful party competition.

The most energetic proponent of the doctrine of political party responsibility was E. E. Schattschneider, a mid-20th-century political scientist. Schattschneider, who was chairman of the Committee on Political Parties and also sat on the report-drafting subcommittee, authored the most persuasive argument in favor of responsible parties, *Party Government*, published in 1942. That book details the theory and logic behind the doctrine of party government, emphasizing that elections should be conducted so that voters can make sense of the competing political parties' agendas. Schattschneider's now famous argument suggested that "democracy is not to be found in the parties, but between the parties." By this he meant that democracy was best served—that voters could make the most meaningful and informed choices between candidates—when those candidates adhered to coherent party platforms that reflected clearly articulated competing policy positions. According to Schattschneider, the goals of democracy are best served by truly COMPETITIVE ELECTIONS in which the parties' opposing positions are plainly obvious to voters.

It has been difficult to fully develop a responsible TWO-PARTY SYSTEM in the United States because the Constitution's framers intentionally structured the federal government to prevent any branch of government or any one group of citizens from becoming too powerful. This "Madisonian constitutionalism," that is, the federal system of checks and balances and separated powers, makes it difficult for political parties to be coherent and cohesive. Different elections—for governor, for senator, for representative, or for president—appeal to different electorates, each with its own set of concerns, attitudes, interests, and preferences. In contrast, in Great Britain governmental power is largely consolidated in one branch, Parliament, and there in the House of Commons. Consequently, the 1950 report presents only a contingent version of the party responsibility doctrine, implicitly arguing that it must be modified to fit the American context. The title of that report uses the comparative "more," which indicates that it was not the intention of the drafters to replicate a British-style parliamentary party system, but rather to approximate only some aspects of the British model.

Still, in what party scholar Gerald Pomper calls a "pattern of undirected implementation," over the years the REPUBLICAN PARTY has adopted 20 of the report's 33 specific party-related proposals, the DEMOCRATIC PARTY has adopted 28 of 33, and 15 of the 20 systemic recommendations have been implemented, at least in part. By the election of 2004, it appeared that the American system had, indeed, moved toward a more responsible two-party system. The parties had clearly defined competing policy positions, both major parties evidenced a significant sustained level of electoral strength, and, by and large, most party identifiers voted for "their" party. Thus, whether because of the 1950 report or in spite of it, the American political party system seems to have become "more responsible."

Further reading: Green, John C., and Paul S. Herrnson, eds. *Responsible Partisanship? The Evolution of American Political Parties Since 1950.* Lawrence: University of Kansas Press, 2002; Ranney, Austin. *The Doctrine of Responsible Party Government: Its Origins and Present State.* Urbana: University of Illinois Press, 1954; Green, John C., and Rick Farmer, eds. *The State of the Parties: The Changing Role of Contemporary American Parties.* 4th ed. Lanham, Md.: Rowman & Littlefield, 2003.

—Marc D. Weiner

Dorr Rebellion

Civil dissatisfaction with Rhode Island's electoral system sparked this brief and largely bloodless uprising around 1842. State representative Thomas Wilson Dorr (1805–54), a native of Providence from a prominent Whig family who studied law under New York supreme court justice James Kent, led the rebellion, in which he and his armed followers sought the adoption of universal male SUFFRAGE in Rhode Island. Under the terms of the 1663 royal charter that still governed the state, only men owning land valued at $134 or more could vote. This requirement disenfranchised most town and city dwellers, whose numbers had grown over the years as industry expanded in the Northeast. By 1830, fully 60 percent of the state's free white males could not vote.

Despite several attempts at reform prior to 1840, changes in voting laws never materialized, since conservative Whigs and rural Democrats controlled the state legislature. Frustrated, Dorr and his followers (who called themselves "Dorrites") founded the reformist PEOPLE'S PARTY and held a convention to revise the state constitution in October 1841. There, they adopted the "People's Constitution," which embraced universal suffrage for all white men who had resided in the state for at least one year. In response, the conservative legislature held a rival convention and drafted the "Freemen's Constitution," which made only some concessions regarding voting eligibility. Voters defeated the Freemen's Constitution and approved the People's Constitution.

Despite Dorrite claims to the contrary, conservatives asserted that the People's Constitution had not been approved by a majority of those entitled to vote under the provisions of the 1663 charter that were still in effect. Though, strictly speaking, both conventions had been extralegal, each side claimed victory and organized a government. Dorr's supporters elected him governor, and both he and rival governor Samuel Ward King pleaded with President John Tyler for recognition. Reluctantly, Tyler sided with King's side and sent federal troops to the area to ease tensions.

In May 1842, frustrated Dorrites took up arms but failed in a bid to seize the state arsenal in Providence. Pursued by King's forces, Dorr's rebels retreated toward the town of Chepachet, where they hoped to regroup. Instead, the rebellion fell apart after only a few minor clashes. King's forces arrested many Dorrites, and King accused Dorr of treason, offering a $5,000 reward for his capture. Dorr fled to New Hampshire and went into hiding.

Though the Rebellion failed, it was significant because it drove home the need for election reform in Rhode Island. Conservatives developed a new constitution that expanded suffrage. Rhode Islanders ratified the new constitution in 1843, the same year that Dorr returned to face trial. He was convicted of treason and sentenced to solitary confinement and hard labor for life, but many believed Dorr to be a hero and condemned this harsh punishment. Responding to this public outcry, Governor Charles Jackson paroled Dorr in 1845. Almost a decade later, the general assembly reversed his treason conviction entirely. Though this fully restored his civil rights, Dorr, who had been in poor health, did not long enjoy them. He died in December 1854.

Further reading: Marvin E. Gettleman. *The Dorr Rebellion: A Study in American Radicalism, 1833–1849.* New York: Random House, 1973.

—Charles H. Wilson, III

Dunn v. Blumstein 405 U.S. 330 (1972)

This was one of a number of cases in the 1960s and 1970s that "incorporated" the Bill of Rights and provisions of the

FOURTEENTH AMENDMENT on the states. James Blumstein moved to Tennessee on June 12, 1970, to begin employment as an assistant professor of law at Vanderbilt University. Intending to vote in the upcoming elections that fall, he attempted to register to vote. The county registrar refused to register him on the ground that Tennessee law allowed registration to persons who had resided in the state for one year and the county for three months. Blumstein's appeal made its way to the Supreme Court, with Justice Thurgood Marshall writing for the majority declaring the Tennessee law to be in violation of the Equal Protection Clause of the Fourteenth Amendment. *Dunn* effectively overturned the Court's previous ruling in *Pope v. Williams* (1904), which had upheld a Maryland law that required one year of residency prior to registration. Echoing *REYNOLDS v. SIMS* (1964), Marshall wrote that "[b]y denying some citizens the right to vote, such laws deprive them of 'a fundamental political right.' "

Tennessee defended the statute on the grounds that it was attempting to "insure purity of ballot box" by preventing fraud in VOTER REGISTRATION and to foster a "knowledgeable voter" who understood the interests of the community. Marshall swept these concerns aside, arguing that an "exacting" test is necessary whenever conditions are placed on the "right to vote." *Dunn* is perhaps most significant because it imposes the high bar of the "compelling-state-interest" test established in *Kramer v. Union Free School District* (1969) and abandons the "rational basis" test, thus making all modifications by states with regard to voting procedures a "suspect" class.

Marshall established 30 days as the standard for voter registration, though as Justice Blackmun observed in his concurrence, the Court was establishing a timeline with little foundation for it. In dissent, Chief Justice Burger argued that it was "reasonable" for states to deny the vote in certain circumstances, as the Court had indicated just two years earlier in *Oregon v. Mitchell*, which upheld age requirements. Most notably, Burger viewed the "compelling" standard as "insurmountable, . . . as it demands nothing less than perfection."

Further reading: Berger, Raul. *The Fourteenth Amendment and the Bill of Rights.* Norman: University of Oklahoma Press, 1989; Fairman, Charles. *The Fourteenth Amendment and the Bill of Rights: The Incorporation Theory.* New York: Da Capo Press, 1970.

—Jeff A. Martineau

Duverger's Law

Duverger's Law claims that electoral laws that apply plurality systems (also referred to as first-past-the-post systems) and single-member districts (SMDs) will produce a TWO-PARTY SYSTEM, whereas electoral laws that use PROPORTIONAL REPRESENTATION (PR), or simple majority system with a second BALLOT, lead to a multiparty system. This assertion was first put forward by Maurice Duverger, a French sociologist, who observed this relationship in democratic countries in the 1950s and 1960s. Duverger's argument was eventually referred to as a "law" by many other social scientists and scholars, who conducted further research on his causal assertion. Duverger also contended that two-party systems generate a more stable political system in comparison to PR systems, especially in countries with parliamentary systems.

There are several implications of Duverger's argument. First, a single-member plurality electoral system can directly lead to a great disadvantage for THIRD PARTIES and consequently encourage "strategic" rather than "sincere" voting among voters. Under such electoral laws, potential supporters and sympathizers of a third party can be encouraged to vote for a less-preferred party that has a better chance of winning, in order to prevent the electoral victory of the least-preferred party. This is also known as a "lesser of evils" attitude. A second consequence of Duverger's Law is the notion called the "SPOILER effect," which refers to the case in which a third party or its candidate takes votes away from one of the candidates from the two major political parties. The existence of a third party can indeed influence the result of an election by shaping the balance between the two relatively close leading parties or candidates.

Social scientists and scholars still debate and test the accuracy of Duverger's Law. Critics of Duverger challenge his argument by asserting that single districts can help two parties to become stronger in particular districts in time, but the two strong parties at a district level may not be the same two strong parties at a national level. Canada and India are two examples that demonstrate this weakness in Duverger's argument. The most important contribution of Duverger's argument is that it demonstrates how arrangements of electoral laws can influence the institutional structure of party systems across contemporary democracies.

Further reading: Duverger, Maurice. *Political Parties: Their Organization and Activity in the Modern State.* New York: John Wiley & Sons, 1963; Riker, William H. "The Number of Political Parties: A Reexamination of Duverger's Law." *Comparative Politics* 9 (1976): 93–106; Riker, William H. "The Two-Party System and Duverger's Law: An Essay on the History of Political Science." *American Political Science Review* 76 (1982): 753–766.

—Odul Celep

E

early voting

Early voting generally refers to any procedure by which a voter may cast a BALLOT before the standard poll opening time on ELECTION DAY. While the term *early voting* is often used broadly to mean voting before election day, it is also used more specifically to refer to voting before election day at an election office or designated polling site. In some states, the designated polling sites have been placed in locations of convenience, such as supermarkets and shopping centers.

Early voting procedures differ from state to state. Texas observes two types of early voting: 1) voting early in person, whereby a registered voter may cast his or her ballot at any polling station convenient to him or her as long as it resides within the voter's political subdivision during a specified period of time prior to election day, and 2) voting early by mail, whereby a person may request a ballot by mail. In Texas, however, early voting by mail is not open to all registered voters and is similar to restrictive ABSENTEE VOTING. In 2004, registered voters in Arizona could cast their ballots at designated polling sites a month prior to election day, whereas in Texas, early voting in person started a little more than two weeks before election day.

Over the last few years, many states have changed their voting procedures to allow citizens to cast ballots before election day, either through absentee or early voting. According to the Committee for the Study of the American Electorate, in 2004 there were 11 states that provided early voting "at a satellite location away from the local registrar" and an additional 12 no-excuse absentee states that provided in-person absentee voting, meaning that a voter could "obtain and cast an absentee ballot in a local registrar's office before polls open." The early voting states included Alaska, Arizona, Colorado, Florida, Hawaii, Iowa, Nevada, New Mexico, North Carolina, Tennessee, and Texas. The no-excuse in-person absentee states included Idaho, Kansas, Maine, Montana, Nebraska, North Dakota, Oklahoma, South Dakota, Utah, Vermont, Washington, and Wisconsin.

Early voting has the potential to change how campaigns are conducted. In some early voting states, voters can cast ballots a month prior to election day. Consequently, political candidates can no longer view election day as the only day on which ballots are cast and must adjust the dissemination of their messages accordingly. Campaigns must target their voter base earlier than before in order to compete against other candidates effectively. Although early voting policies have been adopted as efforts to increase VOTER TURNOUT by making the act of voting easier, there is little evidence to suggest that such policies have increased voter turnout.

Further reading: Kenski, Kate. "The National Annenberg Election Survey 2000." *The Polling Report* 19, no. 15 (2003): 1, 7–8; Neeley, Grant W., and Lilliard E. Richardson. "Who Is Early Voting? An Individual Level Examination." *Social Science Journal* 38 (2001): 381–392; Stein, Robert M. "Early Voting." *Public Opinion Quarterly* 62, no. 1 (1998): 57–69.

—Kate Kenski

earned media

Earned media refers to the highly coveted form of news coverage that elected officials, candidates for public office, and public figures receive without having to pay for through an advertisement. Often referred to as "free media," earned media is typically a product of the work of political consultants, press secretaries, and campaign field workers who actively use strategies that they hope will result in coverage. Seeking earned media has become increasingly popular among political elites, especially during campaign seasons.

In an effort to attract media coverage, elites host photo opportunities, press conferences, and political events; go on talk shows; send out news releases; and try to orchestrate their public schedules in ways that correspond to the needs of reporters' deadlines and to journalistic conventions about what is "news." Elected officials and political hopefuls at every level devote a considerable amount of time and energy toward trying to earn their way into news coverage. Sometimes their efforts can be quite colorful. For example, Ronald Machtley successfully campaigned for office by tooling around the campaign trail with a 250-pound pig named Lester H. Pork ("Less Pork") to symbolize his opposition to the spending policies of his opponent, Fernand St. Germain.

Though government officials need the media to help spread their messages, there are important downsides associated with earned media. Chief among these is that the media have their own interests and needs, which are, of course, not always the same as the needs of those trying to receive favorable news coverage. Put simply, earned media is outside the control of those who seek it. The traditionally adversarial role the media play with those in power makes it difficult for individuals to push an unfiltered message to the public through the media. Additionally, the journalistic convention of objective reporting reduces the likelihood that coverage in a story will be one-sided, representing solely the interested public official's viewpoint. Consequently, media coverage is as likely to disrupt a public official's message with negative coverage as it is to generate support.

Despite the risks, nearly all policy makers have an incentive to engage the media. Research in the mid-1990s found that young, non-southern, liberal Democrats are the most likely to be media entrepreneurs. Among members of Congress, those in the House of Representatives are more likely to seek coverage than are senators. Recent research indicates that members of the House who represent a district that lies in one media market, rather than multiple markets, are more successful than are others at generating news coverage. There are even occasions when these representatives find that their news releases get printed word for word in their local newspapers, providing what is essentially a free commercial about a particular issue. Incumbents are more likely to earn media than their CHALLENGERS.

At the presidential level, recent elections have played host to a great expansion of free media events that developed beyond traditional efforts to appear on the nightly news, in the morning paper, and on Sunday morning talk shows. In 1992, then governor Bill Clinton played his saxophone on the *Arsenio Hall Show* and answered questions about his underwear on MTV. Ross Perot announced his candidacy for president on *Larry King Live*. In 2000, both George W. Bush and Al Gore appeared on late-night programs with David Letterman and Jay Leno. Each also visited Oprah Winfrey's show and made fun of themselves on *Saturday Night Live*. The 2004 election season saw all of the major candidates for the Democratic presidential NOMINATION make the rounds on many of these entertainment programs.

One important general consequence of this phenomenon is that newsmaking helps political elites in the short run but results in news values becoming political values in the long run. As politicians continue to earn media coverage by competing with other politicians for air time and column inches, they frame their messages in a way that is increasingly appealing to the realities of the modern newsroom. This often results in leaders focusing their media strategy on some issues and ignoring other, perhaps more important, ones.

Further reading: Graber, Doris A. *Mass Media and American Politics.* Washington, D.C.: CQ Press, 1993; Jamieson, Kathleen Hall, et al. *The Interplay of Influence: News, Advertising, Politics and the Mass Media.* Belmont, Calif.: Wadsworth Publishing, 2000; Sabato, Larry. *Feeding Frenzy: How Attack Journalism Has Transformed American Politics.* New York: Free Press, 1993.

—Michael W. Wagner

election cycle

An election cycle is the period between two elections for a public office and is often used as a way to measure money raised and spent by candidates, parties, and POLITICAL ACTION COMMITTEES (PACs). The election cycles for members of Congress and the president are outlined in the Constitution. Article I, Section 1 states that House members face election every other year, meaning they operate on a two-year election cycle. Section 3 notes that senators (who have six-year terms) should be divided into three groups, with one group up for election every two years. Article II, Section 1 lists the president's term in office as four years, so presidential campaigns use a four-year cycle. State and local laws determine election cycles for governors, members of state legislatures, and other office holders.

The FEDERAL ELECTION COMMISSION uses election cycles to keep track of how much money federal candidates raise and spend. The commission defines an election cycle as "the period beginning on the day after the date of the most recent election for the specific office or seat that a candidate is seeking and ending on the date of the next election for that office or seat."

In federal races, donors are limited in what they can contribute to individual candidates and party committees in a two-year election cycle. Prior to passage of the Bipartisan Campaign Reform Act of 2002 (known as the MCCAIN-FEINGOLD bill), individuals could donate a total of $2,000 in HARD MONEY per election cycle ($1,000 in the PRIMARY and $1,000 in the GENERAL ELECTION) to a specific candidate. The 2002 act doubled the limits and tied future limits to the inflation rate in odd-numbered years, starting in 2005. During a two-year election cycle, an individual can donate a total of $95,000, or $37,500 to candidates and $57,500 to PACs and parties.

Multicandidate PACs, NATIONAL PARTY COMMITTEES, and state, district, and local party committees can donate a total of $10,000 to a candidate per election cycle ($5,000 during the primary and $5,000 during the general). In the 2002 election cycle, the REPUBLICAN PARTY raised $442 million in hard money, while Democrats raised $217 million, or less than half of the Republican total. Not surprisingly, the parties usually raise more money in election cycles that occur during PRESIDENTIAL ELECTION years. In the 2000 cycle, Republicans took in $466 million, while Democrats raised $275 million.

The election cycle has also become a convenient marker for measuring how much money candidates and parties raise and spend in elections. In the 2000 PRESIDENTIAL ELECTION, George W. Bush raised $193 million and spent $186 million, while Al Gore raised $132 million and spent $120 million. Bush quickened his FUND-RAISING pace in 2004, raising $290 million, while John Kerry raised $251 million. Groups that monitor spending in POLITICS also look at how much donors, industries and businesses, INTEREST GROUPS, PACs, parties, and the candidates themselves spend.

For a typical two-year election cycle, as is the case in the U.S. House, campaign activity starts soon after the newly elected officeholder is sworn into office. Within a few months, a potential candidate will weigh whether to begin his or her campaign for the seat. The candidate may consult with family members and friends, elected officials, PARTY ORGANIZATIONs, interest groups, and CAMPAIGN CONSULTANTs to determine how viable a candidate he or she is. By the end of the first year or the beginning of the second, a candidate will file papers to officially join the race and begin fund-raising. The next goal is to win the party's primary. If successful, the candidate will spend the final stretch of the election cycle campaigning heavily, airing television ads, and debating his or her opponent.

The four-year election cycle for presidential candidates is somewhat different. Behind-the-scenes jockeying among potential candidates of the party not in the White House may begin even before the president is inaugurated. Potential candidates will spend the next two years building fund-raising and GRASSROOTS networks, courting party leaders, delivering policy addresses, and trying to raise their profiles. Shortly after the midterm elections, the candidate will likely announce that he or she is a candidate. However, a formal announcement may take place months later in order to take advantage of additional publicity. After months of campaigning in 2003, John Kerry officially launched his presidential candidacy in September with an aircraft carrier as a backdrop. Presidential candidates typically spend the third year taking part in the preprimary campaign, trying to pull ahead in polls and aggressively fund-raising. The party's nominating contest begins in earnest at the start of the fourth year. After a candidate wins the NOMINATION, he or she spends several months before the convention raising money, trying to attract voters, making speeches about policy agenda, and defending

his or her record against attacks. After the nominating convention concludes, the candidate works in an almost nonstop final push for voter support.

Election cycles also provide a way to track campaign developments and the ELECTORATE's mood. VOTER TURNOUT in an election cycle is a sign of whether the public is feeling apathetic. The success of women and minority candidates can be a sign of larger trends in society. The rising use of the Internet in political organizing and fund-raising was one of the big stories of the 2004 PRESIDENTIAL ELECTION cycle.

Election cycles influence fields other than politics. Many economists contend that the end of the presidential election cycle is generally good news for Wall Street. In the year prior to the election, the Dow Jones Index rose 20 out of 24 times beginning with Theodore Roosevelt's presidency in 1905. Many observers believe that this trend is caused by presidents focusing on economic issues leading up to elections, hoping that people will vote on "pocketbook issues" and either return the president to office or return the president's party.

Further reading: Federal Election Commission. Available online. URL: http://www.fec.gov. Accessed August 10, 2005; Goldstein, Michael L. *Guide to the 2004 Presidential Election.* Washington, D.C.: CQ Press, 2003; Kiefer, David. *Macroeconomic Policy and Public Choice.* Berlin: Springer, 1997.

—Mary Lynn F. Jones

election day

Election day marks the culmination of the campaign season and occurs when voters go to the polls to elect candidates to office. Held every year on the Tuesday after the first Monday in November, it is the time for voters to support the candidates they believe will do a better job governing them, based on the candidates' policy positions and campaign styles.

In 1845, based on the needs of an agrarian and religious citizenry, lawmakers chose to make the Tuesday after the first Monday in November the date for appointing presidential electors. Conducting elections in November allowed farmers to get to the polls after the harvest was complete, and holding elections on a Tuesday allowed them to travel without missing Sunday church services. Choosing the Tuesday after the first Monday allowed lawmakers to guarantee that election day would not fall on November 1, which is All Saints Day, a Catholic holy day. It also took into consideration the fact that many merchants used the first day of the month to tally their books from the previous month. In 1875, election day for House members was established as falling on this date in every even-numbered year; the same was true for senators starting in 1914, after the passage of the SEVENTEENTH AMENDMENT allowing for direct election of senators. In 2004, election day fell on November 2.

The times that polls are open on election day vary depending on the state, but most voting booths are open from early morning to early evening hours, allowing residents to vote on their way to or from work. Polling locations are selected by local election officials. States differ on whether they require voters to show identification, but most states require voters to register before election day. Exceptions include North Dakota, which does not have VOTER REGISTRATION, and Maine, Minnesota, and Wisconsin, which allow same-day registration. States also have different rules on allowing write-in candidates, voting by mail, listing unopposed candidates, and permitting residents to cast a single vote for all candidates of one party. Voters unable to cast their BALLOTs on election day may vote by requesting an absentee ballot before the election.

In presidential campaign years, about half of eligible voters cast their ballots on election day; fewer people vote in other years. In 2000, 54 percent of voters cast ballots in the PRESIDENTIAL ELECTION, up from 51 percent in 1996. In the 1998 midterm election, 36 percent of Americans voted for House candidates. Even fewer people typically show up for SPECIAL ELECTIONs, held to fill an office after a vacancy due to death, resignation, or RECALL. In an effort to increase voter participation, some experts have proposed making election day a holiday or moving it to a Saturday to increase VOTER TURNOUT. While Congress is unlikely to buck history and change the date, some states close schools and give employees time off to vote on election day.

Most candidates take advantage of election day as the last chance to press their case to voters. They and their supporters may appear on television and radio or at schools and subway stops to make last-minute appeals. In the last 30 hours of the 2000 campaign, for example, Al Gore traveled to 15 cities in 11 states. Campaigns and INTEREST GROUPS offer to drive voters to the polls in the hopes of achieving victory. The media also focus attention on candidates, trailing them throughout the day and reporting on their victory or concession parties. Campaign etiquette generally requires that the losing candidate call the winner to concede that night.

Election day does not always run flawlessly, however. In 2000, many African Americans in Florida said they were turned away at the polls because of errors in voting rolls. Other Floridians found their ballots difficult to decipher and accidentally voted for the wrong candidate. Later that night, because of the state's different time zones, some voters complained that press reports called the state for Gore even though polling had not closed in some areas. Due to problems with exit-poll projections, the news media first said Gore won Florida, then moved the state back into the undecided column, then declared Bush the winner of the election, only to move it back into the undecided column. It was not until December that Bush was officially declared the new president.

Further reading: Federal Election Commission. Available online. URL: http://www.fec.gov. Accessed August 10, 2005; Franklin, Mark N. *Voter Turnout and the Dynamics of Electoral Competition in Established Democracies since 1945.* New York: Cambridge University Press, 2004; Sabato, Larry. *The Party's Just Begun: Shaping Political Parties for America's Future.* New York: Longman, 2002; Wayne, Stephen J. *The Road to the White House 2000: The Politics of Presidential Elections.* New York: Bedford/St. Martin's, 2000.

—Mary Lynn F. Jones

election fraud

Election fraud refers to a wide range of practices, but in general it is an attempt to affect the outcome of an election in a manner that violates the agreed-upon rules of fair elections. The spectrum of voter fraud runs from overly aggressive campaigning to attempts to change the outcome of an election by altering results. Election fraud threatens the foundation of democracy by subverting the will of the majority and, when exposed, by eroding the ELECTORATE's faith in the political process.

While the possibility of election fraud is an unavoidable part of democracy, public perceptions of fraud have shifted over time. New issues and questions have been raised, and today, practices that were once commonly accepted have been banned. Participation in elections was once commonly controlled by limiting VOTER REGISTRATION through POLL TAXES, LITERACY TESTS, and by making polling locations inaccessible. Today these practices are illegal. Similarly, the influence of GERRYMANDERing, the drawing of voting districts to ensure a certain political outcome, has been reduced in the last 40 years as a result of the VOTING RIGHTS ACT of 1965 and recent court decisions.

Other forms of election fraud have been universally condemned, if still occasionally practiced. The registration of ineligible or nonexistent voters is a persistent problem that has been reduced by better record keeping and election laws. However, the practice has not been completely eliminated. Yet another form of election fraud is an attempt to "fix" the ballot box either by introducing fraudulent BALLOTs or through a fraudulent counting process. Other issues such as block voting (a "leader" casting votes for a group of people) and voter intimidation, especially of minority groups, have also been widely condemned but have played a real role in American political history.

Accusations and occasionally evidence suggest some level of election fraud in a number of PRESIDENTIAL ELECTIONS and thousands of state and local elections. Tighter election laws and closer public monitoring have increased the accountability and transparency in elections. However,

Two cartoons from *Harper's Weekly* showing politicians trying to buy votes, 1857 *(Library of Congress)*

these developments are relatively recent. For much of America's history, political "machines" dominated the local POLITICS of major cities and occasionally of states. MACHINE POLITICS involve an extremely well-organized political institution that is able to control the distribution of government services, social services, and government jobs. This power combined with a pervasive network that links individuals to the machine through local representatives is then leveraged to control or induce voting behavior. Reform efforts at the start of the 20th century managed to break most political machines. However, New York's Tammany machine survived until 1961, and Chicago was controlled by machine politics until the 1970s.

One of the most blatant instances of election fraud in U.S. history was the Kansas territorial election of 1854–55. A large migration of abolitionists to the Kansas territory threatened to tip its future away from slavery. In response,

residents of Missouri crossed into Kansas to ensure the triumph of pro-slavery forces. Violence, voter intimidation, and ballot box stuffing were rampant. In some areas, the number of votes cast was twice the number of registered voters. So brutal were the Kansas elections that the state became known as Bleeding Kansas.

More recently, the 2002 South Dakota Senate race, which was decided by 524 votes, was the focus of a number of reports related to election fraud. Accusations included paying Native Americans to register, block voting, repeat ABSENTEE VOTING, and absentee voting by ineligible voters. After a detailed investigation, several individuals were charged with a small number of forgery counts. However, the allegations of widespread fraud could not be substantiated.

The "progressive" reform effort at the start of the 20th century focused on addressing some of the most pervasive forms of voter fraud. Similarly, the CIVIL RIGHTS MOVEMENT in the 1960s sought to overcome barriers to political participation and voting faced by African Americans. Today, the FEDERAL ELECTION COMMISSION (FEC), which was established by the 1975 FEDERAL ELECTION CAMPAIGN ACT, works in conjunction with corresponding state offices to monitor and ensure fairness in elections. A combination of better oversight, improved record keeping, and best practice standards have reduced or eliminated some of the more blatant types of election fraud. American election law has also developed to a point where there is usually a legal recourse to address election fraud.

Today, election monitoring has focused on a number of new issues. First, the Bipartisan Campaign Reform Act of 2002 (MCCAIN-FEINGOLD) attempted to restructure how election campaigns are financed. This act further clarifies and enforces the rules of fair elections. Second, attempts to reduce barriers to political participation have expanded to include the disabled and individuals who do not speak English. Third, as voting has become increasingly mechanized and computerized, the FEC has attempted to prevent tampering with the election process by creating voluntary guidelines for the operation of voting machines. The exceptionally close 2000 PRESIDENTIAL ELECTION momentarily focused national attention on the idiosyncrasies of modern voting machines. These idiosyncrasies introduced an element of confusion into the election process and, by default, "fraud." And finally, the development of the Internet has created new concerns about the possibility of on-line voting and the potential for fraud.

Further reading: Jensen, Richard. *The Winning of the Midwest: Social and Political Conflict 1888–1896.* Chicago: Chicago University Press, 1971; Morris, Roy. *Fraud of the Century: Rutherford B. Hayes, Samuel Tilden, and the Stolen Election of 1876.* New York: Simon & Schuster, 2003.

—Brian Urlacher

elections

Elections are the processes by which citizens choose a person to represent them in public office, or by which citizens accept or reject political propositions. People vote in elections to make known their collective preference for an individual, party, IDEOLOGY, or specific public policy. Although elections were used in ancient Greek and Roman societies, the origins of modern political elections can be found in western Europe and North America in the 17th century.

Elections serve a number of practical functions. Regular free elections promote mass political action and allow citizens to affect the actions of their governments. Elections are the means by which public offices are filled, and the elected officials who fill these offices shape the laws that govern the citizens they represent. Elected officials advocate certain policies and ideologies, and elections serve as ways for the public to evaluate (either positively or negatively) the individuals and the parties in power. If the public is pleased with the party or individual in power, the incumbent is rewarded by being reelected and will likely continue his or her policies with a renewed MANDATE from the ELECTORATE. If not, the CHALLENGER is selected to replace the incumbent. Elections, therefore, make candidates and elected officials accountable to the people whom they represent.

Elections also serve a symbolic function. Elections confer legitimacy to the ruling power, and they provide justifiable means for peaceful regime change. It is important, however, to distinguish between the form and the actual substance of elections. Alternatives are central to this concept; elections are about choosing between competing candidates, ideologies, and ideas, and in order for a democracy to have integrity, elections must be fair, competitive, and free from structural bias. Many authoritarian regimes, including those in Singapore and Syria, have often held elections in order to convey legitimacy upon their administrations. However, these elections are held under conditions that do not reflect true competition (including intimidation of opposition candidates and voters and the manipulation of vote counts), and therefore should only cautiously be considered elections in the truest sense.

In the United States, elections vary by type (PRIMARY, GENERAL, initiative or REFERENDUM, and RECALL) and they take place on a variety of levels: local, state, and national. Primary elections are contests in which voters choose which of the candidates within a party will represent that party in the general election. In the general election, the electorate (or citizens qualified to vote) chooses which candidate will actually fill the elective public office. While primary elections are intraparty affairs, general elections are almost always contests among candidates of different parties. Initiative or referendum elections involve voting on issues or specific legislation, instead of voting for candidates. Recall elections, whereby an incumbent can be removed from office by POPULAR VOTE, are quite rare but are allowed in some states.

There is substantial variation in the type of electoral system (ballot types, counting mechanisms, etc.) used throughout the United States and around the world, and the process of elections varies based not only on the formal institutional structure of the state or country but also on the state or country's political culture.

Further reading: Campbell, Angus, Phillip E. Converse, Warren E. Miller, and Donald E. Stokes. *The American Voter.* Chicago: University of Chicago, 1980; Patterson, Thomas E. *The Vanishing Voter: Public Involvement in an Age of Uncertainty.* New York: Vintage, 2003; Weisberg, Herbert F., ed. *Democracy's Feast: Elections in America.* Chatham, N.J.: Chatham House, 1995.

—Joshua J. Scott

elections, gubernatorial

Gubernatorial elections are the means by which voters in a state choose their governor, or chief executive officer of the state. While the individuals who serve as governors vary greatly in personal styles and abilities, as well as in formal powers and responsibilities, governors are almost without exception the main political actors in each state. Gubernatorial elections attract copious attention within the state, and occasionally these races receive national attention.

For much of American history, gubernatorial elections mattered little, mostly because the office of governor mattered little. From the founding through the early 20th century, governors across the country lacked substantial authority to lead, as most of the power was held by state legislatures. Governors were largely figureheads, and many were ineffective because they lacked the formal and informal powers to effect substantive change throughout state government. In the latter part of the 20th century, however, governors evolved into more powerful political players.

Governors currently serve a number of practical and symbolic roles. Some of these roles involve powers specifically granted by state constitutions, while other roles are derived largely out of the force of personality. Governors are their state's strongest advocate and chief public relations person, working to encourage business and tourism for his or her state. Almost all governors appoint a cabinet to run state departments and propose their state's budget and serve in at least an informal way as their party's leader. But perhaps most importantly, governors set the state's agenda, outline broad themes and proposals, and try to influence the state's legislature to pass bills that implement these themes. Most of this agenda is developed during the gubernatorial campaign.

Gubernatorial elections are held on ELECTION DAY in November, but not all states elect governors in the same year. Nine states (Delaware, Indiana, Missouri, Montana,

New Hampshire, North Carolina, North Dakota, Utah, and Vermont) elect their governors during PRESIDENTIAL ELECTION years. The majority of states (34) elect their governors during the second year (or midterm) of a presidential term. A handful of states (Kentucky, Mississippi, and Louisiana) elect governors in the third year of a presidential term, and two states (Virginia and New Jersey) elect their governors in the year immediately following presidential election. A total of 48 of the 50 states elect their governors for four-year terms. Two states (New Hampshire and Vermont) have two-year gubernatorial terms, so they elect their governor every even-numbered year. Two-term limits are very common among the states; 36 states limit governors to two consecutive or nonconsecutive terms. Only Virginia does not allow a governor to be reelected.

Gubernatorial elections generally feature candidates who are middle-aged, white, wealthy, and male, but that is not to say that women and minorities have not found success in gubernatorial elections. Since 1925, 21 states have elected 29 women governors, and in 2004, eight women were serving as governor. Hawaii and Washington have elected Asian-American governors, and Virginia stands alone as the only state to have elected an African-American governor, Douglas Wilder, in 1989. (During RECONSTRUCTION, P. B. S. Pinchback, an African-American lieutenant governor, was appointed acting governor of Louisiana for 43 days.) Most governors have had significant elective experience, with many having served as legislators, lieutenant governor, or attorney general. Exceptions are generally businessmen, such as current Virginia governor Mark Warner, current Massachusetts governor Mitt Romney, and former Texas governor (and current president of the United States) George W. Bush, or occasionally celebrities, such as California governor Arnold Schwarzenegger and former Minnesota governor Jesse Ventura. The vast majority of governors have been from the major parties, although a handful of INDEPENDENT and third-party candidates have been elected in recent years (including Ventura in Minnesota and Angus King in Maine).

Gubernatorial elections are preceded by multimillion-dollar political campaigns that attract a great deal of media attention. In most states, other statewide officials are elected at the same time as the governor, but the number varies. Texas elects 25 statewide officials; New Jersey elects only a governor. In 24 states, the governor and lieutenant governor are elected on the same ticket; in another 18 states, a lieutenant governor is elected separately. In these states, it is not uncommon to see a lieutenant governor and governor of different parties. Many states also elect an attorney general and a secretary of state. Often, lower-ticket statewide officials become candidates for governor.

Given that most states hold elections in off-years, it is not surprising that gubernatorial elections often seem somewhat insulated from national POLITICS. Voters in gubernatorial elections often make their decisions based on factors related to their specific state, rather than federal issues or dominant national candidates. This is not always the case. During the 1994 MIDTERM ELECTIONS, when Republicans took control of the House of Representatives and the U.S. Senate, Republicans also took control of a majority of governorships. But by and large, gubernatorial contests are about state issues and are generally not a REFERENDUM on national issues. Often, the elections are driven more by the appeal of the individual candidates than by party affiliation. This explains, in part, how solidly conservative states such as Kansas, Wyoming, and Virginia currently have Democratic governors, while liberal states such as Massachusetts and California have Republican governors. Governors who run for reelection are also generally successful, not unlike incumbents who hold other offices. Governors are also important political players in national, state, and local races, where they are able to use their NAME RECOGNITION, popularity, and political infrastructures of supporters to affect other elections.

Further reading: Sabato, Larry J. *Goodbye to Good-time Charlie.* Lexington, Mass.: Lexington Books, 1978; Gray, Virginia, and Russell L. Hanson. *Politics in the American States: A Comparative Analysis.* 8th ed. Washington, D.C.: CQ Press, 2003; Beyle, Thad. *State and Local Government 2004–2005.* Washington, D.C.: CQ Press, 2004.

—Joshua J. Scott

elections, House of Representatives

Congressional elections are held every two years. Each House seat represents a geographic CONSTITUENCY, and every member is elected from a unique, or "single-member," district by plurality rule (the candidate with the most votes wins election). Each of the 50 states is assured at least one seat in the House, with the rest allocated to the states by population. For example, Vermont has only one seat in the House, while California currently has 53. The total number of seats in the House of Representatives is 435, with the seats reapportioned among the states every 10 years following the decennial CENSUS.

In order to be elected to the House, candidates must meet the standards set forth in the Constitution. According to Article I, Section 2, Clause 2 of the Constitution: "No Person shall be a Representative who shall not have attained to the Age of twenty five Years, and been seven Years a Citizen of the United States, and who shall not, when elected, be an Inhabitant of that State in which he shall be chosen." It is left to each individual state to determine what constitutes "residency" and how long a person must reside in a state for residency status to be obtained. However, the other two provisions—at least 25 years old, and at least seven years a U.S. citizen—are universal.

Should there by a vacancy in the House, SPECIAL ELEC-TIONS will usually be called to preserve representation until the next regularly scheduled election. According to Article I, Section 2, Clause 4 of the Constitution: "When vacancies happen in the Representation from any State, the Executive Authority thereof shall issue Writs of Election to fill such Vacancies." Furthermore, in 2004, Congress passed legislation mandating that if 100 or more vacancies occur in the House within a short period of time (most likely due to a large-scale terrorist attack), states must hold special elections within 45 days to fill those vacancies. However, under normal circumstances—and for all of U.S. history up to this point—the timing of these special elections is left entirely up to the individual states.

Far more attention is given to PRESIDENTIAL ELEC-TIONS and Senate elections than to House elections. Local newspapers cover presidential races extensively, usually with numerous articles each day. Likewise, a competitive Senate race is likely to average an article a day. Elections to the House of Representatives, on the other hand, receive far less coverage. Given the importance of CONGRES-SIONAL ELECTIONS, it is unfortunate that they receive such scant attention. Some of the most significant policy changes that have occurred in American POLITICS have followed dramatic congressional elections. For example, the congressional elections of 1994, which swept the Republicans into the majority in the House and the Senate, led to a rightward shift in the political scene and the passage of welfare reform and the Defense of Marriage Act, among other pieces of legislation. It also led the country into a showdown over the budget. Likewise, the election of a large number of Democrats in 1964 provided the margin of victory in Congress that Lyndon Johnson needed to pass his landmark Civil Rights Act of 1964 and the VOTING RIGHTS ACT OF 1965.

Several scholars argue that throughout most of this century, congressional elections were "party-centered." Because most voters had long-term loyalties toward one POLITICAL PARTY or the other, they tended to cast their votes along party lines. Members of Congress were often reelected, sometimes holding their position for decades, because a majority of their constituents supported their party. Their efforts as individual candidates often only marginally affected their support.

In the 1960s, however, national elections became increasingly "candidate-centered." The ability to campaign over television, to raise huge amounts of money, to conduct polls, and to wage other aspects of modern campaigning made the voters more aware of the candidate as an individual. As a result, voters began to consider the strengths and weaknesses of the candidates in addition to their party loyalties. In recent elections, this process has further intensified with the rise of the Internet. Barely a factor in 1996, by 2004 the Internet became a major tool of both political

organizing and FUND-RAISING. Candidates with strong messages were able to organize meet-ups and raise millions of dollars online, dramatically changing the nature of politics and political campaigning.

The power of political parties in congressional elections should not be discounted. Party influence is still stronger here than it is at the presidential level. This is chiefly due to the power and influence of CONGRESSIONAL CAMPAIGN COMMITTEES. Congressional Campaign Committees are NATIONAL PARTY COMMITTEES, made up of members of Congress, whose goal is to elect additional members of their own party to national office. There are four major congressional campaign committees that represent the interests of both major parties in both the House and the Senate. In the House of Representatives, Democratic campaign efforts are channeled through the Democratic Congressional Campaign Committee, while the Republicans rely on the National Republican Congressional Committee. On the Senate side, the Democrats have the DEMOCRATIC SENATORIAL CAMPAIGN COMMITTEE, and the Republicans have the NATIONAL REPUBLICAN SENATORIAL COMMITTEE.

Formed in the mid-1970s, in the wake of Watergate and the FEDERAL ELECTION CAMPAIGN ACT, these committees were an attempt to raise funds for congressional and Senate elections and distribute those funds to current members facing reelection as well as to promising CHALLENGERS of their own party. It is through this collection and distribution of campaign funds that the various campaign committees make their most significant impact on the outcomes of congressional elections.

Allocating campaign funds is not the only function of congressional campaign committees. Congressional campaign committees can provide assistance ranging from designing and executing field operations, to polling, creating radio and television commercials, fund-raising, communications, and management consulting. For example, the National Republican Congressional Committee (NRCC) boasts that it supports the election of Republicans to the House through direct financial contributions to candidates and REPUBLICAN PARTY organizations; technical and research assistance to Republican candidates and PARTY ORGANIZATIONS; VOTER REGISTRATION, education, and turnout programs; and other party-building activities. Also, the Democratic Senatorial Campaign Committee is known for helping its candidates with everything from polling and media advice to issues research and the latest techniques for campaigning on the Internet.

This support, both financial and otherwise, can prove crucial in determining both individual races as well as the overall composition and control of Congress itself. For these reasons, congressional campaign committees tend to focus their resources carefully on those select races in which their support could tip the balance in favor of their party's candidate. As a result, this dictates heavy involvement in open-seat races and those select cases of weak opposition incumbents or strong party challengers. Such contests have historically provided the greatest chance of turnover in party control. Hence, both parties focus their resources there in order to either regain the majority or build on their majority in the chamber.

The Republican Party has currently held control of the House for more than a decade, and prior to that, the DEMOCRATIC PARTY controlled the House for 40 years. While due to several factors, one-party control is often associated with the rise of partisan GERRYMANDERing. Gerrymandering is the practice of purposely drawing CONGRESSIONAL DISTRICT lines in order to include, or exclude, certain types of people. Republicans draw districts that are more Republican, and Democrats want districts that are more Democratic. The result is that a large majority of House districts are now dominated by one of the two parties, thus making most House districts virtual "one-party" districts, or "safe-districts." Consequently, it is quite rare that there are significant gains or losses for one party in a given House election.

Further reading: Center for Responsive Politics. Available online. URL: http://www.opensecrets.org. Accessed August 10, 2005; Dodd, Lawrence C., and Bruce I. Oppenheimer. *Congress Reconsidered.* Washington, D.C.: CQ Press, 2000; Fenno, Richard F. *Home Style: House Members in Their Districts.* New York: Longman, 2002; Herrnson, Paul S. *Congressional Elections: Campaigning at Home and in Washington.* Washington, D.C.: CQ Press, 2003; Jacobson, Gary C. *The Politics of Congressional Elections.* 5th ed. New York: Addison-Wesley, 2000; Mayhew, David. *Congress: The Electoral Connection.* New Haven, Conn.: Yale University Press, 1975; University of Virginia Center for Politics Crystal Ball. Available online. URL: http://www.centerforpolitics.org/crystalball. Accessed August 10, 2005; U.S. House of Representatives. Available online. URL: http://www.house.gov. Accessed August 10, 2005.

—Brian DiSarro

elections, judicial

Judicial elections are electoral contests in which judges are selected or retained by POPULAR VOTE. In the United States, judicial elections take place exclusively at the state and local levels. Federal judges, in contrast, are appointed by the president and confirmed by the Senate. As of 2004, 42 states used judicial elections for at least some judges at the trial or appellate level. State supreme court judges are elected in 38 of these states. Of the approximately 30,000 state court judges in the United States, more than 80 percent face election of some kind. There are three basic varieties of judicial elections including partisan, nonpartisan, and retention elections. The use of judicial elections in the

United States has a long history but has recently been a matter of some controversy.

Judicial elections require judges to stand for election at intervals determined in each state. In a number of states, judges initially achieve their seats on the bench by election, while in others they do so by gubernatorial appointment and only later face a contested or retention election. The most basic justification for judicial elections is to hold accountable judges in the same manner as officials of the legislative and executive branches. This is intended to prevent the judiciary from straying unacceptably from standards acceptable to the larger community it serves.

Critics of judicial elections posit that they violate judicial independence, limiting the ability of judges to decide cases on the merits alone or in a potentially unpopular way. In addition, those who find fault with judicial elections cite potential conflicts created by judges raising campaign funds from groups or individuals who may be parties to cases before their courts. This has been problematic with regard to judicial elections, as campaign contributions have historically been dominated by attorneys. Recently, business and special INTEREST GROUPS have also become frequent donors to judicial candidates, supporting those they perceive as being more likely to share their positions on given issues. Another frequent criticism questions the proposition that the general public is sufficiently able to make judgments about who is suited to occupy judicial offices.

The genesis of judicial elections in America came during the democratic movement of the Jacksonian era from the late 1820s through the late 1840s. This period included efforts to enhance the egalitarian nature of American POLITICS by allowing for more popular control and citizen participation. The extension of this movement to the judiciary resulted in state-level elections holding judges accountable to the public. Judicial elections also served as an alternative to impeachment, which had previously been the primary mechanism for punishing judges for what the legislature or public deemed unacceptable behavior. By 1846, more than half the states used judicial elections in some fashion, and all states that joined the Union after that date did so as well. These practices led to a judicial recruitment and selection process dominated by partisan PATRONAGE and cronyism. By 1900, 25 states had partisan elections, and none yet had NONPARTISAN ELECTIONS. The PROGRESSIVE MOVEMENT, prevalent from about the 1880s through 1920, advocated nonpartisan judicial elections, and a dozen states adopted them by 1927.

Further reforms in the latter half of the 20th century brought about the rise of the "Missouri plan" of judicial selection, named after the first state to adopt it. Under the Missouri plan, a nonpartisan merit commission is designated with the power to present to the governor a list of names for consideration for judicial positions. The governor is then assigned the task of choosing from among these recommended candidates. The individuals chosen then face retention elections after a particular duration of tenure. In retention elections, the BALLOT asks voters simply whether a particular judge should be retained rather than pitting him or her against specific opponents in electoral competition. At present, Missouri plan merit selection and nonpartisan elections are the most common methods of selecting state judges in the United States. There is often a mix of judicial election systems within a single state as officials at different levels of the state judiciary are selected by different means.

Proponents of judicial elections tout them as a vital link between the judiciary and the ELECTORATE, providing legitimacy and accountability. For decades the predominant model of judicial elections was partisan. Judicial candidates were recruited by the political parties and listed on the party ticket along with candidates for other elected positions. Ticket-splitting was rarely an option until AT-LARGE ELECTIONS were introduced at the end of the 19th century. PARTY ORGANIZATIONS effectively controlled judicial positions, and they were often given as rewards to party loyalists. While no longer the primary means of judicial selection, partisan judicial elections continue to be used for state supreme court judges in seven states and for lower-level courts in a similar number.

Party labels offer clues as to the potential behavior of a judge on the bench, just as they give voters hints about candidates for legislative and executive offices. This is cited as an advantage of partisan judicial elections because voters often have little information on which to make voting decisions. Some states and organizations have taken steps to provide additional information in judicial elections by circulating voter guides, but the question of whether voters have sufficient information to make educated choices in judicial elections persists.

Controversy has long existed over the propriety of injecting partisan politics into judicial campaigns and elections. Partisan judicial campaigns tend to be more competitive and contentious than nonpartisan or retention elections, and observers have indicated that partisan judicial elections may undermine public confidence in the judiciary or inappropriately influence judges' decisions. The latter could occur if judges attempt to satisfy their PRIMARY or GENERAL ELECTION constituencies rather than deciding cases on the merits or adhering to accepted standards of judicial conduct. Many otherwise qualified potential candidates for judicial positions may also be deterred from public service by the prospect of facing a COMPETITIVE ELECTION fight. Election campaigns can also be a significant demand on the time of sitting judges, possibly detracting from their ability to attend to judicial duties.

Nonpartisan judicial elections came into widespread use in the Progressive Era as a means of removing judges from the political process and party influence. It was thought that nonpartisan elections would increase the quality of the bench and strip the political parties of their ability to use the judiciary as a component of the spoils system. However, partisanship has remained an issue in nonpartisan judicial elections, though in a more nuanced manner. While partisanship may still affect events such as initial ascension to the bench if a potential judge's loyalties are known, nonpartisan judicial elections are much less likely to involve the political parties in electoral competition. Incumbent candidates in nonpartisan judicial elections win reelection in most cases, and quite often do not face a CHALLENGER. Voter ignorance or apathy regarding judicial elections may be even more pronounced in nonpartisan elections, as the voting public is not provided so much as a party label with which to assess candidates.

Retention elections are those under the Missouri plan in which judicial candidates do not face direct competition, but a question appears on voters' ballots simply asking if a particular judge should be retained in his or her office. In addition, retention elections are nonpartisan. Judges are rarely rejected in retention elections. Such electoral defeats tend to occur only when a judge has engaged in highly publicized controversial behavior. This behavior can attract widespread media coverage or organized opposition sufficient to mobilize the public against a particular incumbent. Judges who face retention elections generally enjoy long tenures and substantial electoral security. As retention elections are used in conjunction with a merit selection process, judges who maintain their office by retention are thought to be further removed from partisan politics than are their colleagues in the more overtly political partisan and nonpartisan electoral systems.

In partisan, nonpartisan, and retention judicial elections alike, there is a high degree of ballot "roll-off" as voters fail to participate even while at the polls. This is likely due to the usually nonsalient nature of judicial elections and the voting public's general lack of interest and information pertaining to them. Reform advocates have suggested disclosure of campaign contributors, campaign limits, judicial performance evaluations, and the distribution of voter guides to improve judicial campaigns and elections. Despite the differences in avenues by which state court judges can attain and retain their positions, legal and political science research has failed to find a significant difference in the quality of judges based on the election or selection method used.

A 2002 study by Justice at Stake, a nonpartisan organization that advocates fair and impartial courts, found that the year 2000 was a turning point for escalating costs and conflict in judicial elections. State supreme court candidates in that year alone raised more than $45 million in campaign funds, marking a 61 percent increase over the prior ELECTION CYCLE in 1998. Sixteen individual candidates raised in excess of $1 million for their state supreme court campaigns. Justice at Stake also found that "politics as usual" was seeping into the judicial election process. This included mass media advertisements, heated rhetoric, and large-scale interest group participation. Races in Michigan, Illinois, and Alabama in 2000 were particularly costly, with the candidates in Alabama alone raising more than $13 million in campaign funds. While the Justice at Stake campaign did not find such activities uniform across states, they did warn that they are becoming increasingly more common.

The dynamics of future judicial elections may be significantly influenced by the U.S. Supreme Court's ruling in *Republican Party of Minnesota v. White* 536 U.S. 765 (2002). Prior to this decision, many states had laws governing judicial election campaigns that prevented judicial candidates from publicly commenting on pending cases or issues that may come before courts in the future. These statutes were based on accepted rules governing judicial conduct. These rules disallow judges from discussing pending or potential future case issues to prevent the appearance of bias or a conflict of interest. The Supreme Court's decision struck down these statutes as violations of the First Amendment's protection of free speech. By a 5 to 4 margin, the Court ruled that the speech of judicial candidates could not be so limited, with Justice Antonin Scalia's majority opinion stating that disallowing issue-related political speech was not a constitutionally permissible means of assuring a fair and impartial judiciary. This decision will allow judicial candidates to discuss policy issues more vigorously than ever before in an attempt to sway voters. While the Court's decision did not disallow state regulation of judicial elections altogether, it may have the effect of encouraging a much wider range of political speech in judicial campaigns than had previously been permitted by professional standards and state regulation.

Judicial elections have recently become more contentious, expensive, and caustic. As interest groups and other parties have witnessed the judiciary become an effective force for policy change, they have increased efforts to influence the selection of state judges. Judicial elections remain popular among the public despite a general lack of voter knowledge and recognition of the potential risks associated with a politically indebted judiciary. If recent trends are any indication, judicial elections may become more combative and expensive in many states. It will be left to the individual states to determine if they are satisfied with the balance reached between judicial accountability and judicial independence within their own borders.

Further reading: Baum, Lawrence. "Electing Judges." In Lee Epstein, ed., *Contemplating Courts.* Washington, D.C.: CQ Press, 1995; Champagne, Anthony. "Political Parties and Judicial Elections." *Loyola of Los Angeles Law Review* 34 (2001): 1,411–1,427; Goldberg, Deborah, Craig Holman, and Samantha Sanchez. *The New Politics of Judicial Elections.* New York: Justice at Stake Campaign, 2002; Sheldon, Charles H., and Linda S. Maule. *Choosing Justice: The Recruitment of State and Federal Judges.* Pullman: Washington State University Press, 1997.

—Richard L. Vining, Jr.

elections, local and state

In local elections, residents of a specific locality or jurisdiction vote to elect officials to numerous offices, ranging from mayor to sheriff to school board. In 2002, there were 87,849 units of local government in the United States, according to the U.S. Census Bureau. These substate governments range widely, including counties, towns, cities, school districts, and water districts, to name but a few. They have different structures, election procedures, and responsibilities, although they often overlap. These local governments provide services directly to the citizens living in their boundaries, and the types of officials elected to run the governments vary.

In most counties, the local legislature is called a board of commissioners (or supervisors or selectmen, depending on the state and county). Regardless of what they are called, these individuals are elected to two-year or four-year terms, staggered so that only some members of the board are up for election each year. Some states and counties also elect other officials, including a sheriff, a treasurer, a district attorney, and a tax collector. Cities and other municipalities often elect mayors and city councils, either in ward elections or AT-LARGE ELECTIONS. The power arrangements between the mayor and the city council and the city manager (who is often appointed by the city council to oversee the day-to-day operations of city government) vary depending on each municipality's form of government and charter. In addition, more than 30,000 special districts exist across the country, including school districts, sewer and water districts, and other special purpose districts that cover housing, protection, and sanitation. Many of these special districts are governed by individuals elected at the local level.

What distinguishes local elections from state and national elections is that the vast majority of local elections (more than two-thirds) are nonpartisan in nature. As the old saying goes, "There isn't a Republican or Democratic way to pave a street." This does not necessarily mean that parties cannot or do not endorse candidates in nonpartisan elections, or that informed voters are not aware of partisan leanings or backgrounds of specific candidates. It just means that a partisan identification is not on the BALLOT. It is also important to note that local elective offices often serve as a "proving ground" for many politicians, especially women and minorities.

Turnout for local elections is usually half the average turnout in PRESIDENTIAL ELECTIONS. Despite the fact that local government has more direct impact on their lives than does national POLITICS, most people are less informed about (and less motivated by) local elections. In addition, some localities hold elections for local officials in May, so that they are independent from the highly partisan nature of state and national elections.

In state elections, residents of a state select officials to fill specific offices and act on their behalf by creating laws and setting policy. The U.S. Constitution gives states the authority to determine when and how elections will be held. Each state's election code describes the guidelines for how the elections are conducted (what machinery is used, what the ballots look like, etc.) and also determines who can be a candidate for office. The state, in turn, relies on the counties and cities to run the polls and manage the election. In most states, the secretary of state has the responsibility for conducting elections.

State elections vary greatly across the country, based largely on each state's election laws, history, and political culture. All 50 states elect a governor, who serves as the chief executive officer of the state. Most states also allow for the popular election of a number of other officeholders, including a lieutenant governor, an attorney general (the top law enforcement officer of the state), a state treasurer, and a secretary of state. In some states, the candidates of the same party run as a ticket; in others, they do not. Many states also allow for the election of judges, either in partisan or nonpartisan elections, as well as insurance commissioners and other specialized officers. In other states, many of these positions are appointed by the governor or the legislature.

A total of 49 states elect sets of legislators for two bodies, a state senate and a state house of representatives or DELEGATES. (Nebraska, the lone exception, has a unicameral legislature.) The state house of representatives has more members than the state senate, and the representatives generally serve two-year terms. Members of the state senate usually serve four-year terms. In addition, roughly half the states allow for some form of DIRECT DEMOCRACY, usually through BALLOT INITIATIVES or referenda. California is particularly notorious for its frequency of ballot initiatives, popular referenda, and most recently, a RECALL REFERENDUM of former governor Gray Davis.

Further reading: Smith, Kevin B., Alan Greenblat, and John Buntin. *Governing States and Localities.* Washington, D.C.: CQ Press, 2005; Bowman, Ann O'M., and Richard C. Kearney. *State and Local Government.* 4th ed. Boston: Houghton Mifflin, 1999; Elazar, Daniel. *American Federalism: A View from the States.* 3rd ed. New York: HarperCollins, 1984.

—Joshua J. Scott

elections, U.S. Senate

Elections to the U.S. Senate occur every year that ends in an even number. Senators serve for terms that last six years and that are staggered in such a way that only one-third of the body of the Senate is up for election in any given election. This staggered format was purposefully developed to keep the members of the Senate as far away from the stirred passions of the ELECTORATE as possible, without violating the democratic values of the newly formed nation. This was part of a larger effort on the part of the DELEGATES to the Constitutional Convention to create a Senate that functioned as a small and independent body of legislators composed of wise, independent, and distinguished members.

The Senate has become a responsive legislative chamber, contrary to the original intentions of the architects of the nation's charter. This unforeseen responsiveness is due in large part to the electoral connection that links senators to their constituents. Not only did the framers not expect senators to campaign in closely contested elections as they currently do, but also the original method of senatorial selection did not have senators standing for direct election at all.

The delegates to the Constitutional Convention of 1787 wanted the Senate to serve as a calming influence on the majoritarian impulses that they expected to assault the lower chamber of the legislature, the House of Representatives. In order to do so, they devised an indirect form of senatorial selection. Instead of having the public choose their senators as they chose their representatives, the senators would be chosen by the legislatures of each individual state. Not only did the framers believe that this would temper legislative pandering to the passions of the electorate, they also thought that it would yield more professional and prestigious senators. In addition, they believed that such a selection mechanism would more successfully ensure that senators represented the interests of their respective states, rather than their individual constituents.

The delegates to the Constitutional Convention considered three distinct proposals concerning how best to conduct senatorial selection. These included proposals to allow state legislatures to select senators, to allow the House of Representatives to pick from individuals who were nominated by state legislatures, and to allow senators to be directly elected from massive districts that represented multiple states. Delegates to the convention from smaller states supported the proposal that placed responsibility for senatorial selection in the hands of the state legislatures, largely because they felt that such a process would lead to increased representation of small states in the federal government. Eventually the delegates to the convention compromised between the interests of small state delegates and the preferences of the delegates representing larger states.

Under the indirect, state legislature–based selection process that was eventually agreed upon, the Constitution did not stipulate how the states were to choose their senators; it only ambiguously assigned them the task. By the 1860s, federal legislation was necessary to provide electoral guidance, as some states were having difficulty deciding on their senators even as others were doing so under conditions of dubious legality. Some of this legislation responded to a controversy over the selection of New Jersey senator Robert F. Stockton, which was challenged on the grounds that he was not elected by a majority vote, as the state law required, but rather by a plurality. When the Senate took up the appeal, Stockton's election was certified by a vote of 22 to 21, with Stockton himself casting the deciding BALLOT. Rethinking the appropriateness of allowing Stockton to vote on his own selection, the Senate unseated the senator a short time later. Soon after, the Senate passed legislation providing that in the event that concurrent votes in a state legislature failed to choose the same person, that legislature would be required to meet again in joint assembly every day until someone did receive a clear majority.

Nevertheless, this legislation corrected only one problem in a senatorial selection process that was quickly proving to be full of holes. The inability of states to decide on senators was a chronic problem, with 14 seats going unfilled in as many years (1891–1905). Moreover, when the states were able to send SLATES of senators to the Capitol, they very frequently matched the delegations sent by the same states to the House of Representatives. Given this, the framers' goals of stability and temperance were not met very successfully or often under the indirect selection format.

Regardless of this, the indirect selection mechanism stayed in place until the ratification of the SEVENTEENTH AMENDMENT in 1913. Public disapproval of this electoral arrangement, however, had begun to make itself felt only a few decades after the Constitution was ratified. Beginning in the 1820s, pressure to more fully democratize the Senate began to grow, increasing exponentially as tales of graft, bribery, and corruption in the selection process continued to surface. In the early spring of 1826, a New York congressman put forward a resolution to amend the Constitution in order to provide for direct election to the Senate. The resolution was quickly tabled.

The Progressives of the late 1800s and early 20th century viewed the constitutional structure with suspicion. After 1880 there were 167 attempts to amend the Constitution. The arguments on behalf of direct election centered on legislative impasse, corruption, wealth, and conservatism. Between 1885 and 1912, there were more than 70 deadlocks in state legislatures on the selection of a senator, resulting in delays or no selection for entire legislative sessions—not surprising given that opposing parties often controlled opposing houses. Deadlocks sometimes resulted in a greasing of the process by way of bribes, causing Senate investigations 14 times between 1866 and 1912 for ELECTION FRAUD.

The Populist movement was based largely on the suspicion of wealth and influence and the cleansing powers of democracy. The Senate was described as "too far removed from the people" and their true wishes. The cure was thought to lie in liberalizing the political process—direct democracy. Nebraska senator William Jennings Bryan and others contended that the constitutional structure, as written, might have been needed in the past, but that modern citizens needed a "new system." Simply put, the Progressives believed that the common person was inherently good and, with a more democratic system, could correct the deficiencies in POLITICS and society.

Since 1914, voters have fluctuated in the degree to which they repudiate incumbents. Some elections have seen only a single senator removed from office via the ballot box, while other years have seen as many as 14 incumbents rejected. Numerous scholars have attempted to explain this fluctuation, using many different theoretical explanations and variables. Some of the most solid research has found statistically significant relationships between the electoral outcome and national economic and political conditions, including, for example, changes in real disposable income, national economic indicators, and presidential popularity. Other important predictors include PARTY IDENTIFICATION, issue considerations, sociotropic concerns, and levels of political expertise.

While many different variables have been shown to correlate strongly and significantly with Senate election outcomes, perhaps the most important finding over recent years is that Senate elections have become considerably more competitive than are elections for the House of Representatives. Because senators operate on the basis of an electoral incentive, the upper legislative chamber has also become much more responsive to shifts in public sentiment. This situation is directly counter to the political situation the framers had attempted to engineer during the Constitutional Convention. Nevertheless, while it may be contrary to the spirit of the framers, this unforeseen phenomenon can be explained retrospectively.

A number of different trends have affected Senate elections since the 1960s. One such trend has been the partisan DEALIGNMENT and growth of interparty competition in states that previously were the domain of only one party. A second trend has been the continuing appeal of a Senate seat to ambitious politicians and elites. Third, campaign spending has increased dramatically, making elections closer and thus more competitive. Finally, the rise of television, and with it televised campaigning, has also increased the level of competitiveness in Senate races. Incumbency does not provide nearly the insulation in the Senate, where approximately 20 percent of incumbents lose, as it does in the House of Representatives, where only around 5 percent of the incumbents fail to win reelection. Much of this difference in competitiveness has been caused by the differences in the quality of CHALLENGERS and the intensity of campaigns. Incumbent senators face much more vigorous, better financed challenges from far better-known and qualified candidates. In addition, for the most part, states provide far more heterogeneous constituencies than do CONGRESSIONAL DISTRICTS. As national elections have become increasingly candidate-centered affairs, the burden of this change has been placed on the shoulders of sitting senators.

While it is certain that this current state of affairs conflicts with the goals stated in the U.S. Constitution, it also has important consequences for the decision making that occurs within the Senate and for the politics and policy that come out of it. The increased role that representation has come to play in the job performance of senators has affected how senators approach key institutions within the Senate, as well as the positions they espouse and the votes they cast. In terms of institutions, the increasing demand of responsiveness on the part of senators has affected how senators choose their committee assignments, how they relate to the media, and whether and to what extent they seek leadership positions within their party and the Senate. In terms of policy positions, electorally inclined senators have been forced to follow the views and preferences of their constituents instead of doing what they feel is right. Failure to appease one's constituents can mean almost certain replacement the next time one must face the voters. Due to this, the U.S. Senate has not become the mediating influence on public passions that the framers envisioned it to be. Indeed, quite the opposite is the case.

Further reading: Abramowitz, Alan I., and Jeffrey A. Segal. "Determinants of the Outcomes of U.S. Senate Elections." *Journal of Politics* 48 (1986): 433–439; Abramowitz, Alan I., and Jeffrey A. Segal. *Senate Elections.* Ann Arbor: University of Michigan Press, 1992; Center for Responsive Politics. Available online. URL: http://www.opensecrets.org. Accessed August 10, 2005; Gronke, Paul. *The Electorate, the Campaign, and the Office: A Unified Approach to Senate and House Elections.* Ann Arbor: University of Michigan Press, 2001; Lee, Francis E., and Bruce I. Oppenheimer. *Sizing up the Senate: The Unequal Consequences of Equal Representation.* Chicago: University of Chicago Press, 1999; U.S. Senate. Available online. URL: http://www.senate.gov. Accessed August 10, 2005; Westlye, Mark C. *Senate Elections and Campaign Intensity.* Baltimore: Johns Hopkins University Press, 1991.

—Justin S. Vaughn and Jeff A. Martineau

elector

In its simplest terms, an elector is a voter, although in American POLITICS it formally denotes a member of the ELECTORAL COLLEGE. In the PRESIDENTIAL ELECTION system, an elector is a public official responsible for casting a state's BALLOTS for president and vice president. A state has as many electors as electoral votes, which is equal to its total number of U.S. representatives and senators. The Constitution guarantees each state no less than three electors, two representing the state and one its population. The TWENTY-THIRD AMENDMENT (1961) provides Washington, D.C., a minimum of three electors (though the District does not have any voting members in Congress). The results of the decennial CENSUS reapportion the nation's total number of electors, fixed at 538, among the 50 states and the District of Columbia.

While many DELEGATES to the Constitutional Convention in 1787 apparently backed the office of elector as a compromise between legislative appointment and direct popular election, those promoting the Constitution afterward argued that electors would ensure broad representation. As with Congress, Federalists defended the Electoral College as providing a representative deliberative majority, a means to make choices that the majority of the people would make if they had the time, commitment, and knowledge to weigh the merits of the candidates. As Alexander Hamilton argued in Federalist No. 68, the selection of president would "be made by men most capable of analyzing the qualities adapted to the station and acting under circumstances favorable to deliberation." Advocates of the Constitution held that electors would possess high social standing, education, and a devotion to politics. Moreover, the design of the electoral meeting—having at least three electors; taking place in each state; gathering for no more than one day; converging on the same day (all meetings in the nation); excluding any person having allegiance to Congress, state legislatures, or the president; and preventing electors from casting their two ballots for candidates from the same state—would eliminate political influence and facilitate deliberation among electors about the candidates. Because men of integrity and knowledge would serve as electors within a deliberative structure, "the sense of the people" would inform their decisions, and they would choose presidents possessing "characters preeminent for ability and virtue."

Electors at a few of the early meetings did discuss the candidates. However, the emergence of political parties and the widespread adoption of the winner-take-all method quickly altered these intentions. The Constitution protects the right of each state to determine how to appoint electors. By the 1830s, most states had adopted the UNIT RULE, also known as the winner-take-all system. Under this method, the POLITICAL PARTY of the presidential ticket winning the most POPULAR VOTES in a state in November receives all of that state's electoral votes at the December elector meeting. With this "general ticket," a state does not split its electoral votes among different candidates, and the deliberation discussed by Madison and others as the chief benefit of the Electoral College is essentially removed from the system. Lacking a deliberative element, critics of the current system argue that rather than refining and enlarging the public will, as was the desire of the nation's founders, the system merely distorts voter preference. Today, other than

Maine and Nebraska, all states and the District of Columbia use the winner-take-all selection of electors.

In nearly every state, political PARTY ORGANIZATIONS select the SLATE of people who will serve as electors if their presidential ticket wins the state's popular vote. State party conventions nominate electors in a few more than 30 states, state party committees do so in approximately 10 states, voters select their party's electors in closed primaries in Arizona, and various combinations of these methods exist in the remaining states.

Serving as an elector is essentially a reward for extensive party leadership or support and, in a few cases, financial contributions. For example, some of the more prominent electors of New York included Horace Greeley (1864), Fredrick Douglass (1872), John Jacob Astor (1880), William Steinway (1893), George Eastman (1901), Mario Cuomo (1988, 1992), and Elizabeth Moynihan (1988, 1992).

Electors gather in their respective states on the first Monday after the second Wednesday of December and cast their ballots for president and vice president. In most states, electors meet at their state capitol building. The winning party dominates a state's electoral meeting. High-profile state party leaders and members attend, speakers remind electors about the historic importance of the occasion and that they should "do their duty," and the gathering may extend special recognition to life-long members who have recently passed away. Contrary to the stated expectations of the office, electors do not deliberate over the candidates or decide who to vote for at the meeting.

The TWELFTH AMENDMENT to the Constitution mandates that each elector cast two separate ballots, one for president and another for vice president. After doing so, electors record the results on "Certificates of Vote," which they then mail to the archivist of the United States and other officials. This certificate identifies only the two candidates having won the plurality in a state and the number of electoral votes for each one. Because of the winner-take-all system, a state's electoral college does not assign any electoral votes to candidates in second or third place or list them on the certificate. The two states that use district selection have not as yet divided their electoral votes. Today, the actions of electors are rarely a surprise.

Because the winner-take-all system delivers all of a state's electoral votes to one presidential and one vice presidential candidate, only a "faithless" elector can split a state's vote. Such electors break their pledges to cast their ballots for the presidential ticket that has won the state's GENERAL ELECTION. There is no constitutional or federal provision requiring electors to vote according to their state's popular vote. Several states have measures to fine or replace a faithless elector, although such laws may be unconstitutional. In a close election, just one or two faithless electors could reverse the election results or deny the requisite national majority to a candidate, thereby throwing the election to

Congress. However, a turncoat elector has never resulted in either of these scenarios. In fact, there have been few faithless electors; most scholars agree that only nine of more than 21,000 electors during the last two centuries have voted "against instruction." Nevertheless, the relationship of the elector with democracy remains subject to scrutiny.

Further reading: Congressional Quarterly. "The Electoral College." In John L. Moore, Jon P. Preimesberger, and David Tarr, eds., *Congressional Quarterly's Guide to U.S. Elections.* 4th ed. Washington, D.C.: CQ Press, 2001; Longley, Lawrence D., and Neal R. Peirce. *The Electoral College Primer 2000.* New Haven, Conn.: Yale University Press, 1999; Peirce, Neal R., and Lawrence D. Longley. *The People's President: The Electoral College in American History and the Direct Vote Alternative.* New Haven, Conn.: Yale University Press, 1981.

—Gary Bugh

elector, faithless

Faithless ELECTORS are members of the ELECTORAL COLLEGE who vote against the candidate they were selected to represent. Although electors are bound by law to vote for their party's candidates only in Maine and Nebraska, there is great pressure within POLITICAL PARTY establishments to follow the party's wishes. It is also normally considered a great honor to be chosen as a presidential elector, and as a result, electors are usually the party's most loyal and long-serving activists. Thus, voting against the wishes of the ELECTORATE and the party establishment would tend to alienate one from the party.

The first faithless elector was Samuel Miles of Pennsylvania, who voted for Thomas Jefferson in 1796 instead of John Adams, whom he had been elected to support. A letter published in a newspaper at the time expressed the view many have of faithless electors even today: "What, do I chuse Samuel Miles to determine for me whether John Adams or Thomas Jefferson shall be president? No! I chuse him to act, not to think." Faithless electors are often cited as a reason for abolishing the Electoral College. In a close election, such as 2000, faithless electors could have made the difference, although it is doubtful someone would act faithlessly knowing it would affect the outcome. Other proposals for reforming the Electoral College call for abolishing only the electors, whereby electoral votes would be awarded automatically based on a state's POPULAR VOTE.

There have been only nine cases of faithless electors in recent history. In 2004, a Minnesota elector, apparently by mistake, cast a vote for John Edwards rather than John Kerry. Barbara Lett-Simmons of the District of Columbia chose to abstain in 2000 rather than vote for Democratic nominee Al Gore as a protest against the district's lack of congressional representation. It was the first abstention by an elector since 1872. In 1988, Margarette Leach of West

Virginia reversed the Democratic ticket, voting for Senator Lloyd Bentsen for president and Governor Michael S. Dukakis for vice president. In 1976, Mike Padden of Washington voted for Ronald Reagan instead of President Gerald R. Ford. He claimed this was a protest against winner Jimmy Carter's stance on legalized abortion and not a protest against Ford. Padden at the same time voted for Robert Dole for vice president, making Dole the only vice presidential nominee to receive more votes than the presidential nominee. Padden has fared better than some faithless electors in party circles: He was subsequently elected to the Washington legislature and later became a judge. In 1972, Roger MacBride of Virginia voted for the Libertarian ticket instead of the Republican ticket that he had been elected to support. The LIBERTARIAN PARTY ran a woman for vice president that year, and as a result of MacBride's faithlessness, she became the first woman in history to win an electoral vote. (MacBride, a descendant of Laura Ingalls Wilder, ran as the Libertarian candidate himself in 1976.) Lloyd Bailey of North Carolina voted for George Wallace, the AMERICAN INDEPENDENT PARTY candidate, instead of Richard M. Nixon in 1968, in part because Wallace had been the plurality popular vote winner in Bailey's CONGRESSIONAL DISTRICT. Wallace carried five other states and won a total of 46 electoral votes. In 1960, Henry Irwin of Oklahoma voted for Harry Byrd for president and Barry M. Goldwater for vice president and urged the other electors to do so as well. No other party electors did, although Byrd received 14 votes from electors in Mississippi and Alabama who had been chosen by direct election and not as a result of party election. (Alabama continued to use direct election of electors, whereby voters choose actual electors on the BALLOT instead of presidential candidates, until 1984.) In 1956, W. F. Turner of Alabama voted for a local judge instead of Democratic nominee Adlai E. Stevenson. In 1948, Preston Parks of Tennessee voted for Strom Thurmond, the States' Rights Party candidate, instead of Democratic president Harry S. Truman. Thurmond carried four states and won a total of 39 electoral votes.

Before these recent cases, it had been 116 years since there had been faithless electors for president, except due to death, although they appeared more frequently in the case of vice presidential nominees in that period. In 1872 and 1912, nominated candidates died between the election and the date of the Electoral College voting, and various electors chose to disperse their votes to living persons. The TWENTIETH AMENDMENT to the U.S. Constitution clarified the procedures in case of the death of a nominee, making it rational for electors to vote for a deceased candidate. In 1896, four electors of the PEOPLE'S PARTY voted for the Democratic vice presidential nominee instead of their party's candidate.

The only case in which faithless electors affected the outcome of an election was in 1836, when the Virginia electors abstained rather than vote for Democratic vice presidential nominee Richard Johnson due to his cohabitation with a black woman. These 23 abstentions forced the election into the Senate, which chose Johnson anyway.

Two electors of Maryland in 1832 abstained for president, and all of the Pennsylvania electors voted against Martin Van Buren for vice president in favor of William Wilkins. In 1828, seven electors of Georgia voted for William Smith instead of John C. Calhoun for vice president.

In 1820, William Plummer, Sr., of New Hampshire cast the only vote in the Electoral College against President James Monroe. Plummer felt that George Washington should be the only president ever elected unanimously, so he voted for John Quincy Adams.

In 1812, three FEDERALIST PARTY electors voted for the REPUBLICAN PARTY candidate for vice president instead. (That Republican Party is no relation to the modern Republican Party; in fact, it later changed its name to the DEMOCRATIC PARTY, which is still the country's largest party.) In 1808, several electors refused to vote for James Madison for president and instead voted for the vice presidential nominee, George Clinton.

Further reading: Abbott, David W. *Wrong Winner: The Coming Debacle in the Electoral College.* New York: Praeger, 1991; Longley, Lawrence D., and Neal R. Peirce. *The Electoral College Primer.* New Haven, Conn.: Yale University Press, 1999.

—Tony L. Hill

Electoral College

The Electoral College is the constitutionally mandated mechanism for selecting the president of the United States. A total of 538 votes exist in the Electoral College and are distributed among the American states based on the combined number of senators and representatives each state has in the U.S. Congress. In addition, the District of Columbia possesses three electoral votes. Each state selects the predetermined number of ELECTORS from its population—members of Congress and other federal officers are ineligible for selection—and has the body meet approximately one month after the American ELECTORATE votes in the GENERAL ELECTION. The outcome of the general election governs the votes of the members of the Electoral College, as all states but two (Maine and Nebraska) cast their votes in a winner-take-all fashion based on the winner of the general election in each state.

While electors are not bound by federal law to follow this traditional determinant of their vote, departures from the norm have been infrequent and inconsequential. Those who have diverged from their instructions have been given the label FAITHLESS ELECTORS.

The Electoral College was designed by the framers of the U.S. Constitution as a means of ensuring the selection

In the Texas Electoral College meeting at the Capitol in Austin, the Republican electors vote unanimously for George W. Bush and Dick Cheney, December 18, 2000. *(Corbis)*

of a president who was the most qualified, but not necessarily the most popular. The Electoral College was originally proposed and accepted as an alternative to two other proposed methods of selecting presidents: selection by direct POPULAR VOTE and selection by the legislature. The latter method was rejected because of its potential threat to the separation of powers and checks and balances, whereas the dismissal of the former option was more complex. The framers did not believe that the general public had the ability to choose the best candidate for the presidency, nor were they willing to tolerate the regional confrontations that would arise during the conduct of such a public campaign. While sentiment was generally in favor of an alternative, indirect form of presidential selection, the framers were not able to agree on a method until late in the Constitutional Convention.

With the convention coming to an end, a hasty compromise was reached. It stipulated the selection of electors in each state by rules determined by each state's legislature. The electors would meet at a determined time and send the results to the president of the U.S. Senate for certification and announcement. Whichever candidate received the majority of the votes would be president, and the runner-up would become vice president. If no candidate won a majority of the votes, the determination of the presidency would be thrown into the U.S. House of Representatives, with each state's delegation being accorded a single vote. The Senate would operate in a similar fashion in the selection of the vice president.

The arguments in support of the Electoral College have been romanticized to a great degree over the centuries, but the reality of its adoption as the dominant mode of presidential selection in American POLITICS is of a less distinguished historical reality. In essence, the debate over presidential selection was one of the loose ends remaining to be tied up at the close of the Constitutional Convention. The framers were driven more by pragmatic considerations, based on their contemporary political realities and a desire to end the convention and replace the ARTICLES OF CONFEDERATION, than they were by any ideal theory of presidential selection that necessitated the advent of the Electoral College. The agreement on the form of the Electoral College was a function of pressure on the DELEGATES to reach agreement on the larger constitution itself, a lack of concern for the selection process, and shared misunderstanding of the likely dispersion of support for presidential candidates. Nevertheless, this has not stopped proponents of the Electoral College from trumpeting the institution's value as protector of federalism, small states, and national interest.

Following ratification of the U.S. Constitution, the Electoral College has been employed in every PRESIDENTIAL ELECTION since 1788. Over the decades and centuries since, however, a variety of reforms have been made to the procedural aspects of the Electoral College. As parties began to dominate national politics, something the framers of the Constitution did not envision, the effects of FACTION began to be felt in the Electoral College and on presidential politics more generally. The administration of John Adams was often beset by strife resulting from the attempts of Thomas Jefferson, his political rival and runner-up, to subvert his authority. Moreover, the tied vote in the 1800 contest between Jefferson and Aaron Burr resulted in some last-minute political excitement, but ultimately ended when the Federalist-controlled House of Representatives selected Jefferson as president. This problem was ultimately remedied by the TWELFTH AMENDMENT, which, when passed in 1804, provided for separate balloting for president and vice president.

Controversy and crisis continued to follow the Electoral College into the 1820s. In the election of 1824, the House of Representatives again was forced to follow its constitutional duty and choose among the top three vote getters, since none had received a majority. Henry Clay, who had received the fifth-most votes, threw his considerable clout in the legislature behind John Quincy Adams, who had received the second-most, thus snatching victory away from the leading candidate, Andrew Jackson. Jackson, naturally enraged by this deal making, began a movement to abolish the Electoral College. While ultimately unsuccessful at this venture, several states soon began to choose their electors based on direct election rather than legislative selection, thus making the process at least slightly more democratic.

The next major Electoral College crisis occurred in the election of 1876, when Democrat Samuel Tilden received 19 more Electoral College votes than did Republican Rutherford Hayes but still fell short of a majority. Hayes's supporters contested the outcome in several states, and pressure in Congress led to the creation of an Electoral Commission. The commission, comprised of seven Republicans, seven Democrats, and one nonpartisan judge, eventually sided with the claims of Hayes and his lieutenants, putting the Republican in office despite the victory margin of a quarter-million votes by Tilden in the popular vote and the dubious nature of Hayes's single-vote Electoral College margin.

A decade later, the Electoral College was again tested, when incumbent Democrat Grover Cleveland was pitted against his Republican challenger, Benjamin Harrison. Following a contentious campaign, largely waged as a REFERENDUM on Cleveland's opposition to high protective tariffs, Cleveland won a plurality of votes by a margin of just more than 95,000 votes, but lost the Electoral College contest with only 168 electoral votes, compared to Harrison's 233. Four years later, Cleveland returned to office with a considerable margin of victory.

The 20th century had its fair share of Electoral College controversies. There were several so-called hairbreadth elections in the 20th century, in which a very slight change in the popular vote of one or a few states could have caused yet another Electoral College crisis. Indeed, every presidential election since 1956 has been characterized by such close calls. The elections of 1948, 1960, 1968, and 1976 were especially close calls. In 1948, splinter parties threw the election into disarray, with Strom Thurmond and the Dixiecrats actually siphoning off Electoral College votes in the South, and Henry Wallace stealing votes from Truman in New York, Michigan, and Maryland, giving Thomas Dewey 70 more Electoral College votes than he would otherwise have received. In 1960, an exceptionally close election, fraught with substantiated claims of fraud and deception in places such as Texas and Chicago, proved to be another near miss for the Electoral College. During the election of 1968, the political disarray that characterized the broader electorate was mirrored in the presidential election. Richard Nixon eventually triumphed over Hubert H. Humphrey, the standard-bearer of a staggering DEMOCRATIC PARTY, and George Wallace, the Alabama governor who had run on a platform dominated by segregation. Finally, the election of 1976 featured outsider Jimmy Carter winning an election of beleaguered incumbent Gerald Ford that was largely up in the air as the election loomed closer. In sum, throughout the 20th century, the Electoral College avoided true tests of its procedures, but just barely.

The 21st century, however, does not hold the same prospect. In the election of 2000, the Electoral College once again became the scene of electoral crisis. Despite winning the popular contest by more than a half a million votes, Vice President Al Gore lost the presidency to George W. Bush after the U.S. Supreme Court effectively ended a BALLOT RECOUNT in the state of Florida. The narrowness of Bush's five to four victory in the Supreme Court led to widespread claims of illegitimacy of the Bush presidency, often featuring the refrains of Bush being "selected, not elected" as the nation's 43rd president and mockingly referred to as "his fraudulency." While the terrorist attacks of September 11, 2001, dampened much of this type of criticism, the debacle of the 2000 election prompted much debate over the role of the Electoral College in American politics. Nevertheless, there has been no reform of the process, due in large part to the fear among partisan operatives that any change to the system might upset the balance of power in favor of the other party. With the lack of reform and the persistence of 2000's political conditions, the nation may again see one candidate win the popular vote while the other is proclaimed president by virtue of an Electoral College victory.

There are several other consequences that result from the continued employment of the Electoral College. Specifically, the Electoral College benefits states with the very largest and very smallest amounts of votes, to the detriment of medium-sized states. It magnifies the influence of "swing" states and works against the electoral fortunes of independent THIRD PARTIES, relegating them to the role of SPOILER instead of offering genuine opportunities for victory.

Policy proposals concerning the reform, and often the abolition, of the Electoral College have been percolating among the American polity since long before the debacle of 2000. Among these, several figure prominently, including a direct vote alternative, which would abolish the Electoral College entirely. Other proposals for reform are less dramatic and concern changes to Electoral College procedures that would keep the institution but make it more democratically responsive. One proposal suggests that a state's electoral votes be distributed in proportion with the popular vote outcome, whereas another alternative suggests that the selection of electors should be removed from the state level and determined by special district and statewide elections. Yet another proposal focuses specifically on the problem of faithless electors and suggests automatically applying a state's Electoral College votes to the tally of whatever candidate the plurality of the state's voters cast their ballots for, thereby bypassing the use of actual electors. Without consistent pressure on policy makers, the proposals are at best an academic debate, with little change likely to occur.

Further reading: Federal Election Commission, Guide to the Electoral College. Available online. URL: http://www.fec.gov. Accessed August 10, 2005; Hardaway, Robert M. *The Electoral College and the Constitution: The Case for Preserving Federalism.* Westport, Conn.: Praeger, 1994; Edwards, George C., III. *Why the Electoral College Is Bad for America.* New Haven, Conn.: Yale University Press, 2004; Kura, Alexandra, ed. *Electoral College and Presidential Elections.* Huntington: Nova, 2001; Longley, Lawrence D., and Neal R. Pierce. *The Electoral College Primer.* New Haven, Conn.: Yale University Press, 1996; Pierce, Neal R., and Lawrence D. Longley. *The People's President: The Electoral College in American History and the Direct Vote Alternative.* New Haven, Conn.: Yale University Press, 1981.

—Justin S. Vaughn

Electoral College reform plans
Of the hundreds of ELECTORAL COLLEGE reform plans that members of Congress have introduced, the automatic,

proportional, district, and direct election plans stand out as the most popular. Despite the number of reform plans, Congress has not approved any of the proposed amendments to the Constitution (a process that would require two-thirds support from the House and the Senate). The Senate passed district selection of ELECTORS in 1813, 1819, and 1820. In 1950, the Senate voted in favor of the proportional system, and in 1969 an overwhelming majority of the House endorsed direct election. While neither chamber has recommended the automatic proposal, the Senate considered it in 1934. Reviewing the basic arguments for and against each of these plans may indicate why Congress has not amended the PRESIDENTIAL ELECTION system.

The automatic plan would eliminate the office of elector and mandate the UNIT RULE for each state. With this winner-take-all method, which all states (other than Maine and Nebraska) and the District of Columbia currently use, the presidential ticket winning the plurality of the POPULAR VOTE in a state receives all of that state's electoral votes. Under the automatic system, states would no longer hold elector meetings, avoiding altogether the chance of a "faithless" elector, that is, of an elector casting a BALLOT contrary to expectations. Moreover, by keeping the winner-take-all method, this plan would provide decisive election results, contributing to national unity following a close election. Supporters of the automatic system have also held that it would strengthen the system of federalism by emphasizing the role of states as election units and state and local parties as organizing structures in the presidential election process. Problematic with the plan, however, particularly to those who support minor parties, is that it would cement the two major parties into American POLITICS. Other objections argue that forcing states to use the same electoral method weakens the federal system. Retaining the "constant two" electoral votes helps the smaller states, and using the winner-take-all system sustains influential "pivotal" states. Nevertheless, several presidents, including Thomas Jefferson, Benjamin Harrison, John F. Kennedy, and Lyndon B. Johnson, have favored this reform. In 1826, Representative Charles E. Haynes of Georgia supported the first congressional resolution for this proposal. In 1934, the Senate fell seven votes short of approving the automatic plan by the necessary two-thirds majority.

Reaching further than the automatic proposal, the proportional plan would abolish the office of elector and winner-take-all method, and create a system to disperse each state's electoral votes among the candidates according to their popular vote in the state. Of all the Electoral College reform proposals, Congress has come closest to approving the proportional system. Proponents of this plan have argued that it would equally count every person's vote throughout the nation, since the current winner-take-all method effectively applies all popular votes to the ticket winning a state, arguably "disenfranchising" people who voted for other candidates. At least in the 1950s, advocates also held that abolishing the winner-take-all system would end the enormous influence of pivotal states such as New York and Illinois, as well as the swing power of minority groups within such states. During the 1956 congressional deliberations over this plan, opponents, including the junior senator of Massachusetts, John Kennedy, argued that the current system already provided representation for small states, large states, and, through pivotal states, minority groups. Opponents added that this system would destabilize American politics by fueling the proliferation of splinter parties and increasing the likelihood of a House election, as well as the demand to apply PROPORTIONAL REPRESENTATION to Congress. The earliest introduction of the proportional plan in Congress was in 1848 by Representative William T. Lawrence of New York. On February 1, 1950, the Senate endorsed the "Lodge-Gossett" plan, named for its sponsors, Henry Cabot Lodge, Jr. (R, Mass.), and Ed Gossett (D, Tex.). A few months later, the House defeated this effort. The Senate again considered the plan in 1956 as part of the "Daniel substitute," which stipulated that states adopt either the proportional or the district system, but rejected it.

Similar in intention to the proportional system though different in structure, the district plan would keep the office of elector but replace the winner-take-all method with district selection of electors within each state. Along with using existing CONGRESSIONAL DISTRICTs, most proposals for this reform include two "at-large" electors for each state in order to support federalism, as well as the requirement that electors vote as pledged. Several states have used a district system, including Illinois (1820, 1824), Kentucky (1792–1824), Maine (1820–28, 1972–present), Maryland (1796–1832), Massachusetts (1804, 1812, and 1820), Michigan (1892), Missouri (1824), Nebraska (1992–present), New York (1828), North Carolina (1796–1808), Tennessee (1808–1828), and Virginia (1792, 1796). During the 1950s, proponents argued that the district system would provide an accurate reflection of the popular will and eliminate the undue influence of pivotal states, cities, and minority groups. They also held that because the winner-take-all method would continue to operate within each district, this proposed change would sustain the TWO-PARTY SYSTEM, preventing the growth of splinter parties while also providing reliable election totals. Moreover because districts would serve as the electoral units for both the president and members of Congress, this system would limit divided government, an electoral deadlock, and demands to change the nature of congressional representation. Opponents have charged that using the winner-take-all system at the district level would retain many of the problems of the current system. For example, under such a scheme, only the votes for the candidate winning a district would count, heavily populated areas would have overt influence, organized groups in large competitive districts could swing the

vote, and mistakes and fraud would continue to threaten election outcomes. Additionally, as opponents asserted in the late 1950s, eradicating pivotal states would destroy a method of minority group representation in the presidential election. They also argued that the plan would facilitate the growth of multiple parties, benefit small homogenous states, encourage GERRYMANDERing, and weaken the separation of power between the executive and legislative branches. The first person to offer this proposal was Republican John Nicholas of Virginia in 1800. Many prominent politicians have favored district selection of electors, including James Madison in 1823 and Andrew Johnson (R, Tenn.) as both representative and president. In March 1956, the Senate Judiciary Committee reported this proposal as part of the unsuccessful Daniel resolution.

The proposal that would make the most dramatic change and that has gained momentum since the mid-1960s is direct election. This reform would abolish the Electoral College completely and institute national popular election of the president and vice president. Most proposals for this system would require that a candidate win a predetermined percentage of the popular vote, such as 40 percent, in order to win the presidency, and, in case no candidate achieves this threshold, a RUNOFF ELECTION would be held. Proponents have argued that the recent expansion of SUFFRAGE corresponds with the "one-person, one-vote" element of national direct election, not with the current system's bias toward some states. Along with equally counting every person's vote, this plan would eliminate the chance of the national popular vote loser taking over the executive branch. Because parties would have to work harder in order to win sufficient national support, this system would increase two-party competition and prevent the proliferation of minor parties. The threshold and runoff features would do away with the need for any contingencies involving Congress or the Supreme Court. These democratic and stabilizing aspects of direct election would likely engender greater trust in the electoral system, thereby stimulating VOTER TURNOUT. Opponents disagree that this plan would equally count every person's vote and argue that it would instead entice candidates to campaign in heavily populated areas, ignoring the rest of the country. Direct election would therefore reduce the influence of states, particularly rural states, in the presidential election. Splinter parties would likely form in these areas, weakening the two-party system. Moreover, with changes in the distribution of electoral votes and party competition, the presidential election system now provides representation to minority groups throughout the nation. Some opponents have held that a national popular vote system would compel states to lower voter qualifications in order to increase their number of voters, in turn prompting the federal government to impose greater regulations on election administration. Republican senator Abner Lacock of Pennsylvania initially proposed direct election in 1816. The leading congressional sponsor of this reform in the late 1960s and 1970s was Senator Birch Bayh (D, Ind.). President Jimmy Carter also supported the plan. On September 18, 1969, a large majority of the House approved direct election. The proposal was not as fortunate in the Senate, and a combination of committee delays and filibusters postponed a floor vote until 1979, at which time the Senate rejected the amendment. Appeals to political principles such as federalism and representation, as well as to contemporary features of the electoral landscape, may prevent congressional approval of Electoral College reform.

Further reading: Congressional Quarterly. "The Electoral College." In John L. Moore, Jon P. Preimesberger, and David Tarr, eds., *Congressional Quarterly's Guide to U.S. Elections.* 4th ed. Washington, D.C.: CQ Press, 2001; Lefkowitz, Joel. "The Electoral College: Constitutional Debate, Partisan Manipulation, and Reform Possibilities." In Ronald Hayduk and Kevin Mattson, eds., *Democracy's Moment: Reforming the American Political System for the 21st Century.* Lanham, Md.: Rowman & Littlefield, 2002; Longley, Lawrence D., and Neal R. Peirce. *The Electoral College Primer 2000.* New Haven, Conn.: Yale University Press, 1999; Peirce, Neal R., and Lawrence D. Longley. *The People's President: The Electoral College in American History and the Direct Vote Alternative.* New Haven, Conn.: Yale University Press, 1981; Schumaker, Paul D., and Burdett A. Loomis, eds. *Choosing a President: The Electoral College and Beyond.* New York: Chatham House, 2002.

—Gary Bugh

electorate

An electorate is the body of people in a nation, state, or locality who are qualified and entitled to vote in an election. The electorate does not establish law or policy. Rather, they select officials and confer upon them the authority to make laws and shape policy on their behalf. Over the last 400 years, as democratic theory evolved and the notion of governments deriving their power from the consent of the governed became accepted in Europe and the United States, the question of who constitutes the electorate has evolved as well.

Although the right of individuals in a society to participate fully and equally in the electoral process is considered one of the keystones of democratic societies, universal SUFFRAGE is not necessarily a requisite condition of electoral POLITICS. Deciding who has the right to vote has varied greatly over countries, cultures, and history. Some restrictions are fairly obvious: Few people would argue that a 10-year-old should have a right to vote for president of the United States. Other restrictions, including the permanent prohibition of convicted felons from voting, can be more controversial.

Throughout much of American and European history, the electorate comprised primarily those in the aristocracy, and the power of political participation rested in the hands of very few. Property ownership, age, race, religion, and sex have all been characteristics used to limit the electorate. Over the centuries, however, the electorate has grown gradually, as the notion of who has the right to participate in the electoral process has evolved. In 1870, the FIFTEENTH AMENDMENT gave former slaves the right to vote, although wide-spread systematic abuse (especially in the South) of POLL TAXES, LITERACY TESTS, and other processes greatly restricted the ability of African Americans to vote. By the 1920s, universal white male suffrage was ensured in most Western democracies, and the right of women to vote in the United States was guaranteed by the NINETEENTH AMENDMENT. In 1971, the minimum voting age was lowered from 21 to 18, increasing suffrage for members of the younger generation.

The size and the composition of the electorate matter in campaigns. Unlike Australia and Belgium, voting is not compulsory in the United States, so the number (and type) of people who participate in elections can vary widely. Candidates base their campaign strategies in no small part on what they know about the electorate—what policies they prefer, how strongly they hold their beliefs, how likely they are to vote, and so on. VOTER TURNOUT, or the proportion of the electorate who participate in an election, varies greatly across the United States and around the world; political culture and institutional structure influence voter participation.

Further reading: Wolfinger, Raymond, and Steven Rosenstone. *Who Votes?* New Haven, Conn.: Yale University Press, 1980; Patterson, Thomas E. *The Vanishing Voter: Public Involvement in an Age of Uncertainty.* New York: Vintage, 2003; Verba, Sidney, Norman H. Nie, and Jae-On Kim. *Participation and Political Equality.* Chicago: University of Chicago Press, 1987.

—Joshua J. Scott

EMILY's List

EMILY's List is a POLITICAL ACTION COMMITTEE (PAC) that advocates the election of pro-choice women running for office as members of the DEMOCRATIC PARTY. EMILY's List participates in the campaigns and elections of such candidates by offering financial support, primarily through BUNDLING campaign contributions, as well as strategic assistance through research endeavors, advising, voter education, and voter mobilization. The acronym EMILY means "Early Money Is Like Yeast" as it helps raise "dough." This is indicative of the organization's goal of providing campaign funds to candidates to boost their electoral prospects. EMILY's List focuses on races for the House of Representatives, Senate, and state governorships.

EMILY's List was founded in 1985 by Ellen R. Malcolm to encourage donors to contribute to female Democratic candidates who favor abortion rights. This was a reaction to the small number of American women in high political office, which fueled the determination of Malcolm and her associates to increase the numbers. The membership and electoral capacity of the organization grew steadily from the outset. The period from 1990 to 1992 in particular saw rapid growth, with membership expansion from 3,500 to 23,000. Electoral success for women escalated simultaneously, with 1992 dubbed "The Year of the Woman" due to the large number of electoral victories by women candidates. Since 1994, EMILY's List has also administered a project to mobilize Democratic women voters in battleground states. The steady growth of EMILY's List persisted through the 1990s and continues to date. EMILY's List is headquartered in Washington, D.C.

Through the 2002 ELECTION CYCLE, EMILY's List has participated in the successful elections of 55 House members, 11 senators, and seven governors. In addition, by 2002 EMILY's List had become the most successful FUND-RAISING PAC in American POLITICS, with $16.7 million raised and 73,000 members. This success in fund raising and membership growth has made EMILY's List a key ally of the Democratic Party. This relationship may be enhanced by changes in election laws ushered in by the Bipartisan Campaign Reform Act of 2002, as EMILY's List has long focused on raising HARD MONEY contributions now sought by candidates and parties. However, EMILY's List has on occasion stirred controversy within the Democratic Party by supporting women in PRIMARY elections challenging established male counterparts. Despite such rare spats, EMILY's List is likely to remain an important and powerful actor in Democratic politics for the foreseeable future.

Further reading: Burrell, Barbara C. *A Woman's Place Is in the House: Campaigning for Congress in the Feminist Era.* Ann Arbor: University of Michigan Press, 1994; EMILY's List. Available online. URL: http://www.emilyslist.org. Accessed August 10, 2005; Harrison, Brigid C. *Women in American Politics: An Introduction.* Belmont, Calif.: Thomson Wadsworth, 2003; O'Connor, Karen. *Women in Congress: Running, Winning, and Ruling.* New York: Haworth Press, 2001; Rosenthal, Cindy Simon. *Women Transforming Congress.* Norman: Oklahoma University Press, 2002.

—Richard L. Vining, Jr.

endorsement

An endorsement is a statement of support for a candidate from a person or organization. Endorsements are often touted by candidates as signs of their electability and used to encourage others to back their campaign, but most endorsements have little influence on election outcomes.

The history of endorsements goes back to the nation's earliest days. In 1836, President Andrew Jackson's endorsement of Martin Van Buren helped his vice president win the PRESIDENTIAL ELECTION. Van Buren told voters he would continue the popular Jackson's policies. More recently, in 1988, President Ronald Reagan endorsed his vice president, George H. W. Bush, as his chosen successor, telling Bush to "go out there and win one for the Gipper." Former presidents usually endorse the candidates of their party and are given prominent speaking roles at political conventions.

Early endorsements often act as a seal of approval in helping a candidate attract support from other politicians, groups, and voters who can deliver money and votes. Many pro-choice Democratic women candidates running for federal office seek the support of EMILY's LIST; the group's acronym stands for "Early Money Is Like Yeast" (it helps the dough rise). John Kerry's support from fellow Vietnam veterans in 2004 helped soften his image and provided a powerful network of supporters and voters in the early PRIMARY contests. In 1988, Governor John Sununu (R, N.H.) endorsed Bush in the state's Republican primary, helping to propel Bush to the NOMINATION.

In the 2000 PRESIDENTIAL ELECTION, George W. Bush relied on endorsements from party leaders to create a sense of inevitability about his nomination and defeat of John McCain in the primary. In mid-February, 26 governors, 38 senators, and 175 representatives endorsed Bush, while just a handful of elected officials supported McCain. Although McCain won several contests, Bush was able to wrap up the nomination by March.

Endorsements have additional influence if a well-regarded political figure actively campaigns with the endorsed candidate. During the 2004 election, Republicans dispatched Bush, Vice President Dick Cheney, and First Lady Laura Bush to campaigns across the country for fundraisers costing hundreds of dollars per person. Support from Bush and Senator Rick Santorum (R, Pa.) aided Senator Arlen Specter's (R, Pa.) victory over Representative Pat Toomey (R, Pa.) in the 2004 Republican Senate primary. When a popular incumbent retires, candidates seeking to succeed him or her ask for support and run the endorsement prominently in campaign ads and literature.

Candidates who win their party's primary reach out to losing candidates for their support, though such endorsements often depend on how nasty the primary campaign was and what the relationship is between the candidates. Candidates seek support from party leaders as well. In 2004, former vice president Al Gore gave his nod to Howard Dean, but former president Bill Clinton chose not to endorse a candidate until the party's nomination fight ended. Both Bush and Kerry listed their endorsements from politicians, organizations, and individual voters on their campaign Web sites.

Celebrity endorsements help candidates draw media attention and add a certain star quality to a campaign, though they are generally considered of little value at the ballot box. In the 2004 Democratic primary, Madonna backed Wesley Clark, Moby supported John Kerry, and Martin Sheen endorsed Howard Dean.

Besides seeking support from INTEREST GROUPS, politicians, and celebrities, candidates vie for the endorsements of newspaper editorial pages. Editorial boards usually decide which candidates to endorse based on the candidates' records, agendas, and personalities. Newspapers usually reveal their endorsements on a Sunday shortly before the election. In the 2004 Democratic primary contest, the *Des Moines Register*'s endorsement of John Edwards caused some voters to take a more serious look at his candidacy; Edwards then finished a better-than-expected second in the IOWA CAUCUSes. But newspaper endorsements do not always influence voters. For instance, in 1936, many editorial pages supported Alf Landon, although Franklin Delano Roosevelt won easily.

Candidates may play down or reject endorsements that are viewed as harmful to their campaigns. In 1996, Bob Dole returned a $1,000 check from the Log Cabin Republicans, a gay rights group, but later accepted their support. In 1946, Representative Jerry Voorhis (D, Calif.) declined the endorsement of the CIO-PAC, a LABOR GROUP thought to have communist ties that had supported him earlier. His opponent, Richard Nixon, made an issue of that and other endorsements and eventually won the election.

A poll released in January 2004 by the Pew Research Center for the People & the Press showed that endorsements rarely have little effect on votes. An endorsement by former president Bill Clinton made a person more likely to vote for a candidate by 19 percent, but the same percentage of people said a Clinton endorsement made them less likely to vote for a candidate.

Endorsements by Gore and Governor Arnold Schwarzenegger (R, Calif.) were viewed negatively, while the support of McCain was thought to help a candidate. Support by religious leaders and interest groups, such as the AFL-CIO and the National Rifle Association, made little difference overall among voters. However, endorsements can be helpful when targeted to specific demographic groups. The poll showed that white evangelical Protestants were 37 percent more likely to back a candidate who had won the support of the CHRISTIAN COALITION.

The 2004 Democratic PRESIDENTIAL PRIMARY demonstrated the limit of endorsements. Several powerful labor unions, including the AFSCME and the SEIU, supported Dean, who also enjoyed the backing of Al Gore and Senator Tom Harkin (D, Iowa). Harkin's support in the Iowa caucuses was considered key because of his GRASSROOTS network and popularity, while the unions' large membership and financial support was expected to help Dean cruise to the nomination. Dean's campaign performed poorly in Iowa, coming in third.

Further reading: Herrnson, Paul S. *Congressional Elections: Campaigning at Home and in Washington*. Washington, D.C.: CQ Press, 2004; Lahusen, Christian. *The Rhetoric of Moral Protest: Public Campaigns, Celebrity Endorsement, and Political Mobilization*. New York: W. de Gruyter, 1996.

—Mary Lynn F. Jones

equal time rule

The equal time rule—or, more properly, the equal opportunities provision—requires equal treatment of all candidates for political office by television and radio broadcast stations in terms of airtime. For instance, if a television station sells or gives five minutes of broadcast time to one candidate, it must do the same for all other candidates for that same office. Candidates without the resources to purchase time are given it free if their opponents also receive time at no cost. The purpose of this rule is to prevent stations from selling or giving away airtime to candidates of only one political persuasion. The requirement applies to candidates at all political levels, national, state, and local.

The broadcast requirement for equal time originated with the Radio Act of 1927, yet this law was soon superseded by the COMMUNICATIONS ACT OF 1934. Under Section 315 of the latter statute, if any broadcast station provides "a legally qualified candidate for any political office" airtime, that station must "afford equal opportunities to all other such candidates for that office." This section of the law also prohibits stations from censoring candidates who purchase broadcast time. Consequently, the FEDERAL COMMUNICATIONS COMMISSION (FCC), which enforces the equal opportunities provision, has ruled that candidate advertisements can contain derogatory language as well as disturbing images, such as pictures of aborted fetuses. The Supreme Court held in 1959 that Section 315 protected broadcast stations from liability for statements by candidates exercising their rights under the equal time rule.

Congress amended the equal opportunities provision in 1959 to exempt certain broadcasts from its requirements, including regular news programs, news interviews, news documentaries (if the candidate's appearance is "incidental to the presentation" of the documentary's subject), and coverage of on-the-spot news events (including political conventions). These exemptions freed broadcast journalists from any obligation to provide equal time to CHALLENGERS when reporting an incumbent candidate's official activities as news of the day. Over time, the FCC has expanded the category of exempt broadcast programs to include entertainment shows that regularly provide coverage of current events, such as *Today, Good Morning America*, and *Entertainment Tonight*. Since 1975, the commission also has exempted press conferences by any incumbent or candidate if they were "newsworthy and subject to on-the-spot coverage."

Even though the FCC has exempted many programs, the broadcasting of motion pictures or television shows featuring a qualified political candidate would require equal time for that candidate's competitors. As a result, broadcast stations in California during that state's 2003 gubernatorial RECALL election chose not to run movies starring Arnold Schwarzenegger, a movie star and one of the candidates for governor who would eventually win the election, to avoid triggering equal time requirements. Similarly, the scheduled appearance of Philadelphia mayor John F. Street, who was running for reelection, was cut from an episode of the CBS television drama *Hack* that same year because the network feared it might invoke the equal time rule. A few rerun episodes of *Walker, Texas Ranger* also were preempted by some east Texas television stations in 2000, because one of the actors from the show was running for Congress.

Today broadcast stations are free to stage political debates among a limited number of candidates without violating the equal opportunities provision. This was not always the case. In 1960, Congress needed to pass a bill suspending this provision to allow stations to carry the famous Nixon-Kennedy debates without giving equal time to minor party candidates, of which there were more than a dozen that year. In 1975, the FCC held that debates controlled by someone other than the candidates or the broadcasters were exempt from the equal time rule, opening the door for debates between presidential candidates in 1976 and 1980 sponsored by the LEAGUE OF WOMEN VOTERS. Starting with the 1984 PRESIDENTIAL ELECTION, however, the FCC stopped requiring an outside sponsor to exempt political debates from the obligation for equal time for all candidates.

Section 315 was again amended by Congress in 1971 to require stations to provide federal candidates the right to purchase broadcast time at the lowest rate charged regular advertisers. This requirement reduced the rising costs of campaigns at the expense of the broadcasting industry. A 1990 FCC audit, however, found that political candidates were regularly overcharged for their advertising. In particular, based on a review of 30 television and radio stations in five states across the country, 80 percent of the television and 40 percent of the radio stations failed to give political candidates the lowest available rates. In response to the audit, broadcasters argued that candidates often rejected the "lowest rate available" because it involved the possibility of having their ads bumped; it is common practice in the industry to charge higher rates for fixed commercial broadcast time.

Although Congress and the FCC have been deregulating the broadcast industry in recent decades, the equal opportunities provision remains a staple of broadcasting law. Given that it levels the playing field among political candidates regarding broadcast time, including members of Congress, and that it requires broadcast stations to provide federal candidates with low advertising fees, the equal time rule is unlikely to be repealed any time soon.

Further reading: Carter, T. Barton, Marc A. Franklin, and Jay B. Wright. *The First Amendment and the Fourth Estate: The Law of Mass Media.* 8th ed. New York: Foundation Press, 2001; Donahue, Hugh Carter. *The Battle to Control Broadcast News: Who Owns the First Amendment?* Cambridge, Mass.: MIT Press, 1989.

—Andrew W. Barrett

exit polls

Exit polls are public opinion surveys conducted at voting places on ELECTION DAY. The surveys are usually conducted by media firms to help predict electoral winners, though they are also conducted by academic research teams who are interested in studying voting trends. The surveys are typically conducted by temporary workers who approach randomly selected voters as they leave the voting location to ask them about their voting choices. Additionally, basic questions about such matters as partisan affiliation and political IDEOLOGY are often asked, and basic demographic information is often collected as well.

Exit polls are often quite controversial because they attempt to predict the outcome of an election after it has begun but before it has ended. The exit polling information is theoretically kept confidential until the polls close, but it invariably starts to leak out to the public and influence news coverage while the election is actually underway. In fact, most exit polls are specifically constructed to allow media outlets to report winners and losers of elections before the full official results are available. Consequently, some argue voters who have not yet gone to the polls may be dissuaded from doing so based on exit polling reports.

Exit polling data is a valuable resource for scholars and political analysts, because it enables them to determine with a relatively high degree of certainty who actually turned out to vote on election day. Hence, exit polling data can help to pinpoint whether individuals with particular demographic or ideological characteristics turn out to vote—or cast votes for or against a particular candidate—at lower or higher levels than other voters.

In the 2000 PRESIDENTIAL ELECTION, exit polling led some news organizations to make the controversial prediction that Al Gore had won the PRESIDENTIAL ELECTION, which they were soon forced to retract. Following significant problems with exit polling conducted by VOTER NEWS SERVICE (a private firm that dates back to an exit poll pooling arrangement first formed in 1988), the five major television networks (ABC, CBS, CNN, Fox, and NBC) and the

Associated Press formed a new group known as the National Election Pool to conduct exit polling. The National Election Pool had problems of its own in 2004, inaccurately predicting a lead for John Kerry well into the election night.

Further reading: Milvasy, J Ronald et al. "Early Calls of Election Results and Exit Polls: Pros, Cons, and Constitutional Considerations." *The Public Opinion Quarterly* 49 (1985): 1; Sudman, Seymour. "Do Exit Polls Influence Voting Behavior?" *Public Opinion Quarterly* 50 (1986): 3.

—Brad Alexander

exploratory committee

An exploratory committee is a special legal entity formed by individuals who are considering a run for public office. Exploratory committees are allowed to raise money in order to conduct a limited range of activities directly related to the process of deciding whether to run, giving potential candidates the ability to legally raise funds from donors at an early point in the process.

For candidates at the national level, exploratory committees are authorized by FEDERAL ELECTION CAMPAIGN ACT (FECA) and FEDERAL ELECTION COMMISSION (FEC) regulations. They are allowed to conduct only a limited range of activities—which can be described as "testing the waters"—in consideration of a run for public office. Such activities typically include conducting PUBLIC OPINION POLLING, doing political research, and traveling to speak to groups and individuals. Exploratory committees are not allowed to perform activities that one might traditionally associate with running for office. For example, they cannot raise money beyond what is needed for "testing the waters," nor can they air advertisements.

For strategic purposes, exploratory committees are often used by candidates who have already decided to run for office, because they are regulated more loosely than regular candidate campaign committees. Hence, they enable candidates to perform expensive activities, such as polling, without being subject to a high level of public scrutiny.

In U.S. PRESIDENTIAL ELECTIONS, the formation of an exploratory committee is almost always the first formal step in running for office. Many other candidates for federal office use the committees as a political tool as well. Additionally, state and local candidates may also form exploratory committees, depending on the applicable laws and regulations in their jurisdictions.

—Brad Alexander

F

faction

The most famous and relevant definition of *faction* was written by James Madison and can be found in Federalist No. 10. In essence, Madison saw a faction as any political group that may intentionally or unintentionally oppress the rights of other political groups, individuals, or the nation as a whole. A faction can manifest itself in one of two ways. First, it can rally citizens to petition and lobby those in power to satisfy the faction's demands. Second, a faction can work to have its members, or supporters of its cause, elected to office.

The ultimate aim of factions is political—they desire particular policies to be adopted or rejected. The hazard for a democracy, then, is that if a faction gets its way, it can hurt the rights of others. In a constitutional democracy, the majority does not always rule, because there are institutions, procedures, rights, and principles that are held to be true regardless of what a majority decides. For example, it does not matter if a large percentage of citizens wants to silence a particular instance of free speech; free speech is a right guaranteed by the First Amendment regardless of public opinion. Consequently, some rights and principles must first be guaranteed to a nation's citizens if there can ever be a faction that would seek to limit these rights.

Prior to the U.S. experience, factions were most typically found in monarchies. Here, they represented alternative claims to a monarch's power, or were groups of nobles seeking more power. Factions in this sense were not condoned by the government, and if a monarch discovered such plots, death was the usual penalty for the members of factions.

The Enlightenment, culminating in the 18th century, helped to reveal the importance of factions to democratic government. Enlightenment writers such as John Locke (1632–1704) and others suggested that the best way to keep the well-being of the people protected was by according them freedom to govern. In this way, the people would be safest and most secure through self-government, as there would be less danger that they would oppress one another.

Legitimizing public participation in government also legitimizes factions. Through the usual institutional channels in a democracy, factions can peacefully and legitimately enter the government. This is one of the principle arguments against an openly democratic style of government that was suggested by some of America's founders. Many feared that by giving the people, and factions, power, the government would act irresponsibly (i.e., contrary to the nation's best interest) and ultimately bring down the new government. Madison's solution was not to ban factions and form an undemocratic governmental arrangement, but to create a government in which numerous factions competed with one another, thereby reducing the chance that a single dominant faction would govern. This strategy became one of the key justifications for the system of checks and balances that runs throughout the American political structure.

Since the early 19th century, factions have also been linked to political parties in the United States. In essence, political parties are broad-based factions that tend to focus on numerous issues and to stress electoral change. The earliest instances of partisan factions stemmed from an ideological split between the Federalists and Thomas Jefferson's Democratic-Republicans.

Today factions represent far more than political parties. Any organized collective action among citizens to bring about a particular political end is the work of a faction. The term *faction* applies to groups advocating a specific cause but also to the larger themes and principles that political parties embrace. True to Madison's vision, factions have become a central part of American democracy, providing the people a voice while also checking the power of other factions and providing long-term stability to the large political system.

Further reading: Madison, James, Alexander Hamilton, and John Jay. *Federalist Papers.* New York: Signet Classic, 1999; Wills, Garry. *Explaining America: The Federalist.* New York: Penguin Books, 2001.

—J. Christopher Paskewich

fairness doctrine

The fairness doctrine once required every television and radio broadcast station to devote a reasonable amount of time to the coverage of important public issues in a fair and balanced manner. Emerging from years of regulatory decisions, the first formal description of the doctrine was issued by the FEDERAL COMMUNICATIONS COMMISSION (FCC) in 1949. The purpose of this policy was to help develop an informed public through the "dissemination of news and ideas concerning the vital public issues of the day." The commission repealed the doctrine in 1987, however, claiming that it no longer served the public interest. Several efforts to reinstitute fairness requirements on broadcast stations have failed in subsequent years.

The concept of the fairness doctrine was simple. Broadcast stations needed to provide their viewers and listeners with coverage of important public issues and present contrasting viewpoints. If a station provided only one side of an issue, the FCC could require that station to provide time for an opponent's response. The enforcement of these requirements could be complicated, however. The FCC in 1967, for example, took the position that stations that accepted cigarette advertising were obligated to present public service announcements or other programming describing the health risks of cigarette smoking under the fairness doctrine. This position opened the floodgates for demands to extend this obligation to advertising for other products. In reaction, the FCC reversed itself and removed most product advertising from the requirements of the doctrine in 1974.

The doctrine created several problems and unintended consequences as well. It was difficult to determine who had the right to reply when only one side of a controversial issue was broadcast. In most situations, numerous individuals or groups could claim the right to a response. The process of challenging a station's coverage could be lengthy, sometimes making a response moot before it could be aired. Many also claimed that the doctrine discouraged coverage of controversial issues since stations wanted to avoid demands to air opposing views, which could possibly conflict with regular programming that produced advertising revenue. Similarly, challenges were often costly for stations, which had to hire an attorney to defend themselves. Thus, instead of encouraging debate, it was argued that the fairness doctrine suppressed public discourse in contradiction of the policy's intent and the First Amendment's protections of speech and the press.

As deregulation became the government trend during the late 1970s and throughout the 1980s, the fairness doctrine met its demise. The FCC asked Congress to end the policy in 1981, yet no action was taken. Four years later, the commission issued a report asserting that the doctrine inhibited the broadcasting of controversial public issues, as critics of the policy contended. The FCC also argued that the doctrine was no longer necessary with the rapidly expanding number of information sources available to American audiences, including cable and satellite television. A unanimous Supreme Court had justified the right of the federal government to regulate broadcasters in 1969 as a result of a scarcity of broadcast frequencies (*Red Lion Broadcasting Company v. FCC*).

A federal court of appeals ruled in 1987 that the FCC was not obligated to enforce the fairness doctrine. Many had believed the agency was required by statute to enforce fairness requirements, yet the court ruled that the doctrine had never been actually codified. Hoping to act before the doctrine was repealed, the Democratic-controlled Congress passed broadcasting fairness legislation in June 1987. President Reagan vetoed the bill, arguing that the government's ability to regulate the content of television and radio broadcasts under the fairness doctrine was "antagonistic to the freedom of expression guaranteed by the First Amendment." The FCC repealed the doctrine on August 4, 1987. Congressional attempts to enact fairness requirements later that year and in 1989 both failed.

Even though it was repealed, the courts have never declared the fairness doctrine unconstitutional. Therefore, either the FCC or Congress could resurrect it, though the trend continues toward deregulation of the broadcast industry. A federal appeals court ordered the repeal of two FCC policies similar to the fairness doctrine in 2000. The personal attack rule required broadcast stations to give free reply time to anyone who was the subject of an attack based on "honesty, character, integrity or like personal qualities." The political editorial rule required stations to give opponents of candidates endorsed by broadcasters a reasonable opportunity to reply.

In the years following the repeal of the fairness doctrine, there has been little evidence that broadcast television stations have increased their amount of coverage of issues of the day. Nonetheless, there has been an explosion in the number and popularity of radio talk shows that discuss issues of public importance, particularly with conservative hosts such as Rush Limbaugh. This growth in conservative talk radio would not have been possible under the fairness doctrine (unless radio stations provided equal time to liberal hosts, no easy task considering the two- or three-hour length of many of these programs).

Further reading: Donahue, Hugh Carter. *The Battle to Control Broadcast News: Who Owns the First Amendment?* Cambridge, Mass.: MIT Press, 1989; Jung, Donald J. *The Federal Communications Commission, the Broadcast Industry, and the Fairness Doctrine 1981–1987.* Lanham, Md.: University Press of America, 1996.

—Andrew W. Barrett

favorite son

Favorite son is a term commonly used in describing the presidential nominating process when a candidate is supported by DELEGATES from a particular state or region despite usually lacking a significant national following. By backing such a candidate, the delegation honors the candidate, while delaying the decision on which candidate to throw its weight behind. The term has also been used simply to show the affection of a nation, state, or region for a successful person. It was in this context that the term was first used on May 1, 1789, when the *New York Daily Gazette* refereed to George Washington as "the favorite son of liberty and deliverer of his country."

Abraham Lincoln is an example of a famous candidate who was nominated as a favorite son. Illinois backed Lincoln in 1856 as the vice president in the REPUBLICAN PARTY's first national convention. Lincoln's short-lived candidacy for the number-two slot came to an end when William Dayton was nominated on the first BALLOT. Ronald Reagan was another eventual president whose early foray into presidential POLITICS was as a favorite son. In 1968, California nominated him as a favorite son candidate. Though Reagan could not compete with the major candidates, Richard Nixon and Nelson Rockefeller, he was able to use the considerable support he enjoyed to win an important speaking slot at the convention.

Lincoln and Reagan, however, are the exceptions, as most favorite sons bear names that have now faded into obscurity. For example, in 1964, Colorado Republicans backed Senator Gordon Allott for president. Another was Arkansas senator Joseph T. Robinson, who was a minor contender for the Democratic NOMINATION in 1924. Since they control a number of delegates, favorite sons are not always purely symbolic. The 1948 Republican convention appeared headed for a deadlock with such strong candidates as New York governor Thomas E. Dewey, Ohio senator Robert A. Taft, Harold Stassen of Minnesota, and others contending for the nomination. To capture the nomination the major contenders had to compete for the support of "favorite son" candidates, such as Pennsylvania senator Edward Martin, who controlled 73 delegates. After three ballots, Dewey received enough support for the nomination.

The term has more recently been used to refer to candidates who have an extra advantage with an ELECTORATE. In this context, it is most often used in reference to a geographical advantage, particularly in a presidential race in which the candidate is expected to carry his home state. When Senator Tom Harkin (D, Iowa) ran for the Democratic nomination in 1992, he hoped his favorite son status would garner him an easy win and then boost his candidacy nationwide. In fact, the rest of the Democratic candidates boycotted Iowa, his easy win was seen as insignificant, and his candidacy was short-lived. Another use of the term has been to apply it to religious or ethnic backgrounds. During the 2000 and 2004 PRESIDENTIAL ELECTIONS, Senator Joe Lieberman (D, Conn.) was called the "favorite son" in the Jewish community. Asian-American and Hispanic candidates have also received these tags for expected support in their communities.

Further reading: Ceaser, James W. *Presidential Selection: Theory and Development.* Princeton, N.J.: Princeton University Press, 1979; Cook, Rhodes. *The Presidential Nominating Process: A Place for Us?* Lanham, Md.: Rowman & Littlefield, 2004; Bartels, Larry M. *Presidential Primaries and the Dynamics of Public Choice.* Princeton, N.J.: Princeton University Press, 1988.

—Peter Brownfeld

Federal Communications Commission

The Federal Communications Commission (FCC) is an independent federal agency established by the COMMUNICATIONS ACT of 1934. It replaced the former Federal Radio Commission and is responsible for regulating all non–federal government use of the radio spectrum, interstate telecommunications, and international communications that originate or terminate in the United States. The FCC's jurisdiction covers the 50 states, the District of Columbia, and U.S. possessions. The commission is composed of five members, no more than four members of the same POLITICAL PARTY, appointed by the president with the consent of the Senate.

The 1934 act has been amended considerably since its inception in response to numerous technological advances, including television, satellite communications, cable television, cellular telephone, and PCS (personal communications service). The scope of its activities also expanded when the maximum number of television station licenses that had been set in 1948 was lifted, which caused the number of stations to increase substantially, from 108 to more than 2,000, including almost 250 noncommercial stations. Furthermore, the Communications Satellite Act of 1962 gave the FCC new authority for satellite communications, and the Cable Act of 1992 required similar revisions to the original 1934 act.

The FCC's role in representing the public's interest began to be scrutinized more closely as the nation's communications network matured. A congressional investigation in 1958 led to the resignation of one commissioner over graft in the granting of television licenses. Three years later, chairman Newton Minow stirred up a national debate by declaring television "a vast wasteland." In 1964, court rulings forced the commission to grant the public a larger voice in its consideration of license renewals.

Recent leadership has endorsed a marketplace model. Reliance on the "marketplace rationale" began under chairman Charles Ferris (1977–81), when the commission first started licensing thousands of new stations in an effort to replace behavioral regulation with the forces of competition. Subsequent chairman Mark Fowler (1981–87) more fully endorsed the marketplace model.

Despite the increase of new stations and the hands-off approach of recent leaders of the FCC, the "scarcity rationale," which is based on limitations of the electromagnetic spectrum, remains a primary premise for government regulation over electronic media. The commission has been involved in battles over the regulation of both pricing and content in the cable television industry. With the rapid development of telecommunications technologies, especially mobile communications, in addition to the blurring of distinctions between cable television, telephone companies, and Internet providers, the job of the FCC continues to become more complicated.

Further reading: Besen, Stanley M., et al. *Misregulating Television: Network Dominance and the FCC*. Chicago: University of Chicago Press, 1984; Hilliard, Robert L. *The Federal Communications Commission: A Primer*. Boston: Focal Press, 1991; Ray, William B. *The Ups and Downs of Radio-TV Regulation*. Ames: Iowa State University Press, 1990.

—Taiyu Chen

Federal Corrupt Practices Act of 1910, 1911, and 1925

The Federal Corrupt Practices Act refers to the first comprehensive federal campaign finance reform law enacted in the United States. First passed in 1910, it required federal candidates and their respective national parties to disclose contributions and expenditures. The act was amended in 1911 and, in response to a Supreme Court decision and the Teapot Dome SCANDAL, was expanded and given greater scope in 1925. The legacy of the act was mixed, for despite its longevity—it was the primary CAMPAIGN FINANCE LAW until 1971—it became noteworthy for its loopholes and weak enforcement mechanisms.

The Federal Corrupt Practices Act has its roots in the muckraker and PROGRESSIVE MOVEMENT traditions of the early 20th century, when journalists sought to uncover abuses and wrong-doing in both the business and government sectors. In the realm of POLITICS, journalists and reform-minded politicians fought the influence of financial contributions on politics by seeking and identifying their sources. One of the most notable discoveries occurred in 1905, when it was revealed to a New York state legislative committee that several of the country's largest insurance companies had secretly given to the 1896, 1900, and 1904 Republican presidential campaigns.

The uproar was deafening and immediate as legislation was introduced to prohibit corporate and bank contributions. The author of this legislation, Republican senator William E. Chandler of New Hampshire, could not find support among his Republican allies, so he enlisted the support of South Carolina Democrat Benjamin Tillman. The bill passed in 1907. However, even with the TILLMAN ACT, many reformers were not placated, as they wanted additional legislation that would require all campaign contributions to be publicized.

Two factors led to this change. The first was the revelation in late 1907 that railroad financier E. H. Harriman had given $200,000 to Theodore Roosevelt's 1904 presidential campaign. The second factor was the actions of the National Publicity Bill Organization (NPBO), an organization founded in response to the revelations of the 1905 insurance investigation. The NPBO, a Democrat-dominated organization opposed to the influence of business on politics (particularly corporate contributions to Republican candidates), wrote a bill instituting a disclosure requirement for all federal elections.

The bill, sponsored in the Senate by Republican Samuel McCall of Massachusetts, called for public disclosure of contributions and expenditures for House members and political committees operating in two or more states. The bill passed before the 1910 elections but was slightly different than the one introduced by McCall. Disclosure did not have to be made until after the particular election in question.

The 1911 Congress, a distinctly different landscape from the one a year before, resulted in an expansion of the original legislation. Democrats, the MAJORITY PARTY in the House, sought a preelection filing date for campaign disclosures. Republicans, in a bid to divide the Democrats, sought disclosures for committees for individual campaigns and primaries. In the end, the 1910 bill was amended to include disclosures for Senate campaigns, committees for individual campaigns and primaries, and spending limits for House and Senate campaigns of $5,000 and $10,000, respectively.

The expanded powers of the act did not last long, as the Supreme Court decision in *Newberry v. United States* rendered a part of the 1911 legislation unconstitutional. The case involved Truman Newberry, the victor over automobile pioneer Henry Ford in the Republican PRIMARY for the Senate seat for Michigan, who was convicted of excessive spending under the 1911 act. The Court ruled that the regulation of elections did not extend to primaries, and since Newberry's spending occurred prior to the general election, his conviction was overturned.

Because of the decision and the Teapot Dome SCANDAL of the Harding administration, the Federal Corrupt Practices Act of 1925 included a number of changes. The first was a direct response to the Newberry decision, as disclosure requirements for primary contests were repealed. Second, in response to Teapot Dome, all committees operating in two or more states were required to file quarterly reports listing all contributors that gave more than $100, regardless of whether it was an election or nonelection year. Lastly, the spending limits for Senate races in certain high-population states were raised to $25,000.

While the act provided a number of needed reforms, it failed to provide a detailed description of the enforcement measures. Basic requirements regarding the quarterly reports such as format, accessibility, and punishments for noncompliance were not included in the legislation. As a result, reports, if made, were in a variety of formats and were difficult to access. Many candidates failed or ignored the requirement to file reports, and many also ignored the spending limits put in place by the law. In the entire 45-year life span of the act, no one was prosecuted or fined the $10,000 stipulated by the act for violations, and only two people were excluded from office for violations, both in 1927.

By 1971, the failure of the 1925 act was readily apparent, as years of noncompliance and problematic enforcement attested. Candidates had grown quite adept at circumventing the law. One means by which they avoided the law was by creating multiple organizations that allowed individuals to give several donations of slightly under $100 so they would not be identified, or by having wealthy donors contribute through family members. The rising costs of campaigns, particularly in regard to media expenses, also fueled a desire for new legislation. Finally, in 1972, President Nixon signed the FEDERAL ELECTION CAMPAIGN ACT of 1971, which ended the ambitious, although ineffective, tenure of the Federal Corrupt Practices Act.

Further reading: Alexander, Herbert E. *Financing Politics: Money, Elections, & Political Reform.* Washington, D.C: CQ Press, 1992; Congressional Quarterly. *Dollar Politics.* 3rd ed. Washington, D.C.: CQ Press, 1982; Mutch, Robert E. *Campaigns, Congress, and Courts: The Making of Campaign Finance Law.* Westport, Conn.: Praeger, 1988.
—Stephen Nemeth

Federal Election Campaign Act of 1971 (amended 1974; amended 1976; and amended 1979)

The Federal Election Campaign Act of 1971 and its 1974, 1976, and 1979 amendments consolidated nearly 100 years worth of ineffective federal CAMPAIGN FINANCE LAWS into a comprehensive legislative framework governing the financing of federal elections. These statutes not only limited campaign contributions and expenditures but also required full and timely disclosure of campaign finance activity and established public financing for PRESIDENTIAL ELECTIONS. The act also created the FEDERAL ELECTION COMMISSION (FEC), an independent regulatory agency empowered to enforce campaign finance laws, gather and disclose campaign finance information, and manage the Presidential Public Funding Program.

Congress's first attempts to eliminate corruption in campaign finance came in 1883 in response to abuses of the federal employment system. Andrew Jackson's election to the presidency in 1829 saw the beginning of the practice of rewarding supporters of incoming presidents with government jobs in exchange for a fixed percentage of the employee's salary. The DEMOCRATIC PARTY levied the first assessments on U.S. customs employees in New York City during the 1830s, and by the 1870s the Republican congressional committee raised about 90 percent of its money from these levies. Although several congressmen proposed legislation to end this practice, few politicians wanted to eliminate such a lucrative source of campaign money. The assassination of President James Garfield in 1881 by a disgruntled federal job seeker brought a renewed sense of urgency for reform. In 1883, Congress passed the Civil Service Reform Act, which prohibited solicitation of political contributions from federal workers and created a competitive examination process for federal jobs.

The regulation of campaign donations from businesses and corporations became the next target of reformers at the turn of the century. In 1896, REPUBLICAN PARTY national chairman Mark Hanna directed a number of new FUNDRAISING efforts toward corporate contributors. Hanna instituted a systematic process of gathering corporate donations; the party assessed banks and corporations one-quarter of 1 percent of their capital in exchange for favorable treatment from Republican politicians. Hanna's efforts helped William McKinley beat William Jennings Bryan in the 1896 PRESIDENTIAL ELECTION, but the party received much criticism from Bryan supporters. In 1897 lawmakers in Nebraska, Missouri, Tennessee, and Florida, states whose electoral votes went to Bryan, enacted laws that banned corporate political contributions and required public disclosure of campaign contributions.

Calls for national campaign finance laws peaked in September 1905, after an investigation into questionable financial practices within the insurance industry. New York Life vice president George W. Perkins testified that his company, as regular business practice, made concealed contributions to the Republican presidential campaign during the 1896, 1900, and 1904 PRESIDENTIAL ELECTIONS. The revelations pushed Roosevelt three months later to propose to Congress "that all contributions by corporations to any political committee or for any political purpose should be forbidden by law."

Roosevelt's speech led to the enactment of the nation's first campaign finance laws in 1907 and 1910. The TILLMAN ACT of 1907 prohibited corporations and nationally chartered banks from making direct financial contributions to federal candidates. The FEDERAL CORRUPT PRACTICES ACT of 1910 and its 1911 amendments established disclosure requirements for congressional candidates and set expenditure limits for congressional campaigns.

Passage of the Federal Corrupt Practices Act of 1925, the HATCH ACT of 1939 and its 1940 amendments, and the Taft-Hartley Act of 1947 marked another round of federal campaign finance legislation. The Federal Corrupt Practices Act strengthened disclosure requirements and increased expenditure limits in the GENERAL ELECTION. The Hatch Act gave Congress the power to regulate primaries and limit contributions and expenditures in congressional elections, and the Taft-Hartley Act put a permanent ban on contributions to federal candidates from unions and corporations in both primaries and general elections.

These laws, however, offered the public a weak means of controlling corruption within campaign finance practices. First, no provision created a government agency empowered to administer the laws. By 1970, rampant nonenforcement became obvious when House clerk W. Pat Jenkins sent Attorney General John Mitchell a list of 20 Nixon fund-raising committees that had failed to disclose fund-raising activity during the 1968 presidential campaign. The Justice Department, however, could not prosecute these violators because the government maintained no single campaign disclosure file, nor did it have a standard system of gathering campaign finance data. Moreover, loopholes allowed candidates who claimed no knowledge of spending on their behalf to be exempt from liability under the 1925 law. Finally, despite the Hatch Act's intent to end large contributions and expensive campaigns, legislators inadequately gauged the cost of elections. Almost immediately after Hatch's passage, the 1940 PRESIDENTIAL ELECTION campaign saw both parties significantly exceed the expenditure ceiling.

With these problems in mind, Congress enacted the Federal Election Campaign Act (FECA) and the REVENUE ACT in 1971. FECA repealed the Corrupt Practices Act of 1925 and set more rigorous public disclosure requirements concerning a candidate's CAMPAIGN EXPENDITURES and sources of campaign income. Candidates now had to file full and timely reports and include the names and addresses of individuals who gave more than $100 to the campaign. Here, the law had an immediate impact. In 1968, under the old disclosure requirements, House and Senate candidates reported spending $8.5 million, but in 1972, after the passage of FECA, spending reported by congressional candidates jumped to $89 million. The law also set limits on how much candidates and their families could contribute to their own campaign ($50,000 for president or vice president, $35,000 for senator, and $25,000 for representative). The law also restricted spending on media advertising for congressional and presidential candidates to 10 cents per voter, but this provision was later repealed in the FECA amendments of 1974. The 1971 Revenue Act created the Presidential Public Funding Program. Tax-payers could voluntarily set aside $1 of their annual taxes to a public campaign fund available to eligible presidential candidates. The law also created a $50 individual tax deduction on contributions to candidates in general, primary, or SPECIAL ELECTIONS at the federal, state, or local levels. Congress repealed this provision in 1978.

The 1971 act still did not provide for a regulating agency to monitor and enforce the law. The responsibility for monitoring compliance to the law was split between the two houses of Congress and the Justice Department. The campaign abuses of the 1972 PRESIDENTIAL ELECTION and the rise of COMMON CAUSE, a liberal reform lobby, led to the 1974 FECA amendment. The Watergate SCANDAL revealed that Nixon used a Miami bank account, under the control of G. Gordon Liddy, attorney for the Committee to Reelect the President (CRP), to deposit illegal corporate money that had been laundered through a Mexico City bank, and legal, unlaundered contributions that the CRP did not disclose as required by law. The Nixon campaign's ability to circumvent provisions of the law demonstrated the failure of the oversight process. LOBBYISTS for Common Cause pressured Congress to create a federal agency. On October 15, 1974, President Ford signed into law the 1974 FECA amendments.

The 1974 amendments created the FEC and charged it with disclosing campaign finance data, enforcing limits and prohibitions on contributions, and managing the public funding of presidential elections. It also set spending limits for presidential, House, and Senate primaries and general elections and created individual and POLITICAL ACTION COMMITTEE contribution limits by candidate and by election. Finally, it expanded the Presidential Public Funding Program to provide the option of full public financing for presidential general elections, MATCHING FUNDS for PRESIDENTIAL PRIMARIES, and public funds for presidential nominating conventions.

In 1976 and again in 1979, Congress enacted two additional amendments to FECA. On May 11, 1976, Congress revised campaign finance legislation to comply with *BUCKLEY V. VALEO*, a Supreme Court ruling that found certain provisions of the 1974 amendments unconstitutional. The Court saw contribution limits as a public good, but overturned spending limits that imposed on a candidate's right to free speech. The 1979 amendments simplified reporting requirements, prohibited the FEC from conducting random audits, and allowed state and local parties to promote party activity.

Minor changes to FECA legislation occurred between 1980 and 2002. But in 2002, the Bipartisan Campaign Reform Act (BCRA) brought sweeping changes to how the government regulated SOFT MONEY, previously unregulated money used to promote party activities. Political reform groups and politicians argue that future reforms should include strengthening the Presidential Public Funding Program and also create a funding program for House and Senate races.

Further reading: Alexander, Herbert E., and Anthony Corrado. *Financing the 1992 Election*. Armonk, N.Y.: M. E. Sharpe, 1995; Corrado, Anthony, et al., eds. *Campaign Finance Reform: A Sourcebook*. Washington, D.C.: Brookings Institution Press, 1997; Mutch, Robert E. *Campaigns, Congress, and Courts: The Making of Federal Campaign Finance Law.* New York: Praeger Publishers, 1988.

—Jamie Patrick Chandler

Federal Election Commission (FEC)

This independent regulatory agency was created by Congress in 1975 to administer and enforce the FEDERAL ELECTION CAMPAIGN ACT of 1971 (FECA), which is the statute governing the financing of federal elections. It was created in response to the well-documented campaign abuses in the 1972 PRESIDENTIAL ELECTION to ensure compliance with CAMPAIGN FINANCE LAWS.

The commission comprises six members appointed by the president and confirmed by the Senate who serve a six-year staggered term (every two years two seats are open for appointment). The members select a chairman who serves for one year as the presiding officer and as the commission's spokesperson. The chair and vice chair must be of different political parties, and no more than three members of the commission may be affiliated with the same POLITICAL PARTY. The law also requires four votes for the commission to take action.

The FEC has four major responsibilities: to provide disclosure of campaign finance information; to ensure that candidates, committees, and others comply with the limitations, prohibitions, and disclosure requirements of FECA; to administer the public funding of presidential campaigns; and to serve as a clearinghouse for information on election administration.

To aid in its role as a discloser of campaign finance information, the FEC requires a campaign to file an FEC report disclosing its receipts and disbursements, which is used to maintain a publicly accessible database. The commission's Reports Analysis Division then reviews each report to check for accuracy and monitor compliance. Enforcement cases are initiated by complaints filed by the public, referrals from other federal and state agencies, and the FEC's own monitoring process.

In administering the public funding of PRESIDENTIAL ELECTIONS, the commission first determines which candidates are eligible for public funds and in what amounts. It later audits all the committees that receive public funds to ensure that they use the funds in accordance with the public funding program.

The agency's Office of Election Administration serves as a clearinghouse for information and research on issues related to the administration of federal elections. It conducts research, provides information to state and local election officials, maintains a library of election information, and monitors federal legislation pertaining to the administration of elections.

Critics of the FEC say that is structurally weak and understaffed and point to its budget as evidence that the FEC is incapable of fulfilling its compliance and enforcement responsibilities. Moreover, the FEC has only civil enforcement of FECA, and it does not have the authority to conduct random audits of committees.

Further reading: Jackson, Brooks. *Broken Promises: Why the Election Commission Failed.* New York: Priority Press Publications, 1990; Federal Election Commission. Available online. URL: http://www.fec.gov. Accessed August 10, 2005.

—Meredith Staples

Federalist Papers

The *Federalist Papers* were a set of 85 opinion papers (i.e., polemics) published during the debate in New York in favor of the newly proposed federal constitution of 1787. Published mainly in the *New York Packet* and the *Independent Journal,* the papers, written by Alexander Hamilton, James Madison, and John Jay under the pen name "Publius," were reprinted in other newspapers across New York and in several cities in other states. Now typically reprinted in collected volumes, the *Federalist Papers* represent the first and arguably the finest exposition of American political thought to date.

The framers dictated that the Constitution would go into effect with only nine of the 13 states concurring, but they also knew that all the large states, Massachusetts, New York, Pennsylvania, and Virginia, were needed to make the new government more than mere words on paper. Ratification in New York was by far the most problematic. Two-thirds of the state's delegation had left the convention in July over their objections to the document, leaving only Alexander Hamilton, and him without an official vote. The state economy was booming as a quasi-independent nation, made rich through trade and tariffs on its neighbors. Finally, New York governor George Clinton, the state's powerful leader, was strongly against the proposed document and more than willing to throw his considerable weight behind the anti-Federalist cause.

Hamilton, the lone DELEGATE from the state to attend the Constitutional Convention for the duration, felt strongly that the nation needed the proposed constitution to pass. Anything else might, in his opinion, spell disaster for the fledgling nation. However, the constitution that had been produced by the PHILADELPHIA CONVENTION was in large part a bundle of compromises. While the majority of delegates signed the document in the end, some made a point of not doing so, pointing out what they saw in the document as possessing aristocratic tendencies that would lead the nation down the road to tyranny.

Even the authors of the *Federalist Papers* were not completely sold on the ideas that the constitution contained or on the ability of that document to actually structure a workable government. Hamilton said outright to the convention on the day that he signed for New York that his own ideas on government were most likely the furthest away from the proposed document. Madison later confided to Thomas Jefferson that he felt the new government, as it had been written, would not be able to carry out its own goals, nor would it, he said, be able to distinguish itself from the problems that faced the individual state governments.

These personal misgivings aside, the authors of the *Federalist Papers* successfully explained the provisions of the newly proposed government and addressed effectively the criticisms that were already being published in newspapers across the young nation. Nearly two and a quarter centuries later, the *Federalist Papers* still inform discussions on modern topics. While some of them relate to subjects that are dated, such as the virtue of having the Senate elected by the state legislatures and the fact that the president should be eligible for reelection ad infinitum, others address current problems.

The idea of judicial review is explained quite well in Federalist No. 78. Publius states that the Constitution is the direct embodiment of the will of the people (hence the first words of the Preamble, "We, the People"). Government itself, on the other hand, is merely the elected representative of the people, their servants who are given power through the will of the people. If something they do is in violation of that grant of power, it must be void. To ignore this would be to set the order of precedence on its head, putting the sovereign power in society, the people themselves, subordinate to their own elected representatives, the government.

Other examples of Publius speaking on contemporary issues include a paper on the ability of a large republic to respond to the dangers of FACTIONS (No. 10) by setting competing interests against each other. Factions, Madison writes, are inherent to human nature, and to get rid of them a government would either have to alter human nature itself or destroy liberty. The former being impossible and the latter a cure worse than the disease, it is left to the government to control them. The United States is uniquely capable of this sort of control. Minority factions can be controlled by the democratic principle; being a minority, they will not win enough votes to do much harm. Majority factions are a danger, but Publius argues that a large republic will be able to isolate these factions geographically, and they will not be able to gather a majority, relegating them to minority status. And pitting factions against each other, as the new constitution allowed, was perhaps the greatest check against the influence of any one faction.

The new form of the government was designed with human nature in mind. (No. 51) Humans, the framers believed, were imperfect by nature, and this had to be understood when the operation of government was considered, since it was people who would make up the government. However, being made of imperfect people, the government needs to be able not only to control the people but also protect them from itself. To do this, the framers divided the government and installed checks and balances and gave deliberation a chance at every step. As each branch seeks to enlarge its own power, the competing ambitions of each branch run up against the others. Each branch, jealously protects its sphere of influence against the encroachments of the others. Thus, no single branch of government is able to dominate the others and harm the common good.

Further reading: Hamilton, Alexander, James Madison, and John Jay. *The Federalist Papers*, edited by Clinton Rossiter. New York: Mentor Books, 1999; University of Oklahoma Law Center, *Federalist Papers*. Available online. URL: http://www.law.ou.edu/hist/federalist. Accessed August 10, 2005.

—John P. Todsen

Federalist Party

The Federalist Party was one of the first two political parties in the United States. It dominated POLITICS during the first two administrations, from 1789 to 1801, and remained a potent force through the first quarter of the 19th century. Comprised primarily of wealthy businessmen, conservative merchants and farmers, and large property owners, the party had an aristocratic flavor, favoring a strong executive and scorning egalitarian notions of universal SUFFRAGE and open elections. While the party would be far too conservative to have any real power in the United States today, its policies laid the framework for the country as we know it.

The term *federalist* comes from the *FEDERALIST PAPERS*, which were written in 1787 by Alexander Hamilton, John Madison, and John Jay, who argued for a strong union and the adoption of the Constitution. Other famous members included the first two presidents, George Washington and John Adams, as well as the first Supreme Court chief justice, John Marshall. Geographically, the party was centered primarily in the northeastern New England states, with a strong CONSTITUENCY in the Middle Atlantic states.

While Washington deplored FACTIONS, the Federalist Party itself emerged from the policies of his administration. Alexander Hamilton, who served as Washington's secretary of the Treasury, promoted controversial policies, including the establishment of a national bank, the assumption of the states' debts by the federal government, and the repayment of foreign debt at the original value rather than at its depressed market value. Secretary of State Thomas Jefferson and Congressman James Madison led the charge against these policies, which planted the seeds for the first two parties in the United States. By 1794, following John Jay's treaty with Great Britain, a divide was clearly established between the Federalist Party, led by Alexander

Hamilton, and the Democratic-Republicans, led by Jefferson and Madison.

Members of the Federalist Party argued for strong executive and judicial branches of government. They felt that the early nation needed to be run by the elite aristocracy, who could best foster economic development by encouraging industries with liberal trade policies and a focus on the needs of the largest merchants and landowners. The Federalists argued for the establishment of a strong economy and a well-ordered society above the notions of open elections and a government truly representative of the people. In foreign policy, the Federalist Party advocated diplomatic and commercial harmony with the British, while their opposition favored the French.

During Washington's tenure, the Federalist Party received popular support as it established the strength of the presidency. Washington's farewell address, which was prepared with Hamilton's assistance, is considered a classic text promoting federalism. Washington's successor, John Adams, who was also a Federalist, had less success in maintaining party unity. While Adams initially tried to maintain Washington's policies and cabinet, his unpopular foreign and domestic policies soon caused a fracture in the party. Adams supported the infamous ALIEN AND SEDITION ACTS (1798) and an unpopular and undeclared naval war with France, which caused internal disagreement in the party. After reorganizing the cabinet under his control and refusing to end the naval war with France, the Federalist Party split under the leadership of Alexander Hamilton. This fracture led to the defeat of the party by Democratic-Republican Thomas Jefferson in 1800.

The defeat of John Adams by Thomas Jefferson in 1800 marked the beginning of the end for the Federalist Party. Breaking with the IDEOLOGY of a strong executive, the party protested Jefferson's popular Louisiana Purchase of 1803. After carrying only Maryland, Delaware, and Connecticut against Jefferson in 1804, the party was on the verge of collapse. The demise of the party was hastened by its unpopular opposition to the Louisiana Purchase, the isolation of a party loyalty confined primarily to the New England states, and the untimely death of Alexander Hamilton. However, the party was revived in 1807 with Jefferson's botched embargo of 1807. In the following year, Charles C. Pinckney found renewed support in his unsuccessful bid for the presidency, winning parts of North Carolina and Maryland, Delaware, and all of New England except Vermont. The party gained further strength in the opposition to Madison's War of 1812 against the British, which gained votes from New York, New Jersey, and Maryland. However, the revival of the Federalist Party was short-lived.

While popular at first, the Federalist Party's opposition to the war effort gave it a stigma of secession and treason. Federalist Rufus King managed to carry only Connecticut, Massachusetts, and Delaware in his opposition to the candidacy of Democratic-Republican James Monroe in 1816. The Federalist Party did not offer a candidate for president in 1820 and finally died out in 1824. Ultimately, the failure of the Federalist Party to expand its support geographically and socially led to its demise. While the Democratic-Republicans were able to appeal to the popular democratic spirit spreading through towns and cities, the Federalist Party garnered support primarily from prosperous businessmen, large landowners, and wealthy merchants.

In retrospect, the institutions established by the party's early leaders set the United States on the path of freedom and prosperity. Washington and Adams's emphasis on banking and commerce laid the foundation of today's relatively stable economic system. They also made significant contributions to the judicial system, keeping the ideology of the party alive in constitutional law with Adams's appointment of Federalist John Marshall as chief justice of the Supreme Court. Their foreign policies of open trade gave the young nation a large foreign market for its goods, allowing business to rapidly expand.

Further reading: Banner, James M. *To the Hartford Convention: The Federalists and the Origins of Party Politics in Massachusetts, 1789–1815.* New York: Knopf, 1970; Kurtz, Stephen G. *The Presidency of John Adams: The Collapse of Federalism, 1795–1800.* Philadelphia: University of Pennsylvania Press, 1957; Miller, John C. *The Federalist Era, 1789–1801.* New York: Harper, 1960.

—Clayton L. Thyne

Fifteenth Amendment

Since the FOURTEENTH AMENDMENT did not specifically guarantee blacks the right to vote, Congress attempted to correct this oversight with the Fifteenth Amendment. The amendment was adopted in 1870 and simply states "The right of citizens of the United States to vote shall not be denied or abridged by the United States or any state on account of race, color, or previous condition of servitude" and that Congress shall have the power to enforce the amendment through legislation. The Fifteenth Amendment was the last of the three Civil War amendments (the Thirteenth Amendment abolished slavery and the Fourteenth gave equal protection under the law).

During the period of RECONSTRUCTION following the Civil War, blacks were elected to many political offices in the South: Two black senators were elected from Mississippi, and a total of 14 blacks were elected to the House of Representatives between 1869 and 1877. Southern blacks were helped by the passage of the Reconstruction Acts (1867), which among other things disenfranchised ex-Confederate soldiers. Many of the southern blacks found a home in the REPUBLICAN PARTY, the party of Lincoln and

An 1870 print commemorating the passage and enactment of the Fifteenth Amendment *(Library of Congress)*

the Civil War amendments. After the Civil War, the Republican Party reached out to black voters as a means to build party strength in southern states.

Two seminal events aided in the dissolving of black political power in the South: the withdrawal of federal troops from southern states in 1877 and the disputed 1876 PRESIDENTIAL ELECTION between Rutherford B. Hayes and the Democratic nominee, Samuel Jones Tilden. Southerners and the Republican Party made a compromise. The northern Republicans agreed to relinquish their pursuit of civil rights for blacks in exchange for Hayes becoming president of the United States. With the departure of federal troops from the South in 1877 and weakening support for the rights of African Americans among northern Republicans, the stage was set for a return to white control in the South.

White Democrats regained control of the southern states, and nearly a century passed before the true spirit of the Fifteenth Amendment would be fulfilled. Several southern states adopted such measures as LITERACY TESTS,

GRANDFATHER CLAUSES, and POLL TAXes to ensure obstruction of voting rights for blacks, while terror groups such as the Ku Klux Klan used intimidation and violence to keep blacks from the polls. Eventually, many of the obstructions were removed by the VOTING RIGHTS ACT of 1965, which together with the Fifteenth Amendment, assures that blacks can register and vote without encountering legal or structural impediments.

Further reading: Cornell Law School, Legal Information Center. Available online. URL: http://www.law.cornell.edu. Accessed August 10, 2005; Bailey, Richard. *Neither Carpetbaggers nor Scalawags: Black Officeholders during the Reconstruction of Alabama, 1867–1878.* Montgomery, Ala.: Pyramid Publishers, 1997; Franklin, John Hope. *Reconstruction after the Civil War.* Chicago: University of Chicago Press, 1994; Morris, Roy. *Fraud of the Century: Rutherford B. Hayes, Samuel Tilden and the Stolen Election of 1876.* New York: Simon & Schuster, 2003.

—F. Erik Brooks

fifty-fifty rule

The fifty-fifty rule was established by the two major American political parties to assure equal gender representation and powers on governing committees. Implementation of fifth-fifty rules began at the state level and spread to the national political parties. In 1910, Colorado became the first state to adopt a fifty-fifty rule to assure equal gender representation on all local and STATE PARTY COMMITTEES operating between state conventions. After women gained the right to vote in 11 western states, the Democrats and then the Republicans established women's organizations at the national level. Soon after, women gained the nationwide right to vote in 1920, the Democrats responded by mandating that their national committee would be composed of one man and one woman from each state and territory. In 1923, the Republicans made women nonvoting associated members of their national committee. However, during their convention the following year, the Republicans adopted an equal gender organization similar to their rival party.

The two major national political parties have taken contrasting approaches toward implementing the fifty-fifty rule. During the 1970s and 1980s, the Democrats made several efforts to assure equal gender representation. Rules established by the McGovern-Fraser Commission required PROPORTIONAL REPRESENTATION for men and women during the 1972 national convention. However, in 1980, the party's charter was amended to mandate equal gender representation on all national and state committees, panels, and commissions. In 1988, the party charter was amended to expand the coverage of the fifty-fifty rule to apply to every candidate's delegation within each state. On the other hand, the Republicans have not mandated such fifty-fifty gender representation for national organizations, but allow several state and local PARTY ORGANIZATIONs to do so.

Further reading: Conway, M. Margaret, David W. Ahern, and Gertrude A. Steuernagel. *Women and Public Policy: A Revolution in Progress.* 2nd ed. Washington, D.C.: Congressional Quarterly Press, 1999; Conway, M. Margaret, Gertrude A. Steuernagel, and David W. Ahern. *Women and Political Participation: Cultural Change in the Political Arena.* Washington, D.C.: Congressional Quarterly Press, 1997; McGlen, Nancy E., and Karen O'Connor. *Women, Politics, and American Society.* Englewood Cliffs, N.J.: Prentice Hall, 1995.

—Robert E. Dewhirst

first past the post

First past the post (FPTP) is a vernacular term used to identify a SINGLE-MEMBER DISTRICT plurality electoral system, or what is sometimes referred to as a winner-take-all system. To win in this election system a candidate need only garner the most votes, and is not required to receive a majority of the votes cast in the election. The term is a reference to horse racing, in which the first horse past the post wins the race. It is the most common electoral system worldwide for single-member district elections.

First-past-the-post electoral systems were typically found in Britain and its former colonies, including widespread use in the United States. The system was initially used for three key reasons: It was simple, it provided for stable governments and stable political systems (something seen as good for emerging democracies), and it created a system in which there was a direct relationship between constituents and their elected representatives. After years of use and increasing scrutiny, however, it is considered by many to be a flawed electoral system.

A primary concern about the system is that results are not always representative of the election. The problem arises in spite of the fact that the winners of individual elections are clear; because candidates are not required to garner a majority of the vote there is a chance that a party will win the majority of seats in an election with less than a majority of the total vote of the ELECTORATE. Several examples of this shortcoming can be found in election results from Britain, Canada, and the United States, in which individual election outcomes did not represent election results in aggregate. However, these "failures" are rare and are typically not the norm. A secondary criticism of the system is that it tends to foster a TWO-PARTY SYSTEM, greatly limiting the role of THIRD PARTIES. Support for this criticism is easy to garner, as the majority of countries using first past the post have strong two-party systems, with little opportunity for third-party inclusion.

To address these criticisms, many in these nations are calling for electoral reforms. In many cases countries with this system are moving toward some form of PROPORTIONAL REPRESENTATION. Although these types of systems often address the primary criticisms of the first-past-the-post system, they have their own set of shortcomings. It is worth noting that throughout history countries using the first-past-the-post electoral system have tended to have more stable, longer-lasting political systems than those that have not adopted it.

Further reading: Farrell, David M. *Electoral Systems: A Comparative Introduction.* New York: Palgrave Macmillan, 2001; Keefe, William J. *Parties, Politics, and Public Policy in America.* 8th ed. Washington, D.C.: Congressional Quarterly Press, 1998.

—Derrek M. Davis

focus groups

Focus groups are in-depth group interviews. They are designed to create a climate that allows rich discussion and personal experiences to be expressed and systematically recorded. Group study is used as an alternative to personal interviews, observation, and questionnaires.

Focus group research generally follows a few key steps. Prior to a focus group's initial meeting, the client and researcher establish a purpose for study, that is, the information they want to gain. For instance, a government agency might want to investigate why some people successfully make the transition from prison back into the community and others do not. The study's goal might be to explore "ingredients for successful transitions."

After the initial decision, participant selection begins. Focus groups are often made up of key stakeholders who can address the research topic and who possess specialized insights. Within the target group, it is often beneficial to select a "cross-section" of the population. People are often selected based on their age, sex, race, education, occupation, and so forth, which can improve the discussion and ensure the data collected better relates to those affected by the study.

Once participants are selected, a trained moderator assembles the group. The group, consisting usually of eight to 12 people, will generally meet for around two hours at a neutral site, such as a school, and openly discuss the research topic. The moderator steers the process, describes the group's role, keeps the discussion on track, encourages debate, probes for deeper understanding, and shifts gears when the debate becomes irrelevant or begins to drag on. The process is one in which group members react to one another's opinions, challenge their bases, point out different possibilities, examine misunderstandings, describe unique experiences with the same issue, and generate "cross-communication."

Former political consultant Lee Atwater said "the conversations in focus groups give you a sense of what makes people tick and a sense of what is going on with people's minds and lives that you simply can't get with survey data." The underlying attitudes, opinions, feelings, and beliefs that emerge provide researchers with valuable information about the topic. While focus groups are used for a wide range of reasons, including the marketing of products, candidates and elected officials typically use focus groups to help focus their message, test campaign commercials, and identify hot-button issues. They are a relatively inexpensive way to test ideas before launching a media campaign.

Further reading: Greenbaum, Thomas L. *The Handbook for Focus Group Research.* 2nd ed. Thousand Oaks, Calif.: Sage Publications, 1998.

—John Todd Young

Fourteenth Amendment

The Fourteenth Amendment was one of the three Civil War amendments that were intended to guarantee equal protection and due process to African Americans in the United States. The Fourteenth Amendment was offered by Republicans after the Civil War to ensure that admission of Confederate states back into the Union would be accompanied by a guarantee of equal rights for blacks. It was passed by Congress and ratified by the states in 1868.

This specific amendment reversed the *Dred Scott* (1857) decision, which held that blacks, even free blacks, were not citizens and therefore were not entitled to guarantees under the Constitution. The equal protection clause of the Fourteenth Amendment, Section 1, states, "No State shall . . . deny any person within the jurisdiction the equal protection of the laws." Section 5 of the amendment provides a legal basis for federal CIVIL RIGHTS LEGISLATION when it states, "The Congress shall have power to enforce, by appropriate legislation, the provisions of this article." The equal protection clause has been interpreted by the courts to mean that states must treat all persons in an equal manner and may not discriminate unreasonably against a particular group or class unless there is sufficient reason to do so.

The hopes of blacks seemed fulfilled with the adoption of the three amendments to the Constitution following the Civil War (the Thirteenth Amendment abolished slavery, the Fourteenth gave equal protection under the law, and the FIFTEENTH AMENDMENT gave voting rights to blacks). The struggle for equal protection for African Americans, however, did not end with the Civil War amendments, but instead these amendments provided the legal foundation to build the case for equality. It would take decades of court challenges, civil disobedience, and, ultimately, congressional action for the promises of these amendments to materialize for African Americans, especially African Americans living in the racially divided South. Moreover, passage of the Fourteenth Amendment did little to secure equal rights for other groups, especially women, who were omitted from the protections.

Further reading: Cornell Law School, Legal Information Center. Available online. URL: http://www.law.cornell.edu. Accessed August 10, 2005; Foner, Eric. *Free Soil, Free Labor, Free Men: The Ideology of the Republican Party before the Civil War.* New York: Oxford University Press, 1995; Richards, David A. J. *Conscience and the Constitution: History, Theory, and Law of the Reconstruction Amendments.* Princeton, N.J.: Princeton University Press, 1993; Stamp, Kenneth M. *Era of Reconstruction, 1865–1877: A Revisionist View of One of the Most Controversial Periods.* New York: Knopf, 1972.

—F. Erik Brooks

Free-Soil Party

The Free-Soil Party was a brief-lived political party that grew from the debate between pro- and antislavery forces. The party, created out of opposition to the expansion of slavery, never won an electoral vote. Nonetheless, it was indicative of the growing furor embroiling the country over the issue of slavery.

Martin Van Buren's failure to bridge the gap between abolitionist Whigs and conservative Democrats is portrayed as his downfall in this cartoon from 1848. *(HarpWeek, LLC)*

The main issue that led to the creation of the Free-Soil Party lay in the divisive matter of the expansion of slavery into newly admitted states. While the debate would gradually become one of the issues that led to the secession of the southern states, already in the mid-1840s it was having a disruptive effect on the two major parties of the era, the Whigs and the Democrats. For the Democrats, the division became apparent during the 1844 convention, as proexpansionist candidate James K. Polk won the NOMINATION.

The annexation and statehood of Texas by 1845 renewed the fears that slavery would expand as the country grew to the South and West. In response, antiexpansionists sought a legislative remedy in the Wilmot Proviso. The proviso, an amendment on Polk's fiscal request to purchase land from Mexico, sought to attach a condition that slavery would not be permitted on any new land acquired from Mexico. The proviso predictably split both parties along regional lines, passed the House, but failed in the Senate. Nonetheless, the proviso would continue to be a major force in the creation of the Free-Soil Party.

Both party conventions in 1848 provided the final impetus for the creation of the party. At the Whig convention, Massachusetts Whigs opposed to slavery left the convention when it was revealed that the party would support Zachary Taylor, a general during the Mexican-American War and slaveholder, for president. At the Democratic convention, New York antislavery Democrats, known as "Barnburners," left the convention when their party did not endorse the proviso and when their candidate, Martin Van Buren, failed to win the nomination.

Van Buren's failure to win the Democratic nomination in 1848 and the successful nomination of Taylor caused many antiexpansionist Whigs, Democrats, and supporters of the abolitionist Liberty Party to create the Free-Soil Party. The party, led by Salmon Chase and John P. Hale, organized a convention in Buffalo in August 1848 and nominated Martin Van Buren and Charles F. Adams as its candidates for president and vice president.

The party's major platform was its enthusiastic support of the Wilmot Proviso and its antiexpansionist idea, often with racist overtones for keeping future territories white only. It also advocated internal improvements for trade, a tariff for creating revenue, and a homestead law. The results were disappointing as it became apparent that, despite the fervor that expansion engendered in politicians, most voters in the North lacked the same emotion. The

party garnered nearly 300,000 votes, elected nine congressmen, and threw the election to the Whigs.

The Compromise of 1850 dealt a blow to the party by depriving it of its main issue concerning slavery's expansion. The Free-Soil Party continued to exist, albeit in a smaller form, and those remaining in the party ran John P. Hale for president in 1852. Unfortunately for the party, Hale received only 150,000 votes. In 1854, the remnants of the party were absorbed into the nascent REPUBLICAN PARTY.

Further reading: Blue, Frederick J. *The Free Soilers* Urbana: University of Illinois Press, 1973; Foner, Eric. *Free Soil, Free Labor, Free Men.* New York: Oxford University Press, 1970.

—Stephen Nemeth

front-loading

Front-loading is the process whereby a large number of states move their PRESIDENTIAL PRIMARY elections or caucuses to dates early in the presidential nominating year. Since 1952, the first PRIMARY of the presidential campaign has been held in New Hampshire and the first caucus in Iowa. As a result of their early nominating contests, it is believed that these two states enjoy disproportionate influence in the presidential nominating process and other political benefits. According to William Mayer, states with early primaries enjoy such benefits as prominent press coverage, extensive attention from candidates, disproportionate influence on the NOMINATION race, and economic benefits from campaign and media. Historically, a candidate must finish among the top three in Iowa and among the top two in New Hampshire to have a realistic hope of capturing the party's nomination. The process of front-loading began as other states desired to share in the benefits of early nominating contests.

The first clear instance of this can be seen in the 1980s, when large blocks of southern states began to hold their primary elections on the same day. Known as SUPER TUESDAY, this block of southern primaries played a decisive role in DEMOCRATIC PARTY politics (namely, elevating the candidacies of Jesse Jackson, Michael Dukakis, and Bill Clinton in 1984, 1988, and 1992 and effectively ending the candidacies of Al Gore in 1988 and Jerry Brown in 1992).

The phenomenon of front-loading has rapidly accelerated since the early 1990s. In 1996, both California and New York moved their primaries to early March from mid-June. In 2000, all of the New England states (with the exception of New Hampshire) decided to hold their primaries on the same day at the beginning of March. And by 2004, John Kerry was able to win the Democratic nomination less than six weeks after his victory in the IOWA CAUCUSes.

Parties also favor early primaries because they allow parties to know very early who will win the nomination, they limit interparty strife, and they allow the nominees to focus more quickly on fund-raising and preparing for the GEN-

ERAL ELECTION opponent in November. However, critics of front-loading argue that it tends to favor the candidates who have the most money, most name recognition, and most support from the party establishment. They also argue that the public should be given a much longer span of time in which to evaluate the candidates and that quality is being sacrificed for the sake of speed.

Further reading: Busch, Andrew. *Outsiders and Openness in the Presidential Nominating System.* Pittsburgh: University of Pittsburgh Press, 1997; Cook, Rhodes. *The Presidential Nominating Process: A Place for Us?* New York: Rowman & Littlefield, 2003; Mayer, William G., and Andrew Busch. *The Front-Loading Problem in Presidential Nominations.* Washington, D.C.: Brookings Institution Press, 2003.

—Brian DiSarro

frontrunner

A frontrunner is the candidate seen by the media, PUNDITs, and political observers as most likely to win a party's NOMINATION or the GENERAL ELECTION. Polling and FUNDRAISING numbers, conventional wisdom, incumbency, and party strength are key factors in determining which candidate is dubbed the frontrunner.

The term *frontrunner* reflects the horse race nature of POLITICS, in which one candidate is seen as leading in the early stretch of the campaign. He or she then becomes the yardstick by which other candidates are judged. The word has been used in politics since at least 1960, when Theodore Sorensen discussed the disadvantages of being the "frontrunner" with John F. Kennedy.

Frontrunners, especially in noncompetitive races, tend to win elections easily. In 1996, President Bill Clinton was the frontrunner throughout his reelection campaign against former senator Bob Dole. Being a frontrunner often helps a candidate to raise money and attract large crowds because donors and voters like to support a winner. Incumbents, unless they are tainted by SCANDAL or poor job performance, are almost always considered frontrunners.

Presidential candidates try to establish frontrunner status early and ward off challenges, especially given the compressed PRIMARY calendar. Both Al Gore and George W. Bush met with party officials, strategists, and donors more than a year before the first 2000 primary contests to cement their frontrunner status.

While being the frontrunner brings benefits, there is also a downside. More is expected of the frontrunner than of other candidates. He or she must maintain or increase a lead in the polls, raise more money than competitors, and avoid scandal. While the press often writes glowing profiles of frontrunners early in campaigns, reporters often give frontrunner candidates increased scrutiny, searching for new, and sometimes damaging, information.

The frontrunner can change several times in a single campaign. John Kerry was first considered the frontrunner in the 2004 Democratic primary contest because he enjoyed the support of the party establishment. The title later went to Howard Dean because of his fund-raising prowess, perceived GRASSROOTS support, and ENDORSEMENTS from party leaders such as former vice president Al Gore. After Kerry won the IOWA CAUCUSES, however, Dean lost his frontrunner mantle. Dean complained that as the frontrunner he was the target of attacks by the nine other Democrats seeking the White House and by the media.

It is also possible for there to be no frontrunner in a campaign, especially in an open-seat race. During the final months of the 2000 presidential campaign, neither Bush nor Gore was far ahead, a fact reflected in the postelection RECOUNT. The 2004 PRESIDENTIAL ELECTION also failed to produce a clear frontrunner.

—Mary Lynn F. Jones

fund-raising

The act of requesting and securing campaign donations from individuals, POLITICAL ACTION COMMITTEES (PACs), political parties, and other interested actors for electioneering purposes. Political parties and candidates have long sought out donations from others to operate their campaigns. One of the first examples of excess in campaign fund-raising was Mark Hanna's million-dollar funding of William McKinley's 1896 presidential campaign, whereby Hanna would actually lodge people on trains to travel to McKinley's front porch in Ohio to hear the candidate speak. The widespread use of bribes and questionable donation tactics combined to force a negative image of political fund-raising on the public, which continued until President Richard Nixon's fund-raising tactics spurred action.

While early laws governing political fund-raising have been on the books for nearly a century, most notably the TILLMAN ACT of 1907, it was not until the FEDERAL ELECTION CAMPAIGN ACT (FECA) of 1971 and its 1974 amendments that meaningful limits were placed on federal fund-raising. According to Tillman, registered corporations could not directly contribute to political campaigns. In 1910, the Publicity Act mandated reporting any contribution more than $100 in value. However, the laws were riddled with loopholes and suffered from rampant noncompliance. In 1971, the most comprehensive effort to limit federal campaign contributions came in the form of the Federal Election Campaign Act. Along with amendments in 1974, FECA strengthened disclosure requirements, limited the amount candidates could spend on their own campaigns, and set limits on the amount individuals and groups could spend on campaigns. Individuals were limited to contributing $1,000 to candidates per election, $5,000 to INTEREST GROUPS, and $10,000 to parties. Groups could contribute no more than $5,000 to a candi-

THE "TRUST-BUSTERS" AT WORK

This 1904 cartoon portrays how both political parties solicited campaign funds from business corporations. *(Cartoon by William Allen Rogers, HarpWeek, LLC)*

date, and the parties were limited to contributions of $20,000 or less.

Loopholes existed in the law that allowed some to skirt the limits, and in *BUCKLEY V. VALEO* (1976) the Supreme Court ruled that limits on self-financing and maximum spending ceilings were unconstitutional. In 1996's *Colorado Federal Republican Federal Campaign Committee v. FEC* the Court allowed unlimited donations from unions and corporations for "party-building activities," also known as SOFT MONEY, to pay for ads that avoided expressly advocating the election or defeat of different candidates. In response, candidates and other political actors became increasingly aware of other opportunities to raise money. Instead of limiting the amount of money in campaigns, limits appeared to increase the candidates' general ability to bring cash into the campaign. Through DIRECT MAIL, telephone calls, fund-raising events, and even private outside fund-raising consultants, savvy candidates use every resource possible to bring every possible dollar into their campaign coffers.

The 2002 Bipartisan Campaign Reform Act (BCRA) doubled the possible individual contribution to a campaign but limited the ability of unions and corporations to influence elections as they had during the soft money era of 1996–2002. However, more ideological and independent "527s" (so called due to the section of the IRS tax code that governs them instead of the FEDERAL ELECTION COMMISSION) now raise unlimited amounts from individuals, such as billionaire investment banker George Soros, who contributed more than $23 million in campaign funds to defeat President George W. Bush in the 2004 PRESIDENTIAL ELECTION.

Today campaigns are increasingly turning to the Internet as a source of money, raising small amounts from individuals. In the 2004 Democratic PRESIDENTIAL PRIMARIES, former Vermont governor Howard Dean used the Internet to effectively raise money, inspiring hundreds of other candidates to tap the electronic medium as a funding source. Despite the restrictive laws that have passed at the federal and state levels, public belief that candidates still trade their votes for campaign cash continues.

Further reading: Federal Election Commission. Available online. URL: http://www.fec.gov. Accessed August 10, 2005; Rosencranz, Joshua, ed. *If Buckley Fell: A First Amendment Blueprint for Regulating Money in Politics.* New York: Century Foundation Press, 1999; Malbin, Michael J. *Life after Reform.* Lanham, Md.: Rowman & Littlefield, 2003; Center for Responsive Politics. Available online. URL: http://www.opensecrets.org. Accessed August 10, 2005; Magleby, David, ed. *The Other Campaign: Soft Money and Issue Advocacy in the 2000 Congressional Elections.* Lanham, Md.: Rowman & Littlefield, 2003.

—Chapman Rackaway

fund-raising, Internet

Internet fund-raising is the mechanism whereby nonprofit organizations or political campaigns solicit donations online. Its dramatic speed, low cost, and nationwide scope have both benefits and drawbacks. The advantages of online FUND-RAISING are numerous. First, it has the ability to reach more people than most organizations have historically been able to access. Second, it incurs relatively low expense. Third, it has the potential to target a higher disposable income demographic than traditional marketing methods. Last, it helps to demonstrate an organization's progressiveness.

On the other hand, there are several drawbacks to this type of fund-raising. First, it is difficult for a nascent Web site to be noticed among all the others seeking attention in cyberspace. Second, there is the possibility of technical breakdowns and the fear among donors that their financial information will be misused or illegally obtained from nonsecure sites. Last, there are some legal complexities, as the Internet's underlying infrastructure allows it to easily cross states and borders.

In the United States, Steve Forbes became the first presidential candidate to announce his bid for office over the Internet in 1999. The first large-scale use of the Internet for fund-raising came in 2000, when Senator John McCain raised more than $1 million over the Internet within 48 hours. His accomplishment over the Internet, however, has often been dismissed due to the fact that his online fund-raising took place immediately after an upset win in the NEW HAMPSHIRE PRIMARY, which would have spurred fund-raising regardless of how the contributions were accepted.

Howard Dean, a candidate for the 2004 Democratic Party presidential NOMINATION, brought new sophistication to the use of the Internet for fund-raising and organizing. His campaign, under the direction of Joe Trippi, signed up 640,974 people on his Web site and broke the records for DEMOCRATIC PARTY fund-raising, with more than $40 million in donations. His campaign fund-raising prowess allowed him to forego the need for federal MATCHING FUNDS and to avoid the ceiling placed on campaigns receiving federal funds. Dean's campaign also used Meetup.com to organize meetings of supporters around the country.

As the recent example of Dean's presidential campaign illustrates, the potential of the Internet for fund-raising and mobilizing supporters is only beginning to become clear. These Internet strategies and tools can help modern political campaigns and nonprofit organizations not only to solicit donations but also to generate excitement, participation, urgency, and other forms of support.

Further reading: Burnett, Ken. *Relationship fund-raising: A Donor-Based Approach to the Business of Raising Money.* New York: Jossey-Bass, 2002; Trippi, Joe. *The Revolution Will Not Be Televised: Democracy, the Internet, and the Overthrow of Everything.* New York: Regan Books, 2004.

—Taiyu Chen

fund-raising, mail

Raising money for political campaigns through the mail emerged and grew rapidly as a FUND-RAISING tactic in the last half of the 20th century. It allows candidates to raise large numbers of typically small contributions from individuals who share their views but might not ever meet the candidate in person. DIRECT MAIL fund-raising was largely pioneered by conservative activist Richard Viguerie and originally used to support conservative candidates and causes. However, groups and candidates from one end of the political spectrum to the other now use direct mail fund-raising to help fill their campaign coffers.

Mail fund-raising works through a two-stage process. The first stage is called prospecting, and the second stage is mailing the "housefile." In the prospecting stage, fund-raising consultants select mailing lists of individual donors who are likely to share the views of the candidate for whom they are raising money. Often, these names are identified because the person donated to another candidate, ordered a magazine espousing similar political views, or joined an ideologically aligned organization.

Once the names are identified, each person on the list is mailed a letter outlining the candidate's opinion on a particular issue and asking for funds. The tactics used in such letters vary widely and include everything from asking donors to fill out surveys to offering membership in campaigns, PARTY ORGANIZATIONS, and groups.

Typically, the prospecting phase of direct mail does not generate revenue and, in fact, often loses money. This occurs because only a small percentage, often less than 2 percent, of the individuals who are mailed letters actually mail contributions in return. Therefore, the cost of mailing the letters often exceeds the money raised by them.

It is therefore in the second phase of direct mail fund-raising that most contributions are raised. This phase consists of follow-up mailings to the housefile (i.e., the list of donors generated from the prospect group). This group donates at a much higher rate, typically generating a wide profit margin. The process is then typically repeated, with each round of prospecting being used to make the housefile larger and larger.

Many direct mail fund-raisers also generate additional revenues by renting their housefiles out for other clients to use as prospecting lists. Techniques such as Internet fund-raising and telephone solicitations are frequently used to raise yields from direct mail fund-raising. Direct mail fund-raising is primarily regulated by the Internal Revenue Service and/or the FEDERAL ELECTION COMMISSION, depending on the legal status of the group or candidate doing the fund-raising.

—Brad Alexander

fusion ticket

Generally referred to as a combination of ENDORSEMENTs from two or more major or minor political parties, few states have election laws that allow formal "fusion tickets" or multiple party–provided BALLOT lines. Fusion tickets can consist of one or more candidates but are more often confined to local races. In New York, the BALLOT ACCESS laws typically promote six to eight fixed political parties for each race, with the potential for more. Theoretically, and

usually in judicial races in which the major parties frequently come to consensus, one candidate can occupy every line of the ballot.

In other states, parties will decline to oppose a candidate, giving a de facto endorsement of their opponents' candidacy, particularly in legislative and congressional races, in which districts are drawn on electoral maps to favor one or the other major party. Most states, such as Massachusetts, prevent access to multiple ballot lines by one candidate.

Fusion tickets are almost never formed at the presidential level, at least at the level of the two major parties. Some notable exceptions are the 1872 race, in which the breakaway "Liberal Republican Party," headed by Horace Greeley, was endorsed by the Democratic National Convention, and the 1896 race, in which the small POPULIST PARTY endorsed the Democratic ticket headed by William Jennings Bryan. Frequently, smaller state parties that do not have a NATIONAL PARTY ORGANIZATION or are not affiliated with one will endorse the candidate of another minor party or of a major party. The New York State LIBERAL PARTY, for example, endorsed every Democratic presidential nominee from 1944 until 2000, providing the Democrats with an extra ballot line, with the exception of 1980, in which they endorsed the INDEPENDENT candidacy of Republican John B. Anderson.

Fusion tickets have a mixed degree of success at the local level and an almost universal degree of failure at the national level. Candidates who seek multiple ballot lines at the local level are not guaranteed success. Even in states, such as New York, that allow and even encourage the growth of minor parties that can endorse one another's tickets, the parties with the most significance are the two major parties. If a major party endorses the other's campaign or abstains from opposing it, this will virtually assure victory for the beneficiary. Fusion tickets matter the most when the guaranteed number of votes a secondary party's ballot line can bring to the primary party's nominee is greater than the margin of difference between the two major parties' candidates, and such a margin is virtually impossible to calculate before an election, thus causing the major parties generally to ignore and even avoid any possible benefits a minor party's endorsement might bring.

Further reading: Gould, Lewis L. *Grand Old Party: A History of the Republicans.* New York: Random House, 2003; Witcover, Jules. *Party of the People: A History of the Democrats.* New York: Random House, 2003.

—Daniel T. Kirsch

G

gender gap in U.S. voting

The 1980 PRESIDENTIAL ELECTION marked an important new development in American voting behavior. Before the 1980 election, there had been little difference in the voting behavior between women and men in national elections, and, in the few elections when there was a significant difference, women were more supportive of Republicans than were men. In 1980, in contrast, Democratic president Jimmy Carter received 45 percent of women's votes compared to just 36 percent of men's, creating a pronounced "gender gap" of 9 percentage points, with women voting in a more Democratic and more liberal manner.

The gender gap is the difference in support for a particular candidate between men and women. This gender gap turned out to be far from the idiosyncratic result of candidate personalities or events surrounding the 1980 campaign. In subsequent PRESIDENTIAL ELECTIONS, similar gender gaps existed and even seemed to be growing slightly, as the gender gaps were 12 percentage points in the 1996 and 2000 elections. The gender gap has emerged more slowly in congressional campaigns, but for most of the 1990s it also averaged 10 percentage points. In terms of its size of slightly more than 10 percentage points, the gender gap in voting might appear fairly moderate. Yet, in both the 1996 and 2000 PRESIDENTIAL ELECTIONS, the difference between the voting of women and men approximated such widely perceived cleavages as those associated with income, education, religiosity, community size, and region.

The gender gap in voting, furthermore, reflects similar differences, or gaps, in the attitudes of men and women on a fairly broad array of political issues. Women are more liberal than men on a variety of feminist issues, including support for the women's movement, feminists, and gays and lesbians, but not (perhaps surprisingly) for abortion. In addition to feminist issues, women have also been found to be more liberal than men on many social issues in the sense that they support governmental activism in combating social problems and in providing redistributive aid to the disadvantaged in society.

Women have long been viewed as more strongly opposed to violence than men, as reflected in a variety of issues, such as guns and the environment in domestic affairs and war and peace issues in foreign policy. These fairly long-lasting and stable issue divisions between women and men suggest three major reasons for the gender gap in voting. First, the difference between the sexes on feminist issues and the emergence of the gender gap within a few years of the blossoming of the feminist movement suggest that feminist "consciousness" played a major role in its development. Second, the more liberal attitudes of women about activist government, redistributive social policies, and antiviolence issues imply that the gender gap in voting also derives from women's presumed greater "compassion." This has been explained by women's fairly distinct values compared to men, which may lead them to place more emphasis on "connectiveness" in personal and community relations rather than abstract rights and power considerations. Finally, the growing "feminization of poverty" over the last several decades creates greater "cost-bearing" for women, which gives them a direct interest in liberal government policies.

Perspectives on the gender gap in voting have varied considerably over time. Initially in the early and mid-1980s, feminist politicians and scholars trumpeted women's disproportionate support of Democratic candidates, presumably as a strategy for making that party more responsive to their primary issue concerns. Then, the mainstream press seized on the gender gap in support of Bill Clinton in 1996 to herald "soccer moms" as the key to Clinton's reelection. More sophisticated analysis of public opinion data, incidentally, indicated that the underpinnings of the gender gap were quite complex and went far beyond any single group, such as feminists or soccer moms. Rather than reflecting the voting behavior of a few groups of women, the gender gap in both the 1996 and 2000 presidential elections was the result of significant differences in the voting of men and women for almost all categories of income, education, union membership, religiosity, marital status, family status, community size, region, and race.

Such findings suggested that the gender gap in voting was important and probably stable because it represented the parallel attitudes and actions of quite disparate groups of women, indicating that gender per se had become a factor in American POLITICS. In addition, though, analysis of how women themselves are divided on political issues indicates that, rather than forming a single group with exactly the same opinions, women are better conceptualized as forming a set of overlapping constitutions. For example, feminists and women in disadvantaged social circumstance focus on different issues, but both are generally liberal in their political positions. More surprisingly, some assumedly conservative groups, such as highly religious women, also contribute to the gender gap on voting due to their fairly liberal views on economic issues and the role of government. While this group of women tends to be more conservative than less religious women, they tend to be more liberal than men in the same religious subgrouping.

In stark contrast to the voting patterns of the previous two decades, the gender gap in voting almost completely disappeared in the 2002 CONGRESSIONAL ELECTIONS, primarily due to women's shifting attitudes on security issues following the tragedy of September 11, 2001, but resurfaced in the 2004 presidential race. On most issues (including some aspects of pacifism), the traditional tendency of women to be more liberal than men remains constant. Thus, there appears to be a significant attitudinal basis for the persistence of the gender gap in voting. Given the many important issues on which women have more liberal attitudes than men, it appears that the gender gap will play an important role in electoral politics in the near future.

Further reading: Niemi, Richard G., and Herbert F. Weisberg, eds. *Classics in Voting Behavior.* Washington, D.C.: CQ Press, 1993; Niemi, Richard G., and Herbert F. Weisberg, eds. *Controversies in Voting Behavior.* 4th ed. Washington, D.C.: CQ Press, 2001.

—Cal Clark and Janet Clark

general election

A general election is an election held to determine a winning candidate who will subsequently take office. At the national and state levels, the general election usually involves two or more candidates from different political parties, and it normally follows a PRIMARY election. In most general elections in the United States, the winning candidate is the one who receives the most votes (a plurality of the votes).

For the government of the United States, national elections are held for the presidency and to choose members of the House of Representatives and the Senate. For the office of president, there is a popular general election, followed by a vote by the ELECTORAL COLLEGE to make the final selection. The general election in which the pub-

lic votes contributes to the outcome by selecting "electors" from each state. The electors are pledged to the winning candidate in that state. When the electors from all states vote for president, the winning candidate is the one who receives a majority of the electoral votes. Members of the House of Representatives are elected every two years by POPULAR VOTE. Since U.S. senators have six-year terms, one-third of the Senate is elected every two years. National elections for the president and Congress are held in November of even-numbered years.

In states, general elections for governor, statewide offices, the state legislature, and other offices are held. Gubernatorial elections in most states are held in off-years (even numbered years that do not coincide with the PRESIDENTIAL ELECTION). In some other states, elections are in the presidential year, and five states elect governors in odd-numbered years. Most states elect state legislators every two years, but some of these elections are held at four-year intervals. City elections add another dimension to general elections, with most such contests being conducted on a nonpartisan basis (without party labels). Like states, localities often hold "isolated" elections at times that are separated from national races.

General elections that are fair and open to all adult citizens choosing to participate are essential to a democratic form of government. In these elections, the voters select candidates (representing parties and issue positions), and the choices made among candidates are essential to the process, as the winners will take office and shape policies.

Further reading: Janda, Kenneth, Jeffrey M. Berry, and Jerry Goldman. *The Challenge of Democracy.* 7th ed. Boston: Houghton Mifflin, 2002; Jewell, Malcolm E., and Sarah M. Morehouse. *Political Parties and Elections in American States.* 4th ed. Washington, D.C.: CQ Press, 2001.

—David W. Winder

gerrymander

As specified by the U.S. Constitution, CONGRESSIONAL DISTRICTS are redrawn every 10 years, following the decennial CENSUS. A gerrymander occurs when geographically awkward legislative districts are created to benefit the party in power. Its name derives from an 1811 Massachusetts REDISTRICTING plan signed by Governor Elbridge Gerry that created a district in the shape of a salamander. The district was parodied in a now famous cartoon by Elkanah Tisdale in the *Boston Weekly Messenger* depicting the district complete with fangs, wings, and a tail.

Gerrymanders have caused a great deal of political and legal debate in American history. Prior to the civil rights era, they were created primarily by state parties attempting to "stack," "crack," or "pack" legislative districts for partisan reasons. Stacking refers to combining two districts with opposing party sentiments into a single district, with the majority sentiment favoring the party in power. This MULTIMEMBER DISTRICT would then, theoretically, elect only at-large candidates of that party instead of both parties. Cracking refers to the practice of dividing up a locus of opposition support, while packing refers to the practice of isolating all opposition support in one district. This often entails the overrepresentation of mainly rural groups to support parties sympathetic to agrarian needs. Though many were opposed to the gerrymander on principal, the Supreme Court ruled in 1964 that legislative districts were acceptable as long as they were based approximately on population and were "compact" and "contiguous" (*Wesbury v. Sanders*). This broad definition has done little to quell debate on the subject.

During and following the civil rights era, gerrymanders were used both to discriminate against minorities and to assure minority representation. In a recent case, North Carolina in 1990 created a 160-mile-long ribbonlike district—in many places no wider than the highway it ran along—to assure African-American representation. This district was eventually struck down by the U.S. Supreme Court in *Reno v. Shaw*, which held that equal representation considerations did "not give [North Carolina] *carte blanche* to engage in racial gerrymandering." More recently, Texas Democrats charged that a 2003 Republican redistricting plan deliberately cracked and packed minority support in a manner designed to increase Republican representation in the state. The partisan bickering resulted in Democratic lawmakers leaving the state for Oklahoma in a failed attempt to block passage of the enabling legislation by denying Republicans the necessary quorum to approve the changes. While the plan of the House majority leader, Tom DeLay, to use federal officials to apprehend the renegade Democrats never materialized, the Democrats eventually did return to the state, and the new districts were approved.

Further reading: Lublin, David. *The Republican South: Democratization and Partisan Change.* Princeton, N.J.: Princeton University Press, 2004; Engstrom, Richard L., and John K. Wildgen. "Pruning Thorns from the Thicket: An Empirical Test of the Existence of Racial Gerrymandering." *Legislative Studies Quarterly* 2 (1977): 465–479; Shotts, Kenneth W. "Gerrymandering, Legislative Composition, and National Policy Outcomes." *American Journal of Political Science* 46 (2002): 398–414.

—Jeremy B. Lupoli

get-out-the-vote (GOTV)

Get-out-the-vote (GOTV) refers to a campaign's effort to ensure that more of its candidate's supporters cast votes on ELECTION DAY than supporters for the opposing candidate. GOTV refers specifically to efforts designed to move supporters to the polls on election day, in contrast to more general campaign efforts designed to increase candidate NAME RECOGNITION or to persuade uncommitted voters of the benefits of a candidate's victory.

GOTV has long been a part of democratic processes. Because elections are fundamentally decided by the percentage of votes received by candidates (whether in majority or plurality rule systems), any campaign is concerned with the final tally of votes. Every campaign, therefore, must be concerned with the representation of supporters among the people who actually show up to the polls. A candidate may have substantial, and even overwhelming, support in a polity, but if the vote count goes against the candidate, the election is lost. Thus, there is a simple strategic motivation for developing tactics designed to influence the composition of the election day electorate.

There is an even more pressing need to undertake such activities when the vote division is anticipated to be close; ensuring that core supporters get to the polls is strategically more important when the election may be decided by only a few votes. Similarly, if low VOTER TURNOUT is expected, then each additional supporter's vote becomes more important to an election outcome, and an effective GOTV program can have a profound influence on whether a candidate's supporters will outnumber his or her opponent's on election day.

An early formulation of the strategy of GOTV was articulated during the 1840 PRESIDENTIAL ELECTION. A WHIG PARTY communiqué, cowritten by Abraham Lincoln, laid out four basic steps in organizing states and counties in order to maximize the likelihood of victory, and these steps remain fundamental to modern GOTV campaigns as well. First, counties should be divided into smaller districts; this would divide the labor of the campaign into pieces of manageable size. Modern campaigns utilizing GRASSROOTS efforts rely upon this fundamental plan. Personal contact campaigning such as canvassing, literature drops, and candidate walks are based on geographical divisions of political districts.

Second, the Whigs recommended that within each district, the party should appoint a committee, the task of which would be to make a "perfect list" of all the voters in each district. This list should then be used to identify and keep track of partisan preferences of the voters, so that appropriate campaign materials could be distributed. Even today, PRECINCT "captains" lead local campaign efforts, and voter lists (now maintained electronically) form the basis of mobilization efforts. The fundamental piece of information gathered from voter identification and early canvasses is the candidate or party preference of a prospective voter.

Third, having identified potential voters for whom preferences were in doubt (i.e., undecided, or "swing," voters), the committee should identify individuals in whom the undecideds have confidence; these trusted persons should then, through personal conversation, attempt to influence those preferences. The party also had the responsibility to get persuasive campaign materials into their hands. Note that this was an early effort at voter segmentation—the division of the ELECTORATE by political affinity. The Whigs, like modern campaigners, were concerned about persuading voters who had no strong preferences and made no significant effort to convert voters who already preferred the opposition.

Finally, the party of Lincoln made sure that the members of the committee understood that it was their duty on election day to see that every Whig was brought to the election polls. This was the culmination of their GOTV efforts: Having identified early on partisan preferences, and having made efforts throughout the campaign to influence SWING VOTERs, the final push involved getting those citizens with Whig preferences to show up and vote. The technology and sophistication of voter identification and GOTV methods have evolved over time, but the essential principles have not.

By the middle of the 19th century, the understanding arose that shaping the actual votes cast in an election led to widespread voter fraud. Unscrupulous party organizations would, for example, transport wagons full of men from polling place to polling place, having them vote multiple times (using a party-printed BALLOT) in return for bribes. Such abuses of the political system led to many progressive election reforms, including the introduction of VOTER REGISTRATION lists and the AT-LARGE ELECTION.

Modern efforts to get out the vote involve a variety of techniques and are directly related to the VOTER CANVASS. The canvass is a campaign tactic designed to make personal contact with residents of a particular geographic area early on in a campaign. One main purpose of the canvass is "voter identification," identifying residents as supporters, opponents, and those who are neither. This information is used to prioritize precincts and households for later campaign activities, including get-out-the-vote programs.

GOTV efforts targeted toward voters the campaign knows are supportive can take several forms. Because time is precious as election day approaches, efficiency is the byword of GOTV. The purpose is not to shape preferences, but to move supporters to the polls. Face-to-face contact, while effective early in the campaign, must be supplanted by the ability to contact many people in short periods of time, reminding them to vote. Therefore, GOTV efforts most frequently take the form of phone calls from campaign volunteers. Fast-moving literature drop programs in key neighborhoods (identified and targeted based upon prior election results) distribute cards or door hangers.

Community organizations such as churches may be mobilized to provide transportation to the polls for voters without cars; parties may also rent busses if large numbers of voters lacking transportation are concentrated geographically, such as in apartment complexes or retirement homes. Finally, poll monitoring on election day keeps track of who votes. Poll monitors for a candidate or party periodically contact campaign headquarters with the names of voters who have voted. The campaign compares these names with the targeted voter identification list, and contacts by phone supporters who have not yet voted in an effort to remind them one last time to cast their ballot.

Finally, GOTV also exists as part of nonpartisan voter mobilization efforts. Public INTEREST GROUPS undertake voter registration drives in order to increase participation in elections, regardless of the partisan preferences of those who vote. Generally targeted at segments of the electorate with historically low voter turnout rates, these groups attempt to make it as easy as possible to register to vote, though they tend to leave the substantive mobilization to the parties and candidate campaigns.

Getting out the vote on election day is central to the strategic aims of campaigns, and a large body of experimental and nonexperimental research shows that such efforts tend to increase voter turnout. Campaigns certainly believe that such efforts matter, or else the professionals who manage them would have long since discarded the essential strategies articulated by the Whigs more than 160 years ago.

Further reading: Green, Donald P., and Alan S. Gerber. *Get Out the Vote! How to Increase Voter Turnout.* Washington, D.C.: Brookings Institution Press, 2004; Wielhouwer, Peter W. "In Search of Lincoln's Perfect List: Targeting in Grassroots Campaigns." *American Politics Research* 31 (2003): 632–669.

—Peter W. Wielhouwer

GOPAC

Founded in 1979, GOPAC (Grand Old Party Action Committee) is a national organization focused on electing Republicans to state and local offices. Over its 27 years of operations, GOPAC has concentrated its efforts on building GRASSROOTS Republican leadership and support across the country.

The impetus for GOPAC stemmed from sweeping Democratic victories across local, state, and national government in the late 1970s. The end of the Vietnam War and the Watergate SCANDAL had left conservatives and the REPUBLICAN PARTY in relative disarray. In the aftermath of the November 1978 elections, Delaware's Republican governor, Pierre du Pont, reviewed the electoral landscape for Republicans and found dismaying near-term prospects. Democrats held the White House, both houses of Congress, 38 governorships, and control of nearly 75 percent of state legislatures.

For Governor du Pont, this pattern suggested Democrats would continue to benefit from a "farm team" of experienced candidates ready to pursue national posts. Meanwhile, Republicans' relative inexperience was hindering their electoral hopes. Governor du Pont concluded that the party's primary tenets—lower taxes, limited government, and strong national defense—were often muddled by poor communication.

In its early years, GOPAC focused on making direct contributions to promising candidates in state legislative and municipal elections. However, the Republicans achieved little local success in the first five years, despite sweeping electoral landslides for Ronald Reagan in 1980 and again in 1984. In 1986, Newt Gingrich began five years of transformative leadership at GOPAC, leading it to national prominence by emphasizing and strengthening grassroots organization and communication. Using campaign seminars, workbooks, audio tapes, and other grassroots methods, GOPAC developed a strong education and training center for Republican candidates and activists. By the early 1990s, GOPAC was acknowledged as the most aggressive—and effective—Republican CAMPAIGN ORGANIZATION.

In 1994, Republicans captured control of both houses of Congress and a record number of state legislatures and governorships. GOPAC played a significant role in preparing Republican candidates across the country. The organization sent videotapes to candidates' homes, teaching and stressing the party's CONTRACT WITH AMERICA reform agenda. GOPAC officials also met with candidates in the early stages of their campaigns to discuss the campaign trail protocols and to prepare for likely pitfalls.

Shortly after the 1994 elections, however, GOPAC found itself mired in controversy. In 1995, the FEDERAL ELECTION COMMISSION sued GOPAC in federal court for deliberately subverting federal election statutes. The commission claimed GOPAC made substantial contributions to help Republican candidates for national offices, not just state offices, which requires GOPAC to disclose its finances or observe federal limits on its campaign contributions. In fact, internal GOPAC memos admit that GOPAC contributed $250,000 to help Gingrich's tightly contested 1990 campaign. However, GOPAC was not registered as a federal POLITICAL ACTION COMMITTEE until 1991, allowing Gingrich and GOPAC to avoid the disclosure and limitation requirements. Under public pressure, GOPAC began publicly disclosing donor names in 1994.

For his part, Gingrich insisted he never provided political favors in return for contributions to GOPAC, but organization documents released by the commission fueled speculation that, at the very least, large contributors expected some return. Damage from this and other ethics allegations contributed to his 1995 decision to resign as chairman. After Gingrich's departure, Congressman John Shadegg led GOPAC. He was followed by Congressman David Dreier and Governor Frank Keating, but none were able to sustain the influence and power that GOPAC wielded in the early 1990s. While Gingrich's leadership was missed, the organization also appeared to suffer from its own success. While Republican electoral prospects had changed, new GOPAC officials, still operating under a cloud of scrutiny, struggled to define a clear mission and organizational objectives.

By 1999, GOPAC was a shadow of its former self. Out of the national spotlight, it relinquished its status as a federal political action committee and returned to its roots of local candidate recruitment and training. In March 2003, former congressman J. C. Watts became the new chairman of GOPAC, aiming to return the organization to national power. His strategy is to focus on minorities—a reinvention approach that is proving controversial inside the party. While supporters believe that emphasis is critical to the future of the Republican Party, detractors argue that the new strategy, as well as accompanying staff turnover, is creating instability. Nevertheless, donors have continued to contribute hundreds of thousands of dollars over the last few years, suggesting that Watts has the financial lifeline needed to pursue this new strategy.

Further reading: GOPAC. Available online. URL: http://www.gopac.org. Accessed August 10, 2005.

—Neil J. Beck

grandfather clause

The modern usage of *grandfather clause* refers to provisions in a law exempting certain people from that law. For example, if a city wants to change its regulations on business signs, it might use a grandfather clause to exempt all current signs. This would allow the city to make changes without a great deal of opposition from existing businesses.

The origin of the term goes back to efforts by southern states from 1895 to 1910 to disenfranchise black voters. After 1870, when the FIFTEENTH AMENDMENT to the U.S. Constitution expanded voting rights to include males of any race, many southern states proposed modifying their voting laws to require that voters pass LITERACY TESTS, pay POLL TAXes, or own property in order to register. Though not the intention, these changes would have disenfranchised poor voters regardless of race. As a result, to gain approval of such laws, some southern states added clauses to exempt all those who had been able to vote prior to 1866 or 1867. Also exempt were descendants of those who voted in the past, hence the notion of someone being exempt if his "grandfather" voted. Thus, white residents could vote, but former slaves who did not have such grandfathers were blocked from voting. With the case of *Guinn v. United States,* the U.S. Supreme Court declared these sorts of race-based grandfather clauses unconstitutional in 1915.

Non–race-based grandfather clauses can help make change politically palatable. The use of grandfather clauses is often an issue in the discussion of any cutbacks to Medicare or Social Security to exempt current senior citizens. The usefulness of grandfather clauses is in the balancing of political expediency with long-term ramifications. A grandfather clause with unintended consequences can be seen in the 1979 FEDERAL ELECTION CAMPAIGN ACT, which made 1992 the last year in which members of the House elected before 1980 could retire and still use their campaign funds for personal use. Some believe this resulted in a number of House member retirements in 1992.

Further reading: Groseclose, Timothy, and Keith Krehbiel. "Golden Parachutes, Rubber Checks, and Strategic Retirements from the 102d House." *American Journal of Political Science* 38 (1994): 75–99; Keyssar, Alexander. *The Right to Vote: The Contested History of Democracy in the United States.* New York: Basic Books, 2000; Schmidt, Benno C., Jr. "Black Disenfranchisement from the KKK to the Grandfather Clause." *Columbia Law Review* 82 (1982): 835–905.

—Bonnie J. Johnson

Grand Old Party (GOP)

While the term *GOP* has long referred to the REPUBLICAN PARTY, the acronym that GOP presently represents (i.e., Grand Old Party) is not the original reference. According to the REPUBLICAN NATIONAL COMMITTEE, the first known use of *GOP* occurred in 1875, when an entry in the *Congressional Record* referred to the Republican Party as "this gallant old party." Shortly thereafter, the term *GOP* solidified into the current meaning, Grand Old Party. A *Harper's Weekly* article from 1878 used the term *Grand Old Party,* and the term was repeated several times through 1900, showing its rise in prominence.

It is interesting that the Republican Party would refer to itself as "old." The roots of the DEMOCRATIC PARTY predate those of the Republican Party by more than a half-century. Why the party is "grand" is another mystery, although the common usage of the phrase "Grand Old Man" to describe William Ewart Gladstone, Britain's on-again, off-again prime minister (he served four terms of various lengths from six months to six years during the period from 1868 to 1894) may explain the usage. Gladstone's strong beliefs in individual liberty, limited government, and unrestricted free trade may have led the Republicans to adopt his moniker for their own.

The term *GOP* has undergone rises and falls in popularity. When cars were introduced in the early 1900s, some passengers in horse-drawn carriages would shout "G.O.P.!"—short for "get out and push"—when they saw stranded motorists. Gallup polls conducted in the 1950s showed that less than half of the population knew that *GOP* was another name for the Republican Party. Republicans made various efforts to make the term *GOP* more popular—they referred to themselves as "Go-Party" during the 1964 election, and President Nixon gave numerous speeches that alluded to a "generation of peace." Those efforts, and others, have met limited success. In a 1999 Gallup poll, only 62 percent of Americans knew that *GOP*

referred to the Republican Party. And in 2002, the *Wall Street Journal* publicly announced it would no longer use the term *GOP* in its pages, because it "may seem baffling," though the *New York Times* and the *Washington Post* still enthusiastically use the term.

Further reading: Republican National Committee. Available online. URL: http://www.rnc.org. Accessed August 10, 2005.

—Michael Billok

grassroots

Grassroots is a term that refers to mass-based political activity, that is, any political activity that involves large numbers of "real" people, as opposed to activity that involves mainly political elites. Referring to a campaign as a grassroots campaign is meant to imply that the candidate has wide-ranging popular support and is basing the campaign's activity on the involvement and contributions of large numbers of the public. This is in contrast to a candidate who is perceived as being out of touch with the public, or who is seen as the favorite of political elites (such as a party machine or some other self-serving and nonrepresentative group of political actors).

One of the earliest political articulations of a grassroots strategy was by Abraham Lincoln in a WHIG PARTY campaign memo from 1840. Moreover, the foundation of grassroots campaigning was for many years based on the organizational capacity of urban party machines. Harold Gosnell's 1938 book *Machine Politics* describes, for example, how Chicago Democratic Party PRECINCT captains, in addition to facilitating machine social support activities, participated in a variety of explicitly political activities. These included the traditional canvass for votes, designed to distribute candidate and party information, solidify VOTER REGISTRATION lists, and deliver the votes for machine candidates. The emphasis in these early grassroots political activities was direct, personal contact between local party officials and voters.

Even with the deterioration of the manipulative power of machines in the mid-20th century, LOCAL PARTY ORGANIZATIONS still provided the structure through which campaign information was distributed and by which votes were delivered. While some campaign observers argue that modern campaign technology has eliminated the need for large-scale grassroots campaigning, it is instead the case that campaign technology has also improved the ability of campaigners to undertake these traditional campaign tactics, but with much greater efficiency. For example, rather than relying on boxes of 3 × 5 cards, modern campaigns manipulate large electronic voter databases in order to organize personal contact campaign activities. In spite of the fact that most attention (and money) in campaigns is spent on TV ads, the consensus of political practitioners is that no campaign plan is complete without a comprehensive grass-roots strategy. The evolution of grassroots campaigning continued as candidates (such as Howard Dean) in the 2004 PRESIDENTIAL ELECTION campaign relied on the Internet for large-scale FUND-RAISING and coordination of campaign activities such as meet-ups.

Further reading: McGrath, Dennis J., and Dane Smith. *Professor Wellstone Goes to Washington: The Inside Story of a Grassroots U.S. Senate Campaign.* Minneapolis: University of Minnesota Press, 1995.

—Peter W. Wielhouwer

Greenback Party

The Greenback Party, fueled by agrarian unrest in the late 19th century, called for an expanded supply of paper money. In 1873, Congress demonetized silver, leaving U.S. currency dependent on the gold standard. The supply of gold, however, could not keep up with the growing population and expanding economy after the Civil War. As a result, the nation suffered from deflation, and the South reeled from falling cotton prices, though it remained more profitable than other crops at this time.

Many thought that greenbacks, first issued by the federal government to subsidize the Civil War, provided a flexible supply of money compared to hard money (i.e., paper money backed by gold or silver). To the dismay of agrarian and labor interests who suffered economically from the Panic of 1873, the Grant administration acted to withdraw greenbacks from circulation. Following the labor and agriculture troubles of 1878, labor organizations joined the Greenback Party and established the Greenback-Labor Party.

The party polled nearly 1 million votes in the CONGRESSIONAL ELECTIONS of 1878 and sent 14 party loyalists to Congress while also winning many local elections. In 1880, Greenbackers nominated General James B. Weaver for president. The party's platform included women's SUFFRAGE, federal regulation of interstate commerce, and a graduated income tax. Despite Weaver's assertive campaign tactics, which included stumping over vast expanses of the nation, Weaver won less than 4 percent of the vote.

Americans remained suspicious of the party's reform efforts, and as the national economy improved, support for the party subsided. Moreover, the realization that the Specie Resumption Act would not be repealed further weakened support for the party. The party's last national race occurred in 1884, when it nominated General Benjamin Butler. Butler's failed candidacy marked the Greenback dissolution, though the party's monetary policies persisted and later influenced other reform movements. The POPULIST PARTY in particular shared similarities with the Greenback Party. In 1892, the Populists nominated James B. Weaver, a former Greenback congressman and presidential nominee, to represent their party in that year's presidential race.

THE SELF-MADE PARTY.
The Party that Butler belongs to, and the Party that he serves.

A cartoon satirizing the constantly changing loyalties of political figure Benjamin Butler. He was the presidential candidate of the Greenback Party in 1884. *(Cartoon by Thomas Nast, HarpWeek, LLC)*

Further reading: Barr, Alwyn. *Reconstruction to Reform: Texas Politics, 1876–1906.* Austin: University of Texas Press, 1971; Friedman, Milton. *A Monetary History of the United States, 1867–1960.* Princeton, N.J.: Princeton University Press, 1963; Goodwin, Jason. *Greenback: The Almighty Dollar and the Invention of America.* New York: Henry Holt, 2003.

—Mary L. Fehler

Green Party

The Green Party of the United States is a left-leaning environmental organization. Its organizational structure is based on a confederation of various green parties at the state level. The Green Party collaborates with other green parties in democratic countries, as well as the European Confederation of Green Parties and the Federation of Green Parties of the Americas. The party emphasizes environmentalism, social justice, GRASSROOTS organizing, and peace, while it objects to the influence of big corporations in government and policy making.

The ideological stance of the Green Party is best represented by its "Ten Key Values" that were ratified at the

Green Party Convention in Denver, Colorado, in June 2000. These 10 values are:

1. Grassroots democracy: enhancement of participatory democracy and accountability of representatives to the public
2. Social justice and equal opportunity: objection to barriers against fair and equal treatment of citizens such as racism, sexism, ageism and homophobia
3. Ecological wisdom: respect for the integrity of nature and environment
4. Nonviolence: global peace and de-armament
5. Decentralization: increasing the effect of local-level and individual-level governments on decision making
6. Community-based economics and economic justice: protection of workers' rights, broad citizen participation in economic planning, and enhancement of quality of life
7. Feminism and gender equity: objection to male domination of politics and economics, equal opportunity for different sexes in all domains of social and political life
8. Respect for diversity: respect for cultural, ethnic, sexual, religious, linguistic and racial diversity
9. Personal and global responsibility: encouragement of people to participate in politics for both individual and universal well-being
10. Future focus and sustainability: balancing the requirements and consequences of short-term and long-term goals

In addition to these 10 values, the Green Party is also devoted to other related principles, such as ethical treatment of animals, perception of the drug problem as a social and medical problem rather than an issue of criminal justice, and providing universal health care for all people in the United States. Considering these values and principles that guide the members of the party, the Green Party is accepted as a left-wing alternative in American POLITICS, further to the left than the DEMOCRATIC PARTY.

The history of the Green Party goes back to 1984, when ecologically minded political activists formed the Committees of Correspondence, which were later known as the Green Committees of Correspondence (GCOC). The GCOC began to hold national meetings of green activists starting in 1989. At their gathering in 1991, the GCOC was replaced by a novel organization that was called Greens/Green Party USA (G/GPUSA). At the 1995 national gathering of the G/GPUSA in Albuquerque, New Mexico, the proposal to run a presidential candidate was rejected. Nevertheless, the members who still wanted to support a presidential candidate selected Ralph Nader, a well-known consumer advocate, to run as their first presidential nominee and Winona LaDuke as their first vice-presidential nominee in 1996. The Nader-LaDuke pair

appeared on the BALLOT in 22 states and received 0.7 percent of the national vote in 1996 elections.

In the aftermath of the 1996 election, representatives from 11 state-level Green Parties established the Association of State Green Parties (ASGP), with the purpose of having more Green candidates elected to public office. A considerable number of the local, regional, and state-level Green Parties associated themselves with both the ASGP and the G/GPUSA. In 2000 elections, the Nader-LaDuke pair was once again nominated for president and vice president by the ASGP. The same pair was on 44 state ballots and received 2.7 percent of all the votes cast in the 2000 elections. Even though this 2 percent growth in the electoral vote share of the party signified an almost threefold increase between 1996 and 2000, the party remained a relatively weak third-party alternative. Furthermore, the party could not achieve eligibility for federal funds in 2004 because the Nader ticket failed to receive the 5 percent of the national vote required to receive federal funding.

On October 2, 2000, a joint proposal was put forth by the members of the ASGP and the G/GPUSA to make these two organizations mutually supportive, with the former concentrating on electoral politics and the latter working on ISSUE ADVOCACY. This joint proposal was named the Boston Proposal because it was negotiated in Boston. The proposal mentioned that the G/GPUSA should function as an independent organization rather than a POLITICAL PARTY and adopt a new title without the term *party* in it. Even though the Boston Proposal was passed by the ASGP at its next annual meeting, it did not pass at the congress of the G/GPUSA. The ASGP then changed its official title to the Green Party of the United States and was recognized as the official National Committee of the Green Party by the Federal Election Commission in 2001.

The two like-minded groups still exist as two separate organizations. The G/GPUSA also nominated Nader for president in 2000. Nader refused their offer and accepted the NOMINATION of only the newly renamed Green Party (formerly ASGP). The most significant ideological difference between the two green FACTIONS is that the relatively stronger Green Party emphasizes an environmentalist worldview more and denounces the involvement of big corporations in policymaking, whereas the relatively smaller G/GPUSA follows a more radical leftist IDEOLOGY. Today, the Green Party of the United States is the stronger faction, while the G/GPUSA remains sizably smaller.

Further reading: Green Party. Available online. URL: http://www.gp.org. Accessed August 10, 2005; Nader, Ralph. *Crashing the Party: Taking on the Corporate Government in an Age of Surrender.* New York: St. Martin's Press, 2002.

—Odul Celep

H

hard money

CAMPAIGN FINANCE LAWS limit the amount of money that can be given directly to federal candidates. Direct contributions to candidates—hard money—are subject to strict regulations imposed by law and enforced by the FEDERAL ELECTION COMMISSION. By contrast, SOFT MONEY refers to sums collected by political party committees from INTEREST GROUPS, corporations, labor unions, and individual donors that were largely unlimited and subject to few regulations. While hard money could be used to explicitly advance a specific candidate's campaign, soft money was intended to be used for generic "party-building activities," including VOTER REGISTRATION drives, voter mobilization, and public education programs.

Even as soft money began to outpace hard money in financing campaigns in the 1990s, candidates continued to rely on hard money. In the 2000 PRESIDENTIAL ELECTION, for example, George Bush raised $193 million from donors, and Al Gore raised $133 million in hard money. Moreover, controversy surrounding soft money contributions—permitted by a loophole in the 1974 Federal Elections and Campaigns Act and used primarily in recent campaigns to broadcast issue ads (thinly veiled attacks on opponents) rather than to support intended party activities—renewed calls for reform. The Bipartisan Campaign Reform Act (BCRA) passed by Congress in 2002 called for a complete ban on soft money and pressed for increased individual hard money contribution limits, from $1,000 per candidate per election to $2,000. The Supreme Court upheld both of these key provisions of the law in a 5 to 4 decision on December 10, 2003.

In the 2004 presidential race, Republicans raised more than $286 million in hard money to support George Bush's reelection bid, and Democrats contributed more than $243 million to John Kerry's campaign (through August 2004). In the first six months of the 2004 cycle, NATIONAL PARTY COMMITTEES raised $161 million, 45 percent more hard money than these organizations had received in the 2002 cycle. Indeed, the parties raised $23 million more in hard money during this period than they had collected in hard and soft money combined in the first six months of the last presidential ELECTION CYCLE in 1999. It appears that parties are adapting to new regulations and are successfully replacing soft money revenues with hard money receipts.

The new regulations mandated by the BCRA were intended to make the campaign finance system more transparent and equitable. Despite these efforts, new challenges surfaced during the 2004 election cycle as independent groups called "527s" (after the applicable tax code) emerged as key actors in electioneering. These groups are largely unaffected by the BCRA provisions and can fund activities with unregulated contributions. To be sure, amendments to the campaign finance regulations are certain to address this phenomenon.

Further reading: Magelby, David, ed. *Financing the 2002 Election.* Washington, D.C.: Brookings Institution Press, 2002.

—Costas Panagopoulos

Hatch Act

The Hatch Act is a national law that restricts political activities by federal government employees. It also applies to state and local employees who receive funding from the federal government. Many states and local governments have adopted "mini-Hatch" laws with similar provisions. Professional associations, such as the International City/County Management Association, also have codes of ethics that restrict electioneering by government managers and impose sanctions for violations.

The Hatch Act has its roots in Progressive Era reforms to create merit-based personnel systems in place of PATRONAGE or spoils systems in which employees were selected on the basis of partisan loyalty. The PENDLETON ACT OF 1883 created a federal civil service. Subsequently, the Civil Service Commission established restrictions on partisan activities by federal employees. In response to growth in government during Franklin Roosevelt's presidency, Congress passed bills in 1939 and 1940 to codify and strengthen the restrictions. The legislation originally denied federal employment to former communists or members of any organization supporting the overthrow of the government. The legislation is most commonly known as the Hatch Act, after its sponsor, Senator Carl Hatch, rather than the Act to Prevent Pernicious Political Activities, the original title, or the more standard Political Activities Act.

The constitutionality of the Hatch Act was upheld by a 4 to 3 decision of the Supreme Court in 1947 in *United Public Workers v. Mitchell* (330 U.S. 75) and more decisively in 1973 by a 6 to 3 margin in *National Association of Letter Carriers, AFL-CIO v. United States Civil Service Commission* (413 U.S. 548), ending appeals based on First Amendment rights of free speech and association.

The original Hatch Act prohibited partisan political activities, even if conducted outside the workplace. Federal employees were usually discouraged from being too involved in nonpartisan campaigns as well. Campaign finance legislation in 1974 removed some of the restrictions on political activities by state and local employees. The Hatch Act was substantially amended in 1993, with only law enforcement, legal, national defense, and investigative agencies still subject to the original provisions. Other federal employees can now participate in some campaign activities. Employee political involvement through public sector unions has also increased dramatically over time.

The Hatch Act and related laws continue to set parameters about the types of political activities that can be undertaken by public employees. The U.S. Office of Special Counsel provides online and written guidelines on Hatch Act requirements. State and local employees should seek further guidance about the applicability of the Hatch Act and details about state laws. Incidents still occur on a regular basis in which public employees are unaware of Hatch Act restrictions, run for political office, and are forced to resign their positions.

Further reading: Cayer, N. Joseph. *Public Personnel Administration.* 4th ed. Belmont, Calif.: Wadsworth, 2004; Schultz, David A., and Robert Maranto. *The Politics of Civil Service Reform.* New York: Peter Lang, 1998.
—Marcia L. Godwin

Help America Vote Act of 2002 (HAVA)

The constitutional arrangement that relegates election administration to the states has led to tremendous variation in election management and execution across the United States. The 2000 PRESIDENTIAL ELECTION put the spotlight on imperfections in the electoral system and called attention to irregularities of significant consequence that plague election execution and threaten the credibility of the electoral process. In the aftermath of the 2000 election debacle, Congress asserted its authority over elections and responded to renewed calls for reform by passing the Help America Vote Act (HAVA), a sweeping law that attempted to remedy flaws in the voting process in America and to make the electoral system more accurate and accountable.

On December 12, 2001, the U.S. House of Representatives passed the Help America Vote Act (H.R. 3295). An amended version of the bill was sent to a conference committee after the Senate approved a modified version of the legislation on April 11, 2002. Discrepancies between the two versions were reconciled, and after final passage of the bill in Congress on October 10, 2002, the president signed HAVA into law on October 29, 2002.

The act was designed to upgrade election administration across America. The law provided $3.86 billion to states over four years to help finance improvements to the election process. HAVA authorized $650 million to be used to replace outdated VOTING SYSTEMS nationwide (including punchcards and lever machines). HAVA also established minimum standards for states and local governments to follow in key areas of election administration and required the Department of Justice to monitor and enforce these standards. States were mandated, for instance, to meet uniform and nondiscriminatory election technology and administration requirements, including employing provisional BALLOTS by 2004 (for voters whose eligibility is in question) and developing centralized, computerized statewide VOTER REGISTRATION databases by 2004 (unless states filed for an extension to 2006).

HAVA also created the Electoral Assistance Commission (EAC), an independent, bipartisan agency, to serve as a national clearinghouse for information relating to the administration of federal elections. The EAC was charged with conducting periodic studies about election administration issues, reviewing procedures and reporting on the best practices for effective election execution, and assisting in the administration of federal elections.

The law also funded initiatives intended to provide enhanced access to the voting process for disabled Americans, military personnel, and citizens living overseas. HAVA devoted special attention to young Americans and created the Help America Vote Foundation and College Fund to encourage broader student participation in election administration.

HAVA represents one of the boldest congressional actions to reform voting in America since the VOTING RIGHTS ACT OF 1965. Implementation, however, relies on the states, and the degree of compliance has varied. Some states have enacted significant changes, while others, mired in legislative gridlock or disagreement over specific reform options, lag behind. Despite delays, states are expected to meet compliance deadlines in order to remain eligible for federal funds and to implement changes that improve the voting process in meaningful ways.

Further reading: Crigler, Ann, Marion Just, and Edward McCaffery. *Rethinking the Vote: The Politics and Prospects of American Election Reform.* New York: Oxford University Press, 2004.

—Costas Panagopoulos

home rule

Home rule refers to the delegation of governmental authority from the state level to a regional or local entity. Commonly referred to as devolution, devolved government, local control, or self-government, the most common form of home rule is the delegation of authority by the states to counties, cities, towns, boroughs, and other local municipalities.

There are two primary forms of home rule in the United States, constitutional and legislative. Constitutional home rule, or *imperium in imperio* (state within a state), provides for self-government through a state's constitution. In this form, the municipality is often guaranteed its existence, similar to states in the federalist system of the U.S. Constitution. Legislative home rule provides for self-government through state statute, usually granting the local entity the ability to write and amend its own charter. The primary drawback to this form of home rule, however, is that the legislation often allows for future modifications to the local authority and the possibility of dissolution of the local entity in subsequent legislation.

The home rule movement in the United States began in the late 19th century, spurred on by similar movements for local self-government in the United Kingdom. The first home rule established in the United States was provided for in a constitutional amendment to the Missouri constitution in 1875. Many states followed this lead, primarily due to the common inability or unwillingness of states to address the local concerns of fast-growing cities brought about by continuing suburbanization.

The principal concern with home rule is the state-local relationship, especially when laws come into conflict. Courts today use two differing approaches to address these disputes in accordance with their general perception of state-local relations. One approach, referred to as Dillon's Law, or *ultra vires* (beyond the authority), maintains that municipalities have only those powers expressly granted them, and thus the municipality has no inherent powers. In contrast, the "devolution of powers" approach affirms that a municipality can act in all matters unless clearly prohibited by state laws.

A total of 45 of the 50 states, and an estimated two-thirds of all cities with populations exceeding 200,000, currently have some form of home rule. What remains to be seen is how the state-local relationship will continue to evolve over time. It is unclear if the states will attempt to gain more control over municipalities, or if they will continue to provide increasing autonomy to them.

Further reading: Krane, Dale, et al. *Home Rule in America: A Fifty State Handbook.* Washington, D.C.: CQ Press, 2001; Zimmerman, Joseph F. *State-Local Relations: A Partnership Approach.* 2nd ed. Westport, Conn.: Praeger, 1995.

—Derrek M Davis

horse race journalism

Horse race journalism refers to the media's penchant for covering POLITICS as if it were a competitive sporting event, rather than focusing on the policy stances, philosophical differences, and past records of candidates for office. By focusing on who is winning—the horse race—the media tends to stress coverage dealing with strategy and style over policy and substance. Just as a horse is judged by its relationship to other horses in a race, rather than by its speed or skill, the media often judge politicians by wins and losses in the polls and in political battle, instead of their ideas, arguments, and abilities. Horse race coverage is also the primary way the public develops its perceptions about mass support for candidates. People learn very quickly from the media who is ahead and who is behind in a political campaign, while it takes much longer for voters to learn about particular candidates' stances on political issues.

Horse race journalism is typically decried in academic circles as being lazy, uninformed, and misrepresentative of the democratic process. Nevertheless, it can have a powerful effect on election results. Scholars have shown that voters are likely to cast their BALLOTS in PRESIDENTIAL PRIMARIES on the basis of how well the media say a particular candidate is doing (i.e., the BANDWAGON EFFECT). One reason for this is that people enjoy supporting a winner.

Candidates can benefit or suffer from horse race coverage. First, horse race journalism's reliance on polls can actually influence them. Media coverage has been shown to influence public opinion, so the coverage of polls may actually affect future polls, thus making the polls a kind of self-fulfilling prophecy. In extreme cases, horse race journalism on ELECTION DAY, focused on preliminary EXIT POLLS, can discourage voters from voting if they perceive that their preferred candidate is not faring well, thereby influencing the actual election result. Moreover, coverage of who is winning affects candidates' ability to generate donations for their campaigns. Scholars have shown that candidates who emerge from the horse race as "surging" or "gaining" in polls often experience a significant bump in FUND-RAISING. Sometimes, potential contributors are motivated to send a check to their preferred candidate when the donors are exposed to coverage indicating that their choice for office is losing ground. In other words, horse race journalism forces contributors to make strategic choices about whether to donate money to certain candidates.

The most common type of story written in a horse race fashion uses public opinion polls to determine who is winning and losing in a political campaign or in a debate about an issue. Often, horse race stories focus on a candidate's electability as measured by polls. In the 2004 Democratic presidential PRIMARY, several media outlets aired or printed stories about how well various candidates for the Democratic NOMINATION would stack up against President George W. Bush "if the election were held today." Of course, with the primaries still going on and a winner yet to be determined, these polls were meaningless substantively but important in that they focused voters' attention on who was winning the primary season and who could win the GENERAL ELECTION.

Some argue that horse race coverage is not all bad in that it heightens voter interest in a campaign. Additionally, modern public opinion polls are often so tightly focused that voters in certain demographics can learn what people like them think of candidates for office and then use this information as a shortcut to making an informed decision.

The bulk of scholarship on the topic is critical of horse race journalism and often calls on the media to spend more time covering candidates' issue positions, past records of service, and overall philosophy. Some promote a model of "civic journalism" that uses community forums and nontraditional reporting techniques to learn which issues a community believes are most important for a coming political campaign or issue debate. Most of these media experiments have failed, receded in popularity, or had inconclusive effects. Since the horse race framework of a campaign fits into the journalistic convention of objectivity, as both candidates are given attention in horse race stories, it is an attractive option for reporters to use when characterizing political news coverage.

Further reading: Graber, Doris A. *Mass Media and American Politics.* 6th ed. Washington, D.C.: CQ Press, 2002; Mutz, Diana C. "Effects of Horse-Race Coverage on Campaign Coffers: Strategic Contributing in Presidential Primaries." *Journal of Politics* 57, no. 4. (1995): 1,015–1,042.

—Michael W. Wagner

House of Representatives, leadership   *See* PARTY LEADERSHIP, HOUSE OF REPRESENTATIVES.

House of Representatives, qualifications
The formal qualifications for House members are found in Article I, Section 2, of the Constitution, which states that "no Person shall be a Representative who shall not have attained to the Age of twenty-five Years, and been seven Years a Citizen of the United States, and who shall, when elected, be an Inhabitant of that State in which he shall be chosen." These qualifications are notable for the low threshold they set for entry into the lower chamber. Although the framers believed that representatives needed mature political judgment to fulfill their roles, setting the age requirement four years above the usual age of voters, they explicitly

rejected attempts to add property requirements or other restrictions that would have disqualified poorer or less educated citizens from serving as representatives. Qualifications were kept to a minimum so that "the people's house" could take advantage of the talent and intelligence that were diffused throughout the citizenry. As James Madison wrote in Federalist No. 52, "the door of this part of the federal government is open to merit of every description whether native or adoptive, whether young or old, and without regard to poverty or wealth, or to any particular profession of religious faith."

Although states have sometimes sought to augment the formal requirements for House membership—for example, by adding term limit restrictions—the Supreme Court has declared such attempts to be constitutionally impermissible because they limit citizens' ability to choose their own representatives in Congress. Though the constitutional requirements have remained constant, constituents have in some cases added informal qualifications that House candidates must meet in order to be "electable." For example, most successful House candidates have strong, long-term ties to the state they seek to represent. Newly arrived candidates—sometimes called by the derogatory term *carpetbaggers*—may be viewed by residents as having too little familiarity with the district to represent its interests adequately. And for much of the 20th century, informal partisan qualifications were typical of the one-party regions of the Northeast and South. Southern representatives, for example, were drawn solely from Democratic ranks, in effect making membership in the DEMOCRATIC PARTY a prerequisite for election.

Further reading: Oleszek, Walter J. *Congressional Procedures and the Policy Process.* 6th ed. Washington, D.C.: CQ Press, 2004.

—Celia M. Carroll

House of Representatives, size
As the "people's branch" of the national legislature, the House of Representatives was designed to be responsive to local interests as well as to make decisions on broader national issues. Article II, Section 2, of the Constitution set the initial ratio of representation at one legislator for every 30,000 residents. The number of residents was calculated by a decennial CENSUS of all free and indentured persons (usually white), three-fifths of slaves, and Native Americans who were subject to taxation. Each state was guaranteed at least one representative regardless of population.

The appropriate size of the House was a matter of great controversy during the Constitutional Convention. Both Federalists and ANTI-FEDERALISTS recognized that membership size would play a central role in determining the organizational structures of the institution and shaping the quality of debate and representation. Federalists

Interior view of the House of Representatives showing Congress in session, 1866 *(Prints and Photographs Division, Library of Congress)*

argued that a House with fewer members would promote the election of more qualified candidates and decrease the need for strong political leaders, thereby creating a legislative environment conducive to the thoughtful discussion of national issues. Anti-Federalists, on the other hand, claimed that small legislative chambers inadequately represented the range of interests within the United States and would deposit too much power into the hands of those they feared would become an elite class of legislators. The compromise reached during the Constitutional Convention, a relatively small chamber with the capacity to grow apace with population, attempted to balance these competing visions of representation.

Throughout the 19th century, House membership grew quickly as a result of westward expansion, immigration, and the end of fractional representation for African Americans after the Civil War. From 65 members in 1789, the House grew to 233 members by 1850, and 357 members by 1900. The need to bring order to this large and unwieldy membership led to an increasing reliance on institutions such as the Speaker's list and later the Rules Committee to expedite the discussion of policy and restrict members' access to the floor. Organization came at a price: The influence of rank-and-file members decreased significantly through the period as the prerogatives and powers of party leaders grew. Discontent among the rank and file with the strong-arm tactics used by Speakers Thomas Reed and

Joseph Cannon led to a 1911 "revolt" against the leadership and a more equitable allocation of legislative power.

In 1912, the size of the House was capped by legislative statute at 435 members, with seats apportioned according to state population. As a result of steady growth during the 20th century, the size of each district has radically changed. After the 2000 census, the ratio of representatives was roughly one House member for every 630,000 constituents. Critics claim that the current size of the House has created a legislative chamber that is too large to be organized efficiently but too small to be adequately representative of an increasingly diverse American public. For example, most members rely on "wholesale" campaigning and communication techniques such as mass mailings and television advertisements that provide only a one-way flow of information from Washington to home districts. Constituents rarely meet their representatives, much less have an opportunity to influence their policy choices. At the same time, however, the House is so sizable that most members are plagued by a sense of anonymity and lack routine access to party leaders, the legislative agenda, or the floor. Had the 30,000 to 1 representation ratio in the House been maintained over the years, we would currently have more than 9,000 members of the House of Representatives.

Further reading: Dodd, Lawrence C., and Bruce I. Oppenheimer. *Congress Reconsidered.* 6th ed. Washington,

D.C.: CQ Press, 1997; Oleszek, Walter J. *Congressional Procedures and the Policy Process.* 6th ed. Washington, D.C.: CQ Press, 2004.

—Celia M. Carroll

Hunt Commission

The Commission on Presidential Nominations, otherwise known as the Hunt Commission, was established in 1980 by the DEMOCRATIC NATIONAL COMMITTEE. The commission's goals included strengthening the party, helping the party to win elections, and ensuring that the party could govern once elected. The rules took effect for the 1984 Democratic National Convention.

One key Hunt Commission concern was the role that campaign activists played in presidential nominating contests. Critics argued that DELEGATES selected because of their connection and commitment to a particular candidate were not as concerned with PARTY ORGANIZATION and policy concerns as were party activists and party office holders who were underrepresented at nominating conventions. Critics were concerned that the orientation of these delegates was not focused on party building and was instead focused on supporting their particular candidate. One consequence was that candidates outside the party mainstream were garnering far more support than were party moderates.

One Hunt Commission response was to create SUPERDELEGATES. Superdelegates are persons named as nominating convention delegates by virtue of holding DEMOCRATIC PARTY membership or public office. They are not required to compete for delegate slots. Further, superdelegates come to the convention uncommitted to any particular candidate. At the 1984 Democratic National Convention, superdelegates cast approximately 14 percent of the votes; in 2004 that percentage was 19 percent.

The Hunt Commission also recommended that state parties increase their efforts to include low- and moderate-income persons among their delegate pools. State parties were charged with creating programs encouraging such persons to seek out delegate slots, including helping such persons defray their convention-related expenses.

The commission also addressed concerns about the prenomination calendar. States holding primaries or caucuses earlier in the prenomination season enjoyed more media attention than did states holding later contests. Candidate commitment of resources in early contests meant that those not doing well dropped out long before the NOMINATION contests ended, thereby reducing the number of viable candidates as the season progressed. The Hunt Commission's response was to allow states to hold their primaries and caucuses over a three-month period while also allowing Iowa and New Hampshire to hold their caucus and PRIMARY earlier. New Hampshire was required to hold its primary no earlier than one week before the rest of the states, while Iowa could not hold its caucus more than 15 days before the rest of the states. Finally, the Hunt Commission lowered the percentage of delegates needed to gain representation at the convention. Caucus states required 20 percent, while primary states required 25 percent.

Further reading: Crotty, William J. *Party Reform.* New York: Longman, 1983; Polsby, Nelson W. *Consequences of Party Reform.* New York: Oxford University Press. 1983.

—Terri Fine

I

ideology

The concept of ideology is so basic to the understanding of political life that it is at once both the bedrock of much of our comprehension of POLITICS and a main source of disagreement in scholarly and public discourse. In the broadest sense, an ideology is a set of deeply held beliefs and values that shape the political behavior of individuals and groups. As such, an ideology is also the affirmative expression of what is normatively desirable in the public realm in terms of both goals and the means needed to achieve those goals.

First coming into use in Europe in the late 1800s, the concept of ideology has long been connected with broad views of political philosophy and sweeping theories of the evolution of politics in the modern and postmodern eras. A limited collection of ideologies—communism, capitalism, socialism, and fascism—dominated the thinking and dialogue of scholars and the public for much of the 20th century. Often, these labels were applied to entire nations or even regions of the world. The two major wars of the 1900s, World War I and World War II, have been described as wars fought in the name of ideologies, namely wars waged by the United States and its democratic allies against the forces of antidemocratic imperialism and facism.

The cold war, a global showdown between the world's superpowers that seldom produced actual combat, was easily cast as a fight over ideological positions. The United States, the nations of Western Europe, and additional allies composed a democratic-capitalist COALITION against the "Communist bloc," a set of nations including one true superpower, the Soviet Union, along with the People's Republic of China and other associated and satellite countries. While many factors drove the cold war, including geopolitical motivations over natural resources and responsibilities under international treaties, much of the language supporting the continuation of the struggle on both sides was framed in the words of ideology; one bloc's belief system was a danger to the very existence of the other. For generations, the term *ideology* readily produced thoughts of division and struggle on a global scale. Today, ideologi-

cal idioms are employed in similar ways to explain and support foreign policy goals. The current war on terrorism is, in many ways, a set of policies with ideological roots, featuring dueling belief systems and value configurations.

In terms of domestic politics, U.S. social scientists and the larger public are well versed in the concept of ideology. In the public realm, whether it is liberalism versus conservatism, left versus right, Democrat versus Republican, extremist versus moderate, or some other variation, ideology has often been thought of as a spatial model (i.e., a model of opposing camps with a centrist middle ground separating the true believers at the polar opposites).

The roots of this bifurcation are deep, and the evolution of the American party system provides useful examples of such duality in the ideological makeup of the body politic. The pre-party era featured a struggle between the Federalists and the ANTI-FEDERALISTS over the ratification of the Constitution. The administration of George Washington witnessed an ideological schism personified by the tensions between cabinet members Alexander Hamilton and Thomas Jefferson over the direction of the nation and the true nature of the human condition. From this basic disagreement grew the first fully formed political parties, Jefferson's Democratic-Republicans and Hamilton's Federalists, with each group attempting to grasp control of the government in order to pursue its version of democracy.

The pattern established in the first party system is one that has persisted over time. Occasionally, issues and events, along with social movements and charismatic leaders, do challenge the basic spectrum of American ideology, but these challenges tend to burn brightly before they are ultimately subsumed by the ideological dispositions and institutional mechanisms of the political system in the United States. Americans, having grown accustomed to seeing politics and governing in a binary mode, may not be aware of how institutions such as our FIRST-PAST-THE-POST elections, single-member election districts, and big tent parties limit the likelihood of third- or minor-party activity. What remains is a nation that has been both socialized and institutionally configured to be philosophically and institutionally dualist in its ideological orientations.

The ways that social scientists have constructed the meaning of ideology and the ways they have applied this concept in their thinking have varied over time. In general, however, much of the scholarly activity surrounding ideology in the last 50 years has centered on voting behavior. In the late 1950s, Anthony Downs made the most forceful statement of the early period of research concerning the relationship of ideology to voting behavior. For Downs, individuals arrayed themselves on a continuum of ideology from liberalism to conservativism based on their calculations of self-interested benefit. Trained with a background in economics, Downs's approach focused on ideology as an expression of logically derived choice for the voter, much in the way that economists begin with the assumption that individuals express themselves and behave in self-serving, market-driven ways.

In the late 1950s to the early 1960s, researchers at the University of Michigan produced another groundbreaking refinement in the meaning and use of ideology by social scientists. Rather than approach ideology as the product of a voter's internal cost-benefit analysis, the Michigan model, or social-psychological model, posited that voting behavior and, in a related way, ideology are based on the collection of attitudes toward a variety of objects, notably candidates, issues, and the parties themselves. For the Michigan researchers, the emotional connection, or affect, that the individual had with objects in the political world largely determined voting behavior.

The 1960s and early 1970s brought a broadening view of the meaning of ideology and increasingly diverse use of the concept in social science research. A particularly unique approach was that of Milton Rokeach, a social psychologist. Rokeach had long been interested in the psychological components of concepts such as political dogmatism. He argued that core beliefs, or values, were the controlling variables in the behavior of individuals, groups, and even nations. Moreover, values, unlike attitudes, are enduring and do not need a specific association with an object, such as a candidate or issue, to exist. Rokeach used these hypotheses as the basis for his "two value" model of political ideology that he built on the values of freedom and equality. Using measurements based on the ranking of these values, Rokeach produced four major configurations, which he interpreted as the socialist, communist, capitalist, and fascist ideologies. The debate over the conceptualization and measurement of values has long been a tense one in the social sciences, with some arguing that values are too difficult to measure. With the ascendancy of attitudinally derived conceptions of ideology, the approach developed by Rokeach has largely been ignored.

In an approach related to that of Rokeach, Ronald Inglehart produced a highly influential body of ideologically related work beginning in the 1970s. Inglehart's main argument was that the citizens of Western democracies were evolving new dominant value systems in response to the changes brought on by the success of industrialism in the period following World War II. This "postindustrial" era featured a host of creature comforts along with social and political freedoms that were widely enjoyed by citizens. Inglehart built his approach on Abraham Maslow's hierarchy of needs theory, in which the range of beliefs and behavior of an individual are arranged in a pyramid so that one must first satisfy basic needs, such as food and shelter, before he or she can seek higher-order goals, such as political expression and aesthetic beauty. As modern society readily provided means to acquire the lower-order requirements, Inglehart postulated that individuals and even entire nations were moving toward "postmaterial" value systems, and, because of this value change, postmaterialism was spawning ideological changes as well.

Philip Converse posited one of the most widely accepted versions of ideology in the field of American social science, especially as it is concerned with voting. Converse maintained that individuals behave and think in ways that are directly traceable to their collections of attitudes, beliefs, and values. He called this constellation of dispositions a belief system and was concerned with how much continuity existed among the segments of a person's belief system. The degree of continuity in such a system allowed for the measurement of a person's ideology; the more constraint or continuity, the stronger the ideology. In essence, Converse argued that in order for a person's ideology to function as a useful means of political decision making and guidance, individuals had to make connections between and among the items they held in their minds about politics, government, and policy. Converse found that most Americans lacked constraint among the parts of their belief systems; their opinions and attitudes did not fit together in logical ways, or connections were simply not made at all. In essence, the public was not ideological and often based its voting on illogical or even random decisions. Converse's conclusions continue to produce debate and new research, but his approach has largely become the paradigm for American social scientists concerned with ideology.

The meaning and use of ideology has undergone a transformation in both academia and in wider circles. There is a long, well-established debate within sociology about the importance of ideology. At one end of the continuum are those who argue that ideology is a poor yardstick for measuring American politics. They maintain that most Americans share a similar ideology. Therefore, ideology can do little to explain the motivations for different behaviors. On the other side of the argument are those who view ideology as particular to large subsets of a society, groups such as political parties or even to the level of the individual, making ideology a rich source for the explanation and prediction of political behavior.

Currently, there is a rejuvenation of the use of ideology by academics and, especially, by practitioners of politics and those in the news media. This renewal of interest has come as Americans continue to shed their willingness to link themselves with a POLITICAL PARTY, one of the items long associated with ideology. Presently, the American public is broken into thirds over party affiliation, with a third professing some alliance to the Democrats, a third aligned with the Republicans, and the final and fastest growing third without a party connection at all. While this rough formulation omits those who are members of minor or THIRD PARTIES, their numbers have yet to dent the basic distribution of the ELECTORATE into thirds.

Unfortunately, for those who believe that a democracy is dependent on high levels of citizen participation, the increase in the number of political INDEPENDENTS is associated with a sizable downturn in voting. This loss of partisanship has, oddly enough, tended to exacerbate the ideological divisions in campaigns and governing. Those few who do vote in elections, especially PRIMARY elections to pick candidates for the GENERAL ELECTION, are more ideologically extremist than in the past. This development produces candidates and, ultimately, elected officials who reflect a distinct and often narrower set of beliefs than in the past. As evidence of this change, the measurable amount of party conflict in Congress, known as polarization, has increased as the overall turnout in elections for the national legislature has decreased.

The so-called culture wars begun in the 1980s feature a more simplified version of ideology than that used by social scientists. The combatants in the war over the cultural direction of the United States often use the term *ideology* to signify a set of moral absolutes, which are then used to demonize political opposition. In a similar manner, the flowering of the conservative movement, marked with the election of Ronald Reagan in 1980, developed into a hardened struggle with those on the left of the ideological spectrum for control of the federal and state governments—all while the American public became increasingly disillusioned with the rhetoric of ideological extremism from both sides.

The historic elections that gave control of both houses of Congress to the Republicans for the first time in more than a generation, the two government shutdowns over the federal budget in 1995 and 1996, the impeachment of President Clinton in 1998, the disputed 2000 PRESIDENTIAL ELECTION, and the complex events and policies connected with the war on terrorism have all featured some elements of rhetoric based on a sharpened use of ideological division that is likely to continue for the foreseeable future. Americans may not be getting more ideological—at least not in the ways that social scientists such as Converse use the concept—but Americans will likely be witness to a sustained or increased employment of this more simplified use of ideology as a tool of political rhetoric by candidates and elected officials and as a tool of dramatic license by the mass media.

Further reading: Aldrich, John H. *Why Parties? The Origin and Transformation of Political Parties.* Chicago: University of Chicago Press, 1995; Campbell, Angus, Philip E. Converse, Warren E. Miller, and Donald E. Stokes. *The American Voter.* New York: Wiley, 1960; Converse, Philip E. "The Nature of Mass Belief Systems in Mass Publics." In David Apter, ed., *Ideology and Discontent.* New York: Free Press, 1964; Downs, Anthony. *An Economic Theory of Democracy.* New York: Harper & Row, 1957; Inglehart, Ronald. "Post-Materialism in an Environment of Insecurity." *American Political Science Review* 75 (1981): 880–900; Rokeach, Milton. *The Nature of Human Values.* New York: Free Press, 1973.

—Richard P. Barberio

ideology, type

In the contemporary world of U.S. POLITICS, liberal IDEOLOGY is based on a positive view of human nature (i.e., a belief that people are driven by an innate moral sense) and a desire to overcome societal ills through collective action. Liberal ideology holds that government action should reflect the best qualities of human nature and should actively work to improve society. Modern liberals view government as the primary tool of collective action and, consequently, as a positive agent for a wide range of societal concerns (e.g., civil rights, education, environmental protection, public welfare). Today, many Americans who possess these beliefs eschew the term *liberal* in favor of the term *progressive* because of a commonplace perception that modern liberalism is tainted by connections to overly large and wasteful government.

The term *liberalism*, the foundation for liberal ideology, has its beginnings in the period of Western thought known as the Enlightenment. During this era, a diverse set of political thinkers established a philosophy that stressed individual rights and personal liberty. This philosophy came to be known as classic liberalism. John Locke, an English political philosopher of the time, argued that in a legitimate political system, people are ultimately self-governing because individuals give up some of their freedom to a government for the collective good but retain ultimate sovereignty based on the ownership of their individual rights. In this formulation, government should play only a limited regulatory role and allow the mechanisms of free enterprise to function so as not to unduly limit the rights of citizens who might be disadvantaged by economic regulation.

In the years following the ratification of the U.S. Constitution, many could lay claim to the ideas of classic liberalism. The concepts of individual freedom and a generally laissez-faire approach to economic policy were widely embraced by political parties and candidates from otherwise diverse regions of the country that were often split by other issues. However, by the 1880s, several related factors caused a major rent in the fabric of classic American liberal thought. The economic and political power of a small set of industrialists became increasingly obvious as the industrial revolution bore the fruit of great wealth for some Americans. Additionally, the concentration of political power and outright corruption during this time became increasingly evident.

Two social movements, populism and progressivism, spurred a drive to use government as a way of solving public problems. The New Deal of the 1930s and its progeny of the 1960s, the Great Society, used direct action by the federal government to attempt to right a host of societal and economic wrongs. These popular programs did not bear much resemblance to the ideas of classic liberalism, but because the policy makers saw themselves as the descendants of this line of thinking, they could justly call themselves liberal.

The social, political, and economic upheavals of the late 1960s and early 1970s began to put liberalism on the defensive. Some wondered if government were not contributing to seemingly intractable problems such as poverty and racial division. Those holding this position might have attempted to wrest the title of liberal away from those who held it by arguing that they were nearer to the beliefs of classic liberals. Instead, parts of classic liberalism have found renewed champions in the modern conservative and libertarian movements, while modern liberalism has largely been rechristened as progressivism by its present-day adherents.

In the spatial representation of ideology, featuring liberalism on the left and conservatism on the right, those possessing a moderate ideology populate the middle ground between these two poles. Ideally, moderate ideology mixes elements of conservatism and liberalism into a blend of values, beliefs, attitudes, and positions on a wide range of issues. Because of the strong relationship between ideology and POLITICAL PARTY affiliation in the United States, those holding a moderate ideology are likely to lack a clear and solid connection to either of the two major political parties. In the jargon of modern electoral politics, such individuals are often called SWING VOTERs, INDEPENDENTS, or UNDECIDED VOTERS.

Because the nation was founded on a belief that FACTIONS and parties were suspect and even potentially dangerous because of their tendency to divide the public, the notion of political independence and moderation is an old and in many ways attractive one. George Washington's warning about the "baneful spirit of party" from his farewell address is a touchstone for much of the nation's subsequent experience with political parties; they have often been useful, loved by some but viewed with a degree of suspicion by many. In the 19th century, party affiliation grew steadily as the American party system matured and the ELECTORATE widened by the expansion of SUFFRAGE. The PROGRESSIVE MOVEMENT, spawned by what many viewed as the corrupting influence of overly powerful political parties, won many reforms, such as direct primaries and the creation of the civil service system, that weakened the power of parties in the United States and, in so doing, limited their ability to attract and hold the loyalty of citizens. In the post–World War II era, the continued weakening of parties and the increasing importance of mass communications allowed candidates to run as individuals rather than as the representatives of particular parties. Additionally, an increase in political cynicism, traceable to a series of major crises in political leadership, such as Watergate and Iran-Contra, coupled with a heightened aggressiveness in the news media, helped further distance many Americans from an affiliation with any political party and toward a stance of political moderation.

Recent polls indicate that more than a third of Americans identify themselves as moderates, about the same number of people who have no party affiliation. Traditionally, the moderate-independent was considered the ideal voter, someone who weighed the issues and did not vote on rather irrational connections to a party. In this light, moderates rise above the pettiness of the ideological warfare of partisan politics. In reality, moderates who express independence from partisanship often "lean" toward one party on a consistent basis. "Pure" independents, those who truly do not lean, are among the least politically active members of the electorate. The increase in independence from parties and the associated rise of moderate ideology complicate contemporary politics and governance. Candidates must appeal to the liberal or conservative base of their parties in order to win NOMINATIONs through PRIMARY elections largely populated by voters with strong ideologies and then shift to a GENERAL ELECTION mode that will appeal to moderates with mixed or weak ideologies. Once in office, elected officials must build wide support for policies by appealing to moderates and ideologues alike. These are difficult tasks that are likely to become more problematic as the rise of independence from parties produces a more ideologically mixed electorate.

A conservative ideology is one based on belief in equality of opportunity, freedom expressed as personal liberty, and a preference for private rather than public institutions. In this general regard, the ideology of conservatism has its roots in classic liberalism because the two share key elements concerning the role and power of government. Essentially, conservatism is structured around two core themes: 1) Smaller government is better government, particularly in the area of social policy, and 2) individual liberty outweighs the need for social and economic equality.

This form of conservative thought, closely associated with the Republican presidential nominee in 1964, Barry Goldwater, focused heavily on the reduction of the federal government's social welfare programs and the return of political and economic discretion to the states. The perceived failing of the competing ideology of the time, liberalism, with its emphasis on the use of governmental power to ameliorate public problems, was the target for Goldwater and his contemporary conservatives.

Although he lost the election by a significant margin, Goldwater's ideas were carried forward, albeit in moderated form, by Republican Richard Nixon's successful presidential bid in 1968. The Nixon administration produced a mixed set of results, with some actions and policies reflecting a devolving of power back to the states and others markedly expanding the scope of federal power.

In 1980, the conservative movement had another seminal election that gave Ronald Reagan the chance to redefine the role of government and, ultimately, the meaning of modern conservatism. The Reagan administration made efforts to devolve power to the states by decreasing the role played by the federal government in a host of social welfare programs, while at the same time dramatically increasing the size of military spending. He also tried to limit federal regulations of business and industry.

In these ways, the "Reagan Revolution" of the 1980s was an extension of the philosophy espoused by Goldwater and others in the late 1950s and early 1960s. However, conservative ideology had undergone a shift in the late 1970s and early 1980s that produced a split within the movement. As the "culture wars" began, social conservatives, largely evangelical Christians from the now Republican-dominated South, exerted a major influence on the redefinition of conservatism. These conservatives were generally comfortable with limiting the federal government's social welfare and regulation activities, but also sought the enactment of a social agenda aimed at undercutting or eliminating laws and programs that supported what they considered immoral activities, such as abortion and gay marriage. Social conservatives saw little contradiction in their desire to use the power of government, by executive order, law making, or even proposed amendments to the U.S. Constitution, to achieve their social goals. Economic conservatives, often more socially moderate and less inclined to share the moralistic orientation of their socially conservative brethren, found that their place in American politics was becoming marginalized as social conservatives made gains in the REPUBLICAN PARTY.

Recently, President George W. Bush attempted to redefine, yet again, the meaning of conservatism by creating his own "compassionate" variant that emphasized the role of religious organizations as a means of providing social welfare services. Additionally, neoconservatism, a brand of the core ideology associated with an interventionist foreign policy, has become a potent strain of thought in the modern conservative movement.

Radicalism has long been part of American POLITICS. A nation born in revolution has kept a certain fondness for direct action while at the same time holding revulsion toward less romantic acts of political violence. When a person or group is said to hold a radical ideology, the larger public views the beliefs and values held by the individual or group as outside the norm of what is socially, economically, or politically acceptable at a given time. Social movements and some political parties have been thought to hold radical ideologies. *Radicalism* is often used synonymously with *extremism,* in the sense that the goals, beliefs, strategies, and tactics of individuals and groups holding these views and who favor unconventional modes of achieving them are often viewed as a danger to the existing political, social, and economic order. Simply put, *radical* and *radicalism* are pejorative terms that generally indicate something that is unwelcome and even potentially disruptive.

Because most Americans view contemporary political ideology as existing across a spectrum from left to right, radical ideology and those who espouse views connected to radicalism are often labeled as being from the "far left" or "far right," meaning they are very liberal or very conservative in their ideological dispositions. This view of radicalism assumes two things: first, that political ideology is neatly split into two wings with a large middle ground of ideological moderation, and second, within each of these wings there is a median or average "liberal" and "conservative." It is within the context of this framework that an individual or group's ideas and actions are deemed radical or not.

Given the inexact nature of the boundaries of this spatial framework of ideology, differences of opinion are bound to exist over just which groups and individuals have radical ideologies. For example, many in the widely segregated United States saw the CIVIL RIGHTS MOVEMENT of the 1950s and 1960s as possessing radical or even revolutionary goals and beliefs. In the 1850s, many viewed the newly formed Republican Party as a political aggregation based on the radical concept of abolition. Today, the Civil Rights movement and the antislavery genesis of the Republican Party are commonly seen as hallmarks of social and political progress. Beyond pure anarchy and political violence for its own sake, the concept of ideological radicalism is difficult to map with precision because it is so often dependent on the cultural expectations about political goals and behavior at specific points in time. As time and expectations change, so does the perception of radicalism.

In contemporary U.S. politics, applying the label of *radical* to a person or to a group's ideology is often an attempt to demonize the individual or group's goals and the strategies and tactics used toward reaching those ends. In electoral politics, candidates often seek advantage with voters by describing their opponents as extremist members of their parties. Policy makers also use this method to gain support for their positions by attempting to demonstrate how widely a policy deviates from the norm.

Further reading: Dionne, E. J. *They Only Look Dead: Why Progressives Will Dominate the Next Political Era.* New York: Touchstone, 1996; Euchner, Charles. *Extraordinary Politics: How Protest and Dissent Are Changing American Democracy.* Boulder, Colo.: Westview Press, 1996; Huntington, Samuel P. "The United States." In Michel Crozier, Samuel P. Huntington, and Joji Watnanuki, eds., *The Crisis of Democracy.* New York: New York University Press, 1975; Kristol, Irving. *Neo-Conservatism: The Autobiography of an Idea.* New York: Free Press, 1995; Pateman, Carole. *Participation and Democratic Theory.* Cambridge: Cambridge University Press, 1970. Rawls, John. *Political Liberalism.* New York: Columbia University Press, 1993; Schlesinger, Arthur M. *The Vital Center: The Politics of Freedom.* Somerset, N.J.: Transaction Publishers, 1997.

—Richard P. Barberio

impeachment process

The Constitution provides that an official of the federal government can be impeached and subsequently removed from office for treason, bribery, and "high crimes and misdemeanors." The House of Representatives is vested with sole power of impeachment, and those it impeaches by majority vote are tried in the Senate. If two-thirds of those present in the Senate vote to convict, the official is removed from office. In the country's history, 16 officials have been impeached: Presidents Andrew Johnson and William J. Clinton, Supreme Court justice Samuel Chase, Secretary of War William Belknap, and 12 federal judges. (President Richard M. Nixon resigned after the House Judiciary Committee approved three articles of impeachment, but before the House could vote on them. Although the House subsequently approved the articles of impeachment by a vote of 415–3, the matter was considered moot, and Nixon is not included in the canon of those impeached.) Among the group of impeached officials, only seven were convicted in the Senate and removed from office.

While treason and bribery are well understood concepts, the nature of "high crimes and misdemeanors" is often elusive. English practice prior to colonial times was to treat "high crimes and misdemeanors" as a category of political crime that caused some injury to the state or its constitution. The framers seemed to understand that impeachable offenses were not necessarily offenses for which one could face criminal charges. George Mason wanted to include attempting to subvert the Constitution as an impeachable offense, and also maladministration. James Madison thought the latter term so vague as to suggest that a person could be impeached for anything, and suggested that subverting the Constitution and bona fide maladministration could be impeached under the aegis of "high crimes and misdemeanors."

President Gerald R. Ford, while he was House minority leader, sought the impeachment of Supreme Court justice William O. Douglas, primarily because of the justice's liberal judicial bent and his controversial lifestyle, which included four marriages, the last to a law student 46 years his junior. Douglas had also offended Republican sensibilities by writing an article for an obscure journal that also printed nude photos. Since none of these things are inherently "high crimes and misdemeanors," Ford was pressed to state what the impeachable offense was. He claimed that an impeachable offense is whatever a majority of the House will vote for, and an offense worthy of conviction is whatever two-thirds of the Senate will vote to convict on. This pragmatic approach to impeachment underscores the role of POLITICS in the impeachment process. A committee charged with examining the charges against Douglas recommended that the matter be dropped because no nonpartisan basis for impeachment could be found.

An impeachment begins when someone asks the House to initiate an impeachment investigation. Anyone may do this, although only complaints filed by House members, prosecutors, grand juries, or the Judicial Conference of the United States are apt to lead to investigations. In the past, most impeachments were initiated within the House, but all of the impeachments in recent years began with an outside instigator. Impeachment resolutions are introduced by House members only rarely, sometimes not even one per Congress. In May 2004, Representative Charles Rangel of New York introduced a resolution to impeach Defense Secretary Donald Rumsfeld for his conduct of the war against Iraq. Impeachments of federal judges are ordinarily initiated by the Judicial Conference of the United States. (The three impeachments of judges in the 1980s, all of whom were convicted and removed from office, followed criminal trials.)

Independent counsels (formerly called "special prosecutors") also initiate investigations. The impeachment investigations of Presidents Nixon and Clinton both began this way. Most complaints end when the committee or subcommittee chair to which the matter is assigned decides to drop it. In those few that result in an actual investigation, the House Judiciary Committee and/or one of its subcommittees oversees the work. It is within the committee that actual articles of impeachment are drafted and then voted on. If the committee recommends articles of impeachment, they come before the full House, which then votes on their passage. If any of the articles receives a majority vote in favor, the official is impeached, and the matter then goes to the Senate for trial. In the case of President Clinton, for example, the judiciary committee recommended four articles of impeachment. Two of them were passed by the House, and two were defeated. If articles pass, the House then appoints managers who will serve as prosecutors during the Senate trial.

The House managers present their impeachment articles to the Senate, and a date for trial is set. When a president

Sketch showing the U.S. Senate as a court of impeachment for the trial of Andrew Johnson, 1868 *(Library of Congress)*

is impeached, the chief justice of the United States presides. In other impeachment trials, either the president of the Senate (the vice president of the United States) presides, or senators preside in the vice president's absence. Presumably, the chief justice presides in the case of presidential impeachment so the would-be successor to the president may avoid any conflicts of interest. The Senate can appoint a committee to hear the evidence, or it can try the case as the full Senate. Unlike an ordinary criminal trial, the outcome of Senate impeachment trials is not based on the facts, but rather on senators' perceptions of the significance of the facts. No senator believed, for example, that President Clinton had not committed perjury when he lied to a grand jury about his relationship with a young intern, but only half the senators believed that Clinton deserved to be removed from office on that basis.

The first impeachment was that of a senator, William Blount of Tennessee. He was impeached in July 1797 for trying to involve the United States in a war between Spain and Britain but was not tried until December 1798. The Senate decided the House did not have authority to impeach a senator—the Constitution provides that each chamber is the judge of its own members—and dismissed the charges. Blount had already resigned anyway. No senator has been brought up on impeachment charges since.

The first impeachment leading to removal was that of Judge John Pickering of New Hampshire, who was impeached in March 1803 for improper conduct in a trial pertaining to seizure of a ship. His trial in the Senate began the day after he was impeached, and his son told the Senate that Pickering was insane. Following a trial spanning 10 days, he was convicted and removed from office.

The only Supreme Court justice to be impeached was Samuel Chase, who was impeached in 1804 for a variety of irregular acts committed during several trials. The Senate apparently believed these irregularities did not warrant impeachment because he was acquitted after a trial that spanned five months, with one of the articles receiving not a single vote to convict.

Judge James H. Peck of Missouri was impeached in 1830 for harassing a lawyer who had written a newspaper article critical of Peck's decision against him. Peck was acquitted the next year after a trial that spanned nine months.

Judge West H. Humphreys was impeached in 1862 for supporting the Confederacy. He was not only convicted and removed from office but also disqualified from holding office in the future. On two of the articles, there were no votes to acquit, and on four others there was only one.

President Andrew Johnson was impeached on February 24, 1868, for firing Edwin M. Stanton, his secretary of war, in violation of the Tenure of Office Act, which had been passed specifically to keep Johnson from firing Stanton. His trial began the next day and extended over a three-month period. He was acquitted by a single vote in each of three votes on May 16 and May 26 of that year. His trial adjourned without the Senate having voted on eight remaining articles.

William W. Belknap, secretary of war in the administration of President Ulysses S. Grant, was impeached on March 2, 1876, for five articles of bribery. He was the only person other than a president or judge to be impeached. His trial took five months, and he was acquitted, although nearly all the senators who voted to acquit believed the case to be moot since Belknap had already resigned.

Judge Charles Swayne of Florida was impeached in 1904 for filing false expense reports, residing outside his district, and abuses of contempt of court. He was acquitted after a trial that spanned two and a half months, with none of the 12 charges receiving even a majority to convict.

Judge Robert W. Archibald of the U.S. Commerce Court was impeached in 1912 on 13 articles alleging he used his position to extract payoffs from litigants. He was removed from office and disqualified from holding federal office in the future after a trial that spanned six months.

Judge George W. English of Illinois was impeached in 1926 for a host of judicial malfeasance offenses. He resigned after his trial had been in progress for more than six months. The charges were then dismissed on the motion of the House managers after the House passed a resolution withdrawing the impeachment.

Judge Harold Louderback of California was impeached in 1933 for a variety of acts of favoritism shown on the bench. He was acquitted after a trial that spanned only nine days. Only one of five articles received a majority vote to convict.

Judge Halsted L. Ritter of Florida was impeached in 1936 for accepting kickbacks, tax evasion, and continuing to work as a lawyer. After an 11-day trial, he was acquitted of the first six articles but convicted by a vote of exactly two-thirds on article seven, which alleged that he agreed to recuse himself from a case in exchange for the Miami City Commission passing a resolution praising him. The Senate voted unanimously to bar him from holding office in the future.

Following Judge Ritter's trial, it was more than 50 years before the Senate again sat as a court of impeachment. Then followed three trials in a brief time period. Judge Harry E. Claiborne of Nevada was impeached in 1986 for tax evasion, Judge Alcee L. Hastings of Florida was impeached in 1988 for bribery, perjury, and revealing classified information, and Judge Walter L. Nixon of Mississippi was impeached in 1989 for perjury. All three were convicted and removed from office following trials lasting only three days each. In 1992, Hastings was elected to the House. In 1998, he introduced a resolution to impeach Kenneth W. Starr, independent counsel in the investigation of President Clinton, for usurping the sole prerogative of the House to impeach. (No action was taken on this resolution.)

President William J. Clinton was impeached on December 19, 1998, for perjury and obstruction of justice. His impeachment trial began on January 7, 1999, and ended with his acquittal on two party-line votes on February 12, 1999. Neither article received a majority of votes to convict. No Democrats voted to convict, but 10 Republicans voted to acquit on the first article and five Republicans voted to acquit on the second article.

Further reading: Black, Charles L., Jr. *Impeachment: A Handbook.* New Haven, Conn.: Yale University Press, 1998; Diamond, Robert A., ed. *Impeachment and the U.S. Congress.* Washington, D.C.: Congressional Quarterly Press, 1974; Gearhardt, Michael J. *The Federal Impeachment Process: A Constitutional and Historical Analysis.* Chicago: University of Chicago Press, 2000.

—Tony L. Hill

incumbency advantage

The incumbency advantage refers to the fact that those who already hold a particular seat in government are overwhelmingly likely to be reelected to that seat if they seek to run for another term. This advantage applies to virtually all elective offices, from local positions such as city council members and mayors to state-level offices such as governors and lieutenant governors, to national-level offices such as U.S. representatives and senators. The incumbency advantage became increasingly significant during the second half of the 20th century, as voters' attachments to political parties weakened. Campaigns increasingly focused on the individual candidates in the races. Incumbents benefited disproportionately over their CHALLENGERS from this personal focus of campaigns.

The incumbency advantage is most pronounced in terms of reelection rates for members of Congress, particularly the U.S. House of Representatives. In recent decades, well more than 90 percent of representatives who sought reelection won their races; in 1998, this reached 98 percent of all candidates who were seeking reelection. Candidates for the U.S. Senate are not reelected at quite the same high rate, due in large part to the fact that Senate incumbents typically face more experienced, better-qualified challengers than are common in most House races. However, Senate incumbents still fare quite well, with reelection rates often exceeding 80 percent in recent elections.

Several factors have been identified that help explain why incumbents do so well when they seek reelection. Among the most common explanations are the electoral benefits that officials receive by virtue of already being in office, campaign contributions, and NAME RECOGNITION.

Members of Congress have numerous resources at their disposal not only to help them serve their constituents but also to aid them at reelection time. Each member of the House and Senate has an office in Washington, D.C. In addition, each member of Congress also has several offices in the local community or state that he or she represents. Typically, each of these offices is staffed by several employees. Staffers are paid, and offices are supplied with needed resources through funds that are provided to each member by Congress. Currently, representatives receive funds of approximately $1 million a year to maintain their offices and pay their staff; senators receive proportionately more as the size of their state increases. Through such resources as unlimited long-distance calls, unlimited paid trips between Washington, D.C., and the district or state of the member, and free use of the mail service (a benefit referred to as "franking"), members are able to stay in extremely close contact with their district or state.

The staff members in these offices, both in the district or state and in Washington, D.C., are there to assist citizens in dealing with any governmental issue they might confront. The assistance these staff members perform, which is referred to as CASEWORK, often involves helping constituents cut through bureaucratic "red tape." Casework may involve rushing the processing of a needed passport or advising a constituent about how to appeal a decision from a government agency when individuals are denied benefits for which they believe they qualify. Often, the longer a member has been in Congress, the more adept he or she is at solving such problems. Casework can also involve less serious examples of service to constituents. For example, the staff can set up tours of the Capitol building and other historical sites for constituents who are visiting Washington, D.C., and if the members of Congress are currently in session, they may be able to arrange photo opportunities for constituents with their elected representatives. Another popular service staff can arrange is to have a flag flown over the Capitol building in honor of an individual or to commemorate a special occasion. These types of casework are provided by every member of Congress to any constituent who requests them, regardless of political affiliation. Such examples of casework benefit incumbents when they seek reelection because challengers are generally unable to provide similar types of services to potential voters.

Congressional staffers not only aid constituents directly through casework but also aid congressmen in performing their legislative duties. Members of Congress deal with a tremendous volume of legislation in each Congress; 12,000 pieces of legislation may be introduced over a two-year Congress. Both the House and the Senate are structured in such a way that this workload is divided among relevant committees. Similarly, members assign their staff specific policy issues on which to focus. The staff members in each policy area assist their congressperson in drafting bills related to that topic, in building support among other members for this legislation, and in staying up to date on all relevant legislation that other members are introducing in that policy area. Staff members may attend committee meetings, negotiate with other staffers about the content of legislation, meet with constituents or representatives of INTEREST GROUPS who care about a specific bill, and draft speeches and letters on behalf of the congressperson. As a result of these types of staff assistance, members of Congress are better able to enact legislation that will benefit the voters back home.

Members of Congress also receive important electoral benefits from the structure of Congress itself. As a result of the use of committees in the legislative process, members are able to specialize in issues that are most relevant to their constituents. Congresspersons from farm districts or states will serve on an agriculture committee, and congresspersons who represent districts or states with large numbers of military bases will serve on committees dealing with issues of national defense or veterans affairs. In this way, congresspersons have an active role in shaping legislation that will directly benefit their constituents. The more benefits a congressperson is able to provide to his or her district or state, the greater will be the incentive for voters to support that member in the next election. One very popular type of legislation for an incumbent to provide is referred to as "pork barrel." Pork barrel projects involve members of Congress including in legislation allocations of money that will directly benefit their districts or states. Common examples of pork barrel projects include large sums of money that are allocated to build new roads in a state or district or money that is distributed in order to fund research projects that are vital to the economy in a particular area of the country. Again, challengers are at a major disadvantage in terms of this aspect of the legislative process; they are unable to provide any tangible legislative benefits to voters unless they are already serving in some other office.

Incumbents are also at a distinct advantage over challengers in terms of their financial resources. Interest groups are disproportionately likely to donate campaign contributions to those who are already in office. In fact, many interest groups implement a strategy of donating money to incumbents of either major party rather than donating significant sums of money to a challenger, even if it is a challenger with whom they agree on policy matters. This is particularly true in terms of congresspersons who sit on committees that oversee the groups' concerns. The reality is that most challengers are going to lose. Therefore, it makes more sense to target financial contributions to those who are most likely to be in office. Although campaign contributions may not persuade a member of Congress to vote in a particular way, they do allow interest groups to gain access to representatives of both parties in order to put forth their best cases for representatives voting the way the groups want them to. Interest groups have little incentive in gaining access to a challenger through a financial contribution if that challenger is unlikely to ever be in a decision making position.

Because incumbents are disproportionately likely to receive contributions from interest groups, they are able to build up vast WAR CHESTS, large sums of money they keep on hand to use in upcoming elections. Often, the size of the incumbent's war chest itself will scare away viable challengers. Anyone who faces an incumbent will need an enormous amount of money in order to run a competitive campaign against him or her. Challengers for most seats in the House now need close to $1 million in order to run a competitive campaign. Having that sum available does not guarantee that they will win; it only improves their chances. Senate races are significantly more expensive. Not being able to get the financial backing of interest groups makes it difficult for challengers to obtain the money needed. It is not unusual for challengers to mortgage their homes, to take out loans, or, for those who are wealthy, to donate money to their own campaigns in order to obtain the funds they need to run competitive races.

Another significant advantage that helps incumbents stay in office is largely the result of the congressional benefits and campaign donations previously discussed: Incumbents have significantly higher name recognition than do those who challenge them for their seats. Incumbents have already gained name recognition through running at least one successful campaign. In addition, their recognition increases with their tenure in office and with the supply of benefits they are able to provide to their districts or states. The use of the franking privilege allows members to communicate directly with constituents through either personal correspondence or newsletters typically sent out on a quarterly basis. Such means of communication reinforce for constituents who their representative is, inform them of how the representative has benefited them while in office, and make it easier for voters to recognize the incumbent's name when they see it on a BALLOT in the next election.

Likewise, facilities are available to congresspersons that allow them to broadcast messages to voters in their districts or states through television or radio. In addition, members may be interviewed by broadcast or print journalists regarding their feelings on issues affecting the districts or states. Through all of these means, the incumbent is likely to be much better known than any challenger long before campaign season starts.

Incumbents have a further advantage in name recognition once a campaign starts due to their advantage in bringing in campaign contributions. Incumbents have significantly more money at their disposal to use in campaign commercials and for campaign materials such as bumper stickers and yard signs. Being able to purchase such resources further increases the likelihood that the incumbent will be recognized on the ballot. Particularly in the case of a challenger with little previous political experience or any other form of notoriety, the majority of voters may not even recognize his or her name when they see it on the ballot on ELECTION DAY. Voters are unlikely to vote for a candidate whose name they do not recognize. Because the challenger typically struggles to bring in adequate resources to fund a competitive race, he or she is unlikely to be in a position to purchase adequate television or radio time or other campaign materials.

Through all of these resources, incumbents are not only able to strengthen their own positions in Congress, they are also able to discourage strong challengers from running against them. This is particularly true in terms of House incumbents. A common pattern is that inexperienced, underqualified candidates serve as "sacrificial lambs" in races the incumbents are almost certain to win. Another possibility, though less likely, is for the incumbent in a race to go unchallenged by a candidate of the other major party. Third-party or write-in candidates may face an incumbent in such a situation, but they are even less likely than a major party candidate to defeat the incumbent in such a race. To be a successful challenger and overcome the advantages of an incumbent, one must have valuable political experience in other levels of government, have or be able to raise the necessary sums of money needed to run an effective campaign, and time one's entry into a race at a point when the incumbent is in a weakened position, perhaps as the result of a SCANDAL. These are the most opportune conditions under which to defeat an incumbent.

Further reading: Mayhew, David R. *Congress: The Electoral Connection.* New Haven, Conn.: Yale University Press, 1974.

—Claudia Bryant

independent

An independent is someone who does not affiliate with a particular POLITICAL PARTY. The term *independent* can refer to a political candidate, an elected official, or an ordinary citizen. Independent candidates run campaigns separate from established political parties. They do, however, sometimes receive the ENDORSEMENT of a minor party. Independent candidates seldom win in U.S. elections, and since the turn of the 19th century only a few independent presidential candidates are noteworthy. Eugene McCarthy ran independent campaigns in 1968 and 1976, getting less than 1 percent of the POPULAR VOTE both times. John Anderson in 1980 fared better, with nearly 7 percent of the popular vote. It was Ross Perot who was the most successful in recent years, earning about 19 percent of the vote as an independent in 1992. Finally, Ralph Nader, a GREEN PARTY presidential candidate in 2000, ran as an independent in 2004.

Third-party efforts are often discussed along with independent campaigns. They are natural allies typically challenging the two major parties. Theodore Roosevelt's run for the presidency on the Progressive (Bull Moose) Party ticket earned him about 24 percent of the popular vote. He lost to the Democrat, Wilson, but got more of the popular and electoral vote than his Republican opponent, Taft. In 1968 George Wallace formed the AMERICAN INDEPENDENT PARTY and ran for the presidency as a third-party candidate, gaining about 13 percent of the popular vote. Ross Perot returned to presidential POLITICS in 1996 and ran under the newly formed REFORM PARTY with less success than his prior effort, netting about 8 percent of the popular vote. Although often similar to independents in IDEOLOGY and strategy, these campaigns, like other third-party efforts, are technically partisan.

Independent candidates running for state-level office have been slightly more successful than those running for the presidency. Still, since the turn of the 19th century, the United States has seen only five governors elected as independents: Julius L. Meier in Oregon (1931 to 1935), James B. Longley (1975 to 1979) and Angus S. King, Jr., of Maine (1995 to 2003), Walter Joseph Hickel in Alaska (1990 to 1994), and Lowell P. Weicker, Jr., in Connecticut (1991 to 1995). The 108th Congress includes only two independents: Senator Jim Jeffords and Representative Bernie Sanders, both of Vermont. Sanders entered the House as an independent in 1990. Jeffords changed his party affiliation from Republican to independent in June 2001. While officeholders who are independents are not beholden to any party, they often share interests and tend to align with one of the major parties. This is especially true in the U.S. Congress, where Jeffords and Sanders often side with the DEMOCRATIC PARTY.

Among citizens, there is a substantial population of people who consider themselves independents. These citizens fall into one of two categories: those who tend to lean toward one of the two major parties, often called leaners, and those who express no preference between the Republicans and Democrats, often called pure independents.

While independent leaners are a categorically distinct group, there is little consensus on whether leaners are actually independent or merely partisans reluctant to identify as such. In either case, independent leaners make up a sizable portion of the American public and are a subject of great interest to scholars, analysts, and politicians.

The concept of independent leaners evolved from the classification of PARTY IDENTIFICATION along a continuum, with Democrats on one end and Republicans on the other. Independents were the conceptual midpoint of the continuum. While it is relatively straightforward to classify individuals in these three categories, party identification may be both more complex and subtle than such a measure would reveal. There are likely gradations in between Democrat and independent, or Republican and independent, that are not captured with a single response. Secondary questions in surveys seek to further explore the nature and intensity of party affiliation or independence, asking Republicans and Democrats if they would consider themselves "strong" (strong Republican or Democrat) or "not very strong" (weak Republican or Democrat) partisans and asking of independents whether they consider themselves closer to the Republican or Democratic Party (independent leaning Republicans or Democrats), or neither (pure independent). This series of questions fills in the continuum and produces seven points along the scale, with independent leaners occupying the spaces to the right and left of the midpoint (pure independents).

While the number of individuals who claim independence has indeed increased over the past 50 years, whether this indicates an increase in political independence is questionable. First, most of the increases in independents have been in independent leaners, while aside from the 1970s, the number of pure independents has remained relatively stable at around 10 percent. Some have argued that the independent leaner category is a "holding tank" or "halfway house" for disaffected partisans. This idea is supported by the relative stability of pure independents and the fluctuations among partisans and leaners. Other critics argue that political independence is a completely separate dimension of political attitude than that measured by partisanship and should be analyzed separate from party identification rather than as an element of partisanship.

Another primary question concerning the political behavior of independent leaners is whether their political behavior resembles that of independents or partisans. The differences and similarities between leaners' political behavior and that of partisans and independents has been thoroughly studied with mixed results. Research has found that leaners behave like independents *and* that leaners behave like the partisans they lean toward. For example, if we look merely at presidential voting, mixed results would be gained from an examination of the 1996 and 2000 elections. In 2000, the independent vote edged slightly for

Bush, while approximately 10 percent went for third-party candidates. When leaners are split off from the independents, however, the pure independent vote is split nearly perfectly between Bush and Gore, and slightly more than 10 percent went to third-party candidates. Independents leaning toward Democrats voted solidly for Gore, and independents leaning toward Republicans voted overwhelmingly for Bush. In this case, leaners' voting behavior was much more consistent with partisans' than with pure independents'.

In many ways independents operate in the margins of the political world. At times, however, they are the crucial fulcrum upon which political power shifts. For example, when Jim Jeffords changed from a Republican to an independent in 2001, it created a Democratic majority (50 Democrats, 49 Republicans, and one independent), shifting the leadership in the Senate from the Republicans to the Democrats. This was a dramatic and unusual role for an independent officeholder. However, independents in the electorate are routinely the objects of attention.

In an electoral system dominated by two major parties, a candidate will often count on his or her partisans' votes. It is a successful strategy, then, to appeal to citizens who are not party devotees. In this way, many campaigns by Republicans and Democrats are fashioned to attract moderate and independent voters. In competitive contests this places a considerable amount of electoral clout in the slice of the electorate that is less partisan (i.e., SWING VOTERs), while the strong partisans on either side often receive less attention.

Further reading: Dalton, Russell J. *Citizen Politics: Public Opinion and Political Parties in Advanced Industrial Democracies.* New York: Chatham House, 2000; Keith, Bruce E., et al. *The Myth of the Independent Voter.* Berkeley: University of California Press, 1992; Miller, Warren, and J. Merrill Shanks. *The New American Voter.* Cambridge, Mass.: Harvard University Press, 1996; Wattenberg, Martin P. *The Decline of American Political Parties, 1952–1996.* Cambridge, Mass.: Harvard University Press, 1998.

—Francis Neely and Joel A. Rayan

independent expenditures

Independent expenditures are federal electioneering communications paid for by political parties, INTEREST GROUPS, or individuals without the knowledge or consent of the campaign they are meant to support. Independent expenditures made in support of or opposition to a federal candidate are not limited by law and do not count toward fund-raising limits prescribed by Congress. POLITICAL ACTION COMMITTEES (PACs) and political parties have used independent expenditures to avoid the restrictions and regulations associated with directly contributing to a federal campaign.

The legal rationale behind independent expenditures derives from the Supreme Court's decision in *BUCKLEY V. VALEO* 424 U.S. 1 (1976). In this landmark decision, the Court defined the constitutional limitations, under the First Amendment right of free speech, that Congress must observe in regulating campaign finance. The Court found campaign contributions not to constitute protected free speech, as the act of contributing to a campaign did not directly communicate a political message. Because contributions were actions only related to free speech, the Court considered Congress to have a significant governmental interest in limiting contributions to prevent the appearance of corruption in campaigns. However, the Court held that communications made independently by a party or interest group that were uncoordinated with a candidate or campaign were direct, constitutionally protected free speech and could not be limited.

There is a trade-off to making independent expenditures, as they cannot be directly coordinated with the campaigns they are meant to support. However, PACs and parties have increasingly relied on the independent expenditure to increase the amount of money that may be spent during a single campaign cycle. From 1995 to 2000, independent expenditures by PACs for and against federal candidates more than doubled, to more than $21 million. The Bipartisan Campaign Reform Act of 2002 (BCRA) has placed restrictions on political parties' ability to make independent expenditures. The FEDERAL ELECTION COMMISSION (FEC) has interpreted BCRA to prevent parties from making COORDINATED EXPENDITURES on behalf of candidates if they have previously made an independent expenditure. Moreover, BCRA considers all levels of a national political committee, including associated state and local committees, to constitute a single political committee. Therefore, national parties are now prevented from directing funds to state and local parties for the purpose of making independent expenditures, in addition to making coordinated expenditures at the national level for the same campaign.

Further reading: Bauer, Robert. *More Soft Money Hard Law.* New York: Perkins Coie, 2003; Federal Elections Commission. Available online. URL: http://www.fec.gov. Accessed August 10, 2005; Magleby, David, and Monson, J. Quin. *The Last Hurrah? Soft Money and Issue Advocacy in the 2002 Congressional Election.* Washington, D.C.: Brookings Institution Press, 2004.

—Zachary Courser

interest groups

An interest group is an organization consisting of individuals or institutions that share a common political goal or set of goals and unite for the purpose of influencing government policies to reflect these goals. Interest groups are commonly referred to by journalists and politicians as *special interests,* a term that connotes a negative association between POLITICS and narrow or selfish special interests. Many scholars use the term *organized interest* in place of *interest group* or *special interest* because it is thought to be broader and to capture a wider range of political organizations that are active in politics.

The type of group that most often comes to mind when people think of an interest group is a "citizen group," or a group that is open to any citizen. Examples include the Sierra Club, the National Riffle Association (NRA), and the CHRISTIAN COALITION, but many different types of organizations are considered organized interests, including but not limited to corporations, trade associations, professional associations, labor unions, citizen groups, or public interest groups, think tanks, different levels of government such as states and cities, and foreign governments.

Interest groups make use of a wide range of tools in their attempts to influence government decisions, including making financial contributions to political candidates' campaigns; FUND-RAISING on behalf of a candidate; volunteering time and other resources to assist in political campaigns; providing elected and nonelected officials with information about a particular piece of legislation, potential legislation, policy area, or CONSTITUENCY; and mobilizing public opinion through the use of ISSUE ADVOCACY ADVERTISING and other forms of public mobilization. This list is by no means exhaustive. Interest groups have a variety of formal and informal means to potentially influence the government. In regard to monetary contributions to political candidates, federal CAMPAIGN FINANCE LAWS forbid interest groups from making direct contributions to candidates. Organizations must set up a POLITICAL ACTION COMMITTEE (PAC) to make contributions, and the laws set limits on how much they can give.

Well-financed organized interests, such as corporations, may pay a professional agent, or LOBBYIST, to represent their policy interests, or they may employ lobbyists on their payrolls. However, groups that lack the resources to pay a professional lobbyist have other avenues of participation at their disposal, including lobbying on their own, mobilizing public opinion via protests or the media, and lobbying the courts by submitting amicus curiae briefs, or "friend of the court" briefs, which are short memos providing the court with information about one party or the other in a court case. Moreover, in a federal system such as the one in the United States, interest groups have multiple points of access. Groups can contact an official at the federal level, such as the president, a senator, or a House member. Alternatively, groups can contact someone in the state or local government. The separation of powers also increases the number of access points for interest groups at the state and national levels, as does the existence of the committee system within Congress. At the national level, a group or lobbyist may approach the president, Congress, a federal court, or a federal agency.

Despite multiple points of access, not all groups gain access to governmental decision making. Groups that are well financed and that have political experience generally fare well. Lobbying the government and the public is a sophisticated endeavor, and most organizations that can afford to do so hire a lobbyist and a public relations expert. Moreover, membership in interest groups is biased toward members with higher socioeconomic standing. Despite the rapid growth of interest groups in the past 30 years, there are some groups, such as low-income people, that remain unorganized. It is also important to point out that interest group influence is difficult to demonstrate—scholars interested in studying interest group influence often have difficulty isolating how, when, and under what conditions groups influence the policy process.

Interest groups have always been active in American politics, but the number of groups active in Washington grew steadily from 1900 to 1960 and rapidly from 1960 to the 1980s due to several factors, including the increasing size and complexity of government, the growing religious and social diversity that accompanied immigration, technological changes that made it easier for groups to form, a growing economy that produced new economic interests, and rising affluence, which enabled more individuals to join groups.

Interest groups date back to America's founding. James Madison's Federalist No. 10, one of a series of essays written in support of the Constitution's ratification, remains the foundation of American political theory on interest groups. Madison worried that as society developed and different classes emerged, competing interests, or FACTIONS, would arise. Furthermore, Madison worried that a powerful faction could come to tyrannize others in society. Madison proposed to deal with the problem of factions not by forbidding them, but by designing a government that provided checks and balances. Madison was also confident that the effects of factions would be diluted due to their sheer numbers.

The structure of government has not prevented some groups from gaining more power than others. Generally, those with more resources have done better. Despite this imbalance of influence, interest groups act as an information conduit connecting constituents and government officials. A great deal of the theoretical work on the role of interest groups addresses the tension expressed by Madison in the Federalist No. 10, that is, the tension between the right of people to pursue their interests and the need to protect society from being dominated by one or more interests. This dichotomy is evident in the debates surrounding campaign finance reform today.

The Bipartisan Campaign Reform Act (BCRA) of 2002 significantly restricts interest groups' use of issue advocacy ads, advertisements that are paid for with unregulated funds by interest groups that advocate or oppose a political candidate's position on an issue. In addition, interest groups spending more than $10,000 a year on television ads must disclose who paid for them. The BCRA also bans ads that are paid for by outside groups and identify a particular candidate from being shown 60 days before a GENERAL ELECTION.

The BCRA was the long-awaited result of the McCAIN-FEINGOLD bill, named for its sponsors, Senators John McCain (R, Ariz.) and Russell Feingold (D, Wis.). Both liberal and conservative groups fought provisions in the McCain-Feingold bill that restrict the use of issue ads, including the American Civil Liberties Union, the AFL-CIO, and the U.S. Chamber of Commerce. These groups argued that the provisions infringed on their free speech and their ability to participate in elections. On the other hand, campaign reform groups such as Public Citizen and COMMON CAUSE felt that the McCain-Feingold bill was a necessary step in limiting the influence of powerful organized interests. However, many observers of campaign finance regulation maintain that campaign finance laws have not achieved their desired goals of limiting the influence of well-funded interests. The role of interest groups in the legislative process is likely to be an important part of the campaign finance debate for years to come.

Further reading: Cigler, Allan J., and Burdett A. Loomis. *Interest Group Politics.* 6th ed. Washington, D.C.: CQ Press, 2002; Nownes, Anthony J. *Pressure and Power: Organized Interests in American Politics.* Boston: Houghton Mifflin, 2001; Wright, John R. *Interest Groups and Congress: Lobbying, Contributions, and Influence.* Boston: Allyn & Bacon, 1996.

—Jessica Gerrity

Internet voting

Internet voting, also called I-voting, is the process of casting a secret and secure electronic BALLOT that is transmitted to election officials via the Internet. I-voting is a more specific form of electronic voting, or E-voting, which refers more generally to voting that encompasses a wide range of electronic technology, including telephones, cable, and computers that are not necessarily hooked in to the Internet. According to the California Internet Voting Task Force, there are two types of Internet voting: 1) polling place Internet voting, whereby Internet voting machines are used at traditional polling places staffed by election personnel who help verify or authenticate voters before their ballots are cast, and 2) remote Internet voting, whereby voting takes place over the Internet unsupervised using a computer that is not necessarily owned or operated by election officials. Voting from one's own personal computer at home is an example of remote Internet voting.

The concept of Internet voting is relatively new due to the infancy of the Internet as a medium. The Alaska REPUBLICAN PARTY gave eligible residents in three rural Alaska House districts the opportunity to cast votes over the Internet in the Republican STRAW POLL in January 2000, but only 35 votes were cast via Internet voting. Much higher Internet participation was reached two months later in the first-ever binding Internet election held in Arizona in March 2000. The Arizona Democratic Party gave party members the option of casting their ballots over the Internet in the PRESIDENTIAL PRIMARY between March 7 and March 11 of that year. Voters could also cast their ballots by mail or by voting in person at traditional polling places. Turnout in the Arizona Democratic PRIMARY was higher than in previous years. In March 2000, 85,970 voters cast ballots in the Democratic primary compared to 12,800 voters who cast ballots in the 1996 Democratic primary. It is unclear, however, that Internet voting produced the increase, as the 2000 primary SLATE featured two candidates, Al Gore and Bill Bradley, whereas in 1996 Bill Clinton was the unopposed Democratic candidate. In the 2004 Michigan Democratic caucuses, voters could apply to vote through the Internet in the party caucuses. Of the 163,769 people who participated in the caucuses, 46,543 people, or 28.4 percent of caucus participants, cast their votes online.

The U.S. Department of Defense piloted an Internet voting experiment during the 2000 GENERAL ELECTION involving overseas military personnel. In it, 84 personnel cast ballots over the Internet. For 2004, the Department of Defense had planned a larger pilot test of Internet voting for 100,000 American military personnel and civilians living overseas that was called Secure Electronic Registration and Voting Experiment (SERVE). SERVE was dropped in January 2004, however, after four computer scientists brought to evaluate the program argued that the program should be halted due to concerns over the potential for hackers to steal votes or otherwise harm the integrity of the system.

Concerns over low VOTER TURNOUT rates in the United States have facilitated the adoption of alternative methods of casting ballots, such as liberal absentee and EARLY VOTING, in several states in an effort to make the act of voting more convenient than the traditional method of voting in person at a polling place on ELECTION DAY. Internet voting is another alternative method of voting that has been proposed to make voting easier. Internet voting has the potential to change both when and where people cast their ballots. Like absentee and early voting, the adoption of Internet voting may change elections from a single day to a longer period of time.

The Pew Research Center for the People and the Press asked a nationwide sample of 2,174 adults in June 2000: "There are many ways for people to vote, and some prefer one way over another. If you had the choice of voting in a booth at a polling place on election day, OR over the Internet, OR through the mail during the weeks leading up to election day, which would you prefer?" While a majority of respondents favored the voting booth (52 percent), 26 percent of respondents said they would prefer to vote on the Internet, and 20 percent of respondents said they would prefer to vote by mail (July 13, 2000).

Proponents of Internet voting contend that the Internet will play an important role in revitalizing the American ELECTORATE. Internet voting may increase turnout by minimizing time and travel costs to voters. If barriers to voting are reduced as voting is made more convenient, increased voter participation could enhance the legitimacy of the political system. In addition, Internet voting has the potential to increase the administrative efficiency of election offices by lowering the needs for staffing polling stations, reducing ballot printing costs, and facilitating the speed of vote tabulation.

Opponents counter that Internet voting will benefit already advantaged socioeconomic groups, increasing their representation in government while decreasing the percentage, and thus the voice, of minorities and low-income individuals who are less likely to have access to the Internet. Preventing voter fraud and maintaining the security and integrity of an Internet voting system may also prove difficult due to attacks from hackers who may seek to disrupt or alter the voting process. Drawbacks to Internet voting include potential problems with voter authentication, privacy or secrecy of the ballot, and potential coercion and pressure that may take place when individuals do not vote at the polls. Some opponents to Internet voting argue that alternative methods of voting that take voting away from polling stations on election day erode the significance of voting as a public act by making it into a private one.

Concerns over the integrity of the U.S. electoral system were accentuated by the events following election day on November 7, 2000, when questions about the Florida vote count of the presidential race between Republican George W. Bush and Democrat Al Gore surfaced. More than a month had elapsed before the U.S. Supreme Court ended the RECOUNT of Florida's ballots and Gore conceded the election to Bush. While other states did not have their electoral practices dissected under a public microscope, as did Florida, there was concern that many states would not pass the muster of national scrutiny if put to the test. In the wake of discussions about hanging, dimpled, and pregnant CHADs, Internet voting has a certain elegance and simplicity when compared to visions of poll-workers recounting punch-card ballots. Nevertheless, until concerns over the security of Internet voting are sufficiently addressed, it is unlikely that Internet voting will be adopted by many states in any comprehensive way.

Further reading: Gibson, Rachel. "Elections Online: Assessing Internet Voting in Light of the Arizona Democratic Primary." *Political Science Quarterly* 116, no. 4 (2001): 561–583; Valenty, Linda O., and James C. Brent. "Online Voting: Calculating Risks and Benefits to the Community and the Individual." In Ingo Vogelsang and Benjamin M. Compaine, eds., *The Internet Upheaval: Raising Questions, Seeking Answers in Communications Policy.* Cambridge, Mass.: MIT Press, 2000.

—Kate Kenski

Iowa caucus

The Iowa caucus refers to Iowa's biennial gathering of party activists and party leaders for the purposes of selecting DELEGATES to county conventions and expressing preferences for potential candidates of both the DEMOCRATIC and REPUBLICAN PARTY. Following widespread reforms in the general NOMINATION process in 1968, the caucus system represents a deliberate shift in power from leaders of the PARTY ORGANIZATION to the PARTY IN THE ELECTORATE. As originally designed, caucus meetings represent open and deliberative forums from which citizens determine viable political candidates. After an often highly contentious debate regarding the viability of particular candidates as well as the direction of party POLITICS, delegates are selected to represent individual voters at county conventions. Given that delegates selected to county conventions serve to elect delegates to district, state, and national conventions, caucus meetings represent an influential and highly democratic mechanism for expressing political preferences and setting the party platform.

Generally, caucus meetings are held at various public buildings in more than 2,000 PRECINCTs across the state. While caucuses are open to all citizens of voting age by the GENERAL ELECTION, with most precincts permitting on-site registration, caucus meetings tend to differ according to party rules. For instance, caucus-goers participating in the Democratic caucus must be registered accordingly, while those eligible to participate in the Republican caucus require no formal affiliation with the party. Furthermore, while the Republican Party simply extends a one-person, one-vote policy as designated by a secret BALLOT through the drop of a name in a hat, the Democratic Party requires participants to break into "preference groups" for individual candidates, with the size of such groups determining the percentage of delegates to be represented at county conventions. Preference groups must maintain at least 15 percent of those present to be viable and eligible for sending delegates to the county convention on the candidate's behalf, often leading to serious political lobbying between groups.

In a presidential year, the Iowa caucus is particularly salient due to its "first-in-the-nation" status, with precinct caucuses held in mid- to late January. With both the Democratic and Republican parties holding caucus meetings, the Iowa caucus provides an important staging ground for expressing presidential preferences. Furthermore, given an increasingly shortened nomination calendar, early states such as Iowa tend to have a disproportionate effect on the PRESIDENTIAL NOMINATING PROCESS, with candidates hoping to secure the nomination needing to demonstrate early campaign competitiveness as a means of attracting broad-based support. Indeed, media and news organizations, individual candidates, political parties, local and state officials, and individual supporters tend to spend exorbitant amounts of resources in the months leading up to the Iowa caucus, thereby attracting nationwide interest. While critics tend to argue that relatively unrepresentative results from a single state receive an inordinate amount of national media attention, advocates continually engage in political battles to ensure the Iowa caucus maintains its "first-in-the-nation" status. Thus, while supporters of the Iowa caucus argue that its results tend to reflect mass political attitudes regarding potential presidential nominees, its role as a legitimate predictor of national public opinion remains debatable.

Nevertheless, candidates hoping to fare well in the PRIMARY process often look for a strong caucus showing as a means of providing important political momentum heading into the bulk of the primary season. Furthermore, while a top-three finish among candidates serves to justify individual campaigns, the Iowa caucus also serves as a springboard to primary success and a party's presidential nomination. For instance, in 1976, the Iowa caucus served to provide significant political momentum to the campaign of the relatively unknown former governor of Georgia, Jimmy Carter, ultimately propelling Carter to the nomination and the White House. Indeed, no candidate failing to place in the top three in the Iowa caucus since 1972 has gone on to win the party's presidential nomination. Other candidates who received much-needed support include George H. W. Bush in 1980, Gary Hart in 1984, and initially, George McGovern in 1972, the first year the Iowa caucus received significant national attention. Conversely, the Iowa caucus also serves to effectively spoil struggling campaigns, suggesting the Iowa caucus provides an important and complex role in the nomination process.

Beyond narrowing the presidential field, scholars question whether the Iowa caucus is depreciating in political relevance. Critics point to the 1988 and 1992 caucuses, in which both of the caucus winners for the Democratic Party, including Senator Tom Harkin of Iowa, not only failed to win the party's nomination but also failed to successfully compete throughout the primary season. While the Iowa caucus reemerged with national prominence in 1996 following a political dogfight among eight Republican candidates, the Democratic caucus remained relatively uncompetitive until 2000, when serving vice president Gore defeated former senator Bill Bradley by a more than 2 to 1 margin. Furthermore, given the trend toward "frontloading" in the nomination process, candidates increasingly skip the Iowa

caucus (e.g., Al Gore in 1988 and John McCain in 2000) in order to focus on more substantial and representative states.

The 2004 Iowa caucus, however, while of little importance for the Republican Party, ultimately served to shape the entire primary season for the Democratic Party. Staging an unprecedented turnaround, Senator John Kerry of Massachusetts scored a surprise victory over longtime FRONTRUNNER and former governor of Vermont Howard Dean. Kerry's first-place finish, followed by Senator John Edwards's surprise second-place showing, effectively dismantled the Dean campaign, vaulting Kerry into the frontrunner position and ultimately the party's presidential nomination. Thus, while the role of the Iowa caucus as a precise political barometer for the viability of presidential candidates remains in doubt, its potential influence is indisputable.

Ultimately, given the importance of establishing initial presidential preferences for the upcoming general election, the Iowa caucus serves an important and influential role in the nomination process for both political candidates and citizen activists. Nevertheless, critics argue that the Iowa caucus fails to represent the appropriate level of demographic diversity, providing only a snapshot of mass public opinion. Furthermore, given the open and relatively informal nature of selecting delegates, particularly among the Democratic Party, the Iowa caucus removes citizens from typical mechanisms designed to ensure voter impartiality. Thus, while the caucus system provides a unique format for selecting presidential nominees, in addition to attracting nationwide attention by serving as the first legitimate test of an individual's candidacy and potentially shaping the entire primary season, the Iowa caucus remains subject to political skepticism.

Further reading: Jackson, John S., and William Crotty. *The Politics of Presidential Selection.* 2nd ed. New York: Addison-Wesley Longman, 2001; Wayne, Stephen J. *The Road to the White House: The Politics of Presidential Selection.* Canada: Wadsworth, 2004.

—Christopher Larimer

IRS checkoff

The IRS checkoff refers to the box on an individual tax return (IRS forms 1040, 1040A, and 1040 EZ) that allows the taxpayer to designate $3 of his or her tax liability to the Presidential Election Campaign Fund. If the taxpayer is married and filing a joint return, there is a second box the taxpayer can use to designate $3 of his or her spouse's tax liability to the fund. By checking the box(es), the taxpayer does not increase the amount of tax owed or decrease the amount to be refunded; he or she merely directs $3 (or $6) of taxes already paid to the fund.

Originally, the IRS checkoff allowed taxpayers to designate $1 ($2 on joint returns) to the Presidential Election

Campaign Fund. The fund was established by the REV-ENUE ACT of 1971 and provides for the public financing of presidential campaigns (as well as the party nominating conventions). The law provides funds to qualified presidential candidates (i.e., candidates who abide by certain spending limits, who show a proven FUND-RAISING ability during the nominating process, and who represent established parties). The theory behind the establishment of the fund and the IRS checkoff was that presidential campaigns could be funded by large numbers of small donors, thus freeing presidential candidates from relying on private sources of money, and thereby correct funding disparities between major party candidates.

Unfortunately, use of the fund has steadily declined since its inception. In the late 1970s and early 1980s, around 28 percent of taxpayers were choosing to designate a portion of their taxes to the fund. As a result, between $35 million and $41 million were allocated to the fund each year. But beginning in 1984, participation in the checkoff began to decline, and by 2002 only 11 percent of taxpayers were using it. Since disbursements from the fund greatly increased during the 1980s and 1990s, Congress decided in 1993 to triple the amount of the checkoff. As a result, revenue from the checkoff increased to more than $60 million per year in the late 1990s despite declining participation.

Even with the tripling of the checkoff amount, the funds available in the Presidential Election Campaign Fund have decreased to the point that it is unable to cover the amount owed to presidential candidates. In both 1996 and 2000, several PRIMARY election candidates were forced to wait for money, as the fund awaited replenishment from April tax returns. These shortfalls were the result of the fund's priority system. The fund first provides money for the party nominating conventions, then to GENERAL ELECTION nominees, and finally to primary election candidates. Thus, in the case of a shortfall, primary election candidates may receive only partial MATCHING FUNDS. It is predicted that unless participation in the IRS checkoff increases, the fund will not have enough money to cover disbursements as early as 2008. Moreover, as presidential campaigns become increasingly expensive endeavors, a growing number of candidates, especially well-funded candidates during the nominating season, such as Howard Dean and George W. Bush in 2004, are forgoing the matching funds altogether so as to avoid the limitations that come with accepting federal funds. No major party candidate has yet to forgo the general election federal funding.

Further reading: Corrado, Anthony, Thomas Mann, Daniel Ortiz, and Trevor Potter, eds. *The New Campaign Finance Sourcebook*. Washington, D.C.: Brookings Institution Press, 2004.

—Brian J. Brox

isolationism

Although the origins of isolationism in the United States can be traced back to George Washington, who warned future generations of Americans to avoid entanglement in European affairs, isolationism best describes American foreign policy during the first half of the 20th century. The Monroe Doctrine (1823) and the Atlantic and Pacific Oceans secured the United States a unique place in world affairs, enabling the country, at least for a brief period of time, to focus its attention away from the turbulent affairs of Europe.

Isolationism first failed as a cohesive foreign policy during World War I. The United States had strong cultural and economic ties to the Allied nations and feared that these connections as well as the millions of dollars in loans to these nations would be lost if the Central Powers emerged victorious. Isolationism left the United States ill-prepared for war when it was forced upon the country by German submarine attacks (most notably the sinking of the British liner *Lusitania* in 1915, killing 128 Americans). In 1916, Woodrow Wilson issued his famous Sussex Pledge, vowing to declare war if Germany continued to violate neutral rights by attacking passenger and freight vessels. Germany forced Wilson's hand when it declared unlimited submarine warfare in 1917. The United States followed with a declaration of war on the Central Powers on April 2, 1917.

After World War I the United States again returned to a stance of isolationism. It made few attempts at major foreign policy. The exceptions included the Washington Naval Conference of 1921–22 and the London Naval Conference of 1930, which were designed to limit naval armament. American businessmen Charles G. Dawes and Owen D. Young were instrumental in creating the Dawes Plan in 1924 that scaled back German reparations payments and provided loans. Young also helped fashion the Young Plan in 1929, which further reduced reparations payments. The Kellogg Briand Pact of 1928, fashioned by U.S. secretary of state Frank Kellogg and French foreign minister Aristide Briand, was designed to outlaw all but defensive wars and was signed by every major power of the time except Russia.

During the 1930s, Germany, Italy, and Japan, began to make aggressive maneuvers and violate their international agreements. The major vehicle to enforce these treaties was the League of Nations, but it did little to stop the aggression. The United States relied on the Neutrality Acts of 1935–37.

When World War II (1939–45) began, most of the world, including the United States, was still suffering the effects of the Great Depression. American economic agreements, much like those prior to World War I, favored the Allies, and German and Japanese naval power threatened U.S. foreign interests and domestic security. Isolationism ultimately failed when the Japanese attacked Pearl Harbor on December 7, 1941, and the United States was once again drawn into an international conflict.

The effects of isolationism in both World War I and World War II hindered American preparations for war. The United States, on a peace-time footing, had relatively small military forces prior to its entry into the two world wars. Yet, its industrial capacity, vastly exceeding the expectations of its adversaries, allowed a rapid transition to a major military power.

There was a brief resurgence in isolationist thinking in the United States following the end of the cold war. Proponents of this worldview, often dubbed neoisolationists, share the traditional view of isolationism that focuses attention on domestic issues and calls for a reduction in military spending in order to free up resources for other needs. The events of September 11, 2001, however, have led many to argue against this posture in pursuit of an aggressive foreign policy that promises to "take the war to terrorists."

Further reading: Cohen, Warren I. *Empire without Tears: America's Foreign Relations, 1921–1933.* New York: McGraw-Hill, 1987; Combs, Jerald A. *The History of American Foreign Policy*, Volume II: *Since 1900.* 2nd ed. New York: McGraw-Hill, 1997.

—Antonio Thompson

issue advocacy advertising

Issue advocacy advertising, often referred to as "issue ads," consists of advertisements that are paid for by organized interests and political parties to advocate or oppose a political candidate's position on an issue. They differ from direct political ads in that they are not controlled by the candidate and in that they advocate a candidate's issues, rather than directly endorsing the candidate.

In the early to mid-1980s, political parties and organized interests added issue advocacy to their repertoire of electoral activities as a way to evade the provisions of the FEDERAL ELECTION CAMPAIGN ACT of 1971 (FECA) that limited their financial involvement in federal campaigns. Since then, issue advocacy has evolved into a common lobbying technique and the fastest-growing area of CAMPAIGN EXPENDITURES. Because issue advocacy is not subject to FECA regulations, there is no limit to the amount an organization or party can spend on issue advocacy. Additionally, donors can invest in issue advocacy as a way to influence an election without leaving a financial trace.

Issue advocacy is among the most popular uses of SOFT MONEY because it circumvents FECA and subsequent amendments to it by advocating or opposing a candidate's stance on an issue, rather than urging voters to vote for or against a candidate, or what is often referred to as electioneering. Because issue advocacy does not explicitly contain the words "vote for" or "defeat" candidate X—wording that the Supreme Court ruled constituted direct electoral advocacy in the landmark 1976 case *BUCKLEY V. VALEO*—issue advertisements are not subject to FECA regulations. How-

ever, issue advertisements do implicitly advocate the election or defeat of a candidate, and, as a result, issue advocacy has been the source of much consternation for legislators, individuals, and groups concerned about the exemption of issue ads and, more generally, soft money from FECA regulation.

The roots of issue advocacy can be traced back to 1976, when the U.S. Supreme Court decided *Buckley v. Valeo*. The Buckley court was concerned that the vague statutory language in FECA might inhibit the actions of some political players who were not certain about the law, as well as inadvertently regulate political activity that was not in reality electioneering. In an attempt to both clarify and preserve FECA, the Buckley court interpreted FECA to apply only to communication that "expressly" advocated the defeat or election of a federal candidate. Words such as "vote for," "vote against," "elect," and "cast your ballot" were listed by the Court as examples of express advocacy. Advertising by parties and groups that refrained from using the words that were found to constitute express advocacy were considered issue advocacy. But what originated as examples soon became deemed a test of electioneering by the lower courts. Sometimes referred to as the "magic words test," the test of electioneering adopted by the courts essentially meant that parties and groups could evade legal constraints as long as they did not mention specific words and phrases such as "elect" and "vote against."

Issue advocacy advertising was also propelled by the 1979 amendments to FECA, in which Congress allowed individuals and groups to give unlimited amounts of money to parties in the form of "soft money." In theory, soft money was to be used to fund "party-building activities" and the election of state and local candidates. Party-building activities include VOTER REGISTRATION, voter education, and GET-OUT-THE-VOTE drives. In practice, however, both parties have figured out ways to use soft money to fund CONGRESSIONAL ELECTIONS, and issue advertisements are among the most popular uses of soft money.

Several Supreme Court rulings have been instrumental in expanding the use of soft money to fund issue advocacy in federal elections. In *Colorado Republican Federal Campaign Committee v. FEC* (1996), the Supreme Court ruled that political parties were permitted to spend money on behalf of candidates without using HARD MONEY. Also in 1996, the Federal Election Commission alleged that the CHRISTIAN COALITION used issue ads in a highly partisan way to the benefit of Republican candidates. The case was dismissed when the Court ruled that issue advocacy was illegal only when a group substantially coordinates with the candidate or party. Again, the courts conceptualized "coordination" in a very strict sense—the advertisement must clearly advocate the election or defeat of a candidate, urging voters to vote for or against a particular candidate. These rulings resulted in a marked increase in the use of soft money to fund issue advocacy.

Critics pointed to the dramatic rise in spending on issue advocacy as an example of a major flaw in the way campaigns are financed in the United States. With this concern in mind, the Bipartisan Campaign Reform Act (BCRA) of 2002 significantly restricts the use of issue ads by political parties and organized interests. The BCRA was the long-awaited result of the MCCAIN-FEINGOLD bill, named for its sponsors, Senators John McCain (R, Ariz.) and Russell Feingold (D, Wis.). The BCRA was signed into law by President George W. Bush on March 27, 2002, unsuccessfully challenged as unconstitutional by Senator Mitch McConnell (R, Ky.), and upheld in the Supreme Court on December 10, 2003. The BCRA bans unlimited contributions, or soft money, to the national political parties for "party building" activities. In addition, the BCRA places several key restrictions on issue advocacy that impact the electoral activities of both parties and groups. First, groups spending more than $10,000 a year on television ads must disclose who paid for them. Second, the BCRA bans ads that are paid for by outside groups and identify a particular candidate from being shown 60 days before a GENERAL ELECTION.

Critics of the BCRA claim that the restrictions placed on issue advocacy ads result in unconstitutional limits on free speech. Both liberal and conservative groups fought the provision in the McCain-Feingold bill, including the American Civil Liberties Union, the AFL-CIO, and the U.S. Chamber of Commerce, arguing that the provisions infringed on their free speech and their ability to participate in elections. On the other hand, campaign finance reform groups such as Public Citizen and COMMON CAUSE felt that the McCain-Feingold bill was a necessary step in limiting the influence of powerful organized interests. This debate is certain to continue, as politicians, scholars, and groups continue to debate the goals and boundaries of campaign finance legislation.

Further reading: Cigler, Allan J., and Burdett A. Loomis. *Interest Group Politics.* 6th ed. Washington, D.C.: CQ Press, 2002; Kollman, Ken. *Outside Lobbying: Public Opinion and Interest Group Strategies.* Princeton, N.J.: Princeton University Press, 1998; Nownes. Anthony J. *Pressure and Power: Organized Interests in American Politics.* Boston: Houghton Mifflin, 2001.

—Jessica Gerrity and Edward G. Carmines

K

Kennedy-Nixon debates

The Kennedy-Nixon debates were a series of four one-hour televised debates held in the fall of 1960 in advance of that November's PRESIDENTIAL ELECTION. John F. Kennedy, a senator from Massachusetts, represented the DEMOCRATIC PARTY, and Richard M. Nixon, the sitting vice president under Dwight Eisenhower, represented the REPUBLICAN PARTY. Due to an exemption in the Federal Communication Act's "equal time" provision that was passed by Congress in the summer of 1960, the television networks were not forced to include any other less-well-known candidates in the debates.

The debates are a significant milestone in American political history for two important reasons. They were the first face-to-face PRESIDENTIAL DEBATES in American history, and they were broadcast on television to 70 million viewers across the nation. From the founding of the United States, newspapers had been a vital means of political communication. By the 1930s, technological developments had made radio available to virtually all Americans as a primary source of both entertainment and news coverage. However, by 1960, television had begun to surpass both print media and radio as the preferred source of information for many voters. That preference continues through today, as television remains the primary source of news and political information for nearly two out of three Americans.

Although the debates consisted of four separate encounters between the two candidates, it is the first debate that has tended to be viewed as the most significant of the four, by both political and media analysts as well as by the candidates themselves. It was held on September 26, 1960, in Chicago. Two-thirds of adults in the United States tuned in to the debate either by radio or by television. The most well-known aspect of the night's events is the differences in the public's appraisal of each candidate's performance. Those who listened by radio generally felt that Nixon had won the debate. He had been a skilled debater since his college days and was well prepared, citing facts and figures to support his arguments. However, those who watched the debate on television generally viewed Kennedy as the winner. Kennedy's arguments were equally as well prepared as Nixon's. Nevertheless, Kennedy had a clear advantage in terms of physical presence on screen. While Kennedy wore a dark-colored suit, Nixon wore a gray suit that tended to blend into the gray background of the television studio. Kennedy was well rested, and in the days leading up to the debate, he had spent time in the sun and had a deep, healthy-looking tan. In contrast, Nixon had been ill for a week leading up to the debate and wore an ill-fitting shirt that gaped at the collar, which reinforced the impression that he was unhealthy. To make matters even worse for Nixon, a fresh growth of beard was reappearing on his face by the time of the telecast, which made him look haggard, and the heat from the studio lights caused him to perspire, which caused his makeup to run.

Kennedy's performance in the first debate enabled him to improve his public image, even among many who believed Nixon had performed better in the debate. Not only did it increase the public's knowledge about him by giving him exposure throughout the nation but also, by simply being able to hold his own against the vice president, he exceeded the expectations of many voters. Prior to the debates, many voters had misgivings about Kennedy. Not only was he a Catholic in a nation that had elected only Protestant presidents up to that time, but also there were significant concerns among voters that he was too young and inexperienced to serve as president. He had served six years in the House, but in 1960 he was only two years into his second term as a senator. In contrast, Nixon had served not only as a representative and senator but also was in his eighth year as vice president.

Most research has shown that the debates did not significantly affect vote choice overall. Republicans tended to believe that Nixon won the debates, while Democrats tended to believe that Kennedy had won them. Nevertheless, the debates often are viewed as being a decisive factor in Kennedy's victory that November. The explanation for this contradiction may lie in the fact that the race was extremely close throughout the summer and fall of 1960; any small advantage Kennedy gained from his performance in the debates may have been large enough to seal his victory. As a result of his performance, not only was he able to win over a portion of the UNDECIDED VOTERS, but also he was able to increase enthusiasm for his candidacy among many Democrats who had had their doubts about his qualifications.

The Kennedy-Nixon debates not only solidified the public's preference for television over print or radio media as a source of news, they also marked the beginning of a new era in American POLITICS. The major presidential candidates have debated on television in every election year since 1976. Lyndon Johnson, who became president following Kennedy's assassination in 1963, refused to debate in 1964, as did Nixon when he again ran for president in 1968 and 1972. However, since 1976 presidential debates have become a standard means of informing voters about the candidates' policy positions.

Nevertheless, the effectiveness of debates as teaching tools about presidential candidates can certainly be called into question. The precedent was established in the Kennedy-Nixon debates that candidates will have only a very brief amount of time in which to explain their policy positions, often no more than two to three minutes per issue. Such a brief time period generally does not allow a candidate to fully explain his or her stance on issues, particularly on complex issues that voters may not adequately understand. However, as was also established in the Kennedy-Nixon debates, they do continue to allow voters the opportunity to compare each candidate's response to similar questions and to evaluate the strength of the candidates' overall performances.

Mistakes by the candidates can trigger negative coverage in the press and reinforce any negative perceptions of the candidates that voters may already have. Two such examples occurred in recent campaigns. In 1988 Michael Dukakis bungled his answer in response to a question about whether he would support the death penalty if his wife were raped and murdered. In a similar instance of a momentary lapse in good stage presence, George H. W. Bush was caught on camera looking at his watch during a debate in 1992. Both instances received significant coverage by the media in the days following the debates. Each of these occurrences demonstrates another effect of debates that was also established in 1960: Any miscues that occur during the event can reinforce voters' preexisting negative perceptions of a candidate.

Further reading: Schroeder, Alan. *Presidential Debates: 40 Years of High-Risk TV.* New York: Columbia University Press, 2000.

—Claudia Bryant

keynote address, party conventions

A keynote address is billed as one of the national party convention's most important speeches other than the acceptance speech delivered by the party's presidential nominee. Intended to rouse the party's base to work hard for their candidate's election and to set the tone for the convention, keynote addresses give parties a chance to propel rising stars into the national spotlight, reach out to specific groups of voters, showcase diversity, and eloquently encapsulate the party's message. But the addresses have taken on a lower profile in recent years, especially as television networks have reduced their convention coverage.

An established part of presidential nominating conventions, keynote speeches predate both the time when presidential candidates appeared personally at conventions to accept their party's NOMINATION (as Franklin Roosevelt first did in 1932) and the era when the party's nominee was known before the convention began. The keynoter then spoke for the party and set the tone for the campaign, no matter which candidate was chosen. Arguably the most well-known keynote speech was made by William Jennings Bryan in 1896, when he denounced the gold standard: "You shall not crucify mankind on a cross of gold." Bryan then became the Democratic presidential nominee that year.

Keynote addresses are usually delivered in the first two days of the convention, although Senator Zell Miller (D, Ga.) made his speech to the Republican convention in 2004 on a Wednesday, in part to guarantee greater television coverage. Miller, who also addressed the 1992 Democratic convention as a keynote speaker, is not the first person to address more than one convention, although he is the first to address conventions of opposing major parties. Senator Alben Barkley (D, Ky.) spoke before the Democratic conventions in 1932, 1936, and 1948, when he defined a bureaucrat as "a Democrat who has a job some Republican wants."

While the keynote address is usually delivered by a single person, the REPUBLICAN PARTY in 1972 featured three keynoters, Senator Edward Brooke (R, Mass.), Indianapolis mayor Richard Lugar, and Republican Party chair Anne Armstrong, the first woman to deliver such an address. Four years later, the DEMOCRATIC PARTY's speakers were Senator John Glenn (D, Ohio) and Representative Barbara Jordan (D, Tex.), the first African-American woman to keynote a convention. Keynote addresses are usually delivered by major party leaders—such as governors or senators—or rising party figures who lay out the reasons why their party's candidate should win election and often criticize the opposing party's candidate.

In 2004, Illinois Senate candidate Barack Obama talked about "the audacity of hope" in describing himself as the son and grandson of poor Kenyans who had big dreams for their family. He won election easily in November. Ann Richards's 1988 remarks at the Democratic convention, in which she said Vice President George H. W. Bush had been born with a "silver foot in his mouth," helped her become governor of Texas in 1990. Warren G. Harding's 1916 address, in which he called for the Republican Party to reunite after Theodore Roosevelt's 1912 Bull Moose candidacy, aided his 1920 presidential campaign.

But keynote addresses do not always catapult speakers into higher office. Then-30-year-old representative Harold Ford, Jr. (D, Tenn.), reached out to young voters in 2000, but the speech did not help his bid to become House minority leader in 2002. Several years after Representative Susan Molinari (R, N.Y.) delivered the 1996 keynote address, she left Congress for a job in television.

Keynote speakers help set the tone for the convention by addressing the issues they see as most relevant to voters. Watergate was a central campaign issue in 1976, and the choice of keynote speakers reflected that. Jordan had gained attention as a member of the House Judiciary Committee investigating the break-in and cover-up. Republicans selected Senator Howard Baker (R, Tenn.), who famously asked, "What did the president know, and when did he know it?"

Given the close 2000 PRESIDENTIAL ELECTION, Republicans sought to increase their support among Democratic voters in battleground states by inviting Miller to deliver the keynote address in 2004. After the Democratic convention had touted Senator John Kerry's (D, Mass.) status as a Vietnam War veteran, Zell Miller attacked Kerry's voting record on military issues, calling him "more wrong, more weak and more wobbly than any other national figure." Miller's angry tone led some prominent Republicans, including First Lady Laura Bush and Senator John McCain (R, Ariz.), to distance themselves publicly from some of Miller's comments. In contrast, Obama's speech, in keeping with the Democrats' emphasis on a positive convention, did not mention Bush.

Most keynote addresses are remembered because they contain well-written lines that are delivered in a stirring manner. In 1984, Governor Mario Cuomo (D, N.Y.) took aim at President Ronald Reagan's "shining city on a hill" by declaring, "There is despair, Mr. President, in faces you never see, in the places you never visit in your shining city."

Eight years earlier, Jordan noted that it would have been "most unusual" for a major POLITICAL PARTY to ask her to deliver a keynote speech in 1832, when the Democrats held their first convention. "But tonight here I am," she said.

While the keynoter still enjoys a prominent role, as the choice of a speaker is one of the few surprises between the time a candidate wins his party's nomination and the convention, other speakers often garner more attention. In 2000, Republicans did not feature a keynote speaker at their convention, but instead heavily promoted McCain and former Joint Chiefs of Staff chairman Colin Powell. In 1992, the Republican keynote address was given by Senator Phil Gramm (R, Tex.), but more attention was devoted to Pat Buchanan's controversial remarks about culture wars.

Further reading: DeGregorio, William A. *The Complete Book of U.S. Presidents: From George Washington to George W. Bush.* New York: Barnes & Noble Books, 2004; Milkis, Sidney M. *The President and the Parties: The Transformation of the American Party System since the New Deal.* Oxford: Oxford University Press, 1993.
—Mary Lynn F. Jones

Know-Nothing Party

The Know-Nothing Party was a nativist organization that achieved considerable success during its brief life span in the mid-1850s. Originally created from a fraternal organization known as the Order of the Star-Spangled Banner, the party sought to limit the influence of immigrants and Catholics. Additionally, the party drew many disgruntled voters from both the Democratic and Whig parties and would achieve an antislavery reputation in the fractious environment that characterized POLITICS in the pre–Civil War era.

Nativism grew in 1850s America due to the rapidly growing number of immigrants during this period. Many immigrants, including many Irish fleeing deteriorating conditions at home, arrived in the country lacking both money and specialized skills. Their poverty and Catholicism, coupled with the fact that in many cities immigrants outnumbered native-born residents, bred a resentment that resulted in the creation of politically significant groups.

Politically, the controversies over the issues of the day provided yet another area around which groups such as the Know-Nothings, a name given by their members' feigned ignorance of their political affiliation, coalesced. The failure of the Wilmot Proviso, the passage of the Fugitive Slave Act, and the passage of the Kansas-Nebraska Act in 1854 brought the barbarity of slavery home to many northerners and an inescapable feeling that the North had sacrificed too much politically.

While slavery and antiimmigrant feelings provided groups such as the Know-Nothings with a fertile base to recruit members, the temperance movement was also an important factor. Temperance became extremely popular among Know-Nothings as many religious leaders scorned alcohol, and the failure of temperance legislation was cited as the undue influence of immigrants.

Emboldened by their size, which by October 1854 stood at 1 million, and the political environment, the Know-Nothings quickly became a political force in the North. From 1854 to the end of 1855, the party succeeded in electing to office thousands of local officials, more than 100 members of Congress, eight governors, and the mayors of Boston, Chicago, and Philadelphia.

A pro-nativist cartoon that depicts Irish and German immigrants stealing a ballot box *(Library of Congress)*

In office, Know-Nothings implemented their agenda consisting of temperance, anti-Catholicism, and anti-immigration. In Massachusetts, Know-Nothings sought to reduce the influence of Catholics and immigrants by mandating the reading of the Protestant King James Bible in all public schools. In several New England states, militia units composed of immigrants were disbanded, and LITERACY TESTS were instituted for immigrant voters. In addition, temperance laws were initiated in several northern states through the work of Know-Nothing legislators.

Despite the size of the Know-Nothings, there was a remarkable level of disunity, as the party was comprised of thousands of loosely affiliated councils. As a result, feelings regarding slavery divided northern and southern Know-Nothings and seriously began to upset the effectiveness of the organization.

This came to a head in 1856, when the party endorsed the Kansas-Nebraska Act. Many northern members left the party at this development, with some joining the REPUBLICAN PARTY and supporting John Fremont for president. Southern Know-Nothings, on the other hand, nominated Millard Fillmore for president. During the campaign, Fillmore tried to minimize the issue of slavery and distance himself from the nativist IDEOLOGY of the party. Fillmore carried only Maryland, and Know-Nothings gradually faded into obscurity.

Further reading: Anbinder, Tyler. *Nativism and Slavery.* New York: Oxford University Press, 1992; Billington, Ray A. *The Origins of Nativism in the United States, 1800–1844.* New York: Arno Press, 1974.

—Stephen Nemeth

Ku Klux Klan (KKK)

The Ku Klux Klan (KKK) is one of the oldest, most visible, and most prominent white-supremacist and racist organizations in the United States. Members of the KKK have historically devoted themselves to opposing civil rights and liberties for ethnic, racial, social, and religious groups such as blacks, Hispanics, Jews, Catholics, and homosexuals. They are also against left-wing and libertarian movements such as the Industrial Workers of the World and the gay rights movement.

KKK members believe that racial equality and racial integration of society threaten to destroy the "White Race." Accordingly, they oppose public policies that promote social and political equality for historically disadvantaged groups, such as affirmative action and antidiscrimination laws. Their segregationist opinions with respect to the civil rights and liberties of these social groups have been nourished by a worldview that portrays the nature of humankind as hierarchical and unequal.

Known to be a paramilitary organization, the KKK terrorized blacks and civil rights activists with terrorist tactics and violence, such as lynchings, shootings, whippings, burnings, midnight raids, acid brandings, tar-and-featherings, kidnappings, torture, and castrations. Even though the menace and influence of the KKK has oscillated over the years, it has never vanished completely. In time, the KKK has developed several separate organizational branches, such as American Knights of the KKK, Christian Knights of the KKK, United Klans of America, Southern White Klans, Texas Knights of the KKK, and New York White Knights. Some prominent members of Klan-related organizations are David Duke, Virgil Griffin, Stanley McCollum, James Farrands, Louis Beam, and Robert Miles.

The Ku Klux Klan was originally founded in Pulaski, Tennessee (near the Alabama border), in the aftermath of the American Civil War. On December 24, 1865, General Nathan Bedford Forrest and other Confederate veterans organized the group. The title of the organization comes from the Greek word for circle, *kuklos*, which the members transformed into Ku Klux. The word *Klan* was then incorporated to complete the sound alliteration. An enduring myth has also survived in the United States that the title comes from the sound of the hammer of a rifle being cocked. It has been claimed that the early success of the organization heavily depended on the selection of the title, because the sound aroused curiosity and provided the organization with an immediate image of mystery, as did the initials.

KKK members have described themselves as White Protestant Christians, and their major objection was originally against black emancipation and the expansion of rights for black people after the abolition of slavery in the United States. The organization has had three distinct periods of significant strength in the political history of the United

States: in the late 19th century, in the 1920s, and during the 1950s and 1960s, when the Civil Rights movement was gaining strength.

Historically, black people were the first targets of the KKK. However, Jews, Catholics, socialists, communists, American Indians, Asians, homosexuals, and immigrants have also existed on the long hate list of the organization. Through the mid-1960s, lynching and the threat of lynching was the terror tool of choice for the KKK. Some of the most visible examples of Klan violence were the attack on Nat King Cole (a popular rhythm and blues singer) in 1957, bombings of three black churches in 1962, the murder of Medgar Evers (a civil rights leader) in 1963, and the killing of James Chaney, Andrew Goodman, and Michael Schwerner (civil rights activists) in 1964. Of course, the list is much longer.

The KKK actively participated in electoral POLITICS at various times in the political history of the United States by providing support for Democratic and Republican candidates. David Duke, a former leader of the Klan, ran for office several times in the 1980s and 1990s. The KKK tried a novel method of participation by creating its own legal party in 2003 called the Knights Party. The party refers to itself as "America's Largest, Oldest, and Most Professional White Rights Organization."

The existence of political movements such as the Ku Klux Klan demonstrates that the norms of democracy, egalitarianism, and pluralism are still not accepted by every segment of American society. On the one hand, the decreasing popularity of the KKK also demonstrates that American society is becoming more supportive of racial integration, social and political equality, and democratic norms and values.

Further reading: Lowe, David. *Ku Klux Klan: The Invisible Empire.* New York: Norton, 1967; Wade, Wyn Craig. *The Fiery Cross: The Ku Klux Klan in America.* New York: Simon & Schuster, 1987.

—Odul Celep

L

labor groups

Unlike other nations in which labor parties have been an important part of the electoral system (notably the United Kingdom), a national labor party has not taken root in the United States. Instead, at the national level, labor has attempted to influence the electoral process by supporting "friends of labor." Efforts to form labor parties have taken place primarily at the state and local levels.

In 1828, a Workingmen's Party was established in Philadelphia, and a New York party was created a year later. The party was formed by craftsmen and skilled journeymen who were concerned about their declining socioeconomic status as the young nation moved into the industrial age. The party's platform called for public schools, an end to debtors' prisons, and the enactment of legislation providing for mechanics' liens. While both the Philadelphia and New York parties enjoyed some success in local elections, by 1832 both parties had collapsed due to internal conflict, attacks by political opponents, and the adoption of their proposals by the Jacksonian Democrats.

There were other efforts to form labor parties in cities throughout the Northeast and Midwest during the period before and after the Civil War. All were unsuccessful and short-lived. In the 1870s, unemployed whites in San Francisco formed the Workingmen's Party of California. Led by Denis Kearney, the party denounced Chinese residents of the city, who they blamed for taking jobs and driving down wages. Kearney and his followers denounced San Francisco's business leaders and led violent demonstrations against the Chinese and their largest employer, the Central Pacific Railroad Company. In January 1878, the party held its first statewide convention and released a platform declaring that the U.S. government had been taken over by capitalists and that the rights of the people were being ignored. The platform called for the abolition of "coolie labor," an eight-hour work day, and the abolition of monopolies. In response, the existing political parties joined in a "nonpartisan" alliance to counter the Workingmen's Party. The party won local elections in San Francisco in 1878 and 1879 and dominated the 1879 California Constitutional Convention, forcing the passage of a number of provisions that suppressed the rights of the Chinese. By the end of 1880 the party collapsed due to infighting between FACTIONS loyal to Kearney and to Frank Roney, another founder of the party.

In 1918, the Non-partisan League in Minnesota, along with a number of labor unions, entered a SLATE of candidates in the state's elections under the name of the Farmer-Labor Party. The party became a powerful force in state POLITICS, electing Henrik Shipstead (1922) and Magnus Johnson (1923) to the U.S. Senate, and, as governor, Floyd B. Olson (1930) and Elmer A. Benson (1936). Originally, the party called for government ownership of industry. During the 1930s it supported Franklin Roosevelt's New Deal. In 1943, the party merged with the Minnesota Democratic Party to form the Democratic-Farmer-Labor Party.

Another local labor party was the AMERICAN LABOR PARTY (ALP), which was formed in New York in 1936 by leftists uncomfortable with the DEMOCRATIC PARTY. The party endorsed Roosevelt for president in 1936, 1940, and 1944, but would endorse the PROGRESSIVE PARTY's presidential candidates in 1948 and 1952. The party elected two members to the House of Representatives, Vito Marcantonio (1939–51) and Leo Isacson (1948–49). However, the perception that the party was dominated by communists led to the party's demise in 1956.

In 1944, the LIBERAL PARTY was established as an anticommunist alternative to the ALP. The party was established by David Dubinsky (the president of the International Ladies' Garment Workers' Union), Alex Rose (president of the Hatters' Union), and the theologian Reinhold Niebuhr. While the party generally supported Democrats (New York law allows minor parties to cross-endorse the candidates of other parties), it occasionally supported liberal Republicans. The Liberals supported John Anderson's INDEPENDENT presidential candidacy in 1980 and John Lindsay (1965 and 1969) and Rudolph Giuliani (1989, 1993, and 1997) for mayor of the City of New York.

The Liberal Party's support of Giuliani led to the party's estrangement from African-American Democrats and the formation of the Working Families Party (WFP) in 1998. The WFP was started by a COALITION of unions, community groups, and public INTEREST GROUPS who believed that the Liberal Party no longer represented their interests. In 2003, the party elected its first candidate to the New York City Council. In 2004, it took an active role in supporting a number of candidates in Democratic Party primaries, notably helping defeat the incumbent district attorney in Albany County who opposed reform of the state's draconian Rockefeller-era drug laws. In late 2004, the party's six-year effort to raise the state's minimum wage to $7.15 an hour came to fruition as the state legislature overrode Governor George E. Pataki's veto of the original legislation.

Throughout the 1880s and 1890s, Samuel Gompers, a founder of the Knights of Labor and the American Federation of Labor (AFL), opposed the formation of a national labor party, especially one one with a socialist platform. Such an organization would undermine Gompers's control of the labor movement and threaten the unity of the AFL. Originally, Gompers's strategy was to refrain from getting involved in politics and focus on seeking higher wages and better working conditions. Eventually, Gompers sought to influence Congress to reverse many of the antilabor decisions made by the courts, especially the use of the Sherman Anti-Trust Act to break strikes.

In 1906, the AFL presented a "Bill of Grievances" to Congress and President Theodore Roosevelt and did support a number of candidates; four were elected to Congress. Emboldened, Gompers in 1908 backed Democrat William Jennings Bryan against Republican William Howard Taft for the presidency, though a number of state and local labor federations refused to follow Gompers's lead. The defeat forced Gompers and the AFL to retreat from electoral politics. In 1924, the AFL, reacting to attacks from antiunion groups such as the National Association of Manufacturers and faced with a choice of laissez-faire conservative president Calvin Coolidge and corporate lawyer John W. Davis, endorsed Senator Robert LaFollette, Jr., the Progressive Party candidate for president. This was the first time in 16 years that the AFL endorsed a presidential candidate, and LaFollette polled 17 percent of the POPULAR VOTE.

During the New Deal, the Democratic Party promoted collective bargaining by securing the passage of the National Labor Relations Act (Public Law 74-198) in 1935. A year later, a proposal at the AFL convention to work for the establishment of a labor party was rejected.

In 1938, the Council of Industrial Organizations (CIO) established a COMMITTEE ON POLITICAL EDUCATION (COPE). After Congress prohibited unions from making financial contributions to political campaigns (the War Labor Disputes Act of 1943, also known as the Smith-Connally Act), the CIO established a segregated fund, commonly known as a POLITICAL ACTION COMMITTEE (PAC). After the AFL-CIO merger, COPE had three goals: to make workers aware of the records and promises of candidates running for elective office, to encourage workers to register and vote, and to endorse candidates at local, state, and federal levels.

During the 1960s, labor groups played a significant role in supporting the adoption of a number of "Great Society" policies including Medicare, the Elementary and Secondary Education Act, Civil Rights laws, and the "War on Poverty." During this time, AFL-CIO leader George Meany worked closely with Lyndon Johnson to secure passage of Great Society programs and solidify the alliance between the Democratic Party and organized labor. This relationship became strained during the 1970s as insurgents challenged the leaders of organized labor and the Democratic Party.

In 1977, the Citizen Labor Energy Coalition was formed to build coalitions between labor unions, citizens' groups, and public interest organizations to create a progressive liberal agenda. One of the group's leading figures was William Winpisinger, president of the International Association of Machinists. In 1982, the group supported 35 candidates for the United States Senate and House of Representatives, with 30 winning. By 1985, the group had been absorbed by Citizen Action.

In the late 1980s, the AFL-CIO's Lane Kirkland developed a close relationship with Jim Wright, the Democratic SPEAKER OF THE HOUSE OF REPRESENTATIVES, helping reestablish the alliance between the leading labor organization and the Democratic Party. While generally supporting Democratic candidates, there have been instances when the labor movement was divided. The Teamsters broke with the AFL-CIO to support Richard Nixon in 1972, Ronald Reagan in 1980 and 1984, and George H. W. Bush in 1988. In 1984, the AFL-CIO, hoping to influence the outcome, endorsed former vice president Walter Mondale for president, the first time the federation supported a candidate for president prior to the primaries. While labor's support was crucial to Mondale in securing the Democratic Party's NOMINATION, it became a liability during the GENERAL ELECTION CAMPAIGN as President Ronald Reagan's campaign attacked the "special interests" behind the former vice president.

In 1993, labor groups opposed NAFTA, the North American Free Trade Agreement among the United States, Canada, and Mexico. President Bill Clinton's support of the legislation, in the face of fierce labor opposition, was evidence of the decline in importance of organized labor, even to a Democratic president.

In 2000 and 2004, the AFL-CIO endorsed Democrats Al Gore (2000) and John Kerry (2004) prior to the PRESIDENTIAL PRIMARIES as the movement sought to maintain its influence in the party's selection of its candidate. Other labor groups that were active in the 2004 election were the American Federation of State, County and Municipal Employees and the Service Employees International Union, the American Federation of Government Employees, the Communications Workers of America, the American Federation of Teachers, and the International Brotherhood of Teamsters.

Labor groups have seen their influence in the electoral process diminish. This can be attributed to a number of factors. First, the percentage of union members in the workforce has declined from 35 percent in the mid-1940s to less than 13 percent today. Also, the public's perception of unions has changed, with many seeing unions as just another special interest group, while the number of corporate groups seeking to influence the political process has skyrocketed.

However, unions maintain a degree of influence. The teachers' unions, the National Education Association (NEA) and American Federation of Teachers (AFT), have become quite influential. Overall, labor groups remain influential due to the financial support they provide candidates through their PACs, the paid and volunteer staff they provide to campaigns, their "in-kind" contributions of goods and services, and the higher voter turnout in union households. In 2004, union households accounted for one of four voters, almost 27 million voters.

Further reading: AFL-CIO. Available online. URL: http://www.aflcio.org. Accessed August 10, 2005; Dark, Taylor E. *The Unions and the Democrats: An Enduring Alliance.* Ithaca, N.Y.: Cornell University Press, 1999; Form, William. *Segmented Labor, Fractured Politics: Labor Politics in American Life.* New York: Plenum Press, 1999; Gieske, Millard L. *Minnesota Farmer-Laborism.* Minneapolis: University of Minnesota Press, 1979; Greene, Julie. *Pure and Simple Politics: The American Federation of Labor and Political Activism, 1881–1917.* Cambridge: Cambridge University Press, 1998.

—Jeffrey Kraus

lame duck

Lame duck refers to an elected official who remains in office after having been defeated in an election and before the successor begins his or her new term. The term also includes those elected officials serving out the remainder of their terms having chosen not to run for reelection or, due to TERM LIMITS, facing ineligibility for another term in office. The expression dates back to 18th-century England, in which a defaulter was regarded as a lame duck. Though the term was originally used in America in the early 19th century with respect to a defaulter, the first recorded political use of the phrase was by Vice President Andrew Johnson.

The passage of the TWENTIETH AMENDMENT altered the period of time between elections and inaugurations in an effort to avoid the corruption that had previously surfaced in Congress during the "down" periods following a formal session. Though the amendment sought to end the considerable amount of time before the new session began, it did not directly prohibit Congress from reconvening. Prior to recent elections, it was rare that Congress would convene for a lame duck session following the November elections. With the coming of a highly partisan Congress and the necessity to pass spending bills following the 1994 election, it has become commonplace (with the exception of 1996) for Congress to convene for lame duck sessions.

With respect to a single official qualifying as a lame duck (i.e., the president at the end of his second term or a governor facing term limits), elected officials generally try to distinguish themselves during their final years in office in order to complete their agendas. Often the lame duck will also use this period of time to support causes he or she may have been uncomfortable supporting when facing an election and scrutiny from the public. For instance, he or she may grant pardons and issue executive orders in the remaining months in office.

Further reading: Hedtke, James R. *Lame Duck Presidents: Myth or Reality.* Lewiston, N.Y.: E. Mellen Press, 2002.

—Molly Clancy

Lane v. Wilson 307 U.S. 268 (1939)

Lane v. Wilson saw the U.S. Supreme Court strike down an Oklahoma law that required some voters to register during a 12-day period of time or forever lose their right to vote. In November 1910, the Oklahoma State Constitution was amended to prohibit from voting those who could not pass the state's LITERACY TEST, which required that prospective voters be capable of reading and writing some section of the state's constitution to the satisfaction of election officials. The amendment, however, did make some allowance for those who were illiterate. If either they or their ancestors had been entitled to vote as of January 1, 1866, Oklahoma would not deny them the right to vote regardless of whether they could read or write. While race-neutral on their surface, such GRANDFATHER CLAUSES were commonly used in southern states to discriminate against 20th-century black voters whose enslaved forefathers were not permitted to vote. Ruling in *Guinn v. United States* (1915), the Supreme Court struck down the Oklahoma amendment, holding that the use of grandfather clauses in this manner was an unconstitutional violation of the FIFTEENTH AMENDMENT.

In response, the Oklahoma legislature passed a law that revised VOTER REGISTRATION requirements in the state. According to the statute, all those who had voted in the previous GENERAL ELECTION in 1914 remained on the registration roles as qualified voters. All others desiring to vote were required to register between April 30 and May 11, 1916. Failure to do so would result in the permanent loss of the right to register and, consequently, vote. The issue finally reached the U.S. Supreme Court in 1939 after a black man was denied the opportunity to register to vote in the 1934 election because he had not registered during the 12-day period in 1916.

This law and its narrow 12-day registration window presented obvious difficulties to anyone who had not voted in the previous election. As Justice Felix Frankfurter held in his opinion for the majority in *Lane v. Wilson*, the impact of the law on African Americans in Oklahoma was particularly acute, since the 1914 election had been conducted while the grandfather clause amendment was still in place. Ruling that the Fifteenth Amendment "nullifies sophisticated as well as simple-minded modes of discrimination," the Court struck down Oklahoma's registration scheme as unconstitutional.

—Steven P. Brown

League of Conservation Voters

The primary mission of the League of Conservation Voters (LCV) is to support candidates for federal, state, and local offices who it believes support a pro-environment agenda. The organization targets vulnerable incumbents it would like defeated and supports preferred candidates in key races. The LCV pursues these ends by taking part in voter education, voter mobilization, and direct contributions to candidates through its POLITICAL ACTION COMMITTEE. The group also encourages VOTER REGISTRATION, activism, and GRASSROOTS lobbying by its supporters.

Founded in 1969, the League of Conservation Voters annually publishes its Environmental Scorecard to inform citizens about the voting records of elected representatives in environmental matters. It also publishes a Presidential Report Card each year to grade the environmental policies of the president. Since 1996, the League of Conservation Voters has also published a list of legislators it identifies as the worst environmental offenders in Congress and labels them the Dirty Dozen. These individuals are targeted by the organization for electoral defeat. The LCV also selects candidates each ELECTION CYCLE as Environmental Champions and offers them support when faced with formidable electoral challenges. In addition to its focus on the federal level, the League of Conservation Voters is also affiliated with a number of organizations that perform similar functions at the state and local levels. The LCV is headquartered in Washington, D.C.

In the new era of campaign finance established by the Bipartisan Campaign Reform Act of 2002, the League of Conservation Voters and similar groups may rise in prominence as federal regulations permit them to continue accepting unlimited SOFT MONEY donations from unions, corporations, and individuals, while forbidding political parties from doing so. However, the LCV has historically relied exclusively on donations from individuals. The organization has aided hundreds of candidates in achieving electoral victories and claims a success rate of approximately 80 percent among those it formally endorsed. The League of Conservation Voters has on occasion come under fire from conservatives for supporting more DEMOCRATIC than REPUBLICAN PARTY candidates, but the group regularly expresses opposition and support for individuals from each party, citing their records on environmental issues as justification.

Further reading: Gottlieb, Robert. *Forcing the Spring: The Transformation of the American Environmental Movement.* Washington, D.C.: Island Press, 1993; League of Conservation Voters. Available online. URL: http://www.lcv.org. Accessed August 10, 2005; Rosenbaum, Walter. *Environmental Politics and Policy.* 5th ed. Washington, D.C.: CQ Press, 2001.

—Richard L. Vining, Jr.

League of Women Voters

The League of Women Voters (LWV) was founded February 12–18, 1920, by Carrie Chapman Catt during the national convention of the National American Woman Suffrage Association (NAWSA). As the successor of the NAWSA, the original mission of the LWV was to be a temporary organization to integrate newly enfranchised women into the political system. The league sponsored citizenship schools to educate and mobilize women in 1920, the first election after the adoption of the NINETEENTH AMENDMENT, and offered 13 planks for inclusion in the national party platforms. Initially fearing the power of women's vote, the REPUBLICAN PARTY endorsed five of the positions, and the DEMOCRATIC PARTY, 12.

The LWV was active on many women's issues after SUFFRAGE. It supported protective labor laws for working women, equal pay, jury service for women, and the right of women to retain U.S. citizenship after marriage to an alien. And despite the league's strict policy of nonpartisanship, members were encouraged to become active in the party of their choice, and many women have been trained and motivated to seek elective office.

During much of its history, however, the LWV has preferred to be classified as a public INTEREST GROUP rather than as a woman's group. The league is known for providing objective information on candidates and issues before elections, support of reforms in campaign law and finance, and sponsorship of candidate forums and debates on all levels. Although it does not endorse candidates or political parties, it does select local, state, and national issues for study and takes policy positions. It was a key supporter of the National Voter Registration Act of 1993 (MOTOR VOTER LAW). In

The League of Women Voters registers a group of women to vote, 1923. *(Corbis)*

1976, 1980, and 1984, the league through its education fund sponsored and organized the national PRESIDENTIAL DEBATES, which had not been held since 1960. It withdrew sponsorship in 1988 with rule changes that gave control of the debates to the party nominees.

The LWV, with its 130,000 members (including men since 1974) and 1,000 local chapters, is a respected source for unbiased information on VOTER REGISTRATION, candidates' views, and government structure. The league supports issues such as direct popular election of the president, full voting rights for the residents of the District of Columbia, and public financing for CONGRESSIONAL ELECTIONS. Beginning in the 1970s, the league rejoined the women's rights COALITION with support of the Equal Rights Amendment, legalized abortion, and Title IX, among other issues.

Further reading: Black, Naomi. *Social Feminism.* Ithaca, N.Y.: Cornell University Press, 1989; League of Women Voters. Available online. URL: http://www.lwv.org. Accessed August 10, 2005; Stuhler, Barbara. *For the Public Record: A*

Documentary History of the League of Women Voters. Westport, Colo.: Greenwood Press, 2000; Young, Louise M. *In the Public Interest: The League of Women Voters, 1920–1970.* New York: Greenwood Press, 1989.

—Janet K. Boles

Liberal Party

The New York Liberal Party was born of a dispute that rent the AMERICAN LABOR PARTY in two, and it has participated in every PRESIDENTIAL ELECTION as one of the principal minor parties in New York State since 1944. The party was initially formed by members of the International Ladies Garment Workers Union and endorsed Franklin Roosevelt and the rest of the DEMOCRATIC PARTY's candidates in the 1944 election. Under New York's unique election laws, any party could endorse another party's candidates without any provisos or qualifications, thus allowing for the proliferation of minor political parties that endorsed major party candidates, drawing voters who would vote for the candidates if not for their association with a particular POLITICAL PARTY.

The party was the principal third party in New York State until 1962, when the Conservative Party was formed to be a counterweight to the REPUBLICAN PARTY as a direct response to the counterweight function of the Liberal Party for the Democrats. Liberals endorsed every Democratic Party nominee for president since the party's creation, with the exception of 1980, when they endorsed the NATIONAL UNITY CAMPAIGN of Republican congressman John Anderson. They also provided a ballot line to Republican senator Jacob Javits in the GENERAL ELECTION against Conservative Party endorsee Alfonse D'Amato in 1980, when Javits had lost the Republican PRIMARY to D'Amato. They also endorsed several Republican nominees for mayor of New York City, providing more votes than the margin of victory for Republican mayor Rudolph Giuliani in 1993 and 1997. The media attributed that support less to Giuliani's liberal leanings than to the aid of so-called Liberal Party "boss" Raymond Harding, a longtime Giuliani ally who served in his administration.

In recent years, the Liberals have attempted to accomplish the same goal as that of many minor parties in New York—gain access to as high a line on the BALLOT as possible by winning as many votes as possible in the GUBERNATORIAL ELECTION. In both 1998 and 2002, Liberals endorsed a contender for the Democratic gubernatorial NOMINATION who later lost the primary. In 1998, the party gained more than 75,000 votes (much more than the required 50,000 votes for a ballot line), coming in fifth behind the Republican, Democratic, Independence, and Conservative parties, when its candidate had never formally withdrawn her candidacy, and the party ran ads touting its candidate as a "pro-choice woman." In 2002, the party's nominee formally withdrew from the race days before the Democratic primary and won only 15,000 votes in the general election on the Liberal line, which the party had hoped to avoid by withdrawing its ENDORSEMENT, but the deadline for any replacement had come and gone. Thus, the Liberal Party did not garner the necessary 50,000 votes in a gubernatorial election to gain permanent ballot line status for the next four years. Most of the leaders abandoned the party thereafter, leaving a tiny FACTION to supposedly "reopen" the party's doors after they had been closed by the ballot box.

Further reading: Edwards, Lee. *The Conservative Revolution: The Movement That Remade America.* New York: Free Press, 2002; Javits, Jacob K. *Javits: The Autobiography of a Public Man.* New York: Houghton Mifflin, 1981; Liberal Party. Available online. URL: http://www.liberal party.org. Accessed August 10, 2005.

—Daniel T. Kirsch

Libertarian Party

The Libertarian Party is a minor POLITICAL PARTY in the United States that emphasizes complete personal and economic freedom and a government of greatly reduced and limited powers. A party with a philosophy that mixes an advocacy of free-market economics and a defense of personal freedoms, the Libertarians have often been one of the largest and most active THIRD PARTIES in American POLITICS.

The Libertarian Party was founded on October 11, 1971, in Westminster, Colorado, by a group of eight individuals known as the Committee to Form a Libertarian Party. These early founders created the party as a means to address the perception that the country was drifting from the libertarian ideals set forth by the founding fathers. One of the most significant signs of this drift, according to many of those early Libertarians, was the Nixon administration's imposition in early 1971 of wage and price controls.

Having been founded the previous year, the Libertarian Party fielded its first presidential ticket in 1972. The ticket was led by Joseph Hospers, a philosophy professor at the University of Southern California, and Theodora Nathan, a businesswoman from Oregon. The ticket was on only four state BALLOTs and received 2,600 votes, but the one electoral vote garnered by the team represented the first electoral vote received by a woman on a presidential ticket. By 1976, the Libertarian Party ticket, headed by Roger MacBride and vice presidential candidate David Bergland, achieved BALLOT ACCESS in 32 states and garnered 170,000 votes.

The growth of the early party can be attributed to the work of Edward Crane, one of the founders of the party and the first national chair of the party. It was through his work that the party recruited David Koch and ran a significant campaign in 1980. Koch, a wealthy donor, became the nominee of the party and spent nearly $2 million to run a respectable campaign that gained ballot access in every state, the first party to do so since the Socialists in 1916. Despite the infusion of cash, the ticket of Koch and Ed Clark received only 900,000 votes, or 1.1 percent of the total vote. While Koch's money did not have the intended result, his contributions to the party furthered its aims by helping found the Cato Institute to promote and communicate libertarian ideas.

In 1984, on the ballot in 39 states, the Libertarian SLATE of David Bergland and Jim Lewis received more than 270,000 votes. In 1988, former Republican congressman Ron Paul ran as the party's nominee and received a little more than 421,000 votes. The party had hoped that by nominating Paul, they would receive a boost in votes due to using a candidate with an existing CAMPAIGN ORGANIZATION. In 1992, Andre Marrou, a Libertarian member of the Alaska house of representatives, received 291,000 votes and came in in fourth place behind Perot. In 1996, economist and author Harry Browne ran and received 485,000 votes, a fifth-place finish behind Perot's REFORM PARTY and Ralph Nader's GREEN PARTY. In 2000, Browne ran again and received 384,000 votes, placing him behind Nader's Green Party and Pat Buchanan's Reform Party.

While libertarianism is a unique amalgam of political philosophies, libertarian thought can be characterized by its reliance on two main themes. The first is its reliance on Social Darwinism and its concomitant belief that, much like nature, the strong survive in society. The second is the objectivist philosophy of Ayn Rand, which emphasizes the power of the individual will. Additionally, in order to become a member of the Libertarian Party, one must affirm rejection of the use of force as a means of achieving political or social goals.

The most recent ideals of the Libertarian Party can best be seen through its platform created in Indianapolis in July 2002. Throughout, an emphasis is placed on the ability to make decisions free from government interference, the sanctity of privacy, the inviolability of civil rights, and a minimally regulated free-market economy. As a result, the party advocates a substantial reduction in the size of the federal government through eliminating government involvement and spending in medicine, education, and welfare. By dramatically limiting the size of government, they hope to eliminate the need for a federal income tax, funding government costs instead through existing tariffs and excise taxes.

A controversial aspect of the Libertarian platform is its support of the repeal of existing drug laws and an end to the "War on Drugs." Libertarians advocate an end to drug laws by citing their impact on civil liberties and the growth of government power. By ending drug laws, libertarians hope to reduce the profit of the illicit drug trade and reduce crime. Additionally, libertarians call for freeing more prison space by pardoning convicted nonviolent drug offenders.

While Libertarians do not hold any national office, they have been successful in local elections, with nearly 600 Libertarians holding a variety of offices around the country. In recent years, the Libertarian Party has had to contend with reinvigorated third parties such as Ross Perot's Reform Party and the Green Party. Additionally, it has had to contend with its unique small government, absolute personal freedom message being co-opted by the two major parties. Republicans have been siphoning off supporters from the Libertarian Party by offering a similar ideology and a more politically established organization.

While disenchanted voters have traditionally been the Libertarian Party's greatest strength and reservoir of support, the rise of other third parties has been a significant obstacle to the Libertarians. This, coupled with the ever-present threat that their message may be taken by the major parties, presents the two main dangers to the party. While the Libertarian Party has some difficulties to overcome, the perception that government has continued to grow and that civil liberties are increasingly under attack, especially as a result of recently enacted antiterrorism legislation, is likely to provide the party with the necessary support to remain a meaningful third party in future elections.

Further reading: Libertarian Party. Available online. URL: http://www.lp.org. Accessed August 10, 2005; MacBride, Roger L. *A New Dawn for America: The Libertarian Challenge.* Ottawa, Ill.: Green Hill Publishers, 1976; Ness, Immanuel, and James Ciment, eds. *The Encyclopedia of Third Parties in America.* Armonk, N.Y.: M.E. Sharpe, 2000.
—Stephen Nemeth

A 1976 campaign pamphlet from the Libertarian Party National Convention *(Duke University Special Collections Library)*

likely voter

A likely voter is someone who will probably cast a ballot in an election. Polls of randomly selected respondents that are conducted before an election provide an estimate of the overall support for candidates and ballot measures. However, those estimates may differ from the results on ELECTION DAY since not everyone votes. The ability to gauge the status of an electoral race depends, therefore, on the ability to identify likely voters.

This is why polling results must be scrutinized to determine who the sample includes. If it includes all respondents from a RANDOM SAMPLE, then the results may not predict the outcome of the election very well. If it includes only registered voters, then the results will more accurately reflect the eventual outcome. However, the most accurate predictions will come from polls that report the results from registered voters who are also likely to vote.

The usual method of identifying likely voters is simply to ask the survey respondents who say they plan to vote on election day a follow-up question. For instance, they may be asked if they definitely will vote, if they probably will vote, or if they are leaning toward voting. Likely voters might then be defined as those who say they will definitely vote, or they might be defined as those who say they either definitely or probably will vote. Another criterion that is sometimes used is whether the respondents report having voted in the last national election if they were of voting age.

While every polling organization would like to be able to accurately identify likely voters, they are all subject to limitations. Many people do not know for certain whether they will vote, and even those who say they definitely will vote may fail to cast a BALLOT. Another problem is that voting is a socially desirable act, and surveys are usually conducted through a conversation between two people. This places social pressures on respondents to overstate the likelihood that they will vote.

New technologies in surveying may help attenuate this so-called social desirability problem. Polls conducted over the phone with a computerized interviewer voice and Internet polls that use random sampling methods are more anonymous. Since no living, breathing person is asking the questions, some respondents may feel more comfortable admitting they may not vote. For the foreseeable future, however, the thorny problem of identifying likely voters will continue to challenge political pollsters, leaving some mystery in the projections of electoral outcomes.

Further reading: Asher, Herbert. *Polling and the Public: What Every Citizen Should Know.* Washington, D.C.: CQ Press, 2001; Freedman, Paul, and Ken Goldstein. "Building a Probable Electorate from Pre-Election Polls: A Two-Stage Approach." *Public Opinion Quarterly* 60, no. 4 (1996): 574–587; Kelly, Stanley, Jr. "Pre-Election Polling: Sources of Accuracy and Error." *Public Opinion Quarterly* 53, no. 4 (1989): 613–615; Perry, Paul. "A Comparison of the Voting Preferences of Likely Voters and Likely Nonvoters." *Public Opinion Quarterly* 37, no. 1 (1973): 99–109.

—Francis Neely

Lincoln-Douglas debates

While often mistaken as PRESIDENTIAL DEBATES, the first of which did not take place until a hundred years later in 1960, the KENNEDY-NIXON DEBATES, the Lincoln-Douglas debates were a series of seven senatorial debates that took place in Illinois during the late summer and early fall of 1858. Abraham Lincoln challenged the much better-known incumbent, Senator Stephen Douglas, for the U.S. Senate seat from the state of Illinois. They debated against a backdrop that included the Kansas-Nebraska Act of 1854, the Dred Scott decision of 1857, and the hard-fought and divisive congressional rejection of the pro-slavery Lecompton Constitution for Kansas.

Although it has been cast as a fight between pro-slavery and antislavery forces, the debate was actually a contest between two northern perspectives on slavery in the Union. Lincoln, the Republican, believed that slavery was immoral and should not be permitted to spread into the newly acquired territories of the Union. Douglas, the northern Democrat, adhered to the principle of "popular sovereignty," according to which the people of a state and, more controversially, a territory, which derived its authority from Congress, were free to permit or forbid slavery. Although he is cast as a proponent of slavery, Douglas was hated by the southern slave forces for having broken with the Buchanan administration by leading the fight in Congress against the Lecompton Constitution, which would have admitted Kansas as a slave state.

A corollary of the popular sovereignty argument was the Freeport Doctrine, which was, in effect, an answer to the following question: "Can a territory prevent slavery from taking root?" (The Freeport Doctrine was named for the town in Illinois in which it was supposedly initially enunciated, though Douglas had actually answered this question long before the debate in Freeport.) Though the Dred Scott decision appeared to deny a territorial legislature this power, Douglas asserted that slavery could be excluded from a territory if the territorial legislature refused to pass "friendly legislation," which slavery required to take root, survive, and thrive. Douglas was walking a fine line, attempting to reconcile the doctrine of popular sovereignty, which asserted that territorial legislatures could prevent slavery from taking hold, with the Dred Scott case, which held that territorial legislatures held no such power.

Although the partisan press universally declared its candidate the victor in the debates, it is likely that Lincoln benefited less from his showing in the debates than from the exposure he received by sharing a platform with the better-known senator. While Lincoln won the POPULAR VOTE in the state's November election, Douglas won more legislative districts. The state legislature, which controlled elections to the U.S. Senate until ratification of the SEVENTEENTH AMENDMENT, was in the hands of the Democrats and elected Douglas to the U.S. Senate seat. In 1860, however,

Lincoln got the "bigger game" that he was reportedly after, defeating Douglas, among others, for the presidency.

Further reading: McPherson, James M. *Battle Cry of Freedom: The Civil War Era.* New York: Oxford University Press, 1988; Potter, David M. *The Impending Crisis: 1848–1861.* New York: Harper & Row, 1976; Zarefsky, David. *Lincoln, Douglas and Slavery: In the Crucible of Public Debate.* Chicago: University of Chicago Press, 1990.

—Lawrence Anderson

literacy test

Literacy tests were tests of reading and writing skills given as a condition of voting and were used as part of the systematic practice to disenfranchise African Americans in the South following RECONSTRUCTION. Together with other discriminatory practices, including GRANDFATHER CLAUSES, white primaries, and Jim Crow laws, literacy tests were given by southern state governments to impede voting opportunities for blacks.

At the time literacy tests were used, most southern blacks were either undereducated or not educated at all, making it extremely difficult for them to pass literacy tests. Moreover, most literacy tests were given at the discretion of local election officials, which in practice meant that blacks were required to take the test, while whites, who were often poorly educated in the South at this time, were rarely tested. Officials asked blacks to read long passages from the state constitution or pieces of classical literature. Blacks would also be asked specific questions, such as "Do you know the meaning of the word turpitude? What are interrogatories? What is the FIFTEENTH AMENDMENT to the Constitution? Can you detail the three branches of government?"

In response to literacy tests, some voting rights activists developed "cheat sheets." Their aim was to arm blacks with the correct answers so that they could not be denied the right to vote on the basis of literacy tests. In Dallas County, Alabama, an elderly black woman stated that it took her eight tries and eight years to get registered to vote. She stated that each year after taking the literacy test, she and other blacks would receive a letter in the mail stating that they did not qualify to vote because they had incorrectly answered a question. The VOTING RIGHTS ACT OF 1965 eventually ended the use of literacy tests and many other discriminatory electoral practices in the United States and helped give African Americans equal access to the ballot box.

Further reading: Barker, Lucius Jefferson, Mack Jones, and Katherine Tate. *African Americans and the American Political System.* Upper Saddle River, N.J.: Prentice Hall, 1998; Bennett, Larone. *Before the Mayflower: A History of Black America.* New York: Penguin Group, 2003; Clayborne, Carson, et al. *The Eyes on the Prize Civil Rights Reader.* New York: Penguin Group, 1991.

—F. Erik Brooks

lobbyist

A lobbyist is a person, usually a paid professional, who attempts to influence elected officials in order for the officials to propose, enact, or defeat legislation supporting the lobbyist's interests. The official term dates back to the House of Commons, where members of Parliament met with their constituents in the halls (called louba) and became a commonplace expression in the late 1800s in American POLITICS. Lobbyists play a key function in politics as they attempt to further the goals of specific INTEREST GROUPS.

Lobbyists can be found on the local, state, and federal levels, where they attempt to influence everything from funding playground construction projects to bills proposing restrictions on workman's compensation. Each year, lobbyists spend billions of dollars attempting to gain support for their causes. Often, those familiar with the inner workings of Congress (e.g., former staffers and congresspeople) move from the public sector to lobbying because of their familiarity with the nuances of the governmental system and the lucrative salaries these positions offer. They generally have knowledge of the key issues and acquaintance with the players instrumental in helping their cause. In order to further their goals, they must not only be familiar with the setting but also adept at communicating their interests through both verbal and written material.

Though lobbyists are often seen as trying to "buy" favor within the American political system, they can be beneficial to congresspeople and their staffs, who often do not have the time or experience to learn the minute details of technical subject matter. Though the information may be biased in favor of the lobbyist's organization, it is not unheard of for lobbyists to help members of Congress draft legislation by which they benefit. As a lobbyist's influence is generally a function of his or her ability to persuade elected officials to take action, the primary source of influence comes from the quality of the information provided and the reputation that he or she has developed. While lobbyists may push their agendas on all levels, it is up to the lawmakers to sift through the information they receive in order to develop an agenda that best suits their constituents' interests.

Further reading: Birnbaum, Jeffrey H. *The Lobbyists: How Influence Peddlers Work Their Way in Washington.* New York: Times Books, 1992.

—Molly Clancy

M

machine politics

Machine POLITICS is characterized by "under the table," ward-based control of municipal politics, most notably during the post–Civil War era through the Depression. Machines dominated in a period characterized by rapid urbanization and increased industrialization. In the preindustrial city, political power seekers emerged as demand for a variety of governmental resources soared. Political machines were found mainly in larger cities such as New York, Chicago, and Philadelphia. Each city's machine was run by a "boss," a person who had the loyalty of elected officials and who had the power to effect change and development in the city.

The machines formed in cities mostly as a consequence of the enormous waves of immigration to the United States in the late 19th century and the demands brought on by rapid population increases. For instance, the population of New York City increased by more than 800,000 people from 1820 to 1870. By 1870, Irish and German immigrants composed nearly 50 percent of the city's population. The immigration influx exerted pressure on the inadequate urban infrastructure, from streets and buildings to transportation systems. In certain areas, water shortages combined with a lack of sufficient sewage systems created a formidable public health hazard. The traditionally fragmented nature of local politics made responding to such critical events difficult and slow-going.

In an era when demands for these resources were far outpacing the speed with which traditional routes of government could supply them, bosses and their machines expedited the distribution of resources in exchange for political "favors," such as voting for machine-sponsored candidates and hiring certain individuals for a given job. Bosses thus became formidable power brokers who aided new immigrants in a variety of ways, from handing out private loans and negotiating rent prices with landlords to helping immigrants become naturalized citizens and find PATRONAGE jobs.

Bosses could "make things happen." If there were a pothole on the street, the boss and his underlings had the means to address the problem. If an elected official needed to win an election, he could organize voters at the local level or use illicit tools, such as blackmail or outright ballot box stuffing, to achieve the desired result. Entrepreneurs sought financial and political assistance from the bosses. For instance, they would make arrangements with the boss in order to win a certain franchise or to circumvent restrictions on permits. Individuals more inclined to earn their profits in the black market sought the machine's protection in running gambling and racketeering rings. The entrepreneurs and racketeers would thank the boss by contributing generously to the machine.

In the machine era, urban industrialization and development went hand in hand with the growth of the machine. The politically savvy boss would eagerly adopt new construction projects that modernized the city, for such modernization not only improved the city's landscape overall but also provided vast numbers of patronage jobs for the machine's political supporters. Machine politicians spent and borrowed great sums of money in an effort both to sustain the growing urban landscape and to sustain the machine itself. In fact, a great deal of the work undertaken by the machine was tied back to nourishing the financial and political needs of the machine itself. In order to "stay alive," the machine needed money and strong political support. Money was used in a variety of ways, from supporting the campaigns of machine candidates, to providing loans to needy immigrants, to funding metropolitan projects.

The classic example of a political machine run amok was the notorious Tammany Hall machine in New York City headed by "Boss" Tweed. In 1860, William Marcy Tweed became the chairman of the New York County Democratic Party and the leader of the Tammany Club, a powerful fraternal organization that had long dominated New York politics. An iron triangle developed between the Tammany Club, the DEMOCRATIC PARTY, and the office of the New

York City mayor, giving Boss Tweed unprecedented influence on all aspect of New York politics and making him one of the most powerful figures in the country and also one of the most corrupt. It is estimated that approximately $75 million to $200 million was stolen from city government between 1865 and 1871.

The growing corruption and underhanded dealings of the political machines were anathema to individuals (particularly middle-class and upper-class skilled workers) who did not rely on the machines for their livelihood. The Progressive Era was established by the time Teddy Roosevelt became president of the United States. Progressive reformers successfully instituted both political and social changes that issued critical blows to the increasingly enervated political machines.

At the social level, Progressive reformers were successful at publicizing the wrongdoings of the machines, with MUCKRAKING journalists employing mass media, sensational novels, and other means to "spread the word." As the reputations of the machines became increasingly tarnished, public sentiment increased in favor of political reform. The social change in public perception of the machine truly paved the way for the political reform instituted by the Progressives.

Political institutional reform came in a multitude of ways. In the early 1880s, the Federal Civil Service Reform Act (otherwise known as the PENDLETON ACT) eliminated most patronage jobs at the federal level, replacing them instead with merit-based classified positions. Applicants to certain positions would need to take a standardized test known as the Civil Service Exam and obtain a certain score in order to be considered for a civil service position. The nonpartisan BALLOT and shortened AUSTRALIAN BALLOT were institutional means of reducing the role of the party in electoral politics. On nonpartisan ballots, only candidate names with no partisan identification were present. The Australian ballot was a secret ballot that was not party-specific; it was considerably shorter than the long ballot that listed large numbers of party loyalists running for a variety of offices under the party label. DIRECT PRIMARY elections also served to weaken the party apparatus, as elections became more candidate-centered at the cost of the party. Certain states, starting with Oregon in 1902, enacted the initiative, in which citizens could initiate legislation directly, and the REFERENDUM, in which citizens could directly vote for or against proposed legislation.

In sum, an educated ELECTORATE, the eventual acclimation of immigrants and their families to their new environment, civil service reform, political reform, and large-scale change in social perceptions of the machine all weighed in against the continuation of the political machine in post–World War II America. As the industry-based economy of the United States shifted to postindustrialism, the lifeblood of the political machine was slowly drained. The market was increasingly characterized by fewer unskilled jobs. Businesses and the middle-class workforce moved farther and farther from center cities into the suburbs. All of these forces helped to change the landscape of American politics in the early to mid-20th century and led to the eventual demise of the political machine.

Further reading: Erie, Steven P. *Rainbow's End: Irish-Americans and the Dilemmas of Urban Machine Politics, 1840–1985.* Berkeley: University of California Press, 1990; Riordan, William. *Plunkett of Tammany Hall.* New York: E. P. Dutton, 1963.

—Dari E. Sylvester

machine politics, Byrd

While MACHINE POLITICS often denotes a negative, even unlawful, vision of government control by a single person or entity, Harry Byrd's grip on Virginia politics over the early to mid-20th century was marked by power, influence, and prestige. Indeed, Byrd described his political base not as a machine, but euphemistically as "a loose organization of friends, who believe in the same principles of government."

Harry Flood Byrd was born in 1887 to a middle-class family with a respectable legal and political heritage and quickly made his name known in local politics. Byrd won his first office as city councilman in 1909 and in 1915 successfully ran for the state senate.

During Byrd's rise to power, the Democratic machine, known as the "Organization," was already in place. The organization, which included Harry's father, Henry Byrd, and uncle Hal Flood, maintained power in Virginia by mutual protection, PATRONAGE, disenfranchisement of opponents, and legislative and elective rule making. Harry quickly became an integral member of the organization, fulfilling several roles including fuel administrator, highway administrator, and, of course, state senator.

In 1922, Byrd was unanimously elected chairman of the state committee and effectively took over the leadership of the organization, renewing its fervor with an efficient vote-getting apparatus and tightening its control over all branches of state government. The early years of his chairmanship continued the organization's history of disenfranchising women and minorities to assure an extremely low turnout of swayable voters. He effectively used the organization to become governor of Virginia in 1926, where his use of patronage appointments further cemented his place at the top of Virginia's Democratic political apparatus.

Although hampered by an unsuccessful presidential bid in 1932, Byrd was popular enough in Virginia that Claude Swanson, then the senior U.S. senator, took a cabinet post in the Roosevelt administration to avoid what would have been an embarrassing loss to Byrd in 1934. Being appointed to the position vacated by the senior senator (by the current governor he helped bring to power), Byrd quickly set to work sending patronage jobs back to Virginia, which were particularly needed while the country fought its way out of the Great Depression. It was the start of an extensive career in the U.S Senate, where he was known for "bringing home the bacon" while maintaining his hardened control over Democratic politics in Virginia.

Harry Byrd spent the next 32 years fighting for conservative ideals in Washington while simultaneously assuring Virginia's enlarged slice of federal dollars. While his staunch conservatism alienated him from some of the party faithful over those years, his personal connections, financial sway, and political cunning continued to support the "Organization" until his death in 1966.

Further reading: Heinemann, Ronald L. *Harry Byrd of Virginia*. Charlottesville: University Press of Virginia, 1996; Crawley, William Bryan, Jr. *Bill Tuck: A Political Life in Harry Byrd's Virginia*. Charlottesville: University Press of Virginia, 1978.

—Jeremy B. Lupoli

machine politics, Crump

Edward Hull Crump, also known as "Boss Crump," was the Democratic mayor of Memphis, Tennessee, from 1911 to 1916, U.S. representative from 1931 to 1935, and holder of various local offices from 1905 to 1940. He presided over the Memphis and Shelby County Democratic machine from 1911 until 1954. He dominated Tennessee state POLITICS from 1930 to 1948 and continued to play a leading role in Memphis politics until his death. Often called "wily" or a "sly fox" by admirers and detractors, Ed Crump was the quintessential old-time southern PARTY BOSS. His ability to virtually control elections through manipulation of the large African-American vote via the state's POLL TAX, his carefully cultivated public image as a reformer, his artful selective enforcement of laws and business taxes to keep residential tax rates low and the quality of life in Memphis high, and his control of the vote totals in every election in Memphis and surrounding Shelby County for more than 30 years became key to his success statewide.

Living in a state divided geographically and politically three ways, between eastern Republican, central (Nashville), and west (Memphis), Crump was able to parlay his control of the Memphis Democratic machine into control of the city and, later, the county, due partly to the fact of significantly larger Democratic enrollment in the city and county than Republican. This was also true of the state. As the winning FACTION in the Democratic PRIMARY in Tennessee, as with most southern states in the first half of the 20th century, he invariably won against the Republicans in any statewide election. Crump's organization became a solid bloc that was able to deliver western Tennessee's votes to whichever faction with which he chose to ally himself. The ability to deliver as much as 85 percent of a primary or GENERAL ELECTION vote in Shelby County and western Tennessee to whatever candidate or party he endorsed enabled Crump to build up enough power and influence to virtually select several governors and U.S. senators, as well as completely control the state legislature and most of the congressional delegation for two decades.

Crump's power lasted until several major newspapers began a campaign to rid the state of the poll tax, a restrictive measure disproportionately prohibitive of African-American voters. Crump had used payment of the poll tax as a method of controlling African-American votes since the start of his career, and the public pressure on Crump and his machine officeholders became too great to bury the repeal of the discriminatory law in the business of the legislature. The resulting backlash was evident in the 1948 campaign, in which Crump was not able to deliver a sizable enough majority in western Tennessee for his statewide SLATE of candidates to win for the first time since 1930. He died six years after this defeat, and no leader of the Shelby County organization or the state of Tennessee ever again reached the zenith of power that Edward Hull Crump had exercised. African-American voters, however, had organized both in opposition to and in concert with Crump's organization, and after his death they were considered one of the most politically active African-American communities in the southern states.

Further reading: Miller, William D. *Mr. Crump of Memphis*. Baton Rouge: Louisiana State University Press, 1964; Tucker, David M. *Memphis since Crump: Bossism, Blacks, and Civic Reformers 1948–68*. Knoxville: University of Tennessee Press, 1980; Wright, Susan D. *Race, Power, and Political Emergence in Memphis*. New York: Garland, 2000.

—Daniel T. Kirsch

machine politics, Daley

The *Daley Machine* is the term for DEMOCRATIC PARTY political dominance in Chicago and Cook County, Illinois, from 1953 to the early 1970s, led by Mayor Richard J. Daley. Daley was considered the most powerful political figure in the state of Illinois, earning him the monikers of "boss" and "kingmaker." The Daley Machine was perhaps the most centralized and effective of the metropolitan political machines in the history of the United States, and arguably the most corrupt as well.

Richard J. Daley (1902–76) rapidly rose through the ranks of the existing Chicago Democratic Party machine. He was first elected to the state legislature in 1936, serving 11 years in the house and senate and accumulating political favor within the Cook County Democratic Committee. By 1953, Daley had maneuvered into the committee chairmanship, the pivotal position of power within the machine.

By 1955, Boss Daley had been elected to the first of five terms as mayor of Chicago, establishing himself as the singular leader of the Chicago political machine.

The Daley Machine can be characterized by a series of mutually reinforcing relationships, all designed to accumulate, protect, and consolidate political and economic power. Major contributors to the party were rewarded with lucrative city contracts for public works projects. Government jobs of all levels were given to those who exhibited strong loyalty to Daley and the machine. Loyalty mainly consisted of voting for the Daley-approved Democratic SLATE of candidates or ensuring VOTER TURNOUT and "proper" voting in the many citywide districts. It was not uncommon for money and liquor to be used as voting incentives. Coercion and intimidation were also frequently used, and records show that individuals would even "vote" from the grave. Daley politicians regularly won by large margins, discouraging political rivals from challenging the machine. Opposition often resulted in punishment, such as revocation of business licenses or delay and denial of city-issued permits to those who dared openly contest or disagree with the machine.

Boss Daley had his finger on every aspect of the city: Media feared his tendencies toward retribution, political subordinates dared not attempt to accumulate too much power, the business community's economic health relied on staying in Daley's good graces, and many loyal citizens' livelihoods depended on the success of the machine. The most infamous episode in Daley's legacy was the 1968 Democratic National Convention, an event marred by violence outside the convention hall and political mayhem within. The Daley Machine legacy can be seen everywhere in the city of Chicago, from the elaborate expressway and transportation systems to the high-rise condominiums lining Lake Michigan. The political legacy of the Boss is also evident in his son Richard M. Daley, who has served as the mayor of Chicago since 1989.

Further reading: Biles, Roger. *Richard J. Daley: Politics, Race and the Governing of Chicago.* DeKalb: Northern Illinois University Press, 1995; O'Connor, Len. *Clout: Mayor Daley and His City.* Lincolnwood, Ill.: NTC/Contemporary Publishing, 1984; Rakove, Milton L. *Don't Make No Waves—Don't Back No Losers: An Insider's Analysis of the Daley Machine.* Bloomington: Indiana University Press, 1976; Royko, Mike. *Boss: Richard J. Daley of Chicago.* New York: Plume, 1988.

—Joel A. Rayan

machine politics, Tammany Hall

Tammany Hall refers to the one of the most famous, or infamous, political machines in American history. Tammany Hall was a DEMOCRATIC PARTY machine that existed at its height in New York City from the 1850s until the 1930s.

The Tammany Hall political machine grew from patriotic societies that were formed after the American Revolution. Several of these societies were created in cities scattered across America, with rituals drawing from pseudo–Native American traditions. The group owes it name to the famous Delaware Indian chief Tammany and was originally called the Society of Saint Tammany. The New York branch thrived and eventually became the heart of Jeffersonian POLITICS in New York City. Before the turn of the 19th century, Tammany Hall was controlled by Aaron Burr, who used the organization to help support Thomas Jefferson for president in the election of 1800.

Tammany Hall became a major player in politics after supporting Andrew Jackson for president in 1828 and 1832. Though the organization supposedly stood for common working people, it was largely controlled by those of privilege and power. Tammany Hall expanded its power throughout the 1840s by recruiting newly arrived immigrants into its society.

The social support of new immigrants reflects what most scholars classify as the typical "political machine." The machine would help newly arrived foreigners obtain jobs, CITIZENSHIP, housing, and numerous immediate needs. Prior to the modern welfare state, machines also commonly provided food, clothing, and rent money for families in need. In return, they expected full electoral support. Fraudulent voting practices, graft, corruption, intimidation, and occasionally violence were all negative elements of machines.

The most famous "boss," or leader, of Tammany Hall probably was William M. Tweed. Boss Tweed controlled Tammany Hall from the 1850s until the 1870s. He was remarkable because of his vast power base. Most bosses until Tweed were content with controlling their city. Tweed used the Tammany Hall machine to exert power on the state legislature, influencing financial allocations to New York City as well as other state services. Through the Tweed Ring within New York City, it is estimated he defrauded the city of at least $30 million through fraudulent charges and blatant profiteering. Though Tweed remained popular among his supporters and the poor, by 1870, detractors began to work toward his removal from power. The political cartoonist Thomas Nast published many illustrations critical of Tweed's abuses of power. These humorous, but often scathing, attacks helped sway public support toward the eventual fall of Tweed.

The Tammany Hall machine continued to dominate and corrupt New York City politics until about 1932. The machine lost several key elections that year and never was able to recapture its former strength. Mayor Fiorello LaGuardia (1933–45) was also instrumental in weakening the grip of Tammany Hall on city politics. Eventually, as with many other city machines, the social programs of the New Deal undermined their power. The development of the social welfare state assumed many of the roles machines

A political cartoon portraying William M. Tweed as a bullying schoolteacher giving New York City comptroller Richard B. Connolly a lesson in arithmetic. *(Library of Congress)*

used to ensure voting blocs. In addition, women's SUF-FRAGE and limitations on immigration during the early years of the 20th century further helped weaken the power of the Tammany Hall system.

Tammany Hall machine politics saw a brief revival following World War II under the control of Carmine De Sapio. However, with all the social and economic changes within society, even the Democratic Party was growing tired of the old machine-style system. Reformers within the party increasingly attacked the Tammany Hall machine, and it finally ceased to exert influence on New York politics by the early 1970s.

Further reading: Moscow, Warren. *The Last of the Big-Time Bosses: The Life and Times of Carmine De Sapio and the Rise and Fall of Tammany Hall.* New York: Stein & Day, 1971; Myers, Gustavus. *The History of Tammany Hall.* New

York: Boni & Liveright, 1917; Riordon, William L. *Plunkitt of Tammany Hall.* New York: Knopf, 1948.

—Shannon L. Bow

mail voting

Mail voting refers to voting in elections using the U.S. Postal Service. This type of voting can be accomplished in two ways: ABSENTEE VOTING and vote-by-mail. All states allow for mail voting in cases of absentee voting. If a person will not be able to vote on ELECTION DAY for any of the reasons listed by the elections board, that voter may request an absentee BALLOT. This ballot is equivalent to the ballot the other voters receive on election day. However, the voter must mail it to the elections board, and the elections board must receive it before the appropriate deadline, often 8:00 P.M. on election day. These ballots are then counted, and the totals are added to the regular election returns. Many states reserve the counting of these ballots until after initial returns are counted and count them only in the event that the election is close enough to warrant the extra effort and cost (i.e., if the margin of victory by the winning candidate is less than the total number of absentee ballots).

The second form of mail voting is the vote-by-mail system as practiced in Oregon. In 1981, Oregon initiated a test of the vote-by-mail system. By 1987, the system was made permanent, and the 1993 statewide election was conducted entirely using the vote-by-mail procedure. Finally, through the use of the initiative process, Oregon expanded the vote-by-mail system to include all GENERAL and PRIMARY elections in the state, including the special Senate race of 1996 and the PRESIDENTIAL PRIMARY and election of 2000. In the Oregon system, the elections board mails the ballots to registered voters approximately three weeks before the election. The voter completes the ballot, places it in the secure envelope, signs the outside of that envelope, places the envelope inside a second envelope, and mails it to the county election office. The ballot must be received by 8:00 P.M. on election night. In an effort to avoid the charge that postage acts as a POLL TAX, each voter has the option of depositing the ballot at designated drop-off boxes.

The vote-by-mail system has many advantages over the traditional system. It reduces voting barriers, increases VOTER TURNOUT, and saves taxpayer money. On election day, many people are often unable to take time away from their busy schedules to vote at the PRECINCT. Vote-by-mail makes voting more convenient. Recent studies show that while only 4.1 percent of the voters stated they voted less often under vote-by-mail, 29.3 percent stated they voted more often. Finally, elections are much less expensive to hold when done by the mail. As staffing the precincts is no longer necessary, vote-by-mail reduces the cost of a ballot from $4.33 for traditional elections to $1.24 on average. Critics of this method of voting point to the possibility of voter fraud when voting takes place in a nonsecure location.

Further reading: Magleby, David B. "Participation in Mail Ballot Elections." *Western Political Quarterly* 40 (1987): 79–91; Southwell, Priscilla L. "Five Years Later: A Re-Assessment of Oregon's Vote by Mail Electoral Process." *PS: Political Science and Politics* 37 (2004): 89–93; Southwell, Priscilla L., and Justin Burchett. "Survey of Vote-by-Mail Senate Election in the State of Oregon." *PS: Political Science and Politics* 30 (1997): 53–57.

—Ole J. Forsberg

majority-minority districts

A *majority-minority district* denotes a legislative district that contains a majority of a racial group that exists as a minority in the general population. Majority-minority districts have been used to advance minority representation, particularly in the 1990s. They are created to increase the chance that a member of a minority group will be elected to public office. Majority-minority districts were originally designed to overcome the "first-past-the-post" system of single-member plurality electoral districting systems, most commonly found in districts for the U.S. House of Representatives and state house and senate districts. Using the VOTING RIGHTS ACT OF 1965, advocates of descriptive representation (i.e., representation based on physical characteristics such as race) have pushed for majority-minority districts to increase minority representation in government.

Following passage of the 1965 Voting Rights Act, the percentage of registered black voters skyrocketed, particularly in the southern states that had previously restricted voting among African Americans. Building on the success of the Voting Rights Act, civil rights leaders fought for the creation of majority-minority districts to increase the chance of electing black representatives. Some civil rights leaders interpreted sections two and five of the Voting Rights Act as advocating the creation of majority-minority districts. Section two, as amended in 1982 and interpreted in a series of court decisions, prohibits a state from enacting a REDISTRICTING plan that "results in the denial or abridgement of the right of any citizen of the United States to vote on account of race or color" or because a person is "a member of a language minority group." A "language minority group" is defined as "American Indian, Asian American, Alaskan Native or of Spanish heritage." The 1982 amendments and court decisions did not explicitly mandate that majority-minority districts be drawn. However, states had to justify when they had sufficient minority populations as to why they did not create majority-minority districts. Section five required any changes in voting "standard, practice, or procedure" be preapproved by either the U.S. attorney general or the U.S. District Court for the District of Columbia. The redrawing of district lines following REAPPORTIONMENT and CENSUS reporting is considered to fall under this requirement.

The U.S. Supreme Court in the 1986 case of *Thornborg v. Gingles* (478 U.S. 30) held that in order for such districts to be created, three preconditions must be met. First, it must be possible to create a majority-minority district. This criterion is satisfied if a minority group has a majority of the district's voting age citizens. Second, the minority group must be cohesive in its support of its preferred candidate, that is, that candidate should receive more than half of the minority vote. Third, the majority group must vote sufficiently as a bloc to generally defeat the minority group's preferred candidate. There would be no dilution if minority and majority groups preferred the same candidates or if the minority group's preferred candidate won.

Using these criteria, legislators pressed state legislatures to create majority-minority districts within several of the southern states following the 1990 census. Following reapportionment, 15 new African-American majority-minority districts and 10 new Latino majority-minority districts were created between 1990 and 1992. These districts became the battlegrounds of heated legal challenges over the constitutionality of majority-minority districts.

Most notable in the legal challenges was North Carolina's 12th CONGRESSIONAL DISTRICT. Beginning west of Charlotte, the district stretched 160 miles, snaking up interstate highways from Charlotte through Winston-Salem and Greensboro and ending in Durham. In one part of the district, it was only one lane of Interstate 85. The 12th Congressional District was drawn in order to provide a second majority-minority district in North Carolina, which after the 1990 census had a 20 percent black population. The district was challenged in court, and in the 1993 case of *SHAW v. RENO* (509 U.S. 630), the U.S. Supreme Court held that districts that included voters of a particular race but were drawn in a bizarre manner could be considered racial GERRYMANDERING and that white voters had a right to challenge such districts. The Supreme Court remanded the case to a district court for trial to determine whether North Carolina's 12th and 1st congressional districts were racially gerrymandered. In 1994, a three-judge panel in U.S. district court dismissed the remanded case, saying that while it was racial gerrymandering, North Carolina served a compelling government interest in drawing the districts to advance black representation. While appeals were made of the dismissed case, the U.S. Supreme Court refined the *Shaw* doctrine to focus solely on whether race was the predominant factor in drawing majority-minority districts.

In 1996, the U.S. Supreme Court handed down two important cases. In *Bush v. Vera* (517 U.S. 952 [1996]), the Court ruled that the drawing of majority-minority districts "must not subordinate traditional districting principles to race substantially more than is reasonably necessary." Along with the *Vera* ruling, the Court overturned the lower court's ruling regarding the North Carolina districts and declared that the 12th Congressional District was an unconstitutional racial gerrymandering and must be redrawn (*Shaw v. Hunt,* 517 U.S. 899 [1996]). Following the drawing of a more compact majority-minority district and further legal challenges, the U.S. Supreme Court held that the 12th Congressional District was constitutional. In Associate Justice Steven Breyer's majority opinion, the 12th district was not racial gerrymandering because the district was drawn due to partisanship and that race happened to correlate to partisanship (*Hunt v. Cromartie* 523 U.S. 234 [2001]). Since POLITICS served as the predominate factor in drawing the district's lines, challenges to majority-minority districts faced a heavier burden when using a *Shaw* claim of unconstitutional racial gerrymandering.

The use of majority-minority districts following the 2000 census and reapportionment continues to spark political and legal debates. However, a number of districts are becoming majority-minority status simply due to population changes, particularly among Latinos within the country. As of 2004, the *Almanac of American Politics* found 92 of the 435 U.S. House districts have a population that is majority-minority (non-white), with either a plurality of black, Asian, or Latino residents or a combination of the three minorities constituting a majority within the district.

Further reading: Canon, David T. *Race, Redistricting, and Representation: The Unintended Consequences of Black Majority Districts.* Chicago: University of Chicago Press, 1999; Kousser, J. Morgan. *Colorblind Injustice: Minority Voting Rights and the Undoing of the Second Reconstruction.* Chapel Hill: University of North Carolina Press, 1999; Lublin, David. *The Paradox of Representation: Racial Gerrymandering and Minority Interests in Congress.* Princeton, N.J.: Princeton University Press, 1997; Yarbrough, Tinsley E. *Race and Redistricting: The Shaw-Cromartie Cases.* Lawrence: University Press of Kansas, 2002.

—J. Michael Bitzer

majority party

The term *majority party* simply means the POLITICAL PARTY that has more than 50 percent of the membership of whichever body is under consideration. Most often the term refers to the party that has the majority in a legislative chamber. Thus, from 1954 through 1994, the DEMOCRATIC PARTY was the majority party in the U.S. House of Representatives. That meant that the SPEAKER OF THE HOUSE was a Democrat and the chairpersons of all House committees were Democrats. The majority party in a legislature determines which policy proposals will be considered as well as the schedule for holding hearings on proposals. That party also decides when and if a bill is to be debated, the amount of time for debates, and the fate of the bill, unless there are defections from the majority party that are sufficient to defeat the intention of that party's leaders.

The term *majority party* may also refer to party strength among the ELECTORATE. Thus, it may signify that in a particular state Republicans have a majority of the registered voters. Not all states require registration by party. In a state such as Indiana, where one may not register by party, this basis for determining the majority party is unavailable. The majority party among the electorate can also be based on PARTY IDENTIFICATION, which is the psychological affinity that voters may have for political parties. In this case, the majority party might be determined by public opinion surveys.

Voting statistics are also employed to determine the majority party among the electorate. Thus, if the Democrats, as was the case for many years, persistently win elections by a substantial majority in the southern states, one presumes the majority party in that region is the Democrats. In this situation, persons who would ideologically support the REPUBLICAN PARTY may register as Democrats in order to have a better chance of being elected to office or of influencing who will be nominated by the Democrats and thus be the likely victor in the GENERAL ELECTION. Moreover, with few registered voters, the Republican Party might forgo PRIMARY elections, since the expense of such elections might not be justified. These were practices found in some southern states until Republicans began to be successful at the polls.

Further reading: Aldrich, John. *Why Parties? The Origins and Transformation of Political Parties in America.* Chicago: University of Chicago Press, 1995; Milkis, Sidney. *The President and the Parties: The Transformation of the American Party System since the New Deal.* London: Oxford University Press, 1993; Sabato, Larry, and Bruce Larson. *The Party's Just Begun: Shaping Political Parties for America's Future.* 2nd ed. New York: Longman, 2002.
—Thomas Phillip Wolf

malapportionment

Malapportionment is an unequal distribution of population across a designated political unit. For example, in elections for the U.S. Senate, the state is the political unit, and each state is allocated two senators. In U.S. Senate contests, because state populations are not equal, by definition this is an example of malapportionment. Consider the difference in the number of votes cast in U.S. Senate ELECTIONS in California and Montana. Because there is a smaller ELECTORATE in Montana compared to California, Montana residents are overrepresented. By contrast, California residents are underrepresented since this larger electorate is represented by the same number of senators.

Malapportionment is a phenomenon as old as representative democracy. In the United States at the Constitutional Convention in 1787, the most important compromise centered on how to arrange a system of federal representation acceptable to DELEGATEs from states of small and large populations. The solution, known as the Connecticut Compromise, was to give each state two senators, while each state's number of representatives was determined by population.

The ELECTORAL COLLEGE, the mechanism used for electing presidents, is another example of malapportionment. Each state's number of electoral votes is assigned according to the size of its congressional delegation (U.S. representatives plus U.S. senators). Since small states are overrepresented in the Senate, they are also overrepresented in the Electoral College. Under this system, it is possible to win the POPULAR VOTE and lose the election by failing to win a majority of electoral votes. This happened in 2000 when Democrat Al Gore won the popular vote and Republican George W. Bush won the election by winning the majority of electoral votes.

In the 1960s, several court decisions placed limitations on malapportionment. States that had generally overrepresented rural districts at the expense of representation in urban centers were instructed to redraw their congressional district boundaries to comply with a one-person, one-vote rule. In contemporary U.S. House elections, after every decennial CENSUS, states with enough population for at least two representatives must redraw districts with equal populations.

Malapportionment is generally considered to be harmful to an electoral system because it enables candidates to win elections without capturing the most votes, and this can violate the democratic principle of majority rule. Malapportionment is also controversial because it can lead to an unequal distribution of political power. For example, some federal dollars are allocated according to state population. Before the equal population requirement, politically savvy U.S. representatives who represented sparsely populated CONGRESSIONAL DISTRICTS often secured the lion's share of federal funds.

Despite the negative effects of malapportionment, it is impossible to completely eliminate it. Take the case of U.S. House elections. Because district populations in a state have to be equal, this means that district populations across states will not necessarily be equal. And among states that do not have enough population to have more than one representative, these states will not have equal district populations because no states have the same number of persons. Also, the U.S. Census routinely undercounts certain groups, especially minorities and illegal immigrants. Finally, uneven population growth means that many districts have equal populations only at the time of REDISTRICTING.

Further reading: Ansolabehere, Steven, Alan Gerber, and Jim Snyder. "Equal Votes, Equal Money: Court-Ordered Redistricting and Public Expenditures in the American States." *American Political Science Review* 96 (2002): 767–777; Cain, Bruce E. *The Reapportionment Puzzle.* Berkeley: University of California Press, 1984; Cain, Bruce, and David Butler. *Congressional Redistricting: Comparative and Theoretical Perspectives.* New York: Macmillan, 1992; Cox, Gary W., and Jonathan N. Katz. *Elbridge Gerry's Salamander: The Electoral Consequences of the Reapportionment Revolution.* Cambridge: Cambridge University Press, 2002; Rush, Mark E., and Richard L. Engstrom. *Fair and Effective Representation? Debating Electoral Reform and Minority Rights.* New York: Rowman & Littlefield, 2001.
—Seth C. McKee

mandate

Mandate refers to the idea that votes for a particular politician represent an ENDORSEMENT of his or her ideals and policy ideas or a particular policy idea that he or she espoused during the campaign. When a politician claims to have a mandate, this is considered an electoral justification not only of previously expressed ideas but also a call to particular policy action in accordance with those ideas.

The concept of a mandate comes from the idea of a general will. In this conceptual framework, an election is a chance for "the people" to not only express their preference of a particular candidate but also to express their preferences for the policy direction of the country. Applied to the American context, presidents are said to have a mandate based on the margin of their victory. Presidents and sometimes congressional majorities use the concept of a mandate to justify changes to the status quo, arguing that their electoral victories signal voters' preference for their proposed policies, or policies motivated by a certain ideological orientation.

The concept of a mandate is commonly linked to a demand for a change in the status quo. A specific example of the use of the mandate concept in a congressional context is the 1994 Republican takeover of the House of Representatives and the subsequent push for conservative policies on the grounds that such policies had been endorsed by the ELECTORATE. Similarly, the Clinton administration interpreted the 1992 presidential victory as a mandate for the Clinton national health care plan. In both of these cases it was not clear that the policies supposedly mandated by the electorate actually fit the preferences of the majority of the electorate.

The concept of a mandate has come under criticism on both theoretical and practical grounds. Theoretically, the mandate concept ignores the fact that there is no perfect democratic decision rule. Therefore, the idea of a general or collective will of the people is dubious. The concept of mandates assumes that the result of an election is a perfect reflection of the preferences of the electorate, which is highly unlikely.

On a practical level, this comes up against the question of what kind of victory must be won in order to constitute a mandate. For instance, it is not clear whether a president with a wide margin of victory due to large margins in a few states or districts has a greater mandate than one who won by narrower margins in more states.

Another practical problem with the concept of a mandate is that it may read too much into the meaning of votes. There is no way to be sure that voters are endorsing any particular policy when they support a particular candidate. Since personalities rather than parties and programs are increasingly important in political races, an electoral victory may be less of an endorsement of a candidate's platform and more of a demonstration of his or her personal appeal.

In the American context, the separation of powers allows for "dual mandates"—potentially differing mandates for the legislature and for the president. Under circumstances of divided government, it is unclear which party's agenda has been endorsed by the electorate (ignoring the theoretical problems identified previously). For example, in a midterm congressional election the president's party might lose seats, potentially negating the president's previous mandate. This is particularly problematic in light of the

fact that, like the president, Congress as a whole represents the entire country, but individual members of Congress represent their states or districts.

Since a mandate is a vague concept and difficult to assess or measure, politicians sometimes interpret electoral victories as mandates but discover that their policies do not have popular or congressional support. Another manner in which perceived mandates backfire against politicians is when they are said not to have adequate mandates to enact certain policies given the size of their margins of victory.

Several contemporary examples can illustrate these points. After his 1992 presidential victory, Bill Clinton was said to have interpreted his victory as an endorsement of his health care plan—a mandate to enact a certain proposed policy. Instead, the plan met with opposition from the public and from Congress and failed to become policy. In the absence of a perfect democratic decision rule, winning an election did not mean that President Clinton's ideas were endorsed by the general will. Although Clinton won the election according to the established rules, he received only 43 percent of the POPULAR VOTE, while George H. W. Bush received 37 percent, and H. Ross Perot received almost 19 percent. In other words, more people who went to the polls in 1992 voted for a presidential candidate other than Clinton than voted for him. This arguably did not constitute strong public support for his proposed policies. Furthermore, there is the possibility that voters who chose Clinton did so for reasons other than his policy preferences, such as dislike of the incumbent president or partisan reasons.

An instance in which a president has been accused of overstepping the bounds of his mandate occurred in the early months of George W. Bush's presidency, during which he announced support for government funding for "faith-based" charities, pulled funding for international family planning agencies that performed abortions, and otherwise pursued a strong socially conservative agenda. Commentators criticized these actions on the grounds that Bush's mandate was inadequate because the 2000 PRESIDENTIAL ELECTION was so close (and Bush had, in fact, lost the popular vote).

Further reading: Conley, Patricia Heidotting. *Presidential Mandates: How Elections Shape the National Agenda.* Chicago: University of Chicago Press, 2001; Heith, Diane J. *Polling to Govern: Public Opinion and Presidential Leadership.* Stanford, Calif.: Stanford Law and Politics, 2004.
—Julia R. Azari

marginal district

Legislative districts are generally drawn to reflect dominance by one of the two major parties (i.e., each district has a majority of registered Republicans or registered Democrats that makes them SAFE SEATS for one party or the other). There is no hard and fast rule about the exact percentage that makes a district safe for a party. Some people consider 55 percent, but most seem to think 60 percent or more makes a district safe for one party and at least 55 percent "leaning" to one party. It helps to measure these standards by comparing both party registration and actual voting outcome. Other districts with more closely balanced VOTER REGISTRATION and election outcomes are considered marginal districts that could and do lean in favor of either party at different times.

In marginal districts, candidates tend to win by narrow margins, hence the name. Beyond the fact of balanced party registration, other factors tend to influence the outcome in such districts. The influence of campaign spending, incumbency, third-party (SPOILER) candidates, and outside influences from the state and national parties and special INTEREST GROUPS all become factors. In elections that can be decided by a few hundred votes or less, and certainly by just a few percentage points, smaller issue groups and less-powerful organizations can become viable avenues for electoral success.

The irony of marginal districts is that they would seem to yield "middle-of-the-road" candidates with moderate political views. Nevertheless, such districts also seem to spark highly competitive spirits among the parties, with the outcome being that party primaries often end up choosing more partisan, that is to say liberal and conservative, candidates.

A frequent example used as a marginal district is the Ohio Sixth CONGRESSIONAL DISTRICT, often considered a BELLWETHER for PRESIDENTIAL ELECTIONS. After the 1990 elections, the seat was held by long-time incumbent Bob McEwen, a conservative known both for "bringing home the bacon" (i.e., attracting government spending) to his district and for his willingness to publicly berate liberal causes. But REDISTRICTING threw McEwen into a nasty 1992 PRIMARY with another incumbent that left him stumbling to the victory line with fewer than 300 votes. He was beaten in the GENERAL ELECTION by liberal-leaning Ted Strickland. Strickland, in turn, served one term and was ousted by Frank Cremeans, a staunch conservative who was washed in with the conservative tide of 1994 that gave the House back to Republicans for the first time in 40 years. Cremeans squeaked in over Strickland at 51 percent to 49 percent. Two years later, Strickland would come back for a rematch and win by just 2 percentage points.

It is also important to note that there are relatively few marginal districts. In Gary Jacobson's book *The Politics of Congressional Elections,* he refers to what he calls "the vanishing marginals." Due to incumbency factors and highly fine-tuned redistricting, the number of seats considered competitive between parties is far fewer than in the past, and even those are likely to be competitive only in the absence of an incumbent.

Further reading: Flanigan, William H., and Nancy H. Zingale. *Political Behavior of the American Electorate.* 10th ed. Washington, D.C.: CQ Press, 2002; Jacobson, Gary C. *The Politics of Congressional Elections.* 6th ed. New York: Pearson/Longman, 2004; Thompson, Dennis F. *Just Elections: Creating a Fair Electoral Process in the U.S.* Chicago: University of Chicago Press, 2002.

—Jack St. Croix

matching funds

Matching funds are subsidies to PRESIDENTIAL PRIMARY candidates, financed through a voluntary check-off on individual taxpayers' IRS returns. Presidential primary candidates who raise at least $5,000 in contributions of $250 or less in at least 20 states receive funds matching the first $250 of every contribution from an individual received during the election year. Individuals who receive matching funds must agree to limits on their spending, both nationally and in each state. These amounts are indexed to inflation; for candidates in the 2004 primaries, the limit on total spending was $49 million, and the limits on spending in each state, which are based on the size of the state, ranged from $675,600 in New Hampshire to $13.1 million in California. Candidates lose their eligibility for matching funds if they receive less than 10 percent of the vote in two successive primaries, but matching funds are restored if a candidate receives at least 20 percent of the vote in a later PRIMARY. Candidates who receive matching funds must also agree to limit their personal spending to $50,000. Matching funds are available only during the primary elections; during the GENERAL ELECTIONS, candidates receive full public funding.

Matching funds were introduced as part of the 1974 amendments to the Federal Elections and Campaigns Act. The intent of matching funds was to increase the role of small donors in campaigns and to enable viable candidates to have a steady source of funding throughout the primaries. Virtually all competitive primary candidates received matching funds from 1976 through 1996. Some observers have credited matching funds for the strong primary showings of Jimmy Carter, Ronald Reagan, George H. W. Bush, and Bill Clinton. In recent elections, however, several candidates have forgone matching funds in order to spend as much as they wished overall and in the early primary states. Republican candidate Steve Forbes declined matching funds in 1996 and 2000, and George W. Bush also declined matching funds in 2000. In 2004, Bush's announcement that he again would not accept matching funds led Democratic candidates Howard Dean and John Kerry to also decline matching funds.

There are two current issues of concern regarding matching funds. First, candidates who decline matching funds often have the ability to outraise and outspend their opponents, particularly in the "bridge" period between the point at which a candidate becomes his or her party's presumptive nominee but before the party conventions. Second, taxpayers' willingness to check off the box for matching fund contributions on their returns has declined over the past two decades, leading some to fear that there will not be enough money available in matching funds in the 2008 or 2012 elections. Several proposals have been introduced in Congress to alter the way in which matching funds are raised and distributed.

Further reading: Alexander, Herbert. *Financing Politics: Money, Elections, and Political Reform.* Washington, D.C.: Congressional Quarterly Press, 1984; Corrado, Anthony. *Paying for Presidents: Public Financing in National Elections.* Washington, D.C.: Twentieth Century Fund, 1992; Sorauf, Frank. *Inside Campaign Finance: Myths and Realities.* New Haven, Conn.: Yale University Press, 1992.

—Robert G. Boatright

McCain-Feingold Campaign Finance Reform
(Bipartisan Campaign Reform Act of 2002)

McCain-Feingold, named for sponsoring senators John McCain (R) of Arizona and Russ Feingold (D) of Wisconsin, is the popular name for the Bipartisan Campaign Reform Act of 2002, or BCRA, pronounced "Bikra." It is the most recent and important attempt since the FEDERAL ELECTION CAMPAIGN ACT (FECA) of 1974 to purge national POLITICS of the influence of "big money."

The 1996 ELECTION CYCLE saw unique interpretations of CAMPAIGN FINANCE LAWS and an unprecedented advertising campaign, largely in support of President Bill Clinton's reelection bid against Republican candidate Bob Dole. The campaign highlighted ongoing attempts to circumvent FECA, which had established disclosure requirements and source and amount limitations as well as public financing. Essentially, FECA, buttressed by the landmark Supreme Court decision of *BUCKLEY V. VALEO* (1976), had established limits on HARD MONEY—direct contributions to campaigns. The 1996 election cycle showed how candidates and incumbents were overcoming the hard limits by way of SOFT MONEY. Soft monies are indirect contributions that are not subject to the same restrictions.

The president's campaign made extensive use of POLITICAL ACTION COMMITTEE (PAC), corporate, labor, and foreign support to pay for ISSUE ADVOCACY ADVERTISING. This advertising would typically discuss the president's views on a particular policy area but did not use direct language soliciting viewers' or listeners' votes, though the message was clear. In addition, campaign practices came under scrutiny. The 1996 election is well remembered for "sleepovers" in the Lincoln Bedroom and private "coffee klatches" with the president for donors, solicitation of donations from White House offices, foreign contributions, solicitation of contributions from Buddhist monks, and the receipt of more than $3 million in illegal gifts to the DEMOCRATIC NATIONAL COMMITTEE that were later returned.

Prior to 1996, reformers had focused on extending public financing (MATCHING FUNDS) and strengthening spending limits. Following the 1996 election, they realized that the FECA limits had been overcome by events. The advent of soft money obliterated spending and contribution limits, allowed labor unions and corporate sponsors to give larger amounts than in the past, and effectively eliminated disclosure requirements.

The amount of soft contributions to party committees rose from $86 million in 1992 to $262 million in 1996 and $495 million in 2000. Reform, however, was not easily gained. Between 1985 and 1996, there were 11 major campaign bills considered in Congress. None became law, with only one reaching the president's desk, which was vetoed.

McCain-Feingold's goal was to reestablish the kind of oversight structure that had been established in 1974. It sought to regulate both hard and soft money and bolster disclosure requirements. As the *Congressional Record* indicates, it was tough sledding as various interests sought to push contribution limits higher, whether for unions, individual contributions, or businesses. Others sought higher limits for the parties and third-party groups. Finally, agreement was at hand, in part because of the political capital McCain had gained by running for president in 2000 and because President Bush let it be known that he would not veto the bill, though he thought it presented "constitutional concerns."

The BCRA prohibited the national parties from raising soft funds while allowing limited soft money to state parties and restricting how the funds can be spent. It prohibited corporations and unions from directly creating or funding advertising, though they can contribute via a PAC. Spending of more than $10,000 is to be disclosed. The BCRA largely prohibits candidates from raising soft funds and limits how soliciting can be conducted. Individual contribution limits were raised to $2,000 (indexed to inflation) per candidate, $25,000 to national parties, $5,000 to PACs, and $97,500 per two-year cycle for overall contributions.

The day after President Bush signed the bill, Senator Mitch McConnell (R) of Kentucky, among others, filed a suit challenging the constitutionality of McCain-Feingold. The suit argued that the restrictions were in violation of the First Amendment's freedom of speech clause. In sum, McConnell argued that restricting the money contributed and how it could be spent limited the ability of persons to express their views on politics and that political speech is at the heart of democracy. *McConnell v. FEC* was accepted and handed down by the Supreme Court in the fall of 2003. The Court upheld the legislation, with great deference to Congress. The majority argued that the legislation was warranted in that it would reduce the "appearance of corruption."

Since passage of McCain-Feingold, groups have found a new loophole in the law, namely a provision that allows money to be funneled through what are known as 527 groups. In 2004, over $200 million was funneled through these groups, exposing a loophole at least as large as the soft money loophole closed by McCain-Feingold in 2002.

Further reading: Anderson, Annelise. *Political Money: Deregulating American Politics: Selected Writings on Campaign Finance Reform.* Stanford, Calif.: Hoover Institution Press, 2000; Corrado, Anthony. *Inside the Campaign Finance Battle: Court Testimony on the New Reforms.* Washington, D.C.: Brookings Institution Press, 2003; Malbin, Michael J. *Life after Reform: When the Bipartisan Campaign Reform Act Meets Politics.* Lanham, Md.: Rowman & Littlefield, 2003.

—Jeff A. Martineau

McCarthyism

McCarthyism represented a prolonged effort (1948–54) to expose and root out domestic communism. The effort was championed, but not solely promoted, by the junior Republican senator from Wisconsin, Joseph R. McCarthy. Joe McCarthy was an obscure state judge who in 1946 defeated Senator Robert M. LaFollette, Jr., son of "Fighting Bob" LaFollette, the Progressive senator from Wisconsin. McCarthy entered a Congress narrowly divided between Democrats and Republicans and quickly capitalized on the anxiety of Americans who had successfully fought a two-front war in Europe against Nazi Germany and Fascist Italy and in the Pacific against imperial Japan. American hopes that the postwar world would be a safer place were dashed when the United States' former ally, the Soviet Union, moved into the power vacuum on both continents by stationing its troops in Eastern Europe, abetting the communist takeover of China in 1949, and encouraging North Korea to cross the 38th parallel into South Korea in 1950. Two nations with their contrasting economic and political systems were in conflict with each other, and their mutual suspicions and distrust led to the prolonged geopolitical

Senator Joseph McCarthy gives reporters a list of State Department employees he says are undergoing a security-loyalty check. *(Library of Congress)*

stalemate known as the cold war that was to last for almost 50 years.

Less than five years after the surrender of Japan in 1945, the iron curtain had descended over Eastern Europe, American ally Chiang Kai-shek (Jiang Jieshi) had been defeated in China, and war had engulfed the Korean Peninsula. The further discovery that the Soviets had access to nuclear weapons deepened those fears. The fact that much of the initial information provided to the Soviets came from American communists working in defense industries focused attention on internal adversaries. These were the preconditions that fueled the anticommunist crusade of Joe McCarthy. Aided by Republican allies in the U.S. House such as Representative Richard M. Nixon of California and the House Un-American Activities Committee and in the Senate by William Jenner of Indiana and his Permanent Subcommittee on Investigations, Joe McCarthy was able to parlay American anxieties into a major political force.

Waving lists of purported domestic communists before the news media, Senator McCarthy and his allies created a national climate of fear. The names of government officials and entertainment figures were those most prominently divulged. Eventually, defense industries, Protestant churchmen, academics, and even the American military fell under suspicion. It was a time of great distrust in the United States as loyalty issues seized the agenda.

For Joe McCarthy, anticommunism was a vehicle to advance his political career and to become a power broker within the REPUBLICAN PARTY. For conservative Republican leaders such as Senators Robert Taft of Ohio and Styles Bridges of New Hampshire, McCarthy's anticommunist crusade was an opportunity to stigmatize the DEMOCRATIC PARTY and the previous 20 years of President Franklin Roosevelt's New Deal agenda of economic and social change. They used McCarthyism to gain control of both the House and the Senate in the 1952 election.

Late in 1953, Senator McCarthy overreached when he turned his ire on the Republican Eisenhower administration and brought senior officials of the U.S. Army before his committee to contend that they had been harboring known communists in their midst. The dramatic confrontation between Senator McCarthy and Robert Welch, the army's lead counsel, was televised, and McCarthy's eagerness to engage in reckless accusations cost him support among the American citizenry. In late 1954, McCarthy was censured by the Senate, and the 1954 takeover of the Senate by the Democrats placed him in the minority and rendered him ineffective. Although Joe McCarthy's career was short-lived, his name has become affixed to an era of unfounded accusations, fear, and anxiety, negatively immortalizing him in American political life.

Further reading: Oshinsky, David. *A Conspiracy So Immense: The World of Joe McCarthy.* New York: Free Press, 1983; Rovere, Richard H. *Senator Joe McCarthy.* Berkeley: University of California Press, 1996; Schrecker, Ellen. *Many Are the Crimes: McCarthyism in America.* Boston: Little, Brown, 1998.

—Garrison Nelson

media and elections

Both elections and the media are central to our democracy, as elections determine who represents the citizenry, affecting public policy for years to come, and because the media inform the public, helping it to determine which issues and candidates to support. Interestingly, the media affected the American public even before there was an official country to govern. Publications such as Thomas Paine's *Common Sense* and Alexander Hamilton, James Madison, and John Jay's FEDERALIST PAPERS were widely read and highly influential during the nation's founding period. Paine's work brilliantly argued the case for war with England, while the *Federalist Papers* provided the intellectual basis for adopting the Constitution.

This early period in American history preceded the development of strong political parties. As the press developed, it became standard procedure for political operatives to support newspapers to promote their ideas. In many of these early papers, there was no pretense of objective reporting, as the paper often printed stories beneficial to its patron. In the election of 1824, Andrew Jackson lifted this practice to new heights. Jackson offered papers amenable to his ideas the opportunity to print government documents and laws, while denying the same chance to unfriendly papers.

Over time, and with the PENNY PRESS that made news consumption more affordable to the mass public, newspapers slowly began to become more independent, working to provide objective coverage to candidates. As newspapers gathered more readers, they sought to treat political leaders and ideas more fairly. While newspaper editors and reporters did not remove themselves from POLITICS, they did, in general, make an effort to avoid the perception of being in the pocket of a particular person or party. The founding of the Associated Press in 1848, a wire service that served as a collector of foreign news that was distributed to member papers in the states, increased the need for objectivity in political reporting since the same story would be read in a wide variety of papers across the growing nation.

Radio became an important political tool in 1924, when the first campaign commercials were aired. The first television advertisements appeared in 1952, during Dwight Eisenhower's successful presidential bid. Since then, advertising and regular news coverage have been important, intertwined components of the ELECTION CYCLE. Candidates try to "earn" media coverage, meaning that they attempt to attract news coverage on an issue they want reported to the public, and candidates pay large sums of money for commercial advertising to deliver an unfiltered message to a targeted group of LIKELY VOTERS.

In the modern era, most serious candidates for federal and state offices buy time on local radio and television to air campaign ads while they jointly seek to earn news coverage. Incumbents running for reelection have advantages in both of these areas, as they generally are able to raise more money than CHALLENGERS, enabling them to buy more commercials, and because officeholders are often seen as more newsworthy than challengers. Incumbents can make news by simply doing their jobs as representatives, while challengers rarely have such open access to the press.

One of the factors that influences the level of news coverage dedicated to elections is the amount of overlap a political CONSTITUENCY has with a media market, with political districts residing in a single media market receiving the most attention. Likewise, the more competitive the race, the larger the amount of coverage. As such, what voters are able to learn about candidates in their district, state, and nation from the media often depends on where the voters actually live and how competitive a particular race is in their area.

Today there is a general uniformity found in the coverage patterns of political campaigns. Reporters at different newspapers and television and radio stations often select very similar stories, emphasizing similar facts and interviewing the same people. Studies have shown these similarities at the presidential, congressional, state, and local levels. This phenomenon is called "pack journalism," since the reporters who are covering the story in the same way travel together in "packs" on a campaign bus or plane. In these situations, usually in presidential races, journalists are given tightly controlled access to the candidate. Typically, reporters receive their information in carefully crafted news releases or from a campaign spokesperson.

Often, election reporting is done in what is known as "horse race" fashion, meaning that coverage focuses on who is winning and who is losing. Campaign strategy stories are also a part of horse race reporting. One result of this type of coverage is that voters are less able to learn about candidates' similarities and differences because media stories are dominated by who is leading in the latest poll. The actual issue information covered by the media is often inconsistent and patchy. For example, a story about a candidate's drive to energize the senior citizen vote may make mention of the candidate's position on Social Security and Medicare. While the two issues appear in the story, the focus is not on what the issue positions are and how they differ from opposing candidates. Rather, the story is about how those issues position the candidate to win votes from senior citizens.

Reporters also tend to focus on SCANDALS, resulting in the exclusion of different, and often more relevant, political news. Excessive media coverage of a scandalous event can develop into what one political scientist, Larry J. Sabato, refers to as a "feeding frenzy." While some frenzies cover issues that turn out not to be true, others address issues that, in hindsight, prove to be much less significant than issues left untouched by the media when they are circling in for the proverbial kill. Examples of feeding frenzies include accusations made in 1992 of then candidate Bill Clinton's alleged affair with Gennifer Flowers and the coverage of the O. J. Simpson murder trial.

There are several consequences of the type of pack journalism that engages in horse race coverage between periodic feeding frenzies. Today voters hold politicians in significantly less esteem than they did before the age of the modern media. Moreover, journalism that probes deeply into candidates' personal affairs can dissuade potential candidates from seeking office. Additionally, voters hold the media in less esteem in the 21st century than they did in the 20th century.

Media expert Doris Graber points to four electoral consequences of media politics: the decline of political parties, the role of the media as king maker, the requirement for candidates to be "good on TV," and the age of made-for-TV campaigns. 1) Prior to the 1950s, PARTY IDENTIFICATION was the key determinant in predicting how one would vote on ELECTION DAY. Now, voters' issue positions, opinions of a candidate's personality, and allegiance to a social group all play increasingly important roles in determining vote choice. When voters make political decisions based on a candidate's issue stands and personality, the media become more important in influencing vote choice. Moreover, many newspapers endorse candidates, providing voters guidance about their political decisions that was once reserved for parties. 2) The media have what some scholars call an increasingly powerful role of being "king makers." This means that the media influence the selection of candidates for office and the issues of campaigns. Typically, this is most prevalent at the presidential level during the PRIMARY season, when several candidates seek each party's NOMINATION. The media use public opinion polls, candidates' FUND-RAISING, and other thin evidence to select a FRONTRUNNER and a small number of "viable" candidates. 3) Modern media politics has resulted in the need for most candidates for high office to look good on television. Candidates must seem natural and confident in front of the cameras to be taken seriously in a modern campaign, even if this trait has little bearing on their ability to lead once in office. 4) Candidates work hard to receive the best media exposure possible for themselves. This involves staging visually impressive public events, appearing on a wide variety of talk shows from, *Oprah* to *Larry King Live* to the *Late Show with David Letterman*, and focusing on issues that have media appeal.

Besides the media role in the reported decline in political parties, king making, candidate recruitment, and turning campaigns into media events, modern elections may be influenced by candidates' use of a new medium, the Internet. While most research finds that the Internet has, to date, had either no or small effects on election results, some prognosticators feel that trend could quickly change. Vermont governor Howard Dean's 2004 Democratic PRESIDENTIAL PRIMARY bid captured the attention of the media because of Dean's cutting-edge Web site that played host to record-breaking on-line contributions and popular "web logs," or "blogs," that chronicled various people's experiences on the campaign trail. It is likely that all serious presidential candidates in the future will have features on their Web sites for contributions and blogs.

In short, the media are inexorably linked with the democratic processes of elections. Media coverage affects the kind of information citizens learn about candidates and the choices voters make at the ballot box. Candidates seeking office must contend with the many evolving issues that surround modern media campaigns.

Further reading: Graber, Doris A. *Mass Media and American Politics*. 6th ed. Washington, D.C.: CQ Press, 2002; Lichter, Robert S., and Richard E. Noyes. *Good Intentions Make Bad News: Why Americans Hate Campaign Journalism*. Lanham, Md.: Rowman & Littlefield, 1995; Sabato, Larry J. *Feeding Frenzy: How Attack Journalism Has Transformed American Politics*. New York: Free Press, 1991; West, Darrell M. *Air Wars: Television Advertising in Election Campaigns, 1952–2000*. Washington, D.C.: CQ Press, 2001.

—Michael W. Wagner

media and elections, AM talk radio

Talk radio has been criticized for its tabloid quality, whereby hosts fill airtime by targeting the political extremes and portraying opinion as fact. Nevertheless, talk radio has contributed to the transformation of the workings of the American political system by providing an alternate and perhaps efficacious vehicle for citizen political participation.

AM radio is one part of a growing body of "new media" that include cable news and public access programming, satellite television and radio, Internet-based news organizations, and independent Internet-based reporters commonly known as "bloggers." For its part, commercial AM radio has existed since the 1920s. It was a factor in the political landscape long before the telecommunications revolution of the 1980s and 1990s and the current generation of radio talk show hosts and the all-talk program format.

Throughout his presidency, Franklin Delano Roosevelt used radio to give his fireside chats in the 1930s and early 1940s. Also in the 1930s, Huey Long used radio to communicate with large audiences. In the early days of broadcast, however, AM radio facilitated only one-way communication. Recent changes in communications technology have transformed AM radio into a dynamic "alternative" media source whereby listeners not only receive news and information but also are able to participate more directly in political discourse through telephone calls, e-mails, and faxes to program hosts. AM talk radio has been able to apply both new and older communications technologies to transform the media and political landscape through unprecedented public access to the nation's political institutions, including campaigns and elections.

In 1960, there were only two stations with all-talk formats, KABC in Los Angeles and KMOX in St. Louis. By 1995, there were more than 1,130 talk radio stations. The largest increase in the number of AM radio talk stations happened in the 1980s, with the introduction of cheap satellite transmission technology. By 1993, up to half of Americans were listening to talk radio on a weekly basis. Political actors, especially those to the right of center of the political spectrum, were actively making use of AM radio to funnel information around what they termed the "classic elite media."

A renewed interest in talk radio emerged after the 1994 election, when the REPUBLICAN PARTY gained 52 seats in the House of Representatives and won control of the Senate. According to the Voters News Survey, "talk voters" cast 64 percent of their votes for Republicans in House races and six in 10 voted for Republican Senate candidates. Nonlistening voters cast 51 percent of their BALLOTS for Democratic House and Senate candidates. Moreover, there was a 5 to 1 ratio of conservative to liberal listeners in the 1994 national ELECTORATE. The perceived influence of talk radio was so great that the talk show host with the greatest audience share, conservative Rush Limbaugh, was made an honorary member of the 1994 Republican freshman class in the House in recognition of his support (well publicized through his daily three-hour program) during the campaign.

In the modern context, AM talk radio has become a bastion of conservative dialogue. Influential hosts such as Rush Limbaugh and G. Gordon Liddy dominate the airwaves, rallying their listeners to conservative causes and informing political leaders what the masses are thinking. In this way, Limbaugh and others like him serve a bonding function that connects a significant portion of the electorate to national political life. Given the political behavior and attitudes of many talk radio listeners, it appears that, at least on the conservative side of the political spectrum, talk radio is acting as a two-way link between party elites and the electorate.

The apparent power of AM talk radio in elections since 1994 has led to a concerted effort to establish and develop progressive or liberal AM talk radio programs and networks. Although many areas, particularly urban areas on the East Coast, have thriving liberal FM talk stations, usually in the form of National Public Radio stations, there was no nationally syndicated liberal AM talk radio network. In early 2004, two efforts began to accomplish this objective. By 2005, there was one progressive network with 74 stations and another with 46, including one in the nation's capital.

Given the success of AM talk radio in the past 10 to 15 years, there have been several surveys to find out who listens. In general, talk radio audiences tend to be more ideological, have a stronger sense of citizen duty, and participate more in POLITICS than the general public. Talk radio listeners pay closer attention to politics, vote in higher percentages, and generally stay quite engaged with the policy-making process beyond election campaigns. Supporters of talk radio suggest that unlike the passive medium of television, talk radio is an engaging medium that requires active listening and stimulates critical thought. Opponents suggest that the medium has poisoned political civility and leads listeners to adopt strongly held convictions on topics on which they have little understanding.

Further reading: Bolce, Louis, Gerald De Maio, and Douglas Muzzio. "Dial-In Democracy: Talk Radio and the 1994 Election." *Political Science Quarterly* 111, no. 3 (1996): 457–481; Hofstetter, C. Richard, David Barker, James T. Smith, Gina M. Zari, and Thomas A. Ingrassia. "Information, Misinformation, and Political Talk Radio." *Political Research Quarterly* 52, no. 2 (1999): 353–369; Rozell, Mark J., ed. *Media Power, Media Politics.* Lanham, Md.: Rowman & Littlefield, 2003.

—John W. Carter

media and elections, cable TV

Cable television serves as an option to commercial broadcast television in more than 70 percent of American homes. It provides an alternative method of communicating with potential voters. Successful political campaigns must send the right message to the right people in the right way. Changes in technology and public news gathering behavior patterns force candidates, parties, and INTEREST GROUPS to constantly reconsider the most effective means of transmitting their messages.

In the not so distant past, candidates depended on local newspapers and labor-intensive face-to-face VOTER CANVASSING to present targeted messages to potential voters. The age of mass communication via broadcast radio and television required candidates to either present general messages or carefully select time spots to catch particular kinds of audiences for whom a tailored message could be developed. Virtually all major statewide and national campaigns began to use professional time buyers whose skill lay in determining which type of potential voter tuned in to which particular programs. Their task was more to buy a particular audience than to simply buy a block of time. The growing cost of television advertising and the lack of overlap between electoral constituencies and media markets increasingly drained campaign coffers and resulted in wasted expenditures reaching nonconstituents. In some media markets such as New York City and Los Angeles, more than 90 percent of the audience for a candidate's commercial broadcast advertisement could not vote in that candidate's district.

The arrival of cable television provided a lower-cost alternative to supplement advertising on broadcast channels. The more limited geographic reach of cable systems and their more narrowly defined audiences provided a more cost-effective method of "narrowcasting" targeted messages to local audiences within a CONSTITUENCY. The more clearly defined audiences of CNN (Cable News Network for news junkies), MTV (Music TV for younger voters), and foreign language channels helped define the most appropriate messages and provided a vehicle for transmitting them.

Local requirements for public service broadcasting encouraged cable systems to broadcast candidate forums and interviews, often providing exposure to candidates for lower-level offices who seldom receive broadcast television news coverage. The growing cable audience served as a magnet for increased use by political campaigns. As late as the 1980s, more than 90 percent of people watching television during prime time were watching one of the three major broadcast networks. At the beginning of the 21st century, the figure dropped to below 50 percent, as viewers abandoned the broadcast networks for cable offerings.

In the fading mass media era, it became clear that while the broadcast channels drew more of an inadvertent audience, exposed to whatever was on the air, cable allowed more intentional choices of the kinds of programming the viewer desired. The ability to choose increased with the widespread use of the remote control, allowing considerably more channel surfing. The challenge for political activists, of course, lay in the proliferation of cable channels and the fragmentation of the audience. It was no longer enough to buy *the* right time slot or to get on *the* evening news. Candidates, parties, and interest groups faced the new challenge of appealing to a multitude of channels, recognizing that much of the cable audience would be attuned to channels with no political content.

Cable channels, with their increasingly large programming "hole," had more time for new formats and the motivation for distinguishing themselves from their competitors. Political call-in programs, in-depth interviews with politicians, and a wide variety of programs based on panels of experts are more appealing to cable channels than to the broadcast networks. With breaking news, cable channels are more willing to suspend their regular programming to provide extensive real-time coverage of events. The extensive news gathering reach of cable networks such as CNN encourages government officials to depend on them for their understanding of the world. The agenda-setting role of the media has been heightened by the presence of numerous competing cable networks whose coverage becomes part of the unfolding story.

The proliferation of media sources increases the ability to better understand how choices in the coverage of events change viewers' feelings about them. Watching the 2004 PRESIDENTIAL DEBATES on C-SPAN, whose broadcast showed only the candidate who was speaking, contrasted dramatically with the broadcast networks', which used a split screen to constantly show the opponent's reactions. News stories about George W. Bush's "smirk" and John Kerry's "patrician disinterest" while supposedly off-camera meant little to those who had not seen the split screen version and raised questions about the criteria by which voters should judge candidates.

More broadly, cable television has provided new venues for political education and engagement. CNN pioneered the 24-hour news cycle, forcing candidates to anticipate breaking news stories and react immediately. A number of candidates have chosen to announce their candidacies on CNN, revealing their judgment about the size and political potency of its audience. C-SPAN provided a "window" on the political process, increasing the transparency of government and affecting the behavior of decision makers, encouraging civic involvement, and serving as a vehicle for clever politicians. Fox TV provided a conservative spin on the news, drawing citizens frustrated with the perceived liberal slant of other sources. MTV, with its ROCK THE VOTE campaign, mobilized new voters, particularly in 1992 and 2004. Conservative Christian channels helped focus attention on moral issues during the 2004 campaign, providing a boost to George W. Bush's reelection.

Politicians are strategically conservative, unwilling to bet their futures entirely on new technology. Cable television is currently being used to supplement campaign communications via other means, giving candidates and parties another choice in how they reach the voters.

Further reading: Davis, Richard, and Diana Owen. *New Media and American Politics.* New York: Oxford University Press, 1998; Frantzich, Stephen, and John Sullivan. *The C-SPAN Revolution.* Norman: University of Oklahoma Press, 1996; Kerbel, Matthew. *Edited for Television: CNN, ABC and the American Presidential Elections.* Boulder, Colo.: Westview Press, 1988.

—Stephen Frantzich

media and elections, Internet

In the last decade, the Internet has become an increasingly important part of the media environment in American elections. While the Internet provides much of the same campaign news as do traditional print and broadcast outlets, the recent proliferation of political Web sites and the flexibility of new media have effected profound changes on the availability, timeliness, and volume of election news. Citizens now have access to more political information than at any time in history, and updates on campaign activities and candidate schedules are available from hundreds of sources across the Web. Moreover, the new technology has made it easier for citizens to get involved in campaigns, and some have hoped that the new technology will increase political participation among an apathetic public.

While newspapers, magazines, radio, and television were the sources for virtually all election news in the United States for the first 90 years of the 20th century, the emergence of the World Wide Web has changed the way Americans become informed about the political world. Prior to the early 1990s, the Internet and e-mail were used by just a handful of technological pioneers. Now, research has shown that more than 60 percent of Americans go online every day—a figure that is constantly increasing—and the Internet has become a major source of election news for millions of Americans.

Major news outlets, INTEREST GROUPS, candidates, and ordinary citizens have all made substantial efforts to take advantage of the speed and flexibility of Internet communication. No longer are journalists and candidates bound by the time and physical constraints of traditional communication. The immediacy of Web communication has meant that political actors can provide information to citizens almost as soon as they receive it.

Major American news organizations are the dominant players in the world of Internet election news. Surveys show that the country's biggest and most successful news organizations—the *New York Times,* CNN, Fox News, and their competitors—are also the most popular online sites for political news. While much of what these organizations provide online is identical to their print and broadcast content, there are important distinctions. Newspapers, for example, have begun offering video and audio coverage of major campaign events online, something that simply was not possible prior to the Internet. Likewise, television news sites have used their multimedia capacity to make election news more interesting and accessible to their audiences. Furthermore, journalists now file stories from the campaign trail throughout the day, updating their audiences on events as they occur. No longer do viewers and readers have to wait for the evening news or morning paper.

But national news outlets are by no means the only players in the new media environment. Smaller organizations and individuals maintain Web sites devoted to political and campaign news. The emergence of such entrepreneurs has been notable for three reasons. First, they have provided diversity in political discourse amid the growing consolidation of traditional media outlets. Second, independent and small Web sites have in recent years offered news coverage of campaign events that network television has shied away from, most prominently the presidential nominating conventions. Finally, the emergence of popular Weblogs, or "blogs," in which private individuals provide a running commentary on various social matters, including POLITICS, have exposed previously disinterested observers to politics in an unconventional format.

Many have seen the greatest potential impact of the Internet in its facilitation of political participation. Political participation and VOTER TURNOUT in particular have waned in the United States since the late 1960s, and various reforms have done little to reverse the trend. Scholars who study participation have suggested that making it easier for people to get involved with political campaigns might increase democratic involvement and engagement.

The Internet could make this happen in several ways. First, the explosion of online election information has made it easier than ever for Americans to learn about candidates and the things they stand for. If people are more informed about their choices, they may be more likely to vote and become politically involved. Second, the presence of campaign Web sites has made it easier for interested citizens to volunteer to work for a candidate. Most major campaigns now have online forms for volunteers that allow citizens to get involved with a campaign without having to sign up at a meeting or rally. Third, campaign Web sites make it simple to donate to a candidate. Upstart candidates in recent years have had success raising money and organizing online.

The PRESIDENTIAL PRIMARY campaigns of Republican John McCain in 2000 and Democrat Howard Dean in 2004 demonstrate the ways that the Internet has had an influence on modern elections. McCain, in challenging front-runner George W. Bush, raised millions through his Web site and saw a dramatic upsurge in donations after winning the NEW HAMPSHIRE PRIMARY. Dean's underdog campaign probably best illustrates the potential of the Web to revolutionize campaigns. In raising more than $40 million for his PRIMARY bid, Dean collected most of his donations in small increments pledged through his Web site. His campaign also took advantage of the organizing power of the Web, scheduling "meet-ups" and "house parties" among Dean supporters all over the country. Finally, Dean recruited volunteers through his site, enlisting hundreds, many of them young and new to politics, to travel to Iowa and New Hampshire to help campaign before those states' caucuses and primaries.

While Dean's bid was ultimately unsuccessful, it underscores the potential FUND-RAISING, mobilizing, and organizing power of the Internet. The use of online resources clearly has the power to augment traditional campaign activities and media coverage and is likely to remain an important part of American political campaigns in the 21st century.

Further reading: Anderson, David M., and Michael Cornfield, eds. *The Civic Web: Online Politics and Democratic Values.* Lanham, Md.: Rowman & Littlefield, 2003; Bimber, Bruce A. *Campaigning Online: The Internet in U.S. Elections.* New York: Oxford University Press, 2003;

Klotz, Robert. "Internet Politics: A Survey of Practices." In Roderick P. Hart and Daron R. Shaw, eds., *Communication in U.S. Elections: New Agendas.* New York: Rowman & Littlefield, 2001.

—Danny Hayes

media and elections, network television

Since the 1950s, network television has remained the most important conduit of political information for the American public. The nightly 30-minute news broadcasts on the three major networks, ABC, CBS, and NBC, draw some 30 million viewers. Each network employs hundreds of journalists who report, edit, and air the news stories that the public sees every night. For most Americans, much of their knowledge of campaigns, candidates, and political issues is influenced by what the networks choose to report. For that reason, the networks have a substantial power to shape perceptions of candidates and set the terms of political debate during a campaign.

The emergence of television and its attendant political news coverage had a monumental influence on elections and political parties. Before television, PARTY ORGANIZATIONS in the United States largely controlled the channels of communication with voters. The rise of television, however, helped erode the parties' monopoly over political communication. Beginning in the 1960s, the rise of network television contributed to the creation of an era of candidate-centered POLITICS. Through television advertising and political news coverage, candidates can now take their messages directly to the people, making them less reliant on the party organization.

The centrality of network television in elections has changed the way candidates structure their campaigns. Unlike the print media, television relies on pictures for news. Savvy political candidates now orchestrate events that emphasize visual as well as verbal appeal in the hopes of creating an arresting image that will make it onto the nightly news. For example, candidates might unveil a health care proposal not behind a lectern but in front of a hospital or surrounded by senior citizens. Candidates and their consultants sometimes even provide videotapes of events for the networks to use in their coverage.

With its unique place in American politics, television has a powerful influence on the public's perceptions of the political world. Its greatest power comes in its ability to tell the public which political issues are most important during a campaign. Since most people never meet a candidate or attend a rally, their understanding of elections is filtered through the news media. In choosing which issues to emphasize—or ignore—television reporters and editors strongly influence citizens' beliefs about which issues are important. This is called the media's "agenda-setting" role. For example, during the 1992 presidential campaign, the network newscasts were filled with stories about the sputtering American economy. In public opinion polls, citizens overwhelmingly identified the economy as the most important problem facing the country, reflecting what television news had been telling them for months. This pattern has been shown time and again in experimental and survey research.

While network television's agenda-setting power has been constant since its inception, the content and tone of news coverage has seen major changes. In its early days, coverage of presidential campaigns and elections often focused on the candidates' ideas and policy proposals. News coverage of John Kennedy and Richard Nixon's competing campaigns in 1960 focused on the substantive issues animating each man's vision for America, but since the 1970s, network television election news has become less substantive, more negative, and less friendly to candidate communications.

While the overall amount of campaign coverage has been waning in recent years, the number of election stories that focus on the "horse race," or coverage of candidates' poll standings and campaign strategies, has been steadily climbing. Reporters and editors tend to be more interested in which candidate is "winning" in the polls than in news about public policy problems and the candidates' issue proposals. Research has documented the dramatic growth in recent decades in the amount of time network news reporters spend telling viewers *how* a candidate is doing rather than *what* the candidate is saying. Moreover, the amount of campaign news on the nightly news has been steadily declining, with political coverage taking up an increasingly smaller percentage than it once did.

As the amount of substantive coverage has fallen, the tone of network news coverage has become increasingly critical. This has happened, in part, because reporters have focused intently on SCANDALS on the campaign trail. As network news coverage has turned from issues to mistakes, the tone of coverage has become less favorable to the candidates. For example, Bill Clinton's alleged affair with Gennifer Flowers in the 1992 PRESIDENTIAL ELECTION generated dozens of news stories, including a high-profile interview on CBS's *60 Minutes*. Some scholars have worried that reporters' accentuation of the negative contributes to growing cynicism among the public about candidates and government in general.

With the proliferation of political Web sites and 24-hour cable news channels, many of which devote most of their coverage to politics, some observers have questioned the continued importance of network television. If Americans can now turn elsewhere for their political news and campaign coverage, do the network newscasts continue to carry the same significance as they did 20 years ago? To be sure, candidates and the public both have more outlets for political news, but the influence of the major networks remains robust. Following the terrorist attacks of September 11, 2001, the viewing audiences of ABC, CBS, and NBC shot up, an indication that Americans still see them as particularly credible. And as John Kerry and George W. Bush in 2004 continued to court them, the networks appear to remain key conduits for political information during American elections.

Further reading: Ansolabehere, Stephen, Roy Behr, and Shanto Iyengar. *The Media Game: American Politics in the Television Age.* New York: Macmillan, 1993; Farnsworth, Stephen J., and S. Robert Lichter. *The Nightly News Nightmare: Network Television's Coverage of U.S. Presidential Elections, 1988–2000.* Lanham, Md.: Rowman & Littlefield, 2003; Graber, Doris A. *Mass Media and American Politics.* Washington, D.C.: Congressional Quarterly Press, 1993; Patterson, Thomas E. *Out of Order.* New York: Vintage Books, 1994.

—Danny Hayes

midterm congressional elections and the theory of "surge and decline"

Because CONGRESSIONAL ELECTIONS take place biannually, while PRESIDENTIAL ELECTIONS occur only once every four years, members of Congress face very different electoral environments depending on whether a presidential campaign is occurring simultaneously with the congressional campaigns. Presidential elections attract a great deal of media attention and activate many voters. As citizens turn out to support their preferred presidential candidate, they generally also cast a vote for a congressional candidate. A strong presidential candidate is likely to activate many voters who also support the congressional candidate belonging to the winning presidential candidate's party. This results in the phenomenon known as COATTAILS, whereby a strong presidential candidate benefits his party's SLATE of congressional candidates. The windfall for a party's congressional candidates is the "surge" in the theory of "surge and decline."

During MIDTERM ELECTIONS, however, members of Congress do not benefit from a strong presidential candidate. Indeed, turnout tends to drop in midterm elections because the voters who were activated by the presidential campaign in the previous election are less interested in congressional campaigns. This results in a drop in support for the incumbent president's party relative to its support in the preceding presidential election. This drop is the "decline" in the theory of surge and decline.

This pattern of surge and decline has several significant implications for electoral POLITICS. First, midterm elections are generally marked by congressional seat losses for the incumbent president's party. In nearly every midterm election since the New Deal, the incumbent president's party has lost seats in the House of Representatives. Exceptions to the trend occurred in 1998, when

Democrats gained seats in the House because of a backlash against Republican efforts to impeach Bill Clinton, and in 2002, when the Republicans gained seats, in part because of George W. Bush's high APPROVAL RATING. Additionally, because Bush did not win the POPULAR VOTE in the 2000 elections, there was less of a "surge" from which to "decline."

One consequence of this pattern is that it may lead strategic politicians to time their candidacies at points when they are more likely to be successful. Quality CHALLENGERS from the party that does not control the presidency will be more likely to run in midterm elections, while quality challengers from the president's party may wait for the next presidential election. However, if the president's party is able to mobilize quality challengers for the midterm elections, the party may be able to reduce the loss it would otherwise face.

Further reading: Campbell, Angus. "Surge and Decline: A Study of Electoral Change." In Angus Campbell, Philip E. Converse, Warren E. Miller, and Donald E. Stokes, eds., *Elections and the Political Order.* New York: Wiley, 1966; Jacobson, Gary C. "Party Organization and Distribution of Campaign Resources: Republicans and Democrats in 1982." *Political Science Quarterly* 100 (1985): 603–625.

—Damon Cann

midterm elections

Midterm elections are those elections that fall in even-numbered years that do not feature a PRESIDENTIAL ELECTION. For example, in the decade of the 1990s, the elections held in 1990, 1994, and 1998 were midterm elections, whereas the elections held in 1992 and 1996 were presidential election year elections. While there are a number of different offices up for election in midterm years, including gubernatorial elections, races for state legislatures, and many other state- and local-level posts, the races that consistently receive the most consideration are those for the U.S. Congress.

Considering that midterm elections are essentially defined by the absence of campaigns for the presidency, it is not surprising that a great deal of the scholarly attention paid to midterm elections is dedicated to comparing and contrasting them to presidential elections. In fact, the key characteristic of midterm elections is that they systematically feature significant declines in the number of the current president's fellow partisans in Congress. A number of theoretical explanations have been offered for why this repeatedly occurs. The leading explanations can be roughly grouped into two separate camps: those that subscribe to the referenda hypothesis and those that follow variations of the surge-and-decline hypothesis.

While there are numerous versions of the referenda hypothesis, all share the assumption that votes cast in midterm elections are done so on the basis of the voters'

evaluations of conditions at the time of the election. Generally speaking, the referenda hypothesis posits that a midterm election serves as a referendum on the performance of the sitting president and on his administration's handling of the economy and other important national conditions. Over the past few decades, several scholars have attempted to elaborate upon or refine the general referenda hypothesis. Such efforts include the addition of public evaluations of party competence, while others make the addition of a negative voting hypothesis that supplements the idea of midterm elections as referenda on presidential performance with the argument that voters are more moved by negative impressions of the president than positive impressions. Other scholars have advocated the concept of the strategic politician, which contends that political elites are strategic in their behavior and that politicians also make decisions that affect midterm election outcomes. Yet another enhancement to the referenda theory includes the exposure thesis, which states that parties that are less exposed to the ELECTORATE should find it easier to gain seats.

Critics of this view of midterm elections often deride the referenda hypothesis for its exclusive focus on the midterm election itself and the short-term forces related to midterm campaigning, at the expense of not taking into consideration the full electoral context. Such critics often offer one variation or another of the surge-and-decline hypothesis as an alternative. The surge-and-decline hypothesis considers midterm elections as functions of the prior presidential election. That is, the better the president performed in the previous election, the more potential there is for a drop-off in the votes received by his fellow partisans in Congress. This is because the president's COATTAILS, which many of his colleagues may have ridden into office, are not there to ride on in the midterm election. Moreover, there is less of a stimulus for citizens to vote in midterm elections than there is in presidential election years. As more voters on the periphery flock to the polls during presidential elections and are more susceptible to STRAIGHT-TICKET VOTING, the down-ticket candidates that share party affiliation with the president benefit. These periphery voters are less likely to turn out in lower-stimulus midterm elections. While scholars applying the logic of the surge-and-decline hypothesis to their research have found supportive evidence, critics of this approach contend that it ignores the political context at the time of the actual midterm election. More recent scholarship has attempted to reconcile these two theoretical approaches to explain midterm election outcomes.

Regardless of why midterm elections end up as they do, political elites, and especially presidents, are actively interested in shaping their outcomes. Presidents know that they are more successful in getting their policy goals on the congressional agenda and passed into law when they have more, rather than less, of their fellow partisans in office. As a result, they expend considerable energy and resources attempting to increase their party's number of seats during midterm election campaigns. Despite their efforts, presidents have spent much of the recent past disappointed with the outcomes of midterm elections.

In both 1954 and 1958, defying his label as a nonpolitical president, Dwight Eisenhower went to extensive lengths to improve his party's position in Congress. Nevertheless, he came away suffering considerable losses in both years. John F. Kennedy fared much better in 1962, even though (or perhaps because) he had to curtail his campaigning in the late fall due to the Cuban Missile Crisis. Kennedy's successor, Lyndon Johnson, was not so fortunate, as the congressional Democrats lost a great number of seats, due in part to Johnson's relatively low level of popularity. Richard Nixon was heavily involved in the midterm election campaign of 1970 and did not fare too badly in the outcome. He was, however, punished for his campaign activity by congressional Democrats later as he attempted to pass Welfare reform. The outcome of the midterm elections of 1974 was also a dramatic setback for the incumbent, Gerald Ford, who had been in office for only a short time after Richard Nixon's resignation from office prior to the election.

The pattern from the 1970s to 1990 continued in much the same way, with the president's party losing on average 19 seats in Congress per election. The midterm election of 1994, however, provides another dramatic tale. In the largest shift since the Watergate midterm, House Democrats lost more than 50 seats as well as control of the House of Representatives for the first time in four decades. In the midterm election of 1998, the Democrats managed to buck the historical trend by holding the partisan seat distribution steady in the Senate and actually picking up five seats in the House of Representatives. Congressional Republicans were so shocked and angry at this historical anomaly that they fired the SPEAKER OF THE HOUSE, Newt Gingrich, and many of his lieutenants. The midterm election of 2002 again saw a historical rarity, as Republicans gained seats in the House of Representatives and the Senate.

Further reading: Campbell, James E. "Explaining Presidential Losses in Midterm Congressional Elections." *Journal of Politics* 47 (1995): 1,140–1,157; Campbell, James E. *The Presidential Pulse of Congressional Elections.* 2nd ed. Lexington: University Press of Kentucky, 1997; Edwards, George C., III. *Presidential Influence in Congress.* San Francisco: W. H. Freeman, 1980; Jacobson, Gary C. "Terror, Terrain, and Turnout: Explaining the 2002 Midterm Elections." *Political Science Quarterly* 118 (2003): 1–22; Tufte, Edward R. "Determinants of the Outcomes of Midterm Congressional Elections." *American Political Science Review* 69 (1975): 812–826.

—Justin S. Vaughn

Miller v. Johnson 515 U.S. 900 (1995)

During the process that led to the creation of its congressional REDISTRICTING plan after the 1990 CENSUS, the state of Georgia faced many political, legal, and constitutional constraints. For example, the state sought to reflect traditional redistricting principles, such as compactness, contiguity, and respect for communities of interest. It respected the command of "one person, one vote," and it complied with the Voting Rights Act as interpreted by different political actors, such as the Department of Justice, the federal courts, and the state American Civil Liberties Union. Its plan ultimately reflected these various requirements while also seeking to satisfy the political wishes of those in charge of the process.

Nonetheless, litigants brought a challenge to the redistricting plan in federal court under, among other things, the expressive harm doctrine of *SHAW V. RENO* (1993). Their argument focused on the shape of the challenged districts. Yet, in *Miller v. Johnson,* the Supreme Court dispelled any notions that the shape of a district was central to its expressive harm inquiry. Instead, the Court made clear that the shape of a district is relevant not as an element of the constitutional inquiry but, rather, "because it may be persuasive circumstantial evidence that race for its own sake, and not other redistricting principles, was the legislature's dominant and controlling rationale in drawing its district lines."

This conception of the constitutional wrong placed on plaintiffs challenging a redistricting plan the burden of showing, through circumstantial evidence of shape or demographics, or direct evidence of legislative purpose, "that race was the predominant factor motivating the legislature's decision to place a significant number of voters within or without a particular district." In other words, they must show that the state subordinated traditional race-neutral redistricting principles, such as compactness, contiguity, or respect for political subdivisions, to race. This test is now commonly known as the "predominant factor" test.

—Luis Fuentes-Rohwer

minority-majority district   *See* RACIAL DISTRICTING.

minority party

Unlike the physical sciences, the social sciences do not tightly control the pertinent vocabulary in their areas of knowledge. Instead, journalists, political figures, and other commentators may inconsistently use key terms in the social sciences. *Minority party* is an example of this practice. In nonscholarly usage the term may refer to any party that is less numerous than the main parties within a political system. That includes THIRD PARTIES. Thus, we may find a POLITICAL PARTY such as the Greens labeled a minority party.

Scholars employ the term in two ways. One is that a minority party is the second largest in a nation or a subdivision therein. For example, in the 1930s, during the New

Deal era, the REPUBLICAN PARTY was the minority party in the nation. Similarly, for most of the 20th century the DEMOCRATIC PARTY was the minority party in Kansas.

A second usage defines a minority party as the less numerous of the two largest parties within a legislative chamber. Political parties are the principal organizing mechanisms for legislative bodies. The MAJORITY PARTY in a legislative chamber determines the agenda of that body; the minority party organizes itself parallel to the majority party's structure with a leader of the minority, minority whips, and perhaps other minority party officials. In Great Britain, for example, the minority party has a Leader of Her Majesty's Loyal Opposition, who appoints the Shadow Cabinet, a group of minority party members who have party offices that counterpoise those of the majority party, such as the Shadow Foreign Secretary.

American legislative parties have a less detailed structure, but with the strong committee system of American legislative chambers, the longest-serving minority party member of a committee is designated the "ranking minority member." Because of its four decades as the minority in the U.S. House of Representatives, the Republican Party has been the subject of scholarly inquiries about the operations of a minority party.

Minority party status may grant its leader less job security than that of the majority party's leader. Thus, first in 1959 Joseph Martin of Massachusetts was challenged and replaced by Charles Halleck of Indiana, who in 1965 suffered the same fate when challenged by Gerald Ford of Michigan. Neither loss was a result of ideological differences, but an effort to develop a new strategy for the party.

Further reading: Connelly, William F., Jr., and John J. Pitney, Jr. *Congress' Permanent Minority? Republicans in the U.S. House.* Lanham Md.: Rowman & Littlefield, 1994; Koopman, Douglas L. *Hostile Takeover: The House Republican Party, 1980–1992.* Lanham, Md.: Rowman & Littlefield, 1996.

—Thomas Phillip Wolf

Mississippi Freedom Democratic Party

The Council of Federated Organizations (COFO), a confederation of civil rights organizations in Mississippi, in 1964 established the Mississippi Freedom Democratic Party (MFDP). With especially strong ties to the Student Nonviolent Coordinating Committee (SNCC), the MFDP was an important exponent of the GRASSROOTS activism that carried and defined much of the 1960s CIVIL RIGHTS MOVEMENT. Fannie Lou Hamer, Annie Devine, Unita Blackwell, Victoria Gray, and Ella Baker were among the many women with leading roles in the MFDP. Male leaders included Bob Moses, Lawrence Guyot, Ed King, and Aaron Henry.

At the August 1964 Democratic National Convention in Atlantic City, the MFDP challenged the seating of Mississippi's regular, all-white DEMOCRATIC PARTY delegation. MFDP leaders argued that the regular state party excluded African Americans from participating in the selection of convention DELEGATES. It is uncertain whether MFDP activists were aware of the SOUTH CAROLINA PROGRESSIVE DEMOCRATIC PARTY (PDP), which initiated similar challenges in the 1940s and 1950s.

In Atlantic City, Hamer's dramatic, televised testimony drew the nation's attention. Still, there was enormous pressure on MFDP delegates to accept a compromise proposed by national party leaders, including President Lyndon B. Johnson, who feared losing southern white support. The compromise included at-large convention seats for two MFDP delegates handpicked by national Democratic Party leaders and guest status for the remaining delegates.

Disillusioned, the MFDP delegation rejected the compromise despite pleas to accept it from some of its middle-class, urban members, from white liberal Democrats, and from national civil rights leaders, including Martin Luther King, Jr. The next year, Congress dismissed a seating challenge to Mississippi's congressional delegation by Devine, Gray, and Hamer.

The MFDP convention challenge helped create support for the 1965 Voting Rights Act. The party helped VOTER REGISTRATION skyrocket in Mississippi after 1965, but many activists in the MFDP and SNCC, as well as in the Congress of Racial Equality (CORE), felt betrayed in Atlantic City by national black leaders and white liberals.

The episode contributed to the Civil Rights movement disintegrating from the bottom up from the mid-1960s. SNCC and CORE activists left the South, turning to northern inner cities and increasingly to black nationalism. In Mississippi, they left equally disillusioned local activists with a limited infrastructure and few ties to the national movement.

In 1966, the MFDP contested five congressional races and one for the U.S. Senate with limited success and no victories. In 1968, the party was part of the Loyal Democrats of Mississippi, which successfully challenged the regular state party's seating at the 1968 Democratic National Convention in Chicago. But often overshadowed and outvoted by their more conservative loyalist coalition partners, MFDP delegates returned from Chicago demoralized. After 1968, the party continued to exist in certain counties but no longer on the state level.

Further reading: Dittmer, John. *Local People: The Struggle for Civil Rights in Mississippi.* Urbana: University of Illinois Press, 1995; Payne, Charles M. *I've Got the Light of Freedom: The Organizing Tradition and the Mississippi Freedom Struggle.* Berkeley: University of California Press, 1996.

—Wim Roefs

Aaron Henry, chair of the Mississippi Freedom Democratic Party, speaking at the Democratic National Convention, 1964 (U.S. News and World Report *Magazine Photograph Collection, Library of Congress*)

Mississippi Plan

The Mississippi Plan was the name commonly applied to emotional, often violent, Democratic efforts to overturn the last Republican regimes in the South during RECONSTRUCTION. Although not necessarily devised in Mississippi, it achieved particular force (and notoriety) in that state during the Democrats' successful campaign of 1875. The triumph of the Mississippi Democrats inspired whites in the remaining Republican-controlled states to apply similar strategies during the 1876 elections, which culminated in the Compromise of 1877 and the official end of Reconstruction.

Although it is debatable whether Democrats in Mississippi and elsewhere were conducting a fully organized and articulated plan, a common approach and philosophy pervaded their efforts. Most crucial was the decision to highlight the campaign as a fight between the races. Previously, leading Democrats, fearing that racialized campaigning would invite federal intervention, had stressed the need to accommodate to the reality of biracial POLITICS. In the mid-1870s, with federal resolve clearly fading, more openly racist Democrats, known as white-liners or straightouts, moved to the forefront of the party. Summing up the ascendant philosophy, one Louisiana editorial urged "a fair, square fight, Caucasian versus African." Such an attitude demanded and inspired white unity, pulling in white voters who had chosen to sit out elections rather than accept black political influence. It also marginalized white Republicans, most of whom felt they had no alternative but to acquiesce to the white-line campaign. Through intimidation and social ostracism, Democrats made it too hot (as one Mississippi Democrat put it) for whites to maintain support of the REPUBLICAN PARTY.

The other essential element of the plan was the militarized nature of the campaigns. Local Democratic clubs doubled as militia units, inspiring supporters at dramatic, torch-lit rallies and intimidating Republicans. At the height of Mississippi's 1875 campaign, Democratic intimidation and the violence that such activities sometimes produced forced Republican activities almost completely underground. In 1876, South Carolina and Louisiana Democrats followed suit. Creating an aura of inevitability, red-shirted Democratic militia units essentially asserted control over their local communities before the election, making Republican governments irrelevant. One might characterize the Mississippi Plan as a series of coups that awaited electoral validation.

Black voters did not crumble in the face of the Democratic assault. Democratic myths notwithstanding, very few African Americans marched alongside Democrats, and Republican vote tallies did not shrink appreciably. Blacks remained dedicated Republicans. The main effect of the Mississippi Plan was to unite an overwhelming majority of whites behind an all-or-nothing political strategy. SOUTHERN DEMOCRATS asserted control over their local and state governments and dared the federal government to intervene. The acquiescence of northern voters and politicians to this state of affairs helped set the tone for southern politics and society for the next 75 years.

Further reading: Harris, William C. *Day of the Carpetbagger: Republican Reconstruction in Mississippi.* Baton Rouge: Louisiana State University Press, 1979; Tunnell, Ted. *Crucible of Reconstruction: War, Radicalism and Race in Louisiana, 1862–1877.* Baton Rouge: Louisiana State University Press, 1984; Williamson, Joel. *After Slavery: The Negro in South Carolina during Reconstruction, 1861–1877.* Chapel Hill: University of North Carolina Press, 1965; Zuczek, Richard. *State of Rebellion: Reconstruction in South Carolina.* Columbia: University of South Carolina Press, 1996.

—William Bland Whitley

Motor Voter Law

The National Voter Registration Act (NVRA) of 1993 is a federal law whose key provisions pertain to motor voter registration, agency voter registration, and mail voter registration. It covers 44 states and the District of Columbia. Six states—Idaho, Minnesota, New Hampshire, North Dakota, Wisconsin, and Wyoming—are exempt from the act because either they do not have VOTER REGISTRATION or have ELECTION DAY registration.

The stated objectives of the Motor Voter Law are to establish procedures that will increase the number of eligible voters who register to vote in federal elections, to secure the integrity of the electoral process by maintaining accurate and current voter registration rolls, and to increase participation of eligible voters in federal elections. It pursues these objectives through mandates pertaining to state registration laws and procedures. To increase the number of locations and opportunities whereby eligible citizens can register to voter, the law requires state agencies to register citizens to vote when they get drivers' licenses, food stamps, Medicaid, AFDC (Aid to Families with Dependent Children), and WIC (Women, Infants, and Children) as well as at agencies that provide services to people with disabilities. It also requires states to accept a national mail-in voter registration form.

Along with expanding voter registration opportunities, the law seeks to prevent voter registration fraud in a uniform and nondiscriminatory manner through voter registration file maintenance. Accordingly, it establishes guidelines for maintaining the accuracy of voter registration rolls such as removing names of individuals who are no longer eligible to vote. However, it prohibits states from removing registrants from the rolls for not voting.

To increase voting in federal elections, the Motor Voter Law establishes certain "fail-safe" voting procedures to ensure that an individual's right to vote prevails over current bureaucratic or legal technicalities. For example, the law permits certain classes of registrants to vote even if they failed to reregister after changing their addresses or failed to return certain election office mailings as long as they remain eligible to vote within that jurisdiction.

The Motor Voter Law has substantially increased the number of people registered to vote, though this has not automatically translated into more votes cast during federal elections. In the 1996 PRESIDENTIAL ELECTION, the first PRESIDENTIAL ELECTION following the passage of the Motor Voter Law and considered to be the most dramatic liberalization of voter registration procedures in the United States, only 49 percent of eligible voters went to the polls. Moreover, the turnout rate was lowest among the most "electorally disadvantaged," the very people targeted by the Motor Voter Law. Critics also claim that the law is responsible for faulty voter registration systems resulting in duplicate registrations and registering of noncitizens, while supporters of the legislation point to the spike in voter participation in the 2004 election as evidence of the positive impact of the law.

—Meredith Staples

MoveOn.Org

An online activist network established in 1998 that supports liberal, or progressive, political causes, MoveOn.Org has worked on a variety of issues, including gun control, opposing the war in Iraq, support for campaign finance reform, opposition to media consolidation and deregulation, and trying to prevent oil drilling in the Arctic National Wildlife Refuge. It promotes GRASSROOTS participation by running a POLITICAL ACTION COMMITTEE, ISSUE ADVOCACY ADVERTISING, and producing political advertisements.

MoveOn.Org was founded in 1998 as a bipartisan group during the impeachment investigation of President Bill Clinton when software designers Wes Boyd and Joan

Blades started an e-mail petition urging Congress to censure the president and move on to other more pressing issues. Their Web site was initially called "Censure and Move On." As part of its effort to have bipartisan appeal, Lawrence Rockefeller, a moderate Republican and heir to the Rockefeller fortune, joined the effort to mobilize Republicans opposed to impeachment. Following the September 11 terrorist attacks, Eli Pariser started an online petition calling for a restrained and multilateral response to the attack. Pariser joined with MoveOn.Org and created the MoveOn Peace Campaign.

MoveOn has developed a tripartite structure. MoveOn.Org is a nonprofit organization, formed under section 501c4 of the Internal Revenue Code, that engages in education and issue advocacy. The MoveOn Political Action Committee (PAC), formed in June 1999, raised via small donations over the Internet and contributed more than $2 million to 30 Democratic congressional candidates during the 2000 ELECTION CYCLE, helping elect four new senators and five new members of the House of Representatives. The PAC contributed $3.5 million to congressional candidates during the 2002 cycle. The PAC lets donors select the recipients of their contributions from a list of endorsed candidates. The MoveOn.Org Voter Fund, a 527 organization, educates voters on the positions, records, views, and qualifications of candidates for public office. This can take the form of advocacy advertisements such as those produced by MoveOn.

MoveOn's actions have often aroused controversy. In January 2003, the group remade the "Daisy" spot from Lyndon Johnson's 1964 presidential campaign, the new version warning that a war against Iraq could lead to a nuclear war. CNN, Fox, and NBC all declined to sell airtime for the "Daisy" ad. Later in the year, the organization invited people to create their own anti-Bush ads. The "Bush in 30 Seconds" competition received more than 1,500 entries, two of which compared Bush to Hitler. Following criticism from Republicans, the ads were removed from the MoveOn.org Web site. The winning entry, "Child's Play," was rejected for broadcast during the Super Bowl by CBS, which claimed the spot violated the network's ban on advocacy ads. MoveOn supporters claimed the network was trying to curry favor with the Bush administration.

It was also discovered that Web sites had been set up outside the United States for the receipt of contributions for the purpose of defeating President Bush. Under federal law, foreign nationals cannot make financial contributions to presidential candidates. MoveOn's 527 foundation was not bound by this restriction but shut down the Web sites to avoid the perception of illegality.

In June 2003, the group held an electronic PRIMARY, and former Vermont governor Howard Dean emerged with 44 percent of the more than 300,000 votes that were cast over the Internet. However, the group announced that it would not endorse any candidate since no one had received a majority. Following Dean's withdrawal after poor performances in the IOWA CAUCUS and NEW HAMPSHIRE PRIMARY, the group shifted its support to John Kerry, who had emerged as the Democratic nominee.

The MoveOn PAC presented the Vote for Change Tour, featuring Bruce Springsteen and other performers. The concerts were performed in battleground states with the monies raised benefiting America Coming Together, a 527 organization. The organization claims to have more than 2 million online activists.

Further reading: MoveOn.org. Available online. URL: http://www.moveon.org. Accessed August 10, 2005.

—Jeffrey Kraus

muckraking

Muckraking, a forerunner of today's investigative journalism, was a loosely knit journalistic and literary movement that flourished from 1903 to 1912. Muckrakers sought to expose social ills, political corruption, and corporate abuses of power. Loosely identified with the PROGRESSIVE MOVEMENT, they wrote with a deep faith in progress, believing that exposure of wrong would goad politicians and people to reform. The depth of this faith would be cast in doubt, as later Muckrakers seemed to mirror some of the sensationalistic tactics and profit motives they once attacked.

At the turn of the 20th century, the United States was a nation of severe economic and political contrasts. A laissez-faire approach to POLITICS and business combined with rampant corporate expansion and consolidation seemed incapable of responding to the intense social and infrastructure crises of massive immigration, rapid urbanization, and a proliferating middle class. Numerous middle- and upper-class Americans, who came to be known as Progressives, began searching for means to address these crises. While many Progressives focused directly on policy and structural reform, the Muckrakers made it their goal to root out and publicize the nation's ills.

The first problem the Muckrakers faced was their own journalistic profession. American periodicals were deeply split into two primary media in 1900. On the one hand, this was the heyday of "yellow" journalism. Newspaper publishers such as the notorious William Randolph Hearst reconceived journalism as a big business whose primary goal was mass circulation. To achieve this goal, newspaper publishers engaged in all sorts of questionable tactics: crass sensationalism, publicity stunts, and a questionable commitment to accuracy. On the other hand, the nation's middle-class magazines (such as *Harper's* and the *Century*) attempted to foster a national ethic through a mix of decorous fiction and moderate calls to reform. One of the magazines' chief targets for censure was the daily press. The split between these two media took on a class dynamic due to the fact that the daily papers were cheap and widely popular, while the magazines were relatively expensive and were influential chiefly among social elites.

Magazine editor S. S. McClure is largely credited with founding the muckraking movement by attempting to create a hybrid of the newspapers' topicality and the magazines' virtuous reformism. Founding his self-named magazine, *McClure's*, in 1893, on the model of the established cultural monthly magazines, he quickly joined a group of magazine competitors who discovered that cheaper prices greatly increased circulation. Then, to differentiate his magazine from the other cheap monthlies, McClure searched for a new journalistic angle. He found it in a group of writers who had newspaper experience but magazine credibility.

The first muckraking articles appeared in late 1902 in *McClure's*. Lincoln Steffens's series on corrupt city governments from St. Louis to New York began in October. Ida Tarbell's richly documented exposé of John Rockefeller's Standard Oil Corporation ran for 18 months after its first installment appeared in November. Soon *McClure's* had competitors in the monthly magazine field of journalistic exposure. *Collier's, Cosmopolitan, Everybody's,* and other magazines began running exposés on Congress, police graft, the stock market, the insurance industry, race relations, prisons, child labor, unions, and other social and political problems.

Muckraking journalism was vital to the Progressive movement because of the way it nationalized the news. Daily papers rarely covered national stories beyond PRESIDENTIAL ELECTIONS and war news. By the very nature of their markets, most dailies limited themselves to local social issues concerning vice and MACHINE POLITICS. But muckraking articles appeared in nationally circulating magazines that turned local issues into national problems. Steffens's series on municipal government began with local case studies in a variety of cities and then wove these together to show how parochial conditions reflected national patterns.

Muckraking was not confined to magazines. Several authors turned to literature to create sympathy for Progressive reform. Upton Sinclair's 1906 novel *The Jungle* revealed a disgustingly fetid world in the stockyards and slaughterhouses of Chicago's beef industry. Frank Norris's novels *The Octopus* (1901) and *The Pit* (1903) exposed the bare-knuckled competition in the production and sale of wheat. David Graham Phillips attacked the insurance industry in *Lightfingered Gentry* (1907). Theodore Dreiser's two novels *The Financier* (1912) and *The Titan* (1914) could also be classified as muckraking literature.

Muckraking received a fair amount of criticism in its day. Theodore Roosevelt coined the term in 1906, adapting it from John Bunyan's *Pilgrim's Progress* as an epithet. The muckraker, Roosevelt declared, was a writer who ignored the "celestial crown," preferring instead to "rake to himself the filth of the floor." Elliot Sedgwick's *American Magazine*

decried muckraking as little more than newspaper sensationalism. In the muckraker's court, Sedgwick charged, "men are tried and found guilty in magazine counting rooms before the investigation is begun." (Ironically, Sedgwick's magazine was bought out by several leading muckrakers in 1906, while Sedgwick went on to revive the moribund *Atlantic Monthly* in the 1910s by making it more journalistic.) *Collier's*, which had itself published muckraking articles, condemned Phillips's *Cosmopolitan* series on the Senate as "one shriek of accusations."

Such criticism, however, cannot diminish the political impact of muckraking. Roosevelt himself was powerfully affected by *The Jungle*. He became a major proponent of the two pieces of legislation inspired by the novel, the Pure Food and Drug Act and the Meat Inspection Amendment (1906), and signed both of these monuments of Progressive reform into law. Steffens's series, which gained a wider impact when published in book form as *The Shame of the Cities* in 1906, was instrumental in popularizing the commission form of local government. Phillips's series of articles on Senate corruption, "The Treason of the Senate," contributed to the movement for direct election of U.S. senators that resulted in the SEVENTEENTH AMENDMENT to the Constitution. Other muckraking works bolstered Progressive reform of the insurance industry, labor conditions, advertising, and the trusts.

The politics of the muckrakers, however, never gelled into a coherent IDEOLOGY. McClure's original motivation for publishing Tarbell's series on Standard Oil, for instance, was less to expose Rockefeller than it was to reveal the workings of corporate trusts. Tarbell herself could never decide whether she was a journalist or a historian. Many muckrakers saw themselves as liberal reformers of capitalism, while others, particularly in the literary wing of the movement, were socialists who believed capitalism was the problem.

By 1912, the movement had grown increasingly sensationalistic, to the point that it lost its Progressive aura and seemed to become little more than a magazine version of yellow journalism. Hearst himself bought *Cosmopolitan* magazine in 1906 and published the series that elicited Roosevelt's condemnation of the new magazine journalism, Phillips's inflamed series "The Treason of the Senate." Even Upton Sinclair worried that Phillips "went too far." Readers seemed to tire of the constant discovery of wrongdoing and began to ignore the messenger. Finally, if Sinclair is to be believed, corporate interests sought revenge on the muckraking magazines by putting pressure on advertisers and banks to squeeze the monthlies where it hurt the most, in their sources of capital.

Further reading: Serrin, Judith, and William Serrin. *Muckraking! The Journalism That Changed America.* New York: New Press, 2002; Weinberg, Arthur, and Lila Weinberg, eds. *The Muckrakers.* Urbana: University of Illinois Press, 2001; Wilson, Harold. *McClure's Magazine and the Muckrakers.* Princeton, N.J.: Princeton University Press, 1970.

—Reynolds J. Scott-Childress

Mugwumps

The Mugwumps were Republicans who abandoned their party's nominee and supported the Democratic candidate, Grover Cleveland, in the 1884 PRESIDENTIAL ELECTION. Today the term is applied to any INDEPENDENT voters or political mavericks, especially those who bolt their own party to favor the opposition. It may also describe someone who appears to remain above the fray of conventional POLITICS, focusing instead on their own neutrality or intellectual objectivity.

The word is a derivation of *mugquomp,* a Native American term from the Algonquian tribe meaning "great chief," and was used in John Eliot's Massachusetts Bible (Indian Bible) as early as 1663. The modern spelling dates to the 1830s, when various civic organizations referred to important men, or bosses, as "mugwumps." It entered the political lexicon in June 1884 when a New York newspaper derisively referred to those liberal, independent Republicans who refused to accept the NOMINATION of their party's candidate, James G. Blaine.

Blaine was a senator from Maine and had long served the REPUBLICAN PARTY. Though SCANDALS involving a questionable bond deal, bribery, and marital misconduct had hounded him since 1876, he was supported by Stalwart (conservative) and Half-Breed (moderate) Republicans. They considered him their ablest politician and the most practical choice. These were the very reasons, however, the Mugwumps refused to support him. They were idealistic reformers who scorned his political careerism and his reputation for MACHINE POLITICS. They considered him a politics-as-usual spoilsman with corrupt ties to big business. Though such accusations were undoubtedly exaggerated, the Mugwump defection may have cost the Republicans the election. Cleveland won the POPULAR VOTE by less than three-tenths of 1 percent, with New York casting the deciding vote in the ELECTORAL COLLEGE.

The Mugwumps considered themselves guardians of the public trust, men who valued principles over politics. They emphasized civil service reform and political independence. Political PATRONAGE was despised. They supported sound money, the gold standard, free trade, tariff reform, and an antiimperialist foreign policy. The majority were oldline Anglo-Saxon Protestants from the urban Northeast who were male, college educated, and members of the professional class. Among this group were such luminaries as Charles W. Eliot; George William Curtis, Seth Low, and Carl Schurz; even Samuel Clemens (Mark Twain) claimed membership. Their elitist credentials and aloof attitude set them apart from the American mainstream and often placed them at odds with other Republicans, who considered Mugwumps self-righteous, or worse, hypocritical.

Mugwumpery declined steadily after the 1884 election. The reformers' insistence on political independence hampered their ability to form meaningful COALITIONs. In addition, their inflexible, orthodox views failed to mesh with the growing influence of either the Progressives or the new industrial elites.

However, Mugwump contributions to the modern political landscape are significant. Their efforts helped professionalize the civil service and led to a growing public reliance on specialized, university-trained experts. They increased awareness of political corruption and encouraged honest, virtuous government. More recently, their legacy is seen in politicians such as Senator John McCain of Arizona, who defied many of his party's leaders in his support of the Bipartisan Campaign Reform Act of 2002.

Further reading: Hofstadter, Richard. *The Age of Reform: From Bryan to F.D.R.* New York: Knopf, 1955; McFarland, Gerald W. *Mugwumps, Morals, and Politics, 1884–1920.* Amherst: University of Massachusetts Press, 1995; Sproat, John G. *The Best Men: Liberal Reformers in the Gilded Age.* New York: Oxford University Press, 1968; Tucker, David M. *Mugwumps: Public Moralists of the Gilded Age.* Columbia: University of Missouri Press, 1998.

—R. Matthew Poteat

multimember district

Multimember districts are electoral areas in which more than one candidate is elected to represent a particular CONSTITUENCY. Districts that employ an electoral system of PROPORTIONAL REPRESENTATION use multimember districts to distribute legislative seats. Initially, multimember districts represented the chief means of preserving county boundaries as the defining geographic unit while maintaining equally populated electoral districts. Indeed, prior to the 1970s and 1980s, multimember districts were widely used in state legislatures as the primary method for distributing legislative seats.

Though popular and widely used at the municipal and county levels, multimember districts are in decline at the state level. Critics tend to argue that multimember districts inhibit minority representation, thereby affecting legislative composition. Opponents assert that by diluting minority voting strength within a district, multimember districts potentially dilute the number of minorities likely to serve in a particular state legislature. Following a wave of protest from minority groups contending that multimember districts disproportionately affect the ability of minorities to effectively convey political and policy interests, litigation began to emerge regarding the relationship between electoral structures and legislative composition.

Several court rulings throughout the 1970s and 1980s challenged the use of multimember districts on the grounds that vote dilution of minorities is in direct violation of the Equal Protection Clause of the FOURTEENTH AMENDMENT. Subsequently, the U.S. Supreme Court institutionalized a three-part test to determine whether multimember districts dilute minority voting strength: 1) the minority group must demonstrate that it is sufficiently large and geographically concentrated enough to constitute a majority in a SINGLE-MEMBER DISTRICT, 2) it is demonstrated that the minority group is politically cohesive, and 3) the minority group demonstrates that the majority consistently votes to block and defeat the minority candidate. Nevertheless, while the U.S. Supreme Court and district court rulings have encouraged the use of single-member districts, the Supreme Court has held that multimember districts are not unconstitutional.

Despite the opposition to multimember districts and a general decline in the number of states employing them as well as the size of multimember districts, several states still use these types of districts to distribute legislative seats. Recent scholarly research tends to focus on the effects of multimember districts on both minority and female descriptive representation. While finding that multimember districts tend to disproportionately affect minority representation, research suggests they enhance the opportunities for female descriptive representation.

Further reading: Gerber, Elisabeth R., Rebecca A. Morton, and Thomas A. Rietz. "Minority Representation in Multimember Districts." *American Political Science Review* 92, no. 1 (1998): 127–144; Rule, Wilma, and Joseph F. Zimmerman, eds. *United States Electoral Systems: Their Impact on Women and Minorities.* Westport, Conn.: Greenwood Press, 1992.

—Christopher Larimer

N

name recognition

Name recognition refers to the ability of individuals, usually voters in the political context, to recognize a candidate's name either in print, on radio, or on television. In studies of voter familiarity with candidates, a strong distinction is made between name recognition and name recall. While Americans seem to have a great deal of trouble *recalling* names of candidates or elected officials, they fare much better with regard to *recognizing* the names of such individuals. Early research, which focused strictly on name recall, concluded pessimistically about the political knowledge of Americans. From the early research it appeared that citizens were ill-informed about their representatives.

Later research, which incorporated name recognition as well as recall, produced far more favorable results. For instance, a voter might not be able to remember a candidate's name several weeks prior to an election, but that same person is often capable of recognizing his or her preferred candidate on a BALLOT that stresses recognition rather than recall. Studies suggest that voters use voting heuristics (i.e., information shortcuts) to make informed decisions while possessing limited information about a specific candidate. For instance, a LABOR GROUP endorsement or simple party label is often enough for a voter to vote in a manner that is consistent with his or her preference. In other words, knowing which groups support a candidate is often enough information for a voter to make an informed decision (i.e., the decision he or she would have made with more detailed information).

In modern American POLITICS, a great deal of money is spent by candidates trying simply to get their names across; one need think only of the vast amount of bumper stickers, buttons, and placards in the weeks leading up to an election, often featuring nothing other than a candidate's name. In the end, however, name recognition is but one part, usually a preliminary part, of a general campaign effort. While candidates who have failed to earn name recognition are unlikely to win an election, voters must also be able to associate the candidate's name with a reason to vote for that person, making name recognition a necessary but insufficient end in electoral politics.

Further reading: Jacobson, Gary C. *The Politics of Congressional Elections.* 6th ed. New York: Pearson Longman, 2000; Sidlow, Edward. *Challenging the Incumbent: An Underdog's Undertaking.* Washington, D.C.: CQ Press, 2003.

—Dari E. Sylvester

NASCAR dads

NASCAR dads refers to a popular political and marketing demographic category of mostly white, working-class, conservative male fans of NASCAR racing. Although predominantly southern in character, the NASCAR fan base has experienced significant growth in the past decade in rural and suburban areas across the nation. NASCAR estimates its 2004 fan base at 75 million, of which 45 million are men. A total of 58 percent of NASCAR fans fall into the 18 to 44 age group and have average annual incomes of approximately $55,000.

The term first gained national attention in press coverage of the MIDTERM ELECTIONS of 2002. Democratic pollster Celinda Lake argued in an interview to the Associated Press in June 2002 that Democrats should focus more of their campaign efforts on attracting these voters. During the 2004 campaign, political analysts argued that NASCAR dads constituted an important base of SWING VOTERs much like "Soccer moms" in the 1996 and 2000 campaigns. Although the group traditionally leans Republican, Democrats hoped that by emphasizing economic issues they could increase NASCAR dad support for Democratic candidates. Some 72 percent of NASCAR dads identified economic insecurity in campaign polls as one of the most important political issues influencing their potential 2004 PRESIDENTIAL ELECTION vote.

President George W. Bush and the REPUBLICAN PARTY, however, were most successful in attracting these voters during the 2004 campaign. The Edison Media

Research and Mitofsky International 2004 Presidential election EXIT POLL of 13,360 voters for the National Election Pool found Bush with a 25 percent advantage over John Kerry among white male voters: Bush captured 67 percent of these voters versus Kerry's 37 percent. Additionally, Bush held a large lead in the South, capturing 58 percent of the vote and averaging a 52 percent to 59 percent advantage over Kerry in suburban, small town, and rural communities.

President Bush and Vice President Dick Cheney made several appearances during major NASCAR events. In February 2004, for example, after having Air Force One make a fly-over of the crowded raceway, Bush, dressed in a black NASCAR racing jacket, kicked off the Daytona 500 to an audience of 200,000 attendees and 40 million television viewers. In July, President Bush invited 2004 Indianapolis 500 winner Buddy Rice to the White House for a photo opportunity with the president, complete with NASCAR props. The Bush campaign also developed a line of campaign memorabilia under the label Interstate W'04. Available at GeorgeWBushstore.com, the products included racing caps, t-shirts, and coffee mugs designed to attract NASCAR fans. The Republicans also conducted an aggressive VOTER REGISTRATION drive, opening registration booths at a number of NASCAR events. The Bush campaign's emphasis on national security, gun rights, and socially conservative issues may have also increased NASCAR dad voter loyalty.

Further reading: Kintner, Hallie J., Thomas W. Merrick, Peter A. Morrison, and Paul R. Voss. *Demographics: A Casebook for Business and Government.* Washington, D.C.: Rand, 1997; Michman, Ronald D. *Lifestyle Market Segmentation.* New York: Praeger, 1991; Chiagouris, Larry, and Lynn R. Kahle. *Values, Lifestyle and Psychographics.* Mahwah, N.J.: Lawrence Erlbaum Associates, 1997.

—Jamie Patrick Chandler

National Association for the Advancement of Colored People (NAACP)

The National Association for the Advancement of Colored People (NAACP) is one of the oldest social justice organizations in the United States. It was founded as the National Negro Committee on February 12, 1909, by, among others, Ida Wells-Barnett, W. E. B. DuBois, Henry Moscowitz, Mary White Ovington, Oswald Garrison Villiard, and William English Walling, a multiracial group of national leaders who had met to discuss increasing violence against African Americans. The organization focused its early efforts on antilynching campaigns and protesting against segregation within the federal government. Early leaders of the organization included Walter White, James Weldon Johnson, and Roy Wilkins.

At the core of the NAACP's approach is fighting for the enforcement of the civil rights guarantees contained in the U.S. Constitution. This strategy has manifested itself in a number of legal challenges to discrimination on the basis of race. Perhaps the group's best-known challenge to discriminatory practices was the landmark 1954 Supreme Court case of *Brown v. Board of Education of Topeka, Kansas.* In *Brown,* the NAACP's legal team, led by future Supreme Court justice Thurgood Marshall, argued on behalf of plaintiffs from Delaware, the District of Columbia, Kansas, South Carolina, and Virginia that the principle of "separate but equal," articulated by the Court in 1896 in *Plessey v. Ferguson,* resulted in unconstitutional racial discrimination against black schoolchildren when applied to the nation's public school system. The Court agreed with this argument and found in favor of the petitioners, marking the end of de jure racial segregation in public schools.

Prior to and after the decision in *Brown,* the NAACP achieved important legal victories in cases challenging white primaries, discrimination in public accommodations, and restrictive covenants designed to preclude blacks from owning homes in white neighborhoods. While the NAACP maintains a legal department of its own, the NAACP Legal Defense and Education Fund (LDF), which has been completely independent of the NAACP since 1957, now has primary responsibility for bringing lawsuits to challenge discriminatory practices. The LDF has successfully litigated suits against companies who discriminate against customers and employees on the basis of race, gender, or ethnicity.

In addition to its efforts in the courtroom, the NAACP has devoted much effort to influencing public opinion regarding issues of race. Its journal, *The Crisis,* became an important opinion leader in the early 1900s under the direction of W. E. B. DuBois. Among the writers whose work appeared in *The Crisis* were noted Harlem Renaissance writers Countee Cullen and Langston Hughes. Local NAACP officer Rosa Parks launched the Montgomery, Alabama, bus boycott in 1955 by refusing to yield her seat to a white passenger. Members of the NAACP Youth Council in Greensboro, N.C., led nonviolent sit-ins at segregated lunch counters in the town in 1960. The NAACP also coordinated large-scale VOTER REGISTRATION campaigns and organized marches to protest racial injustice.

During the 1980s and early 1990s, the organization struggled to remain relevant and was beset by SCANDAL, dissension, and mismanagement. Longtime executive director Benjamin Hooks resigned from his post in February 1992 after a 15-year tenure that was marked by conflict with members of the board of directors. His successor, Benjamin Chavis, caused a stir among the group's black and white supporters by associating with Nation of Islam leader, Minister Louis Farrakhan. Chavis, who eventually converted to the Muslim faith, was forced to resign as executive director in 1995 after admitting to using NAACP funds to pay a settlement in a sexual harassment suit that had been filed against him by a former NAACP employee.

In addition to its internal strife, the organization has been criticized for employing outdated methods, such as marches, to achieve social change. In addition, other people of color and marginalized persons have complained that the NAACP focuses on the concerns of African Americans to the exclusion of other groups who suffer from discrimination.

Although its reliance on mass protest has been criticized, the NAACP recently has realized limited success from this traditional form of protest. On January 17, 2000, the NAACP held a march in Columbia, S.C., to protest the flying of the Confederate flag over the statehouse. Although the group was successful in getting the flag removed from the statehouse dome, it continues to protest the flag's presence on the grounds of the state capitol building. The group maintains an economic boycott against the state.

In addition to its activities promoting social justice, the NAACP remains a symbolic representative of the African-American community on the national scene, as evidenced by the importance attached to prospective presidential candidates appearing at the annual NAACP convention. The organization's newfound stability and relevance appear to be largely attributable to the change in leadership after the ouster of Benjamin Chavis in 1995. The current chair of the board of directors, Julian Bond, was the first African American to be elected to the Georgia state legislature. Kweisi Mfume, a former U.S. representative from Maryland and chair of the CONGRESSIONAL BLACK CAUCUS, is the president and CEO. Both have raised the profile and repaired the image of the organization. Included in the NAACP's approximately 500,000 members are more than 400 chapters of youth councils and college chapters, consisting of more than 67,000 members.

Further reading: NAACP. Available online. URL: http://www.naacp.org. Accessed August 10, 2005; Tushnet, Mark V. *NAACP's Legal Strategy against Segregated Education, 1925–1950.* Chapel Hill: University of North Carolina Press, 1987; Williams, Juan. *Thurgood Marshall: American Revolutionary.* New York: Random House, 2000.
—John L. S. Simpkins

National Election Study

The National Election Study (NES) is an ongoing survey research program headquartered at the University of Michigan. NES has conducted national surveys of the American ELECTORATE in every PRESIDENTIAL ELECTION since 1952 and in every midterm congressional election since 1958. Continuity in the content and scope of the NES questionnaires has allowed researchers to examine long-term trends in voting behavior and assess the impact of important political developments and historical events.

NES has provided important innovations in survey design and execution, and perhaps most importantly, it has spawned an international community of students and schol-ars interested in American voting behavior. NES is the single most comprehensive and most widely used source of survey data on the preferences and behaviors of American voters. More than 3,000 books, journal articles, and doctoral dissertations have employed NES data.

In addition to vote choice, the typical NES questionnaire covers a broad range of topics. Many of the specific survey questions have been asked consistently over time, allowing researchers to compare results across elections. At the same time, NES does modify the questionnaire—adding some survey questions, deleting others—to reflect changes in the political landscape. Among the core topics consistently covered by NES are interest in the campaign and attention to media coverage, assessments of national and personal economic conditions, evaluations of political parties and major party candidates, party allegiances, liberal-conservative self-identification, preferences on a variety of policy issues, trust in government, and demographic characteristics of survey respondents.

In presidential election years, NES has drawn national probability samples of 1,800 to 2,500 voting age adults and has interviewed people both before and after the election. Preelection interviews are generally done on a face-to-face basis, though the 2000 NES incorporated telephone interviews as well. Most of the core NES questions are asked in the preelection interview. Respondents are recontacted for a brief postelection interview, typically conducted by phone. The congressional election year surveys are more modest in scale; sample sizes are smaller, and only a postelection interview is conducted.

National Election Study datasets, questionnaires, and other supporting materials are publicly available. They can be obtained through the Interuniversity Consortium for Political and Social Research, or directly from NES. Some data and documentation can be downloaded from the NES Web site.

Further reading: National Election Study. Available online. URL: http://www.umich.edu/~nes. Accessed August 10, 2005.

—Julio Borquez

National Organization for Women (NOW)

The National Organization for Women (NOW) is the largest feminist political group in the United States. As the CIVIL RIGHTS MOVEMENT of the 1950s and 1960s progressed, women also began to focus the nation's attention on issues concerning their status in the country. NOW was formed on October 29, 1966, with the goal of combating discrimination against women in American society. Betty Friedan served as the organization's first president.

Throughout much of the history of the United States, women had been denied equal rights: through laws that prevented women from entering particular fields of study

Betty Friedan, president of the National Organization for Women, tells reporters in the New York state assembly of her intention to "put sex into section I of the New York constitution," 1967. *(Library of Congress)*

and related occupations such as law and medicine; through customs that prevented women from controlling their own property once they married; and, perhaps most visibly, through laws that prevented women from voting. Before the development of NOW and other feminist organizations, the Supreme Court on a routine basis had ruled that laws allowing for gender discrimination were constitutional.

One of NOW's primary concerns is working for the enactment and enforcement of laws that prevent gender discrimination, including sexual harassment. Soon after its creation, NOW turned its attention to ensuring that Title VII provisions of the 1964 Civil Rights Act were appropriately enforced. This legislation required that men and women be treated equally in the workplace. NOW put pressure on agencies such as the Equal Employment Opportunity Commission to ensure that the commission created specific guidelines to allow for the investigation of and solutions to allegations of sexual discrimination in the workplace.

In addition to issues of workplace fairness, NOW also works through the legislative and judicial processes to ensure that women have reproductive freedom, that both mothers and fathers receive fair treatment from their

employers regarding child care responsibilities, that women have the opportunity to be educated in any area of study they choose, and that tax policies are designed in such a way as to treat working women fairly. Perhaps the best example of NOW's efforts in pursuing such legislation was the active role it played in promoting passage of the Equal Rights Amendment in the 1970s and early 1980s. The amendment stated that "Equality of rights under the law shall not be denied or abridged by the United States or any State on account of sex."

Since 1978, NOW has been actively involved in financially supporting candidates for public office through its POLITICAL ACTION COMMITTEE, NOW-PAC. NOW-PAC contributes campaign funds to both male and female candidates who pursue the enactment of feminist policies. More recently, NOW has also begun an initiative to encourage feminist candidates to run for office. Elect Women for a Change provides candidates with assistance in organizing, funding, and running campaigns. Equally important, such initiatives also promote the development of leadership skills.

Further reading: Friedan, Betty. *It Changed My Life: Writings on the Women's Movement.* New York: Random House, 1976; National Organization for Women. Available online. URL: http://www.now.org. Accessed August 10, 2005.

—Claudia Bryant

national party committees

National party committees are the six branches of the Democratic and Republican parties that seek to elect and raise money for their candidates. They include the parties' main committees as well as those that seek to increase their numbers in Congress. The national party committees are the DEMOCRATIC NATIONAL COMMITTEE (DNC) and the REPUBLICAN NATIONAL COMMITTEE (RNC); the DEMOCRATIC SENATORIAL CAMPAIGN COMMITTEE (DSCC) and the NATIONAL REPUBLICAN SENATORIAL COMMITTEE (NRSC); and the Democratic Congressional Campaign Committee (DCCC) and the National Republican Congressional Committee (NRCC).

The first national party committee was the DNC, which was created in 1848. The main party committees plan presidential nominating conventions every four years, raise money, seek to increase VOTER REGISTRATION, conduct voter outreach, work with state and local parties to elect candidates, respond to attacks from the other party, and promote the party's message both in election and non-election years. All party committees offer financial and technical support to their candidates by donating money to their campaigns, offering candidate-training workshops, providing staff members, conducting polls, doing OPPOSITION RESEARCH, distributing voter rolls, producing commercials, and scheduling air dates for ads.

Historically, the party committees have enjoyed an influential role in POLITICS. In 1896, for example, RNC chairman Mark Hanna played a major role in selecting his party's presidential candidate, William McKinley. The committees provided a nationally coherent message that local party leaders could rally around and were expected to support. This top-down system changed, however, with the rise of direct primaries and the weakening of parties, especially from the 1950s to the 1970s. Party committees today wield little influence in choosing which candidates run for office and generally avoid endorsing one candidate during the PRIMARY. In December 2003, then FRONTRUNNER Howard Dean asked DNC chairman Terry McAuliffe to step in and end intraparty squabbling, but McAuliffe refused.

In recent decades, candidates have felt less beholden to the party committees and acted as independent political entrepreneurs, hiring their own political advisers rather than relying on help from party leaders. The diminished number of competitive seats, especially in the House; the growing number of candidates who are able to finance their own campaigns; and the rise of POLITICAL ACTION COMMITTEES (PACs) and leadership PACs—through which candidates donate money to other candidates to increase their own power—have also reduced the committees' influence.

The party committees underwent a profound change in how they raise money following passage of the Bipartisan Campaign Reform Act of 2002. Previously, both parties, especially the Democrats, had relied on SOFT MONEY (i.e., large contributions that were unregulated by the FEDERAL ELECTION COMMISSION) to help fund campaigns. But the party committees adjusted well to the new rules, which barred soft money and increased HARD MONEY contributions from $1,000 to $2,000 per individual in the primary and GENERAL ELECTIONS. According to the Center for Responsive Politics, the RNC raised $330 million in the 2003–04 ELECTION CYCLE, while the DNC took in $299 million. The DSCC brought in $76 million to top the NRSC, which raised $68 million. The NRCC collected $159 million, more than double the DCCC's $76 million.

With a dwindling number of competitive seats in Congress, party committees wield influence by focusing on vulnerable candidates. National party committees can give $20,000 to a House candidate and $17,500 to a Senate candidate in an election cycle, but are allowed to spend additional money on behalf of candidates. Party committees require party leaders, members in SAFE SEATs, and lawmakers who sit on high-profile committees to give money to candidates in MARGINAL DISTRICTS. In 2002, members in safe districts gave more than $30 million to other candidates' campaigns. The candidates donating the money then use that leverage to further their own careers. Before her election to the House in November 2004, Florida Democrat Debbie Wasserman Schultz gained notice by donating $100,000 to the DCCC.

Party leaders also remind vulnerable officeholders of the financial assistance that party committees provide as a way to ensure that members tow the party line. When Representative Rodney Alexander (R, La.) left the DEMOCRATIC PARTY in 2004, DCCC chairman Robert Matsui (D, Calif.) demanded that Alexander return $70,000 Democratic members gave him in the 2003–04 election cycle and the $193,000 the DCCC spent on his 2002 election, which he narrowly won.

National party committees exert more influence when a campaign is nationalized and when party leaders work together. In 1994, Representative Newt Gingrich (R, Ga.) led Republicans in regaining control of the House and Senate by proclaiming a CONTRACT WITH AMERICA and promising to end decades of Democratic rule. The lack of presidential COATTAILS in many recent elections and the individual nature of campaigns today, however, have tested coordination among the committees.

National party chairs must present an image of a unified party to reassure voters, donors, and potential candidates and act as the parties' chief strategist and cheerleader (as well as spokesperson when the party is out of power). Many chairs serve one election cycle, either four years as head of the DNC or RNC, or two years at the helm of the congressional party committees. Chairs who lead party committees in years when their presidential candidate loses can expect to be replaced.

Presidents exert considerable influence in suggesting party committee chairs. Bill Clinton tapped his close friend McAuliffe to head the DNC, although some Democrats complained that McAuliffe was more skilled at raising money than recruiting candidates and helping the party form a cohesive message. George W. Bush suggested that his CAMPAIGN MANAGER, Ken Mehlman, succeed Ed Gillespie in heading the RNC following the 2004 elections.

In Congress, party committee chairs are often awarded to ambitious lawmakers with close ties to party leaders who are able to raise large amounts of money and willing to travel frequently to campaign for candidates. After NRSC chair Bill Frist (R, Tenn.) helped Republicans regain the Senate in the 2002 elections, he was selected to succeed Senator Trent Lott (R, Miss.) as the Senate's Republican leader. Representative Nancy Pelosi's (D, Calif.) success in raising money as the DCCC chair helped her become House minority leader.

Further reading: Jacobson, Gary C. *The Politics of Congressional Elections*. 6th ed. New York: Pearson Education, 2004; Sorauf, Frank J., and Paul Allen Beck. *Party Politics in America*. Glenview, Ill.: Scott, Foresman & Co., 1988.

—Mary Lynn F. Jones

National Republican Senatorial Committee (NRSC)

The National Republican Senatorial Committee (NRSC) supports the election of Republican candidates to the U.S.

Senate by making contributions to candidates, recruiting candidates, and providing technical and research assistance to candidates. The committee is sometimes referred to, along with the National Republican Congressional Committee (NRCC), the Democratic Congressional Campaign Committee (DCCC), and the DEMOCRATIC SENATORIAL CAMPAIGN COMMITTEE (DSCC), as a "Hill committee."

In addition to providing support for incumbents, the committee may recruit Republican candidates (while sometimes discouraging others) in targeted races. Recruitment of candidates might include polls that provide the prospective candidate with an idea of the political landscape, promises of financial and staff support, and entreaties from the chair of the committee and other leading Republicans. FUND-RAISING services provided by the committee to Republican Senate candidates include helping organize fund-raising events and developing DIRECT MAIL campaigns.

The NRSC is headed by a senator elected by the members of the Republican conference in the Senate. The committee chair travels extensively on behalf of Republican candidates, speaking to party groups and contacting major contributors. It is considered a springboard to other leadership positions in the Senate. The current Republican (and Senate Majority Leader) William Frist previously chaired the NRSC.

The committee was established by Republican leaders in the Senate in 1916, after the SEVENTEENTH AMENDMENT to the Constitution changed the manner of election of U.S. senators from election by the state legislatures to direct election by the voters. The committee was founded to assist incumbent Republican senators with their reelection campaigns.

Throughout most of its history the NRSC, as well as the other Hill committees, had little power over state and local POLITICAL PARTY leaders. However, the decline of state and local PARTY ORGANIZATIONs in the years following World War II (as the expansion of the civil service, suburbanization, television, and an increase in the number of two-income households served to undermine party organizations) and the disastrous showing of the REPUBLICAN PARTY in the 1974 (post-Watergate election) midterm elections resulted in the committee expanding its role by increasing its support for candidates as well as state party organizations.

The NRSC emerged, along with the Republican Congressional Campaign Committee, in the 1980s as a significant fund-raising force on behalf of Republican candidates, forcing its Democratic counterparts to match its efforts.

The 1996 U.S. Supreme Court decision in *Colorado Republican Federal Campaign Committee v. FEC* permitted party committees (including the NRSC) to make INDEPENDENT EXPENDITURES in federal elections. This ruling allowed the NRSC to advocate the election or defeat of a federal candidate so long as the expenditure was made without that candidate's knowledge or consent. In 1996, the NRSC made $9.4 million in independent expenditures compared to $1.4 million by its Democratic counterpart.

The Bipartisan Campaign Reform (McCAIN-FEINGOLD) Act outlawed SOFT MONEY contributions to party committees such as the NRSC. Soft money refers to donations that are not earmarked for particular candidates or elections. This prohibition took effect following the 2002 ELECTION CYCLE, during which the NRSC spent $126,600,475.

Further reading: Jacobson, Gary C. "Parties and PACs in Congressional Elections." In Lawrence D. Dodd and Bruce I. Oppenheimer, eds., *Congress Reconsidered.* Washington, D.C.: Congressional Quarterly Press, 1985; Kolodny, Robin. *Pursuing Majorities: Congressional Campaign Committees in American Politics.* Norman: University of Oklahoma Press, 1998; National Republican Senatorial Committee. Available online. URL: http://www.nrsc.org. Accessed August 10, 2005.

—Jeffrey Kraus

National Unity Campaign

The National Unity Campaign was not a true POLITICAL PARTY. Instead it was the 1980 presidential CAMPAIGN ORGANIZATION of INDEPENDENT candidate John Bayard Anderson. The National Unity Campaign did not exist before Anderson declared his candidacy, and it died with his failed election bid.

John Anderson was born in 1922 in Rockford, Illinois, and served for two decades (1960–80) as a Republican member of the U.S. House of Representatives. Anderson held conservative positions on economic policy but was liberal on social issues and foreign policy. Anderson ran for the 1980 Republican presidential NOMINATION but ultimately lost the race to Ronald Reagan. Undeterred, Anderson announced that he would continue running as an independent candidate and selected Wisconsin governor Patrick J. Lucey, a Democrat, as his RUNNING MATE.

The Anderson-Lucey ticket sought to capture the votes of Americans who were tired of Jimmy Carter's presidency and skeptical of Ronald Reagan's staunch conservatism. Anderson defined himself as "The Only Alternative for a Better America." The media referred to him as a SPOILER, to which he replied, "What's to spoil? Spoil the chances of two men at least half the country doesn't want?" The National Unity Campaign emphasized Anderson's support for environmental protection, civil rights, the Equal Rights Amendment, federal abortion funding, and reducing governmental regulation.

Anderson drew much public notice in the summer of 1980. He was featured in the *Doonesbury* comic strip and even appeared on *Saturday Night Live.* In June and July, support for Anderson was as high as 24 percent, and for a time in New England he was ahead of both Carter and Reagan in the polls. Both major party campaigns feared Anderson would cut into their electoral COALITIONS. Anderson challenged Carter and Reagan to a debate in September. Carter demurred, fearing that Anderson's gains would be his losses, but Reagan appeared at the debate and won convincingly. The debate substantially weakened Anderson's campaign and gave Reagan a boost.

On ELECTION DAY, Anderson won more than 5.7 million votes, or 6.6 percent of the POPULAR VOTE (Reagan took 50.7 percent; Carter, 41 percent). He did not win any electoral votes. EXIT POLLS showed that Anderson's supporters were disproportionately liberal, nonsouthern, and of high socioeconomic status.

One of the more important legacies of the National Unity Campaign is the fact that Anderson pushed for public reimbursement of independent presidential candidates' CAMPAIGN EXPENDITURES. The FEDERAL ELECTION COMMISSION ruled by a 5 to 1 vote that even though Anderson's candidacy was not tied to any established party, he would be treated as a third-party candidate for campaign finance purposes. As such, he was reimbursed for $4.2 million in campaign expenditures after the election. Anderson also helped pave the way for future third-party candidates such as H. Ross Perot by fighting a difficult and costly (more than $2.5 million) battle for access to the BALLOT in all 50 states. Anderson retired from political life after the 1980 election.

Further reading: Bisnow, Mark. *Diary of a Dark Horse: The 1980 Anderson Presidential Campaign.* Carbondale: Southern Illinois University Press, 1983; Lipset, Seymour Martin, ed. *Party Coalitions in the 1980s.* New Brunswick, N.J.: Transaction Books, 1981; Rosenstone, Steven J., Roy L. Behr, and Edward H. Lazarus. *Third Parties in America.* Princeton, N.J.: Princeton University Press, 1984.

—Laura R. Olson

Natural Law Party

The Natural Law Party is a minor party established on the principles of the laws of nature and seeks to apply those tenets to governance at the local, state, and national levels. Its philosophy, derived from the transcendental meditation movement, states that natural law is the organizing principle that governs the universe and that adherence to that principle can result in more effective policy and a more peaceful society.

The Natural Law Party was founded in April 1992 in Fairfield, Iowa, by followers of the transcendental meditation movement. Since that time, Dr. John Hagelin, a Harvard-educated quantum physicist, has run as the party's presidential candidate. In 1992, the party gained BALLOT ACCESS in 32 states and received 39,000 votes. Four years later, Hagelin and vice presidential candidate Mike Tompkins won access to the ballot in 44 states and garnered 110,000 votes. In 2000, Hagelin and vice presidential candidate Nathaniel Goldhaber were on the ballot in 39 states and achieved 83,000 votes.

The Natural Law Party's ideological stance can best be seen in its platform and its commitment to "prevention-oriented government and conflict free politics." The means by which party supporters hope to bring about these goals is through the application of alternative techniques such as holistic medicine and transcendental mediation. Through these practices, Natural Law Party supporters claim reduced stress, a healthier lifestyle, and more happiness. Applying these ideas to government, it is claimed, will lead to reduced social problems, a lower tax burden, a government that is more efficient, and an economy that is more productive.

In particular, the Natural Law Party also seeks to encourage the development and expansion of clean energy, the mandatory labeling of genetically altered foods, an elimination of political action committees and SOFT MONEY, and a ban on the development and construction of nuclear energy plants. On the issue of abortion, the party does not explicitly state a preference but instead maintains that it is committed to reducing the number of abortions through educational, not legislative, means.

Organizationally, the Natural Law Party boasts an organization that rivals established THIRD PARTIES. The Natural Law Party of the United States is the largest of approximately 60 Natural Law Parties throughout the world. Within this country, the Natural Law Party is active in all 50 states and runs a large number of candidates for a variety of offices. While Natural Law candidates have not been successful at either national or state level races, a few hold offices at the local level.

Further reading: Natural Law Party. Available online. URL: http://www.natural-law.org. Accessed August 10, 2005; Ness, Immanuel, and James Ciment, eds. *The Encyclopedia of Third Parties in America.* Armonk, N.Y.: M.E. Sharpe, 2000; Roth, Robert. *A Reason to Vote.* New York: St. Martin's Press, 1998.

—Stephen Nemeth

New Alliance Party

The New Alliance Party (NAP) was one of the more controversial minor parties of the 1980s and 1990s. The NAP purported to be a "Black-led, multi-racial, pro-socialist, pro-gay" organization. In reality, it was a front group for Dr. Fred Newman, a New York City psychotherapist. Newman, who had gained a devoted, cultlike following by way of his social therapy practice, aspired to expand his power base through POLITICS.

The party's origins date back to the 1960s, when Newman abandoned an academic career to establish a commune, the Centers for Change (CFC). The commune included a mental health clinic where Newman and his small group of followers practiced a brand of experimental psychology known as social therapy. Melding the ideas of Russian psychiatrist Lev Vygotsky with Marxism-Leninism, social therapy taught patients that they could cure themselves if they rejected "bourgeois" culture and became politically engaged.

Newman's therapists dictated that political engagement should involve recruiting new patients and making large donations to the CFC. The organization enjoyed a steady influx of clients and cash as a result. Emboldened, Newman enlarged his operations, creating the International Workers Party in 1974. Like the CFC, this organization raised money and sought recruits through social therapy. In 1979 Newman created a second party, the NAP.

The party compelled social therapy clients to donate their time and money to the party. On several occasions it infiltrated other political organizations, using their existing infrastructures to advance its cause. It also attacked opponents, suing to keep political rivals off BALLOTs and verbally harassing critics. At the same time, the party publicly promoted a host of democratic causes, winning it support among mainstream leftists.

The NAP began organizing at the national level in 1983 and in 1984 ran its first presidential candidate, Dennis Serrettee, who received approximately 47,000 votes. The party grew during the mid-1980s but became increasingly controversial. Besides questioning the party's FUND-RAISING and recruiting tactics, critics accused the party of anti-Semitism after Newman, Jewish himself, remarked in a 1985 speech that Jews were "the storm troopers of decadent capitalism." Despite the mounting criticism, the NAP achieved BALLOT ACCESS in all 50 states in the 1988 PRESIDENTIAL ELECTION, a rarity for a third party. The party's national chair, Lenora Fulani, received the party's NOMINATION, garnering more than 217,000 votes. In 1992, the NAP again nominated Fulani, but her vote total dropped to 73,714—the controversy surrounding the party had finally taken its toll. Newman disbanded the NAP in 1994.

Although the NAP is officially defunct, Newman, Fulani, and other former party members continue their political operations. Resorting to old tactics, in 1994 Newman's followers captured various leadership posts in the Patriot Party, organized by supporters of Ross Perot's 1992 presidential bid. In 1996, Fulani and cohorts began infiltrating Perot's newly created REFORM PARTY. By 2000, they controlled one-third of the party's national DELEGATEs. Fulani and Newman initially endorsed conservative columnist Patrick J. Buchanan for the Reform Party presidential nomination, but they retracted their ENDORSEMENT when, in a move fraught with irony, Buchanan's supporters seized control of the party apparatus away from Newman and Fulani and other party FACTIONS. In 2004, Newman and Fulani organized some early campaign events for Ralph Nader.

Further reading: Sifry, Micah L. *Spoiling for a Fight: Third-Party Politics in America.* New York: Routledge, 2002.
—John Paul Hill

New Deal Coalition

The New Deal Coalition was the electoral COALITION that formed the DEMOCRATIC PARTY's base and that made the Democratic Party the nation's MAJORITY PARTY for a generation between the 1930s and the late 1960s. The New Deal Coalition included labor unions, African Americans, liberals, white southerners, and new European immigrants. The Democratic Party's strongest regional support between the 1930s and the 1960s came from the South, as well as from major cities and industrial communities. These groups of voters were united by the Democratic Party's support for the social welfare and regulatory programs forged under Roosevelt's New Deal domestic agenda. The national strength of the New Deal Coalition forced the REPUBLICAN PARTY to abandon efforts to dismantle the domestic programs of the Roosevelt presidency. Largely as a result of the strength of this coalition, the Democratic Party won seven out of nine PRESIDENTIAL ELECTIONS between 1932 and 1964. The party also controlled both houses of Congress for all but four years between 1932 and 1980.

Prior to the New Deal Coalition, the Republican Party was the nation's majority party. As the majority party, the Republicans received most of the blame for the economic collapse and human suffering of the Great Depression. At the height of the Depression in 1932, Franklin Delano Roosevelt was elected president in a landslide over Republican president Herbert Hoover. Democrats also won large majorities in both houses of Congress. It was the most sweeping Democratic victory since the presidency of Andrew Jackson, bringing about an electoral REALIGNMENT that established the Democratic Party as the nation's majority POLITICAL PARTY for a generation.

As early as 1948, cracks in the New Deal Coalition began to surface. While most African Americans outside the South supported the Democratic Party (most southern blacks were disenfranchised by complex southern state laws until 1965), the party generally avoided taking a strong stance in favor of CIVIL RIGHTS LEGISLATION. At the 1948 Democratic National Convention, the party took a stance in favor of federal antilynching legislation. Believing this stance to be a violation of the party's traditional deference to states' rights, many southern DELEGATEs walked out of the convention hall and organized a third-party presidential campaign in support of South Carolina governor Strom Thurmond. Thurmond carried four southern states and won 39 electoral votes. The 1948 election was a harbinger of future problems for the maintenance of the New Deal Coalition.

By 1960, with the Democratic Party taking an increasingly supportive position in favor of civil rights, its presidential nominee, Senator John F. Kennedy, worked hard to carry southern states. In 1964, as President Lyndon Johnson was sweeping to victory across the rest of the nation, five Deep South states overwhelmingly cast their votes for the Republican nominee, Senator Barry Goldwater, who strongly opposed Johnson's civil rights agenda. Goldwater also polled above his national average throughout every southern state except for Johnson's home state of Texas.

By 1968, the New Deal Coalition was no longer a majority force in American POLITICS, as INDEPENDENT presidential candidate George Wallace carried five southern states and cut into normally reliable Democratic strongholds in many northern blue-collar communities. Republican Richard Nixon also carried five southern states in 1968, and in 1972 he carried the entire South. In the three presidential elections of the 1980s, Democratic nominees carried only one southern state. Moreover, Republicans in recent elections have significantly eroded the Democrats' strength in southern congressional and state ELECTIONS.

Race and civil rights played a major role in the erosion of the New Deal Coalition in the 1960s and 1970s, but other issues played important roles. The New Deal Coalition lost significant political support from culturally conservative voters in all regions of the country. Many of these voters were working-class Catholics, city dwellers, and labor union members originally drawn to the Democratic Party during the Great Depression. While initially attracted to Roosevelt's New Deal programs, many of them held conservative views on a variety of cultural issues and foreign policy positions. As the Democratic Party adopted more liberal leanings in the late 1960s and 1970s, support from cultural conservatives weakened.

Today the Democratic Party continues to rely on remnants of the New Deal Coalition to win national elections. The party can still count on almost unanimous support from African American voters and Jewish voters, and strong support from union voters, Hispanic voters, liberals, and recently arrived immigrants. Today's Democratic Party also relies on support from gays, nonreligious persons, environmentalists, and women. Democrats run strongest on the West Coast, in the Northeast, in the upper Midwest, and in most major cities.

The strength of the New Deal Coalition between the 1930s and the 1960s represents the last time a majority party dominated American politics for an extended period of time. While the New Deal Coalition began unraveling in the late 1960s, no majority political party has emerged to take its place. After 1968, "divided government"—whereby one party controls Congress and the other party controls the presidency—became the norm in American politics. Nor have Republican presidents and congresses been very successful in their attempts to curtail or abolish many of the social welfare and regulatory programs put in place dur-

ing the New Deal Coalition's more than 30-year period of dominance.

Further reading: Anderson, Kristi. *Creation of a Democratic Majority, 1928–1936.* Chicago: University of Chicago Press, 1979; Petrocik, John. *Party Coalitions: Realignments and the Decline of the New Deal Party System.* Chicago: University of Chicago Press, 1981; Plotke, David. *Building a Democratic Political Order: Reshaping American Liberalism in the 1930s and 1940s.* Cambridge: Cambridge University Press, 1995; Weiss, Nancy. *Farewell to the Party of Lincoln: Black Politics in the Age of FDR.* Princeton, N.J.: Princeton University Press, 1983.

—Donald A. Zinman

New Hampshire primary

New Hampshire is the first state to hold a PRIMARY election in each PRESIDENTIAL ELECTION year. The date of the New Hampshire primary is established by the state legislature, which makes a conscious effort to ensure that its primary will be the first one held in the nation. Iowa voters are actually the first voters in the country to express their views on the presidential candidates in a formal setting. They typically select their DELEGATEs to the presidential nominating conventions at least a week before New Hampshire voters pick their delegates. However, Iowa employs a caucus system, in which voters come together in a series of meetings at venues throughout their communities to debate the quality of the candidates and then decide on whom to support. In contrast, New Hampshire voters choose their delegates to the nominating conventions through the direct election format rather than through a series of meetings.

New Hampshire has a long history of being a state where personal knowledge of the candidates is critical in order to win support from voters. Therefore, candidates devote significant time and financial resources to traveling throughout the state and meeting voters. Candidates will often begin campaigning in the state a year or more before its primary. Some candidates have even been known to take up temporary residence in the state in advance of its primary. Campaigning in New Hampshire has traditionally consisted of meeting with relatively small groups of voters in community centers and in private homes. In these settings, voters have the opportunity to discuss the candidates' positions on issues important to the voters. Such personal modes of campaigning mean that a significant portion of New Hampshire voters typically meet at least one of the presidential candidates.

In addition to personal campaigning, New Hampshire is also well known for the media coverage its PRESIDENTIAL PRIMARY receives both from media sources within the state and from the national media. Within the state, the *Manchester Union Leader* is the most well known media source reporting on the primary. The paper is generally considered to provide a conservative slant to its stories. Because New Hampshire is the first presidential primary, it also receives a significant amount of coverage by the national media outlets. In fact, in some years up to one-fifth of the coverage devoted by the national media to the presidential nominating process has focused on New Hampshire. This is the case despite the fact that New Hampshire residents make up less than 1 percent of the delegates who will formally nominate the presidential candidates, and the state contributes only four of the 270 electoral votes that are needed to win the presidency in the GENERAL ELECTION.

Several disadvantages are commonly discussed in terms of the vast amount of attention that New Hampshire receives in the nominating process. First, New Hampshire is not demographically representative of the U.S. population. New Hampshire is overwhelmingly white, its population tends to be more highly educated and wealthier than the rest of the country, and it is more rural than the United States as a whole. Such demographic characteristics influence the way citizens vote. Therefore, a candidate who does well in New Hampshire may not be supported by voters in other parts of the country. For example, Patrick Buchanan came in an unexpectedly close second to George H. W. Bush in the Republican primary in 1992, despite the fact that he was perceived by many voters nationwide as being overly conservative in his views. His strong challenge to the incumbent president weakened Bush's campaign from the outset. Bush eventually went on to lose his bid for reelection to Bill Clinton that November.

A related disadvantage commonly associated with the importance of the New Hampshire primary is that, despite, the fact that New Hampshire voters are not representative of voters nationwide, if a candidate performs badly in this first race of the election year, his or her chances of winning the party's NOMINATION may be severely reduced. Quality candidates may be prematurely eliminated from the presidential race simply because they did poorly in one small state. The New Hampshire primary is well known for creating a sense of "momentum" for a presidential candidate, which is the idea among the press, the public, and one's opponents that he or she is pulling ahead in the race. The winner of the New Hampshire primary typically receives significant positive coverage by the press in the days following the election. Positive media coverage related to performing well in this race often has a snowball effect on a candidate's future performance—doing well leads to positive media coverage, which encourages voters to donate money to the campaign, enabling the candidate to run more campaign ads than he or she might have been able to afford otherwise, which leads to a better performance in the next primary than he or she might have had otherwise, thus leading to even more positive news coverage as the cycle continues. This momentum effect is particularly important for candidates who are not well known going into a presidential race.

Conversely, doing poorly in an early state such as New Hampshire, or simply not doing as well as had been expected, results in negative press coverage that may discourage voters from contributing to a candidate who is perceived as weak, which limits his or her ability to campaign aggressively in future primaries, thus reducing the likelihood of being able to run a successful campaign for the nomination. The importance of doing well in the New Hampshire primary can be seen clearly in terms of the 1968 Johnson campaign. Lyndon Johnson, the incumbent president, decided not to run for reelection in part because he did not perform as well as had been expected in the New Hampshire race.

The New Hampshire primary remains an important step in the PRESIDENTIAL NOMINATING PROCESS. The nomination process has become increasingly "front-loaded" in recent years. FRONT-LOADING refers to the fact that states are moving the dates of their primaries earlier and earlier in the nominating season. This means that the presidential nominee from a party is often determined by March of the election year. As the dates of primaries are moved up, it becomes more and more important for candidates to do well in the early states, beginning with New Hampshire.

Further reading: Palmer, Niall A. *The New Hampshire Primary and the American Electoral Process.* Westport, Conn.: Praeger, 1997.

—Claudia Bryant

New Jersey Plan (1787)

The New Jersey Plan was a proposal to "revise" the ARTICLES OF CONFEDERATION that would have allowed the states to retain much of the sovereignty they possessed after the War of Independence. The plan, put forth by William Patterson of New Jersey on June 15 during the Constitutional Convention of 1787, was supported by the smaller states and some slave states. It was seen as a "substitute" for the plan under discussion, which had been laid before the DELEGATEs by Edmund Randolph of Virginia on May 29, the first day of deliberations. Randolph's proposals (which in fact had been written mostly by James Madison), known as the Virginia Plan, had been the basis for discussions until the time of Patterson's counter.

At the time of the convention, the new nation had a nominal government under the Articles of Confederation, which had been ratified in the wake of the war with England (1781). The articles were a "league of friendship" among the now free states. The government established under the articles was one of exceptionally limited powers. It consisted of one house, no judiciary, and an executive run by committee. Members were often absent and in some cases did not participate at all during the time of their appointments. This entity had no real ability to compel the states to observe requirements of finance or of law. During the war, a great deal of debt had been acquired. Upon the cessation of hostilities, debtors—individuals as well as the states and central government—often repaid little or nothing toward the debts incurred or simply printed reams of worthless currency to pay creditors. Indeed, state courts and legislatures often cowed under the pressure from debtors to be absolved of their promissory notes.

The specter of renewed hostilities with England lurked in the failure to abide by the peace treaty in the western lands, the confiscation of Loyalist property, and the failure to repay debts. The Congress was further weakened because of the requirement of unanimous consent among the states. In essence, the articles left the states in a powerful position and the union on the brink of collapse. Some of the more public-spirited, such as Alexander Hamilton, thought that if it did fall, the people's love of democracy would go with it, and despotism would emerge in its place.

It was the desire for stability, economic growth, and justice that led some to seek changes and to call for a convention of the states. Upon the commencement, a number of members shared Governor Randolph's view: "Our chief danger arises from the democratic parts of our constitutions." It was excessive democracy and obstinate state sovereignty that many sought to substantially curb. Under the articles, each state had an equal say on the passage of legislation. Georgia's vote, with a 16th the population of Virginia, had the same weight. In the initial Virginia plan, two houses were proposed. The members of the first (House) were to be elected by the people directly, while the members of the second (Senate) were to be appointed by the state legislatures.

The point of contention that nearly led to the collapse of the convention was that both branches were to be "proportioned" based on either population or property. It was also proposed that the national legislature be able to negate state laws. Furthering the attempted jettisoning of the scheme of equal representation under the articles, on May 30, Randolph, seconded by James Madison, moved to have the clause read "Resolved that the rights of suffrage in the national legislature ought to be proportioned *and not according to the present system.*" The line had been drawn—small states as well as slave were concerned about maintaining their control over what they viewed as parochial matters. The delegates would often come back to this during their deliberations.

A consensus arose that the first branch should be elected directly. George Mason argued, "It was to be the grand depository of the democratic principle." James Wilson sought "as broad a basis as possible," to gain "the confidence of the people." James Madison saw popular election of the branch as "essential to every plan of free government."

As the first was to be close to the people, some distance was sought for the second. Randolph sought to "check" the people and the House with the Senate. It was hoped that the wiser and farsighted would be in the Senate to, as Madison put it, "refin[e]" the public voice. It was at this juncture that Madison and others attempted to assuage those fearful of "stripping the States of their powers." While the articles had operated on the states, the new system would operate directly on the people, thus *federalism* rather than nationalism. Roger Sherman contended that by appointing the senators, "the particular states would thus become interested in supporting the National Government."

However, it was the PROPORTIONAL REPRESENTATION of the states and a federal judiciary that caused some states to be concerned. It is important to note that many at that time believed that republican government could succeed only in small states and that the new federal structure would place the government too distant from the people, while others had more parochial concerns such as loss of political power.

On June 9, Patterson claimed that the states were sovereign and that without equal votes among the states, the smaller states would be "destroyed instead of being saved." On June 11, Roger Sherman put on the table that each state have one vote, noting that "[t]he smaller States would never agree to the plan on any other principle." The motion failed. On June 15, Patterson laid his counter before the delegates. He proposed to strengthen the Congress under the articles and to retain equality of state representation, nothing more. John Dickinson summed it up this way: "we would sooner submit to a foreign power, that submit to be deprived of an equality of suffrage."

Three days later, Alexander Hamilton effectively argued that to have a "good" government, the states could not retain their "indefinite power," as they would run counter to "the great purposes" for which the new government was to be established. On June 29, Madison would take a similar line in maintaining that it was the people rather than the states that the new proposals were most concerned with and that the "jealousies" existing in the states "must be done away." Patterson's proposal, however, would bear fruit in the "Great Compromise" brokered by the Connecticut delegation—each state would have equal representation in the Senate, thus giving the states a way to protect their interests.

Further reading: Berkin, Carol. *A Brilliant Solution: Inventing the American Constitution.* New York: Harcourt, 2002; Collier, Christopher. *All Politics Is Local: Family, Friends, and Provincial Interests in the Creation of the Constitution.* Hanover, N.H.: University Press of New England, 2003; Solberg, Winton U., ed. *The Constitutional Convention and the Formation of the Union.* 2nd ed. Urbana: University of Illinois Press, 1990.

—Jeff A. Martineau

Nineteenth Amendment

The Nineteenth Amendment to the U.S. Constitution provides that no person may be denied the right to vote in national or state elections because of gender. The amendment was proposed by Congress on June 4, 1919, and was ratified by the requisite number of states on August 18, 1920.

Although women had the vote in New Jersey from 1776 until 1807, and widows could vote in school elections in Kentucky from 1838, the modern women's suffrage movement can trace its origin to the first women's rights convention in the United States, held in Seneca Falls, New York, in 1848. The organizers of the event were Lucretia Mott and Elizabeth Cady Stanton. Even among the protofeminists who gathered at the convention, the idea of women's suffrage was regarded as outside the mainstream; the suffrage resolution passed with barely a majority, while the other 11 convention resolutions passed unanimously. There was a strong connection between the women's rights movement and the abolition movement, the other great civil rights movement of the time. One of the best-remembered speakers from the SENECA FALLS CONVENTION was the noted abolitionist Sojourner Truth, who had been born a slave.

With the assistance of the National Woman Suffrage Association, the first constitutional amendment to give women the vote was introduced in Congress in 1866 by Representative James Brooks of New York. There was also a failed effort to include women in the FIFTEENTH AMENDMENT (which barred discrimination in voting rights on the basis of race in 1870). The group tried to win the vote through the federal courts in the 1870s, but once again it was unsuccessful. Their argument was based on the idea that even though woman suffrage had been explicitly omitted in the Fifteenth Amendment, it was implicit in the FOURTEENTH AMENDMENT. This was rejected by the Supreme Court in the 1875 case *Minor v. Happersett*. The Court held that suffrage was not a right but a privilege. Interestingly, to this day the Constitution does not state that all citizens have a right to vote, only that one may not be denied the vote on account of race, color, having been a slave (Fifteenth Amendment), sex (Nineteenth Amendment), failure to pay taxes (TWENTY-FOURTH AMENDMENT), or age, if one is 18 or older (TWENTY-SIXTH AMENDMENT).

Susan B. Anthony led a civil disobedience movement in 1872 in Rochester, New York, taking a group of women to vote. She was charged with unlawfully voting. She was not allowed to testify at her trial because she was a woman, and the judge instructed the jury to find her guilty, there being no facts in dispute in the case (juries decide questions of fact, and judges decide questions of law). Despite trying to bait the judge into sending her to jail, Anthony was merely fined $100 plus costs, which she never paid. The judge never held her in contempt for failure to pay, because he knew she wanted to be sent to jail in order to attract sympathy for her cause.

The Women's Christian Temperance Union (which still exists) became the first national women's organization to embrace the cause of suffrage. This may have actually been counterproductive, because it brought liquor interests into the fold in opposition to woman suffrage, on the idea that women might be more likely to favor restrictions on alcohol than male voters, which was, in fact, an important reason why the union wanted women to have the vote.

Other suffragists, under the banner of the American Woman Suffrage Association, organized at the state level. The first entity to grant women the vote was Wyoming Territory in 1869. When Wyoming was admitted as a state in 1890, its constitution gave women suffrage, making it the only state to have never barred women suffrage. This idea was not well received by Congress, which threatened to reject the constitution, but the territorial leaders in Wyoming held firm, and Wyoming was admitted to the Union only by a narrow vote. The two suffrage groups merged in 1890 to form the National American Woman Suffrage Association. Utah was admitted in 1896, with woman suffrage in its constitution, although the territory had not always had it. In 1893, Colorado became the first state to give women the vote by REFERENDUM, in a campaign led by Carrie Chapman Catt. She also led a successful referendum on the subject in Idaho in 1896. The defeat of a suffrage referendum in California that same year was seen as a severe blow to the movement. Liquor interests had pushed for the defeat of the referendum.

A bolder group of feminists, led by Alice Paul, organized the Congressional Union in 1913 to push more aggressively for suffrage than had the National American Woman Suffrage Association. These women also made a point of calling themselves "suffragettes," which, strangely enough, was what opponents of woman suffrage had been calling female suffragists for years. The Congressional Union suffragettes were the first protesters ever to picket the White House. Their protests were outlawed once the United States entered World War I, and Paul and her fellow picketers went to jail.

Although the president has no formal role in the constitutional amendment process, President Woodrow Wilson spoke in favor of the amendment in the Senate in 1918. The amendment was proposed during a special session of Congress that Wilson had called (albeit not for the express purpose of considering the amendment). Although no southern states had yet ratified the amendment, Tennessee was the state whose ratification brought the number to the required three-fourths. Women were thus able to vote in the PRESIDENTIAL ELECTION that year, essentially doubling the size of the ELECTORATE and transforming American electoral POLITICS.

Further reading: Cornell Law School, Legal Information Center. Available online. URL: http://www.law.cornell.edu. Accessed August 10, 2005; Morgan, David. *Suffragists and Democrats: The Politics of Woman Suffrage in America.* East Lansing: Michigan State University Press, 1972; Palmer, Kris E., ed. *Constitutional Amendments: 1789 to the Present.* Detroit: Gale Group, 2000; Scott, Anne F., and Andrew M. Scott. *One Half the People: The Fight for Woman Suffrage,* Philadelphia: Lippincott, 1975; Weatherford, Doris. *A History of the American Suffragist Movement.* Santa Barbara, Calif.: ABC-CLIO, 1998.

—Tony L. Hill

nomination

One of the most important functions of political parties is to select a SLATE of candidates to campaign for public office at all levels of government. Political parties nominate their favored candidate to win a subsequent GENERAL ELECTION and hold office. American political parties commonly have used any one of three methods for selecting their nominees: caucus, convention, or DIRECT PRIMARY.

Caucuses are the oldest method for selecting party nominees. Predating the writing of the U.S. Constitution, caucuses are meetings of party leaders to select candidates to represent the party in upcoming elections. Caucuses dominated state and national party nomination processes through 1824. That system was abandoned amid allegations that caucus members were unrepresentative of either constituents or the party as a whole. Statewide party caucuses still meet today, as popularized by those held in Iowa, but are employed in connection with conventions.

Party conventions were the reform that initially replaced most caucuses. Conventions were thought to be more representative (both literally and by viewpoint) of both the party as a whole and the constituents whose support candidates were seeking to win the general election. Sophisticated convention systems quickly developed at both the state and national levels. Conventions dominated POLITICAL PARTY decision making from the 1830s through the mid-20th century. However, conventions increasingly came under attacks similar to those that felled caucuses. Critics charged conventions with being dominated by a few powerful men—political "bosses"—making secret deals in "smoke-filled rooms" and imposing their wills on the party faithful. Conventions were said to be unrepresentative of the party rank and file.

Reformers successfully replaced conventions with the use of direct primaries to select party nominees. This system featured voters rather than party leaders selecting nominees. PRIMARY elections are governed by state laws. Five basic types of primaries can be found among the states. Open primaries allow all voters to participate in any party's primary election. Closed primaries are limited only to voters registered to that party. Blanket primaries provide one BALLOT on which all voters, regardless of their party preference, may vote for any candidate of their choice, regardless of the candidate's party affiliation. Nonpartisan primaries are held to select nominees running for offices on a nonpartisan basis, such as judges and school board members. Finally, runoff primaries are typically used in one-party-dominant states (such as those in the Deep South) where no candidate is able to attract the majority of primary votes. A second, or runoff, primary is then held between the two leading candidates from the first primary.

Further reading: Cook, Rhodes. *Race for the Presidency: Winning the 2000 Nomination.* Washington, D.C.: Congressional Quarterly Press, 2000; Wayne, Stephen J. *The Road to the White House 2000: The Politics of Presidential Elections.* Boston: Bedford/St. Martin's, 2000.

—Robert E. Dewhirst

nonpartisan election

A nonpartisan election is one in which the candidates are not identified by a POLITICAL PARTY label. BALLOTs for nonpartisan elections simply list candidate names without any reference to partisan identifications, such as Republican or Democratic. Nonpartisan elections are typically found at the local level of government (e.g., city council elections and school board elections), not in state or federal elections. Nevertheless, more than half of the government positions in the United States are currently filled by nonpartisan elections.

Nonpartisan elections were one of the most important and consequential reform measures that came out of the PROGRESSIVE MOVEMENT at the turn of the 20th century. The Progressive movement arose in response to the machine-style POLITICS so common during the post–Civil War period in urban America. Progressives believed that by removing the party label from the voting ballot, voters would be forced to rely on information other than the cues supplied by a candidate's party; the voting ELECTORATE would now be given a "new" responsibility of becoming politically aware of the candidates for whom they would vote. In theory, this would result in a more policy-enlightened electorate along with a substantial blow dealt to the powerful parties who financed and ran the urban machines.

The consequences of nonpartisan elections are many, some of which were unintended. First and foremost, nonpartisan elections are said to have reduced levels of VOTER TURNOUT relative to elections in which candidate party labels are identified. Party labels convey a variety of information to voters, including probable policy stances and candidate IDEOLOGY (e.g., conservative or liberal). For instance, if Candidate A is a known Republican, chances are that she will support measures such as decreased government spending on social programs. Without actually knowing what Candidate A's specific policy preferences are, one can approximately surmise how closely Candidate A's preferences match up with one's own.

Another important consequence of nonpartisan elections is the decline of political party strength in the United States. As more and more candidates run as individuals rather than members of a party, they become less beholden to a party's policy wishes.

Further reading: Garofalo, Jeffrey. *The Struggle for Democracy: The Machines and Reform.* Lincoln, Nebr.: Writers Club Press, 2001; Harrigan, John J., and Ronald K. Vogel. *Political Change in the Metropolis.* New York: Longman Publishing Group, 1999; Pelissero, John P. *Cities, Politics and Policy.* Washington, D.C.: CQ Press, 2002.

—Dari E. Sylvester

open seat elections

Open seat elections are elections in which no incumbent is running for office. This can happen for a variety of reasons, including TERM LIMITS, an incumbent's decision to run for higher office, REDISTRICTING, retirement, resignation, and death. These elections are particularly important because they are often the most competitive and the most susceptible to a party change.

It has been well documented in political science that there is a substantial INCUMBENCY ADVANTAGE that politicians running for reelection enjoy. In the U.S. Congress, this advantage usually results in a biennial incumbency reelection rate of around 90 to 95 percent. This is due mainly to the power of the office, the ready-made campaign staff, the amount of press coverage that an incumbent can generate, high NAME RECOGNITION, and the large amounts of money that an incumbent is able to raise and spend. Therefore, in elections in which no incumbent is on the BALLOT, the OPPOSITION PARTY usually stands a much greater chance of winning the election than would otherwise be the case.

The number of open seat elections can vary greatly from year to year. For example, in 2000, there were 18 open House seats, five open Senate seats, and four open governors' chairs. By contrast, in 2002, there were 45 open House seats, seven open Senate seats, and a remarkable 20 open governors' chairs. And in 2004, there were 31 open House seats, eight open Senate seats, and three open governors' chairs.

Since the power of incumbency is removed in open seat elections, the political parties often aggressively campaign for their nominees in these elections. The party that previously held the seat fights to retain control, while the opposition party sees the open seat contest as a fleeting opportunity to increase its representation in government. The result is that these types of elections often attract the most qualified candidates and disproportionate amounts of campaign funds.

Further reading: Black, Earl, and Merle Black. *The Rise of Southern Republicans.* Cambridge, Mass.: Harvard University Press, 2002; Gaddie, Ronald Keith, et al. *Elections to Open Seats in the U.S. House.* New York: Rowman & Littlefield, 2000; Hawkins, David, et al. *CQ's Politics in America, 2004: The 108th Congress.* Washington, D.C.: CQ Press, 2003.

—Brian DiSarro

opposition party

An opposition party has two characteristics. First, it is a POLITICAL PARTY that is out of power and hence does not have its members in a substantial number of public offices. Second, it supports a different, or at least distinct, vision from the party in power for how POLITICS should be carried out. When an opposition party wins, control of the government is peacefully turned over to the new party. This is a special situation in politics, because many times throughout world history when an opposition is voted into office, the party in control refuses to leave or involves the military to retain its power. The history of peaceful transitions of power is one of the hallmarks of the U.S. political system.

In modern American politics, it is expected that power will frequently change hands between different parties. *Opposition party* is a term most meaningfully applied in a TWO-PARTY SYSTEM, in which one party is generally in control and the other party is the "opposition party." It is also applicable to a multiparty system and would refer to the party or parties that could *seriously* challenge the party in power. Opposition parties do not exist in one-party systems, such as Stalin's Russia or communist China, because political opposition is not allowed in these governments.

While the presence of an opposition party implies that the power in a nation will change hands from time to time, the entire government does not change when an opposition party wins an election and comes into office. The constitution, institutions, procedures, and (some) founding principles remain. An opposition party coming into office must work within the nation's government. Thus, in the United States, it could affect the nation's policies toward defense, welfare spending, and education, but it could not dissolve Congress or disregard the Bill of Rights. The very act of voting means that the candidate in office may lose and the opposition may win, making the opposition party a necessary part of democracy and a key element of popular sovereignty.

Further reading: Bone, Hugh A. *American Politics and the Party System.* 3rd ed. New York: McGraw-Hill, 1965; Eldersveld. Samuel J. *Political Parties in American Society.* 2nd ed. Boston: Bedford/St. Martin's, 2000; Hofstadter, Richard. *The Idea of a Party System.* Berkeley: University of California Press, 1969.

—J. Christopher Paskewich

opposition research

Opposition research is the practice of gathering information about an opposing candidate. It refers to both the tactics employed to collect that information as well as the intelligence produced by those tactics. The sort of information sought can vary widely, as can the intent of the search. Opposition research has become a staple of the modern American campaign at almost every level of government.

In some cases, opposition research simply means compiling and processing the public utterances and actions of one's political opponent. This includes gathering quotes, media clips, and voting records, as well as sifting through public legal documents. This brand of opposition research provides the basic levels of knowledge a campaign needs to properly develop a message aimed at minimizing an opponent's strengths and maximizing his or her weaknesses.

In other instances, the scope of the research can be much broader, reaching into a candidate's personal and professional activities and background. Opposition researchers have been known to look through old yearbooks, interview individuals who know or knew the opponent, look through video rental records, or even dig through trash cans. The goal of these more invasive tactics is often to locate damaging personal information about a candidate. Such information can be damaging either because of its salacious nature (e.g., sexual peccadilloes) or because it suggests hypocritical policy stands (e.g., a history of drug use by a tough-on-crime candidate).

Research may not be limited to the candidate him- or herself, but may extend to family members, business associates, and friends. Opposition research techniques are even used sometimes to affect the decisions of a candidate not yet in a race. A campaign may aggressively and visibly pursue "dirt" on a potential opponent as a means of discouraging that individual from entering the race. Opposition research is by no means unique to electoral settings. The same techniques are often employed to collect potentially damaging information on legislative opponents, judicial nominees, and other political operatives.

Another seemingly paradoxical use of opposition research has also become commonplace. Many campaigns hire independent consultants to conduct research on their own candidate. The goal is to anticipate any possible attack and to know what the opponents are likely to say about their own candidate. A similar process, often referred to as vetting, is used to examine the pluses and minuses of potential RUNNING MATES, appointees, and nominees.

Along with other aspects of the modern campaign, opposition research has become increasingly professionalized. Firms and individuals on both sides of the political aisle peddle their sleuthing services to campaigns and INTEREST GROUPS. During the course of a campaign, the two opposing sides seek to define themselves and each other in hopes of advancing an agenda or gaining electoral advantage. These tasks require at least some amount of opposition research.

Further reading: Sabato, Larry J., and Glenn R. Simpson. *Dirty Little Secrets: The Persistence of Corruption in American Politics.* New York: Times Books, 1996; Shea, Daniel M. *Campaign Craft: The Strategies, Tactics, and Art of Political Campaign Management.* Westport, Conn.: Praeger Publishers, 1996; Thurber, James A., and Candice J. Nelson, eds. *Campaigns and Elections American Style (Transforming American Politics).* Boulder, Colo.: Westview Press, 1995.

—Alex Theodoridis

P

paid media

Paid media is a term for the political advertising that candidates, POLITICAL ACTION COMMITTEES, and independent organizations pay for in order to project their messages via television, radio, newspapers, and the Internet. Paid media is an essential part of any serious campaign for national or state office, as well as most bids for locally elected positions, and campaigners have to spend a great deal of time raising the money necessary to mount large-scale, effective advertising campaigns.

In 1924, radio advertisements first appeared in a presidential campaign with Republicans outspending Democrats about $120,000 to $40,000. A mere four years later, the parties' combined spending total was more than $1 million. The first presidential television advertisements appeared in the 1952 contest between eventual winner Dwight Eisenhower and Adlai Stevenson. Eisenhower ran a series of 20-second spots called "Eisenhower Answers America." Through the 1960s, most campaign commercials were 60 seconds in length. By the early 1970s, the 30-second ad had became the norm, though 15-second and even two-minute ads are still occasionally used. In 1992, REFORM PARTY candidate and multibillionaire H. Ross Perot bought 30-minute blocks of time on television, which he used effectively to introduce himself and his ideas to the American people.

Paid media is not without its problems. Chief among these is that advertising, especially on television, is very expensive. In the 2000 PRESIDENTIAL ELECTION, Al Gore and George W. Bush spent approximately 46 percent of their budgets on media costs from October 1999 to March 2000, some eight months before the election. As elections approach and competition for airtime increases, advertising rates can soar. In the 17 media markets with competitive federal campaigns in 2000, the average cost of a campaign advertisement more than tripled from August to October. The 2000 campaign season saw an estimated $1 billion spent on television ads, four times more than what was spent in 1980, even after the costs are adjusted for inflation. In 2000,

$185 million was spent by George W. Bush and $120 million by Al Gore in the race for president of the United States.

While paid media can also be seen as a less credible source of information than EARNED MEDIA, since the source of the advertisement is the candidate or group that is paying to support the candidate and since it tends to boil complex political issues down to 30-second sound bites, the primary reason paid media has become an essential part of campaigns is because of its effectiveness. Since advertisements are repeated several times and news stories are typically aired or printed only once, paid media is believed to leave a lasting imprint on voters. Moreover, paid media advertising allows candidates to have complete control over the message they send to potential voters. They can select the content, timing, and placement of their advertisements to target particular voters, such as SWING VOTERs. Another reason that presidential candidates are forced to spend large amounts of money on advertising is because the amount of "earned media," or actual news stories about candidates, has dropped 40 percent on the three major networks (ABC, CBS, and NBC) since 1988. Similar trends of decreasing coverage exist at the congressional and gubernatorial levels as well. This trend is especially troublesome for CHALLENGERs, as the average incumbent raises $3 for every $1 the challenger raises.

In recent years, the line between free and paid media has blurred. It is now commonplace for news programs to reply to provocative television ads or to spend entire TV segments or newspaper columns discussing the content of political advertisements, giving candidates more bang for their buck, but also opening up the opportunity for their ads to be scrutinized.

Candidates must make several important decisions when planning to use paid media. First, candidates must decide which issues to emphasize. PUBLIC OPINION POLLING and FOCUS GROUPS can help candidates hone a message that resonates with the ELECTORATE. The goal is to choose a select group of issues, usually only about three in any given advertisement, that the candidate supports and that are popular with the public.

Second, candidates must decide when, or if, they should air attack ads (i.e., ads that cast their opponent in a negative light). Typically, challengers are much more likely to go on the offensive first, as incumbents have an overwhelming likelihood of reelection and thus tend to stick to positive commercials. Sometimes, the attacks can help define a race before the person being attacked can respond, but other times they can backfire if voters see the attacker as being overly aggressive or too negative. Many studies have found that while people do not like negative advertisements, they are often very effective. More recent analysis has greeted this claim with mixed results. Even so, some experimental studies have found that exposure to negative advertisements can demobilize the electorate. In one study, seeing negative advertisements resulted in intentions to vote dropping by 5 percent.

Third, candidates need to decide where, when, and how often to air their ads. Ads can either address issues that are of interest to the general public or can target specific groups. Programs on Spanish-language television, daytime soap operas, or major sporting events, for example, enable candidates to tailor messages for specific groups. Ads that appear early in a campaign tend to be moderate in nature, designed to increase NAME RECOGNITION. Frequency of exposure is also believed to be important, with some studies finding that voters need to see a commercial five or more times before it resonates with them.

Finally, presidential candidates need to choose a mix of local and national advertising buys. Most seekers of the presidency focus their advertisements on battleground states rather than states they are likely to win or likely to lose. Thus, presidential candidates have increasingly "gone local" in their advertisements, targeting areas they have a fighting chance to carry on ELECTION DAY.

What can be done to limit the potentially negative effects of the nation's "air wars?" Journalists such as David Broder of *The Washington Post* and scholars such as Kathleen Hall Jamieson are calling on journalists to more closely scrutinize potentially deceptive claims that candidates often make in their commercials. Others want to continue to amend CAMPAIGN FINANCE LAWS to lessen the impact of money on political elections.

Further reading: West, Darrell M. *Air Wars: Television Advertising in Election Campaigns, 1952–2000.* 3rd ed. Washington, D.C.: CQ Press, 2001; Graber, Doris A. *Media Power in Politics.* 4th ed. Washington, D.C.: CQ Press, 2000.

—Michael W. Wagner

partisan voting in Congress

Partisan voting in Congress refers to House and Senate legislative floor votes that are divided on party lines when a majority of one party in Congress votes in opposition to a majority of the other party in Congress. These votes are often referred to as "party line votes." As a result of changes in the election and committee selection process, the level of partisan voting in Congress has decreased over time, resulting in fewer strict party line votes. As a result of these changes, researchers have also altered the threshold considered to represent a party line vote. What is considered to be a high level of partisan voting in today's Congress is much lower than what was considered to be a high level of partisan voting in the 19th century.

Partisan voting in Congress has decreased over time, but there have been momentary uprisings. Historically, institutional changes have coincided with a decrease. Some argue that these changes influence the level of partisan voting in Congress. One such institutional change was the introduction of a DIRECT PRIMARY system whereby members of the House and Senate are popularly elected rather than selected by party leadership or by state legislatures. A direct primary system was widely adopted by the states in the first two decades of the 20th century. Before the introduction of primaries, party leadership selected candidates for the House, and senators were chosen by their respective state legislatures. Controlling the nominating process, the party leadership had the leverage to hold its nominees to a strict party line on floor votes.

The decline of party control over the nominating process in the 20th century led to CANDIDATE-CENTERED ELECTIONS and contributed to a decline in partisan voting in Congress. These individually focused campaigns combined with technological advancements have encouraged candidates to develop their own organizations using media experts and pollsters and to raise funds on their own. As a result of developing their own organizations, candidates are

A billboard and motion picture truck promoting the candidacy of Herbert Hoover, 1928 *(Corbis)*

no longer forced to rely exclusively on the party. Because members are not as reliant on the party for the above-mentioned campaign resources, members no longer face the same consequences when it comes to voting in opposition to their own party.

The party leadership's power over its members has also dwindled as a result of changes in the way congressional committee members and chairs are selected. The influence of party sanctions on party line voting can be observed cross-nationally as well. Party line voting is higher in Europe because they have stronger party sanctions than exist in the United States. While levels of party voting in the U.S. Congress have probably never been as high as they are in European systems, historical analysis shows that the greater the party sanctions in the United States, the higher the level of partisan voting in Congress. While the party leadership controlled committee appointments in the 19th and early 20th centuries, legislative changes in the early 1900s and then in the 1940s weakened the parties' control over the selection process.

Changing the selection process by taking the direct power to appoint committee chairs and members away from party leadership coincided with a decrease in partisan voting in Congress. In the period of 1910 to 1911, a COALITION of progressive Republicans and Democrats ousted the Speaker of the Rules Committee and broke his stranglehold on committee assignments. Party line voting decreased following these changes. During the 20th century, more reforms were made that continued to alter the ability of party leadership to use committee assignments as sanctions, and partisan voting in Congress has decreased as these changes were enacted. These changes in partisan voting can be observed in the decrease in party line votes across a wide range of legislative policies.

Partisan voting in Congress that results in significant public policy change rarely occurs, and when it does it is usually the result of a critical or realigning election in which there is a durable shift in the ELECTORATE that results in a change of the party in power or of the composition of the party in power. Following a REALIGNMENT of the party system, issues in Congress will be decided in a highly partisan manner resulting in a high occurrence of party line votes. Partisan voting in Congress increases on all floor votes following realignments, but the importance of party is particularly noticeable with regard to the policies associated with these realignments. Party line voting was particularly high with regard to free-coinage votes in the post-1896 era, and party line votes were also high on New Deal votes following the 1932 election. Since realignments are not a regular or frequent occurrence, they do not explain the existence of partisan voting in times with a stable and unchanged party system.

Partisan voting in Congress during eras of electoral stability can often be explained by examining the interests of individual members of Congress. Not only are institutional changes and realignments influential in the level of party line voting, but individual members' personal security in office also plays a role. Members of Congress often pursue policies toward the ideological middle to secure support, and when doing so, partisan voting in Congress is low. Low levels of party line voting also occur when one party has a clear majority within the legislature. If partisans who are part of a super-majority in Congress are electorally motivated, their response to this electoral luxury could be to drift away from their activist positions. While this might seem counterintuitive, the empirical evidence suggests that party line voting decreases in eras with supermajorities in Congress.

The reason party members drift away from their activist positions can be tied to the defining characteristic of parties as tools for office seekers. Simply stated, it is electorally beneficial for elected officials to move toward the middle. Voters toward the middle, or moderate voters, constitute the bulk of the electorate and are vital to a candidate's success in elections in a TWO-PARTY SYSTEM. Core supporters of a party that might be more ideologically extreme have little choice but to support the party's candidate, because even though their representative moved to the middle, he or she is still closer to their views than is the opposition. This offers members a sense of electoral security. The risks of this strategy are small: Liberal party activists have no viable party to turn to if they are displeased with the Democrats, and if conservative voters are dissatisfied with the Republicans, they have no viable alternative, either. Collectively, the electoral benefits of moving to the middle decrease partisan voting in Congress.

Interestingly, the same argument that describes why partisan voting in Congress decreases can explain why it often increases. Evidence has suggested that parties, when faced with stiff competition, have incentives to appeal to their activist core supporters rather than to the median voter. In essence, when one would logically assume it would be a good idea to appeal to the median voter (during a close race or when the partisan composition of Congress is evenly divided), research suggests that party members do the opposite.

Occasionally in the 20th century, there were uprisings in partisan voting in Congress. Without strict party discipline, there are other reasons to explain party line voting during the 20th century. Institutional changes, relationships to realignments, and individual members' levels of security in office can help explain party line voting in the 20th century. The question remains as to whether this pattern will continue in the 21st century. If the final decade of the 20th century is a harbinger of things to come, it would seem that partisan voting in Congress will also fluctuate in the 21st century but is unlikely to reach the levels of the 19th century.

The Republican takeover in 1994 seemed to herald a victory for the "responsible party model." This model suggests that partisan voting in Congress is the optimal condition. The contention is that in our system of separated powers, the party is the glue that can hold together the process of governing by linking the president and both houses of Congress to a coherent agenda. For this to happen, it requires a system of responsible parties that campaign on a common platform, implement it across both houses, and seek reelection based on outcome. Following the takeover, it looked as if Congress had entered a new era in which party differences, party cohesion, and partisan voting in Congress would be high and sustained. Republicans in the House campaigned on a common theme embodied in the CONTRACT WITH AMERICA. They stayed united to pass most of it quickly and showed intent to campaign for reelection on its terms. In the first session of the 104th Congress (1995), 73 percent of House roll call votes met the standard of party line vote, and 69 percent in the Senate.

Yet the patterns of partisan voting that occurred during most of the 20th century eventually prevailed. First, most of the Contract with America did not become law. In part, the failure can be attributed to presidential vetoes as well as to a lack of support in the Senate. More important, it became clear that the public did not approve of the level of partisanship in Congress. Hence, both parties retreated toward the middle. Democrats adopted much of the Republican rhetoric, dropping many ambitious plans and supporting some legislation, such as Welfare reform. Republicans abandoned some of the most conservative proposals and signed on to some of President Clinton's proposals, such as portable health insurance and a minimum wage increase. Members of Congress moved toward the middle, and party line voting dropped to 56 percent in the House and 62 percent in the Senate.

Further reading: Aldrich, John H. *Why Parties? The Origin and Transformation of Political Parties in America.* Chicago: University of Chicago Press, 1995; Barrilleaux, Charles. "Party Strength, Party Change, and Policy Making in the American States." *Party Politics* 6, no. 1 (2000): 61–73.
—Jason Gainous

party boss

Generally, a boss is a domineering leader of a PARTY ORGANIZATION, usually at the local, specifically urban, level, though this type of leadership can exist by extension at the state level, and, much more rarely, at the national level. A party boss exercises regular authority over the choice of party candidates for virtually every election within a jurisdiction, and more often than not leads a party that wins virtually every election within that locale.

Through a prevalent, though not necessarily standard, system of voter graft, voter intimidation, PATRONAGE, electoral fraud, selective law enforcement, and city service delivery, party bosses were able to control local POLITICS, have a variable impact on state politics, and, if they were situated in "swing states," influence PRESIDENTIAL ELECTIONS. Several

attempts to restrain or roll back the power of party bosses and machines generally were made by reformers, made up primarily of journalists and professionals, who saw their influence in government wane as expertise mattered less and personal connections to the party leadership mattered more.

Several theories about the eventual decline of most party machines and bosses, including the influx of different racial and ethnic groups into most large cities in the South and North during the mid-20th century and the growth of the welfare state and its replication of the welfare services delivered by party bosses, exist and have strong backing among scholars. What is uncontested, however, is that very few party bosses of the same type remain in contemporary politics as compared to the bosses of even a generation ago.

Existing predominantly in a vacuum of formal governmental authority, urban party bosses emerged in the late 19th century, though some of their roots, notably those of the New York Tammany Hall machine, can be traced back to the Jeffersonian era. Vice President Aaron Burr set up an organization to deliver votes for the DEMOCRATIC-REPUBLICAN PARTY in the face of landed Federalist opposition, and that organization was active in New York City politics until the 1930s. Tammany Hall is unique in that it had a succession of bosses, while most machines exist for the lifetimes of one or two party bosses. At least one of Tammany's leaders, Boss William Marcy Tweed, went to prison in the late 19th century for activities relating directly to his conduct as the leader of the Tiger, the Tammany organization.

Tammany was particularly notable for its frequent citation as the singularly most helpful organization or institution for immigrants in the half-century after the Civil War. Bosses were able to retain power by granting patronage for immigrant men and welfare services to the indigent immigrant population. "Gentleman Jimmy" Walker was one of the last Tammany mayors of New York City and was defeated in 1933 by Republican congressman Fiorello LaGuardia. LaGuardia had particularly close ties to President Franklin D. Roosevelt, who had been one of the most anti-Tammany politicians from upstate New York during his tenure as state senator and governor. At least in New York, the existence of bosses seemed to wane with the replacement of their services with jobs supplied by the Works Progress Administration (WPA) and various welfare programs furnished by Roosevelt's New Deal.

In Chicago, the machine regime, a COALITION of various immigrant ethnic groups, actually hit its peak of influence after the New Deal and Lyndon Johnson's Great Society, when it set itself up as the chief service delivery mechanism for new social programs offered by the DEMOCRATIC PARTY administrations. Mayor Richard J. Daley is widely regarded as one of the most powerful bosses in American history, and his mayoralty lasted from the late 1950s until his death in 1977. Daley's rise through the ranks of the Democratic Party resulted in his chairmanship of the party in 1955 and his later assumption of the mayor's office.

Initially, Daley's power base consisted of a coalition of white ethnics and African Americans. Typical of his chief lieutenants was Congressman Bill Dawson, an African American who had his own power base in the Second Ward of Chicago, a predominantly black ward. Daley formed his coalition from existing alliances, but quickly overturned those subregimes headed by "bosses" such as Dawson, only to replace them with his own trusted associates. Soon, African Americans were being installed and turned in and out of "office" (unofficial black community leadership subordinate to Daley) on a regular basis, to be replaced at various times by Dawson-esque INDEPENDENT party leaders, loyalist "party hacks," and empty-suit, party-controlled prominent black professionals.

This policy was marginally successful for some time, until such issues as machine-influenced residential segregation (e.g., the zoning of minority housing projects in isolated areas, the construction of highways to favor white neighborhood commuters, and an alliance with the Chicago real estate industry) led to the machine losing favor among minority voters and gaining favor with white voters. Daley's handling of the 1968 Democratic National Convention, in which his police were widely criticized for brutally confronting protesters, marked the period when Daley himself began to be labeled a "conservative" by the major national news media. By the time of his death in 1977, the Daley machine had gone from a "black machine" to a "white machine." Even with the passing of Daley, his machine was not toppled until 1983, when the city elected its first African-American mayor, whose own attempts to construct a minority-based machine met with failure.

Machines do not have to exist in order for a party boss to function as an absolute leader of a party. Several leaders of the New York REPUBLICAN PARTY were labeled bosses at the end of the 19th and start of the 20th century, notably Roscoe Conkling and Thomas Collier Platt. They did not control the New York state polity in the same manner that bosses controlled the electoral mechanisms and overall governmental structures of the city, but they did control the party machinery proper. Their influence was greatest when in control of the state's patronage jobs in New York City and Albany, the state capital. They were still able to single-handedly block legislation by Democratic governors while in control of both houses of the state legislature.

There are examples of lasting party bossism in the southern Democratic Parties during the 19th and 20th centuries, despite the one-party system that dominated the South for much of the period following RECONSTRUCTION. In this region, parties are often taken over periodically by FACTIONS that function like parties in the North and participate in primaries that function like elections in the North. An example of a southern urban party boss can be found in E. H. Crump of Memphis, who, in fact, did gain access to the party machinery in Memphis, Shelby County, and the state of Tennessee, successively, until his regime was toppled in a party PRIMARY in 1948.

Bosses often presume access to patronage bases, as well as other prerogatives, when their support is won during an intraparty or interfactional battle before the GENERAL ELECTION CAMPAIGN. Another example is the case of former president and founder of the Albany Regency, Martin Van Buren, caretaker of the Albany-Richmond axis that formed the core of the Jacksonian Democratic Party. After his defeat for reelection in 1840, Van Buren gained the support of a majority of convention DELEGATEs in 1844 for a third NOMINATION for president, but he was unable to attain the two-thirds majority necessary for nomination. Van Buren acquiesced to Tennessee governor James K. Polk's candidacy, fully expecting his support to translate into absolute control over at least New York state patronage in a Polk administration, if not total deference by Polk to his requests as leader of the party. When Polk did not accede to Van Buren's demands, Van Buren was outraged and withdrew his support for the Polk White House.

When Van Buren was defeated for reelection in 1840, another instance of dissatisfaction of party bosses took place. Henry Clay, who presumed to wield absolute power over the WHIG PARTY, managed to elect his candidate for president in 1840, and for a full month, Clay was called "The Dictator" for his absolute control over patronage, cabinet appointments, and programs of the new Harrison administration. When Harrison died and President Tyler resisted and then refused Clay's demands to sign a new charter for a national bank, Clay forced the entire cabinet (sans the secretary of state, Daniel Webster, in the midst of treaty negotiations) to resign in protest, and he withdrew his support for the Tyler White House.

Party bossism is not, therefore, confined to urban machines, though that is the most common power base for bosses. They will often use an urban base to expand their power, or create a power base within party channels that have little to do with urban administration, if anything. The common denominator is the unchecked authority bosses enjoy within their organizations and the need for continual maintenance of their legitimacy in order to function. Some in the scholarly community believe that bosses are unable to retain power in a polity that now values the telegenic styles of individual candidates, as well as funding apparatuses that are beyond the reach of any absolute authority, instead functioning as vehicles for the influence of several powerful individuals who check one anothers' power. Old-style bossism is difficult to maintain due to the increasing significance of candidate-centered campaigns, FUND-RAISING, and civil service reform that have taken 90 percent of government patronage out of the hands of party leaders and put it in the hands of a merit-based system.

Further reading: Benson, Lee. *The Concept of Jacksonian Democracy: New York as a Test Case.* Princeton, N.J.: Princeton University Press, 1961; Epstein, Leon. *Political Parties in the American Mold.* Madison: University of Wisconsin Press, 1986; Erie, Stephen P. *Rainbow's End: Irish-Americans and the Dilemmas of Urban Machine Politics.* Berkeley: University of California Press, 1988.

—Daniel T. Kirsch

party identification

Party identification is a term used to describe long-term psychological association with a POLITICAL PARTY. Also termed *partisanship,* party identification is considered to be more than legal party affiliation and instead a reflection of voter preference or IDEOLOGY. Party identification is a useful and reliable factor in explaining political behavior. Although there exists debate in political science about the stability of party identification, its sources, and how it is influenced, associations with political parties are considered to be relatively stable throughout the life of an individual and among the ELECTORATE as a whole.

The origins of the concept of party identification stem largely from the emergence of the survey tool in the mid-20th century, most notably the NATIONAL ELECTION STUDY (NES) conducted in election years since 1948. Relationships among attributes, attitudes, and political activities are examined using the survey, and interest in individuals' attitudes toward and associations with political parties has been a key element of the NES since its inception.

The measurement of party identification has developed through a series of items included in the NES. These questions ask respondents to self-identify party association with the Republican, Democratic, or other political party, or if the individual considers him- or herself to be INDEPENDENT of party affiliation. Respondents who self-identify as Republican or Democrat are then asked if they consider their party association as strong or weak; independents are asked if they lean toward one party or the other. This series of questions produces a seven category scale on which respondents are placed as strong Republicans, weak Republicans, independents leaning toward Republicans, pure independents, independents leaning toward Democrats, weak Democrats, and strong Democrats. This measurement continues to be the standard measure of party identification, although experiments and modifications to the measurement have been explored.

The seven-point categorization provides information about individuals' party attachments in a number of ways. Individuals can be classified along their party identification or lack of affiliation with a party, the intensity of their partisan association, or if not attached to a party, if they tend toward one party or the other. The series of surveys has shown significant growth in the number of independents (leaners or otherwise) since the 1960s; for many years in the 1990s and in 2000 and 2002 there were more independents than either Democrats or Republicans. The surveys have also shown that association with the Democratic and Republican Parties has remained relatively stable, although identification with either party has slipped since the 1950s, and that slip is more pronounced among Democrats. The reduction in partisanship coincides with the increase in independents, suggesting that individuals move from partisanship to independence rather than defecting from one party to another.

Because some movement in party identification does occur, political scientists have sought to explain these changes, and how party identification is formed. A traditional approach suggests that partisanship is a product of POLITICAL SOCIALIZATION—the influences on individuals from childhood to adulthood, such as family, religion, and environment. Such influences shape a predisposition to political perceptions, and as a child grows into an adult, these influences, along with his or her own sense and understanding of the world, shape a person's political beliefs and subsequently any attachment to a political party. This attachment becomes more durable and resistant to change as the person ages and produces stable party identification.

While it is apparent that party identification may be stable at the individual level, shifts may be evident at the cumulative, or aggregate, level. One explanation is that there is a generational effect at work in these changes in party identification over time. As the population of voting age citizens is constantly changing, with young people entering the pool of voting age citizens and older persons leaving, aggregate changes in partisan affiliation may be attributed to these continual and individual changes in the electorate.

A further possibility is that the relative stability at the aggregate level may be masking more dramatic change at the individual level. For example, reductions in Democratic identification by one group of individuals may be offset by increased Democratic identification of other groups, or more individuals previously identified as Republicans identifying as independents during that same period. Overall, changes in party identification may appear minimal, but there could be dynamic changes happening within groups and among individuals. This possibility suggests that partisanship is less stable than previously asserted.

Another explanation for changes in party identification further questions stability in partisanship, both at the individual and aggregate levels. Studies that have followed individuals over a series of ELECTION CYCLES have suggested that many respondents displayed a lack of consistency in their responses to questions regarding partisanship. One explanation is that there may be a flaw, or measurement error, in the design of the survey itself, while another implies that there is actual inconsistency in the political beliefs and positions of individuals between one survey period and the next, or respondent error. Yet another approach suggests that there may be short-term forces that influence party identification among individuals. The latter approach calls into question both the stability of party identification and whether party identification is vulnerable to POLITICS and other factors.

It is well established that party identification affects political behavior: Partisanship is a strong predictor of how individuals will vote, their positions on issues, and the way in which political events are interpreted. There is great debate about whether party identification itself is affected by outside forces, and if so, whether these effects are temporary or durable. Early conceptualizations of party identification not only claimed stability but also that it was unaffected by politics and events: Once party identification is established in an individual, it is not typically nor easily altered by political happenings, and individuals do not base their partisan loyalties on the current or recent political environment. Several challenges to this notion arose, arguing that partisanship is subject to political and social currents. One of the most prominent approaches that suggests the fluidity of party identification is that of the "scorecard," whereby voters make retrospective evaluations based on recent past performance. A high degree of partisan stability can be expected from this perspective, because individuals interpret most new information in a way that reinforces partisanship. This approach recognizes the tendency toward stability inherent in party identification, but also provides an explanation for change in partisanship.

Information that is most likely to affect party identification is found in presidential APPROVAL RATINGS, which reflect the perception of presidential performance on a range of current issues, and national economic performance, which some argue contributes to significant shifts in partisanship. For example, Democratic identification spiked in the years following the assassination of President Kennedy and during the CIVIL RIGHTS MOVEMENT of the 1960s, but tapered off as the Vietnam War escalated. Republican affiliation dropped in the years following the Watergate SCANDAL, but surged during the tenure of President Ronald Reagan and jumped again during the REPUBLICAN REVOLUTION of the mid-1990s. These numbers suggest that political events may be related to shifts in aggregate party identification.

There is much debate over the lasting influence of short-term forces on long-term attitudes. If party identification is quite vulnerable to political events, then it would seem unlikely that the impact of an event would have a lasting effect, or that subsequent information might negate any such change. However, there is some evidence that such change can be long-term, particularly when the agents of change are compelling, such as partisan REALIGNMENT, severe economic depression, or war. Those who argue that party identification is characterized by stability claim that stability is typical under normal circumstances; unusual events such as those mentioned above are recognized as possible causes for shifts in aggregate and individual party identification. If the motivation is such that change in party identification is the result, the properties of party identification are such that the new attachment should be strong and resistant to change from other, more typical political events.

Another aspect of party identification is the growth in the number of independents. Between 1952 and 1964, less than 25 percent of respondents claimed independence. Since 1966, that number has increased to the point that more individuals claim independence than identify with either the Republican or Democratic parties. In 2000, 40 percent of the NES sample were independent, compared with 34 percent Democrat and 24 percent Republican. One theory is that individuals do not defect directly from one party affiliation to another, but jump in and out of independence. Another theory suggests that independent leaners, those who claim no party affiliation but lean toward the Republican or Democratic Party, behave more like weak partisans rather than independents. Indeed, if one includes independent leaners in the percentages of partisans from 1952 to 2002, shifts in party identification are not as dramatic as those for partisans alone, although there is still significant fluctuation in aggregate party identification.

There is little doubt that party identification is changeable at both the individual and aggregate levels. The questions that remain unresolved are what causes such change, whether that change is lasting or fleeting, the rate at which shifts occur, and the size and significance of such changes. How these questions are answered can have a notable impact on politics, campaigns, and political behavior. Consider the activities of politicians and parties during political campaigns: If they believe party identification to be unmovable by political forces, perhaps campaign strategy should be to fortify the existing base of party supporters and attempt to sway UNDECIDED VOTERS and independents. There is ample evidence of this occurring in contemporary political campaigns, especially presidential campaigns, as candidates focus on "battleground" states rather than those that historically support one party over the other.

However, there is also evidence that partisan fortunes rise and fall with presidential approval ratings and economic performance, as reflected in the frequent public opinion polls throughout a campaign. Parties in power also seek to enhance their standing or shift the balance of partisan distribution, even if slightly, during the course of a campaign or through emphasizing the progress made under that party's leadership. Consider the 2000 PRESIDENTIAL ELECTION and the MIDTERM ELECTIONS of 2002. Though fewer than 40 percent of the nation identified with the Republican Party (including Republican-leaning independents), Republicans were able to earn the White House and hold on to slim majorities in the House of Representatives and the Senate in the 2000 election. While Democratic affiliation remained steady at nearly 50 percent, in the 2002 NES study, Republican identifiers had increased by 6 percent, while the percentage of pure independents had dropped from 12 to 8 percent, the lowest level in nearly four decades. It is arguable that events of 2001 and partisan unified government response to such events held some influence on both the partisan affiliation of individuals and the midterm elections, in which Republicans retained control of both chambers of Congress.

Further reading: Campbell, Angus, Philip E. Converse, Warren Miller, and Donald Stokes. *The American Voter.* New York: Wiley, 1960; Fiorina, Morris. *Retrospective Voting in American National Elections.* New Haven, Conn.: Yale University Press, 1981; Miller, Warren, and J. Merrill Shanks. *The New American Voter.* Cambridge, Mass.: Harvard University Press, 1996.

—Joel A. Rayan

party in office

This is a term that is not widely used by the public or the media. Instead, it is often used by political scientists and other serious students of political behavior. The term refers to the actions of a POLITICAL PARTY when it holds office. It can be used in two contexts: first, the MAJORITY PARTY that controls the instruments of government, or second, that segment of a political party that holds public office.

In the first instance, it describes the different posture that a political party takes when it controls the major institutions of government, as contrasted with the proposals or criticisms it may offer when it is not the party in power. Since the party in power expects to be held responsible for its actions, it is presumed that it will be less reckless in its policy positions. It is presumed that the party not in office will attack the policy positions of the party in office, although once it becomes the party in office, it may adopt policies similar to, if not identical to, that of its opponent.

For the second use of the term, one refers to the organizational levels of a political party. The broadest level is that of the party's regular voters, or votership, which may be conceptualized as only loosely organized. The next level is that of the party activists, those who contribute time and money to the party. This includes those who hold official party posts, such as PRECINCT committeepersons, as well as officials in volunteer organizations, such as the Federation of Republican Women, the Young Democrats, and the Italian-Americans for Bill Clinton. If one views these organizational levels as concentric rings, the inner ring consists of those party members who actually hold office. Thus, they are the party in office.

This use of the term draws attention to the ideological positions of the three levels of PARTY ORGANIZATION. The votership tends to be less ideological and generally uninformed about these matters. The partisan activists are persistently the most ideological sector of the party. Those party members who hold public office are inclined not to take controversial issue positions or assert extreme views on issues, despite pressure from activists within their party, for the officeholders retain their office only as long as their constituents reelect them.

Further reading: Aldrich, John. *Why Parties? The Origins and Transformation of Political Parties in America.* Chicago: University of Chicago Press, 1995; Milkis, Sidney. *The President and the Parties: The Transformation of the American Party System since the New Deal.* London: Oxford University Press, 1993.

—Thomas Phillip Wolf

party in the electorate

The phrase *party in the electorate* generally refers to a subset of voters who regard themselves, in some formal or informal fashion, as party members. While the term itself is relatively loose, it is generally accepted to denote a group of citizens psychologically and sociologically loyal to a particular POLITICAL PARTY who hold a "standing decision," in the absence of unusual circumstances, to support and vote for that party's candidates. Practically speaking, this means that they will identify themselves as party members and choose candidates on the basis of the party label.

The definition, however, is controversial. The phrase originated in the most common model of political parties, V. O. Key's trinity of party in government, party organization, and party in the electorate. That model gives rise to the well-known mnemonic of political party structure, PIG-PO-PIE. Undergraduate textbooks, generally a good indicator of received wisdom, now routinely speak of party *in* all three entities and give Key credit for that idea. The model, however, has been criticized on the basis that parties do not exist in the ELECTORATE per se, but rather appeal to the electorate for support. As the rising and falling electoral fortunes of American political parties have shown, that support can be either delivered or withheld based on short-term, nonparty-related factors, such as particular candidates, issues, and events. The criticism, then, is that parties that appeal to the electorate for support logically cannot be said to exist "in" the electorate.

Prior to the publication in 1952 of the third edition of Key's book, scholars were aware that voters were typically loyal to one particular political party. That loyalty, however, did not translate to the idea that that party actually manifested, in a definitional sense, "in" the electorate. Several mid-20th-century party scholars, particularly E. E. Schattschneider, argued that the definition of parties could not include the "associations of voters who support the party candidates." In 1960, however, the publication of *The American*

Voter directed scholars' attentions to the concept of PARTY IDENTIFICATION, as measured by the now long-standing core question, "Generally speaking, do you usually think of yourself as a Republican, a Democrat, an independent, or what?" As this measurement device gained currency with researchers, the measurement of party identification became a proxy for the measurement of party in the electorate. Ultimately, levels of party identification came to be thought of as coextensive with levels of party in the electorate.

Scholars have also noted that the three-part model including party in the electorate is a useful teaching tool, particularly in the American political context. It gives form to the otherwise difficult effort to conceptualize political parties, permitting a simple means to promote students' understanding of the diffuse nature of American political parties. In addition, the trinity provides an easy and logical structure for empirical research designs, which, in turn, permit the accumulation of data on which to build comprehensive theories of the scope, nature, and functions of American political parties. The result was a trade-off, as one set of scholars observes, between the utility of the model as a teaching and research tool and the loss of a unified concept of the whole party as more than the sum of these parts.

On the other hand, there has been significant empirical and theoretical criticism of the "in the" conceptualization of the relationship between the party and the electorate. The core of this criticism is that the two major American parties are very much like firms competing for market share. These critics treat party identification as brand loyalty rather than as coextensive with party in the electorate. Under this criticism, if parties are seeking support from the electorate, then it is inconsistent to consider any part of the electorate to actually be a part of the party. Thus, as one scholar has noted, it is more accurate to define party in the electorate as referring to the strength and durability of partisan attachments among the electorate, that is, to the parties' standing among the voters—the bond or connection that they are able to maintain with citizens.

Further reading: Weisberg, Herbert F. "The Party in the Electorate as a Basis for More Responsible Parties." In John C. Green and Paul S. Herrnson, eds., *Responsible Partisanship? The Evolution of American Political Parties since 1950.* Lawrence: University of Kansas Press, 2002; Key, V. O., Jr. *Politics, Parties, and Pressure Groups.* 5th ed. New York: Thomas Y. Crowell, 1964.

—Marc D. Weiner

party leadership, House of Representatives

The Constitution says little about the role of House leadership, only that members "shall choose their Speaker and other Officers." The offices of clerk and assistant clerk, doorkeeper, chaplain, and sergeant at arms were created by members of the First Congress to perform the housekeeping functions necessary for smooth functioning of the legislative process. Even the Speaker was conceived of as a presiding officer, impartially ruling on procedure, order, and debate rather than exercising political leadership. Interestingly, the Constitution does not even require that the Speaker be an elected member of the House of Representatives. The potential for strong political control was soon recognized, and the speakership was transformed into a partisan position by the early 19th century. In the contemporary House, the Speaker is part of an elaborate system of party officials, including majority and minority floor leaders and the whip system, that plans legislative strategy, counts votes, and enforces party discipline. The strength and importance of leaders have fluctuated widely over time as a result of changes in the political environment, increases in workload and membership, and the personality of individual leaders.

The Speakership

Although House rules allowed the Speaker to vote on all bills and to engage in debates when not presiding, most early Speakers chose not to exercise these rights and avoided using committee assignment powers to attain political ends. Legislative leadership, when it existed, was provided by executive branch officials and their agents in the House. By the first decade of the 19th century, three factors converged to alter the Speaker's role and power dramatically.

First, the legislative workload and number of members rapidly increased, creating the need for a more efficient division of labor than that provided by the temporary committee system. Beginning in 1795, the House began to use permanent committees for legislative work. As a result, small groups of members became responsible for drafting bills, thereby exercising a disproportionate influence on legislative outcomes. Through his control of committee appointments, the Speaker could exercise substantial political power over rank and file members.

Second, growing divisions between the President and Congress over how to address British predations against American shipping made it difficult for Speakers to maintain their role as impartial moderator. A large group of aggressive, anti-British representatives—the so-called War Hawks—sought to wrest control of the issue away from the executive branch and centralize power within the House under their control.

Third, the election of Henry Clay to the speakership in 1811 placed an ambitious and charismatic War Hawk leader in a position to take advantage of these new opportunities. Unlike previous leaders, Clay (Speaker, 1811–14, 1815–20, 1823–25) took full advantage of his prerogatives as both member and party leader, participating actively in floor debates, whipping up party support for his proposals,

Speaker of the House and presidential candidate Henry Clay
(Prints and Photographs Division, Library of Congress)

and voting on most legislation. Clay also used the Speaker's power to recognize members during debate, to deny opponents access to the floor, and used his powers of appointment to place War Hawk allies on key foreign policy committees. Finally, Clay expanded the standing committee system, which he then used as a vehicle for promoting his own legislative priorities.

Although Clay set a precedent for strong leadership in the post of Speaker, those who followed him were generally unable to follow his example. Not only did mid-century Speakers lack Clay's personal magnetism, they were also elected by narrow margins in hotly contested elections and served for only short periods of time. As divisions over slavery grew and the major parties lost ideological coherence, Speakers were unable to exercise strong leadership over rank and file members. It was not until after the Civil War that Speakers regained a position of authority comparable to that occupied by Clay at the beginning of the century.

After the Civil War, political circumstances again favored the development of strong party leadership. Republican dominance led to the expansion of PATRONAGE. Thousands of public works positions were created and allocated by party leaders as a means of rewarding the local party faithful. Republican leaders worked closely with large corporations to pass bills that favored industrial interests. Although these practices led to allegations of corruption that reached all the way to the top of party leadership — Speaker James G. Blaine (Speaker, 1869–75) was investigated twice for illicit stock trades—few Republicans pushed to reform the practices that had helped to consolidate the party's control.

Republican Speakers did, however, seek to reform House rules to deal with the growing problem of minority obstructionism. Democratic representatives used delaying tactics including the "silent," or "disappearing," quorum (members refused to answer to their names even when inside the chamber, preventing the House from proceeding to a vote) and continual demands for adjournment to stall the legislative process. Thomas Brackett Reed (Speaker, 1889–91, 1895–99) believed that these dilatory strategies unconstitutionally allowed a handful of members to hold the legislative process hostage. As Speaker, Reed refused to recognize appeals for adjournment, even when they were in order, and counted members of the House as "present" for purposes of the quorum even when they chose not to vote. The "Reed Rules" were formally adopted by the House in 1890 despite heated protests by members of the Democratic minority.

Although these new rules allowed party leaders to organize the House effectively, they also created the potential for abuse, a potential realized under Republican Speaker Joseph Cannon (Speaker, 1903–11). Cannon used his power to reward political friends and punish enemies, mobilize support for conservative bills, and scuttle support for progressive reforms. It was Cannon's use of appointment powers and control over the Rules Committee, however, that drew the sharpest fire from his critics. Committee assignments were doled out according to a member's support of the party agenda, and only laws supported by Cannon were allowed to reach the floor. Called a "tyrant" and "czar" by Democrats and liberal members of his own party, Cannon was removed by a COALITION of these members from his position on the Rules Committee in March 1910. Although the "revolt" was limited—Cannon was not removed from the speakership, and his appointment powers were left untouched—it signaled the end of "Cannonism" and the strong Speakers of the Republican era.

When the Democrats captured control of the House in 1911, the powers of the speakership were further restricted. First, the Speaker no longer exercised the power of committee appointment. Instead, Democratic members of the House Ways and Means Committee determined committee assignments. and promotion within the committee was based strictly on seniority. Second, an increased reliance on the party caucus to determine which bills reached the floor and the rules under which they were discussed meant that the Speaker soon became little more than a figurehead. The real power during this period was exercised by Oscar Underwood, chair of the Ways and Means Committee and majority floor leader.

Although early to mid-20th-century Speakers tried to recentralize power into their own hands, they made little headway in regaining institutional powers. When Speakers were successful, it was usually because they managed to wield influence *in spite of* the limitations of their office. Speakers Nicholas Longworth (Speaker, 1925–31) and Sam Rayburn (Speaker, 1940–47, 1949–53, 1955–61) used informal powers of persuasion and political favors to cultivate a sense of obligation to the leadership among the rank and file. Rayburn, for example, became adept at piecing together compromise legislation that pulled together slim majorities, a task made easier by shifts toward redistributive social spending: Members who chose to work with the leadership could more easily secure for their districts a sizable chunk of money or important federal project.

The election of a more activist Democratic majority in the mid-1970s created a demand for reform of the House rules. Dissatisfied with the inability of party leaders to push through ambitious agendas against the opposition of more senior, conservative committee chairs, liberal Democrats sought to increase leadership prerogatives. The Speaker was given the right to nominate Democratic members of the Rules Committee, was made chair of the Democratic Steering and Policy Committee, and was granted greater discretion to use bill referral and committee appointments to create a coherent legislative policy. At the same time, however, a quasi-independent subcommittee system was established, decentralizing the legislative process among a greater number of representatives. Speakers during this period therefore had to balance members' demands for strong leadership with their desire to act independently on the issues of greatest importance to themselves and their constituents. The tenure of Speaker Thomas P. "Tip" O'Neill (Speaker, 1977–87) is illustrative: At the same time that O'Neill used restrictive rules to limit Republican amendments and ad hoc taskforces to centralize policy information and strategy, he was largely unable to discipline his own rank-and-file. As a result, the Democratic majority was often incapable of generating coherent policy, relying instead on omnibus legislation that purchased legislative support through pork-barrel POLITICS and symbolic displays of party solidarity meant to cover the lack of substantive policy agreement.

The defeat of the long-standing Democratic majority in 1994 led to a radical increase in party loyalty and the Speaker's influence. Newt Gingrich (Speaker, 1995–99), leader of the so-called REPUBLICAN REVOLUTION, pushed through an ambitious legislative agenda in the first 100 days of the session, handpicked chairs for important standing committees, and sometimes skirted the committee system completely to expedite the passage of important bills. Gin-grich used the media effectively to promote his conservative vision and clashed repeatedly with the Clinton administration over budgetary issues. When his popularity within the party waned as a result of declining Republican electoral fortunes, Gingrich resigned from the House. His successor, Dennis Hastert (Speaker, 1999–present), adopted a more low-key public image but nevertheless exercised considerable political muscle behind the scenes. Hastert selected committee chairs through an interview process to determine their views on important policy issues and worked closely with the House Majority Leader and Republican whip system to enforce party discipline.

Majority Leader

In the modern House of Representatives, the Majority Leader serves as the Speaker's chief deputy and floor leader. Usually an experienced legislator, the Majority Leader provides a variety of supportive services for the Speaker. He or she does much of the daily work in promoting the party's policy agenda to audiences outside the chamber and piecing together the coalitions necessary to ensure legislative success.

The Majority Leader's role has changed over time in response to evolving institutions and the political needs of different Speakers. The first Majority Leaders held informal positions and were appointed by the Speaker or selected from within the leadership of important committees, usually Ways and Means or Appropriations. Often political rivals of the Speaker, Majority Leaders were sometimes selected to bring together party FACTIONS or counterbalance the opposition. In 1911, Oscar Underwood became the first elected Majority Leader. A powerful leader, Underwood exercised great influence over the legislative process through the DEMOCRATIC PARTY caucus after the revolt against Cannonism.

In the contemporary House, most Majority Leaders have a close and supportive relationship with the Speaker. Their duties are not spelled out in House rules, and the roles they play are often determined by the specific mix of personalities and talents within the leadership team. For example, Tom DeLay, majority leader under Dennis Hastert until being removed by his party after being formally charged with violating election laws, often played the role of REPUBLICAN PARTY spokesperson in the media and took the lead in campaign activities and establishing ties between the party leadership and Washington LOBBYISTS.

Minority Leader

The Minority Leader is the leader of the "loyal opposition" in the House. First recognized as a distinct position in the 1880s, the Minority Leader is usually viewed as the minority's candidate for Speaker. Minority Leaders serve many of the same functions as the majority leadership team: promoting their party's agenda, seeking support on important bills, and coordinating legislative strategy. Unlike MAJORITY PARTY leaders, however, the Minority Leader also serves as a chief critic of the bills being passed by the opposing party, chief cheerleader to keep the spirits of his rank-and-file members high despite legislative disappointments, and chief campaign strategist in the attempt to "win back" the House. Finally, the Minority Leader may also serve as the chief spokesperson for the administration when they are from the same party.

Minority Leaders have approached these roles in very different ways. Republican Minority Leaders during the long period of Democratic dominance from 1955 to 1995 often acted in a bipartisan fashion in an attempt to secure as many benefits for their members as possible. Given the large Democratic majority, it seemed at the time unlikely that Republicans would ever regain control in the House. Consequently, most Minority Leaders sought to forge occasional majority coalitions with conservative Democrats on issues of importance to both groups. Democratic Minority Leaders since the Republican revolution, however, have taken a more aggressive stance using obstructionism when possible and publicly criticizing both House leaders and the Republican administration of George W. Bush, a strategy driven by the narrow nature of the Republican majority and increasing party polarization.

Whip System

The leadership of both parties are supported by a whip system that tracks support of legislative votes, lobbying members and making sure that they are present on the floor for close votes. Whips are appointed by the leadership for a variety of reasons. Often the whip system is a training ground for those identified as potential party leaders. Dennis Hastert, Newt Gingrich, Tom DeLay, and Nancy Pelosi, for example, all served within the whip system before their election to higher party office. The whip system has expanded in recent years as a means of incorporating rank-and-file members and underrepresented groups such as women and minorities into the leadership structure. Whips promote party discipline as well as providing a channel through which member concerns or complaints are incorporated into the party agenda. Finally, whips provide a variety of services to members such as a job bank and resources for conflict resolution.

Further reading: Davidson, Roger H., Susan Webb Hammond, and Raymond W. Smock. *Masters of the House: Congressional Leadership over Two Centuries.* Boulder, Colo.: Westview Press, 1998; Davidson, Roger H., and Walter Oleszek. *Congress and Its Members.* 9th ed. Washington, D.C.: CQ Press, 2004; Peters, Ronald M., Jr. *The American Speakership: The Office in Historical Perspective.* 2nd ed. Baltimore: Johns Hopkins University Press, 1997.

—Celia M. Carroll

party leadership, Senate

Senate party leadership is a function of the Senate's institutional structure and its membership. The structural hallmarks that are exceptional to the Senate (e.g., small size, unlimited debate, supermajoritarian rules) have determined the extent to which the two political parties, whose dominance virtually excludes splinter party members, are able to shape outcomes. In addition, the members of the Senate govern how much power the leadership has and how leaders are able to use power.

Compared to the House of Representatives, the development of Senate leadership offices is of recent vintage, having emerged to meet members' demands and having evolved, in both scope and function, with those demands. Currently, party leadership in the Senate is relatively strong both because of and resulting from the high level of cohesion within the parties. If the trend toward homogeneity continues, expectations are for continued influence of parties and thus more partisan outcomes, though still within institutional and membership limitations.

The longstanding rules of the Senate, though relatively few, are explicit in their protection of minority rights. The framers' belief that a numerical minority should not be suppressed by a majority run amok resurfaced in the right of individual senators to open debate and freedom of operation on the floor of the Senate. Of course, it is possible for unlimited debate to turn into a filibuster, but even this is protected by a supermajoritarian requirement of three-fifths support to end debate.

The Constitution and other founding documents establish the Senate as the chamber of reason to curb the House of impetuosity, and, consistent with them, reason is brought about by debate. This institutional context of open debate and supermajoritarian rule creates the individualistic nature of the Senate. That one senator can bring business to a halt emphasizes individualism, so that the operating system of the Senate is inherently egalitarian. The individualistic nature of the Senate became all the more apparent in the 1970s and 1980s with the decline of seniority as the criterion for committee assignments and general advancement. Necessarily then, the leadership that emerged was limited by the institutional constraints of the Senate.

The emergence of Senate party leadership positions is recent compared to House party leadership, which began at the founding. It was during the 1890s that Nelson Aldrich (R, R.I.) and Arthur Pue Gorman (D, Md.) began a functional, if not nominal, leadership of their respective parties and the chamber. Both dominated their parties' caucuses but exercised a personality-based leadership that extended to the floor of the Senate. By the time Aldrich and Gorman left the Senate in 1911, a precedent had been established, and senators of both parties expected effective management of party business.

At this time, the first open contest for a Democratic leader occurred, and John Kern (D, Ind.) was elected Democratic caucus chairman in 1913. He was the first Democratic leader since 1895 to preside over a MAJORITY PARTY and was the first Senate leader referred to as Majority Leader. The Republican caucus immediately elected their own party's "floor leader," and thus were born the offices of Majority and Minority Leaders that we know today. Other leadership evolutions and additions followed: Democrats created the office of party whip in 1913 and Republicans in 1915.

The leadership structure of the Senate is based firmly on party. Divided into the majority and minority parties, each has corresponding positions and functions. For the majority party, the chief officer is the Senate Majority Leader; on the minority side, it is the Senate Minority Leader. Each operates in close consultation with the other. The Majority Leader's basic task is to pass majority party legislation. There are many steps to this outcome, but broadly defined, the Majority Leader must schedule votes and manage the floor (in general, ensure the day's business is conducted, but the tasks can be as melodramatic as bargaining for votes or as mundane as responding to points of order).

Votes are scheduled by consultation with the Minority Leader and with input from interested members of the Majority Leader's own party. Scheduling is a strategic resource for the Senate Majority Leader. While official powers are few, the ability to call votes is a necessary if not sufficient tool to ensure outcomes desirable to the party. By rushing or delaying a vote (or even threatening to do so), he or she is able to negotiate and bargain outcomes. Waving the stick of an extended session or dangling the carrot of an early recess breaks the gridlock that sometimes forms when 100 individuals try to influence outcomes.

While the Senate has formal rules regulating floor procedure, these intricacies are set aside, for time's sake, so that the Senate when legislating operates largely by unanimous consent agreements (UCAs). UCAs are a way to expedite floor business by a unanimous agreement to waive the rules of order. While any senator can object to a UCA, these agreements are usually the end product of much negotiation and bargaining between the majority and MINORITY PARTY leaders, and among other senators also, so that by the time a bill reaches the floor, outcomes have been decided and there are few surprises. However, certainty is not always assured, and on the floor the Senate Majority Leader has one important formal power—the right of first recognition. Established by precedent in the 1930s and perfected by Lyndon B. Johnson (D, Tex.) when he was Majority Leader trying to usher through CIVIL RIGHTS LEGISLATION in the 1950s, the right of first recognition gives the Majority Leader priority in being recognized over another senator by the chair. And unlike the SPEAKER OF THE HOUSE, the Senate Majority Leader retains all rights and privileges of a senator. He or she is able to, and ordinarily does, cast votes as well as sit on committees, so his or her influence extends far beyond the floor.

In addition to these narrowly construed legislative duties, the Senate Majority Leader is also spokesperson for the party. He or she is the face of the majority party (under "divided government" at least), which means frequent media appearances. Moreover, he or she undertakes campaign events, including FUND-RAISING, toward the end that his or her party stays in the majority. In addition to party promotional activities, he or she has the institutional obligation to maintain the Senate. Because he or she is not only Majority Leader but leader of the Senate, the leader acts to check and balance the other legislative branch as well as the executive. For example, the Majority Leader selects members for conference committees so that the Senate can discharge its implicit instruction to "cool the tempers of the House." And he or she can use the constitutional order to "advise and consent" on presidential appointments to maintain the Senate's strength against the executive.

Both the majority and minority parties have extensive whip systems. Whips are responsible for counting votes. Theirs is a charge to tally yeas and nays in advance of each vote, and to try to ensure that there is enough in one column or the other to pass the party position. If not, they "whip members into shape" by threats or promises.

Beyond these structural leaders who work to legislate are administrative party leaders who work to maintain and advance the party. These are the chairs of the various party committees, such as the Policy Committee, Steering Committee, and Campaign Committee. These differ from Senate standing committees in that they are devoted exclusively to party business such as assigning committees, electing committee chairs, outlining party agendas, and coordinating campaign activities. There is relatively frequent variation in formation and function and relatively higher turnover in these positions. For the Democrats, the leader serves simultaneously as Chair of the Conference, but for the Republicans, that position is relegated to someone other than the leader. In addition, REPUBLICAN PARTY rules state that the Senate Majority Leader cannot simultaneously serve as chair of a standing committee.

The chairs of the respective party campaign committees have been a prestigious position. They have served as a proving ground for members to move into formal leadership positions, such as Senator Bill Frist's (R, Tenn.) service as chair of the National Republican Senatorial Campaign Committee, which put him in good stead to assume the leadership after Trent Lott (R, Miss.). However, there is some speculation that with the recent banning of SOFT MONEY and other campaign finance regulations, the chief senatorial fund-raiser may prove a less useful office for the ambitious.

Two party–based positions of leadership are largely ceremonial. By constitutional authority, the vice president serves as president of the Senate. Though this role is functionally lame, the vice president will cast a vote if needed to break a tie, but otherwise is seen with the Speaker of the House sitting behind the president during State of the Union addresses. In the vice president's frequent absences from the chamber, the Constitution provides for the Senate to choose a president pro tempore. This customarily is the most senior member of the majority party, but even this position is more honorary than active. For day-to-day business, the chair rotates from one freshman senator to another.

Scholars point roughly to the 1890s as the beginning of party leadership in the Senate (although party caucuses began forming in the 1840s), but vary in their interpretations of causes and effects. Some explanations center on legislative workload, presidential intervention, and party polarization. The most basic contention is that as the business of legislating has expanded (owing to an increased nationalization of problems), so have the development of and expectations for party leaders. More work necessitated a manager for 100 individuals and the issues that occupy them. This view alone is too simple, for it does not explain why the leadership structure that emerged was tied to party.

Another perspective is that the formation of leadership positions, specifically that of Majority Leader, owes not to internal but to external forces. As the job of legislating became more extensive, the president needed a "point man" in the Senate to usher through the executive agenda and to act in an arena from which he was barred. However, a strict interpretation of this explanation violates separation of powers and assumes the Senate Majority Leader is of the same party as the president. Others have linked leadership innovations to levels of interparty polarization—as parties became more divided on more issues and more internally cohesive, leadership strengthened to advance party preferences.

From this, current thinking points to an explanation in principal-agent theory. Leaders are a creation of and draw their powers from party members. Leaders solve collective action problems that individual senators cannot. They formulate and disseminate a party message within and beyond the chamber. Through a wide range of publications, the leaderships provide specific information on each vote to keep party membership abreast of current happenings and upcoming schedules. Highlights of the information flow are weekly party lunches to discuss policy positions. Leaders and their staffs meet formally and informally, regularly and irregularly, with individual senators, committee chairs, and other staff to discuss strategies. In terms of costs and benefits, a single senator could not afford the time and effort to 1) know all the bills, 2) learn about those bills, 3) formulate a party-line position on them, and 4) negotiate with 99 other senators to achieve a favorable outcome. For the benefit of more

and better knowledge and a chance at a favorable outcome, party members sign onto the party line. In short, leadership serves its members and members serve the leadership.

Accordingly, party leadership in the Senate is a function of the institutional structures of the Senate as well as its membership. Rules (such as those governing filibuster and cloture) that emphasize individual senators ensure that leadership is egalitarian rather than hierarchical. Leadership complements rather than conflicts with the structure of the Senate. As party positions became more defined in the ELECTORATE and in Congress, party success was intertwined with individual success. Thus, members, especially in the individualistic Senate, were more likely to accede to a stronger and active leadership to keep members in the party line. However, this grant of authority from members to leaders is revocable but is unlikely to be rescinded if the current state of interparty polarization and intraparty cohesion is sustained.

Further reading: Baker, Richard A., and Roger H. Davidson, eds. *First among Equals: Outstanding Senate Leaders of the Twentieth Century*. Washington, D.C.: Congressional Quarterly, 1991; Gamm, Gerald, and Steven S. Smith. "Emergence of Senate Party Leadership." In Bruce I. Oppenheimer, ed., *U.S. Senate Exceptionalism*. Columbus: Ohio State University Press, 2002; Sinclair, Barbara. "Full Circle? Congressional Party Leadership during the Twentieth Century." In Sunil Ahuja and Robert Dewhirst, eds., *Congress Responds to the Twentieth Century*. Columbus: Ohio State University Press, 2003.

—Andrea C. Hatcher

party organization

The party organization is a committee (or collection of committees) that performs the day-to-day administrative tasks of a POLITICAL PARTY. Prior to 1832, political parties were formless organizations, nothing more than the collected wills and attitudes of their membership. Local political parties were products of their elected (or self-selected) leadership and the lieutenants they chose. Only once, at national presidential nominating conventions, did party membership gather to discuss strategy, organize the party's business, and choose leadership. Even the conventions themselves were planned on an ad-hoc basis by party leadership. Parties had no institutional memory, and conventions were, as a result, chaotic affairs with little grounding in strategy.

The Democratic Party's first nominating convention was in 1832, as Andrew Jackson sought to bypass Congress's self-adopted presidential NOMINATION right, and by the end of that convention the first standing political party organization in America, the DEMOCRATIC NATIONAL COMMITTEE (DNC), existed. Beginning as merely a planning entity for the next convention, the committee was not considered sovereign over the party, the will of the convention retaining that power for itself.

Immediately thereafter, political parties were exercising their power at the local level in machines, another form of informal party organization. Part social welfare agent and part corrupt seller of votes, the machine consisted of elected officials and their patrons in politically appointed jobs. While more nebulous in organization than the national committee, the machine was a powerful organization that ran urban areas under a party organization's aegis.

Following the national parties and machines, state and local parties began to develop their own organizations in a similar vein. Planning has always been central to the party organization's purpose, but more overall authority was granted to state, county, and even the submetropolitan level committees. FUND-RAISING, strategy, and general electoral support gradually found their way into the mix of powers granted these permanent organizations.

Party organizations still call for and organize conventions as their primary mission, but they do much more today. While the Progressive reforms of the early 20th century gutted the party organizations in terms of their formal powers, recent history has shown a significant revival of the party organization's role in American POLITICS. After Rich Bond's ascension to the REPUBLICAN NATIONAL COMMITTEE chair in the late 1970s, he used DIRECT MAIL to build the party's fiscal base and increase the committee's role in electioneering and visibility. As the party built successes in recruitment and electioneering, the DNC and other state parties followed suit.

Today, the party organizations account for more than $500 million in campaign spending and are respected providers of advice and coordination for political candidates at all levels. Party organizations are viewed as valuable by the candidates who run under their party's banner, and so their leadership is also highly valued (and critiqued). Auxiliary and state organizations assist in VOTER REGISTRATION and mobilization efforts, as well. The party organizations at all levels also strategically allocate resources into competitive races in a process known as TARGETING.

Further reading: Aldrich, John. *Why Parties?* Chicago: University of Chicago Press, 1995; Cotter, Cornelius P., and Bernard Hennessy. *Politics without Power: The National Party Committees.* New York: Atherton Press, 1964; Democratic National Committee. Available online. URL: http://www.democrats.org. Accessed August 10, 2005; Katz, Richard S., and Peter Mair. *How Parties Organize.* Thousand Oaks, Calif.: Sage Publications, 1994; Republican National Committee. Available online. URL: http://www.rnc.org. Accessed August 10, 2005; Wattenberg, Martin P. *The Decline of American Political Parties, 1952–1988.* Cambridge, Mass.: Harvard University Press, 1992.

—Chapman Rackaway

party organization, local

The two dominant modern political parties in the United States (i.e., the Democratic and Republican parties) are organized at the local level as well as at the state and national levels. Typically, these parties are organized at the county, city, and sometimes the PRECINCT level.

The beginnings of two-party competition in American POLITICS can be traced to the Jefferson-Adams election of 1800. The period from the 1830s to the 1890s is sometimes described as the "classic period" in American party politics. During that period many voters made a lifelong commitment to "their party" and expected workers for the winning party to seek and sometimes get government jobs. This granting of special job opportunities is called PATRONAGE. Party loyalty declined in the 20th century, especially among younger voters. Patronage hiring now is linked mostly to contested local sheriff elections and elections in a few larger cities.

In the Constitution, states are charged to determine the "time, place and manner" of holding elections. Under state laws, each county and city is divided into election precincts. The county election officer, a paid local government employee, works with the county DEMOCRATIC and REPUBLICAN PARTY chairpersons to assure that elections in each precinct are run as state and federal laws require. The party chairperson is not a public employee and usually works without pay. Most often he or she is elected in the party PRIMARY election.

The county party chairperson is the central figure in local party organization. He or she sometimes recruits and often does BALLOT registration for individuals seeking to run for office, particularly at the county and state legislative levels. He or she presides at the county convention of the party, sometimes speaks for the party to local media, and works with county election officials to assure there are election judges, clerks, and POLL WATCHERS at precincts in the county on ELECTION DAY. Other duties of the COUNTY CHAIRPERSON and other party activists include distribution of CAMPAIGN LITERATURE, FUND-RAISING to help party candidates, distributing posters and lawn signs, and organizing PHONE BANKS and other GET-OUT-THE-VOTE activities.

Formally, the Democratic and Republican parties are organized from the bottom up. A party chooses its candidates in a primary election, and party loyalists meet in a precinct convention to choose DELEGATES to the county convention and approve resolutions. At the county convention, precinct delegates meet, begin the process of selecting delegates to the national political convention, and pass resolutions. Local as well as national party conventions are usually organized by the presidential candidate preference of those attending.

The informal operation of American political parties at the local level differs from the formal structure described above. In some precincts, conventions are not held or are poorly attended. In many counties, the county chairperson is reelected again and again. The county party committee and party election workers are mostly middle-aged or retired and typically have many years of service. At the local level, most Democratic and Republican Party activists are also active in other civic and community activities. Candidates who file and run in the party primary may or may not have been active in local party politics.

Unlike major political parties in Europe, the two major political parties in the United States do not charge dues, usually do not have large or elaborate local offices, and are usually active only around election time. American THIRD PARTIES such as the GREEN PARTY and the LIBERTARIAN PARTY are organized at the national and state levels but are usually organized at the local level only in large metropolitan areas.

Individual-centered media campaigns, recent changes in the campaign finance rules, direct primaries, reductions in patronage positions, and the rise of social welfare programs have all worked to weaken the influence of local political parties in the United States. However, local party organizations and party leaders are still influential at the local level. It is often said that support from the local party is not enough to guarantee a win on election day, but a lack of support can virtually guarantee defeat.

Further reading: Bibby, John F. *Political Parties and Elections in America.* 5th ed. New York: Wadsworth Press, 2002; White, John Kenneth, and Daniel M. Shea. *New Party Politics: From Jefferson and Hamilton to the Information Age.* 2nd ed. Belmont, Calif.: Wadsworth/Thomson Learning, 2004; Maisel, Sandy L., ed. *The Parties Respond: Changes in American Parties and Campaigns.* Boulder, Colo.: Westview Press, 2002.

—Gayle R. Avant

party organization, national

This is a permanent committee designed to formulate and execute the electioneering strategy of a national POLITICAL PARTY. In an effort to plan for the 1836 Democratic National Convention, DELEGATEs to the 1832 nominating meeting formed a permanent organization, the DEMOCRATIC NATIONAL COMMITTEE, to oversee planning and preparation for the next convention. The Democratic National Committee has existed as an organization ever since.

In 1853, after forming at a church in Ripon, Wisconsin, the new REPUBLICAN PARTY immediately formed its own national committee to plan for its premier convention in 1856. Immediately following the Civil War, Republican members of the House of Representatives who impeached President Andrew Johnson were afraid of REPUBLICAN NATIONAL COMMITTEE (RNC) retribution while seeking renomination and founded the Union Congressional Committee (later renamed the National Republican Congres-

sional Committee) as a mirror organization to the RNC, which they saw as controlled by too radical a strain of the party.

Democrats who favored Johnson's removal founded their own rogue organization, the Democratic Congressional Campaign Committee. As post–Civil War tensions eased over time, both congressional committees were folded into the national committee structures of each party to specialize in congressional races while the national committees could concentrate on presidential races. Two new committees emerged in national organizations after the SEVENTEENTH AMENDMENT made senatorial elections popular in 1913.

During the 1972 presidential campaign, the Democratic Party was headquartered in a suite at the Watergate Hotel. A break-in orchestrated by operatives of then President Richard Nixon's reelection campaign eventually brought Nixon's presidency down. The Watergate affair led to both of the parties making efforts to find more secure and stable homes, but until the late 1970s neither had a permanent headquarters. By 1984, both the Republicans and Democrats had their three national committees housed in impressive structures near the Capitol. The stability of the new headquarters allowed the parties to fund-raise better, build institutional memory, and communicate more effectively with their elected officials.

Today, the parties' national headquarters are buzzing centers of political commerce. Staffs of 500 persons and more conduct day-to-day business for the national committees, which includes candidate recruitment, message coordination, FUND-RAISING, and strategic communications. Using DIRECT MAIL as a fund-raising technique, the Republican committee drastically increased its capacity with increased contributions and more aggressive electioneering practices. National party organizations now coordinate POLITICAL ACTION COMMITTEE contributions to candidates and funnel millions of dollars into presidential, congressional, and even state-level campaigns.

Party organizations at the national level do not direct and manipulate all campaigns but nonetheless are powerful participants in the electoral process today. As party organizations strengthened themselves, other tangential groups were added under the party umbrellas, including the Democratic and Republican collegiate and women's auxiliaries. Despite declining voter identification with the parties and the effects of the Bipartisan Campaign Reform Act (BCRA), the national parties remain invaluable parts of the electoral process. From an institutional perspective, the national parties have proved to be remarkably resilient and remain as strong as ever in American electoral POLITICS.

Further reading: Aldrich, John. *Why Parties?* Chicago: University of Chicago Press, 1995; Cotter, Cornelius P., and Bernard Hennessy. *Politics without Power: The National*

Party Committees. New York: Atherton Press, 1964; Democratic National Committee. Available online. URL: http://www.democrats.org. Accessed August 10, 2005; Katz, Richard S., and Peter Mair. *How Parties Organize.* Thousand Oaks, Calif.: Sage Publications, 1994; Republican National Committee. Available online. URL: http://www.rnc.org. Accessed August 10, 2005; Wattenberg, Martin P. *The Decline of American Political Parties, 1952–1988.* Cambridge, Mass.: Harvard University Press, 1992.

—Chapman Rackaway

party organization, state

The state-level PARTY ORGANIZATION consists of a group of party loyalists who guide a state political party's strategy and day-to-day operations. Parties began to organize and contest elections almost from the beginning of the American republic. Pennsylvania was the first state to have recorded some instance of party organization, at first no more than a caucus of like-minded members of the state legislature.

In the early years, party organizations at the state level were nothing more than mobilization efforts orchestrated by the elected officials of the party and their allies. After Andrew Jackson's efforts to bypass the congressional caucus led to the DEMOCRATIC NATIONAL COMMITTEE's formation in 1832, states began to more aggressively contest elections. Simultaneously, the state party organizations became embroiled in local party apparatuses in cities, reinforcing the POLITICS of the urban machine.

State party leaders were often the bosses of MACHINE POLITICS, not only mobilizing voters, but also making PATRONAGE decisions, nominating candidates, and directing the policies of the party machines. George Clinton of New York organized the first state party machine in the late 1700s. State party organizations were the strongest form of political organization during the 1800s and into the 1900s. State organizations revolved around the machines, and so when the machines were severely limited under the Progressive reforms of the late 1800s and early 1900s, state party organizations were decimated. Local party organizations, often autonomous but generally in close allegiance with the state organizations, withered.

Party loyalties decreased steadily nationwide, and the state parties were slow to react. Patronage and NOMINATION power, twin backbones of state party strength, were replaced as parties faded into near-obscurity. Local party organizations that provided jobs and informal welfare provisions through PRECINCT committeemen's "walking around money" during the machine era became inconsequential and disconnected from state party leadership. After the national POLITICAL PARTY organizations began to restructure and strengthen themselves in the late 1970s, state parties began to follow suit.

While the national political party organizations have had great successes in reorganizing and electioneering, the level of state political party organization varies from state to state. State parties with a closed PRIMARY can have more control over the nomination process than states with open primaries, and a number of states are allowed to endorse primary candidates for office. Vagaries in CAMPAIGN FINANCE LAW mean that some state parties have more control over the pipeline of campaign funds, giving them appreciably more power in the craft of electioneering. State party organizations also perform vital election process services, such as choosing NATIONAL PARTY COMMITTEE membership, organizing state conventions, recruiting candidates for office, and selecting national convention DELEGATEs.

While local party organizations are incredibly weak in general, state party organizations also oversee local party politics to an unprecedented extent. Most state party organizations have permanent headquarters, full-time professional staff, and adequate financial resources to both run the party's operations and support electoral efforts by party candidates.

Further reading: Aldrich, John. *Why Parties?* Chicago: University of Chicago Press, 1995.

—Chapman Rackaway

party switchers

Politicians who change partisan affiliations are designated "party switchers." Although voters can do the same, the term *party switcher* generally refers to political elites, typically legislators, who defect from one party to another. Contemporary understanding of party switching pertains more to members of the U.S. Congress than to other positions, although research extends to state legislatures and even to foreign assemblies.

Frequency of cross-party migration among members of Congress is low. From 1876, when the party system stabilized after RECONSTRUCTION, until the 21st century, party switchers numbered 59. This list counts only genuine ideological party switchers, not those who change party label to win renomination or continue to organize and maintain seniority with the original party.

Switching is neither random nor regular but episodic by type of switch, whether between major or minor parties. Party switching increased after 1950, mostly between major parties. In earlier periods, most switches involved movement from a major to a minor party, or vice versa. The decline of major-minor switches is commonly explained by the direct elections of nominees through primaries rather than caucuses or conventions, which weakened minor parties and diminished incentives for elected officials to find comfort in splinter parties.

A principal effect of party switching is a change in roll-call voting behavior. When switchers leave one party for another, their votes are often in sync with their new party. This change is accentuated more when a switcher moves between major parties than from or to a minor party. Party leaders often reward switchers with favored committee assignments. This can be particularly appealing for a moderate member of a POLITICAL PARTY that recently went from majority status to minority status. However, the electoral consequences may not make the trade worth the price. At least among southern state legislators, switching parties made them more susceptible to defeat in subsequent elections.

Reflecting a larger debate on the extent of party influence in Congress, some scholars attribute party switching and its consequences to CONSTITUENCY motivations. Yet, interview evidence from switchers reveals not changing constituencies but increasing pressure to vote party lines. Once, members of Congress could exist on the fringe of parties. Now, the growing divide between parties on a variety of issues forces those members to one side or the other, and some members choose the other side.

Further reading: Hatcher, Andrea C., and Bruce I. Oppenheimer. "Congressional Party Switchers, 1876–2003: The Effects of Party and Constituency on Strategic Behavior." *Legislative Studies Quarterly* 28, no. 3 (2003): 436; Nokken, Timothy P. "Dynamics of Congressional Loyalty: Party Defection and Roll-Call Behavior, 1947–97." *Legislative Studies Quarterly* 15 (2000): 417–444.

—Andrea C. Hatcher

party unity score

The party unity score is the measure of a congressperson's partisan voting record. A maximum score of 100 is given to a congressperson who votes on divisive issues with a majority of his or her party 100 percent of the time, and a minimum score of 0 is given to a congressperson voting for the opposing party on the same issues without fail.

The party unity score is calculated first by determining the number of roll-call votes in which a majority of one party votes opposite to the majority of another party (see PARTISAN VOTING IN CONGRESS); these are labeled "party unity votes." For instance, if 60 percent of Democrats vote for a measure and 60 percent of Republicans vote against it, this measure is considered a party unity vote. However, if 60 percent of both parties vote in the same manner (either both for or both against) on the measure, it is ignored for the purposes of this analysis.

The second and final step in calculating the party unity score for a given congressperson is simply to divide the number of times they have voted with their party on these votes with the total number of party unity votes.

The party unity score is a common variable in congressional studies. Its usage can be traced back to at least 1959, when George Goodwin, Jr., analyzed the effect of party loyalty on the seniority system in Congress. Since that time it has helped explain a variety of phenomena, including shifts in the IDEOLOGY and independence of congresspersons over time.

In modern times, party unity scores rarely reach less than 50 for any given congressperson, though SOUTHERN DEMOCRATS and northern Republicans are apt to have lower scores. In 2002, Ken Lucas of Kentucky, the sole congressional member who received less than a score of 50, bottomed out on the Democratic side of the aisle with a score of 42, while Constance Morella of Maryland crossed party lines more times than any of her colleagues, with a party unity score of 58. Overall, Democrats seem to be less unified than their counterparts, in large part due to the REALIGNMENT of the South.

—Jeremy B. Lupoli

patronage

Patronage refers to an informal system of social organization characterized by reciprocal and unequal transactions between rulers and ruled, involving the exchange of political rights and social and economic benefits. Patronage operates informally, in highly personal, familiar, traditional, and culturally bound settings in which decisions about "who gets what" are made on the basis of implicit understandings and norms. Patronage is unequal and reciprocal in that people or groups of people who are unequal in power provide goods and services to one another for mutual benefit, creating a social compact of utility, security, and meaning. Patronage also functions as a form of social capital by negotiating the boundaries between the public and private spheres. Viewed as a significant driver of societal resource distribution, patronage plays a central role in a wide range of political and electoral contexts.

Patronage as a phenomenon has animated socioeconomic and political relationships from time immemorial, for as long as governance—of nations, communities and villages, institutions, and networks—has pivoted in part on the contestation and disposition of power resources (authority, wealth, and influence). The historical lineage of the word *patronage* can be traced to its etymological root, *patron*, a long-standing reference to someone who sponsors or supports a cause or an institution, such as a benefactor of the arts or an ecclesiastical figure who grants blessings to the faithful. Over time, even as systems of governance have grown increasingly complex, patronage has maintained its fundamental role as an arbiter of power and a fulcrum of distributive POLITICS in traditional, transitional, and modern societies. Examples of patronage abound: 1) vote-buying in free elections, perpetrated by POLITICAL PARTY leaders in control of scarce resources; 2) rule-bending in bureaucracies, engineered to secure particular bureaucratic outcomes; and 3) survival strategies for poor, marginalized groups with no other choices in situations in which official procedures and service delivery are untenable. Patronage in all of its forms has been studied for many years by sociologists, anthropologists, political scientists, and economists, attesting to its persistence across cultures and polities.

The concept of patronage has gained significance in recent years for two principal reasons: Patronage is frequently linked to corruption in representative politics because it is perceived as a variation on a similar theme, the use of asymmetrical power to gain advantage. In light of certain trends in American politics—the influence of monied interests, the rise of incumbency, the "empire" mentality of congressional appropriations committees—any sort of patronage may be cause (like corruption) for the continued estrangement of people from government and the political process. Second, patronage may be useful as a barometer of democratic development around the world. Examination of the historical and cultural expressions of patronage offers "entry points" that can help demystify the political game and illuminate governance structures and functions. With this added analytical dimension, more appropriate democracy assistance interventions may be devised.

Further reading: Brinkerhoff, Derick W., and Arthur A. Goldsmith. "Good Governance, Clientelism and Patrimonialism: New Perspectives on Old Problems." *International Public Management Journal* 7, no. 2 (2002): 163–185.

—Paul J. Nuti

Pendleton Act of 1883

The Pendleton Act of 1883, also known as the Civil Service Act of 1883, emerged as a tool to regulate and improve civil service in the United States. Through the Pendleton Act, the "spoils system" of rewarding political friends and supporters with government jobs was replaced by the "merit system," which provided that federal government jobs be awarded on the basis of merit and through competitive exams. The act also made it unlawful to fire or demote employees covered by the law for political reasons, and it prohibited employers from requiring employees to provide political service or make political contributions as a condition of their employment.

To ensure that the appointments to certain executive branch posts were based on merit, the Pendleton Act also established the Civil Service Commission, a bipartisan commission appointed by the president with Senate approval. Congress abolished the Civil Service Commission in 1978 and replaced it with the Office of Personnel Management, which administers civil service laws, advertises positions, writes civil service exams, and acts as a clearinghouse for agencies seeking employees, and the Merit Systems Protection Board, which settles disputes concerning employee rights and obligations, hears employee grievances, and orders corrective action when deemed necessary.

History has played a key role in the emergence of civil service reform demands. The political adage "to the victor belong the spoils" best describes the method of civil service recruitment and placement employed during the early 19th century. For instance, rather than making federal appointments based on merit, during this period jobs were given as rewards for political support. Consequently, because of presidential TERM LIMITS, workers panicked during each election year, they lacked loyalty to the organization, and the constant civil servant turnover led to a lack of institutional memory. As noted by Henry Clay, after an election, government officials are "like the inhabitants of Cairo when the plague breaks out; no one knows who is next to encounter the stroke of death." Complicating matters were mounting instances of employees being pressured to participate in political activities. In addition, as the federal bureaucracy grew, so did the number of individuals seeking jobs and the number of people demanding political appointments from the president.

To address the mounting problems associated with the spoils system of political appointments, a civil service movement began in New York in 1877. As a result of the considerable success of this movement, civil service reform was introduced and steered through Congress by a longtime civil service reformer, Senator George Hunt Pendleton of Ohio. Though efforts were made to circumvent these reforms, the assassination of President James A. Garfield by Charles Guiteau, a disgruntled individual seeking a job, was the catalyst needed for Congress to finally address civil service reform through the Pendleton Act. In addition to congressional support, Chester A. Arthur also emerged as an ardent civil service reformer after Garfield's assassination and quickly signed this act into law on January 16, 1883.

Although the Pendleton Act helped replace the spoils system with the merit system of recruiting civil servants, a major side effect surfaced. Because political parties could no longer solicit funds from civil servants, their attention turned to corporations as means of financial support. In turn, corporations were happy to donate to political campaigns in hopes of influencing public policy. For instance, during the 1896 PRESIDENTIAL ELECTION campaign between William McKinley and William Jennings Bryant, the REPUBLICAN PARTY spent more than $16 million campaigning, an astronomical amount of money at the time. Consequently, the presidential campaign was wrought with accusations of bribery and unethical contributions when Marcus Alonzo Hanna, a wealthy Cleveland industrialist who made his money in iron and coal, raised more than $6 million for William McKinley—more than $82 million in current dollars. As chairman of the Republican National Committee and as McKinley's chief fund-raiser, Hanna used his power and influence to devise a system of quotas to solicit contributions from large corporations by levying regular assessments on well-off businesses throughout the country. In exchange for these contributions, McKinley vowed to strongly support a big business agenda by establishing silver coinage, supporting protective tariffs, and, on behalf of railroad interests, supporting the replacement of stocks with bonds for the financial backing of corporations.

As a result of significant campaign contributions, McKinley was able to successfully mount a sophisticated presidential race by employing these funds to produce a "Front Porch Campaign," with his face and name appearing on posters, pamphlets, and signs throughout the country. In return for his efforts, the White House raised the profile of Hanna, while the Republican Party continued to promote Hanna as a "lovable character." However, while the White House and Republicans elevated the status of Hanna, the PEOPLE'S PARTY depicted Hanna as "the most vicious, canal and unrelenting oppressor of labor and crusher of its organizations." Consequently, because of the rumors and SCANDALS generated during this campaign, there was a significant growth in public distrust toward campaign financing.

To address campaign finance reform, Theodore Roosevelt's 1904 presidential race focused on a "Clean Government Campaign." Having gained public support and eventually winning the election, Roosevelt adopted many Progressive Era ideas once in office. For instance, with Roosevelt's leadership, Congress passed the TILLMAN ACT in 1907 to prohibit corporations and national banks from contributing to federal campaigns. Though intended to curb attempts to buy political influence through campaign contributions, current proponents of campaign finance reform argue that the Tillman Act has become meaningless because of SOFT MONEY (loosely regulated donations to the parties that are supposedly intended for "party-building," and not specific candidates). In addition, businesses and corporations found ways to circumvent the law by giving their employees large bonuses if the employees endorsed candidates supported by the company. Through this loophole, companies were able to continue to gain political access while gaining tax deductions for employee benefits.

Regardless of its negative side effects on campaign contributions and the ongoing efforts to reform campaign contributions, the Pendleton Act has been quite successful in transforming the nature of public service in the United States. Today many well-educated and well-trained professionals have found rewarding careers in civil service. When the Pendleton Act went into effect, only 10 percent of the government's 132,000 employees were covered; however, this act has grown to cover more than 90 percent of the 2.7 million federal employees.

Further reading: Hoogenboom, Ari Arthur. *Outlawing the Spoils: A History of the Civil Service Reform Movement, 1865–1883.* Urbana: University of Illinois Press, 1961.

—Mitzi Ramos

penny press

Penny press is the term originally coined for newspapers that were sold for 1 cent. The first such newspaper to become popular was the *New York Sun,* which was published by Benjamin H. Day beginning in 1833 and which was closely followed by James Gordon Bennett's *New York Herald* in 1835. The price of a penny represented a significant reduction compared to the price at the time for typical newspapers, which often sold for around 6 cents and which were frequently sold by subscription to be paid in advance. Technological improvements leading to lower costs for printing and paper made this reduction in price possible.

With an eye toward profitability, the penny press emphasized volume for its business strategy and thus was able to depend largely on advertising for its revenue. In order to achieve increased readership in an increasingly competitive environment, the newspapers of the penny press were sold for the first time by "paper boys" on the streets and expanded the use of reporters to cover such subjects as society, crime, and the courts. This more sensational approach to the news, along with the lower price, targeted a mass audience and represented a shift in priorities, as many newspapers up to that point had been affiliated with political parties and were written to appeal to a more politically engaged and upper-class readership. The popularity of the penny press contributed to a broad increase in literacy, as more people became interested in reading the newspaper.

Another lasting effect of the penny press can be seen in the way newspapers are published today. Newspapers continue to rely on advertising for the bulk of their revenues, allowing sales prices to remain comparatively low, and the news coverage continues to focus on local events. The penny press also changed what is considered newsworthy, affecting both the print media and other, more modern, media genres. The more sensational approach to the news might be considered to have been a precursor to the later emergence of "tabloid journalism" and more recently "tabloid television."

Further reading: Crouthamel, James L. *Bennett's New York Herald and the Rise of the Popular Press.* Syracuse, N.Y.: Syracuse University Press, 1989; Huntzicker, William E. *The Popular Press, 1833–1865.* Westport, Conn.: Greenwood Press, 1999.

—Joel Parker

People's Party

On May 19, 1891, the National Union Conference convened in Cincinnati, Ohio, with the goal of creating a national third party that would better represent the American farmer and workingman. More than 1,400 DELEGATES from 33 states and territories (though the majority were from the Midwest) representing various farm alliances, political parties, and organizations met and approved a platform that called for "the formation of what should be known as the People's Party of the United States of America."

On July 4, 1892, the People's Party, also commonly known as the POPULIST PARTY, held its first national convention and selected a former Union general, James B. Weaver of Iowa, as its presidential candidate, and a former Confederate general, James G. Field of Virginia, as his RUNNING MATE. The party platform declared that the candidates met "in the midst of a nation brought to the verge of moral, political, and material ruin" and called for the free coinage of silver and gold at the ratio of 16 to 1; a graduated income tax; the creation of postal savings banks; government ownership of railroads, the telegraph, and telephone; and government reclamation of lands owned but not being used by corporations and aliens to be held for use by settlers only. Additional resolutions that were not part of the official party platform included the secret BALLOT system, restriction of undesirable immigration, an eight-hour workday, the initiative and REFERENDUM, a one-term limit for the president and vice president of the United States, and the direct election of U.S. senators.

In the election of 1892, Weaver carried Kansas, Colorado, Idaho, and Nevada and won electoral votes in three additional states for a total of 22 electoral votes and 9 percent of the POPULAR VOTE. Two Populist governors were elected, 13 Populists participated in the Fifty-Third Congress (1893–95), and several state offices were occupied by Populists. The election of 1894 witnessed more Populist activity in the South, but the People's Party did not make as much progress as it had hoped. In 1896, William Jennings Bryan captured the Democratic ticket for the presidency and centered his campaign on the issue of free silver. For many Populists, free silver was the most important issue, and in the end the party supported Bryan in the PRESIDENTIAL ELECTION. The People's Party lasted until 1908 but did not play as important a role as it had during its first two national campaigns.

It might be argued that the People's Party was a party before its time. While it did not survive as a political entity, many of its proposals were enacted by later generations. The Populists helped kick off a reform movement that drastically changed the face of American government and society.

Further reading: Argersinger, Peter H. *Populism, Its Rise and Fall.* Lawrence: University Press of Kansas, 1992; Hicks, John D. *The Populist Revolt: A History of the Farmers' Alliance and the People's Party.* Minneapolis: University of Minnesota Press, 1931.

—Alan L. Morrell

Philadelphia Convention

The Philadelphia Convention, also known as the Federal Convention or the Constitutional Convention, convened in the Pennsylvania State House (now called Independence Hall) on May 25, 1787, and ran through the summer and

Benjamin Franklin at the convention in Philadelphia, 1787 *(Library of Congress)*

into the fall, ending on September 17, 1787. This single meeting became arguably the most important gathering of political minds in the history of the nation.

It was plain to many citizens and leaders in the early United States that the national government under the ARTICLES OF CONFEDERATION was an ineffectual structure. With no power to compel the states to do anything against their sovereign wills, the Congress was little more than a paper tiger. Great dangers faced the new nation, as the powers of the day (France, England, and Spain) restricted its trade and its westward expansion. Domestically, the government could not resolve border disputes between the states, had no power to stop them from raising tariffs and trade restrictions on each other, and could not do such basic things as raise finances essential to its own operation.

The Philadelphia Convention grew from two previous conventions, the first at Mount Vernon and a second at

Annapolis. The Mount Vernon Convention was a gathering of DELEGATES from Maryland and Virginia that set a precedent for conferences between the states for solving specific problems. The success in calling this convention led to the second convention, called for Annapolis in 1786 for the purpose of discussing the growing economic problems of the nation. While little was accomplished at this convention itself because of a lack of attendance (only five states sent delegates), the report of the commissioners urged that another convention be called early the next May.

It seemed that this new convention, if it was ever officially called, would likely labor under the same burden of poor attendance. Before the Congress could call for the convention, a set of events in western Massachusetts showed how ineffective the central government truly was. Shays's Rebellion began as an orderly petitioning of the Massachusetts government for the issuing of paper money, judicial reform, and lower taxes. When this did not succeed, armed rebellion broke out. The rebels occupied courthouses all over western Massachusetts and later attempted to storm the national arsenal at Springfield, but were defeated by local militiamen. This rebellion, as minor as it was, made it obvious to leaders all over the nation that the national government could do little to stop domestic insurrection. It is ironic that Shays's Rebellion, while unsuccessful, may have led to the transformation of the character of the national government. On February 21, 1787, less than three weeks after Shays's rebels were put down, the Congress authorized the Philadelphia Convention. In the end, only Rhode Island, with its strongly agrarian-dominated government, failed to send delegates.

The delegates that met that spring in Philadelphia came from several professions, but most were members of their respective states' elites. There were state governors, attorney generals, chief justices, and members of state delegations to Congress. Two major political figures, Benjamin Franklin and George Washington, had even come out of their retirements to participate, lending an air of legitimacy and urgency to the proceedings. The groups attending had several major differences to overcome. Some, such as Alexander Hamilton and James Madison, wanted a strong central government. Others, such as Luther Martin and Charles Pinckney, were ardent defenders of states' rights. A number of major figures were not present, however. Thomas Jefferson and John Adams were in Europe as ambassadors to France and England, respectively. Others, such as the Virginia firebrand Patrick Henry, were occupied by local POLITICS, and others, such as John Jay, were occupied by appointments to national office.

On the first day, George Washington was elected as the presiding officer, and two important rules were quickly adopted: secrecy and reconsideration. Secrecy was needed to permit open and frank discussion, and reconsideration was necessary to allow the convention to review and even change its own decisions on the various topics. One of the first things that the convention did behind this veil of secrecy was to throw out the Articles of Confederation. While this was overstepping the official mandate for the convention, the delegates saw the articles as completely unworkable. The first working draft for the new government, the Virginia Plan, proposed a supreme central authority with separate executive, legislative, and judicial branches.

The item that the convention spent the most time on was the design of the national legislature. The general outline of powers was little contested, but huge debates broke out over the issue of SUFFRAGE. The states with large populations and those that expected to soon be in that group felt that equality of suffrage between the states was inherently unfair. They felt that since they carried more of the citizens of the nation, their votes should be stronger. The Virginia Plan proposed a bicameral legislature with votes in both chambers apportioned by population. The smaller states, on the other hand, feared that their influence would be swallowed up by the votes of the larger states. The three biggest states would hold between them nearly half the votes in the proposed congress.

The NEW JERSEY PLAN offered a unicameral legislature with equal votes for each state, similar to the Congress under the Confederation. The debate became so heated that it threatened to tear the meeting, and even the Union itself, apart. However, Roger Sherman from Connecticut finally proposed a compromise, later known as the Connecticut or the Great Compromise, in which the congress would have one chamber in which votes would be distributed based on population and another chamber that would be based on equality of the states. Other problems, though none nearly so divisive, plagued the discussions. What was to be the nature of the executive of this new government? How would that office be elected? How were slaves to count toward representation and taxation, if at all? Should there be a bill of rights? Each of these was solved in turn by intense discussion and much compromise. The final document, seven articles and a little more than 4,000 words, was an outline for a radically new government.

James Madison, dubbed by history the Father of the Constitution, took the most detailed set of notes at the convention. His notes, published posthumously, along with less detailed sets from other authors, the official records of the proceedings, and the arguments put forth in the FEDERALIST PAPERS have given material to modern constitutional lawyers for use in constructing arguments based on original intent.

Further reading: Collier, Christopher. *Decision at Philadelphia: The Constitutional Convention of 1787.* New York: Ballantine Books, 1987; Madison, James. *Notes of the Debates in the Federal Convention of 1787.* New York: Norton, 1987.

National Park Service, Independence National Historical Park. Available online. URL: http://www.nps.gov/inde. Accessed August 10, 2005.

—John P. Todsen

phone banks

A phone bank is a room with several calling stations, as many as 500 in some cases but often as few as 10, that enable callers to reach a large number of people in a short period of time. Political candidates and special INTEREST GROUPS use phone banks to promote a concept, GET OUT THE VOTE, or prospect for new members. In modern American POLITICS, phone banks are a primary means of canvassing voters.

Voter lists with phone numbers are available from political list brokers. The purchase of voter files from brokers may also include voting history and CENSUS data. Vote history, POLITICAL PARTY, gender, date of registration, age, and geographic location are valuable to phone bank workers. Vote history enables callers to contact consistent voters and minimize time spent on unlikely voters. Primary participation, residence in a partisan PRECINCT, and PARTY IDENTIFICATION from an earlier phone call may provide useful background data. Gender, age, geographic information, income, and ethnicity are all important factors to consider when using a phone bank to convey a political message.

The typical phone bank script is very simple: "Hi, I am calling for the Candidate X. Do you plan to vote in the upcoming election?" If no, end the call and call the next LIKELY VOTER. If yes, ask the voter if he or she plans to vote for your candidate. If the voter indicates an opponent, record the answer and end the call. If the voter indicates your candidate, record that as well and ask if the voter is willing to volunteer, make a contribution, or put up a yard sign. If the voter is undecided, read a list of your candidate's main issues and ask the voter about his or her primary concerns. Close the conversation by urging the voter to consider your candidate and follow up by sending relevant campaign materials.

The primary benefit of a phone bank is that a large number of likely voters may be contacted in a relatively short period of time. Volunteer recruitment, voter identification, advocacy calls, survey research, get-out-the-vote efforts, and VOTER TURNOUT are enhanced through an effective phone bank organization.

Further reading: Andreasen, Alan R. *Marketing Research That Won't Break the Bank: A Practical Guide to Getting the Information You Need.* 2nd ed. Hoboken, N.J.: Jossey-Bass, 2002.

—John Rouse

political action committee (PAC)

A political action committee (PAC) is any U.S. committee, association, or organization that accepts contributions or makes expenditures for the purpose of influencing, or attempting to influence, the NOMINATION or election of one or more individuals to elected public office. PACs are an important aspect of American POLITICS and the American electoral system. Legally, they exist as a means for corporations and trade unions, among others, to make contributions to candidates for public office. This allows corporations, trade unions, and others to circumvent what they cannot do directly—finance campaigns.

There is no fixed organizational model for PACs. A PAC's only requirement by law is that it consist of a treasurer and a statement of organization, to be filed with the FEDERAL ELECTION COMMISSION (FEC) at least 10 days after its creation. The term *political action committee* does not appear in U.S. statutes, but one can still turn to the statutes to understand its nature. U.S. statutes spoke only of a "political committee," but Congress sharpened the definition of a "political committee" or a "political action committee" in 2 U.S.C. sec 431 (4).

In order to clarify the definition of a PAC, it is necessary to understand the concept of expenditures. The term *expenditures* does not refer only to cash contributions to candidates. PACs, as well as any group or individual in American society, may try to influence elections with expenditures independent of either a candidate or a party. Some PACs contribute services, goods, or expertise to candidates. PACs may also organize GET-OUT-THE-VOTE campaigns.

PACs exhibit a variety of different organizational structures. Corporate PACs are usually closely tied to the company's chief executive officer (CEO). Generally, the CEO of a company will authorize the formation of a PAC, determine and appoint its governing board's composition and members, specify FUND-RAISING methods, and help in the design of criteria used in determining which candidates receive contributions. In some cases, the CEO may actually specify particular candidates and officeholders as the recipients of donations. The CEO is crucial to the formation and sometimes the operation of a PAC, but in most cases the CEO delegates much of his or her authority to an executive in the company or to the governing board. A corporate PAC's appointed board or committee is usually chaired by the company's public affairs executive and is composed of a wide range of individuals consisting of contributors among the company's administrative personnel, executives, and stockholders.

Most labor union PACs also have a governing board, but union leaders generally have a more direct influence on labor PAC activity than do their counterparts on corporate PAC boards. This makes sense because most labor PACs' membership consists of large groups of contributors that each give a small amount, and for this reason they individually have little say in the dispensing of the collective fund. These conditions provide union PAC leaders with a great amount of autonomy in political decision making, specifically because the PAC board is often made up of state and national union officers. Trade PACs share many of the organizational structures of corporate PACs, but there are differences. Operating a trade PAC is somewhat less complex than operating a corporate PAC due to the corporate committees' need to satisfy its employees, stockholders, and even customers. Trade PACs need worry only about their members.

Although PACs came to the forefront of American public attention in the 1970s, they had been in existence at least 30 years prior. PACs were born out of the American labor movement. At the beginning of the 20th century, Congress prohibited direct contributions to candidates or parties by national banks and corporations. Individuals from these corporate institutions were permitted to make contributions, but there was no real agency to prevent corporations from transferring funds secretly. In the 1940s, the formal prohibition of direct funding from labor unions was also enacted. In 1943, the Congress of Industrial Organizations (CIO) responded with what most observers agree was the first PAC. The CIO established a separate fund set up to receive the voluntary contributions of union members to be spent in campaigns for public office. In 1955, the American Federation of Labor (AFL) merged with the CIO (AFL-CIO) and created its COMMITTEE ON POLITICAL EDUCATION (COPE), which has been referred to as a model for virtually all PACs.

Corporate PACs began forming somewhat later than their labor counterparts. The Business-Industry Political Action Committee (BIPAC) was established by the National Association of Manufacturers in 1963, and the American Medical Political Action Committee (AMPAC) was established in 1962. Both organizations spent more than $600,000 in the 1954 federal elections and more than $1.2 million in the 1968 elections. These combined expenditures almost exactly matched COPE's spending. In its massive overhauling of campaign finance legislation in 1971, Congress authorized corporations and unions to spend their funds on the establishment and administration of segregated funds. This was the first legitimation of PACs in federal legislation. Not only did it allow corporations and labor unions to start fundraising, but also it allowed them to communicate on any subject (including partisan politics) to stockholders and members, respectively, and it allowed them to conduct get-out-the-vote campaigns directed at the same constituencies. This opened the door for the growth of the PAC universe.

The FEDERAL ELECTION CAMPAIGN ACT (FECA) and amendments to it in 1974 and 1976 signified the beginning of the modern era for PACs. Organized labor was instrumental in drafting this legislation. While their hopes were to improve their electoral position, the legislation also provided corporations with the ability to more effectively use PACs as a tool of influence in the electoral process. The amendments to FECA in 1974, written in the troubled aftermath of the 1972 elections and Watergate, included a limit of $1,000 on individual contributions to a candidate. Multicandidate political committees, however, were limited to $5,000 per candidate per election. Individuals were limited to a total expenditure of $25,000, and PACs were not limited, which placed greater constraints on individuals while leaving the door open for PACs to continue their growing involvement.

While the act of 1971 and the amendments in 1974 provided legal authority for the creation of PACs, it was the SUN-PAC/SUN-EPA that truly provided the liberating incentive for the development and widespread use of the PAC mechanism. In 1975, Sun Oil Company proposed expanding general corporate funds to establish, administer, and solicit contributions to their PAC (SUN-PAC). They also proposed creating an employee payroll deduction plan to fund another PAC (SUN-EPA). The Federal Elections Commission ruled that Sun Oil could use general treasury funds, solicit from stockholders and employees, and establish multiple PACs. This allowed corporations the ability to greatly increase their generation of funding, both by increasing solicitation and increasing the number of PACs associated with their company. In turn, the proliferation of PACs began.

In January 1976, in the case of BUCKLEY V. VALEO, the Supreme Court brought the expenditure of money in campaigns under the protection of the First Amendment. Money officially became equated with speech. This allowed candidates to spend increasing amounts and PACs to contribute to political campaigns even though the candidates had accepted public financing. On May 11, 1976, Gerald Ford signed into law the final amendments to FECA. Organized labor won the ability to use payroll deduction plans but also suffered a blow in that labor PACs were to be treated like corporate PACs. They were considered to be a single unit for contribution purposes. Thus, they were subject to the same $5,000 limitation per candidate per election.

It would be decades before any legislation would directly affect the activity of PACs. More recent legislation forces certain tax-exempt political groups to disclose their contributors and expenditures. New legislation requires section 527 groups to make the Internal Revenue Service aware of their existence within 24 hours of forming. Groups that raise $25,000 or more per year must report contributions of $200 or more and spending of $500 or more. Public disclosure may provide light on interactions of big money in politics, but it does not stop money from being an integral, if not the central, part of campaigns. There are also loopholes in the 527 legislation. According to Internal Revenue Service rulings, business COALITIONS, labor unions, and INTEREST GROUPS can conduct the same type of political advertising as section 527 groups and still avoid the new requirements with the stipulation that they cannot spend more than 50 percent of their budget on political activities.

It can indeed be stated that the original PACs that began nearly half a century ago have witnessed many changes that affected their existence. Legislation since the 1970s has affected the way in which PACs have developed and are able to influence the American electoral process. Although legislation, including the 527 legislation, may have been intended to regulate money's involvement in politics, it has not created a system that truly limits money's involvement. PACs grew to more than 4,000 in 1988 and presently number about 3,800. Many represent special interest groups, while others represent large conservative or liberal coalitions. It is a common fear that increased campaign contributions may cause legislators to become less responsive to their constituents and more responsive to these PACs.

The Bipartisan Campaign Reform Act of 2002, the latest in a series of legislative actions aimed at addressing the influence of money in American electoral politics, banned corporations and unions from contributing unregulated SOFT MONEY to political parties and restricted broadcast issue ads that identify candidates in the weeks before elections. Only time will tell what the future holds for PACs, but one thing that is certain is that campaign finance reform will be a debated issue for years to come.

Further reading: Malbin, Michael J. *Life after Reform: When the Bipartisan Campaign Reform Act Meets Politics.* Lanham, Md.: Rowman & Littlefield, 2004; Sabato, Larry J. *PAC Power—Inside the World of Political Action Committees.* New York: Norton, 1984.

—Sherry Walker Gainous

political action committees, corporate

Entities established by corporations to raise money for the purpose of making donations to political candidates, they are a mechanism that allows corporations to legally engage in overtly political activity. Corporations, since the passage of the TILLMAN ACT of 1907, have been prohibited from directly contributing to campaigns of candidates for federal office. This ban came about in the wake of revelations that Marcus Alonzo Hanna, chairman of the Republican National Committee and chief fund-raiser for William McKinley, had raised $6 million to $7 million from corporations during the 1896 campaign. In exchange for these donations, it was claimed that the Republicans pursued a "probusiness agenda," opposing the coinage of silver and supporting protective tariffs.

Theodore Roosevelt made clean government a major issue during the 1904 campaign, although it was discovered after the election that he had received contributions from corporate moguls such as J. P. Morgan and a $50,000 corporate contribution from New York Life. Roosevelt then proposed campaign finance reform, and Congress adopted the Tillman Act in 1907, which prohibited campaign contributions by corporations and federally chartered banks. The

law was sponsored by Senator Benjamin Tillman, a South Carolina Democrat.

Corporations, however, found ways to circumvent the law, making it ineffective. In the wake of the Teapot Dome SCANDAL (1922–23), Congress enacted the Federal Corrupt Practices Act of 1925. One of its provisions prohibited corporate contributions of all kinds to federal candidates. The FEDERAL ELECTION CAMPAIGN ACT (FECA) of 1971, while continuing the prohibition on direct contributions to federal candidates by corporations, exempted from regulation contributions and expenditures for voluntary FUND-RAISING by corporations, paving the way for corporate political action committees (PACs). By establishing PACs, they can make voluntary campaign contributions to federal candidates and seek contributions to the PAC. The corporation forms a PAC composed of corporate officers, who are appointed to the PAC by the corporation's board of directors. Corporate PACs are one type of "connected" PAC, so named because they are affiliated with another entity.

Corporate PACs can solicit contributions from company directors, shareholders, officers, and management employees. The PAC then decides which candidates will receive contributions. They are required to file disclosure reports with the Federal Election Commission (FEC) showing contributions and expenditures.

Contributions are voluntary and are not tax-deductible. Under FECA, a person's contribution to a PAC cannot exceed $5,000 per year. Contributors must be citizens or lawful permanent residents of the United States. Foreign corporations cannot form PACs. A U.S. subsidiary of a foreign parent corporation can form a PAC as long as it does not solicit foreign nationals and no foreign national participates in the PAC's decision making process. The foreign parent corporation cannot provide funds or reimburse the U.S.-based subsidiary for contributions. A joint venture formed in the United States in which a foreign corporation holds an interest can form a PAC.

Federal multicandidate PACs may give $5,000 to each federal candidate per election; $15,000 to NATIONAL PARTY COMMITTEES per calendar year; $5,000 (combined) to state, district, and local party committees per calendar year; and $5,000 to any other PAC per calendar year. FEC regulations state that employers cannot use or threaten physical force, job discrimination, or financial reprisals, and PAC contributions cannot be a condition of employment. The employer is also required to advise employees at the time of solicitation of the PAC's political purposes and of the employees' right to refuse to contribute without any reprisal. The employer must also advise employees that it will not favor or disadvantage anyone by reason of the amount of his or her contribution or decision not to contribute.

As noted earlier, corporations were prohibited by federal law from making contributions to federal candidates, and the earliest POLITICAL ACTION COMMITTEES were established by labor unions, beginning with the formation of the COMMITTEE ON POLITICAL EDUCATION (COPE) by the Congress of Industrial Organizations in 1943.

The first "business PAC" was the Business Industry Political Action Committee (BIPAC), established in 1963 by a group of business leaders led by a Missouri banker, Kenton R. Cravens, and Robert L. Humphrey of the National Association of Manufacturers. The group's objective was to elect probusiness candidates to Congress.

In 1974, in the aftermath of the Watergate scandal, Congress adopted amendments to FECA. One of these provisions, which established contribution limits of $5,000 per election for corporate and labor election committees, had the effect of legitimizing corporate PACs.

In 1975 the FEC explicitly authorized corporate PACs in its Sun Oil Corporation advisory opinion. While corporations and unions had believed that the 1974 statute limited them, respectively, to soliciting stockholders and members, Sun Oil wanted to solicit all of its employees for PAC contributions. In its opinion the FEC stated that "it is the opinion of the Commission that Sun Oil may spend general treasury funds for solicitation of contributions to SUNPAC from stockholders and employees of the corporation."

This opinion served as a catalyst for the increase in the number of corporate PACs. By 1986, a decade after the Sun Oil decision, there were 1,906 corporate PACs, which gave more than $49 million to federal candidates during the 1985–86 campaign cycle.

In 1985, the U.S. Supreme Court, in *FEC v. NICPAC*, held that there should be no limits on the spending of PACs on a candidate provided that the expenditures are not made in collaboration with the candidate, so-called INDEPENDENT EXPENDITURES.

In the 1990s, corporate PACs expanded their participation by making independent expenditures on behalf of favored candidates and engaging in ISSUE ADVOCACY ADVERTISING, so-called SOFT MONEY expenditures. Since these activities were conducted independently of candidates, they were not subject to regulation under existing federal campaign finance statutes. In 2003, there were 1,552 corporate PACs registered with the FEC. Significantly, these committees made more soft money expenditures ($47 million) than direct contributions to candidates ($42.5 million). The Bi-Partisan Campaign Reform Act (McCAIN-FEINGOLD) prohibits corporations and their PACs from giving soft money to political parties and from running "electioneering" issue advertisements except as HARD MONEY expenditures.

Further reading: Clawson, Don. *Money Talks: Corporate PACs and Political Influence.* New York: Basic Books, 1992; Green, Mark. *Selling Out: How Big Corporate Money Buys Elections, Rams through Legislation, and Betrays Our Democracy.* New York: Regan Books, 2002; Morrison,

Catherine. *Managing Corporate Political Action Committees.* New York: Conference Board, 1986; Sabato, Larry J. *PAC Power: Inside the World of Political Action Committees.* New York: Norton, 1984.

—Jeffrey Kraus

political action committees, ideological

A POLITICAL ACTION COMMITTEE, generally referred to as a PAC, is a multicandidate political committee that is organized for the purpose of raising and spending money to elect or defeat political candidates for federal office (five or more). PACs vary greatly in size and organization. An ideological political action committee is one type of PAC. Ideological PACs reach across the entire ideological spectrum and are more comprehensive than single-issue PACs. For example, the American Conservative Union (ACU), one of the oldest conservative lobbying organizations in the United States, takes a position on trade policy, social welfare, environmental, and social and cultural issues. Since 1971 the ACU has published an annual rating of Congress. Members of Congress are rated on a score of 0 to 100. The scores are based on votes cast on a wide range of issues. According to the ACU, the ratings are designed to demonstrate how members vote on all the major policy issues to gauge their adherence to conservative principles. Another example of an ideological PAC is Americans for Democratic Action (ADA), one of the oldest liberal lobbying organizations. In addition to other publications, the ADA publishes scores based on legislators' voting records.

The majority of PACs represent business, labor, or ideological interests. There are, however, important distinctions among the three categories, primarily based on affiliation with a parent organization. Most ideological PACs are classified as independent PACs (also known as nonconnected PACs), as opposed to labor and corporate PACs, which are classified as affiliated or connected PACs. Independent PACs were created following clarification of federal CAMPAIGN FINANCE LAWS in 1976. In addition to ideological PACs, leadership, type-of-candidate, and issue PACs are also included in this category.

In an advisory opinion issued by the FEDERAL ELECTION COMMISSION (FEC), concerning the Sun Oil Company in 1975, the FEC ruled that parent organizations could pay the FUND-RAISING and administrative costs of affiliated PACs. As a result, a connected committee always has a sponsoring corporation or labor organization that establishes, administers, or raises money for it. For example, the General Motors Corporation Political Action Committee is affiliated with General Motors, just as the United Steelworkers of America Political Action Fund is affiliated with the United Steelworkers of America. Although independent PACs may receive limited financial support from sponsoring organizations that are not affiliated with labor unions or corporations, independent PACs are at a distinct disadvantage relative to connected PACs, because independent PACs must pay for fund-raising costs directly from the money they raise.

One advantage that independent PACs have is that they may solicit contributions from anyone in the general public who may lawfully make a contribution. A connected PAC, by contrast, may solicit contributions only from individuals who have a specific relationship with the connected organization, such as stockholders, members, and certain employees of the connected organization. Despite this small advantage, ideological PACs raise and spend the least amount of money on candidates. According to reports filed with the FEC, there were no ideological PACs in the top 20 PAC contributors to federal candidates in 2003–04.

Although PACs existed prior to 1971, they increased rapidly after the 1971 FEDERAL ELECTION CAMPAIGN ACT (FECA) legitimized the use of PACs. Amendments to FECA in 1974, 1976, and 1979 established contribution limits for individuals, parties, and PACs. PACs and lobbying groups are formally distinct organizational entities. PACs serve as fund-raisers for INTEREST GROUPS, but it is important to remember that they may also act independently. Organizations such as labor unions, corporations, and professional associations cannot make campaign contributions out of their general treasuries; they must make contributions from a PAC, which is considered a separate organizational entity. Moreover, when a PAC contributes money to a candidate or an elected official, it does not contribute money to an individual. Rather, it contributes money to the individual's electoral campaign.

All PACs can give $5,000 to a candidate committee per election (including PRIMARY, GENERAL, and RUNOFF ELECTIONS, if necessary). PACs can also give up to $15,000 annually to any NATIONAL PARTY COMMITTEE, and $5,000 to any other PAC. A PAC may receive up to $5,000 per calendar year from individuals, other PACs, and candidate committees. There is no limit to how much a PAC may spend on INDEPENDENT EXPENDITURES, or CAMPAIGN EXPENDITURES that are not coordinated with the candidate or the candidate's campaign committee. PACs' use of independent expenditures to fund ISSUE ADVOCACY ADVERTISING is restricted in the newly passed Bipartisan Campaign Reform Act (BCRA) of 2002. PACs vary in size and organization and represent a broad range of interests. Some PACs are large and well organized, while others are quite modest. PACs have generally come to be thought of as both a symptom and cause of the current problems in the campaign finance system, but not all PACs have the same influence on the legislative process. The larger and more organizationally sophisticated PACs associated with corporations are generally thought to have more influence in the system, but the data are not definitive.

The PACs that make up the ideological sector represent a broad range of issues that encompasses the entire ideological spectrum, including but not limited to social welfare, the environment, education, foreign policy, religion, and family issues. While issue, ideological, type-of-candidate, and leadership PACs are often lumped together because they are all categorized as nonconnected multicandidate committees (as opposed to affiliated PACs) by the FEC, not all of these are, in fact, ideological. Unfortunately, distinctions between PACS are difficult to measure. An important distinction between ideological PACs and the others in the nonconnected category is that ideological PACs take a position on a wide swathe of issues. Rather than focus on one issue, such as abortion or the environment, ideological PACs are broadly defined.

Further reading: Cigler, Allan J., and Burdett A. Loomis. *Interest Group Politics.* 6th ed. Washington, D.C.: CQ Press, 2002; Nownes, Anthony J. *Pressure and Power: Organized Interests in American Politics.* Boston: Houghton Mifflin, 2001; Wright, John R. *Interest Groups and Congress: Lobbying, Contributions, and Influence.* New York: Longman, 2002.

—Jessica Gerrity and Edward G. Carmines

political action committees, leadership

POLITICAL ACTION COMMITTEES (PACs) are the entities formed by individuals, corporations, labor unions, INTEREST GROUPS, and other COALITIONS of individuals to make contributions for political causes. Traditionally, PACs are associated with groups that have a stake in the political process. However, many sitting and former members of Congress now sponsor their own PACs to make contributions to other members of Congress. PACs sponsored by politicians are referred to as leadership PACs. Today, more than 100 members of Congress maintain such organizations.

The first leadership PAC was created in 1978 by Henry Waxman (D, Calif.). Waxman sought a subcommittee chair on the Energy and Commerce Committee over a more senior Democrat. To shore up support for his leadership bid, Waxman formed a PAC and contributed to his colleagues on the Energy and Commerce Committee. His fellow committee members reciprocated by violating the seniority norm and awarding him the chair.

Since Waxman's success, leadership PACs have proliferated to the point that nearly every party leader and committee chair maintains one. In 2002, leadership PACs contributed more than $20 million to the campaigns of other politicians. Leadership PACs serve three primary purposes.

First, politicians with presidential ambitions frequently sponsor leadership PACs. They use the leadership PAC to raise and spend money to begin their presidential campaigns. In the 2000 presidential campaign, Vice President Al Gore and Senators John McCain and Orrin Hatch all used leadership PACs to begin their campaigns. In the 2004 campaign, John Kerry, Dick Gephardt, Dennis Kucinich, John Edwards, and Joseph Lieberman all ran leadership PACs.

Second, members of Congress use it to help elect like-minded representatives. In the 1980s, Newt Gingrich used his leadership PAC (GOPAC) to make contributions to state legislators to create a "farm team" for future congressional candidates. Gingrich funded individuals who shared his IDEOLOGY, expecting that after they served in state legislatures, they would constitute a crop of quality congressional candidates with strong Republican beliefs and loyalty to him. This strategy paved the way to the Republican takeover of Congress in 1994.

Leadership PACs do not only assist in the election of new representatives, but they also help to reelect threatened incumbents. For example, in the 2002 election, Representative Tom Latham (R, Iowa) faced a stiff challenge from a well-known activist in Iowa's state DEMOCRATIC PARTY. Republican leaders targeted Latham's seat as important to maintaining their majority, so they made substantial contributions to his campaign from their leadership PACs. Latham won the election and has proved to be a faithful supporter of Republican legislation throughout the 108th Congress.

Finally, congressional leaders use leadership PAC contributions to help them obtain higher office. Just as Henry Waxman used leadership PAC contributions to shore up support for his 1978 subcommittee chairmanship bid, committee and party leadership aspirants continue to make contributions to buttress their leadership campaigns. For committee chairs, this has become even more important since Republicans placed six-year TERM LIMITS on committee chairs. Knowing that the powerful Ways and Means Committee chair position would open after the 2000 elections, Representative Bill Thomas (R, Calif.) contributed nearly $500,000 to other candidates and to party committees from his leadership PAC and his own campaign funds. As a result, Thomas beat out Phil Crane (R, Ill.) and Clay Shaw (R, Fla.), even though Crane was the most senior member of the committee.

Not only do members use leadership PACs to boost their chances in committee chair contests, but individuals interested in party leadership positions must also demonstrate their FUND-RAISING prowess. In the ELECTION CYCLE before Nanci Pelosi ran to become House Minority Leader, she used her leadership PAC to donate more than $1 million to other candidates and the Democratic Party. When it was time to call back the favors on the leadership vote, Pelosi, a liberal Democrat, was able to win support from many moderate members because she had supported their election campaigns.

Both the propagation of leadership PACs and the dramatic increase in the amounts of money they contribute have significant implications for the campaign finance system and for American POLITICS generally. Leadership

PACs challenge the integrity of contribution limits. Special interests and individuals can give double the legal limit to a member of Congress by contributing once to the member's campaign fund and once to the member's leadership PAC. Congressional leaders can give twice the legal limit to other members of Congress by donating once from their leadership PAC and again from their personal campaign funds. In this way, special interests and congressional leaders can potentially yield even more influence over the political process.

Further reading: Currinder, Marian L. "Leadership PAC Contribution Strategies and House Member Ambitions." *Legislative Studies Quarterly* 28 (2003): 551–577; GOPAC. Available online. URL: http://www.gopac.org. Accessed August 10, 2005; Wilcox, Clyde. "Share the Wealth: Contributions by Congressional Incumbents to the Campaigns of Other Candidates." *American Politics Quarterly* 17, no. 4 (1989): 386–408.

—Damon M. Cann

political action committees, single-issue groups

A POLITICAL ACTION COMMITTEE, generally referred to as a PAC, is a multicandidate political committee that is organized for the purpose of raising and spending money to elect or defeat political candidates for federal office. PACs vary greatly in size and organization. An issue PAC is one type of PAC. Issue PACs typically focus on a single issue or a narrow set of issues. The types of concerns around which issue PACs are organized are quite extensive and include, but are not limited to, the environment, taxes, consumer rights, gun rights and gun control, abortion, civil liberties, and women's issues. An example of an issue PAC is EMILY's LIST. The name is an acronym that stands for "early money is like yeast" (it makes the dough rise). Emily's List was founded in 1985 by Ellen Malcolm to fund female, Democratic, pro-choice candidates. In this case, the issue PAC is concerned with a very specific goal. Other issue PACs are organized around a bundle of issues that all relate to a similar theme. An example of this type of PAC is the Eagle Forum PAC. The Eagle Forum is a conservative group concerned with pro-family issues.

PACs represent a broad range of interests. Some are large and well organized, while others, such as those that fall into the issue PAC category, are quite modest. PACs have generally come to be thought of as both a symptom and cause of the current problems in the campaign finance system, but not all PACs have the same influence on the legislative process. The larger and more organizationally sophisticated PACs associated with corporations are generally thought to have more influence in the system, but the data are not definitive.

The PACs that make up the issue sector represent a broad range of interests, including but not limited to human rights, abortion, the environment, gun control and gun rights, conservative issues, gay and lesbian rights, and women's issues. While issue, ideological, type-of-candidate, and leadership PACs are often lumped together because they are all categorized as nonconnected multicandidate committees (as opposed to affiliated PACs) by the FEC, there are important differences among them. While distinctions between political action committees are difficult to measure, an important distinction between issue PACs, and the others in the nonconnected category is that issue PACs are focused on a single issue or a limited set of issues. Issue PACs stand in contrast to ideological PACs, which take positions on a wide range of issues.

Further reading: Cigler, Allan J., and Burdett A. Loomis. *Interest Group Politics.* 6th ed. Washington, D.C.: CQ Press, 2002; Nownes, Anthony J. *Pressure and Power: Organized Interests in American Politics.* Boston: Houghton Mifflin, 2001; Wright, John R. *Interest Groups and Congress: Lobbying, Contributions, and Influence.* New York: Longman, 2002.

—Jessica Gerrity and Edward G. Carmines

political action committees, union/labor groups

Entities established by labor organizations to raise money from union members for the purpose of making donations to political candidates, POLITICAL ACTION COMMITTEES (PACs) are a mechanism through which labor organizations can engage overtly in the political process. Labor unions cannot, by federal law, contribute to campaigns of candidates for federal office. By establishing PACs, they can make voluntary campaign contributions to federal candidates and seek contributions to the PAC from union members. Labor union PACs are one type of "connected PAC," so named because they are affiliated with another organization.

Members of unions and their families may contribute to a union/labor PAC. Contributions are voluntary and are not tax-deductible. The amount contributed, or the decision not to contribute, cannot be the basis for the union to benefit or disadvantage a member or his or her family. Under the FEDERAL ELECTION CAMPAIGN ACT (FECA), a person's contribution to a PAC cannot exceed $5,000 per year. Contributors must be citizens or lawful permanent residents of the United States. Federal multicandidate PACs may give $5,000 to each federal candidate per election; $15,000 to a NATIONAL PARTY COMMITTEE per calendar year; $5,000 (combined) to state, district, and local party committees per calendar year; and $5,000 to any other PAC per calendar year.

In addition to providing financial assistance, unions provide "in-kind" goods and services to union-supported candidates. These activities are not subject to disclosure requirements under federal law (although some states require candidates and/or unions to disclose in-kind contributions). Such activities include VOTER REGISTRATION drives, telephone PHONE BANKS, union staff time, and publicity.

The Smith-Connally Act of 1943 (also known as the War Labor Disputes Act) barred labor unions from contributing to federal candidates, placing them on a "level playing field" with corporations, which had been prohibited from making such contributions in 1907. The measure was intended to be temporary. In response, the Council of Industrial Organizations (CIO), founded in 1938, established the first separate segregated fund, commonly known as a PAC.

The COMMITTEE ON POLITICAL EDUCATION (COPE) was seen as a vehicle for union members to pool their resources in order to support the political candidates of their choice. In 1944, it raised $1.2 million, primarily to support Franklin D. Roosevelt's campaign for a fourth term. In 1947, the Taft-Hartley Act made the temporary wartime prohibition permanent and expanded it to include PRIMARY elections. Over the next three decades, other labor organizations recognized their utility and established PACs of their own: 17 national labor PACs gave $2.1 million to federal campaigns in 1956, and 37 PACs spent $7.1 million in 1968. By 1974 there were 201 labor PACs.

For three decades organized labor enjoyed a near monopoly on PACs. During this time, most labor PAC contributions went to DEMOCRATIC PARTY candidates. In 1963, the first business PAC, the Business Industry Political Action Committee, was established. Corporate PACs were authorized by the FEDERAL ELECTION COMMISSION in its 1975 Sun Oil Company decision.

In 1971, Congress enacted the FECA, which exempted from regulation contributions and expenditures made for voluntary FUND-RAISING by unions. The law also permitted unions to use their funds for nonpartisan voter registration and GET-OUT-THE-VOTE drives. In 1972, the Supreme Court held, in *Pipefitters Local Union Number 562 et al. v. United States*, that the FECA "plainly permits union officials to establish, administer and solicit contributions for a political fund."

Following the Watergate SCANDAL, Congress adopted amendments to FECA (1974). The act legitimated PACs by establishing the $5,000-per-election contribution limit for union or corporate election committees. When the Federal Election Commission first started keeping track of PAC activity in January 1975, unions accounted for almost one-third (201 of 608) of the PACs. In January 2004, labor PACs accounted for less than 10 percent (308 of 4,023) of the registered PACs.

While labor PACs do not play as large a role as they once did, they have remained important by giving larger contributions than most PACs. They still direct most of their giving to Democratic candidates.

In 1988, the U.S. Supreme Court, in *Communications Workers of America v. Beck* (487 U.S. 735), held that a union could not, over the objections of dues-paying nonmember employees (employees who do not join a union but are required to pay agency fees as a condition of employment), spend funds collected from them on activities unrelated to collective bargaining. As a result, objecting employees could get a pro-rated refund of their agency fees representing the costs of non–collective bargaining activities.

In the 1990s, labor PACs expanded their activities by making INDEPENDENT EXPENDITURES on behalf of favored candidates and by engaging in ISSUE ADVOCACY ADVERTISING. These so-called SOFT MONEY expenditures were not regulated by existing federal CAMPAIGN FINANCE LAWS. The Bi-Partisan Campaign Reform Act of 2003 prohibits unions and their PACs from giving soft money to political parties, and from running "electioneering" issue advertisements except as HARD MONEY expenditures through their PACs.

In 2003, there were 308 labor PACs registered with the Federal Election Commission. During the period January 1, 2002, to December 31, 2003, they collected $87,961,863, with disbursements of $61,205,772, of which $18,705,430 was made in direct contributions to federal candidates.

Further reading: Sabato, Larry J. *PAC Power: Inside the World of Political Action Committees.* New York: Norton, 1984.

—Jeffrey Kraus

political cartoons

Political cartoons are illustrations that provide commentary about social and political issues. The artist may use humor as well as symbolism, irony, and sarcasm to support a particular view and to elicit a response from the reader. Modern political cartoons appear in newspapers and magazines, usually on the editorial page. In addition, certain comic strips that appear in a newspaper's entertainment section may delve into political issues.

Cartoons are composed of two elements, caricature, which parodies an individual, and allusion, which provides the political context for the drawing. A cartoonist creates a recognizable image of an individual using particular facial features, props, or mannerisms. For instance, President George W. Bush is frequently portrayed wearing a cowboy hat, President Richard Nixon was often shown with bushy eyebrows, a long nose, and a five o'clock shadow, and President Franklin Roosevelt was shown with a cigarette holder and round glasses. Not all political cartoons contain specific individuals. Instead, a cartoonist may choose to draw a generic "everyman" or a representative of a particular political group. Finally, a cartoonist may use symbols such as the Statue of Liberty, Uncle Sam, or a bald eagle to represent the United States.

The roots of modern political cartoons can be traced back to the 15th century and the Renaissance, when caricature was popularized by Leonardo da Vinci. However, it was during the Protestant Reformation in Germany, when editorial illustrations were developed by Martin Luther, that it flourished. By using simple broadsheet posters and illustrated pamphlets, Luther was able to recruit a large number of supporters despite the high illiteracy rates of the 16th century. Editorial drawings were later applied to POLITICS during the Thirty Years' War (1618–48).

By the 18th century, political cartoons had grown into an important venue for social commentary. James Gillray, known for his drawings that ridiculed the ruling class, was the most important British caricaturist during this period. The British were also responsible for introducing a new meaning for the term *cartoon*; prior to the 1840s, this term had been used to describe a preliminary sketch for a fresco or painting.

Individuals such as Benjamin Franklin and Paul Revere used political cartoons in the United States in colonial times. Franklin's *Join or Die* (1754) is considered to be

Political cartoon making fun of presidential candidate Grover Cleveland, who fathered a child out of wedlock, 1884 *(HarpWeek, LLC)*

the first American cartoon. The illustration, which shows a snake severed into eight parts to represent the colonies, was used to rally support for an intercolonial association to deal with the Iroquois. The snake icon reappears in other early American illustrations and was eventually incorporated into the Don't Tread on Me battle flag.

Throughout American history, political cartoons have been characterized by conflict and confrontation. During the early years of the republic, political illustrations were used to attack the Stamp and Intolerable Acts and to express fear over the establishment of a strong national government. In the years leading up to and following the Civil War, artists focused on concerns over slavery, racism, and immigration.

Thomas Nast, the "grandfather" of newspaper editorial cartoonists, modernized the art of the political cartoon during the mid- to late 1800s. Nast is most famous for his cartoons in *Harper's Weekly* (1871) that documented the corruption of Boss Tweed and New York's Tammany Hall. He is also responsible for popularizing the Republican elephant and the Democratic donkey symbols and for creating the modern image of Santa Claus.

Due to the extensive labor needed to create woodblock engravings of these political illustrations, the cartoons appeared only in weekly and monthly magazines from the revolutionary era through the 1880s. In 1884, political cartoons debuted in the daily newspapers when the *New York World* published a cartoon by Walt McDougall. In the following year, political cartoons became an issue in the circulation war between the *World* and the *New York Evening Journal*.

In the years that followed, political cartoonists have provided observations on the issues of temperance and SUFFRAGE, World Wars I and II, the Great Depression and FDR's New Deal, the Vietnam War, the cultural revolution of the 1960s, and the oil crisis of the 1970s. Some of this political commentary made its way into the comic strips as early as 1934, when Harold Gray provided conservative commentary in his cartoon *Little Orphan Annie*. This trend continues today, with Garry Trudeau's *Doonesbury*, Bruce Tinsley's *Mallard Fillmore*, and Aaron McGruder's *The Boondocks*. Political cartoons have also migrated to new media venues. Bill Mitchell, a former print cartoonist, now publishes his cartoons exclusively on the Internet.

Modern political cartoons are well respected as a form of news medium. This is demonstrated by the amount of annual awards given for editorial cartoons. These include the Pulitzer Prize, the National Headliner Award, the National Society of Professional Journalists Award, the Scripps-Howard Award, the Berryman Award, the Overseas Press Club Award, and the Fischetti Award.

One of the most well known modern editorial cartoonists is the late Herblock (Herbert Block), who worked for the *Washington Post*. Herblock defined many of the issues of the 20th century, including the rise of Hitler, the cold war, and the Clinton SCANDALS. He drew every president from Hoover to George W. Bush, personified the threat of nuclear war with "Mr. Atom," and originated the term MCCARTHYISM. During his career, Herblock won three individual Pulitzers for editorial cartooning, received the Presidential Medal of Freedom (1994), and was named a "living legend" by the Library of Congress.

Other prominent political cartoonists include the late Jeff MacNelly, who won three Pulitzers and the Sigma Delta Chi National Award for editorial cartooning; Pat Oliphant, who has been called the "most influential cartoonist now working" by the *New York Times;* and Ted Rall, whose provocative work following the September 11 bombings led to calls for new censorship laws. Even Dr. Seuss (Theodor Geisel) was an editorial cartoonist in the 1940s; these cartoons were recently chronicled in Richard Minear's *Dr. Seuss Goes to War* (1999).

Political cartoons continue to play a significant role as a critic of the government. In 2004, Garry Trudeau's Memorial Day comic strip, which listed the names of more than 700 U.S. military personnel who have been killed in Iraq, was the subject of debate among many newspaper editors including Doug Clifton of the *Cleveland Plain Dealer.*

Further reading: Block, Herbert. *Political Cartoons from the Crash to the Millennium: Herblock's History*. Washington, D.C.: Library of Congress, 2000; Brooks, Charles. *Best Editorial Cartoons of the Year*. Gretna, La.: Pelican Publishing, 2004; Hess, Stephen, and Milton Kaplan. *The Ungentlemanly Art: A History of American Political Cartoons*. New York: Macmillan, 1975.

—Mary Hallock Morris

political party

A political party is a group united by common political beliefs in pursuit of political office and public policy objectives. In a parliamentary system of government, political parties often represent a discrete interest, such as the environment or labor. The United States has two dominant parties, the REPUBLICAN PARTY and the DEMOCRATIC PARTY, each of which represents a broad spectrum of beliefs both at the national and local levels. THIRD PARTIES such as the GREEN PARTY and the LIBERTARIAN PARTY also are active in American POLITICS, but their membership is limited and their representation in elective office very small.

Political parties were not originally intended to be part of American government, but the advantages parties provide to the people who belong to them has made them an essential ingredient to modern American democracy. Ideally, parties are independent organizations that work at the periphery of government, directing the needs and beliefs of the people to the actual machinery of government. Political parties provide distinct advantages to helping coordinate and maintain effective democratic rule. They help mobilize and educate voters by informing their members on the issues, encouraging them to vote in elections, and continually seeking to register more voters friendly to their political outlook. Parties help to coordinate the constitutionally separated powers of American government, allowing the president and Congress to work together toward specific policy goals. Moreover, parties help voters to hold the government accountable for its actions by voting out or retaining a party on the basis of its performance. Parties give individual citizens an entryway into political service and participation at all levels of government.

The set of political principles and beliefs that unite parties and help define their stance on issues is called IDEOLOGY. The ideology of the two major American political parties has changed significantly over the course of American history, and opinion is divided on what drives parties to change their political agendas and continue the struggle for political power. Anthony Downs in *An Economic Theory of Democracy* (1957) suggested the primary objective of parties is to attract the largest number of voters possible in order to win political power. This view posits that parties are little more than a conspiracy to gain and maintain power. Ideology plays a subordinate role as a motivator for change in Downs's account of party politics; parties act primarily as maximizers of political advantage given the perceived preferences of the ELECTORATE, and are less interested in political principle. This economic account of parties also views citizens as primarily motivated by self-interest to make rational political decisions that will tend to maximize their material benefits.

Economic theory helps to explain the inconsistency of party platforms and the constant changes in party makeup over time, but tends to discount the strength of political principles directing party behavior. Some political scientists suggest that American parties are primarily ideological, strongly committed to political ideals and beliefs that motivate them to win power to achieve their political vision. In this account of party ideology, many different causes may affect change in party ideology such as conflict between elite and popular interests, conflict over religious and moral beliefs, and exogenous factors such as economic crises and wars.

The founders did not intend for political parties to play a role in American government. Most DELEGATEs to the Constitutional Convention believed parties to be FACTIONS allied by private interests and at odds with the public good. In fashioning the Constitution, they conceived of a nonpartisan government that based electoral appeal on reputation and public standing instead of the divisiveness of political parties. George Washington was particularly wary of what he called "the baneful effects of the spirit of party" in his farewell address of 1796. Washington was steadfast in maintaining a nonpartisan administration and worked to keep members of his cabinet from dividing along partisan lines. Despite his best efforts, two members of Washington's cab-

inet, Alexander Hamilton and Thomas Jefferson, constantly quarreled over national policy, and gradually two distinct visions of the Constitution developed.

The rift between Jefferson and Hamilton finally developed into a public political divide in the election of 1800, with Jefferson organizing a national OPPOSITION PARTY to the Federalist administration of John Adams. Jefferson's DEMOCRATIC-REPUBLICAN PARTY won handily, and within a very few years the FEDERALIST PARTY died out as a national political force. For a short period after 1800, Jefferson's party dominated national politics, but by the late 1820s problems began to develop in the absence of an opposition party. Without any strong opposition, Jefferson's party began selecting presidential candidates from within its congressional caucuses, a practice that became known as "King Caucus." Compounding this problem was the crowded field of candidates for president and the difficulty in developing a consensus of opinion among the people for a particular candidate.

Due to the Constitution's requirement of a majority vote of the ELECTORAL COLLEGE to win the presidency, the House of Representatives was continually being drawn into the presidential selection process. After the House chose John Quincy Adams to be president over Andrew Jackson in 1824, despite Jackson's having won a plurality of votes, Martin Van Buren was inspired to reinvigorate the spirit of partisanship. Van Buren convinced Jackson to run in the next election as a member of the Democratic Party, and not as a candidate independent of a party. Jackson wielded a great deal of power as president thanks to the coordination the Democratic Party allowed and the offices he was able to distribute on the basis of party loyalty. Jackson strongly believed in the "spoils system," that party loyalists should be rewarded with government offices, and his administrations were dominated by members of his party. Within a short while the WHIG PARTY developed, initially in opposition to what it considered Jackson's monarchical exercise of presidential power. Since the founding of the Whig Party, America has been dominated by a TWO-PARTY SYSTEM.

The late 19th century was a high-water mark for the strength and influence of political parties in America. The habit of voting as an indication of how deeply parties affected the lives of average Americans stands unrivaled in this period. A constant of around 80 percent of the eligible population cast a vote in PRESIDENTIAL ELECTIONS from 1872 to 1896. During this same period, the eligible voting population nearly doubled, and despite this dilution of the voting base, interest in elections never flagged. Campaigns were grand civic productions orchestrated by political parties involving entire communities in firelight parades and other well-attended outdoor gatherings. The political machine became a dominant force within political parties during this era. Powerful political bosses dictated party policy and distributed offices and other privileges as PATRON-

AGE for party loyalists. Many citizens felt political machines to be corrupt and inept at administering government, especially within major cities.

The PROGRESSIVE MOVEMENT developed out of a popular sentiment that the major political parties had become corrupt private cabals, interested only in self-enrichment and detached from public opinion. Progressives saw the party system as too diffuse, conservative, and parochial to ever provide effective leadership to a modern industrialized nation. Many DIRECT DEMOCRACY reforms passed during the beginning of the 20th century by Progressives, such as the initiative, direct primaries, and the RECALL, sought to undermine the influence of parties. A chief political goal of the Progressive movement was to increase the ability of individual voters to directly influence the course of government outside the influence of political parties.

President Theodore Roosevelt's charismatic leadership during his presidency helped to shape Progressive thought about alternatives to party leadership. Progressives such as Herbert Croly and Woodrow Wilson believed strong, assertive, popular presidents could more effectively lead government toward social reform and effective administration than could parties. Woodrow Wilson saw parties as a means of weakening the separation of powers among American political institutions, thus allowing for centralized authority and energy in government. Wilson attempted to place himself in control of the Democratic Party in order to direct policy and used the office of the president to directly influence public opinion. Wilson suffered serious political setbacks toward the end of his administration in his quest to consolidate party power within the presidency, and by the time of the election of Franklin Roosevelt in 1932, the die had been cast in favor of presidential leadership over party government.

The Great Depression gave Franklin Roosevelt an opportunity to fundamentally change the course of party politics during the 1930s. Roosevelt ran in 1932 promising a "New Deal" for America that would guarantee economic rights to the people. In order to achieve this goal, Roosevelt set about expanding the size and scope of the federal government to include an alphabet soup of different agencies and departments and centering federal power within the presidency. After Roosevelt's unprecedented four election triumphs, the role of parties would be forever transformed. Parties would cease to be the primary mobilizers of public opinion and agenda setters in national politics. After Roosevelt, the people would increasingly look to the president to perform these roles. As federal administration grew during the 20th century, parties became partners within a large administrative bureaucracy, led by the president and focused on managing national economic security. Parties lost much of their influence within the electorate as independent popular political institutions thanks to Progressive reforms and the expansion of presidential power.

In recent decades, the strength of political parties in mobilizing and influencing public opinion has declined significantly. In the NATIONAL ELECTION STUDY (NES) of 2000, nearly 40 percent of American voters declared themselves to be independent of political parties, almost double the number of independents measured by the NES in 1950. Parties today play an increasingly smaller role in the political life of the average citizen. Participation in elections has also declined precipitously during the 20th century. Despite a political system that enfranchises virtually all citizens of legal age and offers a widening array of direct democratic tools such as primaries, initiatives, recalls, and the REFERENDUM, Americans are retreating from the ballot box.

With the exception of an uptick in the 2004 presidential race, turnout has declined steadily in recent presidential and CONGRESSIONAL ELECTIONS, with an almost 12 percent decline in turnout among the voting age population between 1960 and 2000. One explanation for declining participation lies in the ebbing of opportunities provided the electorate to engage in politics through parties. The decline in participation can be linked, in part, to a decline in the effectiveness of political parties in engaging citizens in the political process. Passage of the Bipartisan Campaign Reform Act (BCRA) of 2002, which makes it more difficult for political parties to raise funds, is likely to increase this trend. Independent groups not directly associated with political parties and candidates who are not subject to many of the restrictions of BCRA are likely to grow in importance in the future and many of the roles previously served by the parties.

Further reading: Aldrich, John. *Why Parties? The Origins and Transformation of Political Parties in America.* Chicago: University of Chicago Press, 1995; Gerring, John. *Party Ideologies in America, 1828–1996.* London: Cambridge University Press, 1998; Milkis, Sidney. *The President and the Parties: The Transformation of the American Party System since the New Deal.* London: Oxford University Press, 1993; Sabato, J. Larry, and Bruce Larson. *The Party's Just Begun: Shaping Political Parties for America's Future.* 2nd ed. New York: Longman, 2001.

—Zachary Courser

political socialization

Political socialization is the process through which people learn about the political world and begin to develop values, beliefs, and opinions about POLITICS. The process of political socialization is often described in terms of how various "agents of socialization" within society are able to teach individuals about the political system. There are several agents of socialization that are especially significant in the United States: the family, schools, the church, mass media, friends and community members, and government officials and institutions.

The family is generally viewed as the most significant agent of political socialization. Socialization begins within the family when children are quite young, and it often occurs in very subtle ways. For example, when parents teach their children to respect the authority of police officers, they are engaging in political socialization by teaching the importance of obedience to government officials. When families gather together on July 4 to watch fireworks shows in the shadow of an American flag, they are teaching their children about the significance of historic national events. When parents take their children to the polls on ELECTION DAY, and perhaps even let them go into the voting booth with them to flip a switch or push a button, parents are socializing their children about the importance of voting. As children grow older, the patterns of political socialization may become more specific. While sitting around the dinner table, parents may discuss the policies of officials currently serving in or running for office. Such conversations not only develop within the young person the belief that politics matters, but in many cases they also shape the child's views toward the various political parties. At least early on, most children adopt the same political affiliation as their parents.

Schools are also especially important agents of political socialization. Schools teach students facts about our system of government: our political history, the three branches of government, and who our elected officials are and how they were selected to represent us. Particularly in the early years, schools often teach students respect for political leaders, for example by telling students about the honesty of political figures such as George Washington and Abraham Lincoln. In addition, they routinely encourage respect for the nation by displaying the American flag in the classroom and by having students recite the Pledge of Allegiance at the start of the school day. By the time students reach middle school and high school, schools are engaged in the socialization process in other ways as well. By this age, students are often encouraged to participate in student government associations, allowing students the opportunity to campaign, to hold debates, and to vote on which of their classmates they prefer to represent them. Another means through which schools socialize students about the value of our political system is by routinely using schools as polling places in city, state, and national elections. Not only do students have the opportunity throughout an election day to see adults coming to their school to vote, but also students are often allowed to vote in mock elections, particularly when a president is being elected.

Churches can also play a significant role in political socialization through both subtle and direct means. In many denominations, it is not unusual to see an American flag displayed at the front of the church along with a cross. Some churches may also become involved in the political process as a result of particular policy issues. For example, the CIVIL RIGHTS MOVEMENT of the 1950s and 1960s was based in the African-American churches of the South. In more recent years, conservative churches—what many political analysts refer to as the religious right—have become politically active in response to various social movements, such as the women's movement, that gained momentum in the 1970s, and the gay rights movement, which has gained strength in recent years. Many of these churches campaigned against passage of the Equal Rights Amendment for fear of what it would mean for the stability of the traditional American family and because it would have guaranteed women reproductive rights, including abortion rights. Particularly since 1993, when state courts began addressing issues such as marriage rights for homosexuals, these churches have also been actively involved in promoting the maintenance of traditional definitions of marriage and preventing the expansion of rights to cover individuals regardless of their sexual orientation. These churches have been active in accomplishing their political objectives both in terms of involvement in the electoral arena and by boycotting services from companies whose policies they oppose, for instance, companies that extend benefits to partners of gay and lesbian employees. They have also played a part in political socialization through members of the clergy running for political office themselves. In recent elections, both Reverend Jesse Jackson and Reverend Pat Robertson have been candidates for president.

The mass media are also a vital agent of political socialization for Americans, particularly once they leave school. Relatively few Americans have direct contact with elected officials, particularly on the federal level. Therefore, most Americans must rely on the mass media to obtain the majority of their information about government and politics. The media can shape Americans' opinions about the political system in a number of ways: through bias, slant, and the content of coverage they choose. One well-known concept in discussing the influence of the media is "liberal bias." Both print and television news reporters working for the major news organizations have allegedly tended to be more liberal in their political opinions than average Americans. Their personal attitudes are said to influence the tone of the coverage they provide, giving more supportive coverage to the liberal side in political arguments. In recent years, this alleged liberal bias has been offset somewhat as more conservative media outlets have emerged, especially on cable television and AM radio programs. Radio commentators in particular have traditionally been more conservative than mainstream print or television journalists.

The media also play a significant role in socializing citizens through the slant they give to stories, particularly regarding international news events. U.S. involvement in the politics, economics, and national security efforts of other nations around the world has tended to be portrayed in the American media in a positive light, as an example of

U.S. efforts to spread democracy. Often this is a result of the fact that journalists receive from government officials much of the information they report to the public. International news sources often report similar events from a much different perspective.

A final aspect of media coverage that analysts find increasingly significant is its role in setting the political agenda. It is often said that the media has little power over what people think, but that it has tremendous influence over what people think about. The public thinks about and talks about the issues the media has reported in recent days. A significant aspect of the media's agenda-setting role that has been noted in recent decades is the media's increasing tendency to focus on uncovering political SCANDALS. Particularly since the Vietnam War and Watergate in the late 1960s and early 1970s, media coverage of political officials has become more focused on uncovering wrongdoing. Another popular focus of the media is HORSE RACE JOURNALISM, the tendency of the media to cover who is ahead and who is trailing in a campaign. Both of these trends in coverage have reduced the amount of time the media are able to devote to reporting on politicians' issue positions.

Friends and the wider community can also play a significant role in socializing individuals about the political world. Friends often reinforce for each other the opinions each holds. This influence is particularly significant if they hold opinions that are not popular within the larger community. People within communities have tended to share similar opinions on political matters. This has been the case because people raised in the same area have been exposed to similar kinds of influences—they have experienced political socialization in a similar way. In tight-knit communities, it can often be difficult or uncomfortable to express opinions that are contrary to what the majority believes. The reluctance to express contrary opinions has been referred to as the "spiral of silence."

Political leaders and the parties they represent can also be significant influences in shaping one's political socialization. Both individuals and their parties attempt to mold public opinion and increase support for policies by giving press conferences, issuing statements, and running ads in the media. Two examples of this phenomenon are the press conferences held by Presidents Bill Clinton and George W. Bush before sending American troops into combat situations in Bosnia and Kosovo and into Afghanistan and Iraq, respectively.

The effects of these agents and the process of political socialization can be debated. Despite the variety and scope of socialization agents in the United States, Americans tend to vote less frequently than citizens of almost every other Western democracy. This is particularly true in terms of younger voters between the ages of 18 and 25; this group of citizens is the least likely of any group in society to vote. However, Americans overall do tend to participate at higher rates than citizens of other nations in activities such as community organizations and through donating money to such groups.

Further reading: Gimpel, James, J. Celest Lay, and Jason Schuknecht. *Cultivating Democracy: Civic Environments and Political Socialization in America.* Washington, D.C.: Brookings Institution Press, 2003.

—Claudia Bryant

politics

The term *politics* is derived from the classical Greek term *polis,* which means city-state, and is closely associated with the classical Greek words for citizen and citizenship. The term demonstrates the connection between power and the populace that was established in ancient Greece.

In the modern context, the term refers to the means by which power is distributed and exercised. Looked at this way, one may refer to the pace or tone of politics. One may also refer to the level of politics (e.g., local, state, national, or international politics) or refer to politics in geospacial terms (e.g., American, European, or southern politics). The concept is also useful when considering specific issue areas, such as environmental politics, racial politics, or welfare politics. What the concept has in common when discussed in this way is that it refers to the exercise of power (i.e., the process by which decisions are made). The political process includes any activities related to elections, legislation, or policy formation.

The term has also taken on a negative connotation, referring to the making of decisions on the basis of narrow interests rather than on the broader merits of an issue. The term is invoked when policy is scuttled or pushed through the political process due to the influence of special interests, which can mean anything from POLITICAL PARTIES, INTEREST GROUPS, FACTIONS, LOBBYISTS, campaign donors, or moneyed interests. Fiscal decisions are frequently charged with politics. For example, to fund a project in Rhode Island might have more merit (by whatever standard) than to fund a competing project in Arizona, but since Arizona has more members in the House of Representatives than does Rhode Island, and more of them are members of the MAJORITY PARTY, the Arizona project might be funded due to politics.

—Tony L. Hill

poll tax

The poll tax was a charge levied on individuals of voting age by state and local governments. Prospective voters were required to pay the tax before they would be allowed to vote in any election. The poll tax became especially common in the post-RECONSTRUCTION South as a way to deny poor whites and African Americans access to the ballot box.

The first poll taxes were levied in the United States just after independence. Some states granted the franchise to all white male residents who paid a poll tax. This practice actually expanded the ELECTORATE by eliminating property ownership by white males as a prerequisite for eligibility to vote.

After the Civil War, however, the poll tax was employed for discriminatory purposes. States throughout the former Confederacy used the tax to prevent African Americans and poor whites from voting. In order to cast a BALLOT, individuals had to present proof that they had paid the poll tax. Along with the GRANDFATHER CLAUSE, LITERACY TESTS, and the WHITE PRIMARY, the poll tax severely limited the number of qualified black and poor white voters in states where both groups made up significant portions of the population.

As part of a general effort to eliminate discriminatory practices in the United States, civil rights groups successfully lobbied against the levying of poll taxes throughout the South. Several southern states repealed the tax in response to entreaties from voting rights groups. In the wake of many of these changes, the TWENTY-FOURTH AMENDMENT to the U.S. Constitution was ratified in 1964. The amendment eliminated the poll tax in national elections. Ruling that the right to vote was a fundamental right of all citizens, the U.S. Supreme Court followed the adoption of the amendment by ruling in 1966, in *Harper v. Virginia Board of Elections,* that the use of poll taxes in state elections violated the Equal Protection Clause of the FOURTEENTH AMENDMENT.

While the issue of imposition of poll taxes is largely a settled question today, it did resurface in the case of *Morse v. Republican Party of Virginia,* which the Supreme Court heard in 1996. In a plurality opinion, the Court ruled that a state party requirement that registered voters pay a fee before they would be considered as DELEGATEs to the state party nominating convention was an unconstitutional imposition of a poll tax and was prohibited by Section 10 of the 1965 Civil Rights Act.

Further reading: Key, V. O. *Southern Politics in State and Nation.* New York: Knopf, 1949; Lawson, Steven F. *Black Ballots: Voting Rights in the South, 1944–1969.* New York: Columbia University Press, 2000.

—John L. S. Simpkins

poll watcher

A poll watcher is a person who protects against voter fraud by ensuring that only those eligible to vote are allowed to cast votes on ELECTION DAY and that those who are eligible to vote do so at their proper polling location. The term had negative connotations during the period of minority voter suppression following RECONSTRUCTION and during the CIVIL RIGHTS MOVEMENT, when poll watchers fought to suppress black voters.

Though poll watchers are now meant to be overseers of elections, some worry that they continue to be placed in particular PRECINCTs in order to intimidate voters whose views may be unaligned with their own. This became a hotbed of an issue following the 2000 PRESIDENTIAL ELECTION, in which minority voters claimed they were intimidated when they arrived at their polling locations to vote. The issue intensified during the 2004 race, leading to a decision in the 6th Circuit Court in Ohio, where the justices overturned an order barring Republican poll watchers in a heavily Democratic district. The decision again prompted calls of voter intimidation.

Today poll watchers continue to serve as challengers to citizens who, as they see it, may be ineligible to vote. They are allowed in polling precincts in order to observe the voters as well as the officials conducting the elections. Poll watchers may not interfere with a voter's BALLOT casting unless that voter specifically asks them for help. Though they often work for partisan organizations, they may not wear political paraphernalia. Poll watchers are unable to directly interfere with the voting process, though some believe their presence influences not only the voting population but also the poll workers, who may fear that their actions will be questioned by the watchers. As elections continue to be hard-fought and hard-won, so also will be the issues surrounding poll watchers.

—Molly Clancy

popular vote

The popular vote represents the number of all eligible voters who voted for a particular candidate. While the term is rarely controversial, it is associated with many controversial aspects of American democracy. It is most likely to receive attention when the "winning" candidate takes office without winning a clear majority of the popular vote.

Winning an election without majority support can happen for several reasons in the United States. For example, the FIRST PAST THE POST voting system, whereby three or more parties compete for one seat, can result in a "minority winner." This is quite likely in elections such as California's 2003 election, in which the ultimate victor, Arnold Schwarzenegger, faced nearly 130 other candidates. In such an election, the winner could conceivably be elected with less than 1 per cent of the popular vote, though Schwarzenegger received a far greater portion of votes than his competitors.

Another controversy arises in cases in which the candidate with the lower popular vote count actually wins the election, as George W. Bush did in 2000. This is most likely to happen as a consequence of the winner-take-all ELECTORAL COLLEGE system, in which states allocate all of their Electoral College votes to the winning candidate, rather than using a proportional allocation.

Further reading: Neubauer, Michael G., and Joel Zeitlin. "Outcomes of Presidential Elections and the House Size." *Political Science & Politics* 36, no. 4 (2003): 721–725.

—Samuel Millar

Populist Party

The Populist Party was the common name for the PEO-PLE'S PARTY of America that existed from 1892 to 1908. The generally accepted story of the name's origin holds that while traveling home from the Cincinnati conference in 1901 at which the new party had been launched, William F. Rightmire complained to David Overmeyer that it was awkward to refer to a member of the new party. For example, a member of the REPUBLICAN PARTY was a Republican, a member of the DEMOCRATIC PARTY was a Democrat, but it did not make sense to call a member of the People's Party a People or a Person. Overmeyer thought for a moment and came up with the Latin word *populace*, which means people. Journalists traveling with the delegation adopted the new name of Populist, and it appeared in the next day's edition of the *Kansas City Star*. The name stuck, and it became the generally accepted name of the party across the nation.

The name of the party was meant to encompass the average American worker, who party organizers felt was being abused by the moneyed class and who was not justly represented in government. Mary Lease, a leading speaker for the Populists, captured the essence of the party when she said, "Wall Street owns the country. It is no longer a government of the people, for the people, by the people, but a government of Wall Street, for Wall Street, and by Wall Street. . . . The West and South are bound and prostrate before the manufacturing East."

The party was most successful among American farmers, who had experienced great changes in the years after the Civil War. An understanding of their history provides greater insight into the meaning of the Populist Party and its goals. The Homestead Act of 1862 that provided 160 acres to anyone willing to improve the land drew farmers west in the decades following the war. These years also witnessed advances in farm machinery that made the American farm far more productive than ever before but also made it necessary for farmers to upgrade or be left behind. Initially, farm prices remained stable and high, encouraging many farmers to go into debt to establish or improve their farms. Increased grain production, a more competitive world market, and deflation caused by the government switching to currency based solely on gold in 1873 devastated American farmers. Organizations such as the Patrons of Husbandry (the Grange), the Farmers Alliance, and several new political parties tried to improve the condition of the American farmer, leading to the organization of the People's Party of America in 1892.

While the Populist Party died in 1908, the idea of populism continued throughout the 20th century. Both conservatives and liberals have used populist rhetoric to claim that they best represented the needs and desires of America's common person.

Further reading: Clanton, Gene. *Populism: The Human Preference in America, 1890–1900.* Boston: Twayne Publishers, 1991; Kazin, Michael. *The Populist Persuasion: An American History.* New York: Basic Books, 1995; McMath, Robert C., Jr. *American Populism: A Social History 1877–1898.* New York: Hill & Wang, 1993.

—Alan L. Morrell

precinct

The precinct is the fundamental electoral unit in the United States, with each precinct containing at least one polling place where residents cast their votes on ELECTION DAY. The precinct serves as the building block for district-based election units. Most notably, precincts combine into congressional and state legislative districts but also form local districts, such as school, county, and city districts (also known as wards).

The states control the formation and maintenance of precincts, which range in size from smaller than city blocks in some urban areas to large portions of the Nevada desert. The number of precincts in a state ranges from more than 10,000 in states such as New York, California, and Illinois to less than 100 in Delaware. The number of voters in a precinct varies depending on the population of the state and the area where the precinct is located. Typically, urban precincts have around 2,000 voters, while some rural precincts may have less than 50 voters. While similar in size, precincts are not the same as census blocks, the fundamental unit used by the Census Bureau while collecting population data. Though the Census Bureau is attempting to work with the states in matching census blocks and voting precincts for easier reporting of population, electoral, and demographic information, to date the match is not perfect.

Local PARTY ORGANIZATIONS often build around precincts by forming precinct committees headed by precinct captains. Generally, these precinct committees work to recruit and organize poll workers, oversee the election process, provide political information, and help local candidates campaign. Prior to public welfare programs, the precinct committees also provided assistance to the needy in an attempt to garner electoral favor. Today precinct committees are far more likely to oversee election procedures than provide welfare assistance. The 2000 PRESIDENTIAL ELECTION is a good example, as precinct workers in south Florida made national news in their attempt to resolve voting problems that resulted from hanging CHADS and BUTTERFLY BALLOTS.

Further reading: Conway, M. Margaret, and Frank B. Feigert. "Incentives and Task Performance among Party Precinct Workers." *Western Political Quarterly* 27, no. 4. (1974): 693–709; Wolfinger, Raymond E. "The Influence of Precinct Work on Voting Behavior." *Public Opinion Quarterly* 27, no. 3 (1963): 387–398.

—Jonathan Winburn

precinct committee officer

A precinct committee officer (PCO) represents the most localized level of political PARTY ORGANIZATION. A PRECINCT is the smallest political division, numbering about 500 to 1,000 voters and primarily used to coordinate polling places. A PCO is a party's representative within each precinct. PCOs are usually elected by voters registered with their party within their precinct to serve two-year terms, acting as GRASSROOTS party operatives during their tenure. When called upon by a candidate or the party, PCOs often disseminate party literature door-to-door, solicit potential new recruits to the party, and coordinate volunteers for campaign activities within their precincts. Candidates will often turn first to PCOs when looking for volunteers, and local party committees rely on PCOs to serve as a point of first contact between neighborhood voters and the party. PCOs also form the foundation of the party caucus system by administering precinct caucuses and serving as DELEGATES to county conventions.

The usefulness and function of PCOs has become diluted as political parties have weakened during the 20th century. As elections have become increasingly candidate-centered, and electoral POLITICS has shifted away from party politics, the purpose of PCOs has become obscured and perhaps outmoded. In the era of strong parties during the late 19th and early 20th centuries, PCOs and their equivalents served a vital role in party politics. During this time party PATRONAGE was strong, and caucuses were the chief means of nominating candidates. The predecessors of PCOs, the "ward healers" of Chicago and New York, made sure that the number of voters from their neighborhood needed for a party win would show up on ELECTION DAY. They had the resources of the party machine at their command and were rewarded with patronage for ensuring the party's success at the polls. They also exercised real influence over party nominees in the caucus system, and their support was indispensable to potential candidates.

Today most party nominees are chosen by DIRECT PRIMARY, and the focus of attention has shifted away from electing a SLATE of party candidates and toward individual candidates' campaigns. Whereas potential party nominees used to campaign solely within their party's caucus for the NOMINATION, now they are forced to appeal to the ELECTORATE as a whole. As a result, the loyalties of PCOs are often conflicted among several of their party's candidates vying for resources and volunteers during a PRIMARY election. Additionally, as the influence and importance of their office has declined, many party committees find it difficult to recruit and maintain reliable PCOs in every precinct.

Further reading: Riordan, William, and Plunkitt, George Washington. *Plunkett of Tammany Hall.* New York: Signet Classics, 1995; Skocpol, Theda. *Diminished Democracy: From Membership to Management in American Civic Life.*

Norman: University of Oklahoma Press, 2003; Wattenberg, Martin. *The Decline of American Political Parties, 1952–1992.* Cambridge, Mass.: Harvard University Press, 1994.

—Zachary Courser

preprimary endorsements

It is standard procedure in many states for political parties to refrain from explicitly supporting a specific candidate until after the PRIMARY election, when voter preferences have designated a party nominee. In some states, however, party assemblies (or conventions) endorse one or more candidates before the primary election. This practice typically aids incumbents and FRONTRUNNERS and challenges candidates who may be less connected to the local party elite. Preprimary ENDORSEMENTS can affect the degree of public support for a candidate as well as the ability to fund-raise and to mount a viable campaign against competitors within the party.

Colorado's system of preprimary endorsements is a compelling example. Each party designates one or more aspirants to run in the primary at a convention. Anyone who receives at least 30 percent of the vote at the convention is endorsed, and names appear on the BALLOT in the order of share of votes received at the convention. Others who are interested in appearing on the primary election ballot must petition separately.

Preprimary endorsements are a mechanism used by party elites to exert greater influence over the NOMINATION process. Greater control over nominations is also more likely to result in the ultimate election of candidates beholden to and supported by the party apparatus, not necessarily by partisans or voters more broadly. Critics argue that preprimary endorsements foment tensions within the party and unfairly disadvantage nonentrenched candidates.

Evidence that many view preprimary endorsements uneasily surfaced in the 2004 presidential campaign when Vice President Al Gore, the 2000 Democratic nominee, threw his support behind Vermont governor Howard Dean during the early phase of the primary campaign. Gore's decision surprised many and was criticized widely as premature and miscalculated. This appeared justified when Dean abandoned the race early on as it became clear that Massachusetts senator John Kerry was favored for the nomination. Gore ultimately supported Kerry in the race.

Further reading: Cook, Rhodes. *Race for the Presidency: Winning the 2004 Nomination.* Washington, D.C.: CQ Press, 2004; Lorch, Robert. *State and Local Politics: The Great Entanglement.* 6th ed. Upper Saddle River, N.J.: Prentice Hall, 2001.

—Costas Panagopoulos

presidency qualifications

Article II of the U.S. Constitution details the formal qualifications for the U.S. presidency, naming three primary requirements. Eligible individuals must be natural-born citizens or citizens of the United States at the time of adoption of the Constitution, must be age 35 or older, and have been a U.S. resident for at least 14 years.

Though the time required to agree on these three qualifications was considerable, the ultimate justifications for each qualification reflected careful consideration of public fears, pragmatic governance, precedence, and simple self-interest. The natural-born citizen requirement guarded against the newly formed government importing a foreigner—a European monarch, for example—to serve as the president, a popular concern of the day. Residency requirements ruled out those British sympathizers or others who came to the United States after the Revolution intent on undermining the fledgling government from the top down. (Conveniently, the 14-year bar was set sufficiently low so as not to exclude various DELEGATEs themselves from the new nation's highest office.) An age requirement ensured the wisdom of maturity as well as a thorough record of accomplishment on which electors could judge the candidate's presidential potential. As John Jay argued in Federalist No. 64, an age requirement of 35 years would confine the electors "to men of whom the people have had time to form a judgment" and who would "not be liable to be deceived by those brilliant appearances of genius and patriotism which like transient meteors, sometimes mislead as well as dazzle." Though the delegates considered additional qualifications—that of property ownership, for example—none of the additional qualifications made the final document.

Article II also establishes an implicit qualification for the presidency. Section 4 clearly delineates that the president shall be removed from office after impeachment and subsequent conviction for "treason, bribery, or other high crimes and misdemeanors." Though not a qualification for entrance into office, abstinence from treason, bribery, or other high crimes and misdemeanors is a requirement to remain in office.

The TWENTY-SECOND AMENDMENT, added to the Constitution in 1951, adds additional qualifications to the presidency, prohibiting election to the presidency more than twice. Also, no one who has "held the office of President, or acted as President, for more than two years of a term to which some other person was elected president" shall be elected to the presidency more than once.

Further reading: Nelson, Michael, ed. *Guide to the Presidency.* 3rd ed. Washington, D.C.: CQ Press, 2002.

—Chris Mandernach

presidential campaigns, public financing

U.S. election law provides taxpayer dollars to match small political contributions to any qualified PRESIDENTIAL PRIMARY candidate, as long as the candidate's campaign agrees to abide by caps on its spending. To qualify for the public financing, a candidate must raise $100,000 ($5,000 in each of 20 states) in contributions of $250 or less. Qualified candidates receive taxpayer-supported payments that match the first $250 received from any contributor during the presidential PRIMARY season. In addition to voluntary spending limits, qualified campaigns also agree to submit to federal audits.

Public financing is also available for presidential candidates in the GENERAL ELECTION. In the general election, major-party candidates are eligible for full public funding, originally set at $20 million and indexed for inflation. (In 2000, George W. Bush and Al Gore each received $67.6 million.) Recipients may spend only that sum, excepting legal and accounting costs. New minor-party candidates who receive at least 5 percent of the general election POPULAR VOTE are eligible for postelection funds proportionate to their vote share; they also qualify for prorated funds in the subsequent presidential election.

Major parties can receive a public grant—$4 million in 1974 dollars, indexed for inflation—to finance their quadrennial nominating conventions. Parties that accept the grant may spend only those funds on their conventions. Minor parties are eligible for pro-rated convention funding.

Public financing first emerged in the United States when Congress passed the REVENUE ACT of 1971 and the 1974 amendments to the 1971 FEDERAL ELECTION CAMPAIGN ACT (FECA), which together established public funding for PRESIDENTIAL ELECTIONS and nominating conventions. The program's aims include limiting the apparent influence of large political contributions by encouraging campaigns to raise smaller amounts from larger numbers of individual donors across the country, and controlling the costs of the primary campaign seasons by encouraging candidates to adhere to voluntary spending limits.

In the eight presidential campaigns since the program was created, nearly every major-party candidate who has qualified has participated in the matching fund system. But the demands of an extended presidential race, with an increasingly compressed primary calendar and the early start of the GENERAL ELECTION campaign, have put pressure on many candidates to opt out of the primary financing system in order to avoid the program's spending limits. In the 2004 presidential primaries, the FEDERAL ELECTION COMMISSION (FEC) distributed just less than $30 million in MATCHING FUNDS. However, three of the major-party primary candidates, including the eventual Democratic and Republican nominees and another top Democratic CHALLENGER, decided to forgo the taxpayer money.

Public financing is funded through a voluntary check-off on U.S. tax forms. Taxpayers who select the check-off set aside a small portion of their tax dollars to support various federal financing programs for presidential campaigns. It is important to note that the program does not increase one's tax burden. In 1994, the amount of the voluntary taxpayer contribution increased from $1 for an individual taxpayer to $3. Participation peaked in 1980, when nearly a third of taxpayers (29 percent) selected the check-off. In more recent years, check-offs have waned, with slightly more than one in 10 taxpayers participating.

Low taxpayer participation sparked warnings from the FEC starting in the 1990s that the demand for federal campaign funds would exceed available money for the program. However, the decisions of several prominent Democratic and Republican primary candidates to forgo matching funds have helped keep the program solvent.

At the same time, decisions to give up the matching funds to avoid spending caps also have raised doubts about the system's goals of controlling CAMPAIGN EXPENDITURES and limiting political contributions. The most prominent major-party candidate to forgo federal funds since the program was created was Republican George W. Bush, who ran without the matching payments in 2000 and 2004. Two of the major Democratic primary candidates in 2004, Massachusetts senator John F. Kerry and former Vermont governor Howard Dean, also opted out of the matching funds system to avoid the financial caps that some Democrats feared hampered Vice President Al Gore, Bush's Democratic opponent in 2000. However, all of Kerry and Dean's Democratic rivals stuck with the program, as did INDEPENDENT candidate Ralph Nader.

Another concern about the public financing system has been whether the threshold for candidates to qualify for the matching funds is too low. Lyndon LaRouche, a convicted felon and perennial presidential candidate known for his extremist views, has qualified for millions of dollars in federal matching funds since 1980, including about $1.5 million in 2004. Moreover, after Ross Perot won 18.9 percent of the vote in 1992, guaranteeing his REFORM PARTY roughly half the level of public funding as the two major parties in the next presidential race, the public was committed to allocating millions of dollars in support of a party that had little support by 1996.

Further reading: Corrado, Anthony. *Paying for Elections: Public Financing in National Elections.* New York: Twentieth Century Fund Press, 1993; Green, John C., and Anthony Corrado. "The Impact of BCRA on Presidential Campaign Finance." In Michael J. Malbin, ed., *Life after Reform: When the Bipartisan Campaign Reform Act Meets Politics.* Boulder, Colo.: Rowman & Littlefield, 2003; Malbin, Michael J., and Thomas L. Gais. *The Day after Reform: Sobering Campaign Finance Lessons from the American States.* Albany, N.Y.: Rockefeller Institute Press, 1998; Norrander, Barbara. "Presidential Nomination Politics in the Post-Reform Era (in Field Essay)." *Political Research Quarterly* 49, no. 4 (1996): 875–915.

—Mark Stencel and Bruce A. Larson

presidential debates

Presidential debates allow candidates to appeal to the ELECTORATE on the basis of their policy positions and ideas as well as their personalities and intelligence. Presidential debates typically occur two or three times (with an additional vice presidential debate) in the months leading up to an election, moderated by prominent members of the media. While the format of the debates varies, it typically allows candidates to answer questions and then issue a rebuttal to their opponents' responses.

Presidential debates were not a part of early American POLITICS, as electioneering was not seen as appropriate activity for presidential candidates. Debates were more common in elections for Congress, such as the famous LINCOLN-DOUGLAS DEBATES, which lasted three hours each and led to election for an Illinois seat in the U.S. Senate. With the advent of radio, candidates for presidential NOMINATION began to debate on the radio as part of the competition to win state primaries. An intraparty primary debate (aimed at winning the Florida PRIMARY) between Estes Kefauver and Adlai Stevenson was televised in 1956, four years prior to the famous 1960 debate between Richard M. Nixon and John F. Kennedy. Presidential candidates in the television era have demonstrated ambivalence about participating in debates, particularly when incumbents do not want to concede media time to their CHALLENGERS.

Although the idea for televised presidential debates was first suggested in 1952, the first face-to-face debate between the two major party nominees for the presidency did not occur until 1960. This famous debate between Nixon and Kennedy, which was broadcast from coast to coast, introduced the importance of appearance into PRESIDENTIAL ELECTION campaigns in a new way. Nixon appeared pale and sweaty, had refused makeup, and had lost weight recovering from an injury. Kennedy was relaxed and able to project an image of charisma. Those who watched the debates were generally convinced that Kennedy had won, while most who listened to the debate on the radio felt that Nixon had won.

Following the 1960 election, there were no presidential debates for 16 years. One reason for this was the equal time provision in the COMMUNICATIONS ACT OF 1934, which had been temporarily suspended by Congress in 1960. This provision stipulated that networks that provided free airtime to political candidates had to provide equal time to all candidates for that office. Before the presidential election in 1976, a loophole was created in the law that designated presidential debates as "news events," meaning that media could cover them without such coverage being considered airtime for political candidates, and thus they were not covered by the equal time clause.

After the creation of this loophole, which allowed only the major candidate debates to be televised, the LEAGUE OF WOMEN VOTERS undertook the responsibility of plan-

1992 presidential debate between incumbent George Bush (left), independent candidate Ross Perot (center), and Democratic candidate Bill Clinton (right) *(Wally McNamee/Corbis)*

ning debates. In 1988, the COMMISSION ON PRESIDENTIAL DEBATES (CPD) was created to manage presidential debates. The inclusion of minor candidates continues to be a question in the planning of presidential debates. The CPD has three criteria for inclusion in the debates: constitutional eligibility to hold the office of president, evidence of BALLOT ACCESS, and indicators of electoral support. The first and second criteria are relatively straightforward: The Constitution lays out the requirements for eligibility, and ballot access requirements are determined by whether the candidate appears on the BALLOT in enough states to have a mathematical chance of winning an ELECTORAL COLLEGE majority. The third criterion, indicators of electoral support, is more subjective. The current measure used to determine a candidate's electoral support is whether he or she has 15 percent support in five selected national polling organizations, using the average of the most recently reported results from each.

The format for televised debates has departed significantly from the three-hour, alternating speeches format used by Lincoln and Douglas in their Senate contest. The first televised GENERAL ELECTION debate in 1960 lasted an hour, and subsequent debates have typically lasted one and a half hours. The debates include a moderator and a set of panelists, who ask the questions. Moderators and panelists are usually members of the media, working for outlets such as PBS, *Newsweek*, CNN, ABC, and NBC. Variations on this format have been the town hall meeting, as in a 1996 debate between incumbent president Bill Clinton and challenger Robert Dole, and a single moderator with no panel. The single-moderator format has been more popular since 1996, while panel debates dominated from 1976 to 1992.

Candidates from outside the major parties have participated in several recent debates. In 1980, INDEPENDENT candidate John Anderson debated Ronald Reagan in a separate debate from the one Reagan had with incumbent president Jimmy Carter. In 1992, independent candidate H. Ross Perot participated in all three presidential debates along with challenger Bill Clinton and incumbent president George H. W. Bush, although Perot was unable to secure a spot in the 1996 debates. Ralph Nader was not included in the 2000 debates.

In terms of substantive content in presidential debates, the 1960 debate between Kennedy and Nixon placed great emphasis on cold-war issues and issues of international competition. Because there was a high degree of consensus between the two candidates about the pressing need for international primacy and the general nature of domestic problems in need of attention, such as poverty, racial inequality, and better health care for the elderly, the basic tone of the debates centered on the ability to achieve these shared goals based on differences in party and experience.

When televised debates were revived 16 years later, the topics covered in presidential debates were clearly influenced by recent struggles with Watergate, the Vietnam War, and economic problems. The incumbent president, Gerald Ford, and challenger, Jimmy Carter, debated about the specifics of economic policy, including tax structures and plans to increase employment. Carter also brought up Ford's decision to issue a pardon for former president Richard M. Nixon after the Watergate SCANDALS led to Nixon's resignation in 1974, in reference to whether President Ford supported pardons for draft evaders from the Vietnam War. The candidates also clearly had fundamental differences in their ideas about foreign policy and the role that the United States should play in the international conflicts of the day. President Ford made the notorious statement that there was "no Soviet domination of Eastern Europe," which was then interpreted as a sign of Ford's incompetence in the realm of foreign policy.

During the 1980 election campaign, two debates occurred. One was between Republican challenger Ronald Reagan and independent challenger John Anderson, and the other was between Reagan and incumbent Democratic president Jimmy Carter. The debate between Anderson and Reagan, in which Carter chose not to participate, included issues such as tax cuts, energy usage, and defense. Anderson denounced Reagan's failure to comprehend the severity and scope of the energy crisis, pointing out that it was beyond a national problem and arguing that Americans would have to make lifestyle changes, while Reagan refuted this point. Anderson also criticized Reagan's tax cut plan as inflation-causing. This debate highlighted the tendency of candidates from outside the two major parties to be more willing to express potentially unpopular views such as opposing tax cuts and insisting on material sacrifices in the service of more long-term goals. The debate between Carter and Reagan focused on Carter's defense of his record against questions from panelists as well as from Reagan.

In 1988, there was no incumbent president, so the debate took a different tone than those conducted in 1976 and 1980, when the debates called on a sitting president to defend his record. However, since George H. W. Bush was a sitting vice president, the administration's record was still brought up, as Democratic challenger Michael Dukakis attempted to use the Reagan administration's involvement in the Iran-contra scandal against Bush. Another key issue in these debates was the balance between decreasing taxes and resolving the budget deficit. More so than in the debates previously described, the candidates engaged in personal and fundamental conflict, with then vice president Bush making reference to Dukakis as a "card-carrying member of the American Civil Liberties Union" and to the Willie Horton incident. Instead of focusing solely on policy issues, issues of values and culture were increasingly important in this set of debates.

In 1992, the format changed from a panel to a single moderator, Jim Lehrer of PBS. In the first of the three debates, Lehrer presented a question and all three candidates took a turn answering it. They covered such general topics as their own experience and qualification as candidates, as well as more specific plans for defending national interests and encouraging job growth. In the second debate, questions were directed at specific candidates, with the other two candidates then given a chance to respond. This debate touched on some of the controversial issues of the day: the North American Free Trade Agreement, the line item veto proposal, and the proposal for a Balanced Budget Amendment to the Constitution. Yet another format was used for the third debate, in which a single moderator asking questions, with time for rebuttal and follow-up questions, was used for the first half, and panelists posed the questions, with no follow-up option, during the second half of the debate.

In the 1996 debates, Bob Dole, the Republican challenger, emphasized that while he shared the goals of his opponent, he trusted the people rather than the government to achieve these goals. Dole also questioned the state of the economy, including the change in real income during Clinton's first term. The second debate was a town hall meeting, with questions asked by members of the audience. As such, the questions covered a variety of topics, but some important themes were expansion of health care programs such as Medicare, prevention of drug use and tobacco use, and the fate of Social Security.

In 2000, there were three debates between Vice President Al Gore and Texas governor George W. Bush, all of which used the single-moderator format. Similar to 1988, there was no incumbent president, but Gore was a member of the Clinton administration and as such was forced to defend its record (and was able to try to use its record to his advantage). The discourse between Bush and Gore was more tense than that between Clinton and Dole in 1996, with Bush accusing Gore of using "fuzzy math" and Gore questioning the objectivity of data that Bush cited to support his claims about the federal budget.

In the current political world, presidential debates are expected and considered a normal part of the process. But the strength of their influence remains a point of controversy. In 2000, the number of viewers of the presidential debates had decreased by half since 1992, from about 60 million watching each debate to about 30 million watching each debate. Public opinion polls also often reveal that viewers generally believe their preferred candidate to have won. It has been called into question whether the debates, particularly if they are viewed by only a narrow and attentive audience, play a role in truly shaping the voters' opinions.

In theory, debates should be an excellent way for voters to obtain information about candidates. However, as well as imparting information about the candidates' positions, debates create another forum for election campaigns to be candidate centered and allow factors such as appearance, stage presence, and charisma to become influential in modern campaigns. Presidential debates have great promise to inform citizens and allow candidates to consider and communicate their stances on issues but also may contribute to a more shallow and personality-based mode of campaigning.

Further reading: Kraus, Sidney, ed. *The Great Debates: Carter vs. Ford, 1976.* Bloomington: Indiana University Press, 1979; Kraus, Sidney, ed. *The Great Debates: Kennedy vs. Nixon, 1960.* Bloomington: Indiana University Press, 1962; Minow, Newton N., and Clifford M. Sloan. *For Great Debates: A New Plan for Future Presidential TV Debates.* New York: Priority Press, 1987.

—Julia R. Azari

presidential elections

Presidential elections are the method by which the president and vice president, who run as a unified ticket, are selected. The winner of the POPULAR VOTE in each state (with the exception of Maine and Nebraska, which allow their electoral votes to be allocated by CONGRESSIONAL DISTRICT, although neither state has ever split its electoral votes) wins all of the state's electoral votes. In order to win the presidency, a candidate must win 270 electoral votes (i.e., a majority of the 538 total ELECTORAL COLLEGE votes), which are allocated to each state according to their number of representatives in Congress (House and Senate), plus three electors for the District of Columbia.

The concept of a popularly elected executive was not the original vision when the Constitution was initially debated and constructed. The current system of presidential elections is the result of a compromise between elite selection of the president (seen as a potential compromise of the separation of the three branches of government) and direct popular election.

Presidential elections occur every four years on the Tuesday following the first Monday in November. Nominating procedures have changed over the course of American history. Currently, state primaries begin around February of an election year, and nominating conventions occur over the summer, in July or August, though nominees had been informally chosen by late March in the 2000 and 2004 elections, and by June during the late 1980s and early 1990s. At this time, presidential election campaigns consist of television advertising, campaign tours, and intense attention in "swing states" such as Michigan, Ohio, Pennsylvania, and Illinois. These are states that do not consistently vote for a particular party in presidential elections and have a considerable number of electoral votes.

Several institutional factors have changed presidential elections over time. The development of political parties in the 1790s, the shift from state nominating conventions to national party conventions, and the establishment of direct primaries have all affected the content and length of the presidential election season. Presidential elections have been opened up to more meaningful public participation due to the adoption of AT-LARGE ELECTIONS, state laws that require electors to vote in a way that is consistent with the popular vote in the state, and the expansion of the franchise to African Americans, women, and 18- to 20-year-olds.

Another institutional factor that has changed considerably is the selection of the vice president. The TWELFTH AMENDMENT established that the vice president would be elected separately by the Electoral College instead of chosen in the same race. Prior to the Twelfth Amendment, electors cast two votes for president and made no distinction between their votes for president and vice president. The role of vice presidential selection in presidential election campaigns has evolved in a fashion somewhat parallel to the overall process. Party leaders selected vice presidential nominees at nominating conventions in order to maximize electoral advantage until recent decades, when presidential nominees began to select their own RUNNING MATES.

Much debate has taken place in both scholarly and journalistic contexts over which factors influence election outcomes. The role of the economy is often invoked as a determinant of voting behavior and has played a prominent role in several campaigns in which the incumbent was defeated. Ronald Reagan used the slogan "Are you better off today than you were four years ago?" in his 1980 challenge against incumbent president Jimmy Carter, to call voter attention to economic problems such as inflation. In a more direct approach, Bill Clinton used the slogan "It's the economy, stupid," in his 1992 bid for the presidency against incumbent George H. W. Bush. Both challenges were successful.

Issues such as crime, defense, and personal character have also played prominent roles in presidential elections in the latter half of the 20th century. The prevalence of television advertising may have facilitated such themes due to their compatibility with short and compelling advertisements. In 1964, Johnson used the concern about military issues in the famous "Daisy" advertisement featuring a child counting the petals of a daisy, and then the counting turning into a countdown to a nuclear explosion, in order to emphasize Barry Goldwater's positions on nuclear weapons.

Crime was a prominent issue in the 1988 election and came up in several advertisements and debates. A POLITICAL ACTION COMMITTEE supporting the Bush campaign made an advertisement featuring the story of a Massachusetts prisoner, Willie Horton, who was issued a weekend furlough and committed two violent crimes during the time he was out of prison. The advertisement was criticized for its (allegedly intentional) attempt to evoke a race-based reaction among voters because it showed both the criminal, who was African American, and his victims, who were white. Dukakis's stance against the death penalty was also criticized, and he was asked in a PRESIDENTIAL DEBATE if he would favor the death penalty if his wife, Kitty Dukakis, were raped and murdered.

Character issues have influenced the POLITICS of presidential elections in recent decades as well. Gary Hart, a senator from Colorado, suffered damage to his 1984 bid for the Democratic NOMINATION for the presidency because of accusations of marital infidelity, and ultimately his NOMINATION CAMPAIGN was unsuccessful. Bill Clinton's 1992 and 1996 campaigns brought character issues, particularly those involving marital fidelity, to the forefront of presidential elections.

Since the TWENTY-SECOND AMENDMENT to the Constitution was ratified in 1951, limiting presidents to two terms in office, presidential incumbents have often defeated their CHALLENGERs handily. This occurred in 1956, 1964, 1972, 1984, and 1996. Incumbent presidents were defeated in 1976, 1980, and 1992. Typically, in elections in which the incumbent was constitutionally barred from running again, the candidate from the nonincumbent party has fared better. In 1960, John F. Kennedy prevailed after eight years of Republican rule under Dwight D. Eisenhower. In 1968, Republican Richard Nixon became president after Lyndon Johnson's decision not to run for reelection. In the controversial and closely contested election of 2000, George W. Bush became president after eight years of a Democratic White House under William Jefferson Clinton. And in 2004, George W. Bush, running as an incumbent, won against Democratic challenger John Kerry from Massachusetts. The counterexample was 1988, when George H. W. Bush became the first sitting vice president since Martin van Buren to win the presidency.

The 1972 and 1984 elections represent several themes that dominated presidential elections in the last three decades of the 20th century. First, they were extreme examples of landslide victories for incumbent presidents. The challenger in 1972, George McGovern, managed to win only 38 percent of the popular vote. He carried only the state of Massachusetts and the District of Columbia, which together contributed a total of 17 electoral votes. The second trend is the dominance of Republicans in recent presidential races. Between 1952, when Dwight D. Eisenhower won the presidency, and 1994, when the Republicans won a majority in the House of Representatives for the first time since 1954, the usual configuration of power was for the Democrats to control Congress and the Republicans to control the White House. The 1984 election exemplifies these two trends as well. After a divisive PRIMARY, Walter F. Mondale won the Democratic nomination. Mondale was disadvantaged at the outset by his association with the Carter administration, in which he had served as vice president, and he was running against a popular incumbent, Reagan. He made several decisions that did not make his task any easier. He made statements indicating that he would favor increasing taxes, and his selection of Geraldine Ferraro as a running mate proved controversial not only because of her gender but also because of her husband's financial history. Mondale ended up losing the election, receiving only 42 percent of the popular vote and winning only the electoral votes of his home state of Minnesota.

Attempts to explain the trend of Republican dominance in presidential elections have pointed to the fact that Republicans are perceived as being stronger and closer to the preferences of the public on issues such as defense and foreign policy, which are in turn perceived as the domain of the presidency. The Democrats, on the other hand, are perceived as stronger on social issues, which are seen as the domain of Congress. Some obvious explanations for the advantage afforded to incumbent presidents seeking reelection are the visibility and free publicity of the office, as well as connection to popular policies and the demonstration of experience.

Third-party and INDEPENDENT candidates have also occasionally used presidential elections to rise to national prominence, if not electoral success. Such candidacies often reflected the prominence of particular issues, as well as bringing the issues into the national public agenda, and highlighting areas that were neglected or agreed on by the major parties. The U.S. PROGRESSIVE PARTY (nicknamed the Bull Moose Party), led by Theodore Roosevelt (and later Robert M. La Follette), as well as the Social Democratic and Socialist parties that ran Eugene V. Debs as a presidential candidate, highlighted the importance of labor issues in the early decades of the 20th century. George Wallace, a former Democrat and governor of Alabama, ran for president in 1968 as a candidate for the AMERICAN INDEPENDENT PARTY. Wallace was best known for his opposition to integration in public education, and his candidacy reflected the importance of issues surrounding civil rights and integration during that era and the controversy caused by changes in the status quo of racial laws.

While John Anderson, a former Republican, did not focus on any particular issues in his 1980 presidential bid as an independent, subsequent third-party candidacies were more ideological or issue-based. H. Ross Perot, a former businessman who was new to politics, ran in 1992 on a campaign that honed in on economic issues, promising to balance the budget and decrying the North American Free Trade Agreement as bad for American jobs. Perot was able to garner 19 percent of the popular vote (though no electoral votes) in the 1992 election, when economic and employment issues were particularly salient. His 1996 bid was less successful, however, and he received about 8 percent of the vote. In the 1992 contest, Perot was seen as a viable candidate to some extent, appearing on the BALLOT in all 50 states and participating in presidential debates. Perot eschewed ideological appeals and instead drew supporters who felt that mainstream parties and politicians were unresponsive to their demands. In 1996 and 2000, Ralph Nader ran for president as a GREEN PARTY candidate, though he never passed the 5 percent threshold to gain federal MATCHING FUNDS for the Green Party. Aside from the Green Party's signature environmental issues and standard leftist positions, Nader's campaign focused on trade and globalization issues. In his failed 2004 bid for the presidency, this time as an independent, Nader argued that the two major parties were too similar and offered the voters little real choice.

The significance of third-party and independent candidacies is not limited to the introduction of new issues on the political agenda. The presence of third-party candidates in certain elections is said to have influenced the outcome of several elections, usually by dividing the ELECTORATE on one side of the ideological spectrum. Theodore Roosevelt's defection from the REPUBLICAN PARTY and subsequent third-party candidacy led to the victory of Democrat Woodrow Wilson in 1912. Perot's candidacy was said to have influenced the electoral outcome by detracting from the CONSTITUENCY that would otherwise have supported then president George H. W. Bush. Finally, and perhaps most controversially, Ralph Nader's candidacy in the closely contested 2000 election may have crucially tipped the balance of several states, splitting voters on the left and leading to victories for George W. Bush in several close states and ultimately deciding the outcome of the election in Bush's favor. While the winner-take-all system by which most states allocate electoral votes serves to greatly diminish the chances of third-party candidates to actually win presidential elections, it also allows them to exert influence on electoral outcomes.

In the broader context of American politics, presidential elections serve to influence the directions of party platforms and publicize vital issues. Turnout in presidential elections is typically higher than in MIDTERM ELECTIONS, and scholars have found evidence of a presidential COATTAIL effect, in which popular presidential candidates can help win votes for congressional candidates from the same party.

Presidential elections serve as rallying points for the two major parties, opportunities to increase the salience of WEDGE ISSUES (such as abortion), to celebrate success in handling the economy (such as in 1984 and 1996, both handy victories for the incumbent), or to decry the weakness of the incumbent on the important issues of the day and assert the need for change (as in 1976 and 1992, when incumbents were defeated). However, presidential elections also have significance for the paradigms of political culture that transcend pure partisan politics. Trying to capture the character of "swing" voters has been a primary task for parties as well as the media, leading to the development of certain archetypes, such as the "soccer mom" and the "NASCAR DAD." Attempts to understand the SWING VOTE involve deeper probing into American political culture and into the priorities of the electorate. As presidential candidates attempt to attract swing voters, more attempts are made to understand the political preferences of citizens who do not identify strongly with either of the major parties.

Presidential elections also serve to reveal and influence the ideological direction of national politics. Ronald Reagan in the 1980 Republican primary and in the GENERAL ELECTION represented the emerging prominence of the New Right and its socially conservative values. The triumph of Bill Clinton in the 1992 Democratic primary and in the general election was considered a major victory for the DEMOCRATIC LEADERSHIP COUNCIL and its "third way" ideals, a turn to the center for the Democrats.

Further reading: Ceaser, James W. *Presidential Selection: Theory and Development.* Princeton, N.J.: Princeton University Press, 1979; Cook, Rhodes. *The Presidential Nominating Process: A Place for Us?* Lanham, Md.: Rowman & Littlefield, 2004; Bartels, Larry M. *Presidential Primaries and the Dynamics of Public Choice.* Princeton, N.J.: Princeton University Press, 1988; Wayne, Stephen J. *The Road to the White House: The Politics of Presidential Elections.* New York: St. Martin's Press, 2000.

—Julia R. Azari

presidential election 1788–89

Winning President and Vice President: George Washington and John Adams
Number of States: 11
Major Candidates (Party Affiliation): George Washington (Federalist), no opposition
Electoral College Votes: George Washington: 69; John Adams: 34; John Jay: 9; Robert Harrison: 6; John Rutledge: 6; John Hancock: 4; (six others): 10
Popular Vote: unavailable

On May 25, 1787, the Constitutional Convention began in Philadelphia with the hope of curing the ills of the ARTICLES OF CONFEDERATION. Under those articles, the lack of a central authority figure to execute the laws passed by the national legislature rendered the national government largely impotent and able to do little more than suggest policies for the states to consider; states could then dismiss or adhere to these suggestions as they so chose. It was unanimously decided in the first week of the convention that the nation needed a chief executive to execute and enforce the laws passed by the legislative branch.

However, the powers, tenure, and election of that executive (or in the case of the NEW JERSEY PLAN, a multiple executive) were major points of debate. Was the executive to be chosen by the people, whose whims, fancies, and uninformed nature would, as one DELEGATE expressed, make choosing the president similar to "a blind man picking colors?" Was the president to be selected by the national legislature? Madison proposed that legislative selection would not only create divisiveness within the chamber but also that the president could be manipulated by money or the promise of power, or the legislature could produce an executive who felt subservient to those who voted him into office. In addition, would the president hold his term for a single period of seven years with no possibility for reelection, or should he be granted shorter terms with the chance to seek the office for a second term?

Almost four months later, the initial discussions that had engaged the convention delegates concerning the executive were still unresolved. In early September, a committee of a single delegate from each state met to discuss the issue and later proposed to the whole convention that the president not only be chosen by a group of special presidential electors from each state, but that the duration of the presidential term be four years with a possibility for reelection.

In late 1788, after the PHILADELPHIA CONVENTION had concluded its debate and the Constitution had been ratified by 11 of 13 states (North Carolina and Rhode Island would wait a while longer), it was generally assumed by the citizens of the country and delegates to the convention alike that one man would be the country's first president— George Washington. In fact, before the convention discussion of the executive branch began in Philadelphia, there was an awkward pause as delegates wondered how to discuss the office that the chief presiding officer of that gathering, General Washington, would undoubtedly hold. As willing as the rest of the delegates were to make him the chief executive, Washington himself had hesitations about taking the office, such as his age (56), the power of his enemies in government, and the fact that he would be the first president of a new nation. However, chief among his concerns was that there would be competition for the office and that he would be forced to degrade himself through a campaign and to defend himself on his previous actions and positions. This hesitancy set precedent for the future, as other candidates of high standing down the road would likewise express reluctance.

Washington's worries of presidential competition were unfounded, although a partisan battle was pitched for the vice presidential position. The Federalists needed a vice presidential candidate who could garner northern support as well as work congenially and supportively with the new first president. Henry Knox, Benjamin Lincoln, Samuel Adams, and John Hancock were all considered by the Federalists as possibilities for the position. However, in the end, Alexander Hamilton and other prominent Federalists decided on John Adams for the party's nominee. In turn, the ANTI-FEDERALISTS, also seeking a northern candidate, nominated Governor George Clinton of New York as their candidate. The problem faced by the Anti-Federalists, however, was that they were unable to criticize a government that had not been commenced; how could one protest something that might or might not occur?

Another dilemma of this inaugural election was that the newly developed constitutional system lacked the specification of the TWELFTH AMENDMENT (passed in 1804) that would force the parties to specify their candidates for the office of the presidency and the vice presidency. Under the constitutional format in 1789, the winner of the largest number of electoral votes was to be the president, and second place became vice president. There was little question that Washington would have his name written down by every one of the electors. However, there was the possibility that the electors would all demarcate Adams as their second choice, understanding that he would be vice president, while, due to the Constitution, there would be nothing suggesting that Adams could not be president if he had fulfilled the same requirements as another candidate (namely Washington). As a fail-safe against Adams receiving the same or more votes than Washington and thereby becoming president, Hamilton persuaded Pennsylvania and Connecticut electors to vote for lesser candidates for vice president, effectively throwing them away and preventing a presidential quagmire.

Except for a snag in New York, the election went smoothly, as Hamilton had planned. In New York, the electors were chosen by the legislature (as with Connecticut, Delaware, Georgia, New Jersey, and South Carolina; Pennsylvania and Maryland had popular election of electors), and the lower house proposed that Clinton be vice president while the senate selected Adams. As the state's bicameral nature required that both houses concur on their decision for electors to be chosen, the division between the two on the choosing of Federalist or Anti-Federalist electors could not be resolved. The result was that New York forfeited its electoral votes for the election (and incidentally its right to senators in the first Congress). Despite the slight problems of the first election in America's history, Washington won the presidency by a unanimous 69 of 69 electoral votes. Adams, however, received only 34 of 69 votes but was still elected vice president.

Further reading: Milkis, Sidney, and Michael Nelson. *The American Presidency: Origins and Development, 1776–1998.*

Washington, D.C.: Congressional Quarterly Press, 2003; Schlesinger, Arthur M., Jr., and Fred I. Israel, eds. *History of American Presidential Elections*, Volume I, *1789–1844*. New York: Chelsea House Publishers, 1971.

—Ryan Teten

presidential election 1792

Winning President and Vice President: George Washington and John Adams
Number of States: 15
Major Candidates (Party Affiliation): George Washington (Federalist), no opposition
Electoral College Votes: George Washington: 132; John Adams: 77; George Clinton: 50; Thomas Jefferson: 4; Aaron Burr: 1
Popular Vote: unavailable

In all respects, Washington's first term was a success. He had added a Bill of Rights to the Constitution to please ANTI-FEDERALISTS, he had seen Rhode Island, North Carolina, Vermont, and Kentucky enter the Union, and he had surrounded himself with brilliant men as his advisers and cabinet. However, Washington witnessed infighting between Alexander Hamilton and Thomas Jefferson over the financial matters of the nation (the establishment of a national bank), and Washington was confronted with the Whiskey Rebellion, in which the militia was needed to quell a citizen uprising.

In 1792, Washington was tired of the quibbling. At 60 years old, he had suffered serious illness in 1790 and 1791, was going deaf and losing his eyesight, was worried about his reputation being assailed in the political realm, had not been able to return to Mount Vernon as often as he would have liked, and had family (a nephew) facing serious infirmity. However, his letters back to Mount Vernon, providing specific and detailed agricultural prescriptions for his land, suggest that he may have been suffering less from the ailments of old age and more from the frustrations and exasperations of being the president.

He would be convinced to govern for a second term, however, by the united pleadings of the bitter enemies Jefferson and Hamilton that Washington remain at the helm of the nation to act with authority and quell the domestic conflicts within the country. They also told Washington that the problems across the Atlantic necessitated a stability and continuity in the nation that could be provided only by his continuance as president. In addition, Washington personally reflected on the absence of a unifying successor. Neither John Jay, John Adams, nor Thomas Jefferson would be able to command universal support from every region of the new country that was necessary during its fledgling years. On the basis of these ponderings, and despite his growing apprehension and dissatisfaction with the office, Washington gave his consent to seek the presidency for a second term.

As in the election of 1789, with the presidency assumed to be entirely in the capable (and unopposed) hands of George Washington, the political battle for vice president took center stage. John Adams, though considered by some to be monarchical, was a logical and widely supported choice for vice president. Endorsed by both Hamilton and Jefferson, Adams's FEDERALIST PARTY concluded that maintaining Adams as vice president was just as important as ensuring that Washington remain chief executive.

The Anti-Federalists had disappeared into the political landscape, and opposition to Adams came instead from the DEMOCRATIC-REPUBLICAN PARTY of Jefferson. Although Jefferson himself had little aspiration to seek the vice presidency at this time, as in 1788, Governor George Clinton of New York appeared as the CHALLENGER to Adams. Electioneering (in its earliest forms) was waged in earnest against Adams from the Democratic-Republican side with such vehemence that Adams retreated to his Massachusetts farm to avoid becoming embroiled in the fray. Despite being implored by both Hamilton and other politicians to return to Philadelphia to confront any misrepresentations of character or policy, Adams remained in Quincy, Massachusetts, until well after the contest had been decided in late November.

As the election neared, and amid Democratic-Republican murmurings that Clinton wished to withdraw from consideration as a candidate for the vice presidency, Aaron Burr emerged as another possible choice for the second-highest office in the land. However, due to Democratic-Republican indecision as well as Hamilton's aggressive pamphleteering against Burr (a conflict of personalities that would cost him his life years later in a duel with Burr), the movement for a Burr vice presidency was brief and soon replaced by Democratic-Republican unity behind Clinton.

The 1792 election would bring the same result as the initial election in 1788, namely that Washington would be reelected unanimously and Adams would be reelected after competition. Washington received all 132 electoral votes to continue his tenure as president. Adams again received 77 electoral votes to Clinton's 50 to win the vice presidency for another four years.

Although the outcome of the election in 1792 was identical to that of four years earlier, the distribution of electoral votes for the vice presidency suggested that the political battle lines were becoming much more cohesive in the new nation. During Washington's presidency, the nation did not witness a complete polarization of opposing parties or divisive issues that would threaten to unhinge the Union. Instead, Washington's tenure delayed the rise of political parties by his tentative nature and unwillingness to begin or enter a political fray. His farewell address, a strong expression of his opposition to FACTIONS, exemplified his presidency as a whole: He had worked for unity, and general unity had prevailed at the cost of strong and divisive factions or parties. However, the distribution of electoral votes for the vice presidency told a different story. New Hampshire, Massachusetts, Connecticut, New Jersey, Pennsylvania, Delaware, Maryland, South Carolina, Vermont, and Kentucky had each given almost unanimous support to the Federalist candidate, John Adams. Virginia, Georgia, New York, and North Carolina had solidly supported the Democratic-Republican candidate, George Clinton. The era of POLITICAL PARTY nonactivity and disorganization was nearing a close. And, despite the warnings of Washington to America, partisan POLITICS had emerged in the new democratic nation.

Further reading: Milkis, Sidney, and Michael Nelson. *The American Presidency: Origins and Development, 1776–1998.* Washington, D.C.: Congressional Quarterly Press, 2003; Schlesinger, Arthur M., Jr., and Fred I. Israel, eds. *History of American Presidential Elections,* Volume I, *1789–1844.* New York: Chelsea House Publishers, 1971.

—Ryan Teten

presidential election 1796

Winning President and Vice President: John Adams and
    Thomas Jefferson
Number of States: 16
Major Candidates (Party Affiliation): John Adams
    (Federalist); Thomas Jefferson (Democratic-
    Republican); Thomas Pinckney (Federalist);
    Aaron Burr (Democratic-Republican);
    Samuel Adams; Oliver Ellsworth
Electoral College Vote: John Adams: 71; Thomas Jefferson:
    68; Thomas Pinckney: 59; Aaron Burr: 30; Samuel
    Adams: 15; Oliver Ellsworth: 11; (seven others): 22
Popular Vote: unavailable

The presidential election of 1796 was the first test of the PRESIDENTIAL SUCCESSION system. George Washington, the hero of the War for Independence and the first president of the republic, had stated that he would not stand for reelection, opting instead to return to private life at Mount Vernon.

The social climate of the nation was chaotic. The uniting spirit of jubilation from the War for Independence and the establishment of the new government eight years prior had worn off, and there was little else to unite the citizens of the young country. Some looked for a stronger government, while others decried that the government they had was already too strong. Parts of the nation's population looked to Britain for aid, while others hoped for support from the revolutionary government in France. The economy, having turned around in the Washington administration's first term, had since fallen into a depression. Partisan divisions were inflamed by the Jay Treaty and were becoming much more pronounced. Settlers on the frontier felt little if any loyalty to the government of a country in which

two-thirds of the population lived within a hundred miles of the coast. Europe had descended again into war, and the United States, with an army numbering less than 2,000 men and a navy totaling one ship with no guns, was caught between the powers of England and France and with no realistic way to protect itself or its commerce.

The campaign started in earnest in the fall of 1796 with the release of Washington's farewell address. In the manner of the time, neither candidate was much involved with the campaign himself. To do such was considered unethical by both men. However, this did not stop their supporters from doing so. Adams, who hoped for victory, was exactly as uninvolved in the campaign as was Jefferson, who had been drafted and was a quite unwilling candidate.

The major issues of the election focused on foreign affairs. The main divisive issues were the Jay Treaty with the British and the French Revolution. Adams and the Federalists supported the Jay Treaty, while Jefferson and the Democratic-Republicans denounced it as favoring the British over the nation's erstwhile supporters, the French. Related to this were the positions of the parties on the revolution in France. Adams did not want to support France, as he felt that the nation could not afford to be drawn into another costly war with Great Britain. On the other hand, the Democratic-Republicans felt that it was the honor-bound duty of the United States to support the French in return for their aid, so essential in winning the colonies' independence from England.

The campaign itself, however confined it was to newspaper editorials, leaflets, and political rallies, was nasty. Compared even to modern attack strategies, the 1796 election is still considered one of the most virulent and personally abusive campaigns in the history of American POLITICS. Jefferson was branded by the Federalists as an atheist who would campaign to do away with all organized religion. He was also accused of being a friend of France who would draw the young nation into a war with Great Britain. Adams, on the other hand, was dubbed a monarchist and a friend of Britain. He did not, according to the Democratic-Republican handbills, believe in democracy or in the federal Constitution.

One of the most remarkable aspects of the election was the direct support by the French government, run now by the Directorate, for Jefferson. The French leadership made no doubt which candidate it preferred and endeavored to do anything within its power to bring about the defeat of Adams and the Federalists. The French attitude came both as a result of the pro-British Jay Treaty and the idea that Jefferson, who had been for a number of years the American ambassador to Paris and a friend of the Revolution, would favor France. The French minister to the United States, Pierre Adet, made a point of being particularly active in public circles of the day. Adet even went so far as to publicize a proclamation from the French government that France would treat American ships in the same way that the

English were allowed to treat American ships. Finally, he released in delayed manner news of his own recall to France because the American government was becoming too pro-British. This release, in mid-November, was timed in such a manner as to be as large an influence on the electors as possible.

The Federalists in the campaign were divided against themselves. Alexander Hamilton, the leading Federalist politician, would have preferred anyone to Adams. However, the prestige of being Washington's vice president and his popularity with the common people made it impossible for Hamilton to exclude Adams completely from the government. The scheming to relegate Adams to a third term as vice president seems to have started in the spring and summer of 1796, well before Washington's official withdrawal from the race. The man chosen by Hamilton was the less experienced and probably more pliable Thomas Pinckney of South Carolina. It was thought that if the North could be persuaded to vote solidly for both Adams and Pinckney, the few votes that the latter would pull away from Jefferson in the southern states would swing him, rather than Adams, into the lead. The election was such, in fact, that Adams himself was convinced as late as mid-December that Pinckney, rather than himself, had won.

When finally the electoral vote was tallied in Congress on February 8, Adams had carried the day. However, because the Constitution laid out a system by which the man who received the second-highest total of electoral votes for president would then become vice president, Jefferson, the leader of the OPPOSITION PARTY, was inaugurated as Adams's vice president. This was a sort of shock to the system, revealing a flaw in the framers' plan that would be further emphasized in 1800 and corrected by the TWELFTH AMENDMENT. After a few short discussions about the looming crisis with France in the first two days of the administration, Adams excluded Jefferson from any meaningful play in the administration for the balance of his term.

Further reading: Brown, Ralph Adams. *The Presidency of John Adams.* Lawrence: University of Kansas Press, 1975; Russell, Francis. *Adams: An American Dynasty.* New York: American Heritage Publishing, 1976; Ryerson, Richard Alan, ed. *John Adams and the Founding of the Republic.* Boston: Massachusetts Historical Society, 2001.

—John P. Todsen

presidential election 1800

Winning President and Vice President: Thomas Jefferson and Aaron Burr
Number of States: 16
Major Candidates (Party Affiliation): Thomas Jefferson (Democratic-Republican); Aaron Burr (Democratic-Republican); John Adams (Federalist); Charles Cotesworth Pinckney (Federalist)

Electoral College Vote: Thomas Jefferson: 73; Aaron Burr: 73; John Adams: 65; Charles Cotesworth Pinckney: 64; John Jay: 1
Popular Vote: unavailable

The election of 1800 can truly be seen as one of the most significant in U.S. history. First, it marked the first peaceful transfer of power from one party to another in the history of America. Second, the election was important because the tranquillity and peaceful operation of government that the fledgling government had originally enjoyed was put to the test. The election of 1800 was entirely a party contest, with the party of Jefferson, the Democratic-Republicans, facing off against the party of Adams, the Federalists, for control of the White House and Congress. The differences between the two candidates and their parties were quite clear. Adams had a long history of supporting aristocratic ideals and cautioning against the will of the people. On the other hand, Jefferson swore allegiance to his belief in the rights and powers of the common man. In the election of 1796, Jefferson attempted to paint Adams as a monarchist who favored titles and class distinctions. In 1800, the Jefferson camp was able to extend these attacks to Adams's record as well as his philosophy.

For the first time in American history, there was no revolutionary hero to head the government as president. As such, Adams was forced to stand on the positions and operations of his tenure. This record was largely a consequence of interactions and activity on the international stage that had occurred while Adams was vice president. As a result of the Jay Treaty with Great Britain, France had halted trade with America. In addition, Congress released dispatches from France (nicknamed the XYZ Affair) that expressed anti-American sentiment. Adams and the Federalists benefited from the anti-French sentiment that occurred as a result of the memos and greatly increased their numbers in Congress during the midterm elections of 1798–99. With the members of Congress behind him and anti-French sentiment growing within the American people, Adams established the Department of the Navy and raised the issue of the propriety of a permanent standing army. In addition, the Adams administration passed the controversial ALIEN AND SEDITION ACTS and the Naturalization Act of 1798.

In response to this record, Democratic-Republican opponents attacked the navy and standing army propositions as attempts to increase taxes. In addition, the combination of a standing army with the Alien and Sedition Acts and Naturalization Act was viewed by Democratic-Republicans as a possible attempt to eliminate dissent or opposition from parties that did not adhere to the Federalist proposals.

In addition to attacking Adams's record, Democratic-Republicans examined the ways in which states chose their presidential electors, as Jefferson had lost the election of

1796 by only three electoral votes (one each from Virginia, Pennsylvania, and North Carolina). The three states provided ELECTOR allocation by district, thereby allowing the possibility that a state might split its electoral votes between several presidential candidates. However, in many other states the presidential candidate receiving the majority of the vote won all of the state's electoral votes. Therefore, the electoral vote would almost certainly be distributed to the presidential candidate whose party had control of that state's legislature (as it was the case in almost every state where the state legislature, not the people, chose the electors). Both FEDERALIST and DEMOCRATIC-REPUBLICAN PARTY leaders seized on these differences illustrated by the election of 1796 and attempted to influence states to change their form of appointing presidential electors to either POPULAR VOTE or legislative appointment as best would suit the party in power and secure votes for the presidency. After all of the state changes and raising of democratic questions, only five of 16 states decided to choose their electors by popular vote; the election of 1800 was truly out of the hands of the people and dependent upon the predispositions of the state legislatures. The Democratic-Republican Party, however, was much better organized than its Federalist counterpart and began to organize formal party machinery, from committees of correspondence to GRASSROOTS campaigns, for the first time in American history.

The candidates for the election of 1800 were determined by congressional caucus, with Democratic-Republican national legislators selecting Jefferson as presidential nominee and Aaron Burr as his vice president, and their Federalist counterparts choosing John Adams as the presidential nominee and Charles Cotesworth Pinckney as the vice presidential candidate (this was the origin of the caucus nominating system, which would continue until 1824). Although the Democratic-Republican machinery posed a strong obstacle, the primary threat to Adams came from within his own party. Alexander Hamilton so disliked Adams that he worked to take the election from Adams by attempting to influence votes in South Carolina, Massachusetts, and other states, as well as releasing scathing letters to the public that attacked Adams more devastatingly than Democratic-Republicans had ever attempted. Hamilton proposed that members of his party vote for Pinckney with as much, if not more, fervor as John Adams. As a result, because of the lack of differentiation in the Constitution between the votes for the president and the vice president, a tie between Adams and Pinckney could lead to a Hamilton-pleasing Pinckney presidency.

After all the electoral votes were counted, Jefferson and Aaron Burr had tied, with 73 electoral votes each. Adams ran a distant third, with 65, and Pinckney finished fourth, with 64 votes. The tie in the ELECTORAL COLLEGE between Jefferson and Burr forced the vote to the House of Representatives, where each state would receive one vote

for its choice of president. Balloting began on February 11, 1801, and Hamilton lobbied continuously against the selection of Burr for president (another event that would lead to his demise in a duel with Burr years later). On February 17, 1801, on the 36th BALLOT, Jefferson received the votes of 10 states, making him the victor. As a result of the tie for the presidency, the TWELFTH AMENDMENT was passed in 1804, which separated the balloting for presidential and vice presidential elections.

Further reading: Milkis, Sidney, and Michael Nelson. *The American Presidency: Origins and Development, 1776–1998.* Washington, D.C.: Congressional Quarterly Press, 2003; Schlesinger, Arthur M., Jr., and Fred I. Israel, eds. *History of American Presidential Elections*, Volume I, *1789–1844.* New York: Chelsea House Publishers, 1971.
—Ryan Teten

presidential election 1804

Winning President and Vice President: Thomas Jefferson and George Clinton
Number of States: 17
Major Candidates (Party Affiliation): Thomas Jefferson (Democratic-Republican); Charles Cotesworth Pinckney (Federalist)
Electoral College Vote: Thomas Jefferson: 162; Charles Cotesworth Pinckney: 14
Popular Vote: unavailable

The election of 1804 stands in sharp contrast to the election that occurred only four years earlier. In 1800, the presidential vote saw a tie between Thomas Jefferson and Aaron Burr that was sent to the House of Representatives for a decision, made on the 36th BALLOT in favor of Jefferson. However, the PRESIDENTIAL ELECTION only four years later was a near landslide, as witnessed by the number of electoral votes garnered by Jefferson versus those for Pinckney. There were several reasons for this one-sided contest and lopsided victory for the Democratic-Republicans.

In 1804, Jefferson had an outstanding record of governance and accomplishment, built upon many contributions made materially and politically to the new nation. Jefferson doubled the size of the United States by negotiating the Louisiana Purchase from Napoleon and France and expanded settlement possibilities far into the new western frontier. In addition, stemming from his longstanding support for agrarian interests in the states, he proposed and executed new programs that offered opportunities for land ownership and development, expanded the national educational system to rural areas, and enacted many internal improvements in roads and canals in order to increase commerce and provide a better way of life for all Americans.

Jefferson also made significant political moves that gained the support of Federalists and Democratic-

The PRAIRIE DOG sickened at the sting of the HORNET — or a Diplomatic Puppet exhibiting his Deceptions!

An anti-Jefferson cartoon criticizing his somewhat underhanded negotiations for and purchase of West Florida from Spain in 1804 *(Cartoon by James Atkins, HarpWeek, LLC)*

ery of the Annual Message (which would become the State of the Union Address) because he felt it resembled a speech given by a king to his subjects. Not a terribly gifted orator, his writings seemingly more than made up for this fact. His well-articulated and persuasive commentaries were viewed as so important to the American people that the press consistently published them so that they could be disseminated to the larger public.

The landslide victory was not the result only of sound policy and lucid communication. The organization of the Democratic-Republican Party at the national, state, and local levels enabled some of the first party machines to effectively GET-OUT-THE-VOTE and publicize the accomplishments of Jefferson. The Democratic-Republicans chose campaign committees for each state, set up local committees in closely contested states, used strong Democratic-Republican daily presses, and directed news to the average person. To renominate Jefferson, the party held a congressional caucus, where he was the unanimous decision for president. However, the Democratic-Republicans decided to switch the vice presidential nominee from Aaron Burr to George Clinton of New York. This was due largely to Burr's refusal to withdraw from presidential consideration when the electoral vote was sent to the House of Representatives in 1800, as well as Jefferson's complaint that he was little help while in office. In the congressional caucus, he received no votes for vice president.

Lacking the general support enjoyed by Jefferson, the Federalists also lacked PARTY ORGANIZATION at the many different levels exhibited by the Democratic-Republicans. For a short time, the Federalists in New York were considering support of Aaron Burr, until vicious attacks on his character by Hamilton ended the consideration and led to a duel between Burr and Hamilton in which the latter was killed. Failing to have any type of organization for presidential contention such as a congressional caucus, the Federalist newspapers were largely responsible for providing the presidential contender. This medium witnessed the inaction of the party in the election year and in the October immediately preceding the election and posited to its readers that General Charles Cotesworth Pinckney should be the man for presidential office. In a private gathering unrepresentative of the nation as a whole, the Federalists proposed General Pinckney as the presidential nominee and Rufus King of New York as the vice presidential hopeful.

In September of the election year, the TWELFTH AMENDMENT to the Constitution was passed, demarcating electoral votes for president and vice president in the hope of preventing an electoral quagmire like that of four years earlier. In total, reflecting the organization of the parties, the Federalists received only 14 electoral votes (only the states of Connecticut and Delaware and two of nine from Maryland), while Jefferson won handily with 162 votes. The credit for the sweeping victory can be laid to the ability of the Democratic-Republican Party to mobilize when neces-

Republicans alike. During the Adams administration, the ALIEN AND SEDITION ACTS as well as the establishment of the Department of the Navy and the push for a standing army had concerned Democratic-Republicans and average citizens alike, who worried that these policies were attempts to stifle the dissenting political voice in the country. To respond to these concerns, Jefferson not only allowed the Alien and Sedition Acts to expire without renewal, he also issued pardons to all those who had been convicted under its tenets. This move not only solidified the ability for an opposition POLITICAL PARTY to be lawfully established in the United States without fear of prosecution for dissenting opinions, it also opened the door for the development of the freedom of the press and media provision of governmental accountability. He also limited defense spending, reducing military expenditures by nearly two-thirds.

In addition to addressing those policies that concerned DEMOCRATIC-REPUBLICAN PARTY members, Jefferson acknowledged Federalist interests by refusing to provide opposition to the national charter of the Bank of the United States and even opened a new branch in New Orleans. Jefferson also cut spending, reduced the national debt, and almost completely eliminated internal revenue taxes. These moves strengthened his standing among the OPPOSITION PARTY and made many Federalists in Congress willing to work with Jefferson on policies and programs that he attempted to pursue within the legislature.

In addition to political popularity, Jefferson had an almost undefeatable personal appeal with the general public. He was a handsome, athletic president who stood more than six feet tall. He believed in the power of the people above that of the elite in society and eliminated oral deliv-

sary, the incapacity and decline of the FEDERALIST PARTY, and the administration's record, which pleased both Democratic-Republicans and Federalists alike.

Further reading: Genovese, Michael A. *The Power of the American Presidency, 1789–2000*. Oxford: Oxford University Press, 2001; Roseboom, Eugene H. *A History of Presidential Elections*. New York: Macmillan, 1964; Schlesinger, Arthur M., Jr., and Fred I. Israel, eds. *History of American Presidential Elections*, Volume I, *1789–1844*. New York: Chelsea House Publishers, 1971.

—Ryan Teten

presidential election 1808

Winning President and Vice President: James Madison and George Clinton
Number of States: 17
Major Candidates (Party Affiliation): James Madison (Democratic-Republican); George Clinton (Democratic-Republican); Charles Cotesworth Pinckney (Federalist)
Electoral College Vote: James Madison: 122; Charles Cotesworth Pinckney: 47; George Clinton: 6; (not voted): 1
Popular Vote: unavailable

In the presidential contest of 1808, James Madison of Virginia resoundingly defeated George Clinton of New York and General Charles C. Pinckney of South Carolina. Madison's victory continued a period both of Democratic-Republican domination of national POLITICS as well as a political structure known as "the first party system." Yet Madison's clear victory in 1808 masks a host of political developments that produced the so-called Era of Good Feelings and, eventually, the dissolution of the first party system.

Madison garnered 122 electoral votes, winning Virginia, Pennsylvania, North Carolina, Vermont, Georgia, Kentucky, New Jersey, and Ohio entirely and a majority in Maryland and New York. Fellow Democratic-Republican George Clinton gained New York's remaining votes, while Federalist Charles Pinckney won Connecticut, Delaware, Maryland, Massachusetts, and Rhode Island plus a minority in North Carolina, for a total of 47. These regional voting blocs—the Federalist Northeast and the Democratic-Republican West, Midwest, and South—were characteristic of what scholars call "the first party system." A geographically expanding ELECTORATE, incrementally organizing party structures, and a dominant system of party caucus NOMINATIONS characterized the electoral process in the election of 1808, as it had since 1796, and as it would until 1828. Also continued was the "Democratic-Republican revolution," which had carried Thomas Jefferson into office in 1800.

The central issue of the contest was the 1807 Embargo Act, a brainchild of Madison and Jefferson's that effectively shut down American exports by prohibiting American vessels from leaving domestic ports. Although it was an immediate response to a British attack on the USS *Chesapeake* in 1807, British and French policy had neglected the neutrality of American merchant vessels since 1802. As Madison emerged as the presidential nominee, then, it appeared that his political fortunes would be deeply connected to an Embargo Act that had contracted American export revenues and wrought discontent among agrarian and mercantile interests alike.

Powered by New England merchants' criticism of the Embargo Act of 1807, the declining Federalists experienced resurgence. Voicing strong support for Great Britain, Federalists claimed that the embargo had been enacted only to compensate for Madison's ineffectual tenure as secretary of state. In March 1808, leading Federalist Timothy Pickering devised the Federalist platform: The Democratic-Republicans, he claimed, were "instruments" of French tyranny, aiming to start a war with Great Britain. In the end, this platform failed to expand Federalist appeal beyond its stronghold in New England. General Pinckney would handily win these states, but it was clear as early as January 1808 that the Federalists could not win the presidential election.

Yet the Federalist critique of Madison's embargo policy encouraged the fragmentation of the DEMOCRATIC-REPUBLICAN PARTY. Led by John Randolph, a clique of libertarians within the party calling themselves the Tertium Quids echoed the Federalist claim that Madison and Jefferson were irrational supporters of Napoleon's France. Infuriated by Jefferson's use of French mediators in the U.S. purchase of west Florida from Spain in 1806, the Quids threw their support behind Virginian James Monroe, only to see his candidacy fail to materialize. A second FACTION aligned behind Vice President George Clinton, a New Yorker, whose supporters included the growing mercantile interests of the middle states. For this group, the Embargo Act appeared to extend the possibility of defeating Madison. In the end, George Clinton's candidacy fell victim to a combination of both poor strategy and the caucus system.

Under the caucus system, congressmen enjoyed the ability to nominate official presidential and vice presidential candidates. Congressional Republicans strongly backed Madison, but they feared that Clinton's support would grow the longer the party lacked an official nominee. The congressional Madisonians thus hurriedly convened the caucus and nominated Madison in January 1808. Clinton's supporters made the fatal error of boycotting the caucus, opening the door for a clever strategic move by the Madisonians. By nominating Clinton for vice president, they removed much of the antiestablishment sting from Clinton's platform. That is, a Madison-Clinton ticket papered over the Democratic-Republican fragmentation and presented, instead, a confident face of party unity.

In February 1808, Clinton committed a blunder, conscious or accidental, that all but sealed his electoral fate.

Seeking to capitalize on the rising Federalist critique that Madison was but a shill for the French, Clinton obtained diplomatic dispatches from the secretary of state's office that made it appear that Jefferson and Madison were bent on an anti-British commercial and military policy. Yet these documents were classified as "confidential," and by reading them aloud, Clinton drew criticism about his capacity to lead virtuously. Worse yet for Clinton, a month later Jefferson sent Congress Madison's correspondence with European officials in the hope of dispelling the idea that Madison was a French "instrument." These letters were read continuously for six days as Clinton angrily observed from the vice president's chair. As the reading concluded, congressional Democratic-Republicans had already united behind Madison.

The March 1808 congressional reading of Madison's correspondence also magnified his domination over the print media, perhaps the most important political resource during the early republic. As the FEDERALIST PARTY resurrected itself in 1807, Democratic-Republican newspapers proliferated, bringing new members into the Democratic-Republican Party and spreading its geographical reach. This trend continued during the election year, fueled in part by the Democratic-Republicans' distribution of Madison's foreign correspondence to loyal printers. For a few months, these newspapers hammered home the message that Madison had been strong and decisive, effectively drawing the electoral contest to a close well before the first vote was cast.

The implications of these events were significant. Newspapers would continue to grow in significance in antebellum America, anchoring citizens' interactions with national politics. While Madison's election continued the Virginian dynasty, it was clear that the Jeffersonian COALITION between moderate and "old" Democratic-Republicans could not remain intact. These fissures would become full-blown faults after 1812, as the first party system dissolved in 1816. Finally, the electoral process itself began to change as the problems of the caucus system came into view.

Further reading: Bryant, Irving. *James Madison: Secretary of State, 1800–1809.* Indianapolis: Bobbs-Merrill, 1953; Buel, Richard, Jr. *Securing the Revolution: Ideology in American Politics, 1789–1815.* Ithaca, N.Y.: Cornell University Press, 1972; Chase, James S. *The Emergence of the Presidential Nominating Convention, 1789–1832.* Urbana: University of Illinois Press, 1973; Cunningham, Noble E., Jr. *The Jeffersonian Republicans in Power: Party Operations, 1801–1809.* Chapel Hill: University of North Carolina Press, 1963.

—Gautham Rao

presidential election 1812

Winning President and Vice President: James Madison and Elbridge Gerry
Number of States: 18

Major Candidates (Party Affiliation): James Madison (Democratic-Republican); DeWitt Clinton (Federalist)
Electoral College Vote: James Madison: 128; DeWitt Clinton: 89; (not voted): 1
Popular Vote: unavailable

The 1812 presidential election pitted incumbent James Madison against his Federalist CHALLENGER DeWitt Clinton. The major issue in the campaign was the war against Great Britain. Madison, a Democratic-Republican, defeated Clinton in a closely contested race. Madison won 11 of 18 states and captured 128 electoral votes, while Clinton took seven states with a total of 89 electoral votes.

In June 1812, the U.S. Congress declared war on Great Britain. The conflict between the two nations had been growing steadily for a time. When he took office in 1809, President Madison inherited from his predecessor, Thomas Jefferson, a dangerous situation. Britain was harassing American ships and impressing American sailors into the British navy. Madison attempted to forestall any war by prohibiting trade with Britain. However, the drumbeat for war in America grew, especially after the election of "War Hawks" in the 1810 CONGRESSIONAL ELECTIONS. These members of Congress urged Madison to take a tougher line against England. After failed negotiations, Madison asked for a war declaration in June 1812.

The members of Madison's party generally supported the war. Ever since Madison had helped create the DEMOCRATIC-REPUBLICAN PARTY in the early 1790s, the Democratic-Republicans had voiced opposition to Great Britain and sided with France during the continental wars. During the PRESIDENTIAL ELECTION the Democratic-Republicans sought to exploit the war for their own political purposes.

Most Federalists opposed the conflict. The Federalists were largely centered in New England, and they believed a war with Britain would damage that region's economy. As descendants of the party established by Alexander Hamilton, the Federalists looked favorably upon Britain, and the New England Federalists caustically described the conflict as "Mr. Madison's War." Every Federalist in the House of Representatives and the Senate voted against the declaration of war.

The news from the front initially benefited Madison's opponents. The country was ill-prepared for war, and in the first few months, the military suffered several humiliating defeats. An alliance developed between the Federalists and dissident Republicans, and the two groups worked together in an effort to defeat Madison. Leading Federalists made a calculated decision not to nominate a candidate of their own and instead threw their support behind DeWitt Clinton, a former New York senator and mayor of New York City. Clinton came from one of the nation's most prominent families; his uncle George (who died in April 1812) served as vice president under Thomas Jefferson and James Madison. Elected New York's lieutenant governor in 1810, Clinton was a very appealing candidate. He was tall (his supporters called him the Magnus Apollo), a good public speaker, and a successful politician. New York Republicans who opposed the war pushed for him as a presidential candidate, and he accepted the call. In September, after the Federalists held a convention and decided to go with Clinton as their candidate, they put forward Jared Ingersoll of Pennsylvania as the vice presidential nominee.

The Democratic-Republican Party backed James Madison for reelection. The 61-year-old Virginian was at the pinnacle of his illustrious political career. He had been a DELEGATE to the Constitutional Convention, served as a member of Congress, and had been Thomas Jefferson's secretary of state. Madison also played an instrumental role in the formation of the Democratic-Republican Party during the 1790s. Madison was an extraordinarily skillful legislator and politician, but he lacked Clinton's dynamism. Short (only five feet four inches) and sickly, Madison was a poor public speaker who shied away from public appearances. Madison benefited from the custom of the time that dictated that candidates for elected office did not give addresses or attend rallies. For his part, Madison pretended to be too consumed by the responsibilities of his office to pay any attention to the campaign. Behind the scenes, however, Madison played a vital role in the shaping of the reelection effort. In an effort to help his chances in the Northeast and New England, the Democratic-Republican congressional caucus nominated Massachusetts governor Elbridge Gerry to serve as his RUNNING MATE.

The war overshadowed all other issues. Since neither man openly campaigned, the burden of getting their messages out fell to the parties. The Democratic-Republicans presented a united front and a unified message. The war was just, Democratic-Republicans argued, and necessary to secure independence from Britain once and for all. But DeWitt Clinton and his followers lacked a coherent message, and they offered different positions to different audiences. To northerners Clinton was portrayed as a staunch opponent of "Mr. Madison's War" and a friend to commercial interests. In states where the war was more popular, Clinton tried to sway voters by contending Madison was an incompetent commander in chief and that Clinton would end the conflict sooner by waging it more vigorously.

The voting transpired over two months during the fall. Of the 18 states in the Union, half allowed for a POPULAR VOTE, while the other nine chose their electors in the state legislatures. The early returns were from New England, an area in which Clinton did very well. He won all of New England except Vermont. The results from other states slowly trickled in, with Madison capturing most of the South and the West. The election hinged on the tallies of New York and Pennsylvania. Clinton won his home state,

taking 29 electoral votes, but Madison carried Pennsylvania, and with it, reelection.

The 1812 election was the first contest to be held during a time of war. President Madison and his supporters linked the two and used the war to gain political advantage, yet the bad news blunted much of the support Madison received from the general willingness of the American public to rally around a president during a crisis. The Federalists and renegade Republicans such as Clinton did not shy away from criticizing the war, and they might have gained as much from the unpopularity of the war as Madison benefited. Although no records were kept of the popular vote, it is likely that the final results mirrored the ELECTORAL COLLEGE, with Madison winning by a relatively narrow margin. The 1812 election is also significant in that it was the last campaign in which the FEDERALIST PARTY would be a major factor. Their opposition to war cost them dearly when in December 1814 a group of 26 Federalists met in Hartford, Connecticut. The delegates at the convention offered a resolution in support of secession, and even though the measure failed, it cast them as unpatriotic, especially after news of a dramatic victory by American forces at the Battle of New Orleans.

Further reading: Cogliano, Francis D. *Revolutionary America, 1763–1815: A Political History.* New York: Routledge, 1999; Hickey, Donald R. *The War of 1812: A Forgotten Conflict.* Urbana: University of Illinois Press, 1989.

—Justin P. Coffey

presidential election 1816

Winning President and Vice President: James Monroe and Daniel D. Tompkins
Number of States: 19
Major Candidates (Party Affiliation): James Monroe (Democratic-Republican); Rufus King (Federalist)
Electoral College Vote: James Monroe: 183; Rufus King: 34; (not voted): 4
Popular Vote: unavailable

The 1816 presidential election matched Democratic-Republican James Monroe of Virginia against Federalist Rufus King of New York. Monroe defeated King in a landslide. The Virginian won 16 of 19 states and 183 electoral votes. King, the standard-bearer of the Federalists, managed to take only Massachusetts, Delaware, and Connecticut, for a total of 34 electoral votes.

The 1816 campaign was the last in which the Federalists fielded a candidate for the presidency. Their support had been dwindling, and their fierce opposition to the War of 1812 decimated the party. Since Alexander Hamilton created the FEDERALIST PARTY in the 1790s, the Federalists had always sought close relations with Great Britain. When the war between the United States and Britain broke out in 1812, most Federalists staunchly opposed the war. In December 1814, a small group of prominent Federalists from five states met in Hartford, Connecticut. The members of the convention assembled after the Massachusetts legislature urged New England states to meet to discuss the problems confronting the region. During the convention, the DELEGATES debated a plank calling for secession from the union. The proposal was voted down, and the final resolutions merely condemned the war and its impact on the New England economy and called for the adoption of several constitutional amendments. However, shortly after the convention, the United States and Great Britain signed a treaty ending the conflict, and Americans received word of a tremendous victory by General Andrew Jackson in New Orleans. The timing of these events was extremely damaging to the Federalists, as they seemed unpatriotic.

By the 1816 election season, the Federalists were in serious decline. The remaining party members resided in a few New England states. They decided to launch a half-hearted campaign for the presidency. No candidate stepped forward for the Federalist NOMINATION, but a small group initiated a plan to back New Yorker Rufus King. The 61-year-old King had an illustrious political career. King served as a delegate from Massachusetts at the Constitutional Convention. He then moved to New York and was elected a senator. Following his appointment as ambassador to Great Britain, King ran as the Federalist vice presidential nominee in 1804 and 1808, losing both times. In 1813, King returned to the Senate but suffered another political defeat in the 1815 New York gubernatorial contest. King did not seek the Federalist nomination for the presidency in 1816 and made no effort to campaign. He had actually supported the war, but his position did not garner him any support outside New England.

The Democratic-Republicans nominated James Monroe of Virginia. The incumbent, James Madison, following the precedent established by George Washington and continued by Thomas Jefferson, voluntarily stepped aside after serving two terms. His handpicked successor was Monroe, Madison's secretary of state and fellow Virginian. At the age of 18, Monroe had volunteered for service in the Virginia infantry and served under George Washington at Valley Forge. After the War for Independence, Monroe became active in POLITICS and was elected to the U.S. Senate in 1790. President Washington appointed Monroe minister to France. After being recalled in 1796, Monroe briefly retired from politics, but in 1800 he ran successfully for governor of Virginia. Monroe served again as minister to France under Jefferson. He retuned in 1808 in time to run for the Democratic-Republican nomination for president against James Madison. He lost the contest and suffered a breach with Madison. The two men eventually reconciled, and Madison picked Monroe as his secretary of war and secretary of state. Monroe was a diligent man of whom Jef-

ferson once claimed, "If you turned his soul inside out there would not be a spot on it." As the vice presidential candidate, the Democratic-Republicans selected New York governor Daniel Tompkins.

From the beginning of the race, there was virtually no doubt of the outcome, as Rufus King himself knew when he wrote to a friend in September 1816: "So certain is the result, in the opinion of friends in the measure, that no pains are taken to excite the community on the subject." The Federalists were divided and disgraced, while the Republicans were united. The Democratic-Republicans also had an effective PARTY ORGANIZATION, and their members worked diligently to secure voters for Monroe. In sharp contrast, the Federalists barely waged a campaign. There were few issues to debate. The United States was at peace and the economy, which had suffered before and during the war, was beginning to expand. Monroe sailed to an easy victory.

With James Monroe's victory, Virginia's hold on the presidency continued. Four of the first five chief executives were from Virginia. Monroe was also the last member of the Revolutionary generation to hold the office. The 1816 election is significant because it spelled the end of the Federalist Party. The first party system, which began in the 1790s, came to an end in that election. The Democratic-Republicans were firmly entrenched as the only major POLITICAL PARTY, a position they would hold for nearly 20 years.

Further reading: Cunningham, Noble E., Jr. *The Presidency of James Monroe.* Lawrence: University Press of Kansas, 1996; Skeen, C. Edward. *1816: America Rising.* Lexington: University Press of Kentucky, 2003.

—Justin P. Coffey

presidential election 1820

Winning President and Vice President: James Monroe and Daniel Tompkins
Number of States: 24
Major Candidates (Party Affiliation): James Monroe (Democratic-Republican)
Electoral College Vote: James Monroe (231); John Quincy Adams (1)
Popular Vote: unavailable

The election of 1820 was a unique election in American history because James Monroe, the incumbent president, was virtually unopposed in the contest. The DEMOCRATIC-REPUBLICAN PARTY had dominated POLITICS for the past two decades, and its opposition, the FEDERALIST PARTY, had become obsolete. The "Era of Good Feeling," following the War of 1812, carried Monroe into a second term as president of the United States.

The power of the Federalist Party, which had dominated politics in the first decade of the new nation, had been usurped by the Democratic-Republicans with the election of Thomas Jefferson in 1800. The Federalists retained some political force, but their power continued to diminish and was extinguished after the plans of the Hartford Convention were revealed, which showed that the Federalist Party opposed the War of 1812 and had met in Hartford to consider seceding from the United States. With the signing of the Treaty of Ghent and victory in New Orleans, opposition to the war appeared treasonous. The death of the Federalists left the Democratic-Republicans as the only POLITICAL PARTY in 1820.

James Monroe, the only president besides George Washington who fought in the American Revolution, joined the Continental Army at the age of 18. He fought at White Plains, Trenton, Brandywine, Germantown, and Monmouth, ending the war as a well-respected lieutenant colonel. He studied law under Thomas Jefferson and then served in the Continental Congress from 1783 to 1786. Monroe was sent to Paris as ambassador by Washington in 1794 but was removed in 1796. He returned to France in 1803 and negotiated the purchase of Louisiana.

Monroe was asked to join Madison's administration in 1811 as secretary of state. When the British forces attacked Washington, D.C., and burned the White House, Madison appointed Monroe the additional duty of secretary of war. By the end of the war, Monroe's reputation had grown throughout the United States, and with the support of Madison, he was elected to the presidency in 1816.

During Monroe's first two years in office, the country experienced a period of growth and prosperity. During a trip through New England, the Boston *Columbia Centinel* pronounced his visit an "era of good feeling." This term soon became synonymous with Monroe's administration. Despite the Panic of 1819 and the bitter debates over Missouri statehood, James Monroe emerged as the only candidate in the next PRESIDENTIAL ELECTION. Opposition to Vice President Daniel Tompkins failed to block his NOMINATION, and he, too, remained on the ticket.

The forgone conclusion of the election of 1820 prevented excitement over the vote. Apathy suppressed VOTER TURNOUT. For example, in Virginia, with 600,000 white residents, only 4,321 were reported to have voted. The ELECTORAL COLLEGE cast 231 votes for the incumbent. The one outstanding vote, from William Plumer of New Hampshire, went to the unexpecting John Quincy Adams. Plumer, a former Federalist, disliked Monroe and cast his lone protest vote. Ironically, John Adams, former Federalist president and a head of the Massachusetts electors, readily cast his vote for Monroe. Opposition to Tompkins as vice president was greater. He received only 218 electoral votes.

The election of 1820, although uneventful, was the calm before the storm. The election of 1824 witnessed four Democratic-Republicans running for the presidency. The Era of Good Feeling would fade away by the mid-1820s, as

would the Democratic-Republican Party itself. While Madison and Monroe easily won their terms in the presidency, FACTIONs within the party developed around issues such as states' rights and, most importantly, slavery. Although Monroe was able to temporarily squash the slavery dilemma with the Missouri Compromise, it would revive itself shortly.

James Monroe's presidency offered the Rush-Bagot Treaty, which neutralized the northern boundary with Canada, still owned by Great Britain. It accepted the Adams-Onis Treaty, in which the Spanish gave up rights to Florida. And most notable, Monroe lent his name to the protection of Latin American states from European colonization. The Monroe Doctrine made the United States the leading force in the Western Hemisphere. Monroe presided over a relatively tranquil time of American political history. The Era of Good Feeling made the election of 1820 one of the least riveting elections in American history.

Further reading: Ammon, Harry. *James Monroe: The Quest for National Identity.* New York: McGraw-Hill, 1971; Dangerfield, George. *The Era of Good Feeling.* Chicago: Ivan R. Dee, 1952.

—Sarah Miller

presidential election 1824
Winning President and Vice President: John Quincy Adams and John C. Calhoun
Number of States: 24
Candidates (Party Affiliation): John Quincy Adams (Democratic-Republican); Andrew Jackson (Democratic-Republican); William H. Crawford (Democratic-Republican); Henry Clay (Democratic-Republican); John C. Calhoun (Democratic-Republican); DeWitt Clinton (Democratic-Republican); William Lowndes (Democratic-Republican)
Electoral College Vote: John Quincy Adams: 84; Andrew Jackson: 99; William H. Crawford: 41; Henry Clay: 37
Popular Vote: John Quincy Adams: 108,740; Andrew Jackson: 153,544; Henry Clay: 47,136; William H. Crawford: 46,618

Following the Era of Good Feeling was the election of 1824, in which many contenders came forward to succeed Monroe. The FEDERALIST PARTY was largely defunct following the War of 1812, and each candidate in 1824 was a member of the DEMOCRATIC-REPUBLICAN PARTY. Because of the lack of a party difference to aid voters, candidates attempted to distinguish themselves on the basis of personality as well as sectional issues. The candidates addressed the Missouri Compromise, which established demarcations of slavery for the northern and southern sections of the Louisiana Purchase, and attempted to marshal support for its protest or advocacy on the basis of their regional loyalties and constituencies. In addition, candidates dealt with issues such as tariffs, internal improvements, banking, and public land policy.

The candidates made no effort to establish a Democratic-Republican platform, and each ran on the merits of his own record instead. These candidates also represented a new generation of leaders. They were men who were not part of the generation of elder statesmen. In addition, there were no candidates from Virginia. In the beginning there were seven prominent nominees. Three of those nominees, DeWitt Clinton, William Lowndes, and John C. Calhoun, either withdrew or died before the end of the campaign. The remaining four nominees, John Quincy Adams, Henry Clay, William Harris Crawford, and Andrew Jackson, were all qualified nominees in a race whose result would not be determined until three months after the GENERAL ELECTION by the House of Representatives.

Elimination of the Democratic-Republican congressional caucus was perhaps one of the biggest changes seen during this election. Due to the decline and disappearance of the Federalist Party, it no longer provided the unity necessary to beat an opponent. As a result, every candidate but Crawford looked elsewhere for the party NOMINATION in 1824. Moreover, Crawford, nominated by only 66 Democratic-Republican congressmen who showed up (out of 261), signified that the caucus had lost its power and prominence among the Democratic-Republican Party members and congressional leaders.

Due to the expiration of the usefulness of the congressional caucus, the other Democratic-Republican contenders used party conventions, legislative state caucuses, straw votes, and mass meetings to officially become candidates in the race for president. As an example, Calhoun was endorsed by the South Carolina legislature as early as December of 1821. Jackson was endorsed and supported by Tennessee in July 1822, but this was done more from the belief that his name would help other state politicians rise to congressional office than from a deep-seated conviction that Jackson was the man for the presidency. Clay obtained nominations and ENDORSEMENTs from Missouri in 1822, Kentucky in 1822, and Ohio in January 1823. Adams received a legislative endorsement by Maine and Massachusetts in January 1823. In this way, all the major presidential hopefuls became legitimate contenders.

Without the presence of party as an identifier in the elections, personal attacks were frequent in pamphlets and newspaper publications. Adams was criticized for his dress, Calhoun was portrayed as a young man consumed with ambition, Clay was depicted as a drunkard and a gambler, Crawford's honesty was questioned in light of the last election, and Jackson was portrayed as a simplistic military man.

As state after state allocated their electoral votes, it became clear that the contest was between Adams and Jackson for the presidency, although Clay remained a constant contender, garnering several states' electoral support. The results illustrated regional differences as well as support for each candidate. Overall, the southern states solidly voted for Jackson, and the North turned out almost exclusively for Adams. However, there were several states where close competition between Adams and Jackson emerged, and strong lobbying gained Jackson some much-needed electoral support in states such as New Jersey and Pennsylvania.

As the electoral votes returned and with the return of Congress in December 1824, the results illustrated that no one candidate had won the majority of electoral votes (Jackson 99, Adams 84, Crawford 41, and Clay 37). As a result of no single contender receiving 51 percent of the electoral votes, the election was thrown to the House of Representatives. The House members were, in effect, given carte blanche to make a decision as to who would be the next president of the United States. Because each state received only one vote for president in the House regardless of the number of representatives, small states such as Rhode Island had the

John Quincy Adams *(Library of Congress)*

same sway as the larger states such as Virginia and New York. Clay, having extraordinary influence as the SPEAKER OF THE HOUSE and no longer a contender in the election for president (as only the top three electoral vote recipients were considered and voted on by the House), found himself courted by the supporters of each candidate. After long thought, Clay threw his support behind Adams. He asserted that Jackson had too little experience in POLITICS and too much of a temper to successfully be president. However, there were allegations that Adams had agreed to make Clay secretary of state in exchange for his support. With the support and influence of Clay, Adams went on to win with the necessary 13 states. Surprisingly or not, his first appointment immediately thereafter, for better or more damagingly worse, was Clay to secretary of state.

In the election of 1824, no candidate (of the seven from the Democratic-Republican Party) received a majority of the electoral vote, and the office was closely decided by the House of Representatives, with charges of impropriety and PATRONAGE. As a result of this tumultuous and patronage-driven election, Jackson vowed to unseat Adams, and the competition for the presidential office in 1828 began almost immediately.

Further reading: Genovese, Michael A. *The Power of the American Presidency, 1789–2000.* Oxford: Oxford University Press, 2001; Milkis, Sidney, and Michael Nelson. *The American Presidency: Origins and Development, 1776–1998.* Washington, D.C.: Congressional Quarterly Press, 2003; Schlesinger, Arthur M., Jr., and Fred I. Israel, eds. *History of American Presidential Elections,* Volume I, *1789–1844.* New York: Chelsea House Publishers, 1971.

—Ryan Teten

presidential election 1828

Winning President and Vice President: Andrew Jackson and John Calhoun
Number of States: 24
Major Presidential Candidates (Party Affiliation): Andrew Jackson (Democratic-Republican); John Quincy Adams (National Republican)
Electoral College Vote: Andrew Jackson: 178; John Quincy Adams: 83
Popular Vote: Andrew Jackson: 647,286; John Quincy Adams: 508,064

The Election of 1828 took place between Andrew Jackson, a Democratic-Republican, and John Quincy Adams, a National Republican. Jackson and Adams also ran against each other in 1824. Even though Jackson won the popular and electoral vote in 1824, Adams was proclaimed the victor by the House of Representatives when three states that had voted for Jackson and three states that had voted for Henry Clay changed their votes to Adams. Jackson claimed that the states originally for Clay changed their votes as part of a corrupt bargain struck between Adams and Clay. He said that Clay agreed to support Adams in exchange for an appointment. When Adams appointed Clay secretary of state, Jackson felt this was proof of the corrupt bargain.

The corrupt bargain was one of the many charges Jackson made against Adams in his 1828 campaign. The 1828 presidential election was called one of the first true mudslinging contests and also one of the dirtiest elections in American history. Both Jackson and Adams made vehement charges against each other. Besides the corrupt bargain, Adams was also accused of misusing public funds when he supposedly bought gambling devices for the White House. However, it turned out the supposed gambling devices he bought were actually a chessboard and a pool table. Adams was also called an aristocrat and charged with treating the White House as his palace.

The charges made against Jackson were in some ways more damaging. Some of Jackson's actions in the military were questioned, and he was accused of executing militia deserters and of dueling. One pamphlet distributed was known as the "Coffin Hand Bill." It featured pictures of six coffins and gave a mostly one-sided story of six soldiers Jackson had court-martialed and executed during the Creek War in 1813. However, the most detrimental accusations involved Jackson's wife, Rachel.

Rachel Donelson Jackson was a divorcée, and it turned out that the paperwork for her divorce was incomplete when she married Jackson, making their marriage illegitimate. When the Jacksons continued to live together until they were lawfully married, Jackson's opponents branded them adulterers. The criticism of Jackson's wife was so great that it caused her much distress. She ended up dying before Jackson was inaugurated into office, and Jackson claimed that it was the humiliation from the accusations that killed her.

In order to spread the allegations against each other, Jackson and Adams both used their party's presses. The main newspapers used by the Democratic-Republicans were the Washington-based *United States Telegraph*, the *New-Hampshire Patriot*, and the *Argus of Western America*, based in Frankfort, Kentucky. The National Republicans relied mainly on the *National Intelligencer* and the *National Journal*. To make sure members of the ELECTORATE had access to these newspapers, congressmen frequently used their franking privileges to mail them. Both parties used their papers as a means to spread stories about the opposition as well as a way to disperse party news. Newspapers were also used to portray personal attributes of the two candidates. Referred to as "Old Hickory" or "Old Hero," Jackson was seen as a patriotic war hero who was a down-to-earth man with Jeffersonian Republican beliefs. In contrast, Adams was regarded as a more reserved man who was often thought of as being cold and austere.

Besides helping to print and disperse newspapers, the parties also increased their roles during the campaign in other ways. Although both parties held local rallies and county meetings, the Democratic-Republicans were much better at organizing than were the National Republicans. The Democratic-Republicans were led by two central committees, one in Nashville led by John Overton, and one in Washington chaired by banker John P. Van Ness. Also, a caucus of Jacksonians in Congress was coordinated by Martin Van Buren. From these central PARTY ORGANIZATIONS, local party organizations were created. The local organizations were often called "Hickory Clubs," and their purpose was to increase voter interest and participation. They did this using a variety of techniques, from town meetings, to barbecues and parades, to hickory pole raisings. The party organizations were especially good at identifying Jackson as "Old Hickory." Besides the hickory pole raisings, they also used small hickory poles to hold signs and used hickory brooms as a symbol for Jackson sweeping out filth and corruption.

Besides the amplified role of parties, the election of 1828 was also significant because of the increase in voter participation. The number of voters participating in the 1828 election nearly quadrupled from 1824. One of the reasons for this was because states started lowering VOTING REQUIREMENTS. Many states removed the property requirements that had been necessary to vote, which resulted in SUFFRAGE for virtually all white males. Also noteworthy was the way candidates were selected for the 1828 election. Instead of using congressional caucuses to choose the candidates, as had been done in the past, candidates were chosen by state conventions and state legislatures.

Although the 1828 contests focused more on the candidates than on issues, one issue that was particularly controversial was tariffs. Americans had different opinions regarding tariffs depending on the area of the country in which they resided. In the North, which was dominated by manufacturing interests, people favored high protective tariffs. However, the South was largely anti-tariff, and the West wanted protection of its raw materials. Jacksonians in Congress tried to accommodate these varying interests in the Tariff of 1828, also known as the Tariff of Abominations. The Tariff of 1828 placed heavy duties on imported raw materials, particularly hemp, wool, and iron. While this pleased people in the West, it was damaging to those in New England. New Englanders were further displeased because the tariff also levied a 10 cent per gallon duty on molasses and raised the duty on distilled spirits by 10 percent. By placing a high duty on iron products, the tariff gained support from Pennsylvania. The bill also safeguarded wool producers. However, it only partially protected manufacturers of woolen commodities.

The Tariff of 1828 was successful in gaining support from protectionist farmers in New York and Pennsylvania, and also from westerners, many of whom had voted for Clay in 1824. Even though the bill upset many New Englanders, Jacksonians were willing to sacrifice support there, as they were confident that Adams already had assured victory there. While the high protectionist rates also upset people in the South, the Democratic-Republicans were confident that southerners would not retaliate by voting for Adams.

In the end, the strategy proved successful, as Jackson won the South, West, Pennsylvania, and New York, while Adams won most of New England. Jackson received 178 electoral votes and 56 percent of the POPULAR VOTE, while Adams won only 83 electoral votes and 44 percent of the popular vote. Jackson had finally defeated his nemesis and won the presidency.

Further reading: Cole, Donald B. *The Presidency of Andrew Jackson.* Lawrence: University of Kansas Press, 1993; Roseboom, Eugene H. *A History of Presidential Elections.* New York: Macmillan, 1957; Skowronek, Stephen. *The Politics Presidents Make.* Cambridge, Mass.: Harvard University Press, 1997.

—Allison Clark Odachowski

presidential election 1832

Winning President and Vice President: Andrew Jackson and Martin Van Buren
Number of States: 24
Major Presidential Candidates (Party Affiliation): Andrew Jackson (Democratic); Henry Clay (National Republican); John Floyd (Independent); William Wirt (Anti-Masonic)
Electoral College Vote: Andrew Jackson: 219; Henry Clay: 49; John Floyd: 11; William Wirt: 7; (not voted): 2
Popular Vote: Andrew Jackson: 687,502; Henry Clay: 530,189; William Wirt: 101,051

Andrew Jackson originally said that he would serve only one term as president. However, when a falling-out took place between Jackson and his vice president, John Calhoun, Jackson decided to seek reelection in order to keep Calhoun from running. In many ways the election of 1832 was a seminal election, especially in terms of party structure and organization. It marked the first time that parties held national conventions to nominate candidates, as well as the first time party platforms were developed. It also was the first time that there was a viable third party in a presidential contest. Besides the progress made in the development of political parties, the election of 1832 was also significant because of the debates that took place regarding the Second Bank of the United States.

In 1832, political parties held national nominating conventions for the first time. Before 1832, nominees were chosen either by congressional caucuses, state legislatures, or nonrepresentative political meetings. The DELEGATES to the national conventions were chosen in a variety of ways depending on the organization and strength of the party in each state. Some of the ways delegates were selected included state or district conventions, local meetings, and informal caucuses.

The ANTI-MASONIC PARTY was the first of the parties to hold a nominating convention. They held their convention in Baltimore with 116 delegates representing 13 states. Although it was thought that John McLean would be nominated, the night before the convention he decided not to accept, which left the NOMINATION open for William Wirt. The National Republicans (not to be confused with the modern Republican Party) were next to hold their convention. Also holding their convention in Baltimore, they received a higher turnout than the Anti-Masons, with 168 delegates from 18 states and the District of Columbia. The Democrats were the last to hold their convention and never bothered to vote for their presidential nominee because there was such a large consensus that it would be Jackson. Instead, they focused on nominating a vice presidential candidate, which turned out to be Martin Van Buren. The Democratic convention was the largest held, with 334 delegates representing 23 states.

Besides being the first time parties held national nominating conventions, the 1832 election was also significant because it was the first time parties developed platforms. However, the platforms were not nearly as complex as the current ones. The platform of the National Republicans consisted of 10 separate resolutions regarding various issues, from protection of American industry to the spoils system. Some of the resolutions were debated by the delegates before being adopted by the full convention. The Democrats developed their platform in a somewhat different manner. Instead of deciding upon resolutions at their convention, newspapers encouraged local groups to meet and pass resolutions. The resolutions were then often published in newspapers and sent to nearby communities and states. Regardless of how the platforms were devised, they still set a precedent for future elections.

The 1832 election also marked the first time there was a viable third party. Animosity toward the Masons started with the disappearance of William Morgan in 1826, when he was about to write a book exposing the secrets of Masonry. The anti-Masonic movement continued to grow, eventually encompassing much of New England. Since Jackson and Clay were both high-ranking Masons, the anti-Masons thought the 1832 election would be a good time to enter a presidential candidate. Although the Anti-Masonic Party managed to win few votes outside New York and New England, it had an impact on the election by inadvertently weakening Clay's campaign by splitting the anti-Jackson vote.

PARTY ORGANIZATIONS also continued to grow stronger during this period. However, the parties were still not strong enough to outweigh the candidates. The parties were getting better at running campaigns, particularly the Democrats. They focused on mobilizing voters through various campaign activities such as parades, barbecues, pamphlets, and newspapers. Though the other parties were not as well organized, the National Republicans were excellent at political cartooning. They published a number of POLITICAL CARTOONS mocking Jackson, particularly regarding the relationship between Jackson and Van Buren and pertaining to the Second Bank of the United States.

The National Bank was the major issue of the 1832 campaign. Jackson was known to be largely against the bank, and often questioned its constitutionality. Even though the bank's charter did not expire until 1836, Clay was anxious to push the bank issue, hoping it would end Jackson's reelection bid. Nicholas Biddle, the president of the bank, asked Congress for a recharter early in 1832 even though he was warned not to by the Democrats. When the recharter passed both houses of Congress, Jackson vetoed the legislation. In his veto message, Jackson claimed that there were too many foreign investors in the bank and that it gave an unfair advantage to elite foreign and domestic institutions. About 30,000 copies of Jackson's veto message were distributed by the National Republicans in hopes that his own words would hurt him.

Besides debate surrounding the bank, there were a few other key issues in the election. One involved the treatment of Native Americans. Clay accused Jackson of refusing to enforce John Marshall's decision regarding Native Americans. Jackson refuted by claiming he had never been asked to enforce it. Another issue was Jackson's use of the spoils system. Even though Jackson was clearly in favor of rotation, it is estimated that he replaced only about one of 10 people, which was much less than his opponents claimed. Finally, tariffs were once again an issue, as they had been in the 1828 election. Southerners felt they were being unfairly disadvantaged by the Tariff of 1832. Leaders from South Carolina became so upset that they threatened to nullify the tariff or possibly secede from the Union if the South's interests were not taken into consideration. While these issues played a role in the 1832 election, they were second to the bank issue.

Ultimately, Jackson prevailed in the election. However, it was the only time in history that a president won reelection while receiving less of a percentage of the POPULAR VOTE than he had in the previous election. In 1832, Jackson received about 55 percent of the vote compared to 56 percent in 1828. Nevertheless, Jackson won with 219 electoral votes compared to Clay's 49 and Wirt's 7. John Floyd of Virginia received 11 electoral votes when South Carolina's electors, who had been chosen through its legislature, voted for him. In the end, Jackson felt his victory was an approval from the people of his handling of the bank situation and gave him a MANDATE to continue on a similar course.

Further reading: Cole, Donald B. *The Presidency of Andrew Jackson.* Lawrence: University of Kansas Press, 1993; Roseboom, Eugene H. *A History of Presidential Elections.* New York: Macmillan, 1957; Skowronek, Stephen. *The Politics Presidents Make.* Cambridge, Mass.: Harvard University Press, 1997.

—Allison Clark Odachowski

presidential election 1836

Winning President and Vice President: Martin Van Buren and Richard M. Johnson

Number of States: 26

Major Candidates (Party Affiliation): Martin Van Buren (Democrat); William Henry Harrison (Whig); Hugh L. White (Whig); Daniel Webster (Whig); Willie P. Mangum (Independent Democrat)

Electoral College Vote: Martin Van Buren: 170; William Henry Harrison: 73; Hugh L. White: 26; Daniel Webster: 14; Willie P. Mangum: 11

Popular Vote: Martin Van Buren: 764,176; William Henry Harrison: 550,816; Hugh L. White: 146,107; Daniel Webster: 41,201; Willie P. Mangum: unavailable

The presidential election of 1836 was a watershed in the development of American political parties. That year, for the first time since the days of the Federalist and Jeffersonian-Republican rivalry, two clearly identifiable parties, now the Democrats and the Whigs, actively campaigned against each other. Or at least this is the common interpretation. In reality, one of the "parties" in the equation was so disorganized as to hardly deserve the label of *party* at all. Animated as the Whigs were by their vehement and overwhelming dislike of Andrew Jackson, such a disposition provided the only real cement holding together what were, in fact, wildly disparate and only loosely organized political FACTIONS.

Ironically, given the temper and energy of the campaign, the most important figure in the presidential election of 1836 was not one of the candidates. He was outgoing president Andrew Jackson, and more than any other single person, he had been responsible for the reemergence of the often bitter party spirit. His opponents reviled him every bit as much as his followers loved him. The election was, in many ways, a referendum on the Jacksonian political agenda and Andrew Jackson in particular.

The salient question in 1836 seemed to be whether the political organization that had grown up under Jackson would continue to rule, and whether the policies that had emerged as "Jacksonian" would themselves continue. Probably the best known of these policies was Jackson's proclaimed "war" on the Second Bank of the United States. Henry Clay of Kentucky, in many eyes the leader of the Whigs in Congress, was the man most identified with the bank. Clay and his supporters believed that a national bank would best serve to guide, direct, and assist economic development throughout the nation.

Following the Panic of 1819, however, and amid the growing egalitarian spirit taking root in the 1820s, Jackson and others came to believe that the bank had been responsible for the economic depression and that, through its power to restrict loans, it worked only to the financial benefit of eastern and northern elites, purposefully excluding the interests of the South and West. To open economic opportunity to the "people," Jackson had vetoed a bank recharter bill in 1832 and then proceeded to remove all government funds from the bank. It made him wildly popular with his supporters, but utterly alienated politicians such as Clay and those who favored a more activist and energetic national government. In 1836, the bank episode still irritated Jackson's opponents, and many northern Whigs hoped eventually to reestablish the idea of a national government that could charter a bank and generally wield more power.

Another lingering bitterness from the Jackson administration had to do with the Nullification Crisis of 1832–33, in which South Carolina attempted to declare a federal tariff null and void, to which Jackson answered with a threat to use the army to see to it that national law was upheld. Jackson believed in states' rights, but he was also a patriotic nationalist, and he had no problem with the apparent dichotomy these positions involved. No state would be leaving the Union while he was president. South Carolina backed down. Burned by the failure of nullification and Jackson's response, anti-Jackson southerners flocked to the WHIG PARTY simply because it opposed Jackson, and not for any political positions their fellow northern Whigs might espouse.

Related to the nullification standoff was the increasing feeling in the South that the national government would bow to growing abolitionist pressure in the North and pass legislation against either slavery or the spread of slavery. During the election, Whig candidate Hugh White capitalized on this fear, warning that as the only true southerner, his election was the surest way to protect the institution of slavery. Democratic candidate Martin Van Buren, he reminded voters, was a New Yorker who might be sympathetic to abolitionist pressures.

Citizens who opposed Jackson during his two terms as president reflexively opposed Van Buren, Jackson's handpicked successor. Van Buren had served in the first Jackson administration as secretary of state and later minister to Great Britain. In Jackson's second term, he replaced John C. Calhoun as vice president, thereby becoming heir-apparent to the presidency. Everyone knew that Van Buren had the ENDORSEMENT of Jackson, and that simple fact was enough for many people to oppose him.

Democrats emerged from Jackson's two terms well organized as a party; Whigs, on the other hand, were quite the opposite. Nevertheless, to defeat Van Buren, they felt they had little alternative other than to downplay their differences and attempt to band together. As a result, even though the Democrats lined up their unified support behind Martin Van Buren at a formal nominating convention a full 18 months before the election, the divided Whigs were forced to offer up several legitimate candidates, distinguished primarily by sectional identification: Daniel Webster from Massachusetts, Hugh White from Jackson's home state of Tennessee, and William Henry Harrison of Indiana. The tactic they hoped to put in place was to flood the field with candidates and thus prevent any one man from receiving a majority of votes—in essence a replay of the election of 1824. Then the House of Representatives, where Whigs felt they had a greater voice, would step in to decide the election.

There was much organized campaigning by all sides. Party newspapers heralded their own candidates and lambasted the opposition. Countless political pamphlets explained the candidates' positions. Rallies, parades, and picnics took place throughout the Union. Because of their disparate nature, Whigs, however, operated at a disadvantage. As a party, they staged no convention, an acknowledgement, perhaps, of their widely differing views. After all, there were ardent abolitionists who called themselves Whigs alongside slaveholders who identified themselves in the same way. Webster was the "official" Whig candidate, though his name was on the BALLOT only in Massachusetts. White was identified as the Whig candidate in nine states, all of which were slave states. Harrison was on the ballot in 15 states. The lone indication of PARTY ORGANIZATION was that the party had been able to ensure that only one of these candidates was on any single state's ballot.

In the end, Jackson's legacy coupled with a broad suspicion on the part of voters of the centralizing tendencies apparent in many of the Whig policies won out. Martin Van Buren became the eighth president. He was immediately faced with a grave economic crisis that had been aggravated by Jackson's financial policies. He never quite recovered politically. He also proved that he possessed none of Jackson's appeal to the "common man" and, unlike his predecessor, would be elected to only a single term.

Further reading: McCormick, Richard P. *The Presidential Game: The Origins of American Presidential Politics.* New York: Oxford University Press, 1982; Remini, Robert V. *Andrew Jackson and the Bank War: A Study in the Growth of Presidential Power.* New York: Norton, 1967; Silbey, Joel H. *Martin Van Buren and the Emergence of American Popular Politics.* Lanham, Md.: Rowman & Littlefield, 2002.

—David A. Smith

presidential election 1840

Winning President and Vice President: William Henry Harrison and John Tyler
Number of States: 26

Candidates (Party Affiliation): William Henry Harrison (Whig); Martin Van Buren (Democratic)
Electoral College Vote: William Henry Harrison: 234; Martin Van Buren: 60
Popular Vote: William Henry Harrison: 1,274,624; Martin Van Buren: 1,127,781

Historians remark that the presidential election of 1840 represented the first modern presidential campaign in American history because of the nationwide excitement that the campaign generated among the American public. On December 4, 1839, members of the WHIG PARTY convened in Harrisburg, Pennsylvania, to select a candidate for the upcoming PRESIDENTIAL ELECTION. As the DELEGATES arrived at the convention, a number of them thought that Henry Clay of Kentucky would receive the NOMINATION because of his political experience and leadership skills within the Whig Party. On the first BALLOT, Clay was the FRONTRUNNER among the other candidates. However, some delegates expressed apprehensions in selecting Clay to head the Whig ticket for the upcoming election because he had suffered numerous defeats in previous presidential elections. Therefore, a number of delegates who supported General William Henry Harrison of Ohio promoted him for the party nomination. The delegates believed that Harrison, who had gained national fame for defeating Indian forces under the leadership of the Shawnee chief Tecumseh during the Battle of Tippecanoe and securing the Old Northwest at the Battle of the Thames during the War of 1812, would appeal to the American public because of his military record. The pro-Harrison delegates also noted that he made a strong showing in the 1836 PRESIDENTIAL ELECTION.

Clay's chances of winning the nomination dwindled away as the pro-Harrison delegates garnered support for their candidate. On the final ballot, Harrison won the nomination by receiving 148 votes, while Clay received 90 votes. General Winfield Scott of Virginia received only 16 votes. The delegates also nominated John Tyler of Virginia, who had defected from the DEMOCRATIC PARTY, for vice president. While Tyler's views differed from a majority of the Whig leaders', the delegates believed that nominating Tyler as Harrison's RUNNING MATE would strengthen the ticket because of his pro-southern IDEOLOGY.

The Whigs supported a variety of issues ranging from the establishment of a third national bank, high protective tariffs, internal improvements, and the sale of public lands. With the party representing such a diversified group, the delegates could not agree on which planks to put in the party platform. Thus, the delegates did not construct a party platform at the convention. Instead, the Whigs unified themselves under the idea that they opposed the Democratic Party and its ideology.

In May 1840, delegates of the DEMOCRATIC NATIONAL CONVENTION assembled in Baltimore, Maryland, to select

Woodcut created for the Whigs' "log cabin" campaign of 1840 for candidate William Henry Harrison   *(HarpWeek, LLC)*

a candidate for the upcoming presidential election. During the convention, the delegates renominated President Martin Van Buren of New York to head the Democratic ticket. They also constructed the first national party platform at the convention. Among the planks of the platform were a strict construction of the U.S. Constitution, support for federally funded internal improvements, federal assumption of state debts, and opposition to the resurrection of the Bank of the United States. At the conclusion of the convention, the delegates renominated Richard M. Johnson of Kentucky as Van Buren's running mate.

Upon learning of Van Buren's nomination, the Whigs sensed that they could win the presidential election. Prior to the election of 1840, the nation had entered into a severe financial depression. Ruin had spread throughout every major city as banks and businesses closed, unemployment rose, and farmers received low prices for their crops. The economic depression had resulted from an imbalance of trade between the United States and England, the collapse of cotton prices in the South, and land speculation. The Whigs ignored these various elements that caused the financial depression and blamed Van Buren for the country's economic condition. Members of the Whig Party maintained that Harrison would stabilize the American economy, but they remained vague on the policies he would use to accomplish this feat. Nevertheless, the Whigs' claim won Harrison support from western farmers and eastern businessmen in his bid for the presidency.

The Whigs' desire to win the presidential election of 1840 caused party leaders to stress Harrison's military career and his western background instead of discussing political and economic issues. They also developed slogans, songs, and symbols to promote Harrison's bid for the presidency.

For instance, "Tippecanoe and Tyler too" represented one of the many slogans the Whigs used throughout the 1840 campaign. Ironically, the Democrats' constant attacks against Harrison's character allowed the Whigs to develop their most successful campaign theme. For example, the editor of the Democratic *Baltimore Republican* maintained that if Harrison received a pension, he would spend the rest of his life sitting in a log cabin drinking hard cider. Upon learning of the newspaper article, the Whigs turned the editor's slanderous remarks into a campaign motto. Therefore, members of the Whig Party began to refer to Harrison as "the log cabin and hard cider" candidate. Capitalizing on their candidate's new image, the Whigs held great parades with log cabins and rolled hard-cider barrels down the streets. As Whigs served hard cider during these pro-Harrison rallies, individuals sang songs about pioneer days. The Whigs were successful in their campaign tactics as thousands of individuals attended these rallies.

During the campaign, the Whigs discredited Van Buren by portraying him as an aristocrat. They maintained that he spent large amounts of money on fine wines, foreign foods, and imported clothing. Van Buren, who was the son of a New York innkeeper, denied these allegations. Ironically, Harrison, who came from one of the first families in Virginia, represented the true aristocrat in the presidential campaign. Nevertheless, the tactic utilized by the Whigs caused the American public to oppose Van Buren because they regarded him as part of the eastern elite.

Nearly 80 percent of the eligible voters cast their ballots in the presidential election of 1840. After the votes had been tabulated, Harrison won the presidential election by receiving 234 electoral votes to Van Buren's 60 votes. Although Harrison defeated Van Buren by a landslide in the ELECTORAL COLLEGE, the POPULAR VOTE was rather close. Harrison received 1,274,624 of the popular votes, while Van Buren gained 1,127,781 of the popular votes. Among the states that Harrison carried were Connecticut, Delaware, Georgia, Indiana, Kentucky, Louisiana, Maine, Maryland, Massachusetts, Michigan, Mississippi, New Jersey, New York, North Carolina, Ohio, Pennsylvania, Rhode Island, Tennessee, and Vermont. The extent of Van Buren's unpopularity among the American public was illustrated by the fact that he failed to carry New York, which was his home state. During the election, Van Buren was able to carry only Alabama, Arkansas, Illinois Missouri, New Hampshire, South Carolina, and Virginia.

Further reading: Cleaves, Freeman. *Old Tippecanoe: William Henry Harrison and His Times.* New York: Scribner's Sons, 1939; Gunderson, Robert G. *The Log-Cabin Campaign.* Lexington: University of Kentucky Press, 1957.
—Kevin M. Brady

presidential election 1844

Winning President and Vice President: James K. Polk and George M. Dallas
Number of States: 26
Major Candidates (Party Affiliation): James K. Polk (Democrat); Henry Clay (Whig); James G. Birney (Liberty)
Electoral College Vote: James K. Polk: 170; Henry Clay: 105; James G. Birney: 6
Popular Vote: James K. Polk: 1,338,464; Henry Clay: 1,300,097; James G. Birney: 2,300

For American voters in 1844, the lingering issue of Texas annexation (the republic had won its independence from Mexico in 1836) demonstrated how sectional tensions were not far from the surface in antebellum national POLITICS. Since the 1830s, both Democrats and Whigs had attempted to fight political battles over nonsectional issues relating to economic recovery, such as banking, tariffs, and internal improvements. Beginning in 1844, however, a persistent effort to expand the boundaries of the United States westward would slowly push the issue of slavery to the center of presidential politics.

In the spring of 1844, President John Tyler and Senator John C. Calhoun submitted an annexation treaty to the U.S. Senate at the same time that Calhoun publicly informed the British that the expansion of slavery was "essential to the peace, safety, and prosperity" of the United States. Such an open statement linking slavery with annexation did not sit well with many Whigs and northern Democrats concerned about sectional strife, and the treaty to annex Texas went down to defeat. However, the annexation issue would not rest with the treaty's rejection, and the DEMOCRATIC PARTY's presidential victory in the fall of 1844 demon-

strated the resolve of many southerners to fight for an empire friendly to the rights of slaveholders.

Both of the leading contenders for the Democratic and Whig NOMINATIONS in the spring of 1844, Martin Van Buren and Henry Clay, had opposed the Texas annexation treaty. Initially, this was more of a problem for Van Buren than for Clay, since large numbers of "Calhoun" Democrats from the South clamored for a nominee who would champion the Texas cause. At the DEMOCRATIC NATIONAL CONVENTION in the late spring, southern DELEGATEs blocked Van Buren's nomination through eight BALLOTs due to the former president's lack of the necessary two-thirds majority to secure the nomination. On the ninth ballot, weary Democrats nominated the first "dark-horse" candidate in presidential history, James K. Polk of Tennessee. Polk was a strong advocate of Texas annexation, and after his nomination, a close associate of John Calhoun exulted: "We have triumphed. . . . Polk is nearer to us than any public man who was named. He is a large Slave holder and [is for] Texas . . . out and out."

During the course of the campaign, Polk and the Democrats evinced clear support for territorial expansion in both the South and North by endorsing in their platform the annexation of the Oregon Territory, a region ill-suited for slavery. The Democrats also had some success at playing on the racial fears of northerners who disliked free blacks with the bizarre claim that Texas would attract free blacks away from border states. Additionally, Polk was able to convince some protectionist Democrats in the North that he was not a doctrinaire supporter of free trade. In contrast, Clay and the Whigs suffered from their candidate's apparent shifting of positions on Texas that alienated more voters than it attracted.

By the summer of 1844, the Whigs faced an antislavery insurgency from the newly formed Liberty Party, led by its nominee, abolitionist James Birney. Even as Clay had come out against Texas annexation, he also claimed in the summer of 1844 that he had no problem with annexation as long as it did not lead to sectional discord. Many antislavery Whigs joined with the recently formed Liberty Party to register their distaste for Whig politicians such as Clay, who, besides being a slaveholder, had appeased the southern "slave power" by refusing to speak decisively against Texas annexation. The Liberty Party's platform of 1844 (like its platform in 1840) boldly called for the abolition of slavery in the District of Columbia as well as in interstate slave trading, and called on Congress to bar the admission of new slave states into the Union. While these ideas occupied the fringe of national politics in 1844, they caused problems for the Clay campaign. If Clay had won the Liberty Party votes in New York State, he would have won both the state and the GENERAL ELECTION.

The Democrats, on the other hand, were able to solidify support for their party from among the largely Catholic foreign-born element in the North by criticizing the Whig's nomination of Theodore Frelinghuysen, a leading Presbyterian clergyman and temperance activist. The issue of Frelinghuysen's nomination convinced many immigrants that the WHIG PARTY belonged solely to moralizing, orthodox Protestants. On the eve of the election, so many Irish Americans registered for the Democrats that one Whig asserted "Ireland has reconquered the country which England lost."

The results of the election of 1844 demonstrated that the annexation of Texas commanded widespread support in the country. Many Americans in the North and South believed that the United States possessed a "manifest destiny" to expand to the Pacific and did not see a potential conflict between free labor and slaveholders over the nature of the West's development. Instead, Americans frequently viewed westward expansion as an attempt to repel the influence of monarchies and to provide for the country's economic future. In the short term at least, such expansionism risked war with Mexico, even as it spoke to the almost inevitable future prospect of the United States extending to the western coast of North America.

Further reading: Bergerson, Paul H. *The Presidency of James K. Polk.* Lawrence: University Press of Kansas, 1987; Merk, Fredrick. *Slavery and the Annexation of Texas.* New York: Knopf, 1972.

—Ryan Jordan

presidential election 1848
Winning President and Vice President: Zachary Taylor and Millard Fillmore
Number of States: 30
Candidates (Party Affiliation): Zachary Taylor (Whig); Lewis Cass (Democrat)
Electoral College Vote: Zachary Taylor: 163; Lewis Cass: 127
Popular Vote: Zachary Taylor: 1,360,967; Lewis Cass: 1,222,342

While the status of slavery in the territory newly acquired from the Mexican War represented a key issue among the American public during the presidential election of 1848, Whigs and Democrats remained vague on this question throughout the campaign in an attempt to appeal to both northerners and southerners. Therefore, the presidential campaign was fought with limited enthusiasm and practically without an issue.

In June 1848, members of the WHIG PARTY convened in Philadelphia, Pennsylvania, to nominate a candidate for the upcoming PRESIDENTIAL ELECTION. Among the leading candidates at the convention were General Zachary Taylor, Henry Clay of Kentucky, General Winfield Scott of New Jersey, and Senator Daniel Webster of Massachusetts.

Many Whig politicians feared that nominating Clay would cost their party another chance at winning an election, so they seized upon Taylor as a candidate. Even though Taylor represented a clear favorite among a majority of the DELEGATES at the convention, some Whigs expressed apprehension in selecting Taylor for the NOMINATION because he had never held a political office. Additionally, others expressed concern that Taylor remained indifferent toward their party's principles. Nevertheless, pro-Taylor supporters reassured the delegates that their candidate epitomized their beliefs and IDEOLOGY. They also maintained that Taylor's military victory at the Battle of Buena Vista during the Mexican War had made him a national hero. The Whig Party had gained success in the 1840 PRESIDENTIAL ELECTION with William Henry Harrison, who was a military hero, and the delegates hoped to repeat this triumph in the 1848 election. Taylor won the Whig nomination on the fourth BALLOT, and Millard Fillmore of New York was selected as Taylor's RUNNING MATE.

While delegates at the Whig National Convention united in selecting a candidate for the upcoming presidential election, they divided over the question of the Wilmot Proviso, a bill designed to ban slavery in any territory that the United States acquired from the Mexican War. As proslavery and antislavery delegates argued over whether the Whigs should support this measure, party leaders avoided a sectional split by refusing to write a party platform at the convention.

As the Democrats convened in Baltimore, Maryland, to attend the DEMOCRATIC NATIONAL CONVENTION, Governor Lewis Cass of Michigan was the FRONTRUNNER among the candidates. Throughout the nomination process, Senator James Buchanan of Pennsylvania, John C. Calhoun of South Carolina, and Supreme Court justice Levi Woodbury received some consideration from the delegates, but they failed to receive enough support to defeat Cass. On the fourth ballot, Cass won the Democratic nomination. The delegates also selected General William Butler as Cass's running mate.

During the Democratic National Convention, the party experienced a split between the Barnburners and the Hunkers, who were New York FACTIONs of the DEMOCRATIC PARTY. The Barnburners, who supported the antislavery movement, opposed Cass's nomination because they viewed him as a "doughface," a northerner who favored southern principles. Nevertheless, the Hunkers, who supported the extension of slavery, favored Cass as a nominee because of his southern beliefs. Fearing that this divisiveness would hinder the party in the upcoming presidential election, the delegates at the convention attempted to ease the tension by avoiding any discussion of slavery. For example, delegates expressed delight over the French Republic that emerged amid the various revolutionary movements in Europe. Unfortunately, these efforts by the delegates failed to unite the Democratic Party, as the antislavery Barnburners defected from the party.

As the issue of slavery continued to divide members of both the Whig and Democratic parties, antislavery Democrats, abolitionists from the Liberty Party, and "Conscience" Whigs joined forces to form the FREE-SOIL PARTY in 1848. Members of the Free-Soil Party opposed the admission of any new slave states into the Union. In the summer of 1848, the party was strengthened with the addition of the Barnburners, who had recently defected from the Democratic Party.

At the Free-Soil Party's founding convention in Buffalo, New York, delegates nominated former president Martin Van Buren as their presidential candidate. Although Van Buren had a long association with the Democratic Party, members of the Free-Soil Party still favored him as their candidate because of his antislavery position. The CAMPAIGN SLOGAN of the Free-Soilers was "Free Soil, Free Speech, Free Labor, and Free Men." Before the delegates concluded their convention, they nominated Charles Francis Adams, son of John Quincy Adams, as Van Buren's running mate.

During the 1848 presidential campaign, Taylor refused to comment on the Wilmot Proviso because he did not want to alienate southern or northern voters. Unlike Taylor's vague stance on the slavery issue, Cass spoke out against the Wilmot Proviso because he opposed the federal government interfering with states' rights. As an alternative to the proviso, he proposed popular sovereignty, which would allow the individuals residing in the new territories that the United States acquired from Mexico to determine whether to permit slavery within their borders.

Throughout the campaign, Taylor opposed taking more territory from Mexico to compensate Americans for claims against the Mexican government. He believed that the acquisition of additional territory by the United States would increase the sectional struggle within the nation. Cass's position in regard to territorial expansion was in marked contrast to Taylor's because Cass openly advocated the acquisition of additional territory from Mexico. Cass viewed himself as an imperialist, and he believed the United States needed to expand its boundaries in order to improve its status among other nations. Throughout the presidential campaign, the Whigs attacked Cass's position because they believed his aggressive foreign policy would endanger the security of the nation.

The election of 1848 marked the first presidential election in which voting occurred nationwide on the same day. After the votes had been tabulated, Taylor won the presidential election by receiving 163 electoral votes to Cass's 127 votes. Taylor received 1,360,967 POPULAR VOTES, while Cass won 1,222,342 popular votes. Van Buren received 291,263 popular votes, but he failed to win any electoral votes. Even though Van Buren failed to carry a single state in the election, he received enough votes to tip the election in favor of Taylor. The states that Taylor carried during the election were Connecticut, Delaware, Florida, Georgia, Kentucky, Louisiana, Maryland, Massachusetts, New Jersey, New York, North Carolina, Pennsylvania, Rhode Island, Tennessee, and Vermont. Cass garnered support in the South and Northwest, but this combination of states was not enough to defeat Taylor. The states that Cass carried during the election were Alabama, Arkansas, Illinois, Indiana, Iowa, Maine, Michigan, Mississippi, Missouri, New Hampshire, Ohio, South Carolina, Texas, Virginia, and Wisconsin.

Further reading: Dyer, Brainerd. *Zachary Taylor.* Baton Rouge: Louisiana State University Press, 1946; Hamilton, Holman. *Zachary Taylor: Soldier in the White House.* Indianapolis: Bobbs-Merrill, 1941; McKinley, Silas Bent, and Silas Bent. *Old Rough and Ready: The Life and Times of Zachary Taylor.* New York: Vanguard Press, 1946.

—Kevin M. Brady

presidential election 1852

Winning President and Vice President: Franklin Pierce and William R. King
Number of States: 31
Major Candidates (Party Affiliation): Franklin Pierce (Democrat); Winfield Scott (Whig)
Electoral College Vote: Franklin Pierce: 254; Winfield Scott: 42
Popular Vote: Franklin Pierce: 1,601,117; Winfield Scott: 1,385,453

By 1852, many of the earlier political squabbles that had been so divisive, such as the protective tariff and a national bank, were retreating into the background, while the issue of slavery was beginning to dominate political discussion. Party leaders of both the Whigs and the Democrats were finding it increasingly difficult to keep their ranks in order over the issue, and crafting a national platform that could appease both pro-slavery and antislavery wings of a party was becoming nearly impossible.

Two years before the election, Congress had passed a handful of programs known collectively as the Compromise of 1850 providing for the admission of California as a free state, the organization of the other territories gained via the Mexican War by the principle of "popular sovereignty" (that is, the territories themselves decided whether to allow slavery or not), the abolition of slave trading in Washington, D.C., and a far tougher fugitive slave law. It was a true compromise in the sense that no one was happy with it, and in the next PRESIDENTIAL ELECTION, its most controversial elements would loom large in deciding the candidates.

As early as 1846, when Pennsylvania Democrat David Wilmot introduced a motion to ban slavery in any territory gained in the Mexican War, the Democrats had to deal with a forceful free-soil movement in opposition to the pro-slavery wing. In the election of 1848, in fact, many Democrats bolted the party to vote for Free-Soil candidate Martin Van Buren rather than support Senator Lewis Cass of Michigan, who favored popular sovereignty. As a result of this party split, the Whig candidate and Mexican War hero Zachary Taylor won the White House. In July 1850, Taylor died suddenly, and Vice President Millard Fillmore of New York, a pro-slavery Whig, became the chief executive.

Losing the election of 1848, however, did not cause the Democrat FACTIONS to make peace with each other. On the contrary, by the 1852 convention to nominate the presidential candidate, the factions were strong enough to block any particular nominee. Dedicated supporters of Lewis Cass, those of his fellow senator Stephen Douglas of Illinois, along with those of former secretary of state James Buchanan of Pennsylvania, forced the convention to take almost 50 BALLOTS before finally picking a compromise candidate. On the 49th ballot the DELEGATES chose Franklin Pierce of New Hampshire, a handsome and well spoken, if relatively unknown, former senator, regarded to be sympathetic to southern interests, as the candidate. William King of Alabama accepted the NOMINATION for vice president, ensuring at least the appearance of a national ticket.

Many influential Whigs, meanwhile, especially men such as William Seward of New York, were working hard to make their party fully embrace a dedicated free-soil position, if only because abolition remained out of the question. The Fugitive Slave Law—an element of the complicated Compromise of 1850 that in essence made assisting an escaped slave a federal crime—rankled many northern Whigs, while southern Whigs eyed men such as Seward and his followers with deep suspicion at best. For their part, they demanded that whoever the nominee was, he vigorously endorse the Compromise of 1850, particularly the Fugitive Slave Law, for which they had labored hard.

Eventually, the two most promising candidates who emerged were the sitting Whig president, Millard Fillmore, and another heroic general from the Mexican War, Winfield Scott. Like Taylor before him, Scott's political opinions were not widely known, although he privately supported the compromise. Fillmore had already alienated many Whigs, particularly Seward's allies, by his ardent support of the Compromise of 1850 and his later purge from his administration of anyone who had opposed it. At any rate, it took 53 ballots before the delegates agreed on Scott, and that only after his supporters agreed to southern demands that the Whig platform pledge the party to the strict enforcement of the Fugitive Slave Law.

Outraged by these proceedings, ardent free-soil Whigs soon after held their own convention and nominated their own antislavery ticket headed by New Hampshire senator John P. Hale. Predictably, this faction took votes away from Scott. But Scott's pledge to enforce the Fugitive Slave Law did not necessarily endear him to southern Whigs, either, who still feared the influence of men such as Seward on any possible Scott administration.

Again there were pamphlets, newspapers, rallies, and all types of hyperbole and spectacle engineered either to the support of one candidate or to frighten voters away from him. The actual candidates, however, took little part in these events, although Scott's advisers, hoping to capitalize on his service in the army and desperately hoping to avoid having to concentrate on anything regarding slavery, did convince him to go on a tour of military hospitals. The results were poor at best due to Scott's awkwardness before a crowd.

When the results finally came in, it was noticeable how poorly the Whig ticket had done in the southern states. Of slave states, Scott carried only Kentucky and Tennessee. This is not to say the Whigs fared much better among free states, where they won only Massachusetts and Vermont. Despite the poor showing, Pierce won the presidency by only about 50,000 votes of more than 3 million cast. All in all, the election was the beginning of the end for the Whig COALITION, which never quite overcame its inherent sectional qualities and which finally and decisively broke apart two years later over the Kansas-Nebraska Act.

Further reading: Smith, Elbert B. *The Presidencies of Zachary Taylor & Millard Fillmore.* Lawrence: University Press of Kansas, 1988.

—David A. Smith

presidential election 1856

Winning President and Vice President: James Buchanan and John C. Breckinridge
Number of States: 31
Major Candidates (Party Affiliation): James Buchanan (Democrat); John C. Fremont (Republican); Millard Fillmore (American, Know Nothings)
Electoral College Vote: James Buchanan: 174; John C. Fremont: 114; Millard Fillmore: 8
Popular Vote: James Buchanan: 1,832,955; John C. Fremont: 1,339,932; Millard Fillmore: 871,731

The campaign of 1856 commenced against the backdrop of sectional violence over the question of slavery's expansion into western territories. After Congress allowed settlers of the Nebraska Territory (present-day Kansas, Nebraska, and parts of the Dakotas and Montana) to determine by election the future of human bondage within their prospective states, violence soon erupted in eastern Kansas when some settlers were determined to circumvent the ballot box in support of slavery. Antislavery residents responded in kind, and one of them, John Brown, led a murderous nighttime raid in Pottawatomie Creek, Kansas, that resulted in five deaths. This act set off a full-scale guerrilla war in the territory, and many newspapers throughout the United States headed their news items from Kansas in 1855 with the phrase "Progress of the Civil War."

The sectional crisis over the Nebraska Territory precipitated the formation of the REPUBLICAN PARTY in 1854. Disgusted by politicians (both Democratic and Whig) who had allowed the potential expansion of slavery into territories previously set aside as free by an act of Congress (such as Kansas and Nebraska), the Republican Party committed itself to oppose any further extension of slaveholding. The Republicans were the first party in American history ever to assert this, and the party was therefore the first purely sectional party in U.S. history. Republicans also represented the dominant, northern, evangelical Protestant culture viewed by many as the conduit for the rise of industrial capitalism in the United States.

The Republicans, in addition to opposing the extension of slavery, advanced unabashed support for government subsidies to railroads and other agents of the transportation revolution. Furthermore, they roundly condemned the "relic of barbarism" represented by Mormon polygamy. However, those who advanced economic modernization and a cohesive Protestant national culture did not all unify politically behind the Republicans in the 1850s; many, called alternatively KNOW-NOTHINGS or Americans, led a crusade against the political power of immigrants (especially Catholics) who were then beginning to stream into an industrializing North. The divided nature of those opposed to the Democrats likely prevented the Republicans from gaining the presidency in 1856, but the ominous consequences of a singularly southern victory for Democrats in 1856 could hardly be ignored by contemporaries who saw the formation of the Republican Party as an act of revolution.

Holding their convention in Philadelphia in June, the first REPUBLICAN NATIONAL CONVENTION nominated for the presidency the leader of the 1846 Bear Flag Revolt in California, John C. Frémont. By choosing an inexperienced politician lacking a detailed public record, the Republicans took a calculated gamble to broaden support for their fairly radical platform. Passed over for the NOMINATION were men such as William Seward and Samuel Chase, who were widely known in the country for their strong antislavery beliefs. Among the Democrats, the convention rejected both President Franklin Pierce and the recognized party leader, Senator Stephen Douglas, and instead selected the former congressman and ambassador James Buchanan. Buchanan's main attribute was having had the good fortune to be out of the country during the Nebraska controversy, and therefore he had no public record to criticize regarding the slavery issue. The American Party, appealing primarily to former Whigs in the southern states, nominated President Millard Fillmore, even while many American Party members in the North chose to join the Republican Party.

The issues of slavery and the Union's future rarely left center stage in the 1856 presidential campaign. At a meeting of Frémont supporters in Buffalo, Republican Party members demanded a new government maintaining "before the world the rights of men rather than the privilege of masters. The contest ought not to be considered a sectional one but the war of a class—the slaveholders—against the laboring people of all classes." In what would become a rather famous chant, thousands of Republican faithful marching in torch-lit parades throughout the North in 1856 intoned "Free Soil, Free Labor, Free Men, Frémont!" Throughout the free states, many newspapers, universities, and intellectual leaders took part in what was termed a "great moral crusade" to stop the "slaveocracy" and its attempt to overrun the Kansas Territory.

For their part, the Democrats hammered away at the Republicans' support for sectional POLITICS that threatened to destroy the American nation. Frémont's own father-in-law, Thomas Hart Benton, supported Buchanan because he believed the Republicans were "treading upon a volcano that is liable at any moment to burst forth and overwhelm the nation." Democrats also played upon racist fears of millions of slaves being liberated by "Black Republicans." The election, read one party document, would determine whether white Americans preferred African-American rights above "their own race . . . color, and Union."

Besides using the issues of race and disunion to discredit the opposition, Buchanan supporters also attempted to take votes away from the Republicans in favor of the American Party by claiming that Frémont was secretly a Catholic. Indeed, Frémont's father had been a Catholic, and the former general had been married by a Catholic priest, but by the 1850s Frémont worshipped at an Episcopalian church. Nonetheless, the Republican nominee would not openly disavow his Catholic past out of a personal belief that religious convictions should not prevent an American from reaching the presidency. In a further effort to discredit Frémont personally as an incompetent upstart, the Democrats attacked Frémont's dealings with a defaulted California financial firm, Palmer, Cook, and Company, that owed nearly $100,000 in debt to the state. Democrats also claimed that Frémont had acted in a cruel and rapacious manner with native Californians during the Bear Flag Revolt.

Working in the Democrats' favor had been the fact that by the fall of 1856 the Kansas situation had been pacified by a new territorial governor, John Geary. This reduced the immediacy of the crisis over slavery in the West. By October, it was clear from state ELECTIONS in Indiana and Pennsylvania that Buchanan and the Democrats had the upper hand. Many former Whigs turned to Fillmore and the American Party because they believed the Republicans were irresponsibly driving a wedge between the two sections over slavery. The PRESIDENTIAL ELECTION was in actuality two elections, between Frémont and Buchanan in the North and between Fillmore and Buchanan in the

South. The crucial struggle between Buchanan and Frémont took place in the lower North (i.e., New Jersey, Pennsylvania, Indiana, and Illinois). In part with Fillmore's help, Buchanan won all four states and was therefore elected president.

Further reading: Nevins, Allan. *Fremont: Pathmaker of the West.* New York: Appleton-Century, 1939; Klein, Philip S. *President James Buchanan.* University Park: Pennsylvania State University Press, 1962.

—Ryan Jordan

presidential election 1860

Winning President and Vice President: Abraham Lincoln and Hannibal Hamlin
Number of States: 33
Major Candidates (Party Affiliation): Abraham Lincoln (Republican); Stephen A. Douglas (Democrat); John C. Breckinridge (southern Democrat); John Bell (Constitutional Union)
Electoral College Vote: Abraham Lincoln: 180; Stephen A. Douglas: 12; John C. Breckinridge: 72; John Bell: 39
Popular Vote: Abraham Lincoln: 1,865,593; Stephen A. Douglas: 1,382,713; John C. Breckinridge: 848,356; John Bell: 592,906

The presidential election of 1860 shattered the delicate political balance between southern (slave) states and northern (free) states that had existed since the earliest days of the United States. The election was a four-way political match. The young REPUBLICAN PARTY nominated Abraham Lincoln to face off against a splintered DEMOCRATIC PARTY. Stephen Douglas led the northern Democrats, and the southern FACTION nominated John Breckinridge. A fourth party, the Constitutional Union Party, fielded John Bell to challenge the SOUTHERN DEMOCRATS.

The presence of four viable political parties prevented any one party from winning the nationwide POPULAR VOTE, though Abraham Lincoln's Republican Party managed a solid victory in the ELECTORAL COLLEGE. The Republican Party swept the northern and western states, earning 180 electoral votes, almost 60 percent of the 303 total electoral votes. Breckinridge's southern Democrats finished second, with 72 electoral votes that came mainly from the Deep South. The northern Democrats managed just 12 electoral votes, winning only Missouri and splitting the vote in New Jersey. The Constitutional Union Party collected 39 electoral votes from the "border states," Tennessee, Virginia, and Kentucky.

Lincoln emerged the clear winner in the Electoral College even though the Republican Party won only 40 percent of the popular vote. The northern Democratic Party, which won the fewest electoral votes, was second in the popular vote, with 30 percent. Not only did no party manage to win a majority of the popular vote, but the Republican Party was not even on the BALLOT in nine southern states. The Republicans managed to win not as a national party but as a regional party, which reflected the geographic cleavages of the time.

In 1860, the United States was a nation divided along geographic lines. Economic and social differences had become deeply entrenched. Technology was steadily reinforcing these differences. The northern states experienced industrialization and a large influx of immigrants, while improvements in transportation allowed continued westward expansion that enabled agrarian states in the Midwest to ship crops back east. The South also responded to technological change. The demand for cotton increased dramatically in the first half of the 19th century, and technology allowed the South to produce and process even greater amounts of cotton. The southern economy became increasingly dependent on the production of cotton, and as a result, the institution of slavery.

These changes also altered the demographics of the United States and as a result the political balance of power. Urbanization and immigration swelled the populations of northern states, while the agrarian southern states experienced no comparable increase in population. Similarly, admission of western free states into the Union threatened to even further destabilize the balance between slave and free states.

As the South's reliance on slavery increased, the objections of northerners and westerners to slavery increased as well. For decades, the political tension between slave states and free states had been carefully balanced, but by 1860 low-level fighting was already breaking out. Kansas's election of 1855 had turned violent, and radical abolitionists attempted an uprising at Harpers Ferry in 1859.

The election of Lincoln without the support of a single southern state convinced many southern voters that their rights were in jeopardy and that they had been politically marginalized. In late December 1860, South Carolina seceded from the Union, citing the election of Lincoln as the solidification of geographic battle lines. South Carolina was joined by other southern states, and the civil war that followed claimed the lives of 600,000 Americans.

The forces that divided the United States after Lincoln's election also divided the Democratic Party throughout the election. Stephen Douglas and his supporters argued that states should be free to decide on domestic issues such as slavery without federal involvement. This noninterventionist approach was rejected by supporters of John Breckinridge, who believed that this would even further tip the balance of power against the slave states. They advocated for active federal involvement to ensure the institution of slavery.

While the Democratic Party split over the slavery debate, the Republican Party, which had a strong abolition-

A nonpartisan satire of the 1860 presidential race portraying a map of the United States being torn apart by candidates Lincoln, Douglas, Breckinridge, and Bell *(HarpWeek, LLC)*

ist component, chose to play down the slavery issue. Instead, the Republicans built a party platform that emphasized westward expansion, railroad construction, and protective tariffs. The Constitutional Union platform centered on principles of "reconciliation, fraternity, and forbearance," but outlined few concrete proposals.

The field of candidates was as diverse as the party platforms. Three of the four presidential candidates had extensive experience on the national stage. Douglas was a prominent senator from Illinois. Bell had served multiple terms in the House of Representatives and as secretary of war. Breckinridge also served multiple terms in the House before becoming vice president. Only Abraham Lincoln had limited political experience. His one term in the House of Representatives was accompanied by a failed Senate bid against Stephen Douglas. For this reason, Lincoln was not the leading candidate for the Republican NOMINATION, but Lincoln supporters flooded the convention, which was held in Lincoln's home state of Illinois, and a comparatively inexperienced Lincoln won the nomination. While Lincoln

was the least experienced of the candidates, his oratorical abilities were a valuable asset on the campaign trail. The election of 1860 proved to be a catalytic moment that altered POLITICS in the United States. Lincoln's election sparked secession and civil war. It also transformed the Republican Party into a major national party that dominated U.S. politics during much of the post–Civil War era.

Further reading: Jaffa, Hary V. *A New Birth of Freedom: Abraham Lincoln and the Coming of the Civil War.* Lanham, Md.: Rowman & Littlefield, 2000; Luthin, Reinhard H. *The First Lincoln Campaign.* Englewood Cliffs, N.J.: Prentice Hall, 1960.

—Brian Urlacher

presidential election 1864

Winning President and Vice President: Abraham Lincoln and Andrew Johnson

Number of States: 36 (states that had seceded did not take part in the election)

Major Candidates (Party Affiliation): Abraham Lincoln
  (Republican); George B. McClellan (Democrat)
Electoral College Vote: Abraham Lincoln: 212; George
  McClellan: 21; not voted: 81
Popular Vote: Abraham Lincoln: 2,206,938; George
  McClellan: 1,803,787

As the 1864 election approached, the Civil War showed few signs of ending, though it had dragged on since April 1861. "Good riddance" was the frank opinion of many in 1861 when the southern states withdrew from the Union, particularly for those who had grown weary of either the political or moral strains that southern slavery had caused the nation over the years. Just as many, both North and South, were surprised at Lincoln's emerging determination and tenacity to hold the Union together—by war if necessary—when the southern states left. Then, in the midst of the fighting, Lincoln injected the idea of emancipation into the war, gladdening the hearts of abolitionists but at the same time angering the significant number of northerners who had little or no desire at all to fight for the freedom of black slaves.

An especially striking blow to the president's popularity came through the inconsistent and often downright poor battlefield performance of the Union army. Once the fighting commenced, most assumed it would be a short war. Hundreds of Washington's socialites flocked to the fields of northern Virginia in the summer of 1861 to watch their army humiliate the rebels and slam the door on secession. Their panicked flight back to the capital city when the Confederate army won the day became almost as famous as the battle itself. Shortly after, there began a seemingly endless chain of military reversals, with each reversal accompanied by the unceremonious firing of another Union general. Despite isolated successes, the Lincoln administration seemed utterly unable to manage the war and appeared to be drifting from humiliation to humiliation. As time wore on, more and more people questioned the wisdom of the war and felt that a negotiated peace and a simple end to the fighting was the only answer.

Lincoln, however, held to his convictions. In the wake of the Union victory at Gettysburg and the fall of the Confederate stronghold of Vicksburg, both coming in early July 1863, there was great hope that the tide was at last turning. It was, but not fast enough for Lincoln's detractors. By spring 1864, the Union army had again suffered terrible losses in the fields of Virginia, and even Lincoln's own REPUBLICAN PARTY wondered whether he was capable of winning reelection. Names of potential CHALLENGERS were whispered, including Treasury Secretary Samuel Chase, former Republican presidential candidate John C. Frémont, and even General Ulysses S. Grant, who, unlike the others, voiced no desire at all to have Lincoln's job.

But, as many were prone to forget, Abraham Lincoln was an adept politician and knew how to exert control over his party, especially at the all-important state and local levels at which he enjoyed great and broad support. By the time of the convention in June, Lincoln's NOMINATION was a certainty. Hoping, however, to win over those who considered themselves "Unionists" more so than Republicans, the convention reached outside the Republican ranks to nominate Unionist Democrat and former Tennessee senator Andrew Johnson as vice president. The ticket would therefore seem less strictly Republican and more broadly "Unionist," a label many party leaders thought would attract more support.

Two problems remained: the sizable population of Democrats who still had little personal regard for the president, and the unpredictable tides of the war. Bad news from the front could scuttle Lincoln's standing with the people faster than anything else. Into July and August there was little progress to report. Grant was stalled in his siege of Petersburg, Virginia, and General William T. Sherman was as yet unable to capture Atlanta, the key city of the Deep South. Consequent talk of another military draft galvanized the Democrats, who began to demand a negotiated end to the war. Frustratingly, Lincoln knew that such talk only encouraged Confederate president Jefferson Davis to hang on and prolong the struggle. By the end of August, he was convinced that he would not be reelected.

At their convention in Chicago that summer, the Democrats nominated General George B. McClellan as their candidate, with George Pendleton from the key state of Ohio as vice president, and adopted a platform calling for an immediate truce. Personally, George McClellan had nothing but disdain for Lincoln. Much of this came from Lincoln's having removed him from command of the Union army not once but twice, but McClellan had never thought much of the president or his abilities. While McClellan generally repudiated the calls for peace before reunion, he nevertheless loudly condemned Lincoln's handling of the war.

At last there came the definitive battlefield successes for which Lincoln had hoped. In the first days of September Sherman captured Atlanta. Northerners were jubilant at the news, and many rightly saw it as a defeat from which the Confederacy could not recover. News of Sherman's subsequent unopposed and destructive march to the Atlantic confirmed the scope of the Confederate collapse in Georgia. Lincoln's campaign was revived. Republican newspapers from big cities to small towns offered ringing ENDORSEMENTs of the president intended to energize supporters. Northern churches, especially Protestant congregations, actively campaigned for Lincoln's reelection. The army put together a program of temporary leave for soldiers to go home and vote, and when they did so, they voted overwhelmingly for Lincoln. Even as the popular tide seemed to turn, Democrats alternately condemned Lincoln's incompetence, his threats to civil liberties, and the goal of emancipation itself.

In the end, Lincoln was reelected, but McClellan carried New Jersey, Delaware, and Kentucky and garnered nearly 45 percent of the votes out of 4 million that were cast. Lincoln would live only a few weeks after his second inauguration, however, and in the wake of his assassination, Andrew Johnson became the new president.

Further reading: Carwardine, Richard J. *Lincoln.* Essex, England: Pearson-Longman, 2002; Donald, David Herbert. *Lincoln.* New York: Simon & Schuster, 1995.

—David A. Smith

presidential election 1868

Winning President and Vice President: Ulysses S. Grant and Schuyler Colfax

Number of States: 37 (the "unreconstructed" states of Virginia, Mississippi, and Texas did not participate in the election)

Major Candidates (Party Affiliation): Ulysses S. Grant (Republican); Horatio Seymour (Democrat)

Electoral College Vote: Ulysses S. Grant: 214; Horatio Seymour: 80; (not voted): 23

Popular Vote: Ulysses S. Grant: 3,013,421; Horatio Seymour: 2,706,829

The election of 1868 marked the first presidential contest to be held following the Civil War, and yet problems stemming from the war remained unresolved. Having won the war, Republican leaders faced the difficult task of reconstructing southern society, restoring the seceded states, and determining the status of 4 million newly emancipated African Americans.

Congressional Republicans united to enact moderate legislation aimed at disenfranchising former southern political and military leaders, establishing pro-Republican southern state governments, and securing a minimum of civil, legal, and political rights for blacks before readmitting the southern states into the nation. Alleging Republican RECONSTRUCTION subverted the Constitution, Democratic supporters rallied around President Andrew Johnson, who favored a lenient and rapid restoration of the southern states with little concern for minority rights. This political struggle pitted Congress against Johnson over Reconstruction policy and resulted in the first impeachment of a U.S. president in May 1868. REPUBLICAN and DEMOCRATIC PARTY leaders searched among a short list of candidates not tainted by disloyalty during the Civil War, extremist Reconstruction policies, or by the gloom of impeachment for their party's presidential nominee.

The main campaign issue centered on whether Reconstruction would proceed under a Republican presidency or be rolled back under a Democratic presidency. As the ELECTORATE cast their BALLOTs at the polls in 1868, the future of Reconstruction lay in the balance.

In May 1868, the Republican Convention assembled in Chicago, adopted a platform, and nominated a presidential candidate. They considered only one person for the NOMINATION, General Ulysses S. Grant. The nation's most popular citizen, Grant escaped Johnson's impeachment without harm to his reputation. Throughout Johnson's administration, the general walked a political tightrope, keeping his ambition for the presidency and his political views on Reconstruction private. Publicly, Grant appeared reluctant to accept the nomination but noted he would do so out of a sense of duty. On the first ballot, the DELEGATES nominated Grant unanimously. They then chose House Speaker Schuyler Colfax as the general's RUNNING MATE. The Republican platform upheld congressional Reconstruction, denounced the Johnson administration's obstructionism and corruption, and pledged equalization and reduction in taxes. In a decision that generated controversy among Republicans and Democrats alike, party leaders guaranteed SUFFRAGE for the freedmen in the South. However, the question of black suffrage in the northern and border states was left to the electorate of those states. Grant's CAMPAIGN SLOGAN, "Let us have peace," promised an end to bitter partisan POLITICS and signaled a new era of national peace and economic prosperity.

The Democratic Convention assembled in New York City in early 1868. A multitude of possible candidates confronted the Democrats. However, sectional differences divided the delegates and complicated the balloting process. Western Democrats supported soft money, paper currency known also as greenbacks, to spur inflation in an effort to assist indebted farmers. Eastern Democrats favored "hard money," specie backed by gold and silver, to maintain a stable economy. The leading candidates were Ohio representative George Pendleton, a soft money supporter, and Indiana senator Thomas Hendricks, a hard money candidate. Deadlocked, party leaders then turned to the ambitious Supreme Court chief justice, Samuel P. Chase, ironically a founding member of the Republican Party. Yet Chase's advocacy for black suffrage presented a major obstacle to his nomination. General Winfield Hancock offered Democrats a military hero to run against the Republicans, but Hancock could not match Grant's popularity. After 22 ballots, the delegates selected DARK-HORSE CANDIDATE former New York governor Horatio Seymour, to be the Democratic presidential nominee. Although a reluctant candidate, Seymour was respected and had the fewest enemies of the Democratic office-seekers. For Seymour's running mate, the delegates unanimously chose Frank Blair, Jr., of Missouri. The drafting of the platform took a considerable amount of time. The Democratic platform insisted on immediate restoration of the southern states, amnesty for all political officials, payment of the public debt, equal taxation, a sound money policy with one currency, and equal rights and protection for all naturalized and native-born citizens. The platform assailed Republican congressmen for imposing a policy of "military despotism and negro supremacy."

Republicans held an enormous advantage over their Democratic opponents. They reminded voters that they had preserved the nation and had freed approximately 4 million blacks from slavery with the passage of the Thirteenth Amendment. The adoption of pro-Republican state governments and the extension of suffrage to the freedmen increased the party's chances in the South. Republican leaders waved the "bloody shirt," that is, reminding voters of who had instigated the war and hinting at Democratic disloyalty. Despite Republican advantages, Democrats labeled all Republicans as radicals, although moderates constituted the majority of the party. Moreover, Democrats accused Grant of drunkenness, anti-Semitism, fathering an illegitimate Indian child, and being a "black" Republican bent on "Africanizing the South." Colfax was susceptible to allegations of anti-Catholicism as a result of his membership in the KNOW-NOTHING PARTY during the 1850s.

Questions of inconsistency and loyalty hindered the Democratic Party's ticket. Initially supportive of hard money, Seymour moderated his views and campaigned on a sound economic policy criticizing Republicans for doing nothing to eliminate the national debt. Republican officials reminded voters of Seymour's refusal as New York governor to furnish Lincoln with troops as well as his ardent opposition to emancipation. Republicans attacked Seymour's running mate, Blair, as a revolutionary, seeking another war to overthrow Republican Reconstruction.

As was customary in 19th-century American presidential politics, Grant did not campaign. Seymour, on the other hand, took to the stump to invigorate Democrats and appeal to border-state and midwestern voters more concerned about the slumping economy than southern Reconstruction. On November 3, 1868, Grant defeated Seymour by 300,000 votes to become the 18th president, and at that time, the youngest, at 46 years old. He received 214 electoral votes to Seymour's 80. Virginia, Mississippi, and Texas, not yet readmitted to the nation, did not participate in the election.

Republican success in the 1868 election may be credited to Grant's popularity. With an estimated 500,000 southern blacks exercising their right to vote (even with acts of terror and threats of violence keeping many from the polls), it is clear that Grant, who failed to receive a majority of the white vote, owed his victory to black voters. As a result, the Republican Congress passed and sent to the states for ratification the FIFTEENTH AMENDMENT, which declared that the states could not deny the vote on the basis of race, to protect these new Republican voters. Disappointing to radical Republicans, the election signified no clear MANDATE to continue Reconstruction. Although Republicans secured victory in the ELECTORAL COLLEGE, Democrats might have won the POPULAR VOTE if the states of Virginia, Mississippi, and Texas had been allowed to vote and if the freedmen had not voted in overwhelming numbers for Grant.

Further reading: Foner, Eric. *Reconstruction: America's Unfinished Revolution, 1863–1877.* New York: Harper & Row, 1988; Schlesinger, Arthur M., Jr., and Fred L. Israel, eds. *History of American Presidential Elections*, Volume II, *1789–1968.* New York: Chelsea House Publishers, 1971.

—William Hardy

presidential election 1872

Winning President and Vice President: Ulysses S. Grant and Henry Wilson
Number of States: 37
Major Candidates (Party Affiliation): Ulysses S. Grant (Republican); Horace Greeley (Democrat)
Electoral College Vote: Ulysses S. Grant: 286; Horace Greeley: 0; Horace Greeley died shortly after the election with his electoral votes divided: Thomas Hendricks (42), Benjamin G. Brown (18), Charles J. Jenkins (2), and David Davis (1); (not voted) 17
Popular Vote: Ulysses S. Grant: 3,596,745; Horace Greeley: 2,843,446

The presidential election of 1872 was marked by dissent within the incumbent party, disarray within the challenging party, and RECONSTRUCTION. The two major party candidates were incumbent Ulysses Grant (Republican) and Horace Greeley (Democrat and Liberal Republican).

President Ulysses Grant was first elected in 1868. He was a popular president, having led the Union army to victory in the American Civil War just a few years earlier. During the presidency of his predecessor, Andrew Johnson, Grant supported the actions of the Radical Republicans in Congress. These Republicans passed laws that supported voting rights and civil right for African Americans. They also passed laws that punished former rebels.

The laws passed without support from President Johnson. Congress had also passed restrictions on the office of the president. Based on these disagreements and an action by the president that violated one of these new restrictions, the House of Representative impeached President Johnson in 1868, while the Senate acquitted him by one vote. The impeachment sealed Johnson's fate, and he was not nominated as the Republican candidate for election in 1868. Also, the president pro tem of the Senate, Benjamin Wade, who had been floated as a potential nominee, had been defeated in his previous election. This series of events made Grant the presumptive Republican nominee.

Grant's first term highlighted his political inexperience. Among his problems was a reliance on friends and army colleagues. He appointed a number of inexperienced acquaintances to political posts, which angered some of Grant's fellow Republicans who hoped to have some of those political positions offered to their cronies, or at the very least to professionals. Lack of a professional civil service and dependence on political allies caused a major rift in the REPUBLICAN PARTY. This conflict within the Republican Party, as well as a disagreement regarding the failed annexation of Santo Domingo, led to a split between the two FACTIONS. The radicals remained committed to Reconstruction and to the freedmen. The newly formed Liberals took up the standard of civil service reform as their main issue.

The Liberal Republicans were led by Missouri senator Carl Schurz and Massachusetts senator Charles Sumner. In Missouri, Senator Schurz had orchestrated a defeat of the Radicals by aligning Liberals and Democrats. In early May 1872, the Liberal Republican Party began its party convention in Cincinnati to nominate an alternative to Grant. Voting for the nominee began on May 2. Charles Francis Adams, the son of John Quincy Adams and the grandson of John Adams, was the FRONTRUNNER. He was not a very popular man, but given his family history, he was believed to be the best option. One of the other candidates withdrew his NOMINATION and threw his support to Horace Greeley, a newspaper publisher from New York. Thus, Greeley was the Liberal Republican nominee.

The DEMOCRATIC PARTY was also in disarray. It was obvious that a majority of Republicans still favored Grant and that he would be the Republican nominee for reelection. Schurz believed that if the Liberal Republicans and the Democrats could merge, they could defeat the corruption of the Grant administration. With Schurz's goal in mind, the Democratic Party nominated Horace Greeley as their candidate for the presidential election of 1872. The Liberal Republicans' cause was then almost totally absorbed by the better-organized Democrats.

Horace Greeley did support civil service reform. His campaign motto was "More Honest Government." And, although he had railed against SOUTHERN DEMOCRATS in his newspapers, Greeley also supported an end to carpetbagger rule in the South. In direct opposition to the Liberals, Greeley supported high tariffs.

One feature of this campaign was the influence of the media, most noticeably of Thomas Nast, a political cartoonist for *Harper's Weekly*. Nast, an illiterate immigrant, was wholly supportive of Grant. He regularly drew cartoons in which Senators Schurz and Sumner were depicted as Iago and Brutus, treacherous characters from Shakespearian dramas. Likewise, Grant was shown as a defender of liberty and freedom.

The paper for which Nast drew took a similar position in the election. On March 30, 1872, *Harper's Weekly* read, "It [the New Hampshire election] shows that the people do not believe that parties should be dissolved, and the higher welfare of the country abandoned to a scrub-race of new organizations. It shows a profound conviction that the defeat of the Republican Party, under whatever fair name and fine promise and by whatever coalition that defeat should be secured, would be a peril not to be tolerated."

In the end, Grant won by a wide margin. He garnered 56 percent of the POPULAR VOTE and 286 of the 349 electoral votes. Greeley received just 44 percent of the popular vote, which would have earned him 45 of the electoral votes. Unfortunately, Horace Greeley died just weeks after his humiliating loss, causing his electoral votes to be split among lesser-known contenders.

Further reading: Korda, Michael. *Ulysses S. Grant: The Unlikely Hero.* New York: HarperCollins, 2004; Maihafer, Harry J. *The General and the Journalists: Ulysses S. Grant, Horace Greeley, and Charles Dana.* Washington, D.C.: Brassey's, 1998; Perret, Geoffrey. *Ulysses S. Grant: Soldier & President.* New York: Random House, 1997.

—Lisa Kimbrough

presidential election 1876

Winning President and Vice President: Rutherford B. Hayes and William A. Wheeler
Number of States: 38
Major Candidates (Party Affiliation): Rutherford B. Hayes (Republican); Samuel J. Tilden (Democrat)
Electoral College Vote: Rutherford B. Hayes: 185; Samuel J. Tilden: 184
Popular Vote: Rutherford B. Hayes: 4,036,572; Samuel J. Tilden: 4,284,020

The election of 1876 took place during one of the most volatile periods in American history, in the long shadow of the Civil War and RECONSTRUCTION. The Reconstruction period that followed the South's surrender in 1865 had caused considerable tension between the North and South. Federal troops remained in the region to ensure that the Reconstruction process proceeded without resistance. These troops protected newly freed blacks who voted in massive numbers for the REPUBLICAN PARTY. Between 1863 and 1877, Republicans in the South held power in the region, while the DEMOCRATIC PARTY, comprising former secessionists and Confederate government officials and military officers, was barred from voting or holding office.

The PRESIDENTIAL ELECTION pitted Democrat Samuel J. Tilden, former New York governor, against Ohio Republican Rutherford B Hayes, with no significant third-party CHALLENGER. Rutherford B. Hayes was something of a DARK-HORSE CANDIDATE at the REPUBLICAN NATIONAL CONVENTION and was selected because he was seen as a "cleaner" politician than the FRONTRUNNER, James G. Blaine, who had been tainted by corruption charges. It was hoped that the clean Hayes candidacy would divert attention from the SCANDAL-plagued Grant administration. As Hayes's RUNNING MATE, the convention selected William

A. Wheeler of New York. The Democrats selected New York's Samuel J. Tilden with Indiana's Thomas Hendricks as his running mate. A significant issue in this election was the effort of SOUTHERN DEMOCRATS to regain political power in the South. Consequently, it was no surprise that of the three states with contested vote counts, two were from the South.

Tilden held a lead of 250,000 POPULAR VOTES and an electoral lead in winning New York, Connecticut, Indiana, and the South. However, Republicans disputed returns from South Carolina (seven electoral votes), Florida (four electoral votes), Louisiana (eight electoral votes), and Oregon (one disputed electoral vote), which left Tilden a vote shy of the necessary electoral vote majority needed for victory. Republicans in the disputed southern states effectively eliminated enough Tilden votes to give Hayes the win. In Oregon, the governor disqualified a Republican ELECTOR and replaced him with a Democrat, in violation of the law.

The Constitution prescribed that presidential electoral votes be opened and counted by the president of the U.S. Senate in the presence of the House of Representatives and Senate. But Republicans controlled the Senate, and Democrats ruled the House, compounding the controversy over how the votes would be counted. To resolve the issue Congress appointed an electoral commission consisting of five House members, five senators, and five Supreme Court justices to determine who actually won the election. Composed of seven Republicans and seven Democrats with a mutually agreed upon independent 15th member, the commission was split evenly along political lines. The independent member was to be David Davis of Illinois, who, as fate would have it, had just won election to the U.S. Senate from Illinois, which effectively eliminated him. Into his place walked Republican justice Joseph P. Bradley.

The commission heard testimony recounting fraud on the part of both Republicans and Democrats in the states under dispute. It became clear that while Democrats had outpolled Republicans in those states, they also were guilty of driving thousands of African Americans from the polls. It became hard to imagine a situation that did not occur in these contested states: Dead people voted, some people voted more than 10 times in multiple places, election officials tampered with voting sheets, and whites paid for black votes.

On February 9, 1877, the commission voted 8 to 7 along party lines not to investigate the returns too deeply and awarded the Florida votes to Hayes. Over the next three weeks, they awarded Hayes the remaining disputed states, giving Hayes the victory with 185 electoral votes to Tilden's 184. By the resolution creating the commission, the only way to void the commission decision was a veto agreed upon by both chambers of Congress, which was not likely. The electoral crisis might have continued under claims that Bradley was "controlled" by Republicans, but southern

GO SOUTH, YOUNG MAN.
The latest and most reliable news.

Cartoon portraying the controversy surrounding the outcome of the 1876 election. Voting results were disputed in the southern states of Florida, Louisiana, and South Carolina. *(Cartoon by Thomas Nast, HarpWeek, LLC)*

Democrats put their support behind the commission's decision after reaching a compromise in late February at the Wormley Hotel in Washington, D.C. In exchange for supporting the commission, the South would receive one or two cabinet seats in the Hayes administration, a withdrawal of federal troops from the region (and an effective end of Reconstruction), hefty federal appropriations for internal improvements and reconstruction, and the passage of the Texas Pacific Railroad Bill to achieve a southern transcontinental railroad line.

LOBBYISTS had succeeded in convincing many southern congressmen that a Hayes victory was crucial to the survival and success of the Texas Pacific, and thus it became attached to the compromise measure. Hayes took the oath of office on March 3 and quickly appointed Tennessean David Key postmaster general, giving the South its coveted cabinet position. Federal troops evacuated the South by April. The South did receive a larger share of appropriations for internal improvements, but Hayes failed to give money to the Texas Pacific Railway.

Who really won the election remains a controversial question among historians. The consensus today is that Hayes most likely won South Carolina and Louisiana, while Tilden probably won Florida, which would have given him the victory. The historian C. Vann Woodward wrote that five times in the 19th century sectional conflict threatened the nation. In four instances compromise prevailed: the Missouri Compromise of 1820, the nullification crisis in the 1830s, the compromise of 1850, and the one in 1877. In the fifth instance, the Civil War defeated compromise. This latest compromise, Woodward asserted, restored the tradition of "expediency and concession" as opposed to violence and bloodshed.

Further reading: Foner, Eric. *Reconstruction: America's Unfinished Revolution, 1863–1877.* New York: Harper-Collins, 1989; Morris, Roy, Jr. *Fraud of the Century: Rutherford B. Hayes, Samuel Tilden and the Stolen Election of 1876.* New York: Simon & Schuster, 2003; Woodward, C. Vann. *Reunion and Reaction: The Compromise of 1877 and the End of Reconstruction.* Boston: Little, Brown, 1951.

—Gordon E. Harvey

presidential election 1880

Winning President and Vice President: James A. Garfield and Chester A. Arthur

Number of States: 38

Major Candidates (Party Affiliation): James A. Garfield (Republican); Winfield S. Hancock (Democrat)

Electoral College Vote: James A. Garfield: 214; Winfield S. Hancock: 155

Popular Vote: James A. Garfield: 4,453,295; Winfield S. Hancock: 4,414,082

In the first election after the end of postwar Reconstruction, Republicans faced Democrats on an electoral map that appeared evenly divided. Democrats controlled both houses of Congress, and the Republicans held the presidency, with Rutherford B. Hayes of Ohio, who, despite his status as the incumbent president, was never considered for renomination by his party. He had spurned his congressional Republican allies by denying them the PATRONAGE resources at his disposal. Hayes issued a call for civil service reform coupled with his denial, so that the presidency would not remain a mere "patronage-brokerage." Hayes had pledged not to run for a second term after his dubious election in 1876, and Republicans did not presume to support him for further service.

At their respective conventions, neither party chose longtime leaders or perennial candidates, although they nearly pitted two old soldiers who served closely together in the Civil War against each other. Instead, the losing candidate in the 1880 Republican presidential NOMINATION was retired general Ulysses S. Grant, the former president. Grant was backed by the self-styled "Stalwarts," whose support was among the larger states and several southern state delegations. Senator Roscoe Conkling of New York, national REPUBLICAN PARTY chairman Simon Cameron of Pennsylvania, and Don Logan of Illinois, calling themselves the "Triumvirate" that purported to wholly control the

Republican Party, sought to impose a UNIT RULE on the convention (binding individual DELEGATE votes to the choice of a majority of state delegates) in the absence of an outright majority in favor of nominating Grant.

Several delegates opposed Grant only on the principle that no president should serve more than two terms, and none had, though it was constitutionally permissible. Grant, however, was a national and even international icon, a war hero and successful former president who had, after his recent departure from the White House and two-year journey around the world, achieved much notoriety, and was more popular than ever. His convention support, virtually unwavering but devoid of growth, ranged from 304 to 313 of the 756 total votes, painfully short of the 378 needed to nominate. His Stalwart supporters were consistent, but without the unit rule, lacked a majority as well as a viable COALITION partner in either of the two other candidates.

Republicans voted a record 36 times before they decided on a compromise nominee, James Abram Garfield, a prominent senior congressman and senator-elect from Ohio, and a decidedly minor commander in the Civil War with the rank of major general. Garfield was supported primarily by the more liberal, northern, progressive elements in the party who had earlier backed the leader of the "Half-Breed" FACTION, Senator and former house speaker James G. Blaine of Maine. This coalition also included elements, notably Garfield himself, who had supported incumbent secretary of the Treasury and former senator John Sherman of Ohio, whose brother, William Tecumseh Sherman, had been a commanding general in the Civil War.

Democrats decided on their second BALLOT on General Winfield Scott Hancock of Pennsylvania, a commanding general for the Union in the Civil War who was wounded in the Battle of Gettysburg, but a relative newcomer to POLITICS. Democrats campaigned on a platform not entirely different from the Republicans', with the exception of their stance on the tariff and their posturing about 1876. Their platform called for a tariff "for revenue only," devolution of powers to state and local government, "honest money consisting of gold and silver," an end to Chinese residential immigration, and civil service reform. They denounced the distribution of party patronage after the "great fraud" of the 1876 election in particular as a "reward for political crime," issued a call for an end to the "threat of military violence" as a guarantor of elections, and pledged themselves to the cause of representative government.

The Republicans campaigned on what had been and would continue to be a familiar plank of theirs in the late 19th century, a protective tariff "so as to favor American labor," one of their prime constituencies being industrial wage workers in the northern states. They also professed support for moderate Chinese immigration reform, racial equality, an assertive national government supreme over the states, and, following the lead of incumbent President

Hayes, civil service reform. The popularity of this facet of their program was being driven primarily by the courts, the media, and religious organizations, all of whom were ashamed of what they saw as a system of organized graft.

From their promotion of the protective tariff, Republicans counted on the support of industrial capitalists who wanted to protect their products from foreign competition, commercial farmers for the same reason, urban laborers for their dependence on industry for their employment, and Civil War veterans. Veterans' groups, particularly the Grand Army of the Republic, actively campaigned for the Republican ticket because of the Republicans' support for liberalized pension benefits for veterans (costing a full 20 percent of the federal budget in 1880 and supporting one-third of male senior citizens in the North) and the high protective tariffs needed to finance them.

The minor GREENBACK PARTY and its nominee, James B. Weaver, campaigned mostly on a liberalized currency, fairness in labor laws, and reviews in the implementation of RECONSTRUCTION's "Homestead Act," claiming land was being distributed in excess to corporations for railroad construction when its purpose was for residential settlers. They also called for a graduated income tax and the regulation of monopolies. They did not take a position on the protective tariff because many of their supporters were Civil War veterans dependent on the revenue from the tariff for their pensions.

James Garfield conducted what would later be called a "front-porch campaign," staying primarily at his homestead in Mentor, Ohio (dubbed "Lawnfield" by the press), at which he had spent theretofore little time, continuing the tradition of presidential candidates abstaining from "the stump" while allowing surrogates to campaign for him. Roscoe Conkling, whose close ally, Chester Alan Arthur of New York, had been selected as Garfield's RUNNING MATE, campaigned very late in the election season, but still made several hours-long speeches that drew crowds from New York to Baltimore to Chicago and possibly decided the election for Garfield in New York, without which the Republicans would have lost to the Democrats in the ELECTORAL COLLEGE. General Grant denounced General Hancock, the Democratic standard-bearer, as media-hungry and a mere puppet of the Democratic elites who would do anything for the spotlight, despite his valiant and extremely able service during the Civil War. It was the first time a former president had actively campaigned for another candidate for president.

Arthur also took the opportunity in his position as New York state Republican Party chairman to finance the Republican PRESIDENTIAL ELECTION effort through "assessments," that is, mandatory contributions to the campaign till from patronage-appointed federal and state workers. A central component of a major civil service reform bill that Arthur would later, as president, sign into law, was the prohibition of these assessments. Garfield and the Republicans assembled a nearly contiguous electoral majority that pitted the mostly industrialized core of the North, West, and Midwest plus California and Nevada in their camp, against the entire South, Deep and Outer, as well as border states of the Midatlantic, and also Oregon. Republicans counted on several constituencies in the North, all of them supporting the protective tariff for various reasons, thereby wedding their fortunes to a Republican victory and, perhaps more importantly, a Democratic loss.

Greenback votes were presumably drawn from the constituencies of both major parties, and Weaver's vote total was greater than the plurality won by Garfield only in Indiana (15 electoral votes), but in two states, California (six) and New Jersey (nine), Hancock's plurality was reduced by a sizable Weaver showing, and thus the Greenbacks were not a SPOILER for the Republicans or the Democrats in the election.

Garfield's victory in one of the closest presidential elections in history carried COATTAILS. The Republicans also captured the House of Representatives, picking up 17 seats, and nabbed a narrow working majority in the Senate, picking up four seats to deadlock at 37 for each party, Vice President Arthur cast the tie-breaking vote for the Republicans. Republicans also picked up several governorships.

Republicans also won the governorships of all the northern and western states where Garfield won, with the exception of Maine, which, in addition to the element of a FUSION TICKET between the Greenbacks and the Democrats that occurred on the state level but not the presidential level, also voted in September rather than November, when the presidential election was held. Democrats also won every governorship in the South and Midatlantic in the states where Hancock won, with the exception of Tennessee, which suffered a schism in the DEMOCRATIC PARTY that year that allowed the Republicans to win with a low plurality over both Democratic candidates.

Further reading: Abramson, Paul R., John H. Aldrich, and David W. Rohde. *Change and Continuity in the 1996 Elections.* Washington, D.C.: CQ Press, 1998; Ackerman, Kenneth A. *Dark Horse: The Surprise Election and Political Murder of James A. Garfield.* Washington, D.C.: Free Press, 2003; Bensel, Richard Franklin. *The Political Economy of American Industrialization, 1877–1900.* Cambridge: Cambridge University Press, 2000.

—Daniel T. Kirsch

presidential election 1884

Winning President and Vice President: Grover Cleveland and Thomas Hendricks
Number of States: 38
Major Candidates (Party Affiliation): Grover Cleveland

(Democrat); James G. Blaine (Republican)
Electoral College Vote: Grover Cleveland: 219; James G.
    Blaine: 182
Popular Vote: Grover Cleveland: 4,879,507; James G.
    Blaine: 4,850,293

In summer of 1884, that year's presidential campaign seemed destined to play out along traditional party lines. But by July it erupted with charges and countercharges of political corruption, sexual dalliance, and moral debauchery. Underneath the mudslinging, the campaign represented two major changes in American POLITICS. The election of the Democrat Grover Cleveland spelled the end of the Civil War as a Republican campaign issue, and it put the problem of reforming the federal spoils system at the forefront of American politics. The mudslinging itself indicated cultural changes that would increasingly alter American politics.

The two major party candidates, Democrat Grover Cleveland and Republican James G. Blaine, were mirror opposites of each other. The heavyset and resolute Cleveland was new to public office. Elected mayor of Buffalo, New York, in late 1881, he captured the governorship of the state the following year. Dubbed the "Veto Mayor," Cleveland developed a reform reputation that put him at odds with the powerful Tammany Hall political machine of New York City. Blaine was an energetic and wily veteran of the U.S. Congress. A former SPEAKER OF THE HOUSE, he had served as Maine's senator since 1876. His nickname, the "Plumed Knight," cut in two directions. On the one hand, Blaine's magnetic personality attracted fervent followers, popularly known as "Blainiacs." On the other, critics believed the Plumed Knight to be insincere, insecure, vainglorious, and corrupt.

In the early stages, the campaign was Blaine's to lose. No Democrat had won the presidency since the Civil War. Cleveland was unknown to the national ELECTORATE and was a poor speaker who disliked the rigors of campaigning. His DEMOCRATIC PARTY was fragmented. Outside the solid South, the Democrats seemed to be little more than affiliated state parties, and new political fissures were opening along urban and rural lines. These divisions mandated that the Democrats choose a little-known candidate who would carry few factional ties. The only advantage the Democrats seemed to enjoy was the mild economic recession of 1884. This economic downturn highlighted what many observers thought would be the major issue of the campaign: the tariff.

The election of 1884 was practically a referendum on the tariff. But the issue went far deeper than an argument over the rates at which the federal government should assess imported goods. The tariff was a code word for the two parties' fundamentally different visions of the duties of federal government. The Republicans—the party of Civil War–era reform, big business, and nationalism—saw the tariff as the foundation for a neo-Whig program of internal improvements and federal control over government programs. The Democrats—the party of individual liberty (at least for whites), limited federal government, and localism—argued that the tariff threatened what their platform called "personal rights" and "the reserved rights of the states."

A campaign based solely on these distinctions would likely have sent Cleveland down to defeat, but he made a key strategic move. He attacked the Republicans as "a vast army of officeholders" bent on making the government a tool for both partisan and personal gain. Cleveland called for an overhaul of the civil service to dismantle the spoils system.

The tactical key to victory in 1884 was Cleveland's home state of New York. New York was almost equally divided between the two parties. A shift of only a few hundred votes might determine the outcome of the election. Blaine faced two major hurdles in New York. First, the "MUGWUMP" reformers of the REPUBLICAN PARTY made civil service reform their battle cry. Reviling Blaine as the exemplar of the evils of federal PATRONAGE, the Mugwumps bolted the party and threw their support to Cleveland. Second, Blaine had a mortal enemy within the ranks of the New York Republican Party. Roscoe Conkling, the still-powerful former senator from central New York state, had hated Blaine since a bitter debate in 1866. Cleveland's potential stumbling block was Tammany Hall: Could the New York City machine swallow its distaste for the reform governor in the name of party victory?

Before the campaign was hardly underway, it devolved into a vituperative battle of character assassination. Cleveland's Democratic operators attacked Blaine's under-the-table dealings with the railroads. On July 21, Republicans counterattacked by revealing that Cleveland had fathered a child out of wedlock. The scathing report was given great credence because it appeared in a Buffalo newspaper and was written by a minister (who was nonetheless a staunch Republican). To fan the fear of the relatively unknown Cleveland, Republican foot soldiers paraded through various cities taunting Democrats with chants of "Ma! Ma! Where's My Pa!" Republican newspapers ran story after story depicting Cleveland as a whoremonger and moral demon.

Cleveland astutely blunted the accusations in two ways. First, he admitted his responsibility for the affair while demonstrating that he had taken care to support both mother and child. Second, he admonished his CAMPAIGN MANAGERS in a telegram to "tell the truth" as he had done. Democrats soon played tit-for-tat, revealing that Blaine had fathered his firstborn before marrying the child's mother. In one last scurrilous moment, Blaine's plans for countering the Mugwumps in New York failed when a religious supporter overzealously smeared the Democrats as the party of "Rum, Romanism, and Rebellion" (that is, alcoholics, Irish

Catholics, and Confederates). Blaine's failure to repudiate the remark seems to have cost him any Irish votes he hoped to attract by playing up his own Irish heritage.

While it is unclear how these moral attacks and parries affected the election, it is certain that the election was very close. The final tally was not known for a week as the votes were counted and RECOUNTED. As expected, the election turned on the results in New York. Cleveland won there by 1,149 votes, a margin of 0.1 percent. A shift of 575 votes would have thrown New York and its electoral votes to Blaine, handing him the presidency. The key factor seems not to have been either the mudslinging or the Mugwump defection, but rather Conkling's betrayal. Whereas Garfield in 1880 had carried Oneida County (Conkling's base) with a plurality of 1,946 votes, Cleveland won the county with a plurality of 69 votes. Tammany turned out not to be a Cleveland impediment: It had paid a high cost for bolting the Democrats in 1879 and now decided that any Democrat was better than Blaine.

The election of 1884 reveals a nation embroiled in cultural upheaval. Traditionally, historians have focused on Cleveland's victory as the end of the "bloody shirt" in presidential politics. This is certainly true, but a closer look reveals that a new moral culture was beginning to reshape American politics. The Republican smear campaign focused not on Cleveland's sex outside of marriage, but on the claim that he had abandoned the mother and child. The Republicans were in essence trying to play on class perceptions of the two parties. Underlying the Republican attack was the charge that Democrats were an antifamily rabble who advocated license rather than liberty in both personal and economic transactions.

If voters bought this depiction, Republicans would then appear as the party of moral and economic order. Cleveland confused the labels and expectations by admonishing his supporters not to make excuses for his behavior or try to cast the blame elsewhere. His directive to "tell the truth" demonstrated to enough voters that while he had erred, he was not craven. No coward or lecher would take such a principled stand. Cleveland used the mudslinging to prove that although a sinner, he was honorable nonetheless. Just enough Americans forgave or ignored the mud to vote for the Democrat.

Further reading: Summers, Mark Wahlgren. *Rum, Romanism, and Rebellion: The Making of a President, 1884.* Chapel Hill: University of North Carolina Press, 2000; Welch, Richard E., Jr. *The Presidencies of Grover Cleveland.* Lawrence: University Press of Kansas, 1988.

—Reynolds J. Scott-Childress

presidential election 1888

Winning President and Vice President: Benjamin Harrison and Levi P. Morton

Number of States: 38
Major Candidates (Party Affiliation): Benjamin Harrison (Republican); Grover Cleveland (Democrat)
Electoral College Vote: Benjamin Harrison: 233; Grover Cleveland: 168
Popular Vote: Benjamin Harrison: 5,447,129; Grover Cleveland: 5,537,857

The presidential election of 1888 was one of the closest races in American history. It was also one of the few elections in which the winner received fewer POPULAR VOTES than the looser. The Democrats nominated incumbent Grover Cleveland, while the Republicans turned to Benjamin Harrison as their candidate. Cleveland received 5,537,857 votes, but finished second in the ELECTORAL COLLEGE, with a total of 168. His Republican CHALLENGER, Harrison, garnered 5,447,129 popular votes but won a decisive victory in the Electoral College, with 233 votes.

The two candidates had somewhat similar backgrounds, in that both men were reared by devout Presbyterian fathers and both became lawyers. Born in New Jersey in March 1837, Cleveland was one of 11 children of a Presbyterian minister. After earning his law degree, Cleveland moved to Buffalo. During the Civil War, Cleveland opted out of military service by paying a replacement $300 to serve in his stead. Cleveland prospered as a lawyer and served as an assistant district attorney. He was elected mayor of Buffalo in 1881. A year later, Cleveland won election as New York governor, and he captured the Democratic NOMINATION for the presidency in 1884. Cleveland was elected president in 1884 after narrowly defeating James G. Blaine by less than 50,000 votes. During this presidency, Cleveland unsuccessfully pushed for civil service reform, lower tariffs, and a bill that required the government to buy and coin as much silver as possible. Despite these setbacks, Cleveland was unanimously renominated in 1888.

Benjamin Harrison came from a prominent political family. His great-grandfather signed the Declaration of Independence and his grandfather, William Henry Harrison, was the nation's ninth president. Born in Ohio in 1833, Harrison was reared in a strict Presbyterian household. An intensely religious man, Harrison thought of becoming a minister before embarking on a legal career. Harrison moved to Indianapolis, where he established a law practice and raised his family. When the Civil War broke out, Harrison volunteered for service and rose to the rank of brigadier general. After the war, the Republican Harrison reluctantly agreed to run for Indiana governor in 1876. He lost the race but won election to the U.S. Senate in 1880. Defeated for reelection in 1886, Harrison still had a national following, and his chances for the Republican nomination were greatly aided when Senator James Blaine of Maine, the party's 1884 candidate for president, backed Harrison. At the Republican convention in 1888, Harrison was nominated on the eighth BALLOT, along with vice presidential candidate Levi Morton.

The tariff question dominated the campaign. President Cleveland devoted his entire 1887 State of the Union Address to that issue. The Democrats favored a lower tariff, while the Republicans, who drew much of their support from eastern industrialists, supported high rates in order to protect American manufacturers. Harrison and the Republicans also criticized Cleveland's veto of a pension bill for Civil War soldiers and promised to provide more money for veterans.

Neither man actively campaigned. Harrison made most of his speeches from his porch at his Indianapolis home, while Cleveland spent his time at the White House. Surrogates hit the campaign trail for the two men, making speeches before large and enthusiastic crowds. Senators Roscoe Conkling of New York and Matthew Quay of Pennsylvania managed much of the Republican campaign. The Republicans raised enormous amounts of money for the race, primarily from businessmen who wanted to keep high tariff rates. The Democrats, however, were far less successful in raising money and running a coordinated campaign.

The 1888 election differed greatly from the 1884 contest. That race, one of the dirtiest in American history, featured the Republicans accusing Cleveland of fathering a child out of wedlock and of being a coward for not having fought in the Civil War. One Republican slogan stated that the Democrats were the party of "Rum, Romanism, and Rebellion." In contrast, the 1888 election was tame, with little of the mudslinging that characterized the 1884 race. There was one dirty trick in the race, however. A few weeks before the election, a California Republican wrote a letter to the British ambassador to the United States. The man claimed to be a British immigrant and wanted the ambassador's opinion about who he should vote for. The minister stated that the British government favored Cleveland. The *Los Angeles Times* printed the letter, and the resulting uproar may have harmed Cleveland's chances.

What most hurt Cleveland, however, was his inability to wage an effective campaign. Since Cleveland disdained the give-and-take of POLITICS, it fell to Vice President Allen Thurman to tour the country in support of the president. Yet Thurman was old and in declining health, and he was not up to the task. The Democrats were also divided, and Cleveland was unable to unite the party.

As ELECTION DAY neared, the race was still very close. Like almost all presidential contests in the Gilded Age, the outcome hinged on a few states that could swing the race. In 1888 New York and Indiana were the key battleground states. VOTER TURNOUT in those states was very high, as it was across the country. Cleveland lost his home state of New York by 13,000, and with it, New York's 34 electoral votes. Harrison narrowly carried Indiana and its 15 elec-

toral votes. With those two states, which had both gone for Cleveland four years earlier, Harrison won the election.

The 1888 election was significant in several ways. It was one of the last contests in which the candidates would do little active campaigning. The race was also one of the few elections in which the candidate with the most popular votes lost the Electoral College. The results denied Harrison any claim to a MANDATE and also made Cleveland the likely Democratic nominee in 1892.

Further reading: Brodsky, Alyn. *Grover Cleveland: A Study in Character.* New York: St. Martin's Press, 2000; Socolofsky, Homer E., and Allan B. Spetter. *The Presidency of Benjamin Harrison.* Lawrence: University of Kansas Press, 1987.

—Justin P. Coffey

presidential election 1892

Winning President and Vice President: Grover Cleveland and Adlai E. Stevenson
Number of States: 44
Major Candidates (Party Affiliation): Grover Cleveland (Democrat); Benjamin Harrison (Republican); James B. Weaver (Populist); John Bidwell (Prohibition)
Electoral College Vote: Grover Cleveland: 277; Benjamin Harrison: 145; James B. Weaver: 22
Popular Vote: Grover Cleveland: 5,555,426; Benjamin Harrison: 5,182,690; James B. Weaver: 1,029,846

If not terribly remarkable for the contest of candidates or even the issues they campaigned about, the 1892 election was perhaps significant for the seemingly marginal constituencies of small farmers and professional political reformers that played a pivotal, and possibly a decisive role, in the election. The MUGWUMPS, liberal reformers who typically leaned Republican but who were known to switch their allegiances, supported Cleveland in 1892, as they had in 1884, due to the incumbent Republican administration's unsatisfactory performance in the area primarily of civil service reform. The National Civil Service Reform League (NCSRL), made up of professional journalists, lawyers, and clergy, with a growing business contingent, felt Harrison had resisted the recommendations of the three-member U.S. Civil Service Commission and its highest-profile member, Theodore Roosevelt. Roosevelt's primary focus was on PATRONAGE abuse in the post office, the head of which, John Wanamaker, had been and continued to be Harrison's chief fund-raiser and the most prolific dispenser of patronage appointments. The number of federal civil service positions classified as merit appointees (as opposed to party patronage appointees) nearly doubled during Harrison's administration, though not because of, and even in spite of, the efforts of Harrison.

The NCSRL and its Mugwumps were disappointed when the Republican Roosevelt did not support the Democrat Cleveland, as most of Roosevelt's supporters had. Cleveland clearly welcomed their support again and took careful policy stands, such as his opposition to the high "McKinley tariff" signed into law by Harrison with the proviso that he favored only a moderate reduction, and his sop to eastern industrial core interests that favored the gold standard. Republicans, normally the party of the gold standard in currency, controlled the first administration forced to answer for an experiment in silver coinage, in which a limited but large quantity of silver was purchased by the Treasury, with notes redeemable in gold. This was part of the legislative trade with Democrats that allowed Harrison to raise tariff rates. Harrison had also signed into law the Sherman Antitrust Act. "Deliberately vague" and "narrowly applicable," the bill fined corporations engaged in commerce in transit but not in manufacturing.

At the Republican convention, there was a movement by New York PARTY BOSS Thomas C. Platt to deny Harrison renomination and replace him with longtime party leader James G. Blaine, only to see the president renominated on the first BALLOT, with 536 out of 900 votes. William McKinley, chairman of the House Ways and Means Committee and author of the "McKinley Tariff" that raised the average rate on imported duties to 48 percent, showed a surprising amount of strength on that ballot, garnering slightly less DELEGATE votes (182) than the seasoned Blaine (183). The Republican platform praised the Harrison administration, endorsed gold and silver as the "hard money" standard, called for civil service reform and praised the protective tariff, and liberalized the veterans' benefits that Harrison had signed into law. Harrison hewed closely to the Republican platform, and his letter of acceptance to the party for renomination merely restated his commitment to party principles.

Cleveland won his third consecutive NOMINATION from the party, this time on the first ballot. The original Democratic platform had called for ambivalence on the gold and silver standards, but a motion to install a plank endorsing silver passed overwhelmingly. It also called for Chinese immigration reform, a tariff for revenue only, and civil service reform. It denounced the patronage of the Harrison administration and called for stronger ethics in government. Cleveland felt the need to distance himself from the party platform on two central issues: the tariff and silver. Cleveland felt the silver standard was dangerous and would later, as president, restore the gold standard, as had been his position for many years. The tariff, he felt, should be kept at a relatively high rate; it was only the abnormally high rate of the McKinley tariff that had touched off inflation, and it should be returned to its previous average rate.

The election turned on the tariff, and the Populists could have capitalized on some discontent about its height, but there were several constituencies in the dominant electoral COALITION and the larger ELECTORATE who depended on the tariff for revenue for social programs, such as war veterans' pension benefits and the protection of various eastern manufacturing interests, such as steel, and western farming interests, such as the special protection afforded wool in the West. Weaver, the Populist Party candidate, seized on western discontent with Cleveland's stance on currency, and Cleveland was denied the opportunity to compete in five western states, surely a blow to the Democratic electoral coalition. The absolute poorest in the country, most of them subsistence farmers and small commercial farmers in the western states, voted for Weaver, who won four states and 22 electoral votes. The strong Populist showing in 1892 signaled that there was a large degree of discontent with the profits supported by the gold standard and select manufacturing interests in the East, and the West was growing poorer. Farmers saw silver currency and a looser money supply as a panacea for their sagging fortunes, and both parties had nominated candidates hostile to its broad-based implementation.

Cleveland won his third consecutive popular plurality in three consecutive PRESIDENTIAL ELECTIONS, but only his second ELECTORAL COLLEGE majority, and thus his second victory. Harrison suffered his second consecutive popular loss, but his first in the Electoral College. Populist Weaver won 8.5 percent of the vote and 22 electoral votes, and John Bidwell of the PROHIBITION PARTY won 2.25 percent, but no electoral votes. A total of 78.3 percent of eligible voters participated in the election nationwide, but due mainly to the lack of racial and gender liberalization of voting rights, 34.9 percent of the voting age population voted.

The Senate changed hands, the Democrats gaining five seats. Republicans, however, gained 39 seats in the House, weakening the Democrats' majority from 235 to 218. Republicans won the gubernatorial elections held in states that Harrison won in 1892, with the exceptions of Massachusetts and Wyoming, no doubt because Cleveland was not on the ballot in Wyoming, and Weaver supporters as well as regular Democrats supported the Democratic candidate in the gubernatorial election. The ardent opposition of many western Democrats to Cleveland was primarily due to his support of the gold standard. The Democrats' wholesale adoption of the silver platform in 1896 and the logic of William Jennings Bryan's candidacy can easily be gleaned from the division evident in the 1892 election.

Further reading: Bensel, Richard Franklin. *The Political Economy of American Industrialization, 1877–1900*. Cambridge: Cambridge University Press, 2000; Skocpol, Theda. *Protecting Soldiers and Mothers: The Political Origins of Social Policy in the United States*. Cambridge, Mass.: Belknap Press of Harvard University Press, 1992; Skowronek, Stephen. *Building a New American State: The Expansion of*

National Administrative Capacities 1877–1920. Cambridge: Cambridge University Press, 1982.

—Daniel T. Kirsch

presidential election 1896

Winning President and Vice President: William McKinley and Garret A. Hobart
Number of States: 45
Major Candidates (Party Affiliation): William McKinley (Republican); William Jennings Bryan (Democrat); William Jennings Bryan (Populist)
Electoral College Vote: William McKinley: 271; William Jennings Bryan: 176
Popular Vote: William McKinley: 7,102,246; William Jennings Bryan: 6,492,559

The election of 1896 can be seen as a watershed election. The presidential contest of that year ended a period of political parity between the two major parties that had begun at the close of RECONSTRUCTION. The 1896 election ushered in an era of Republican dominance at the national level that remained almost unbroken until 1932. The DEMOCRATIC PARTY divided along sectional and ideological lines and descended into a long period as the MINORITY PARTY. This election also saw the end of the third-party movement know as the PEOPLE'S PARTY, or the Populists, when they fused with the Democrats and backed the candidacy of Bryan.

The depression of 1893 and the seeming inability of President Grover Cleveland and the Democrats to manage the crisis gave the Republicans hope as the presidential election of 1896 loomed. The Republicans had done quite well in the CONGRESSIONAL ELECTIONS of 1894, and the presidential race looked promising. William McKinley, governor of Ohio, with the help of his political manager, Marcus Hanna, gained the Republican presidential NOMINATION. McKinley, a Civil War veteran addressed by his military rank of major, had enjoyed a lengthy career as a congressman before his election to the governorship. His career had been marked by his long advocacy of high tariffs on imported goods that protected American manufacturers, and he enjoyed widespread support in the business community.

One other issue involved the availability of cash and credit. William McKinley backed the gold standard and rejected the unlimited coinage of silver. Many felt that silver, in the wake of the economic crisis of the 1890s, offered a solution to those who could not acquire capital or could not pay their debts. This issue cut across party lines with Silver Democrats and Republicans pitted against Gold Democrats and Republicans. This divide occurred across sectional lines, as gold supporters were located in the East, and silver advocates came from the West and South.

These ideological and sectional splits plagued the Democrats. Cleveland, a committed Gold Democrat, became convinced that mandated purchases of silver by the government had led to the depression and sought to reverse this process. He called for and achieved a repeal of the Sherman Silver Purchase Act, the law that had mandated the purchases, and set off a firestorm in his own party. In the end, Democrats from the South and West repudiated Cleveland and denied him any chance at the presidential nomination in 1896.

William Jennings Bryan, a 36-year-old onetime congressman from Nebraska, captured the Democratic nomination. He achieved this by encouraging the efforts of Silver Democrats in the West and South to take over STATE PARTY COMMITTEES, which sent pro-silver DELEGATES to the nominating convention in St. Louis. Bryan then electrified the gathering with his famous "Cross of Gold" speech, in which he stated that business and banking interests were interested in building their fortunes on the backs of hard-pressed farmers and laborers. Bryan and the Democrats offered the unlimited coinage of silver as the solution to the problem for those who could not accumulate cash and credit.

The POPULIST PARTY also offered its nomination to Bryan. Western and southern farmers victimized by the economic downturns of the 1880s and 1890s had turned to collective self-help as a remedy for their problems. First in the form of INTEREST GROUPS such as the Farmers' Alliances, they sought to exert pressure on the major parties to address their economic distress. However, finding that the Democrats and Republicans remained unresponsive, they turned to the formation of an INDEPENDENT third party as an alternative.

The third party, known as the People's Party, or Populists, ran its own candidate in the 1892 PRESIDENTIAL ELECTION. They ran far behind the two major party candidates, and like many THIRD PARTIES, debated the best way to have their concerns addressed. The solution for many was fusion with the Democrats. Bryan, though not a Populist himself, shared many of their ideas and endorsed one of their major platform planks when it came to the advocacy of silver. In 1896, after much debate, the Populists endorsed a FUSION TICKET with the Democrats. Bryan then secured the nomination of not only the Democrats but also the People's Party. However, the Populists, unhappy with Bryan's RUNNING MATE, Maine businessman Arthur Sewall, selected Georgia Populist Tom Watson to run as vice president on the ticket. Bryan never formally accepted the nomination nor acknowledged Watson's participation in the presidential campaign.

The Republicans had some advantages as the GENERAL ELECTION approached in November of 1896. Hanna, armed with large amounts of campaign contributions, paid for extensive advertising via billboards, handbills, and newspaper ads that assailed Bryan and the Democrats. McKinley's campaign also paid for campaign surrogates who fanned out across the country to attack Bryan. They were also aided by business leaders, who also assailed the Democratic candidate's economic policy. These two allies emphasized the inflationary effect that the unlimited coinage of silver would have on the American economy. While farmers might have backed inflationary policies so they could get a better return on their crops, many Americans did not share that view. Political advertisements targeted the urban middle and working classes, who rented and bought their goods from merchants. Any increase in pricing could have adversely affected those groups' economic health. These coordinated campaign attacks portrayed Bryan as reckless and McKinley as a steady and strong leader.

McKinley reinforced this image by the nature of the campaign that he waged in 1896. He conducted a "front porch" campaign from his home in Canton, Ohio. Republican groups would come to McKinley's house, where he would make carefully constructed speeches on his stands on the tariff and currency issues. The Republicans presented McKinley as dignified and presidential.

Bryan and the Democrats had a different approach. The Democratic candidate mounted a cross-country train trip and gave numerous speeches urging voters to support him. He was criticized for not acting presidential because a candidate in that time did not beg for votes. Rather, the candidate was expected to wait for the voters to call upon him to serve. The Democrats also had trouble raising money to mount a response to Republican accusations about Bryan's perceived recklessness. The campaign eventually degenerated into a discussion about the competing gold and silver standards. Bryan was unable to focus the debate on any other issues, and his candidacy became tied to the issue of silver.

In the end, the Republicans and McKinley won a solid victory. McKinley outpolled Bryan by 600,000 votes, which was a wide margin in the wake of several close presidential elections of the era. The Democratic ticket carried the South solidly, augmented by some support in the West, which were the regions most identified with the silver cause. The Populists were spent as a distinct political force, though their positions on economic justice and greater political access for common people were adopted by the two major parties. Consequently, the 1896 presidential election installed the REPUBLICAN PARTY as the MAJORITY PARTY in American POLITICS until the landmark election of 1932.

Further reading: Coletta, Paolo E. *William Jennings Bryan: Political Evangelist 1860–1908.* Lincoln: University of Nebraska Press, 1964; Goodwyn, Lawrence. *The Populist Moment: A Short History of the Agrarian Revolt.* Oxford: Oxford University Press, 1978; Hollingsworth, J. Rogers. *The Whirligig of Politics: The Democracy of Cleveland and Bryan.* Chicago: University of Chicago Press, 1963; Morgan, Wayne H. *William McKinley and His America.* Rev. ed. Kent, Ohio: Kent State University Press, 2003.

—Robert Butts

presidential election 1900

Winning President and Vice President: William McKinley and Theodore Roosevelt
Number of States: 45
Major Candidates (Party Affiliation): William McKinley (Republican); William Jennings Bryan (Democrat/Populist); John G. Woolley (Prohibition)
Electoral College Vote: William McKinley: 292; William Jennings Bryan: 155
Popular Vote: William McKinley: 7,218,491; William Jennings Bryan: 6,356,734

A protectionist president, an imperialist foreign policy, and the entrance of a Roosevelt into the presidential arena were the oddly juxtapositioned realities Americans faced in the election of the first president of the 20th century. William McKinley, defeated for reelection to Congress 10 years before after sponsoring the highest-rated tariff bill in American history, which caused sharp inflation, now rode a wave of public approval ideal for reelection to the presidency after signing a similar bill only six years after the first. This time,

An 1896 Republican campaign poster with portraits of McKinley and Hobart surrounded by symbols for businesses and commodities *(Gillespie, Metzgar & Kelly, Library of Congress)*

improving overall economic conditions followed passage of the bill, and regardless of the causal relationship, McKinley took credit for the recovery. McKinley had also spearheaded the United States' first venture into extracontinental imperialism, invading Cuba and fighting the Spanish-American War, despite his best diplomatic efforts to avoid it. Gold had also been struck during his inaugural term in the presidency, and thus the proposition of the unlimited and free coinage of silver virtually disappeared as a realizable platform plank for William Jennings Bryan and the Democrats.

In contrast to 1896, when the DELEGATES explicitly refused to praise outgoing Democratic president Grover Cleveland because of his adherence to the gold standard of currency valuation and the free coinage of silver plank was overwhelmingly adopted, Democrats were more reticent in 1900, some in the minority even calling for removal of the silver plank. The party tried to put on a united front, calls for factional reconciliation drawing the largest applause, and its most eloquent affirmative speaker was almost nominated for the vice presidency, David Hill of New York. Bryan promised to refuse the NOMINATION if the silver plank was removed, despite the discovery of gold reserves in Alaska, the economic recovery, and overall, a lack of urgency in the West and South about the free coinage of silver or any other emergency measures to redistribute wealth in the country. A "Gold Democrat," Adlai E. Stevenson, the former vice president under Cleveland, was nominated as Bryan's RUNNING MATE, which he grudgingly accepted, though he had clearly wanted another vice presidential nominee more sympathetic to his own views and those of a majority of western delegates.

Both the Democrats and the Republicans counted one woman delegate among their ranks. The Democratic platform also railed against the "militarism" of the Spanish-American War and its underlying meaning of "conquest abroad." Notably, the Democrats subtly opposed the military reforms called for by Emory Upton in his 1881 book *The Military Policy of the United States*, which proposed, among other reforms, a professional standing army of 100,000 soldiers by noting that if the nation were threatened by external threat, "the volunteer soldier is the country's best defender," echoing the calls of state governors and state militia promoters, who opposed the permanent expenditure of a standing army. The antiimperialist plank, in general, was the most popular part of the platform, and Democrats tried to make it a central issue of the campaign, which perhaps backfired due to the country's regard of the recent war as a "splendid little war" and advantageous to its economic and international well-being.

The Republican platform praised the economic recovery begun under McKinley in marked contrast to the downturn during the Cleveland administration, though their economic policies (the gold standard) without respect to the tariff were relatively the same. The platform praised the president's conduct during the Spanish-American War, reit-erated its support for construction of a canal across Central America, favored more immigration restriction, and called for continuation of the protective tariff, urged raising the age for children to be classified as involved in "child labor," and also condemned trusts and monopolies. It generally praised McKinley's policies of postwar imperialist expansion as favorable to business and proposed a Department of Commerce.

The surprise at the convention was the addition of young New York governor Theodore Roosevelt to the ticket. Roosevelt, at 41, had been a party maverick for many years, nipping at the heels of those party leaders who purported to be reformers, such as James G. Blaine and Benjamin Harrison, but had always loyally supported the REPUBLICAN PARTY during elections. Roosevelt had resigned his position as assistant secretary of the navy in the first half of McKinley's term to accept a commission as a lieutenant colonel (later rising to colonel) in charge of a band of volunteer Rough Riders in Cuba, who later stormed San Juan Hill (actually a nearby hill called Kettle Hill). Roosevelt gained enormous popularity and notoriety from the event, which was, symbolically, indicative of the United States' triumph despite its lack of readiness and actually an example of the Democrats' charge that volunteers were more suited to U.S. military policy than a standing army. Roosevelt was given the opportunity to run for vice president primarily because New York boss Thomas C. Platt wanted him out of the governor's chair in Albany, where Roosevelt had refused to cater to Platt's demands for PATRONAGE. As a former civil service commissioner who had publicized patronage abuses in the Harrison and Cleveland administrations, this was to be expected. McKinley's principal adviser, Senator Mark Hanna of Ohio, is purported to have told McKinley that his only occupation for the next four years ought to be to "stay alive," because he was now the only obstacle "between that madman and the White House!"

Roosevelt campaigned tirelessly in 1900, promising "four more years of the full dinner pail" to voters, while McKinley himself repeated his strategy of four years before, in which he conducted his James Garfield-inspired "front porch campaign." Bryan crossed the country as he had in 1896, when he had traveled 18,000 miles and made some 600 speeches by some accounts. Bryan was the first major party presidential candidate in history to make a concerted effort to campaign in all parts of the country. The competition between two of the greatest orators in American history undoubtedly made for one of the most vigorous campaign seasons in American POLITICS.

Republicans gained seats in the election of the 57th Congress, as well. They picked up 12 seats in the House of Representatives, the new makeup becoming 197 to 151 to nine of Republicans, Democrats, and Populists, respectively. Republicans in the Senate saw gains to their already massive majority, now housing 55 Republicans, 31

Democrats, and four independents. Republicans won the contested governorships of all the states in the North, West, and Midatlantic in which McKinley won a plurality of the POPULAR VOTE, and Democrats won the contested governorships of all the states in the South and West in which Bryan won a plurality of the popular vote.

Voting participation was high among those eligible, at a robust 73.7 percent, but this followed a pattern of relative decline among eligible voters in participation since the years immediately after the Civil War, besides the fact that, counting all voting age adults of the time, 34 percent of the voting age population participated in the voting that led to McKinley's second election. McKinley expanded his 1896 majority, clearly and convincingly winning the popular and electoral votes. Minor party candidates warrant an honorable mention in this election, as well: John C. Woolley of the PROHIBITION PARTY won 1.5 percent, doing its best in Delaware, where the party won nearly 6 percent of the popular vote. Eugene V. Debs, leader and candidate of a new SOCIALIST PARTY, made his first of five appearances on a national BALLOT, garnering a modest percentage and showing greatest strength in Massachusetts, where the labor-based party gained 2.5 percent (nearly 10,000 votes). Bryan won only the South and several states in the West, including some of the states that had gone for Weaver in 1892. Bryan's base CONSTITUENCY of disaffected southern voters and rural western farmers proved no match for the engine of prosperity and economic model of the northern industrial core that McKinley had. In addition to this, McKinley had had a campaign spending advantage of nearly 10 to one in 1896, and party financing was still as strong for the Republicans four years later.

Further reading: Bensel, Richard Franklin. *Sectionalism and American Political Development, 1880–1980*. Madison: University of Wisconsin Press, 1984; Skowronek, Stephen. *Building a New American State: The Expansion of National Administrative Capacities 1877–1920*. Cambridge: Cambridge University Press, 1982; Skocpol, Theda. *Protecting Soldiers and Mothers: The Political Origins of Social Policy in the United States*. Cambridge, Mass.: The Belknap Press of Harvard University Press, 1992.

—Daniel T. Kirsch

presidential election 1904

Winning President and Vice President: Theodore Roosevelt and Charles Fairbanks

Number of States: 45

Major Candidates (Party Affiliation): Theodore Roosevelt (Republican); Alton B. Parker (Democrat)

Electoral College Vote: Theodore Roosevelt: 336; Alton B. Parker: 140

Popular Vote: Theodore Roosevelt: 7,628,461; Alton B. Parker: 5,084,223

The presidential election of 1904 became a referendum on the policies and personality of Theodore Roosevelt. Roosevelt brought renewed energy and vitality to the presidency, which had long lain dormant since the administration of Abraham Lincoln. In the domestic realm, Roosevelt used his office to put Progressive reform on the national agenda. In foreign relations, Roosevelt, an unabashed imperialist, pushed the United States further onto the international stage as the country developed into an emerging power. The Democrats, split between the reform followers of William Jennings Bryan and the conservative remnants of the Grover Cleveland wing of the party, offered little as an alternative to Theodore Roosevelt and the Republicans.

The ascension of Theodore Roosevelt to the presidency was a dizzying one. He had risen to national celebrity by his service with the Rough Riders in Cuba during the War of 1898. He had parlayed his service into a term as New York's Republican governor pursuing a Progressive reformist agenda. This, in turn, led him to clash with the conservative Republican machine in the state, which led the successful effort to place Roosevelt on the Republican presidential ticket with William McKinley in 1900. McKinley's assassination by an anarchist in September 1901 elevated the young vice president into the presidency. He began an energetic pursuit of domestic and foreign policies that set the stage for the election of 1904.

On the domestic side, Roosevelt breathed new life into the Sherman Anti-Trust Act. The act had been intended to combat the growth of monopolies in the American economy during the late 19th century. However, the act was rendered toothless by lax enforcement and narrow interpretations of the law by conservative courts. Roosevelt ordered his Justice Department to invoke the act against financier J. P. Morgan and his attempts to consolidate his railroad holdings. The Northern Securities case signaled that the federal government would take a more proactive stance when it came to the scrutiny it applied to the acquisition of trusts. Roosevelt also intervened in a threatened coal strike in the Pennsylvania coalfields and brokered an agreement between management and labor. He altered the perception of many in labor by departing from the outright hostility that the federal government had shown to unions and labor in other strikes of the period. Roosevelt, fearful of class conflict, wanted to use the government as a kind of umpire or referee to bring the upper and lower classes closer together to build a more harmonious society. His most innovative program was the commitment of the national government to a program of conservation by expanding the National Park System. These actions defined the program of the "Square Deal" on which Roosevelt based his presidential campaign.

Roosevelt also built a dynamic foreign policy record. He ended the Filipino Insurrection that had grown out of the War of 1898, which he had inherited from the McKinley administration. He reiterated America's claim on the islands and a continued commitment to imperialism. Roosevelt also aided Panamanian rebels in their struggle against Colombia. In turn, he negotiated with the newly independent Panamanian government for the building of a transisthmian canal. The canal idea had been the dream of many Americans, and Roosevelt made that dream a reality.

Roosevelt, however, was not unopposed in his own party. Marcus Hanna, McKinley's former CAMPAIGN MANAGER and U.S. senator from Ohio, had opposed Roosevelt's place on the Republican ticket in 1900 and hinted he might block the president's NOMINATION in 1904. Roosevelt then carefully in the year before the Republican convention lined up support among DELEGATES that assured his nomination. The threat also disappeared with Hanna's death in early 1904. Roosevelt was then easily nominated, with conservative senator Charles Fairbanks of Indiana placed on the ticket as the vice presidential nominee. This added a balance with the reformist Roosevelt at the top of the ticket.

The Democrats, as the election approached, fell to fighting among themselves. The conservative wing of the party, tired of the consecutive defeats of Bryan by the Republicans, gained control of the nominating convention. The party chose as its presidential nominee New York state judge Alton B. Parker and West Virginia millionaire Henry Gassaway Davis as vice president. The Democrats could never gain any traction in the course of the GENERAL ELECTION. The trust issue that Democrats had hoped to use against the Republicans was rendered moot by the administration's actions against Northern Securities. Parker, a tepid and colorless campaigner, offered little resistance to the dynamic Roosevelt.

Roosevelt ran well in almost all sections of the country. Parker carried the South but little else and failed to gain even 40 percent of the POPULAR VOTE. The Republicans continued their dominance started with the 1896 PRESIDENTIAL ELECTION. Roosevelt, gratified by his landslide victory, pledged to not seek another term. This led to the grooming of his handpicked successor, William Howard Taft, to continue the Progressive agenda set forth by the Roosevelt administration. This decision by Roosevelt would lead to a temporary end to Republican dominance in presidential POLITICS.

Further reading: Blum, John M. *The Republican Roosevelt.* New York: Atheneum, 1967; Cooper, John Milton, Jr. *The Warrior and the Priest.* Cambridge, Mass.: Belknap, 1983; Hollingsworth, J. Rogers. *The Whirligig of Politics: The Democracy of Cleveland and Bryan.* Chicago: University of Chicago Press, 1963; Morris, Edmund. *Theodore Rex.* New York: Random House, 2001.

—Robert Butts

presidential election 1908

Winning President and Vice President: William Howard Taft and James S. Sherman
Number of States: 46
Major Candidates (Party Affiliation): William Howard Taft (Republican); William Jennings Bryan (Democrat)
Electoral College Vote: William Howard Taft: 321; William Jennings Bryan: 162
Popular Vote: William Howard Taft: 7,765,320; William Jennings Bryan: 6,412,294

In the 1908 presidential race, Republican presidential nominee William Howard Taft of Ohio and vice presidential RUNNING MATE James J. Sherman of New York handily defeated their opponents. The Democrats nominated William Jennings Bryan of Nebraska and John W. Kern of Indiana as Bryan's running mate. There were four different THIRD PARTIES that ran candidates: The SOCIALIST PARTY of America nominated Eugene V. Debs of Indiana and Benjamin Hanford of New York as his running mate, the PROHIBITION PARTY nominated Eugene W. Chafin of Illinois and Aaron S. Watkins of Ohio as his running mate, the Independence Party nominated Thomas L. Hisgen of Maine and John T. Graves of Georgia as his running mate, and the POPULIST PARTY nominated Thomas E. Watson of Georgia and Samuel Williams as his running mate.

Taft had been secretary of war under President Theodore Roosevelt. Roosevelt had earlier vowed not to seek another term, though he would have likely won reelection. Instead, Roosevelt urged his supporters to back Taft and the REPUBLICAN PARTY. Taft had a massive physical presence, weighing more than 300 pounds. Taft was forced to install an oversize bathtub in the White House. One popular story suggested that this was the result of getting stuck in the previous one and being freed only through the exertion of several men. Campaigning under the slogan "Get on the Raft with Taft," Progressives and other Roosevelt supporters flocked to Taft and hoped that his presidency would be a continuation of Roosevelt's reforms without Roosevelt's heavy-handedness. With this support and backed by his jovial personality, Taft was easily elected.

William Jennings Bryan had received much fame during his campaigning as Democratic nominee during the election of 1896, when he toured the country and delivered his "Cross of Gold" speech. He was also supported by the Populist Party in the election of 1896. His penchant for stopping at seemingly any town, large or small, earned him the moniker "boy orator of the Platte." His detractors claimed, however, that the Platte "was only six inches deep, but a milewide at the mouth." He was nominated a second-time as Democratic candidate for the election of 1900. Bryan attempted to maintain his Progressive and reformist platform but was competing against the proven reform

William Jennings Bryan *(Library of Congress)*

as the Populist presidential candidate in 1904 and again in 1908. After 1900, however, the Populists lost much of their former power, and Watson received only a small number of POPULAR VOTES in both elections. Watson would be the last Populist presidential candidate.

Eugene W. Chafin was the Prohibition Party's nominee for the election of 1908 and he would be again in 1912. The party was founded in 1869 and enjoyed only small success in national POLITICS. Its basic ideas, however, helped shape the platforms of the major parties and helped gain support for the Eighteenth Amendment.

The results of the election of 1908 overwhelmingly favored William Howard Taft. Taft received 7,765,320 popular votes, or 51.7 percent, and 321 electoral votes. William Jennings Bryan garnered 6,412,294 popular votes, or 43 percent, and 162 electoral votes. Eugene V. Debs trailed behind in third with less than 500,000 popular votes, or 2.8 percent.

Further reading: Anderson, Donald. F. *William Howard Taft: A Conservative's Conception of the Presidency.* Ithaca, N.Y.: Cornell University Press, 1973; Ashby, LeRoy. *William Jennings Bryan: Champion of Democracy.* Boston: Twayne Publishers, 1987; Minger, Ralph Eldin. *William Howard Taft and United States Foreign Policy: The Apprenticeship Years, 1900–1908.* Urbana: University of Illinois Press, 1975.

—Antonio Thompson

presidential election 1912

Winning President and Vice President: Woodrow Wilson and Thomas R. Marshall
Number of States: 48
Major Candidates (Party Affiliation): Woodrow Wilson (Democrat); Theodore Roosevelt (Progressive); William Howard Taft (Republican)
Electoral College Vote: Woodrow Wilson: 435; Theodore Roosevelt: 88; William Howard Taft: 8
Popular Vote: Woodrow Wilson: 6,296,547; Theodore Roosevelt: 4,118,571; William Howard Taft: 3,486,720

In the election of 1912, former president Theodore Roosevelt left retirement to challenge his handpicked successor, William Howard Taft, for the Republican NOMINATION. Roosevelt and Taft were close during Roosevelt's administration, but this familiar relationship evaporated once Roosevelt left office. Roosevelt was disappointed that Taft did not conform to his vision of the presidency. Taft embraced a constructionist outlook on the powers of the presidency and did not carry on many of the progressive reforms from the previous administration. Throughout 1910–11, the two grew increasingly adversarial. Roosevelt supported the more moderate Progressive elements within the REPUBLICAN PARTY, while Taft maintained strong support from the

legacy of the Roosevelt administration and its hand-picked successor. The 1908 election marked Bryan's third NOMINATION and third defeat in the bid for the presidency. This was the last time that he would seek the office.

Eugene V. Debs, best known for his role in the Pullman Strike (1894) and as a founder the Socialist Party of America, was again the Socialist candidate for president. He was the 1900 and 1904 nominee and would be again in 1912 and 1920, when he campaigned from prison. Debs was a fiery and flashy campaigner. One of his tactics was the Red Special Train, on which he toured the nation and gave speeches. Debs, however, was unable to compete against the two major parties for votes.

Tom Watson was the presidential nominee for the Populist Party. Watson was a founding member of the Populist Party (1891) and was also chosen to be the party's vice presidential nominee for the election of 1896. This was a decision that not all Populists, including presidential nominee William Jennings Bryan, agreed on, and this split the party. The Populist defeat nearly destroyed the party. Watson ran

conservative wing. Their relationship strained to the point that Roosevelt decided to challenge Taft for the Republican Party's nomination in 1912.

Roosevelt was still a hugely popular figure in America and won 10 of the 12 Republican state primaries. However, while Roosevelt may have had support of the Republican rank and file, those in control of the party still supported their incumbent, Taft. The Republican Convention, held in June in Chicago, was probably one of the most dynamic, fractious, and memorable conventions in American history. Taft and Roosevelt DELEGATES got into fistfights and brawls all throughout Chicago when they encountered one another on the streets, in hotels, or in bars. With the backing of the Republican Party, Taft won the nomination, but the process was contentious enough for Roosevelt to contend he was robbed. In fact, the night before the convention, Roosevelt gave a speech in Chicago accusing Taft of breaking the 8th Commandment, "Thou shall not steal." When it was clear Roosevelt would not win the nomination at the convention, he encouraged his supporters to leave with him and form a new party free of the perceived corruption within the Republican Party. This new party, the Progressives (or commonly called the BULL MOOSE PARTY), held its convention in August and nominated Roosevelt for president.

The deep division within the Republican Party was a boon for the Democrats. It meant the Republicans were likely to split their vote, allowing a Democrat to be elected for the first time since Grover Cleveland in the 1890s. However, this opportunity for the Democrats meant their convention was also highly contentious. Many Democrats saw this opportunity as perhaps their best chance ever to win the presidency. Several men including Champ Clark (U.S. House Speaker), Thomas Marshall, Judson Harmon, and Oscar W. Underwood all sought their party's nomination in Baltimore. After a very long and difficult balloting process, Woodrow Wilson gained the nomination on the 46th BALLOT.

The nomination of Woodrow Wilson placed Theodore Roosevelt at a disadvantage. Roosevelt knew he could carry the Progressives and many moderate Republicans. He was hopeful moderate Democrats would also vote for him. Unfortunately, Wilson also held the reputation of a progressive reformer and kept many moderate Democrats loyal to their party. Throughout most of the election season, Roosevelt and Taft primarily attacked each other, leaving Wilson unscathed by their assaults. Most important, the 1912 election campaign marked the first time an incumbent president campaigned for himself. Taft hit the campaign trail and made a few unsuccessful speeches in an attempt to rally support.

The two main platforms during this election were Roosevelt's "New Nationalism" and Wilson's "New Freedom" programs. At the heart of this election was the fate of America's political future. The New Freedom platform endorsed

Cartoon portraying Theodore Roosevelt during the 1912 election. Roosevelt was the only major-party candidate to support women's suffrage. (HarpWeek, LLC)

by Wilson called for increased individualism along with stronger states' rights. New Nationalism, on the other hand, was inspired by Herbert Croly's 1909 book *The Promise of American Life*. Roosevelt claimed "old" nationalism was a party to special interests. He argued that while economic concentration was inevitable, giant corporations should be brought under federal control. By doing so, the government would balance corporate power and protect the rights of both labor and the common man. Though elements within Roosevelt's platform were part of the genesis for the modern welfare state, he was frequently accused of socialism, and his views were very controversial among the conservative elements of the Republican Party and even among Progressives.

Ultimately, the Republican Party did exactly what was predicted following the Progressive split. Its voters divided their support between Roosevelt and Taft, ensuring Wilson the majority of the popular and ELECTORAL COLLEGE votes. Together, Roosevelt and Taft won a majority of the POPULAR VOTE, but their division allowed Wilson to dominate the Electoral College.

The PROGRESSIVE PARTY was unable to turn itself into a fully viable third party, and many of its supporters eventually rejoined the Republicans or Democrats. The importance of this election involves the fate of the Republicans. If Roosevelt had been able to win the nomination, the conservative wing of the party would have been forced to become more moderate or perhaps join the DEMOCRATIC PARTY. However, with the reformers and moderates leaving the party during the 1912 convention, the Republican Party fell firmly under the control of conservative elements, a fact that shaped the party's policy platforms for most of the 20th century.

Further reading: Genovese, Michael A. *The Power of the American Presidency, 1789–2000*. Oxford: Oxford University Press, 2001; McPherson, James M. *To the Best of My Ability: The American Presidents*. New York: Dorling Kindersley, 2001; Milkis, Sidney, and Michael Nelson. *The American Presidency: Origins and Development, 1776–1998*. Washington, D.C.: Congressional Quarterly Press, 2003.

—Shannon L. Bow

presidential election 1916

Winning President and Vice President: Woodrow Wilson and Thomas R. Marshall
Number of States: 48
Major Candidates (Party Affiliation): Woodrow Wilson (Democrat); Charles Evans Hughes (Republican)
Electoral College Vote: Woodrow Wilson: 277; Charles Evans Hughes: 254
Popular Vote: Woodrow Wilson: 9,127,695; Charles Evans Hughes: 8,533,507

Democratic incumbent president Woodrow Wilson from New Jersey and vice president Thomas R. Marshall from Indiana won the presidential election of 1916. The Republicans nominated Charles Evans Hughes from New York and Charles W. Fairbanks from Indiana as his RUNNING MATE. The Socialists were the major third party in the race and chose A. L. Benson from New York and George R. Kirkpatrick from New Jersey as his running mate.

Wilson had been elected president of Princeton University in 1902 and was elected governor of New Jersey in 1910, where he demonstrated his Progressive leanings. He left that position to seek the presidency in 1912. Wilson's 1912 campaign, dubbed the "New Freedom," promised numerous Progressive reforms and to keep the United States out of war. During his first term, Wilson succeeded

in keeping the country out of World War I despite his own pro-British sentiment. This was remarkable considering the tensions that were mounting between the United States and Germany over submarine warfare. Wilson's antiwar attitude was in line with the majority of the nation, which preferred a policy of ISOLATIONISM. It was also in line with his personal experience, having witnessed the devastation of the American Civil War while a young boy living in Richmond, Virginia, and later in Columbia, South Carolina. Despite Wilson's antiwar leanings and his slogan "He kept us out of war," Wilson was aware that American entry into the war was likely in the near future.

Prior to his NOMINATION by the REPUBLICAN PARTY, Charles Evans Hughes had served as governor of New York from 1907 to 1910 and then on the Supreme Court from 1910 to 1916 before stepping down to accept the presidential nomination. Much like Wilson, Hughes had earned a reputation as a Progressive reformer. Hughes also ran on an antiwar platform and was supported by Irish and German Americans, who opposed American aid to Britain, as well as by other Progressives. Hughes, however, faced two major obstacles in the election. The first was defeating the popular incumbent. The second stemmed from the support that Hughes received from Theodore Roosevelt.

Roosevelt refused to run as a nominee for the BULL-MOOSE PARTY, as he had in the election of 1912. Instead he chose to support Hughes and prevent splitting the Republican Party, as had been the case in 1912. As a former vice-secretary of the navy, war hero, vice president (1901), and president (1901–08), Roosevelt was well known, and many Americans associated him with militarism. Roosevelt felt that the United States was not prepared for war and should take stronger measures. This ran counter to the strong antiwar sentiment that prevailed in the United States and probably damaged Hughes's campaign.

Allan Louis Benson (A. L. Benson) was a newspaper reporter and editor and later wrote many books with a socialist agenda, including *A Way to Prevent War*, published in 1915. He was nominated as the SOCIALIST PARTY candidate after Eugene V. Debs, a founder of the Socialist Party of America and Socialist candidate in the presidential elections of 1904, 1908, and 1912, declined to be nominated in the election of 1916. Benson also ran on an antiwar platform and accused Wilson and American industry of being overly eager for war.

The results of the election were very close between the two major party candidates. Wilson received 277 of the electoral votes and 9,127,695, or 49.4 percent, of the POPULAR VOTE. Hughes garnered 254 electoral votes and 8,533,507, or 46.2 percent, of the popular vote. Benson won 3.2 percent of the popular vote. This close election came down to the vote in California, where one city claimed that its votes swung the election in Wilson's favor, and its citizens renamed it Wilsonia. Wilson's second term ended the validity of "He kept us out of war" after German submarine warfare prompted the United States to declare war on the Central Powers on April 2, 1917.

Further reading: Ambrosius, Lloyd E. *Wilsonian Statecraft: Theory and Practice of Liberal Internationalism during World War I.* Wilmington, Del.: SR Books, 1991; Ambrosius, Lloyd E. *Wilsonianism: Woodrow Wilson and His Legacy in American Foreign Relations.* New York: Palgrave Macmillan, 2002; Heckscher, August. *Woodrow Wilson.* New York: Scribner, 1991; Lovell, S. D. *The Presidential Election of 1916.* Carbondale: Southern Illinois University Press, 1980.

—Antonio Thompson

presidential election 1920

Winning President and Vice President: Warren G. Harding and Calvin Coolidge
Number of States: 48
Major Candidates (Party Affiliation): Warren G. Harding (Republican); James M. Cox (Democrat)
Electoral College Vote: Warren G. Harding: 404; James M. Cox: 127
Popular Vote: Warren G. Harding: 16,153,115; James M. Cox: 9,133,092

The first PRESIDENTIAL ELECTION after World War I offered weak leadership from both political parties. The war had not produced a hero ready for national POLITICS, the mood of the country was moving to the right, and President Woodrow Wilson was making the Democrats' job of choosing a nominee more difficult by refusing to endorse a successor as the party's standard bearer.

The REPUBLICAN NATIONAL CONVENTION was held in Chicago in early June and, lacking an obvious FRONTRUNNER, was strongly influenced by Senate "bosses." Legend has it that the bosses picked the nominee, but that is generally considered inaccurate. Harry Daugherty, acting on behalf of Warren G. Harding, had positioned Harding to be the viable alternative to the big names—General Leonard Wood of New Hampshire, Senator Hiram Johnson of California, and Governor Frank Lowden of Illinois. Harding was both available and acceptable, particularly because he had no ties to the bosses, and secured the NOMINATION on the 10th BALLOT.

The Democrats held their convention in San Francisco in late June. The three candidates thought to have the best chance for nomination were former secretary of the Treasury in the Wilson administration William McAdoo of California, Wilson's attorney general, A. Mitchell Palmer, and the three-term governor of Ohio, James M. Cox. Immigration and Prohibition dominated the convention, with divisions in the convention running along the lines of "wet vs. dry," "Northeast and Midwest vs. South and West," and, to a lesser extent, "Catholic vs. Protestant." Cox obtained the nomination on

the 44th ballot, and a young New Yorker, Franklin D. Roosevelt, was chosen as his vice presidential RUNNING MATE.

The general campaign of 1920 was the first presidential election since 1908 in which the Republicans were solidly united. The Republicans dominated the campaign from the start, with Cox and Roosevelt immediately facing great odds. Harding employed a "front-porch" campaign strategy from his home in Marion, Ohio, welcoming a wide variety of potential voters from all parts of the country. There were visits to Marion by celebrities, and a Major League baseball game was played in Marion with Harding throwing out the first pitch. Much of the publicity the Republican ticket received, with the first presidential candidate to give a speech over the radio, was due to the efforts of the Republican National Party.

The Democrats, lacking money for a "modern" campaign such as the Republicans were running with paid advertising and large staffs of publicity agents, resorted to William Jennings Bryan's technique of marathon whistle-stop trips. The press coverage of the Democratic campaign was limited almost to the point that it took a train derailment to make the front pages of the California newspapers. The Democrats' message did not appeal to the ELECTORATE, and there was lingering dissension among Democrats over Prohibition. Cox adopted a timid stance on the League of Nations, which did not endear him to Wilsonian Democrats. While the Democrats' message was not resonating with the public, Harding was calling for higher tariffs, criticizing socialism, and calling for lower taxes as well as limits on immigration.

The outcome of the election was never in much doubt. Harding became the first Republican to carry New York City and Boston. He also carried all of the "border states" except Kentucky, as well as the entire North and West, including Oklahoma. His percentage of more than 60 percent was the largest in presidential elections up to that time. In the ELECTORAL COLLEGE he tallied 404 votes to Cox's 127.

The cause of the defeat was not necessarily Cox or his platform, but a backlash from Wilsonism. The *Nation* called it an election by "disgust." Voters, wanting the hopeful and secure world of 1913, voted their resentments. The election was a referendum on Woodrow Wilson and the problems that had plagued the United States between the Armistice and the election.

Further reading: Cooper, John Milton. *Pivotal Decades.* New York: Norton, 1990; Goldinger, Carolyn, ed. *Presidential Elections since 1789.* Washington, D.C.: Congressional Quarterly Press, 1987; Roseboom, Eugene H. *A History of Presidential Elections.* New York: Macmillan, 1957.

—J. Mark Alcorn

presidential election 1924

Winning President and Vice President: Calvin Coolidge and Charles G. Dawes
Number of States: 48

Major Candidates (Party Affiliation): Calvin Coolidge (Republican); John William Davis (Democrat); Robert Marion LaFollette (Progressive)

Electoral College Vote: Calvin Coolidge: 382; John William Davis: 136; Robert Marion LaFollette: 13

Popular Vote: Calvin Coolidge: 15,719,921; John William Davis: 8,386,704; Robert Marion LaFollette: 4,832,532

While the Election of 1924 was not a close one, it nevertheless proved to be a dramatic one, as demonstrated by the political reversals of fortune that befell both parties. It was the Democrats, beneficiaries of the electoral results of 1922 and the SCANDALS of the Harding administration, who entered 1924 with hopes to regain the White House. Republicans, on the other hand, reeling from the shocking losses of 1922, the loss of Harding, and initial wariness over Coolidge, seemed to be teetering on the brink of defeat. The contest also saw the reemergence of the Progressives, this time under the leadership of Wisconsin senator Robert LaFollette. In the end, Republicans united behind Coolidge and won a decisive victory. Democrats, initially hopeful, fell victim to internecine warfare and a bland candidate and suffered a crushing loss. The Progressives could not replicate the success they had enjoyed in 1912 and won only Wisconsin.

The unexpected death of President Warren Harding provided an unanticipated early beginning to the 1924 campaign. Republicans, despite having Vice President Calvin Coolidge ascend to the office, began discussing who would become the party's nominee. Coolidge's liberal record as governor of Massachusetts did not sit well with the party's conservatives, nor did he have the confidence of Republican liberals, either. As a result, Republican senator Hiram Johnson of California announced his candidacy in fall 1923. However, Coolidge quickly dampened the PUNDITS' speculation by running an efficient administration that was politically conservative and conscientious in eliminating any vestige of scandal from his administration. To the public, Coolidge displayed competence in the way he handled the Pennsylvania coal miners strike and with his appointment of a special counsel to investigate the Teapot Dome scandal.

The Democrats saw the Teapot Dome scandal as an excellent opportunity to recapture both houses of Congress and the White House. Their optimism was well placed, as the MIDTERM ELECTION of 1922 whittled Republican majorities in the House and Senate to a small 18 and eight, respectively. Their obstacle lay in choosing the correct candidate who could unite the party, use the anger created from the scandals, and parlay both into a November victory.

However, the Democrats suffered from a paralyzing enmity that existed between rural and urban Democrats. Rural Democrats, characterized by hostility to immigrants, Catholics, alcohol, cities, and the POLITICS that existed within them, were represented by former secretary of the Treasury William Gibbs McAdoo. Urban Democrats, made up of immigrants, opponents of Prohibition, and machine members supported the liberal governor of New York, Al Smith.

Not only was the party crippled by its division, it also began to be tarnished by the scandals that plagued Harding. It was revealed that during the Teapot Dome scandal, one of the private developers to whom naval oil reserve lands were leased was Edward Doheny. Doheny was highly placed in the DEMOCRATIC PARTY in California and had employed as consultants the services of several Wilson cabinet officials, including McAdoo. Nor was Smith spared, as it was revealed that he had appointed Harry F. Sinclair, the other major developer in the scandal, to the New York State Racing Commission.

Despite McAdoo's connection with the Teapot Dome scandal and swirling rumors of backing by the KU KLUX KLAN, he continued to campaign and participate in the Democratic primaries. He easily won nine of the 17 primaries. McAdoo appeared to have wide appeal, as his victories were not limited to a particular region. Smith, on the other hand, did not perform so well in the primaries but could not be ignored because he was strong in the new power centers of the party, mainly the industrialized areas and the cities.

Coolidge remained untouched by the scandals, and he worked to undermine Johnson to ensure the Republican NOMINATION. His first move was to organize the party in such a way as to render his opponent powerless. First, Coolidge consolidated the South by limiting the influence of African-American Republican leaders to attract more white votes. In Indiana, Coolidge discouraged FAVORITE SON candidacies. In the Midwest, Coolidge reduced Johnson's popularity by increasing wheat tariffs and the availability of farm loans. Coolidge went on to defeat Johnson in 16 primaries, including Johnson's home state of California. After that loss, Johnson withdrew from the race.

The Republican convention, held in Cleveland, opened on June 10. It marked the first convention to be broadcast by radio and the first to elect women to the national committee. Coolidge won the nomination easily, garnering 1,065 votes to LaFollette's 34 and Johnson's 10. The nomination of the vice president was less clear-cut, as eight candidates were forwarded. The first nominee to win a majority was former Illinois governor Frank Lowden, who subsequently declined. The second choice fell between former general Charles Dawes and Secretary of Commerce Herbert Hoover. Dawes was well liked by the convention, while Hoover was the object of scorn for his role in fixing the price of wheat during the war. On the third BALLOT, Dawes defeated Hoover. The last outcome of the convention was the platform, which focused on the administration's role in the economy, the need for tax cuts, and a general satisfaction in the status quo.

The Democratic convention, which opened in New York on June 24, failed to live up to the order and civility demonstrated by its Republican counterpart. Much of this disorder can be traced to the lack of a strong leader and the unreasonable burden created by the two-thirds rule. The first crucial moment occurred when the platform committee issued a report debating whether to censure the Ku Klux Klan by name. McAdoo controlled the committee and through his influence got a report without a mention of the Klan.

On June 30, the balloting for president began. The two-thirds rule crippled the proceedings, and a drawn-out and combative stalemate developed. Smith reached his highest point with 368 votes, and McAdoo reached his at 528. Democrats from Tammany Hall tried to prolong the debacle until hotel bills became too expensive for many of the conventioneers. Forces on both sides desperately sought an end to the spectacle. Smith was reportedly offered second place on the McAdoo ticket. At one point, Smith offered to withdraw if McAdoo did the same, but he refused. By the 99th ballot, McAdoo withdrew, with many of his DELEGATES flocking to Ambassador John W. Davis. Finally, on the 103rd ballot, Davis won the nomination. Charles W. Bryan, governor of Nebraska and brother of William Jennings Bryan, won the vice presidential nomination on the first ballot. The impasse marked the most ballots cast in a political convention and resulted in the longest convention on record (June 24–July 10).

The Progressives met for their convention in Cleveland on July 4. Not surprisingly, the convention's 1,200 delegates chose LaFollette as the party's presidential nominee. Their platform included tenets similar to those of the earlier BULL MOOSE PARTY, such as a repeal of Prohibition, an end to monopolies, conservation of natural resources, an end to child labor, and the right of collective bargaining. LaFollette chose Democratic senator Burton K. Wheeler as his RUNNING MATE.

The issues that confronted the candidates were vastly different from those that confronted candidates in later elections. The economy, a dramatic and critical issue in times of economic downturn, was booming and a nonissue for the CHALLENGERS. Republicans stressed the prosperity of the "Roaring Twenties" as a result of their policies and their general laissez-faire orientation toward business. Second, Coolidge's adept handling of the Harding scandals and the prosecution of the guilty participants nullified the issue for the voting public. The issue that seems notable in its absence today is foreign policy, as the times were characterized by a general embrace of ISOLATIONISM.

Davis, the Democratic nominee, can be described as bland and colorless. His nomination represented a victory for the Smith forces and the urban Democrats. Much of Davis's trouble lay in the times. Davis did not offer much, nor did he have many to offer to. Farmers, labor, and radicals had Lafol-lette, and businessmen had Coolidge. Davis was also conservative, at least more so than the two former FRONTRUNNERS. It was the subsequent nomination of Bryan, a move many believed was a way to placate the radicals, that made the Democratic ticket particularly unattractive. The Bryan name frightened business, and the conservative leanings of Davis offended labor and Progressive voters. Lastly, his personality as a candidate left much to be desired. He failed to excite voters, and many, not knowing his record, wrote him off as a shadow of the Republican Coolidge.

Coolidge ran his campaign much like he presented himself—silent and unremarkable. Little attention was paid to either competitor, and Coolidge stuck to the issues of common sense and the economy. Also, saddened by the death of his son, Coolidge limited himself to just a few outside ventures, preferring to stay at his father's Vermont farm or in Washington, D.C. It was Dawes, often with the approval of the president, who launched into political attacks on the two other candidates. The most effective Republican attack centered on the possibility of LaFollette's candidacy throwing the election to the House. In that situation, they argued, the House would be deadlocked over the selection of a president. The Senate, with a COALITION of Democrats and progressive Republicans, would select Bryan for vice president. The absence of a result from the House would mean that Bryan would become president. Thus, Republicans focused on Bryan as a way to scare voters from casting a ballot for either Davis or LaFollette.

The Progressives focused their campaign on the issues presented in their platform. However, while the Progressive candidacy featured a viable option other than the two major parties as well as the first successful alliance of farm and labor interests, it suffered from a variety of weaknesses. The first lay in its nominee. LaFollette had a history of ill health and was not suited for the rigors of the campaign trail. Second, Progressives failed to achieve the type of press coverage and funds afforded the other parties. Last, a rise in agricultural prices and the weakness of organized labor reduced the effectiveness of the party.

By ELECTION DAY, prospects for the Republicans were dramatically different than they had been the previous year. Republicans had raised nearly $4 million compared to $1 million for the Democrats and less than a quarter-million for the Progressives. PATRONAGE had kept most Republicans in line, and the failure of the corruption issue to catch on with the public meant an easy victory for the GRAND OLD PARTY. The final totals were impressive: Coolidge dominated, outpacing Davis by more than 7 million votes. In the ELECTORAL COLLEGE, Coolidge earned 382 votes to Davis's 136 and LaFollette's 13.

The significance of the 1924 election transcends its temporal results. While the dramatic Republican victory of 1924 has been overshadowed by the Great Depression and the REALIGNMENT caused by Franklin Roosevelt and the

New Deal, the election has continued to have ramifications that affect the present. This contribution can be seen in the pioneering use of photojournalism and radio for campaign coverage. This development, a modest forerunner to today's coverage, has influenced the way candidates are conveyed and the way campaigns are conducted.

Further reading: Schlesinger, Arthur, and Fred L. Israel. *History of American Presidential Elections, 1789–1968.* New York: Chelsea House, 1971.

—Stephen Nemeth

presidential election 1928

Winning President and Vice President: Herbert C. Hoover and Charles Curtis
Number of States: 48
Major Candidates (Party Affiliation): Herbert C. Hoover (Republican); Alfred E. Smith (Democrat)
Electoral College Vote: Herbert C. Hoover: 444; Alfred E. Smith: 87
Popular Vote: Herbert C. Hoover: 21,437,277; Alfred E. Smith: 15,007,698

In the latter part of President Calvin Coolidge's third year in office, he stunned most, if not all, people, including his wife, by sending a wire from his summer residence in the Black Hills of South Dakota: "I do not choose to run for President in 1928." Only Coolidge's private secretary, Everett Sanders, had known of the decision.

Secretary of Commerce Herbert Hoover, well known as the food administrator during World War I, was the logical successor. He was considered the "class" of the Coolidge administration, and though he was not popular with the political bosses, he was admired around the country by the common people. Hoover had long been planning for this moment and immediately had his people start the search for DELEGATES. He secured delegates without the help of the heavy hitters in the administration and despite not having a blessing from Coolidge in his quest for the NOMINATION. His campaign spent nearly $400,000 in the preconvention phase.

The Republicans held their national convention in Kansas City in early June 1928. The nomination, for all practical purposes, was settled prior to the convention, with Hoover winning on the only BALLOT cast for president. The only opposition to him came from die-hard party regulars who would not accept him as an authentic Republican. The platform pushed the idea of contentment with the prosperity generated from the Harding-Coolidge years as well as Prohibition. The platform committed the party to the "observance and vigorous enforcement" of the Eighteenth Amendment. Senator Charles Curtis was nominated as the vice presidential candidate of the REPUBLICAN PARTY.

The Democrats held their convention in Houston in late June and nominated four-term New York governor Al Smith. His support came from the East as well as city-controlled state organizations. His campaign was able to establish Smith organizations throughout the country and secure delegates. Smith's main obstacles were that he was Roman Catholic, had a Tammany Hall background, was "wet," and, to rural America, was too "big city."

In his favor in his quest for the nomination was the lack of a strong candidate in opposition who could draw together the anti-Smith elements in the West and South. All of the other well-known candidates were opposed for one reason or another—being wet, opposing the League of Nations, and so on—and thus lacked support. Smith gained the nomination for all intents and purposes on the first ballot after Ohio switched to Smith from its nominal choice of former Ohio senator Atlee Pomerene. In an attempt to add balance to the Democrat ticket, Arkansas senator Joseph Robinson was nominated as the vice presidential candidate.

Farm relief occupied a significant portion of the platform, as well as an acknowledgment that work needed to be done on the country's unemployment problem. Prohibition was addressed by criticizing the Republicans for being inconsistent and by the Democrats promising an honest effort in enforcement of the Eighteenth Amendment.

Radio was prominent in a presidential campaign for the first time, with the dry, humorless Hoover coming across well over the radio. He portrayed himself as a self-made man who was born an orphan, worked his way through Stanford, and believed in American individualism, free enterprise, and small government. He was the businessman's ideal candidate: a self-made millionaire who rejected anything suggesting socialism, paternalism, or a planned economy. As secretary of commerce, however, he had endorsed some Progressive measures, such as support for federal regulation of the fledgling radio broadcasting industry, and he had endorsed some labor unions.

Immediately after the national convention, Republicans went to work raising money, and the national committee spent a record $6 million. In Hoover's acceptance speech, broadcast from Palo Alto, California, he stressed the prosperity the country was enjoying, accomplishments of the Harding-Coolidge years as well as the abolition of poverty, and sang the praises of "rugged individualism."

Hoover surrogates traveling throughout the country displayed considerably more charisma than the candidate himself. They were dispatched to regions of the country where they would be most helpful. Charles Evans Hughes pushed the prosperity and achievement themes in the East, where Prohibition was unpopular, while Senator William Borah of Idaho, a Republican progressive, used Prohibition, farm relief, and Tammany Hall in the farm belt.

Al Smith was a far more charismatic and dynamic person than Hoover. He delivered his acceptance speech from Albany, New York, and then went on the road, giving major

Herbert Hoover campaigning from the back of a railroad car during the 1928 presidential election *(Library of Congress)*

addresses throughout the country while tailoring the message to his audience. He spoke of farm relief in Omaha, Prohibition in Milwaukee, and religious tolerance in Oklahoma City. His campaign was the best financed in Democratic history, raising and spending $5.3 million.

The Democrats had several problems. First, they had to contest the prosperity appeal. Second, they had to overcome the triple objections to Smith (i.e., his "wetness," religion, and Tammany Hall associations). Prosperity served the Republicans where it existed. Where it did not, emotional appeals to bigotry and prejudice took its place. In the Democratic South, the Republicans kept quiet and let the anti-Smith Democrats, or Hoovercrats, fight their battles. There was a serious movement against Smith because he was a Roman Catholic. Stories circulated that the pope would move from the Vatican to the United States if Smith

were to be elected. Others attacked Smith's "wetness," claiming he was a drunkard and could not serve as president. When Smith had a chance to speak, he explained himself well. In the end, however, his obstacles proved insurmountable.

November 6, 1928, provided the Republicans with a significant victory. Hoover won the East with two exceptions, the entire West, the border South, as well as Texas, Florida, North Carolina, Tennessee, and Virginia from the old South. The POPULAR VOTE was 21 million to 15 million, with the ELECTORAL COLLEGE vote at 444 for Hoover and 87 for Smith.

Further reading: Hinshaw, David. *Herbert Hoover, American Quaker.* New York: Farrar Straus, 1950.

—J. Mark Alcorn

presidential election 1932

Winning President and Vice President: Franklin D.
    Roosevelt and John N. Garner
Number of States: 48
Major Candidates (Party Affiliation): Franklin D.
    Roosevelt (Democrat); Herbert C. Hoover
    (Republican)
Electoral College Vote: Franklin D. Roosevelt: 472;
    Herbert C. Hoover: 59
Popular Vote: Franklin D. Roosevelt: 22,829,501;
    Herbert C. Hoover: 15,760,684

National POLITICS in the 1930s were dominated by the Great Depression, the worst economic downturn in American history. Beginning with the stock market crash in October 1929, the economy deteriorated quickly: On the eve of the 1932 elections, nearly a third of the national workforce was unemployed, thousands of banks and farms had failed, and personal incomes had fallen by almost half. This economic collapse was even more disorienting because, to most Americans, it was entirely unexpected. The 1920s had been a period of unprecedented prosperity and seemingly permanent economic growth. In his 1929 inauguration address, incoming Republican president Herbert Hoover echoed the generally shared belief that the United States had been liberated from "widespread poverty" and "reached a higher degree of comfort and security than ever existed before in the history of the world."

The prosperity of the "Roaring Twenties," however, was based on unsound economic footing: Stock prices were greatly overvalued, and American families had sunk deeply into debt to purchase the cars, household appliances, and houses upon which the industrial economy depended. When stock and credit systems crumbled, the entire economic structure of the United States was also pulled down. The prospects for recovery became even bleaker as the remainder of the industrialized world succumbed to recession. Indeed, the global economic disintegration was so severe that many observers feared that capitalism itself was on the verge of collapse.

Despite the magnitude of the Depression, Hoover continued to claim that the country's economic structure was basically sound and was unwilling to diverge from the economic orthodoxy of balanced budgets, protectionism, and the gold standard. Moreover, because Hoover was dedicated to individualism and states' rights, he minimized federal involvement in economic relief, relying instead on voluntary cooperation from business leaders to maintain employment and wage levels. Only near the end of his term did Hoover begin to experiment on a larger scale with job programs, business loans, and modest tax reductions to expand consumer purchasing power.

Hoover's reluctance to act decisively made him seem cold and unconcerned about the problems of average Americans. As a result, he bore the brunt of public anger about continuing economic woes, and his name became almost synonymous with poverty. For example, dumps and abandoned buildings where the homeless gathered for shelter were called "Hoovervilles," and newspapers used for warmth became "Hoover blankets." This negative opinion was reinforced by the administration's treatment of the "Bonus Army." The army consisted of thousands of unemployed veterans who assembled in Washington, D.C., to petition Congress for early payment of the "bonuses" promised to them as a reward for service in World War I. When the veterans refused to disband, Hoover ordered the U.S. Army to force protesters out of the abandoned government buildings in which they had set up residence. In the ensuing conflict, two veterans and a baby were killed, a public relations nightmare for the already weakened administration.

Despite these problems, Hoover won the REPUBLICAN PARTY NOMINATION without serious opposition—but also without much enthusiasm or expectation of victory in the November GENERAL ELECTION. By contrast, the DEMOCRATIC PARTY nomination was the object of fierce competition. Three major contestants—Al Smith, former governor of New York and Democratic presidential nominee in 1928, Franklin Roosevelt, current governor of New York, and John Nance Garner, SPEAKER OF THE HOUSE OF REPRESENTATIVES—vied for votes at the Chicago convention. Smith and Roosevelt, once political allies in New York, represented very different groups of voters. Smith was popular with urban Democrats but disliked by southern and rural voters, who were suspicious of his Catholicism and opposition to Prohibition. Moreover, Smith's loss in the 1928 election, including a loss of his home state to Hoover, convinced many Democrats that Smith was unelectable in a national contest.

Roosevelt's campaigning skills and immense popularity even among rural New Yorkers convinced party leaders that Roosevelt was a better candidate, and he quickly became the FRONTRUNNER for the nomination. On the first BALLOT, Roosevelt won 666 1/2 votes to Smith's 202 3/4 and Garner's 90 1/4. Despite this clear majority, Roosevelt fell short of the two-thirds majority required to win the nomination and made little headway on the second and third ballots. Fearing that a deadlocked convention would nominate a weak compromise candidate, Garner released his votes to Roosevelt in return for the vice presidential slot, allowing Roosevelt to win on the fourth ballot. Breaking precedent, Roosevelt flew to Chicago to accept the nomination in person, pledging his administration to "a new deal for the American people."

The general campaign was determined as much by style and personality as by party platform. Hoover seemed to offer the public little that was new, merely repeating the claim that "prosperity is right around the corner" and insisting that too much federal involvement would destroy individual liberty and the work ethic. In public, Hoover appeared tired and lacking confidence; in private, he complained of exhaustion and an inability to cope with the demands of leadership.

By contrast, Roosevelt projected an image of youthfulness, optimism, and a willingness to use whatever power or policy was necessary to end the Depression. As a result, although Roosevelt's platform established general priorities—shoring up market and banking systems, providing economic security for all Americans, and more equitably distributing wealth—it was not specific about how such goals should be accomplished. Indeed, it was often difficult for observers to sort out Roosevelt's economic policy. For example, on the one hand Roosevelt supported the regulation of utilities (a liberal stance), while at the same time he maintained a vague support for balanced budgets (a conservative position). On the tariff, usually a central issue within Democratic politics, Roosevelt was evasive and failed to stake out any clear position at all. The lack of an unambiguous economic agenda irritated critics on the left, who believed that a more thoroughgoing reform of the capitalist system was needed. SOCIALIST PARTY candidate Norman Thomas stressed Roosevelt's ideological inconsistencies throughout the campaign, using them as evidence that both major parties were too tied to the market system to bring about long-term recovery.

As expected, the November elections were a repudiation of Hoover's economic conservatism. Roosevelt won a healthy majority of the POPULAR VOTE and was awarded a landslide in electoral votes. Although the Socialist Party candidacy was never a real threat to Roosevelt, Thomas's ability to win almost 1 million votes made it clear that Roosevelt had not convinced a large bloc of voters that he was truly dedicated to economic and social equality. This lesson would shape the policy choices of Roosevelt's first term and push him further to the left for the 1936 election.

Roosevelt's obvious popularity intimidated even the Republican members of Congress, setting the stage for an unprecedented burst of legislative activity in early 1933. A spate of important policies passed in the first hundred days of Roosevelt's term, including emergency banking legislation, abandonment of the gold standard, and the establishment of the Tennessee Valley Authority, Federal Deposit Insurance Corporation, and Civilian Conservation Corps. A "hundred-days" measure has since been applied to each president's freshman term as a standard for judging the new administration's ability to pass its legislative agenda.

The election of 1932 was important for several reasons. First, it was a "realigning" election that ended more than half a century of Republican domination of the White House. Between 1860 and 1932, Democrats had won the presidency only four times, and one of those elections, in 1912, had resulted from the split between progressive and conservative Republicans rather than Democratic strength. Roosevelt's elevation to the presidency therefore signaled the reemergence of Democrats as a viable national party.

Franklin D. Roosevelt giving a campaign speech in 1932 *(Franklin D. Roosevelt Presidential Library and Museum)*

Second, Roosevelt changed the way presidential campaigns were run. He successfully used new forms of transportation and communication to craft a "candidate-centered" campaign that emphasized personality as well as (or perhaps more than) substance. By concentrating on character—geniality, optimism, confidence—while finessing divisive issues such as the tariff, Roosevelt had greater flexibility once in office. Because he had not tied himself to a specific policy agenda during the campaign, Roosevelt could experiment with different policies without appearing to renege on campaign promises. This candidate-centered strategy did have negative consequences, however. To voters with strong ideological preferences, Roosevelt's cultivation of public image seemed shallow at best and demagogic at worst.

Third, the economic crisis created the opportunity for an expansion of the presidential role beyond traditionally recognized constitutional limits. Roosevelt exploited public demand for strong leadership to direct the legislative agenda and establish a system of executive agencies that institutionalized long-term presidential influence over a variety of issues. As "chief bureaucrat," the presidents who followed Roosevelt controlled significantly more power in national policy making. By the late 20th century, presidents would become the primary leaders of their parties, displacing congressional leadership within the legislative process.

Further reading: Fausold, Martin. *The Presidency of Herbert C. Hoover.* Lawrence: University Press of Kansas, 1985; Lisio, Donald. *Hoover, MacArthur and the Bonus March.* New York: Fordham University Press, 1994; Neal, Steven. *Happy Days Are Here Again: The 1932 Election, the Emergence of FDR—and How America Was Changed Forever.* New York: William Morrow, 2004.

—Celia M. Carroll

presidential election 1936

Winning President and Vice President: Franklin D.
    Roosevelt and John N. Garner
Number of States: 48
Major Candidates (Party Affiliation): Franklin D.
    Roosevelt (Democrat); Alfred M. Landon
    (Republican)
Electoral College Vote: Franklin D. Roosevelt: 523; Alfred
    M. Landon: 8
Popular Vote: Franklin D. Roosevelt: 27,757,333; Alfred
    M. Landon: 16,684,231

The election of 1936 clarified and strengthened the partisan REALIGNMENT that had begun with the election of Franklin Roosevelt in 1932. New Deal policies had proven very popular with the American public and deepened the attachment of voters to Franklin Roosevelt and the DEMO-

CRATIC PARTY more generally. Many of the new Democratic voters came to the party out of a sense of gratitude to the Roosevelt administration. New Deal policies offered a degree of economic security to many previously Republican-leaning groups. Federal home, business, and farm loan programs helped to stem the tide of foreclosures, and agricultural price supports propped up failing farmers. Both of these programs brought large portions of the Midwest and the middle class into the Democratic fold.

Even groups that had first viewed the Roosevelt administration with skepticism were attracted by New Deal policies. For example, passage of the National Labor Relations Act in 1935 affirmed the rights of workers to bargain collectively and join independent, or "nonshop," unions. This helped Roosevelt win union votes and diminished support for the SOCIALIST PARTY. Businesses that benefited indirectly from public works policies also became Roosevelt supporters. Retail companies such as J.C. Penney's defended public works programs such as the Civilian Conservation Corps and the Civil Works Administration because they increased consumer demand by putting money in the hands of public employees and their families.

The most impressive change in voting behavior, however, was the shift away from the REPUBLICAN PARTY by African Americans. Since RECONSTRUCTION, African Americans had been steadfast supporters of "the party of Lincoln," and it was conventional wisdom that this allegiance was inalterable. Roosevelt's willingness to make federal relief monies available to blacks, although usually at lower levels than to whites, began to chip away at this group's support for Republicans. Roosevelt's support for antilynching legislation and his wife, Eleanor's, vocal sympathy for black political goals brought even greater numbers of African Americans into the Democratic fold. By 1936, a majority of politically active blacks voted for Roosevelt's reelection.

As a consequence, the Democratic COALITION grew beyond its traditional bases of support within the urban areas of the North and among southern whites and made the New Deal the central political issue of the 1936 election. The general popularity of the Roosevelt administration presented potential political opponents with a strategic dilemma: To reject the New Deal entirely alienated groups that had come to depend on government subsidies for economic security. On the other hand, to acknowledge the accomplishments of the Roosevelt administration provided little incentive for voters to defect from the Democratic ranks.

Republicans, especially, were divided about how to run against Roosevelt. Most believed that increased federal spending and growing budget deficits would stall economic recovery, depress business activity, and increase dependence on government handouts. Party members strongly disagreed, however, about how far to go in criticizing Roosevelt. Progressive Republicans such as Senator William E.

Borah were sympathetic to the goals of the New Deal but felt that it was poorly administered and wasteful. More conservative members such as Herbert Hoover worried that the centralization of power and money at the federal level was a prelude to the creation of a totalitarian state such as the Soviet Union or Fascist Italy.

A successful Republican candidate therefore faced the daunting task of bridging intraparty divisions even before facing Roosevelt in the GENERAL ELECTION. Alfred M. Landon, governor of Kansas, struck this balance by supporting sizable relief programs combined with spending limits and state-level administration. Styling himself a "constitutional liberal," Landon sought to create an image of the Republican Party as one concerned with long-term fiscal responsibility and individual liberty as well as short-term economic relief. Many party leaders supported the Landon candidacy from an early date, believing that his support for agricultural programs would appeal to farmers, that his business experience would soothe the fears of eastern financiers, and that his support of a balanced budget would attract those who feared the economic effects of a ballooning federal deficit. Landon also seemed to have the golden touch in POLITICS, surviving the anti-Republicanism prevalent in the 1930s. For example, he had been the only incumbent Republican governor to win reelection in 1934. For these reasons, Landon was widely viewed as the Republicans' best chance at halting the Roosevelt juggernaut and was chosen to represent the party with little opposition.

A second set of critics, on the other hand, felt that the New Deal had not gone far enough to relieve the economic woes of average Americans. By concentrating too heavily on business recovery and public employment, they argued, the Roosevelt administration had ignored the stark economic inequalities and most vulnerable groups within American society. Under the guidance of popular speakers and politicians, a number of public movements were established during Roosevelt's first term to voice this discontent. California physician Francis Townsend, for example, organized an "old people's movement" to petition for pension payments to the elderly. Huey Long, senator from Louisiana and popular southern politician, promoted a program to radically redistribute income ("share the wealth") among Americans. Catholic priest Father Charles Coughlin used weekly radio sermons as a national platform from which to oppose the New Deal. Although he had supported Roosevelt in the 1932 elections, Coughlin had soured on the New Deal, claiming that it was controlled by Jewish "banking interests."

By 1935, these protest movements had reached their fullest strength: Hundreds of Townsend Clubs and Share-the-Wealth Clubs had been organized throughout the United States, and Coughlin's listeners routinely sent telegrams and letters to Washington to protest Roosevelt policies. Despite their differing agendas (and personal disdain for one another), Coughlin, Townsend, and Long's succes-

sor, Gerald L. K. Smith, decided to pool their resources and create a third-party alternative, the UNION PARTY, to both major parties. If successful, the Union Party would combine Coughlin's support among Catholics, Smith's following in the South, and Townsend's popularity among older voters into a formidable voting bloc. By selecting North Dakota congressman and agricultural reformer William Lemke as its presidential candidate, the Union Party hoped to round out its anti-Roosevelt coalition with the votes of midwestern farmers.

Roosevelt's strategy in the face of these political challenges was twofold. First, Roosevelt successfully portrayed the Republican attempt to strike a balance among party FACTIONS as a capitulation to business interests. As a result, Landon was unable to separate himself from Hoover and the conservative wing of the Republican Party and failed to capitalize on the political potential of his moderate agenda. Second, Roosevelt "stole the thunder" of his populist critics by enacting a series of new programs, the Second New Deal, that coopted the attractive features of the Share-the-Wealth and Townsend programs.

For example, the Revenue Act of 1935 raised tax rates sharply on incomes above $50,000 and increased estate, corporation, and gift taxes. Called the "Soak-the-Rich Tax" by conservative critics, the Revenue Act appealed to voters who wanted a more equitable distribution of wealth. The Social Security Act of 1935 established an unemployment insurance program and charged the government with a responsibility for helping "dependent" members of society—children, the blind and disabled, and, significantly, the elderly. Although neither of these programs promised (or delivered) the scope of benefits originally espoused by Townsend and Long, they were adequate to slow Union Party momentum.

Roosevelt enjoyed an overwhelming victory in the November elections, winning almost 61 percent of the POPULAR VOTE and taking all but eight electoral votes. The Union Party ticket was an almost complete failure, winning fewer than 1 million votes nationwide. Democrats also swept the CONGRESSIONAL ELECTIONS; in the new Congress, Republicans found themselves outnumbered 107 to 328 in the House of Representatives and 19 to 77 in the Senate. These results were interpreted as a wholesale reaffirmation of the New Deal, greatly strengthening Roosevelt's political stature at the beginning of his second term.

Further reading: Brinkley, Alan. *Voices of Protest: Huey Long, Father Coughlin, and the Great Depression.* New York: Knopf, 1982; Schlesinger, Arthur M. *The Politics of Upheaval: The Age of Roosevelt.* Vol. 3. Boston: Houghton Mifflin, 1960. Weiss, Nancy J. *Farewell to the Party of Lincoln: Black Politics in the Age of FDR.* Princeton, N.J.: Princeton University Press, 1983.

—Celia M. Carroll

presidential election 1940

Winning President and Vice President: Franklin D.
Roosevelt and Henry A. Wallace

Number of States: 48

Major Candidates (Party Affiliation): Franklin D.
Roosevelt (Democrat); Wendell Willkie (Republican)

Electoral College Vote: Franklin D. Roosevelt: 449;
Wendell Wilkie: 82

Popular Vote: Franklin D. Roosevelt: 27,313,041; Wendell
Wilkie: 22,348,480

This election was the first time an incumbent president ran for a third term and won. This election also marked the change from John Nance Garner, Franklin Roosevelt's vice president during his first two terms, to Henry A. Wallace. Garner, a conservative southerner, was instrumental in the success of the early New Deal programs. However, the two began to grow apart during the second term. Garner opposed some of the president's labor and social programs and strongly objected to his decision to run for a third term. In fact, Garner unsuccessfully challenged him for the 1940 DEMOCRATIC PARTY NOMINATION.

The election of 1940 was rife with politicians who swapped party for political advantage. Henry A. Wallace, Roosevelt's RUNNING MATE in 1940, was a former Republican from Iowa. Needless to say, he was not a popular choice for a running mate among those in charge of the Democratic Party. Roosevelt made it well known he would resign the nomination if Wallace was not approved as his running mate. He sent Eleanor Roosevelt to give a speech to the DELEGATES in an attempt to garner their support. Her speech was successful, and Wallace was voted in as the vice presidential nominee.

Both conventions in 1940 were remarkable, but for different reasons. The 1940 Democratic Convention in Chicago was perhaps one of the first conventions where the president actively manipulated the delegates in his favor. During 1940, Roosevelt was keenly planning to depart from the two-term principle set forth by George Washington. He felt that with the United States poised to enter World War II, the country needed consistent and strong leadership. While he had the support of many Democrats, others opposed his nomination simply for the precedent it would set for the presidency. Roosevelt chose to take the public position that he was not going to actively seek the nomination. However, he wanted the Democratic Party's delegates to instinctively and fully support him without any active cajoling on his part.

During the convention, the mayor of Chicago, Ed Kelly, fully supported Roosevelt. Kelly, unbeknownst to the delegates on the floor, wired a microphone in the basement into the public address system. When Roosevelt's memo was read announcing he would not actively seek the nomination, Kelly had Thomas D. Garry (Chicago's superintendent of

sewers) break in on the microphone shouting "No! No! No! We want Roosevelt!" The attendees of the convention spontaneously and positively reacted to that shout, sweeping Roosevelt into the Democratic nomination with 946 votes.

The 1940 Republican Convention in Philadelphia was equally memorable. Right before the convention convened in Philadelphia, the zoo's oldest elephant, 42-year-old Lizzie, suddenly died. Newspapers throughout the United States used that tidbit to poke fun at the upcoming Philadelphia Republican Convention. More important, the 1940 Republican Convention was the first time a political convention was broadcast on television. At the time, televisions were rare and not even for sale to most of the general public. NBC estimated that approximately 40,000 to 50,000 people saw part of the Republican Convention coverage on television, mostly in Pennsylvania or selected parts of the Northeast.

Many Republicans saw this election season as their best chance to win the presidency since Hoover in 1928. The initial FRONTRUNNERS were Senator Arthur A. Vandenberg, Senator Robert A. Taft (son of the former president), and Manhattan district attorney Thomas E. Dewey. Early in the convention, even former president Herbert Hoover was considered. The eventual party nominee, Wendell Willkie, was not the favorite among party leaders, as he had switched from the Democratic Party in 1939 because of his opposition to the New Deal.

Willkie was an attractive nominee because he was quite different from the rest of the field. Taft, Vandenberg, and Dewey were all isolationists (Taft and Vandenberg extremely so), and their position ran against mainstream public opinion. All three, however, received support from the conservative Republican leadership. Willkie was the favorite among the Republican rank and file because of his more liberal positions. He was strongly in favor of America supporting the Allies and argued that the country was foolish for ignoring the growing crisis in Europe. By the time of the convention in June, Hitler had invaded Belgium and France and reached the English Channel. With America's entrance into war seemingly more and more likely, the Republican delegates were uneasy with the candidates who embraced an isolationist platform. Willkie eventually carried the REPUBLICAN PARTY nomination on the sixth BALLOT.

Wendell Willkie ran on an outsider platform for president. He received generous press coverage that built up the image of a charismatic GRASSROOTS candidate. He embarked on a train campaign that covered 31 states in seven weeks. Though Willkie had an engaging conversational style, he would often make remarks off the cuff that damaged his popularity. Willkie's voice also gave out during the campaign, and he never gave it proper time to recover. The scratchy voice that remained disappointed many potential voters and made him a less effective public speaker. Additionally, Willkie failed to have a consistent theme on which to attack Roosevelt. He bounced between attacks on the third term attempt, foreign policy positions, and New Deal programs.

Roosevelt initially paid little attention to the Willkie campaign, but by late October he launched a more aggressive campaign. Much of the campaign before the election was extremely personal from both camps, making this election unforgettable for its acrimony. Perhaps some of the most memorable events of the campaign were the various objects thrown at Willkie during his speeches, including eggs (most common), oranges, tomatoes, potatoes, cantaloupes, ashtrays, rocks, and chairs. The most serious incident happened at Madison Square Garden when a man pulled a loaded gun while approaching Willkie.

Ultimately, Roosevelt easily defeated Willkie on ELECTION DAY. In fact, Roosevelt carried every large city in America with the exception of Cincinnati, Ohio. Roosevelt's successful New Deal, coupled with his desire to maintain consistent leadership in the face of war, proved to be too large a hurdle for Willkie to overcome.

Further reading: McPherson, James M. *To the Best of My Ability: The American Presidents.* New York: Dorling Kindersley, 2002; Milkis, Sidney, and Michael Nelson. *The American Presidency: Origins and Development, 1776–1998.* Washington, D.C.: Congressional Quarterly Press, 2003.

—Shannon L. Bow

presidential election 1944

Winning President and Vice President: Franklin D.
    Roosevelt and Harry S. Truman
Number of States: 48
Major Candidates (Party Affiliation): Franklin D.
    Roosevelt (Democrat); Thomas E. Dewey
    (Republican)
Electoral College Vote: Franklin D. Roosevelt: 432;
    Thomas E. Dewey: 99
Popular Vote: Franklin D. Roosevelt: 25,612,610;
    Thomas E. Dewey: 22,017,617

World War II was the dominant national concern in the early 1940s. President Franklin D. Roosevelt, elected to an unprecedented third term in 1940, had presided over the transformation of the United States from a peacetime footing to full mobilization for the war effort. By 1944, 11 million men and women were in military service, and the nation's industrial might was heavily focused on production of equipment and supplies for national defense. Domestically, while the basic elements of the New Deal remained intact, the Roosevelt administration diverted almost all its attention to the armed conflict. In a 1943 press conference, the president himself said that "Dr. New Deal" was now replaced by "Dr. Win-the-War."

In the years immediately prior to American entry into the war, a key national debate had emerged over the extent to which the United States should aid Great Britain and other nations in fighting German aggression. Secondarily, there was concern over how the United States should respond to Japanese threats in the Far East. The Japanese attack on Pearl Harbor on December 7, 1941, and Germany's declaration of war on the United States a few days later ended the debate. Though political leaders expressed differing views on how the postwar world should be organized and on certain tactical considerations during the war itself, there was overwhelming bipartisan support for the war effort by 1941. Despite vigorous disagreements over matters of taxation and labor relations, there was also far less dissension than in the 1930s over the basic premise of the New Deal—that the federal government had a role to play in promoting a strong economy and protecting the social welfare of individuals. Both Roosevelt and his 1944 Republican opponent, Thomas E. Dewey, agreed on these fundamental issues. The campaign itself focused on narrower concerns.

The 1944 election maintained the incumbent party in power and produced no major foreign or domestic policy departures. Nevertheless, the election was significant for three reasons. First, it demonstrated that a democratic society could engage in a political contest during wartime without endangering national consensus about the war effort. Second, in reelecting Roosevelt, the nation reaffirmed its support for an activist government. Third, the fact that the Republican nominee accepted the basic premises of the New Deal (though he strongly criticized specific measures) helped institutionalize Roosevelt's domestic program for at least a generation.

The key issues raised by Dewey in 1944 related to the competence of the Democratic administration and, though it was discussed only indirectly by the Republicans, Roosevelt's age and health. Other issues included the conditions under which the United States should be involved in a postwar multilateral organization (which both Roosevelt and Dewey advocated, though with Dewey more vague on details), expansion of postwar social programs (with Roosevelt unequivocally supportive and Dewey more wary), and the role of organized labor in the economy and POLITICS, with the Republicans alleging excessive labor power over the Roosevelt administration. A further charge was that some key union leaders close to the president were influenced by the Communist Party.

Dewey summarized his basic arguments in a speech in Philadelphia on September 7. "This . . . is a campaign to displace a tired, exhausted, quarreling and bickering Administration . . . which has been the most wasteful, extravagant and incompetent Administration in the history of the nation. . . ." But he assured his audience that he would not repeal the New Deal: "Of course we need security regulation. Of course we need bank deposit insurance. . . . Of course we need unemployment insurance and old-age pensions and also relief whenever there are not enough jobs. Of course the rights of labor to organize and bargain collectively are fundamental." His premise was that the REPUBLICAN PARTY could more effectively provide these guarantees and administer the war effort.

Roosevelt responded in a classic speech to the Teamsters Union on September 23. Characterizing Republican support for major New Deal measures as an example of "their insincerity and of their inconsistency," Roosevelt defended organized labor's war effort, cast aside Republican suggestions that he had grown too old for his job, and refuted a charge, then circulating in the media, that the president had sent a destroyer to pick up his dog, accidentally left behind during a war visit to the Aleutian Islands. "These Republican leaders have not been content with attacks on me, or on my wife, or on my sons," he said. "No, not content with that, they now attack my little dog Fala." A few weeks later, Roosevelt (who was, in fact, suffering from heart disease) again demonstrated his physical health by riding in an open car through a rainstorm in a lengthy New York City parade.

Dewey, who pledged in his successful 1942 campaign for governor of New York that he would serve a full term, did not actively seek the NOMINATION. But the defeat of 1940 nominee Wendell Willkie in the Wisconsin PRIMARY, and the failure of a movement to draft General Douglas MacArthur, left Dewey the choice of Republican organizations, and he won the nomination on the first BALLOT. To balance the ticket, he chose conservative Ohio governor John Bricker as his RUNNING MATE.

Roosevelt generated some opposition in Democratic ranks, mostly from southern conservatives, though once he agreed to run for a fourth term he was the overwhelming choice. The real battle was for the vice presidency. Incumbent vice president Henry Wallace was an unabashed liberal and internationalist, strongly supported by the left wing of the party. Wallace generated opposition not only from southern conservatives but also from some northern organization politicians, who persuaded Roosevelt that his presence would weaken the ticket among moderate voters. At the convention Roosevelt mildly endorsed Senator Harry Truman of Missouri, who won the vice presidential nomination on the second ballot. Truman, a pro-labor moderate, was acceptable to all FACTIONS of the party.

By 1944, Roosevelt had already won three PRESIDENTIAL ELECTIONS by large margins. Though the popularity of the New Deal had waned somewhat, he was nevertheless viewed as a successful commander in chief whose world stature was itself a national asset. Once questions about his running mate and his health were resolved, Roosevelt's political position was secure.

Dewey, then 42 years old, was respected as an effective executive but was considered to be lacking in personal appeal. His aggressive campaign against Roosevelt, grounded not in underlying philosophy but in charges of poor administration, roused Republican faithful but did little to reach beyond the party's core supporters.

The election itself represented a substantial victory for the Democrats. Roosevelt carried the South, the West, the Northeast, and every major industrial state except Ohio. Dewey won in most of the Midwest. Ohio, Wisconsin, and Wyoming had supported Roosevelt in 1940 but now went Republican; Michigan, Republican four years earlier, went for Roosevelt by a narrow margin. Democrats increased their margin of control in the Senate and House of Representatives.

Roosevelt's health deteriorated in the months following the election. He was inaugurated for a fourth time on January 20, 1945, but died 82 days later and was succeeded by Vice President Truman.

Further reading: Burns, James MacGregor. *Roosevelt: The Soldier of Freedom.* New York: Harcourt Brace Jovanovich, 1970; Goodwin, Doris Kearns. *No Ordinary Time.* New York: Simon & Schuster, 1994; Smith, Richard Norton. *Thomas E. Dewey and His Times.* New York: Simon & Schuster, 1982.
—Ronald C. Schurin

presidential election 1948

Winning President and Vice President: Harry S. Truman and Alben W. Barkley
Number of States: 48
Major Candidates (Party Affiliation): Harry S. Truman (Democrat); Thomas E. Dewey (Republican); Strom Thurmond (Dixiecrat); Henry A. Wallace (Progressive)
Electoral College Vote: Harry S. Truman: 303; Thomas E. Dewey: 189; Strom Thurmond: 39
Popular Vote: Harry S. Truman: 24,179,345; Thomas E. Dewey: 21,991,291; Strom Thurmond: 1,176,125

The election of 1948 was most notable due to Truman's surprise victory and because it was the first election after both the Great Depression and World War II. The country was coming out of one of its most tumultuous times and had just risen to become one of the world's superpowers. America was shifting its focus away from its traditional isolationist policies, giving special attention to the rise of the Soviet Union. Moreover, Americans also had a litany of economic and social concerns to contend with on the domestic front. The election of 1948 was also unusual in that it was one of the few PRESIDENTIAL ELECTIONS in which two minor party candidates played a significant role. One of the minor party candidates, Strom Thurmond, received 39 ELECTORAL COLLEGE votes.

Harry Truman had become president after the death of Franklin Roosevelt in 1945. Most in the DEMOCRATIC

PARTY never expected Truman to become president, and Truman himself had never had any strong personal desires to be president. The first years in office for Truman were rather difficult. As the economy transitioned from wartime to peacetime, prices soared, rising 30 percent after the wartime price controls were lifted. There were also consumer shortages, labor disputes arising from the Taft-Hartley Act, and significant unrest among minority populations.

The REPUBLICAN PARTY felt that the election was theirs for the taking. They had a strong candidate in Thomas Dewey of New York, who had held his own in the 1944 presidential race against Franklin Roosevelt and fared well in his 1946 congressional election. After 16 years of Democratic control, Republicans believed that the American people would be ready for a change in leadership. With MINORITY PARTY candidates Henry Wallace and Strom Thurmond courting the far left and far right of the Democratic Party, the Republicans' confidence continued to grow.

The Democratic Party entered the election season fully aware that it was in trouble, and had even gone so far as attempting to replace Truman on the ticket with former World War II commander and future president Dwight Eisenhower. However, after aggressive courting from both parties, Eisenhower refused the NOMINATION from either side, and Truman won the Democratic Party nomination with ease.

Thomas Dewey was a strong candidate for the Republicans. In the 1944 PRESIDENTIAL ELECTION, Dewey had won more than 22 million votes and became the closest competitor that Franklin Roosevelt faced in his four GENERAL ELECTIONS. Dewey was an internationalist and moderate on domestic issues. He had established a strong record as an attorney in New York City, was widely considered to be an effective governor of New York, and was an able communicator.

The DEMOCRATIC NATIONAL CONVENTION was the most eventful convention of 1948 because of two major events. First, a stirring speech delivered at the Democratic convention by the young mayor of Minneapolis, Hubert Humphrey, called for the Democratic Party to become the standard bearer for CIVIL RIGHTS LEGISLATION and reform. Truman himself had delivered a civil rights message to Congress the previous February but had been slow to act on any measures in an attempt to placate SOUTHERN DEMOCRATS. Despite pleading from a number of party leaders, Humphrey continued to push the civil rights issue and forced its inclusion on the party's platform, causing many southern DELEGATEs to walk out of the convention.

The second major event of the Democratic convention occurred when Truman announced that he would call Congress back into session. This was all part of the Democratic political strategy. Truman and the Democrats predicted that with Republicans under the leadership of the conservative senator from Ohio, Robert Taft, very little would be accomplished in the special session. Truman designed and promoted legislation for the special session that would supposedly be a stimulus for the American economy. When few measures were passed in the special session, Truman had the ammunition he needed when campaigning across the country. He accused the 80th Congress of being the worst Congress ever, a "do nothing" Congress. Truman claimed that the Republicans failed to help the American people when they had an opportune chance to do so.

The Democrats' new stand on civil rights, as well as a perceived dilution of state power and continued growth of the federal government, resulted in the rise of the Dixiecrat Party. The Dixiecrats were led by Governor Strom Thurmond of South Carolina, who had previously been a Democrat. Despite receiving less than 3 percent of the POPULAR VOTE, Thurmond was able to win 39 electoral votes (Louisiana, Mississippi, Alabama, South Carolina, and one electoral vote from Tennessee). Thurmond and his followers never expected to win the election, but instead hoped to draw enough votes to bring the election to the House of Representatives, which they believed would choose a president more sympathetic to southern prerogatives. In the end, it is likely that the Dixiecrats actually helped Truman by providing convincing evidence to the African-American population that the Democrats, many of whom had resisted civil rights legislation previously, now represented the civil rights cause.

Henry Wallace and the Progressives felt that the country was going in the wrong direction in regard to its foreign policy initiatives. Wallace represented the far political left of the country in his campaign for the presidency. Far from a fringe candidate, Wallace was a seasoned public official, having previously held the positions of secretary of agriculture, secretary of commerce, and vice president. Wallace was forced out at commerce when he continued to take strong public stances in opposition to Truman's actions against the Soviet Union.

Wallace was opposed to the Marshall Plan and favored working in harmony with the Soviet Union. Although Wallace himself was not a communist and indeed had made a fortune developing new agricultural products, accusations that Wallace was sympathetic to communists continued to plague his campaign. Truman was especially vehement in his accusations against Wallace. Once again, the minor party candidacy by a former Democrat probably helped Truman. This time the minor party showed the voters that the Democrats were not soft on communism and would stand up to the Soviets.

Dewey's campaign platform stressed national unity. After a tough mudslinging campaign against Franklin Roosevelt in the 1944 election, Dewey decided to run a campaign that stayed above the political fray. Despite having a strong speaking voice, he was considered rather boorish according to political observers of the day. On the campaign trail he gained the reputation of being an elitist and was seen as catering to the needs of the wealthy. When Truman went on the attack against the "do nothing" Congress, Dewey failed to respond. In fact, Dewey rarely mentioned Truman's name while on the campaign trail, a fatal mistake for someone running against an incumbent.

Truman became the first sitting president to extensively campaign across the country. Despite advances in air travel, the Truman campaign decided to use train travel by conducting a "whistle-stop" tour of the country. Truman drew huge crowds, and the tour catered to Truman's strength as an off-the-cuff speaker.

As ELECTION DAY approached, most in the press believed that Dewey would win the election handily. The press discounted the indications that Truman was making a strong comeback, such as the large crowds that Truman was drawing. The pollsters were also part of the prediction problem, using a flawed methodology that over-sampled wealthy voters. Moreover, most pollsters had stopped conducting polls two weeks before the election, at the very time Truman's campaign was gaining momentum. The 1948 election will also always be remembered for one of the most memorable political images in American history. With a firm belief that Dewey would defeat Truman, the *Chicago Daily Tribune* went to press with the headline "Dewey Defeats Truman." When the vote was determined, Truman held up the newspaper with the incorrect headline in celebration.

Politically, the 1948 election can be considered the starting point of a 20-year trend of the traditionally "solid South" breaking away from the Democratic Party and turning into the Republican stronghold that we see today. The election also established the Democratic Party as the dominant party for African Americans and other minority populations.

Further reading: Gosnell, Harold. *Truman's Crises: A Political Biography of Harry S. Truman.* Westport, Conn.: Greenwood Press, 1980; Karabell, Zachary. *The Last Campaign.* New York: Knopf, 2000.

—Daniel Ballard

presidential election 1952

Winning President and Vice President: Dwight D. Eisenhower and Richard M. Nixon

Number of States: 48

Major Candidates (Party Affiliation): Dwight D. Eisenhower (Republican); Adlai E. Stevenson (Democrat)

Electoral College Vote: Dwight D. Eisenhower: 442; Adlai E. Stevenson: 89

Popular Vote: Dwight D. Eisenhower: 33,936,234; Adlai E. Stevenson: 27,314,992

President-elect Harry Truman holding up the infamous *Chicago Tribune* headline declaring his defeat by Dewey, 1948 *(New York World-Telegram and Sun Newspaper Photograph Collection, Library of Congress)*

The presidential election of 1952 signaled a major shift in the American political landscape, reflecting changes in both the domestic cultural climate and the country's international stance. Dwight D. Eisenhower's victory marked the first selection of a Republican to the nation's highest office in 24 years and reflected a different set of priorities for the United States.

Having weathered World War II, America was not eager to continue fighting battles on foreign soil. Even given the anticommunist sentiment pervasive at the time as a consequence of the cold war, an isolationist mood settled on the country once again, making the Korean War an unpopular conflict. Yet the fervent anticommunist movement was heating up domestically. Meanwhile, after enduring the Great Depression and the social programs employed to address it by the Roosevelt and Truman administrations, America was ready to enjoy a guilt-free return to prosperity. Moreover, deficit spending by the federal government and resultant inflation had become a concern, thanks largely to the wars and the programs that targeted the Depression. Adding to this list of advantages handed the Republicans, bribery SCANDALS besmirched some Truman appointees during his tenure.

Given the difficulties encountered during his first full term in office, President Harry S. Truman decided not to run for reelection and tapped Governor Adlai Stevenson of Illinois as his chosen successor. However, once Truman took himself out of the race, both parties initially tried to convince General Dwight Eisenhower to run for their respective NOMINATIONS, on the expectation that the former overall commander of the armed forces in World War II would prove a formidable candidate for either party. Eisenhower, born in Texas, considered a resident of New York, and headquartered at the time in Paris, finally decided to run for the Republican nomination on the premise that 20 straight years of Democratic presidents was enough and that change was due. He defeated Senator Robert Taft of Ohio for the REPUBLICAN PARTY's nomination, winning on the first BALLOT at its convention in Chicago in early July (845 votes to Taft's 280; California governor Earl Warren and General Douglas MacArthur also received votes).

Later that month, also in Chicago, Stevenson, whose grandfather had been vice president during President Grover Cleveland's second term, claimed the spot at the top of the Democratic ticket. His nomination was less easily secured than Eisenhower's, as 14 candidates received votes at the convention, and Stevenson actually finished second on the first ballot, behind Senator Estes Kefauver of Tennessee. Stevenson finally secured the DEMOCRATIC PARTY's nomination on the third ballot, thereby fulfilling Truman's wishes.

In the campaign for the GENERAL ELECTION, Stevenson was hamstrung by the difficulties in challenging an American war hero. The Democratic Party platform was constructed largely of esoteric notions such as "world peace with honor" and "a high level of human dignity." The campaign centered on the success of the previous two presidents in dealing with the events that America and the world faced during their terms, and contrasted the economic growth underway in the early 1950s with the record of economic failure and corporate malfeasance experienced during the last Republican administrations.

The Republican campaign ran under the memorable slogan, "I Like Ike," and Eisenhower, for his part, presented a friendly face and played the part of the nonpolitician. He allowed other ranking Republicans, including 1948 Republican presidential nominee Thomas E. Dewey, Senator Joseph McCarthy, and vice presidential candidate Richard M. Nixon, to handle the dirty work for him. The Republican campaign focused primarily on a message of change from the priorities of the Truman administration, promising to clean up the government, reduce spending, control inflation, get tougher on communism, and get out of Korea.

The bribery scandals and budgets of the Truman administration, as well as the public's increasing weariness with war, provided fodder for the Republican campaign on these points. Further, the Republican Party, with its hard-line anticommunists in Joseph McCarthy and Nixon, was able to paint the Democrats as "soft" on communism. Stevenson had not been part of the Truman administration, so he was to some degree immune from direct attack by the Republicans on these policies. Yet Nixon, undeterred, at one point called Stevenson an "egghead," a term that referred both to his baldness and to his positions, which appealed largely to the intellectual elite.

In an example of the new and prominent role that television played in the campaign, Nixon himself provided the most lasting image of the race. Faced with charges of misuse of campaign funds, Nixon made a televised speech in which he featured his dog, Checkers. The appearance has since become known as the "Checkers speech" and preserved Nixon's place on the ticket and his political career. The Republicans also used television to play up the family angle, as both Eisenhower and Nixon campaigned very visibly with their wives, in itself a relatively new technique, while Stevenson was vulnerable on this front due to his status as a divorcé. This family-based approach, combined with an emphasis on fiscal responsibility by the government, allowed the Eisenhower campaign to attract a large share of the women's vote.

Ultimately, Eisenhower won the election handily. He was a favorite from the moment he entered the race and likely could have won for either party. In the general election, Stevenson managed to take only nine states, all located in or near the Southeast, where Democratic hegemony traced back to the late 19th-century post-RECONSTRUCTION era. Stevenson won no state north of West Virginia and no state west of Arkansas, and lost even in his home state of Illinois. The win for Eisenhower was one of the largest in American history.

Further reading: Eulau, Heinz. *Class and Party in the Eisenhower Years: Class Roles and Perspectives in the 1952 and 1956 Elections.* New York: Free Press of Glencoe, 1962; Greene, John Robert. *The Crusade: The Presidential Election of 1952.* Lanham, Md.: University Press of America, 1985; Johnson, Walter. *How We Drafted Adlai Stevenson.* New York: Knopf, 1955; Pickett, William Beatty. *Eisenhower Decides to Run: Presidential Politics and Cold War Strategy.* Chicago: Ivan R. Dee, 2000.

—Joel Parker

presidential election 1956

Winning President and Vice President: Dwight D. Eisenhower and Richard M. Nixon
Number of States: 48
Major Candidates (Party Affiliation): Dwight D. Eisenhower (Republican); Adlai E. Stevenson (Democrat)
Electoral College Vote: Dwight D. Eisenhower: 457; Adlai E. Stevenson: 73; Walter B. Jones: 1
Popular Vote: Dwight D. Eisenhower: 37,590,472; Adlai E. Stevenson: 26,022,752

The presidential election of 1956 saw a rematch of the 1952 PRESIDENTIAL ELECTION, with Republican president Dwight D. Eisenhower squaring off against Democratic nominee Adlai Stevenson. In the 1952 contest, Eisenhower easily defeated Stevenson, and the reelection four years later was even more lopsided. Eisenhower and his RUNNING MATE, Vice President Richard Nixon, won 57 percent of the POPULAR VOTE, and in the ELECTORAL COLLEGE, Eisenhower won overwhelmingly, 457 to 73. In the process, the incumbent president won every state he had won in 1952, and picked up three states he had lost in his first election—Louisiana, Kentucky, and West Virginia.

The 1956 election was considerably different than its predecessors. The campaigns of the previous two decades had been fought in the context of economic depression and amid debates over World War II and the Korean War. After a brief downturn during Eisenhower's first term, the economy in 1956 was healthy, and American troops were not involved in large-scale armed conflict. Incumbent presidents tend to do well in such scenarios, and Eisenhower sought to make the election a referendum on his stewardship of the country during his first term. Stevenson, however, preferred to focus on those who had been left behind in the last four years.

The slogan for the president's reelection campaign was "Peace, Prosperity, and Progress." The line was an attempt to highlight what Eisenhower regarded as the key achievements of his first four years, maintaining peace and economic health, while also looking to the future. Stevenson, meanwhile, refused to concede that the country could not be improved. Instead, he called for a "New America," a program of liberal policies that sought to protect the interests of working-class and poor Americans. The central argument in his proposal was that the recent economic success had benefited the wealthy, but not the poor. Working-class people in the United States were being left behind, and Stevenson saw his proposal as a way to address growing inequity. The argument seemed promising in light of polls that showed the public believed the Republican Party to be the party of big business. But with a robust economy, the appeal apparently did little to persuade voters that a change was needed.

Domestic policy was not the only area of difference between the candidates. Despite the absence of a war footing, foreign policy was central to the campaign. With the cold war of paramount concern, Stevenson called for a ban on aboveground nuclear weapons testing, a proposal that ultimately was put into place six years later during the administration of John F. Kennedy. Eisenhower, a former general and war hero, refused to debate nuclear policy publicly and focused on dealing with the foreign policy issues confronting the world at the time. Late in the campaign, conflict erupted in the Middle East over the Suez Canal, and Soviet tanks began rumbling into Hungary, two crises that consumed most of the president's time and caused him to cut back on campaigning in the last week before the election.

Stevenson also faced a major obstacle in overcoming Eisenhower's popularity. The rallying cry of Eisenhower's supporters—"I Like Ike"—was grounded in the president's remarkably high APPROVAL RATINGS. Public opinion surveys taken throughout 1956 showed Eisenhower's job approval in the 60s and 70s, suggesting that relatively few Americans were looking for a change in leadership. Questions about Eisenhower's fitness to lead did arise, however, after the president suffered a heart attack in 1955 and underwent surgery in June 1956 for inflammation of the small intestine, a side effect of his Crohn's disease, called ileitis at the time. To call attention to Eisenhower's health troubles, Stevenson mounted a vigorous campaign, traveling across the country on a grueling schedule. In doing so, he hoped to highlight his energy level and create a contrast with Eisenhower, whom he frequently referred to as a part-time president. The Democrats also created advertisements reminding the public that Eisenhower's running mate, Vice President Richard Nixon, with whom many moderate Americans felt uncomfortable, would succeed the president should he die.

The 1956 election also foreshadowed the era of modern media campaigns. Eisenhower and Stevenson both took advantage of the relatively new technology of television in their 1956 campaigns, pouring millions into broadcasting commercials across the country. The Republicans spent $2.8 million on television and radio ads in 1956, while the Democrats spent $1.7 million, figures that represented about 35 percent of total spending in the election. In conjunction with the national parties, both candidates sought to use the power of mass communication to burnish their images at the national conventions. The Republicans in particular tried to turn their convention into a made-for-TV event, limiting the length of speeches and scheduling sessions to accommodate the viewing patterns of residents of different time zones across the country.

One stark difference between the campaign of 1956 and those that followed was the absence of debates. Seeking to put Stevenson on the same stage with the president, the Democrats were eager for a series of televised debates. The Republicans, however, never agreed to do so, deciding that such a move would only erode Eisenhower's sky-high popularity and give Stevenson free media exposure. Thus, televised PRESIDENTIAL DEBATES would not take place until the famous KENNEDY-NIXON DEBATES of 1960.

Further reading: Allen, Craig. *Eisenhower and the Mass Media: Peace, Prosperity, and Prime-Time TV.* Chapel Hill: University of North Carolina Press, 1993; Ambrose, Stephen E. *Eisenhower: The President.* New York: Simon & Schuster, 1984.

—Danny Hayes

presidential election 1960

Winning President and Vice President: John F. Kennedy
and Lyndon B. Johnson
Number of States: 50 (plus D.C.)
Major Candidates (Party Affiliation): John F. Kennedy
(Democrat); Richard M. Nixon (Republican); Harry
Flood Byrd (Independent)
Electoral College Vote: John F. Kennedy: 303; Richard M.
Nixon: 219; Harry Flood Byrd: 15
Popular Vote: John F. Kennedy: 34,226,731; Richard M.
Nixon: 34,108,157

Perhaps a harbinger of things to come, the presidential
election of 1960 left an indelible mark on American history
and contemporary POLITICS. Not only did the election feature one of the closest results in history, but also the men
who led the campaigns would both leave lasting imprints on
the political landscape. In addition, the events of the campaign proved significant and a predecessor to the ways in
which modern campaigns are conducted and conveyed.

The campaign season of 1960 opened with the Republicans bidding farewell to President Dwight Eisenhower
and preparing the way for his heir-apparent, Vice President
Richard Nixon. As a result, Nixon had an unencumbered
path to the NOMINATION. Virtually unchallenged, Nixon
coasted easily through PRIMARY season, winning nearly 90
percent of votes cast. The only noteworthy resistance was
encountered before the Republican convention and was
effectively neutralized with the negotiation of the "Compact of Fifth Avenue" with the liberal Republican governor
of New York, Nelson Rockefeller.

The Democrats, while enjoying nearly 20 years in the
White House with the Roosevelt and Truman administrations, were anxious to reclaim the office after eight years on
the outside during the Eisenhower administration. No less
than five candidates embarked on the trail for the nomination. Senators Hubert Humphrey of Minnesota, Stuart
Symington of Missouri, Lyndon Johnson of Texas, and John
F. Kennedy of Massachusetts sought the nomination. Adlai
Stevenson, the party's nominee in 1952 and 1956, waited in
the wings but never formally initiated a campaign.

For the Democrats, winning the nomination was vastly
more difficult. Kennedy and Humphrey decided to campaign through the primary process, despite living in a time
when a candidate could win the nomination by appealing to
state and local PARTY BOSSES who controlled each state's
nominating conventions. Kennedy's advisers believed that
his competing in the 16 available primaries was the best
way they could garner attention for their candidate. On the
other hand, Johnson and Symington chose the traditional
route.

From a modern perspective, Kennedy's victories in the
primaries seem almost as if they were predetermined, due
to his talent in campaigning and his excellent speaking abil-

ities. They were, however, less certain. One of the most
ominous clouds surrounding Kennedy was his Catholicism,
as no president had ever been a Catholic and the ghost of
the 1928 Smith candidacy still loomed.

The two most critical primaries in that year occurred in
Wisconsin and West Virginia. Humphrey, a native of neighboring Minnesota, mounted a serious effort in Wisconsin to
derail the Kennedy campaign but lost, with the Massachusetts senator winning 56 percent of the vote. A convincing 61 percent of the vote in Protestant West Virginia
garnered the Catholic Kennedy the victory, the requisite
number of DELEGATEs, and the subsequent withdrawal of
Humphrey from the race.

On July 11, Kennedy entered Los Angeles and the
Democratic convention with the number of delegates
needed to win and held off late surges from Johnson and a
nostalgic rally for Stevenson to ensure the result. In a surprising political move, Kennedy extended the opportunity
to be the vice presidential RUNNING MATE to Lyndon Johnson. While there was some underlying hostility for a Texan
in the Kennedy camp, Johnson was chosen because he
could help win the South. Almost equally surprising was
Johnson's acceptance.

Two weeks later, the Republicans gathered for their
convention in Chicago. The convention was initially characterized by the divisiveness among the disparate elements of
the party. Members of the Republican Platform Committee
balked when some sought to include elements of the Compact of Fifth Avenue in the platform. Senator Barry Goldwater, a conservative, called the compact a "surrender" and
"the Munich of the Republican Party." A compromise was
later agreed to as elements of the original civil rights and
defense planks were reworked to appease the New York
governor. Also during the convention, Ambassador Henry
Cabot Lodge was named the Republican vice presidential
nominee. The naming of Lodge appeased the wounded
sensibilities of both the moderates and conservatives.

The issues confronting both parties' nominees were
characterized by two elements. First, 1960 was a particularly low point in the cold war relationship between the
United States and the Soviet Union. The nation was still
reeling from the shock inflicted on it by the 1957 launch of
the Soviet Sputnik satellite. More recently, the downing of
a U-2 spy plane on a reconnaissance mission within the
Soviet Union and the resultant cancellation of a summit
between Khrushchev and Eisenhower added to anxieties
about national security. The other element was the home-
front and the sluggish economy. The second term of the
Eisenhower administration had done little to stimulate the
economy, and the term *stagflation,* a term coined by the
press combining the words stagnation and inflation,
became the dominant characterization of the economy.

One of the most important developments of the 1960
campaign was the first face-to-face general election PRESI-

DENTIAL DEBATE and the first use of televised presidential debates. This was a unique opportunity in history, as it presented Kennedy the opportunity, with a good performance, to catapult his stature to a position equal to that of the more experienced vice president. Such a result did occur and more. Visually, the juxtaposition between the candidates was remarkable. Kennedy looked confident and composed, and Nixon, ill and tired, looked unshaven and pale. Kennedy directly answered the moderator's questions and, Nixon, many times in a rambling way, merely echoed the senator's sentiments. Nearly 70 million watched the debates, and Kennedy demonstrated that, despite his youth and lack of experience compared to Nixon, he was capable of handling the responsibilities of president.

Nixon's campaign hampered him and often restricted his message. His promise during the convention to visit all 50 states put him in a difficult position; during the last week of the campaign Nixon visited Alaska while Kennedy campaigned in the electorally lucrative state of New York. Additionally, Nixon fell victim to the attacks of the insurgent Goldwater Republicans, as he did not share their conservative position regarding the economy. Last, President Eisenhower did not prove to be as beneficial to Nixon as was originally hoped. The president's health restricted his advocacy for Nixon, and his less-than-glowing appraisal of Nixon's experience hurt the candidate. However, the few times Eisenhower did campaign for Nixon did help the candidate and tightened the race considerably.

Kennedy campaigned on his youth, drawing a subtle yet distinct contrast with the Eisenhower years. He spoke of a "missile gap" and the need to strengthen the military. In addition, Kennedy called for the creation of the Peace Corps, the institution of a minimum wage, and the creation of an economic policy that would result in a 5 percent growth rate. Kennedy also continued to confront the issue of his Catholicism throughout the campaign. While 1960

President John F. Kennedy greets Peace Corps volunteers, 1962 *(Library of Congress)*

was more than a generation removed from 1928, the specter of anti-Catholicism and fears of a president controlled by the pontiff were still visible. Kennedy directly addressed the issue in a speech to a group of Houston clergymen in September. In the speech, Kennedy defined a strict separation of his views and his public duties and pledged to carry out his duties according to the Constitution. Kennedy was also effective in wooing the votes of African Americans, particularly with his successful negotiation to release Dr. Martin Luther King, Jr., from prison in Georgia. Nixon, fearful of a conservative backlash, could only watch.

On the eve of the election, the race was a dead heat. Nixon, through some of Eisenhower's help and despite conservative sniping, had overcome his performance in the debates and several errors to pull even with Kennedy. ELECTION DAY proved no different, as Kennedy defeated Nixon by a margin of less than 115,000 votes out of 68.8 million. Kennedy's ELECTORAL COLLEGE victory was more decisive; even though Nixon won four more states, the Massachusetts senator garnered 303 electoral votes to Nixon's 219. Segregationist candidate Harry F. Byrd of Virginia received 15 Electoral College votes, one from an ELECTOR pledged to Nixon and 14 from unpledged Democratic electors. In the end, it is quite possible that some of the margins by which Kennedy won in several states were engineered by a number of Democratic machines, particularly Daly's in Chicago, but Nixon, wanting to avoid a lengthy and divisive constitutional crisis, conceded the election to Kennedy.

The significance of the election lay not only in the future events that the two candidates would become involved in but also in the consequences of the election itself. Televised debates became a critical, as well as a feared, part of future elections. Their ability to legitimatize a trailing candidate and harm a favored one led to their not being used again until 1976. More recently, debates are seen as a necessary and important milepost in the election season. The 1960 campaign also led to the wider use of the primary. Kennedy had parlayed primary support into a successful candidacy. In subsequent decades, primaries became the principal means of selecting a party's nominee.

Further reading: Parmet, Herbert. *JFK: The Presidency of John F. Kennedy.* New York: Dial Press, 1983; White, Theodore. *The Making of the President—1960.* New York: Atheneum, 1961.

—Stephen Nemeth

presidential election 1964

Winning President and Vice President: Lyndon B. Johnson and Hubert H. Humphrey
Number of States: 50 (plus D.C.)
Major Candidates (Party Affiliation): Lyndon B. Johnson (Democrat); Barry M. Goldwater (Republican)

Electoral College Vote: Lyndon B. Johnson: 486; Barry M. Goldwater: 52
Popular Vote: Lyndon B. Johnson: 43,129,566; Barry M. Goldwater: 27,178,188

In 1964, incumbent Democratic president Lyndon Johnson stood for election against Republican senator Barry Goldwater from Arizona. The election was held just a little more than a year after President John F. Kennedy's assassination, which had elevated Johnson to the presidency. While the nation was experiencing peace and prosperity in 1964, the United States stood on the precipice of a major war in Indochina and significant turmoil at home.

After Kennedy's assassination, President Johnson fully committed himself and the national DEMOCRATIC PARTY to the cause of civil rights for African Americans. The Democratic Party had previously taken ambiguous, cautious stances in support of civil rights for fear of offending the important southern wing of the party. Johnson abandoned this approach. Much to the chagrin of white southerners, Johnson signed the Civil Rights Act in July of 1964, which effectively ended legally sanctioned racial segregation in the South. Johnson also supported an expansive social welfare state, a legislative program he called the Great Society.

The REPUBLICAN PARTY took a sharp turn to the right in 1964. Republican presidential nominees between 1936 and 1960 had avoided taking rigid stances in opposition to existing social welfare programs and regulatory agencies, due to the popularity of Franklin Roosevelt's New Deal policies of the 1930s. In 1964, conservative activists within the Republican Party succeeded in nominating a candidate who promised to stringently oppose the social welfare state and regulatory agencies. Goldwater defeated several moderate Republicans for the party NOMINATION through the GRASSROOTS strength of his CAMPAIGN ORGANIZATION, which was full of deeply ideological conservative activists. The Goldwater activists challenged local power brokers within the Republican Party to substantially shift the party's principles to the right. Goldwater scored respectable showings in party primaries, including a key victory in California, and arrived at the party convention with enough DELEGATES to win the nomination on the first BALLOT. He chose William Miller, a congressman from upstate New York, as his RUNNING MATE. Many moderate Republican politicians and party activists either refused to endorse Goldwater outright or gave him only lukewarm support.

Goldwater's campaign did little to shed his reputation as a temperamental right-wing extremist. He called for making participation in the Social Security program voluntary, suggested that the Tennessee Valley Authority be abolished, and contended that farm subsidies might be reduced. His statements on foreign policy issues made him appear reckless and unstable, given the delicacy of U.S. relations with the Soviet Union. He was prone to talking casually about nuclear war and even joking about it. He once joked that he would "lob one [a nuclear missile] into the men's room of the Kremlin." Goldwater opposed federal CIVIL RIGHTS LEGISLATION and actively campaigned in the South for support, yet he also refused to run an explicitly racist campaign. He contended that while he personally opposed racial segregation, the federal government had no authority to bar states from enacting racial segregation statutes.

Johnson and his running mate, Minnesota senator Hubert Humphrey, ran an equally aggressive campaign. Johnson sought to build a national MANDATE for his policies. Not only did his campaign gleefully exploit Goldwater's frequent verbal outbursts, it also appealed to moderate Republican voters throughout the nation who were troubled by their party's direction. Johnson's folksy, down-home, and simple appeals to the American people contrasted considerably with Goldwater's perceived abrasiveness. Johnson campaigned in full support of his Great Society programs and the Democratic Party's traditional commitment to aid the underprivileged. In contrast to Goldwater, Johnson campaigned as the peace candidate who could be trusted with the awesome powers of the cold war presidency. Johnson campaigned against a more active role for the United States in Vietnam, though in August he asked Congress to enact a resolution giving him the authority to use greater military force after an engagement in the Gulf of Tonkin between U.S. warships and North Vietnamese patrol craft.

Throughout the election, public opinion polls showed Johnson leading by a large margin, and on ELECTION DAY the polls were proven correct. Johnson won 61.1 percent of the POPULAR VOTE, the largest ever in American history. He won 486 electoral votes, carrying normally Republican states such as Vermont, Indiana, and all the states of the Great Plains. Goldwater won just 38.5 percent of the popular vote and 52 electoral votes. He narrowly carried his home state of Arizona, as well as the Deep South states of Louisiana, Mississippi, Alabama, Georgia, and South Carolina.

While Johnson's victory was overwhelming and substantial, the 1964 presidential election was a harbinger of danger for the Democratic Party. Goldwater's solid victories in five southern states began that region's gradual but certain march away from the Democratic Party, first in PRESIDENTIAL ELECTIONS and later at the congressional and state levels. Goldwater also ran competitively in every other southern state except for Johnson's home state of Texas. The Democrats' pro–civil rights stance was the major reason for the South's defection from its ancestral party, but in subsequent elections the South would also drift away from the Democrats because of the party's increasingly liberal stances on cultural and foreign policy issues. In the aftermath of the Goldwater defeat, the Republican Party increasingly drew its electoral strength from the South and the interior West. At the same time, African-American voters became even more heavily Democratic than they had been between the 1930s and early 1960s. African Americans typically voted Democratic by about a two to one margin during this period, and following the 1964 election African Americans typically voted about nine to one Democratic.

Further reading: Donaldson, Gary. *Liberalism's Last Hurrah: The Presidential Campaign of 1964.* Armonk, N.Y.: M.E. Sharpe, 2003; Johnson, Lyndon Baines. *The Vantage Point: Perspectives of the Presidency, 1963–1969.* New York: Holt, Rinehart & Winston, 1971; Perlstein, Rick. *Before the Storm: Barry Goldwater and the Unmaking of the American Consensus.* New York: Hill & Wang, 2001.

—Donald A. Zinman

presidential election 1968

Winning President and Vice President: Richard M. Nixon and Spiro T. Agnew
Number of States: 50 (plus D.C.)
Major Candidates (Party Affiliation): Richard M. Nixon (Republican); Hubert H. Humphrey (Democrat); George Wallace (American independent)
Electoral College Vote: Richard M. Nixon: 301; Hubert H. Humphrey: 191; George Wallace: 46
Popular Vote: Richard M. Nixon: 31,785,480; Hubert H. Humphrey: 31,275,166; George Wallace: 9,906,473

In 1968, the United States was experiencing severe domestic turmoil and was beset by a war in Indochina that appeared endless to many Americans. The Vietnam War took a deadly turn for the worse, and the nation's streets were rocked by rising rates of crime and riots. In the midst of all this, the United States held one of the most significant PRESIDENTIAL ELECTIONS in its history.

Democratic President Lyndon Johnson planned to run for reelection in 1968, but his popularity flagged in 1967 and early 1968. Casualties from the Vietnam War were mounting, and the war was becoming more and more unpopular. In January 1968, Vietnamese communists launched a major offensive against South Vietnamese cities. U.S. forces and their South Vietnamese allies beat back the offensive but sustained major casualties. This episode was known as the Tet Offensive because it commenced on the first day of Tet, the lunar new year holiday. In America, public support for Johnson's handling of the war dropped, and Johnson shocked the nation when he went on television on March 31 to announce that he would not seek reelection.

Johnson's decision came shortly after the NEW HAMPSHIRE PRIMARY, which he had narrowly won. Senator Eugene McCarthy of Minnesota, an antiwar candidate, finished a very strong second to the incumbent president. Robert F. Kennedy entered the race later that month, and Vice President Hubert Humphrey declared his candidacy after Johnson's abdication. Humphrey, who supported Johnson's Vietnam policy, had his support, as well as the support of the DEMOCRATIC PARTY establishment. Nonetheless, other Democratic candidates put together formidable CAMPAIGN ORGANIZATIONS to compete for the NOMINATION. Kennedy performed well during the primaries, and he may have been a contender for the nomination. On the same night in early June that he was celebrating his victory in the California PRIMARY, Kennedy was assassinated. McCarthy also commanded significant support from antiwar liberals and young college students.

The Democratic convention of 1968, held in Chicago, was a disaster for the party. Humphrey, with the full backing of the White House and the traditional power brokers of the Democratic Party, won the nomination, but only after the DELEGATES were torn apart by floor fights over credentials and procedures as well as the party's platform plank on the Vietnam War. Outside the convention hall, antiwar protesters, many of whom supported McCarthy, clashed with Chicago police. Humphrey chose Maine senator Edmund Muskie as his RUNNING MATE.

Republicans gave their nomination to former vice president Richard Nixon, a compromise candidate with support from both the right and center of the REPUBLICAN PARTY. Nixon had been challenged within the party by New York governor Nelson Rockefeller, representing the moderate wing, and California governor Ronald Reagan, representing the conservative wing. Nixon worked hard to rehabilitate his image after losing the presidency to John F. Kennedy in 1960 and the California governorship in 1962. Nixon shored up his credentials with the leadership of the party in 1966 by campaigning for Republican candidates in that year's midterm congressional elections. Nixon chose Maryland governor Spiro Agnew as his running mate.

George Wallace, who served as governor of Alabama between 1963 and 1967, declared his intention to run as an INDEPENDENT candidate, causing headaches for both Republicans and Democrats. Wallace was nationally known for his clashes with the Kennedy and Johnson administrations over civil rights issues and his stringent opposition to federal interference with state laws pertaining to racial segregation. Democrats feared the Wallace vote would cut into traditionally Democratic strongholds in white, working-class communities in northern states, while Republicans feared Wallace would win southern votes won by their nominee, Barry Goldwater, four years earlier. In 1968, Republicans hoped to replicate Goldwater's success in the South. Wallace ran under the banner of the AMERICAN INDEPENDENT PARTY and succeeded in obtaining BALLOT ACCESS in all 50 states. Wallace chose former air force general Curtis LeMay as his running mate.

The Vietnam War was the major foreign policy issue of the campaign. At first, Humphrey supported Johnson's policy, a position that earned him the wrath of liberals and college students, many of whom regularly jeered and booed him at campaign rallies. Nixon maintained an ambiguous stance. Observers in the media hinted that Nixon had a "secret plan" to end the war. Law and order also resonated deeply in the campaign. Many Americans were troubled by the rising rates of crime and the almost regular occurrence of urban riots and noisy antiwar demonstrations, which often resulted in violence. Nixon charged the Democrats with being soft on crime and promised to restore peace and order to the nation's cities. But it was Wallace who made the most out of the law and order issue, using it to harshly denounce the two major parties as ineffective, and suggesting in not so subtle ways that racial integration was responsible for rising crime rates. Using sharp, arguably demagogic rhetoric, Wallace energized crowds at campaign rallies with his attacks on government bureaucrats, student leftists, and "pointy headed" intellectuals. Public cynicism of government institutions began to rise in the 1960s, which played right into Wallace's hands. He argued that the federal government under Johnson assumed powers that properly belonged to the states, especially in the area of education.

Throughout the campaign, most public opinion polls showed Nixon in the lead. In late September, however, Humphrey began distancing himself from Johnson's Vietnam policy, arguing that he would support halting the bombing of North Vietnam to achieve a peace settlement with the North Vietnamese. Humphrey's support from liberals returned, the heckling at his campaign rallies dwindled, and he closed the gap in the polls with Nixon.

But Humphrey came up short. Nixon was narrowly elected with 43.3 percent of the POPULAR VOTE and 301 electoral votes. He swept the states of the interior West, California, and the Great Plains. He polled respectably in the South and won most of the industrial Midwest. Humphrey won 42.7 percent of the popular vote, but only 191 electoral votes. His strength was greatest in the Northeast. Wallace carried five southern states, winning 46 electoral votes. He polled strongly throughout the South and in neighboring border states. Wallace also polled strongly in many predominantly white, working-class PRECINCTs in northern states.

The election of 1968 ushered in an era of divided government. After this election, the normal state of affairs in American POLITICS was for one party to control the presidency, while the other party would control at least one house of Congress. The movement of the South into the Republican Party, which had begun in 1964, accelerated in 1968. In 1972, an overwhelming majority of Wallace voters in the South cast their BALLOTs for Nixon. The Democrats ceased to be a national MAJORITY PARTY after this election, although Republicans did not replace them as the majority party, either, as more and more voters began to identify themselves as independents and split their tickets between the two parties in elections.

Further reading: Chester, Lewis, Godfrey Hodgson, and Bruce Page. *An American Melodrama: The Presidential Campaign of 1968.* New York: Viking Press, 1969; Gould, Lewis. *1968: The Election That Changed America.* Chicago: Ivan R. Dee, 1993; Phillips, Kevin. *The Emerging Republican Majority.* New Rochelle, N.Y.: Arlington House, 1969.
—Donald A. Zinman

presidential election 1972

Winning President and Vice President: Richard M. Nixon and Spiro T. Agnew
Number of States: 50 (plus D.C.)
Major Candidates (Party Affiliation): Richard M. Nixon (Republican); George McGovern (Democrat)
Electoral College Vote: Richard M. Nixon: 520; George McGovern: 17; John Hospers: 1
Popular Vote: Richard M. Nixon: 47,169,911; George McGovern: 29,170,383

The 1972 presidential election pitted Republican incumbent Richard M. Nixon against Democratic CHALLENGER senator George McGovern of South Dakota. The result was a landslide of historic proportions for Nixon and Vice President Spiro T. Agnew. The Nixon-Agnew ticket carried 49 states and won 521 electoral votes. McGovern managed to win only Massachusetts and the District of Columbia. In the POPULAR VOTE, Nixon received 47,169,911 votes, while McGovern won 29,170,383 votes and finished with only 37.5 percent of the total vote.

Nixon's victory was marred by allegations of corruption leveled against his administration. On June 17, 1972, five men were arrested in the headquarters of the DEMOCRATIC NATIONAL COMMITTEE in the Watergate Hotel in Washington. The administration denied having any ties to the break-in, and White House press secretary Ron Ziegler dismissed the incident as a "third-rate burglary." However, several media organizations, primarily the *Washington Post*, reported that the burglars had ties with Nixon's CAMPAIGN ORGANIZATION, the Committee to Reelect the President (CREEP). The *Post* detailed how members of CREEP used money to harass the leading Democratic candidates. The publicity created questions about the methods employed by Nixon's aides, but Nixon was not personally charged with any wrongdoing. The news stories about Watergate, as the brewing SCANDAL became known, did not significantly harm his reelection effort.

By the time of the Watergate break-in, Nixon was in a commanding political position. The first half of 1972 was a period of startling achievement by the 37th president. After a long and difficult political career, Nixon was at the pinnacle of power. He had been a national figure for more than 20 years. He had served two terms as vice president under Dwight Eisenhower. In 1960, he was narrowly defeated by John F. Kennedy in the PRESIDENTIAL ELECTION, and two years later he suffered a crushing loss in his race for governor of California. Many PUNDITs believed Nixon's political career was over, but he embarked on a remarkable comeback that culminated in his election to the presidency in 1968. The staunchly anticommunist Nixon became the first American president to visit communist China. Three months after his China trip, in May 1972, Nixon traveled to Moscow to sign an arms control treaty with the Soviet Union. The diplomatic initiatives boosted Nixon's APPROVAL RATINGs and enhanced his reelection chances.

The most important issue in the race, however, was the Vietnam War. When Nixon took office in 1969, the United States had more than 500,000 troops in Vietnam. Nixon pledged to find an honorable end to the war, but in his first two years in office the conflict dragged on, with the fighting expanding into Cambodia. However, by 1972, American involvement was winding down, and Nixon had brought home most of the troops. Critics of the Vietnam War attacked Nixon's policy of gradual withdrawal and continued bombing of North Vietnam, but public opinion polls showed that a majority of Americans supported the president. Polls also demonstrated a concern among the public about George McGovern's proposals for ending the war.

McGovern ran as a peace candidate, and his stance helped him win the Democratic NOMINATION. When the PRIMARY season opened, McGovern was viewed as an underdog, but after FRONTRUNNER senator Edmund Muskie of Maine slipped, McGovern captured the nomination. A two-term senator from South Dakota, McGovern was an unabashed liberal who staked out controversial stands on a host of issues. During the campaign, he called for a guaranteed national income for the poor, promised amnesty for draft dodgers, and also pledged to go to Hanoi, the capital of North Vietnam, to ask for peace.

These views were outside the political mainstream, and the Nixon campaign had little trouble convincing voters that McGovern was a radical. While Nixon ignored McGovern by not mentioning him by name and refusing to debate McGovern, his election team hammered away. Members of McGovern's own party deserted him, including most southern members of Congress. Whatever small chance he may have had to win the election was blown away by his own ineptitude. McGovern ran a disastrous campaign. At the Democratic National Convention in July, he selected Missouri senator Thomas Eagleton as his vice presidential RUNNING MATE without conducting a background check. Six weeks later Eagleton admitted that he had been treated for depression with electric shock therapy. McGovern at first supported his beleaguered running mate, defiantly announcing that he was "1,000 percent" behind Eagleton. But McGovern quickly distanced himself from Eagleton, and Eagleton quit the race. McGovern spent the next few weeks trying to find another running mate, but the Democrats he approached refused his entreaties. Finally, McGovern settled on Sargent Shriver, a former director of the Peace Corps.

In comparison to the McGovern candidacy, the Nixon campaign operated smoothly. Nixon conducted a "Rose Garden" strategy, in which he tried to appear presidential and above POLITICS. Nixon also downplayed his partisan affiliation, a move that attracted Democrats but alienated Republican officials, who believed that he could help elect more Republicans to the House and the Senate. Nixon sought a personal victory, and he concentrated on winning INDEPENDENTs and Democrats. With his foreign policy achievements and a prosperous economy, Nixon sailed to a landslide reelection.

Richard Nixon won a decisive but ultimately costly victory. In their zeal for reelection, Nixon aides and campaign workers engaged in tactics that were illicit and illegal. The break-in at the Watergate Hotel was only one of a number of "dirty tricks" perpetrated by members of CREEP. While Nixon did not have advanced knowledge of the break-in, he directed the White House effort to contain any further political damage by trying to prevent an FBI investigation into the break-in. This strategy worked during the election, but just a few months into Nixon's second term the cover-up unraveled. Because of the ensuing revelations about his role in the cover-up, Nixon was forced from office. On August 9, 1974, Nixon became the first president ever to resign the office.

Further reading: Ambrose, Stephen E. *Nixon: The Triumph of a Politician.* New York: Simon & Schuster, 1987; White, Theodore. *The Making of the President, 1972.* New York: Scribner, 1972.

—Justin P. Coffey

presidential election 1976

Winning President and Vice President: Jimmy Carter and Walter F. Mondale
Number of States: 50 (plus D.C.)
Major Candidates (Party Affiliation): Jimmy Carter (Democrat); Gerald R. Ford (Republican)
Electoral College Vote: Jimmy Carter: 297; Gerald R. Ford: 240; Ronald Reagan: 1
Popular Vote: Jimmy Carter: 40,830,763; Gerald R. Ford: 39,147,793

The presidential election of 1976 marked the first time an incumbent president ran for reelection without previously being elected either president or vice president. When Spiro Agnew resigned as vice president in 1973, Richard Nixon appointed then congressman Gerald Ford as vice president. Ford then became president when Nixon resigned on August 9, 1974, following the Watergate SCANDAL. With Ford assuming the presidency, he became the first nonelected vice president to become president.

As the 1976 election season began, Ford decided to run for the presidency on his own merit, and was quickly anointed as the party FRONTRUNNER despite a challenge mounted by California governor Ronald Reagan. Ford then chose Senator Robert Dole of Kansas as his RUNNING MATE and prepared to run as the incumbent.

For the DEMOCRATIC PARTY, the race for the party's NOMINATION was wide open. Six candidates began the PRIMARY season with a chance to be the Democratic presidential nominee, Governor Jimmy Carter (Georgia), Senator Birch Bayh (Indiana), Senator Fred Harris (Oklahoma), Senator Henry "Skip" Jackson (Washington), Representative Mo Udall (Arizona), and Sargent Shriver (Massachusetts). All six individuals had a chance to win the nomination, but the eventual winner, Jimmy Carter, was initially seen as a long shot. Carter was a popular southern governor, but many outside the South did not know who he was or what he stood for. Once he received the nomination, Carter chose Walter Mondale (Minnesota) as his running mate.

When the votes were counted on November 2, 1976, Carter-Mondale defeated Ford-Dole, with Senator Eugene McCarthy finishing a distant third. Carter-Mondale received 50 percent of the POPULAR VOTE to Ford-Dole's 48 percent. McCarthy and other third-party candidates combined to receive the remaining 2 percent.

The ELECTORAL COLLEGE vote mirrored the popular vote in its closeness. Carter-Mondale received 297 electoral votes, while Ford-Dole received 240. Ronald Reagan received one Electoral College vote from a dissatisfied Republican ELECTOR. The total turnout for the election was 53.6 percent of voters nationwide (voting statistics from U.S. Office of Federal Registry).

The 1976 election was one of the closest PRESIDENTIAL ELECTIONS in the 20th century. Its significance derives from unique factors that occurred leading up to and during the election. Perhaps the election's greatest significance is that it was the first election to happen after President Nixon resigned as a result of the Watergate scandal. As the first post-Watergate election, 1976 provided the voters with their first opportunity to have a say in the events that led up to and occurred after Nixon resigned. Voters also had the opportunity to comment on Ford's policies and his decision to pardon Nixon shortly after the resignation.

The election also served as one of the first opportunities for a Washington outsider to succeed in a national election. Carter, as governor of Georgia, was a virtual unknown in many Washington circles. This led many within the Democratic Party to question his experience as governor and his more moderate stances compared with the traditional New England wing of the party. Carter was able to seize on these themes and mold his campaign to compete in states outside the South early during the primary season. He was then able to solidify his standing among the candidates by virtually sweeping the southern primaries.

Carter used his success in the primaries to jump-start his campaign. Both Carter and Ford used traditional presidential themes as well as issues such as foreign and economic policy. Carter ran his campaign as an outsider and as the morally upright candidate who could provide a change to the corrupt Republican administration that had been in office since 1968. Ford tried to use the strength of the office of the presidency to focus the election on the accomplishments of his administration.

While the biggest issue in the campaign was the debate over insider experience versus change as an outsider, the single defining moment probably came during a debate about foreign policy between Carter and Ford. During the debate, Ford made the claim that the Soviet Union did not have an influence over Eastern Europe. Ford's comment made him seem out of touch and unaware of the world situation and allowed Carter's inexperience to fade to the background.

Throughout the entire election process, both the Republican and Democratic parties had influence over the election, but in different ways. The REPUBLICAN PARTY was initially divided between supporting the sitting president and backing the popular former governor of California. In the end, it chose the sitting president in an attempt to move beyond the Watergate scandal.

The primary contests allowed Democratic voters to choose between longtime party loyalists and a southern outsider with bold new ideas and a connection to the "average voter." Carter was able to use the relatively new party nomination system to his advantage and prove that he had appeal outside the South by winning primaries in the Northeast and Midwest "Rust Belt."

Overall, the 1976 presidential election marked a temporary shift back to New Deal principles that still coursed through the Democratic Party. The election was a final statement against those involved in the Watergate scandal and a chance for an outsider to make a difference by bringing fresh blood and ideas to Washington.

Further reading: Anderson, Patrick. *Electing Jimmy Carter: The Campaign of 1976.* Baton Rouge: Louisiana State University Press, 1994; Miller, Warren E., and Teresa E. Levitin. *Leadership & Change: Presidential Elections from 1952 to 1976.* Lanham, Md.: University Press of America, 1984; Stroud, Kandy. *How Jimmy Won: The Victory Campaign from Plains to the White House.* New York: Morrow, 1977.

—Jacob R. Straus

Celebration for incumbent Gerald Ford and his running mate, Robert Dole, on winning the nomination at the Republican National Convention, Kansas City, Missouri *(Yanker Poster Collection, Library of Congress)*

presidential election 1980

Winning President and Vice President: Ronald Reagan and George H. W. Bush
Number of States: 50 (plus D.C.)
Major Candidates (Party Affiliation): Ronald Reagan (Republican); Jimmy Carter (Democrat)
Electoral College Vote: Ronald Reagan: 489; Jimmy Carter: 49
Popular Vote: Ronald Reagan: 43,904,153; Jimmy Carter: 35,483,883

The 1980 election now appears as a watershed REALIGNMENT, but at the time the outcome was close and almost uneventful. The results ran counter to one of the proverbs of national POLITICS, that incumbents enjoy a decided advantage in American elections. In reality, the questionable nostrum of incumbent invulnerability was largely outdated in a television age, especially when the CHALLENGER,

Ronald and Nancy Reagan campaigning for election during the 1980 presidential race *(Ronald Reagan Library)*

Ronald Reagan, was a charismatic actor. Jimmy Carter, in contrast, presented himself as a victim of events beyond his control, but on election day voters held him responsible for the condition of the country.

The dominant event of the election occurred on November 4, 1979, exactly one year before the vote, when a terrorist cell that supported the overthrow of the Shah of Iran and the ascension to power of Ayatollah Ruhollah Khomeini seized 52 hostages in the American embassy in Tehran. No event in the election, with the possible exception of the economy, had more importance than the hostage crisis. Political opportunism ran in the face of patriotic responsibility, and eventually a candidate's stand on the crisis determined his success, or lack of same. In the first flush of rage after the seizure of the American embassy, a patriotic fervor washed over the country, and President Jimmy Carter enjoyed some much needed popularity. The effect did not last for long.

Four years earlier, Carter lost a sizable lead over Gerald Ford but came back to narrowly beat the incumbent president. The Carter administration promised a vigorous defense of its policies, and used an unabashed "Rose Garden" incumbent strategy when it came to his reelection campaign. Two Democrats opposed Carter in 1980. Ted Kennedy was the heir to a family legacy that stretched back 20 years and gripped the heartstrings of the American

ELECTORATE like few politicians in the nation's history. The early polls showed him a favorite again, with 62 percent of Democrats supporting Kennedy compared to Carter's paltry 24 percent support. The other candidate was Jerry Brown, the governor of California, whose name suggested another West Coast family legacy. Against these two party rivals, Jimmy Carter played the powers of his office to perfection, skipping a scheduled debate in Iowa and using the White House news-making machine to dominate the daily agenda with the Iran crisis.

The hostage emergency frustrated Carter's Democratic opponents but was less of a hindrance to the Republicans. While there were several Republican candidates in 1980, the FRONTRUNNER was Ronald Reagan, whose good-natured aura and plain-spoken style hid a personal toughness and conservative convictions. He pressed Carter on the issue of American vulnerability in foreign affairs and economic weakness at home. George Herbert Walker Bush was a man of impressive origin, the scion of a wealthy eastern Republican family, a millionaire oilman who had been director of the Central Intelligence Agency, ambassador to the United Nations, and special envoy to China. The third major candidate in the race was John Bowden Connally, a former governor of Texas and secretary of the Treasury and navy, who characterized himself as a wheeler-dealer. The trailing pack consisted of John Anderson, Bob Dole, Phil Crane, and Howard Baker.

After stumbling in Iowa, Reagan's campaign regained momentum in New Hampshire, and he began an affable march to the NOMINATION. The Reagan message was tailored directly to the malaise of the Carter era. The present condition of the country, said the Republican frontrunner, required a new approach of lower taxes, less government, and a strong national defense. The former governor of California was the perfect person by experience and conviction to lead the transition. In an act of pragmatism and party unity, which would affect American politics for three decades to come, Reagan chose George H. W. Bush as his RUNNING MATE.

While Republicans sought a champion, the Democratic president fended off competitors from his own party. The Carter campaign took electioneering seriously, and even without an appearance by the president, he beat Ted Kennedy by a two to one margin in Iowa. No matter how hard he tried, Kennedy was never able to resurrect the glories of his family's past to defeat the incumbent president. Carter easily won renomination at the Democratic convention.

With the hostage crisis as a backdrop, Reagan ran a campaign of upbeat optimism, complete with a promise of a more aggressive foreign policy. The contrast was sharp with the disquiet of the Carter years and the president's apparent impotence in the face of terrorist hostility. The Republican candidate never led in the polls until the last days of the election. Reagan promised an end to "big government," a restoration of economic health through supply-side economics, and a renewed respect for U.S. foreign policy. Although his candidacy was burdened by the third-party effort of John B. Anderson, a moderate Republican who ran as an INDEPENDENT, the twin issues of the economy and the hostage crisis continually favored Reagan.

Polls in the weeks before the election still had the outcome a tossup, but in the end Reagan won a landslide victory, and the Republicans gained control of the U.S. Senate for the first time in 25 years. The Reagan conservative COALITION and its legacy would influence American politics for decades to come. The Republican president garnered 489 electoral votes to Carter's 49. John Anderson won no electoral votes but had more than 5 million POPULAR VOTES.

Further reading: Cannon, Lou. *President Reagan: The Role of a Lifetime.* New York: Public Affairs, 2000; Jordan, Hamilton. *Crisis: The Last Year of the Carter Presidency.* New York: Putnam Group, 1982; Sick, Gary. *October Surprise: America's Hostages in Iran and the Election of Ronald Reagan.* New York: Random House, 1992.

—J. David Woodard

presidential election 1984

Winning President and Vice President: Ronald Reagan and George H. W. Bush
Number of States: 50 (plus D.C.)
Major Candidates (Party Affiliation): Ronald Reagan (Republican); Walter Mondale (Democrat)
Electoral College Vote: Reagan: 525; Mondale: 13
Popular Vote: Reagan: 54,455,075; Mondale: 37,577,185

Although the reelection of Ronald Reagan in 1984 was largely a forgone conclusion, the magnitude of his victory was truly astounding. Reagan eclipsed Walter Mondale with 58 percent of the POPULAR VOTE, carrying 49 states. Reagan's landslide performance confirmed his status as one of the towering figures of contemporary American POLITICS and sent shockwaves through the DEMOCRATIC PARTY, creating a movement to retool the party's image and issue platform.

Two elements of the political environment, Ronald Reagan's popularity and the state of the economy, assured that any Democratic candidate would have great difficulty unseating the president. Gallup Poll data in February of 1984 showed that 55 percent of Americans approved of Reagan's handling of his job as president, marking a significant comeback from an APPROVAL RATING of 35 percent just a year earlier. In particular, Reagan received high marks for his leadership qualities. Reagan's robust approval ratings heading into the 1984 campaign owed to favorable economic trends. Real disposable income rose 5.8 percent in the year before the 1984 election, compared to only 0.7 percent in the year preceding the 1980 election. Although the average unemployment rate in 1983–84 was higher than in 1979–80 (7.8 percent vs. 6.9 percent), unemployment was decreasing in 1983–84 rather than increasing as it was four years earlier.

Ronald Reagan faced no opposition for the REPUBLICAN PARTY NOMINATION, but there was a spirited battle within the Democratic Party. Former vice president Walter Mondale was widely recognized as the FRONTRUNNER for the Democratic nomination, but he faced several notable opponents, including Senators Edward Kennedy, Gary Hart, and John Glenn, as well as the Reverend Jesse Jackson. Mondale had been laying the groundwork for his campaign since 1981, securing commitments from a wide variety of Democratic Party constituencies, including organized labor, feminists, civil rights groups, and Democratic elected officials. His aim was to assemble a broad COALITION of party support that would ensure success in early primaries and caucuses. Gary Hart, by contrast, presented himself as the candidate of "new ideas," hoping to appeal to professional, baby boom voters. Jesse Jackson sought to construct a RAINBOW COALITION of African Americans, Hispanics, women, and other groups outside the Democratic Party establishment.

Mondale started strongly with a victory in the IOWA CAUCUSES, but lost to Gary Hart a week later in the NEW HAMPSHIRE PRIMARY. Thus began a protracted two-man struggle for the nomination. Neither Mondale nor Hart clearly prevailed in the cluster of SUPER TUESDAY primaries in early March. Mondale's attention to traditional Democratic constituencies, notably organized labor, paid dividends later as he scored a string of victories in the DELEGATE-rich industrial states of Michigan, Illinois, New York, and Pennsylvania. Although Hart triumphed in California in June, Mondale's win in New Jersey clinched the Democratic nomination.

Along the way, Jesse Jackson's support among African-American voters gave him victories in Louisiana and the District of Columbia, and enabled him to collect enough convention delegates to sustain viability and media attention throughout the nomination season. At the time, Jackson's campaign was the most successful foray into presidential politics by an African-American candidate.

The highlight of the DEMOCRATIC NATIONAL CONVENTION was Mondale's selection of New York congresswoman Geraldine Ferraro as his vice presidential RUNNING MATE. Ferraro became the first woman to run on a major party ticket. Excitement over the Ferraro nomination, along with a display of party unity at the convention, provided Mondale with an encouraging, though temporary, bump in the polls; some trial heat surveys showed him within 7 percent of Reagan.

Reagan and Mondale entered the GENERAL ELECTION CAMPAIGN with starkly different strategies and themes. A reservoir of popular support and a healthy economic climate gave Reagan wide strategic berth and severely ham-

pered Mondale's case for turning him out of office. The Reagan campaign avoided discussions of specific policies, and instead emphasized the general themes of economic recovery, peace through strength, and leadership. Its strategic goal was to make the election a referendum on the president's recent successes and to remind voters of Mondale's connection to the failings of Jimmy Carter. The overall tenor of the Reagan campaign was perhaps best illustrated by its "Morning in America" television ad; against a visual backdrop of contented everyday Americans, viewers were reminded that compared to four years earlier, the economy was stronger, the nation was at peace, and people felt better about their lives.

Mondale was left with the unenviable task of convincing voters that the economy was not as strong as it appeared, and that while "Morning in America" appeared to be bright, storm clouds were on the horizon. Mondale argued that Reagan policies had left unemployment uncomfortably high and had created troublesome budget deficits that would haunt future generations. He stated that tax increases would be needed to address the deficit and challenged Reagan to admit as much; Reagan declined the invitation. More generally, the Mondale campaign tried to highlight considerations of "fairness," arguing that Reagan policies neglected too many segments of the population. Mondale also tried to stir doubts about Reagan's foreign policy by raising the specter of nuclear conflict. Although Mondale's "fairness" theme resonated with some voters, his campaign made little headway during the general election campaign. Reagan enjoyed double-digit leads in most pre-election polls throughout the fall. Mondale closed the gap briefly following Reagan's lackluster performance in their first nationally televised debate, but Reagan's margin in the polls rebounded quickly.

On ELECTION DAY, Reagan won handily, thanks in part to many votes from former Democratic bastions. One in four white Democrats defected to Reagan, fueling speculation that REAGAN DEMOCRATS might become a permanent part of the Republican base. Reagan also won 80 percent of the vote among white southerners, and 45 percent of the vote in union households, underscoring the inroads that the Republican Party had made in traditional Democratic constituencies. There was a notable GENDER GAP in the vote, but it offered little comfort to Democrats, as Reagan won 54 percent of the vote among women; with 62 percent of men voting for Reagan, it became clear that the gender gap signaled a Democratic weakness among men rather than a Republican weakness among women. Reagan's share of the vote varied only slightly across age groups, and his appeal among young voters further encouraged talk of an impending Republican REALIGNMENT. However, poll data suggested that votes for Reagan were motivated primarily by economic appraisals and judgments of Reagan's leadership rather then considerations of policy.

Walter Mondale and Geraldine Ferraro during the 1984 Democratic National Convention. Ferraro was the first woman to run for the White House on a major-party ticket. (Bettmann/Corbis)

Thus, most analysts concluded that Reagan's victory was largely an ENDORSEMENT of his first term performance rather than a MANDATE for conservative policy in his second term.

Further reading: Abramson, Paul R., John H. Aldrich, and David W. Rohde. *Change and Continuity in the 1984 Elections.* Washington, D.C.: CQ Press, 1986; Nelson, Michael, ed. *The Election of 1984.* Washington, D.C.: CQ Press, 1985; Pomper, Gerald, et al. *The Election of 1984: Reports and Interpretations.* Chatham, N.J.: Chatham House, 1985.

—Julio Borquez

presidential election 1988

Winning President and Vice President: George H. W. Bush and J. Danforth Quayle
Number of States: 50 (plus D.C.)
Major Candidates (Party Affiliation): George H. W. Bush (Republican); Michael Dukakis (Democrat)
Electoral College Vote: George H. W. Bush: 426; Michael Dukakis: 111; Lloyd Bentsen: 1
Popular Vote: George H. W. Bush: 48,886,097; Michael Dukakis: 41,809,074

The 1988 presidential election marked an important transition point in contemporary American POLITICS. As the presidency of Ronald Reagan drew to a close, several questions provided the backdrop for the 1988 campaign: How long a shadow would Reagan cast over the campaign? Were voters looking for a continuation of the Reagan years, or were they ready to take the country in a new direction? Could the Democrats regroup after their 1984 debacle?

Although Reagan's reelection in 1984 was largely predetermined, 1988 was an election in which the campaign itself might matter. On the one hand, Democrats had reason to believe that they could reclaim the White House in 1988. Reagan was unable to run for a third term, and most Democratic strategists viewed Vice President George H. W. Bush as a relatively ineffectual campaigner with a strong public résumé but weak public image. On the other hand, Republicans were confident of their prospects due to Reagan's strong APPROVAL RATINGS (55 percent in September 1988) and increased parity with the Democrats in PARTY IDENTIFICATION. In the end, Bush maintained Republican control of the presidency after a hard-fought and decidedly negative campaign.

Reagan's departure set the stage for a competitive NOMINATION process, especially on the Democratic side. Throughout 1987, a crowded field of candidates began jockeying for the Democratic nomination. Active candidates included Senators Gary Hart, Joseph Biden, Al Gore, and Paul Simon, Congressman Richard Gephardt, and the Reverend Jesse Jackson. When New York governor Mario Cuomo announced that he would not seek the nomination, Massachusetts governor Michael Dukakis soon entered the fray.

A distinctive feature of the 1988 PRIMARY season was the cluster of March 8 SUPER TUESDAY primaries, many held in southern states. Engineered by moderate Democrats, Super Tuesday was intended to produce a centrist nominee who could appeal to REAGAN DEMOCRATS and counter Republican strength in the South. Anticipation of Super Tuesday diminished the impact of Gephardt's win in the IOWA CAUCUSES and Dukakis's win in the NEW HAMPSHIRE PRIMARY. Gore and Jackson, who had passed over Iowa and New Hampshire, were counting on strong showings on Super Tuesday to bolster their candidacies. Indeed, Super Tuesday appeared to be tailor-made for the Tennessean, Gore.

The Super Tuesday results did help winnow the field but failed to produce a moderate FRONTRUNNER. Although Gore won five southern primaries, he was unable to parlay that into significant support outside the region. Jackson's support among African Americans gave him victories in Georgia, Louisiana, and Virginia and ensured that he would be a factor going into the DEMOCRATIC NATIONAL CONVENTION. Dukakis won Florida and Texas and did well enough in other southern states to stake a claim as a viable national candidate. He established himself as the clear frontrunner by winning the New York primary, and went into the Democratic convention seeking to unite his party and frame his GENERAL ELECTION CAMPAIGN. Dukakis tried to set a moderate tone by selecting Senator Lloyd Bentsen of Texas as his RUNNING MATE and by declaring that "this election is not about ideology, it's about competence." Dukakis emerged from the Democratic convention with a 17-point lead over Vice President Bush in national polls, an advantage that would soon evaporate.

Vice President Bush enjoyed frontrunner status for the Republican nomination but was challenged early by Senator Robert Dole and the Reverend Pat Robertson. The Bush campaign was temporarily derailed by Robertson's victory in an early Michigan caucus and by Dole's win in Iowa. Bush rebounded by winning New Hampshire and sweeping the Republican primaries on Super Tuesday. The remaining contests were a formality for the Bush campaign. Bush's principle task at the Republican convention was to step out of Ronald Reagan's shadow while still exploiting the president's popular support. For instance, Bush's call for a "kinder, gentler nation" was an attempt to distance himself from one of Reagan's political weaknesses, a perceived lack of concern for the less fortunate. By contrast, Bush's exhortation "Read my lips, no new taxes" was a pledge to carry on Reagan's mission of lower taxes and smaller government. Despite controversy surrounding the military record of vice presidential nominee Dan Quayle, Bush enjoyed a 46 to 40 trial heat advantage over Dukakis immediately after the Republican convention.

As the general election campaign began, it was clear that Michael Dukakis was still an unknown quantity to many Americans. Thus, the Bush campaign embarked on an effort to define Dukakis's public image before he did it himself. The aim was to portray Dukakis as an elitist liberal who was soft on crime, weak on defense, disdainful of mainstream American values, and far too risky for the presidency. In campaign appearances and television advertisements, the Bush campaign criticized Dukakis's membership in the American Civil Liberties Union, his veto of state legislation requiring schoolchildren to recite the Pledge of Allegiance, and a Massachusetts prison furlough program. This last point was especially controversial, as it involved the infamous Willie Horton case and opened the Bush campaign to charges that it was exploiting racial tensions for electoral advantage. For its part, the Dukakis campaign was slow to respond to Bush's criticisms, allowing the vice president to set the terms of campaign discourse through much of the fall. That discourse centered on "values" (patriotism, family, fear of crime) more than specific policy and was distinctly negative in tone. Negative television ads constituted more than 80 percent of the ad content in 1988.

The Bush campaign successfully shaped public perceptions of Dukakis. In an early September CBS/*New York Times* survey, 37 percent of respondents labeled Dukakis a liberal. By early November, 56 percent considered him liberal. Dukakis never led in a trial heat poll during the fall, though he closed to within 2 percent after the first nationally televised debate. By late October, he trailed Bush 51 to 38. Dukakis took a more aggressive stance late in the campaign, but even then he still faced a 48 to 40 deficit on the eve of the election.

Bush was elected president with a comfortable 8 percent margin in the POPULAR VOTE and a nearly 4 to 1 margin in the ELECTORAL COLLEGE tally. The vote represented a general ENDORSEMENT of the Reagan record rather than a concrete policy MANDATE for the incoming Bush administration. In several ways, the outlines of Bush's support confirmed trends evident in the Reagan elections and underscored the weakening of the Democrats' NEW DEAL COALITION. Bush maintained Republican ascendancy in the South, winning 67 percent of the vote among white southerners. By winning 81 percent among evangelical Christians, he solidified Republican strength in a critical, emerging voting bloc. Bush won easily among traditional Republican constituencies such as upper-income and rural voters.

In other ways, Bush was less successful in capitalizing on Reagan's appeal. Among voters aged 18 to 29, Bush received 52 percent of the vote, 7 percent less than Reagan received in 1984. Republican support among voters earning less than $30,000 a year dropped 10 percent from 1984; support among union members dropped by a similar amount.

All told, Bush lost about half of the Reagan Democrats who had voted Republican four years earlier, giving Democrats a glimmer of hope as they looked ahead to 1992.

Further reading: Goldman, Peter, and Tom Matthews. *The Quest for the Presidency 1988.* New York: Touchstone, 1988; Pomper, Gerald, et al. *The Election of 1988: Reports and Interpretations.* Chatham, N.J.: Chatham House, 1989; Runkel, David R. *Campaign for President: The Managers Look at '88.* Dover, Mass.: Auburn House, 1989.

—Julio Borquez

presidential election 1992

Winning President and Vice President: William Jefferson Clinton and Albert Gore, Jr.
Number of States: 50 (plus D.C.)
Major Candidates (Party Affiliation): William Jefferson Clinton (Democrat); George H. W. Bush (Republican); Ross Perot (independent)
Electoral College Vote: William Jefferson Clinton: 370; George H. W. Bush: 168
Popular Vote: William Jefferson Clinton: 44,909,326; George H. W. Bush: 39,103,882; Ross Perot: 19,742,240

Profound changes in the international environment as well as domestic economic concerns dominated the political landscape before the 1992 presidential election. In 1989, the Soviet bloc of Eastern Europe began to crumble in a series of largely nonviolent revolutions, capped by the dissolution of the Soviet Union itself in 1991, officially ending the cold war. Also in 1991, the United States led Operation Desert Storm, building an international COALITION to remove Saddam Hussein from Kuwait. President George H. W. Bush reaped significant political benefits from these international victories, attaining extraordinarily high job APPROVAL RATINGS in early 1991. Bush seemed positioned to dominate in 1992.

These international victories, however, proved a double-edged sword for President Bush. Caught up in his stellar approval ratings, President Bush seemed content to rest on his accomplishments and ride his wave of success into the elections. And, as economic conditions sagged at home, the public became less concerned with events overseas and more concerned with their own pocketbooks. Public perception solidified around the notion that Bush was spending greater attention on international affairs than on domestic affairs.

Growing dissent led some Republicans to challenge President Bush for the NOMINATION. Former Nixon White House adviser and conservative writer Patrick Buchanan accused Bush of ignoring his conservative roots. Echoing popular sentiment, Buchanan argued that Bush placed internationalism ahead of domestic priorities and that the president's 1990 tax increases were a betrayal of the party's base, as well as a clear violation of Bush's "no new taxes" pledge from the 1988 campaign.

Buchanan waged a fierce PRIMARY fight against Bush. Buchanan's strong second-place finish in the early NEW HAMPSHIRE PRIMARY attracted considerable media attention, even though, by the numbers, he never seriously threatened President Bush's lead in the polls. Buchanan failed to repeat his strong showing in subsequent contests, however, and by June had dropped from the race.

Early in the campaign, few Democrats sought to challenge the incumbent president, though more entered the arena as Bush's approval ratings fell. Former governors William Clinton of Arkansas, Jerry Brown of California, and Douglas Wilder of Virginia, as well as Senators Tom Harkin of Iowa and Robert Kerrey of Nebraska and former senator Paul Tsongas of Massachusetts all entered the race before the start of the primary season.

No clear FRONTRUNNER emerged in the early stages of the Democratic primaries. Senator Tom Harkin won a sizable victory in his home state of Iowa, while Paul Tsongas won the New Hampshire primary in his New England backyard. Bill Clinton, though originally polling well, did not break from the pack until the race moved to Georgia and the southern states in early March. By late April Clinton was the clear frontrunner among the Democratic candidates.

Character questions dogged Clinton throughout the primary season. Charges of extramarital affairs, questionable actions to avoid service in Vietnam, and marijuana use during his college days hampered Clinton's early efforts. A January appearance with his wife, Hillary Rodham Clinton, on *60 Minutes* helped calm some of the uproar, though Clinton never fully escaped the questions surrounding his character.

Outside the two major parties, Texas billionaire H. Ross Perot campaigned as an INDEPENDENT. His antiestablishment message was largely concentrated on the failing economy and deficit reduction. Lacking a major PARTY ORGANIZATION to solidify his status, Perot waged a nearly self-financed, GRASSROOTS campaign built around his "United We Stand America" organization.

Perot's simple, populist style played well early in the campaign. The public seized on his antiestablishment message, at one point buoying him to the number-two position in some national polls. In time, however, questions surfaced regarding Perot's background and qualifications for the presidency. For many, Perot lacked experience and detailed solutions to address the nation's policy problems. Perot's various conspiracy theories regarding Vietnam-era prisoners of war led his political rivals to raise damaging questions about his qualifications. As his poll numbers fell, Perot

Democratic candidate Bill Clinton campaigning at a pro-choice rally in Washington, D.C., 1992 *(Owen Franken/Corbis)*

ended his candidacy in mid-summer, only to reenter the race in the fall.

The major party conventions set the stage for the GENERAL ELECTION season. The Republicans officially chose President Bush and Vice President Dan Quayle to face Democrats Bill Clinton and Albert Gore, a well-respected Democratic senator from Tennessee. Perot chose retired admiral James Stockdale, a Vietnam War hero, as his RUNNING MATE.

Issues similar to those of the primary season dominated the general election. Bush continued to attack Clinton's character, while playing to his experience as the incumbent. Bush addressed the concerns of his conservative political base, many such concerns identified by his early competitor, Patrick Buchanan, highlighting "family values" and a return to fiscal discipline. Bush also offered tax cuts coupled with government spending cuts to pull the economy out of recession and to diminish the impact of breaking his "no new taxes" pledge.

The Clinton campaign focused on change. Embracing the 1960 Kennedy campaign spirit, Clinton focused on creating a better America through domestic issues, including health care and education, as well as targeted tax increases to strengthen the economy. He used the catchphrase "It's the economy, stupid" to portray Bush as out of touch with the common American's condition and to keep his own campaign focused. Clinton also embraced the Perot antiincumbency message, campaigning as a Washington outsider to tap voter antiestablishment antipathy.

The campaign reflected the generational difference dividing America. Whereas Bush represented the World War II generation, Clinton was a "baby boomer," part of the post–World War II generation for which Vietnam was the defining military conflict. The younger generation appeared more willing to forgive character flaws than older generations and seemed less concerned with a president's lack of military service.

VOTER TURNOUT was relatively high on ELECTION DAY, with more than 55 percent of the ELECTORATE voting. Clinton won the POPULAR VOTE with a 43 percent plurality over Bush and Perot, with 38 and 19 percent, respectively. The ELECTORAL COLLEGE vote was not as close, with 370 votes for Clinton, 168 for Bush, and 0 for Perot.

Further reading: Nelson, Michael, ed. *Guide to the Presidency.* 3rd ed. Washington, D.C.: CQ Press, 2002.

—Chris Mandernach

presidential election 1996

Winning President and Vice President: William Jefferson Clinton and Albert Gore, Jr.
Number of States: 50 (plus D.C.)
Major Candidates (Party Affiliation): William Jefferson Clinton (Democrat); Robert Dole (Republican); H. Ross Perot (Reform)
Electoral College Vote: William Jefferson Clinton: 379; Robert Dole: 159
Popular Vote: William Jefferson Clinton: 47,401,054; Robert Dole: 39,197,350; H. Ross Perot: 8,085,402

The year 1996 dawned on the heels of the REPUBLICAN REVOLUTION of 1994, when Republicans took control of Congress for the first time in 40 years. Having helped to orchestrate the Republican victory in 1994, the powerful new SPEAKER OF THE HOUSE, Newt Gingrich, spent most of 1995 leading a headfirst charge against Democratic president Bill Clinton in an attempt to unravel the legacy of President Lyndon Johnson's Great Society programs of the 1960s. Senate Majority Leader Bob Dole was Gingrich's collaborator throughout, although he clearly played second fiddle for most of 1995.

Ongoing battles through the year climaxed in a budgetary showdown when Republicans threatened to shut down the government if President Clinton did not agree to a balanced budget program to their liking. When Clinton vetoed the Republican plan, there were two separate shutdowns from December 1995 into January 1996. Clinton and the DEMOCRATIC PARTY mounted an all-out attack in the media against "Gingrich-Dole" Republicans, tying the eventual Republican nominee to the highly effective, though unpopular, Speaker. Clinton came out more popular than ever while at the same time weakening the Republicans.

Clinton faced no serious PRIMARY opponent and cruised to his party's NOMINATION. The Republican contest went through a series of twists, starting from when the candidate with the most money, Senator Phil Gramm of Texas, dropped out before the IOWA CAUCUS due to a loss in virtually irrelevant Louisiana. Billionaire businessman Steve Forbes entered the primaries and drove much of the debate with his proposal for a "flat tax." Forbes also spent millions savagely attacking Dole, though his own poll numbers remained low. Senator Dole squeaked by with a close victory in Iowa over conservative PUNDIT Pat Buchanan and former governor (and federal secretary of education) Lamar Alexander of Tennessee. But the biggest shock came the next week, when Buchanan stunned the political world with an upset victory over Dole in the much touted NEW HAMPSHIRE PRIMARY. However, Buchanan failed to keep the momentum, losing to Dole in South Carolina within the month and eventually dropping out of the race.

Dole had exhausted most of his money to win the nomination, allowing Clinton and the DEMOCRATIC NATIONAL COMMITTEE to run ads against him throughout the summer, while the Republicans were forced into virtual silence. He resigned from the Senate upon clinching the nomination to focus full time on his campaign. Dole briefly gained a lead after picking former congressman and Housing and Urban Development secretary Jack Kemp as his RUNNING MATE at the San Diego convention, and after one of Clinton's top aides, Dick Morris, resigned due to a sex SCANDAL. However, after the Democratic convention in Chicago, Clinton jumped ahead again and stayed in front for the rest of the campaign.

President Clinton based his campaign on a promise to "build a bridge to the 21st century," a slogan with little substance but much appeal to the public in a time of strong economic growth and peace. H. Ross Perot, who drew 19 percent of the popular vote in 1992 as a third-party candidate focusing on the budget deficit and trade, ran again as the leader of his newly created REFORM PARTY, though with a much lower profile. Dole was left without much to complain about, so he focused on a range of issues including welfare reform, but primarily spent large amounts of time addressing the incumbent's personal character. While the issue of welfare reform died after Clinton signed a

Republican-sponsored reform bill, character questions only intensified toward the end of the contest. In addition to the Whitewater real estate scandal and the ongoing Paula Jones sex scandal, several media outlets broke a story involving foreign money sent to the Clinton campaign, as well as other potential campaign finance violations, just two weeks before ELECTION DAY. The latest scandal brought Clinton's numbers down, keeping him under his desired goal of at least 50 percent (a number he received neither for his first or second term, thanks to Ross Perot) and making his margin of victory over Dole only 8 percentage points, when most polls just weeks earlier had him with a 15 to 20 point lead.

Clinton's victory made him the first Democratic president since Franklin Roosevelt to be reelected to a second term. However, his victory was primarily a personal one, not a win for his party. Under direction from soon-to-be-disgraced aide Dick Morris, Clinton developed a strategy nicknamed "triangulation," under which he could take the middle road between left-wing congressional Democrats and right-wing Republicans. This crafty strategy made Clinton seem above the fray and a national leader. The strategy, however, did little to help congressional Democrats, who made few gains in their attempt to regain the House or Senate.

Another important feature of Clinton's reelection campaign was his reliance on so-called SOFT MONEY, or money directed to the party instead of to his personal reelection campaign fund. These soft money donations were legally unlimited, so corporations, unions, and some wealthy individuals donated hundreds of thousands, if not millions, of dollars to the president's reelection effort in the guise of donations to the entire Democratic Party. The Democratic National Committee and the Clinton-Gore campaign coordinated their activity in unleashing one of the most spectacular media bonanzas ever witnessed in American POLITICS. All this activity came to a head in 1997 as the burgeoning campaign finance scandal became the latest in a series of scandals endured by the administration. No administration officials were directly implicated in any wrongdoing, although Vice President Gore's FUND-RAISING calls from his West Wing office created much embarrassment. Republicans copied many of the same tactics in the 2000 election, with a few innovations of their own. The sight of virtually unlimited amounts of money pouring into the system eventually led Congress in 2002 to pass the MCCAIN-FEINGOLD campaign finance reform bill, which had languished in Congress for several years.

Further reading: Caesar, James W., and Andrew E. Busch. *Losing to Win: The 1996 Elections and American Politics.* Lanham, Md.: Rowman & Littlefield, 1997; Crotty, William J., and Jerome M. Mileur, eds. *America's Choice: The Elections of 1996.* Guilford, Conn.: McGraw-Hill, 1997; Woodward, Bob. *The Choice: How Clinton Won.* New York: Touchstone Books, 1997.

—William D. Adler

presidential election 2000

Winning President and Vice President: George W. Bush and Richard Cheney
Number of States: 50 (plus D.C.)
Major Candidates (Party Affiliation): George W. Bush (Republican); Al Gore (Democrat)
Electoral College Vote: George W. Bush: 271; Al Gore: 267
Popular Vote: Al Gore: 50,996,582; George W. Bush: 50,456,062

The presidential election of 2000 was one of the longest GENERAL ELECTION CAMPAIGNS in U.S. history, and it culminated in the longest election "night" (36 days) in modern history. Only the presidential election of 1876 comes close to the 2000 election in terms of postelection drama. In the 2000 election, Democratic vice president Albert Gore had been the presumptive nominee of his party for nearly eight years. Although he faced a challenge from former senator Bill Bradley, Gore triumphed in early primaries and had the NOMINATION wrapped up in March. The Republican candidate was not nearly so certain. The REPUBLICAN PARTY has a tradition of giving an open nomination (i.e., no incumbent running) to whomever has been seeking it the longest—Richard Nixon in 1968, Ronald Reagan in 1980, George H. W. Bush in 1988, Robert Dole in 1996—and by that paradigm the 2000 nomination belonged to either former congressman and cabinet secretary Jack Kemp or former vice president J. Danforth Quayle. But it was clear fairly early in the long prenomination period that neither of their efforts had much traction. Instead, there was a burning desire for revenge against Gore and President William J. Clinton in many Republican circles for their having ousted Bush in 1992. The best revenge, many opined, was to elect Bush's son, George W. Bush. By mid-1999, Bush was the FRONTRUNNER (albeit with huge numbers of Republicans undecided). Bush's only serious competition was Senator John McCain of Arizona. But this race, too, was ended in March, and since it is usually June before both nominees are known (sometimes not until late August), this set up the longest general election campaign in history.

The U.S. economy was remarkably strong in 2000, as it had been for six years running. The country was also at peace, with no war looming on the horizon and no major domestic terrorism since the Oklahoma City bombing five years earlier. This would have been an ideal landscape for the incumbent vice president to run, but the Republicans had neutralized Gore's ability to run on the Clinton-Gore record by eight years of demonizing Clinton and his wife, Hillary, and ultimately by exposing the president's extramarital affair with a young intern and then impeaching him after he was caught lying about it under oath. Although the Republicans knew from the outset the impeachment would fail, many believe it had the desired effect on the 2000 election campaign. Gore, indeed, did not run on the administration's record and barely mentioned he had been part of it. Gore was also hampered by his tendency to make overstatements, such as suggesting he was the "father of the Internet," rather than making the more modest and accurate statement that he had led efforts to fund the expansion of Internet connections beyond the small group of universities and defense installations that were using them. His generally quiet style and nonenergetic speaking manner did not serve him well in the national campaign.

Bush had problems of his own. He was hampered throughout the early nomination race by reports of past cocaine use and alcohol abuse. He failed to make a clean admission of his history and instead allowed rumors to fuel press stories. Bush was hit with a bombshell going into the final weekend. A drunk driving charge of which he had been convicted in Maine in 1976 was revealed. Gore, by contrast, was frank about his marijuana use while in college and the army, thereby defusing the issue. Democrats also tried to raise the question of Bush's leadership during five years as governor of Texas. This had serious implications, since Bush's chief merit to seek the presidency was his governorship, and if that was attacked, his aspirations were greatly undermined. He also had the problem, which continued into his presidency, of being cast not as a man of ideas but instead as one dominated by advisers, many of them left over from previous administrations. This tendency was confirmed for many by his choice of his father's defense secretary, former representative Richard Cheney, as his RUNNING MATE.

Gore, on the other hand, made a bold stroke by choosing as his running mate Senator Joseph Lieberman of Connecticut, the first Jewish person on a major party ticket. This underscored his principal electoral target of urban voters, particularly in highly urbanized states. Lieberman became the first candidate in history to campaign outside the United States, traveling to Israel to urge U.S. citizens to cast BALLOTS.

With the candidates known months in advance, the national party conventions were reduced to nonevents. Gore was nominated at the DEMOCRATIC NATIONAL CONVENTION in Los Angeles, and Bush was nominated at the REPUBLICAN NATIONAL CONVENTION in Philadelphia. The general election campaign was also lackluster. In the debates the candidates were apparently so afraid of making serious blunders that they moderated their attack styles to nonattacks and spent much time agreeing with each other on side points of national issues rather than engaging in a serious debate about national priorities. Gore, with his reputation as an excellent debater, failed to meet the high expectations that were made for him. Expectations for Bush, on the other hand, were so low that almost any performance was seen as a victory.

The election will forever be remembered in U.S. history for the fight over the RECOUNT in Florida. We will probably never know which candidate, George W. Bush or Albert Gore, actually carried the POPULAR VOTE in Florida in that election. The debacle involved all three branches of government of both the United States and Florida and included major roles for the news media.

The kernel of the controversy was a flawed ballot design in Palm Beach County, a traditional Democratic stronghold. The key feature of the BUTTERFLY BALLOT is that it is spread across two facing pages, like a butterfly with its wings open. The voters indicate their choices by punching a hole between the two pages. It happened that the top hole, referenced by the top line on the left page, was to vote for Bush. The second hole, referenced by the top line on the right page, was to vote for Gore. Many people had trouble understanding the butterfly design and voted for the candidate on the third line, Patrick M. Buchanan, whose hole was adjacent to the name of Gore's RUNNING MATE, Senator Joseph Lieberman. This was evidenced by the large number of voters who punched the hole for Buchanan for president and then voted for Democrats in other races on the ballot. Another group of voters punched two holes, apparently thinking they had to vote for both president and vice president. By voting for both Gore and Buchanan, they spoiled their presidential vote. Again, the "overvotes," as these ballots are known, were disproportionately cast by people who voted Democratic on the rest of the ballot.

These spoiled votes were not reflected in the EXIT POLLS the television networks conducted. Television networks routinely interview voters leaving the polls about their votes so they can declare the election immediately after polls close. So exit pollers working Palm Beach County were provided with information about how voters intended to mark their ballots, not how they actually did. On election night, relying on their exit polls, major media outlets declared Gore the presumptive winner in Florida shortly after the polls closed in the eastern time zone. However, these same outlets either forgot that part of the Florida panhandle is in the central time zone, or they disregarded their policies not to declare statewide winners while the polls are open. (These policies were adopted after the 1980 election, when NBC in particular was criticized for declaring winners in states where polls were still open, and declaring Ronald Reagan the national winner before 7:30 P.M. ET.) Although evidence of voters leaving the polls or choosing not to vote in the panhandle is scant, the difference between Bush and Gore was so small that even a tiny number of votes or nonvotes could have made the difference.

The Bush campaign, relying on its own polling and aware of what the public perception would be if Gore were deemed to have won, immediately moved to advise the broadcast networks that its own data indicated the exit polls were wrong. The networks took an especially close look at incoming election results from Florida and soon decided to withdraw their call of Florida for Gore. As election night progressed, the networks declared winners in every other state, but neither candidate had a majority in the ELECTORAL COLLEGE. The importance of Florida was obvious to the entire world at that point. The pattern of incoming election results gave Bush a lead, which increased to some 50,000 votes by 2:15 A.M. eastern time, and Fox News declared Bush the winner of Florida and the PRESIDENTIAL ELECTION. The other networks followed suit within minutes. Everyone waited for the candidates to make their respective speeches, but neither Bush nor Gore appeared. Although Gore called Bush to concede, he learned while on his way to make his speech that the election was too close to call, and he called Bush to retract his concession. Soon the broadcasters became aware of the tightness of the race, with Bush's lead having evaporated from the 50,000 that led to the declaration of his victory to less than 1,000. The networks, for the second time since the election ended, withdrew their call of Florida. At the same time, it became clear as a result of actual returns from California and other states in the West that no matter what happened in Florida, Gore would be the winner of the national popular vote. This set the stage for an electoral inversion, whereby one candidate or party wins the popular vote but another wins the election through the Electoral College.

The battle was thus on for a RECOUNT in Florida. The problem was not only the butterfly ballot in Palm Beach County but also other problems with computer punch-card voting throughout Florida. This is an antiquated voting system, having been developed in the 1960s and having been replaced in most of the United States by more sophisticated voting machines, notably optical scanners, which are highly sensitive to even the slightest mark on a ballot. The punch-card system, as indicated, involves the voter making a hole in a card by punching through a small perforation called a CHAD. Not every hole is fully punched, owing to a light touch on the part of the voter. If the chad is not completely punched, the tabulating machines will not read every intended vote as a vote.

The remedy proposed by the Gore campaign was to manually recount every undervoted ballot in the presidential race and look for evidence that the voter tried to punch out the chad and then count that as a vote. The operative idea was that very few people vote in an election and skip the presidential race—usually 1 percent or less. The Gore campaign created a problem for itself by not asking every punch-card undervote in the state be recounted, but by picking four key counties, all of which had large, urban Democratic bases. This led to the charge from Republicans that Gore was "cherry-picking" for votes. The process was complicated by the undervoted ballots having chads in various states. Some were adhering to the ballot by only one corner and were called "hanging" chads. Others were holding on by two corners and were called "swinging" chads. Others were separated only at one corner and were called "tri-tip" chads. Yet others remained connected at all corners but had an indentation, suggesting the voter inserted his or her stylus for a particular candidate but did not punch. These were called "dimpled" or "pregnant" chads. There was no agreement as to what constituted a vote, other than that a fully punched chad was a vote. This would prove to be a serious bone of contention when the case made it to the U.S. Supreme Court.

Florida ordered a machine recount of all counties (meaning only that the ballots would be fed through a machine a second time), but even this simple act was not carried out in nearly 20 counties. The machine recount gave Bush a lead of 327 votes.

While Gore pushed all out for a recount, the Bush campaign moved to delay and obstruct whatever recounting was done. Several of the counties Gore wanted recounted started on their own. Bush went to court to stop these manual recounts. Bush had key help inside the Florida government. The Florida secretary of state, Katherine Harris, the chief elections officer in the state, was cochair of the Bush campaign in Florida, as was the governor, Bush's brother Jeb Bush. Harris was widely criticized for acting not as an impartial elections official, but as a partisan, throughout the recount period. She decided she would not accept certified county totals after the November 14 deadline but would continue to accept overseas military ballots.

Bush had two key reasons for trying to obstruct the recount. First, Bush was ahead in the official tally after election night, so stopping the counting would leave him in the lead. Second, nearly every stage in the recount process resulted in an increase in votes for Gore. Part of this was a result of who had cast those faulty ballots. Many were from senior citizens who were not computer savvy and many of whom lacked the mere physical strength needed to fully punch the ballots.

Four other states, New Mexico, Wisconsin, Iowa, and Oregon, had results close enough in the presidential balloting that in any other year, recounts would have been conducted there too. But Gore won all of those states, and the Bush campaign could hardly push for the Florida recount to be shut down while pursuing a recount in other states. Furthermore, those states generally used more modern and sophisticated voting methods so that there would be fewer faulty ballots to be found. And none of them had the electoral votes needed to put Bush over the top.

Harris went to the state supreme court to stop the manual recounts, and the Bush campaign went to federal court to pursue a similar course. This was the beginning of the landmark lawsuit BUSH V. GORE. Many noted the irony of the Republicans, long champions of "states' rights," going to

Supporters of candidates Al Gore and George W. Bush rallying in front of the Supreme Court during the 2000 election recount (Reuters/Corbis)

federal court to stop a state court, and Democrats, long trumpeters of federal intervention, touting the opposite. The Florida supreme court let the recounts proceed, finally giving the counties five more days, and issued an injunction to stop Harris from certifying the election in the meantime. The Bush campaign also initially failed in federal court.

The overseas absentee ballots were Bush's best gain in the recount process; they raised his lead to 930 votes. Several county canvassing boards failed to meet the deadline, and Harris refused to extend it. Harris certified Bush as the winner by 537 votes after the partial recounts were tallied. Gore pledged to continue with the recount, and by this time, the U.S. Supreme Court had agreed to hear Bush's appeal. Meanwhile, the Florida legislature got ready to appoint its own set of (presumably Republican) electors.

Gore made a late push to have only the undervotes counted in two of the counties that did not finish their recounts. Bush urged every vote be recounted, but Demo-

crats retorted that there was no need to recount fully punched ballots and that the Republicans were seeking only to delay the process. But Democratic lawsuits in some predominately Republican counties attempted to disqualify absentee votes as well. The Florida supreme court next ordered a manual recount in those counties with an unusually large number of undervotes. Bush appealed this to the U.S. Supreme Court, which, in an unprecedented move, ordered a halt to the manual recounts a day later. On December 11, the case was argued before the Supreme Court. One key swing justice, Anthony Kennedy, was reportedly troubled by Gore's failure to pronounce a uniform statewide standard for what counted as a vote, relying on individualistic opinions in each county and situation.

The Court ruled late in the evening that the Florida supreme court could resolve the matter, but it had to do so before midnight. This essentially ended Gore's chances at prevailing in a recount. The Court ruling, on a 5 to 4 vote on the Court's usual conservative-moderate faction lines, was condemned by many as an unnecessary act of partisanship, abrogating a democratic process in the state of Florida. Gore conceded the election the next evening in a nationally televised address. He carefully avoided calling Bush the winner and instead congratulated him for "becoming president." Democrats protested Florida's vote in the U.S. House and Senate when the electoral votes were counted on January 6, 2001, but the Republicans prevailed, and Bush became president two weeks later.

Some news outlets later counted the ballots that the U.S. Supreme Court had ordered go uncounted. Results were inconclusive. Some analyses found that Bush had indeed won the popular vote, but others drew contrary conclusions, including that the key to Gore's victory might not have been undervotes but overvotes, whereby a person votes for too many candidates. This was the case not only in Palm Beach County, where many people had voted for both Gore and Buchanan, but also in every county where people voted for a candidate and then also filled in the oval for a write-in candidate and wrote in the same candidate's name or left the space blank. Ordinarily, these are counted as valid votes for the intended candidate in a hand count. There were enough in Florida for Gore to have won.

Further reading: Abramson, Paul R., John H. Aldrich, and David W. Rohde. *Change and Continuity in the 2000 Elections.* Washington, D.C.: CQ Press, 2002; Dover, E. D. *Missed Opportunity: Gore, Incumbency, and Television in Election 2000.* Westport, Colo.: Praeger, 2002; Dover, E. D. *The Disputed Presidential Election of 2000: A History and Reference Guide.* Westport, Conn.: Greenwood Press, 2003; Jamieson, Kathleen Hall. *Electing the President 2000: The Insiders' View.* Philadelphia: University of Pennsylvania Press, 2001; Simon, Roger. *Divided We Stand: How Al Gore Beat George Bush and Lost the Presidency.* New York: Crown, 2001. Toobin, Jeffrey. *Too Close to Call: The Thirty-six Day Battle to Decide the 2000 Election.* New York: Random House, 2001.

—Tony L. Hill

presidential election 2004

Winning President and Vice President: George W. Bush and Richard Cheney

Number of States: 50 (plus D.C.)

Major Candidates (Party Affiliation): George W. Bush (Republican); John F. Kerry (Democrat)

Electoral College Vote: George W. Bush: 286; John F. Kerry: 252

Popular Vote: George W. Bush: 62,028,285; John F. Kerry: 59,028,109

The 2004 presidential election was a highly divisive contest that reflected a serious fracture within the American ELEC-

TORATE. For many voters, incumbent Republican president George W. Bush suffered from a legitimacy problem, as he had not won the POPULAR VOTE in the 2000 election, and there was unease over the circumstances that led to him winning the electoral vote in 2000. Some Democrats, therefore, never accepted Bush as the legitimate winner of the 2000 election. The controversial war against Iraq, which Bush initiated in March 2003, further fueled discontent among the Democratic faithful, setting the stage for a strongly partisan battle.

Bush was unopposed for NOMINATION within the REPUBLICAN PARTY. The Democratic contest effectively began in December 2002, when Albert Gore, Jr., the Democratic nominee in 2000, announced he would not run again in 2002. Democrats who had been waiting for a decision from Gore began campaigning more publicly at that point. Senator John F. Kerry of Massachusetts was perceived as the early FRONTRUNNER. However, polls in late 2003 suggested that former Vermont governor Howard Dean had taken the lead. Dean, however, polled poorly in the IOWA CAUCUSES and then gave a bizarre election night speech that ended with a scream. His campaign soon petered out, as did the campaigns of Senator Joseph Lieberman of Connecticut and Representative Richard Gephardt of Missouri.

The DARK-HORSE CANDIDATE was Senator John Edwards of North Carolina, but the movement he needed in key PRIMARY states to overtake Kerry failed to materialize, leaving Kerry the clear frontrunner. By March, it appeared that Kerry had locked up the nomination, challenged at that point only by former Cleveland mayor Dennis Kucinich, who garnered support among those Democrats who were most outspoken about the Iraq war and Bush's leadership. Kucinich continued his moribund but vocal campaign until the DEMOCRATIC NATIONAL CONVENTION.

Kerry chose Edwards as his RUNNING MATE at the convention in Boston, Kerry's hometown. Republicans renominated George W. Bush and Vice President Richard Cheney in New York City. Ralph Nader ran again, but his campaign, which had siphoned enough liberal votes from Gore to give Bush the election in 2000, proved inconsequential in 2004.

The election proved to be a referendum on the Bush presidency. There was little focus on Senator Kerry in the campaign. Most of the dialogue and talk of the campaign focused on the incumbent and the war in Iraq. The election was the first presidential contest after the September 11, 2001, terrorist attacks on the Pentagon and the World Trade Center. Bush was able to campaign on reforms he had made to streamline governmental actions to combat terrorism and to invoke powerful images of September 11 to the advantage of his presidency.

Democrats hammered hard on the failure of the war in Iraq to uncover weapons of mass destruction and the growing casualty rate among the U.S. and other coalition forces in Iraq. Left-of-center filmmaker Michael Moore came out with one of the most talked-about films of the year, *Fahrenheit 9/11*, which focused on the aftermath of the terrorist attacks and Bush's decision to go to Iraq.

Both candidates faced intense scrutiny of their military records. A controversial book, *Unfit for Command*, claimed that Kerry had exaggerated his military heroics in the Vietnam War. Bush was accused of being AWOL from his National Guard duty, also during the Vietnam War, and it was also alleged that persons influenced by Bush's powerful family had covered up these transgressions. In a bizarre sidebar to the campaign, CBS News aired a story critical of Bush's National Guard record that was later determined to have been based on fabricated documents. As a result, anchorman Dan Rather, after having apologized for the story on the air, agreed to retire from CBS, and several high-ranking officials within CBS were fired.

By November 2004, most of the electorate was either strongly in favor of Bush or strongly opposed to him. The president did well by appealing to cultural conservatives in the face of an increasing leftward drift on social issues by the Democrats. Some credited BALLOT INITIATIVES in 13 states to prohibit gay marriage with mobilizing conservatives to turn out who also voted for Bush, but most analysts doubted the issue was pivotal in the presidential race. Kerry's message regarding the poor performance of the economy and the sinking value of the American dollar was drowned out by issues of security and personal character.

The candidates held three debates (Cleveland, St. Louis, and Tempe, Arizona). The conventional wisdom was that Kerry won all three, but his margin of victory was greatest in the first, smaller in the second, and rather narrow in the third. Thus, the closing debates did not give Kerry the decisive wins he needed to reverse the assumption that Bush would be reelected. Polls throughout the fall showed very close races in many key states, while Bush enjoyed a comfortable lead over Kerry in safe states that had supported him in 2000. This meant that Kerry had to win nearly all of the close states to win the election and that Bush needed to capture only a few swing states to win reelection.

Despite early EXIT POLLS that indicated a strong showing for Kerry, as PRECINCTs closed in key states it became clear that the exit polls were flawed and that Bush was leading the contest. Bush's reelection became more certain once Florida was recorded in his column. Around midnight, Kerry's last chance was Ohio, and it was tilting more toward Bush by the minute. The wild card was the estimated 175,000 provisional votes in the state—BALLOTs that would remain sealed, like absentee votes, until the voter's eligibility was determined, perhaps 10 days after the election. It was widely believed that these votes would be more Democratic than Ohio's votes as a whole. With Bush's lead in the state up to 135,000 by mid-morning, Kerry had little choice but to concede the election. The provisional votes would have to run over three to one for Kerry in order for him to win, and no one believed the proportion would be that large.

In the ELECTORAL COLLEGE, election 2004 was eerily similar to election 2000. Only three states switched parties: Iowa and New Mexico (which Gore had won by narrow margins) went for Bush, and New Hampshire switched from Bush to Kerry. Kerry swept the Northeast, won every Pacific state except Alaska, and won four midwestern states: Illinois, Michigan, Minnesota, and Wisconsin. Bush won the rest: the entire South (including West Virginia), all of the Great Plains and mountain states, and four other midwestern states: Indiana, Iowa, Missouri, and Ohio. This gave Bush 286 electoral votes. There were 251 for Kerry and one faithless elector in Minnesota who voted for Edwards. A very small number of Democrats in the House of Representatives (and one Democratic senator) protested Ohio's electoral votes for Bush, but the challenge went nowhere.

In the aftermath of the election, many noted the stark geographic contrast between the Bush and Kerry states—the so-called RED STATES–BLUE STATES divide. A more salient split in the country was urban-rural. Major cities went quite heavily for Kerry, while rural areas went heavily for Bush. Suburbs held the balance of power in this election, and by narrowly going for Bush, they gave him the presidency. After four years in office, Bush had won a majority vote, but from a country deeply polarized on partisan, geographic, and social lines.

Further reading: Sabato, Larry J. *Presidential Election 2004 Recap.* Boston: Longman Publishers, 2005; Wayne, Stephen. *The Road to the White House 2004: The Politics of Presidential Elections.* 7th ed. Boston: Wadsworth Publishing, 2004.

—Tony L. Hill

presidential nominating process

The presidential nominating process is the method by which political parties select a candidate to run for president of the United States. Several candidates in each party may seek their party's NOMINATION, but only one from each party will become the nominee, earning the right to represent his or her POLITICAL PARTY on the BALLOTs in the PRESIDENTIAL ELECTION. There are three basic elements to the contemporary nominating process: candidate announcement, when individuals make known their intent to seek the nomination; the PRIMARY season, in which the candidates from each party battle for votes and support in state contests; and, finally, the nominating conventions, where the nominee is officially named and the vice presidential selection is announced.

The process has undergone significant change over more than two centuries. The founders created the ELECTORAL COLLEGE as the method for selecting the president, but because political parties had not yet developed, the Constitution is silent as to procedures for nominating candidates. For the first eight years this was not problematic, as George Washington was the consensus choice for president. As the party system began to develop, the FACTIONS within the U.S. government at the time, the Federalists and ANTI-FEDERALISTS, began to coordinate among themselves to select candidates that would represent their factional interests.

When partisan divisions in government became more established, nomination of candidates was conducted by way of party caucus. The procedures of the caucus were never formalized, however, and congressional leadership from each party held great influence in the selection of party nominees. Many criticized this method as being at odds with the principle of separation of powers, as Congress was essentially choosing the president. The lack of institutional structure for the process, along with the demise of the FEDERALIST PARTY, leaving the DEMOCRATIC-REPUBLICAN PARTY (Anti-Federalists) as the single dominant party, and the eventual fragmentation of the Democratic-Republicans caused the party caucus to fall out of use in the 1820s.

State-level institutions contributed to the decentralized nature of the nomination process of the 1820s. STATE PARTY COMMITTEES and state legislatures would nominate candidates for the presidency from their parties, emphasizing regional and local interests. While this method distributed influence over nominations more broadly than did the congressional party caucus approach, it also made for a daunting task to unite those interests behind a single nominee. The idea to involve regional interests in a forum whereby a national consensus could be produced for a party nominee resulted in the creation of national nominating conventions. Nominating conventions came into use sporadically in the early 1830s, and by 1840 the major political parties exclusively employed the nominating convention for nominee selection. The convention system provided a means to produce agreement on a nominee among varied interests within the political parties, but perhaps more importantly, a set of principles and positions for the party could be established in what has become known as the party platform.

Each state sends DELEGATES to the convention, in general proportion to a state's congressional representation. How delegates are selected is left for each state to decide, and through the 19th century, delegate selection was made by the state party organizations through caucuses, conventions, or committees. The delegates authorize the rules by which the convention will be run, decide the party platform, and select a nominee. The nominee is selected on the basis of delegate votes. Therefore, if no candidate receives the required number of votes to secure the nomination, a second ballot is required, and balloting continues until the required number of votes is secured. While repeat balloting is not typical, there are numerous instances in which several

ballots were required to make a nomination. In 1920, Republicans required 10 ballots to nominate Warren Harding, and three weeks later the Democrats nominated James Cox after 44 ballots. In 1924, the Democrats were unable to settle the nomination until John W. Davis was finally nominated after two weeks and a remarkable 103 ballots.

Delegate support for candidates in nominating conventions was influenced heavily by state party leaders. One consistency between the party caucus and the nominating convention was that nominee selection was controlled exclusively by the leadership of the parties, and ordinary party members had little say in party nominating decisions. Calls for change to break the grip of powerful state and local party machines were heeded during the Progressive Era at the beginning of the 20th century. The use of primary elections for delegate selection or for voter preference of candidates was intended to alleviate the domination of the process by powerful and well-organized state political machines. By the election of 1916, more than half of the delegates necessary for nomination were awarded in primary elections. As many of the primary contests were nonbinding, most of the influence on nominations still resided with the party elite. Even if candidates succeeded in winning delegates in a number of primaries, party leaders were able to quash the hopes of such CHALLENGERS, as the leadership controlled the rules and credentialing (official recognition of delegates) in the conventions. This allowed the party elite to manipulate the proceedings in favor of FAVORITE SON candidates whose loyalty and support among party leaders served as a barrier to would-be challengers within the party.

Ineffectiveness, high costs to candidates and parties, and low turnout from the general public caused use of the primary election to decline after 1920. The reforms aimed at opening the process to a wider range of candidates and voters had not provided the antidote to concentration of power among the party elite and at best became an alternate route to nomination for "outsider" candidates. Incumbents and favorite son candidates did not have to enter these contests, as their support lay not in the POPULAR VOTE but in the support of the party leadership at the state and national levels. In addition, fewer than half the total available delegates were awarded via the primary between the years 1920 and 1968. Even if a candidate were to win every delegate in every primary held in those years, it would not have been enough to achieve the nomination against the wishes of the PARTY BOSSES.

The DEMOCRATIC NATIONAL CONVENTION of 1968 provided the catalyst for change in the process that elevated primary contests to the pivotal role held in the contemporary nomination process. The decision of incumbent president Lyndon Johnson not to seek another term and the assassination of Robert Kennedy left the party with no clear favorite candidate. Influential party leaders supported Vice

President Hubert Humphrey, while a swelling antiwar movement, prominent among the rank-and-file membership and some party leaders, favored Eugene McCarthy. While McCarthy had successfully waged a number of primary contests, Humphrey did not compete in any of the contests. The convention itself was marred by chaos outside, as police and antiwar protesters clashed, while inside, factions within the party quarreled over the selection of a nominee and the violence occurring on the streets of Chicago. Ultimately, Humphrey, the choice of the party establishment, won the nomination handily, despite the large number of delegates supporting McCarthy. The lack of representation among rank-and-file members and minority delegates, coupled with the dominance of party bosses, compelled the DEMOCRATIC PARTY to reform the methods of delegate allocation to ensure broader representation and participation in the selection process. The REPUBLICAN PARTY followed suit with similar reforms to encourage the use of the primary election as the principal method for allocating delegates to the nominating conventions.

The reforms of 1972 have had tremendous impacts on how presidential NOMINATION CAMPAIGNS are run. They are no longer merely a testing ground for candidates to measure popularity or strength, but an essential component to securing the nomination. Approximately three-quarters of the states employ primary elections for presidential nomination purposes, while the remaining states hold statewide caucuses. Delegate allocation is determined by these contests, yet a few in each state are unpledged, or SUPERDELEGATES, reserved for the party to allocate. In the postreform process, the selection of the eventual nominee is no longer brokered by the party leaders, but directed by the rank-and-file of the party, delegates who are committed to specific candidates. In this regard, the process is said to have opened up to a wider range of candidates, giving a chance to candidates who would not otherwise be able to compete for the nomination under the boss-dominated system, such as Democrats Jesse Jackson in 1984, Dennis Kucinich and Al Sharpton in 2004, and Republicans Pat Robertson in 1992 and 1996 and Gary Bauer in 2000. In many other ways, these reforms have fundamentally altered how the presidential nominating process is conducted.

Since the 1972 reforms, the timing of candidate announcements has been accelerated. Candidates traditionally announced the intention to run in the spring of the election year. Currently, major party candidates officially announce their candidacy more than a year before the GENERAL ELECTION but really begin the process much earlier. Typically, candidates seeking the nomination begin to build their campaign organizations at least two years prior to the election, putting together exploratory commissions, developing campaign and FUND-RAISING staff, and developing a base of support. In the 2004 contest, former Vermont governor Howard Dean filed his candidacy for the Democratic nomination on March 31, 2002, and by February 2003, nine Democratic challengers had announced intentions to enter the race.

Early preparation has become extremely important given the changes to the primary season. The process, now decided by a series of contests rather than by back room dealing among party leaders, has been lengthened. Whereas the prereform process began in the late spring of election year and culminated in the summer conventions, the postreform contests begin in January of the election year with the NEW HAMPSHIRE PRIMARY and IOWA CAUCUS. Primary contests are spread out, some not occurring until June, but the presumed nominee is known long before the conventions state the official nominations in late summer.

While the primary season is longer, at the same time the primary calendar has been compressed. The emphasis on early contests has produced a front-loaded primary schedule: states holding their contests earlier and earlier in the season in order to have greater impact on the nomination. Since 1988, several states have held primaries on the same day, in early March, providing a pivotal point in the process. On SUPER TUESDAY, as this joint primary day is known, approximately half the delegates necessary to earn the nomination are at stake, and it is the point at which the presumptive nominee solidifies his or her status. The front-loaded primary season places difficulties on candidates regarding effective campaigning in a large number of states over a short period of time, and states that hold later primaries generally see limited numbers of candidates and have very little impact on the outcome of the process.

For example, in 2000, Republican George W. Bush and Democrat Al Gore were recognized as the parties' presumptive nominees by early April, more than three months prior to the nominating conventions and seven months prior to the election, while approximately one-quarter of the states had yet to hold contests. The 2004 Democratic contest produced the earliest nominee in history: Senator John Kerry had secured the necessary number of delegates in the second week of March. By early March, campaign ads from both the Bush and Kerry campaigns for the general election were airing in several states, more than eight months prior to the election and four months prior to the official nominations at the conventions.

While nominations have become known much earlier, the nominating conventions have lost much of the prominence they held in the prereform era and are often considered a "rubber stamp" for what is already known months in advance. Several aspects of conventions remain important in the postreform era. The conventions signify the official start of the election. Party platforms are decided, the vice presidential candidate is unveiled, and the party nominee is officially named. The conventions redirect what is often a divisive intraparty struggle to a battle focused on the opposing party. Conventions serve as a venue to project party unity to the nation.

In the media-driven primary season, prime-time television coverage of the conventions provides a way for parties to reach the ELECTORATE. Events such as keynote speakers, vice presidential nomination, and the nominee's acceptance speech are often criticized as being "made-for-television" events but serve to solidify support and provide a "bounce" in popularity among the voting public. In the 2000 campaign, Democratic candidate Al Gore had been trailing Republican nominee George W. Bush in the polls by double digits for much of the summer. After the Democratic National Convention, Gore pulled even with Bush in national polls, and the race remained close through the election.

Other aspects of the nomination process have evolved as well. At the same time that delegate selection rules were changing, so were laws regarding the financing of presidential campaigns. New CAMPAIGN FINANCE LAWS placed limits on campaign contributions, required public disclosure of campaign revenues and expenditures, established public MATCHING FUNDS for campaigns, and set spending ceilings for those candidates who accept matching funds. These laws recognized the nomination period as a crucial aspect of the election process and emphasized the role of the primary election by making public funding available in the prenomination period to eligible candidates. Generally, more total funds are raised and spent in the prenomination period than in the general election, largely due to the larger number of participants. More than $200 million had been spent by Kerry and Bush alone by June 2004, nearly three months prior to the conventions. The dependence on such large amounts of money emphasizes the necessity of launching campaign efforts, particularly fund-raising activities, early in the cycle.

Media coverage has also changed in the postreform era. The emergence of 24-hour cable television news channels has altered the way political events are covered. The media have been criticized for covering the nomination contests in "horse-race" fashion, giving unequal media attention (good and bad) to the FRONTRUNNER while neglecting trailing candidates and providing analysis of the process and campaign strategy rather than issues. The proliferation of the Internet and modern communications have further altered the nomination process, as candidates can look to the Internet for disseminating information and fund-raising efforts with little financial expense or use of the candidates' valuable time. Howard Dean embraced the Internet as a campaign tool in the 2004 nomination process and was able to raise more than $10 million over the Internet and to build a grassroots organization of Internet users. The nature of the presidential nominating process has evolved significantly over the past two centuries, and as

rules, technology, and expectations of society continue to change, so will the process of nominating presidential candidates.

Further reading: Cook, Rhodes. *The Presidential Nominating Process.* Lanham, Md.: Rowman & Littlefield, 2004; Kirkpatrick, Jeanne J. *The New Presidential Elite: Men and Women in National Politics.* New York: Russell Sage Foundation and Twentieth Century Fund, 1976; Wayne, Stephen J. *The Road to the White House 2004: The Politics of Presidential Elections.* Florence, Ky.: Wadsworth/Thomson Learning, 2004.

—Joel A. Rayan

presidential polls

Since about 1950, the American public's satisfaction with the president has been regularly measured by periodic presidential polls, also known as presidential approval polls. Presidential approval polls are conducted by media organizations and polling firms. Perhaps the most well known and longest-running presidential approval poll is that conducted by the Gallup organization, which asks respondents, "Do you approve or disapprove of the way" the current president "is handling his job as president." The percentage of respondents who report that they approve of the way the president is handling his job is known as the president's APPROVAL RATING. For instance, if 55 percent of respondents indicate that they approve of the way the president is handling his job, then the president is said to have an approval rating of 55 percent at that particular moment in time.

Presidential approval polls, and the president's resulting approval ratings, play two important roles in American POLITICS. First, the president's approval rating can have a great effect upon his ability to lead the government. A president with very high approval ratings, for example, is likely to meet with more success in promoting and enacting those policies he favors than is a president with very low approval ratings. Indeed, in some cases, high approval ratings may even have the power to save the president's job. It is quite possible to imagine, for instance, that had Bill Clinton not enjoyed the support of the American people as expressed in high job-approval ratings, then the Monica Lewinsky SCANDAL could have spelled the end of his presidency (because the Senate may have been more willing to remove an unpopular president from office than it was to expel a very popular president).

Second, presidential approval ratings are one important indicator of the likelihood that a sitting president will be reelected. Scholars have found that high approval ratings in an election year are a good indication that the incumbent president (or the candidate of the same party as the incumbent) has a good chance of being reelected, whereas low approval ratings in an election year can portend trouble for the incumbent (or his party).

Presidential approval polls are inherently unpredictable to some extent, as the president's approval rating moves in response to the way he handles events and issues as they arise. Nevertheless, political scientists have been able to discern some noticeable patterns in the movement of presidents' approval ratings over the course of a term of office. Specifically, many have noticed that most presidents experience an initial "honeymoon" period upon first taking office, and that, after the honeymoon period has ended, presidential approval ratings are particularly responsive to two main issue areas, foreign policy (especially war) and the economy.

The term *honeymoon period* refers to the weeks and months immediately after the president first takes office, during which his approval ratings are generally quite high. In fact, many presidents, including Dwight D. Eisenhower, John F. Kennedy, Lyndon B. Johnson, and Jimmy Carter, have experienced approval ratings in excess of 70 percent during their respective honeymoon periods. In essence, during the honeymoon period, a large percentage of the American public, including members of the opposing party, unite in support of the new president. (One interesting possible exception to this general rule is George W. Bush. While it might not be accurate to claim that Bush had no honeymoon, it is true that after the controversy and acrimony that surrounded the 2000 election and especially the Florida RECOUNT, George W. Bush's honeymoon period was subdued and short-lived.)

Within a few months of taking office, however, the president's honeymoon period comes to an end, and presidential approval ratings become much less predictable. Few presidents are able to sustain high approval ratings for the entire duration of their term in office, though Dwight Eisenhower and Bill Clinton consistently enjoyed approval ratings in excess of 50 percent. In fact, it is common for presidential approval ratings to demonstrate a relatively high degree of variability throughout a president's term, though the general pattern seems to be for presidents to lose support over the course of their terms. Indeed, except for two cases (Gerald Ford and Bill Clinton), every president since Harry S. Truman has had a lower approval rating upon leaving the White House than he did when he entered.

Two issues that have a dramatic impact on approval ratings, are foreign policy and the economy. Generally speaking when important foreign policy events come to pass, presidents enjoy an immediate upsurge in their approval ratings. This is known as the "rally around the flag" effect and is often particularly pronounced when the United States is engaged in military action or war. President George H. W. Bush, for example, enjoyed an approval rating in excess of 85 percent following the 1991 Gulf War. Similarly, following the terrorist attacks on the World Trade Center and the Pentagon in September 2001, approval ratings for George W. Bush rose from about 55 percent to more than 80 percent. It should be pointed out that though the "rally around the flag" effect following important foreign policy events is often dramatic, it is also often quite temporary. President George H. W. Bush, for instance, saw his approval rating drop from 87 percent in March 1991 to just more than 40 percent at election time in 1992. Not surprisingly, Bush lost the 1992 PRESIDENTIAL ELECTION to Bill Clinton.

The other major issue that is known to have an important effect on presidential approval ratings is the economy. Basically, when the economy is strong and improving, the sitting president is rewarded with high approval ratings, and if the economy is strong and improving at election time, the president is typically rewarded with reelection. If, on the other hand, the economy is weak or declining, the president's approval rating, and his chances for successfully seeking reelection, also decline.

Further reading: Asher, Herbert. *Polling and the Public: What Every Citizen Should Know.* Washington, D.C.: CQ Press, 2001; Erikson, Robert S., and Kent L. Tedin. *American Public Opinion.* New York: Longman, 2001; Holbrook, Thomas M. "Campaigns, National Conditions, and U.S. Presidential Elections." *American Journal of Political Science* 38 (1994): 973–998.

—Gregory A. Smith

presidential primaries

Presidential primaries are state contests in which candidates compete for their POLITICAL PARTY'S NOMINATION for president of the United States. Presidential primaries are intraparty contests whereby candidates from the same party vie for their party's nomination. Candidates for the nomination seek to win DELEGATEs in each state through a PRIMARY election, and a majority of the total delegates available in all 50 states (and the District of Columbia) is necessary to earn the party's nomination. Although not every state holds primaries, between two-thirds and three-quarters of the states use this method to indicate preference and award delegates for presidential nominees. The presidential primary election has been used for much of the 20th century, although the significance of the primary to the nominating process was not great until the 1970s following reforms to the nominating process in the Democratic and Republican Parties.

The presidential primary election came into use as a Progressive Era response to the dominance of party elites in selecting nominees to the presidency. Nominating conventions that selected the parties' nominees were controlled by the leadership of state party organizations at the expense of ordinary party members. The delegates to the conventions were selected by party leaders and represented the interests of the party elites rather than the preferences of party members within the state. States soon began to enact laws that required delegates to be directly elected to the conventions, and shortly thereafter, to directly select candidates. Beginning with Florida in 1904, the presidential primary election emerged in a number of states, and by 1916, 20 states held some form of presidential primary election. In the 1916, presidential nominating process, more than half the delegates necessary for the nomination were awarded through primary elections.

The presidential primary did little to curb the influence of PARTY BOSSES in the selection of party nominees, however. While several states required a binding primary vote, whereby delegates were required by law to carry out the will of the primary voters of their state, many of the states' primary contests were advisory contests only. As such, delegates were free to exercise their own judgment, or that of the state party leaders, and the influence of presidential primaries was minimal in the selection of party nominees. The presidential primary did lay the groundwork for CHALLENGERS to FAVORITE SON candidates to contest the nomination and to show support from the voting public, although the primary was not a crucial element of the nomination process.

The significance of presidential primaries began to change following the 1968 PRESIDENTIAL ELECTION. Growing discontent with the influence of powerful party leaders and a lack of representation for the rank-and-file membership encouraged the DEMOCRATIC PARTY to undertake a series of reforms designed to widen participation and representation among party supporters. These rule changes reduced the number of state party leaders who had previously gained automatic selection as delegates. The reforms, implemented by the national party organization, also promoted primaries as the preferred method of delegate selection, prompting states to adopt presidential primaries to avoid eligibility challenges to their delegations at the national conventions. The reforms placed a time frame specifying the earliest and latest dates that the contests could be held and imposed rules requiring gender equity among state delegations.

The national party organization also addressed how delegates were awarded in the state contests. Typically, states employed a winner-take-all allocation, in which the candidate who earned the most electoral support in the primary election earned all of the delegates from that voting district or even from the state. Critics argued that this approach did not accurately reflect the wishes of the party within a state, and the party adopted a rule mandating allocation of delegates be based upon PROPORTIONAL REPRESENTATION of the vote that a candidate earned. Subsequent reforms have modified each of these reforms, including the creation of SUPERDELEGATES, delegates reserved for members of the state party organizations to ensure adequate

Vermont governor Howard Dean campaigning during the presidential primaries in hopes of capturing the Democratic nomination *(Reuters/Corbis)*

representation of party leadership among state delegations. The DEMOCRATIC NATIONAL COMMITTEE continues to reevaluate its procedures following each PRESIDENTIAL ELECTION.

The REPUBLICAN PARTY did not enact such sweeping reforms on a national level. The rules governing the process leading to the next convention are set at each convention and cannot typically be altered by the REPUBLICAN NATIONAL COMMITTEE. However, the Democratic rules changes did affect the process for the Republicans. While the parties are responsible for determining who can participate at the conventions, state legislatures enact laws regarding presidential primaries. At the time of the reforms, many state houses were controlled by Democrats, who implemented many of the changes to delegate selection rules through election laws.

Although the Republican Party has not implemented national standards for the state parties to follow, reforms have been made to widen representation, to promote primary contests as the preferred method for delegate selection, and to encourage states to hold contests later in the year. The Republican National Committee does not impose gender equity, nor is there a rule preventing states from awarding delegates in a winner-take-all format, but the state party organizations are empowered to make these determinations.

The reforms in both parties have had the consequence of both lengthening the process and creating a front-loaded schedule. As states have consistently moved their primaries forward to gain influence and media attention, the process is now stretched out over a lengthy period: six months for primaries, and the conventions are held in the mid- to late summer. While the first primary contest of the season has traditionally been held in New Hampshire, more and more states are holding primaries earlier in the year, compressing most of the primary contests into a relatively short period between January and April.

In 1988, several states held simultaneous primaries in March to gain advantage and influence in the nominating process. This has become known as SUPER TUESDAY, and often the party nominees become known shortly after this date. The process became even more front-loaded in 2004, when seven states staged "Mini-Tuesday" primaries on February 3, four weeks before Super Tuesday. The FRONT-LOADING of the primary calendar has raised several criticisms, including a lack of fairness to states that hold their contests later, increasing expense of campaigning in a compressed time frame, and an extended gap between the effective end of the primary season and the GENERAL ELECTION.

Aspects of presidential primaries may also contribute to voter fatigue. Presidential primaries and primary elections for state offices are not typically held at the same time, and the parties can also hold their presidential primaries at different times, creating the potential for confusion among voters. States employ different rules for participation in presidential primaries, whether the primary is open to all voters, closed, or limited to registered party members only, or some method in between. The complexity and length of the process, as well as multiple elections, the timing of the contests, and barriers to participation can potentially deter many from participating in the process of selecting presidential nominees.

The presidential primary has become a highly important aspect of the nominating process: Candidates seeking the nomination of their party must enter and succeed in primary contests to have a chance at earning the nomination. Although incumbent presidents are generally safely assured of their party's nomination, serious challenges to the incumbent can and have been made through the primary contests, such as those against Gerald Ford in 1976 and Jimmy Carter in 1980. While the presidential primary has evolved to be a central aspect of the selection of presidential nominees, the problems that have emerged are bound to prompt further reforms to the process.

Further reading: Cook, Rhodes. *The Presidential Nominating Process.* Lanham, Md.: Rowman & Littlefield, 2004; Kirkpatrick, Jeanne J. *The New Presidential Elite: Men and Women in National Politics.* New York: Russell Sage Foundation and Twentieth Century Fund, 1976; Wayne, Stephen J. *The Road to the White House 2004: The Politics of Presidential Elections.* Florence, Ky.: Wadsworth/Thomson Learning, 2004.

—Joel A. Rayan

presidential succession

Succession in case of the death, resignation, or disability of the president is now one of the most carefully detailed areas of American law. These details came about as a result of several crises and hypothetical crises made imaginable by real ones. The original constitution provided that in case of a vacancy in the office, the vice president would assume the powers and duties. Many believed this to mean that the vice president would not assume the presidency, but would be acting president until a president was elected. When the situation first arose in 1841 upon the death of President William H. Harrison, Vice President John Tyler insisted on being sworn in as president. This precedent has lasted, and it was institutionalized by the Twenty-fifth Amendment.

Beyond the vice president, the order of presidential succession is not fixed in the Constitution but is set by federal law. Title 3, Section 19 of the U.S. Code provides that in the event of a vacancy in the presidency and the vice presidency, the SPEAKER OF THE HOUSE OF REPRESENTATIVES, if qualified, shall act as president upon resignation from the speakership and the House of Representatives. If the speakership is vacant or the Speaker does not qualify, the president pro tempore of the Senate, if qualified, shall act as president upon resignation from the Senate. If the presidency pro tempore is vacant or the president pro tem does not qualify, then the highest-ranking cabinet officer (in the order listed here) shall act as president: secretary of state, Treasury, defense; attorney general; secretary of the interior, agriculture, commerce, labor, health and human services, housing and urban development, transportation, energy, education, and veterans affairs. (Although the secretaries of environmental protection and homeland security are cabinet level, they have not been added to the presidential succession.) When Secretary of State Henry Kissinger was fourth in line of succession (including two periods when the vice presidency was vacant), he would have been ineligible to succeed to the presidency because he was an immigrant. Although there has never been a cabinet secretary too young to be president (the youngest was Robert F. Kennedy, who became attorney general at age 35), it is not inconceivable that someone too young to serve as president will serve in a position in the succession. As recently as 2003, the president pro tempore (third in succession) was 100-year-old J. Strom Thurmond. All but one of the people in the succession attend the president's State of the Union address. There is a tradition that one of the cabinet members stays away from the speech to avoid a crisis of succession in case all of the others are killed in some catastrophe during the event. In order to prevent both offices from being vacant at once, federal law prohibits the president and vice president from traveling in the same vehicle.

The Twenty-fifth Amendment to the U.S. Constitution was passed to resolve some long-standing questions of disability of the president. Part of the impetus for its passage were hypothetical questions arising from the assassination of President John F. Kennedy in 1963. The third bullet fired by assassin Lee H. Oswald killed the president, but Oswald's second shot pierced his neck and would have left him incapacitated but not mortally wounded. (The first shot missed.) If Kennedy had not been killed, he might have been permanently unable to be president, yet there was no provision for removing him from office under those circumstances. Similarly, President James A. Garfield was shot on July 2, 1881, but he did not die until September 19 of that year. President Woodrow Wilson and President Dwight D. Eisenhower each experienced several illnesses while in office that left them incapacitated for a matter of days, weeks, and (in Wilson's case) even months. The amendment was proposed by Congress on July 6, 1965, and was ratified by the requisite number of states on February 10, 1967. Upon President Richard M. Nixon's resignation on August 9, 1974, Gerald R. Ford became the first vice president to accede to the presidency under Section 1 of the amendment, which clarifies the practice that John Tyler had begun. Only eight months earlier, Ford had become the first vice president appointed under Section 2 of the amendment, replacing Spiro T. Agnew, who resigned in the wake of a SCANDAL. Ford would shortly nominate Nelson A. Rockefeller to replace him as vice president. Less than a decade after the amendment had been proposed, the country was headed by two people who had been appointed under it rather than elected. Had the amendment not been passed, upon Agnew's resignation the vice presidency would have remained vacant until January 20, 1977, and upon Nixon's resignation, Speaker of the House Carl Albert of Oklahoma would have become acting president.

Sections 3 and 4 of the amendment provide for temporary replacement of the president in case "he is unable to discharge the powers and duties of his office." Section 3 provides for the manner in which the president may do this voluntarily and then revoke his instruction when he is again able. Section 4 provides for the involuntary invocation of presidential disability by "the Vice President and a majority of either the principal officers of the executive departments [the cabinet] or of such other body as Congress may by law provide." The amendment also provides a process by which a dispute between the president and the others over the disability can be resolved. Section 3 was first invoked by President George W. Bush on June 29, 2002, when he underwent anesthesia. President Ronald Reagan used a similar process (notification by letter) when he underwent surgery for colon cancer on July 13, 1985, but in his letter he specifically said he was not invoking the amendment.

Further reading: Corwin, Edwin S. *The President: Office and Powers, 1787–1957: History and Analysis of Practice and Opinion.* New York: New York University Press, 1959; Robert E. Gilbert. *Managing Crisis: Presidential Disability and the Twenty-fifth Amendment.* New York: Fordham University Press, 2000; Witcover, Jules. *Crapshoot: Rolling the Dice on the Vice Presidency: From Adams and Jefferson to Truman and Quayle.* New York: Crown, 1992.

—Tony L. Hill

primary

A primary is an election held to select a party's candidates for public office. In a DIRECT PRIMARY, voters select candidates directly. In an indirect primary, voters select DELEGATES who then select candidates at a nominating convention. Primaries are held at various times in the calendar year before the GENERAL ELECTION and are used in all 50 states to select party candidates for virtually all state and local offices and most national offices.

The first direct primary was held in Crawford County, Pennsylvania, where in 1842, DEMOCRATIC PARTY leaders allowed voters to select their choice of party candidates for assemblymen and county officers in a primary election. But it was not until the turn of the century that the primary system for selecting presidential candidates emerged. Florida passed legislation in 1901 giving members of the Democratic Party the option of selecting delegates to the national convention in a primary election. Following Florida's lead, Wisconsin in 1905, Pennsylvania in 1906, and Oregon in 1910 each adopted election laws that permitted primary elections for the presidential nominating process.

By 1912, seven states had passed legislation establishing PRESIDENTIAL PRIMARIES that allowed for a presidential preference vote, the selection of delegates to the national convention, or both. In 1912, an additional five states established primaries in response to Theodore Roosevelt's challenge of then president William Howard Taft for the Republican presidential NOMINATION. His strategy was to use primaries to demonstrate to party leaders he was the more electable candidate. Although Roosevelt beat Taft in nine of the 10 primaries in which he faced him, Taft eventually secured the nomination by stacking the convention in his favor.

As the popular response to direct primaries remained favorable, the 1916 election saw 20 states hold presidential primaries, the high-water mark until the 1970s. For the next several decades primaries were optional, used by candidates like Roosevelt to demonstrate their electability to party leaders. This was the strategy, for example, of the DARK-HORSE CANDIDATES Wendell Willkie (1944), Dwight Eisenhower (1952), and John Kennedy (1960), whose primary win in Protestant West Virginia proved to party leaders that his Catholicism would not hinder his electability.

The 1968 Democratic nomination was the beginning of the end of the convention system of presidential nominations. Eugene McCarthy made a strong showing in that year's NEW HAMPSHIRE PRIMARY, and as a result, President Lyndon Johnson announced he would not seek the Democratic nomination. This opened the field, and Vice President Hubert Humphrey and Robert Kennedy subsequently entered the race. Humphrey was favored by party regulars, while Kennedy ran an extremely successful primary campaign. When Kennedy was assassinated immediately following his victory in California's primary, Humphrey, who had not entered a single primary, secured the nomination at what was a very contentious convention.

To heal the wounds from the nomination struggle and unite the party for the upcoming election season, the party agreed to review its nominating procedures. Two commissions were appointed, and the proposals of one, the McGovern-Fraser commission, were responsible for 21 states (up from 15) establishing presidential primaries in 1972. More importantly, the percentage of convention delegates selected at these events and pledged to support a particular candidate jumped from about 40 percent in 1968 to roughly two-thirds in 1972.

Thus, 1972 was the first year that the presidential nomination was not decided by the convention, marking the transition to the primary system of presidential nominations. Since then there has been a steady increase in the number of states that hold presidential primaries and the number of delegates pledged to support candidates selected in these primaries. There were 21 such events in 1972, 27 in 1976, and 36 in 1980. There were 43 in 2000. It is now impossible to capture the party nomination without winning presidential primaries in many states.

There has also been an increase in the number of states that hold their primaries earlier in the year, a phenomenon known as FRONT-LOADING. In 1968, only New Hampshire held its primary before the end of March; by 1988, 20 states did so. In 2004, 21 primaries (and nine caucuses) were held between January 19 and March 2, when the nomination was effectively decided. Being competitive in the primary season means organizing, campaigning, and continuing to raise money in several states simultaneously. This front-loading puts a premium on early success. Those who do not do well in the first few primaries face an uphill struggle, and less successful candidates find it harder to effectively compete in other states.

These early contests also make it imperative for candidates to raise a large sum of money the year before the primaries. In fact, FUND-RAISING success in the preprimary season is a fairly reliable predictor of who will win the nomination. Only twice since 1980 has the candidate with the most money going into the primary season lost the nomination (Republican John Connally in 1980 and Democrat Howard Dean in 2004).

The importance of early primary success makes what happens in New Hampshire's primary, the first in the nation, critical to primary success. New Hampshire held its first presidential primary in 1916, and from 1920 to 1996, it was the first primary of the season. A 1977 state law (and subsequent revisions) mandates this status, and although the DEMOCRATIC NATIONAL COMMITTEE sets a window for when primaries and caucuses are to take place, New Hampshire is exempt. The New Hampshire primary is a fairly strong predictor of who the eventual nominee will be, or, at a minimum, who the nominees will not be. In 14 contested nominations from 1972 to 2004, the eventual nominee won the New Hampshire primary nine times and placed second five times; no candidate placing third or lower ever went on to win the nomination.

The campaign for New Hampshire typically starts two years before the primary, often earlier. For example, shortly after returns were in for the 1998 CONGRESSIONAL ELECTIONS, Vice President Al Gore made roughly 200 telephone calls to people throughout the state to enlist their aid in his 2000 campaign. In 2003, the 10 Democratic candidates spent a combined total of 300 days campaigning in the state (and 65 days from 2001 to 2002). Candidate attention to New Hampshire is matched by media attention. Journalists flock to the state in droves to cover the event. By one measure, the 1996 Republican New Hampshire primary received more than one-quarter (28.9 percent) of the stories devoted to primary elections around the country on ABC, CBS, CNN, and NBC from January 1995 through June 1996.

Although primaries are ostensibly party affairs, states are responsible for regulating elections, and thus primaries. One reason for this is the potential for abuse by party leaders, perhaps most evident in Texas's white primaries. Starting in 1923, blacks were barred from participating in Democratic Party primaries. Since Texas, like all other southern states at the time, was a solidly Democratic state, the WHITE PRIMARY thus had the effect of disenfranchising blacks. In 1944 the Supreme Court held white primaries were unconstitutional, and this discriminatory practice was put to an end.

Today, there are three main types of primaries, distinguished according to who may participate: open, closed, and semiopen. In a closed primary, participation is limited to those registered with the respective party. For example, in a closed Democratic primary, only registered Democrats may vote. In an open primary, any registered voter may participate. In semiopen primaries, any registered voter can participate in a party's primary, including INDEPENDENTS and those registered with another party, provided they change their registration to the party in whose primary they wish to vote.

The merits of open versus closed primaries are widely debated. Proponents of open primaries argue, in short, that they are more democratic and more likely to nominate candidates with broad-based appeal. Party leaders generally prefer closed primaries, arguing that the choice of party candidate should be a party decision. Moreover, they fear the possibility of CROSSOVER VOTING, also know as raiding, whereby, for example, Democratic Party regulars might vote in a Republican primary to support a weaker Republican candidate that they believe will be easier for their Democratic candidate to defeat in the general election. There is little evidence that this type of strategic voting occurs.

Until recently a few states (notably, California and Washington) held a fourth type of primary known as a blanket primary, in which all registered voters, regardless of party registration, were presented with a single BALLOT. Voters could then select any candidate from any party for any office. California's blanket primary was ruled unconstitutional by the Supreme Court in 2000. In 2003 a federal appeals court made a similar ruling about Washington's blanket primary, holding that parties should have some control over their own affairs.

The two parties differ in how delegates are allocated to presidential candidates in primaries. In most REPUBLICAN PARTY primaries, delegates are awarded to the plurality winner. The Democratic National Committee, on the other hand, mandates that delegates be awarded in proportion to the percentage of votes candidates receive.

Turnout in primaries is lower than general election turnout, hovering at about 15 percent of eligible voters. This is because most people are not paying a great deal of attention to the campaign in the spring. Moreover, primary voting is fairly challenging: Voters must choose between several candidates all within the same party. To make an informed choice, individuals must take the time to learn something about several candidates. Thus, those who vote in primaries are generally better educated, more politically aware, come from higher-income brackets, and are slightly older than other party identifiers or voters. In addition, they tend to be more ideologically extreme (more liberal or conservative) than the average party identifier or voter.

In addition to being used to select presidential candidates, primaries are used to select congressional candidates in all 50 states. In one-party-dominant areas, the winner of the dominant party's nomination is virtually assured of election in November. However, most congressional primaries are not competitive. For example, from 1982 through 1996, almost 60 percent of House incumbents and 70 percent of Senate incumbents faced no primary challenge. Most competitive congressional primaries are those in which there is no incumbent running. Some congressional primaries are quite costly, especially for Senate seats. In 1994 California Republican Michael Huffington spent more than $10 million in the Senate primary, and in 2000, Jon Corzine spent approximately $30 million to win the Democratic senatorial primary in New Jersey.

Although a product of the United States, primaries are increasingly being used in other countries as well. Throughout the 1990s, parties in Argentina, Chile, Uruguay, Mexico, Bulgaria, Taiwan, and Finland held primaries to select their presidential candidates. In addition, some parties in a few parliamentary systems have begun holding primaries to select their party's prime ministerial candidate. These pre-selections, as they are known, are held in Australia and by both main parties (Likud and Labor) in Israel.

By wrestling control from domineering and often corrupt party leaders, primaries democratized and added an element of accountability to the process of selecting candidates for public office in the United States. However, they are not without detractors. Parties resent the loss of control over the nomination process. Also, contentious primaries can divide parties and make victory in November more difficult. Other criticisms include the fact that primaries are rather elitist, since so few citizens vote. Primaries have also driven up the cost of campaigns, since there are now two elections held for most public offices. Frontloading, in which candidates are winnowed from the field very quickly, means that voters' choices are narrowed at a very early stage. And the media now play a major role in that winnowing, since the amount of coverage they decide to give to a candidate affects campaign efforts.

Further reading: Buell, Emmett H., Jr. "The Changing Face of the New Hampshire Primary." In William G. Mayer, ed., *In Pursuit of the White House 2000: How We Choose Our Presidential Nominees.* Chatham, N.J.: Chatham House, 2000; Ceaser, James W. *Presidential Selection: Theory and Development.* Princeton, N.J.: Princeton University Press, 1979.

—Jody Baumgartner

primary, blanket

The blanket, or jungle, primary was a PRIMARY system that included all candidates on a single BALLOT but was determined by the U.S. Supreme Court to be unconstitutional on freedom of association grounds. A voter could select one candidate for each office, regardless of party affiliation. For example, the same voter could select a Democratic candidate in the race for governor, a Libertarian for U.S Senate, and a Republican for state senate. The top candidate within each party then advanced to the GENERAL ELECTION for a given office, such as one Democrat, one Republican, one Libertarian, and one GREEN PARTY candidate.

The blanket primary was first adopted by Washington state in 1935 and later used in Alaska and California. In Washington, voters did not register with political parties, and there were only eight weeks between the primary and general elections, creating a runoff type political environment. The Washington version also required INDEPENDENT and political parties without statewide qualification to receive at least 1 percent of votes in the primary to advance to the general election. The California version was adopted via a BALLOT INITIATIVE and went into effect in 1998. California voters could continue to register by party or decline to state a party preference. Since registered Republicans could vote for Democrats or vice versa, political parties filed lawsuits about the constitutionality of the

California blanket primary. In addition, because of national party restrictions, crossover votes in the 2000 California PRESIDENTIAL PRIMARY were not counted.

The U.S. Supreme Court ruled on June 26, 2000, that the blanket primary was unconstitutional in *California Democratic Party v. Jones* (530 U.S. 567). The Court ruled in a 7 to 2 decision, with Justice Antonin Scalia writing the opinion, that the blanket primary violated political parties' freedom of association and right to select their own nominees for political office. Justices John Paul Stevens and Ruth Bader Ginsburg dissented. Alaska and California then adopted modified closed primary systems. Washington adopted a nonpartisan primary in 2004 after additional federal litigation and a protracted stalemate in the state legislature.

The blanket primary gave maximum freedom of choice to voters, provided independent voters with improved opportunities to participate in primary elections, and, thus, may have increased primary election VOTER TURNOUT. Evidence from studies of open and blanket primaries suggests that most crossover voters vote sincerely, increasing the probability of more moderate candidates advancing to general elections in competitive primaries. Crossover voters also tend to vote for popular incumbents, weakening political parties and promoting candidate-based campaigns. The popularity of the blanket primary in those states that implemented it may lead to further attempts to design more open primary systems.

Further reading: Cain, Bruce E., and Elisabeth R. Gerber, ed. *Voting at the Political Fault Line: California's Experiment with the Blanket Primary.* Berkeley: University of California Press, 2002; Labbe, John B. "Louisiana's Blanket Primary after California Democratic Party v. Jones," *Northwestern University Law Review* 96, no. 2 (2002): 721–753; Sabato, Larry J., and Bruce A. Larson. *The Party's Just Begun: Shaping Political Parties for America's Future.* 2nd ed. New York: Longman, 2002.

—Marcia L. Godwin

primary, mixed

A mixed, or modified, primary is a PRIMARY that is neither a fully closed primary, restricted to POLITICAL PARTY members, nor an open primary, with voters allowed to select any party's BALLOT. There is not a consensus on which terms to use to describe all of the variations in primary systems. Some scholars and election officials designate a "modified closed primary" as one with a party registration requirement that gives voters the opportunity to change registration on ELECTION DAY. A mixed primary may be one in which different parties have different requirements for authorizing voters to participate in their primaries.

The diversity in primary systems results from the decentralization of elections administration in the United States, as specified in the Constitution. In addition, both states and political parties have a role in setting up primary systems. State governments can set up the procedures and deadlines for VOTER REGISTRATION by political party and even decide whether to sponsor partisan primaries. Political parties, under First Amendment freedom of association guarantees, can decide whether to close their primaries to party outsiders. The Supreme Court ruled in 1986 that political parties also have the discretion to open up their primaries to nonparty members, even if state law establishes a closed system (*Tashjian v. Republican Party of Connecticut,* 479 U.S. 208).

Because of the differences in definitions, the number of mixed primaries in the United States is difficult to identify. It appears that about 41 percent of primaries in the 2000 PRESIDENTIAL ELECTION were open, and that another 24 to 28 percent were partially open. The trend toward open primary systems is continuing into the 21st century, and additional variation in primary system design by state is likely as well.

Further reading: Ceaser, James. *Presidential Selection.* Princeton, N.J.: Princeton University Press, 1979; Cook, Rhodes. *The Presidential Nominating Process: A Place for Us?* Lanham, Md.: Rowman & Littlefield, 2003; Sabato, Larry J., and Bruce A. Larson. *The Party's Just Begun: Shaping Political Parties for America's Future.* 2nd ed. New York: Longman, 2002.

—Marcia L. Godwin

primary, nonpartisan

A nonpartisan primary is a PRIMARY election in which all candidates appear on the same BALLOT. Voters select one candidate per office. A RUNOFF ELECTION is held between the top two candidates only if the top candidate does not receive a majority.

The nonpartisan primary has been used in a variety of local governments, including hundreds of cities. In California, the nonpartisan primary is used for such positions as members of the Los Angeles City Council, county boards of supervisors, and one statewide office, the state superintendent of schools. The nonpartisan primary was adopted at the statewide level by Louisiana in the 1970s, replacing a runoff primary system. In Louisiana's version, POLITICAL PARTY affiliations are listed on the ballot. Mississippi attempted to adopt a nonpartisan primary as well, but it was overturned in court on the grounds that it would discriminate against racial minorities. The state of Washington adopted a nonpartisan primary system in 2004 after its blanket primary was ruled to be unconstitutional.

The effects of the nonpartisan primary have been studied mainly for Louisiana, and the results may not be representative. However, it appears to give incumbents an advantage since voters may vote largely on NAME RECOGNITION. CHALLENGERS have to do well enough in the primary to trigger a runoff and have enough funds to continue campaigning past the primary, which deters competition. It also appears to increase probability of extreme candidates emerging. The most infamous example was Louisiana's 1991 gubernatorial election, which featured a runoff between a candidate who had previously been a KU KLUX KLAN leader and a former governor accused of political corruption. Critics of the Louisiana system also attribute Louisiana's low VOTER TURNOUT to the nonpartisan primary system and point out that turnout usually drops considerably between a primary and runoff election, raising concerns about the representativeness of the ELECTORATE.

Because the U.S. Constitution gives Congress the authority to set the ELECTION DAY for federal offices, the Supreme Court overturned Louisiana's original October primary schedule in late 1997. Since then, Louisiana has scheduled its nonpartisan primary on the national Election Day in early November and its runoff some weeks later. When incumbent Democratic senator Mary Landrieu was forced into a runoff in 2002 against one of three Republican challengers, the runoff election attracted attention from national party organizations and out-of-state donors. If a future runoff election in a nonpartisan primary state could decide the partisan majority in the House or Senate, there would likely be even more outside influence.

Further reading: Cain, Bruce E., and Elisabeth R. Gerber, ed. *Voting at the Political Fault Line: California's Experiment with the Blanket Primary.* Berkeley: University of California Press, 2002; Labbe, John B. "Louisiana's Blanket Primary after *California Democratic Party v. Jones*," *Northwestern University Law Review* 96, no. 2 (2002): 721–753; Sabato, Larry J., and Bruce A. Larson. *The Party's Just Begun: Shaping Political Parties for America's Future.* 2nd ed. New York: Longman, 2002.

—Marcia L. Godwin

primary, open

An open primary is a PRIMARY election in which voters are not required to be party members in order to participate. Voters decide at the polls which party primary to participate in; they may not vote in more than one party's primary at the same election. In some open primary states, voters do have to register in advance or do have to declare a party preference. In effect, voters declare themselves members of particular political parties for the day of the election only.

Open primary systems have become more common in recent decades. As of the 2000 election, a little more than 40 percent of primaries could be classified as open. There have been more open primary systems in southern states, but they are becoming more prevalent in other regions of the United States as well. Open primaries have not been subject to the same constitutional challenges as blanket primaries because political parties technically limit voting to their sup-

porters. On the whole, open primary systems provide less control to political parties than do closed primaries.

Open primary systems are believed to attract a more moderate and somewhat younger ELECTORATE. Since nonparty members are not excluded, primary VOTER TURNOUT is somewhat higher than occurs with closed primaries. Crossover or SWING VOTERs can have a moderating effect, increasing the probability of selecting nominees who are more centrist and have a better chance of appealing to the broader electorate that will vote in a GENERAL ELECTION. For example, Senator John Edwards (D, N.C.) received relatively strong support from moderates and INDEPENDENTs in open primary states in the 2004 PRESIDENTIAL ELECTION. Even though he did not win, these results contributed to his selection as the vice presidential candidate by Democratic nominee John Kerry.

Several studies have found that crossover voters select sincerely, choosing candidates who are close to their own views rather than trying to sabotage another party's primary by selecting an extremist candidate. However, they may revert to candidates of their own party in the general election. The competitiveness of primaries has a strong effect on how many and which types of voters cross over to vote in another party's primary. In the 2000 PRESIDENTIAL ELECTION, it would have been rational for Democratic voters to cross over and vote in the more competitive Republican primary between George W. Bush and John McCain. Republicans might have had an incentive in 2004 to vote in Democratic primaries since President George W. Bush was running unopposed.

One of the major concerns with the open primary system is that there can be unintended impacts if there are multiple positions on the same BALLOT. Independent and crossover voters tend to choose a party ballot based on the most visible campaign. These voters may not make informed choices in other races. If moderate voters participate mainly in one primary, a more ideologically extreme electorate may be left in the other party's primary.

Further reading: Cain, Bruce E., and Elisabeth R. Gerber, ed. *Voting at the Political Fault Line: California's Experiment with the Blanket Primary.* Berkeley: University of California Press, 2002; Karen M. Kaufmann, James G. Gimpel, and Adam H. Hoffman. "A Promise Fulfilled? Open Primaries and Representation," *Journal of Politics* 65, no. 2 (2003): 457–476; Sabato, Larry J., and Bruce A. Larson. *The Party's Just Begun: Shaping Political Parties for America's Future.* 2nd ed. New York: Longman, 2002.

—Marcia L. Godwin

primary, regional

A regional primary is a PRESIDENTIAL PRIMARY in which several states schedule their primaries on the same day. States thus try to maximize their influence over selection of a presidential nominee. In principle, candidates will devote greater time and resources toward campaigning in states and regions where there are the most DELEGATES. The adoption of a regional primary could increase the probability that presidential nominees will come from that region and create an incentive for candidates to focus more on regional concerns.

Traditionally, Iowa held the first PRIMARY caucus and New Hampshire the first primary election during each presidential ELECTION CYCLE. Other primaries were spread out over the next several months, culminating in the original SUPER TUESDAY, the first Tuesday in June, with the California and New York primaries. By 1988, a large number of southern states had moved their primaries to early March, which became the new Super Tuesday. In subsequent elections, additional states moved up their primaries in a process that became known as FRONT-LOADING. There are now several early primaries, with several state primaries at the same time.

There have been a number of proposals to spread out the primary election calendar and have more systematic regional primaries. The order of regions would be established by lottery under most of the proposals. Senator Robert Packwood (R, Ore.) proposed legislation in the early 1970s that would have created five regions, with monthly voting on the second Tuesday of each month through July. There have also been proposals to establish regions by time zone, although there would be an unequal number of states in each region, and it is unclear how states with more than one time zone would be categorized. The Delaware Plan, considered by a REPUBLICAN PARTY commission in 2000, would establish four groups of states by population, with smaller states having their primaries first. This plan would make later primaries more meaningful and allow less-funded candidates to build momentum in the earlier, smaller states. However, the overall system could create logistical and campaign cost problems with candidates having to travel from state to state.

The National Association of Secretaries of State (NASS), which includes the elections officials of each state, adopted its own regional primary proposal in 2000, reaffirmed it in 2003, and attempted to gain POLITICAL PARTY and state support in 2004 for implementation as early as 2008. The NASS proposal would keep the early IOWA CAUCUS and NEW HAMPSHIRE PRIMARY. The remaining 48 states would be divided into four regions. Primaries would be held the first Tuesday after the first Monday of each month from March through June. The order of regions would rotate each election cycle.

Regional primary plans attempt to rotate regional influence over presidential selection, more adequately season candidates, and keep campaign costs below what they would be with a national primary. However, political parties, FRONTRUNNERS, and incumbents usually prefer to have shorter primary seasons, and resistance to the regional plans persists. The selection of which regions go first also has the potential to favor some types of candidates over others and adds to the controversy.

Further reading: Cain, Bruce E., and Elisabeth R. Gerber, ed. *Voting at the Political Fault Line: California's Experiment with the Blanket Primary.* Berkeley: University of California Press, 2002; Mayer, William G., and Andrew E. Busch. *The Front-Loading Problem in Presidential Nominations.* Washington, D.C.: Brookings Institution Press, 2004; Sabato, Larry J., and Bruce A. Larson. *The Party's Just Begun: Shaping Political Parties for America's Future.* 2nd ed. New York: Longman, 2002.

—Marcia L. Godwin

primary, runoff

Runoff primaries are PRIMARY elections that take place in nine mostly southern states with a law that requires a majority (50 percent plus one) vote to win an electoral NOMINATION. When no candidate receives a majority of the votes, a second election, or runoff primary, occurs between the top two vote finishers to determine the nominee. This practice is a clear exception to the plurality rule that is prevalent in most American constituencies.

Runoff primaries were instituted in the South at the beginning of the 20th century, when Democrats were enjoying a lengthy period of dominance in southern POLITICS. In order to preserve and strengthen this powerful political position, DEMOCRATIC PARTY officials instituted runoff primaries to unite a potentially disparate base of support and thwart any prospective CHALLENGERS. Because the practice began in the South, where racial tensions have historically been prevalent, this practice has been criticized as an attempt to dilute the influence of black voters.

In 1984, Reverend Jesse Jackson pointed to North Carolina's second CONGRESSIONAL DISTRICT election as proof of prejudice and a violation of both the Constitution and the Voting Rights Act. H. M. "Mickey" Michaux, Jr., running against two white candidates, captured 44 percent of the votes in the first Democratic primary. However, he lost the runoff primary, winning only 46 percent of votes, to a white candidate. Jackson claimed that in districts with significant, but minority, black voting populations, a single black candidate could easily lead the first primary against two or more white candidates, as Michaux did, but lose in the runoff, when the majority white population votes en masse for the white candidate.

In response, a handful of the nine states that continue to support runoff primaries have taken legislative measures to reduce the threshold needed to win a primary to 40 percent from a true majority of 50 percent plus one. Most notably, North Carolina, probably in response to the public controversy led by Jackson, amended its runoff primary law accordingly in 1989.

Racial discrimination in runoff primaries, although consistently alleged, has never been categorically proven or adjudicated. Opposing arguments insist that the antithesis of Jackson's argument holds true. In those districts where any minority population—black, Hispanic, or any other—constitutes a majority of the population, some scholars argue that runoff primaries would ultimately work to their advantage, not disadvantage.

Further reading: Maisel, L. Sandy. *Parties and Elections in America*. 2nd ed. New York: McGraw-Hill, 1987; Thurber, James A., and Candice J. Nelson, eds. *Campaigns and Elections American Style*. 2nd ed. Boulder, Colo.: Westview Press, 2004.

—Costas Panagopoulos

Progressive movement

The Progressive movement was a social, political, and economic movement that emerged toward the end of the 19th century and ended by the end of World War I in 1918. The term itself was used because of the movement's progressive goals. The Progressive movement was never considered a distinct organization, although the PROGRESSIVE PARTY that evolved toward the end of the Progressive movement shared the movement's goals. The Progressive movement was a nonpartisan effort that attracted Republicans, Democrats, and members of THIRD PARTIES. The multiplicity of changes due to industrialization, immigration, and urbanization that had not been effectively addressed by the government in a manner consistent with democratic, egalitarian, and individualistic principles spurred the Progressive movement.

Progressives were strong supporters of democratic ideals and social justice. Major accomplishments included the introduction of numerous political and economic reforms all having in common more public involvement in political decision making and access to economic opportunities. The Progressive movement strongly believed that the means to address the ills that emerged from an unregulated economic and political system were through legislation. While the Progressive movement was concerned with various problems at the local, state, and national levels, the movement operated largely at the national level.

The Progressive movement was mostly an urban movement, although it had some support in agrarian areas. Between 1900 and 1910, 8.8 million immigrants entered the United States. Most of these immigrants lived in large, growing urban centers and were unable to speak, read, or write English. Coupled with a lack of political and economic empowerment, these immigrants were readily exploited by their employers and the political system. Immigrants provided a steady supply of cheap labor in growing industrial centers. Local political party machines provided help for these immigrants in exchange for their support. Immigrants received help from local party machines and bosses in their efforts to secure housing, jobs, and other benefits.

Progressives believed that the political and economic practices of an earlier time were not appropriate once the nation had grown in size and diversity. City governments had difficulty functioning efficiently and in a socially responsible manner. Growing urban centers were unable to respond effectively to burgeoning public needs for transportation, fire and police protection, lighting, sanitation, and education. Population density and growth contributed to widespread disease, congestion, and poverty in rapidly developing slums. Compounding these social problems were long-standing practices that included bribery, corruption, and crimes that took advantage of the powerless and the poor while they benefited political leaders and corporate bosses.

The Progressive movement emerged out of the middle and upper class, which, once aware of these conditions, causes, and the lack of political and economic response to them, fought for more citizen participation in government and economic regulation. The Progressive movement is well known for its role in introducing many instruments of DIRECT DEMOCRACY. These include PRESIDENTIAL PRIMARIES, the direct primary, the direct selection of U.S. senators, the initiative, the REFERENDUM, and the RECALL. All of these efforts gave citizens a voice in political decision making that had previously been exercised by PARTY BOSSES or political elites. Progressives also played a role in securing the ratification of three constitutional amendments: Prohibition (which was later repealed), women's suffrage, and the direct election of senators. The Progressive movement also introduced the notion that citizens should have the right to recall public officials.

Economic regulations introduced by the Progressives include antitrust legislation. Progressives are also known for their efforts in strengthening the Sherman Anti-Trust Act (1890) as a way to maximize economic competition and reduce the formation of corporate trusts. The Progressives also worked for improving working conditions in order to minimize worker exploitation as well as improving public health through the Pure Food and Drug Act and the Meat Inspection Act in 1906.

Journalists assisted the Progressive agenda through their efforts to highlight the social ills that resulted from the concentration of economic and political power in the hands of an insensitive elite. These journalists argued that the comfortable relationship between big business and machine politicians served their own interests to the detriment of the people.

The Progressive movement was helped by its key leaders ascending to the presidency, such as Theodore Roosevelt in 1901 and Woodrow Wilson in 1912. Roosevelt, a Republican, broke with his own party in order to regulate big business. He targeted monopolistic business practices for reform and asked Congress to create the Bureau of Corporations that would investigate and regulate big business. He also brought an antitrust lawsuit against the Northern Securities Company, a railroad trust controlled by industrialist J. P. Morgan. Later in Roosevelt's administration, the U.S. Supreme Court dissolved the trust in the case of *Northern Securities Co. v. United States.* In 1912, Roosevelt ran for president on the Progressive Party ticket and lost.

A second well-known progressive was Democrat Woodrow Wilson. Due largely to the earlier Progressive successes and growing public concerns with the Great War (later known as World War I), Wilson's contribution to the Progressive agenda as president was largely associated with his efforts to bring moralism to issues of world conflict and human rights. This included Wilson's authorship of the League of Nations, a world body meant to mediate and prevent future wars that the U.S. Senate rejected. Wilson also supported women's suffrage during the last stages of his presidency. Progressive ideals lost public and political favor once national attention focused on the role of the United States in world affairs.

The Progressive legacy is still felt today. Presidential primaries have become more widespread. Since 1972, both major parties have increased their use of presidential preference primaries, while fewer states use caucuses for NOMINATION purposes. Arguments for limiting the number of legislative and executive terms and campaign finance reform are often presented as Progressive measures because they may reduce electoral advantages linked to incumbency and wealth.

Further reading: Grantham, Dewey W., Jr. "The Progressive Era and the Reform Tradition." *Middle America* 46, no. 4 (1964): 227–251; Hofstadter, Richard. *The Progressive Movement, 1900–1915.* Englewood Cliffs, N.J.: Prentice Hall, 1963; Scott, Andrew M. "The Progressive Era in Perspective." *Journal of Politics* 21, no. 3 (1959): 685–701.

—Terri Fine

Progressive Party

The Progressive Party has had three separate manifestations in the 20th century. The first came in 1912, when Theodore Roosevelt left the White House after anointing his successor, William Howard Taft, to take over as the REPUBLICAN PARTY nominee for president in 1908. Roosevelt returned from a safari in Africa to discover a bitter struggle between "Old Guard" and progressives for control of the party. He also realized that Taft was not quite the reformer he had portrayed himself to be before Roosevelt

left office. Convinced to once again run for president, Roosevelt failed to secure the Republican NOMINATION at the party convention in the summer of 1912. Determined to win back the presidency, Roosevelt and his followers bolted the party and established the Progressive Party, with Roosevelt and Hiram Johnson of California as the party's first presidential ticket.

The party found a fitting nickname when Roosevelt declared that he was as "strong as a bull moose." Roosevelt's attempt at a political comeback denied Taft another term and propelled Woodrow Wilson to the White House. He may have lost the election, but Roosevelt outpolled Taft. Roosevelt won 27 percent of the popular vote to Taft's 23 percent and won 88 electoral votes to Taft's 8. In 1916, the Progressives nominated Roosevelt once again, but Roosevelt withdrew and threw his support behind the Republican candidate Charles Evans Hughes, who eventually lost to Wilson.

The second manifestation of the Progressive Party came in 1924, when the Conference for Progressive Political Action nominated Wisconsin senator Robert "Battling Bob" LaFollette (who had sought the Republican nomination in 1908 and 1912) for the presidency. The LaFollette nomination was supported by farmers and LABOR GROUPS, who believed that government was hopelessly controlled by business interests. LaFollette became the first presidential candidate ever endorsed by the American Federation of Labor. The Progressive Party stood on a platform that called for land conservation, collective bargaining for unions, child labor legislation, and public ownership of railroads. Although he finished third behind Democrat John W. Davis and Republican Calvin Coolidge, LaFollette won 13 electoral votes and nearly 5 million POPULAR VOTES.

In 1948, the Progressive banner was once again unfurled in support of Henry Wallace. Wallace had been Franklin Roosevelt's vice president from 1941 to 1945 and a cabinet member for both Roosevelt and Truman. Wallace criticized Truman for inactivity on civil rights and publicly opposed the cold war containment policy and the formation of NATO, the North Atlantic Treaty Organization, for fear that it might bring about another world war. Wallace and his RUNNING MATE, Idaho senator Glen Taylor, garnered only 1.1 million votes and no electoral votes.

Further reading: Hesseltine, William B. *Third-Party Movements in the United States.* Princeton, N.J.: D. Van Nostrand, 1962; Mowry, George E. *Theodore Roosevelt and the Progressive Movement.* New York: Hill & Wang, 2000; Thelen, David P. *Robert M. LaFollette and the Insurgent Spirit.* Madison: University of Wisconsin Press, 1986; White, Graham, and John Maze. *Henry A. Wallace: His Search for a New World Order.* Chapel Hill: University of North Carolina Press, 1995.

—Gordon E. Harvey

Prohibition Party

In its various forms and entities, the Prohibition Party has existed from 1854 to the present (2006), and of minor parties in the United States, it had the longest history of participation in PRESIDENTIAL ELECTIONS, entering a candidate in each presidential election between 1872 and 2004, with 1980 as the only exception. Emerging as part of the reform-minded COALITION that helped form the REPUBLICAN PARTY in 1854, the Prohibition Party coalesced from three temperance movements in the Northeast. Three people formed the early leadership of the party, each of whom had led prohibition efforts in their respective states: Neal Dow of Maine, Gerrit Smith of New York, and James Black of Pennsylvania.

The motivation for organizing such a party arose from humanistic concerns of the day expressed by wives, mothers, and social reformers who believed that alcohol consumption was a bane to society, led to absenteeism from work, and fostered family crises. Women played a central role in the party, such political participation being allowed because of women's society-defined role as "nurturers."

One woman especially played an important role in the course of the party: Frances E. Willard, president of the Women's Christian Temperance Union (WCTU). The party often found itself split between "narrow gaugers," who wanted to emphasize only one issue, temperance, and "broad gaugers," who resisted such limitations. The party solidly supported the women's suffrage movement, most likely due to the large and influential presence of women within the temperance movement.

The Prohibition Party never fared well in national elections. It wielded more influence at the state and local levels, including forcing several states to go "dry" before the implementation of a national prohibition policy. Notable state victories under the Prohibition Party banner included Sidney J. Catts's election as governor of Florida in 1916. The highest vote total in a presidential campaign for Prohibition Party candidates came in the election of 1892, when the John Bidwell and James B. Cranfill ticket garnered 264,133 votes. The party saw its greatest success between 1900 and 1933, culminating in the outlawing of the production and consumption of alcoholic beverages in the 1920s.

Further reading: Flynt, J. Wayne. *Cracker Messiah: Governor Sidney J. Catts of Florida.* Baton Rouge: Louisiana State University Press, 1977; Sinclair, Andrew. *The Era of Excess: A Social History of the Prohibition Movement.* New York: Harper & Row, 1964.

—Gordon E. Harvey

proportional representation

Proportional representation is an electoral system in which the seats held by a POLITICAL PARTY in a legislature are proportional to the votes that party received in the last election. For example, if a party received 40 percent of the vote, it would be allotted roughly 40 percent of the seats in the legislature. This system was developed in Europe in the mid-19th century in order to guarantee minority groups representation in the legislature. In this system, any group of like-minded voters can elect candidates proportionate to their vote rather than have their vote discarded in the winner-take-all, or FIRST-PAST-THE-POST, system.

In the proportional representation system, there are several methods for apportioning seats. One of the more popular of these methods is that of the single transferable vote, in which the voter ranks the candidates by preference on the BALLOT. If this were to be done on a national level in the United States, CONGRESSIONAL DISTRICT lines would have to be redrawn in order to produce fewer but larger districts. As a result, there would not be one seat per district, but several, and seats would be allocated to party members in proportion to the party's vote share in each district.

Though it does not exist on the national or state level in the United States, proportional representation can be found at the municipal level. One such case is the town of Cambridge, Massachusetts, where voters use a complex form of proportional representation to elect the city council and school committee members. They use a system that ensures representation of minorities and protects majority control. In Cambridge, any group that numbers at least one-tenth of the aggregate population is assured of electing at least one of the nine council members on the board, yet the majority group is also assured of receiving the majority of seats. The voters may vote for as many candidates on the ballot as they choose, but then they must rank them according to order of preference. The candidate must then win a quota, or required number of votes, to be elected. The quota itself is determined by dividing the total number of valid ballots cast by the number of positions to be elected plus one and then adding one to the resulting dividend.

Though it is not used as widely in the United States, proportional representation offers what others systems have been accused of lacking: the certainty of representation for minorities. While other cities in the United States such as Cincinnati, Seattle, and San Francisco have attempted to pass initiatives of proportional representation, Cambridge is one of the few areas with an established tradition of proportional representation.

Further reading: Powell, G. Bingham, Jr. *Elections as Instruments of Democracy: Majoritarian and Proportional Visions.* New Haven, Conn.: Yale University Press, 2000; Lijphardt, Arendt. *Patterns of Democracy: Government Forms and Performance in Thirty-Six Countries.* New Haven, Conn.: Yale University Press, 1999.

—Jeremy B. Lupoli

public opinion polling

Modern public opinion polling is a scientific effort to estimate what an entire population thinks about an issue by asking a smaller sample of that group for its opinion. Polling has become increasingly important in American POLITICS, as nearly every media report about an election contains the results of a poll, and candidates rely heavily on polls when crafting their campaign messages.

Jean-Jacques Rousseau coined the term *public opinion* (*l'opinion publique*) in 1744, but the first modern opinion poll did not appear until 1936. Prior to that, several media outlets conducted nonscientific STRAW POLLS with varying degrees of success. Straw polls went out of favor in 1936, when *Literary Digest* used a straw poll to incorrectly predict that Republican Alf Landon would beat incumbent President Franklin Roosevelt 57 percent to 43 percent. Roosevelt won with 62.5 percent of the vote, and *Literary Digest* went bankrupt.

Led by George Gallup and Elmo Roper, polls became more scientific in the years to follow, though both men's firms incorrectly predicted the 1948 PRESIDENTIAL ELECTION would go to Thomas Dewey rather than Harry Truman. Subsequently, the Social Science Research Council called for pollsters to use probability sampling, a much more accurate method of polling than earlier techniques. Probability sampling requires that every member of a population have an equal probability of being selected to take a survey, assuring that even a small sample (often less than 1,500 individuals) can be representative of a population as large as that of the United States, with over 280 million people. While not entirely accurate, such surveys typically have a margin of error of plus or minus 3 to 4 percentage points.

Sampling is not the only area in which polls can run into trouble. Questions early in a survey may influence responses later in the survey, the gender or race of the interviewer may influence responses in unpredictable ways, leading questions can lead to misleading results, and poorly worded questions can lead to faulty conclusions.

While modern surveying is firmly based in science, it remains an imperfect science. Because of important information that they provide at relatively low cost, surveys remain an indispensable part of American electoral journalism and campaign strategizing.

Further reading: Eisinger, Robert Martin. *The Evolution of Presidential Polling.* New York: Cambridge University Press, 2003; Lavrakas, Paul J. *Election Polls, the News Media, and Democracy.* New York: Chatham House Publishers, 2000; Warren, Kenneth F. *In Defense of Public Opinion Polling.* Boulder, Colo.: Westview Press, 2001.

—Michael W. Wagner

pundit

Pundits are media commentators who are frequently called on by journalists to explain issues and events, sometimes in areas beyond the expertise on which the commentators' reputations were built. The term was once a lighthearted honorific reserved for influential senior journalists and columnists whose analysis often swayed public policy and POLITICS. Now the term is applied to a broader range of "talking heads," including media savvy authors and academics and former professional political operatives. In an era of 24-hour talk radio and cable television news, *pundit* increasingly carries a derogatory edge with implications of glibness, partisanship, and even ignorance. It also has spawned many popular derivations, such as *punditry,* a word used to describe the art of political analysis, especially in broadcast media.

Derived from *pandita,* a Sanskrit word for a learned person, *pundit* has been in use in English as a way to denote a kind of expertise for nearly two centuries. *New York Times* columnist William Safire, a pundit who also has written about the word's origins both in his renowned political dictionary and his weekly column, "On Language," attributes its contemporary use to *Time* magazine founder Henry R. Luce (1898–1967). According to Safire, Luce borrowed the word from a group of Yale undergraduates called the Pundits to use as a respectful title for leading observers of the day, such as Walter Lippmann (1889–1974), the widely read and respected syndicated newspaper columnist.

Over time, the pundit label has been applied to a growing list of influential journalists and commentators, such as syndicated columnists David S. Broder of the *Washington Post,* George F. Will of *Newsweek,* Robert Novak of the *Chicago Sun-Times,* and Jack W. Germond of the *Baltimore Sun.* Increasingly, any news analyst who appears on televised political talk shows, such as NBC's *Meet the Press,* ABC's *This Week,* PBS's *Washington Week in Review,* and the syndicated *McLaughlin Group,* is called a pundit.

The rise of 24-hour cable TV news in the 1980s and political talk radio in the 1990s created a growing reliance on expert analysis to help broadcast producers bridge coverage of news events and fill increasing amounts of airtime. Former political operatives, whom news radio and TV producers once sought primarily as guests, were instead tapped as regular on-air analysts. These professional analysts included onetime CAMPAIGN MANAGERS, party officials, pollsters, consultants, and even candidates and elected officials. In presidential politics, former campaign officials have been hired by TV news networks to provide exclusive expert commentary within days of their candidates dropping out of the race.

Prominent examples of such pundits have included Bob Beckel, a television commentator who was the campaign manager for Democrat Walter F. Mondale's losing presidential campaign in 1984; Patrick J. Buchanan, a former White House speechwriter whose popularity as a conservative newspaper columnist, author, and TV commentator inspired two presidential runs of his own in 1992 and 1996; William Krystal, editor of the conservative *Weekly Standard* magazine and a TV commentator who was once Republican vice president Dan Quayle's chief of staff; and James Carville, the Democratic political consultant who ran Bill Clinton's 1992 presidential campaign before becoming a regular media commentator on NBC's *Meet the Press*. Both Carville and Buchanan have been cohosts of CNN's *Crossfire*, a daily political talk show that has turned numerous political figures into media commentators. Other pioneers in this form of punditry included Safire, who was a New York publicist and a campaign aide and White House adviser to Richard M. Nixon before becoming a newspaper columnist, and Will, who served on the staff of Senator Gordon L. Allott (R, Colo.) before becoming Washington editor of the conservative *National Review*, a *Newsweek* columnist, a syndicated newspaper columnist, and a regular commentator and interviewer on ABC's *This Week*.

Before becoming a kind of pundit himself, scholar and media critic Eric Alterman coined the term *punditocracy* in the late 1980s to describe the political and policy influence of some prominent commentators. For example, while working as a columnist, George Will also advised Ronald Reagan during the Republican presidential candidate's preparations to debate President Jimmy Carter in 1980. Alterman's term became widely used after he published *Sound and Fury: The Making of the Punditocracy*, a 1992 book on the influence of political analysts such as Will.

Further reading: Alterman, Eric. *Sound and Fury: The Making of the Punditocracy*. Rev. ed. New York: Cornell University Press, 2000; Safire, William. *Safire's New Political Dictionary: The Definitive Guide to the New Language of Politics*. New York: Random House, 1993.

—Mark Stencel

push poll

A push poll is a controversial political tool used by some political operatives to spread negative information about the opposing side. Thus, a push poll may be defined as a poll in which questions are prefaced by misleading, inaccurate, or provocative information about the sponsoring candidate's opponent. The primary purpose of this negative campaign tactic is not to measure public opinion, but to change it. Push polls are characterized by one or more of the following qualities. Respondents are not selected at ran-

dom; rather, a directory or mailing list is used to TARGET voters who belong to a particular demographic or political group. The pollster or polling organization does not record or process the responses they receive from respondents. Most important, push polls contain a message or negative information about one candidate that is designed to weaken support for that candidate.

A push poll differs from a traditional poll in several important ways. Traditional political polls are conducted over the telephone, whereby blocks of prospective voters are randomly selected and asked questions that help politicians identify issues, themes, and opinions in the early stages of a political campaign. Often these polls include questions designed to test respondents' reactions to potential CAMPAIGN SLOGANS or messages. Their primary purpose is to collect information and to measure public opinion. Results are tabulated and totaled, and this information is presented by the polling firm to the political candidate who sponsored the poll.

Push polls, on the other hand, are designed to weaken support for the political candidate about whom negative information is being spread. An example of a push poll question may take the following form: "Given Senator X's arrest for cocaine use, are you more or less likely to support him in the November election?" Such questions, if not based in fact, more closely resemble a telemarketing ploy than a poll. This technique is often conducted toward the end of a close political contest, making it particularly effective and difficult to detect.

While push polling has been practiced at least since the 1940s, when Nixon is believed to have used it in his inaugural congressional campaign, it did not become a regular part of electoral POLITICS until the 1990s. During the 1996 presidential race, a group of political operatives working for Robert Dole's presidential campaign publicly acknowledged that the technique had been used against Dole's PRIMARY opponents. While such admissions are rare, and it is impossible to know how prevalent the practice has become in American campaigns, the secrecy and effectiveness of the practice assures that it will continue to be used by political campaigns in the future.

Further reading: Lavrakas, Paul J. *Election Polls, the News Media, and Democracy*. New York: Chatham House, 2000; Sabato, Larry J. *Dirty Little Secrets: The Persistence of Corruption in American Politics*. New York: Times Books, 1996.

—James B. Tuttle

R

racial districting

Racial districting occurs when district lines are drawn to favor or disadvantage a particular racial or ethnic group. Racial GERRYMANDERing is the general method used to accomplish the goals of racial districting by the creation of MAJORITY-MINORITY DISTRICTS. Majority-minority districts are those that have a majority of the population from a group that consists of a minority in the larger population. The idea is that with a majority of the population, the minority group can elect a representative of its choosing, in most cases someone from that minority group.

While legislative districts are based on total population, the voting age population is important when considering racially based districting. It is also important to note that members of minority groups tend to vote less frequently than do whites, and this may hinder the ability of voters in majority-minority districts to successfully elect a minority representative. When a majority-minority district is not feasible, racial districting can also produce influence districts. Influence districts tend to have between 40 and 50 percent of a group population in a district and give the minority group the chance of electing a representative of its choice or at least of having a strong influence on the electoral outcomes.

Racial districting in the United States is generally thought of in terms of African-American communities, although it applies to other groups as well, most notably Hispanics. However, the African-American population is the best suited for racial gerrymandering because of the geographic concentration of many communities within a state and the general political cohesiveness of the community. On the other hand, Hispanics tend to be less geographically concentrated and politically cohesive, making racial districting more difficult in most cases.

While today racial districting is used to help minority groups elect representatives, southern states originally drew district lines to ensure black voters did not constitute a majority in a district and effectively helped keep African Americans from winning legislative seats. This changed beginning with the 1982 Voting Rights Act and the Supreme Court's 1986 ruling in *Thornburg v. Gingles*. In the *Thornburg* case, the Court ruled the Voting Rights Act required legislative districts not discriminate against racial minorities, even if the discrimination was an unintended consequence of the districting plan. This was a switch from earlier decisions in which the Court ruled plans were discriminatory only if the intent of the plan was to limit minority representation.

The *Thornburg* decision led mapmakers to pursue majority-minority districts where geography and residency patterns permitted. The 1990 round of REDISTRICTING saw the first widespread use of affirmative racial gerrymandering, and the results were increases in minority representation and criticism for the creative district designs used to produce some of the majority-minority districts. After the 1992 elections, African Americans gained 13 seats, from 25 to 38, while Hispanics gained seven seats, from 10 to 17. However, the bizarre shapes of many of the districts stirred controversy as critics called into question the fairness of relying on race when determining district boundaries. The most notorious example was the 12th district in North Carolina, also known as the I-85 district. The mapmakers in North Carolina attempted to draw a majority-minority district by connecting African-American communities in several of the state's largest cities since none of the minority populations was large enough to create a district within any of the individual cities. To avoid picking up the largely white suburbs, the district boundaries followed along I-85, in some cases as narrowly as the northbound lanes. The Supreme Court first got involved in 1993 (*SHAW V. RENO*) by ruling bizarrely shaped districts designed to create majority-minority districts might violate the constitutional rights of white voters and in 1995 (*MILLER V. JOHNSON*) by striking down a Georgia congressional plan on the grounds that any map in which race was the "predominant factor" was unconstitutional on equal protection grounds. This ruling forced amendments to districts in Florida, Georgia, Louisiana, New York, Texas, and Virginia in the 1990s.

While these court decisions appeared to weaken the ability to racially gerrymander, the Court ruled in 1999 (*Hunt v. Cromartie*) that race could be used when drawing districts if the primary objective was not racially motivated but rather partisan in nature. This is important given that blacks tend to overwhelmingly support the DEMOCRATIC PARTY and every African-American representative in Congress comes from the Democratic Party. Despite the apparent Democratic gains from majority-minority districts, Republicans also appear to gain from the use of majority-minority districts. By packing many Democratic supporters into a few racially based districts, the surrounding districts tend to become more favorable to the Republicans. According to political scientist Gary Jacobson, racial gerrymandering in the South was responsible for as many as 10 House seats the Republicans gained in the area in the 1990s. During the 2000 round of state legislative redistricting, several states saw Republicans come out in favor of more majority-minority districts, while Democrats tried to produce maps with fewer such districts. This has important implications for the type of representation minorities receive. The advantage to majority-minority districts is the ability to produce symbolic representation for minority groups by electing their candidates of choice, who presumably identify with their common values as a CONSTITUENCY. The Democrats' argument is that too many majority-minority districts may hurt substantive representation by decreasing the number of Democrats, who in the African-American case are more likely to pass important policies favorable to the group when more Democrats are in the legislature.

The legal questions surrounding racial districting are far from over as the courts must face continued questions of majority-minority districts, partisanship, and gerrymandering. Heading into the 2004 elections, the Court's decision to limit race as a predominant factor has not appeared to hurt minority representation, as the number of minority members in Congress has held steady since 1992.

Further reading: Lublin, David. *The Paradox of Representation: Racial Gerrymandering and Minority Interests in Congress.* Princeton, N.J.: Princeton University Press, 1997; Jacobson, Gary. *The Politics of Congressional Elections.* 5th ed. New York: Longman, 2001.

—Jonathan Winburn

Rainbow/PUSH Coalition

The Rainbow/PUSH Coalition (RPC) is a multiracial, multiissue, international membership organization founded by Reverend Jesse L. Jackson in 1996. The RPC is an amalgamation of two organizations founded by Jackson: Operation PUSH and the National Rainbow Coalition. Operation PUSH (People United to Serve Humanity) was founded in Chicago in December 1971 to promote economic empowerment and expand educational, business, and employment opportunities for the disadvantaged and people of color. The National Rainbow Coalition was founded in 1985 to serve as a Washington, D.C., based national social justice organization devoted to education, political empowerment, and public policy changes.

In September 1996, Operation PUSH and the National Rainbow Coalition merged to form the Rainbow/PUSH Coalition in order to strengthen the work of both groups and to maximize their resources. RPC's mission is to move the nation and the world toward social, racial, and economic justice. Through its national headquarters in Chicago, satellite headquarters in New York and Los Angeles, and bureau in Washington, D.C., the RPC continues to strive to unite people of diverse ethnic, religious, economic, and political backgrounds in order to promote America's promise of "liberty and justice for all."

In order to generate public support, the RPC employs traditional CIVIL RIGHTS MOVEMENT mobilization strategies, in addition to state-of-the-art communication tools. For instance, through the Rainbow/Push Coalition Internet Web site, listserv, mass e-mail mailings, and the "Jackson Fax," the RPC continues to educate, demonstrate, boycott, and litigate minority causes. Through these efforts, the RPC strives to protect the interests of minorities and share in the power, benefits, and responsibilities of being an American citizen.

Through its mobilization efforts and activism, the RPC has achieved major accomplishments, including registering thousands of voters, assisting in elections at all levels of government, mediating labor disputes, promoting equal employment opportunity in media broadcasts, lobbying to increase minority representation in the entertainment industry and professional sports, increasing minority representation in university administrative posts, increasing minority business opportunities, and promoting South African and Haitian public policy.

The RPC continues to strive toward socioeconomic and political equality by promoting employment, economic and political empowerment, employee rights and livable wages, affirmative action and equal rights, educational access, fair and decent housing, fairness in the media and sports, criminal and environmental justice, electoral law reform, and increases in VOTER REGISTRATION and civic education.

Further reading: Rainbow/PUSH Coalition. Available online. URL: http://www.rainbowpush.org. Accessed August 10, 2005.

—Mitzi Ramos

random sample

Random sample is a statistical term to describe a method for selecting participants in surveys, experiments, or other scientific studies in which a target population (people,

African Americans voting in Washington, D.C., 1964 *(U.S. News and World Report Magazine Photograph Collection, Library of Congress)*

events, cities, etc.) is to be examined using a portion of the population. There are several types of random sampling techniques, and all random sampling requires that members of the sample be selected by chance and that the probability of selection to the sample be equal for all members of the population. Random sampling allows researchers to conduct studies in which the information used is representative of a population without having to interview or observe every member of the population. Surveys that use random sampling techniques require only a few hundred to a thousand respondents to attain accuracy with a level of certainty and a known level of inaccuracy (referred to as sampling error or margin of error). The use of random sampling in the social sciences has become standard procedure with the development and widespread use of public opinion surveys since the 1930s.

While scientific surveys and polls (those in which random sampling methods are employed) provide a fair assessment of the target population's positions, nonscientific polls (those that use nonrandom, or nonprobability, sampling), such as Internet polls and person-on-the-street interviews, are highly subject to sample bias (i.e., the chance that the sample is not representative of the target population). Respondents in nonscientific polls are often self-selected; they actively choose to include themselves in the surveys. However, there are segments of the population that cannot be involved in these samples, such as those without television, telephone, or Internet access, those who do not care

enough to call in, and those who do not watch a particular news program or channel. The information received from nonscientific polls or surveys is applicable only to those who participated rather than the public at large. In political news coverage, scientific and nonscientific polling data are frequently presented to illustrate public opinion. Use of both types of polls without explanation of the differences often presents conflicting, confusing, and sometimes misleading information to viewers.

Although surveys and polls that use random sampling are always more accurate than those that use nonrandom sampling, there are some limitations to the accuracy of random sampling. For example, if there are specific subgroups in the target population, simple random sampling may undersample some of the smaller groups. One remedy to this problem is stratified random sampling, whereby the population is divided along such subgroupings, and random sampling is performed on each of the subgroups to approximate the proportion of members of the subgroups in the sample to the population at large. Other types of weighting mechanisms are used to retain the value of a probability sample while interviewing a sufficient number of representatives of subgroups.

Further reading: Agresti, Alan, and Barbara Finlay. *Statistical Methods for the Social Sciences.* 3rd ed. Upper Saddle River, N.J.: Prentice Hall, 1997.

—Joel A. Rayan

Reagan Democrats

Ronald Reagan's victories in the 1980 and 1984 PRESIDENTIAL ELECTIONS were due in part to the votes of large numbers of self-identified Democrats, namely white, blue-collar, middle- and working-class Democrats. These defecting Democrats came to be known as "Reagan Democrats." During the 1980s and 1990s, Reagan Democrats were considered a crucial "swing" group, and the battle over Reagan Democrats was a strategic priority for both major parties. Some analysts saw Reagan Democrats as key to victory in 1988, with George H. W. Bush hoping to inherit their support, and Michael Dukakis striving to bring them home. Bill Clinton's New Democrat agenda in 1992 was clearly aimed at Reagan Democrats.

Reagan Democrats were thought to be more than simply Democrats who voted for Ronald Reagan. Reagan Democrats were defined by a cluster of conservative policy preferences that set them apart from other rank-and-file Democrats and put them at odds with DEMOCRATIC PARTY leadership. In polls and FOCUS GROUPS, Reagan Democrats expressed hostility toward affirmative action, Welfare, food stamps, and redistributive policy more generally, as well as the expansion of rights to ethnic and cultural minorities. Reagan Democrats felt abandoned by a Democratic Party that, in their view, had moved too far to the left.

Republicans were hopeful that in voting for Ronald Reagan, these disaffected Democrats would develop a long-term affinity toward the party and contribute to a Republican REALIGNMENT. Some Democrats, fearful of that development, sought to reshape their party's image by promoting a more centrist policy agenda. The establishment of the DEMOCRATIC LEADERSHIP COUNCIL and the New Democrat platform was largely a response to the Reagan Democrat phenomenon.

But the Reagan Democrat phenomenon also owed much to the singular appeal of Ronald Reagan as a candidate. Without Reagan on the Republican ticket, many Reagan Democrats returned to the Democratic fold. In 1988, George H. W. Bush won only 50 percent of the vote among Democrats who had voted for Reagan in 1984. Similarly, in 1992 he lost 50 percent of his Democratic support from 1988.

Further reading: Edsall, Thomas Byrne, and Mary D. Edsall. *Chain Reaction: The Impact of Race, Rights, and Taxes on American Politics.* New York: Norton, 1991; Greenberg, Stanley B. *Middle Class Dreams: The Politics and Power of the New American Majority.* New York: Times Books, 1995.

—Julio Borquez

realignment

Realignment is the term that is generally used to describe the quick, durable, and meaningful change in the party preferences of the general public that occurs after a CRITICAL ELECTION. Realigning elections are typically thought to be dominated by discussion of new political issues that crosscut the existing political alignment. Voters choose partisan sides based on their views of those new issues. According to realignment theory, this produces rapid and dramatic changes in the party system, followed by significant changes in public policy. Thus, realignment has often been associated with "conflict displacement," whereby one dominant party cleavage is simply replaced by another or a new collection of issues becomes more important to the public than the issues that made up the previous alignment. Other scholars call realignment a wholesale change in the partisan balance of power, with the MINORITY PARTY replacing the MAJORITY PARTY in the White House and both chambers of Congress.

To understand the meaning of realignment, it is useful to briefly consider the meaning of alignment. Alignments represent the issues that give political conflict substantive and symbolic meaning. For example, the most documented alignment is the New Deal alignment that was formed after the 1932 election. With the election of President Franklin Roosevelt, political conflict organized itself around two related sets of issues: the extent to which the government should intervene in the economy and the degree to which

the government should provide social welfare aid to the citizenry. As long as elections were contested along this political dimension, with Democrats generally supporting economic intervention and the provision of social welfare and Republicans generally opposing such measures, instead relying on private markets, Democrats were generally in control of Congress and often occupying the White House. The alignment remained stable via three simple, related forces: the salience of the alignment's issue agenda to the public, the vividness of the alignment to its founding generation, and the constraints the alignment held on partisan politicians.

Over time, the intensity of a political alignment often wanes as new generations emerge onto the political scene, and strategic politicians introduce new issues to try to disrupt the existing alignment and wrestle power from the majority party. The traditional way of defining these changes has been via the critical elections perspective. Pioneered by V. O. Key in 1955, critical elections were defined as elections dominated by a new issue(s), having unusually high turnout, resulting in a new partisan majority, having lasting consequences, and spurring major policy changes. Critical elections can be the result of built-up tension regarding a single issue or one party swallowing up an upstart third party's positions on a set of new issues.

Many scholars have argued that 1932 was not the first recorded realignment, citing the elections of 1789, 1828, 1856, and 1896 as other possible examples of realignment. One interesting observation made by political scientist Walter Dean Burnham is that these realignments seemed to happen about every 30 to 38 years, suggesting a cyclical pattern.

Other scholars, such as Edward Carmines and James Stimson, have critiqued the entire realignment perspective. They argue that the dichotomous nature of the realignment theory (either an election is or is not a realigning one) results in political scientists missing other important, perhaps more consequential, political changes. As an alternative to the realignment perspective, Carmines and Stimson offer the idea of "issue evolution," which claims that political elites and then the general public choose sides on a new set of issues that gradually come to dominate political debate. This idea closely resembles another idea developed by V. O. Key only a few years after he wrote about critical elections (i.e., the notion of a secular realignment). In this work, Key discussed secular realignment as important partisan changes that take place slowly over a long period of time.

An example of issue evolution, an issue that slowly transformed American POLITICS, is the politics of race. From the 1960s to the 1980s, racial issues gradually came to redefine national politics. During this period, SOUTHERN DEMOCRATS who retained a conservative stance on civil rights issues left the DEMOCRATIC PARTY for the REPUBLICAN

PARTY. Gradually, the mass public recognized this change (whereby the Democratic Party, once dominated by racial conservatives from the South, became the party of the federal CIVIL RIGHTS MOVEMENT). The lasting result was the weakening of electoral support in the "solid south" for Democrats. Whether one accepts the realignment perspective, issue evolution, or some other description of meaningful political change, the concepts provide useful frames of reference for those trying to make sense of the political world before them.

Further reading: Carmines, Edward G., and James A. Stimson. *Issue Evolution: Race and the Transformation of American Politics.* Princeton, N.J.: Princeton University Press, 1989; Key, V. O., Jr. "A Theory of Critical Elections." *Journal of Politics* 17 (1955): 3–18.

—Michael W. Wagner

reapportionment

Reapportionment refers to the reallocation of congressional seats among the states every 10 years based on the population figures provided by the decennial CENSUS. Reapportionment and REDISTRICTING, while often used interchangeably, are two distinct concepts. Redistricting refers to the redrawing of district lines, and reapportionment refers to the reallocation of congressional seats based on each state's population. Reapportionment applies only to the House of Representatives and not to the Senate. As stated by the Constitution, representation in the House is based on population, while the Senate provides equal representation for each state.

After each census, the 435 seats in the House of Representatives are reallocated to the states based on population growth or decline from the past 10 years. States that undergo the largest population increases gain seats from those states that lost population or did not grow as fast during the period. Once reapportionment is complete, the states redraw their legislative districts (i.e., redistrict) to adjust for population shifts within the state. The 2000 census produced a population of just more than 281 million for the purposes of reapportionment with an ideal CONGRESSIONAL DISTRICT size of just more than 632,000.

From the first census in 1790 until 1910, reapportionment involved increasing the size of Congress as the population of the nation increased. Congress increased the number of seats during this period to accommodate the new states added to the Union and the increasing population. The number of seats grew from 105 in 1790 to the current 435 in 1910. In the early 1900s, Congress permanently fixed the number of districts at 435, recognizing the fact that too many members would lead to an unwieldy and inefficient body. The number has remained at 435 except for a three-year period between 1959 and 1962, when it rose to 437 to account for Hawaii and Alaska gaining statehood.

For the most part, reapportionment does not generate much political controversy, since population is the sole criteria for assigning seats and no other factors go into the formula. However, the method used to assign seats has occasionally generated debate over the years. While the concept is simple, with the number of districts in a state being proportional to the population, practically this is more complicated, since a state cannot receive a fraction of a seat. Over the years, Congress has used five different formulas for apportioning seats among the states. Each method is similar and basically changes the formula for how to deal with the fractions of seats produced by the proportions of a state's population to total seats. The changes in the method represent attempts to make the process as fair as possible. From 1790 to 1830, a fixed ratio method, known as the "Jefferson method," was used, which ignored any fractions as Congress continually increased the number of seats to fit the population growth and addition of new states. In 1840 only, the "Webster method," or fixed ratio with major fraction method, was used, which assigned additional seats to states based on the largest fractions above one-half. The third method, known as the Vinton system, was in use from 1850 to 1900. Under this system, districts were allocated to states based on a quota, with the extra seats distributed among the states with the largest fraction left over. From 1910 to 1940, the major fractions method replaced the Vinton system, which moved away from the ratio system and replaced it with a priority system that assigned each state one seat and then distributed the remaining seats in succession to the state with the largest remaining quota. Since 1950, the Huntingdon, or equal proportion, system has been in place and is a more complex version of the major fractions method. This system allocates one seat per state and then assigns each state a priority number by dividing the state's population by the square root of n $(n - 1)$, with n being the number of seats given so far to the state. The priority numbers are then ranked, and the top 385 priority numbers, in which a state is assigned to every number, receive additional seats. There are few objections to this complex system, although some argue the Huntingdon system favors less populated states. In comparison to the Vinton system, small states tend to receive two or three more seats than the large ones.

The politically sensitive issue of sampling arose during the preparation for the 2000 census. Democrats wanted to use a sampling method for counting population since they claimed it was a more precise way to count the entire population, including those often missed in the actual count. The Republicans challenged this proposal, and the Supreme Court agreed that the Constitution required an actual count and not a statistical estimation for the purposes of reapportionment. In terms of reapportionment, the sampling count, if used, probably would have added population to the more populated states with large urban centers and immigrant populations. Any additional districts the sampling count would have added would have potentially helped the Democrats gain a few seats in the House since the populations added with the sampling tend to support the Democrats.

Reapportionment is not to be confused with MALAPPORTIONMENT, which is the unequal distribution of population among districts. While states receive districts based on an equal division of the population, and districts are, in turn, supposed to have equal populations, this was not always the case. In the first half of the 20th century, many states had congressional districts that had much smaller populations than other districts and the ideal size of a district. This represented an unfair advantage for those citizens in the smaller districts by giving them greater representation for their vote. Often, this malapportionment represented attempts to keep political advantage for those in power by not distributing districts within a state to represent population shifts. Starting in 1964, the Supreme Court started what has become known as the "Reapportionment Revolution" by enforcing the one-person, one-vote mandate of equally populated congressional districts. Malapportionment is essentially an issue of the past, as the courts have enacted strict population standards for congressional districts. The seven states (Alaska, Delaware, Montana, North Dakota, South Dakota, Vermont, and Wyoming) that do not have populations large enough to require a second seat are, in a sense, malapportioned compared to the other states. However, this does not represent an intentional attempt to limit the influence of some districts.

The 2000 census produced patterns of reapportionment similar to the last several decades reflecting the continuing population shifts within the country from the Rust Belt of the Midwest and New England to the Sun Belt states of the South and Southwest. Four states (Arizona, Florida, Georgia, and Texas) were the big winners in the latest reapportionment by picking up two seats each. California, Colorado, Nevada, and North Carolina each picked up a seat as well. To make up for these seat gains, 10 states lost at least one seat. New York and Pennsylvania each lost two seats, while Connecticut, Illinois, Indiana, Michigan, Mississippi, Ohio, Oklahoma, and Wisconsin each lost one seat. The 2000 census reinforced trends evident since around 1940. During that 60-year span, California went from 23 seats in 1940 to 53 seats in 2000, more than doubling its congressional delegation. Texas also experienced double-digit seat gains by going from 21 in 1940 to 32 in 2000. However, Florida showed the fastest growth by quadrupling the number of House districts from six in 1940 to 25 in 2000. New York and Pennsylvania saw the greatest loss in seats during this same time period. New York, which had the most seats in 1940 with 45, fell to only 29 seats in 2000. Pennsylvania had the secondmost seats in 1940 with 33 and now has only 19 seats. For the most part, states have either lost a few seats or gained a few seats over the years, with generally stable patterns of growth or decline based on the region in which the state is located. These trends should continue over the next 10 years as the big winners in 2000 continue to gain population, especially California, Texas, and Florida, while many of the Rust Belt states continue to either lose population or not grow at very fast rates.

Reapportionment has several significant implications for POLITICS. The size of a state's delegation in Congress is important, as this has a direct influence on the types of policies and benefits directed toward the state or region. The more members from the state, the more likely it is that a state will receive the benefits of allocative representation, or pork barrel politics, such as funding for special projects. Regional issues can also be important. As the Sun Belt areas gain seats at the expense of the Rust Belt, policies and programs benefiting these areas become more likely as the delegations gain voting strength in Congress. Historical examples of this include the ability of southern representatives to block CIVIL RIGHTS LEGISLATION, as they were able to put together strong regional voting COALITIONs in the House.

A change in the number of districts in a state has important implications for redistricting. While all states except for those with only one seat must redraw their districts due to population shifts to produce equally sized districts, states that either gain or lose a seat tend to have a tougher time completing this process. Given the inherently political nature of redistricting, the addition of a district is a way for the party drawing the lines to try to pick up a seat in Congress. For states losing a district, those drawing the lines must find a way to eliminate an existing House member's seat. This often involves the contentious process of drawing two incumbents into the same district.

Finally, reapportionment has a direct effect on PRESIDENTIAL ELECTIONS. The number of ELECTORAL COLLEGE votes a state receives comes from the size of the state's congressional delegation. Therefore, all 50 states are guaranteed three electoral votes from the two senators and mandatory one representative, with additional votes coming from the extra House seats apportioned to the state. Given the importance placed on the electoral map during presidential elections, the more Electoral College votes a state has, the bigger part that state plays during the campaign. For the 2004 election, if either George W. Bush or John Kerry carried the 13 largest states, he would have won the needed 270 Electoral College votes to win the election. While this was unrealistic based on the partisan division across the country, it demonstrates the importance of reapportionment to presidential politics.

Further reading: Anderson, Margo, and Stephen E. Fienberg. "History, Myth Making, and Statistics: A Short Story about the Reapportionment of Congress and the 1990

Census." *PS: Political Science and Politics* 33, no. 4 (2000): 783–792; Butler, David, and Bruce Cain. *Congressional Redistricting: Comparative and Theoretical Perspectives.* New York: Macmillan, 1992; Lyons, Michael, and Peter F. Galderisi. "Incumbency, Reapportionment, and U.S. House Redistricting." *Political Research Quarterly* 48, no. 4 (1995): 857–871.

—Jonathan Winburn

recall

A recall is the removal of an elected official by vote of the ELECTORATE, usually at a SPECIAL ELECTION, following a successful voter petition. The recall is one of three DIRECT DEMOCRACY tools, including the initiative and REFERENDUM, that have been adopted by many state and local governments. Provisions such as which officeholders are subject to recall, the number of signatures required for a recall to qualify for the BALLOT, signature circulation deadlines, whether grounds are needed for the recall, prohibitions on initiating recalls near regular elections, scheduling of a recall election, and whether a replacement is selected at the same election vary by jurisdiction.

Some scholars trace the roots of the recall to early Greek democracy and the practice of banishing or ostracizing politicians from Athens. Others have asserted that the first documented recall took place in Rome with the removal of Tribune Octavius in 133 B.C. With the rise of modern nation-states, the term *recall* seems to have been most closely associated with the recall of diplomats and elected officials back to their home countries and districts, respectively. In America, the first formal adoption of a recall procedure was probably by the Massachusetts Colony in the 17th century. A recall provision was also included in Pennsylvania's 1776 constitution. The ARTICLES OF CONFEDERATION of 1781 to 1787 had an indirect recall procedure allowing states to replace their legislators.

In the period after the American Revolution, many states had short terms for elective office and restrictions on running for reelection that minimized the need for a recall procedure as a safeguard against malfeasance in office. The U.S. Constitution, with longer terms for elected offices and lifetime appointments for the Supreme Court, contains provisions for expulsion of legislators along with impeachment and conviction trial procedures for the president, vice president, and federal judges. The ANTI-FEDERALISTS cited the lack of a recall as a reason to oppose adoption of the Constitution.

States and cities began adopting the recall in the late 19th and early 20th centuries as part of Progressive Era reforms to reduce corruption in government by political machines and special interests, such as railroads. John Randolph Haynes, sometimes called the "Father of the Recall," modeled the city of Los Angeles' recall, adopted in 1903, after Switzerland's recall procedure, which had been formalized in the 1850s. Oregon became the first state to add the recall to its constitution in 1908.

The majority of states that currently have the recall for statewide offices adopted it during the Progressive Era, and the recall is still more common in western and midwestern states compared to other regions. Even determining the number of governments with recall procedures is difficult because some states have adopted the recall by statute, not by constitutional amendment, and local jurisdictions in some states can adopt the recall through HOME RULE charters. References vary on the total number of states with the recall, but it appears that at least 36 states, the District of Columbia, Guam, and the U.S. Virgin Islands have the recall for some offices. According to the National Conference of State Legislatures, 18 states had allowed the recall of state officials as of 2004: Alaska, Arizona, California, Colorado, Georgia, Idaho, Kansas, Louisiana, Michigan, Minnesota, Montana, Nevada, New Jersey, North Dakota, Oregon, Rhode Island, Washington, and Wisconsin. Virginia also has a recall petition process that requires a trial instead of a recall election.

Only two governors have been recalled in the last 100 years, North Dakota's Lynn Frazier in 1921 and California's Gray Davis in 2003, neither for criminal wrongdoing. State officials who have been accused of criminal activity or major malfeasance have usually resigned or been removed from office before a recall process could take place. Arizona governor Evan Mecham was convicted by the state legislature in 1988 just ahead of a scheduled recall election. Other officials have automatically relinquished their positions upon conviction of a crime. The expense, time, and logistical effort required to qualify a recall for a statewide ballot is simply too burdensome in most cases. A total of 117 recall drives against state officeholders and legislators were initiated in California before 2003, but the seven that qualified for election were targeted toward state legislators with smaller constituencies.

Recall elections take place more often at the local government level, although there has been limited research on how often recall petitions are initiated, how many qualify for the ballot, and the percentage of recalls that are successful. An International City/County Management Association 2001–02 survey of cities with populations of more than 2,500 found that 61 percent of jurisdictions were subject to recall provisions. About 5 percent of the responding jurisdictions had had a recall petition filed against one or more elected officials within the last five years, with 29 percent resulting in a successful recall. Other scholars have estimated that a third to a half of the recalls that qualify for the ballot are successful. Historically, there seem to have been considerably more local government recalls in California, Oregon, and Michigan compared to other states.

The most famous local government recalls include the 1909 recall of the mayor of Los Angeles; the 1959 recall of segregationist school board members in Little Rock, Arkansas; the 1971 recall of several "radical" Berkeley, California, city council members; the 1978 recall election against Cleveland mayor Dennis Kucinich that failed by less than 300 votes; and the unsuccessful attempt by a gun rights group to recall San Francisco mayor Dianne Feinstein in 1983. Recall elections have been based on relatively minor reasons along with more serious charges. For example, a mayor of Chino, California, was easily recalled in 1911 for cursing in the presence of women at a contentious meeting, while council members in the city of South Gate, California, were recalled in 2003 amid allegations of widespread corruption.

Supporters claim that the recall makes officeholders more accountable to the electorate and allows for the removal of officials who break campaign promises or are found to be corrupt. The threat of a recall petition, even in states with more stringent qualifying elections, may serve to deter officials from engaging in inappropriate behavior. Critics argue that the recall restricts the ability of a governing body to enact policies that serve a long-term public purpose but are unpopular in the short term, such as tax increases. The mere initiation of a recall drive may also disrupt necessary government functions. The recall may also be used for partisan reasons or by special interests, contrary to the original purpose.

Further reading: Cronin, Thomas. *Direct Democracy: The Politics of Initiative, Referendum, and Recall.* Cambridge, Mass.: Harvard University Press, 1989; Farmer, Rod. "Power to the People: The Progressive Movement for the Recall, 1890s–1920." *New England Journal of History* 57, no. 2 (2001): 59–83; Zimmerman, Joseph F. *The Recall: Tribunal of the People.* Westport, Conn.: Praeger, 1997.

—Marcia L. Godwin

recall, California (2003)

The California recall refers to the October 7, 2003, SPECIAL ELECTION that resulted in the removal of California governor Gray Davis from office and the election of actor Arnold Schwarzenegger as his replacement. The RECALL was significant as the first successful gubernatorial recall in the United States since that of North Dakota governor Lynn Frazier in 1921 and the only successful statewide recall in the history of the nation's most populous state. The level of media attention was also extremely high due to the unusual recall procedure, the 135 candidates on the replacement BALLOT, the successful candidacy of an iconic movie star, and the level of litigation attempting to postpone the election.

The recall was adopted into California's state constitution in 1911. There have been numerous successful recalls of local officials in California, and two Republican state legislators were recalled in 1995 for cooperating with Democrats over partisan control of the California assembly.

Republican activists began efforts to recall Democratic governor Gray Davis soon after his relatively narrow reelection win in 2002. With major donations from Representative Darrell Issa (R, Vista), proponents were able to easily gather the 897,158 required signatures (12 percent of the ELECTORATE in the last statewide election) through paid signature gatherers and direct mailings to Republican voters.

Arnold Schwarzenegger, who had been active in Republican POLITICS and had sponsored a BALLOT INITIATIVE in the 2002 election, announced his candidacy in early August 2003 in a *Tonight Show* interview. The visibility of the recall election and lenient candidate qualifying requirements resulted in an unprecedented number of other candidates filing to run for governor as well. A federal appeals court ruling in mid-September threatened to postpone the election until after the complete phaseout of punch-card ballots, but the original date was restored after review by a larger panel of judges.

Governor Davis was recalled by a 55 percent to 45 percent margin. Voters cited the state's budget crisis, energy problems, and management concerns as reasons for voting for the recall. Schwarzenegger received a solid plurality and came close to winning an outright majority, with almost 49 percent of the vote. Schwarzenegger received more votes than Davis received in favor of retaining him in office, which added to the legitimacy of Schwarzenegger's election.

PUNDITs and scholars initially speculated about whether the success of the California recall would create an incentive for an increased use of the recall in other states. Instead, the lasting lessons of the recall relate more to celebrity politics, the role of the media, and the use of litigation as a political strategy. In addition, the election set a precedent with the inclusion of INDEPENDENT and minor party candidates in debates. The absence of a PRIMARY and shortened campaign season also made it easier for a moderate Republican to gain office in a Democratic state.

Further reading: Gerston, Larry N., and Terry Christensen. *Recall! California's Political Earthquake.* Armonk, N.Y.: M.E. Sharpe, 2004; Lubenow, Gerald C. *California Votes: The 2002 Governor's Race and the Recall That Made History.* Berkeley, Calif.: Berkeley Public Policy Press/Institute of Governmental Studies, 2004.

—Marcia L. Godwin

Reconstruction

Reconstruction refers to the period immediately following the Civil War in which attempts were made to politically, economically, and socially "reconstruct" the Union and the 11 defeated ex-Confederate states. The era was marked by horrific racial violence, widespread southern poverty, and general political unrest. Reconstruction lasted from the end of the Civil War in 1865 to the withdrawal of the last federal troops from the South in 1877.

By the end of the Civil War, the South was devastated. The Union army had burned cities, uprooted train tracks, and destroyed plantation homes and cotton gins to suppress Confederate resistance. At least 4 million newly emancipated slaves sought food, shelter, and work alongside an impoverished and resentful white community. Fears persisted among whites that freed slaves would revolt against them, and in the first postwar Reconstruction governments (still consisting of Confederate representatives), "black codes" were passed to severely limit the economic, social, and political mobilization of freed blacks.

In June 1866, Congress passed the FOURTEENTH AMENDMENT, which extended CITIZENSHIP to blacks. In response to the empowerment of ex-Confederate politicians in new state offices and the emergence of "black codes" in southern states, northern Republicans in Congress refused to recognize the immediate postwar southern governments (initially allowed by President Lincoln and by Johnson's administrative policies). Congress instead developed its own standards for Reconstruction and readmission to the Union. It initiated an era of congressional dominance over Reconstruction policy (Congressional Reconstruction, also known as Republican Reconstruction or Radical Reconstruction) with the Reconstruction Acts of 1867. Under the acts, passed over the veto of President Andrew Johnson, the ex-Confederate states were separated into five districts to be occupied by the U.S. Army. Conditions were set for readmission to the Union and included acceptance of the Fourteenth Amendment (and FIFTEENTH AMENDMENT, if admitted after its passage), disenfranchisement of ex-Confederate soldiers, and the establishment of a new state constitution. Under this agreement, every one of the ex-Confederate states was readmitted to the Union by 1880, though readmission to the Union did not signify the end of Reconstruction for southern states.

With ex-Confederates barred from political activity, Congressional Reconstruction governments in the South were composed of blacks, southern Unionist whites (derided as "scalawags" by white secessionists), and northern whites (derided as "carpetbaggers"). The disenfranchised white community accused the Reconstruction governments of ineptitude, corruption, and graft. Early Reconstruction historians—disproportionately southern and white—reinforced this portrayal for many years. Although there was some corruption within Reconstruction governments, it appears picayune measured by the standards of its day. In light of the egregious excesses of MACHINE POLITICS in northern cities and the numerous SCANDALS surrounding the Grant administration, the bad behavior of Reconstruction governments appears quite insignificant.

Furthermore, Reconstruction governments, although short-lived, ushered in substantial progressive reform. The political gains made during Reconstruction for emancipated blacks were profound. Black politicians emerged throughout the South to assume judgeships, law enforcement positions, and nearly all other forms of elected office. In South Carolina, blacks held a majority of seats in the state house of representatives. Reconstruction afforded blacks a degree of political freedom that they would not enjoy again for nearly 100 years.

Other important reforms marked the Reconstruction era, such as the establishment of free public schools, the abolishment of debt imprisonment, the curbing of capital punishment, and the drafting of state constitutions that incorporated the concept of equal protection. Congress also created the Freedman's Bureau to aid and protect emancipated blacks in the aftermath of the war. The bureau issued 20 million rations to needy Americans in the four years after the war, with a quarter of this aid provided to whites. The Freedman's Bureau also built hospitals and schools and helped establish institutions of higher learning, including some that continue today.

From the beginning of Congressional Reconstruction, disenfranchised southern whites violently opposed the Reconstruction governments and their supporters. They focused their aggression primarily on blacks, and through lynchings, beatings, arson, vandalism, and a host of other intimidation tactics, sought to keep black voters away from the polls. These terror campaigns were conducted across the South through secret organizations such as the KU KLUX KLAN and Knights of the White Camellia. In some areas, federal presence was so scarce that similar organizations were able to conduct themselves in public under the auspices of "rifle clubs." Their violent campaigns to end Reconstruction government in southern states were ultimately successful.

By 1876, the combination of voter intimidation, racist terror, and dwindling congressional interest in the affairs of the southern states had returned all but three to white Democratic rule. That same year, the disputed Hayes-Tilden election brought about the end of the remaining Republican Reconstruction governments. Although Democrat Samuel Tilden needed just one electoral vote to win the presidency, Republican Rutherford B. Hayes was able to capture the 22 disputed electoral votes he needed to secure the election by making a deal with white Democrats in each of the three remaining Reconstruction government states. In return for the votes, Hayes agreed to remove the last occupying federal troops from the South, and thus the last vestige of protection for the Republican Reconstruction governments. Through this final action, white Democrats returned to power in these southern states for the first time since 1867.

The racial violence of the Reconstruction era foreshadowed the systematic removal of voting rights and civil liberties from blacks by southern state governments. Marked by extreme violence, political upheaval, sectional bitterness, economic ruin, and social oppression, Reconstruction remains one of the most tragic episodes in U.S. history.

Further reading: Foner, Eric. *Reconstruction: America's Unfinished Revolution, 1863–1877.* New York: Harper & Row, 1988; Franklin, John Hope. *Reconstruction after the Civil War.* Chicago: University of Chicago Press, 1994.

—Brook B. Andrews

recount

A recount is an additional tabulation of votes cast in an election, which takes place following the original vote count when certain circumstances are met. Every state has different laws relating to elections and recounts, and therefore the methods for initiating a recount are not the same across the country. Typically, recounts take place when an election is extremely close or when there are extenuating circumstances that call into question the validity of the election results.

American history is filled with instances in which election results have been contested, and that tradition continues up to the present day. As early as the late 18th century, states—and before them, colonies—would routinely place the examination of disputed local elections at the top of their business agenda upon convening. Even founding fathers such as Thomas Jefferson and George Washington interceded in questionable elections during their times in the Virginia legislature.

While recounts have always been part of the American political system, they have evolved over time. With the importance of accurate election results in mind, the U.S. Constitution was written to give Congress the authority to determine the dates of elections and when the members of government would be sworn in, and these dates were initially established with ample time for the proper calculation, verification, announcement, and recounts, if necessary, of votes in federal elections.

Without today's voting technology, recounts were time consuming endeavors in the 18th and 19th centuries, and Congress initially established the first Wednesday in March as the date on which the president, vice president, and members of Congress would begin their terms. As voting and communication technology improved over time, this long span of time between ELECTION DAY and the installation of newly elected officials was no longer necessary. On January 23, 1923, the Twentieth Amendment to the Constitution was ratified, and it stipulated that the new Congress would meet on January 3 of the year following the election, and the president and vice president's term would commence on January 20 of the same year.

Examples of election recounts are plentiful over the years, but the 20th century offers some of the more interesting and significant cases. The closest Senate race in American history involved several recounts and eventually an entirely new election. In 1974, Democrat John Durkin and Republican congressman Louis Wyman ran for the U.S. Senate in New Hampshire. After the first count, Wyman was ahead by 542 votes, but a recount led to Durkin being certified the winner by a mere 10 votes. Still another recount reversed this certification and awarded the seat to Wyman with a two-vote margin. Eventually, the race was

The Supreme Court–ordered manual recount of ballots cast in Miami-Dade County, Florida, December 2000 *(Reuters/Corbis)*

referred to the U.S. Senate, which, according to ARTICLE I of the Constitution, is "the Judge of the Elections, Returns, and Qualifications of its own members." The Senate did some private opinion polling, deliberated, and eventually decided in August 1975 that New Hampshire should hold another election for the seat. That election took place in September 1975, and due in large part to the recent Watergate SCANDAL and then president Gerald Ford's pardon of former president Richard Nixon, Durkin defeated Wyman by nearly 10 percentage points. He would serve only one partial term, however, and he was swept out of office in the landslide created by Ronald Reagan's presidential victory in 1980.

On the House side, a slightly more recent election involved a recount with more significant long-term consequences for the parties involved. In 1986, Rick McIntyre ran as the Republican nominee for Indiana's 8th District seat in the U.S. House of Representatives. His opponent was first-term, incumbent Democratic congressman Frank McCloskey. When the votes were initially counted, Republican McIntyre was certified the winner by a margin of 34 votes by a Republican secretary of state. The Democratic-controlled U.S. House, using the same provision of the Constitution as the Senate in the Durkin-Wyman race, took up this election and ordered a recount that resulted in a four-vote lead for McCloskey. The House then voted along party lines to seat McCloskey as the winner, and the entire Republican delegation promptly walked out of the House chambers in protest. This made front-page headlines across the country, and even some of the most liberal newspaper editorial boards came out strongly against this action. The result was a more unified and motivated REPUBLICAN PARTY, and this contributed to the eventual Republican majority, led by Newt Gingrich in the early 1990s.

Concerning the race for the presidency, no recount drew more attention than the one that took place in Florida in 2000. Due to the closeness of the margin between then vice president Al Gore and former Texas governor George W. Bush, Florida state election law mandated an automatic recount of the results. While the mechanisms for this recount were set in motion, Democrats also demanded hand counts of BALLOTS in several counties, and Republicans filed suits attempting to prevent further recounts. Contributing to the controversy surrounding the election results was the fact that George Bush's brother, Jeb Bush, was governor of the state at the time. While the Gore campaign successfully appealed to the Florida state supreme court for recounts to continue, the Bush campaign took its case to the U.S. Supreme Court, and eventually it ruled 5 to 4 in Bush's favor on December 12. The final margin ended up being 537 votes, and further investigation revealed thousands of ballots without any votes for president (undervotes) or with multiple votes for president (overvotes).

The situation in Florida in 2000 demonstrates that having different recount laws in each state provides insurance against the need for a nationwide recount in these kinds of circumstances. In a handful of states, recounts take place automatically, often at random, to determine that certain voting machines or systems are operating properly. In a majority of states, currently 37, recounts can be initiated at the request of candidates provided the vote margin is within a certain range. Also, one or more voters may request recounts in 20 states. Finally, the closeness of an election result mandates that a recount take place without any other action in 15 states.

Further reading: Kutner, Luis. "Due Process in the Contested New Hampshire Senate Election: Fact, Fiction, or Farce." *New England Law Review* 11 (1975): 25–54; Sabato, Larry J. *OVERTIME! The Election 2000 Thriller.* New York: Longman, 2001.

—Matt Smyth

redistricting

Redistricting refers to the redrawing of legislative district lines after the decennial CENSUS to keep districts as equally populated as possible. The most visible redistricting usually occurs at the congressional and state legislative levels, although many local districts, such as school boards and county and city commissioners, also redistrict. Redistricting and REAPPORTIONMENT are oftentimes thought of synonymously. Although interrelated, they are two distinct concepts. Redistricting refers to the redrawing of district lines, and reapportionment refers to the reallocation of congressional seats based on each state's population, not how the districts are drawn.

With redistricting often comes GERRYMANDERing, or the drawing of district lines to benefit specific parties, incumbents, or racial groups, depending on the goals of those in charge of drawing the maps. The term dates back to 1812, when Governor Elbridge Gerry of Massachusetts signed a redistricting plan that packed, or concentrated, FEDERALIST PARTY supporters in a few districts with the hope of electing more Democratic-Republicans to office. A famous POLITICAL CARTOON by Elkanah Tisdale was published in the *Boston Weekly Messenger* depicting one of these districts in the shape of a salamander, and the term *gerrymandering* was born. The common gerrymandering techniques include packing, cracking, and stacking districts. For example, under a Democratic gerrymander the goal when packing a district would be to concentrate Republican supporters into a few districts, therefore allowing the Democrats a better chance at winning a majority of districts. Cracking districts usually involves targeting specific incumbents for defeat. For example, the Republicans may try to crack a Democratic incumbent's district into several districts to dilute the incumbent's support. Stacking refers to combining two districts with opposing party sentiments into a single district, with the majority sentiment favoring the party in power.

While the traditional American method of redistricting is for the state legislatures to redraw both their own districts and the congressional maps, a recent trend has been for redistricting to be completed by commissions or bodies independent of the legislature. The purpose of these commissions, which are used widely in other Western democracies, is to take the POLITICS out of redistricting and to overcome the inherent conflict of interest that occurs when legislators determine the districts from which they are elected. Currently, four states use commissions for congressional redistricting, and 14 states use commissions in some form for state legislative redistricting. At this early stage, the effects of commission-based redistricting in the United States are not fully known, especially in regard to partisan gerrymandering. When either the legislature or commissions cannot agree on new maps or they produce unconstitutional plans, the courts have regularly entered the redistricting fray. Following the 2000 round of redistricting, court-ordered plans were used in seven states.

While achieving equally populated districts has always been the main justification for redistricting, through the 1960s this guiding criteria was often ignored, as political operatives were more worried about incumbent, partisan, and regional goals than population equality. This led to MALAPPORTIONMENT, or the unequal distribution of population among districts, especially between rural and urban districts. As urban areas gained population, many rural legislators failed to redraw districts with equal population for fear they might lose power in the legislatures to the ever-expanding cities. The Supreme Court finally ruled on the issue in 1962 in BAKER V. CARR, when it moved from its original position that redistricting was strictly a legislative matter and not a judicial one. This ruling allowed legal challenges to state redistricting practices based primarily on the Equal Protection Clause of the FOURTEENTH AMENDMENT that guarantees everyone's vote be counted equally. This landmark case entered the Court into the political thicket and transformed how legislatures redistricted. With what became known as the Reapportionment Revolution, throughout the 1960s and early 1970s the courts established the "one person-one vote" doctrine, which mandated population equality as the dominant and overriding criterion for drawing legislative districts.

Over the years, the Court has established separate laws for congressional and state legislative redistricting. At the congressional level, the courts have ruled against population deviations, with the exception of small states in which the necessity to allocate each state at least one CONGRESSIONAL DISTRICT makes malapportionment unavoidable. For state legislative redistricting, the courts have been more lenient. Through a series of cases, a 10 percent population deviation standard now governs state districts. Essentially, state legislative districting plans may have up to a 10 percent population disparity between districts and still

be considered constitutional under the one person-one vote standard. The main difference for these standards is the legal requirements governing the plans. The courts have ruled that congressional redistricting is governed by the Constitution, which requires strict equal population, whereas state-level plans fall under the Fourteenth Amendment, with the key requirement being fairness to all voters.

The Court continued its involvement in redistricting during the 1970s and 1980s. While continuing to shape the definition of one person–one vote, the Court also moved into questions concerning the legality of gerrymandering. The Court avoided directly ruling on partisan gerrymandering until 1986, when in *Davis v. Bandemer* it ruled that political gerrymandering was justiciable based on the Equal Protection Clause. However, the ruling was so vague that no clear definition of unconstitutional partisan gerrymandering was established. Since the *Davis* case, the Court has not ruled any plans unconstitutional on the grounds of partisan gerrymandering.

For racial gerrymandering, both the courts and the Department of Justice have played important roles. The Voting Rights Act (VRA) passed in 1965 disallowed discriminatory practices in elections and allowed challenges to redistricting plans that limited minority representation. For redistricting plans, initially the courts ruled the VRA made plans unconstitutional only when they had intentionally been drawn to disadvantage minorities. However, amendments to the VRA in 1982 established that any plans that had the effect of disadvantaging minorities, whether intentional or not, could be overruled by the courts. Along with these changes in the 1980s, the courts ruled that redistricting could attempt to improve minority representation by maximizing MAJORITY-MINORITY DISTRICTS (districts that have a majority population from a group that consists of a minority in the larger population). However, the 1990s saw a more conservative Supreme Court revisit this issue. In *MILLER V. JOHNSON*, a case involving Georgia congressional districts, the Court ruled that race may not be the predominant factor in drawing congressional districts. Mapmakers may consider race for establishing majority-minority districts, but they cannot circumvent other traditional factors.

While the courts set the constitutional framework from which states redistrict, each state sets its own guidelines and laws for redistricting. In addition to equal population, the states also rely on other factors for redistricting. Every state has laws on what factors can or cannot be considered during redistricting. These factors tend to be more important in state legislative districting, in which the courts allow more leeway in the adherence to population equality but may become more important for congressional redistricting since the *Miller* ruling. These traditional redistricting principles include compactness, contiguity, and respect for communities of interest. Compact districts are those that minimize the geographic size of the district. Contiguous districts are connected throughout, and a person should be able to walk the entire district without leaving it. Neither of these are highly controversial, but occasionally a dispute arises over how to measure and maximize compactness and how to deal with districts that are connected only by a point on a map, a body of water, or a highway. The communities of interest principle holds that districts should not split natural communities or political subdivisions. Usually the law defines these in terms of local government units, such as counties and townships, but can also include ethnic neighborhoods or areas with similar economic interests. Additionally, partisanship, minority strength, and incumbency are allowable considerations in some states.

Redistricting is one of the most contentious and controversial aspects of politics and the latest round highlighted these issues. Many redistricting disputes center on the partisan control and competition in a state. States with divided government, in which political control of the executive and one or both branches of the legislature is divided between the political parties, tend to have partisan disputes over redistricting, as do states with competitive legislatures where a few seats could swing the power between the parties. Further, advances in the computer technology used to produce new maps make it easy to manipulate district boundaries for political gain. This technology allows legislators, individuals, or INTEREST GROUPS to craft plans that maximize their political interests. The resulting disputes often boil down to raw issues of power, as the ability to draw the lines and receive the potential gains in representation from the lines can make the difference in legislative agendas and public policies.

The battle over Texas congressional redistricting following the 2000 census highlights an extreme example of the type of disputes that may erupt. Heading into the 2000 census, the Democrats held a 17 to 13 seat advantage in the Texas house. Due to population gains, Texas gained two seats during reapportionment, and the state legislature had the task of redrawing the existing 30 districts along with two new districts. In 2001, a divided Texas state legislature, with Republicans controlling the senate and Democrats controlling the house, could not reach an agreement on a new congressional map in time for the 2002 elections. As a result, a group of federal judges produced a map that resulted in minimal changes to the existing lines. However, as Republicans gained control of both chambers of the Texas legislature in 2002, the issue was bound to be readdressed.

The Majority Leader of the U.S. House, Republican Tom DeLay questioned the judicial map on grounds it did not accurately reflect the true partisanship of the state. This was a major departure from years past, when redistricting was done once every 10 years and not more. Since Texas law did not specifically prohibit this, the newly unified Republican Texas legislature pushed for new plans in 2003. The Texas senate Democrats balked and walked out of the legislature and the state, once to Oklahoma and once to New Mexico, in an attempt to stop the Republicans. DeLay and the Texas Republicans eventually won out and passed a new congressional plan that many experts expect to swing the Texas House delegation to 22 to 10 in favor of the Republicans. While the Texas case is an extreme example, many states go through similar partisan fights over redistricting, and almost all redistricting plans are changed in the courts.

Further reading: Butler, David, and Bruce Cain. *Congressional Redistricting: Comparative and Theoretical Perspectives.* New York: Macmillan, 1992; Epstein, David, and Sharyn O'Halloran. "A Social Science Approach to Race, Redistricting, and Representation." *American Political Science Review* 93, no. 1 (1999): 187–191. Swain, John W., Stephen A. Borrelli, and Brian C. Reed. "Partisan Consequences of the Post-1990 Redistricting for the U.S. House of Representatives." *Political Research Quarterly* 51, no. 4 (1998): 945–967.

—Jonathan Winburn

red states

A term derived from the graphics used by the television and cable news networks during their coverage of the 2000 PRESIDENTIAL ELECTION, where red states voted for George W. Bush, the Republican candidate, while BLUE STATES supported Democrat Al Gore. These electoral maps depicted a sharply divided ELECTORATE, with the largely rural states being red and the urban states blue. This divide has been described as being a cultural as well as a political divide.

The red states, located primarily in the South, the Great Plains, and lower Midwest, are states with electorates dominated by people of faith (those who attend religious services on a regular basis), white males (so called NASCAR DADS as opposed to soccer moms targeted by the Democrats), people who are married, and gun owners. These voters have been attracted to the REPUBLICAN PARTY by its emphasis on "traditional values."

While the red state–blue state dichotomy emerged following the 2000 election, its origins date back to the 1970s. The SOUTHERN STRATEGY, developed by Richard Nixon, emphasized WEDGE ISSUES designed to alienate white ethnic and southern white voters from the NEW DEAL COALITION that had established the Democrats as the MAJORITY PARTY since the 1930s. By focusing on the national DEMOCRATIC PARTY's support for civil rights, abortion rights, and gay rights, the Republicans were able to move socially conservative Democrats to the Republican column.

The 2000 election, held following the Clinton impeachment, highlighted the differences between what political analysts describe as a closely divided, highly polarized electorate. The Bush campaign, highlighting morality and traditional family values, attracted the votes of more conservative voters from rural areas. Gore attracted the votes of those living in blue states, who supported the party's emphasis on the environment, gun control, and civil rights.

Demographically, the red states tend to be more rural than the blue states, with agriculture being among the most important industries. Red states tend to have fewer college graduates than blue states and also are home to more military personnel and veterans than are blue states. Red states also tend to have larger white and Christian populations than do blue states. As a result, the red-blue dichotomy has come to represent a cultural as well as a political divide in American life. Solid red states include Alaska, Idaho, Indiana, Kansas, Nebraska, Oklahoma, South Dakota, Utah, Virginia, and Wyoming, which have not voted for a Democratic presidential candidate since Lyndon Johnson's 1964 landslide victory over Republican Barry Goldwater.

Further reading: Brooks, David. "One Nation, Slightly Divisible." *Atlantic Monthly* 288, no. 5 (2001): 53–65; Fiorina, Morris P. *Culture War? The Myth of a Polarized America*. New York: Longman, 2005; Frank, Thomas. *What's the Matter with Kansas? How Conservatives Won the Heart of America*. New York: Metropolitan Books, 2004; Greenberg, Stanley B. *The Two Americas: Our Current Political Deadlock and How to Break It*. New York: Thomas Dunne Books, 2004; Zogby International. *America: Blue vs. Red States, Republicans vs. Democrats; Two Separate Nations in a Race for the White House*. Utica, N.Y.: Zogby International, 2003.

—Jeffrey Kraus

referendum

Referenda are legislative proposals or state constitutional amendments that are "referred" to the ELECTORATE. There are a number of different forms of referenda. Automatic, or mandatory, referenda are passed first by the legislature and then are required to be approved by citizen vote. A total of 49 states require referenda for state constitutional amendments, and many states also require referenda for certain types of tax increases. The term *legislative referendum* includes both the automatic form and when a legislative body voluntarily decides to put a measure on the BALLOT. Popular, or protest, referenda are initiated by voters to overturn legislation, with fairly restrictive time periods given between initial passage of a law and qualifying it for the ballot. The referendum can be used in some local jurisdictions to overturn a development project or zoning decision, and the timing of a referendum election is thus critical. If there is not an urgent need to act, a referendum might be scheduled for the next regular election, or opponents may choose to pursue a BALLOT INITIATIVE instead.

Early use of the legislative referendum can be traced to the 15th century in Switzerland, and it has a long history of use in America. Town meetings have been used in New England since the 1600s to adopt ordinances and other policies, although some communities have moved to separate votes as town meeting participation declined. States began using referenda for ratification of their state constitutions in the late 18th century. Only the state of Alabama did not have a requirement for a referendum for state constitutional amendments as of the early 21st century. Referenda or plebiscites may also be held related to statehood or form of government. The most significant plebiscites in recent decades have been the 1967 and 1993 votes concerning statehood for Puerto Rico. The percent in favor of keeping commonwealth status (48 percent) was just more than the votes for statehood (46 percent) in 1993, indicating that there may be support in the future for another referendum on statehood.

The popular, or protest, referendum was first adopted in the Progressive Era as part of a package of DIRECT DEMOCRACY reforms modeled after those used in Switzerland. Nebraska authorized the use of the referendum by local governments in 1897, and South Dakota in 1898 became the first state to adopt the popular referendum for statewide use. Today 24 states allow the use of the popular referendum: Alaska, Arizona, Arkansas, California, Colorado, Idaho, Kentucky, Maine, Maryland, Massachusetts, Michigan, Missouri, Montana, Nebraska, Nevada, New Mexico, North Dakota, Ohio, Oklahoma, Oregon, South Dakota, Utah, Washington, and Wyoming. Of these, 14 states had some restrictions on the types of referenda allowed, mostly prohibitions against overturning appropriations or budget decisions. However, Ohio directly allows appropriations referenda. The legislative referendum (72 percent) has also been more common than the popular referendum (47 percent) at the local government level according to a 2001–02 survey of cities by the International City/County Management Association. The most common actions subject to automatic referenda requirements included bond or debt financing measures and amendments to HOME RULE charters.

Some scholars and activists have called for a national referendum process, pointing to increases in the use of direct democracy in other countries and the referenda held in many European countries over admittance to the European Union and approval of a common currency. Political scientists Bruce Ackerman and James Fishkin have been the most prominent advocates of reforms to increase nationwide public deliberation about policy issues. They have designed deliberative public opinion poll experiments with small groups and have called for a national "Deliberation Day" holiday in PRESIDENTIAL ELECTION years to serve as an advisory tool for voters and candidates. Nevertheless, the adoption of a constitutional amendment that would allow a formal version of a national referendum process does not seem likely for at least the near future.

The referendum has not attracted nearly the level of criticism or scholarly attention as has its counterpart, the initiative (legislation or constitutional ballot measures that originate from the public through petition drives). The legislative referendum is the type most commonly used, has a longer political tradition, and has been more universally adopted. There is a deliberative process in state legislatures before referenda are placed on the ballot. The major criticism is that large numbers of constitutional amendment ballot measures can appear on the same ballot, potentially causing voter fatigue. Depending on ideological perspective, there may also be some concern about how referenda requirements for tax measures constrain budget decisions.

The popular, or protest, referendum seems to be used only when legislation is extremely unpopular, and therefore the number of popular referenda has lagged considerably behind the number of initiatives. California, the initiative leader, requires referenda for bond measures and constitutional amendments proposed by the state legislature, but the last successful state-level popular referendum was in 1950. None have qualified for the ballot since 1982. The popular referendum was resurrected in 2003 by foes of a recently adopted bill that would have issued driver licenses to illegal immigrants. However, the bill was repealed by the state legislature following the RECALL of California governor Gray Davis with the consent of the bill's sponsor, and the signature drive was suspended.

On the whole, the referendum at the state and local levels has been accepted as a legitimate tool for the electorate to participate in policy making. In a sense, it is more of an extension of representative democracy than other direct democracy tools. The referendum provides an additional safeguard and role for citizens on matters that directly affect their level of taxation and the scope of government.

Further reading: Ackerman, Bruce, and James S. Fishkin. *Deliberation Day.* New Haven, Conn.: Yale University Press; Initiative & Referendum Institute. Available online. URL: http://www.iandrinstitute.org. Accessed August 10, 2005; Sabato, Larry J., Howard R. Ernst, and Bruce A. Larson, eds. *Dangerous Democracy? The Battle over Ballot Initiatives in America.* Lanham, Md.: Rowman & Littlefield, 2001; Waters, M. Dane. *Initiative and Referendum Almanac.* Durham, N.C.: Carolina Academic Press, 2003.
—Marcia L. Godwin

Reform Party

The predecessor to the Reform Party, United We Stand America (UWSA), came into being in early 1992. The initial purpose of the organization was to gather signatures so that Ross Perot's name could appear on the BALLOT. The GRASSROOTS organization, headquartered in Dallas, Texas, was organized on a state-by-state basis, which facilitated the collection of signatures under state BALLOT ACCESS laws.

Following the 1992 election, Perot decided to maintain the organization as an "educational group," appointing Russell Verney executive director. The organization appeared to lack any clear purpose, aside from serving as a vehicle for Perot's opposition to the North American Free Trade Agreement (NAFTA).

The organization was credited with helping Republicans win a number of CONGRESSIONAL ELECTIONS in 1994, notably the SPECIAL ELECTION victories of Ron Lewis in Kentucky and Frank Lucas in Oklahoma. Perot founded the Reform Party in 1995, which was eligible for $30 million in federal funding as a result of Perot's obtaining 19 percent of the POPULAR VOTE in the 1992 election. While Perot's intent was to subsume United We Stand America into the Reform Party, appointing Verney the Reform Party's national chairman, there was opposition within the organization to this plan. Some opposed the plan because they did not wish to see the nonpartisan organization become a partisan organization. Others opposed the plan because they had supported former Colorado governor Richard Lamm for the party's presidential NOMINATION and believed that Perot's supporters (who controlled the PARTY ORGANIZATION) had rigged the Reform Party primary. This resulted in the creation of competing organizations: the Reform Party and United We Stand America in a number of states.

The stated mission of the Reform Party is to reform the current system of government by electing individuals who will pass policies that will make government more fiscally responsible and more responsive to citizens. The key issues of interest to Reform Party members are campaign finance, TERM LIMITS, a balanced budget, foreign trade, employment, and programs such as Social Security and Medicare.

Similar to other political parties, the Reform Party has a national committee consisting of four officers and 50 committee members. It also has state-level party organizations in all 50 states plus the Virgin Islands, Guam, Puerto Rico, American Samoa, and the District of Columbia. Estimates of party membership are hard to obtain, as those who vote for Reform Party candidates may come from registered Democrats, Republicans, or INDEPENDENTs who may affiliate with another third party such as the GREEN PARTY. It is clear, however, that support for the party has declined substantially since its inception in 1992.

The history of the party is tumultuous. The party gained more legitimacy after Perot garnered 19 percent of the popular vote in 1992, making the party eligible for federal funds in the 1996 PRESIDENTIAL ELECTION. However, early in the 1996 ELECTION CYCLE a significant power struggle emerged within the party over who should be nominated for that year's presidential contest (Ross Perot or Richard Lamm). While Perot beat Lamm by a significant margin in the party's PRIMARY, the struggle weakened the party. In contrast to the 1992 election, Perot obtained only 8 percent of the vote in 1996, and after the November election the party leadership broke with Perot in an attempt to broaden its appeal.

In 1998, the party became more involved in state elections, endorsing Jessie Ventura in his bid for the governorship of Minnesota. While Ventura won his election as a Reform Party candidate, he broke with the party in 2000, stating that the party lacked the necessary organizational leadership and seemed unable to move beyond the shadow of Perot. Although the Reform Party has never been able to achieve as much media attention or political salience as it did with Perot in 1992, it continues to endorse candidates in presidential races, endorsing Pat Buchanan in 2000 and Ralph Nader in 2004.

United We Stand America initiated a number of grassroots projects, notably the Electronic Town Hall Initiative Comprehensive System (ETHICS), becoming one of the first organizations to recognize the role the Internet could play in grassroots mobilization. It was also the first to use the Internet to raise money and coordinate activity by members, tactics that would become the hallmark of the Howard Dean campaign in 2004.

Further reading: Andryszewski, Tricia. *The Reform Party: Ross Perot and Pat Buchanan.* Brookfield, Conn.: Millbrook Press, 2001; Gross, Ken. *Ross Perot: The Man behind the Myth.* New York: Random House, 1992; Perot, H. Ross. *United We Stand: How We Can Take Back Our Country.* New York: Hyperion Books, 1992; Posner, Gerald. *Citizen Perot: His Life and Times.* New York: Random House, 1996; Reform Party. Available online. URL: http://www.reform party.org. Accessed August 10, 2005; Silfry, Micah. *Spoiling for a Fight: Third Party Politics in America.* New York: Routledge, 2002.

—Jeffrey Kraus and Jamie Pimlott

Republican National Committee

The Republican National Committee (RNC) is the organization responsible for promoting Republican elected officials at all levels of government. It is also considered the governing body of the REPUBLICAN PARTY in the United States, whose membership currently consists of 165 members representing all 50 states, the District of Columbia, and a variety of U.S. territories. In each state and territory, the delegation to the RNC consists of a national committeeman, national committeewoman, and the state party chair. Each of these is an elected office consisting of a four-year term. The RNC leadership consists of the national chair and a co-chair, each of whom is elected by members of the RNC. According to RNC rules, the chair is required to be of the opposite sex of the co-chair. Rank and file membership of the Republican Party trickles down to the neighborhood level, where a Republican PRECINCT captain organizes Republican workers to GET OUT THE VOTE on ELECTION DAY.

The first official Republican Party meeting took place on July 6, 1854, in Jackson, Michigan. Many historians argue that the Republican Party arose out of a strong opposition to the westward expansion of slavery in the United States after the passage of the Kansas-Nebraska Act two months prior. At the Jackson, Michigan, meeting, the Republican Party adopted its first party platform and nominated candidates for office in the state of Michigan. The Republican National Committee was founded two years later in 1856 as a body to organize and prepare for the party's quadrennial national nominating convention. The permanent headquarters of the RNC was established in Washington, D.C., in 1918.

Contemporary national nominating conventions continue to this day and consist of three main functions. The first is the NOMINATION of candidates for the offices of president and vice president, which is an important, albeit symbolic, function of the conventions. Analogous to the ELECTORAL COLLEGE, which decides the general PRESIDENTIAL ELECTION, the party primaries and caucuses do not constitute a direct election; rather than voting directly for candidates, people vote for a DELEGATE who is allied with that candidate. As opposed to the DEMOCRATIC PARTY, which favors proportional elections, in which multiple candidates can share a portion of a state's delegates, the Republican Party employs "winner-take-all" elections, in which all of a state's delegates are compelled to vote for the candidate who earns the most votes. About two-thirds of the delegates are selected in primaries held in the first six months of presidential election years. Therefore, by convention time, the candidates have been effectively selected.

The second main function is the creation and adoption of a party platform, one of the critical functions of the nominating conventions. The Republican Party platform consists of the governing principles and objectives of the party for the next four years (until the next nominating convention). The third main function includes the ratification of official procedures governing party activities, such as the nomination process for presidential candidates in a future ELECTION CYCLE.

The Republican National Committee has three standing committees. The Committee on Resolutions, otherwise known as the Platform Committee, is responsible for articulating the values and views of the Republican Party through the party's most visible declaration of these principles, the Republican Party platform. Since 1968, the chair of the Platform Committee has rotated among governors and members of the House and Senate. One male and one female delegate from each state serve on the Committee on Resolutions. The second standing committee is the Committee on Permanent Organization. The Permanent Organization Committee works during and between convention years primarily to select convention officers. The third standing committee in the Republican National Committee is the Committee on Credentials. The CREDENTIALS COMMITTEE certifies all delegates and alternates to the national convention.

In summary, the primary goal of the RNC is to elect Republicans who are running for elected offices. The committee has greatly expanded its operations to include a variety of services to the state parties. These include state representatives and senators, county officials, and a variety of judgeships. The RNC attempts to turn out voters in an effort to get Republican candidates elected. Though the mechanism by which the RNC turns out voters varies depending on the state and the office, it works to spread the Republican message using all forms of media in every state in the country. The RNC handles communications, political education, FUND-RAISING, legal assistance, and strategic planning for parties at multiple levels of government.

Further reading: Cotter, Cornelius P., and Bernard Hennessy. *Politics without Power: The National Party Committees.* New York: Atherton Press, 1964; Gerring, John. *Party Ideologies in America, 1828–1996.* Cambridge: Cambridge University Press, 2001; Republican National Committee. Available online. URL: http://rnc.org. Accessed August 10, 2005.

—Dari E. Sylvester

Republican National Committee, chair

The REPUBLICAN PARTY grew out of the collapse of the WHIG PARTY following the loss of the 1852 presidential contest. That collapse created a vacuum within the party system that was competed for by two new political parties, the antiimmigrant American Party and the Republicans. Founded in Ripon, Wisconsin, in 1854 and representing a fusion of northern Whigs and Free Soilers, the new Republican Party captured 11 states and 114 electoral votes in the 1856 PRESIDENTIAL ELECTION. The American Party faded after 1856, and the Republicans first gained the U.S. House speakership in 1859 and the presidency in 1860 with the candidacy of Abraham Lincoln, barely six years after its founding. It emerged as the most successful new party in American history.

As a late arrival in party POLITICS, the Republicans had existing models of PARTY ORGANIZATION to emulate, such as a national nominating convention and a national committee. Their first convention in 1856 nominated John C. Frémont of California for president, and they named Edwin D. Morgan of New York as their first national chair. Morgan was the first Republican state chair in New York and was subsequently elected governor and U.S. senator. Morgan presided over the party's fortunes for 12 years and for four nominating conventions in 1856, 1860, 1864, and 1876. Morgan's stewardship was the longest ever. In this capacity Morgan mentored two key New York politicians, U.S. senator Roscoe Conkling and President Chester Arthur. Morgan was succeeded by publisher Henry J. Raymond, founder of both the *New York Times* and *Harper's Magazine.* Raymond departed the chairmanship for the U.S. House in 1866.

Early Republican chairs were politically prominent, and many served in the U.S. Senate and the cabinets. Following Raymond in succession were New Jersey governor Marcus Ward, 1866–68; Massachusetts governor William Claflin, 1868–72; U.S. senator Zachariah Chandler of Michigan, 1876–79; U.S. senator J. Donald Cameron of Pennsylvania, 1879–80; former Connecticut governor Marshall Jewell, 1880–83; and U.S. senator Dwight M. Sabin of Minnesota, 1883–84. Encouraged by his allies such as National Chair Morgan and Senator Conkling, President Grant named Chandler, Cameron, and Jewell to his cabinet as secretaries of the interior and war and postmaster general, respectively. These men were the linchpins of the Stalwart FACTION of the party, and they enhanced their power by linking the presidential and organizational Republicans.

Intraparty conflict between the Stalwarts and the party's "Half-Breeds" led by President James A. Garfield and U.S. senator James G. Blaine of Maine led to a minor party functionary, Pennsylvania's B. F. Jones, holding the chairmanship (1884–88). Regaining the White House with Benjamin Harrison in 1888 brought a new wave of major Republican leaders into the party's chairmanship, including U.S. senators Matthew S. Quay of Pennsylvania, 1888–91; Ohio-born Thomas H. Carter of Montana, 1892–96; and the indomitable Mark Hanna of Ohio, 1896–1904. Serving simultaneously as national chair and U.S. senator, Mark Hanna was able to rehabilitate the political career of former U.S. representative William McKinley by helping him win the governorship of Ohio in 1891 and the presidency in 1896. Hanna prevented eastern Republican leader, House Speaker Thomas B. Reed, from gaining the 1896 NOMINATION. But Hanna was unable to prevent Spanish-American War hero and New York governor Theodore Roosevelt from obtaining the 1900 vice presidential nomination. Upon learning of McKinley's assassination in 1901, Hanna apparently exclaimed, "That damned cowboy is in the White House." Hanna maintained the national chairmanship and flirted with challenging Roosevelt for the nomination until his death in February 1904.

Hanna's death led Teddy Roosevelt to place his postmaster general, Henry C. Payne of Wisconsin, in the post, but Payne's untimely death in October 1904 led to the selection of Secretary of Commerce and Labor George Cortelyou of New York as chair. Cortelyou succeeded Payne as both postmaster general and as national chair. Cortelyou left to become secretary of the Treasury and was succeeded in 1907 by Harry S. New of Indiana, who, like Roosevelt, was a Spanish-American War veteran. New was elected to the U.S. Senate in 1916 and later served as postmaster general under both Presidents Harding and Coolidge.

The 1908 election of William Howard Taft brought two New Englanders into the chair, Frank Hitchcock of Massachusetts (1908–09) and John F. Hill, the former governor of Maine (1909–12). Hill's death in 1912 led to the selection of Victor Rosewater of Nebraska, the first Jewish chair, who chaired during the 1912 fratricidal battle between Taft and Teddy Roosevelt. Taft's disastrous showing of 23.2 percent and eight electoral votes led to Rosewater's replacement by Charles D. Hilles of New York (1912–16), followed by William R. Willcox, also of New York (1916–18).

Indiana state chair Will Hays replaced Willcox, was named postmaster general by President Warren Harding, and served until he was named head of the Motion Picture Producers and Distributors of America. During Hays's 23-year stint in that post (1922–45) he sought to "clean up" Hollywood by instituting the Hays Code in 1930 to bring "moral obligations" to the movies. Hays's departure led to the assumption of the post by its vice chair, John T. Adams of Iowa (1920–24), who in turn was followed by U.S. senator William M. Butler of Massachusetts (1924–28), a long-time ally of President Calvin Coolidge. Butler was succeeded by Hubert Work of Colorado (1928–29) who had followed Hays as postmaster general and was named secretary of the interior by Coolidge. Work's successor, Claudius H. Huston of Tennessee, was the first southern chair (1929–30) and was rewarded for the party's strong showing in the South in the 1928 contest against Democratic governor Al Smith of New York, but the 1929 stock market crash and its ensuing political difficulties led to his replacement by U.S. senator Simeon D. Fess of Ohio (1930–32). Former U.S. representative Everett Sanders of Indiana, who had served as secretary to President Coolidge, was chair during the dismal early days of the New Deal (1932–34) and was succeeded by career diplomat Henry P. Fletcher of Pennsylvania (1934–36). Yet another landslide defeat for the party in 1936 led to Fletcher's replacement by former Kansas state chair John Hamilton, who presided during its late 1930s comeback.

A key architect of that comeback, House Minority Leader Joseph W. Martin, Jr., of Massachusetts, a protégé of Calvin Coolidge, had been responsible for cobbling together the "Conservative Coalition" alliance with SOUTHERN DEMOCRATS that thwarted much of Franklin Roosevelt's liberal legislation in his second term. Martin served as the permanent chair of the 1940 convention that nominated utility executive Wendell Willkie, the party's DARK-HORSE CANDIDATE, and Senate minority leader Charles L. McNary of Oregon. Martin was named permanent chair in the four subsequent conventions through 1956. It was in the 1940 campaign that Roosevelt made his famous remark about the firm of "Martin, Barton and Fish," linking Joe Martin to New York congressmen Bruce Barton and Hamilton Fish. Martin was replaced in 1942 by former Iowa state chair Harrison E. Spangler, the last Spanish-American War veteran in that post. The nomination of New York governor Thomas E. Dewey in 1944 led to Nebraska-born Herbert Brownell of New York becoming chair.

Brownell stepped aside in 1946 and later served as President Dwight Eisenhower's first attorney general. Succeeding Brownell was B. Carroll Reece, a long-time House member from Tennessee and the second southerner to lead the party. Reece had to deal with the 1948 political fallout from the battle between moderate Governor Dewey and conservative U.S. senator Robert A. Taft of Ohio.

Governor Dewey's renomination in 1948 led to U.S. representative Hugh D. Scott of Pennsylvania being named chair. Scott returned to the House in 1949 after Dewey's second defeat, was elected to the U.S. Senate in 1958, and succeeded U.S. senator Everett Dirksen of Illinois as Minority Leader in 1969.

Guy Gabrielson of New Jersey (1949–52) followed Scott in the post and presided over the fractious conflict between Senator Taft and General Eisenhower at the 1952 convention. After his nomination, Eisenhower named auto dealer Arthur E. Summerfield of Michigan to be chair for the campaign (1952–53), and Summerfield was rewarded with the job of postmaster general in his first cabinet. C. Wesley Roberts of Kansas passed briefly through the post in 1953 and was quickly succeeded by former U.S. representative Leonard W. Hall of New York (1953–57). It was Hall who saved Vice President Nixon from the "Dump Nixon" movement of 1956. Hall's successor, H. Meade Alcorn, Jr., of Connecticut (1957–59), led the party during the disastrous 1958 midterm election that gave Democrats solid majorities in both houses of Congress and the nation's governorships.

U.S. senator Thruston B. Morton of Kentucky succeeded Alcorn and was responsible for extending the party's influence into the South. Morton (1959–61) successfully navigated the 1960 convention through the potentially dangerous shoals of the conflict between Vice President Nixon and Governor Nelson A. Rockefeller of New York.

Morton's successor, William E. Miller, a Catholic congressman from western New York, delighted in tweaking Democratic presidents Kennedy and Johnson. Miller was so successful at unnerving President Johnson that U.S. senator Barry M. Goldwater of Arizona named Miller to be his running mate in 1964 precisely for that reason. Miller turned the chairmanship over to a young Arizona attorney and Goldwater loyalist, Dean Burch, in 1964. Goldwater's 44-state defeat led to a call for a nonideological "nuts and bolts" manager for the party. Named to the post in 1965 was longtime Ohio chair Ray C. Bliss. Bliss's strategy worked. He helped make large gains in the 1966 CONGRESSIONAL ELECTIONS and recapture the presidency with Richard Nixon in 1968. Bliss was replaced in 1969 by U.S. representative Rogers C. B. Morton of Maryland, the younger brother of former chair Thruston Morton, who served until 1971, when he was named secretary of the interior. He later served as President Gerald Ford's secretary of commerce. Morton was chair during the unfortunate 1970 midterm election that cost the party several governorships and further cemented its minority status in the U.S. Congress.

Replacing Morton was U.S. senator Robert Dole of Kansas (1971–73), who assumed the post in 1971, apparently unaware of the machinations in the Nixon White House concerning "dirty tricks" and "enemies lists." President Nixon ignored the party in his 1972 reelection campaign by creating the "Committee to Re-elect the President." Known to reporters as "CREEP," the president's committee operated independently of the party, and thus it (and Senator Dole) escaped responsibility for the "Watergate crisis" that would end the Nixon presidency in August 1974.

Following Dole as chair was Massachusetts-born former U.S. representative George H. W. Bush of Texas. Bush had lost his second U.S. Senate contest in 1970, and as chair he had to defend Nixon throughout the nightmarish Watergate hearings. Bush was also on the job early in the disastrous 1974 congressional elections that led to the "Watergate babies" giving Democrats a veto-proof Congress. Bush turned over the party's reins in 1974 to Mary Louise Smith of Iowa (1974–77), the first female chair.

President Ford's defeat in 1976 led to the 1977 naming of defeated U.S. senator William Brock of Tennessee, who held the post until 1981. Brock served in President Reagan's cabinet as U.S. trade representative and later as secretary of labor. It was during the Reagan administration that the chairmanship was altered. Reagan loyalist Richard Richards of Utah (1981–83) was the first to serve under a Reagan-dominated party. In 1983, the party named two chairs, a national chair to manage the party's business and a general chair to be its public spokesman. Both chairs were from Nevada, with longtime Reagan ally U.S. senator Paul Laxalt serving as general chair while businessman and fund-raiser Frank Fahrenkopf, Jr., served as national chair. The two-chair experiment did not last long, but Fahrenkopf did. His six-year stint (1983–89) was the longest in the 20th century and the third-longest in history, behind those of Edwin Morgan and Mark Hanna. Fahrenkopf's most important legacy was to create the COMMISSION ON PRESIDENTIAL DEBATES with Democratic chair Paul Kirk in 1988.

The 1988 nominating battle matched former chairs Bob Dole and George H. W. Bush, a bitter contest won by Bush. During the 1988 presidential contest between Vice President Bush and Governor Michael Dukakis of Massachusetts, a young South Carolina political strategist, Lee Atwater, led the Bush campaign to victory. Atwater's hardball tactics earned him the nickname of "Bad Boy," but the Bush campaign was so impressed that he was named chair in 1989. However, cancer ended Atwater's life in 1991, and he was replaced by Clayton Yeutter of Nebraska (1991–92), the secretary of agriculture. Yeutter was no Atwater, and he and Rich Bond, the chair for 1992 to 1993, were no match for Bill Clinton's skilled operatives in 1992.

Named to confront the Clinton presidency in 1993 was Haley Barbour of Mississippi, further evidence of the Deep South's growing influence on the party. Barbour had served as Reagan's director of political affairs and had assisted U.S. representative Newt Gingrich of Georgia's Republican takeover of the U.S. House in 1994. Barbour was elected governor of Mississippi in 2003. Jim Nicholson, a Colorado realtor, succeeded Barbour in 1997 and withstood a challenge to his leadership in 1999. Since then, the tenure of chairs has been short, with Jim Gilmore of Virginia (2001–02), Governor Marc Raciot of Montana (2002–03), and Ed Gillespie of the District of Columbia chairing the party for the 2004 election.

Following the reelection of President George W. Bush, Maryland lawyer Ken Mehlman was named head of the RNC. Like Haley Barbour, Mehlman had worked as the White House's director of political affairs (2001–03) and was widely credited with mobilizing 1.4 million volunteers in the 2004 contest to bring about the highest voter turnout since 1968 and to give President Bush the 51 percent majority that had eluded him in 2000.

Further reading: Bone, Hugh A. *Party Committees and National Politics.* Seattle: University of Washington Press, 1958; Brady, John. *Bad Boy: The Life and Politics of Lee Atwater.* Reading, Mass.: Addison-Wesley, 1997; Cotter, Cornelius P., and Bernard C. Hennessy. *Politics without Power: The National Party Committees.* New York: Atherton Press, 1964; Goldman, Ralph M. *The National Party Chairmen and Committees: Factionalism at the Top.* Armonk, N.Y.: M.E. Sharpe, 1990; Klinkner, Philip A. *The Losing Parties: Out-Party National Committees.* New Haven, Conn.: Yale University Press, 1994.

—Garrison Nelson

Republican National Convention

The Republican National Convention occurs every four years to officially nominate candidates for president and vice president, adopt the party platform, settle party rules, and provide a place for party activists and leaders from around the country to build the party and plan for the upcoming election. In their heyday, party nominating conventions were the battlegrounds for choosing the party's presidential ticket, but they now serve as a four-day media extravaganza to showcase a unified party and to introduce the presidential nominee and his campaign message.

The history of the Republican National Convention is a history of the methods used by the party to select its presidential and vice presidential nominees, or more accurately, the methods used to select convention DELEGATEs. Since the first Republican convention in 1856, delegates have been the official nominating body for the party's presidential ticket, selecting the nominees by a simple majority. The delegates were not representative of the vox populi. Rather, they were selected by either state and local caucuses and conventions or appointed by the state party. Conventions in the 19th century were raucous affairs in which the convention chair exercised considerable power through his ability to interpret party rules and recognize—or refuse to recognize—motions from the floor. Although most were not divisive enough to tank the GOP's fortunes in the GENERAL ELECTION, a growing sentiment of "one man, one vote" and the demand for broader participation set the stage for a new means of choosing convention delegates.

Suspicions of smoke-filled rooms and demands for direct voter participation fueled by the PROGRESSIVE MOVEMENT paved the way for the first PRESIDENTIAL PRIMARY between Republicans William Howard Taft and Theodore Roosevelt. In 1905, Wisconsin became the first state to legislate the election of Republican electors through PRIMARY voting. By the start of Taft and Roosevelt's 1912 contest, seven states had established primaries with direct election of delegates and/or presidential preference votes, and five others would follow suit before the end of the campaign. Roosevelt won landslide victories against the incumbent president, including in Taft's home state of Ohio, taking nine of the 10 primaries where both were on the BALLOT.

Roosevelt's success in these early contests was no match for Taft's control of the REPUBLICAN NATIONAL COMMITTEE and hence control of the convention that year in Chicago. With a temporary convention chair allied to Taft, Roosevelt's fate was sealed as the incumbent president went on to win his party's NOMINATION that year. The 1912 Republican convention in many ways is illustrative of today's conventional wisdom. Taft's inability to attract primary voters spelled disaster in his GENERAL ELECTION CAMPAIGN: He finished third in the popular and electoral votes that November. It became known that whoever controlled the party machinery controlled the nomination, regardless of the primary results. But perhaps most portentous, primaries were popular, and voters would cast a ballot when they saw it had a real consequence. Although newly elected president Wilson would call for the establishment of primaries and the abolition of conventions in his inaugural address, the primary season would not play a role again until 1952, when a rematch of sorts of the 1912 contest was set to take place.

Robert Taft, the Republican leader in the Senate, and Dwight Eisenhower, the widely admired supreme commander of NATO and leader of the Allied forces in World War II, went head-to-head in only a few primaries that year. Eisenhower picked up a decisive win in the first primary in New Hampshire and made a surprise showing in Minnesota, while Taft took almost all of the midwestern primaries. Unlike his father 40 years earlier, Taft did not have the advantage at the convention. Eisenhower was much more popular, both with Republicans around the country and with Republican governors who could help him orga-

President Gerald Ford's supporters at the Republican National Convention, Kansas City, Missouri *(Prints and Photographs Division, Library of Congress)*

nize at the state level. Further sealing Taft's fate was polling that showed Eisenhower would fare better in the November general election. With the television lights illuminating him for the country to see, Taft watched as Eisenhower's popularity allowed him to take control of the party machinery and eventually secure the nomination.

The greatest impetus for change to both parties' nominating processes and subsequent conventions came from the 1968 Democratic convention. With the conflict in Vietnam and sorrow over the assassination of Robert Kennedy lingering in the air, Hubert Humphrey was named the party's nominee despite skipping every state primary. As a concession to ensure his ascension to the nomination, Humphrey allowed a minority report from the Rules Committee to pass calling for the creation of a commission to study and suggest reforms to the nominating process. With Humphrey's narrow loss in the general election that year, two commissions were eventually established to enact reforms, the most powerful of which was the McGovern-Fraser Commission.

The commission's final report, *Mandate for Reform*, outlined 18 steps for the state parties to take in anticipation of the 1972 election that would strip the traditional party "kingmakers" of their power and hand it to the voters. While their intent was to create more of a caucus or convention system within each state, the local Democratic parties found it easier to establish primaries. When the primary season opened in 1972, more than 20 states had enacted primaries to select delegates to the national conventions. In 1976, six more primaries were added, and more than 26 million ballots were cast between the two parties' competitive contests. That year marked the end of the era of conventions and the beginning of true presidential primaries.

The call for reform of the Republican National Convention was not heard again until the 1990s. Changes to party rules and demands for reform are more frequently heard from the losing party in the last PRESIDENTIAL ELECTION; Republicans had lost only once since the onset of the primary era, in 1976.

The modern-day Republican National Convention has the same ostensible purpose as the conventions of the late 19th and early 20th centuries, but practically is for an entirely different purpose. Round-the-clock news coverage ensures that the convention is planned to run smoothly. Platform debates are saved for committees far removed from the convention floor, and the party's nominations for president and vice president are decided well in advance. To be sure, the campaign team of the presumptive nominee has great sway in the arrangements, the speakers, and any other facet that may attract the attention of the media's careful eye.

Conventions in both parties begin with the "call," an announcement 18 months prior, specifying the date and location. For the 2004 Republican National Convention in New York City, the call was a document some 32 pages long detailing the rules for delegate and alternate allocation and election. The party in power in the White House holds its convention in mid- to late August, while the out-of-power party convenes in mid- to late July. Following the call, the nonprofit host committee that was established to attract a political convention to its city begins to work in coordination with the party to host the event. This host committee commits to privately fund the costs associated with holding a national political nominating convention. Its goal is to promote the city while connecting businesses with the national party to provide the goods and services needed for a successful convention.

The FEDERAL ELECTION COMMISSION (FEC) provides both the Democrats and the Republicans with federal funding. In 2004, both parties were provided with approximately $15 million in FEC funds. The host committee raised the remainder of the $80 million budget in private donations, with $27 million for security provided by New York City.

The Committee on Arrangements (COA), a committee of the Republican National Committee, plans for and manages the Republican National Convention. By law, the COA is separate from the host committee and is prohibited from raising money to fund the convention. The COA issues credentials to members of the media, convention delegates and alternates, and special guests. It is also responsible for logistical arrangements during the convention, including coordinating security. In order to provide continuity from convention to convention, the Permanent Organization Committee of the Republican National Committee is charged with selecting convention officers.

The temporary rules of the national convention listed in the rules of the Republican National Committee require reports from the following committees: the Committee on Credentials, the Committee on Rules and Order of Business, and the Committee on Resolutions. Once the reports of these committees are acted on and disposed, the convention proceeds to the nomination of a presidential and then vice presidential candidate.

The Committee on Credentials is responsible for certifying the state and territorial delegations to the convention and hearing and acting on any challenge to a delegation. In modern times, this has become a mere formality. The Committee on Rules and Order of Business is responsible for adopting and amending the official rules of the Republican National Committee and the rules of the convention.

The Platform Committee, also known as the Committee on Resolutions, drafts the platform for approval during the convention. As with all committee assignments, each state and territory elects one man and one woman to serve on the Platform Committee, with the chairs and cochairs rotating among serving members in the House and Senate and a Republican governor. The committee chair will create subcommittees—in 2004, Chair Bill Frist created five—to focus on the major themes of the platform. These subcommittees flesh out the details of their respective topics and report back to the Platform Committee. Upon completion of the platform and approval by the committee, the document is sent to the floor of the convention.

Even while the national nominating conventions in both parties have become more and more a media extravaganza, networks have reduced their television coverage as television ratings have dropped. Composite Nielsen ratings for both the Republican and Democratic conventions reached their zenith in 1968, the year of the contentious Democratic convention in Chicago, and have declined steadily ever since. The major networks—ABC, NBC, and CBS—cover the speeches of the most prominent politicians, which are intentionally scheduled during the prime time hours of 7 P.M. to 11 P.M. Eastern Standard Time. The cable television networks—CNN, Fox News, and MSNBC—cover these and will cut in from time to time during the day for important convention votes and activities, as well as the less prominent speeches. C-SPAN covers the entire convention's proceedings from start to finish.

News executives and producers attribute the decline in coverage to lower ratings, which for television stations means smaller advertising revenue during the conventions. The parties contend that the conventions are still important events in the political process and deserve around-the-clock attention from all stations. Furthermore, they argue that the news media are shirking their duty to the American public. But today's conventions are not the exciting affairs of the past. The presidential and vice presidential nominees of the parties are determined well in advance; drama and spectacle are never seen on the convention floor, nor should they be, as the parties have intentionally scripted each day's events to show party unity in preparation for the November general election.

Media coverage of the conventions is only the first sign in a growing trend of irrelevance for the national nominating conventions of both parties. Growing antipathy toward the nominating process has fueled renewed calls for reform. Recent presidential primaries demonstrate the power that the IOWA CAUCUSES and the NEW HAMPSHIRE PRIMARIES have in determining a party's nominee. Since the primary era began in 1972, no candidate in either party has finished lower than second place in the New Hampshire primary and then gone on to win his party's nomination. With the exception of Democrats Bill Clinton in 1992 and George McGovern in 1972, no party has nominated a candidate who did not win either in Iowa or New Hampshire.

Three viable proposals for reforming the nomination process have emerged: a one-day national primary, a regional primary in which Iowa and New Hampshire would retain their first-in-the-nation status and regions would rotate in order every four years, and the so-called Delaware Plan of the Republicans, whereby states would vote in groups arranged in inverse order according to their populations.

Although the conventions of today and in coming years certainly will not play the role in selecting a party's nominee as did the conventions through 1968, they remain a vital part of America's presidential elections. With or without reforms to the nominating process, conventions still serve for most voters as an introduction to the candidates, a reminder of the values and platforms of the parties, and a crucial time to prepare for the upcoming election.

Further reading: Cook, Rhodes. *The Presidential Nominating Process: A Place for Us?* Lanham, Md.: Rowman & Littlefield, 2004; Shafer, Byron E. *Bifurcated Politics: Evolution and Reform in the National Party Convention.* Cambridge, Mass.: Harvard University Press, 1988; Sabato, Larry J., and Bruce Larson. *The Party's Just Begun: Shaping Political Parties for America's Future.* 2nd ed. New York: Longman, 2001.

—Peter Jackson

Republican Party

At the 2004 presidential convention, the Republican Party observed its 150th birthday as a political organization in the United States. During that span, it has won 22 PRESIDENTIAL ELECTIONS to 15 for the Democrats, a winning percentage of nearly 60 percent. A century and a half of POLITICS has seen the Republican philosophy undergo dramatic changes. Abraham Lincoln's vigorous leadership during the Civil War established nationalism as a means to abolish slavery and save the Union. The party became synonymous with the promotion of business interests in the 19th and 20th centuries. By the 1980s, Ronald Reagan was contending that the proper role of Washington was to cede power back to state capitols. At the turn of the century, the Republicans were the party of smaller national government (at least for social programs), lower taxes, increased spending for national security, and individual responsibility.

From the period of the party's founding in 1854 to the CRITICAL ELECTION of 1896, the Republicans were concerned with issues of race and RECONSTRUCTION. They won the Civil War, garnered enough votes to approve the FOURTEENTH AMENDMENT to the Constitution, and passed acts ensuring the rights of black Americans in the defeated southern states. Thaddeus Stevens, a radical Republican, summarized the spirit of the age when he said, "The whole fabric of southern society *must* be changed, and never can it be done if this opportunity is lost." The Republican Party of the mid- to late 19th century was the civil rights party.

As the Civil War faded into memory, the issues of the American South seemed less important than the spreading economic hard times. The party moved away from Reconstruction and toward an agenda emphasizing finance and trade. In 1870, the national income stood at $7 billion, and when the century closed, that figure had grown to $17 billion. The Republicans were the party of governmental activism and economic nationalism during this time. They used the same arguments employed during the Civil War to contend that the national government should be used to distribute public lands, promote the expansion of railroads, and encourage the growth of industry through protective tariffs.

The Republicans controlled the presidency for all but four years between 1876 and 1892. The only elections to escape them were the two terms of Grover Cleveland, and they had a majority in Congress for all but four of these years. Mark Twain and Charles Dudley labeled the period the Gilded Age, and it became synonymous with opulence and economic inequality. The Republican Party's strength was rooted in the Northeast and industrial Midwest, while the

Democrats had the South. States such as Indiana, Ohio, and Illinois were disputed battleground states, along with the Atlantic states of New York, New Jersey, and Pennsylvania.

The success of the Republican Party led to the origin of the term *GOP* in these years. The *New York Herald* newspaper on October 15, 1884, used the acronym for GRAND OLD PARTY to describe the nation's governing majority. It was an ironic label, since the DEMOCRATIC PARTY was founded some 22 years before the Republicans, but the failure of the Democrats to win office led to their derision in the popular press. A joke at the time said the Democratic Party was like alcohol: It killed everything that was alive and preserved everything that was dead. In the late 19th century, the GOP elected Rutherford B. Hayes, James A. Garfield and Benjamin Harrison. The party had a higher degree of internal unity that its opponents and waged expensive and successful election campaigns.

The Panic of 1893, during Democrat Grover Cleveland's administration, led to a Republican landslide in the MIDTERM ELECTION the next year and was a prelude to Republican William McKinley's defeat of Populist William Jennings Bryan in 1896. Voters believed that Bryan's cheap-credit platform threatened their savings and the national economy. The election witnessed the nation's first modern CAMPAIGN MANAGER, Marcus A. Hanna, who collected money from industrial leaders to buy newspaper ads that portrayed Bryan as an enemy of the urban worker. The Republicans strengthened their hold on the urban areas of the Northeast and the Midwest in this critical realigning election.

During the next four decades, between the 1890s and the 1930s, the Republicans held the presidency for every election except Woodrow Wilson's two terms and had a majority in Congress for all but six years. In November 1904, the Republican Party stood at the apex of power in American politics. Theodore Roosevelt's defeat of Alton B. Parker was the first true landslide in the modern sense of the term. The Republican nominee swamped his rival in both the popular and electoral votes, and the GOP held secure majorities in the House and Senate at the same time. The Roosevelt presidency became synonymous with the Progressive Era, when corrupt practices were reformed, large corporations were corralled, and the powers of the federal government were expanded. Midwestern Republicans regarded themselves as the progressive wing of the party, and they applauded Roosevelt's actions. But their ambitions led to a division within the GOP, and Woodrow Wilson became a minority president in 1912 with 41.9 percent of the POPULAR VOTE, but 435 electoral votes from 40 states.

The outbreak of World War I in late July 1914 galvanized the ELECTORATE in support of the Democratic president. Republicans were ineffective opponents until Wilson presented the Senate with the Versailles Treaty in 1919. Henry Cabot Lodge summarized the isolationist sentiments of the country when he declared, "we would not have our country's vigor exhausted, or her moral force abated, by everlasting meddling and muddling in every quarrel, great and small, which affects the world." The Versailles Treaty came up seven votes short of approval, and the Republicans used the victory to elect Warren G. Harding to office by 7 million votes in 1920. "It wasn't a landslide," said Wilson's secretary, "it was an earthquake."

Republicans ruled during America's Jazz Age. The 1920 CENSUS revealed a nation whose population was increasingly urban, with half of its population living in cities and towns of 2,500 or more. After a slow start in the first two years of Harding's presidency, the economy boomed through 1927. The presidencies of Harding, Coolidge, and Hoover ushered in an age of Republican dominance. In this time, no star shone brighter than that of Herbert Hoover, who in 1928 was one of the dazzling success stories of the Republican Party. Orphaned at a young age, he amassed a personal fortune and devoted his life to philanthropy and public service. As commerce secretary and public person, Hoover became the best-known government official in Washington. In 1928, he overwhelmed Al Smith in the election. The Republican president won nearly 60 percent of the popular vote and beat the Democrat by 357 electoral votes.

The triumph was short-lived. Under Hoover's watch on October 24, 1929, Wall Street traders found that there were no buyers for their stocks, and with the collapse of Wall Street came the Great Depression. In the 1930 midterm election the GOP suffered a 51-seat loss in the House. In 1932, Franklin Roosevelt (FDR) out-polled Hoover by 7 million votes, and the Democrats gained big majorities in both houses of Congress. The ghost of Herbert Hoover would haunt the Republican Party for 30 years.

The NEW DEAL COALITION of urban workers, ethnic minorities, African Americans, Catholics, and the Democratic South would be the base of Democratic support in the coming years. The Democrats became the country's MAJORITY PARTY, and their political and policy agenda favored a significant social and economic role for the national government. FDR's election began a 36-year period of Democratic presidencies that was interrupted only by Dwight D. Eisenhower's two terms in the 1950s. In this period, the Democrats dominated Congress, losing control only twice, in 1947–48 and 1953–54.

Republicans learned to live their political lives as a permanent minority, walking into the chamber to face inevitable defeat on floor votes. Occasional victories were won by making alliances with conservative SOUTHERN DEMOCRATS, and defining themselves as being against communism, budget deficits, and the expansion of the federal government. The Democratic New Deal Coalition began to erode in the mid-1960s, as conservative southern Democrats became disenchanted with the party's pro–civil rights agenda and began to change parties.

The New Deal Coalition, however, was not replaced by Republican hegemony. Instead, voters tended to reduce their partisan identification and began to support individual candidates rather than parties. In the 1970s and 1980s the country experienced divided government, defined as a time when one POLITICAL PARTY controls one branch of government and the other political party controls a different branch. The electorate deadlocked the process by selecting Republicans to executive offices and Democrats to legislative majorities. Divided government was the norm in the Nixon (1968–74), Ford (1974–76), Reagan (1980–88), and Bush (1988–92) administrations.

The modern Republican Party was born in the rubble of Barry Goldwater's lopsided defeat in 1964. "The GOP will either go forward as the conservative party or it will disappear," wrote the *National Review* after the vote, "and conservatism will be forced to create another vehicle." The conservative core IDEOLOGY was adopted by the party in the election and defended by a Hollywood actor named Ronald Reagan. Following the Watergate SCANDAL and the political demise of President Richard M. Nixon, a rebirth was spawned in the "malaise" of the Carter administration and realized in the election of Ronald Reagan in 1980.

The triumph of the Republicans in 1980 was across the board. The GOP turned out 12 Democratic senators and regained control of the U.S. Senate for the first time since 1955. The party platform reflected Reagan's conservative political beliefs. Another characteristic of the time was the president's attraction among religious conservatives and his stances against abortion and for prayer in public schools. Republican foreign policy advocated a military presence against terrorism and a challenge to communism.

At the end of Reagan's eight years, the Republican Party's future was open and bright, but some question remained as to who would pick up the legacy. George H. W. Bush stepped into the limelight and established a family legacy that would stretch 20 years into the future. The most memorable line from the Republican convention was the phrase, "Read my lips. No new taxes." The phrase, borrowed from Hollywood star Clint Eastwood's films, produced exuberant applause at the time but also made Bush hostage to unexpected events when he became president. Economic troubles in 1990 produced a compromise in which the president went back on his pledge and learned that raising taxes as a Republican was tantamount to political suicide. The high levels of approval that Bush achieved after the Gulf War victory slipped away in 1991 as the White House was immobilized by economic woes.

A brief downturn in the economy in 1991 and a third-party challenge by billionaire H. Ross Perot opened the door for Democrat Bill Clinton to become president in 1992 with only 43 percent of the popular vote. The election showed that the GOP was solidly in control of two geographical areas, the Rocky Mountain West and the Deep South. Democrats ruled in the Northeast and the Pacific Coast, while the Ohio River valley and states in the Midwest were battleground contests in each election. As the Clinton administration struggled to gain momentum early in his first term, Congressman Newt Gingrich saw a chance to accomplish what had previously seemed politically unthinkable: winning a GOP majority in the House of Representatives.

The 1994 midterm elections saw the Republicans gain 52 seats in the House of Representatives and regain control of it for the first time in 40 years. The GOP also won back the Senate, and Republicans took key governors' races in New York and Texas, where George W. Bush ousted rival Ann Richards. In 1996, Clinton seemed vulnerable, but Republican nominee Bob Dole was unable to overcome the power of incumbency and the influence of a booming economy.

The 2000 PRESIDENTIAL ELECTION was the closest in the nation's history. Democratic nominee Al Gore won the popular vote, only to have George W. Bush achieve victory in the ELECTORAL COLLEGE following a controversial Supreme Court decision. The televised vote-counting in Florida divided the nation. The dispute reached the Supreme Court, where the Florida election vote for Bush was sustained by a 5 to 4 decision. On January 21, 2001, George W. Bush became the 18th Republican chief executive since the party's founding.

At its 150th birthday, the Republican Party represented itself as the sustainer of American values and conservative ideals. GOP ideology is unabashedly conservative, pro-business, favoring states' rights, military spending, fewer social programs, and free trade. The party opposes abortion, pornography, and homosexual rights.

Further reading: Foner, Eric. *Free Soil, Free Labor, Free Men: The Ideology of the Republican Party before the Civil War.* New York: Oxford University Press, 1995; Gould, Lewis. *Grand Old Party: A History of the Republicans.* New York: Random House, 2003; Republican National Committee. Available online. URL: http://www.rnc.org. Accessed August 10, 2005.

—J. David Woodard

Republican Party, platforms

The REPUBLICAN PARTY platform is considered to be the most prominent and nationally approved "guide" to issues that are adopted by the Republican Party. The party platform is created and ratified at the REPUBLICAN NATIONAL CONVENTION, which meets every four years, in a PRESIDENTIAL ELECTION year. At the Republican National Convention, DELEGATES from all 50 states and U.S. territories meet to establish the party platform that will direct the party's broad issue priorities for the next four years. It is considered the primary instrument of the party's governing philosophy.

A party platform is meant to be a unifying thread among members of the party and to convey broad party directives. However, the creation of the party platform is often characterized by a fair amount of compromise as differing interests vie to have issue priorities highlighted. The party's many constituencies and COALITIONS have a hand in developing the platform, each hoping it can advocate its position and turn it into a priority for the rest of the party.

A number of issues contained in the platform are chosen with little debate among delegates; other issues, nevertheless, are more divisive and have historically caused schisms within the party. However self-interested each coalition is in its approach to the creation of the platform, each knows that ultimately the platform is considered a document that binds all members of the Republican Party. For instance, in the weeks leading up to the Republican National Convention in 2004, Republicans faced some minor opposition in their ranks. Religious conservatives expressed concern that they were not accorded the same level of priority and recognition as other interests within the convention program. The religious conservative members of the Republican Party are often among the most ideologically conservative members of the party. A party that seeks to represent diverse interests (particularly in a TWO-PARTY SYSTEM such as the United States) will always have the challenge of wanting to satisfy the more ideologically "extreme" members while not alienating more moderate members.

The Platform Committee is a standing committee of the REPUBLICAN NATIONAL COMMITTEE. Its main task is to help craft and obtain adequate support for the passage of the party platform at the nominating convention. While the party platform is prepared in advance by the Platform Committee, it sometimes undergoes a variety of changes on the convention floor through "minority reports." These reports are filed by those who were unsuccessful in incorporating their views into the main draft version. The extent to which such minority reports are successfully integrated into the final platform is fully contingent upon obtaining a minimum threshold level of delegate support. This procedure prevents the "fringes" of the party from gaining control of the party's agenda.

Several of the Republican Party's basic principles have remained constant in recent years. For instance, particularly with regard to the economic rights of people and companies, the party has often stood for issues on the basis that individuals, not government, can make the best decisions, and they therefore often call for a reduced role of the national government in market-related issues. The modern Republican Party has a great deal of faith in the unfettered forces of the market and has adopted a pro-defense posture that often calls for increased military spending and reductions in social welfare spending.

The 2004 platform, entitled "2004 Republican Party Platform: A Safer World and More Hopeful America," focused on five broad goals for the Republican Party. The first was "winning the war on terror." Second, the Republican Party emphasized its desire to usher in an "ownership era," in an effort to spark entrepreneurial spirit that keeps the economy strong. Third, the party maintained a commitment to the principles of "building an innovative economy to compete in the world," recognizing that as technology expands, the economy is increasingly global in character. A fourth concentration of the party platform was to "strengthen communities" through a variety of medical insurance initiatives and to focus on a healthy environment and urban revitalization. Finally, "protecting families" included initiatives such as protecting against identity theft and the continuation of the "Do Not Call" registry for individuals who wish to be permanently removed from telemarketing lists.

Further reading: Gerring, John. *Party Ideologies in America, 1828–1996.* Cambridge: Cambridge University Press, 2001; Republican Party Platforms. Available online. URL: http://www.rnc.org. Accessed August 10, 2005.

—Dari E. Sylvester

Republican Party, symbol

What became the Republican Party symbol, the elephant, was originally drawn to insult Republicans by *Harper's Weekly* cartoonist Thomas Nast, who used the donkey to insult Democrats as well. The Republican elephant has become a universally recognized graphic representation of one of the two largest political parties in the United States. In 1874, the *New York Herald* published an editorial accusing President Ulysses S. Grant of trying to become a Caesar in considering a third term as president. Shortly thereafter, Democratic politicians charged Grant with empire-building and with breaking the tradition of two terms established by George Washington.

Their protests successfully scared Republican voters away from supporting the party in the MIDTERM ELECTIONS of 1874. The ploy worked, as Republicans lost four seats to a Democratic gain of 10 seats in the U.S. Senate. In the House of Representatives, Republicans lost 25 seats to a Democratic gain of 17. Although Republicans maintained a majority in both chambers, Nast expressed his disgust with Republicans for being so easily frightened away and expressed his displeasure in a cartoon that portrayed a jackass wearing the lion skin of "Caesarism" (to symbolize Democrats) frightening a group of animals in a forest, including an elephant, which implicitly symbolized Republican voters. Although it seems apparent that Nast did not intend to invent symbols for the parties, they nonetheless remained and have been easily recognizable ever since.

Further reading: Neal, Harry Edward. *Diary of Democracy: The Story of Political Parties in America.* New York:

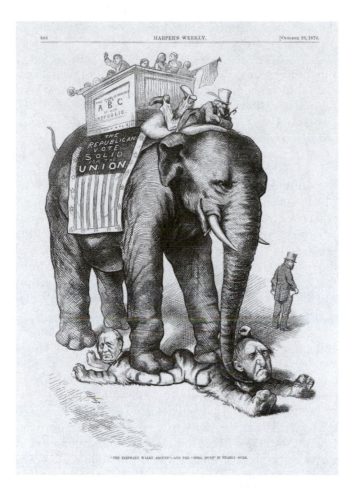

868   HARPER'S WEEKLY.   [OCTOBER 28, 1876.

"THE ELEPHANT WALKS AROUND"—AND THE "STILL HUNT" IS NEARLY OVER.

A cartoon portraying the elephant as a symbol for the Republican Party. The elephant became a widely known symbol for the party between 1860 and 1872, when a number of magazines popularized the association. *(Cartoon by Thomas Nast, HarpWeek, LLC)*

Julian Messner, 1962; Safire, William. *New Language of Politics.* Rev. ed. New York: Collier Books, 1972; Keller, Morton. *Affairs of State: Public Life in Nineteenth Century America.* Cambridge, Mass.: Harvard University Press, 1977.

—Gordon E. Harvey

Republican revolution

The Republican revolution refers to the victories of the REPUBLICAN PARTY over Democrats in the MIDTERM ELECTIONS of 1994. On November 8, 1994, Republicans took control of Congress, ending a 42-year Democratic majority. No incumbent Republican running for office that year was defeated.

In the House of Representatives, Republicans added 52 seats, resulting in a 230 to 204 majority. In the Senate, Republicans took nine seats from Democrats, giving them a 53 to 47 edge. Republicans had achieved their greatest electoral net gain since 1946, and Speaker Newt Gingrich,

considered one of the chief architects of the Republican revolution, had a policy MANDATE to implement the party's CONTRACT WITH AMERICA.

The term first appeared in the popular press around 1985. Republicans, like Gingrich, feeling frustrated over their failure to wrest control of Congress from the Democrats despite Ronald Reagan's landslide victories in 1980 and 1984, called for a revolution that would supplant the party's conservative COALITION with a younger, more unified, rightward-leaning party and end the DEMOCRATIC PARTY's control of Congress.

Gingrich saw the need to build a GRASSROOTS Republican movement in order to realize the Republicans' vision of a partisan REALIGNMENT. He used his position as head of GOPAC, the Republican Party POLITICAL ACTION COMMITTEE, to recruit loyal, conservative-minded Republicans to run for state and local office. Gingrich's farsighted vision created a strong offense, a team of experienced Republican politicians who could run for Congress in the 1990s.

The Republicans' decisive moment came in 1994; the party had a unique opportunity to hold the Democrats accountable for the nation's problems, since Democrats controlled both Congress and the presidency. Gingrich and his band of young Republicans built their campaign around the Contract with America, a 10-point plan, seeking TERM LIMITS and ethics rules in the House and a conservative legislative agenda of balanced budgets and Welfare reform. Republicans targeted their efforts on winning open seats formerly controlled by Democrats, defeating freshman Democrats elected in 1992, and challenging key Democratic leaders. The result was the first election leading to a Republican majority in the house since 1952 and the largest partisan swing since 1948.

The Republicans' early successes in the 104th Congress were tempered by their later failures that slowed the Republican revolution. At first, Gingrich and his leadership team successfully shifted control over the flow of legislation from the committee system to the party leadership and select House members. The Republican majority also guaranteed Republican dominance of floor debates and the policy process. Welfare reform, tax cuts, regulatory overhaul, and budget resolutions passed the House as products of party, not committee, negotiations. But later, Gingrich and House Republicans suffered public disfavor after their failure to compromise with President Clinton over the federal budget led to two federal government shutdowns. And, once many of the more popular items of the Contract with America had passed, Gingrich failed to expand his revolution into other policy areas. He and other House Republicans became more occupied by the Monica Lewinsky SCANDAL.

Republican electoral success since 1994 has been mixed. From 1996 to 2000, it was difficult for the party to solidify its majority in Congress. Dissatisfaction over Republicans' handling of the budget crisis partly led to a nine-seat loss by Republicans in the 1996 midterm elections, and 1998 saw Democrats gain four house seats buoyed by a fast-growing U.S. economy. In 2001, the Democrats briefly retook control of the Senate after Senator Jim Jeffords left the Republican Party and became INDEPENDENT. Since 2002, however, Republicans have seen a steady flow of electoral successes partly due to the public's homeland security concerns, congressional REDISTRICTING, a wave of generational retirements by SOUTHERN DEMOCRAT senators, and initial popular support for President George W. Bush's handling of the war on terror. On November 2, 2004, Republicans retained control of the White House and gained four seats in the House and four seats in the Senate, giving them a 231 to 200 margin and a 55 to 45 margin, respectively, over Democrats.

Further reading: Killian, Linda. *The Freshman: What Happened to the Republican Revolution?* Boulder, Colo.: Westview Press, 1998; Klinker, Philip A. *Midterm: The Elections of 1994 in Context.* Boulder, Colo.: Westview Press, 1996.

—Jamie Patrick Chandler

retirement slump

The retirement slump refers to the decrease in votes a party's candidate receives in the election after an incumbent retires and a nonincumbent of the same party seeks to fill the seat. The retirement slump is most commonly used to measure the INCUMBENCY ADVANTAGE in CONGRESSIONAL ELECTIONS. Measures of the incumbency advantage that are based solely on the vote share of incumbents ignore the fact that some voters would vote for any candidate of their party, regardless of their incumbency status. The retirement slump avoids this problem because it compares the votes a single party receives with a nonincumbent and an incumbent.

While the retirement slump seems superior to simply using incumbent vote shares, the measure has certain limitations. Most important, there is a selection bias problem. Incumbent candidates almost always receive at least 50 percent of the vote share, at least in a two-candidate race, or they would not be incumbents. If the party's next candidate has anything less than a perfect chance of victory, there will appear to be an incumbency advantage.

In spite of its limitations, the retirement slump is still used as an intuitive way to understand and measure the incumbency advantage. While the retirement slump can be used alone as a measure of incumbency advantage, researchers frequently average it with the SOPHOMORE SURGE (the increase in votes an incumbent receives in his or her second election). Together, the retirement slump and sophomore surge have increased dramatically through the second half of the 20th century, suggesting a strengthening in the power of incumbency over this period. While there has been a slight decline since the peak in the 1980s, the evidence suggests a robust incumbency advantage in American electoral POLITICS today.

Further reading: Gelman, Andrew, and Gary King. "Estimating Incumbency Advantage Without Bias." *American Journal of Political Science* 34, no. 4 (1990): 1,142–1,164; Jacobson, Gary C. *The Politics of Congressional Elections.* 5th ed. New York: Longman, 2001.

—Damon M. Cann

Revenue Acts (1971 and 1978)

The Revenue Acts of 1971 and 1978 marked a shift in federal policy from support for progressive taxation to a strategy of government-sponsored economic stimulation achieved by reducing the tax burden on corporations and the nation's wealthiest citizens. By the end of the century, this strategy came to be associated with fiscal conservatives and the REPUBLICAN PARTY. However, passage of both acts occurred while Democrats controlled Congress.

Faced with an anemic economy, runaway inflation, and a growing trade deficit, President Nixon announced that he supported Keynesian economic policies. Previous adherents of Keynes's economic theory nurtured growth through direct federal spending. However, with the Revenue Act of 1971, Nixon and the 92nd Congress increased the national debt as a means to keep money under the control of those most likely to invest in job development. A major component of the act was the creation of domestic international sales corporations (DISC). In addition to tax credits for investment, deferment of taxes on earnings, accelerated depreciation schedules, and the reduction of certain excise taxes, DISCs enjoyed permanent deferrals on one-half of earnings. Although the 1971 act also altered income tax brackets, thereby reducing taxes for some, a 20 percent increase in Social Security benefits resulted for those at the lower end of the spectrum facing higher overall payroll taxes.

The shift toward a less progressive tax structure (i.e., away from a system in which the wealthy pay a higher percentage of their income in taxes) accelerated with the Revenue Act of 1978. Reluctantly signed by President Carter, the act further reduced corporate taxes and established tax savings on long-term capital gains, leading to further red ink and increased taxes for the less affluent. Making this palatable to the majority of voters were reforms rewarding home ownership, provisions that were criticized for favoring white voters, as home ownership among white citizens exceeded home ownership among minorities.

The effects of these revenue acts were modest compared to what followed but paved the way for the Economic Recovery Tax Act of 1981 and "Reaganomics." With mixed results, this use of tax policy preceded increases in the standard of living for many Americans, while the trade surplus in 1970 of $2.5 billion shrank to a deficit of nearly

$450 billion by the end of the century. Similarly, a tenfold increase in the gross national product over those three decades coincided with a nearly 1,500 percent increase in the federal debt, to more than $5.7 trillion.

Further reading: Goldberg, Sanford, and Paul Farber. *Revenue Act of 1971.* New York: Practicing Law Institute, 1972.

—Bret A. Weber

Reynolds v. Sims 377 U.S. 533 (1964)

The U.S. Supreme Court opened the federal courts to voting rights litigants in 1962 in BAKER V. CARR. But this was only the beginning of a much larger crusade, as many challenges remained. The biggest challenge lay in determining how lower courts should interpret *Baker*'s mandate. This issue was at the heart of the Court's involvement in REAPPORTIONMENT questions. The Court addressed this issue in *Reynolds v. Sims*, a 1964 case involving a Tennessee REDISTRICTING process after the 1960 CENSUS.

The challenge in *Reynolds* was similar to the challenge the Court faced in *Baker*: how to evaluate a districting plan crafted decades before and whose population disparities defied rationality? The Court answered this question while explicitly invoking the equal population principle, a concept that lay dormant in *Baker* yet served as the implicit force behind Justice Brennan's majority opinion. In the Court's words, it is "the basic principle of representative government" that "the weight of a citizen's vote cannot be made to depend on where he lives. Population is, of necessity, the starting point for consideration and the controlling criterion for judgment in legislative apportionment controversies." This was the constitutional rule of "one person, one vote." The reasons for the rule were obvious. After all, "legislators represent people, not trees or acres."

In demanding population equality, the Court sought to curtail the practice of political GERRYMANDERing. The standard also forced jurisdictions to redistrict decennially. Rather than applying the standard as a straitjacket, however, the Court ultimately settled on a pragmatic compromise. For state redistricting plans, the maximum deviation between districts allowed by the Equal Protection Clause was 10 percent; states enacting a districting plan with deviations above this threshold must offer valid justifications for the difference. For congressional plans, any deviation must be explained, particularly if plans with smaller deviations are possible.

Further reading: Dixon, Robert G., Jr. "The Warren Court Crusade for the Holy Grail of 'One Man–One Vote.'" *Supreme Court Review*, 1969, p. 219; Issacharoff, Samuel. "Judging Politics: The Elusive Quest for Judicial Review of Political Fairness." *Texas Law Review* 71 (1993): 1,643.

—Luis Fuentes-Rohwer

Rock the Vote

Rock the Vote is a not-for-profit organization geared toward engaging American youths in the political process. The nonpartisan organization was originally founded in 1990 as part of the entertainment community's response to what was considered a "wave of attacks on freedom of speech and artistic expression," according to its Web site. Rock the Vote encourages young citizens to participate in POLITICS by using celebrity actors, artists, athletes, and other entertainers to make active political engagement seem cool.

The primary goal of Rock the Vote is to increase VOTER TURNOUT. The organization mobilizes young voters through an outreach strategy that employs media campaigns, street teams, voter registration drives, GET-OUT-THE-VOTE events, and voter education efforts. A key early component of this strategy was the organization's intense lobbying for the National Voter Registration Reform Act, otherwise known as the MOTOR VOTER LAW. This legislation was initially vetoed by President George H. W. Bush in 1991 but later signed into law by President Bill Clinton in 1993.

Clinton's support of the Rock the Vote–favored legislation was not surprising, considering his positive interaction with the organization during the 1992 campaign. In addition, the organization's Web site claims that it helped register more than 350,000 young voters and helped lead more than 2 million new young voters to the ballot booths. According to the organization, "On Election Day, these young people reversed a 20-year cycle of declining participation with a 20 percent increase in youth turnout compared to the previous Presidential election."

Following this success, Rock the Vote continued to work toward liberalization of voter registration laws through efforts such as enacting programs that enabled citizens to register to vote over the phone and online. The organization also began to provide information to voters through nonpartisan voting guides, public service announcements, and awards ceremonies honoring celebrities who took on leadership roles in encouraging greater political participation among the nation's youngest voters.

In the most recent PRESIDENTIAL ELECTIONS, Rock the Vote has taken a leading role in humanizing candidates and helping them relate to younger voters. A classic example of this occurred in 1992, when Clinton was asked whether he preferred boxers or briefs before an MTV crowd. Similarly, in November 2003, Rock the Vote sponsored a debate among candidates for the DEMOCRATIC PARTY nomination for president. The debate featured several questions that appealed to younger viewers, including whether the candidates had ever smoked marijuana.

Further reading: Rock the Vote. Available online. URL: http://www.rockthevote.org. Accessed August 10, 2005.

—Justin S. Vaughn

running mate

The term *running mate* usually refers to the person chosen by a party's presidential nominee to run with him or her in the GENERAL ELECTION as the vice presidential choice. Governor's choices for lieutenant governor in the states are also called running mates, but the colloquial usage of the term refers to national candidates.

Running mates have had a wide variety of impacts on PRESIDENTIAL ELECTIONS, more often through their mistakes than through their successes. John C. Calhoun was vice president during Andrew Jackson's first term as president, but resigned in 1832 in opposition to Jackson's support for higher tariffs. Calhoun, who hailed from South Carolina, believed that tariffs hurt the agricultural South in favor of the industrializing North, and in response wrote a treatise explaining why states had the right to "nullify" federal laws. Calhoun's replacement was a northerner, Martin Van Buren of New York, who helped the DEMOCRATIC PARTY overwhelm the Whig candidate, Senator Henry Clay of Kentucky. Van Buren later succeeded Jackson as president in 1836. In an interesting twist, his running mate, Richard M. Johnson of Kentucky, became the only vice president in history chosen by the Senate (as provided by the TWELFTH AMENDMENT in cases in which no vice presidential candidate has a majority in the ELECTORAL COLLEGE), when some southern electors refused to vote for him on the grounds that his wife and children were free blacks. This entire period helped to crystallize the sectional divisions that later turned the Democrats into a southern party, as well as presaging the Civil War.

Another famous running mate of the era was John Tyler of Virginia, who ran for vice president with General William Henry Harrison of Ohio on the Whig ticket in 1840. Harrison won a famous military campaign in 1811 against Native Americans at the Battle of Tippecanoe, and the politically inexperienced war hero was balanced by Governor Tyler. Tyler formerly belonged to the Democratic Party, leaving it in 1833 due to policy differences with then president Jackson. This unity ticket won an overwhelming majority in the Electoral College, 234 to 60, over the incumbents Van Buren and Johnson. However, Harrison caught pneumonia during his inaugural speech and died just one month later, the shortest term of any president in history. Tyler became the first vice president to be elevated to the presidency. As a strong believer in the principle of states' rights, he clashed repeatedly with congressional Whigs over establishing a national bank and other issues, and, not surprisingly, the Whigs decided not to nominate him for president in 1844.

The next dubious milestone in vice presidential history occurred when Andrew Johnson of Tennessee took office as president after Abraham Lincoln's assassination. Johnson was one of the few Democrats who did not join the Confederacy during the Civil War, and he was rewarded with

the vice presidency in the 1864 election as part of a UNION PARTY ticket. Johnson took office in 1865 but quickly earned the ire of so-called radical Republicans for not taking a hard-line approach to reconstructing the South and providing aid to the freed slaves. Johnson vetoed legislation giving civil rights to African Americans, dividing the South into military districts for an indefinite period of time, and opposed the FOURTEENTH AMENDMENT because of its Equal Protection Clause. All of his vetoes were overridden by huge Republican majorities in Congress. The final showdown came over the Tenure of Office Act of 1867, which prohibited the president from removing cabinet officials without Senate approval. President Johnson argued that the act was unconstitutional and fired Secretary of War Edwin M. Stanton without consulting the Senate. The House impeached Johnson, using this power for the first time in history, and in an extraordinary last-minute vote the Senate acquitted Johnson by a margin of only one vote.

President William McKinley was not the next president to be assassinated (that distinction belongs to James

John C. Calhoun was Andrew Jackson's running mate and vice president during Jackson's first term, but he resigned the position in opposition to Jackson's support of higher tariffs. *(Library of Congress)*

Garfield), but his successor, Theodore Roosevelt, has entered the annals of history as one of the most active presidents of all time. His impact on the election of 1900 was minimal, since he was chosen for balance (he was governor of New York and McKinley was from Ohio) and because REPUBLICAN PARTY bosses thought he would do no harm. But his impact on the presidency was tremendous: He pioneered the use of rhetoric as a tool to move public opinion behind his policies, negotiated the treaty ending the Russo-Japanese War, moved to bust the large trusts, and called on the United States to have a "speak softly but carry a big stick" foreign policy.

Modern-day running mates have occasionally swung elections for their party, though perhaps not as often as people believe. The most famous example of a running mate making the key difference comes from the 1960 election between sitting vice president Richard M. Nixon and Senator John F. Kennedy of Massachusetts. The Democratic Party had a bitterly contested PRIMARY election between Kennedy and Senate Majority Leader Lyndon B. Johnson of Texas. After clinching the presidential NOMINATION, Kennedy chose Johnson as his running mate because of the geographical balance he provided. Kennedy's gambit worked, as he won Texas along with much of the South and beat Nixon in one of the closest national elections in history.

Two more milestones in this history should be mentioned. Congresswoman Geraldine Ferraro was chosen by Walter Mondale as the Democratic Party's vice presidential nominee in 1984, becoming the first woman on a major party ticket. The 2000 election saw another landmark when Vice President Al Gore chose Senator Joseph Lieberman as his running mate. Lieberman was the first Jewish candidate on a national party ticket.

Further reading: Witcover, Jules. *Crapshoot: Rolling the Dice on the Vice Presidency, From Adams and Jefferson to Truman and Quayle.* New York: Crown Publishers, 1992.

—William D. Adler

runoff elections

Runoff elections are elections held to resolve a previous election that failed to produce a clear winner. They are most commonly used in single-member elections in which more than two candidates are vying for the elected position. In this case, the initial election rarely produces a majority winner. Therefore, the two candidates with the most votes move on to a runoff election to obtain a clear majority winner for the elected position. Runoff elections are most prevalent in state and local elections, elections to determine party candidates for national elections, and elections for offices in groups such as unions, organizations, and schools.

There are two primary reasons for runoff elections. Most important is the fulfillment of majoritarian democracy, a foundation of U.S. electoral POLITICS. Majority rule states that elected representatives should have the support of a majority of their constituents. A plurality vote, or selecting the candidate with the most votes from multiple candidates, rarely provides a majority outcome. Second, candidates need a legislative mandate. If a representative is elected with less than a majority of constituency support, which is typically the case in plurality elections, he or she often finds it hard to act with strength in the government, as he or she appears weak or even illegitimate to other representatives.

Runoff elections have been criticized in American politics because they are costly and because VOTER TURNOUT tends to drop dramatically. These concerns have led to several electoral reform movements proposing electoral systems that remain democratic but avoid the need for separate runoff elections. The most popular is instant runoff voting, which allows voters to cast a vote for their runoff choice at the same time they cast their vote for their favorite candidate. They do this by ranking candidates in order of choice. The rankings are then used in a series of runoffs to determine a winner with majority support. Places such as Vermont and San Francisco already use this system, and others are considering it.

Further reading: McGann, Anthony, et al. "How an Ideologically Concentrated Minority Can Trump a Dispersed Majority: Nonmedian Voter Results for Plurality, runoff, and Sequential Elimination Elections." *American Journal of Political Science* 46, no. 1 (2002): 134.

—Derrek M. Davis

runoff primaries   *See* PRIMARY, RUNOFF.

S

safe seat

Safe seats, also known as safe districts, refer to noncompetitive legislative seats (congressional or state) in which the incumbent or a party is unlikely to lose the seat in future elections. Generally, a seat is considered safe if more than 55 percent of the vote regularly goes to one party in the district. Seats become safe for several reasons, such as when the incumbent has gained the trust of the district and remains relatively popular or the district is composed of an overwhelming number of people from the same POLITICAL PARTY, virtually guaranteeing one party control. Often, candidates in these seats run unopposed in GENERAL ELECTIONS because potential opponents recognize that winning such a seat is a long shot and unlikely to be worth the time or resources required to vie for the seat.

The House has proportionally more safe seats than the Senate, which allowed Democrats to hold control of the House from 1954 to 1994. Over the last decade, reelection rates in the House have regularly exceeded 90 percent, while in the Senate the reelection rate has been slightly lower. There are several factors that contribute to the higher reelection rates and larger number of safe seats in the House than the Senate. In comparison to the Senate, House seat districts tend to be smaller in geographic size and population and far more homogenous in composition. Moreover, partisan REDISTRICTING can help to secure a House seat in ways that do not apply to the Senate. The more general benefits of incumbency play a central role in maintaining safe seats and help to explain high reelection rates in both the House and the Senate.

Further reading: Fenno, Richard F. *Home Style: House Members in Their Districts.* Boston: Little, Brown, 1978; Fiorina, Morris P. *Congress: Keystone of the Washington Establishment.* New Haven, Conn.: Yale University Press, 1977; Mayhew, David R. *Congress: The Electoral Connection.* New Haven, Conn.: Yale University Press, 1974.

—Marija Bekafigo

scandals

Political scandals are as old as the practice of POLITICS, but the nature of these phenomena has changed over the years. John Thompson contends that scandal involves 1) a transgression of moral codes, 2) an element of secrecy or concealment, 3) disapproval of the action by observers (nonparticipants), 4) expressed disapproval of the event by nonparticipants, and 5) disclosure and condemnation of the action that may damage the reputations of the individuals involved in the transgression.

Thompson categorizes three types of political scandal: those involving the violation of sexual mores, those pertaining to financial matters, and those seeking to enhance political power. It is not uncommon to find these three types intermixed. The affair of President Bill Clinton and Monica Lewinsky was a violation of sexual mores, but as it became part of an attempt to impeach Clinton, it evolved into one of political power: Would the Republican-controlled Congress remove the president from office? The "Keating Five" scandal involved five members of the Senate who intervened with a regulatory agency on behalf of Charles Keating, who had made large contributions to the senators' campaigns. This was both a financial and political scandal. The Watergate scandal, perhaps the most notorious of all American political scandals, was primarily about protecting and increasing the power of President Richard Nixon (i.e., a political scandal).

Whether an action is scandalous is very much a consequence of the scope of media coverage as well as the social mores of the historical period. For example, medieval rulers as a matter of custom had their way with women to whom they were not married, but those actions did not become scandalous, unlike the intimate relations between President William Clinton and intern Monica Lewinsky. Medieval rulers, especially those that held office by divine right, were granted broad privileges, and there were no media to report and evaluate their actions. As recently as the 1960s, journalists were reluctant to report what later would be considered scandalous. Thompson argues that as journalism became more professional and independent of political officials, reporters were less likely to protect public servants from scrutiny. Of course, in authoritarian regimes in which the media are tightly controlled, scandal does not occur: The emperor may have no clothes, but no one is free to comment on the fact.

It is ironic that as the public has become more tolerant in its attitudes about sexual relations, such as homosexuality, the private sexual practices of politicians have become less acceptable. This is mainly because such relationships, even if known to journalists but considered by them not to be pertinent to an office holder's duties, were not reported in prior times. In 1952, the fact that Adlai Stevenson was divorced was a source of commentary, yet from the 1960s to the 1980s, when Ronald Reagan sought election as governor and then president, his divorce and the fact the first child of his second marriage was born less than the usual gestation period after that marriage warranted not even a footnote.

The line between political corruption and political scandal is not always clear and changes with time. At the opening of the 21st century, the employment of a relative in a paid position on a public official's staff is less acceptable than it was in earlier times. Thus, in the first half of the 20th century, when Margaret Chase Smith and other congressmen's wives were aides to their husbands, there was little criticism. At a later point, when New York congressman Adam Clayton Powell's wife held a paid position on his staff, this was considered both scandalous and corrupt. The situation was compounded by the fact that she was often absent from work, although it was not evident that other congressional wives punched a time clock. By the end of the 20th century, spouses of elective or appointed officials in Washington were less likely to be hired by their husbands or wives. Instead, they would be employed in other governmental agencies or private entities, such as consulting firms.

Without question, the most significant scandal of the last half of the 20th century was Watergate, named for the apartment and office complex along the Potomac River in Washington, D.C., where a group of Republican operatives broke into the DEMOCRATIC PARTY campaign headquarters during the 1972 presidential campaign. Their intention was to wiretap these offices so that Democratic presidential campaign plans could be monitored. The subsequent criminal investigations, trials, and congressional hearings lead to the resignation of President Richard M. Nixon and the convictions of several of his aides, among the most prominent of whom were John Ehrlichman, H. R. "Bob" Haldeman, Charles Colson, and Jeb Magruder. The hearings of the Senate committee chaired by Sam Ervin of North Carolina discovered that the president had an "enemies list" and a sound recording system in the Oval Office. The recorded tapes from that system would prove to be the crucial element in his decision to resign. In addition to these consequences, the scandal popularized investigative journalism, as practiced by Bob Woodward and Carl Bernstein, but also increased politicians' distrust of the media. It also disillusioned many citizens about politics.

Given less attention but ranking just behind Watergate in its political significance and abuse of power was the Iran-contra scandal. This involved illegal, secret sales of arms to post-shah Iran via Israel in an effort to influence the release of American hostages, whose captors, although in Lebanon, presumably were operating in cooperation with Iran. The funds from the arms sales were used to finance the operations of the contras, American-sponsored rebels seeking to overthrow the left-wing Sandinista government of Nicaragua. The announcement of this conspiracy was shocking since it was widely believed that President Reagan would never negotiate with hostage takers.

Investigation of the Iran-contra conspiracy exemplifies conflicting demands in the American governmental system. On the one hand, illegal behavior should be punished. On the other hand, Congress needs to investigate in order to determine if new laws are required to exercise oversight. Because key American officials, notably John Poindexter and Oliver North, were granted legal immunity as a condition for testifying before a joint congressional committee and President Reagan did not recall authorizing the arms sales or channeling of funds to the contras, the convictions of central figures in this undercover operation were ultimately reversed on appeal. Given Reagan's practice of delegating authority and his sympathetic denial of knowledge about the plot, no impeachment proceedings were initiated, although one could argue that these actions were as impeachable as those of Watergate and certainly as impeachable as the grounds for the Clinton impeachment.

The misbehaviors of members of Congress tend to receive less attention than do those of the White House. In addition to the Keating Five, several other scandals arose in the last decades of the 20th century. In the early 1980s, FBI agents were successful while posing as Arab nationals to secretly videotape members of Congress taking bribes as inducement for their support on immigration and business problems of their "client" with the government. Known as "Abscam" (Arab scam), the scandal resulted in the convictions of one senator and six congressmen. All had already either lost reelection or had resigned from Congress. One became the first member to be expelled from Congress since 1861.

Less egregious, but reflecting the changing standards of Congress, was the case of Wilbur Mills of Arkansas, chairman of the powerful Ways and Means Committee, who was arrested for cavorting in the Tidal Basin in the nation's capital while obviously intoxicated and accompanied by a well-known striptease performer. Mills did not seek reelection and concentrated on overcoming his alcoholism.

Both Jim Wright of Texas and Newt Gingrich of Georgia, while serving as SPEAKER OF THE HOUSE, were charged with improper behavior in conjunction with the sale of books that each wrote. This led to Wright's fall from power, but Gingrich survived.

The Clinton administration was notable for the number of scandals in which it was allegedly involved. Even more notable was the fact that the primary investigation, Whitewater, or "Whitewatergate," dealt with events that occurred before he became president. While governor of Arkansas, he and his wife invested in a plan for a land development in that state. Although tens of millions of dollars of government funds were expended to investigate this matter, no indictments were handed down for either Clinton. Kenneth Starr, who replaced the initial independent counsel for Whitewater, expanded his authority to pursue other matters. Material from these non-Whitewater incidents became the basis for the impeachment of Clinton.

The impact of media coverage is illustrated by noting a parallel event to the impeachment proceedings against Clinton. While Congress was indicting and trying Clinton, the Speaker of the House, Newt Gingrich, who was married, was having an affair with a House committee staff member, whom he later married after divorcing his second wife. Gingrich's behavior was not reported until after the Senate failed to remove Clinton from office. Gingrich's resignation as Speaker was followed by the resignation of his apparent successor, Robert L. Livingston, Jr., of Louisiana, who had previously been intimate with a woman that was not his wife. The American response to such matters contrasts with reactions in Europe, where it is not uncommon for political leaders to have illicit sexual liaisons of which the public is aware.

Further reading: Dudley, William, ed. *Political Scandals: Opposing Viewpoints.* San Diego, Calif.: Greenhaven Press, 2001; Thompson, John B. *Political Scandal: Power and Visibility in the Media Age.* Malden, Mass.: Polity Press, 2000.
—Thomas Phillip Wolf

Senate, qualifications

Qualifications for the U.S. Senate were put forward in the Constitution of the United States in 1787 and ratified in 1789. The Constitution specifies that senators must be 30 years old, citizens of the United States for at least nine years, and residents of the state from which they are elected. Senators serve six years that are staggered so that only one-third of the chamber runs for reelection every two years. Originally elected by the state legislatures, the Seventeenth Amendment to the Constitution, ratified on April 8, 1913, initiated popular election of the Senate.

Debate in the Constitutional Convention about the distribution of congressional representation was resolved by the Great Compromise presented by Roger Sherman. It was agreed that the House of Representatives would be apportioned by population and that each state would be represented in the Senate with two members. Qualifications for the Senate were set slightly higher than those of the House of Representatives because the Senate would be a more stately office, filtered from the passions of the people. The bicameral legislature mimicked the British Parliament, and the old idea of protected property in the House of Lords carried over in the Constitution.

Although the constitutional qualifications for the Senate make many Americans eligible for office, few run and even fewer are elected. Senatorial campaigns are expensive and require much time from the candidate. Senators are older than the average American and are usually established in a lucrative occupation or a position that provides them fame prior to taking office. About a third of the Senate consists of millionaires, compared to 1 percent of the general population. The majority of the Senate is white, male, and Protestant, which does not reflect the makeup of American society. While these are not actual qualifications for the Senate, it does suggest the existence of an economic, cultural, and racial bias in the selection for this prestigious office.

Further reading: Wirls, Daniel, and Stephen Wirls. *The Invention of the United States Senate (Interpreting American Politics).* Baltimore: Johns Hopkins University Press, 2004.
—Sarah Miller

Seneca Falls Convention

The Seneca Falls Convention, held July 19 and 20, 1848, in the Wesleyan Chapel at Seneca Falls, New York, is recognized as the birthplace of the U.S. feminist movement and the site of the first organized call for women's suffrage. The meeting was motivated by an incident at the World Anti-Slavery Convention in London in 1840. Elizabeth Cady Stanton, Lucretia Mott, and four other U.S. women were denied DELEGATE status and forced to sit silently in the balcony. Stanton and Mott agreed to hold a convention upon their return home to form a society to advance the rights of women. Their family duties and other commitments delayed the event, which was announced in the July 14, 1848, issue of the *Seneca County Courier.*

The convention was attended by approximately 300 people, who adopted the Declaration of Sentiments, written by Stanton and Mott, who used the language of the Declaration of Independence to demand equal CITIZENSHIP rights for women. A total of 13 resolutions on topics such as married women's property rights, divorce, and increased educational and employment opportunities for women were passed without dissent, with one exception. The ninth resolution stated "that it is the duty of the women of this country to secure to themselves their sacred right to the elective franchise." Approval by a small majority came after Stanton and former slave and abolition leader Frederick Douglass argued that the vote was essential for attaining other rights.

The demand for the vote was controversial because it was the most specific and affected white women of all classes, not simply women of property and education. Mott and Stanton's own husband, Henry (who left town), opposed the suffrage resolution, fearing that such a radical stance would defeat other goals and discredit the movement. Only 68 women and 32 men signed the Declaration of Sentiments and Resolutions. Amelia Bloomer, later a suffrage leader, attended but refused to sign the document. Some signers later withdrew their signatures because of negative press coverage of the convention.

Despite the controversy in Seneca Falls, the division over women's suffrage among supporters of the women's rights movement was short-lived. Another convention was held two weeks later in Rochester, New York, where the suffrage resolution was adopted by a wider margin. The franchise came to be recognized as the symbol of and route to all other rights in a democracy and was the central issue of the women's agenda after Seneca Falls.

Further reading: Bernhard, Virginia, and Elizabeth Fox-Genovese, eds. *The Birth of American Feminism: The Seneca Falls Woman's Convention of 1848*. St. James, N.Y.: Brandywine Press, 1995; DuBois, Ellen Carol. *Feminism and Suffrage: The Emergence of an Independent Women's Movement in America, 1848–1869*. Ithaca, N.Y.: Cornell University Press, 1978; Gurko, Miriam. *The Ladies of Seneca Falls: The Birth of the Women's Rights Movement*. New York: Macmillan, 1974.

—Janet K. Boles

Seventeenth Amendment

The Seventeenth Amendment to the U.S. Constitution was ratified on April 8, 1913. By adopting the Seventeenth Amendment, as Ralph Rossum recently remarked, "they leveled the walls of federalism." The amendment states: "The Senate of the United States shall be composed of two Senators from each State, elected by the people thereof, for six years; and each Senator shall have one vote. The electors in each State shall have the qualifications requisite for electors of the most numerous branch of the State legislatures. When vacancies happen in the representation of any State in the Senate, the executive authority of such State shall issue writs of election to fill such vacancies: Provided, That the legislature of any State may empower the executive thereof to make temporary appointments until the people fill the vacancies by election as the legislature may direct. This amendment shall not be so construed as to affect the election or term of any Senator chosen before it becomes valid as part of the Constitution."

The process of ratification culminated in 1913, taking only 330 days to receive adoption from the states. The state legislatures had increasingly faced state-level reform pressures from Progressives who sought direct election by the people. Additionally, state legislatures had dealt with increasingly difficult partisan struggles to select U.S. senators, and often states had undergone extended vacancies, being unrepresented or under-represented in the U.S. Senate during such times. These circumstances made many state legislatures eager to capitulate in passing perhaps the most fundamental transfer of power ever witnessed in American federalism.

The U.S. Senate elections by state legislatures were the result of the Connecticut Compromise. This compromise between large states and small states, between those seeking preservation of the ARTICLES OF CONFEDERATION and those seeking a more democratic government and proponents of the new federalist Constitution, would preserve states' rights with equal SUFFRAGE of states in the U.S. Senate. This states' rights protection was twofold: It featured equal representation of two senators from each state, but it also protected states structurally through allowing the state legislatures to select the senators.

Direct election of senators was first proposed in 1826, and from 1893 until it passed Congress on May 13, 1912, an amendment was proposed to allow direct election of the U.S. Senate. George Anastaplo dates the anticipation of nationalization in Senate selection to the mid-19th century, when the movement for direct elections was witnessed in races such as Lincoln and Douglas in Illinois in 1858, and such debates were "intended to influence the choice by the people of the members of the State legislature that would in turn choose a [U.S.] Senator." By 1912, 29 of the 48 states allowed popular (PRIMARY or GENERAL ELECTIONS) and binding mechanisms to select U.S. senators.

Direct election was promoted by Progressives as a means of reducing corruption and reducing the influence of the wealthy and corporations. Additionally, proponents argued the direct election of the Senate would free state legislatures from national political influence while allowing a greater voice for the people and more democratic governance.

The impact was profound, as noted by Ralph Rossum, "By ratifying the Seventeenth Amendment, the people in their pursuit of more democracy inattentively abandoned what the framers regarded as the primary constitutional means for the protection of the federal-state balance and the interest of the states as states."

The political legacy has been one of unbalancing the Founding Fathers' federalism and a long-term centralization of power in the national government. Despite an intense period of devolution reflected by the incorporation of new federalism by both the Republicans and the Democrats, the persistent importance of this amendment is demonstrated in the entropy of centralized federalism and an enduring struggle of rebalancing federalism.

Further reading: Anastaplo, George. *The Amendments to the Constitution.* Baltimore: Johns Hopkins University Press, 1995; Rossum, Ralph A. *Federalism, the Supreme Court, and the Seventeenth Amendment: The Irony of Constitutional Democracy.* Lanham, Md.: Lexington Books, 2001.

—Michael W. Hail

Shaw v. Reno **509 U.S. 630** (1993)

After the 1990 REDISTRICTING round, the courts faced a myriad of constitutional challenges to the political lines drawn by political actors. The first major challenge surfaced in North Carolina, where Democrats controlled the redistricting process. As a covered jurisdiction under Section 5 of the Voting Rights Act, North Carolina must submit its redistricting plans for preclearance to the Justice Department (as an alternative, it could seek a declaratory judgment in the U.S. district court in Washington, D.C.). The Department of Justice objected to the state's initial plan, contending that Section 2 of the act demanded the creation of a second MAJORITY-MINORITY DISTRICT. The North Carolina Democrats complied with this request while also attempting to preserve their perceived political advantage as reflected in their original plan. This led to the creation of districts of unusual shape.

In *Shaw v. Reno*, the Supreme Court concluded that such districts were subject to strict scrutiny irrespective of the state's motivation for their enactment. To the Court, the shape of the district made all the difference. After all, "redistricting legislation that is so bizarre on its face that it is 'unexplainable on grounds' other than race . . . demands the same close scrutiny that we give to other state laws that classify citizens by race." The Court was particularly troubled by the message sent by these districts to elected officials. Such bizarre districts, the Court noted, "reinforce the perception that members of the same racial group . . . think alike, share the same political interests, and will prefer the same candidates at the polls."

In subjecting these districts to strict scrutiny, the state must proffer a compelling interest in defense of its redistricting plan, and the means used must be narrowly tailored to the proffered end. Of note, simply pointing to the Voting Rights Act or to the requests by the Department of Justice would not satisfy this exacting test.

Further reading: Pildes, Richard H., and Richard G. Niemi. *"Expressive Harms, 'Bizarre Districts,' and Voting Rights: Evaluating Election-District Appearances after Shaw v. Reno." Michigan Law Review* 92 (1993): 483.

—Luis Fuentes-Rohwer

single-issue voter

A single-issue voter is one who determines his or her opinion of a candidate based solely on that candidate's position on one issue, and then votes accordingly. While the single issue on which the vote is determined may vary from voter to voter, the issue is generally one with which some controversy is associated, and there are generally single-issue voters on both sides of an issue.

Single-issue voters are not necessarily partisans, although they tend to vote consistently for one party or another based on that party's platform. That is to say, a voter who supports abortion rights and bases his or her vote on that issue will probably consistently vote Democratic because that position is a plank of the DEMOCRATIC PARTY platform. Of course, there are occasions on which a candidate departs from the official party platform, and as a result, both candidates agree on a particular issue that forms the basis of a single-issue voter's preference. In those instances, the voter is still likely to vote for the party whose platform matches the voter's position.

Single-issue voters can affect elections in two ways. First, single-issue voters can steer campaigns to their issue and force the election to be a sort of REFERENDUM on that issue. Single-issue voters do this by forming INTEREST GROUPS and banding together to push their issue to the fore. They can keep their issue in the public eye and make the candidates address their positions on the issue. An effective interest group will keep the media spotlight on its issue throughout the campaign and make the election not between two candidates, but between two opposing positions on the same issue.

Single-issue voters can also influence an election by not voting. For example, a pro-life voter might be reluctant to vote for a pro-life Democrat over a pro-choice Republican, as the Democratic platform specifically supports the pro-choice position. In this situation, a pro-life voter must choose between supporting a particular candidate who supports his or her position and supporting the POLITICAL PARTY that supports his or her position. Forced to choose between two unsatisfactory options, the single-issue voter may choose not to participate.

Further reading: Niemi, Richard G., and Herbert F. Weisberg, eds. *Controversies in Voting Behavior.* Washington, D.C.: CQ Press, 2001; Niemi, Richard G., and Herbert F. Weisberg, eds. *Classics in Voting Behavior.* Washington, D.C.: CQ Press, 1993.

—Lisa Kimbrough

single-member districts

Single-member districts (SMDs) refer to a geographically based districting design that elects one member from a defined district boundary. This is the districting method currently used in the American representative system.

The Apportionment Act of 1842 was the first congressional mandate for using SMDs. However, in a series of apportionment acts up through 1901, the use of SMDs was changed and reinterpreted to mean districts with equal population of both contiguous and compact territory, and several states continued to use at-large districts. In 1967, Congress passed additional legislation, PL 90-196, which reasserted the legal requirement for SMDs in states with more than one House seat. Congress passed this law to limit southern states from diluting minority voting strength by resorting to winner-take-all elections and to prevent AT-LARGE ELECTIONS in states that could not reach agreements on new REDISTRICTING plans.

While CONGRESSIONAL DISTRICTS must be SMDs, state legislative districts are not covered under the law. Currently, nearly a third of the states use MULTIMEMBER DISTRICTS (MMDs) in at least one chamber, with 15 percent of all state legislative districts being MMDs. However, this has decreased greatly over the past 40 years.

The use of SMDs has both advantages and disadvantages. The advantages include providing constituents with a single, generally easily identifiable district representative, which encourages CONSTITUENCY service. The disadvantages include the need to redraw the districts every 10 years based on population shifts and the tendency to reinforce majority interests and underrepresent minority interests. The growing use of MAJORITY-MINORITY DISTRICTS is one attempt to help better represent minority interests within SMDs. Overall, the use of SMDs is the traditional and dominant method of electing representatives in the American electoral system.

Further reading: Adams, Greg D. "Legislative Effects of Single-Member vs. Multi-Member Districts." *American Journal of Political Science* 40, no. 1 (1996): 129–144; Welch, Susan, and Donley T. Studlar. "Multi-Member Districts and the Representation of Women: Evidence from Britain and the United States." *Journal of Politics* 52, no. 2 (1990): 391–412.

—Jonathan Winburn

slate

A slate is a list of candidates for election nominated by a POLITICAL PARTY or group, such as a union, board, or association. Loosely synonymous with *ticket* in its generic sense, *slate* has also found usage as a marker distinguishing a range of election systems and processes, particularly with regard to the issue of direct vs. indirect representation. The slate concept figures prominently in a set of key questions that lie at the heart of debates on the competing merits of election systems: For what purposes are slates of candidates or delegates assembled? To what degree can a slate accurately reflect the wishes of the ELECTORATE? How does a slate influence the democratic choices of voters?

In U.S. PRESIDENTIAL ELECTIONS, slates of electors are chosen by each state to the ELECTORAL COLLEGE. These electors, in turn, cast the official votes for president. It is, essentially, an indirect vote. In all but two states, the party that wins the most POPULAR VOTES becomes that state's electors—a winner-take-all result. The germane point here is whether a given slate of electors does or does not disenfranchise those voters who cast their votes for the candidate or party receiving fewer votes, or by reducing their proportional contribution to the final election result. In short, the slate-voter-outcome linkage in this election process may legitimately be considered incongruous.

A second usage of the term *slate*, in PRIMARY election contexts, spotlights similar issues. A central difference between a proportional primary (used by the DEMOCRATIC PARTY NOMINATION process) and the winner-take-all primary (used principally by the REPUBLICAN PARTY nomination process) is that the latter results in an unlisted slate of DELEGATES automatically being awarded to the winner of a state's presidential preference vote. By contrast, the proportional primary allows for more direct delegate apportionment in response to voter preference at district or state levels. Again, a slate may be associated with an incongruity between delegate allocation and voter representation.

More broadly, *slate* is employed as a common referent to identify some PROPORTIONAL REPRESENTATION voting systems, party-list systems in particular. It is argued, for example, that closed party-list systems of proportional representation give voters little power over which candidates on the party slate (list) are elected. In this case, a slate determined by the party ultimately diminishes the degree of choice held by the voter.

Further reading: *Congressional Quarterly's Guide to U.S. Elections.* 4th ed. Washington, D.C.: CQ Press, 2001; Cook, Rhodes. *The Presidential Nominating Process: A Place for Us?* Lanham, Md.: Rowman & Littlefield, 2004.

—Paul J. Nuti

Smith v. Allwright 321 U.S. 649 (1944)

Smith v. Allwright was a landmark case in which the U.S. Supreme Court struck down the WHITE PRIMARY in Texas in 1944. As a reaction to the requirements of the FOURTEENTH and FIFTEENTH AMENDMENTS to the Constitution, many southern states adopted strategies to deny blacks the right to vote. In 1923, Texas became the first state to enact a white primary statute, which denied blacks the opportunity to vote in DEMOCRATIC PARTY PRIMARY elections. Because there was no real opposition to the Democratic Party in Texas at that time, the candidate who emerged from the primary election would, for all intents and purposes, win the GENERAL ELECTION. In order to prevent blacks from participating in the primary and thus affecting the outcome of the general election, the Texas legislature enacted a statute that stipulated that "in no event shall a Negro be eligible to participate in a Democratic Party primary election held in the State of Texas and should a Negro vote in a Democratic Party primary election such ballot shall be void and election officials are herein directed to throw out such ballot and not count the same."

When the law was initially challenged in the 1927 case of *Nixon v. Herndon,* the U.S. Supreme Court ruled unanimously that the Texas statute violated the Equal Protection Clause of the Fourteenth Amendment because the state's extension or denial of primary voting privileges to Democratic Party members was based solely on race. In response, the Texas legislature delegated the power of determining the qualifications for participating in primary elections to the Democratic Party itself.

On July 24, 1940, a Houston dentist, Dr. Lonnie E. Smith, attempted to vote in the Democratic primary. When he was denied a BALLOT under the white primary rules adopted by the Democratic Party, he secured the assistance of the NAACP and its lead counsel, future Supreme Court justice Thurgood Marshall. Smith questioned how his Fifteenth Amendment rights were any less violated when party rules denied him the right to vote in a primary election than when the state legislature had mandated such exclusion as a matter of law.

By an 8 to 1 margin, the Supreme Court held that the relationship between parties and the state in the selection of party officers, the administration of primary elections, and judicial oversight of contested election results implicated the state in such a manner that the party's discriminatory rules could not be viewed as merely private action that was not subject to constitutional review. The Court ruled further that the right to vote protected by the Fifteenth Amendment applied to both primary and general elections. Thurgood Marshall, incidentally, maintained that this case was the most important of all the landmark decisions in which he participated as counsel for the NAACP because of the participatory voice it gave blacks in the selection of public officials.

Further reading: Hine, Darlene Clark. *Black Victory: The Rise and Fall of the White Primary in Texas.* Columbia: University of Missouri Press, 2003.

—Steven P. Brown

Socialist Party

Over the last century, the Socialist Party has pushed for public control of the market, social equality, and peace in American POLITICS. The origins of the Socialist Party in the United States can be traced to the formation of the Socialist Labor Party, founded in 1877, and the Social Democratic Party, founded in 1898. In 1901, the two organizations merged to form the Socialist Party under the leadership of lawyer Morris Hillquit, labor leader Eugene Debs, and legislator Victor Berger. The peak of the Socialist Party's electoral strength came in 1910–12 as party membership grew to nearly 120,000. In the 1912 PRESIDENTIAL ELECTION, Debs received nearly 1 million votes (6 percent) as the

Eugene V. Debs, a founding member of the Socialist Party and presidential candidate in 1912 *(Prints and Photographs Division, Library of Congress)*

party's presidential candidate. The party also had roughly 1,000 members in public office at this time.

Electoral strength for the Socialist Party declined rapidly, however, with Allan Benson receiving around 3 percent of the presidential vote in 1916. Strength further declined with the party's unpopular decision to oppose World War I, which led to expulsion of Socialists from public office, banning of Socialist press from the mails, and eventually the landing of Debs and other Socialist leaders in prison. The most significant blow to the party came in 1919 as radical members, inspired by the Russian Revolution, split from the Socialist Party to form the Communist Party. This fractionalization decreased membership to roughly a fourth of its former size. Despite its decline, the Socialist Party nominated Norman Thomas for president in 1928 and the following five PRESIDENTIAL ELECTIONS. In 1960, the party decided to withdraw from national politics due to steadily declining support. In 1972, the Socialist Party changed its name to the Social Democratic Party of the United States.

While its role as an important political actor was short-lived, the Socialist Party played an important role in promoting political reforms throughout the century. The Socialist labor movement of the 1930s paved the way for the New Deal reforms such as unemployment compensation and labor law reform. Socialist participation in the CIVIL RIGHTS MOVEMENT of the 1960s helped usher in Johnson's Great Society. Over the years, the Socialists played influential roles as leaders of organizations such as the AFL unions and the NAACP and in smaller groups on college campuses, in church groups, and among the women's rights movements. Today the Social Democratic Party is primarily concerned with social rights such as labor, education, and civil rights. For practical reasons, many Socialists align themselves with the larger and more powerful DEMOCRATIC PARTY during elections, while generally pushing a far more leftist agenda than either mainstream POLITICAL PARTY.

Further reading: Chester, Eric Thomas. *True Mission: Socialists and the Labor Party Question in the U.S.* Sterling, Va.: Pluto Press, 2004; Fried, Albert. *Socialism in America from the Shakers to the Third International.* Garden City, N.Y.: Anchor Books, 1970.

—Clayton Thyne

socialization   *See* POLITICAL SOCIALIZATION.

soft money

Soft money refers to unrestricted political contributions to political parties for the purpose of party-building activities such as GET-OUT-THE-VOTE drives and GRASSROOTS development. It cannot be spent in direct advocacy or in opposition to specific candidates and is not subject to the same limits and restrictions as so-called HARD MONEY. Soft money developed out of a long, contingent process of the FEDERAL ELECTION COMMISSION's (FEC) implementation of CAMPAIGN FINANCE LAWS in the face of the shifting funding strategies of the national political parties.

When initially created as a category by a 1978 FEC ruling, soft money was of little importance. By 1992, soft money contributions totaled $86.1 million, about 16 percent of each party's total FUND-RAISING. Soft money had ballooned 10 years later to a combined total of $496.1 million, accounting for 53 percent of all funds raised by Democrats and 36 percent of all Republican fund-raising. In 2002, after a long struggle for reform in Congress, the Bipartisan Campaign Reform Act (BCRA) banned national parties from raising soft money and placed restrictions on state and local parties' use of the funds.

The origins of soft money date back to the first modern American attempt to limit the influence of money in the electoral process. In 1971, Congress passed the FEDERAL ELECTION CAMPAIGN ACT (FECA) in response to the growing role campaign contributions were playing in elections. The act required campaigns and national committees to report contributions and set moderate spending limits on advertising. In 1974, after a fund-raising SCANDAL associ-

ated with Richard Nixon's 1972 presidential campaign, Congress passed several amendments to FECA that severely limited the role money could play in federal elections. Congress added contribution limits, further restricted campaign spending, and established the FEC as a regulatory agency to oversee and enforce campaign finance laws.

The law was challenged and modified by the landmark decision *BUCKLEY V. VALEO*, 424 U.S. 1 (1976). The Supreme Court declared Congress had a sufficient governmental interest in limiting the role of money in elections to reduce the appearance of corruption, and therefore could limit contribution amounts. Contributions themselves, the Court stated, did not, in fact, constitute direct political speech but were indirectly related. However, spending limits were declared unconstitutional and in violation of the First Amendment due to their limiting of direct political speech.

After 1976, it was up to the FEC to make sense of the FECA amendments, modified by the *Buckley* decision, and issue regulations for federal candidates and national parties to follow in their fund-raising activities. In 1978, the FEC issued an advisory opinion that state parties were not required to adhere to federal campaign finance laws in financing party-building activities, even if federal candidates were involved. This decision was followed the next year by another decision that declared national parties were also not subject to federal law in financing party-building activities. Thus, the distinction between "hard" and "soft" money was born. State and national parties would be allowed to raise unlimited amounts of money (soft money) from a variety of previously forbidden sources, such as general treasury funds of corporations and unions, provided the money was used only for party-building activities and not for expressly advocating the election of a particular candidate.

National parties were slow to realize the potential the new soft money category held for increasing the amount of money they could raise and spend during an ELECTION CYCLE. Republicans were the first to actively seek out soft money donations during the 1980 and 1984 PRESIDENTIAL ELECTIONS. After a 1984 lawsuit filed by COMMON CAUSE against the FEC to restrict the new practice of using soft money was dismissed in federal court, both parties began to actively pursue soft money contributions.

What made soft money so attractive to parties was not the party-building they could fund with it, but the ability to spend it on ISSUE ADVOCACY ADVERTISING. Beginning in the 1980s, parties began to increasingly push the envelope on allowable uses of soft money. It became increasingly common for parties to place election time advertisements funded with soft money dollars. These issue advocacy advertisements were clearly meant to influence the outcome of elections, but did not expressly advocate for or against a particular candidate and therefore remained within FEC rules.

By the late 1990s, many in Congress believed soft money to contravene the intent of the original FECA laws to reduce the role of money in federal elections. In 1997, Senators Russell Feingold of Wisconsin and John McCain of Arizona took the lead in the fight by introducing a bill to end soft money. The MCCAIN-FEINGOLD bill proposed further amendments to FECA that would ban the use of soft money by national parties and restrict its use by state and local parties, in addition to placing restrictions on when issue advocacy ads could be broadcast. By the 1999–2000 election cycle, soft money contributions totaled $495.1 million, or 40 percent of all national party fund-raising. With increasing pressure mounting from the press, especially in the wake of the collapse of the Enron Corporation, a soft money contributor that had relied heavily on good government relations to operate, Congress approved the McCain-Feingold bill and President George W. Bush signed the Bipartisan Campaign Reform Act (BCRA) into law in March 2002.

Almost immediately, Senator Mitch McConnell of Kentucky, a former staunch opponent of the McCain-Feingold bill, challenged the BCRA in court. Several disparate INTEREST GROUPS, including the National Rifle Association (NRA), the American Civil Liberties Union (ACLU), AFL-CIO, and both major political parties joined McConnell in attempting to overturn BCRA. The appellants claimed many constitutional arguments against the BCRA, but McConnell's argument centered on the act's violation of parties' First Amendment right of free speech. By banning the use of soft money, McConnell claimed, Congress undermined the ability of parties to participate in the political process. The Supreme Court decided in *McConnell v. FEC*, 124 S. Ct. 619 (2003) that the BCRA did not violate the First Amendment, and found that, as in *Buckley*, Congress was exercising a legitimate governmental interest by reducing the appearance of corruption in banning the use of soft money. The Court having upheld the soft money ban in *McConnell*, the FEC has issued revised rules that currently ban the collection or use of soft money by national political parties.

Further reading: Bauer, Robert. *More Soft Money Hard Law.* New York: Perkins Coie, 2003; Federal Elections Commission. Available online. URL: http://www.fec.gov. Accessed August 10, 2005; Magleby, David, and Quin J. Monson. *The Last Hurrah? Soft Money and Issue Advocacy in the 2002 Congressional Election.* Washington, D.C.: Brookings Institution Press, 2004; Slaback, Frederick. *The Constitution and Campaign Finance Reform.* Durham, N.C.: Carolina Academic Press, 1998.

—Zachary Courser

sophomore surge

The sophomore surge refers to the increase in vote share experienced by an elected official the first time he or she runs as an incumbent. Candidates seeking an office for the first time do not enjoy the benefits of the INCUMBENCY ADVANTAGE. However, after running successfully as a CHALLENGER or open seat candidate, they gain incumbency status. The difference in their vote share when they run the first time (as a nonincumbent) and when they seek reelection (as an incumbent) is the sophomore surge.

The sophomore surge is most commonly used to measure the incumbency advantage in CONGRESSIONAL ELECTIONS. Measures of the incumbency advantage that are based solely on the vote share of incumbents ignore the fact that some voters would vote for any candidate of their party, regardless of their incumbency status. The sophomore surge avoids this problem because it compares the vote a candidate of a given party receives as a nonincumbent and as an incumbent.

While the sophomore surge seems superior to simply using incumbent vote shares, the measure has certain limitations. One does not observe the performance of a candidate who runs as an incumbent and as a nonincumbent in the same election. Further, there is a significant amount of variability in the size of the sophomore surge across candidates in a given year.

In spite of its limitations, the sophomore surge is used as an intuitive way to understand and measure the incumbency advantage. Frequently, the sophomore surge is averaged with the RETIREMENT SLUMP (the decrease in votes a party's candidate receives in an election after an incumbent retires and a nonincumbent seeks to fill the seat) measure referred to as the slurge. Together the retirement slump and sophomore surge have increased dramatically through the second half of the 20th century, suggesting a strengthening in the power of incumbency over this period of time. While there has been a slight decline since the peak in the 1980s, the evidence suggests a robust incumbency advantage in American electoral POLITICS today.

Further reading: Gelman, Andrew, and Gary King. "Estimating Incumbency Advantage without Bias." *American Journal of Political Science* 34, no. 4 (1990): 1,142–1,164. Jacobson, Gary C. *The Politics of Congressional Elections.* 5th ed. New York: Longman, 2001.

—Damon M. Cann

South Carolina Progressive Democratic Party

The South Carolina Progressive Democratic Party (PDP) in the 1940s and 1950s forced the national DEMOCRATIC PARTY to address the exclusion of African Americans from the party's southern primaries. The PDP in 1944 contested the seating of the regular state delegation at the DEMOCRATIC NATIONAL CONVENTION in Chicago. That challenge, the first by an all-black delegation, caused considerable consternation within the national party.

Also in 1944, the PDP's Osceola McKaine was the first African American in the 20th century to run for a major federal office as a Democrat in the South. McKaine ran for the U.S. Senate against South Carolina governor Olin D. Johnston.

State NAACP leaders in 1944 formed the PDP while campaigning for President Franklin D. Roosevelt. Suspecting that the state's Democratic Party would not support Roosevelt for a fourth term, black leaders worked to create a pro-Roosevelt ELECTORAL COLLEGE SLATE, as permitted under state law. McKaine and John H. McCray supported the effort in McCray's newspaper, the *Lighthouse and Informer.* The enormous response among South Carolina blacks led to the formation of the PDP.

In May 1944, 172 local DELEGATEs and observers from eight southern states attended the PDP's first convention, in Columbia. McCray was elected party chairman and McKaine, secretary. Within months, the PDP claimed 45,000 members.

National Democratic leaders failed to prevent the PDP's Chicago challenge. PDP leaders insisted the national party deal with discrimination in its southern ranks. The PDP challenged again at the 1948 and 1956 Democratic conventions.

The PDP delegations were never seated. Still, McCray claimed that in 1956 the national party promised PDP leaders an end to all-white delegations from state parties discriminating against potential black delegates. This, McCray argued, opened the door for the MISSISSIPPI FREEDOM DEMOCRATIC PARTY's 1964 convention challenge.

The PDP became the state NAACP's VOTER REGISTRATION arm. Local official George Elmore was the plaintiff in *Rice v. Elmore*, which followed the U.S. Supreme Court's SMITH V. ALLWRIGHT decision and was crucial in ending the exclusion of blacks from Democratic primaries in South Carolina and other southern states. In 1950, in a U.S. Senate race, PDP and state NAACP officials delivered the black vote and decisive margin for Johnston's defeat of Governor Strom Thurmond, the DIXIECRAT presidential candidate in 1948.

After 1956, the PDP gradually merged into the state Democratic Party. Some of its officers gained local and county Democratic offices. McCray became vice chairman of a majority-white Democratic ward.

Further reading: Roefs, Wim. "Leading the Civil Rights Vanguard in South Carolina: John McCray and the Lighthouse and Informer, 1939–1954." In Adam Green and Charles Payne, eds., *Time Longer than Rope: A Century of African-American Activism.* New York: New York University Press, 2003.

—Wim Roefs

southern Democrats

The concept of *southern Democrats* has been transformed during the 20th century from a term that described conservative and segregationist "politicos" in the American South, to a term that described elected officials who adhere to more liberal policies and attract more than just white support. From the end of RECONSTRUCTION to the end of World War II, Democrats were the only political players in the South, due in large part to anti-Republican feelings following the Civil War and the presence of "black-belt" officials, or those who came from majority-black counties. These black-belt politicians dominated the DEMOCRATIC PARTY in the old Confederacy. Following World War II and the advent of the modern CIVIL RIGHTS MOVEMENT, southern Democrats became more racially diverse due to the influence of northern Democrats, who advocated civil rights for blacks, the influx of southern black voters following the passage of the 1965 Voting Rights Act, and the subsequent realigning of southern conservative whites to the REPUBLICAN PARTY.

In the period following the Reconstruction era, white southerners used the Democratic Party to instill the "Solid South." This development of a Democratic Solid South was shaped by elite whites, notably from counties with large black populations, to re-create a segregated society where only whites would be allowed to cast BALLOTs. Using such restrictive techniques such as POLL TAXes, LITERACY TESTS, and other discriminatory devices, white southerners all but locked out black participation in elections. Another reason for white southerners to align themselves with the Democratic Party was due to the history of the Republican Party supporting civil rights for blacks during and after the Civil War.

With control of a major region, southern Democrats became the majority FACTION within the national party and used their power and seniority to stave off attempts to promote civil rights for blacks. This domination within the region by the Democrats was most vividly seen in PRESIDENTIAL ELECTIONS. On all but two occasions between 1876 and 1948, the Democratic Party received virtually unanimous support by all the southern states at the presidential level. Nevertheless, Republicans dominated the White House from the end of Reconstruction to the 1930s, save for the presidency of southern-born Woodrow Wilson. At the congressional level, southerners overwhelmingly elected Democrats to the U.S. House and Senate. For some political observers, the real election did not usually occur in November of the election year, but in the Democratic PRIMARY earlier in the summer. This dominance in the South created a power base for southern politicians to control both chambers through the power of seniority and COALITIONs with conservative Republicans to defeat liberal attempts to advance civil rights for blacks.

For most scholars, 1948 signaled a critical fissure in the Democratic South. This can be traced back to the NEW DEAL COALITION, put together by President Franklin D. Roosevelt (FDR) in 1932. Along with the Democratic South, FDR's coalition comprised northern liberal, Catholic, and Jewish voters, as well as some blacks. By 1934, however, black voters began to desert the party of Lincoln for the party of FDR, and southern Democrats began to come into conflict with both blacks and northern liberals over issues of civil rights. This fissure was dramatically played out in 1948, when southern Democrats left the party's nominating convention over civil rights and formed their own "Dixiecrat" party. While unable to throw the presidential election into the House of Representatives, white southern Democrats no longer felt strong adherence to the national party.

This defection by Dixiecrats signaled the opening crack in the Democratically Solid South, and also signaled a shift in the composition of southern Democrats. With the advent of the modern Civil Rights movement and advocacy by northern Democratic liberals, black voters began to become more vocal and active in the Democratic Party. This was particularly evident when white southern Democrats failed to stop the 1957, 1960, and 1964 Civil Rights Acts, as well as the 1965 Voting Rights Act. Following the passage of that landmark enfranchisement legislation, southern Democrat and president Lyndon Johnson remarked that with the passage of the Voting Rights Act, Democrats had turned the South over to the Republicans. Johnson's remarks proved to be prophetic in that black voters would eventually come to play a major role in the Democratic Party in the South, while white southerners would align themselves with the growing conservative movement in the Republican Party.

With the presidential candidacies of Barry Goldwater in 1964, Richard Nixon in 1968 and 1972, and Ronald Reagan in 1980, former white conservative southern Democrats found a new home in the Republican Party, leading to a regional REALIGNMENT of the South. Since 1980, Republicans have been able to dominate the formerly Democratic Solid South at the presidential level, while Democrats have fought to break the Republican grip on the South in order to win the White House. At the congressional level, there appears to be two forms of southern Democrat. One form is a white moderate who must build a biracial electoral coalition between black voters and moderate whites in order to win against a Republican opponent, who generally attracts conservative whites. The other form of southern Democrat is usually a minority candidate who wins an election in a majority-minority CONGRESSIONAL DISTRICT in the South.

Further reading: Black, Earl, and Merle Black. *Politics and Society in the South.* Cambridge, Mass.: Harvard University Press, 1987; Black, Earl, and Merle Black. *The Vital South: How Presidents Are Elected.* Cambridge, Mass.: Harvard University Press, 1992; Berard, Stanley P. *Southern Democrats in the U.S. House of Representatives.* Norman: University of Oklahoma Press, 2001; Rae, Nicol C. *Southern Democrats.* New York: Oxford University Press, 1994.

—J. Michael Bitzer

southern strategy

The southern strategy, often identified with Republican presidential candidate Richard M. Nixon in 1968, sought to capitalize on the defection of conservative white southerners from the DEMOCRATIC PARTY to win the White House. With the aid of U.S. senator Strom Thurmond (South Carolina), Nixon and his campaign put together a successful plan that endured through the end of the 20th century and serves as the basis for the modern REPUBLICAN PARTY's strategy for winning the White House.

The southern strategy was born out of the 1964 PRESIDENTIAL ELECTION. Even though southerner Lyndon B. Johnson, the Democratic incumbent, won in a landslide over his conservative Republican opponent, U.S. senator Barry Goldwater (Arizona), the election activated Republican support in the South. It was in that election that Goldwater won four southern states that constituted the original Solid South for the Democratic Party. Goldwater's conservative message reshaped the Republican Party, and once he secured the presidential NOMINATION in 1964, Goldwater used the adage of "going hunting where the ducks are" and campaigned in the heartland of conservative thinking, the white South. With a message of states' rights, Goldwater sought to capitalize on the disenchantment of white conservative southerners, who were seen as reliable Democratic voters. But with the advent of the modern CIVIL RIGHTS MOVEMENT, and in particular the vocal support of civil rights for blacks and liberal appeals to blacks to vote Democratic, white southerners became increasingly disenchanted with the party that they had once called home. Goldwater's calls for a strong military, coupled with votes against the 1964 Civil Rights Act and ENDORSEMENTs by conservative leaders such as Strom Thurmond, appealed to conservative southern whites.

Four years later, seeking to capitalize on this attraction to a conservative Republican Party, Richard M. Nixon solidified a deal with Thurmond: In exchange for gaining southern support for his nomination bid and his presidential run, Nixon promised to lighten federal pressure that forced southern schools and other institutions to desegregate. Campaigning on a "law and order" platform following the violent protests against the Vietnam conflict and racial unrest, Nixon won the White House with the aid of southern whites.

However, the southern strategy did not end with the success of Nixon in 1968. Democrats, sensing the defection of their once Solid South, nominated Georgia governor Jimmy Carter to hold back the Republican intrusion in the South. Yet, in 1980, Ronald Reagan created his own southern strategy by molding what was left of the Goldwater and Nixon COALITION and combining them with a conservative appeal based on social and religious issues.

This southern strategy has become the modern-day Republican tactic to winning the White House. It begins at the Canadian border in the Rocky Mountains and runs south into the desert Southwest, then proceeds toward the Atlantic Ocean and picks up the old Confederacy states. For modern Republican strategies in capturing the White House, this block of southern states often creates a successful foundation for winning the presidency. For Democrats, some believe that it takes a few southern states from the Republican column to aid in their strategy to win the White House.

Further reading: Aistrup, Joseph A. *The Southern Strategy Revisited: Republican Top-Down Advancement in the South.* Lexington: University Press of Kentucky, 1996; Murphy, Reg, and Hal Gulliver. *The Southern Strategy.* New York: Charles Scribner's Sons, 1971.

—J. Michael Bitzer

Speaker of the House of Representatives

The Speaker of the House refers to the presiding officer within the U.S. House of Representatives. One of only four positions detailed in the Constitution, it is an office that has developed and evolved over the course of time. The origins of the position of Speaker of the House lie within the Constitution. Its inclusion along with the offices of president, vice president, and chief justice of the Supreme Court, provides an indication of the importance that the founders placed on the position of Speaker of the House. While it is indicated that the Speaker is the leadership position of the House and that it is to be voted on by the entire membership of the House, the founders failed to define the duties that accompany the position or the qualifications for the position.

It is difficult to ascertain the intent of the founders, but it is believed that they sought to emulate similar positions in the colonial legislatures as well as in the British House of Commons. In either case, the Speaker was a partisan position and one that often represented opposition to executive authority. By creating the position it is likely that the founders hoped that a Speaker, by both leading the House and representing local constituents, would provide an effective opponent to an aggressive executive branch. Nevertheless, the need to ensure that the House ran effectively while constituent needs were served continued to be a dilemma that hung over the first Speakers.

The original rules of the House gave the Speaker a variety of powers, some of which have been limited and reinstated in subsequent years. As the presiding officer, the Speaker was directed to maintain order and decorum within the House, to provide rulings on points of order, to determine violations of rules, and to appoint members to committees. In a less concrete, though no less important, way, the Speaker had a ceremonial role as the public face of the institution of the House.

The first Speaker was Frederick Muhlenberg of Pennsylvania, elected to the position on April 1, 1789. Despite the conflicting responsibilities as leader of the House and as a district representative, Muhlenberg performed well. In leading the House, he remained outside of most partisan debates, committing himself only to the issue that a location in Pennsylvania be the site of the national capital. While he appointed members to committees, he appeared to limit his involvement in their discussions. Last, Muhlenberg had a social role, inviting representatives and senators to events in order to discuss political issues.

Henry Clay is perhaps the most well known of the early Speakers. On his first day as a representative in 1810, he was elected with a large majority that encompassed not only his Democratic-Republican colleagues but also the Federalist opposition. Clay was a charismatic individual who dominated the House by his personality. One of Clay's enduring legacies was the growth in the size and power of the committee system. From 1811 to the end of his intermittent tenures as Speaker in 1825, the number of standing committees grew from nine to 25. Additionally, Clay skillfully used his appointment powers to appoint like-minded colleagues to important committees within the growing House bureaucracy.

The years after Clay's rule and prior to the Civil War were absent a man of Clay's stature, but several Speakers nonetheless provided effective leadership. The defining characteristic of those days was not the occupants of the position but the fractious environment that characterized the POLITICS of the era. Clay's legacy, particularly that regarding committees, contributed much to the acrimony of the era, as a party's control of the Speakership allowed it to determine committee assignments and the House agenda, especially in regard to issues such as slavery. As a result, during the period from 1832 to 1860, 12 men served as Speaker, with only two serving for two successive sessions. In addition, the House was witness to protracted and acrimonious elections for Speaker. The longest of these lasted from December 1855 to February 1856, a span of 63 days and 133 BALLOTs that finally resulted in Nathaniel Banks of Massachusetts becoming the Speaker.

After the Civil War, the office of Speaker began a slow ascent to finally reach its pinnacle during the era of "czar" rule from 1890 to 1910. Part of this ascent lay in the tremendous growth of the country that created a concomitant need for more legislation. During this time, the Speaker wielded control through the power of floor recognition. Republican Speaker James G. Blaine of Maine pioneered the use of this power through the creation of a "Speaker's list" of members who sought floor recognition. Blaine developed the list by asking members to come to him for clearance prior to floor recognition. If the Speaker did not approve the purpose, the member then failed to achieve recognition to address the House.

The event that finally led to czar rule occurred with the creation of the Rules Committee. By 1880, under Democratic Speaker Samuel J. Randall of Pennsylvania, reforms within the House led to the abandonment of the "Speaker's list" and instead led to the creation of the Rules Committee. This new committee, which the Speaker chaired, structured the rules by which each piece of legislation would be considered and debated. This meant that the Speaker now had control over the way legislation would be considered in addition to floor recognition and the power to appoint individuals to committees.

The end of czar rule finally occurred in 1910, when Progressive Republicans led by George Norris of Nebraska mounted a campaign to wrest control of the Rules Committee away from Speaker Joseph "Uncle Joe" Cannon. While Cannon kept his post as Speaker, the "uprising" led to an agreement in which the Rules Committee was reorganized without the Speaker as a member. Cannon's successor, Democrat Champ Clark of Missouri, acceded to further reduction in the Speaker's powers by allowing Democrats to have their committee assignments determined by the Democratic members of the Ways and Means Committee.

Their powers diminished, the Speakers after the end of czar rule had to contend with the strengthened committee chairmen. In this new era, the proliferation of committees and the inability of the Speaker to appoint members to committees resulted in the increased ability of chairmen to determine the business of the House. As a result, Speakers during the 1920s and the Roosevelt administration were weak, with Nicholas Longworth and John Nance Garner providing exceptions.

The end of czar rule did not mean the end of the powerful Speaker, as influence and control had to be wielded in different ways. While the awesome array of powers and sanctions were no longer at his control, Sam Rayburn of Texas provided the best example of the new Speaker. Rayburn (1941–61), the longest-serving speaker in the history of the House, used persuasion and worked with committee chairmen to advance his agenda. Instead of command and control, Rayburn worked toward policy goals by creating friendships and loyalty.

The 1970s heralded another wave of reform in the office of Speaker. Democrats gave their speaker, Carl Albert of Oklahoma, the power to nominate the chairman and all Democratic members of the Rules Committee and to make committee assignments through the Democratic Steering and Policy Committee, which he led. In essence, the reforms under Albert reinstituted much of what was lost during the revolt against Cannon.

Albert's successor, Tip O'Neill, benefited greatly from the expanded powers of the reinvigorated office. Unlike Albert, O'Neill more actively used the Democratic Steering and Policy Committee to make committee assignments. While O'Neill supported President Carter in his policies, O'Neill achieved noteworthy status as a Speaker through his staunch opposition and frequent legislative battles with President Ronald Reagan.

While floor responsibilities are paramount, more recent Speakers have engaged in a policy-making role. Jim Wright's tenure as Speaker began with a call toward addressing the budget deficit, social problems, and the issues stemming from the Iran-contra affair. Additionally, Wright broke new ground for the Speaker when he became involved in peace negotiations for Central America. The Speakership of Newt Gingrich was ushered in and began with an ambitious legislative program known as the CONTRACT WITH AMERICA. Gingrich also provided a dramatic example of the Speaker as tactician, often leading to titanic struggles with the Clinton administration.

The Speakership is a position that can be defined by two parameters—those determined by institutional constraints and, perhaps more importantly, those by its occupant. While the strength of the office has alternated throughout history between weak and strong, its only constant is that it is an office that does not define those who attain it, but rather, is defined by them.

Further reading: Cooper, Joseph, and David Brady. "Institutional Context and Leadership Style: The House from Cannon to Rayburn." *American Political Science Review* 75 (1981): 411–425. Office of the Speaker of the House. Available online. URL: http://speaker.house.gov. Accessed August 10, 2005; Peters, Ronald M. *The American Speakership: The Office in Historical Perspective.* Baltimore: Johns Hopkins University Press, 1997.

—Stephen Nemeth

special election

A special election is held when an incumbent dies, chooses to or is forced to resign, or is RECALLed by voters. Special elections tend to be highly competitive because no candidate enjoys the benefits of incumbency and because they offer the party out of power an unexpected chance to pick up a seat and increase its numbers.

The procedure for House special elections is laid out in Article I, Section 2, of the Constitution, which states, "When vacancies happen in the Representation from any State, the Executive Authority thereof shall issue Writs of Election to fill such Vacancies." Governors usually set the date for special elections in accordance with state law. If a House member leaves during the first session of a Congress, a special election will likely be held to succeed him or her. If a House member leaves during the second session, the governor may wait to hold the special election until the regularly scheduled ELECTION DAY, depending on how long the seat will remain vacant.

The Senate procedure for special elections was updated in 1913 with the SEVENTEENTH AMENDMENT, which allows for the direct election of senators. It states:

"When vacancies happen in the representation of any State in the Senate, the executive authority of such State shall issue writs of election to fill such vacancies: Provided that the legislature of any State may empower the executive thereof to make temporary appointments until the people fill the vacancies by election as the legislature may direct."

Usually the appointed senator serves until the next GENERAL ELECTION, at which time he or she vacates the seat to the newly elected senator. But when Senator Paul Wellstone (D, Minn.) was killed in a plane crash on October 25, 2002, Governor Jesse Ventura (I, Minn.) appointed INDEPENDENT Dean Barkley to take Wellstone's seat; Barkley remained there until January 7, 2003, when the new Congress began.

The governor, secretary of state, or other election official may determine the date of special elections for other offices, depending on state law. Historically, several women have come to Congress by running in special elections to succeed their deceased husbands. Arkansas Democrat Hattie Caraway became the first woman to win a Senate special election on January 12, 1932, when she took the seat of her late husband, Thaddeus Caraway. Later that year, she was the first woman to win a Senate seat in her own right. Among the current women House members who first won special elections to succeed their late husbands are California Republican Mary Bono, Missouri Republican Jo Ann Emerson, and California Democrat Lois Capps. Widows, however, do not always win special elections. Marta Macias Brown failed to win the seat of her late husband, California Democratic representative George Brown, in 1999. Democrat Jean Carnahan was appointed to her husband's seat when Governor Mel Carnahan (D, Mo.) was elected posthumously to the Senate after being killed in a plane crash shortly before election day in 2000. Jean Carnahan was defeated in the 2002 special election to fill out the remaining four years of her husband's term by Republican Jim Talent.

Because of their unique nature, special elections often attract a large number of candidates. A total of 135 candidates ran for governor in California's 2003 special election. In Hawaii, 44 candidates ran in January 2003 to succeed veteran Democratic representative Patsy Mink, who died the previous September. Many politicians have used special elections to advance their careers. Future president Lyndon Baines Johnson began his House career in 1937 by winning a special election in Texas.

With party representation in Congress closely divided, special elections have become a prime opportunity for the party out of power to pick up an additional seat. Special elections often attract high-profile candidates because they are already known to voters and can raise money easily, both important qualities given the limited time period in which many special elections occur. Party leaders, including the president and vice president, may campaign for candidates. Elected officials often lend candidates their staff members and advisers to aid campaigns. INTEREST GROUPS pour hundreds of thousands of dollars into the contests in hopes of currying favor with the winner.

GET-OUT-THE-VOTE efforts are also a key factor in special elections because fewer voters participate generally in special elections than in regularly scheduled elections. In the February 2004 special election to fill the House seat of Kentucky Republican Ernie Fletcher (who was elected governor in 2003), 34 percent of voters turned out to elect Democrat Ben Chandler, with 55 percent of the vote. Chandler became the first Democrat in 13 years to win a special election in a seat previously held by a Republican.

Some candidates who lose special election races run again in regularly scheduled elections. In 1996, Republican Gordon Smith lost the special election to replace Senator Bob Packwood (R, Ore.) to Democrat Ron Wyden. Smith used the visibility and support he gained in the special election to succeed retiring senator Mark Hatfield (R, Ore.) that fall. Other special election winners choose not to run for office in their own right. Democrat Zell Miller of Georgia was elected to complete the term of Senator Paul Coverdell, who died in 2000, but Miller opted not to run again in 2004.

—Mary Lynn F. Jones

split-ticket voting

Split-ticket voting (or ticket-splitting) occurs when an individual votes for candidates of different parties across various offices in the same election. Examples of split-ticket voting include someone who votes for the Democratic presidential candidate but for the Republican candidate for the U.S. House of Representatives, someone who votes for the Republican presidential candidate but the Democratic gubernatorial candidate, and someone who votes for the Democratic candidate for the U.S. House but for the Republican U.S. Senate candidate. Ticket-splitting attracts the attention of scholars and politicians alike because it is considered to be a major contributor to divided government and symptomatic of a general erosion in the influence of political parties in American POLITICS.

Split-ticket voting became a prominent feature in the American ELECTORATE in the latter half of the 20th century. Only about 15 percent of voters split their presidential and House votes during the 1950s. The incidence of ticket-splitting rose sharply in the 1960s and hit a peak in 1972, when 30 percent of voters split their tickets. More than a quarter of the electorate split their presidential-House votes during the 1980s. Although the 1990s saw a decline in ticket-splitting, it is still the case that about 20 percent of voters split their presidential-House vote.

Several explanations have been offered for split-ticket voting. The "party balancing" explanation states that voters strategically split their tickets in order to divide party control of the executive and legislative branches; voters favor divided government as a way to keep the major parties in check and encourage moderation in policy making. The "institution matching" explanation posits that many voters split their party votes because they focus on different issues and attributes when voting for presidential and congressional candidates. More specifically, presidential campaigns often revolve around economic and foreign policy issues, which tend to be REPUBLICAN PARTY strengths. By contrast, House campaigns often emphasize domestic policy concerns, many of which are DEMOCRATIC PARTY strengths. The INCUMBENCY ADVANTAGE explanation highlights the many ways in which congressional incumbents can cultivate support among their constituents and protect themselves from electoral forces that might shape the accompanying presidential race. The "party decline" explanation posits that party allegiances are generally less important to voters, thus making them more willing to cross party lines as they cast votes for different offices on the BALLOT. Because split-ticket voting has important consequences for patterns of divided government and the partisan composition of congress, it will continue to be closely monitored by party strategists and academic observers.

Further reading: Burden, Barry C., and David C. Kimball. *Why Americans Split Their Tickets: Campaigns, Competition, and Divided Government.* Ann Arbor: University of Michigan Press, 2002.

—Julio Borquez

spoiler

A spoiler in general is considered to be a third-party candidate in a race dominated by two parties in a plurality-style election. The third candidate is seldom considered to have a viable chance of winning but rather is in the race for the strategic reason of siphoning votes from one of the two dominant party candidates. Particularly in a close race, a spoiler who diverts votes from the "leading candidate" can affect the outcome, and when successful, deny the once leading candidate the election.

At this point in U.S. history, the most famous spoiler candidate is Ralph Nader of the GREEN PARTY, who ran as a third candidate in the 2000 presidential contest. In the end, the race hinged on the state of Florida, where Gore was eventually ruled to have lost by 537 votes in the final RECOUNT. Nader, who ran much to the political left of Gore, won 96,837 votes, the vast majority of which likely would have gone to Gore and not to Bush had Nader not been in the race. In this case, Nader arguably spoiled the race for Gore. Nader was not the only third-party candidate on the presidential BALLOT that year: three INDEPENDENTS and one REFORM PARTY candidate were also third-party candidates. The other four candidates gained a total of about 42,000 votes among them, but it is Nader's presence on the ballot that is widely believed to have affected the outcome.

A spoiler may not always aid one of the two major parties. In the 1994 Maine gubernatorial race, Independent Angus King was elected rather than the Republican or the Democrat. The presence of a Green Party candidate on the ticket is thought to have taken enough votes away from the Democrat to push King over the finish line. In this case, the Green Party candidate was again the spoiler siphoning votes away from the Democrat. However, the Republicans did not benefit, and the Independent candidate advanced to office.

Third-party candidates are not always strategically placed on the ballot specifically to be spoilers. In some states, smaller parties nominate candidates because of adherence to strict ideologies. In states such as New York, the Conservative and Right-to-Life parties have a fairly strict orthodoxy for candidates to gain their ENDORSEMENTS. While frequently placing the name of the Republican nominee on their ballot lines, these parties will only qualify candidates who adhere to and commit to their core principles. While occasionally achieving the spoiler effect as described above, these smaller parties often do not affect the final outcome of the elections at municipal, state, or federal levels.

—Jack St. Croix

state party committees

These are permanent committees designed to formulate and execute the electioneering strategy of a state POLITICAL PARTY. Parties formed during the earliest days of the republic, though those PARTY ORGANIZATIONS were primarily legislative caucuses. State party committees did not begin to form until after the first national committee, the DEMOCRATIC NATIONAL COMMITTEE, was formed in 1832. Immediately thereafter, parties at the state level began to form their own permanent committees. Mostly, those committees were crony organizations for powerful party leaders who integrated their local party machines with state party mechanisms.

Party committees were occasional organizations, meeting to handle NOMINATIONS and prepare state conventions, but did little more and would disappear as soon as an election season ended. Some states had no formal party committees, relying solely on the leadership of chairmen. By 1930, though, all states had committees for both of the major political parties.

The Progressive reforms undermined local machine powers, and state party committees were some of the hardest hit by the reforms. Stripped of PATRONAGE and nomination power, both loyalists in the ELECTORATE and candidates had little use for the organization of their political party. Therefore, throughout most of the 20th century state party committees were committees in name only. NATIONAL PARTY COMMITTEES suffered nearly as much but were still able to revive themselves in the 1970s. During this period, however, most state parties had no permanent headquarters and sporadic leadership and were active only when elections approached. State party committees lagged behind their national counterparts but still embarked on a state-by-state self-renewal process in the 1980s and 1990s.

State party committees lack the nomination and patronage powers of their forebears but have managed to mimic the national committees in reinventing themselves as election support committees. Expanded FUND-RAISING and permanent headquarters laid the groundwork for the states, like the national committees before them, to recruit candidates for office, coordinate campaign efforts with the national party committees and POLITICAL ACTION COMMITTEES, target resources to competitive races, and generally support the party's SLATE of candidates in a given state. Not all state committees have fully developed, but all have some manner of permanent facility, and all participate in campaigns. More powerful than they had been throughout most of the 20th century, state party committees are once again significant parts of the electioneering process.

Further reading: Jewell, Malcolm, and Sarah Morehouse. *Political Parties and Elections in American States.* Washington, D.C.: CQ Press, 2001; Katz, Richard S., and Peter Mair. *How Parties Organize.* Thousand Oaks, Calif.: Sage Publications, 1994; Reichley, A. James. *The Life of the Parties.* 2nd ed. Lanham, Md.: Rowman & Littlefield, 2002.

—Chapman Rackaway

States' Rights Democratic Party   *See* DIXIECRATS.

straight-ticket voting

Voting a "straight ticket" means that a person votes for the same POLITICAL PARTY for all positions listed on a BALLOT. The term dates from the 19th century. Before the 1890s, there was not one ballot for all voters in a given electoral PRECINCT. Instead, each party issued a long ticket, or party strip, listing all of the party's candidates running for different positions. Voters were encouraged to "vote a straight party ticket."

Beginning in 1889, states began to print nonpartisan ballots. The ballots now included the names of all candidates running for all offices, regardless of partisan affiliation. With the introduction of this new system, voters were now confronted with long lists of candidates from different parties for the various offices. One outcome of this long ballot was voter roll-off, in which voters cast votes for high-profile offices, but failed to vote for offices lower down on the ballot. To combat this problem, often called voter fatigue, many state legislatures adopted a straight-ticket option, which allows voters to cast a single vote for all candidates from their preferred party. Studies have found that the straight-ticket option makes voting easier and quicker and increases turnout for lower-level offices.

Since the 1960s, there has been an overall decline in straight-ticket voting and a rise in SPLIT-TICKET VOTING among voters. This is when voters cast their votes for candidates from different parties. Scholars have argued that this decrease in straight-ticket voting is due to a decline in partisanship, or attachment to a political party, among voters and the rise of CANDIDATE-CENTERED ELECTIONS.

In recent years, many states have taken up the issue of straight-ticket voting in legislatures and on referenda to eliminate its use. Many of its detractors argue that straight-ticket voting benefits only one political party and is used more by particular groups in the ELECTORATE. The use of the straight-ticket option on ballots is decreasing. In the 2002 GENERAL ELECTION, only 16 states allowed voters to cast a straight-party ticket. The states that still use the straight-party option are concentrated in the South and former Rustbelt states of the Midwest and Northeast, with a few exceptions.

Further reading: Rusk, Jerrold G. "The Effect of the Australian Ballot Reform on Split Ticket Voting: 1876–1908." *American Political Science Review* 64 (1970): 1,220–1,238.

—Jae-Jae Spoon

straw poll

Straw polls are perhaps best understood in relation to scientific polls. Scientific polls are designed to learn about the collective opinion of a population by asking questions of a small subgroup (called a sample) of people that is known to be representative of the larger population. For example, in order to measure what proportion of registered voters intended to vote for George W. Bush in the PRESIDENTIAL ELECTION, a scientific pollster would ask a small group of registered voters (usually around 1,000 people) who they intend to vote for. The key point to understand is that for scientific polls the sample is selected by the pollster in such a way as to ensure that it is representative of the larger population of interest. The fundamental characteristic of straw polls is that, in contrast to scientific polls, they have samples that are not representative of the larger group of interest. As a result, straw polls cannot be relied upon to reveal the collective opinion of the larger population.

One of the most famous examples of the characteristics and dangers of straw polls was the 1936 *Literary Digest* poll. The *Literary Digest* was a popular magazine that, prior to the 1936 election, sent a poll to a sample of people picked from telephone directories and automobile registration lists. The results of the poll, based on responses from more than 2 million people, suggested that the Republican candidate, Alf Landon, would win the 1936 PRESIDENTIAL ELECTION in a landslide. Of course, as it turned out, it was actually Democrat Franklin Roosevelt who won the election. Why was the *Literary Digest* prediction so wrong? In 1936, when telephones and automobiles had not been around for long and were quite expensive, people who appeared in telephone directories and automobile registration lists were likely to be much wealthier than the average American. In short, the sample drawn from 1936 telephone directories and automobile registration lists was not representative of the overall American ELECTORATE.

Straw polls were much more common in the days prior to the 1930s, which is when scientific polling techniques were applied to POLITICS. Nevertheless, straw polls still exist. Many Web sites, for example, ask visitors to complete online surveys. Of course, the Web site does not control the sample; any visitors to the Web site can choose to complete the survey if they are so inclined. As a result, the sample is not necessarily representative of any larger population, making this type of Internet survey a modern-day straw poll. Though they can be fun to participate in, these Internet straw polls should not be used to draw conclusions about the collective opinions of any population.

Further reading: Lavrakas, Paul J., Michael W. Traugott, and Peter V. Miller, eds. *Presidential Polls and the News Media.* Boulder, Colo.: Westview Press, 1995.

—Gregory A. Smith

suffrage

Suffrage refers to the right of citizens to vote. In the early decades of the nation's history, suffrage rights were stringently limited. Many of the founding fathers believed it an appropriate requirement that citizens should own property in order to vote, and particularly so if they wanted to hold elective office. However, they were unable to agree on how the precise wording of such a requirement should be incorporated into the Constitution. Therefore, Article 1, Section 4, of the Constitution left it up to the states to establish their own requirements regarding suffrage rights. For much of the early history of the country, the states generally limited suffrage rights to white male property owners. Over time, suffrage rights have been extended to larger portions of the population through five major reform movements aimed at incorporating the following groups: the lower classes, African Americans, women, residents of the District of Columbia, and 18-year-olds.

The founders supported the notion of establishing property qualifications for voting based on the rationale that only those who had a real stake in the government should play a part in the selection of its leaders. Many believed that if an individual was not successful in his own financial endeavors, he was not worthy of being involved in developing the policies of the government. In addition, many elitists feared that if the poor had equal rights in terms of political participation, including voting rights, they would enact policies that benefited themselves at the expense of the wealthier population. On this basis, denial of voting rights was a form of self-protection.

Over time, the society and its political views changed. Thomas Jefferson's influence was particularly significant in contributing to this change in philosophy. He had great faith in the common man and believed that the common man should be an active participant in his community. Similarly, Andrew Jackson during his presidency also stressed the importance of allowing the common man to be a part of government. As Jefferson and Jackson's philosophy spread, financial qualifications were relaxed. By 1840, such qualifications had been removed from most state constitutions, allowing all white males over the age of 21 to vote.

Nevertheless, financial qualifications for voting in the United States were not removed entirely until 1966. The TWENTY-FOURTH AMENDMENT to the U.S. Constitution, ratified in 1964, prohibits the federal or state governments from imposing POLL TAXes in federal elections for offices such as the presidency, the Senate, or the House of Representatives. A poll tax is a fee that must be paid before a citizen is allowed to vote. In addition, the amendment also prohibits these governments from barring citizens from voting in such elections because they have not paid any other form of tax that they owe. It was not until 1966, when the Supreme Court handed down its decision in the case of *Harper v. Virginia State Board of Elections*, that the use of poll taxes was outlawed in all other elections.

African Americans have endured a long struggle in the quest to attain full CITIZENSHIP rights, including voting rights. In the 1857 Supreme Court case of *Dred Scott v. Sanford*, Chief Justice Roger Taney ruled that slaves were the property of their owners and therefore lacked standing as citizens of the United States. The Court's decision in the case upheld slavery as an institution in the United States. It was not until the conclusion of the Civil War in 1865 that African Americans began, technically at least, to attain greater rights. The Thirteenth Amendment, ratified in 1865, made slavery illegal unless it was used as a form of punishment against one convicted of a crime. The FOURTEENTH AMENDMENT, ratified in 1868, granted full citizenship rights to former slaves, thereby reversing the Court's decision in *Dred Scott*. The amendment extended voting rights to all males over the age of 21, regardless of race. It went so far as to mandate that if a state denied its citizens the right to vote in any election, it risked losing its representation in Congress in proportion to the percentage of its adult male population that was denied the right. To address even more directly the issue of voting rights of former slaves, the FIFTEENTH AMENDMENT was ratified in 1870. Section 1 of the amendment extends voting rights to all regardless of race, color, or previous condition of servitude. Section 2 grants Congress the authority to enact legislation needed to enforce the amendment.

The reality of African-American voting rights has been much more complicated than the texts of these amendments would indicate. African Americans were able to exercise voting rights in the years immediately after the conclusion of the Civil War. However, RECONSTRUCTION came to an end in 1877. At that point, the federal troops who had ensured African Americans' access to the public realm in the South were withdrawn from the region. Whites began to engage once again in practices that discriminated against African Americans, including interfering with their right to vote through a variety of means. Most basic of all, whites often used fear and intimidation as a means of preventing African Americans from voting. The "Jim Crow" laws of the time segregated whites and blacks. African Americans who violated these laws or otherwise attempted to fully exercise their rights of citizenship risked physical abuse or even death through lynching.

More directly, limitations and/or additional requirements were imposed on African Americans who attempted to vote. One common strategy was for southern officials to implement what came to be known as the WHITE PRIMARY. These officials simply refused to allow African Americans to vote in PRIMARY elections. At the time, the DEMOCRATIC PARTY was the dominant party in the region. Despite the fact that African Americans technically could vote in the GENERAL ELECTION later in the year, their votes were essentially meaningless because they had no voice in selecting who the Democratic nominee would be. Given the strength of the Democratic Party at the time, there was little chance that the Republican candidate would win in the general election. The white primary was not made illegal until 1944, when the Supreme Court declared it unconstitutional in the case of SMITH V. ALLWRIGHT.

Other common methods of denying African Americans the right to vote were through the use of LITERACY TESTS, poll taxes, and other unfair registration procedures. Literacy tests often required prospective voters to interpret legal documents rather than simply demonstrate one's ability to read, and any small error in completing necessary forms constituted sufficient grounds to deny the right to vote. The poll tax, as discussed above, required the payment of a fee in order to vote. White citizens were exempted from such requirements through what became known as GRANDFATHER CLAUSES: If one's grandfather had been eligible to vote in 1860, meaning that only whites met the exemption, they were not required to fulfill any of these additional requirements. In less formal ways, white officials also denied African Americans the opportunity to vote by delaying the processing of their registration forms or by simply closing their offices when African Americans came to register.

Despite the ratification of the Fifteenth Amendment in 1870, the vast majority of African Americans did not vote as late as 1964. It was not until 1965 that Section 2 of the amendment became relevant. Congress began to enforce the amendment through appropriate legislation: the VOTING RIGHTS ACT (VRA) OF 1965. The VRA grants authority to federal officials, including federal registrars and the U.S. Justice Department, to monitor voting participation among African Americans in the South. It prohibits government officials in these areas from using any methods to prevent African Americans from voting, including the use of literacy tests. As a result of the VRA, African Americans now regularly vote at higher rates than white citizens with comparable levels of education.

Before the Civil War, women in the United States were actively involved in the abolitionist movement to end slavery. It was through their involvement in this issue that women began to confront their own inferior political status. Both Lucretia Mott and Elizabeth Cady Stanton were denied the opportunity to participate as American DELEGATEs in the 1840 World Anti-Slavery Convention in London. Eight years after the convention, Mott and Stanton organized the SENECA FALLS CONVENTION to address the rights of women, including the first call for women to have suffrage rights. With the exception of women in some western states, females were not allowed to vote in the United States. Women in some western states did receive the right to vote on a state-by-state basis as early as 1869. Women in these areas generally made up only a small portion of the population, but their scarcity actually worked to their political advantage in terms of gaining rights. Because these women were needed for companionship and to raise children, they tended to be more highly valued and therefore granted more rights, including voting rights.

Many members of the National American Woman Suffrage Association, which formed in 1890, supported the state-by-state expansion of voting rights. However, its first two leaders, Stanton and Susan B. Anthony, believed that suffrage must be granted on a nationwide basis. In 1878, an amendment that Anthony wrote granting women voting rights was introduced in Congress for the first time. Though it was voted down a number of times over the next 40 years, it finally passed by the required two-thirds margin in both the House and the Senate by June 1919. It was ratified by the necessary three-fourths of the states by 1920, becoming the NINETEENTH AMENDMENT to the Constitution.

Unlike citizens of states, residents of the District of Columbia do not have voting representation in the U.S. House or Senate. Instead, they are represented in these chambers by a nonvoting delegate in the House, a "shadow" representative, and two "shadow" senators. The TWENTY-THIRD AMENDMENT grants to citizens of the District a formal role in electing the president every four years. The amendment grants the District the same, but no more than, number of electors in the ELECTORAL COLLEGE as has the smallest state; at present, that number stands at three. With the addition of the District in 1961, the total number of votes cast in the Electoral College increased to 538, representing one for each of the 435 House districts, 100 for the two Senate seats from each of the 50 states, and the District's three electoral votes.

The final major expansion in suffrage rights was a reaction to the antiwar protests conducted by the nation's young people during the Vietnam War. In public schools and on college campuses across the nation, young people protested U.S. involvement in Vietnam. Sometimes these protests were peaceful, as in the wearing of armbands in silent protest. At other times they turned violent, as happened in 1968 in Chicago and in 1970 in Ohio. During the 1968 Democratic convention in Chicago, held to nominate the party's candidate for president in that year's race, antiwar protesters collided with the city's police force. The events were covered live by the network reporters who were on the scene to report on the political developments regarding the convention. In 1970, four Kent State University college students who were protesting the war were shot and killed by members of the Ohio National Guard during a confrontation on that campus.

Many in the nation believed that the frequency and intensity of the antiwar protests would be reduced if young people had the right to vote. Young people were engaging in vocal protests because they and/or their classmates were being drafted into military service, yet they did not have a voice in electing the representatives who were authorizing the military's actions. The voting age in most states at that time was set at 21, although males were eligible for the military draft at the age of 18. The TWENTY-SIXTH AMENDMENT, ratified in 1971, reduced the voting age to 18 nationwide in all elections. Supporters of the amendment believed that if young people were granted a right to vote, they would express their political beliefs through the BALLOT as opposed to the bullhorn. This has been only partly true; while today's young people are less likely to engage in the violent protest activities that were more common in their parents' generation, they are also unlikely to express their attitudes in a voting booth. Voters aged 18 to 21 have the lowest rate of VOTER TURNOUT of any demographic group.

Despite the expansion of suffrage rights to more and more groups of voters over the course of U.S. history, Americans continue to vote at lower rates than citizens of other nations. In part, this is due to differences in how voter turnout rates are calculated in the United States compared to other nations. In the United States, voter turnout rate is determined by comparing the percentage of the voting age population in the country to the percentage that casts a ballot. This number includes many who are, in fact, ineligible to vote: those who are in prison or who have felony records, those who are not legal citizens of the country, and those who are eligible to vote but who are not registered to do so. In fact, the largest drop in voter turnout rates occurred following the 1971 ratification of the Twenty-sixth Amendment, when 18-year-olds were added to the voting rolls. Their inclusion on the rolls as "eligible voters" increased significantly the number of people in the nation who could vote. However, because young people are much less likely than older people to vote, or even to be registered to vote, the nation's overall voter turnout rate has declined since they became eligible to participate. In many other nations, in contrast, the turnout rate is calculated based on the number of registered voters who turn out to vote on ELECTION DAY. This results in an artificially high turnout rate in these nations.

Further reading: Arrington, Karen McGill, and William L. Taylor, eds. *Voting Rights in America: Continuing the Quest for Full Participation.* Lanham, Md.: University Press of America, 1992.

—Claudia Bryant

suffrage, African-American

The U.S. Constitution, and Supreme Court interpretation of that document, legalized the notion of African Americans as second-class citizens. The U.S. Constitution allowed slaves to be imported into the United States until 1808. The THREE-FIFTHS COMPROMISE allowed southern states more representation in the U.S. House of Representatives by including African Americans in their CENSUSES at the rate of three-fifths. In 1857, the U.S. Supreme Court determined that Dred Scott, a slave, did not have the right to sue because he was not a citizen. Chief Justice Roger Taney reasoned that African Americans (whether enslaved or not) were not meant to be citizens according to the Constitution. There is no definition of CITIZENSHIP in the original Constitution.

Following the abolition of slavery in 1863 and the "Civil War Amendments," legal avenues were created for African Americans to enjoy SUFFRAGE. The Thirteenth Amendment (1865) outlawed slavery, while the FOURTEENTH AMENDMENT (1868), among other things, defined citizenship and extended it to "all persons born or naturalized in the United States." The FIFTEENTH AMENDMENT, ratified two years after the Fourteenth, explicitly granted African-American males the right to vote.

The U.S. Constitution is vague when it comes to voting and voting rights. There are no provisions for matters such as registration, NOMINATION, or qualifications for office (other than federal office). The Constitution gives state governments the power to make these decisions. There is no mention of political parties in the Constitution. This means that a key component of the elections process (nominations) is not regulated or otherwise stipulated by the Constitution.

In former southern slave states, barriers to participation were erected against African Americans once the Civil War Amendments were ratified. These barriers included POLL TAXES that required citizens to pay a tax in order to be able to vote. African Americans were also subjected to literacy and good citizenship tests in order to be able to register. While some whites (especially poor whites) were also subjected to literacy and good citizenship tests, the tests were generally given at the discretion of local voting officials, and invariably the tests for African Americans were more difficult to complete than were those given to whites.

African Americans were also subject to GRANDFATHER CLAUSES. Grandfather clauses required that citizens prove that their grandfathers had been eligible to vote in order to be able to vote themselves. For several decades following RECONSTRUCTION (the period immediately following the Civil War), thousands of African Americans were denied the right to vote because their grandfathers, who had been slaves, had not been allowed to vote. The U.S. Supreme Court outlawed grandfather clauses in *Guinn v. U.S.* in 1915.

African-American suffrage was also denied through the white primary. The WHITE PRIMARY was practiced by Democratic parties in the South as a way to prevent African Americans from voting in their primaries. These practices had the effect of denying African Americans voting rights altogether because southern whites strongly opposed Abraham Lincoln's REPUBLICAN PARTY. It was rare for Republican parties to exist or be organized at the state or local levels in the South. This meant that the only party holding primaries or putting candidates forward was the DEMOCRATIC PARTY. Without competition in the GENERAL ELECTION, whoever won the Democratic primary won the election by default. In preventing African Americans from participating in Democratic primaries, African Americans were effectively frozen out from voting altogether. The U.S. Supreme Court outlawed white primaries in *SMITH V. ALLWRIGHT* in 1944.

This combination of barriers, coupled with violent intimidation, kept African Americans from the voting rights guaranteed them in the Fourteenth and Fifteenth Amendments. The push for full enjoyment of voting rights took root during the CIVIL RIGHTS MOVEMENT. In 1963–64, Dr. Martin Luther King, Jr., along with hundreds of African Americans, went to the Selma, Alabama, courthouse in order to register to vote. They were all turned away. King's organized protests of African Americans being denied the right to register or vote ultimately resulted in the ratification of the TWENTY-FOURTH AMENDMENT in 1964 and passage of the Voting Rights Act in 1965.

The Twenty-fourth Amendment bans the practice of requiring poll taxes, while the Voting Rights Act codifies the Fifteenth Amendment by breaking down existing voting barriers. The Voting Rights Act eliminated the use of literacy or good citizenship tests as voting conditions. The Voting Rights Act also authorized the use of Department of Justice examiners to oversee registration and voting, particularly in those areas where registration and turnout did not reach 50 percent. The Voting Rights Act also outlawed other barriers to voting, such as requiring that any meaningful changes in election procedures be cleared by the Jus-

tice Department. Since passage of the Voting Rights Act, African-American registration and voting have increased significantly, particularly in the South.

The Voting Rights Act was amended in 1982 in part to address the notion of "vote dilution," whereby election districts are organized in a way that minimizes the impact of African-American voters. In *Thornberg v. Gingles* (1986), the U.S. Supreme Court encouraged states to minimize vote dilution by promoting increased African-American representation in the U.S. House of Representatives through the creation of districts that included a majority of minority group members. These MAJORITY-MINORITY DISTRICTS have resulted in significant increases in the number of African-American congressional members, but have resulted in a legal backlash in more recent cases in which whites have successfully argued that racial GERRYMANDERING has resulted in reverse discrimination.

Discrimination toward African Americans in their efforts to secure voting rights has been addressed through a

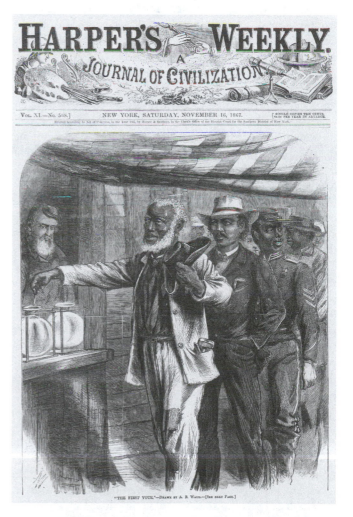

A cover of *Harper's Weekly* depicting blacks voting for the first time, 1867 *(Library of Congress)*

series of state and federal laws, amendments to the Constitution, and Supreme Court decisions. More recent questions have arisen regarding whether practices that encourage increased representation among African Americans in elected office constitute discrimination against whites.

Further reading: Baker, Lucius J., Mack H. Jones, and Katherine Tate. *African-Americans and the American Political System.* 4th ed. Upper Saddle River, N.J.: Prentice Hall, 1999; Gilliam, Franklin D., Jr. *Farther to Go: Readings and Cases in African American Politics.* Fort Worth, Tex.: Harcourt College Publishers, 2002.

—Terri Fine

suffrage, age requirements

The question of who should be granted the right to vote has triggered much debate throughout American history. While the practice of withholding SUFFRAGE on the basis of race, gender, or wealth has been discredited, the idea that there should be a minimum age for the exercise of voting rights has near-universal acceptance. The question that has confronted the American people and policy makers is not whether to use age as a criterion for suffrage, but rather which age is the appropriate threshold.

Throughout the American colonies, the age of 21 was widely established for voting rights, based on the English practice granting knighthood to no one younger than 21 years of age. But even in the early days of the republic, this threshold was not uncontested. Thomas Jefferson was among the notable advocates of lowering the age of suffrage so that those in military service to their state and country could vote for their elected officials. Indeed, the argument that a person who is old enough to fight in the military and die for the country should be old enough to vote has long resonated, as attempts to lower the voting age have been made during or in the aftermath of wars throughout American history.

Advocates of a legal voting age of 18 had to battle two significant obstacles. First, doubts about lowering the long-standing tradition that set 21 as the threshold for political maturity, and thereby suffrage, were widespread. Second, states' rights proponents contended that voting rights should be left to and determined by the states and were concerned that national efforts to intrude on the prerogatives of the states in this regard would lead to additional encroachments in other matters.

The large numbers of military personnel under 21 who served in World War II led to renewed calls for a lowering of the voting age, but a proposed constitutional amendment that was introduced in 1942 was never considered on the floor of the Senate. The war did lead to change on the state level, however. In 1943, Georgia amended its constitution to establish 18 as the state's legal voting age.

The national movement gained a high-profile ENDORSE-MENT on January 7, 1954. President Dwight D. Eisenhower neatly summed up arguments in favor of a lower voting age when he declared before a joint session of Congress, "For years our citizens between the ages of 18 and 21 have, in time of peril, been summoned to fight for America. They should participate in the political process that produces this fateful summons. I urge Congress to propose to the States a constitutional amendment permitting citizens to vote when they reach the age of 18." In May of 1954, the Senate considered Eisenhower's proposal, but failed to muster the two-thirds vote needed. SOUTHERN DEMOCRATS who defended states' rights were the strongest opponents of the measure.

The Vietnam War brought the gap between the right to vote and the obligation to serve in the military to the forefront of the nation's attention. Widespread opposition to the war led many young people to protest and resist the military draft, which required male Americans to register at age 18. Organizations that promoted the cause of lowering the voting age came together in the Youth Franchise Coalition, which counted among its members established groups such as the National Education Association, the American Legion, Veterans of Foreign Wars, B'nai B'rith, YMCA, and the NATIONAL ASSOCIATION FOR THE ADVANCEMENT OF COLORED PEOPLE. New organizations emerged as well, such as Let Us Vote (LUV) and COMMON CAUSE, and lobbied for their cause at both the national and state levels.

By 1970, their efforts had yielded several successes. Three states—Alaska, Georgia, and Kentucky—allowed 18-year-olds to vote. Three other states—Massachusetts, Minnesota, and Montana—had set their minimum age for suffrage at 19. An additional three states—Hawaii, Maine, and Nebraska—had established 20 as their voting age. The other 41 states still did not grant the franchise to anyone under 21 years old.

That year, Congress attempted to lower the voting age nationally through ordinary legislation, in spite of the widespread belief that the only way it could constitutionally do so was by amending the U.S. Constitution. The Senate attached a provision lowering the voting age to 18 in all U.S. elections to a bill that would extend the Voting Rights Act. The bill passed both the Senate and House, and President Richard M. Nixon, who endorsed the idea of lowering the voting age but thought that it would be unconstitutional to do so via regular legislation, signed the bill into law in spite of his reservations.

The issue reached the Supreme Court in the case of *Oregon v. Mitchell*, and in December 1970, the Court, in a sharply divided decision, held that Congress could alter the voting age only for federal elections. The decision left the country with a voting age of 18 years in federal elections and of 21 years in much of the country for state and local elections. As the logistical challenges and financial implications of the decision became clear—states would need to maintain separate voter lists and use distinct sets of voting machines for voters of different ages—pressure built for a constitutional amendment that would apply a uniform national standard for suffrage.

One month after the decision in *Oregon v. Mitchell*, a constitutional amendment was introduced in the Senate to lower the voting age to 18 in all U.S. elections. It was approved without dissent on March 10, 1971. The House followed suit on March 23, 1971, by a vote of 400 to 19. When Ohio became the 38th state to ratify the amendment on June 30, 1971, providing the necessary three-fourths of all the states, the TWENTY-SIXTH AMENDMENT became the fastest-ratified amendment in U.S. history, just 100 days after Congress had passed it. The text of the amendment reads, "The right of citizens of the United States, who are eighteen years of age or older, to vote shall not be denied or abridged by the United States or by any state on account of age." With the ratification of the amendment, the ages at which the United States asks its citizens to fight and allows them to vote at last became aligned.

Further reading: Cultice, Wendell W. *Youth's Battle for the Ballot: A History of Voting Age in America.* New York: Greenwood Press, 1992; Keysarr, Alexander. *The Right to Vote: The Contested History of Democracy in the United States.* New York: Basic Books, 2000.

—Brendan J. Doherty

suffrage, District of Columbia

Unlike other American citizens who pay income taxes, residents of the District of Columbia do not elect voting members to the U.S. Congress. Also, there have been times in its history when the District's residents did not elect their local government or cast BALLOTs for presidential electors.

The Constitution (Article I, Section 2, Clause 2) provides that members of the House of Representatives be chosen "by the People of the Several states," and allocates electoral votes based on a state's total representation in Congress (Article II, Section 1, Clause 2). Since the District is not a state, it is not entitled to representation in the House or the Senate. Article I, Section 8, Clause 17 of the Constitution gives Congress power to "exercise exclusive legislation in all Cases whatsoever over such capital district . . . as may . . . become the seat of Government of the United States."

Prior to the arrival of the federal government in 1801 from the temporary capital of Philadelphia, residents of Washington voted for members of the House of Representatives from Maryland. In 1801, Congress passed the Organic Acts of 1801 (2 Stat. 103), which stripped the residents of the District of the right to vote for members of Congress. In 1802, a charter was granted to the City of Washington. It provided for an elected 12-member city council and a mayor appointed by the president of the United States. By 1820, residents of Washington could vote for mayor.

In 1871, the city governments of Washington and Georgetown were abolished and replaced by a territorial government with a governor and an 11-member council appointed by the president. An elected 22-member House of Delegates and a nonvoting DELEGATE to the House of Representatives were created. This government's excessive spending pushed the District to the verge of bankruptcy, and it was abolished in 1874. Congress then created a three-member board of commissioners, appointed by the president, to run the District. The residents of Washington, D.C., would not elect another local government for 100 years.

The TWENTY-THIRD AMENDMENT was added to the Constitution in 1961. The amendment granted the District of Columbia a number of electoral votes equal to that of the least populous state (three votes). Three years later, the District's residents voted in their first PRESIDENTIAL ELECTION.

In 1967, Congress approved the District of Columbia Elected Board of Education Act. The following year, voters elected an 11-member school board. In 1970, Congress reestablished the position of nonvoting delegate (Public Law 91–405). Walter Fauntroy was elected in 1971. In 1973, Congress enacted the District of Columbia Self-Government and Government Reorganization Act (Public Law 93-198). The act provided for an elected mayor and a 13-member city council. The following year, Walter Washington became the city's first elected mayor in more than 100 years.

In 1972, the platforms of the Democratic and Republican parties supported congressional representation for the District of Columbia. In 1978, Congress proposed the D.C. Voting Rights Constitutional Amendment. The amendment would have given the District representation in both houses of Congress, as if it were a state, granted the District electoral votes equal in number to its total representation in Congress, given the District government the power to ratify amendments to the U.S. Constitution as if it were a state, and repealed the Twenty-third Amendment. The amendment was not ratified by the requisite 38 states and expired in 1985. In 1982, the voters of the District approved a constitution for the state of New Columbia. Since 1990, the District has elected shadow senators and a shadow representative, who are not allowed onto the floor of the House or Senate and who function as unpaid LOBBYISTS for SUFFRAGE.

In 1993, the delegate from the District of Columbia (as well as those representing Puerto Rico, Guam, the Virgin Islands, and American Samoa) was given the right to vote in the Committee of the Whole House on the State of the Union in the House of Representatives (House Rule XXIII). This committee is composed of all members of the House and considers most bills before they are formally debated by the House. However, this privilege was limited in that the committee would automatically be dissolved if the votes of the delegates provided the margin of victory on a motion. Following the Republican takeover of the House in 1995, this rule was rescinded.

Since the failure of the amendment, there have been a number of unsuccessful legislative efforts to extend the franchise to residents of the District of Columbia. A bill has been introduced in Congress that would allow District residents to vote for representatives from Maryland; statehood bills have been introduced (the state of New Columbia); there has been a proposal to balance a likely Democratic house seat from the District with an additional likely Republican seat from the state of Utah, and a bill was introduced that would have exempted residents of the District from paying federal income taxes until the District received voting representation.

In 2000, the District government placed the motto "Taxation without Representation" on the District's license plates. President William Jefferson Clinton had the new plates placed on the presidential limousine. President George W. Bush, upon taking office in 2001, had the plates removed.

In 2001, a federal appeals court ruled against District residents who had brought a lawsuit in an effort to gain voting representation in Congress (*Adams v. Clinton,* 90 F. Supp 2d 35). Subsequently, the Inter-American Commission on Human Rights found that the U.S. government had denied the citizens of the District of Columbia "an effective right to participate in the Federal legislature" (IACHR, 2003; paragraph 117). The rulings of the commission, an organ of the Organization of American States (OAS), are not binding.

In 2004, in an effort to draw attention to its situation, the District held an unsanctioned "first in the nation" PRIMARY to draw presidential candidates to the District in order to gain their support for full suffrage. The Democratic candidates, fearful of offending voters in Iowa and New Hampshire, ignored the primary since the DEMOCRATIC NATIONAL COMMITTEE did not recognize the primary. Just under 13 percent of the District's 342,000 voters participated.

Further reading: Best, Judith. *National Representation for the District of Columbia.* Frederick, Md.: University Publications of America, 1984; Inter-American Commission on Human Rights. *Statehood Solidarity Committtee, United States,* Case 11.204; Report 98/03. Washington, D.C.: Organization of American States, 2003; Markman, Stephen J. *Statehood for the District of Columbia: Is It Constitutional? Is It Wise? Is It Necessary?* Washington, D.C.: National Legal Center for the Public Interest, 1988.

—Jeffrey Kraus

suffrage, Native American

Though the right to vote is fundamental in that it is preservative of other basic civil and political rights, the franchise has been denied to blacks, women, Native Americans, Hispanics, and various immigrant groups throughout various periods of American history. While the right of African Americans to vote was constitutionally protected in 1870 with the enactment of the FIFTEENTH AMENDMENT, and women's suffrage was secured in 1919 with the TWENTIETH AMENDMENT, the right of Native Americans to vote has never been formally protected or secured by a constitutional amendment.

Subject to certain rules regarding the electoral process and specific federal constitutional prohibitions against the denial or abridgment of the right to vote on account of "race, color or previous condition of servitude" (Fifteenth Amendment, 1870), sex (NINETEENTH AMENDMENT, 1920), failure to pay POLL taxes (TWENTY-FOURTH AMENDMENT, 1964), and age (TWENTY-SIXTH AMENDMENT, 1971), all states have the power to set "reasonable" requirements in determining who is eligible to vote in local, state, and national elections. Consequently, many local, state, and national officials have historically used this power to deny the franchise to Native Americans.

For example, state officials in California, Minnesota, Oklahoma, North Dakota, and Wisconsin denied the right of Indians to vote by adopting provisions in their state constitutions requiring that all voters be "civilized." The Minnesota supreme court defined this requirement more specifically in 1917 in *Opshal v. Johnson.* There, the justices declared that "tribal Indians" might "prove to the satisfaction of the courts" that they are civilized "by taking up [their] abode outside the reservation and there pursuing the customs and habits of civilization" for a period of several years.

State taxation laws and residency requirements have also been used to deny or abridge the right of Indians to vote. The states of New Mexico, Idaho, and Washington, for example, barred from the polls all "Indians not taxed." And despite an 1881 U.S. Supreme Court decision that held that all Indians were residents of the state in which their reservations were located, the Utah supreme court ruled in 1956 in *Allen v. Merrill* that Indians living on reservations did not meet residency requirements as defined in state law and were therefore ineligible to vote.

Similarly, the states of Colorado, Montana, Nebraska, Oregon, South Dakota, and Wyoming denied Indian suffrage by adopting provisions in their state constitutions requiring that all voters be "citizens." The constitutions of Arizona, Nevada, and Utah imposed even stricter restrictions requiring that all voters not only be citizens, but "residents" and "taxpayers" as well. Prior to 1924, such requirements effectively denied the franchise to thousands of Native Americans who had not been granted CITIZENSHIP. Yet even after Congress passed the Indian Citizenship Act of 1924, which granted citizenship to all Native Americans born in the United States, the right of Indians to vote continued to be denied or abridged by other means, such as the use of poll taxes and LITERACY TESTS, the manipulation of election laws by local registrars, as well as voter intimidation, fraud, and harassment.

Congress declared all these practices to be illegal, however, when it passed the VOTING RIGHTS ACT OF 1965. Although its express legislative intent was to prohibit black disenfranchisement, the Voting Rights Act had significant implications for Indian suffrage. When the act was renewed and amended in 1975, Congress adopted a provision that required certain states to provide bilingual BALLOTS and voter assistance to Native Americans, Hispanics, and other linguistic minority voters. When the act was renewed again in 1982, Congress amended Section 2 so as to prohibit any voting practice or procedure, including any REDISTRICTING plan, that results in a denial or abridgement of the right to vote on account of race or color. As amended, Section 2 also provides federal redress for Native Americans and other racial, ethnic, and language minority voters injured by discriminatory voting practices or procedures.

Since 1965, discriminatory practices and procedures resulting in "vote dilution," as opposed to vote denial, have been the predominate method of disenfranchising American Indians. Vote dilution occurs when the political representation of a politically unified minority is obstructed, diminished, or weakened by a particular election system or redistricting plan. The manipulation and misuse of "at-large" election systems is perhaps the most common vote dilution practice in the United States today. In districts with AT-LARGE ELECTIONS, the majority of residents in that district can, provided they vote as a bloc, prevent minority voters from electing the candidates of their choice. This voting system was challenged in Montana in 1986 by a group of Crow and Northern Cheyenne Indians in *Windy Boy v. County of Big Horn*. In that case, the federal district court of Montana ruled that the county's at-large election system violated Section 2 of the Voting Rights Act and ordered that all districts in the county be reorganized into SINGLE-MEMBER DISTRICTS.

But the use of single-member districts—defined as election systems in which only a single representative resides, and is elected from, a specified jurisdiction—are not always effective in preventing vote dilution, especially when minority populations are dispersed. In those situations, CUMULATIVE VOTING systems, which allow voters to cast multiple votes, are perhaps the most effective method for preventing vote dilution. Yet another common contemporary method of vote dilution is the misuse of REAPPORTIONMENT plans. In those circumstances, courts can step in and impose their own redistricting plan so as to bring the offending jurisdiction into compliance with the requirements of the Voting Rights Act and other state and federal election laws.

Despite the enactment of the Voting Rights Act and other election laws designed to protect the voting rights of minorities, and despite the fact that Native Americans have been elected to prominent local, state, and national office, the right of Indians to vote continues to be diluted, abridged, or denied by opponents of Indian suffrage, and the struggle for equal Native American voting rights continues.

Further reading: Grinde, Donald A., Jr., ed. *Native Americans.* Washington, D.C.: CQ Press, 2002; Keysarr, Alexander. *The Right to Vote: The Contested History of Democracy in the United States.* New York: Basic Books, 2000; Wofley, Jeanette. "Jim Crow, Indian Style: The Disenfranchisement of Native Americans." *American Indian Law Review* 16 (1991): 167.

—Suzanne E. Evans

suffrage, nonlandowners

In the colonies, as well as England, property requirements had long been acceptable to ensure that only those who had a stake in the community and those who had adequate independence would vote. Only three of the original 13 states—Georgia, New Hampshire, and Pennsylvania—did not have such landowning requirements. In fact, owning land was one of the most consistent prerequisites throughout the 13 states in terms of being enfranchised, with other requirements being quite varied throughout the states.

States admitted to the Union after 1790 did not have property-owning qualifications in their initial constitutions, and support for landowning qualifications began to weaken following the Revolution, a trend that continued into the 19th century. The idea expressed in the Declaration of Independence that "all men were created equal" made it difficult to deny the franchise to otherwise qualified citizens. On the East Coast, urban areas were growing rapidly, and this increased by a considerable number the adult males who were unable to meet the existing landowning requirements. Because of the increased urban population that was developing, especially in the East, a growing class of men who participated socially and contributed to the economic stability of the society were denied voting rights because they were nonlandowners.

During the first 40 years of the 19th century, debates occurred at state constitutional conventions, state legislatures, and other forums on the topic of increasing the size of the ELECTORATE, with landowning qualifications often the provision most criticized. Delaware eliminated its landowning requirements in 1792, with Maryland following nine years later. In 1821, Massachusetts and New York eliminated their requirements on land, with the latter maintaining a stipulation applying only to African Americans. Virginia was the last state to have a real property requirement in all elections held in the state, and North Carolina finally eliminated its landowning requirement for Senate elections in the mid-1850s. On the eve of the Civil War, only two property requirements remained in existence in the United States, one applying to foreign-born residents of Rhode Island and the other New York's race-based provision.

While the states were dropping property requirements through new constitutions or statutes, the courts fairly consistently upheld the legality of selective economic prerequisites for voting, including some landowning requirements. In 1902, the New York Court of Appeals (that state's highest court) upheld a law that permitted the village of Fulton to restrict voting on financial matters to those owning property in Fulton. In the next decade, the U.S. Supreme Court, in *Myers v. Anderson*, 238 U.S. 368 (1915), emphasized it did find unconstitutional taxpaying or property requirements in voting. During the second half of the 20th century, landowning requirements met with mixed results in the courts, particularly the U.S. Supreme Court. In 1969, in *Kramer v. Union Free School District*, 395 U.S. 621 (1969), the Court ruled that the Equal Protection Clause of the FOURTEENTH AMENDMENT made unconstitutional a New York law permitting school districts to allow just those who owned taxable property or had children in the schools to vote in school elections. In *Cipriano v. Houma*, 395 U.S. 701 (1969), the Court struck down a Louisiana law allowing only property taxpayers to vote on revenue bond issues in municipal elections.

In the 1970s and 1980s, the Supreme Court established some circumstances in which property requirements would be tolerated. In a series of cases, the Court ruled that participation in elections for such units as water storage districts could be based on the ownership of property. While there are still some relatively minor landowning requirements in existence today, those instances are few, as landownership has ceased to be a widespread restriction since the late 19th century.

Further reading: Keyssar, Alexander. *The Right to Vote: The Contested History of Democracy in the United States.* New York: Basic Books, 2000; Gettleman, Marvin E. *The Dorr Rebellion: A Study in American Radicalism, 1833–1849.* New York: Random House, 1973.

—J. Mark Alcorn

suffrage, women

Women in the United States have endured a long struggle to attain equality in the public sphere. Since the earliest days of the nation's history, women have been denied rights and freedoms that have been enjoyed by many men. Among the most important rights that women were once denied is the right to vote. This has been the case despite the fact that Dolly Madison, the wife of James Madison, the so-called father of the Constitution, cautioned her husband to "remember the ladies" as he and his colleagues drafted the U.S. Constitution in the summer of 1787. However, rather than confront the controversial concept of granting SUFFRAGE rights to women in the Constitution, the founders chose instead to allow states to determine for themselves who would be allowed to vote within their bor-

A parade in support of women's suffrage, New York, 1912 *(Prints and Photographs Division, Library of Congress)*

ders. The end result was that women were denied the right to vote in the majority of states for most of the first 100 years of the nation's history.

Despite the fact that women lacked the right to vote, by early in the 1800s many American women were becoming actively involved in public affairs, particularly by working to improve the status of disadvantaged groups within society. They organized to address the conditions of child workers, the mentally ill, those who were imprisoned, and slaves, among others. It was as a result of women's participation in the abolition movement, which culminated in the mid-1800s, that women were compelled to address their own political inequality. Lucretia Mott and Elizabeth Cady Stanton both served as American DELEGATES to the World Anti-Slavery Convention in London in 1840. However, because they were women, both were denied the opportunity to participate in the proceedings.

In 1848, Mott and Stanton organized the SENECA FALLS CONVENTION, which is considered to be the beginning of the women's movement in the United States in order to address the issue of women's rights. Stanton prepared a statement summarizing the women's concerns. The document, called the Declaration of Sentiments, was modeled on the Declaration of Independence. In it, Stanton noted many of the ways women in the United States were denied equal rights, among them divorce and child custody laws, being barred from working in certain occupations, lack of protection from physically abusive husbands, and lack of suffrage rights.

With the ratification of the Civil War Amendments, particularly the FOURTEENTH and FIFTEENTH AMENDMENTS, women hoped their status as voters would be ensured. In the end, the Fourteenth Amendment, which granted CITIZENSHIP to former slaves, was phrased in such a way that it ensured voting rights for males only; the Fifteenth Amendment also was phrased in such a way that it presented the denial of voting rights based only on race, color, or previous condition of servitude. Discrimination against voters based on their sex was still legal under the Constitution.

Following the ratification of the Civil War Amendments, proponents of women's suffrage split into two separate groups. In 1869, Stanton and Susan B. Anthony organized the National Woman Suffrage Association (NWSA) in order to work for the extension of voting rights to women across the country. The NWSA was considered a radical group at the time: It excluded men from its membership and was focused on attaining voting rights for women nationwide. In fact, Anthony drafted a constitutional amendment extending voting rights to women that was first introduced to Congress in 1878. A more moderate group, the American Woman Suffrage Association (AWSA), was formed under the leadership of Lucy Stone. The AWSA did allow men to work within the group, and rather than trying to achieve a nationwide right to vote, it focused instead on achieving voting rights on a state-by-state basis.

The state-by-state strategy proved to be moderately successful as women challenged state laws that prevented them from voting. In 1869, Wyoming became the first state to grant women the right to vote. Over the next 50 years, almost 30 states extended at least some degree of voting rights to women. However, the state-by-state strategy was not without setbacks. In 1874, the Supreme Court decided in the case of *Minor vs. Happersett* that Reese Happersett, the registrar of voters in St. Louis, Missouri, had not violated any laws by barring Virginia Minor from registering to vote. The Court ruled in its decision that merely being a citizen did not guarantee one the right to vote.

In 1890, the splinter groups that had been the American Equal Rights Association, the NWSA, and the AWSA, reunited as the National American Woman Suffrage Association (NAWSA). The NAWSA was initially headed by Stanton and then by Anthony. Despite the fact that both women supported a national approach to voting rights, the larger membership of the group preferred to stick with the state-by-state strategy. Eventually, Anthony stepped down as president and was replaced by a leader more in tune with the wishes of the entire group, Carrie Chapman Catt. Catt continued to work for nearly two decades to extend voting rights on a state-by-state basis.

Nevertheless, by the mid-1910s, more and more members of the NAWSA were becoming convinced that Stanton and Anthony had been correct in their focus on a constitutional amendment. Alice Paul, a member of the NAWSA, organized a parade of suffragists in advance of President Woodrow Wilson's 1913 inauguration in order to draw attention to the need for a constitutional amendment. The event began to galvanize public attention on the issue of women's voting rights. By 1917, even Catt had come to believe that the only realistic hope of attaining voting rights was by pushing for a constitutional amendment.

On May 21, 1919, the House of Representatives approved an amendment granting women the right to vote by the necessary two-thirds margin; the Senate followed suit several weeks later. The necessary three-fourths of the states ratified the amendment by August 26, 1920. On that date, the NINETEENTH AMENDMENT was formally added to the Constitution, granting women nationwide the right to vote.

Further reading: Frost, Elizabeth, and Kathryn Cullen-DuPont. *Women's Suffrage in America: An Eyewitness History.* New York: Facts On File, 1992.

—Claudia Bryant

superdelegate

A superdelegate is an unelected at-large delegate to the DEMOCRATIC NATIONAL CONVENTION. Each state party organization is responsible for selecting these DELEGATES, which can constitute up to 20 percent of a state's delegation. Superdelegates are thus not elected through primaries or caucuses. The idea of the superdelegate is that these delegates have the party's best interests in mind. Superdelegates are often elected officials or political professionals, such as governors, members of Congress, DEMOCRATIC NATIONAL COMMITTEE members, and state party officials. They are unpledged, or uncommitted, delegates, which means that they are supposed to come to the convention not having decided who they will support. However, they often declare their support long before the convention.

Superdelegates were one of the reforms to the PRESIDENTIAL NOMINATING PROCESS proposed by the HUNT COMMISSION in 1982, established and led by Governor James Hunt of North Carolina. Although used before 1984, the Democratic convention of that year saw the largest increase of superdelegates from previous years. The introduction of superdelegates was a reaction to the earlier post-1968 reforms of the McGovern-Frasier (1969–72) and Mikulski Commissions (1972–73). These reforms attempted to reduce the presence of party professionals, make the delegate selection process more democratic, and increase the diversity of delegates. For example, delegates are now allocated proportionally to all candidates who received a minimum of 15 percent of the vote in a given state's caucus or PRIMARY. In addition, each state organization now implements an affirmative action plan for the selection of delegates to include African Americans, women, and youths in proportion to their presence in the Democratic ELECTORATE. The Hunt Commission reversed the trend of these earlier reforms by introducing the concept of superdelegates to ensure the participation of more experienced members of the party at the convention.

In 2004, the superdelegates accounted for a substantial portion of the votes needed for the nomination and often constituted a large percentage of a state's delegation. Of California's 440 total delegates in 2004, 70 were superdelegates, for example. There were 24 superdelegates in Florida's total delegation of 201. In practice, however, the superdelegates have had little influence over the nominating process. This is the case because the nomination process has become front-loaded in recent years, and concludes long before the national convention. Hence, the superdelegates have been unable to play an independent role in the nomination process. They typically support the presidential candidate who is the FRONTRUNNER and presumed winner.

In some cases, superdelegates will have to change their candidate choice before the convention. In 2004, for example, Howard Dean obtained the support of many superdelegates even before their states' primaries were held. However, once he dropped out of the race, these superdelegates then had to give their support to another candidate.

Further reading: Herrera, Richard. "Are 'Superdelegates' Super?" *Political Behavior* 16, no. 1 (1994): 79–92; Southwell, Priscilla L. "The 1984 Democratic Nomination Process: The Significance of Unpledged Superdelegates." *American Politics Quarterly* 14 (1986): 75–88.

—Jae-Jae Spoon

Super Tuesday

Super Tuesday is a phrase for PRESIDENTIAL PRIMARY elections and caucuses held by several states on a Tuesday in early March of the PRESIDENTIAL ELECTION year. *Super* refers to the importance of the event: Approximately half of the DELEGATEs necessary to gain the major parties' NOMINATION can be won in the contests on Super Tuesday. Although the states involved vary with each election period, Super Tuesday is an important element of the nominating process to candidates, states, and voters alike.

The first Super Tuesday was March 8, 1988, when nine southern states chose to hold their primaries on the same day in an effort to have greater influence in the nomination process. Since then, Super Tuesday has become a focusing event in the process. Strong performances on Super Tuesday can catapult trailing candidates past FRONTRUNNERS to claim the nomination, or seal the fate of CHALLENGERs who do not fare well. In 2000, 16 states held PRIMARY contests on Super Tuesday, and 10 states scheduled Super Tuesday contests on March 2, 2004, including delegate-rich California and New York.

The emergence of Super Tuesday has produced "front-loaded" primaries, increasing numbers of contests earlier in the season as states vie for influence in the selection of the nominees. As a result of FRONT-LOADING, the field of candidates can shrink rapidly in a number of closely packed early primaries. Voters in later contests may have a limited choice of candidates or little say in who wins the nomination, as the nomination may be secured early in the year. Moreover, front-loading is believed to drive up the cost of primaries and increase the need to raise money early in the process, potentially increasing the influence of early campaign contributions and media ENDORSEMENTs. In 2004, Democratic nominee John Kerry had mathematically eliminated all other challengers shortly after Super Tuesday, while 13 states had yet to hold their contests.

Some proposals made to offset the problems of a compressed primary calendar have been a single national primary; regional primaries; equal distribution of available delegates over a series of weeks; and plans that limit the number of delegates available in the earliest contests, progressively increasing the number of delegates available in later weeks. Advocates of such proposals claim that geographic and regional interests will remain relevant, voters will have more choices, and the effect of early contests and the influence of larger states will be held in check. While none of these plans has been implemented, the 2004 primaries did see further evidence of front-loading, with the emergence of "Mini-Tuesday": Several states that had previously held primaries or caucuses on Super Tuesday held their primaries even earlier, on February 3, 2004.

While Super Tuesday is not the earliest date on the primary calendar, there are typically more delegates at stake than on any other primary ELECTION DAY, and as such, the race for the nomination can be either defined or decided with the results from Super Tuesday.

Further reading: Norrander, Barbara. *Super Tuesday: Regional Politics and Presidential Primaries*. Lexington: University Press of Kentucky, 1992; Wayne, Stephen J. *The Road to the White House 2000: The Politics of Presidential Elections*. Boston: Bedford/St. Martin's, 2000.

—Joel A. Rayan

swing ratio

The swing ratio refers to the change in legislative seats associated with a 1 percent change in POPULAR VOTE share for a party's candidates. It is derived by dividing the change in percentage of seats a party wins by the change in the share of votes it receives. The swing ratio is a measurement of how legislative votes are translated into congressional seats and is primarily associated with SINGLE-MEMBER DISTRICT plurality (SMDP) electoral systems in which a party's seat share is likely to differ from its share of the vote partly because minor-party support is absorbed by the two largest parties. The swing ratio shows the extent to which electoral districting benefits a certain party in elections by giving it disproportionate (usually more) representation in the legislature.

Though election results and consequent seat distribution are closely associated, the two are not as correlated in SMDP systems as they are in PROPORTIONAL REPRESENTATION systems. In many elections, the party that wins a majority of votes does not win a majority of seats. The swing ratio highlights well, however, the fact that in most elections the party that wins a majority of votes wins an even larger portion of legislative seats.

The swing ratio brings to light the extent to which the two largest parties are insulated from minor party influence. GERRYMANDERING and REDISTRICTING, intended ideally to bring the ratio as close to one as possible, however, can bias the swing ratio in favor of a particular party.

There is considerable disagreement among scholars about the methodology used to measure the swing ratio, and critics assert that the ratio can be inaccurate, misleading, and extremely sensitive to small changes that render such irrational outcomes as negative ratios (implying gains in seats by winning fewer votes). Despite these considerations, the swing ratio is a useful indicator that helps researchers analyze the translation of votes into legislative seats and its implications.

Further reading: Jacobson, Gary. *The Electoral Origins of Divided Government: Competition in U.S. House Elections, 1946–1988.* Boulder, Colo.: Westview Press, 1990; Niemi, Richard G., and Patrick Fett. "The Swing Ratio: An Explanation and an Assessment." *Legislative Studies Quarterly* 11 (1986): 75–90; Tufte, Edward R. "The Relationship between Seats and Votes in Two-Party Systems." *American Political Science Review* 67, no. 2 (1973): 540–554.

—Costas Panagopoulos

swing vote

The term *swing vote* refers to a group of voters who, depending on their voting decision, have the capability of effectively deciding a given election. A true swing vote possesses two key characteristics. First, to constitute a swing vote, a group of voters must be large enough to exercise a substantial amount of political power. Second, in order to be considered a true swing vote, a group of voters must have the potential to support either POLITICAL PARTY. In short, a swing vote is a group of voters who could end up voting either way (supporting either major party candidate) in any given election and whose support has the potential to propel the supported candidate to victory.

Some scholars argue that in modern times Roman Catholics represent a key group of swing voters. Catholics meet both of the criteria mentioned above. As the single largest religious denomination in the United States, they certainly have the potential to exercise significant political power. And, though Catholics were once solid supporters of Democrats, the Catholic vote has shown the potential to go either way in recent elections (in the 1980s, for instance, Republican Ronald Reagan won a majority of the Catholic vote, whereas in the 1990s Democrat Bill Clinton was supported by a majority of Catholics). Due to their status as a group of key swing voters, Catholics have in recent years been wooed by both major parties. Both political parties are aware that the Catholic vote is up for grabs and also know that winning support from Catholics could be the key to winning any given election. As a result, both parties campaign hard to try to garner the support of Catholic voters.

Another group that has been identified as a key swing vote in recent years is "soccer moms." Especially in the 1996 election, these soccer moms (relatively prosperous, suburban women with children) were thought to be one of the groups with the potential to decide the election. Their support of Bill Clinton was an important factor in his victory over Republican Bob Dole. Looking to the future, some analysts predict that "NASCAR DADS" could become the next important group of swing voters. The party and the candidate that wins the support of these conservative-leaning, white male automobile racing fans should have an advantage in upcoming elections. Another likely swing vote in the future is the Hispanic vote. This group has grown substantially in recent years, and while it still tends to favor the DEMOCRATIC PARTY, the REPUBLICAN PARTY has been aggressively campaigning for the Spanish-speaking vote in recent elections.

Further reading: Kenski, Henry C., and William Lockwood. "Catholic Voting Behavior in 1988: A Critical Swing Vote." In James L. Guth and John C. Green, eds., *The Bible and the Ballot Box: Religion and Politics in the 1988 Election.* Boulder, Colo.: Westview Press, 1991.

—Gregory A. Smith

T

targeting

Targeting, a prevalent and powerful political tool used extensively by modern candidates and their campaign strategists, strategically preselects voters through research and tailors political messages to the interests of that CONSTITUENCY. This method is particularly valuable because campaign resources are finite, and it permits customized messages to be directed toward the most receptive voters. In contrast to mass messages, targeting helps candidates to deliver the most effective message to the right voters. These voters may change at certain points in a campaign as campaigns first attempt to solidify their base by communicating with partisans and later try to persuade UNDECIDED VOTERS to support the candidate. Knowing precisely who these voters are, what kinds of communications will appeal to them, and how to reach them is a key goal of any modern campaign.

Campaigns can target voters using a variety of electoral, demographic, and even psychographic (lifestyle) characteristics. A host of independent commercial firms and targeting specialists are increasingly hired by political campaigns to compile lists on nearly every plausible demographic variable. Elaborate targeting plans and lists are developed using voter files, U.S. Census Bureau statistics, public opinion polls, and field work. Targeting information, dependant on the message and the level of office sought by the candidate, is organized by any combination of, but not limited to, PARTY IDENTIFICATION, voting frequency and history, geography, age, sex, race, marital status, religion, household income, education, profession, IDEOLOGY, and lifestyle. Once this data is compiled, extraordinarily precise (and stereotypical) categories emerge, such as "check-writing evangelical activist," "soccer mom," and "NASCAR DAD."

Although telephone lines and the Internet are prevalent in the majority of modern American homes with registered voters, the most effective form of targeting in terms of response rate is DIRECT MAIL, which originated in 1908 when William Jennings Bryan made his third bid for the presidency. Over time, technology has increasingly revolu-tionized the way the information about voters and potential voters is culled and refined. The Claritas lifestyle targeting system, ground-breaking when it was introduced in 1978, used multivariate analysis to sort America's 36,000 zip codes into 40 demographic clusters, using amusing names such as, "furs and station wagons" and "Norma Rae-ville." As technology improved, so did the quality and quantity of information available to candidates through these systems. The recently introduced Chi-Square Automatic Interaction Detection (CHAID), reportedly 15 percent more effective than traditional targeting methods, incorporates more than 60 different predictor variables in order to identify the combinations that produce the highest percentages of undecided or SWING VOTERs.

Targeting is an expensive venture for any candidate. In addition to the obvious costs of technology, the nature of the information needed to create and maintain target lists is inherently fluid and needs to be updated constantly to be accurate. In terms of running a successful campaign, however, targeting costs are warranted because the investment reduces the potential for wasted resources. Electoral targeting, which is used to varying degrees in local, regional, state, and national elections, has revolutionized the way a candidate develops and presents messages, to whom a message is presented, and the mechanisms through which messages are delivered. Targeting is a precise and sophisticated process that uses modern data management technology to assure that messages with maximum effect are disseminated to the desired ELECTORATE.

Further reading: Johnson, Dennis W. *No Place for Amateurs.* New York: Routledge, 2001; Thurber, James A., and Candice J. Nelson, eds. *Campaigns and Elections American Style.* 2nd ed. Cambridge, Mass.: Westview Press, 2004.
—Costas Panagopoulos

term limits

The limitation on the number of terms lawmakers can hold a specific office is known as a term limit. For example, in

452

1990 voters in the state of California passed by initiative a state constitutional amendment limiting the number of terms for state assemblypersons and state senators. Assembly members were limited to three terms or six years, and senators were limited to eight years or two terms. The U.S. Constitution prohibits limiting the number of congressional terms without a constitutional amendment, though states have tried to limit the terms of their own U.S. representatives, only to rebuffed by the Supreme Court in *U.S. Terms Limits v. Thornton* (1995). The TWENTY-SECOND AMENDMENT (1951) to the Constitution is the only form of term limit for federal lawmakers. It prohibits the president from being elected more than twice or from serving more than 10 total years in the event of the death or removal of the previous president.

Recent years have seen an unprecedented movement toward limiting terms of office. Between 1950 and 1989, for example, the number of states that limited the terms for governors rose from 27 to 46. As one source has put it: "Term limitation involves a simple idea that summarizes and expresses a deep public dissatisfaction with Congress and state legislatures." In fact, Colorado and Oklahoma voters in 1990 instituted term limits with 67 and 71 percent of the vote, respectively. Many people are uneasy with high rates of reelection and long terms in office. Reelection rates for members of the U.S. Senate, to take but one example, historically average 85 percent, with some elections returning more than 98 percent of incumbent senators. The length of service for many members runs into the decades. But the lack of turnover is not the central issue. The concern lies with a latent feeling among the ELECTORATE that politicians with long service time are unresponsive, corrupt, and incompetent. Of course, the high reelection rates for legislators runs against the popular refrain "Throw the bums out!" Accordingly, while many like to complain about Congress members, voters rarely turn them out. Indeed, the American people seem to dislike legislatures as institutions while at the same time reelecting their own legislators at historically high rates. It is this paradox that makes term limits an interesting aspect of American POLITICS.

Term limits, or "rotation" in office, has a long lineage in America. Rotation was alive and well in colonial America, which had imported the practice from the English and Dutch. The colonists saw rotation as encouraging participation, checking possible tyranny, and enhancing representation. The first national governmental scheme, the ARTICLES OF CONFEDERATION (1781), limited members to serving no more than three out of every six years. It should be no surprise, then, that during the Constitutional Convention (1787), DELEGATEs discussed making members of the House "incapable of reelection" out of concern for corruption. While the president is now limited to two full terms, the founders decided against such a restriction, though it was discussed at length. It was decided that by fixing each term to four years—not too long to put up with a lesser president—and with the creation of the ELECTORAL COLLEGE, good would come from allowing the president to seek further terms. In essence, ambition would cause presidents to seek the public good and thus reelection. George Washington retired after two terms, setting an unofficial standard that was not exceeded until Roosevelt in 1940 in the midst of a worldwide depression and war. In fact, it was Roosevelt's four election victories that initiated the Twenty-Second Amendment. Washington stated his view to James Madison: "The spirit of the government may render a rotation in the elected officers of it most congenial with the ideas of liberty and safety."

The proposal to limit members of the House during the convention was likely dropped because the House was viewed by many as "the grand depository of the democratic principle," that is, reflective of the people. The issue, however, lived on in the debate over the Senate. Defenders of the Senate saw the body as a needed filtration of public sentiments. The Senate was viewed by both admirers and critics as distant from the people and consisting of those more virtuous. The members were not to be directly elected, and they were to have long six-year terms (Alexander Hamilton suggested lifetime appointments). They were to be involved in confirming presidential appointments and ratification of treaties.

The ANTI-FEDERALISTS, those in opposition to varying aspects of the Constitution, were concerned that rotation in office had not been applied to the Senate. The *Federal Farmer* stated their general view: "[I]n a government consisting of but few members, elected for long periods, and far removed from the observation of the people, but few changes in the ordinary course of elections take place among the members; they become in some measure a fixed body, and often inattentive to the public good, callous, selfish, and the fountain of corruption." The cure was for a senator "to return home, mix with the people, and reside some time with them; this will tend to reinstate him in the interests, feelings and views similar to theirs, and thereby confirm in him the essential qualifications of a legislator."

The Anti-Federalists thought that tight control of politicians by a virtuous and vigilant public was needed for good government. Patrick Henry went further in saying the people would "be undone" if they were less than vigilant. One can see in today's debate similar concerns. New York's "Brutus" advocated rotation as it would allow more people to serve: "It would give opportunity to bring forward a greater number of men to serve their country, and would return those, who had served, to their state, and afford them the advantage of becoming better acquainted with the condition and politics of their constituents." Richard Henry Lee of Virginia maintained that long service would cause senators to "lose sight of the people, and gradually fall into measures prejudicial to them."

The defenders of the constitutional structure defended the lack of rotation, or what James Madison, writing in *The Federalist,* called "an excess of refinement," on three general grounds: The people have a right to decide who they will elect, rotation reduces the incentive for responsible action, and rotation punishes experience. Roger Sherman put the argument succinctly: "It is proposed to make the president and senators ineligible after certain periods. But this would abridge the privilege of the people and remove motive to fidelity in office, and renders persons incapable of serving in offices, on account of their experience, which would best qualify them for usefulness in office." While the critics often thought the people easily duped, the defenders of the Constitution maintained that the people would do a reasonable job of watching the politicians. Human ambition was acknowledged and used by the framers in the constitutional structure in an attempt to benefit the whole. Interestingly, during much of the 19th century, in the wake of Jeffersonian and Jacksonian democracy, there was an informal system of rotation, due to the strong party system, with turnover in Congress averaging between 40 and 50 percent per term. As the *Democratic Review* put it in 1836: "We have no great faith in professional politicians." Faithful party followers often rotated through a variety of state, congressional, and executive positions. Ironically, however, it may have been the early strength of parties and the "spoils system" that Andrew Jackson encouraged that led to the professionalism of politics and the bureaucracy. Nevertheless, by the end of the 1800s, the average congressman served about five years, while today the number exceeds 10 years.

Some observers today argue that the informal party-driven rotation system prohibited the career politician, and that congressmen were more responsive to the people. Beginning in the 1880s, however, a forceful voice emerged that argued against this view. The Progressives, intellectually led by Woodrow Wilson, suggested that the party system was corrupt and, in fact, was not responsive to the people. Rather, congressmen concerned themselves with various "interests." Wilson's prescription, as outlined in his *Congressional Government* (1885), was to move Congress in the direction of the British parliamentary system. The parties would stake out clear positions for the electorate, and party leadership would seek to enforce party discipline. Wilson disliked the give-and-take that the founder's design encouraged. It was Wilson's view that the MAJORITY PARTY should have near complete control over legislation for the period in which it held the majority. Wilson also sought to open up the process through "sunshine" rules. Too many decisions were made hidden from the public view—"smoke-filled" back room deals. More debates and votes should take place in public view. Wilson, following his German education, strongly advocated a professional bureaucracy as an alternative to politics. However, as many critics today point out, the creation of a national bureaucracy directly led to an increase in the size of Washington and its power, and it encouraged a "career" attitude toward public "service." Ironically, with the career bureaucrat and Congress member came erosion of party power, as Congress members came to see themselves as "free agents" rather than party members. After the turn of the century, reforms such as the RECALL, initiative, and term limits were successfully sought at the state level.

As noted above, in the present era politicians serve longer and are reelected at increasing rates. Given the public's generally poor view of Congress, how can this be explained? A number of answers are generally accepted. David Mayhew has identified one problem as "vanishing marginals," which is the decline of competitive races in most districts. Most congresspeople win by large margins or go unopposed. One reason for this is that state legislatures GERRYMANDER districts after each CENSUS to lock in incumbents. Another is the privilege of office—being able to communicate with the electorate back home at taxpayer expense. But research suggests these factors are not strong enough by themselves. Morris Fiorina has argued that the keys for longevity in office are constituent service and bringing "pork" ($) back to the district. As the federal government has expanded since the 1930s and taken on more responsibilities that were once the purview of states, Congress members have had a greater opportunity to impress the locals. Mayhew further argues that as the "faceless" bureaucracy has expanded, voters have sought the help of their congresspeople. Polling bears this trend out. Voters overwhelmingly approve of their representative but have a less positive view of Congress as a whole.

In recent years, various limits on congresspeople have been suggested—generally along the lines of 10 years or five terms. The last issue that must be addressed, then, is the effect that might be expected. The experience of the states that have imposed limits provides examples to look at. There seems to have been little change of public views on state legislators. If limits are imposed at the national level, we should not expect the approach of representatives to change; they will still address constituent needs to ensure reelection, including the interests of businesses in their districts—one of the principle cries of those who want limits. It must be remembered that businesses employ the people of the district. To forgo taking into account the wants of business owners or of those holding company stock (think of 401k accounts) runs the risk of alienating those employed. It has been persuasively argued that term limits have strengthened bureaucrats and LOBBYISTS, as a large number of new members lack knowledge upon entering office. Indeed, new members may have an incentive to turn to knowledgeable professionals to stave off potential CHALLENGERS who might take advantage of their naïveté. This concern with ensuring reelection, albeit for a shorter time, could lead to one of Alexander Hamilton's concerns about rotation in 1787: "a diminution of the inducements to good behavior." The limits of tenure may lead to, as Gouverneur Morris put it at the time, "make[ing] hay" while one can. Perhaps most important, term limits would limit experience at a time when the burdens of national office are the weightiest. One must remember the founders' thought that good government required ambitious, as well as good, wise, and farsighted persons to serve.

—Jeff A. Martineau

third parties

Third parties in contemporary American POLITICS are all parties that are not one of the two major parties (DEMOCRATIC PARTY and REPUBLICAN PARTY). They are sometimes referred to as minor parties. There have been third-party CHALLENGERS since the early days of the nation. Third parties are formed by individuals who are dissatisfied with the two major parties of the day. The dissatisfaction could be due to disagreements over policy positions, leaders, or unaddressed issues. The term *third party* dates from 1806, when John Randolph, a member of President Jefferson's DEMOCRATIC-REPUBLICAN PARTY, opposed the president's land policy. Randolph and his supporters said they sought a "tertium quid," or a third position, and came to be known as the Quids.

Some third parties have formed around issues. These have included opposition to slavery, Prohibition, environmental protection, the economic plight of farmers, and states' rights. Other third parties have focused more on a single individual. These include Theodore Roosevelt's BULL MOOSE PARTY, George Wallace's AMERICAN INDEPENDENT PARTY, and Ross Perot's United We Stand.

Most third parties have not lasted for more than two ELECTION CYCLES. However, there are exceptions. The Republican Party formed in 1854 in opposition to the Kansas-Nebraska Act. This act overturned the limits on the extension of slavery to the territories enacted earlier in the Missouri Compromise of 1820 and the Compromise of 1850. Although it was founded primarily on the slavery issue, the Republican Party also promised protective tariffs, a transcontinental railway, and free land for homesteading. These were issue positions that the two dominant parties of the time, the Democrats and Whigs, did not possess. By 1860, the Whigs had disappeared, and the party system took on its present two-party formation of competition between the Democrats and Republicans. Thus, the United States has had nearly 150 years of experience as a two-party dominant system. Other exceptions to the two-party rule include the PROHIBITION PARTY, which has fielded candidates since 1872, and the SOCIALIST PARTY, which has done so since 1900. These two parties continue to run candidates at the presidential, congressional, state, and local levels to this day.

There are many barriers that third parties face. These constraints make it difficult for third parties to succeed at the gubernatorial, congressional, and presidential levels. The first of these barriers is the SINGLE-MEMBER DISTRICT system. Under this system, only one person is elected from each district. Since there is no reward for coming in second or third, as there often is in parliamentary systems, this creates a difficult situation for a minor party. A party that consistently comes in in third place finds it difficult to increase its electoral momentum and grow as a political force.

A second difficulty at the presidential level is the nature of the ELECTORAL COLLEGE. The candidate who receives the majority of votes in a given state receives all of that state's electoral votes. They are not divided up among all of the candidates. For example, Ross Perot won 19 percent of the national vote in 1992, but he did not win any electoral votes. Some third-party candidates have, however, succeeded in gaining electoral votes. Theodore Roosevelt, for example, won 28 percent of the vote and 88 electoral votes in 1912. Oftentimes, the electoral votes of a third-party contender are concentrated in one region. This was the case with George Wallace, who won 13 percent of the national POPULAR VOTE in 1968 and 48 electoral votes, which were predominately in the South. Another example was Strom Thurmond's run as a Dixiecrat in 1948. He won 2.4 percent of the national vote, but 23 percent in the South. His 38 electoral votes were concentrated in only four states.

A third barrier for third parties is the cost of campaigns. Third parties typically cannot raise the large sums of money required for high-level offices. In addition, funding from the FEDERAL ELECTION COMMISSION is available only for Democrats and Republicans. Third parties are eligible for public funds after the PRESIDENTIAL ELECTIONS and only if their candidate appeared on the BALLOT in at least 10 states and obtained a minimum of 5 percent of the national popular vote. Third-party candidates often receive less media coverage than their larger-party counterparts. Without a media presence and lacking funds, voters rarely have enough information regarding third-party contenders to cast a vote in their favor.

It is also difficult for third-party candidates to qualify for the ballot. In presidential races, in which one must qualify in 50 different states, this is particularly problematic. Each state has its own BALLOT ACCESS requirements. These usually include a certain number of signatures from registered voters and filing fees. Only three third-party candidates have been able to get on the ballot in all 50 states. These were George Wallace of the American Independent Party in 1968, Lenora Fulani of the NEW ALLIANCE PARTY in 1988, and Ross Perot in 1992 of United We Stand and in 1996 of the REFORM PARTY.

Third parties have also not been electorally successful because the major parties will often co-opt their issues and convince voters that voting for a third-party candidate is a "wasted" vote. While it is rare for third-party candidates to win elections, their presence on the ticket can often pull votes away from one party more than the other and help to determine the outcome of the election. This is often referred to as the SPOILER and causes the two major parties to give careful consideration to third-party candidates even if the third-party candidate is unlikely to win the election.

Some voters, nevertheless, do vote for third-party candidates, and third parties are a regular part of the political process. Third parties often have more success at the state and local levels. In these elections, candidates have to appeal to fewer voters, and personal contact is often more important than PARTY IDENTIFICATION. Also, voters tend to be more homogeneous in smaller constituencies. Thus, it is easier for a third-party candidate to appeal to one group of voters.

Even with all of these constraints and barriers to success, third parties are an essential part of party politics in the United States today. They remain an alternative choice for those dissatisfied with the two major parties. In 1996, Perot won 8.0 percent of the national vote in the presidential election. In 2000, Ralph Nader received 2.7 percent. There are Greens, Libertarians, and other third-party members on city councils, county commissions, and in some state legislatures across the country.

Further reading: Eldersveld, Samuel J., and Hanes Walton, Jr. *Political Parties in American Society.* 2nd ed. Boston: St. Martin's Press, 2000; Rosenstone, Steven J., Roy L. Behr, and Edward H. Lazarus. *Third Parties in America: Citizen Response to Major Party Failure.* 2nd ed. Princeton, N.J.: Princeton University Press, 1996.

—Jae-Jae Spoon

third rail issues

The term *third rail* is a metaphor for a dangerous political issue that politicians must avoid "touching" at all cost. The phrase originates from the railway term for the conduit that carries electric current to power a train's engines. In the United States, such electric-powered train systems are primarily found in subway and commuter rail networks in big cities. In popular stories, the third rail was the place onto which the urban hopeless flung themselves to commit suicide. Likewise, touching on a third rail issue, suggestion, or comment means almost certain death for wayward leaders. Third rail political issues tend to be those of a serious, contentious nature.

Third rail issues are traditionally defined as highly toxic issues for which suggested policy solutions or legislation will so enrage a swath of the ELECTORATE that they will refuse to vote for a candidate, regardless of the candidate's other policy positions. This is a type of single-issue voting taken to an extreme. The concept is widely associated with Social Security reform in the United States. In a historical sense, this has to do with the centrality that Barry Goldwater

gave to the issue in his failed PRESIDENTIAL ELECTION campaign. Since then, most presidential candidates have made vague promises on Social Security reform but offered few specifics and subsequently enacted little in the way of reform.

But the term, thanks to being a highly descriptive metaphor, sees frequent use and wide application to many issues. There are a host of issues deemed poisonous enough to be called third rail. On a national level, public health care, restrictions on immigration, limiting abortion rights, and gun control have all been dubbed third rail issues at some point. Third rail issues can also be local or particular to a state. Raising tobacco taxes in tobacco-producing Kentucky, workers' compensation in Oregon, and adding a sales tax in New Hampshire are examples of local third rail issues.

—Samuel Millar

three-fifths compromise

The three-fifths compromise grew out of the Great Compromise at the Constitutional Convention of 1787. Under the terms of the Great Compromise, the national government would be structured with a bicameral legislature with representation in one chamber, the House of Representatives, based on population, and representation in the other chamber, the Senate, equally divided among all states. The three-fifths compromise was an agreement by which three-fifths of all slaves were to be counted for tax purposes and representation in the House of Representatives.

Conflicts emerged at the Constitutional Convention between slave and nonslave states that pitted southern planters against northern merchants. At the time of the founding, slaves accounted for 30 percent of the nation's population, with 90 percent of slaves residing in five states—Georgia, Maryland, North Carolina, South Carolina, and Virginia. In some places, slaves outnumbered nonslaves by a margin of 10 to one.

The southern states wanted slaves to be counted equally in determining representation in Congress, not because they desired slaves to have equal rights, but so the South could have greater representation in Congress and thereby help to retain the privileged position of whites in the American South. Representatives from the northern states argued that since slaves were considered property according to the law of the time and not granted the basic rights of citizens, including the right to vote, they should not be included when deciding issues of representation. The three-fifths compromise essentially stated that a slave was to be counted as three-fifths of a person.

The problem of representation was one of several issues regarding slavery that had to be addressed during the Constitutional Convention. While many DELEGATES wanted the slave trade banned outright in the United States, the delegates compromised on this issue as well by agreeing that Congress could limit the number of slaves imported to the United States. All told, the Constitution's many compromises regarding slavery did less to resolve the slave issue in the United States than they did to put the issue off for a later generation.

Further reading: Urosky, Mel, and Paul Finkleman. *A March of Liberty: A Constitutional History of the United States.* New York: Oxford University Press, 2002.
—F. Erik Brooks

Tillman Act (1907)

The Tillman Act, passed by Congress in 1907, prohibits banks and corporations from making political contributions to candidates for federal office. Named for its most vocal sponsor, Senator Benjamin Ryan Tillman (D, S.C.), the act was a Progressive Era reform designed to curb increasing campaign finance abuses by political operatives and corporate donors. In its present form, the Tillman Act (2 U.S.C. Sec. 441b) bars both direct contributions and indirect INDEPENDENT EXPENDITURES by corporations on behalf of federal political candidates.

The Tillman Act was in large part a response to the escalation in extortion as a political FUND-RAISING practice during the late 19th century. As national parties grew and solidified, they assumed ever-increasing campaign costs. In order to ensure a reliable stream of resources, the parties developed systematic formulas to assess and extract campaign contributions from donors.

During the 1896 PRESIDENTIAL ELECTION, the extortion of corporate political contributions reached unprecedented heights. Mark Hanna, Republican candidate William McKinley's chief fund-raiser and political operative, assessed pledge amounts from businesses and banks at one-quarter of 1 percent of their capital. Hanna assessed contributions according to a "stake in the general prosperity." Standard Oil, the largest corporation of its day, was charged $250,000. During McKinley's reelection campaign in 1900, Hanna raised $2.5 million through his fund-raising assessments, obliterating all existing fund-raising records of the time.

By the 1904 PRESIDENTIAL ELECTION, Progressives and journalists were decrying the "corruptive" influence of corporate money in POLITICS. Presidential candidate Judge Alton Parker accused his opponent, Theodore Roosevelt, of inappropriate dealings with corporate financiers. Although Parker lost the election, he was able to shed light on Roosevelt's campaign finances. Indeed, Roosevelt received substantial donations from corporations—three-quarters of his campaign money came from oil and railroad companies—as well as a $150,000 donation from financier J. P. Morgan.

When news of Roosevelt's campaign finances broke after his election, public reaction was severe. Nevertheless, in 1905 Roosevelt was able to redeem himself politically by embracing election reform as one of the central pieces of his legislative agenda. His quick turnaround was both a brilliant political stroke and the impetus for the Tillman Act, which became the first major CAMPAIGN FINANCE LAW.

Aside from being one of the oldest standing campaign finance laws, the Tillman Act is also one of the most steadfast. Since the landmark campaign finance decision of BUCKLEY V. VALEO in 1976, the Supreme Court has struck down every limitation on corporate independent expenditures that it has reviewed except for one, the absolute ban on direct contributions to federal candidates included in the Tillman Act.

Further reading: Luna, Christopher, ed. *Campaign Finance Reform.* New York: H.W. Wilson, 2001; Yearly, C. K. *The Money Machines: The Breakdown and Reform of Governmental and Party Finance in the North, 1860–1920.* Albany: State University of New York Press, 1970.
—Brook B. Andrews

tracking poll

A daily small-sample public opinion poll intended to describe the pattern of change in responses over time, usually used during PRESIDENTIAL ELECTIONS. Tracking polls are a relatively new phenomenon, entering the sphere of political consciousness during the 1996 PRESIDENTIAL ELECTION. An evolution from traditional opinion polling on election campaigns, the tracking poll takes results from smaller samples on a daily or nearly daily basis. Tracking polls often use a rolling sample, meaning that a set of 100 people are interviewed over a span of time, such as three days. After the three-day span is complete, the first 100 respondents are removed and replaced with an additional 100 respondents.

The result is a small-sample measure of trends in public opinion, useful for measuring day-to-day changes in favorability of candidates as a campaign garners daily media attention and UNDECIDED VOTERS begin to make up their minds about the campaign and candidates. Tracking polls are not limited to use within a campaign context, as presidential APPROVAL RATINGS, political efficacy feelings, and trust of others are tracked by polling companies such as Gallup, Rasmussen, Zogby, and Harris.

Tracking polls are useful for campaigns to determine which strategies and events are effective at changing voters' minds, since the numbers are computed daily. Tracking polls informed voters in 2000 that Al Gore began the campaign with a sizable lead, only to see it erode through August. In 2004, like 1996, the incumbent president was regularly ahead in tracking polls. However, since tracking polls measure the national POPULAR VOTE and not a state-by-state breakdown of the electoral vote, the polls are an imperfect measure of a candidate's success during a campaign.

Some polling firms, such as Rasmussen, run separate tracking polls in "battleground" states where the popular vote outcome is in question, thereby making the electoral votes from those states more influential in the eventual outcome of the campaign. As of 2004, tracking polls were popular for presidential, senatorial, and some gubernatorial races, but were rare for less expensive state and local races.

Further reading: Asher, Herbert. *Polling and the Public: What Every Citizen Should Know.* 6th ed. Washington, D.C.: CQ Press, 2004; Bardes, Barbara, and Robert Oldendick. *Public Opinion: Measuring the American Mind.* Belmont, Calif.: Thomson/Wadsworth, 2003; Gallup Polling Corporation. Available online. URL: http://www.gallup.com. Accessed August 10, 2005; Moore, David W. *The Superpollsters.* New York: Four Walls Eight Windows, 1992; Real Clear Politics. Available online. URL: http://www.realclear politics.com. Accessed August 10, 2005; Romer, Daniel, et al. *Capturing Campaign Dynamics: The National Annenberg Election Survey.* New York: Oxford University Press, 2003; Traugott, Michael W., and Paul Lavrakas. *The Voter's Guide to Election Polls.* 3rd ed. Lanham, Md.: Rowman & Littlefield, 2004; Zogby Poll. Available online. URL: http://www.zogby.com. Accessed August 10, 2005.

—Chapman Rackaway

Twelfth Amendment

The Twelfth Amendment to the Constitution, ratified in September 1804, fundamentally altered the operation of the ELECTORAL COLLEGE and had a profound effect on PRESIDENTIAL ELECTIONS and the operations of political parties. Despite hundreds of attempts over the last 200 years to reform the way the Electoral College works, the Twelfth Amendment has been the only reform to successfully pass the hurdles to amending the Constitution. It requires electors to vote separately for president and vice president, and it reduces the number of candidates eligible for consideration in the House-contingent election from five to three. The amendment also made arrangements for the vice president to act as president if, under a House contingent election, no president has yet been picked.

Prior to the Twelfth Amendment, electors cast two votes for the executive without making a distinction between their votes for president or vice president. Whoever received the second-highest amount of electoral votes would be named vice president. It is likely that many of the Founding Fathers at the Constitutional Convention believed that the Electoral College would act as a sort of nominating forum for presidential candidates and that most elections would end up in the House. The Panglossian aspirations of the Founding Fathers were that electors would be disinterested citizens who would choose men of "continental reputation." They naively thought that electors would gather around the country at their state capitols and deliberate intelligently before casting their votes for president. Moreover, they did not consider that parties would submit SLATES of candidates for president and vice president.

But as many of the Founders themselves began to disagree on the role of the federal government shortly after the Constitution was ratified, they began to form FACTIONS. James Madison and Thomas Jefferson lined up against Alexander Hamilton and John Adams, eventually leading to the formation of the Democratic-Republican and Federalist Parties, respectively. The Founders failed to foresee the almost immediate development of these political parties in the 1790s, and unfortunately, the original design of the Electoral College did not operate to the benefit of these parties. In reality, no electors deliberated about whom they would vote for president. Rather, the electors simply became mechanical and automatic vote-casters for their parties.

This lack of deliberation was all too apparent in 1796. Federalist electors voted for their presidential nominee, John Adams, and Democratic-Republicans voted for their presidential nominee, Thomas Jefferson. The Federalists won the most electoral votes. However, they faced a dilemma whereby if all Federalists cast both their votes for Adams and his vice presidential candidate, Thomas Pinckney, then a tie would occur. This would throw the election into the House of Representatives. In strategizing, the Federalists blundered and held back too many votes for their vice presidential candidate. Consequently, Jefferson came in second in the Electoral College balloting and became vice president.

Clearly, before the Twelfth Amendment, the parties faced two unsavory possibilities. If the party that won the most electors withheld too many of its votes for vice president, the OPPOSITION PARTY could end up in second place and win the vice presidency. On the other hand, if the winning party gave all its votes to both candidates, and a tie resulted between a party's vice president and president, the election could be thrown into the House of Representatives. In case of a tie, only those two candidates would be considered in a House-contingent election. However, this would give the opposition party the chance to influence the winning party's ticket and turn the winning party's vice president into president.

The catalyst for the adoption of the Twelfth Amendment arose out of the fiasco of the 1800 election. In this rematch between Adams and Jefferson, the Democratic-Republicans won a majority of the Electoral College vote but failed to withhold at least one of their votes from their vice presidential nominee, Aaron Burr. As a result, Burr was tied with Jefferson for votes in the Electoral College. The election was thrown into the House of Representatives. At the time, the Federalists controlled the House, and many did not want to see Jefferson become president. The House began voting by state on February 11, 1801. Jefferson received the votes of only eight states, one shy of a majority, because many Federalist representatives were throwing their support in the balloting to Burr. If the voting had been on the basis of each congressman rather than by state delegation, Burr would have received 53 House votes compared to 48 for Jefferson.

Balloting continued for six days—36 votes in all. Some Federalists suggested that they stall until inauguration day, March 4, so that when no president could assume office, a new presidential election would be required by statute. As such, these Federalists hoped to get another chance at the office. Some Democratic-Republicans spoke of open rebellion if such a move were attempted by Federalists. Before such a disastrous scenario could happen, Hamilton helped break the deadlock. While Hamilton intensely disliked Jefferson on a personal level, he was on cordial relations with Burr. But he thought Burr was ambitious and corrupt, describing him in letters to colleagues as a person whose ascendancy to the presidency could "only promote the purposes of the desperate and the profligate" and that, "Mr. Burr [was] the most unfit man in the United States for office of the President." Burr ended up as vice president.

The elections of 1796 and 1800 illustrated the problems with the original Electoral College system after the rise of the TWO-PARTY SYSTEM. The Twelfth Amendment, which was passed in time for the 1804 election, remedied these problems and bolstered the two-party system. This amendment fostered a more convenient process for the parties by guaranteeing both the president and vice president would be from the same party. Thus, there was no chance for the MINORITY PARTY to gain entry into the executive by taking the vice presidency.

This reform tended to lead to two-party competition by encouraging parties and interests to merge in order to form the broadest COALITIONS possible to give them a better chance of winning the presidency. Moreover, the change made the executive department more partisan because it was now always unified in the hands of one party. Furthermore, by changing the House-contingent election (when no candidate received an Electoral College majority) from the top five to the top three finishers in electoral voting, the amendment decreased the chance that a small minority party might throw the election into the House of Representatives and still be considered for the presidency.

Finally, the Twelfth Amendment made it less likely an opposing party would stall the voting during a House-contingent election because the amendment requires the vice president to assume the office of president if no president has been selected by the House. Since the vice presidency in a contingent election procedure would be determined between only the top two candidates by the Senate, the possibility of a deadlock in the Senate would be nearly impossible. In the end, by reinforcing the two-party system, the Twelfth Amendment helped insulate the Electoral College from later attempts at reform.

Further reading: Peirce, Neal R., and Lawrence D. Longley. *The People's President: The Electoral College in Ameri-* can History and the Direct Vote Alternative. New Haven, Conn.: Yale University Press, 1981; Lutz, Donald, et al. "The Electoral College in Historical and Philosophical Perspective." In Paul D. Schumaker and Burdett A. Loomis, eds., *Choosing a President: The Electoral College and Beyond.* New York: Chatham House Publishers, 2002; Wilmerding, Lucius. *The Electoral College.* New Brunswick, N.J.: Rutgers University Press, 1958.

—Mark J. McKenzie

Twentieth Amendment

The Twentieth Amendment to the U.S. Constitution, known popularly as the Lame Duck Amendment, provides that the presidential and vice presidential terms of office will begin on January 20 following their election, and the terms of office for senators and representatives in Congress will begin on January 3. The amendment also provides for succession to the presidency in case the president-elect dies or fails to qualify. (This section gained importance in 2000 when the outcome of the PRESIDENTIAL ELECTION remained in doubt for more than a month.)

The amendment was passed because of the length of service of senators and members of Congress after their election. Before the amendment, congressional sessions began on the first Monday in December in the year after an election. This meant that those who had been voted out of office (or chose not to seek reelection) served for more than a year after the election. These "lame duck" sessions were notorious for passing pork-barrel legislation aimed at serving the interests of members who had been defeated. By shortening the interim period to approximately two months, lame duck sessions were eliminated, or at least made much shorter.

Though not the first person to propose eliminating lame duck sessions, the Twentieth Amendment was primarily the work of Senator George W. Norris of Nebraska, who took umbrage at a bill subsidizing the shipbuilding industry in 1922. The amendment, which Norris originated in the agriculture committee, passed the Senate five times in the 1920s but each time failed in the House, four times without even coming to a floor vote. The amendment finally passed when Democrats gained control of the House after the 1930 election. Although Norris was a Republican, he blamed Republicans in the House, working with Republicans in the three Republican administrations of the period, for obstructing the amendment.

The shipbuilding bill was a minor problem of lame duck government. Following the election of Abraham Lincoln in 1860, seven southern states seceded from the Union. The lame duck president and Congress were passive in their response. The first secession took place in December, even before the modern dates for congressional and presidential inaugurations, but it could be argued that the seceding states might have acted more cautiously had they known an active government would soon be in place.

The change in date of the presidential and vice presidential inauguration might not have been practical at earlier periods of American history. In the 18th century, when the Constitution was written, mail delivery and travel took much longer than they do today. An early inauguration might not have provided enough time for one to be notified of one's election and to travel to the nation's capital. This was not a problem by 1932 with the advent of electronic communication and air travel. The presidential inauguration is held 17 days after the congressional session begins to give Congress time to count the electoral votes and, if necessary, elect a president or vice president.

The amendment was proposed by Congress on March 2, 1932, and was ratified by the requisite number of states on January 23, 1933. Pursuant to the language contained in the amendment, it became effective on October 15 of that year. The first Congress to take office under the amendment began on January 3, 1935, and the first presidential inauguration under the amendment was held on January 20, 1937. The amendment began to show its impact immediately. President elect Franklin D. Roosevelt was the target of an assassination attempt less than a month after the amendment was ratified. Had he died, the amendment makes it clear that the vice president elect would have become president. The amendment is unusual in that three of its provisions are subject to modification by legislative will: the date for Congress to assemble annually, the provision for who will act as president if neither president elect nor vice president elect can qualify, and the provision in case of the deaths of the candidates for president and vice president (i.e., the top three candidates in the ELECTORAL COLLEGE for president and the top two for vice president). Congress held hearings in 1995 on legislation to cover scenarios not anticipated by the amendment, but the legislation was not passed.

The provision regarding the death of the president elect was motivated by the death of Horace Greeley after the 1872 election but before the Electoral College had voted. Although Greeley had not won the election, the scenario has provided a challenging hypothetical scenario ever since. In the 1872 case, Greeley's electors scattered several different ways, meaning none of those they voted for could win. Under the Twentieth Amendment, it would have been rational for electors in such an instance involving a winning ticket to vote for the deceased candidate, insofar as the vice president elect would automatically become president, which is exactly what would happen if the president died in office. On the other hand, if the electors scattered, the election of the president would be thrown to the House of Representatives, and the results could be unpredictable.

The amendment became controversial during the impeachment of President William J. Clinton. Some legal scholars maintained that the impeachment would not be valid if carried from one Congress into the next, which was the plan of the Republicans in Congress who impeached Clinton. Clinton chose not to bring the question to court, in part because no one believed the president would be convicted in the Senate. Nevertheless, the controversy illustrates how a normally noncontroversial constitutional provision can suddenly become debatable.

The amendment largely accomplished its goals, though there are those who would go further and move the inauguration date back even closer to the election. There continue to be pork barrel bills passed during lame duck sessions, often known as "Christmas ornaments," but their scope and intensity is less than before the Twentieth Amendment was in place.

Further reading: Ackerman, Bruce. *The Case against Lameduck Impeachment.* New York: Seven Stories Press, 1999; Anastaplo, John. *The Amendments to the Constitution: A Commentary.* Baltimore: Johns Hopkins University Press, 1995; Cornell Law School, Legal Information Center. Available online. URL: http://www.law.cornell.edu. Accessed August 10, 2005; Palmer, Kris E., ed. *Constitutional Amendments: 1789 to the Present.* Detroit: Gale Group, 2000.

—Tony L. Hill

Twenty-fourth Amendment

The Twenty-fourth Amendment to the U.S. Constitution abolished the POLL TAX in federal elections. It states: "The rights of citizens to vote in any primary or other election for President or Vice President . . . shall not be denied or abridged by the United States or any state for failure to pay any poll tax or other tax." The amendment was ratified on January 23, 1964, nearly two years after the proposal passed in the U.S. House and Senate.

While the FIFTEENTH AMENDMENT (1870) prohibited the federal government or the states from denying the right to vote based on "race, color or previous condition of servitude," by the late 1880s, whites in the South had found numerous ways to stop African Americans from voting. The poll tax was one of many measures with which white southerners denied African Americans the ability to vote in elections. The tax, along with the GRANDFATHER CLAUSE, LITERACY TESTS, and outright intimidation, essentially stripped blacks in the South of the opportunity to vote. A poll tax required all citizens to pay an annual fee before voting. The first taxes were introduced in the South during the late 19th century. The tax was applied to all voters, both black and white. Since it was meant to be prohibitive, that meant it could prevent a large number of whites from casting their BALLOTS. The solution the southerners developed was to add a grandfather clause to the poll tax. The grandfather clause exempted citizens from poll taxes and other restrictive measures if they could prove that their grandfather had voted. Because almost all blacks in the South were descendants of slaves who had no voting rights, the poll tax accomplished the goal.

For more than a decade, Senator Spessard Holland, a Democrat from Florida, waged a campaign to end the tax. Beginning in 1949, Holland presented on the Senate floor a proposed constitutional amendment that would ban the poll tax in federal elections. Even though Holland was a conservative Democrat from a southern state who argued that civil rights was a state and not a federal issue and eventually voted against the 1964 Civil Rights Act, he fought hard to achieve his goal. However, his strenuous efforts were in vain, as were other early attempts to abolish the tax.

By the early 1960s, the tax existed in only five southern states: Alabama, Arkansas, Mississippi, Virginia, and Texas. However, when Holland offered his proposed amendment in 1962, members of Congress from other Jim Crow states rushed to defend the tax. Senators Richard Russell of Georgia and John Stennis of Mississippi were two of the most prominent and vocal opponents of Holland's proposal. President John F. Kennedy, who up until that time had been reluctant to oppose his party's powerful congressional delegation from the South, actively supported an amendment and urged his fellow Democrats to do so. Every single Republican in the Senate, with the exception of John Tower of Texas, voted in favor of the bill. The measure easily passed the House of Representatives, with the final vote 295 to 86.

The amendment went to the states for ratification in December 1962. In January 1964, the South Dakota legislature voted to ratify the legislation. President Lyndon Johnson lauded the action and described the vote as a measure of the progress the country had made in race relations. He also declared: "There can be no one too poor to vote."

The Twenty-fourth Amendment was in many ways more a symbolic victory in the struggle for full equality for African Americans. By the time the amendment made its way through Congress, most of the southern states no longer required the tax to vote. It was not the most effective way of prohibiting blacks from casting their ballots, something that both civil rights activists and segregationists understood. In the 1964 election, the first GENERAL ELECTION after its ratification, the percentage of black voting barely increased from 1960. Whites were still able to use the grandfather clause and literacy tests to deny African Americans the franchise. Not until the 1965 Voting Rights Act would African Americans fully have the opportunity to vote.

Further reading: Cornell Law School, Legal Information Center. Available online. URL: http://www.law.cornell.edu. Accessed August 10, 2005; Lawson, Stephen F. *Black Ballots: Voting Rights in the South, 1944–1969.* New York: Columbia University Press, 1976; Lusane, Clarence. *No Easy Victories: Black Americans and the Vote.* New York: Franklin Watts, 1996; Mann, Robert. *The Walls of Jericho: Lyndon Johnson,* *Hubert Humphrey, Richard Russell and the Struggle for Civil Rights.* New York: Harcourt, Brace & Co., 1996.

—Justin P. Coffey

Twenty-second Amendment

The Twenty-second Amendment to the U.S. Constitution provides that no person may be elected president more than twice, or more than once if he or she has served more than two years of someone else's presidential term by succession. The amendment was proposed by Congress on March 21, 1947, and was ratified by the requisite number of states on February 27, 1951. Other than the Twenty-seventh Amendment, which was ratified 202 years after being proposed, this amendment took the longest of any successful constitutional amendment to be ratified.

The chief sponsor of the amendment was Representative Earl Michener, Republican of Michigan. Several other proposals were introduced, including one for a single six-year term, but opinion in Congress crystallized around Michener's amendment. The original bill limited the term not only of the president but also the vice president. An amendment to the bill by Senator Robert Taft of Ohio allowed for a president who had served no more than half of someone else's term to serve two full terms. It was passed by party-line votes in each chamber, with Republicans voting for it unanimously in both chambers, while Democrats opposed it 47-121 in the House and 13-23 in the Senate. Only 83 Republican state legislators in the country voted against its ratification.

The amendment's purpose was to limit the power of the presidency, and it was passed in response to Franklin D. Roosevelt being elected four times from 1932 to 1944. Prior to Roosevelt, no president had sought a third term, although supporters of Ulysses S. Grant had urged him to, and Grover Cleveland had flirted with the idea of running for a third nonconsecutive term in 1904. In effect, the amendment institutionalized George Washington's dictum upon his retirement that no one should serve more than eight years as president. The amendment encapsulates congressional desires for an earlier age when Congress, rather than the president, dominated the national government.

The amendment contained a proviso that it would not apply to the person who was president when it was proposed (Harry S. Truman) nor to the person who was president when it was ratified (also Truman). Although eligible, Truman did not seek a third term in 1952 but later called for repeal of the amendment. So the amendment effectively came into force when Dwight D. Eisenhower was elected in 1952. One historical irony is that the amendment was proposed by a Republican Congress in order to punish the already-deceased Roosevelt, but it has forced the retirements of three Republican presidents (Eisenhower, Richard M. Nixon, and Ronald Reagan) but only one Democratic president (William J. Clinton).

TERM LIMITS for the president were proposed in Congress as early as 1789. Alexander Hamilton argued against a limit on presidential tenure in Federalist No. 72, stating, "nothing appears more plausible at first sight, nor more ill founded upon close inspection, than a scheme . . . of continuing the Chief Magistrate in office for a certain time, and then excluding him from it, either for a limited period, or forever after." The Senate passed a term limits amendment in 1824 and again in 1826, but both bills failed in the House of Representatives. The Congress that finally passed the amendment acted in a narrow window of opportunity; it was the only Congress in which both chambers were controlled by Republicans between 1931 and 1995. The bill was introduced on the first day of the congressional session.

Many political scientists and other scholars and observers of the presidency have called for repeal of the amendment. They argue that it has had the effect of rendering presidents virtually impotent in their second terms. Prior to the amendment, presidents enjoyed greater political capital in their second terms even though it was generally known there would be no third term. Since senators and representatives know at the start of the second term that the president will not be heading the ticket again, they show the president less deference in legislative matters. This was presaged by the experience of Theodore Roosevelt, who, upon being elected to a full term of his own in 1904 (having served three and a half years of the assassinated William McKinley's second term), announced that he regarded the term as his second and would not seek a third in 1908. He found that his clout was greatly reduced as a result of this announcement and wished he had left Congress and the voters wondering about whether he would seek another term. After four years of retirement, Roosevelt ran as a third-party candidate in 1912. This time he tried to maintain that he had really served only one term, but his pronouncement from 1904 came back to haunt him. A button that year read "Washington Wouldn't, Grant Couldn't, Roosevelt Shouldn't."

Ronald Reagan enjoyed a remarkable decline in political capital from his first to his second term. After leaving office, he signed his name to an article calling for repeal of the amendment, calling it "a perversion of the constitution's sound design for a limited but energetic government." The amendment is also criticized as an abrogation of the democratic process, preventing voters from reelecting an incumbent to a third term. Others maintain that no one can effectively maintain personal health in more than eight years in office, let alone serve effectively. State efforts to impose term limits on Congress and the House of Representatives were overturned by the U.S. Supreme Court in 1995, the same year the House rejected a constitutional amendment on congressional term limits. The president remains the only federal elected official with a term limitation.

Further reading: Anastaplo, John. *The Amendments to the Constitution: A Commentary.* Baltimore: Johns Hopkins University Press, 1995; Cornell Law School, Legal Information Center. Available online. URL: http://www.law.cornell.edu. Accessed August 10, 2005; Mayer, Jane, and Doyle McManus. *Landslide: The Unmaking of the President, 1984–1988.* Boston: Houghton Mifflin, 1988; Palmer, Kris E., ed. *Constitutional Amendments: 1789 to the Present.* Detroit: Gale Group, 2000.

—Tony L. Hill

Twenty-seventh Amendment

The Twenty-seventh Amendment, the most recent addition to the U.S. Constitution, prohibits Congress from passing any pay raise that takes effect before the next election for the House of Representatives is held. The theory is that the ELECTORATE should have an opportunity to vote members of Congress out of office before they receive a newly passed pay increase. The purpose of the amendment is to prevent members of the House and Senate from taking advantage of the system to raise their own salaries.

This amendment was originally proposed along with 11 others and submitted to the states for ratification on September 25, 1789. By 1791, 10 of those proposed amendments were approved and became the Bill of Rights, while the other two failed to receive the approval of the required three-fourths of the states. The proposed congressional pay limitation amendment was approved only by six states as of 1791. As late as the early 1980s, only two additional states had voted to ratify it. Unlike many later proposed amendments, the pay raise amendment did not include a stipulation that it had to be ratified within a certain time limit or become void.

This came to the attention of University of Texas student Gregory Watson, who argued in an academic paper that the amendment could still be added to the Constitution if enough of the remaining states approved it. Watson's instructor disagreed and gave the paper a "C." Watson sought to prove his instructor wrong and campaigned over the next decade to have the amendment approved. His work was rewarded in 1992, when the 38th state voted to ratify it. It took 203 years for the amendment to go through the process of proposal and ratification—the longest the process has ever taken. The passage of the amendment after 200 years left open the question of whether other proposed amendments without time limit stipulations could also be ratified.

Several attempts have been made in recent years to apply the Twenty-seventh Amendment to the Ethics Reform Act of 1989, which set an automatic increase in congressional salaries unless both houses voted to reject the increase in a particular year. In a 1992 case, *Boehner v. Anderson,* the federal court ruled that the act did not violate the Constitution because raises provided for by the act did not take effect until after House elections. In 1999, the courts also rejected a similar attempt to invalidate the automatic pay increases because the members of Congress who initiated the case could not show any injury, and thus they were declared to have no standing in the case. Moral outrage, the courts argued, was not enough to prove injury, and the effect of the law was to increase the salaries of members of Congress, something that could not be shown to injure those members.

Further reading: Anastaplo, George. *The Amendments to the Constitution: A Commentary.* Baltimore: Johns Hopkins University Press, 1995.

—Kenneth Quinnell

Twenty-sixth Amendment

The Twenty-sixth Amendment to the U.S. Constitution, giving 18-, 19-, and 20-year-old citizens the right to vote, was proposed by Congress on March 23, 1971, and declared ratified shortly thereafter on June 30, 1971. It is one of 26 amendments to the U.S. Constitution that have been ratified by state legislatures in at least three-fourths of the states (the Twenty-first Amendment was ratified by state conventions in three-fourths of the states). Moreover, it is one of four amendments that extended the right to vote (the others are the Fifteenth, Nineteenth, and Twenty-fourth Amendments).

Historically, citizens were required to attain the age of 21 before they enjoyed the right to vote. The war in Vietnam caused a critical push to extend the vote to younger Americans, since 18-year-olds were old enough for conscription (the draft), but not yet old enough to vote for representatives who would support their positions on the war. In 1970, Congress passed the Voting Rights Act that gave 18-year-olds the right to vote, but only in federal elections starting January 1, 1971. A provision allowing 18-year-old citizens the right to vote in state elections was also included, but this provision was ultimately struck down by the Supreme Court. In December 1970, *Oregon v. Mitchell* was handed down by the Supreme Court, ruling that Congress did not have the power to compel states to guarantee voting rights to citizens aged 18. In response to the Supreme Court decision, Congress proposed and the states ratified the Twenty-sixth Amendment in 1971.

This amendment has become a symbol of the final legislative authority that rests with Congress and its ability to nullify a Court decision with the help of state governments; while checks and balances provide for some overlap in the law-making process, it is ultimately Congress along with the various state legislatures that have the ability to make dramatic changes to the Constitution of the United States.

Richard Nixon, then president of the United States, and a variety of other high-ranking elected officials had high expectations for the new infusion of voting-age Americans. The outcome of the constitutional amendment passage, however, was far less than those expectations. In the years following passage of the amendment, less than half of the newly eligible population actually exercised the vote. In the 1972 presidential election between Nixon and McGovern, young people who did vote tended to support Nixon, except for college students, who tended to support McGovern in greater numbers.

The newly enfranchised population of voters turned out to be the least electorally active. The 1990s witnessed a small increase in the percentage of younger voters, and optimism about the youth vote ensued. An attempt was made to address the issue by passing the Motor Voter Law to try to increase the number of registered voters, particularly young voters, and ultimately increase voting rates among this group. Get-out-the-vote groups such as Rock the Vote voiced the importance of young voters exercising their right to vote. Such efforts have been instrumental in registering hundreds of thousands of young voters, yet the act of registering to vote does not necessarily ensure voting come election day. The Bureau of the Census reports that in 2000 only 36 percent of voters aged 18 to 24 voted. While the voting rate of young voters increased in the 2004 presidential election, this group still votes at a far lower rate than do older voters. Youths continue to represent the group with the lowest rates of voter turnout among all age groups, and their inclusion in the eligible voting age population had the effect of lowering national turnout overall.

Further reading: Eisner, Jane. *Taking Back the Vote: Getting American Youth Involved in Our Democracy.* Boston: Beacon Press, 2004; U.S. Census Bureau. Available online. URL: http://www.census.gov. Accessed August 10, 2005; Wolfinger, Raymond. *Who Votes?* New Haven, Conn.: Yale University Press, 1980.

—Dari E. Sylvester

Twenty-third Amendment

The Twenty-third Amendment to the Constitution gave citizens living in the District of Columbia the right to vote in presidential elections. This amendment allows Washington, D.C., to be represented in the Electoral College by the number of electors of the least populous state, which is three. Washington, D.C., however, is still not to be considered a state and is not provided full representation in Congress. Congress passed the amendment on June 17, 1960; it was ratified on March 29, 1961. The Twenty-third Amendment is composed of two sections. The first section explains what the amendment does, and the second section confers on Congress the power to enforce the amendment.

Washington, D.C., was designated as the permanent seat of the U.S. government in 1800. It was created from land ceded by Maryland and Virginia and named after George Washington and Christopher Columbus. When first established, it was a town of 5,000. By 1900, more than a quarter of a million people lived within its bounds, and by 1960, 760,000 people lived in the District. In 1960, American citizens living in Washington were required to pay taxes and were subject to the the military draft, but were not allowed to vote in national elections. The Twenty-Third Amendment partially changed this by allowing residents of the District to participate in presidential elections.

According to Section I, Article 8, of the Constitution, Congress shall have exclusive power of legislation in all cases over a district that shall be the seat of government. The "district" described in Section I, Article 8, was to become the District of Columbia in 1800. The idea that the federal government should have exclusive jurisdiction over the space in which it gathers has historical roots. In 1783, Congress, meeting in Philadelphia, was threatened by disgruntled veterans demanding the pay still owed them from the American Revolution. The situation became dangerous when the state of Pennsylvania refused to step in between the veterans and the Congress. From this experience, Congress determined that it could not rely on the states for protection, and therefore it was necessary that the permanent seat of government be under congressional control.

Though the Twenty-third Amendment significantly expanded the SUFFRAGE of the residents of Washington, many individuals and groups are still working to achieve full representation. In 1983, Congress proposed a constitutional amendment that would have extended full congressional voting rights to the citizen residents of Washington, D.C., but this proposal was not ratified by the three-fourths of the states needed to amend the Constitution, receiving only 16 of the 38 states needed. The effort to achieve full suffrage for the citizens of Washington, D.C., is unlikely to succeed in the near future for many reasons. Many believe that it would be imprudent to alter the unique status of the District and thereby compromise the neutrality of the capital city. Perhaps the biggest obstacle to suffrage, however, is partisan POLITICS. Washington, D.C., has voted for the DEMOCRATIC PARTY candidate in every election since 1964, and congressional representation would almost certainly add to the number of representatives in Congress who belong to the Democratic Party. The effort to achieve congressional representation for Washington gained a significant ally when, late in his second term, President Bill Clinton had the presidential limo outfitted with D.C. license plates declaring "taxation without representation." President George W. Bush had the plates replaced soon after taking office in 2001.

Further reading: Abbot, Carl. *Political Terrain: Washington, D.C., from Tidewater Town to Global Metropolis.* Chapel Hill, N.C.: University of North Carolina Press, 1999.

—Ryan Rakness

two-party system

The two-party system refers to the dominance of American POLITICS by two parties offering alternative opinions about governing. The two-party system traces its roots to the 1800s. The DEMOCRATIC-REPUBLICAN PARTY and the FEDERALIST PARTY opposed one another in the early 1800s, although there was a brief period in which Democratic-Republicans were the only major party. From 1833 to 1856, the Democratic and Whig Parties battled each other, followed by the Democratic and Republican Parties since 1856.

With one party in charge and the other in opposition, the two-party system gives voters a choice in how they want to be governed. Competing interests among Americans, whether economic, social, or geographic, have contributed to its success. In recent years, Americans have favored dividing power between the parties, with one controlling the White House and the other at least one house of Congress. One party has occasionally dominated the political landscape by winning a landslide election, such as in 1964.

The Democratic and Republican Parties run sophisticated FUND-RAISING and GRASSROOTS organizations in all 50 states, enjoy high NAME RECOGNITION among voters, and have a steady stream of candidates seeking the parties' ENDORSEMENT, making it difficult for an outside party to gain electoral traction. Most state election officers are members of one of the two parties, and election laws and regulations favor maintaining the two-party system. Democrats and Republicans are the only parties guaranteed to receive federal funding in elections and participation in PRESIDENTIAL DEBATES.

Candidates of other parties enjoy more success at the local and state levels. Representative Bernie Sanders (I, Vt.) won four terms as mayor of Burlington, Vermont, as a socialist. They can tip national election outcomes, however. Fearing a repeat of 2000, when many Democrats believed Ralph Nader, then the GREEN PARTY candidate, cost them the White House, Democrats brought lawsuits in battleground states in 2004 to keep Nader, the REFORM PARTY nominee, off the BALLOT. Democrats argued that the Reform Party was not a legitimate national party.

Critics of the two-party system, such as Nader, complain that Democrats and Republicans put their self-interest above "a working, deliberative democracy" by favoring business interests that give money to their candidates and that the two-party system offers voters few real choices. Although some voters lament their lack of choice in elections, they have not shown widespread support for changing the system. While the most successful third-party candidate was former president Theodore Roosevelt in 1912 (his BULL MOOSE PARTY captured 88 electoral votes and 27 percent of the POPULAR VOTE), most THIRD PARTIES have failed to wield much influence beyond a single election and have dissolved.

Other critics of the two-party system argue that the system is not the consequence of voter choice, but rather the logical outcome of the single-member plurality districts that dominate American politics. Unlike PROPORTIONAL REPRESENTATION, as is the norm in many parliamentary systems, it is believed that single-member plurality districts work against minority parties. Supporters of the two-party system justify the lack of choice by pointing to the political stability that a two-party system offers over multiparty systems that are the norm under proportional representation.

Further reading: Nader, Ralph. *Crashing the Party: How to Tell the Truth and Still Run for President.* New York: Thomas Dunne Books, 2002; Sorauf, Frank J., and Paul Allen Beck. *Party Politics in America.* Glenville, Ill.: Scott, Foresman & Co., 1988.

—Mary Lynn F. Jones

U

uncontested election

An uncontested election occurs when a candidate, usually an incumbent, faces no opposition. Often enjoying advantages in NAME RECOGNITION, FUND-RAISING, and poll numbers, the candidate in an uncontested election successfully dissuades potential CHALLENGERS, leaving the other party unable to recruit a candidate.

The nation's first uncontested election occurred in 1789, when George Washington was unanimously elected president. Since then, however, every presidential candidate has faced opposition. Uncontested elections are much more common at lower levels in the political system, as higher offices often attract several well-qualified candidates.

The number of uncontested CONGRESSIONAL ELECTIONS has risen in recent years due to REDISTRICTING efforts that have left fewer competitive seats and to the impressive electoral power of incumbency. In 2002, 78 House members were unopposed by a major-party nominee, up from 63 in 2000. Four senators were given a free pass by major-party challengers in 2002, up from just one in 2000.

Many incumbents who run unopposed are veterans of Congress and/or represent districts that closely match their political ideologies, making it next to impossible for a candidate from a different party to win. In 2002, six of Massachusetts's 10 representatives ran unchallenged; all of the state's House members are Democrats. The number of House incumbents who won at least 60 percent of the major-party vote during reelection was 77.3 percent in 2000, up from 59.1 percent in 1956.

Incumbents who recently survived tough elections may be unopposed the next time because they demonstrated their strength as tested candidates. For example, Senator John Warner (R, Va.) did not face a Democratic challenger in 2002 after defeating a formidable opponent, Mark Warner, in 1996.

Candidates who run in uncontested elections are often asked by party leaders and committees to hold down their own spending and donate resources to candidates in tight elections. In 2002, Democratic and Republican members of Congress donated $7.8 million from their campaigns to other candidates, up from $2 million in 1990.

Besides uncontested GENERAL ELECTIONS, many incumbents run unopposed during party primaries. In 2002, 71 percent of House members and 69 percent of senators had uncontested PRIMARY elections. In their presidential reelection campaigns in 1996 and 2004, neither Bill Clinton nor George W. Bush faced a primary challenger.

Further reading: Herrnson, Paul S. *Congressional Elections: Campaigning at Home and in Washington.* Washington, D.C.: CQ Press, 2004; Jacobson, Gary C. *The Politics of Congressional Elections.* Boston: Pearson Addison-Wesley, 2003.

—Mary Lynn F. Jones

undecided voters

Undecided voters are potential voters in an election who have not yet decided on a particular candidate. They are an influential lot in American POLITICS because they hold the focus of most electoral campaigns. Candidates have three ways of increasing their share of the votes. The first is to inspire their supporters to turn out and cast a vote. The second is to weaken support among the opposition's supporters. The third is to gain the support of undecided citizens.

Early in the campaign cycle, the percentage of undecided citizens may be relatively high, even one-fourth or one-third of the ELECTORATE. As ELECTION DAY draws near, that percentage decreases. Political events often help citizens choose among their options. In a PRESIDENTIAL ELECTION, for instance, many people who are undecided before the national conventions pick a favorite candidate soon after the conventions. The PRESIDENTIAL DEBATES also help many undecided voters make up their minds. Others, however, will find it more difficult to choose and may remain undecided until the day of the election.

Undecided voters are usually citizens who have weak partisan ties or are INDEPENDENTS. Most strong partisans vote for their party's nominee, regardless of who it is. By contrast, citizens who are less loyal to a party tend to base their preference on evaluations and impressions of the particular candidates in the race. While some of these citizens make up their minds early in the campaign, soon after they learn who is competing for the office, others do not. It is this group of uncommitted potential voters that campaigns spend much of their resources attempting to reach.

The independent nature of most undecided voters is one reason cited for the moderate tone of campaign discourse in large GENERAL ELECTIONS. It is also noted as a reason why candidates' messages may become less ideologically extreme from the PRIMARY season to the general election season. In most primaries, undecided voters are still partisans, and many are strong partisans. Therefore, appeals to undecided voters in the primary election phase are naturally more ideological. By contrast, once the NOMINATION is won, the pool of undecided voters is made up of nonpartisans and weak partisans. Since one of the main goals of the general election campaign is to successfully attract members of this group, the campaign message usually becomes more moderate.

Further reading: Lavrakas, Paul J., and Jack K. Holley, eds. *Polling and Presidential Election Coverage.* Newbury Park, Calif.: Sage Publications, 1991; Fenwick, Ian, Frederick Wiseman, John F. Becker, and James R. Heiman. "Classifying Undecided Voters in Pre-Election Polls." *Public Opinion Quarterly* 46, no. 3 (1982): 383–391.

—Francis Neely

Uniformed and Overseas Citizens Absentee Voting Act

The Uniformed and Overseas Citizens Absentee Voting Act (UOCAVA) was enacted into law in 1986 to facilitate voting by civilians and members of the U.S. military living abroad. The core provisions of this law set forth procedures governing how Americans residing overseas who no longer maintain a U.S. address can register and vote by absentee ballot in elections for federal offices.

The UOCAVA was a response to the challenges that confront Americans living abroad who attempt to vote in U.S. elections. These citizens must plan ahead to register to vote and request an absentee ballot, taking into account lengthy delays in international mail service and shifting military deployments. Legal requirements governing signatures, witnesses, postmarks, and deadlines that vary across states and localities contribute to further confusion about voting from overseas.

The procedures set forth by the UOCAVA received a great deal of attention during the contested 2000 PRESIDENTIAL ELECTION, as Florida was one of 14 states that counted overseas absentee ballots received after ELECTION DAY and had almost 177,000 military personnel among its registered voters. With Texas governor George W. Bush holding an unofficial lead of 1,784 votes after BALLOTS were initially tallied, a fierce public relations and legal battle ensued to determine the disposition of the ballots that would arrive before the state deadline, 10 days after election day.

While Florida law required that all late-arriving ballots be postmarked from abroad on or before election day, the UOCAVA stipulated that voting materials under this act "shall be carried expeditiously and free of postage." When many absentee ballots sent through military mail arrived with no postmark, election officials could not ascertain when or from where they had been mailed. Additionally, many ballots lacked required witness signatures or dates. The Bush campaign argued that uniformed personnel should not be disenfranchised because of such technicalities, and after an initial protest, the campaign of Vice President Al Gore did not contest this point.

Though elections officials in each county were the arbiters of which overseas ballots were counted, the constitutionality of using different standards to determine the validity of overseas absentee ballots was not among the issues the U.S. Supreme Court was asked to consider in *BUSH V. GORE,* the decision that concluded the electoral standoff. Without counting the overseas ballots received after election day in the state's final tally, Gore edged Bush in Florida by 202 votes. With those overseas ballots, Bush's official final margin of victory in Florida was 537 votes, earning him the presidency.

In the aftermath of the 2000 election, the UOCAVA was amended by the National Defense Authorization Act of 2002 and the HELP AMERICA VOTE ACT of 2002 to increase the chances that the votes of Americans living abroad would be counted. Among its numerous provisions, procedures

Petty Officer 3rd Class Candie Thompson assists fireman Paul Byrd in filling out an absentee ballot. *(Photographed by Raul Quinones, U.S. Navy)*

were established to ensure that information about voting regulations and deadlines would be spread more effectively and that military absentee ballots would bear proof of the date on which they were mailed.

Further reading: Coleman, Kevin J. "The Uniformed and Overseas Citizens Absentee Voting Act: Background and Issues." *Congressional Research Service Report for the Congress,* January 30, 2003. Order Code RS20764; Federal Voting Assistance Program. Available online. URL: http://www.fvap.gov. Accessed August 10, 2005.

—Brendan J. Doherty

Union Party

The Union Party was organized June 20, 1936. It was a COALITION of Depression-bred political movements, united primarily by common dissatisfaction with Franklin Roosevelt, whose New Deal, they claimed, was inadequate to meet the challenge of the Great Depression.

William Lemke, U.S. representative from North Dakota and leader of the agrarian movement called the Nonpartisan League, was the party's presidential candidate. Its leader, however, was Charles Coughlin, the "radio priest" from Michigan, who claimed 10 million listeners to his weekly political broadcasts. Despite initially supporting Roosevelt, in 1934 Coughlin labeled the president a tool of business and founded the National Union of Social Justice to oppose "Franklin 'Double-Crossing' Roosevelt." Coughlin recruited Lemke and looked to other movements for support.

If Huey Long had not been assassinated in September 1935, he likely would have been the candidate. The Louisiana senator advocated radical income redistribution and had made a national base by founding the Share Our Wealth Society. The preacher Gerald Smith claimed leadership of its 7 million members in 1936. Dr. Francis Townsend proposed a $200 monthly pension for Americans more than 60 years of age to stimulate the economy. By 1936, there were thousands of Townsend Clubs with millions of members.

That summer the National Union and the Townsend movement drew a total of 20,000 people to conventions in Cleveland, Ohio. The four men addressed the gatherings, convinced that their broad coalition—Lemke and Long's farmer supporters, Townsend's aged followers, and Coughlin's northern listeners—would bring victory. Their platform was as much an amalgam as the party. It urged, among other things, a national bank, help for bankrupt farmers, pensions, and capping incomes to redistribute wealth.

Autumn brought predictions that the party would deny Roosevelt reelection. However, problems appeared. In September, Townsend ceased campaigning, distancing his movement from Coughlin's party. In mid-October, Smith was forced from the party after apparently advocating fascism. The party proved unable to mobilize local organization, and Lemke failed to make the BALLOT in 14 states.

Increasingly, the party's leaders depended on their personal abilities to influence voters.

It was not enough. Lemke won 892,378 votes, 2 percent of the national total, and did not carry a single state. Coughlin was stunned and disbanded his National Union; Townsend refocused his efforts on Congress. Only Lemke continued to speak of the Union Party as a force, but it was never again more than a name. Its office closed in 1938.

Further reading: Bennett, David. *Demagogues in the Depression: American Radicals and the Union Party, 1932–1936.* New Brunswick, N.J.: Rutgers University Press, 1969; Brinkley, Alan. *Voices of Protest: Huey Long, Father Coughlin, and the Great Depression.* New York: Knopf, 1982; Schlesinger, Arthur. *The Politics of Upheaval.* Boston: Houghton Mifflin, 1960.

—Matthew Bowman

United We Stand America   *See* REFORM PARTY.

unit rule

The unit rule refers to a controversial practice at the DEMOCRATIC PARTY's national nominating conventions that enabled a plurality of a state's delegation to dictate the allotment of all of the state delegation's votes to one candidate or position. Believed to distort DELEGATES' actual preferences, this "winner-take-all" scheme was abolished by the 1968 convention. After a series of reforms intended to "democratize" convention and NOMINATION rules was proposed by a commission led by Senator George McGovern (the McGovern-Fraser Commission), the Democratic Party adopted proportional allocation of delegates at conventions.

The unit rule also refers to the "winner-take-all" scheme of allocating electoral votes in PRESIDENTIAL ELECTIONS in the United States. As a result of the unit rule, all states (except Nebraska and Maine) allot all of their electoral votes to the candidate who receives a plurality of the POPULAR VOTE in that state. Maine and Nebraska can split their electoral votes; each distributes two electoral votes to the winner of the popular vote in the state and then by CONGRESSIONAL DISTRICT to the candidate with the largest share of votes.

The U.S. Constitution is notoriously vague with respect to detailed instructions for ELECTORAL COLLEGE procedures. Many of the specifics are left up to individual state legislatures, which have granted control over selection procedures for electors largely to the parties. Parties call for electors to pledge support for candidates, and 29 states plus the District of Columbia legally bind electors to vote for the popular winner. Five states provide sanctions for defection (there have been only eight defections since 1948), but they are constitutionally questionable and rarely enforced. In actuality, there is no federal law that requires electors to remain faithful to their pledges.

The unit rule has serious implications for presidential POLITICS in America. To begin with, this feature sets up a situation in which a candidate can win the presidency by winning the popular vote in as few as a handful of the country's most populous states. Scholars have shown that the winner-take-all feature of the Electoral College disproportionately advantages states with larger populations. It also boosts attention to swing states. Strategic decisions about resource allocation in national campaigns typically involve ignoring states that candidates are likely to lose and likely to win. Resources (time and money) are devoted primarily to battleground (swing) states, where the election outcome is not a foregone conclusion. Ordinarily, most of the country (that part outside swing states) is neglected by both nominees in presidential campaigns, and critics argue that the unit rule permits violation of the constitutional mandate for "one person, one vote."

The unit rule has been a standard feature of presidential campaigns despite the fact that public opinion nationwide appears to support reform. Moreover, legislators in 29 states have proposed bills to eliminate the "winner-take-all" system since the election debacle in 2000, but not one has passed. In 2004, reformers in Colorado attempted to circumvent the legislature entirely and to change the state's electoral system by passing a BALLOT INITIATIVE. If the reform (Amendment 36) had passed, it would have taken effect immediately and required Colorado to divide its nine electoral votes proportionally among candidates based on the state's overall popular vote. Interestingly, had the measure been in place in Colorado in 2000, where Gore received 42 percent of the popular vote, the Democrat would have won the White House with 270 electoral votes (Bush would have won 268). The ballot initiative ultimately failed in 2004.

Increased attention to the unit rule and its consequences for presidential elections (especially close races) may sustain a serious reform movement that ultimately alters the method of presidential selection. To be sure, such an enterprise is likely to be long and complex.

Further reading: Brams, Steven J., and Morton D. Davis. "The 3/2's Rule in Presidential Campaigning." *American Political Science Review* 68 (1974): 113–134; Colantoni, Claude S., Terence Levesque, and Peter C. Ordershook. "Campaign Resources under the Electoral College." *American Political Science Review* 69 (1975): 141–154.

—Costas Panagopoulos

U.S. Taxpayers Party

One of the more prominent minor parties, the U.S. Taxpayers Party champions a conservative Christian agenda. Its preamble states "that the foundation of our political position and moving principle of our political activity is our full submission and unshakable faith in our Savior and Redeemer, our Lord and Savior Jesus Christ." The party is pro-life,

pro–school prayer, pro–states' rights, anti–gay rights, anti-welfare, and anti–free trade. It fields candidates at both the local and national levels.

The party dates to 1992, when several INDEPENDENT state political parties, including the remnants of the arch-conservative AMERICAN INDEPENDENT PARTY, united to enhance their political viability. Former Nixon administration official and Conservative Caucus chairman Howard Phillips spearheaded the movement. Throughout the party's existence, Phillips has unsuccessfully attempted to convince a prominent, nationally known conservative to run for president under the party's label. Phillips made overtures to conservative columnist Patrick J. Buchanan in 1992 and 1996, but Buchanan declined each time. In 2000, U.S. senator Bob Smith of New Hampshire bolted the REPUBLICAN PARTY to seek the party's NOMINATION, but he returned to the Republicans after only a matter of weeks. Phillips and the party have also courted two-time Republican presidential hopeful Alan Keyes.

With no other candidate emerging, Phillips accepted the party's nomination in 1992, 1996, and 2000. In 1992, he appeared on the BALLOT in 21 states, garnering approximately 43,000 votes. Over the next four years, the party became larger and better organized. In 1994, the party began running candidates at the local level. Two years later, Phillips gained BALLOT ACCESS in 39 states and received about 185,000 votes. In 2000, Phillips made 41 state ballots, but his vote total fell to 98,000. This decline in support was due in part to the REFORM PARTY presidential candidacy of Patrick Buchanan.

The U.S. Taxpayers Party (renamed the Constitution Party in 1999) remains an important outlet for conservatives who are disgruntled with moderate Republicans. The party is particularly active in California and Pennsylvania. In 2004, it selected conservative activist Michael Peroutka as its presidential nominee and Chuck Baldwin, a Baptist pastor and radio talk show host, as its vice presidential candidate.

Further reading: Phillips, Howard, ed. *The Next Four Years.* Franklin, Tenn.: Adroit Press, 1992.

—John Paul Hill

U.S. Term Limits v. Thornton 514 U.S. 779 (1995)

On November 3, 1992, voters in Arkansas adopted an amendment to the state constitution that limited the number of terms individuals may serve in public office. The first two sections of the amendment pertained to individuals elected to state office, and the remaining sections limited individuals to no more than three terms in the U.S. House of Representatives and two terms in the U.S. Senate.

Approximately two months before the amendment went into effect, U.S. representative Ray Thornton, along with the LEAGUE OF WOMEN VOTERS and various citizens of Arkansas, filed suit in state court asking judges to declare the amendment unconstitutional. The primary argument was that Amendment 73 violated ARTICLE I of the U.S. Constitution, because the state amendment altered the qualifications for federal office. In response, the organization U.S. Term Limits argued in support of the amendment. It noted that the U.S. Constitution stipulates state regulation of the time, place, and manner for holding elections. Since the state amendment prohibited individuals only from appearing on the BALLOT (and these individuals could consequently run for office as write-in candidates), it operated as a manner of restriction and not as a qualification for office. Additionally, since the Constitution did not explicitly prohibit the states from setting qualifications for office, this was a power reserved to them under the Tenth Amendment.

The courts of Arkansas rejected the argument from U.S. Term Limits and struck down the amendment as a violation of Article I. On certiorari to the U.S. Supreme Court, Justice Stevens, writing for a 5 to 4 majority, affirmed this decision. He stated, "allowing individual States to adopt their own qualifications for congressional service would be inconsistent with the Framers' vision of a uniform National Legislature representing the people of the United States. If the qualifications set forth in the text of the Constitution are to be changed, that text must be amended." In dissent, Justice Thomas wrote, "nothing in the Constitution deprives the people of each state of the power to prescribe eligibility requirements for the candidates who seek to represent them in Congress. The Constitution is simply silent on this question. And where the Constitution is silent, it raises no bar to action by the States or the people."

The decision in *U.S. Term Limits v. Thornton*, combined with the Supreme Court's decision in *Powell v. McCormack* (1969), authoritatively resolved the issue of congressional qualifications. The age, residency, and CITIZENSHIP requirements in Article I provide a complete declaration for eligibility. Neither Congress nor the states can alter these requirements without the passage of an amendment to the U.S. Constitution.

Further reading: Epstein, Lee, and Thomas G. Walker. *Constitutional Law for a Changing America: Institutional Powers and Constraints.* 5th ed. Washington, D.C.: CQ Press, 2004; Gunther, Gerald, and Kathleen M. Sullivan. *Constitutional Law.* 13th ed. Westbury, N.Y.: Foundation Press, 1997.

—Kirk A. Randazzo

V

vice presidency qualifications

When the U.S. Constitution was originally drafted, the framers did not include any qualifications for the office of vice president. The authors of the Constitution gave very little thought to the office, and the Constitution specified only that the powers of the office were to serve as the presiding officer of the Senate, to cast a vote in the case of a tie, and to assume the office of the presidency upon the death of the president. Not until the TWELFTH AMENDMENT of the Constitution was ratified in 1804 were the qualifications for the office detailed.

The Twelfth Amendment mandates that "no person constitutionally ineligible to the office of the President may be eligible to that of the Vice President." Just as the president, the vice president must be a natural-born citizen, a resident of the United States for 14 consecutive years prior to holding the office, and at least 35 years of age. The amendment also prohibits presidents and vice presidents from residing in the same state. In the 2000 election, Texas governor George W. Bush selected Richard Cheney as his RUNNING MATE. At the time, Cheney was a resident of Texas, but he quickly changed his address and VOTER REGISTRATION to Wyoming.

The qualifications for the vice presidency have not changed since 1804. However, the clause requiring the vice president, and of course the president, to be natural-born citizens is being questioned, particularly in light of the election of two foreign-born politicians. In 2002, Democrat Jennifer M. Granholm was elected governor of Michigan. Democrats and political PUNDITs heralded Granholm as a rising star in American POLITICS, but since Granholm was born in Canada (she moved to the United States at age five), she was constitutionally ineligible to run as a vice presidential candidate. Similarly, in October 2003, the actor Arnold Schwarzenegger, a native of Austria, won election as California's governor. Shortly after his victory, Schwarzenegger called for an amendment to the Constitution allowing foreign-born citizens to be eligible for the presidency and vice presidency.

Changing the requirements for the vice presidency would necessitate the passage of a constitutional amendment. Enacting any amendment is difficult, but with the increasing political power of immigrants in the United States, a possibility exists that the qualifications for the vice presidency may be altered.

Further reading: Goldstein, Joel K. *The Modern American Vice Presidency: The Transformation of a Political Institution.* Princeton, N.J.: Princeton University Press, 1982; Vice President. Available online. URL: http://www.white house.gov/vicepresident. Accessed August 10, 2005; Witcover, Jules. *Crapshoot: Rolling the Dice on the Vice Presidency: From Adams and Jefferson to Truman and Quayle.* New York: Crown Publishing, 1992.

—Justin P. Coffey

vice presidency selection

Article II, Section 1, of the Constitution specified the original method for selecting vice presidents: Whoever finished second in the ELECTORAL COLLEGE became the vice president. If there was a tie for second place, then the Senate would choose the winner. The framers expected that the Electoral College would regularly be unable to choose a president by majority vote, letting the House of Representatives select the president and the Senate the vice president. The original plan did not anticipate the subsequent development of political parties, as the framers of the Constitution were philosophically opposed to partisan POLITICS.

But after George Washington's two virtually uncontested terms as president, with John Adams serving as his vice president, the 1796 election produced an unusual result. Adams, the choice of the nascent FEDERALIST PARTY, succeeded Washington as president, but his archrival, Thomas Jefferson of the DEMOCRATIC-REPUBLICAN PARTY, came in second, making him the vice president. The two had once been friends, but the developing TWO-PARTY SYSTEM estranged them, filling Adams's term as president with tension.

Retiring vice president John Garner administering the oath of office to his successor, Henry Wallace (second from left), as President Roosevelt looks on, 1941. *(New York World-Telegram* and Sun *Newspaper Photograph Collection, Library of Congress)*

By 1800, both parties had become better organized, and each ran one man for president and another for vice president. This time the Democratic-Republicans won, but the quirky Electoral College led to a tie between Jefferson and his RUNNING MATE, Aaron Burr, which threw the election into the House. The temperamental Burr surprisingly refused to concede, and only the intervention of Federalist leader Alexander Hamilton eventually gave the presidency to Jefferson. After two consecutive near-disasters, Congress passed the TWELFTH AMENDMENT in time for the 1804 election, which separated the vice presidential vote from the presidential vote, making either of these odd scenarios impossible in the future.

Candidates for president and vice president in the early 19th century were selected primarily by congressional party leaders, a time later dubbed "King Caucus" for its reliance on these caucuses of members. Democratic-Republicans (later shortened to Democrats) won every PRESIDENTIAL ELECTION from 1800 until the election of Whig leader William Henry Harrison in 1840. The vice presidency was not considered an important office. John Adams once remarked of it, "In this I am nothing, but I may become everything." Elder statesman George Clinton of New York served as vice president under both Jefferson and his successor, James Madison. Few vice presidents played any significant role in the executive branch, instead spending most of their time presiding over the Senate.

With the development of national party conventions, PARTY BOSSES from Congress as well as local party leaders chose the vice presidential candidate with little input from the man who was nominated for president. Usually they chose someone who would "balance" the ticket in some way by comparison with the man at the top, either geographically, ideologically, or to unite two warring party FACTIONS for the election's duration. For example, sitting vice president Martin Van Buren of New York ran in 1836 with Richard M. Johnson of Kentucky. Such considerations remained important through the 20th century, though they diminished somewhat in importance as the vice presidency became a more powerful office.

Presidential nominees nowadays are expected to choose a person whose main qualification is having the stature to become president on a moment's notice, if necessary. This lesson has been repeatedly reinforced, starting with Harry Truman's rise to power after the death of Franklin D. Roosevelt in 1945. Truman, who had been in office for barely three months, was unaware of the atom bomb's existence until Roosevelt's death. Truman then faced the wrenching decision of whether to drop the A-bomb on Japan, ordering its use twice. This awesome responsibility in the hands of one person put questions in many people's minds over how Truman was selected in 1944 to run with Roosevelt. DEMO-CRATIC PARTY bosses knew that Roosevelt was on death's door and did not want sitting vice president Henry Wallace, considered by many too liberal, to become president. After repeated urging, the frail president agreed to dump Wallace from the ticket and put Truman on instead for the 1944 election. Truman himself, however, was kept in the dark about the president's condition.

Roosevelt's time in office was also marked by another significant innovation in vice presidential selection. John Nance Garner of Texas, who had been SPEAKER OF THE HOUSE, served as vice president during Roosevelt's first two terms. (Garner is best remembered for saying that his new office was "not worth a pitcher of warm spit.") Garner was originally chosen because he was a conservative southerner, but as Roosevelt geared up to run for an unprecedented third term in 1940 he was so popular that such "balance" was no longer necessary. Instead he wanted then secretary of agriculture Henry Wallace as his running mate and told the Democratic Convention that if it did not accede to his wishes he would refuse to accept renomination. Roosevelt thus became the first presidential nominee to choose a running mate on his own, the precedent that now governs such selections.

In recent years, vice presidential nominees were often chosen for characteristics other than geographic location or "balance" of some kind. Bill Clinton, for example, was a young southerner who chose as his running mate another young southerner, Al Gore. Governor George W. Bush of Texas selected Dick Cheney of Wyoming, a choice that added no electoral votes but counteracted Bush's perceived lack of "gravitas," or stature, to become president. Increasingly, national campaigns run through nationalized media outlets require the two candidates on each party's ticket to reinforce a common message that they are trying to promote throughout the country.

Further reading: Purcell, L. Edward, ed. *The Vice Presidents: A Biographical Dictionary.* New York: Facts On File, 1998; Vice President. Available online: URL: http://www. whitehouse.gov/vicepresident. Accessed August 10, 2005; Witcover, Jules. *Crapshoot: Rolling the Dice on the Vice Presidency: From Adams and Jefferson to Truman and Quayle.* New York: Crown Publishers, 1992.

—William D. Adler

voter canvass

Voter canvass refers to two activities related to campaigns and elections. The first kind of voter canvass is a campaign tactic designed to make personal contact with residents of a particular geographic area (such as a PRECINCT or neighborhood) early on in a campaign. This activity supports several of the campaign's goals. One main goal is voter identification. Voter identification involves a campaign's early efforts to identify residents as opponents, supporters, or undecided. (Catherine Shaw, in her campaign manual *The Campaign Manager,* describes these three types of

people as "sinners, saints, and savables.") Strategically, this information is used to prioritize precincts and households for later campaign activities, such as distributing campaign information (for example, a literature drop), FUND-RAISING, or conducting a candidate "walk" in a neighborhood. This information may also be used for later voter canvasses as part of a GET-OUT-THE-VOTE program for mobilizing supporters at the very end of a campaign.

Historically, this voter canvass was organized and managed by local party officials, such as those in political machines. Even with the deterioration of the manipulative power of machines in the mid-20th century, local PARTY ORGANIZATIONS still provided the structure through which campaign information was distributed and by which votes were delivered. In modern times, canvassing is run by a candidate's campaign team as part of the campaign's voter contact plan, or "field operations." While some campaign observers argue that modern campaign technology has eliminated the need for large-scale GRASSROOTS campaigning such as the canvass, campaign technology has also improved the ability of campaigners to undertake these traditional campaign tactics, but with much greater efficiency.

The second kind of voter canvass takes place after an election has occurred and is the official counting of BALLOTS in order to determine the winner of that election. This canvass is usually conducted by local boards of elections and is the time when any legal challenges to election procedures and outcomes can be made. The 2000 PRESIDENTIAL ELECTION RECOUNT controversy in Florida highlighted many of the problems associated with aging vote-counting technology.

Further reading: Shaw, Catherine M., and Michael E. Holstein. *The Campaign Manager: Running and Winning Local Elections.* 2nd ed. New York: Westview Press, 1999.

—Peter W. Wielhouwer

Voter News Service (VNS)

Voter News Service (VNS) was a consortium created in 1993 by ABC, CBS, CNN, Fox News, NBC, and the Associated Press that forecast vote counts by conducting EXIT POLLS in presidential, congressional, and gubernatorial races. Member media organizations then used the data when reporting election results and political analysis. VNS was intended to pool media resources to economically collect information on voter choices throughout the United States. Specifically, it was believed that the larger sample of voter preferences would yield a more accurate view of trends in races on ELECTION DAY, thus making it easier to predict winners as soon as possible after the polls closed.

VNS came under intense scrutiny and criticism during the 2000 PRESIDENTIAL ELECTION when errors in the statistical models used by the service caused member news outlets to receive inaccurate predictions of the winner of the election in the state of Florida. Thus, Al Gore was first projected to have won Florida, then, several hours later, George W. Bush was projected to be the winner in the state.

In addition to its inability to accurately predict the eventual winner in Florida, VNS was plagued by systemic deficiencies in the information it provided. Specifically, the VNS exit polling data did not explain voter behavior. There was no way to know why voters voted the way they did. This problem was exacerbated by the inability of VNS to identify discrete blocs of voters (e.g., by race, PARTY IDENTIFICATION, gender, etc.) among exit poll respondents. Therefore, analysts were unable to determine whether voter preferences among a particular racial group, party affiliation, or gender, for instance, were affecting the outcome of specific contests.

Chastened by the debacle in the PRESIDENTIAL ELECTION, VNS pledged an overhaul of its system ahead of the 2002 midterm CONGRESSIONAL ELECTIONS. The service, however, performed worse than during the 2000 election, failing to deliver vote counts or exit poll results to member media outlets. The deterioration of the credibility of VNS resulted in its demise. The media companies who formed the consortium voted to disband it in late 2003.

Further reading: Mitofsky, W. J. "Voter News Service after the Fall." *Public Opinion Quarterly* 67, no. 1 (2003): 45–58; Wardle, C., et al. "The Voter News Service and the 2000 Election Night Calls." *American Behavioral Scientist* 44, no. 12 (2001): 2,306–2,313.

—John L. S. Simpkins

voter registration

Voter registration is the process by which a state's citizens enfranchise themselves through an enrollment process. State regulated voter registration laws vary substantially across states. Registration is voluntary in America, but citizens in all states are required to be registered in order to vote on ELECTION DAY. Registration requirements were designed partly as a means to safeguard the voting process from fraud and can prevent, among other things, citizens from repeatedly casting votes in different PRECINCTS.

Voter registration has changed dramatically over the years as there has been a steady expansion of voter eligibility requirements. Early on, most states limited voting privileges to white property-owning males at least 21 years of age. Property ownership requirements were considerably lessened (though not entirely abolished) by the early 1800s. All adult white males had the ability to vote by 1860, though the exclusion of women and blacks continued to effectively silence the political voices of a significant segment of the population. The FIFTEENTH AMENDMENT enfranchised black males in 1870. After it was enacted, however, discriminatory practices such as LITERACY TESTS and POLL TAXES by white election authorities kept many black citizens

away from the polls, particularly in the South. Women's suffrage was granted in 1920 with the ratification of the NINETEENTH AMENDMENT.

A series of additional changes expanded the pool of eligible voters and addressed access to the voting process. The District of Columbia received the right to vote for presidential electors in 1961 with the passage of the TWENTY-THIRD AMENDMENT. Poll taxes were abolished when the TWENTY-FOURTH AMENDMENT was ratified on January 23, 1964. From the 1940s to the 1960s, Congress evaluated voter registration laws and held hearings intended to expose voting obstructions common primarily with minority voters. A voting rights bill to rectify the system's shortcomings was drafted and referred to the House Judiciary Committee in early 1965, but the bill was met with strong resistance from southern members of Congress and conservative northerners.

The bill aimed to address inequalities in poll access between whites and blacks in the South. Resistance to the bill diminished when national sentiment turned to outrage following the murder of Viola Liuzzo, a white, middle-class mother from Michigan who was working on voter registration in Alabama when she was shot by a member of the KU KLUX KLAN. The Voting Rights Act was ultimately passed in 1965. The law prohibited states from requiring literacy tests as a prerequisite for voting and required states to get "pre-clearance" from the federal government before altering their electoral systems.

As a result of the Twenty-fourth Amendment, the Voting Rights Act, and other court decisions and legislation, poll taxes and literacy tests have been abolished, state and local residency requirements have been shortened, and registration has become simpler and more convenient. After protests during the Vietnam War, the TWENTY-SIXTH AMENDMENT, adopted in July 1971, reduced the legal voting age to 18.

Still, registration requirements are a major impediment to electoral participation in American elections. One reason why registration presents formidable challenges is the high rate of mobility in America. One in three citizens changes his or her address every two years, according to some estimates. This mobility, combined with voter registration requirements, is believed to depress participation. In a seminal study of the impact of registration laws on turnout, political scientists Rosenstone and Wolfinger demonstrated that if all citizens who moved registered to vote in their new communities, national turnout rates would rise by 9 percent. They also indicated that such a change would benefit both major parties roughly evenly.

To reduce the deleterious impact of mobility, Congress passed the National Voter Registration Act (NVRA) in 1993. The MOTOR VOTER LAW, as it is called, requires states to allow citizens to register to vote by mail or at government offices when they renew their driver's licenses and car registrations. It also requires states to offer national mail voter registration forms. The NVRA covers 44 states and the District of Columbia and exempts the states of Idaho, Minnesota, New Hampshire, North Dakota, Wisconsin, and Wyoming.

A 1998 report prepared by the Office of Election Administration found that voter registration rose in 1996 by 1.82 percentage points in states covered by the law. Scholars have continued to debate the impact of the law, but several studies provide evidence that the legislation may be boosting voter registration. Even as some states have witnessed increases in registered voters, however, VOTER TURNOUT rates have not necessarily risen.

In many countries, including the United Kingdom, Spain, and Japan, eligible voters are automatically registered to vote. In the United States, however, citizens must register voluntarily. As it turns out, this additional requirement appears to prevent many potential voters from registering. Studies do show, however, that the level of voter registration influences voter turnout more than any other variable. Thus, politicians in states across the country can affect participation by altering local registration requirements including deadlines and locations, among other things.

Some states have introduced innovations to reduce barriers to participation erected by voter registration requirements. Besides the Motor Voter Law, states including Maine, Minnesota, and Wisconsin allow voters to register on the day of the election, and one state (North Dakota) does not even require voters to register. Turnout in these states is generally higher. Other states have relaxed eligibility for absentee ballots. California even allows voters to register as "permanent absentees" and to receive BALLOTS automatically in the mail. Many states permit EARLY VOTING, and Oregon has replaced voting booths entirely and adopted a vote-by-mail system.

Further reading: Polsby, Nelson W., and Aaron Wildavsky. *Presidential Elections: Strategies and Structures of American Politics.* 11th ed. Lanham, Md.: Rowman & Littlefield, 2004; Wolfinger, Raymond E., and Steven J. Rosenstone. "The Effect of Registration Laws on Voter Turnout." *American Political Science Review* 72 (1978): 22–45.

—Costas Panagopoulos

voter turnout

Democracy functions when the voice of the people is heard and policies are enacted that reflect the will of the people. Elections are the main vehicle for determining the will of the people. The higher the percentage of eligible voters who vote, the more reflective the election is of public opinion. Thus, the importance of voter turnout is manifest, and the fact that voter turnout has been steadily declining since the 1890s is cause for great concern among many political observers.

VOTER TURNOUT OF EUROPEAN DEMOCRACIES AND THE UNITED STATES

Country	Average
Italy	90%
Iceland	89%
Greece	85%
Belgium	84%
Sweden	84%
Denmark	83%
Argentina	81%
Turkey	80%
Portugal	79%
Spain	79%
Austria	78%
Norway	76%
Netherlands	75%
Germany	72%
United Kingdom	72%
Finland	71%
Ireland	71%
France	61%
Luxembourg	60%
United States	45%
Switzerland	38%

Data are based on Voting Age Population (VAP).
Source: International Institute for Democracy and Electoral Assistance. URL: http://www.fairvote.org/turnout/intturnout.htm. Accessed August 10, 2005.

The highest turnout rate is in PRESIDENTIAL ELECTION years. The importance of the office and the visibility of the nationwide campaigns increase voter interest and mobilization. The lack of nationwide candidates and issues reduces the turnout rates for MIDTERM ELECTIONS. The turnout rates are generally at least 10 percentage points lower than for presidential election years. However, turnout is still generally higher in off-year GENERAL ELECTIONS than in PRIMARY elections. SPECIAL ELECTIONS, runoffs, and local elections fall at the bottom of the turnout scale. While generally the higher the office the greater the voter turnout, even gubernatorial elections often suffer from poor turnout when the elections are held between presidential elections and midterm elections.

Within a given election, there are also demographic variations in voter turnout. Higher-educated, higher-income people tend to vote more than those with lower incomes and education levels. Moreover, strong partisans tend to vote more than INDEPENDENTS. Caucasians have the highest turnout rate compared to other races. Although historically women have had lower turnout rates than men, since 1988 women have had higher turnout rates than men. Finally, older people (until about 70 years of age) have higher turnout rates than do younger people. Those between the ages of 18 and 24 have the lowest turnout rates.

Despite efforts to expand SUFFRAGE to virtually all citizens aged 18 or more, the percentage of eligible voters who vote has been steadily declining since the 1890s. While there are fluctuations from year to year, the general trend over time has been downward. In 1960, 63 percent of eligible voters voted. In the 2000 PRESIDENTIAL ELECTION only 51 percent of eligible voters cast BALLOTS. The 1998 CONGRESSIONAL ELECTIONS had one of the lowest turnout rates in American history.

There are several explanations for the low voter turnout rates in the United States. One explanation concerns the expansion of suffrage. The Constitution originally left the question of who could vote up to the individual states. Voting at that time was limited almost exclusively to white, property-owning males. However, as the country grew and expanded, property ownership requirements were slowly eliminated. By the time of the Civil War, suffrage had been expanded to include all free white males over the age of 21. With the ratification of the FIFTEENTH AMENDMENT, all males were granted the right to vote. Voter turnout was high during this period. Turnout remained high through the 19th century because the wealthy and more highly educated elements of society, who were the only ones eligible to vote, recognized the efficacy of voting. As suffrage was expanded, voting turnout remained high because of PATRONAGE. Thus, until the advent of the PENDLETON ACT (1883), AT-LARGE ELECTIONS (1890s), the various New Deal programs of the 1930s, and the HATCH ACT (1939), citizens had tangible incentives (e.g., government jobs and largesse) for voting.

Suffrage was further expanded with the ratification of the NINETEENTH AMENDMENT (1920), essentially giving all men and women age 21 and over the right to vote. The federal elections immediately after the ratification of the amendment saw a precipitous decline in voter turnout. Whereas the turnout rate had been more than 60 percent, with the inclusion of this new and inexperienced voting block, the 1920 and 1924 elections saw the turnout rate drop by more than 10 percent, to just less than 50 percent.

Suffrage was further expanded in 1924, when Native Americans were granted CITIZENSHIP and voting privileges by the TWENTY-THIRD AMENDMENT, which also granted Washington, D.C., residents the right to vote in federal elections, and, finally, the TWENTY-SIXTH AMENDMENT, which gave 18-year-olds the right to vote.

Other efforts to expand suffrage included the ratification of the TWENTY-FOURTH AMENDMENT, which prohibited the use of POLL TAXES, and the passage of the Civil Rights Act of 1965, which removed restrictions aimed at keeping African Americans from voting. The Civil Rights Act of 1965 banned literacy requirements, eased registration requirements, and allowed for the replacement of local election officials with federal registrars where discrimination had been the most blatant. While these actions did not grant suffrage to previously ineligible voters, they did attempt to eliminate official and unofficial hurdles to VOTER REGISTRATION and voting for African Americans.

An alternative explanation for the lower voter turnout in the United States is the requirement that almost all voters register to vote. Many other Western democracies have automatic registration—and much higher voter turnout rates. Turnout rates in the United States are as much as 30 percent lower than in European democracies. Switzerland is the only European democracy with a lower turnout rate than the United States.

Today, every state except North Dakota requires voters to register in order to be able to vote. While three states allow citizens to register on the day of the election, most states require that citizens be registered at least 30 days before an election. Requiring registration makes citizens do additional work to make sure they can vote. Eligible citizens need to remember to actually register as well as find and go to the proper location to register. If registration locations are not convenient, it creates a difficult hurdle for those without a reliable source of transportation to register and an excuse for apathetic individuals to opt out of the process.

In 1993, President Clinton signed the National Voter Registration Act, or the MOTOR VOTER LAW. This act allowed citizens to register to vote when they renewed their driver's licenses. The idea was to make registering to vote less burdensome. The Motor Voter Law also increased the number of sites that could register voters. Places such as disability offices, Welfare offices, libraries, public schools, and clerk's offices can also be registration sites. While the Motor Voter Law has increased the number of registered voters by approximately 12 million, thus far it has not substantially increased voting rates in the United States.

A third explanation for low turnout rates in the United States has been attributed to the TWO-PARTY SYSTEM. Most democracies, especially democracies based on PROPORTIONAL REPRESENTATION, have more than two dominant political parties. Where there are more parties, voters have more candidates from which to choose. The greater number of candidates provides a wider diversity of options on issues for voters and is believed to increase participation. In the United States, voters typically have only Republicans and Democrats from which to choose. The parties, of necessity, have to appeal to as broad a base as possible. The result is often political stances that differ little in the eyes of many voters. Perceiving a lack of difference, voters may decide not to vote. In 1992, when Ross Perot ran as an independent candidate for president, voters had a highly visible third option. Turnout rates increased to 55 percent, an increase of 5 percent from the 1988 PRESIDENTIAL ELECTION.

The lack of a "voting holiday," or day off for elections, is also argued by some scholars to diminish voter turnout. Whereas many democracies hold elections on weekends or on a national holiday, elections in the United States are typically held on a workday.

It is also believed that electoral reforms have contributed to the decline in voter turnout. During most of the 19th century, political parties conducted elections. The parties printed what were often color-coded ballots, which they distributed to party "members." This allowed party organizers to monitor how people voted. It also provided easy opportunities for multiple voting and other fraudulent electoral activities. A reform movement managed to bring about the use of the AUSTRALIAN BALLOT, a secret ballot printed by the state, and voter registration. While these changes made it much more difficult to engage in voter fraud, they also decreased voter turnout.

Another fact that is associated with low voter rates in the United States is the large number of elections that are held. Given the federal system in the United States, voters are asked not only to select the candidates for the parties in primary elections, they must also select officials at the national, state, and local levels of government, and in some jurisdictions vote on state and local ballot measures. The number of elected positions and ballot measures complicates the act of voting and suppresses the vote.

Low participation rates represent a major challenge to the democratic process. Legal action requiring citizen participation in the electoral process, as is the case in countries such as Australia, is highly unlikely in this country. Less extreme actions such as providing a modest tax incentive to vote, a national holiday to vote, MAIL VOTING, same-day registration, EARLY VOTING, and electronic voting are likely to be more fully tested in the future. The existing government actions, such as the Motor Voter Act, have attempted to increase voter registration and by extension voter turnout but have had limited success.

Nongovernmental actors have also been created to encourage higher voter turnout. Partisan and nonpartisan groups such as BeAVoter.org, Strive for Five, 10 For Change, the DEMOCRATIC NATIONAL COMMITTEE, the REPUBLICAN NATIONAL COMMITTEE, and Project Vote Smart aim to increase voter participation, or at least the participation of certain subgroups within the larger population. A number of groups focusing on youth voter mobilization have also arisen to address the particularly low turnout rates of the youngest voters. Groups such as Youthvote.org, Declare Yourself, ROCK THE VOTE, Hip Hop Summit Action Network (HSAN), Smackdown Your Vote, and the Youth Leadership Initiative all appeal specifically to the 18- to 24-year-old age group to try to increase voter turnout rates.

Further reading: Flanigan, William H., and Nancy H. Zingale. *Political Behavior in Midterm Elections.* Washington, D.C.: CQ Press, 2003; Flanigan, William H., and Nancy H. Zingale. *Political Behavior of the American Electorate.* 10th ed. Washington, D.C.: CQ Press, 2002; Patterson, Thomas E. "The Vanishing Voter: Why Are the Voting Booths So Empty?" *National Civic Review* 91, no. 4 (2002): 367–378; Wattenberg, Martin P. *Where Have All the Voters Gone?* Cambridge, Mass.: Harvard University Press, 2002.
—Scott Dittloff

voter turnout, age

VOTER TURNOUT and age are highly correlated in the United States. In general, older Americans register and vote in larger numbers than their younger counterparts. While voter turnout in American elections has declined in recent years, the drop in voter participation has been especially pronounced among voters under the age of 25. In addition, turnout among senior citizens has actually increased since 1972.

The problem of low voter turnout among young Americans dates back to the ratification of the TWENTY-SIXTH AMENDMENT on July 1, 1971, which lowered the voting age from 21 to 18. According to a 2002 study by the Center for Information and Research on Civic Learning and Engagement, voter turnout among Americans between the ages of 18 and 24 has dropped approximately 15 percent since the 1972 PRESIDENTIAL ELECTION, though younger Americans are more likely to participate in political protests.

Several factors have been cited for the lower turnout rates among younger Americans, including the weakening of family and neighborhood ties as Americans become more mobile in their lifestyles, lower voter turnout rates among their parents, and the need to register prior to ELECTION DAY. When asked, young Americans say that they feel largely ignored by politicians, that their vote does not count, and that they do not have the kind of information they need to make an informed choice.

Some researchers have cited the early experiences of the baby boomer and X generations as curtailing their voter turnout rates while contributing to a growing sense of political mistrust among young people. Whereas three out of four members of the World War II generation voted regularly by midlife, the rates were much lower among the baby boom generation, who witnessed the Vietnam War, the assassinations of Martin Luther King, Jr., and the Kennedy brothers, and the Watergate SCANDAL during the Nixon administration. In addition, the younger generations have also been exposed to political campaigns that are infused with scandals and attack advertisements.

Concerns over the issue of a decline in young voter turnout have launched a series of organizations dedicated to the problem, including ROCK THE VOTE, the New Millennium Young Voters Project, Declare Yourself, and Youth04. Of these groups, Rock the Vote is the most established. Founded in 1990 by members of the recording industry to protect artistic expression, the group expanded its mission during the 1992 PRESIDENTIAL ELECTION when it helped to register 350,000 new voters. In 1996, the group developed an on-line voter registration program and has since created a public education campaign.

Youth04 and Declare Yourself also focus on voter participation, using different methods to bring young Americans to the polls. A project of the Center for Democracy and Technology, Youth04 is primarily an Internet project that encourages candidates and the media to pay attention to the beliefs and values of young voters. Declare Yourself is a broad-based campaign that uses a mix of college tours, high school programs, concerts, and public service announcements to "energize" young voters.

The New Millennium Young Voters Project was launched by the National Association of Secretaries of State in 1998 with the goals of improving voter turnout rates among 18- to 24-year-olds and raising public awareness about the importance of youth participation in government and the political process. The group has pushed for more youth-oriented content in candidate debates and works toward implementation of civic education and voting skills workshops in the public schools. The program is similar to programs started by academic centers such as the University of Virginia's Youth Leadership Initiative.

Groups such as these have experienced some success in bringing attention to the problem of low voter turnout among young Americans. During the 2004 PRESIDENTIAL ELECTION, the media developed its coverage of youth-oriented issues. For example, CNN created a "Campus Vibe" component as a part of its America Votes 2004 election coverage. Presidential candidates also attempted to appeal to young voters through the use of the Internet and Web "blogs." Although unsuccessful in his bid for the Democratic NOMINATION, former Vermont governor Howard Dean was the first candidate during the 2004 PRIMARY season to significantly draw high school and college voters through his "Generation Dean" campaign. Other candidates followed suit, and both the Kerry and Bush campaigns included young voter "blogs" on their Web sites.

During the 2004 presidential elections, college-aged voters were expected to act as a SWING VOTE. A 2003 study conducted by the Harvard University Institute on Politics found that nearly 60 percent of young voters polled said they would vote during the 2004 election, compared to the 32 percent that voted in 2000. However, exit polls show that the number of votes cast by people under the age of 30 was actually down during the Democratic primaries and showed little change during the general election.

The problem of low turnout among young voters is especially significant due to the size of the new millennium generation, which is one of the largest generations of young people in U.S. history and is almost as large as the baby boom generation. The continued anxiety about young vot-

ers has actually led to calls to once again lower the voting age to 17 in an attempt to instill a "voting habit" in teenagers before they become involved with job searches, military service, and college. Legislation to this effect has been considered in Maine, Texas, and California. In addition, youth voting rights activists have campaigned to lower the voting age in the states of Florida, Hawaii, and North Dakota and in New York City and Anchorage, Alaska.

Further reading: Center for Information and Research on Civic Learning and Engagement at the University of Maryland School of Public Affairs. Available online. URL: http://www.civicyouth.org. Accessed August 10, 2005; Patterson, Thomas E. *The Vanishing Voter: Public Involvement in an Age of Uncertainty.* New York: Knopf, 2002; MTV's Rock the Vote. Available online. URL: http://www.rockthevote.com. Accessed August 10, 2005; Youth Leadership Initiative at the University of Virginia Center for Politics. Available online. URL: http://www.centerforpolitics.org/programs/yli.htm. Accessed August 10, 2005.
—Mary Hallock Morris

voter turnout, economic status

Voter turnout in the United States can be explained in many ways, but perhaps the most revealing manner to analyze turnout is in its relationship to an individual's annual income. The choice an individual makes to vote in an election as well as his or her choice of candidate in that election are both heavily influenced by income.

In recent years, voters with high income levels have voted at higher rates than voters in lower economic groupings. There are numerous explanations for the relationship. Some observers believe that high-income voters feel they have more at stake in the outcomes of elections and are thus more involved in the political process. Others attribute the relationship to education levels, knowledge levels, and news consumption levels that also closely correlate with economic status and voting rates. Others argue that there are tangible costs to voting (i.e., the time and expense of developing knowledge about and an interest in POLITICS and the time and expense of participating in the process) that could make the act of voting more rational for high-income voters than for low-income voters, since these costs would constitute a smaller percentage of a high-income person's disposable time and income than that of a low-income person.

There was not always a strong correlation between income and voter turnout. In the early 20th century, the slums of major cities such as New York and Chicago were politically active areas. At that time political machines and PARTY BOSSES were able to activate and influence the inner-city vote, which was, of course, heavily composed of poor immigrants. The manner in which party bosses were able to exercise such influence was through the system of PATRONAGE, in which party bosses were able to pay for the support of lowly immigrants. However, with the political reforms of the Progressive Era during the early 1900s, the party bosses of the inner city were no longer able to exert their influence.

According to the U.S. Census Bureau (2000), of citizens at the lowest income level, 55.87 percent registered to vote, and 38.45 percent actually cast BALLOTS. In the middle level, 71.34 percent registered, and 60.41 percent voted. In the highest income level, 82.08 percent registered to vote, and 74.94 percent eventually cast ballots. These statistics reveal that citizens with the highest income levels were almost twice as likely to vote as citizens in the lowest level.

It is believed that shifts in average incomes in the United States, coupled with the higher voting rates among people at higher income levels and their general preference for the REPUBLICAN PARTY have altered the outcome of elections and given an advantage to Republican versus Democratic candidates. The results of the 2004 PRESIDENTIAL ELECTION typify voting patterns by income level. The majority of voters with an annual income less than $50,000 (55 percent) voted for Democratic candidate John Kerry. These voters constituted 45 percent of the total voting population. The largest margin of support for Kerry was in the voting population with an annual income of less than $15,000, from whom he received 63 percent of votes. However, this group makes up only 8 percent of all voters. Incumbent George W. Bush received the majority of votes from voters with annual incomes of $50,000 or more (55 percent). This group constituted the majority of all voters (55 percent). His largest support came from voters with annual incomes of $200,000 or more (63 percent support), but these voters made up only 3 percent of the voting population.

There are exceptions to strictly voting by political PARTY IDENTIFICATION. While voters with lower income levels tend to vote Democratic, they will vote against a Democratic incumbent if they view unemployment as a major issue. Those with higher income levels tend to vote Republican but will vote against a Republican incumbent if they view taxes as being too high or if they feel the country is headed in the wrong direction.

Further reading: Brooks, Clem, and David Brady. "Income, Economic Voting, and Long-Term Political Change in the U.S., 1952–1996." *Social Forces* 77, no. 4 (1999): 1,339; Filer, John, Lawrence Kenny, and Rebecca Morton. "Redistribution, Income, and Voting." *American Journal of Political Science* 37, no. 1 (1993): 63–87; Harrigan, John J. *Empty Dreams, Empty Pockets: Class and Bias in American Politics.* 2nd ed. New York: Addison-Wesley Longman, 2000; Tullock, Gordon. *Wealth, Poverty and Politics.* New York: Basil Blackwell, 1988; U.S. Census Bureau. *Voting and Registration in the Election of November 2000.* Washington, D.C.: U.S. Census Bureau, 2002.

—Glenn L. Starks and Matthew DeSantis

voter turnout, education

Education has become a primary predictor of voting in the United States. The turnout rate of voters with the highest levels of education far exceeds that of voters with lower levels of education. In recent PRESIDENTIAL ELECTIONS, the percentage of eligible voters with at least a bachelor's degree had a turnout rate that was more than double that of voters with no high school diploma.

The U.S. Census Bureau defines educational achievement across five categories: less than a ninth-grade education, ninth- to 12th-grade education (with no diploma), high school graduate or graduate equivalency degree (GED), some college or associate's degree, and bachelor's degree or more (including master's, professional, and doctoral degrees). During the 1964 PRESIDENTIAL ELECTION, approximately 59 percent of those in the lowest category cast BALLOTS, 65 percent of those with between a ninth- and 12th-grade education voted, 76 percent of those with a high school education or GED voted, 82 percent of those with some college or associate's degree voted, and 88 percent of those with bachelor's degree or more voted.

Between the 1964 and 2004 PRESIDENTIAL ELECTIONS, the average VOTER TURNOUT rates in all five categories decreased, though the general relationship between education level and voting remains strong. By 2000, the respective voting rates in each category (and the percentage decrease from 1964) were 26.8 percent (–54.58%), 33.6 percent (–48.62 percent), 49.4 percent (–35.09 percent), 60.3 percent (–26.55 percent), and 72.0 percent (–17.71 percent). These percentages show that although the percentage of eligible voters casting ballots has decreased over time, the disparity in voting by education has consistently widened over the past four decades. The comparable percentage decreases in voter turnout rates for each category grew smaller as the level of voters' education increased. The turnout rate for those with the highest levels of education was 59 percent greater than that of voters with the least amount.

There are several reasons that help to explain the voting disparity among education groups. It is generally believed that education enhances civic duty, political efficiency, political skills, and political awareness. Those with lower levels of education may find it difficult to understand the VOTER REGISTRATION process, the process for casting ballots, and complex ballot issues. Some may not comprehend major political issues and the stances or political platforms of candidates on these issues. While some may comprehend debated issues, they may feel these issues have little direct effect on their daily lives. Moreover, those with higher levels of education tend to earn larger incomes and feel they are more affected by such issues as taxation and inflation. They also have a greater identification with and loyalty to political parties and feel the need to get involved in the political process. They are taught that voting is a primary aspect of their civic duty.

Further reading: Jackson, Robert A. "Clarifying the Relationship between Education and Turnout." *American Politics Quarterly* 23, no. 3 (1995): 279–300; U.S. Census Bureau. *Reported Voting and Registration by Region, Educational Attainment and Labor Force: November 1964 to 2002. Current Population Survey, November 2002 and Earlier Reports.* Washington, D.C.: United States Census Bureau, 2004.

—Glenn L. Starks

voter turnout, gender

Voter turnout by gender refers to the percentage of women who cast BALLOTS and the percentage of men who cast ballots in a given election. The VOTER TURNOUT by gender percentages are related to, but not synonymous with, the percentage of ballots that are cast by women versus the percentage cast by men. In 2000, 56.2 percent of female voting-age adults (59,284,000 of 105,523,000) cast ballots in the November election compared to 53.1 percent of male voting-age adults (51,542,000 of 97,087,000). Given that women made up a larger percentage of voting-age adults in the population and voted at a slightly higher rate than men, 53.5 percent of ballots were cast by women, and 46.5 percent of ballots were cast by men—a difference of 7,742,000 votes.

During the 1800s, women's involvement in U.S. POLITICS was severely hampered by their disenfranchisement. In 1838, Kentucky became the first state to grant some women voting rights in school elections. These rights were restricted to widows with school-age children. In 1861, 23 years later, Kansas also granted school election SUFFRAGE to women. When the Wyoming Territory was established in 1869, the first woman suffrage law was passed. When Wyoming became a state in 1890, it became the first state to grant women the right to vote in all elections. By 1916, all West Coast and Rocky Mountain states (except New Mexico) and Kansas had granted women full suffrage rights. In 1893, New Zealand became the first nation to grant full voting rights to women. All women in the United States did not receive full voting rights until August 18, 1920, with the ratification of the NINETEENTH AMENDMENT to the U.S. Constitution, which states that "The right of citizens of the United States to vote shall not be denied or abridged by the United States or by any State on account of sex."

As demographic information often has not been collected from voters as they cast their ballots at the polls, it is difficult to estimate the voter turnout percentages by gender prior to the systematic collection of data by the U.S. Bureau of the Census and Bureau of Labor Statistics' Current Population Survey. Data collected from 1968 to the present show that men were registered to vote and voted at higher rates than women until 1980. In 1980, these trends reversed, with women registering and voting in slightly higher percentages than men. In every PRESIDENTIAL ELECTION since that time, women have continued to have some advantage over men in registration and voter turnout rates. In 2000, women's higher voting rates cut across racial and ethnic groups, with white Hispanic, white non-Hispanic, Hispanic (all races), and black women voting at slightly higher rates than their male counterparts.

Part of the gender difference in turnout rates may be explained by VOTER REGISTRATION. Voter registration is a precursor to voting in an election. In 2000, women were registered more than men by 3.4 percent and therefore more likely to be eligible to vote.

TABLE OF REPORTED REGISTRATION AND VOTING IN PRESIDENTIAL ELECTION YEARS BY SEX, 1968 TO 2000

Year	Men		Women		Difference (men–women)	
	% Registered	% Voted	% Registered	% Voted	% Registered	% Voted
1968	76.0	69.8	72.8	66.0	3.2	3.8
1972	73.1	64.1	71.6	62.0	1.5	2.1
1976	67.1	59.6	66.4	58.8	0.7	0.8
1980	66.6	59.1	67.1	59.4	–0.5	–0.3
1984	67.3	59.0	69.3	60.8	–2.0	–1.8
1988	65.2	56.4	67.8	58.3	–2.6	–1.9
1992	66.9	60.2	69.3	62.3	–2.4	–2.1
1996	64.4	52.8	67.3	55.5	–2.9	–2.7
2000	62.2	53.1	65.6	56.2	–3.4	–3.1

Source: U.S. Department of Commerce, U.S. Census Bureau, Current Population Reports, *Voting and Registration in the Election of November 2000.* Series P20-524, February 2002, Tables C and D.

Three women casting their ballots in New York City, 1917 *(Prints and Photographs Division, Library of Congress)*

One explanation for gender differences in voter turnout rates between men and women prior to 1980 has to do with generational differences in POLITICAL SOCIALIZATION. When women received the right to vote in 1920, many women were not inclined to exercise that right, as they had not been socialized into viewing themselves as political beings. As time passed and older generations of women were replaced with younger ones for whom voter participation no longer seemed controversial or inappropriate, women's participation in elections increased. Women's increased presence in higher education may be a part of this change in political socialization.

The association of age and turnout may explain the current higher turnout rates of women compared to men, as women tend to live longer than their male counterparts. Age has long been shown to be associated with voter turnout rates: Older citizens tend to vote at higher rates than younger ones. The 2000 U.S. CENSUS data show that the male-female ratio (the number of males in the popula-

tion for every 100 females) was 96.3. This ratio is much lower in higher age categories. For example, the male-female ratio for 65- to 74-year-olds was 82.3, 75- to 84-year-olds was 65.2, and 85 year olds and older was 40.7.

Differences in voter turnout rates between men and women are consequential because of GENDER GAPs in PARTY IDENTIFICATION and candidate preference. In the last 25 years, men and women have exhibited different proclivities toward candidates and party identification. Therefore, if women and men vote at different rates, the differences may have consequences for which candidates are selected to hold political office and which public policies are adopted.

Further reading: Federal Elections Commission. Available online. URL: http://www.fec.gov. Accessed August 10, 2005; Kenski, Henry C. "The Gender Factor in a Changing Electorate." In Carol M. Mueller, ed., *The Politics of the Gender Gap: The Social Construction of Political Influence.*

Newbury Park, Calif.: Sage Publications, 1988; Stucker, John J. "Women as Voters: Their Maturation as Political Persons in American Society." In Marianne Githens and Jewel L. Prestage, eds., *A Portrait of Marginality: The Political Behavior of the American Woman*. New York: David McKay, 1977.

—Kate Kenski

voter turnout, race

A historical disparity exists between the VOTER TURNOUT rates of whites in comparison to minorities, particularly African Americans, Hispanics, and Asians/Pacific Islanders. While nearly two-thirds of whites who are eligible to vote actually register and approximately 60 percent eventually cast BALLOTs, approximately 50 percent of eligible blacks vote compared to less than one-third of Hispanics and only a quarter of Asians and Pacific Islanders. These rates have held constant over the last two decades even though the percentage of minorities in the United States has constantly increased. Lower voter turnout rates for minorities are directly tied to their lower propensity to register to vote in comparison to their white counterparts.

The Census Bureau categorizes voters by race as white (non-Hispanic), black (non-Hispanic), Hispanic (of any race), and Asian or Pacific Islander. The percentage of registered voters within each category has remained relatively constant since 1978, while the total voting age population has risen constantly each year. The racial disparity remains constant across election years. During recent PRESIDENTIAL ELECTION years, an average of 62 percent of the eligible white population actually cast ballots, while in nonpresidential election years (off-years), an average of 57 percent of this group voted. During years when presidential elections were held, 53 percent of blacks voted, while in off-years only 47 percent of blacks voted. The percentages for Hispanics and Asians/Pacific Islanders have historically been almost half those of blacks. On average, during presidential election years, only 29 percent voted. During off-years, only 26 percent voted. Asians/Pacific Islanders have historically had the worst voting rates. During presidential election years, only 26 percent voted, and during off-years, 20 percent voted.

There are numerous explanations regarding levels of voter turnout by race. Many believe that the leading factor that causes lower voter turnout rates for minorities is lower percentages registering to vote. There are several factors that have a negative impact on VOTER REGISTRATION rates. First, the location in which registration takes place is rarely the same location where votes are cast. These registration locations may be less convenient for voters to visit than polling locations. Registration must take place a specific time before elections take place, requiring potential voters to make a commitment to vote even before final candidates are chosen. Moreover, legal and illegal barriers have histor-

ically been used to keep minorities (especially African Americans in the South) from registering and voting. These barriers include the use of POLL TAXes, LITERACY TESTS, WHITE PRIMARIES, and physical intimidation. Since the 1960s, efforts have been made to remove these obstacles, and a growing number of groups now seek to increase the number of registered voters among minority groups.

Minorities also have lower voting rates than whites due to lower average incomes, lower average levels of education, and a lack of identification with candidates (particularly presidential candidates). In the last two decades, as legal barriers to minority voting were eliminated, candidates began to recognize the voting power of blacks. Moreover, as Hispanics are replacing African Americans as the nation's largest minority group, they are likely to attract far more political attention among candidates. As this group is less fully committed to a single party than are African Americans, the Democratic and Republican Parties have begun all-out efforts to attract members of this quickly growing group of SWING VOTERs.

Over the next two decades the voter turnout of minorities is expected to increase as their percentage of the population continues to grow and their income and average education levels also increase. Concurrently, minorities are gaining political power in local, state, and federal positions and providing minority voters with candidates they can relate to on a cultural level.

Further reading: Leege, David C., Kenneth D. Wald, Brian S. Krueger, and Paul D. Mueller. *The Politics of Cultural Differences: Social Change and Voter Mobilization Strategies in the Post-New Deal Period*. Princeton, N.J.: Princeton University Press, 2002; U.S. Census Bureau. *Reported Voting and Registration by Race, Hispanic Origin, Sex and Age Groups: November 1964 to 2002. Current Population Survey, November 2002 and Earlier Reports*. Washington, D.C.: United States Census Bureau, 2004.

—Glenn L. Starks

voting requirements

Voting requirements are imposed by states to determine which residents are eligible to vote in local, state, and federal elections. The federal government has greatly expanded SUFFRAGE through amendments to the Constitution and federal law despite Article I, Section 4, of the Constitution, which delegates to the states the role of prescribing "the Times, Places, and Manners of holding elections."

Considered one of the many necessary aspects of a modern democracy, universal suffrage is the extension of voting rights, regardless of race, sex, belief, or status, to citizens of a certain age. Although federal and state laws ensure that all eligible voters are able to cast BALLOTs, there are claims of disenfranchisement to this day, albeit less common than during the country's battles with voting rights in the 19th and 20th centuries. Currently, any full citizen at least 18 years of age who has not had his or her voting rights revoked for the commission of a felony is eligible to vote.

From the inception of the Union, the right to vote was restricted to white, property-owning men. The history of black and women's suffrage is intrinsically tied to the abolition of slavery and the enactment of CIVIL RIGHTS LEGISLATION. Until the passage of the Thirteenth Amendment, blacks were almost entirely disenfranchised at the polls. Following their readmission to the Union after the Civil War, most Confederate states passed the "Black Codes," sets of laws denying blacks the legal rights given to whites. In response, the RECONSTRUCTIONist Congress passed the Civil Rights Act of 1866, formally granting CITIZENSHIP to African Americans and giving federal courts the power to enforce their right to vote. Whereas state court judges were elected locally—and therefore more sympathetic to the slaveholder mentality—federal judges were appointed by the president and thus provided a more realistic venue for challenging violations of the newly enacted federal statutes.

The Civil Rights Act of 1866 was controversial, however, seen by some as unconstitutionally overriding the power of states to determine voter qualifications. In response, Congress passed and states ratified the FOURTEENTH and FIFTEENTH AMENDMENTs, prohibiting states from abridging "the privileges or immunities of citizenship" or depriving "any person of life, liberty, or property without due process of law," and prohibiting the national and state governments from denying the right to vote based on "race, color, or previous condition of servitude." White southerners were still determined to deprive their black neighbors of the right to vote. Avoiding the Fifteenth Amendment's proscription against using race or color, southern state legislatures used three methods to keep blacks away from the polls: POLL TAXes, property ownership requirements, and LITERACY TESTS.

Poll taxes amounted to a petty sum for white former slaveholders but were prohibitive to poor black sharecroppers. Property-owning qualifications were also enacted to keep poorer blacks from voting. Finally, local registrars used literacy tests to weed out black voters, who were often poorly educated. In addition to discriminating against blacks, literacy or comprehension tests allowed SOUTHERN DEMOCRATS to retain control of some state legislatures well into the 20th century.

GRANDFATHER CLAUSES were passed to help stem the disenfranchisement of white voters who could not afford the poll tax, who did not own property, or who could not pass a literacy test. These laws granted voting privileges to anyone whose grandfather voted before Reconstruction.

In 1890, the National and American Woman Suffrage Movements merged, creating the National American Woman Suffrage Association (NAWSA) and reigniting the march for the vote. While women's movement pioneers such as Elizabeth Cady Stanton were allied with African Americans in their struggle to gain freedom and equality before the Civil War, their cause departed from the abolitionist movement after the passage of the Fourteenth Amendment. Angered that the amendment applied only to men—in fact, the amendment contains the Constitution's first use of the word *male*—women later pressed their argument using racist rhetoric. When arguing for the vote, some women employed the argument that if uneducated black men had the right to vote, why should they be deprived the right. Nevertheless, a broad-based group of women's associations that sprang from the PROGRESSIVE MOVEMENT and included NAWSA was able to secure passage of the NINETEENTH AMENDMENT in 1920, granting women the right to vote.

While passage of the Nineteenth Amendment came 50 years after black men were given the same right under the Fifteenth Amendment, it would be almost another 50 years until blacks became fully enfranchised at the polls. The Supreme Court's decision in *Plessy v. Ferguson* (1896), which established a separate-but-equal doctrine, not only galvanized anti-African-American sentiment but also provided a legal justification for other forms of discrimination against blacks. The same Progressive movement that fueled women's suffrage, combined with a changing Supreme Court composition following Franklin Roosevelt's court packing plan, paved the way for the NATIONAL ASSOCIATION FOR THE ADVANCEMENT OF COLORED PEOPLE (NAACP) to launch an all-out challenge to the Court's jurisprudence in *Plessy*. Beginning with cases of discrimination in professional and graduate education, the NAACP, and later the NAACP Legal Defense and Education Fund, brought challenges in federal courts eventually resulting in the Court's landmark ruling in *Brown v. Board of Education* (1954). Thurgood Marshall, who would eventually sit on the bench of the Supreme Court, argued on behalf of Brown and the NAACP that the separate-but-equal doctrine was unconstitutional under the equal protection clause of the Fourteenth Amendment. The Court agreed.

The CIVIL RIGHTS MOVEMENT rolled forward when in 1963 President John F. Kennedy called on Congress to pass legislation banning public discrimination. Later that year, more than 250,000 people marched on Washington, D.C., and heard Martin Luther King, Jr., deliver his "I Have a Dream" speech from the Lincoln Memorial in support of this cause. Although Kennedy was assassinated later that year in Dallas, his successor, Lyndon B. Johnson, put civil rights reform at the top of his domestic agenda, eventually securing passage of the Civil Rights Act of 1964. The act outlawed discrimination in local registrars' offices, expedited voting rights lawsuits, and, in time, secured enfranchisement for black voters.

In the 2004 election, African Americans in Cleveland, Ohio, bemoaned excessively long voter lines at polling places, while white voters in other areas of the state benefited from more voting machines and shorter waits. As in 2000, some voters claimed they were intimidated at the polls or told beforehand they were not eligible, when, in fact, they were. Even so, the effects of relaxed voting requirements have been felt throughout the ELECTORATE, as was the case in the 1990s, when African Americans and women formed the core of the DEMOCRATIC PARTY.

Further reading: Baker, Jean H., ed. *Votes for Women: The Struggle for Suffrage Revisited.* New York: Oxford University Press, 2002; Goldman, Robert Michael. *Reconstruction and Black Suffrage: Losing the Vote in Reese and Cruikshank.* Lawrence: University Press of Kansas, 2001; Williams, Juan. *Eyes on the Prize: America's Civil Rights Years, 1954–1965.* New York: Penguin, 1987.

—Peter Jackson

Voting Rights Act of 1965 (amended 1970; amended 1975; amended 1982)

The Voting Rights Act of 1965, along with its amendments in 1970, 1975, and 1982, represents the statutory embodiment of the FIFTEENTH AMENDMENT to the U.S. Constitution and its protection of the right to vote. Created and passed during the height of the U.S. CIVIL RIGHTS MOVEMENT, the 1965 Voting Rights Act sought to enfranchise black and other minority voters, most notably in the South. Along with the three amending laws to the original measure, the Voting Rights Act has been among the most significant pieces of legislation to extend the right to vote to minorities in U.S. history.

The original piece of legislation was born out of the growing conflict between white southern political officials and leaders of the Civil Rights movement. From the end of RECONSTRUCTION through the 1940s, white southerners sought to limit the power of blacks, most notably by denying them the right to vote. Through such "Jim Crow" measures as the POLL TAX, LITERACY TESTS, GRANDFATHER CLAUSES, a WHITE PRIMARY system, and economic and physical intimidation, white southerners effectively kept blacks from participating in the electoral system. By 1940, only 3 percent of the 5 million black southerners of voting age were registered to vote; far fewer blacks actually cast BALLOTS.

With the advent of the NATIONAL ASSOCIATION FOR THE ADVANCEMENT OF COLORED PEOPLE's (NAACP) strategy of legally contesting segregation in the 1930s and 1940s, the Civil Rights movement began to challenge Jim Crow laws through the courts and congressional action. With the 1954 U.S. Supreme Court decision in *Brown v. Board of Education* and the adoption of federal civil rights acts in 1957, 1960, and 1964, the conflict over segregation by whites and blacks in the South reached a boiling point, most notably with the Selma march across the Edmund Pettus Bridge and the reaction by white officials. The use of excessive force by white officials prompted then president Lyndon B. Johnson to order his attorney general, Nicholas Katzenbach, to write the "god-damnedest, toughest voting rights act." The resulting act placed the burden on white southern officials to justify the use of discriminatory tactics against black voters.

Using the power of the Fifteenth Amendment, the 1965 Voting Rights Act prohibited the use of discriminatory techniques that denied or abridged the right of a voter to cast a ballot. Specifically, the use of literary tests was suspended, and the act allowed for federal "registers," or examiners, to register qualified citizens to vote through sections two and four of the act. In addition, section five of the act required several states (Alabama, Alaska, Georgia, Louisiana, Mississippi, South Carolina, Virginia, 40 counties in North Carolina, and parts of Arizona, Hawaii, and Idaho) to gain approval, or "preclearance," by the U.S. Department of Justice or the U.S. District Court for the District of Columbia before the states could change their voting practices or procedures. Sections six and seven required federal registrars to go into areas where complaints were made regarding the ability of minorities to register to vote, as well as POLL WATCHERS to oversee election practices in the covered areas to ensure the exercise of voting rights. Finally, section three of the act allowed the courts to impose sections four through seven on an area if the judges deemed it necessary to enforce the Fifteenth Amendment.

The 1970 amendments to the original act extended the act by another five years, as well as banned literacy tests nationwide and included additional jurisdictions under the act's coverage. In 1975, the act was extended another seven years, with the literacy test ban made permanent. In addition, minority voters who used another language than English were granted protection.

In 1982, amendments were added to the original legislation that continued section five for another 25 years. However, after much debate and controversy by the Reagan administration, a new "bail-out" procedure was adopted for states subject to the "preclearance" requirement. If a state or covered jurisdiction could demonstrate that it had not engaged in discriminatory practices and had promoted minority voting practices for a 10-year period, a state could be removed from the "preclearance" section of the act. In addition, a new provision was added to the original act that resulted from a U.S. Supreme Court case, *City of Mobile v. Bolden* 446 U.S. 55 (1980). In the *Bolden* case, the city of Mobile had been under a court order to restructure its at-large electoral system to ensure that black voters, who made up 40 percent of the city's population, would gain representation. The U.S. Supreme Court overturned that court order and held that because blacks could register to vote, no discriminatory intent was implied by the at-large system. Congress responded with a revised section two of the act, which held that voters could challenge that an electoral system was discriminatory based solely on the practice or procedures, and not necessarily the intent of the electoral system. However, the revised section two could not be used to create an electoral system based on racial quotas or to create a system that protected minorities from defeat at the polls.

The effect of the 1965 Voting Rights Act and its subsequent amendments has led many scholars to characterize the legislation as among the most successful laws to ensure civil rights by the federal government. For example, black eligible voters who have been registered under the act went from just 12 percent in 1947 in the 11 southern states to 43 percent in 1964, to 63 percent in 1976. Today, the gap between registered eligible white voters and registered eligible black voters is within single digits.

In addition to increasing the numbers of eligible black voters who are registered, the Voting Rights Act and its various amendments have had a tremendous impact as well on the role of the judiciary in civil rights litigation. Numerous cases have been filed challenging the Voting Rights Act and its progeny. In 1967, the basic premise that the federal government could adopt legislation protecting voters' rights was resolved through one of the first cases to challenge the act, *South Carolina v. Katzenbach* 383 U.S. 301 (1966). In addition, the Voting Rights Act has been interpreted, both by judges and others through the original law and subsequent amendments, as advocating the creation of MAJORITY-MINORITY DISTRICTS, which are designed to enable racial minorities to be joined within a district so that they may elect one of their own to represent them.

Further reading: Davidson, Chandler, and Bernard Grofman, eds. *Quiet Revolution in the South: The Impact of the Voting Rights Act, 1965–1990.* Princeton, N.J.: Princeton University Press, 1994; Keyssar, Alexander. *The Right to Vote: The Contested History of Democracy in the United States.* New York: Basic Books, 2000; Kousser, J. Morgan. *Colorblind Injustice: Minority Voting Rights and the Undoing of the Second Reconstruction.* Chapel Hill: University of North Carolina Press, 1999; Lawson, Steven F. *Black Ballots: Voting Rights in the South 1944–1969.* Lanham, Md.: Lexington Books, 1999; U.S. Department of Justice, Introduction to the Federal Voting Rights Laws. Available online. URL: http://www.usdoj.gov/crt/voting/intro/intro_b.htm. Accessed August 10, 2005.

—J. Michael Bitzer

voting systems

Voting systems prescribe the means by which a community expresses its political preferences and elects its representa-tives to office. How communities design their voting systems structures the voting process, from the design of BALLOTS and the means for casting votes to the vote count and how winners are decided. This structure has a far-reaching impact: It not only helps to determine who represents the ELECTORATE but also which policies get attention and which segment(s) of the population reap the benefits of those policies.

The dominant voting system in the United States is the "winner-take-all system," or the single-member plurality district system. In this system, each candidate campaigns to win one representative seat in each geographically defined legislative district; the candidate who gains the most votes wins the election and represents a specific area. An alternative to the winner-take-all system, common in many European countries, is the PROPORTIONAL REPRESENTATION system. Proportional representation systems elect representatives to MULTIMEMBER DISTRICTS, and those seats are distributed according to the percentage of the vote won by political parties or political groups.

Recent developments in American voting behavior (e.g., VOTER TURNOUT rates hovering at 50 percent in PRESIDENTIAL ELECTIONS and 30 percent in CONGRESSIONAL ELECTIONS and growing dissatisfaction with the limited candidate choices associated with the TWO-PARTY SYSTEM) have fueled discussion of alternative voting systems. One example, "preferential voting," is employed to elect a single officer who has the support of the majority of the voters and to mitigate the need for RUNOFF ELECTIONS. Here voters have multiple votes instead of one vote, and indicate a gradation of preferences by placing a number next to the name of a candidate. If a candidate receives a majority of the first-rank votes, he or she is elected. If not, then the candidate with the lowest number of first-rank votes is eliminated, and ballots are counted according to the next rank, and so on, until a majority is achieved.

It was not until 1843, when Congress passed the Congressional Redistricting Act, that all states shifted to SINGLE-MEMBER DISTRICTS. From 1787 to 1843, only five states elected its members of Congress this way. The rest opted for representation based on one statewide at-large district. The effect of the 1843 act was that it prevented any one party from gaining a hegemonic hold on all congressional seats in each state. The transition to single-member districts on the state level, however, took much longer to become the norm. Between the mid-19th century and the mid-20th century, a majority of states filled their state legislative seats in one statewide at-large district.

The single-member plurality district system offers democratic communities a number of advantages, but it is also not without criticism. The system is the simplest, and it also promotes geographic representation. Voters can simply cast their ballots for their preferred candidate, and the winners from each district help ensure, at the broadest level, that the various geographical differences of the electorate are expressed in the legislative system. Moreover, the system promotes enduring party COALITIONS, because it leads to single-party legislative majorities. The government is more stable and efficient since the possibility for the collapse of governing coalitions dissipates. At the same time, single-member pluralities tend to underrepresent minorities. Historical patterns in GERRYMANDERing of CONGRESSIONAL DISTRICTS have often yielded districts where the voting power of racial minorities gets diluted by the white majority vote. MAJORITY-MINORITY DISTRICTS, however, have become a common means of mitigating this problem in the United States over the last several decades. Here, congressional districts are constructed in such a way as to ensure that minority voters have more influence in elections.

Proportional representation systems first appeared in 19th-century Europe to help resolve some of the weaknesses of winner-take-all systems. Ethnic and religious tension within the populations of Belgium and Switzerland pushed the two countries to adopt proportional representation systems in 1899. Finland and Sweden adopted the system in 1906 and 1907, respectively, and by the 1920s most European countries had followed suit. For the remainder of the 20th century the trend toward proportional representation systems continued in the newly democratized former republics of the Soviet Union and eastern Europe. In the 1990s, New Zealand switched its single-member plurality system to proportional representation after a national REFERENDUM.

Proportional representation systems promote fair representation of political parties and fewer wasted votes, and they give political parties the number of seats they merit based on voting strength. If 50 percent of voters vote for candidates from a party, that party gains 50 percent of the seats in the legislature. A POLITICAL PARTY needs only a small number of votes in a proportional representation system to gain representation, but in a single-member plurality system, a party that wins lower than a majority of votes wins no representation. Researchers on proportional representation systems have also found evidence that the system decreases the amount of negative advertising candidates rely on to win an election, promotes better representation of women, and offers voters more choice at the polls. At the same time, proportional representation systems have been criticized for promoting unstable coalitions, legislative gridlock, and too many concessions to small parties. Italy, for example, has encountered significant instability in its government since it instituted a proportional representation system in the 1940s. In Israel, small radical religious parties have won support for their policy proposals by threatening to pull out of the ruling coalition, even though those proposals lacked approval by a majority of the population.

Further reading: Kelppner, Paul, Walter Dean Burnham, Ronald P. Formisano, Samuel P. Hays, Richard Jensen, and William G. Shade. *The Evolution of American Electoral Systems: (Contributions in American History)*. Westport, Conn.: Greenwood Press, 1981; Douglas, Amy J. *Behind the Ballot Box: A Citizen's Guide to Voting Systems*. Westport, Conn.: Praeger, 2000.

—Jamie Patrick Chandler

voting trends, African-American

Voting trends among African Americans have been the subject of analysis by scholars since the inception of PUBLIC OPINION POLLING. This type of analysis examines the historical and current voting trends of African Americans. In this context, voting analysis addresses how African Americans vote, often in comparison to how white voters vote in the same election.

African Americans have had a long-standing history of political participation and mobilization in the United States. African Americans have become a key voting bloc for the DEMOCRATIC PARTY, especially in the urban Northeast and throughout the South. Today the African-American vote is the most reliable CONSTITUENCY for the Democratic Party.

Early in the history of the REPUBLICAN PARTY, in the mid-1850s, African Americans identified the Republican Party as the party of Lincoln and generally supported Republican candidates. As conservative Democrats left the Democratic Party in favor of the Republican Party, mostly in the South, and the Democratic Party adopted civil rights legislation in the mid-1960s, African Americans changed their allegiance to the Democratic Party.

Throughout much of the early 20th century, the partisan preferences of African Americans were of little electoral consequence, as the group was systematically denied a voice in the electoral process. They faced significant barriers such as being denied the right to vote, disenfranchisement, redistricting barriers, and living in impoverished neighborhoods. These barriers were impediments to their right to be participants in the American political system.

Seeing the racial barriers that impeded the rights of African Americans, President Lyndon B. Johnson worked to reform the process and open the door to African-American voter participation. The U.S. Congress passed the VOTING RIGHTS ACT OF 1965, which removed racial barriers to voting and allowed African Americans to vote. This act not only granted African Americans access to polls, it also fostered and mobilized INTEREST GROUPS that were created to advance the civil rights cause. As a consequence of Johnson's work and the exodus from the party of SOUTHERN DEMOCRATS, the Democratic Party became viewed as the right party to improve the social, economic, and political environment of African Americans.

Today African Americans are voting in larger numbers than at any other time in American history. As party loyalists, African Americans continue to vote in support of the Democratic Party. In 1996, 84 percent of registered African Americans voted for Bill Clinton for president, a trend that continued in the 2000 election, in which African Americans overwhelmingly supported Al Gore, and in 2004, when this group threw its support behind John Kerry. Within the African-American constituency, African-American women are believed to be a particularly important voting group, as they have voted in higher numbers than their male counterparts, and their loyalty to the Democratic Party has remained solid.

In recent years, however, a growing number of African Americans have become discontented with the Democratic Party. It is believed that the Democratic Party has taken advantage of the "black vote," or at least taken it for granted, and has focused less campaign efforts addressing the salient issues affecting this group. Since the mid-1990s, the Republican Party has attempted to court African-American voters, believing that the strength of religious values within the African-American community and the growing number of affluent and middle-class African Americans should lead this group to increasingly support the Republican Party in the future. While the Republican Party has rekindled the interests of African-American voters, to date the group remains loyal to the Democratic Party.

Further reading: Bibby, John F. *Politics, Parties, and Elections in America.* Belmont, Calif.: Thomson-Wadsworth, 2003; Day, Jennifer, Amie Jamieson, and Hyon B. Shin. *Voting and Registration: The Election of November 2000.* Washington, D.C.: U.S. Census Bureau, 2002; McKinnon, Jesse. *Current Population Reports: The Black Population in the United States: March 2002.* Washington, D.C.: U.S. Census Bureau, 2002.

—William L. Barnes

voting trends, economic issues

Studies of voting behavior have demonstrated that the economy plays an important role in determining how people vote. Typically, the economy is the dominant issue for most Americans and the top policy concern that drives their voting decisions. It is generally believed that voters reflect retrospectively and prospectively on the incumbent party.

Prospective economic voting refers to evaluation of candidates for office based on perceptions of how the candidates would influence the performance of the economy. Candidate pronouncements, including statements regarding tax policy, income redistribution, and trade policy, may provide voters with information regarding how a candidate would influence key economic variables such as rates of growth, unemployment, and inflation.

According to this theory of voter behavior, citizens consider how each candidate's preferred policies would influence their economic well-being and cast their BALLOTS for the candidate they believe will most positively affect their welfare. For example, prospective considerations may have played an important role in the 2004 elections. Voters likely considered the potential impact of party differences with respect to several policy issues. Republican support for lower marginal tax rates was likely compared with Democratic support for increased spending on several programs. Voters evaluated which policy platform was most likely to increase their future welfare.

Proponents of prospective economic voting argue that citizens use information provided by candidates during a campaign to update their expectations about economic conditions likely to prevail in the future, rather than relying solely on past experiences. Further, prospective evaluations allow a voter to consider which of the candidates would generate a better outcome rather than focusing only on the performance of an incumbent or an incumbent's party. Critics of prospective economic voting argue that it is difficult to forecast the impact of differing policy positions on economic variables such as unemployment and inflation. Further, voter decisions may be influenced by a number of other factors, including prospective evaluations of social and foreign policy issues as well as retrospective evaluations of incumbent performance.

Retrospective economic voting refers to evaluation of incumbent politicians on the basis of the economic conditions prevailing during their term. General measures of economic performance including rates of growth, unemployment, and inflation may be combined with a voter's personal experience (i.e., pocketbook issues) to assess an incumbent's performance during his or her term of office.

According to this theory of voter behavior, a positive evaluation translates into a vote for the incumbent, whereas a negative evaluation leads to a vote for the CHALLENGER. For example, economic conditions may have played an important role in the 1992 PRESIDENTIAL ELECTION, contested between incumbent George H. W. Bush and challenger William J. Clinton. Slow economic growth, combined with increasing unemployment rates during the election campaign, led to the famous campaign theme "It's the economy, stupid." Negative voter perception of economic performance during the Bush administration may have influenced voter decisions on ELECTION DAY.

Proponents of retrospective economic voting argue that past performance may provide an indication of the conditions likely to prevail if an incumbent is reelected. Further, reliance on personal experience during the course of an incumbent's term allows voters to focus on what they know rather than make predictions about the future based on campaign promises or policy pronouncements. Critics of retrospective voting argue that economic conditions are the result of several complicated forces and cannot reasonably be attributed to the performance of an individual politician. Further, voter decisions may be influenced by a number of other factors, including performance on social and foreign policy issues as well as prospective evaluations of conditions likely to prevail under alternative electoral outcomes.

Early studies of economic voting suggested that voters considered primarily their own economic circumstances (i.e., pocketbook issues) in making up their minds about economic performance. They simply asked themselves if they were personally better off financially than they were before the incumbent party held office. Such information is, after all, readily available to voters and requires little awareness of broader economic conditions besides knowledge about personal finances.

An alternative conceptualization of how voters incorporate evaluations about the economy in their personal voting calculus is sociotropic voting. Sociotropic voters determine their political preferences by assessing national economic conditions rather than personal finances. Less preoccupied with their own economic interests, sociotropic voters are influenced by their understanding of how the incumbent party has fared with respect to the nation's economic life. Sociotropic voters consider such factors as the national rate of unemployment, inflation, job growth, and per capita income and arrive at voting decisions accordingly.

Scholars have debated which of these characterizations best describes the type of economic information voters process in their individual voting calculus. Some critics believe sociotropic voting is unrealistic because it imposes far too high demands on voter information about complex matters related to the nation's economy. If so, pocketbook voting would represent a more reasonable understanding of economic voting behavior. Other analysts believe that sophisticated analyses of economic conditions are not necessary. They argue that the average voter can develop rough measures of national economic conditions and use these evaluations to guide vote choices.

Further reading: Fiorina, Morris P. *Retrospective Voting in American National Elections.* New Haven, Conn.: Yale University Press, 1981; Key, V. O. *The Responsible Electorate.* Cambridge, Mass.: Harvard University Press, 1966; Kinder, Donald R., and D. Roderick Kiewiet. "Sociotropic Politics: The American Case." *British Journal of Political Science* 11, no. 2 (1981): 129–161; Miller, Warren E., and J. Merrill Shanks. *The New American Voter.* Cambridge, Mass.: Harvard University Press, 1996; Niemi, Richard G., and Herbert F. Weisberg. *Controversies in Voting Behavior.* 4th ed. Washington, D.C.: CQ Press, 2001.

—John Cadigan and Costas Panagopoulos

voting trends, Hispanic

Hispanics are persons from 22 countries of origin including Mexico and those in Central and South America, the Spanish-speaking Caribbean, and the Iberian Peninsula as well as those from U.S. communities dating back to the 17th century. The Hispanic population in 2000 was 35 million (12.5 percent of the total U.S. population), a figure that slightly exceeded the number of African Americans. Almost 75 percent of Hispanics are Mexican, Puerto Rican (10 percent), or Cuban (4 percent) in origin. Around 90 percent live in 10 states. Though this population is rapidly dispersing, it forms a sizable bloc in the large ELECTORAL COLLEGE states of California, Texas, New York, Florida, and Illinois.

Hispanics contribute around 7 percent of the vote in national elections. The rate of Hispanic VOTER TURNOUT (among registered voters only) is lower (10 to 12 percent) than for non-Hispanic whites. Even though this gap has not significantly closed, from 1968 to 2000 the number of Hispanics in the voting population has greatly increased. Although Puerto Ricans are U.S. citizens, about half of nonvoting Hispanics are not citizens. Low Hispanic turnout is also linked to a younger median age (10 years below the national median age), low education and income, and a high number of non- or limited-English speakers. The 1975 amendments to the Voting Rights Act, however, require bilingual voting materials and assistance to linguistic minorities and are credited with increasing Hispanic registration and voting.

The Hispanic vote is traditionally Democratic and has averaged 63 percent, from 1976 to 2000, for the Democratic candidate in PRESIDENTIAL ELECTIONS. In a 2002 poll of registered Hispanics, 49 percent identified with the DEMOCRATIC PARTY and 20 percent with the Republicans. There are differences among groups, with Puerto Ricans most aligned with the Democratic Party, followed by Mexican Americans, and then Central and South Americans, who "lean" Democratic. Cuban Americans in the early 1960s were also Democrats, but now a majority of Cubans are Republicans because of that party's stronger stance against Fidel Castro and communism. Hispanic voters make distinctions between presidential and other candidates. Ronald Reagan received almost 40 percent of the Hispanic vote in 1984 even though the levels of support for Democratic candidates for all other offices were uniformly high. In 1996, Bill Clinton received 50 percent of the Cuban vote, which provided his winning margin in Florida.

Despite lower voting turnout, Hispanics are viewed as a key SWING VOTE whose support for the Democratic Party has been declining. Since 1988, both parties have aired Spanish-language advertisements, and candidates have appeared on Spanish-language television to discuss Hispanic issues. Neither party finds it easy to appeal to Hispanics, who are not easily categorized in ideological terms. The Democratic Party is closer to Hispanics on economic issues, bilingual education, affirmative action, immigrant rights, health care, and affordable housing. Republicans are closer on defense, crime, abortion, educational vouchers, and family values. Since a 1967 decision by the U.S.

Supreme Court, dual CITIZENSHIP for naturalized citizens has been allowed, and naturalization petitions have greatly increased. With a rapidly growing (and aging) population, concentration in large states and metropolitan areas, an increasing middle-class, and more effective mobilization by Hispanic groups and leaders, the Hispanic vote will be a major force in U.S. elections in the future.

Further reading: DeSipio, Louis. *Counting on the Latino Vote: Latinos as a New Electorate.* Charlottesville: University of Virginia Press, 1996; García, John A. *Latino Politics in America.* Lanham, Md.: Rowman & Littlefield, 2003; De la Garza, Rodolfo, Louis DeSipio, F. Chris García, John A. García, and Angelo Falcón. *Latino Voices: Mexican, Puerto Rican, and Cuban Perspectives on American Politics.* Boulder, Colo.: Westview, 1993.

—Janet K. Boles

voting trends, religious

Religious affiliation began to have a visible influence on partisan alignment in the United States during the 20th century. Historically, little differentiation could be seen between Catholics and Protestants until the 1920s. The key exception was the rise of the KNOW-NOTHING PARTY in the 1850s, which opposed the influx of Catholic immigrants into the United States. This party declined quickly because of the issues of secession that were dominating political discourse during the pre–Civil War period.

In 1928, however, the Catholic versus Protestant divide at the voting booths became significant. The DEMOCRATIC PARTY became the first major party to nominate a Roman Catholic to be president when it chose Governor Al Smith of New York. An anti-Catholic backlash against this choice convinced more Catholics to vote with the Democratic Party. A similar incident arose in 1960, when John F. Kennedy, a Catholic, was nominated to be president by the Democratic Party. Whereas 50 percent of Catholics in 1956 voted for Adlai Stevenson, the Democratic nominee, 80 percent of Catholics voted for John F. Kennedy in 1960.

This cleavage remained steady throughout the 1900s as Catholics predominantly identified with the Democratic Party while Protestants tended to favor the REPUBLICAN PARTY. The strict divide was blurred somewhat by the tendency of higher-income religious adherents to vote Republican and lower-income members to vote Democratic and by the tendency of African Americans to overwhelmingly support the Democratic Party regardless of religious association.

Since the New Deal era, Jewish voters have maintained consistently firm ties to the Democratic Party. Notwithstanding the influence of education levels or socioeconomic status, Jewish voters have, by and large, identified with the Democratic Party. This is dissimilar to the tendency of higher-income Catholics to vote Republican, for example.

In recent elections, some REALIGNMENT has taken place. Party COALITIONs in 2000 revealed less differentiation between Catholics and Protestants and more differentiation between regular and irregular churchgoers. Among white regular churchgoers, the Republican nominee, George W. Bush, was the candidate choice of 84 percent of evangelical Protestants, 66 percent of mainline Protestants, and 57 percent of Roman Catholics. Among whites who attended church less regularly, Bush's support dropped to 55 percent of evangelical Protestants, 57 percent of mainline Protestants, and 41 percent of Roman Catholics. Therefore, increased frequency of church attendance was related to a voter being more likely to vote for George W. Bush. Attendance or nonattendance at religious services was not statistically significant among African American voters, 90 percent of whom voted for the Democratic nominee, Al Gore.

EXIT POLLS in 2000 revealed that approximately 63 percent of those who attended religious services more than weekly voted for George Bush, while Al Gore received support from 61 percent of those who never attended religious services. Bush received support from 80 percent of those whites who identified with the Religious Right and only 42 percent of those whites who did not consider themselves members of the Religious Right.

The support of weekly church attendees for the Republican Party remained consistent in 2002, as 62 percent of LIKELY VOTERs from this demographic planned to vote for the Republican congressional candidates. Meanwhile, 60 percent of likely voters who attended church monthly and 57 percent of those who seldom or never attended church planned to vote for Democratic congressional candidates in 2002.

There was somewhat less religious differentiation in 2000, when the survey questions dealt with PARTY IDENTIFICATION. Of mainstream Protestants, 40 percent declared themselves to be Republicans, while 44 percent declared themselves Democrats. Of evangelical Protestants, 39 percent were Republicans, while 48 percent were Democrats. Of Catholics, 40 percent were Republicans, while 45 percent identified themselves as Democrats. Of Jewish voters, 13 percent were Republicans, while 65 percent were Democrats.

The case of evangelical Christians in particular shows that more complexity is present within religious groups than can be ascertained from most quantitative survey results or exit poll statistics. Evangelicals for Social Action, an activist group on the Christian left, was inspired by Democratic candidates such as George McGovern due to their opposition to the Vietnam War. As a result, members participated in voter mobilization drives to encourage Christian pacifists to support McGovern.

Evangelical Christians with more right-wing political ideologies, however, have shifted back and forth between the major parties. Jimmy Carter's humanitarian ideals and the fact that he was a born-again Christian inspired many evangelical Christians to support the Democratic Party. The arrival of Ronald Reagan and his conservative emphasis on issues dealing with abortion and families led many evangelical Christians to support the Republican Party. While members of the Religious Right were not immediately a major force in the Republican Party, the rise of the CHRISTIAN COALITION in 1989 led many to become even more politically active in this party.

Other evangelical Christians have taken more of an abstinence approach to voting. Although the Mennonites were the first group in the North American colonies to verbalize an opposition to slavery and were later active in securing conscientious objector status for religious members opposed to war, they have also traditionally abstained from voting and holding political office. Therefore, they are not usually factored into most surveys or exit polls and illustrate the complexity of measuring religious voting trends.

Further reading: Bibby, John F. *Politics, Parties, and Elections in America.* Belmont, Calif.: Thomson-Wadsworth, 2003; Petrocik, John R. *Party Coalitions: Realignments and the Decline of the New Deal Party System.* Chicago: University of Chicago Press, 1981; Sabato, Larry, and Bruce Larson. *The Party's Just Begun: Shaping Political Parties for America's Future.* New York: Longman, 2002; White, John Kenneth, and Daniel M. Shea. *New Party Politics: From Jefferson and Hamilton to the Information Age.* Belmont, Calif.: Thomson-Wadsworth, 2003.

—Nathan Zook

voting trends, urban/suburban/rural

Party professionals look closely at voting patterns and public opinion in urban, suburban, and rural regions of the country. This regional dimension highlights some important developments in the electoral landscape and underscores the close partisan balance in contemporary American POLITICS.

Since the 1980s, both parties have been keenly interested in suburban voters because they constitute the largest segment of the ELECTORATE. In the 2000 PRESIDENTIAL ELECTION, 42 percent of voters came from the suburbs, compared to 28 percent from urban areas and 30 percent from rural regions. Despite their smaller numbers, party strategists recognize that urban and rural voters still play an important part in ELECTORAL COLLEGE strategies.

Voting patterns in suburbs and central cities have undergone some important changes over the past 20 years. During the1980s, the REPUBLICAN PARTY enjoyed significant advantages in suburban areas. Compared to their urban neighbors, suburban voters were more apt to identify themselves as Republicans, were more likely to vote Republican in presidential and CONGRESSIONAL ELECTIONS, and tended to profess more conservative policy preferences, especially on Welfare and other redistributive programs. By contrast, urban voters went solidly Democratic during the 1980s, with Democratic presidential candidates receiving 60 to 62 percent of the vote.

Democratic dominance in central cities has increased since then, with 71 percent of the urban vote going to Al Gore in 2000. At the same time, the suburbs have become more competitive. Bill Clinton won small majorities in suburbs in 1992 and 1996, while Al Gore and George W. Bush battled to a 50 percent to 50 percent draw in 2000.

Many analysts attribute the Republican suburban advantage in the 1980s to the appeal of Ronald Reagan, to a general distaste for government activism, and to racial resentment among some white suburbanites. Research has shown that Republican advantages were strongest in suburbs adjacent to central cities with the highest percentages of poor and African-American residents. The increased suburban competition beginning in the 1990s has been explained by the appeal of Bill Clinton, voter apprehension of the REPUBLICAN REVOLUTION following the 1994 elections, as well as the increasing ethnic and class diversity of many suburban areas. The stereotypical portrayal of suburban voters as affluent, white, and conservative is no longer especially true.

Rural areas have gone Republican in recent PRESIDENTIAL ELECTIONS. Although Bill Clinton ran even with his Republican opponents in 1992 and 1996, George W. Bush won 59 percent of the rural vote in 2000. Some research suggests that Republican support among rural voters is driven by conservative policy preferences on noneconomic issues such as abortion and gun control.

Further reading: Gainsborough, Juliet F. *Fenced Off: The Suburbanization of American Politics.* Washington, D.C.: Georgetown University Press, 2001; McKee, Seth C., and Daron R. Shaw. "Suburban Voting in Presidential Elections." *Presidential Studies Quarterly* 33 (2003): 125–144.

—Julio Borquez

voting trends, women

When women's SUFFRAGE was adopted in the United States in 1920 with the ratification of the NINETEENTH AMENDMENT, it was expected (and feared by some) that women would enter the ELECTORATE on an equal basis with men, vote as a bloc, and even form a women's party to contest elections. In practice, women long trailed men in turnout. Women joined the two major parties in roughly the same proportions as men. And no distinctive women's vote emerged in American elections. However, there have always been gender differences in PARTY IDENTIFICATION, issue preferences and saliency, and candidate evaluations. These differences have created GENDER GAPS in voting that have varied over time.

These gaps have assumed greater importance in recent years. Beginning with the 1964 PRESIDENTIAL ELECTION, women, due to their preponderance in the voting-age population, have cast more total votes than have men. Women make up a slightly larger segment of the electorate (due to their longer life expectancy), and since 1980 women as a group have had slightly higher rates of voting participation. In situations in which a majority of male and female voters choose different candidates, the election could be determined by women's votes even though women do not constitute a unified bloc of voters.

Although women joined political parties after 1920 in percentages mirroring those of men, more affluent and better-educated women were more likely to enter the electorate, and thus women probably identified more with the REPUBLICAN PARTY from 1920 to 1932. With the coming of the New Deal, poorer and immigrant women tended to join the electorate as Democrats. Until the 1970s, there was no strong gender gap in party identification. A small gender gap in candidate choice (the difference between the percentage of men who vote for a particular candidate and the percentage of women who vote for that same candidate) in PRESIDENTIAL ELECTIONS from 1920 to 1960 favored the Republican Party among women. During this period, most women were housewives and more conservative.

Since 1964 (except for 1976) women have cast a higher percentage of their votes for the Democratic candidate than have men. The contemporary gender gap ranges between 7 and 12 percentage points in CONGRESSIONAL ELECTIONS and has averaged 6 percentage points in presidential elections. This voting trend became an issue only when women began to identify with the DEMOCRATIC PARTY more than men, who began leaving that party in the early 1970s. The primary change in party identification has been the male shift to the Republican Party. In 2003, about 33 percent of women aligned with the Democratic Party, compared with 25 percent of men.

This electoral REALIGNMENT of the sexes has been attributed to IDEOLOGY and issues. Before 1980, most women were more likely than men to be conservative; the exceptions were younger, college-educated, and working-class (employed) women. Since then, women in all cohorts have become more liberal. Currently, men are much more likely and women are less likely to self-identify as conservative. Men have been attracted to the Republican Party and its support for a strong defense and opposition to Welfare and affirmative action. Women perceive the Democratic Party as being more concerned about women's issues and closer to them on other issues such as war and peace and the needs of others (e.g., social welfare, education, health care, unemployment, poverty, and civil rights). The gender gap in public opinion on these issues has not changed much over time. However, the salience of some of these issues did change from 1976 to 1992, as women stressed economic benefits and abortion in their voting decisions and men focused on defense, taxation, and the budget deficit in forming their choices.

A third factor in voting decisions, in addition to the roles of party identification and issue preferences, is personal evaluation of the candidates. Although scholars once expected that women would be more likely to vote on the basis of the personal characteristics of the candidate, men and women evaluate candidates similarly and are equally issue oriented. Competence, trust, and issue positions are more important than a candidate's personality to both sexes. As more women have sought elected office, however, a new voting trend has emerged. Women voters have a stronger preference for a representative of their own sex than do men and are more likely to vote for a woman and view them as sharing their concerns. The average gender gap (with women voters favoring the Democratic candidate) is several points higher if the Democratic candidate is a woman and several points lower if the Republican candidate is a woman than in races in which two men are competing. Even so, party membership and incumbency have a greater impact on voting than does candidate sex. And in elections in which there is a high focus on gender issues, women candidates may be advantaged. Conversely, in elections in which the salience of national security is high, women candidates may face barriers because of gender-role stereotyping within the electorate.

The gender gap in voting behavior and public opinion is real. Because women make up 52 percent of the electorate, these gender-based patterns should not be ignored but should be viewed in perspective. The gender gap is much smaller than that between the races and economic classes. Intragender differences are also much greater, as women (and men) differ among themselves along lines of race, ethnicity, class, sexual orientation, age, education, and marital status. Many of these demographic characteristics also explain the gender gap, which is larger among young, single, college-educated, professional, affluent, and poorer women as well as women of color. Women's voting trends continue to be based in their different experiences and statuses.

Further reading: Andersen, Kristi. *After Suffrage: Women in Partisan and Electoral Politics before the New Deal.* Chicago: University of Chicago Press, 1996; Dolan, Kathleen A. *Voting for Women: How the Public Evaluates Women Candidates.* Boulder, Colo.: Westview, 2004; Seltzer, Richard A., Jody Newman, and Melissa Voorhees Leighton. *Sex as a Political Variable: Women as Candidates and Voters in U.S. Elections.* Boulder, Colo.: Lynne Rienner, 1997.

—Janet K. Boles

W

war chest

A war chest refers to a store of funds that candidates and political parties assemble in anticipation of an election campaign. A war chest is most commonly associated with the campaigns of political incumbents seeking to secure a financial head start and advantage and discourage potential CHALLENGERS. The war chest often incorporates leftover funds from the previous election as well as money raised early in the term. Building a war chest is a routine task related to the notion of the permanent campaign—the practice of FUND-RAISING throughout one's term of office in order to have as much money on hand as possible in advance of the next election.

The origins of the war chest idea can be traced to the large-scale soliciting of voluntary contributions by allied charitable organizations in American communities to fund social welfare initiatives and community development programs during the pre–World War I era. This brand of "federated" giving came to be known as the community chest movement and proved to be a highly popular and efficient method of raising money at low cost. With the onsets of World War I and World War II, established community chests across the country redirected their fund-raising drives to generate funds for purposes related to the war efforts. These drives became known as war chest campaigns. Over time, as the term *war* has come to suggest general contestation of all kinds, including electoral POLITICS, the phrase *war chest* has been adapted to election contexts to denote a concentrated political fund-raising campaign.

The war chest idea is significant for three principal reasons. First, the contemporary necessity for political candidates to amass a sizable war chest is indicative of how expensive electoral campaigns have become. The ascendancy of polling, television advertisement production, and media buying as the core elements of campaigns has driven costs so high that candidates unable to raise large war chests are unlikely to succeed. Second, and more generally, the war chest notion is emblematic of the profound and growing influence of money in electoral politics. Despite regulatory measures, the nexus of influential monied interests and candidates for elective office continues to expand, prompting campaigns to seek ever greater sums of campaign cash to fill their war chests. Finally, the relative ease with which an incumbent can build a war chest underscores the power of incumbency as a decisive electoral edge. An incumbent has built-in institutional advantages such as a fund-raising operation and established relationships with political donors. The net effect of this trend is to render many campaigns virtually noncompetitive.

Further reading: Anderson, Annelise, ed. *Political Money: Deregulating American Politics: Selected Writings on Campaign Finance Reform.* Stanford, Calif.: Hoover Institute Press, 2000; Kobrak, Peter. *Cozy Politics: Political Parties, Campaign Finance, and Compromised Governance.* Boulder, Colo.: Lynne Rienner Publishers, 2002.
—Paul J. Nuti

wedge issues

Wedge issue is a popular, not technical, term describing tactics employed by a party to divide its opposition's COALITION, forcing some of the opposition's members to switch allegiances. In the perfect scenario for the user of the wedge, his or her coalition remains united, but the other team is badly divided as a result of the wedge issue. The user of the wedge will increase support relative to the opposition.

The person credited with coining the phrase was an adviser to the Carter administration, Stuart E. Eizenstat, who used the term in 1990 to describe President George H. W. Bush's use of affirmative action as a wedge issue, attempting to separate the traditional coalition of voters on the left. His intention in coining the phrase was, in his own words, to "illustrate the attempt to split the coalition of working-class whites and blacks, the two constituencies Roosevelt unified on economic grounds."

The person most renowned for the etymology of contemporary political language, William Safire, notes that this new term was the logical heir of the earlier expressions *hot-*

button issue and *polarizing issue*. This new term represented a more politically nuanced expression of the tactical considerations in a political campaign. Despite its very specific early meaning, the term *wedge issue* has often been confused with these earlier concepts, especially *polarizing*.

Employing a hot button issue will cause a high degree of voter agitation. The nature of this agitation is predictable and is likely to afflict members of both coalitions. Furthermore, the hot button does not necessarily imply that voters will reach the "point of switching allegiance." On the other hand, the polarizing issue will generally serve only to entrench current membership in each coalition and so does not have the same kind of tactical value to political campaigns. Polarizing issues can sometimes be related to THIRD RAIL ISSUES like Social Security, which are deemed too dangerous to touch.

Though intensely sought, pure wedge issues are relatively rare. American POLITICS, with its two "big tent" political coalitions, makes finding a wedge issue like discovering the Holy Grail. It remains a remote possibility since, for party strategists, any issue likely to change the minds of voters in the other party could very well change some minds in their own as well. In 2004, President George W. Bush and the Republicans thought they might have a wedge in banning gay marriage. They believed a constitutional amendment might bring Democrats with conservative social values into the Republican fold. But its wedge potential was weakened since some traditional Republican voters, especially Republican-inclined libertarians who want to limit state interference in private affairs, were turned off by the issue. Correctly understood, gay marriage is most likely a hot-button issue.

For the Democrats, one important wedge device has been the abortion issue. While Democrats are generally united behind abortion rights, particularly unmarried female Democrats, this issue can divide Republicans. Knowing that within the Republican coalition there exists a rift between a vocal pro-life segment and pro-choice conservative women, President Bill Clinton, advised by James Carville, nominated Henry Foster as surgeon-general in 1996. Dr Foster was a known proponent of choice and brought the right to choose to the fore of Clinton's administration.

A unique tactic related to the wedge has been used in California with its allowance for referenda and BALLOT INITIATIVES. Parties in this state discovered that VOTER TURNOUT and the type of voter can vary depending on the type of issue on the BALLOT. Several propositions have been drafted to mobilize particular groups of voters. Increased participation in the proposition has an add-on effect to the GENERAL ELECTIONS held simultaneously. This turnout bulge benefits those candidates sympathetic to the issues at stake in the propositions. This might be characterized as a "positive" wedge, since it brings new voters into the fray rather than merely redistributing the original complement.

Further reading: Smith, Daniel A., and Caroline J. Tolbert. "The Initiative to Party: Partisanship and Ballot Initiatives in California." *Party Politics* 7, no. 6 (2001): 739–757.
—Samuel Millar

Whig Party

The Whig Party existed as a major POLITICAL PARTY in the United States from 1834 until 1860. The Whigs developed from the FEDERALIST PARTY and generally represented the aristocratic establishment and business interests. The Whig Party formed the major rival party of the Democrats. The Whigs were a national party formed from the remnants of the Federalist and National Republican parties along with Abolitionists, or Conscience Whigs, Cotton Whigs, and Anti-Masons. The Cotton Whigs are understood in contradistinction to the Conscience Whigs as constituting major FACTIONS within the national Whig Party throughout the period, with the Cotton Whigs supporting the constitutionality and, at times, expansion of slavery, and the Conscience Whigs opposing slavery.

Throughout its existence, the challenge of the national Whig Party was to ameliorate the often divergent and complex heterogeneity of its constituent interests into a governable unity with a national party identity. An example of problems within the Whig Party is illustrated by the NOMINATION of Zachary Taylor in 1848. The Whig editor of the *Independent Democrat* in New Hampshire believed that Taylor was a captive of Cotton Whig southerners and attacked him, saying he was "one of the greatest slaveholders" in the United States who "raises babies for the market and makes merchandize of his fellow men!" In contrast, Abolitionist Whig Abraham Lincoln thought Taylor was a man of great integrity, and Lincoln formed an early organization of supporters within Congress to assist with electing Taylor.

The period leading to the American Civil War saw factionalism and increased conflict within the Whig Party. There was increasingly limited ground for compromise, and compromise was the hallmark of Whig POLITICS. Through this period of heightened sectional polarization, the Whig record of compromise left Whig partisans suspect throughout both northern and southern sections, and this growing suspicion served as a catalyst for the disintegration of the party and the development of a new party system.

Among the most important policy positions that defined the Whig Party was the area of economic development, in which Whig policies were most distinct from the rival Democrats. The American System was an economic development program that became the cornerstone of the Whig Party platform in the 19th century. Actuated by Henry Clay of Kentucky, the American System had three essential components: federal aid for internal improvements, a protective tariff for industry, and a national bank. The Whig Party political legacy is reflected by the incorporation of the

An 1848 campaign banner for Whig candidate Zachary Taylor *(Library of Congress)*

core elements of the American System by both the Republicans and the Democrats and in the bipartisan consensus that the Whig economic development paradigm enjoys today.

Further reading: Bauer, K. Jack. *Zachary Taylor: Soldier, Planter, Statesman of the Old Southwest.* Baton Rouge: Louisiana State University Press, 1985; Burnham, Walter Dean. *Presidential Ballots 1836–1892.* Baltimore: Johns Hopkins University Press, 1955; Howe, Daniel Walker. *The Political Culture of the American Whigs.* Chicago: University of Chicago Press, 1979; Rosenstone, Steven J., Roy L. Behr, and Edward H. Lazarus. *Third Parties in America.* Princeton, N.J.: Princeton University Press, 1996.

—Michael W. Hail

white primary

The white primary was used primarily in the South by the DEMOCRATIC PARTY at the turn of the 20th century to bar African Americans from participating in the selection of party candidates to run in local, state, and national GENERAL ELECTIONS. In the heavily Democratic South, this practice effectively disenfranchised southern blacks.

The racially exclusive PRIMARY was a reaction by whites to the political gains realized during the RECONSTRUCTION era by southern African Americans, who won election to local, state, and federal offices after being granted the franchise by the FIFTEENTH AMENDMENT to the Constitution. Because most African Americans were elected to office from the REPUBLICAN PARTY, the party of Lincoln, whites began to flock to the Democratic Party in the early 1900s to consolidate their electoral strength. As a result, the almost all-white Democratic Party came to dominate southern POLITICS by the beginning of the 20th century.

With the rise of the Democratic Party in the South, general elections were virtually meaningless. The Democratic Party primary emerged as the most important election, and African Americans sought to participate in the primary to have a voice in choosing their elected officials. White southerners responded to black attempts to vote in the Democratic primary by barring black voters, claiming that the Democratic Party was a private organization. Party officials contended that because the Democrats were a private group, they could exclude whoever they chose from participating in the internal business of the organization. By the party's reasoning, the primary was an internal, and therefore private, function of the organization.

Challenges to the white primary abounded. The NATIONAL ASSOCIATION FOR THE ADVANCEMENT OF COLORED PEOPLE (NAACP) brought several cases, many of which reached the Supreme Court, that questioned the constitutionality of restricting access to the candidate selection process. Some of the most significant matters in this line of white primary cases originated in Texas. Among the first was *Nixon v. Herndon,* in which the Supreme Court ruled unanimously in 1927 that the Texas law barring blacks from voting in the Democratic primary violated the Equal Protection Clause of the FOURTEENTH AMENDMENT. In response to the Court's decision, the Texas legislature redrafted the original white primary statute in an attempt to preserve its discriminatory intent. When the new legislation was challenged in 1932, the Court determined, in *Nixon v. Condon,* that the redrafted Texas law, which granted authority to the Democratic Party executive committee to exclude blacks, violated the Fourteenth Amendment because the executive committee required party consent to take such action.

In response to the *Herndon* decision, the Texas Democratic Party voted as a body to maintain the white primary. A 1935 challenge to the decision was denied by the Supreme Court in *Grovey v. Townsend,* in which the Court held that a private organization such as the Democratic Party had a right to determine eligibility for membership within the group. A reconstituted World War II–era Court overturned the *Grovey* decision in 1944 in *SMITH V. ALLWRIGHT.* In *Smith,* the Court found the primary process to be a critical step in the eventual election of candidates to public office.

Because of this, any attempts to prevent African Americans from participating in the selection process—whether by party leadership or rank-and-file members—were unconstitutional. Although white primaries remained in other states in the South, the Texas cases served as the beginning of the end of this discriminatory voting practice.

Further reading: Hine, Diane Clark. *Black Victory: The Rise and Fall of the White Primary in Texas.* Columbia: University of Missouri Press, 2003; Klarman, Michael J. "The White Primary Rulings: A Case Study in the Consequences of Supreme Court Decisionmaking." *Florida State University Law Review* 29 (2001): 55–107.

—John L. S. Simpkins

Y

Yellow Dog Democrat

Yellow Dog Democrat is a term used to describe someone who is fiercely loyal to the DEMOCRATIC PARTY. In its common usage, this breed of Democrat professes to vote Democratic as opposed to Republican even if a yellow dog were the Democratic Party's nominee. In other words, a Yellow Dog Democrat is faithful to the party no matter how unattractive the Democratic Party's candidate is versus a candidate of another party.

The origins of the term date back to the 1928 PRESIDENTIAL ELECTION. Alabama senator Tom Heflin, a Democrat, chose to support Republican presidential candidate Herbert Hoover over the Democratic candidate, New York governor Al Smith. Given the fact that he was a Catholic and a Yankee, it is not surprising that Al Smith appeared to be a hard sell in a Deep South state such as Alabama. Nonetheless, Alabama was a Democratic bastion, and the Democratic Party was essentially the only party in the South since the end of RECONSTRUCTION. Particularly in the Deep South states of Alabama, Georgia, Louisiana, Mississippi, and South Carolina, the Democratic Party served as a defender of white dominance. Prior to the passage of the Voting Rights Act in 1965, hardly any African Americans in the Deep South states were eligible to vote. And so, despite his religious profile and northern stock, white Alabamians backed Al Smith in 1928, declaring they would even "vote for a yellow dog if he ran on the Democratic ticket!"

The rise of the REPUBLICAN PARTY in southern POLITICS has placed Yellow Dog Democrats on the list of endangered species. In today's South, most whites identify with the Republican Party and vote Republican in high-profile elections such as for president, U.S. Senate, and U.S. House. Furthermore, younger generations of white southerners are very supportive of Republicans.

The historical origins of the term *Yellow Dog Democrat* are clearly southern and connote a racial distinction. However, casting aside the heritage of the term, the most loyal Democrats today are African Americans. Southern whites have found a new home in the Republican Party, and southern blacks, like northern blacks, are overwhelmingly Democratic. Therefore, in contemporary American politics, African Americans are the most qualified to claim the label Yellow Dog Democrats.

Further reading: Black, Earl, and Merle Black. *The Rise of Southern Republicans*. Cambridge, Mass.: Harvard University Press, 2002; Key, V. O., Jr. *Southern Politics in State and Nation*. Knoxville: University of Tennessee Press, 1949; Phillips, Kevin P. *The Emerging Republican Majority*. New Rochelle, N.Y.: Arlington House, 1969.

—Seth C. McKee

Young Democrats of America

Young Democrats of America (YDA) is the official youth arm of the DEMOCRATIC PARTY. The organization encourages individuals under 36 years of age to join and become active members of the Democratic Party. YDA members participate in electoral activity, lobbying, skill development, training, and social networking intended to further Democratic Party growth and success. The group's membership is comprised primarily of students at the high school and college levels and young workers and professionals. YDA members take part in federal, state, and local electoral contests and offer logistical support by providing campaign assistance and youthful enthusiasm.

The YDA traces its roots to the 1932 establishment of the Young Democratic Clubs of America (YDCA). Several such Democratic state youth clubs had existed for some time, but no national organization existed prior to the YDCA's founding. The group's name was later shortened to its current moniker. The YDA is institutionally structured similarly to the DEMOCRATIC NATIONAL COMMITTEE (DNC), with the national organization coordinating the actions of state-level clubs and their lower-level units. Also like the DNC, the YDA has an elected leadership structure and maintains a platform agreed upon at its conventions. Conventions are held biennially in odd years, as they have been since 1933.

These events are attended by YDA members from across the United States who debate party issues and select leaders. In addition, eight geographic regions are designated by the YDA, each made up of several states. These regional bodies also hold biennial conventions to discuss issues of particular interest to the member states. The YDA is headquartered in Washington, D.C., as it has been since its inception.

As of 2004, the YDA had chartered state organizations in 42 states, with nearly 800 local chapters and more than 43,000 official members. Aside from providing support for Democratic Party candidates, many members and alumni of YDA run for office themselves, while others become staffers or political operatives. The success of YDA in recruiting and mobilizing members is an aid to the Democratic Party, as it provides GRASSROOTS support and offers an entry point for young adults who aspire to become involved in party activities. The YDA remains an important organization within the Democratic Party fold, serving as a vehicle for recruitment and encouragement of both dedicated partisans and the party's future leaders and elected officials.

Further reading: Kim, Jee, et al. *Future 500: Youth Organizing and Activism in the United States.* Atlanta: New Mouth from the Dirty South, 2002; Witcover, Jules. *Party of the People: A History of the Democrats.* New York: Random House, 2003; Young Democrats of America. Available online. URL: http://www.yda.org. Accessed August 10, 2005.

—Richard L. Vining, Jr.

Young Republican Club

Young Republican Clubs are official youth organizations of the REPUBLICAN PARTY. These organizations encourage individuals from 18 to 40 years of age to join and become active members of the Republican Party. For those under age 18, there is also a National Teen Age Republicans organization that welcomes their membership. Young Republican Club members participate in electoral POLITICS, lobbying, skill development, and social networking intended to involve young Republicans in the political process and encourage interest in the party. The group's membership is comprised primarily of college students and young professionals. Young Republican Club members take part in federal, state, and local electoral contests by acting as volunteers and staffers for Republican candidates.

The earliest founding of a local Young Republican Club took place in New York City in 1911. The Young Republican National Federation (YRNF) was later founded in 1931 and is the oldest and largest youth political organization in the United States. Young Republican Clubs are established at the local and state levels, with the national-level YRNF overseeing the various lower-level organizations. The YRNF is institutionally structured similarly to the REPUBLICAN NATIONAL COMMITTEE (RNC), with which it is affiliated. Like the RNC, the YRNF has an elected leadership structure and standing committees and maintains a platform agreed upon at its conventions.

Young Republican Club members from across the United States attend national conventions to debate party issues and select party leaders. These conventions are held biennially in odd years, as they have been since 1947. In addition, six geographic regions of several states are designated by the YRNF, with each having a regional council responsible for activities within it. The YRNF is headquartered in Washington, D.C.

As of 2004, there were chartered Young Republican Clubs in 48 states with tens of thousands of members nationwide. Aside from providing support for Republican Party candidates, many members and alumni of Young Republican Clubs pursue careers as elected officials, staffers, and political operatives. The ability of Young Republican Clubs to recruit and mobilize members provides GRASSROOTS support for the Republican Party and offers an entry point for young adults to become involved in party activities. Young Republican Clubs remain important organizations for the Republican Party as a means of recruiting and fostering dedicated partisans and the party's future leaders and elected officials.

Further reading: Kim, Jee, et al. *Future 500: Youth Organizing and Activism in the United States.* Atlanta: New Mouth from the Dirty South, 2002; Young Republicans. Available online. URL: http://www.youngrepublicans.com. Accessed August 10, 2005.

—Richard L. Vining, Jr.

Z

Zapple Doctrine

The Zapple Doctrine is a FEDERAL COMMUNICATIONS COMISSION (FCC) policy that requires broadcasters to give supporters of a political candidate equal airtime if supporters of the opposing candidate are given time on their station. On May 6, 1970, Nicholas Zapple, a U.S. Senate communications counsel, opened debate when he asked the FCC in a letter: Should broadcast stations give equal airtime to supporters of a political candidate if supporters of the opposing candidate used spots in which their candidate did not appear? The FCC responded by stating that all parties should receive equal airtime. The FCC based its decision on the FAIRNESS DOCTRINE, a long-standing policy that encourages broadcasters to present contrasting viewpoints to the American public.

The Zapple Doctrine has come under attack in recent years. Opponents of the doctrine have pointed out that it is a violation of the First Amendment. Others have argued that, due to the many news outlets available today, it is impossible for the public to be exposed to only one political viewpoint and thus the FCC should discard the Zapple Doctrine. Even after the fairness doctrine became defunct in 1987, FCC commissioners insisted that the doctrine was necessary to ensure that broadcasters continued to present contrasting viewpoints. Nonetheless, the Zapple Doctrine holds little weight. In the past 30 years, the FCC has refused to enforce it.

Further reading: Brinson, Susan L. *Personal and Public Interests: Frieda B. Hennock and the Federal Communications Commission.* Westport, Conn.: Praeger, 2002; Einstein, Mara. *Media Diversity: Economics, Ownership, and the FCC.* Mahwah, N.J.: L. Erlbaum Associates, 2004; Parker, Richard A. *Free Speech on Trial: Communication Perspectives on Landmark Supreme Court Decisions.* Tuscaloosa: University of Alabama Press, 2003.

—Bruce E. Stewart

Bibliography

Abbott, David W. *Wrong Winner: The Coming Debacle in the Electoral College.* New York: Praeger, 1991.

Abraham, Henry J. *The Judiciary.* 8th ed. Dubuque, Iowa: Wm. C. Brown, 1987.

Abramowitz, Alan I., and Jeffrey A. Segal. "Determinants of the Outcomes of U.S. Senate Elections." *Journal of Politics* 48 (1986): 433–439.

———. *Senate Elections.* Ann Arbor: University of Michigan Press, 1992.

Abramson, Paul R., John H. Aldrich, and David W. Rohde. *Change and Continuity in the 1984 Elections.* Washington, D.C.: CQ Press, 1986.

———. *Change and Continuity in the 2000 Elections.* Washington, D.C.: CQ Press, 2002.

———. *Change and Continuity in the 1996 Elections.* Washington, D.C.: CQ Press, 1998.

Ackerman, Bruce. *The Case against Lameduck Impeachment.* New York: Seven Stories Press, 1999.

Ackerman, Bruce, and James S. Fishkin. *Deliberation Day.* New Haven, Conn.: Yale University Press, 2004.

Ackerman, Kenneth A. *Dark Horse: The Surprise Election and Political Murder of James A. Garfield.* Washington, D.C.: Free Press, 2003.

Adams, Greg D. "Legislative Effects of Single-Member vs. Multi-Member Districts." *American Journal of Political Science* 40, no. 1 (1996): 129–144.

Adams, Willi Paul. *The First American Constitutions.* Lanham, Md.: Rowman & Littlefield, 2001.

Ader, Emile B. "Why the Dixiecrats Failed." *Journal of Politics* 5, no. 3 (1953): 356–369.

AFL-CIO. Available online. URL: http://www.aflcio.org. Accessed August 10, 2005.

Agresti, Alan, and Barbara Finlay. *Statistical Methods for the Social Sciences.* 3rd ed. Upper Saddle River, N.J.: Prentice Hall, 1997.

Aistrup, Joseph A. *The Southern Strategy Revisited: Republican Top-Down Advancement in the South.* Lexington: University Press of Kentucky, 1996.

Aldrich, John. *Why Parties? The Origins and Transformation of Political Parties in America.* Chicago: University of Chicago Press, 1995.

Alexander, Herbert. *Financing Politics: Money, Elections, and Political Reform.* Washington, D.C.: Congressional Quarterly Press, 1984.

Alexander, Herbert E., and Anthony Corrado. *Financing the 1992 Election.* Armonk, N.Y.: M.E. Sharpe, 1995.

Allen, Craig. *Eisenhower and the Mass Media: Peace, Prosperity, and Prime-Time TV.* Chapel Hill: University of North Carolina Press, 1993.

Allen, W. B., and Gordon Lloyd, eds. *The Essential Anti-Federalist.* Lanham, Md.: Rowman & Littlefield, 2002.

Alterman, Eric. *Sound and Fury: The Making of the Punditocracy.* Rev. ed. New Ithaca, N.Y.: Cornell University Press, 2000.

Ambrose, Stephen E. *Nixon: The Triumph of a Politician.* New York: Simon & Schuster, 1987.

———. *Eisenhower: The President.* New York: Simon & Schuster, 1984.

Ambrosius, Lloyd E. *Wilsonianism: Woodrow Wilson and His Legacy in American Foreign Relations.* New York: Palgrave Macmillan, 2002.

———. *Wilsonian Statecraft: Theory and Practice of Liberal Internationalism during World War I.* Wilmington, Del.: SR Books, 1991.

American Association of Retired Persons. Available online. URL: http://www.aarp.org. Accessed August 5, 2005.

American Independent Party. Available online. URL: http://www.aipca.org. Accessed August 5, 2005.

American Museum of the Moving Image. Available online. URL: http://livingroomcandidate.movingimage.us. Accessed August 5, 2005.

Ammon, Harry. *James Monroe: The Quest for National Identity.* New York: McGraw-Hill, 1971.

Amy, Douglas James. *Behind the Ballot Box: A Citizen's Guide to Voting Systems.* Westport, Conn.: Greenwood Press, 2000.

Anastaplo, John. *The Amendments to the Constitution: A Commentary.* Baltimore: Johns Hopkins University Press, 1995.

Anbinder, Tyler. *Nativism and Slavery.* New York: Oxford University Press, 1992.

Andersen, Kristi. *After Suffrage: Women in Partisan and Electoral Politics before the New Deal.* Chicago: University of Chicago Press, 1996.

Anderson, Annelise. *Political Money: Deregulating American Politics: Selected Writings on Campaign Finance Reform.* Stanford, Calif.: Hoover Institution Press, 2000.

Anderson, David M., and Michael Cornfield, eds. *The Civic Web: Online Politics and Democratic Values.* Lanham, Md.: Rowman & Littlefield, 2003.

Anderson, Donald. F. *William Howard Taft: A Conservative's Conception of the Presidency.* Ithaca, N.Y.: Cornell University Press, 1973.

Anderson, Kristi. *Creation of a Democratic Majority, 1928–1936.* Chicago: University of Chicago Press, 1979.

Anderson, Margo J. *The American Census: A Social History.* New Haven, Conn.: Yale University Press, 1988.

Anderson, Margo, and Stephen E. Fienberg. "History, Myth Making, and Statistics: A Short Story about the Reapportionment of Congress and the 1990 Census." *PS: Political Science and Politics* 33, no. 4 (2000): 783–792.

Anderson, Patrick. *Electing Jimmy Carter: The Campaign of 1976.* Baton Rouge: Louisiana State University Press, 1994.

Andreasen, Alan R. *Marketing Research That Won't Break the Bank: A Practical Guide to Getting the Information You Need.* 2nd ed. Hoboken, N.J.: Jossey-Bass, 2002.

Andryszewski, Tricia. *The Reform Party: Ross Perot and Pat Buchanan.* Brookfield, Conn.: Millbrook Press, 2001.

Angel, William D., Jr. *Not All Politics Is Local: Reflections of a Former County Chairman.* Kent, Ohio: Kent State University Press, 2002.

Ansolabehere, Stephen, et al. "Does Attack Advertising Demobilize the Electorate?" *American Political Science Review* 88 (1994): 829–838.

Ansolabehere, Stephen, and Shanto Iyengar. *Going Negative: How Attack Ads Shrink and Polarize the Electorate.* New York: Free Press, 1995.

Ansolabehere, Stephen, Roy Behr, and Shanto Iyengar. *The Media Game: American Politics in the Television Age.* New York: Macmillan, 1993.

Ansolabehere, Stephen, Alan Gerber, and Jim Snyder. "Equal Votes, Equal Money: Court-Ordered Redistricting and Public Expenditures in the American States." *American Political Science Review* 96 (2002): 767–777.

Argersinger, Peter H. *Populism, Its Rise and Fall.* Lawrence: University Press of Kansas, 1992.

Arnold, R. Douglas. *The Logic of Congressional Action.* New Haven, Conn.: Yale University Press, 1992.

Arrington, Karen McGill, and William L. Taylor, eds. *Voting Rights in America: Continuing the Quest for Full Participation.* Lanham, Md.: University Press of America, 1992.

Ashby, LeRoy. *William Jennings Bryan: Champion of Democracy.* Boston: Twayne Publishers, 1987.

Asher, Herbert. *Polling and the Public: What Every Citizen Should Know.* 6th ed. Washington, D.C.: CQ Press, 2004.

Baer, Kenneth S. *Reinventing Democrats: The Politics of Liberalism from Reagan to Clinton.* Lawrence: University of Kansas Press, 2000.

Bailey, Michael A., Ronald A. Faucheux, Paul S. Herrnson, and Clyde Wilcox. *Campaigns and Elections: Contemporary Case Studies.* Washington, D.C.: CQ Press, 2000.

Bailey, Richard. *Neither Carpetbaggers nor Scalawags: Black Officeholders during the Reconstruction of Alabama, 1867–1878.* Montgomery, Ala.: Pyramid Publishers, 1997.

Baker, Jean H., ed. *Votes for Women: The Struggle for Suffrage Revisited.* New York: Oxford University Press, 2002.

Baker, Lucius J., Mack H. Jones, and Katherine Tate. *African-Americans and the American Political System.* 4th ed. Upper Saddle River, N.J.: Prentice Hall, 1999.

Baker, Richard A., and Roger H. Davidson, eds. *First among Equals: Outstanding Senate Leaders of the Twentieth Century.* Washington, D.C.: Congressional Quarterly Press, 1991.

Banks, Christopher P., and John C. Green, ed. *Superintending Democracy: The Courts and the Political Process.* Akron, Ohio: University of Akron Press, 2001.

Banner, James M. *To the Hartford Convention: The Federalists and the Origins of Party Politics in Massachusetts, 1789–1815.* New York: Knopf, 1970.

Bardes, Barbara, and Robert Oldendick. *Public Opinion: Measuring the American Mind.* Belmont, Calif.: Thomson/Wadsworth, 2003.

Barker, Lucius Jefferson, Mack Jones, and Katherine Tate. *African Americans and the American Political System.* Upper Saddle River, N.J.: Prentice Hall, 1998.

Barr, Alwyn. *Reconstruction to Reform: Texas Politics, 1876–1906.* Austin: University of Texas Press, 1971.

Barrilleaux, Charles. "Party Strength, Party Change, and Policy Making in the American States." *Party Politics* 6, no. 1 (2000): 61–73.

Barrilleaux, Charles, Thomas Holbrook, and Laura Langer. "Electoral Competition, Legislative Balance, and American State Welfare Policy." *American Journal of Political Science* 46 (2002): 415–427.

Bartels, Larry M. *Presidential Primaries and the Dynamics of Public Choice.* Princeton, N.J.: Princeton University Press, 1988.

Basu, Kaushik. *Prelude to Political Economy: A Study of the Social and Political Foundations of Economics.* Oxford: Oxford University Press, 2000.

Bauer, K. Jack. *Zachary Taylor: Soldier, Planter, Statesman of the Old Southwest.* Baton Rouge: Louisiana State University Press, 1985.

Bauer, Robert. *More Soft Money Hard Law.* New York: Perkins Coie, 2003.

Baum, Lawrence. "Electing Judges." In Lee Epstein, ed., *Contemplating Courts.* Washington, D.C.: CQ Press, 1995.

Beck, Paul Allen. "The Dealignment Era in America." In Russell J. Dalton, Scott C. Flanagan, and Paul Allen Beck, eds., *Electoral Change in Advanced Industrial Democracies: Realignment or Dealignment?* Princeton, N.J.: Princeton University Press, 1984.

Behr, Joshua. *Race, Ethnicity, and the Politics of City Redistricting: Minority Opportunity Districts and the Election of Hispanics and Blacks to City Councils.* New York: State University of New York Press, 2004.

Bennett, David. *Demagogues in the Depression: American Radicals and the Union Party, 1932–1936.* New Brunswick, N.J.: Rutgers University Press, 1969.

Bennett, Larone. *Before the Mayflower: A History of Black America.* New York: Penguin, 2003.

Bensel, Richard Franklin. *Sectionalism and American Political Development, 1880–1980.* Madison: University of Wisconsin Press, 1984.

———. *The Political Economy of American Industrialization, 1877–1900.* Cambridge: Cambridge University Press, 2000.

Benson, Lee. *The Concept of Jacksonian Democracy: New York as a Test Case.* Princeton, N.J.: Princeton University Press, 1961.

Berard, Stanley P. *Southern Democrats in the U.S. House of Representatives.* Norman: University of Oklahoma Press, 2001.

Berger, Raul. *The Fourteenth Amendment and the Bill of Rights.* Norman: University of Oklahoma Press, 1989.

Bergerson, Paul H. *The Presidency of James K. Polk.* Lawrence: University Press of Kansas, 1987.

Berkin, Carol. *A Brilliant Solution: Inventing the American Constitution.* New York: Harcourt, 2002.

Bernhard, Virginia, and Elizabeth Fox-Genovese, eds. *The Birth of American Feminism: The Seneca Falls Woman's Convention of 1848.* St. James, N.Y.: Brandywine Press, 1995.

Beschloss, Michael. *American Heritage Illustrated History of the Presidents.* New York: Crown Publishers, 2000.

Besen, Stanley, M., et al. *Misregulating Television: Network Dominance and the FCC.* Chicago: University of Chicago Press, 1984.

Best, Judith. *National Representation for the District of Columbia.* Frederick, Md.: University Publications of America, 1984.

Beyle, Thad. *State and Local Government 2004–2005.* Washington, D.C.: CQ Press, 2004.

Bibby, John F. *Political Parties and Elections in America.* 5th ed. New York: Wadsworth Press, 2002.

Biersack, Robert, Paul S. Herrnson, and Clyde Wilcox. *After the Revolution: PACs, Lobbies, and the Republican Congress.* Boston: Allyn & Bacon, 1999.

Biles, Roger. *Richard J. Daley: Politics, Race and the Governing of Chicago.* DeKalb: Northern Illinois University Press, 1995.

Billington, Ray A. *The Origins of Nativism in the United States, 1800–1844.* New York: Arno Press, 1974.

Bimber, Bruce, and Richard Davis. *Campaigning Online: The Internet in U.S. Elections.* New York: Oxford University Press, 2003.

Birnbaum, Jeffrey H. *The Lobbyists: How Influence Peddlers Work Their Way in Washington.* New York: Times Books, 1992.

Bisitis, David. *The Congressional Black Caucus in the 103rd Congress.* Lanham, Md.: Rowman & Littlefield, 1994.

Bisnow, Mark. *Diary of a Dark Horse: The 1980 Anderson Presidential Campaign.* Carbondale: Southern Illinois University Press, 1983.

Black, Charles L., Jr. *Impeachment: A Handbook.* New Haven, Conn.: Yale University Press, 1998.

Black, Earl, and Merle Black. *The Rise of Southern Republicans.* Cambridge, Mass.: Harvard University Press, 2002.

———. *The Vital South: How Presidents Are Elected.* Cambridge, Mass.: Harvard University Press, 1992.

———. *Politics and Society in the South.* Cambridge, Mass.: Harvard University Press, 1987.

———. *The Rise of Southern Republicans.* Cambridge, Mass.: Harvard University Press, 2002.

Black, Naomi. *Social Feminism.* Ithaca, N.Y.: Cornell University Press, 1989.

Blahous, Charles P., III. *Reforming Social Security for Ourselves and our Posterity.* Westport, Conn.: Praeger, 2000.

Block, Herbert. *Political Cartoons from the Crash to the Millennium: Herblock's History.* Washington, D.C.: Library of Congress, 2000.

Bloom, Allan, ed. *Confronting the Constitution.* Washington, D.C.: AEI Press, 1990.

Blue, Frederick J. *The Free Soilers.* Urbana: University of Illinois Press, 1973.

Blue Dog Democrats. Available online. URL: http://www.bluedogdemocrats.com. Accessed August 5, 2005.

Blum, John M. *The Republican Roosevelt.* New York: Atheneum, 1967.

Bolce, Louis, Gerald De Maio, and Douglas Muzzio. "Dial-In Democracy: Talk Radio and the 1994 Election." *Political Science Quarterly* 111, no. 3 (1996): 457–481.

Boller, Paul F. *Presidential Campaigns.* New York: Oxford University Press, 1996.

Bone, Hugh A. *Party Committees and National Politics.* Seattle: University of Washington Press, 1958.

Bowler, Shaun, Todd Donovan, and Caroline J. Tolbert, eds. *Citizens as Legislators: Direct Democracy in the United States.* Columbus: Ohio State University Press, 1998.

Bowman, Ann O'M., and Richard C. Kearney. *State and Local Government.* 4th ed. Boston: Houghton Mifflin, 1999.

Bradford, M. E. *Original Intentions: On The Making and Ratification of the United States Constitution.* Athens: University of Georgia Press, 1993.

Brady, David W. *Critical Elections and Congressional Policy Making.* Stanford, Calif.: Stanford University Press, 1988.

Brady, John. *Bad Boy: The Life and Politics of Lee Atwater.* Reading, Mass.: Addison-Wesley, 1997.

Brams, Steven J., and Morton D. Davis. "The 3/2's Rule in Presidential Campaigning." *American Political Science Review* 68 (1974): 113–134.

Branch, Taylor. *Parting the Waters: America in the King Years, 1954–63.* New York: Simon & Schuster, 1988.

———. *Pillar of Fire: America in the King Years, 1963–65.* New York: Simon & Schuster, 1998.

Brewer, Cynthia A. *Mapping Census 2000: The Geography of U.S. Diversity.* Washington, D.C.: U.S. Dept. of Commerce, Economics and Statistics Administration, U.S. Census Bureau, 2001.

Brinkerhoff, Derick W., and Arthur A. Goldsmith. "Good Governance, Clientelism and Patrimonialism: New Perspectives on Old Problems." *International Public Management Journal* 7, no. 2 (2002): 163–185.

Brinkley, Alan. *Voices of Protest: Huey Long, Father Coughlin, and the Great Depression.* New York: Knopf, 1982.

Brinson, Susan L. *Personal and Public Interests: Frieda B. Hennock and the Federal Communications Commission.* Westport, Conn.: Praeger, 2000.

Brockington, David, Todd Donovan, Shaun Bowler, and Robert Brischetto. "Minority Representation under Cumulative and Limited Voting." *Journal of Politics* 60 (1998): 1,108–1,125.

Broder, David S. *Democracy Derailed: Initiative Campaigns and the Power of Money.* New York: Harcourt, 2000.

Brodsky, Alyn. *Grover Cleveland: A Study in Character.* New York: St. Martin's Press, 2000.

Brooks, Charles. *Best Editorial Cartoons of the Year.* Gretna, La.: Pelican Publishing Company, 2004.

Brooks, Clem, and David Brady. "Income, Economic Voting, and Long-Term Political Change in the U.S., 1952–1996." *Social Forces* 77, no. 4 (1999): 1,339.

Brooks, David. "One Nation, Slightly Divisible." *Atlantic Monthly* 288, no. 5 (2001): 53–65.

Brown, Clifford Waters, Lynda W. Powell, and Clyde Wilcox. *Serious Money: Fund=raising and Contributing in Presidential Nomination Campaigns.* Cambridge: Cambridge University Press, 1995.

Brown, Ralph Adams. *The Presidency of John Adams,* Lawrence: University of Kansas Press, 1975.

Bryant, Irving. *James Madison: Secretary of State, 1800–1809.* Indianapolis: Bobbs-Merrill, 1953.

Buckley, William F. *Up From Liberalism.* New York: Stein & Day, 1984

Buel, Richard, Jr. *Securing the Revolution: Ideology in American Politics, 1789–1815.* Ithaca, N.Y.: Cornell University Press, 1972.

Buell, Emmett H., Jr. "The Changing Face of the New Hampshire Primary." In William G. Mayer, ed., *In Pursuit of the White House 2000: How We Choose Our Presidential Nominees.* Chatham, N.J.: Chatham House, 2000.

Burden, Barry C., and David C. Kimball. *Why Americans Split Their Tickets: Campaigns, Competition, and Divided Government.* Ann Arbor: University of Michigan Press, 2002.

Burnett, Ken. *Relationship Fund=raising: A Donor Based Approach to the Business of Raising Money.* New York: Jossey-Bass, 2002.

Burnham, Walter Dean. *Presidential Ballots 1836–1892.* Baltimore: Johns Hopkins University Press, 1955.

Burns, James MacGregor. *Roosevelt: The Soldier of Freedom.* New York: Harcourt Brace Jovanovich, 1970.

Burrell, Barbara C. *A Woman's Place Is in the House: Campaigning for Congress in the Feminist Era.* Ann Arbor: University of Michigan Press, 1994.

Burton, Michael John, and Daniel M. Shea. *Campaign Mode: Strategic Vision in Congressional Elections.* Lanham, Md.: Rowman & Littlefield, 2003.

Busch, Andrew. *Outsiders and Openness in the Presidential Nominating System.* Pittsburgh: University of Pittsburgh Press, 1997.

Butler, David, and Bruce Cain. *Congressional Redistricting: Comparative and Theoretical Perspectives.* New York: Macmillan, 1992.

Cain, Bruce E. *The Reapportionment Puzzle.* Berkeley: University of California Press, 1984.

Cain, Bruce, and David Butler. *Congressional Redistricting: Comparative and Theoretical Perspectives.* New York: Macmillan, 1992.

Cain, Bruce E., and Elisabeth Gerber. *Voting at the Political Fault Line: California's Experiment with the Blanket Primary.* Berkeley: University of California Press, 2002.

Campaign Finance Institute. *Participation, Competition, and Engagement: How to Revive and Improve Public Funding for Presidential Nomination Politics.* Washington, D.C.: Campaign Finance Institute, 2004.

Campaigns & Elections Magazine. Available online. URL: http://www.campaignline.com. Accessed August 5, 2005.

Campbell, Andrea Louise. *How Policies Make Citizens: Senior Political Activism and the American Welfare State.* Princeton, N.J.: Princeton University Press, 2003.

Campbell, Angus. "Surge and Decline: A Study of Electoral Change." In Angus Campbell, Philip E. Converse, Warren E. Miller, and Donald E. Stokes, eds., *Elections and the Political Order.* New York: Wiley, 1966.

Campbell, Angus, Philip E. Converse, Warren E. Miller, and Donald E. Stokes. *The American Voter.* New York: Wiley, 1960.

Campbell, James E. "Explaining Presidential Losses in Midterm Congressional Elections." *Journal of Politics* 47 (1995): 1,140–1,157.

———. *The Presidential Pulse of Congressional Elections.* 2nd ed. Lexington: University Press of Kentucky, 1997.

Cannon, Lou. *President Reagan: The Role of a Lifetime.* New York: Public Affairs, 2000.

Canon, David T. *Race, Redistricting, and Representation: The Unintended Consequences of Black Majority Districts.* Chicago: University of Chicago Press, 1999.

Carey, John M., Richard G. Niemi, and Lynda W. Powell. *Term Limits in State Legislatures.* Chicago: University of Chicago Press, 2000.

Carlson, Jody. *George C. Wallace and the Politics of Powerlessness: The Wallace Campaigns for the Presidency, 1964–1976.* New Brunswick, N.J.: Transaction Books, 1981.

Carmines, Edward G., and James A. Stimson. *Issue Evolution: Race and the Transformation of American Politics.* Princeton, N.J.: Princeton University Press, 1989.

Carp, Robert A. *Judicial Process in America.* Washington, D.C.: CQ Press, 2004.

Carter, Stephen. *Integrity.* New York: HarperCollins, 1996.

Carter, T. Barton, Marc A. Franklin, and Jay B. Wright. *The First Amendment and the Fourth Estate: The Law of Mass Media.* 8th ed. New York: Foundation Press, 2001.

Carwardine, Richard J. *Lincoln.* Essex, U.K.: Pearson-Longman, 2002.

Cayer, N. Joseph. *Public Personnel Administration.* 4th ed. Belmont, Calif.: Wadsworth, 2004.

Ceasar, James W. *Presidential Selection: Theory and Development.* Princeton, N.J.: Princeton University Press, 1979.

Ceaser, James W., and Andrew E. Busch. *Losing to Win: The 1996 Elections and American Politics.* Lanham, Md.: Rowman & Littlefield, 1997.

———. *The Perfect Tie.* Lanham, Md.: Rowman & Littlefield, 2001.

Center for Information and Research on Civic Learning and Engagement at the University of Maryland School of Public Affairs. Available online. URL: http://www.civicyouth.org. Accessed August 5, 2005.

Center for Responsive Politics. Available online. URL: http://www.opensecrets.org. Accessed August 5, 2005.

Champagne, Anthony. "Political Parties and Judicial Elections." *Loyola of Los Angeles Law Review* 34 (2001): 1,411–1,427.

Chase, James S. *The Emergence of the Presidential Nominating Convention, 1789–1832.* Urbana: University of Illinois Press, 1973.

Chester, Eric Thomas. *True Mission: Socialists and the Labor Party Question in the U.S.* Sterling, Va.: Pluto Press, 2004.

Chester, Lewis, Godfrey Hodgson, and Bruce Page. *An American Melodrama: The Presidential Campaign of 1968.* New York: Viking, 1969.

Chiagouris, Larry, and Lynn R. Kahle. *Values, Lifestyle and Psychographics.* Mahwah, N.J.: Lawrence Erlbaum Associates, 1997.

Christian Coalition. Available online. URL: http://www.cc.org. Accessed August 5, 2005.

Cigler, Allan J., and Burdett A. Loomis. *Interest Group Politics.* 6th ed. Washington, D.C.: CQ Press, 2002.

Clanton, Gene. *Populism: The Human Preference in America, 1890–1900.* Boston: Twayne Publishers, 1991.

Clawson, Don. *Money Talks: Corporate PACs and Political Influence.* New York: Basic Books, 1992.

Clayborne, Carson, et al. *The Eyes on the Prize Civil Rights Reader.* New York: Penguin, 1991.

Cleaves, Freeman. *Old Tippecanoe: William Henry Harrison and His Times.* New York: Scribner's Sons, 1939.

Cogliano, Francis D. *Revolutionary America, 1763–1815: A Political History.* New York: Routledge, 1999.

Cohen, Lee M. *Justice across Generations: What Does It Mean?* Washington, D.C.: Public Policy Institute, American Association of Retired Persons, 1993.

Cohen, Warren I. *Empire without Tears: America's Foreign Relations, 1921–1933.* New York: McGraw Hill, 1987.

Colantoni, Claude S., Terence Levesque, and Peter C. Ordershook. "Campaign Resources under the Electoral College." *American Political Science Review* 69 (1975): 141–154.

Cole, Donald B. *The Presidency of Andrew Jackson.* Lawrence: University of Kansas Press, 1993.

Coleman, Kevin J. "The Uniformed and Overseas Citizens Absentee Voting Act: Background and Issues." *Congressional Research Service Report for the Congress,* January 30, 2003. Order Code RS20764; Federal Voting Assistance Program. Available online. URL: http://www.fvap.gov. Accessed August 10, 2005.

Coletta, Paolo E. *William Jennings Bryan: Political Evangelist 1860–1908.* Lincoln: University of Nebraska Press, 1964.

Collier, Christopher. *All Politics Is Local: Family, Friends, and Provincial Interests in the Creation of the Constitution.* Hanover, N.H.: University Press of New England, 2003.

———. *Decision at Philadelphia: The Constitutional Convention of 1787.* New York: Ballantine Books, 1987.

Combs, Jerald A. *The History of American Foreign Policy,* Volume II: *Since 1900.* 2nd ed. New York: McGraw-Hill, 1997.

Commission on Presidential Debates. Available online. URL: http://www.debates.org. Accessed August 10, 2005.

Common Cause. Available online. URL: http://www.common cause.org. Accessed August 10, 2005.

Commoner, Barry. *The Politics of Energy.* New York: Knopf, 1979.

Communist Party of the United States. Available online. URL: http://www.cpusa.org. Accessed August 10, 2005.

Congressional Black Caucus. Available online. URL: http://www.house.gov/cummings/cbc/cbchome.htm. Accessed August 10, 2005.

Congressional Quarterly Press. *Dollar Politics.* 3rd ed. Washington, D.C.: CQ Press, 1982.

———. "The Electoral College." In John L. Moore, Jon P. Preimesberger, and David Tarr, eds., *Congressional Quarterly's Guide to U.S. Elections.* 4th ed. Washington, D.C.: CQ Press, 2001.

———. *Congressional Quarterly's Guide to U.S. Elections.* 4th ed. Washington, D.C.: CQ Press, 2001.

Conley, Patricia Heidotting. *Presidential Mandates: How Elections Shape the National Agenda.* Chicago: University of Chicago Press, 2001.

Connelly, William F., Jr., and John J. Pitney, Jr. *Congress' Permanent Minority? Republicans in the U.S. House.* Lanham, Md.: Rowman & Littlefield, 1994.

Converse, Philip E. "The Nature of Mass Belief Systems in Mass Publics." In David Apter, ed., *Ideology and Discontent.* New York: Free Press, 1964.

Conway, M. Margaret, and Frank B. Feigert. "Incentives and Task Performance among Party Precinct Workers." *Western Political Quarterly* 27, no. 4 (1974): 693–709.

Conway, M. Margaret, David W. Ahern, and Gertrude A. Steuernagel. *Women and Public Policy: A Revolution in Progress.* 2nd ed. Washington, D.C.: Congressional Quarterly Press, 1999.

Conway, M. Margaret, Gertrude A. Steuernagel, and David W. Ahern. *Women and Political Participation: Cultural Change in the Political Arena.* Washington, D.C.: Congressional Quarterly Press, 1997.

Cook, Rhodes. *Race for the Presidency: Winning the 2000 Nomination.* Washington, D.C.: Congressional Quarterly Press, 2000.

———. *Race for the Presidency: Winning the 2004 Nomination.* Washington, D.C.: CQ Press, 2004.

———. *The Presidential Nominating Process: A Place for Us?* Lanham, Md.: Rowman & Littlefield, 2004.

Cooper, John Milton. *Pivotal Decades.* New York: Norton, 1990.

Cooper, John Milton, Jr. *The Warrior and the Priest.* Cambridge, Mass.: Belknap, 1983.

Cooper, Joseph, and David Brady. "Institutional Context and Leadership Style: The House from Cannon to Rayburn." *American Political Science Review* 75 (1981): 411–425.

Cornell Law School, Legal Information Center. Available online. URL: http://www.law.cornell.edu. Accessed August 10, 2005.

Corrado, Anthony. *Inside the Campaign Finance Battle: Court Testimony on the New Reforms.* Washington, D.C.: Brookings Institution Press, 2003.

———. *Paying for Elections: Public Financing in National Elections.* New York: Twentieth Century Fund Press, 1993.

Corrado, Anthony, et al., eds. *Campaign Finance Reform: A Sourcebook.* Washington, D.C.: Brookings Institution Press, 1997.

Corrado, Anthony, Thomas Mann, Daniel Ortiz, and Trevor Potter, eds. *The New Campaign Finance Sourcebook.* Washington, D.C.: Brookings Institution Press, 2004.

Corwin, Edwin S. *The President: Office and Powers, 1787–1957: History and Analysis of Practice and Opinion.* New York: New York University Press, 1959.

Cotter, Cornelius P., and Bernard C. Hennessy. *Politics without Power: The National Party Committees.* New York: Atherton Press, 1964.

Cox, Gary W., and Jonathan N. Katz. *Elbridge Gerry's Salamander: The Electoral Consequences of the Reapportionment Revolution.* Cambridge: Cambridge University Press, 2002.

Crawley, William Bryan, Jr. *Bill Tuck: A Political Life in Harry Byrd's Virginia.* Charlottesville: University Press of Virginia, 1978.

Crigler, Ann, Marion Just, and Edward McCaffery. *Rethinking the Vote: The Politics and Prospects of American Election Reform.* New York: Oxford University Press, 2004.

Cronin, Thomas E. *Direct Democracy: The Politics of Initiative, Referendum and Recall.* Cambridge, Mass.: Harvard University Press, 1989.

Crotty, William J. *Party Reform.* New York: Longman, 1983

Crotty, William J., and Jerome M. Mileur, eds. *America's Choice: The Elections of 1996.* Guilford, Conn.: McGraw Hill, 1997.

Crouthamel, James L. *Bennett's New York Herald and the Rise of the Popular Press.* Syracuse, N.Y.: Syracuse University Press, 1989.

Cultice, Wendell W. *Youth's Battle for the Ballot: A History of Voting Age in America.* New York: Greenwood Press, 1992.

Cunningham, Noble E., Jr. *The Jeffersonian Republicans in Power: Party Operations, 1801–1809.* Chapel Hill: University of North Carolina Press, 1963.

———. *The Presidency of James Monroe.* Lawrence: University Press of Kansas, 1996.

Currinder, Marian L. "Leadership PAC Contribution Strategies and House Member Ambitions." *Legislative Studies Quarterly* 28 (2003): 551–577.

Curry, George, and West, Cornel. *The Affirmative Action Debate.* Reading, Mass.: Addison-Wesley, 1996.

Curtis, Michael Kent. *Free Speech, "The People's Darling Privilege:" Struggles for Freedom of Expression in American History.* Durham, N.C.: Duke University Press, 2000.

Dalton, Russell J. *Citizen Politics: Public Opinion and Political Parties in Advanced Industrial Democracies.* New York: Chatham House, 2000.

Dangerfield, George. *The Era of Good Feeling.* Chicago: Ivan R. Dee, 1952.

Danish, Max D. *The World of David Dubinsky.* Cleveland: World Publishing, 1957.

Dark, Taylor E. *The Unions and the Democrats: An Enduring Alliance.* Ithaca, N.Y.: Cornell University Press, 1999.

Davidson, Chandler, and Bernard Grofman, eds. *Quiet Revolution in the South: The Impact of the Voting Rights Act, 1965–1990.* Princeton, N.J.: Princeton University Press, 1994.

Davidson, Chandler, and George Korbel. "At-Large Elections and Minority-Group Representation: A Re-Examination of Historical and Contemporary Evidence." *Journal of Politics* 43 (1981): 982–1,005.

Davidson, Roger H., Susan Webb Hammond, and Raymond W. Smock. *Masters of the House: Congressional Leadership over Two Centuries.* Boulder, Colo.: Westview Press, 1998.

Davidson, Roger H., and Walter Oleszek. *Congress and Its Members.* 9th ed. Washington, D.C.: CQ Press, 2004.

Davis, Richard, and Diana Owen. *New Media and American Politics.* New York: Oxford University Press, 1998.

Day, Jennifer, Amie Jamieson, and Hyon B. Shin. *Voting and Registration, the Election of November 2000.* Washington, D.C.: U.S. Census Bureau, 2002.

DeGregorio, William A. *The Complete Book of U.S. Presidents: From George Washington to George W. Bush.* New York: Barnes & Noble Books, 2004.

———. *The Complete Book of U.S. Presidents.* New York: Dembner Books, 1989.

De la Garza, Rodolfo, et al. *Latino Voices: Mexican, Puerto Rican, and Cuban Perspectives on American Politics.* Boulder, Colo.: Westview, 1993.

Democratic Leadership Council. Available online. URL: http://www.ndol.org. Accessed August 10, 2005.

Democratic National Committee. Available online. URL: http://www.democrats.org. Accessed August 10, 2005.

Democratic Party. Available online. URL: http://www.democrats.org. Accessed August 10, 2005.

Democratic Senatorial Campaign Committee. Available online. URL: http://www.dscc.org. Accessed August 10, 2005.

DeSipio, Louis. *Counting on the Latino Vote: Latinos as a New Electorate.* Charlottesville: University of Virginia Press, 1996.

Diamond, Edwin, and Stephen Bates. *The Spot.* Cambridge, Mass.: MIT Press, 1984.

Diamond, Robert A., ed. *Impeachment and the U.S. Congress.* Washington, D.C.: Congressional Quarterly Press, 1974.

Dionne, E. J. *They Only Look Dead: Why Progressives Will Dominate the Next Political Era.* New York: Touchstone, 1996.

Dittmer, John. *Local People: The Struggle for Civil Rights in Mississippi.* Urbana: University of Illinois Press, 1995.

Dixon, Robert G., Jr. "The Warren Court Crusade for the Holy Grail of 'One Man-One Vote.'" *Supreme Court Review* (1969): 219.

Dodd, Lawrence C., and Bruce I. Oppenheimer. *Congress Reconsidered.* 6th ed. Washington, D.C.: CQ Press, 1997.

Dolan, Kathleen A. *Voting for Women: How the Public Evaluates Women Candidates.* Boulder, Colo.: Westview, 2004.

Donahue, Hugh Carter. *The Battle to Control Broadcast News: Who Owns the First Amendment?* Cambridge, Mass.: MIT Press, 1989.

Donald, David Herbert. *Lincoln.* New York: Simon & Schuster, 1995.

Donaldson, Gary. *Liberalism's Last Hurrah: The Presidential Campaign of 1964.* Armonk, N.Y.: M.E. Sharpe, 2003.

Douglas, Amy J. *Behind the Ballot Box: A Citizen's Guide to Voting Systems.* Westport, Conn.: Praeger, 2000.

Dover, E. D. *Missed Opportunity: Gore, Incumbency, and Television in Election 2000.* Westport, Conn.: Praeger, 2002.

———. *The Disputed Presidential Election of 2000: A History and Reference Guide.* Westport, Conn.: Greenwood Press, 2003.

Downs, Anthony. *An Economic Theory of Democracy.* New York: Harper & Row, 1957.

Dubin, Jeffrey A., and Gretchen A. Kalsow. "Comparing Absentee and Precinct Voters: A View over Time." *Political Behavior* 18, no. 4 (1996): 369–392.

Dubinsky, David. *David Dubinsky: A Life with Labor.* New York: Simon & Schuster, 1977.

DuBois, Ellen Carol. *Feminism and Suffrage: The Emergence of an Independent Women's Movement in America, 1848–1869.* Ithaca, N.Y.: Cornell University Press, 1978.

Dudley, William, ed. *Political Scandals: Opposing Viewpoints.* San Diego: Greenhaven Press, 2001.

Dulio, David A. *For Better or Worse?: How Political Consultants Are Changing Elections in the United States.* Albany: State University of New York Press, 2004.

Duverger, Maurice. *Political Parties: Their Organization and Activity in the Modern State.* New York: Wiley, 1963.

Dwyre, Diana, and Robin Kolodny. "Throwing out the Rule Book: Party Financing of the 2000 Elections." In David B. Magleby, ed. *Financing the 2000 Election.* Washington, D.C.: Brookings Institution Press, 2002.

Dyer, Brainerd. *Zachary Taylor.* Baton Rouge: Louisiana State University Press, 1946.

Edsall, Thomas Byrne, and Mary D. Edsall. *Chain Reaction: The Impact of Race, Rights, and Taxes on American Politics.* New York: Norton, 1991.

Edwards, George C., III. *At the Margins: Presidential Leadership of Congress.* New Haven, Conn.: Yale University Press, 1989.

———. *On Deaf Ears: The Failure of the Bully Pulpit.* New Haven, Conn.: Yale University Press, 2003.

———. *Presidential Influence in Congress.* San Francisco: W. H. Freeman, 1980.

———. *The Public Presidency.* New York: St. Martin's Press, 1983.

———. *Why the Electoral College Is Bad for America.* New Haven, Conn.: Yale University Press, 2004.

Edwards, George C., III, and Stephen J. Wayne. *Presidential Leadership: Politics and Policy Making.* 6th ed. Belmont, Calif.: Wadsworth, 2003.

Edwards, George C., III, with Alec M. Gallup. *Presidential Approval: A Sourcebook.* Baltimore: Johns Hopkins University Press, 1990.

Edwards, Lee. *The Conservative Revolution: The Movement that Remade America.* New York: Free Press, 2002.

Einstein, Mara. *Media Diversity: Economics, Ownership, and the FCC.* Mahwah, N.J.: L. Erlbaum Associates, 2004.

Eisinger, Robert Martin. *The Evolution of Presidential Polling.* New York: Cambridge University Press, 2003.

Eisner, Jane. *Taking Back the Vote: Getting American Youth Involved in Our Democracy.* Boston: Beacon Press, 2004.

Elazar, Daniel. *American Federalism: A View from the States.* 3rd ed. New York: HarperCollins, 1984.

Eldersveld, Samuel J., and Hanes Walton, Jr. *Political Parties in American Society.* 2nd ed. Boston: St. Martin's Press, 2000.

Elkins, Stanley, and Eric McKitrick. *The Age of Federalism.* New York: Oxford University Press, 1993.

Emery, Fred. *Watergate: The Corruption of American Politics and the Fall of Richard Nixon.* New York: Times Books, 1994.

EMILY's List. Available online. URL: http://www.emilyslist.org. Accessed August 10, 2005.

Engstrom Richard L., and John K. Wildgen. "Pruning Thorns from the Thicket: An Empirical Test of the Existence of Racial Gerrymandering." *Legislative Studies Quarterly* 2 (1977): 465–479.

Epstein, David, and Sharyn O'Halloran. "A Social Science Approach to Race, Redistricting, and Representation." *American Political Science Review* 93, no. 1 (1999): 187–191.

Epstein, Lee, and Thomas G. Walker. *Constitutional Law for a Changing America: Institutional Powers and Constraints.* 5th ed. Washington, D.C.: CQ Press, 2004.

Epstein, Leon. *Political Parties in the American Mold.* Madison: University of Wisconsin Press, 1986.

Erie, Stephen P. *Rainbow's End: Irish-Americans and the Dilemmas of Urban Machine Politics.* Berkeley: University of California Press, 1988.

Erikson, Robert S., and Kent L. Tedin. *American Public Opinion.* New York: Longman, 2001.

Euchner, Charles. *Extraordinary Politics: How Protest and Dissent Are Changing American Democracy.* Boulder, Colo.: Westview Press, 1996.

Eulau, Heinz. *Class and Party in the Eisenhower Years: Class Roles and Perspectives in the 1952 and 1956 Elections.* New York: Free Press, 1962.

Fair, Ray C. *Predicting Presidential Elections and Other Things.* Stanford, Calif.: Stanford University Press, 2002.

Fairman, Charles. *The Fourteenth Amendment and the Bill of Rights: The Incorporation Theory.* New York: Da Capo Press, 1970.

Farmer, Rod. "Power to the People: The Progressive Movement for the Recall, 1890s–1920." *New England Journal of History* 57, no. 2 (2001): 59–83.

Farnsworth, Stephen J., and S. Robert Lichter. *The Nightly News Nightmare: Network Television's Coverage of U.S. Presidential Elections, 1988–2000.* Lanham, Md.: Rowman & Littlefield, 2003.

Farrell, David M. *Electoral Systems: A Comparative Introduction.* New York: Palgrave Macmillan, 2001.

Faucheux, Ronald A., ed. *Winning Elections: Political Campaign Management, Strategy, and Tactics.* New York: M. Evans, 2001.

Fausold, Martin. *The Presidency of Herbert C. Hoover.* Lawrence: University Press of Kansas, 1985.

Federal Election Commission. Available online. URL: http://www.fec.gov. Accessed August 10, 2005.

Federal Election Commission, Guide to the Electoral College. Available online. URL: http://www.fec.gov/pages/ecmenu2.htm. Accessed August 10, 2005.

Felknor, Bruce L. *Dirty Politics.* New York: Norton, 1966.

———. *Political Mischief: Smear, Sabotage, and Reform in U.S. Elections.* New York: Praeger, 1992.

Fenno, Richard F. *Home Style: House Members in Their Districts.* Boston: Little, Brown, 1978.

Fenwick, Ian, Frederick Wiseman, John F. Becker, and James R. Heiman. "Classifying Undecided Voters in Pre-Election Polls." *Public Opinion Quarterly* 46, no. 3 (1982): 383–391.

Ferejohn, John A., and Randall L. Calvert. "Presidential Coattails in Historical Perspective." *American Journal of Political Science* 28 (1984): 127–146.

Filer, John, Lawerence Kenny, and Rebecca Morton. "Redistribution, Income, and Voting," *American Journal of Political Science* 37, no. 1 (1993): 63–87.

Finley, M. I. "Athenian Demagogues." *Past and Present* 21 (1962): 3–24.

Fiorina, Morris. *Congress: Keystone of the Washington Establishment.* New Haven, Conn.: Yale University Press, 1977.

———. *Retrospective Voting in American National Elections.* New Haven, Conn.: Yale University Press, 1981.

Flanigan, William H., and Nancy H. Zingale. *Political Behavior of the American Electorate.* 10th ed. Washington, D.C.: CQ Press, 2002.

———. *Political Behavior in Midterm Elections.* Washington, D.C.: CQ Press, 2003.

Flynt, J. Wayne. *Cracker Messiah: Governor Sidney J. Catts of Florida.* Baton Rouge: Louisiana State University Press, 1977.

Foner, Eric. *Free Soil, Free Labor, Free Men: The Ideology of the Republican Party before the Civil War.* New York: Oxford University Press, 1995.

———. *Reconstruction: America's Unfinished Revolution, 1863–1877.* New York: Harper & Row, 1988.

Form, William. *Segmented Labor, Fractured Politics: Labor Politics in American Life.* New York: Plenum Press, 1999.

Francia, Peter L., et al. *The Financiers of Congressional Elections.* New York: Columbia University Press, 2003.

Frank, Thomas. *What's the Matter with Kansas? How Conservatives Won the Heart of America.* New York: Metropolitan Books, 2004.

Franklin, John Hope. *Reconstruction after the Civil War.* Chicago: University of Chicago Press, 1994.

Franklin, Mark N. *Voter Turnout and the Dynamics of Electoral Competition in Established Democracies since 1945.* Cambridge: Cambridge University Press, 2004.

Frantzich, Stephen, and John Sullivan. *The C-SPAN Revolution.* Norman: University of Oklahoma Press, 1996.

Frederickson, Kari. *The Dixiecrat Revolt and the End of the Solid South, 1932–1968.* Chapel Hill: University of North Carolina Press, 2001.

Fredman, Lionel E. *The Australian Ballot: The Story of an American Reform.* East Lansing: Michigan State University Press, 1968.

Freedman, Paul, and Ken Goldstein. "Building a Probable Electorate from Pre-Election Polls: A Two-Stage Approach." *Public Opinion Quarterly* 60, no. 4 (1996): 574–587.

Frendreis, John P., James L. Gibson, and Laura L. Vertz. "The Electoral Relevance of Local Party Organizations." *American Political Science Review* 84, no. 1 (1990): 225–235.

Fried, Albert. *Socialism in America from the Shakers to the Third International.* Garden City, N.Y.: Anchor Books, 1970.

Friedan, Betty. *It Changed My Life: Writings on the Women's Movement.* New York: Random House, 1976.

Friedman, Milton. *Capitalism and Freedom.* Chicago: University of Chicago Press, 1962.

———. *A Monetary History of the United States, 1867–1960.* Princeton, N.J.: Princeton University Press, 1963.

Frost, Elizabeth, and Kathryn Cullen-DuPont. *Women's Suffrage in America: An Eyewitness History.* New York: Facts On File, 1992.

Gable, John A. *The Bull Moose Years: Theodore Roosevelt and the Progressive Party.* Port Washington, N.Y.: Kennikat Press, 1978.

Gaddie, Ronald Keith, et al. *Elections to Open Seats in the U.S. House.* New York: Rowman & Littlefield, 2000.

Gallup Polling Corporation. Available online. URL: http://www.gallup.com. Accessed August 10, 2005.

Gamm, Gerald, and Steven S. Smith. "Emergence of Senate Party Leadership." In Bruce I. Oppenheimer, ed., *U.S. Senate Exceptionalism.* Columbus: Ohio State University Press, 2002.

García, John A. *Latino Politics in America.* Lanham, Md.: Rowman & Littlefield, 2003.

Garofalo, Jeffrey. *The Struggle for Democracy: The Machines and Reform.* Lincoln, Neb.: Writers Club Press, 2001.

Gearhardt, Michael J. *The Federal Impeachment Process: A Constitutional and Historical Analysis.* Chicago: University of Chicago Press, 2000.

Gelman, Andrew, and Gary King. "Estimating Incumbency Advantage without Bias." *American Journal of Political Science* 34, no. 4 (1990): 1,142–1,164.

Genovese, Michael A. *The Power of the American Presidency, 1789–2000.* Oxford: Oxford University Press, 2001.

Gerassi, John. "The Comintern, the Fronts, and the CPUSA." In Michael E. Brown, Randy Martin, Frank Rosengarten, and George Snedeker, eds., *New Studies in the Politics and Culture of U.S. Communism.* New York: Monthly Review Press, 1993.

Gerber, Elisabeth R., Rebecca A. Morton, and Thomas A. Rietz. "Minority Representation in Multimember Districts." *American Political Science Review* 92, no. 1 (1998): 127–144.

Gerring, John. *Party Ideologies in America, 1828–1996.* London: Cambridge University Press, 1998.

Gerston, Larry N., and Terry Christensen. *Recall! California's Political Earthquake.* Armonk, N.Y.: M.E. Sharpe, 2004.

Gibson, Rachel. "Elections Online: Assessing Internet Voting in Light of the Arizona Democratic Primary." *Political Science Quarterly* 116, no. 4 (2001): 561–583.

Gieske, Millard L. *Minnesota Farmer-Laborism.* Minneapolis: University of Minnesota Press, 1979.

Gilbert, Paul. *Peoples, Cultures and Nations in Political Philosophy.* Washington, D.C.: Georgetown University Press, 2000.

Gilbert, Robert E. *Managing Crisis: Presidential Disability and the Twenty-fifth Amendment.* New York: Fordham University Press, 2000.

Gilliam, Franklin D., Jr. *Farther to Go: Readings and Cases in African American Politics.* Fort Worth: Harcourt College Publishers, 2002.

Gimpel, James. *Fulfilling the Contract: The First 100 Days.* Boston: Allyn & Bacon, 1995.

Gimpel, James, J. Celest Lay, and Jason Schuknecht. *Cultivating Democracy: Civic Environments and Political Socialization in America.* Washington, D.C.: Brookings Institution Press, 2003.

Gingrich, Newt, et al. *Contract with America: The Bold Plan by Rep. Newt Gingrich, Rep. Dick Armey and the House Republicans to Change the Nation.* New York: Times Books, 1994.

Goldberg, Deborah, Craig Holman, and Samantha Sanchez. *The New Politics of Judicial Elections.* New York: Justice at Stake Campaign, 2002.

Goldberg, Sanford, and Paul Farber. *Revenue Act of 1971.* New York: Practicing Law Institute, 1972.

Goldinger, Carolyn, ed. *Presidential Elections Since 1789.* Washington, D.C.: Congressional Quarterly Press, 1987.

Goldman, Peter, and Tom Matthews. *The Quest for the Presidency 1988.* New York: Touchstone, 1988.

Goldman, Ralph M. *The National Party Chairmen and Committees: Factionalism at the Top.* Armonk, N.Y.: M.E. Sharpe, 1990.

Goldman, Robert Michael. *Reconstruction and Black Suffrage: Losing the Vote in Reese and Cruikshank.* Lawrence: University Press of Kansas, 2001.

Goldstein, Joel K. *The Modern American Vice Presidency: The Transformation of a Political Institution.* Princeton, N.J.: Princeton University Press, 1982.

Goldstein, Ken, and Paul Freedman. "Lessons Learned: Campaign Advertising in the 2000 Elections." *Political Communication* 19 (2002): 5–28.

Goldstein, Michael L. *Guide to the 2004 Presidential Election.* Washington, D.C.: CQ Press, 2003.

Goldwater, Barry. *The Conscience of a Conservative.* Washington, D.C.: Regnery Publishing, 1990.

Goodwin, Doris Kearns. *No Ordinary Time.* New York: Simon & Schuster, 1994.

Goodwin, Jason. *Greenback: The Almighty Dollar and the Invention of America.* New York: Henry Holt, 2003.

Goodwyn, Lawrence. *The Populist Moment: A Short History of the Agrarian Revolt.* Oxford: Oxford University Press, 1978.

GOPAC. Available online. URL: http://www.gopac.org. Accessed August 10, 2005.

Gosnell, Harold. *Truman's Crises: A Political Biography of Harry S. Truman.* Westport, Conn.: Greenwood Press, 1980.

Gottlieb, Robert. *Forcing the Spring: The Transformation of the American Environmental Movement.* Washington, D.C.: Island Press, 1993.

Gould, Lewis. *1968: The Election That Changed America.* Chicago: Ivan R. Dee, 1993.

———. *Grand Old Party: A History of the Republicans.* New York: Random House, 2003.

Graber, Doris A. *Mass Media and American Politics.* 6th ed. Washington, D.C.: CQ Press, 2002.

———. *Media Power in Politics.* 4th ed. Washington, D.C.: CQ Press, 2000.

Grantham, Dewey W., Jr. "The Progressive Era and the Reform Tradition." *Middle America* 46, no. 4 (1964): 227–251.

Gray, Virginia, and Russell L. Hanson. *Politics in the American States: A Comparative Analysis.* 8th ed. Washington, D.C.: CQ Press, 2003.

Green, Donald P., and Alan S. Gerber. *Get Out the Vote! How to Increase Voter Turnout.* Washington, D.C.: Brookings Institution Press, 2004.

Green, John C., and Anthony Corrado. "The Impact of BCRA on Presidential Campaign Finance." In Michael J. Malbin, ed., *Life after Reform: When the Bipartisan Campaign Reform Act Meets Politics.* Boulder, Colo.: Rowman & Littlefield, 2003.

Green, John C., and Rick Farmer, eds. *The State of the Parties: The Changing Role of Contemporary American Parties.* 4th ed. Lanham, Md.: Rowman & Littlefield, 2003.

Green, John C., and Paul S. Herrnson, eds. *Responsible Partisanship? The Evolution of American Political Parties Since 1950.* Lawrence: University of Kansas Press, 2002.

Green, Mark. *Selling Out: How Big Corporate Money Buys Elections, Rams through Legislation, and Betrays Our Democracy.* New York: Regan Books, 2002.

Greenbaum, Thomas L. *The Handbook for Focus Group Research.* 2nd ed. Thousand Oaks, Calif.: Sage Publications, 1998.

Greenberg, Ellen. *The House and Senate Explained: The People's Guide to Congress.* New York: Norton, 1996.

Greenberg, Stanley B. *Middle Class Dreams: The Politics and Power of the New American Majority.* New York: Times Books, 1995.

———. *The Two Americas: Our Current Political Deadlock and How to Break It.* New York: Thomas Dunne Books, 2004.

Greene, Abner. *Understanding the 2000 Election: A Guide to the Legal Battles That Decided the Presidency.* New York: New York University Press, 2001.

Greene, John Robert. *The Crusade: The Presidential Election of 1952.* Lanham, Md.: University Press of America, 1985.

Greene, Julie. *Pure and Simple Politics: The American Federation of Labor and Political Activism, 1881–1917.* Cambridge: Cambridge University Press, 1998.

Green Party. Available online. URL: http://www.gp.org. Accessed August 10, 2005.

Grey, Lawrence. *How to Win a Local Election.* New York: Evans, 1994.

Grinde, Donald A., Jr., ed. *Native Americans.* Washington, D.C.: CQ Press, 2002.

Gronke, Paul. *The Electorate, the Campaign, and the Office: A Unified Approach to Senate and House Elections.* Ann Arbor: University of Michigan Press, 2001.

Groseclose, Timothy, and Keith Krehbiel. "Golden Parachutes, Rubber Checks, and Strategic Retirements from the 102d House." *American Journal of Political Science* 38 (1994): 75–99.

Gross, Ken. *Ross Perot: The Man behind the Myth.* New York: Random House, 1992.

Guber, Deborah. "Environmental Voting in the American States: A Tale of Two Initiatives." *State and Local Government Review* 33, no. 2 (2001): 120–132.

Gunderson, Robert G. *The Log-Cabin Campaign.* Lexington: University of Kentucky Press, 1957.

Gunther, Gerald, and Kathleen M. Sullivan. *Constitutional Law.* 13th ed. Westbury, N.Y.: Foundation Press, 1997.

Gurko, Miriam. *The Ladies of Seneca Falls: The Birth of the Women's Rights Movement.* New York: Macmillan, 1974.

Hake, Ted. *Encyclopedia of Political Buttons: United States 1896–1972.* York, Pa.: Hake's Americana & Collectibles, 1985.

Hale, Jon F. "Making of the New Democrats." *Political Science Quarterly* 110, no. 2 (1995): 207–232.

Hall, Kermit L., ed. *The Oxford Companion to the Supreme Court of the United States.* New York: Oxford University Press, 2002.

Hamilton, Alexander, James Madison, and John Jay. *The Federalist Papers.* New York: Mentor Books, 1999.

Hamilton, Holman. *Zachary Taylor: Soldier in the White House.* Indianapolis: Bobbs-Merrill, 1941.

Hammond, Susan Webb. *Congressional Caucuses in National Policy Making.* Baltimore: Johns Hopkins University Press, 1998.

Hardaway, Robert M. *The Electoral College and the Constitution: The Case for Preserving Federalism.* Westport, Conn.: Praeger, 1994.

Harrigan, John J. *Empty Dreams, Empty Pockets: Class and Bias in American Politics.* 2nd ed. New York: Addison Wesley Longman, 2000.

Harrigan, John J., and Ronald K. Vogel. *Political Change in the Metropolis.* New York: Longman Publishing Group, 1999.

Harris, William C. *Day of the Carpetbagger: Republican Reconstruction in Mississippi.* Baton Rouge: Louisiana State University Press, 1979.

Harrison, Brigid C. *Women in American Politics: An Introduction.* Belmont, Calif.: Thomson Wadsworth, 2003.

Hatcher, Andrea C., and Bruce I. Oppenheimer. "Congressional Party Switchers, 1876–2003: The Effects of Party and Constituency on Strategic Behavior." *Legislative Studies Quarterly* 28, no. 3 (2003): 436.

Hawkings, David, et al. *Politics in America 2004: The 108th Congress.* Washington, D.C.: CQ Press, 2003.

———. *CQ's Politics in America, 2004: The 108th Congress.* Washington, D.C.: CQ Press, 2003.

Heckscher, August. *Woodrow Wilson.* New York: Scribner, 1991.

Hedtke, James R. *Lame Duck Presidents: Myth or Reality.* Lewiston, N.Y.: E. Mellen Press, 2002.

Heinemann, Ronald L. *Harry Byrd of Virginia.* Charlottesville: University Press of Virginia, 1996.

Heith, Diane J. *Polling to Govern: Public Opinion and Presidential Leadership.* Stanford, Calif.: Stanford Law and Politics, 2004.

Herrera, Richard. "Are 'Superdelegates' Super?" *Political Behavior* 16, no. 1 (1994): 79–92.

Herrnson, Paul S. *Congressional Elections: Campaigning at Home and in Washington.* Washington, D.C.: CQ Press, 2004.

Hess, Stephen, and Milton Kaplan. *The Ungentlemanly Art: A History of American Political Cartoons.* New York: Macmillan, 1975.

Hesseltine, William B. *Third-Party Movements in the United States.* Princeton, N.J.: D. Van Nostrand, 1962.

Hickey, Donald R. *The War of 1812: A Forgotten Conflict.* Urbana: University of Illinois Press, 1989.

Hicks, John D. *The Populist Revolt: A History of the Farmers' Alliance and the People's Party.* Minneapolis: University of Minnesota Press, 1931.

Hill, Kim, Tom Leighley, and Angela Hinton-Andersen. "Lower Class Mobilization and Political Linkage in the United States." *American Journal of Political Science* 39, no. 1 (1995): 73–86.

Hill, Steven. *Fixing Elections: The Failure of America's Winner-Take-All Politics.* New York: Routledge, 2003.

Hilliard, Robert L. *The Federal Communications Commission: A Primer.* Boston: Focal Press, 1991.

Himmelfarb, Gertrude. *One Nation, Two Cultures: A Searching Examination of American Society in the Aftermath of Our Cultural Revolution.* New York: Knopf, 1999.

Hinckley, Kathleen. *Your Guide to the Federal Census.* Cincinnati: Betterway Books, 2002.

Hine, Diane Clark. *Black Victory: The Rise and Fall of the White Primary in Texas.* Columbia: University of Missouri Press, 2003.

Hinshaw, David. *Herbert Hoover, American Quaker.* New York: Farrar Straus, 1950.

History of Campaign Web sites. Available online. URL: http://iml.jou.ufl.edu/projects/fall01%5CDuBose. Accessed August 10, 2005.

Hofstadter, Richard. *The Age of Reform: From Bryan to F.D.R.* New York: Knopf, 1955.

———. *The Idea of a Party System.* Berkeley: University of California Press, 1969.

———. *The Progressive Movement, 1900–1915.* Englewood Cliffs, N.J.: Prentice Hall, 1963.

Hofstetter, C. Richard, et al. "Information, Misinformation, and Political Talk Radio." *Political Research Quarterly* 52, no. 2 (1999): 353–369.

Holbrook, Thomas M. "Campaigns, National Conditions, and U.S. Presidential Elections." *American Journal of Political Science* 38 (1994): 973–998.

Hollingsworth, J. Rogers. *The Whirligig of Politics: The Democracy of Cleveland and Bryan.* Chicago: University of Chicago Press, 1963.

Holman, Craig, and Luke McLaughlin. *Buying Time 2000: Television Advertising in the 2000 Federal Elections.* New York: Brennan Center for Justice at New York University, 2001.

Hoogenboom, Ari Arthur. *Outlawing the Spoils: A History of the Civil Service Reform Movement, 1865–1883.* Urbana: University of Illinois Press, 1961.

Howe, Daniel Walker. *The Political Culture of the American Whigs.* Chicago: University of Chicago Press, 1979.

Hrebenar, Ronald J., Matthew J. Burbank, and Robert C. Benedict. *Political Parties, Interest Groups, and Political Campaigns.* Boulder, Colo.: Westview Press, 1999.

Huntington, Samuel P. "The United States." In Michel Crozier, Samuel P. Huntington, and Joji Watnanuki, eds., *The Crisis of Democracy.* New York: New York University Press, 1975.

Huntzicker, William E. *The Popular Press, 1833–1865.* Westport, Conn.: Greenwood Press, 1999.

Inglehart, Ronald. "Post-Materialism in an Environment of Insecurity." *American Political Science Review* 75 (1981): 880–900.

Initiative and Referendum Institute. Available online. URL: http://www.iandrinstitute.org. Accessed August 10, 2005.

Institute for Money in State Politics. Available online. URL: http://www.followthemoney.org. Accessed August 10, 2005.

Inter-American Commission on Human Rights. *Statehood Solidarity Committee, United States,* Case 11.204, Report 98/03. Washington, D.C.: Organization of American States, 2003.

Issacharoff, Samuel. "Judging Politics: The Elusive Quest for Judicial Review of Political Fairness." *Texas Law Review* 71 (1993): 1,643.

Iton, Richard. *Solidarity Blues: Race, Culture and the American Left.* Chapel Hill: University of North Carolina Press, 2000.

Iyengar, Shanto, and Richard Reeves. *Do the Media Govern?: Politicians, Voters, and Reporters in America.* Thousand Oaks, Calif.: Sage Publications, 1997.

Jackson, Brooks. *Broken Promises: Why the Election Commission Failed.* New York: Priority Press Publications, 1990.

Jackson, John S., and William Crotty. *The Politics of Presidential Selection.* 2nd ed. New York: Addison-Wesley Longman, 2001.

Jackson, Robert A. "Clarifying the Relationship between Education and Turnout." *American Politics Quarterly* 23, no. 3 (1995): 279–300.

Jacobson, Gary. *The Electoral Origins of Divided Government: Competition in U.S. House Elections, 1946–1988.* Boulder, Colo.: Westview Press, 1990.

Jacobson, Gary C. "Terror, Terrain, and Turnout: Explaining the 2002 Midterm Elections." *Political Science Quarterly* 118 (2003): 1–22.

———. *The Politics of Congressional Elections.* 6th ed. New York: Pearson/Longman, 2004.

———. "Parties and PACs in Congressional Elections." In Lawrence D. Dodd and Bruce I. Oppenheimer, eds., *Congress Reconsidered.* Washington, D.C.: Congressional Quarterly Press, 1985.

———. "Party Organization and Distribution of Campaign Resources: Republicans and Democrats in 1982." *Political Science Quarterly* 100 (1985): 603–625.

Jaffa, Hary V. *A New Birth of Freedom: Abraham Lincoln and the Coming of the Civil War.* Lanham, Md.: Rowman & Littlefield, 2000.

Jamieson, Kathleen Hall. *Dirty Politics: Deception, Distraction, and Democracy.* Oxford: Oxford University Press, 1992.

———. *Packaging the Presidency: A History and Criticism of Presidential Campaign Advertising.* 3rd ed. New York: Oxford University Press, 1996.

———. *Electing the President 2000: The Insiders' View.* Philadelphia: University of Pennsylvania Press, 2001.

Jamieson, Kathleen Hall, et al. *The Interplay of Influence: News, Advertising, Politics and the Mass Media.* Belmont, Calif.: Wadsworth Publishing, 2000.

Janda, Kenneth, Jeffrey M. Berry, and Jerry Goldman. *The Challenge of Democracy.* 7th ed. Boston: Houghton Mifflin, 2002.

Javits, Jacob K. *Javits: The Autobiography of a Public Man.* New York: Houghton Mifflin, 1981.

Jensen, Merrill. *The Articles of Confederation: An Interpretation of the Social-Constitutional History of the American Revolution.* Madison: University of Wisconsin Press, 1970.

Jensen, Richard. *The Winning of the Midwest: Social and Political Conflict 1888–1896.* Chicago: University of Chicago Press, 1971.

Jewell, Malcolm E. and Sarah M. Morehouse. *Political Parties and Elections in American States.* 4th ed. Washington, D.C.: CQ Press, 2001.

Johnson, Dennis W. *No Place for Amateurs: How Political Consultants Are Reshaping American Democracy.* New York: Routledge, 2001.

Johnson, Lyndon Baines. *The Vantage Point: Perspectives of the Presidency, 1963–1969.* New York: Holt, Rinehart & Winston, 1971.

Johnson, Walter. *How We Drafted Adlai Stevenson.* New York: Knopf, 1955.

Jordan, Hamilton. *Crisis: The Last Year of the Carter Presidency.* New York: Putnam Group, 1982.

Jung, Donald J. *The Federal Communications Commission, the Broadcast Industry, and the Fairness Doctrine, 1981–1987.* Lanham, Md.: University Press of America, 1996.

Kahn, Kim Fridkin, and Patrick J. Kenney. "Do Negative Campaigns Mobilize or Suppress Turnout?" *American Political Science Review* 93 (1999): 877–889.

Kamber, Victor. *Poison Politics: Are Negative Campaigns Destroying Democracy.* New York: Insight Books, 2003.

Kaplan, Dave. "Alternative Election Methods: A Fix for a Besieged System?" *Congressional Quarterly Weekly Report* 52, no. 13 (1994): 812.

Kaplan, David A. *The Accidental President: How 413 Lawyers, 9 Supreme Court Justices, and 5,963,110 (Give or Take a Few) Floridians Landed George W. Bush in the White House.* New York: William Morrow, 2001.

Karabell, Zachary. *The Last Campaign: How Harry Truman Won the 1948 Election.* New York: Knopf, 2000.

Karp, Jeffrey A., and Susan A. Banducci. "Absentee Voting, Mobilization and Participation." *American Politics Research* 29, no. 2 (2001): 183–195.

Katz, Richard S., and Peter Mair. *How Parties Organize.* Thousand Oaks, Calif.: Sage Publications, 1994.

Katzenbach, Nicholas B. "Some Reflections on Baker v. Carr." *Vanderbilt Law Review* 15 (1962): 829, 832–833.

Kaufmann, Karen M., James G. Gimpel, and Adam H. Hoffman. "A Promise Fulfilled? Open Primaries and Representation." *Journal of Politics* 65, no. 2 (2003): 457–476.

Kavanagh, Dennis. *Election Campaigning.* Oxford: Blackwell, 1995.

Kazin, Michael. *The Populist Persuasion: An American History.* New York: Basic Books, 1995.

Keefe, William J. *Parties, Politics, and Public Policy in America.* 8th ed. Washington, D.C.: Congressional Quarterly Press, 1998.

Keith, Bruce E., et al. *The Myth of the Independent Voter.* Berkeley: University of California Press, 1992.

Keller, Morton. *Affairs of State: Public Life in Nineteenth Century America.* Cambridge, Mass.: Harvard University Press, 1977.

Kelly, Stanley, Jr. "Pre-Election Polling: Sources of Accuracy and Error." *Public Opinion Quarterly* 53, no. 4 (1989): 613–615.

Kelppner, Paul, et al. *The Evolution of American Electoral Systems*. Westport, Conn.: Greenwood Press, 1981.

Kenski, Henry C. "The Gender Factor in a Changing Electorate." In Carol M. Mueller, ed., *The Politics of the Gender Gap: The Social Construction of Political Influence*. Newbury Park, Calif.: Sage, 1988.

Kenski, Henry C., and William Lockwood. "Catholic Voting Behavior in 1988: A Critical Swing Vote." In James L. Guth and John C. Green, eds., *The Bible and the Ballot Box: Religion and Politics in the 1988 Election*. Boulder, Colo.: Westview Press, 1991.

Kenski, Kate. "The National Annenberg Election Survey 2000." *Polling Report* 19, no. 15 (2003): 1, 7–8.

Kerbel, Matthew. *Edited for Television: CNN, ABC and the American Presidential Elections*. Boulder, Colo.: Westview Press, 1988.

Kernell, Samuel. *Going Public: New Strategies of Presidential Leadership*. 3rd ed. Washington, D.C.: Congressional Quarterly, 1997.

Key, V. O., Jr. *Southern Politics in State and Nation*. New York: Knopf, 1949.

———. "A Theory of Critical Elections." *Journal of Politics* 17 (1955): 3–18.

———. *Politics, Parties, and Pressure Groups*. 5th ed. New York: Thomas Y. Crowell, 1964.

———. *The Responsible Electorate*. Cambridge, Mass.: Harvard University Press, 1966.

Keysarr, Alexander. *The Right to Vote: The Contested History of Democracy in the United States*. New York: Basic Books, 2000.

Kiefer, David. *Macroeconomic Policy and Public Choice*. Berlin: Springer, 1997.

Killian, Linda. *The Freshman: What Happened to the Republican Revolution?* Boulder, Colo.: Westview Press, 1998.

Kim, Jee, et al. *Future 500: Youth Organizing and Activism in the United States*. Atlanta: New Mouth from the Dirty South, 2002.

Kinder, Donald R., and D. Roderick Kiewiet. "Sociotropic Politics: The American Case." *British Journal of Political Science* 11, no. 2 (1981): 129–161.

Kintner, Hallie J., Thomas W. Merrick, Peter A. Morrison, and Paul R. Voss. *Demographics: A Casebook for Business and Government*. Washington, D.C.: RAND, 1997.

Kirkpatrick, Jeanne J. *The New Presidential Elite: Men and Women in National Politics*. New York: Russell Sage Foundation and Twentieth Century Fund, 1976.

Klarman, Michael J. "The White Primary Rulings: A Case Study in the Consequences of Supreme Court Decisionmaking." *Florida State University Law Review* 29 (2001): 55–107.

Klein, Philip S. *President James Buchanan*. University Park: Pennsylvania State University Press, 1962.

Klinkner, Philip A. *Midterm: The Elections of 1994 in Context*. Boulder, Colo.: Westview Press, 1996.

———. *The Losing Parties: Out-Party National Committees*. New Haven, Conn.: Yale University Press, 1994.

Klotz, Robert. "Internet Politics: A Survey of Practices." In Roderick P. Hart and Daron R. Shaw, eds., *Communication in U.S. Elections: New Agendas*. New York: Rowman & Littlefield, 2001.

Kluger, Richard. *Simple Justice: The History of Brown v. Board of Education and Black America's Struggle for Equality*. New York: Knopf, 1975.

Kobrak, Peter. *Cozy Politics: Political Parties, Campaign Finance, and Compromised Governance*. Boulder, Colo.: Lynne Rienner Publishers, 2002.

Koch, Jeffrey W. "Political Cynicism and Third Party Support in American Presidential Elections." *American Politics Research* 31 (2003): 48–65.

Kollman, Ken. *Outside Lobbying: Public Opinion and Interest Group Strategies*. Princeton, N.J.: Princeton University Press, 1998.

Kolodny, Robin. *Pursuing Majorities: Congressional Campaign Committees in American Politics*. Norman: University of Oklahoma Press, 1998.

Koopman, Douglas L. *Hostile Takeover: The House Republican Party, 1980–1992*. Lanham, Md.: Rowman & Littlefield, 1996.

Korda, Michael. *Ulysses S. Grant: The Unlikely Hero*. New York: HarperCollins, 2004.

Kornbluh, Mark Lawrence. *Why America Stopped Voting: The Decline of Participatory Democracy and the Emergence of Modern American Politics*. New York: New York University Press, 2000.

Kousser, J. Morgan. *Colorblind Injustice: Minority Voting Rights and the Undoing of the Second Reconstruction*. Chapel Hill: University of North Carolina Press, 1999.

Krane, Dale, et al. *Home Rule in America: A Fifty State Handbook*. Washington, D.C.: CQ Press, 2001.

Krasno, J., and D. Seltz. *Buying Time*. New York: Brennan Center for Justice, 2000.

Kraus, Sidney, ed. *The Great Debates: Carter vs. Ford, 1976*. Bloomington: Indiana University Press, 1979.

———. *The Great Debates: Kennedy vs. Nixon, 1960*. Bloomington: Indiana University Press, 1962.

Kristol, Irving. *Neo-Conservatism: The Autobiography of an Idea*. New York: Free Press, 1995.

Kura, Alexandra, ed. *Electoral College and Presidential Elections*. Huntington, N.Y.: Nova, 2001.

Kurian, George T., ed. *A Historical Guide to the U.S. Government*. New York: Oxford University Press, 1998.

Kurland, Philip, and Ralph Lerner. *The Founders' Constitution.* Vol. 4. Chicago: University of Chicago Press, 1987.

Kurtz, Stephen G. *The Presidency of John Adams: The Collapse of Federalism, 1795–1800.* Philadelphia: University of Pennsylvania Press, 1957.

Kutler, Stanley I. *The Wars of Watergate.* New York: Knopf, 1990.

Kutner, Luis. "Due Process in the Contested New Hampshire Senate Election: Fact, Fiction, or Farce." *New England Law Review* 11 (1975): 25–54.

Labbe, John B. "Louisiana's Blanket Primary after California Democratic Party v. Jones." *Northwestern University Law Review* 96, no. 2 (2002): 721–753.

Lahusen, Christian. *The Rhetoric of Moral Protest: Public Campaigns, Celebrity Endorsement, and Political Mobilization.* New York: W. de Gruyter, 1996.

Lavrakas, Paul J. *Election Polls, the News Media, and Democracy.* New York: Chatham House Publishers, 2000.

Lavrakas, Paul J., and Jack K. Holley, eds. *Polling and Presidential Election Coverage.* Newbury Park, Calif.: Sage, 1991.

Lavrakas, Paul J., Michael W. Traugott, and Peter V. Miller, eds. *Presidential Polls and the News Media.* Boulder, Colo.: Westview Press, 1995.

Lawson, Kaye. "How State Laws Undermine Parties." In A. James Reichley, ed., *Elections American Style.* Washington, D.C.: Brookings Institution Press, 1987.

Lawson, Stephen F. *Black Ballots: Voting Rights in the South, 1944–1969.* New York: Columbia University Press, 1976.

League of Conservation Voters. Available online. URL: http://www.lcv.org. Accessed August 10, 2005.

League of Women Voters. Available online. URL: http://www.lwv.org. Accessed August 10, 2005.

Lee, Francis E., and Bruce I. Oppenheimer. *Sizing up the Senate: The Unequal Consequences of Equal Representation.* Chicago: University of Chicago Press, 1999.

Leege, David C., Kenneth D. Wald, Brian S. Krueger, and Paul D. Mueller. *The Politics of Cultural Differences: Social Change and Voter Mobilization Strategies in the Post–New Deal Period.* Princeton, N.J.: Princeton University Press, 2002.

Lefkowitz, Joel. "The Electoral College: Constitutional Debate, Partisan Manipulation, and Reform Possibilities." In *Democracy's Moment: Reforming the American Political System for the 21st Century,* Ronald Hayduk and Kevin Mattson, eds. Lanham, Md.: Rowman & Littlefield, 2002.

Lewis, Anthony. "Legislative Apportionment and the Federal Courts." *Harvard Law Review* 71 (1958): 1,057.

Liberal Party. Available online. URL: http://www.liberal party.org. Accessed August 10, 2005.

Libertarian Party. Available online. URL: http://www.lp.org. Accessed August 10, 2005.

Lichter, Robert S., and Richard E. Noyes. *Good Intentions Make Bad News: Why Americans Hate Campaign Journalism.* Lanham, Md.: Rowman & Littlefield, 1995.

Lijphardt, Arendt. *Patterns of Democracy: Government Forms and Performance in Thirty-six Countries.* New Haven, Conn.: Yale University Press, 1999.

Lipset, Seymour Martin, ed. *Party Coalitions in the 1980s.* New Brunswick, N.J.: Transaction Books, 1981.

Lisio, Donald. *Hoover, MacArthur and the Bonus March.* New York: Fordham University Press, 1994.

Lockerbie, Brad. "Prospective Voting in U.S. House Elections, 1956–88." *Legislative Studies Quarterly* 16, no. 2 (1991): 239–261.

Lokos, Lionel. *Hysteria 1964.* New Rochelle, N.Y.: Arlington House, 1967.

Longley, Lawrence D., and Neal R. Peirce. *The Electoral College Primer 2000.* New Haven, Conn.: Yale University Press, 1999.

Lorch, Robert. *State and Local Politics: The Great Entanglement.* 6th ed. Upper Saddle River, N.J.: Prentice Hall, 2001.

Lovell, S. D. *The Presidential Election of 1916.* Carbondale: Southern Illinois University Press, 1980.

Lowe, David. *Ku Klux Klan: The Invisible Empire.* New York: Norton, 1967.

Lubenow, Gerald C. *California Votes: The 2002 Governor's Race and the Recall That Made History.* Berkeley, Calif.: Berkeley Public Policy Press/Institute of Governmental Studies, 2004.

Lublin, David. *The Paradox of Representation: Racial Gerrymandering and Minority Interests in Congress.* Princeton, N.J.: Princeton University Press, 1997.

———. *The Republican South: Democratization and Partisan Change.* Princeton, N.J.: Princeton University Press, 2004.

Luna, Christopher, ed. *Campaign Finance Reform.* New York: H.W. Wilson, 2001.

Lusane, Clarence. *No Easy Victories: Black Americans and the Vote.* New York: Franklin Watts, 1996.

Luthin, Reinhard H. *The First Lincoln Campaign.* Englewood Cliffs, N.J.: Prentice Hall, 1960.

Lutz, Donald, et al. "The Electoral College in Historical and Philosophical Perspective." In Paul D. Schumaker and Burdett A. Loomis, eds., *Choosing A President: The Electoral College and Beyond.* New York: Chatham House Publishers, 2002.

Lyons, Michael, and Peter F. Galderisi. "Incumbency, Reapportionment, and U.S. House Redistricting." *Political Research Quarterly* 48, no. 4 (1995): 857–871.

MacBride, Roger L. *A New Dawn for America: The Libertarian Challenge*. Ottawa, Ill.: Green Hill Publishers, 1976.

Madison, James, Alexander Hamilton, and John Jay. *Federalist Papers*. New York: Signet Classic, 1999.

Madison, James. *Notes of the Debates in the Federal Convention of 1787*. New York: Norton, 1987.

Magee, James. *Freedom of Expression*. Westport, Conn.: Greenwood Press, 2002.

Magleby, David B. "Participation in Mail Ballot Elections." *Western Political Quarterly* 40 (1987): 79–91.

———. *Direct Legislation: Voting on Ballot Propositions in the United States*. Baltimore: Johns Hopkins University Press, 1984.

Magleby, David, ed. *Financing the 2002 Election*. Washington, D.C.: Brookings Institution Press, 2002.

———. *The Other Campaign: Soft Money and Issue Advocacy in the 2000 Congressional Elections*. Lanham, Md.: Rowman & Littlefield, 2003.

Magleby, David, and Quin J. Monson. *The Last Hurrah? Soft Money and Issue Advocacy in the 2002 Congressional Election*. Washington, D.C.: Brookings Institution Press, 2004.

Maihafer, Harry J. *The General and the Journalists: Ulysses S. Grant, Horace Greeley, and Charles Dana*. Washington, D.C.: Brassey's, 1998.

Maisel, L. Sandy. *Parties and Elections in America: The Electoral Process*. 3rd ed. Lanham, Md.: Rowman & Littlefield, 2002.

Maisel, Sandy L., ed. *The Parties Respond: Changes in American Parties and Campaigns*. Boulder, Colo.: Westview Press, 2002.

Malbin, Michael J. *Life after Reform: When the Bipartisan Campaign Reform Act Meets Politics*. Lanham, Md.: Rowman & Littlefield, 2003.

Malbin, Michael J., and Thomas L. Gais. *The Day after Reform: Sobering Campaign Finance Lessons from the American States*. Albany, N.Y.: Rockefeller Institute Press, 1998.

Mann, Robert. *The Walls of Jericho: Lyndon Johnson, Hubert Humphrey, Richard Russell and the Struggle for Civil Rights*. New York: Harcourt, Brace, 1996.

Markman, Stephen J. *Statehood for the District of Columbia: Is It Constitutional? Is It Wise? Is It Necessary?* Washington, D.C.: National Legal Center for the Public Interest, 1988.

Marvin, E. Gettleman. *The Dorr Rebellion: A Study in American Radicalism, 1833–1849*. New York: Random House, 1973.

Mayer, Jane, and Doyle McManus. *Landslide: The Unmaking of the President, 1984–1988*. Boston: Houghton Mifflin, 1988.

Mayer, Kenneth R., and John M. Wood. "The Impact of Public Financing on Electoral Competitiveness: Evidence from Wisconsin, 1964–1990." *Legislative Studies Quarterly* 20 (1995): 69–88.

Mayer, William G. "Caucuses: How They Work, What Difference They Make." In William G. Mayer, ed., *In Pursuit of the White House: How We Choose Our Presidential Nominees*. Chatham, N.J.: Chatham House, 1996.

Mayer, William G., and Andrew E. Busch. *The Front-Loading Problem in Presidential Nominations*. Washington, D.C.: Brookings Institution Press, 2004.

Mayhew, David R. *Congress: The Electoral Connection*. New Haven, Conn.: Yale University Press, 1974.

McChesney, Robert W. *Telecommunications, Mass Media, and Democracy: The Battle for the Control of U.S. Broadcasting, 1928–1935*. New York: Oxford University Press, 1993.

McCormick, Richard P. *The Presidential Game: The Origins of American Presidential Politics*. New York: Oxford University Press, 1982.

McFarland, Gerald W. *Mugwumps, Morals, and Politics, 1884–1920*. Amherst: University of Massachusetts Press, 1995.

McGann, Anthony, et al. "How an Ideologically Concentrated Minority Can Trump a Dispersed Majority: Nonmedian Voter Results for Plurality, Run-Off, and Sequential Elimination Elections." *American Journal of Political Science* 46, no. 1 (2002): 134.

McGlen, Nancy E., and Karen O'Connor. *Women, Politics, and American Society*. Englewood Cliffs, N.J.: Prentice Hall, 1995.

McGrath, Dennis J., and Dane Smith. *Professor Wellstone Goes to Washington: The Inside Story of a Grassroots U.S. Senate Campaign*. Minneapolis: University of Minnesota Press, 1995.

McKee, Seth C., and Daron R. Shaw. "Suburban Voting in Presidential Elections." *Presidential Studies Quarterly* 33 (2003): 125–144.

McKinley, Silas Bent. *Old Rough and Ready: The Life and Times of Zachary Taylor*. New York: Vanguard Press, 1946.

McKinnon, Jesse. *Current Population Reports: The Black Population in the United States: March 2002*. Washington, D.C.: U.S. Census Bureau, 2002.

McMath, Robert C., Jr. *American Populism: A Social History 1877–1898*. New York: Hill & Wang, 1993.

McPherson, James M. *Battle Cry of Freedom: The Civil War Era*. New York: Oxford University Press, 1988.

———. *To the Best of My Ability: The American Presidents*. New York: Dorling Kindersley, 2002.

Merk, Fredrick. *Slavery and the Annexation of Texas*. New York: Knopf, 1972.

Merriam, Charles E., and Louise Overacker. *Primary Elections*. Chicago: University of Chicago Press, 1928.

Michman, Ronald D. *Lifestyle Market Segmentation.* New York: Praeger, 1991.

Milkis, Sidney M. *The President and the Parties: The Transformation of the American Party System since the New Deal.* Oxford: Oxford University Press, 1993.

Milkis, Sidney, and Michael Nelson. *The American Presidency: Origins and Development, 1776–1998.* Washington, D.C.: Congressional Quarterly, 2003.

Miller, John C. *The Federalist Era, 1789–1801.* New York: Harper, 1960.

Miller, Warren E. "Presidential Coattails: A Study in Political Myth and Methodology." *Public Opinion Quarterly* 19 (1955): 353–368.

Miller, Warren E., and Teresa E. Levitin. *Leadership & Change: Presidential Elections from 1952 to 1976.* Lanham, Md.: University Press of America, 1984.

Miller, Warren, and J. Merrill Shanks. *The New American Voter.* Cambridge, Mass.: Harvard University Press, 1996.

Miller, William D. *Mr. Crump of Memphis.* Baton Rouge: Louisiana State University Press, 1964.

Milvasy, J. Ronald, et al. "Early Calls of Election Results and Exit Polls: Pros, Cons, and Constitutional Considerations." *Public Opinion Quarterly* 49 (1985): 1.

Minger, Ralph Eldin. *William Howard Taft and United States Foreign Policy: The Apprenticeship Years, 1900–1908.* Urbana: University of Illinois Press, 1975.

Minogue, Kenneth R. *Politics: A Very Short Introduction.* Oxford: Oxford University Press, 1995.

Minow, Newton N., and Clifford M. Sloan. *For Great Debates: A New Plan for Future Presidential TV Debates.* New York: Priority Press, 1987.

Mitofsky, W. J. "Voter News Service after the Fall." *Public Opinion Quarterly* 67, no. 1 (2003): 45–58.

Moore, David W. *The Superpollsters.* New York: Four Walls Eight Windows, 1992.

Moos, Malcolm. *Politics, Presidents, and Coattails.* Baltimore: Johns Hopkins University Press, 1952.

Morgan, David. *Suffragists and Democrats: The Politics of Woman Suffrage in America.* East Lansing: Michigan State University Press, 1972.

Morgan, Wayne H. *William McKinley and His America.* Rev. ed. Kent, Ohio: Kent State University Press, 2003.

Morris, Aldon D. *The Origins of the Civil Rights Movement.* New York: Free Press, 1984.

Morris, Dick. *Power Plays: Win or Lose. How History's Great Leaders Play the Game.* New York: Reagan Books, 2002.

Morris, Dwight, and Murielle Gamache. *Gold Plated Politics: The 1992 Congressional Races.* Washington, D.C.: Congressional Quarterly Press, 1994.

Morris, Edmund. *Theodore Rex.* New York: Random House, 2001.

Morris, Roy, Jr. *Fraud of the Century: Rutherford B. Hayes, Samuel Tilden and the Stolen Election of 1876.* New York: Simon & Schuster, 2003.

Morrison, Catherine. *Managing Corporate Political Action Committees.* New York: Conference Board, 1986.

Moscow, Warren. *The Last of the Big-Time Bosses: The Life and Times of Carmine De Sapio and the Rise and Fall of Tammany Hall.* New York: Stein & Day, 1971.

MoveOn.org. Available online. URL: http://www.moveon.org. Accessed August 10, 2005.

Mowry, George E. *Theodore Roosevelt and the Progressive Movement.* Madison: University of Wisconsin Press, 1946.

MTV's Rock the Vote. Available online. URL: http://www.rockthevote.com. Accessed August 10, 2005.

Murphy, Reg, and Hal Gulliver. *The Southern Strategy.* New York: Charles Scribner's Sons, 1971.

Mutch, Robert E. *Campaigns, Congress, and Courts: The Making of Federal Campaign Finance Law.* New York: Praeger, 1988.

Mutz, Diana C. "Effects of Horse-Race Coverage on Campaign Coffers: Strategic Contributing in Presidential Primaries." *Journal of Politics* 57, no. 4. (1995): 1,015–1,042.

Myers, Gustavus. *The History of Tammany Hall.* New York: Boni & Liveright, 1917.

NAACP. Available online. URL: http://www.naacp.org. Accessed August 10, 2005.

Nader, Ralph. *Crashing the Party: How to Tell the Truth and Still Run for President.* New York: Thomas Dunne Books, 2002.

Nader, Ralph. *Crashing the Party: Taking on the Corporate Government in An Age of Surrender.* New York: St. Martin's Press, 2002.

Nakashima, Ellen, et al. *Deadlock: The Inside Story of America's Closest Election.* New York: Public Affairs, 2001.

National Election Study. Available online. URL: http://www.umich.edu/~nes. Accessed August 10, 2005.

National Organization for Women. Available online. URL: http://www.now.org. Accessed August 10, 2005.

National Park Service, Independence National Historic Park. Available online. URL: http://www.nps.gov/inde. Accessed August 10, 2005.

National Republican Congressional Committee. Available online. URL: http://nrcc.org. Accessed August 10, 2005.

National Republican Senatorial Committee. Available online. URL: http://www.nrsc.org. Accessed August 10, 2005.

Natural Law Party. Available online. URL: http://www.natural-law.org. Accessed August 10, 2005.

Neal, Harry Edward. *Diary of Democracy: The Story of Political Parties in America.* New York: Julian Messner, 1962.

Neal, Steven. *Happy Days Are Here Again: The 1932 Election, the Emergence of FDR—and How America Was Changed Forever.* New York: William Morrow, 2004.

Neeley, Grant W., and Lilliard E. Richardson. "Who Is Early Voting? An Individual Level Examination." *Social Science Journal* 38 (2001): 381–392.

Nelson, Candice J., David A. Dulio, and Stephen K. Medvic. *Shades of Gray: Perspectives on Campaign Ethics.* Washington, D.C.: Brookings Institution Press, 2002.

Nelson, Michael, ed. *Guide to the Presidency.* 3rd ed. Washington, D.C.: CQ Press, 2002.

———. *The Election of 1984.* Washington, D.C.: CQ Press, 1985.

Neubauer, Michael G., and Joel Zeitlin. "Outcomes of Presidential Elections and the House Size." *Political Science & Politics* 36, no. 4 (2003): 721–725.

Nevins, Allan. *Fremont: Pathmaker of the West.* New York: Appleton-Century, 1939.

Newman, Bruce I. *The Marketing of the President: Political Marketing as Campaign Strategy.* Thousand Oaks, Calif.: Sage Publications, 1994.

Niemi, Richard G., and Patrick Fett. "The Swing Ratio: An Explanation and an Assessment." *Legislative Studies Quarterly* 11 (1986): 75–90.

Niemi, Richard G., and Herbert F. Weisberg, eds. *Classics in Voting Behavior.* Washington, D.C.: CQ Press, 1993.

———. *Controversies in Voting Behavior.* 4th ed. Washington, D.C.: CQ Press, 2001.

Nokken, Timothy P. "Dynamics of Congressional Loyalty: Party Defection and Roll-Call Behavior, 1947–97." *Legislative Studies Quarterly* 15 (2000): 417–444.

Norrander, Barbara. "Presidential Nomination Politics in the Post-Reform Era (in Field Essay)." *Political Research Quarterly* 49, no. 4 (1996): 875–915.

———. *Super Tuesday: Regional Politics and Presidential Primaries.* Lexington: University Press of Kentucky, 1992.

Nownes, Anthony J. *Pressure and Power: Organized Interests in American Politics.* Boston: Houghton Mifflin, 2001.

O'Connor, Karen. *Women in Congress: Running, Winning, and Ruling.* New York: Haworth Press, 2001.

O'Connor, Len. *Clout: Mayor Daley and His City.* Lincolnwood, Ill.: NTC/Contemporary Publishing, 1984.

Office of the Speaker of the House. Available online. URL: http://speaker.house.gov. Accessed August 10, 2005.

Oleszek, Walter J. *Congressional Procedures and the Policy Process.* 6th ed. Washington, D.C.: CQ Press, 2004.

Ornstein, Norman J., Thomas E. Mann, and Michael J. Malbin. *Vital Statistics on Congress, 2001–2002.* Washington, D.C.: American Enterprise Institute, 2002.

Oshinsky, David. *A Conspiracy So Immense: The World of Joe McCarthy.* New York: Free Press, 1983.

Ottanelli, Fraser M. *The Communist Party of the United States: From the Depression to World War II.* New Brunswick, N.J.: Rutgers University Press, 1991.

Paglin, Max D. *A Legislative History of the Communications Act of 1934.* New York: Oxford University Press, 1989.

Paletz, David L. *The Media in American Politics: Contents and Consequences.* 2nd ed. New York: Longman, 2002.

Palmer, Kris E., ed. *Constitutional Amendments: 1789 to the Present.* Detroit: Gale Group, 2000.

Palmer, Niall A. *The New Hampshire Primary and the American Electoral Process.* Westport, Conn.: Praeger, 1997.

Parker, Richard A., ed. *Free Speech on Trial: Communication Perspectives on Landmark Supreme Court Decisions.* Tuscaloosa: University of Alabama Press, 2003.

Parmet, Herbert. *JFK: The Presidency of John F. Kennedy.* New York: Dial Press, 1983.

Pateman, Carole. *Participation and Democratic Theory.* Cambridge: Cambridge University Press, 1970.

Patterson, James T. *Congressional Conservatism and the New Deal; The Growth of the Conservative Coalition in Congress, 1933–1939.* Lexington: University of Kentucky Press, 1967.

Patterson, Thomas E. "The Vanishing Voter: Why Are the Voting Booths So Empty?" *National Civic Review* 91, no. 4 (2002): 367–378.

———. *Out of Order.* New York: Vintage Books, 1994.

———. *The Vanishing Voter: Public Involvement in an Age of Uncertainty.* New York: Knopf, 2002.

Payne, Charles M. *I've Got the Light of Freedom: The Organizing Tradition and the Mississippi Freedom Struggle.* Berkeley: University of California Press, 1996.

Pelissero, John P. *Cities, Politics and Policy.* Washington, D.C.: CQ Press, 2002.

Perlstein, Rick. *Before the Storm: Barry Goldwater and the Unmaking of the American Consensus.* New York: Hill & Wang, 2001.

Perot, H. Ross. *United We Stand: How We Can Take Back Our Country.* New York: Hyperion Books, 1992.

Perret, Geoffrey. *Ulysses S. Grant: Soldier & President.* New York: Random House, 1997.

Perry, Paul. "A Comparison of the Voting Preferences of Likely Voters and Likely Nonvoters." *Public Opinion Quarterly* 37, no. 1 (1973): 99–109.

Peters, Ronald M., Jr. *The American Speakership: The Office in Historical Perspective.* 2nd ed. Baltimore: Johns Hopkins University Press, 1997.

Petrocik, John R. *Party Coalitions: Realignments and the Decline of the New Deal Party System.* Chicago: University of Chicago Press, 1981.

Phillips, Howard, ed. *The Next Four Years.* Franklin, Tenn.: Adroit Press, 1992.

Phillips, Kevin. *The Politics of Rich and Poor: Wealth and the American Electorate in the Reagan Aftermath.* New York: Random House, 1990.

———. *The Emerging Republican Majority.* New Rochelle, N.Y.: Arlington House, 1969.

Pickett, William Beatty. *Eisenhower Decides to Run: Presidential Politics and Cold War Strategy.* Chicago: Ivan R. Dee, 2000.

Pierce, Neal R., and Lawrence D. Longley. *The People's President: The Electoral College in American History and the Direct Vote Alternative.* New Haven, Conn.: Yale University Press, 1981.

Pildes, Richard H., and Richard G. Niemi. "Expressive Harms, 'Bizarre Districts,' and Voting Rights: Evaluating Election-District Appearances after *Shaw v. Reno.*" *Michigan Law Review* 92 (1993): 483.

Pilon, Roger. *The Politics and Law of Term Limits.* Washington, D.C.: Cato Institution, 1994.

Pitkin, Hanna. *The Concept of Representation.* Berkeley: University of California Press, 1967.

Plotke, David. *Building a Democratic Political Order: Reshaping American Liberalism in the 1930s and 1940s.* Cambridge: Cambridge University Press, 1995.

Polsby, Nelson W. *Consequences of Party Reform.* New York: Oxford University Press, 1983.

Polsby, Nelson W., and Aaron Wildavsky. *Presidential Elections: Strategies and Structures of American Politics.* 11th ed. Lanham, Md.: Rowman & Littlefield, 2004.

Pomper, Gerald. *Nominating the President: The Politics of Convention Choice.* New York: Norton, 1996.

Pomper, Gerald, et al. *The Election of 1984: Reports and Interpretations.* Chatham, N.J.: Chatham House, 1985.

———. *The Election of 1988: Reports and Interpretations.* Chatham, N.J.: Chatham House, 1989.

Popkin, Samuel L. *The Reasoning Voter.* Chicago: University of Chicago Press, 1993.

Posner, Gerald. *Citizen Perot: His Life and Times.* New York: Random House, 1996.

Posner, Richard. *Breaking the Deadlock: The 2000 Election, the Constitution, and the Courts.* Princeton, N.J.: Princeton University Press, 2001.

Potter, David M. *The Impending Crisis: 1848–1861.* New York: Harper & Row, 1976.

Powell, G. Bingham, Jr. *Elections as Instruments of Democracy: Majoritarian and Proportional Visions.* New Haven, Conn.: Yale University Press, 2000.

Price, David Eugene. *The Congressional Experience.* Boulder, Colo.: Westview Press, 2000.

Purcell, L. Edward, ed. *The Vice Presidents: A Biographical Dictionary.* New York: Facts On File, 1998.

Rae, Nicol C. *Southern Democrats.* New York: Oxford University Press, 1994.

Rainbow/PUSH Coalition. Available online. URL: http://www.rainbowpush.org. Accessed August 10, 2005.

Rakove, Jack N., ed. *The Unfinished Election of 2000.* New York: Basic Books, 2001.

Rakove, Milton L. *Don't Make No Waves—Don't Back No Losers: An Insider's Analysis of the Daley Machine.* Bloomington: Indiana University Press, 1976.

Ranney, Austin. *The Doctrine of Responsible Party Government: Its Origins and Present State.* Urbana: University of Illinois Press, 1954.

———. *Curing the Mischiefs of Faction: Party Reform in America.* Berkeley: University of California Press, 1975.

Rapoport, Ronald B. *The Life of the Parties: Activists in Presidential Politics.* Lexington: University Press of Kentucky, 1986.

Ratner, Lorman. *Antimasonry: The Crusade and the Party.* Englewood Cliffs, N.J.: Prentice Hall, 1969.

Rawls, John. *Political Liberalism.* New York: Columbia University Press, 1993.

Ray, William B. *The Ups and Downs of Radio-TV Regulation.* Ames: Iowa State University Press, 1990.

Real Clear Politics. Available online. URL: http://www.realclearpolitics.com. Accessed August 10, 2005.

Reed, Ralph. *Active Faith: How Christians Are Changing the Soul of American Politics.* New York: Free Press, 1996.

Reform Party. Available online. URL: http://www.reformparty.org. Accessed August 10, 2005.

Reichley, A. James. *The Life of the Parties.* 2nd ed. Lanham, Md.: Rowman & Littlefield, 2002.

Remini, Robert V. *Andrew Jackson and the Bank War: A Study in the Growth of Presidential Power.* New York: Norton, 1967.

Republican National Committee. Available online. URL: http://www.rnc.org. Accessed August 10, 2005.

Richards, David A. J. *Conscience and the Constitution: History, Theory, and Law of the Reconstruction Amendments.* Princeton, N.J.: Princeton University Press, 1993.

Riker, William H. "The Number of Political Parties: A Reexamination of Duverger's Law." *Comparative Politics* 9 (1976): 93–106.

———. "The Two-Party System and Duverger's Law: An Essay on the History of Political Science." *American Political Science Review* 76 (1982): 753–766.

Riordon, William L. *Plunkitt of Tammany Hall.* New York: Knopf, 1948.

Roberts, Robert N., and Scott J. Hammond. *Encyclopedia of Presidential Campaigns, Slogans, Issues, and Platforms.* Westport, Conn.: Greenwood Press, 2004.

Rock the Vote. Available online. URL: http://www.rockthevote.org. Accessed August 10, 2005.

Roefs, Wim. "Leading the Civil Rights Vanguard in South Carolina: John McCray and the Lighthouse and Informer, 1939–1954." In Adam Green and Charles Payne, eds., *Time Longer than Rope: A Century of African-American Activism.* New York: New York University Press, 2003.

Rokeach, Milton. *The Nature of Human Values.* New York: Free Press, 1973.

Romer, Daniel, et al. *Capturing Campaign Dynamics: The National Annenberg Election Survey.* New York: Oxford University Press, 2003.

Roper Center for Public Opinion Research. Available online. URL: http://roperweb.ropercenter.uconn.edu. Accessed August 10, 2005.

Roseboom, Eugene H. *A Short History of Presidential Elections.* 3rd ed. New York: Collier Books, 1967.

Rosen, Philip. *The Modern Stentors: Radio Broadcasters and the Federal Government, 1920–1934.* London: Greenwood Press, 1980.

Rosenbaum, Walter. *Environmental Politics and Policy.* 5th ed. Washington, D.C.: CQ Press, 2001.

Rosencranz, Joshua, ed. *If Buckley Fell: A First Amendment Blueprint for Regulating Money in Politics.* New York: Century Foundation Press, 1999.

Rosenstone, Steven J., and John Mark Hansen. *Mobilization, Participation, and Democracy.* New York: Macmillan, 1993.

Rosenstone, Steven J., Roy L. Behr, and Edward H. Lazarus. *Third Parties in America: Citizen Response to Major Party Failure.* 2nd ed. Princeton, N.J.: Princeton University Press, 1996.

Rosenthal, Cindy Simon. *Women Transforming Congress.* Norman: Oklahoma University Press, 2002.

Rossum, Ralph A. *Federalism, the Supreme Court, and the Seventeenth Amendment: The Irony of Constitutional Democracy.* Lanham, Md.: Lexington Books, 2001.

Roth, Robert. *A Reason to Vote.* New York: St. Martin's Press, 1998.

Rovere, Richard H. *Senator Joe McCarthy.* Berkeley: University of California Press, 1996.

Royko, Mike. *Boss: Richard J. Daley of Chicago.* New York: Plume, 1988.

Rozell, Mark J., ed. *Media Power, Media Politics.* Lanham, Md.: Rowman & Littlefield, 2003.

Rule, Wilma, and Joseph F. Zimmerman, eds. *United States Electoral Systems: Their Impact on Women and Minorities.* Westport, Conn.: Greenwood Press, 1992.

Runkel, David R. *Campaign for President: The Managers Look at '88.* Dover, Mass.: Auburn House, 1989.

Rush, Mark E., and Richard L. Engstrom. *Fair and Effective Representation? Debating Electoral Reform and Minority Rights.* New York: Rowman & Littlefield, 2001.

Rusk, Jerrold G. "The Effect of the Australian Ballot Reform on Split Ticket Voting: 1876–1908." *American Political Science Review* 64 (1970): 1,220–1,238.

Russell, Francis. *Adams: An American Dynasty.* New York: American Heritage, 1976.

Ryerson, Richard Alan, ed. *John Adams and the Founding of the Republic.* Boston: Massachusetts Historical Society, 2001.

Sabato, Larry J. *PAC Power: Inside the World of Political Action Committees.* New York: Norton, 1984.

———. *Feeding Frenzy: How Attack Journalism Has Transformed American Politics.* New York: Free Press, 1991.

———. *Goodbye to Good-time Charlie.* Lexington, Mass.: Lexington Books, 1978.

———. *OVERTIME! The Election 2000 Thriller.* New York: Longman, 2001.

———. *Presidential Election 2004 Recap.* Boston: Longman, 2005.

———. *The Rise of Political Consultants: New Ways of Winning Elections.* New York: Basic, 1981.

Sabato, Larry J., and Bruce Larson. *The Party's Just Begun: Shaping Political Parties for America's Future.* 2nd ed. New York: Longman, 2001.

Sabato, Larry J., and Glen R. Simpson. *Dirty Little Secrets: The Persistence of Corruption in American Politics.* New York: Random House, 1996.

Sabato, Larry J., Howard R. Ernst, and Bruce A. Larson, eds. *Dangerous Democracy? The Battle over Ballot Initiatives in America.* Lanham, Md.: Rowman & Littlefield, 2001.

Safer, Byron E. *Bifurcated Politics: Evolution and Reform in the National Party Convention.* Cambridge, Mass.: Harvard University Press, 1988.

Safire, William. *New Language of Politics.* Rev. ed. New York: Collier Books, 1972.

———. *Safire's New Political Dictionary: The Definitive Guide to the New Language of Politics.* New York: Random House, 1993.

Saltman, Roy G. *Accuracy, Integrity, and Security in Computerized Vote-Tallying.* Gaithersburg, Md.: National Bureau of Standards, 1988.

Sarbaugh-Thompson, Marjorie. *The Political and Institutional Effects of Term Limits.* New York: Palgrave Macmillan, 2004.

Schlesinger, Arthur M. *The Vital Center: The Politics of Freedom.* Somerset, N.J.: Transaction Publishers, 1997.

———. *The Politics of Upheaval: The Age of Roosevelt,* Volume III. Boston: Houghton Mifflin, 1960.

Schlesinger, Arthur M., Jr., ed. *History of U.S. Political Parties.* New York: Chelsea House, 1973.

Schlesinger, Arthur, and Fred L. Israel. *History of American Presidential Elections, 1789–1968.* New York: Chelsea House, 1971.

Schmidt, Benno C., Jr. "Black Disenfranchisement from the KKK to the Grandfather Clause." *Columbia Law Review* 82 (1982): 835–905.

Schmidt, David D. *Citizen Lawmakers: The Ballot Initiative Revolution.* Philadelphia: Temple University Press, 1989.

Schneider, Jerrold E. *Campaign Finance Reform and the Future of the Democratic Party.* New York: Routledge, 2002.

Schrecker, Ellen. *Many Are the Crimes: McCarthyism in America.* Boston: Little, Brown, 1998.

Schroeder, Alan. *Presidential Debates: 40 Years of High-Risk TV.* New York: Columbia University Press, 2000.

Schultz, David A., and Robert Maranto. *The Politics of Civil Service Reform.* New York: Peter Lang, 1998.

Schumaker, Paul D., and Burdett A. Loomis, eds. *Choosing a President: The Electoral College and Beyond.* New York: Chatham House, 2002.

Schumpeter, Joseph. *Capitalism, Socialism, and Democracy.* New York: Harper, 1942.

Schwadron, Terry, and Paul Richter, eds. *California and the American Tax Revolt.* Berkeley: University of California Press, 1984.

Scott, Andrew M. "The Progressive Era in Perspective." *Journal of Politics* 21, no. 3 (1959): 685–701.

Scott, Anne F., and Andrew M. Scott. *One Half the People: The Fight for Woman Suffrage.* Philadelphia: Lippincott, 1975.

Sears, David, and Jack Citrin. *Tax Revolt.* Cambridge, Mass.: Harvard University Press, 1982.

Seltzer, Richard A., Jody Newman, and Melissa Voorhees Leighton. *Sex as a Political Variable: Women as Candidates and Voters in U.S. Elections.* Boulder, Colo.: Lynne Rienner, 1997.

Senior, E. D. *Australian Systems of Voting: The Ballot and the Scrutiny.* Sydney: Current Book Distributors, 1946.

Serrin, Judith, and William Serrin. *Muckraking! The Journalism that Changed America.* New York: New Press, 2002.

Shafer, Byron E. *The Quiet Revolution: The Struggle for the Democratic Party and the Shaping of Post-Reform Politics.* New York: Russell Sage, 1983.

———. *Bifurcated Politics: Evolution and Reform in the National Party Convention.* Cambridge, Mass.: Harvard University Press, 1988.

Shaw, Catherine M., and Michael E. Holstein. *The Campaign Manager: Running and Winning Local Elections.* 2nd ed. New York: Westview Press, 1999.

Shea, Daniel M. *Campaign Craft: The Strategies, Tactics, and Art of Political Campaign Management.* Westport, Conn.: Praeger, 1996.

Sheldon, Charles H., and Linda S. Maule. *Choosing Justice: The Recruitment of State and Federal Judges.* Pullman: Washington State University Press, 1997.

Shotts, Kenneth W. "Gerrymandering, Legislative Composition, and National Policy Outcomes." *American Journal of Political Science* 46 (2002): 398–414.

Sick, Gary. *October Surprise: America's Hostages in Iran and the Election of Ronald Reagan.* New York: Random House, 1992.

Sidlow, Edward. *Challenging the Incumbent: An Underdog's Undertaking.* Washington, D.C.: CQ Press, 2003.

Sifry, Micah L. *Spoiling for a Fight: Third-Party Politics in America.* New York: Routledge, 2002.

Sighn, Robert. *The Congressional Black Caucus: Racial Politics in the U.S. Congress.* Thousand Oaks, Calif.: Sage Publications, 1998.

Silbey, Joel H. *Martin Van Buren and the Emergence of American Popular Politics.* Lanham, Md.: Rowman & Littlefield, 2002.

Simon, Roger. *Divided We Stand: How Al Gore Beat George Bush and Lost the Presidency.* New York: Crown, 2001.

Simpson, Dick. *Winning Elections.* New York: Longman, 1996.

Sinclair, Andrew. *The Era of Excess: A Social History of the Prohibition Movement.* New York: Harper & Row, 1964.

Sinclair, Barbara. "Full Circle? Congressional Party Leadership during the Twentieth Century." In Sunil Ahuja and Robert Dewhirst, eds., *Congress Responds to the Twentieth Century.* Columbus: Ohio State University Press, 2003.

Sitkoff, Harvard. *The Struggle for Black Equality: 1954–1992.* New York: Hill & Wang, 1993.

Skeen, C. Edward. *1816: America Rising.* Lexington: University Press of Kentucky, 2003.

Skocpol, Theda. *Diminished Democracy: From Membership to Management in American Civic Life.* Norman: University of Oklahoma Press, 2003.

———. *Protecting Soldiers and Mothers: The Political Origins of Social Policy in the United States.* Cambridge, Mass.: Belknap Press of Harvard University Press, 1992.

Skowronek, Stephen. *Building a New American State: The Expansion of National Administrative Capacities 1877–1920.* Cambridge: Cambridge University Press, 1982.

———. *The Politics Presidents Make.* Cambridge, Mass.: Harvard University Press, 1997.

Slaback, Frederick. *The Constitution and Campaign Finance Reform.* Durham, N.C.: Carolina Academic Press, 1998.

Smelser, Marshall. *The Democratic Republic 1801–1815.* Prospect Heights, Ill.: Waveland Press, 1968.

Smith, Daniel A. *Tax Crusaders and the Politics of Direct Democracy.* New York: Routledge, 1998.

Smith, Daniel A., and Caroline J. Tolbert. "The Initiative to Party: Partisanship and Ballot Initiatives in California." *Party Politics* 7, no. 6 (2001): 739–757.

Smith, Elbert B. *The Presidencies of Zachary Taylor & Millard Fillmore.* Lawrence: University Press of Kansas, 1988.

Smith, Judith G. *Political Brokers: Money, Organizations, Power and People.* New York: Liveright, 1972.

Smith, Kevin B., Alan Greenblat, and John Buntin. *Governing States and Localities.* Washington, D.C.: CQ Press, 2005.

Smith, Richard Norton. *Thomas E. Dewey and His Times.* New York: Simon & Schuster, 1982.

Socolofsky, Homer E., and Allan B. Spetter. *The Presidency of Benjamin Harrison.* Lawrence: University of Kansas Press, 1987.

Solberg, Winton U., ed. *The Constitutional Convention and the Formation of the Union.* 2nd ed. Urbana: University of Illinois Press, 1990.

Sorauf, Frank J. *Inside Campaign Finance: Myths and Realities.* New Haven, Conn.: Yale University Press, 1992.

Sorauf, Frank J., and Paul Allen Beck. *Party Politics in America.* Glenville, Ill.: Scott, Foresman, 1988.

Southwell, Priscilla L. "Five Years Later: A Re-Assessment of Oregon's Vote by Mail Electoral Process." *PS: Political Science and Politics* 37 (2004): 89–93.

———. "The 1984 Democratic Nomination Process: The Significance of Unpledged Superdelegates." *American Politics Quarterly* 14 (1986): 75–88.

Southwell, Priscilla L., and Justin Burchett. "Survey of Vote-by-Mail Senate Elections in the State of Oregon." *PS: Political Science and Politics* 30 (1997): 53–57.

Sowell, Thomas. *Affirmative Action around the World: An Empirical Study.* New Haven, Conn.: Yale University Press, 2004.

Spinner, Jeff. *The Boundaries of Citizenship: Race, Ethnicity and Nationality in the Liberal State.* Baltimore: Johns Hopkins University Press, 1996.

Sproat, John G. *The Best Men: Liberal Reformers in the Gilded Age.* New York: Oxford University Press, 1968.

Stamp, Kenneth M. *Era of Reconstruction, 1865–1877: A Revisionist View of One of the Most Controversial Periods.* New York: Knopf, 1972.

Stein, Robert M. "Early Voting." *Public Opinion Quarterly* 62, no. 1 (1998): 57–69.

Storing, Herbert J., ed. *The Complete Anti-Federalist.* Chicago: University of Chicago Press, 1981.

Stratmann, Thomas. "Ballot Access Restrictions and Candidate Entry in Elections." *European Journal of Political Economy* 18 (2004): 1–15.

Stroud, Kandy. *How Jimmy Won: The Victory Campaign from Plains to the White House.* New York: Morrow, 1977.

Stucker, John J. "Women as Voters: Their Maturation as Political Persons in American Society." In Marianne Githens and Jewel L. Prestage, eds., *A Portrait of Marginality: The Political Behavior of the American Woman.* New York: David McKay, 1977.

Stuhler, Barbara. *For the Public Record: A Documentary History of the League of Women Voters.* Westport, Conn.: Greenwood Press, 2000.

Sudman, Seymour. "Do Exit Polls Influence Voting Behavior?" *Public Opinion Quarterly* 50 (1986): 3.

Summers, Mark Wahlgren. *Rum, Romanism, and Rebellion: The Making of a President, 1884.* Chapel Hill: University of North Carolina Press, 2000.

Supreme Court Historical Society. Available online. URL: http://www.supremecourthistory.org. Accessed August 10, 2005.

Swain, John W., Stephen A. Borrelli, and Brian C. Reed. "Partisan Consequences of the Post-1990 Redistricting for the U.S. House of Representatives." *Political Research Quarterly* 51, no. 4 (1998): 945–967.

Swint, Kerwin C. *Political Consultants and Negative Campaigning: The Secrets of the Pros.* Lanham, Md.: University Press of America, 1998.

Tenpas, Kathryn Dunn. "Words vs. Deeds: President George W. Bush and Polling." *Brookings Review* 21 (2003): 32–35.

Thelen, David P. *Robert M. LaFollette and the Insurgent Spirit.* Madison: University of Wisconsin Press, 1986.

Thompson, Dennis F. *Just Elections: Creating a Fair Electoral Process in the U.S.* Chicago: University of Chicago Press, 2002.

Thompson, John B. *Political Scandal: Power and Visibility in the Media Age.* Malden, Mass.: Polity Press, 2000.

Thurber, James A., and Candice J. Nelson. *Campaign Warriors.* Washington, D.C.: Brookings Institution Press, 2000.

Thurber, James A., and Candice J. Nelson, eds. *Campaigns and Elections American Style.* 2nd ed. Boulder, Colo.: Westview Press, 2004.

Toobin, Jeffrey. *Too Close to Call: The Thirty-Six Day Battle to Decide the 2000 Election.* New York: Random House, 2001.

Traugott, Michael W., and Paul Lavrakas. *The Voter's Guide to Election Polls.* 3rd ed. Lanham, Md.: Rowman & Littlefield, 2004.

Trent, Judith S., and Robert V. Friedenburg. *Political Campaign Communication.* Westport, Conn.: Praeger, 2000.

Trippi, Joe. *The Revolution Will Not Be Televised: Democracy, the Internet, and the Overthrow of Everything.* New York: Regan Books, 2004.

Tucker, David M. *Memphis since Crump: Bossism, Blacks, and Civic Reformers 1948–68.* Knoxville: University of Tennessee Press, 1980.

———. *Mugwumps: Public Moralists of the Gilded Age.* Columbia: University of Missouri Press, 1998.

Tufte, Edward R. "Determinants of the Outcomes of Midterm Congressional Elections." *American Political Science Review* 69 (1975): 812–826.

———. "The Relationship between Seats and Votes in Two-Party Systems." *American Political Science Review* 67, no. 2 (1973): 540–554.

Tullock, Gordon. *Wealth, Poverty and Politics.* New York: Basil Blackwell, 1988.

Tunnell, Ted. *Crucible of Reconstruction: War, Radicalism and Race in Louisiana, 1862–1877.* Baton Rouge: Louisiana State University Press, 1984.

Tushnet, Mark V. *NAACP's Legal Strategy against Segregated Education, 1925–1950.* Chapel Hill: University of North Carolina Press, 1987.

UCLA Online Campaign Literature Archive. Available online. URL: http://digital.library.ucla.edu/campaign. Accessed August 10, 2005.

University of Oklahoma Law Center, Federalist Papers. Available online. URL: http://www.law.ou.edu/hist/federalist. Accessed August 10, 2005.

University of Virginia Center for Politics Crystal Ball. Available online. URL: http://www.centerforpolitics.org/crystalball. Accessed August 10, 2005.

Urosky, Mel, and Paul Finkleman. *A March of Liberty: A Constitutional History of the United States.* New York: Oxford University Press, 2002.

U.S. Census Bureau. Available online. URL: http://www.census.gov. Accessed August 10, 2005.

———. *Reported Voting and Registration by Race, Hispanic Origin, Sex and Age Groups: November 1964 to 2002. Current Population Survey, November 2002 and Earlier Reports.* Washington, D.C.: U.S. Census Bureau, 2004.

———. *Reported Voting and Registration by Region, Educational Attainment and Labor Force: November 1964 to 2002. Current Population Survey, November 2002 and Earlier Reports.* Washington, D.C.: U.S. Census Bureau, 2004.

———. *Voting and Registration in the Election of November 2000.* Washington, D.C.: U.S. Census Bureau, 2002.

U.S. Department of Justice, Introduction to the Federal Voting Rights Laws. Available online. URL: http://www.usdoj.gov/crt/voting/intro/intro_b.htm. Accessed August 10, 2005.

U.S. House of Representatives. Available online. URL: http://www.house.gov. Accessed August 10, 2005.

U.S. Senate. Available online. URL: http://www.senate.gov. Accessed August 10, 2005.

Valenty, Linda O., and James C. Brent. "Online Voting: Calculating Risks and Benefits to the Community and the Individual." In Ingo Vogelsang and Benjamin M. Compaine, eds., *The Internet Upheaval: Raising Questions, Seeking Answers in Communications Policy.* Cambridge, Mass.: MIT Press, 2000.

Van Atta, Dale. *Trust Betrayed: Inside the AARP.* Washington, D.C.: Regnery Publications, 1998.

Vaughn, William Preston. *The Antimasonic Party in the United States, 1826–1843.* Lexington: University Press of Kentucky, 1983.

Verba, Sidney, Kay Lehman Schlozman, and Henry E. Brady. *Voice and Equality: Civic Voluntarism in American Politics.* Cambridge, Mass.: Harvard University Press, 1995.

Verba, Sidney, Norman H. Nie, and Jae-On Kim. *Participation and Political Equality.* Chicago: University of Chicago Press, 1987.

Vice President. Available online. URL: http://www.whitehouse.gov/vicepresident. Accessed August 10, 2005.

Wade, Wyn Craig. *The Fiery Cross: The Ku Klux Klan in America.* New York: Simon & Schuster, 1987.

Walker, David B. *The Rebirth of American Federalism.* Chatham, N.J.: Chatham House, 1995.

Wardle, C., et al. "The Voter News Service and the 2000 Election Night Calls." *American Behavioral Scientist* 44, no. 12 (2001): 2,306–2,313.

Warren, Kenneth F. *In Defense of Public Opinion Polling.* Boulder, Colo.: Westview Press, 2001.

Waters, M. Dane. *Initiative and Referendum Almanac.* Durham, N.C.: Carolina Academic Press, 2003.

Watkins, William. *Reclaiming the American Revolution: The Kentucky and Virginia Resolutions and Their Legacy.* New York: Palgrave Macmillan, 2004.

Watson, Justin. *The Christian Coalition: Dreams of Restoration, Demands for Recognition.* New York: St. Martin's Press, 1996.

Wattenberg, Martin P. "From Parties to Candidates: Examining the Role of the Media." *Public Opinion Quarterly* 46 (1982): 216–227.

———. "The Decline of Political Partisanship in the United States: Negativity or Neutrality?" *American Political Science Review* 75 (1981): 941–950.

———. *The Decline of American Political Parties, 1952–1996.* Cambridge, Mass.: Harvard University Press, 1998.

————. *The Rise of Candidate-Centered Politics: Presidential Elections of the 1980s.* Cambridge, Mass.: Harvard University Press, 1991.

————. *Where Have All the Voters Gone?* Cambridge, Mass.: Harvard University Press, 2002.

Wayne, Stephen J. *The Road to the White House 2000: The Politics of Presidential Elections.* New York: Bedford/St. Martin's, 2000.

Wayne, Stephen J. *The Road to the White House 2004: The Politics of Presidential Selection.* Belmont, Calif.: Wadsworth, 2004.

Weatherford, Doris. *A History of the American Suffragist Movement.* Santa Barbara, Calif.: ABC-CLIO, 1998.

Weinberg, Arthur, and Lila Weinberg, eds. *The Muckrakers.* Urbana: University of Illinois Press, 2001.

Weisberg, Herbert F. "The Party in the Electorate as a Basis for More Responsible Parties." In John C. Green and Paul S. Herrnson, eds., *Responsible Partisanship? The Evolution of American Political Parties since 1950.* Lawrence: University of Kansas Press, 2002.

Weisberg, Herbert F., ed. *Democracy's Feast: Elections in America.* Chatham, N.J.: Chatham House, 1995.

Weiss, Nancy J. *Farewell to the Party of Lincoln: Black Politics in the Age of FDR.* Princeton, N.J.: Princeton University Press, 1983.

Welch, Richard E., Jr. *The Presidencies of Grover Cleveland.* Lawrence: University Press of Kansas, 1988.

Welch, Susan. "The Impact of At-Large Elections on the Representation of Blacks and Hispanics." *Journal of Politics* 52 (1990): 1,050–1,076.

Welch, Susan, and Donley T. Studlar. "Multi-Member Districts and the Representation of Women: Evidence from Britain and the United States." *Journal of Politics* 52, no. 2 (1990): 391–412.

West, Darrell M. *Air Wars: Television Advertising in Election Campaigns.* 3rd ed. Washington, D.C.: Congressional Quarterly Press, 2001.

Westlye, Mark C. *Senate Elections and Campaign Intensity.* Baltimore: Johns Hopkins University Press, 1991.

White, Graham, and John Maze. *Henry A. Wallace: His Search for a New World Order.* Chapel Hill: University of North Carolina Press, 1995.

White, John Kenneth, and Daniel M. Shea. *New Party Politics: From Jefferson and Hamilton to the Information Age.* 2nd ed. Belmont, Calif.: Wadsworth/Thomson Learning, 2004.

White, Theodore. *The Making of the President, 1960.* New York: Atheneum, 1961.

————. *The Making of the President, 1972.* New York: Scribner, 1972.

Wielhouwer, Peter W. "In Search of Lincoln's Perfect List: Targeting in Grassroots Campaigns." *American Politics Research* 31 (2003): 632–669.

Wilcox, Clyde. "Share the Wealth: Contributions by Congressional Incumbents to the Campaigns of Other Candidates." *American Politics Quarterly* 17, no. 4 (1989): 386–408.

Wilcox, Clyde, and Joe Wesley. "Dead Law: The Federal Election Finance Regulations, 1974–1996." *PS: Political Science and Politics* 31 (1998): 14–17.

Williams, Juan. *Eyes on the Prize: America's Civil Rights Years, 1954–1965.* New York: Penguin, 1987.

————. *Thurgood Marshall: American Revolutionary.* New York: Random House, 2000.

Williams, T. Harry. *Huey Long.* New York: Vintage Books, 1969.

Williamson, Joel. *After Slavery: The Negro in South Carolina during Reconstruction, 1861–1877.* Chapel Hill: University of North Carolina Press, 1965.

Wills, Garry. *Explaining America: The Federalist.* New York: Penguin Books, 2001.

Wilmerding, Lucius. *The Electoral College.* New Brunswick, N.J.: Rutgers University Press, 1958.

Wilson, Harold. *McClure's Magazine and the Muckrakers.* Princeton, N.J.: Princeton University Press, 1970.

Wirls, Daniel, and Stephen Wirls. *The Invention of the United States Senate.* Baltimore: Johns Hopkins University Press, 2004.

Witcover, Jules. *Crapshoot: Rolling the Dice on the Vice Presidency from Adams and Jefferson to Truman and Quayle.* New York: Crown, 1992.

————. *Party of the People: A History of the Democrats.* New York: Random House, 2003.

Wofley, Jeanette. "Jim Crow, Indian Style: The Disenfranchisement of Native Americans." *American Indian Law Review* 16 (1991): 167.

Wolfinger, Raymond E. "The Influence of Precinct Work on Voting Behavior." *Public Opinion Quarterly* 27, no. 3 (1963): 387–398.

Wolfinger, Raymond E., and Steven J. Rosenstone. "The Effect of Registration Laws on Voter Turnout." *American Political Science Review* 72 (1978): 22–45.

————. *Who Votes?* New Haven, Conn.: Yale University Press, 1980.

Woodward, Bob. *The Choice: How Clinton Won.* New York: Touchstone Books, 1997.

Woodward, C. Vann. *Reunion and Reaction: The Compromise of 1877 and the End of Reconstruction.* Boston: Little, Brown, 1951.

Wright, John R. *Interest Groups and Congress: Lobbying, Contributions, and Influence.* Boston: Allyn & Bacon, 1996.

Wright, Susan D. *Race, Power, and Political Emergence in Memphis.* New York: Garland, 2000.

Yarbrough, Tinsley E. *Race and Redistricting: The Shaw-Cromartie Cases.* Lawrence: University Press of Kansas, 2002.

Yearly, C. K. *The Money Machines: The Breakdown and Reform of Governmental and Party Finance in the North, 1860–1920.* Albany: State University of New York Press, 1970.

Young Democrats of America. Available online. URL: http://www.yda.org. Accessed August 10, 2005.

Young Republicans. Available online. URL: http://www.youngrepublicans.com. Accessed August 10, 2005.

Youth Leadership Initiative at the University of Virginia Center for Politics. Available online. URL: http://www.centerforpolitics.org/programs/yli.htm. Accessed August 10, 2005.

Zaller, John R. *The Nature and Origins of Mass Opinion.* New York: Cambridge University Press, 1992.

Zarefsky, David. *Lincoln, Douglas and Slavery: In the Crucible of Public Debate.* Chicago: University of Chicago Press, 1990.

Zimmerman, Joseph F. *State-Local Relations: A Partnership Approach.* 2nd ed. Westport, Conn.: Praeger, 1995.

———. *The Recall: Tribunal of the People.* Westport, Conn.: Praeger, 1997.

Zogby International. *America: Blue vs. Red States, Republicans vs. Democrats; Two Separate Nations in a Race for the White House.* Utica, N.Y.: Zogby International, 2003.

Zogby Poll. Available online. URL: http://www.zogby.com. Accessed August 10, 2005.

Zuczek, Richard. *State of Rebellion: Reconstruction in South Carolina.* Columbia: University of South Carolina Press, 1996.

Index

Note: **Boldface** page numbers indicate extensive treatment of a topic. *Italic* page numbers denote illustrations. In the alphabetization of subheadings, numbers precede letters, and articles and prepositions are ignored.

A

AARP. *See* American Association of Retired Persons

abortion
 EMILY's List on 138–139
 single-issue voters on 428
 as wedge issue 493

Abscam scandal 425

absentee voting **1–2,** 211–212
 early voting in 118
 in military 1–2, 467–468
 in 2000 presidential election 2, 374, 467

Ackerman, Bruce 407

ACU. *See* American Conservative Union

ADA. *See* Americans for Democratic Action

Adams, Charles Francis 155, 316, 324

Adams, John
 Constitutional Convention and 272
 Electoral College and 135, 458, 471
 in Federalist Party 150, 151
 nomination of 42
 in 1788–89 presidential election **295–297**
 in 1792 presidential election **297–298**
 in 1796 presidential election **298–299**
 in 1800 presidential election 299–300
 on vice presidency 472

Adams, John Quincy *307*
 and Democratic Party 102
 in Democratic-Republican Party 108
 Electoral College and 135
 nomination of 42
 in 1824 presidential election **306–308**

in 1828 presidential election 308–309

Adams, John T. 411

Adet, Pierre 298–299

advertisements **2–5**
 campaign expenditures on 54, 217, 251
 dirty campaign tricks in 112
 effectiveness of 4–6, 251, 252
 and election themes 4, 293–294
 ethics in 53
 fairness doctrine in 144
 financing of, limits on 56
 by interest groups 186–187, 191–192
 v. Internet campaigns 40
 issue advocacy 2, 186–187, **191–192,** 217, 431–432
 in media campaigns 41
 media consultants and 48
 media coverage of 4–5, 251, 252
 media intertwined with 219–220, 251
 by MoveOn.Org 231
 negative 2, 3, 4, **5–6,** 252
 as paid media **251–252**
 truth in 53

"advice and consent" role of Senate 14

affirmative action 22–23, 492

AFL. *See* American Federation of Labor

AFL-CIO. *See* American Federation of Labor–Congress of Industrial Organizations

African Americans
 in census 66
 in Congress 77–78, 151
 in Democratic Party 347, 486–487, 496
 disenfranchisement of 112–113, 442–443. *See also* African-American suffrage

equal rights for 154. *See also* civil rights
 Ku Klux Klan on 196–197
 in machine politics 209, 255
 in majority-minority districts 212–213
 Mississippi Plan and 229–230
 racial districting for 394–395
 in Reconstruction 402
 runoff primaries and 388–389
 in South Carolina PDP 432–433
 voter registration for 70–71, 200–201, 474
 voter turnout by 482
 voting trends among **486–487**
 as Yellow Dog Democrats 496

African-American suffrage 440–441, **442–444**
 barriers to 112–113, 442–443, 483–484
  grandfather clauses as **164–165,** 441, 443
  literacy tests as 113, **206,** 441
  poll taxes as **285–286,** 460–461
  by southern Democrats 433–434
  white primaries as 384, 429–430, 441, 443, **494–495**
 Fifteenth Amendment on 151–152, 440, 442
 gerrymandering and 162

age, and voter turnout 463, **477–478,** 481

age requirements
 for candidates 61, 124, 171, 289
 for suffrage 442, **444–445,** 463, 477

Agnew, Spiro T.
 in 1968 presidential election **359–361**

in 1972 presidential election **361–362**
 resignation of 383

agriculture, Populist Party on 287

AIP. *See* American Independent Party

Alabama
 Civil Rights movement in 70–72, 236, 484
 referenda in 407

Alaska, Internet voting in 187

Albany Regency 9, 255

Albert, Carl 383, 436

Alcorn, H. Meade, Jr. 411

Aldrich, Nelson 262

Alexander, Lamar 370

Alexander, Rodney 239

Alien Act (1798) 6

Alien and Sedition Acts (1798) **6–7,** 299, 301

Alien Enemies Act (1798) 6

alignments 397. *See also* dealignment; realignment

Allen v. Wright 15

allocative representation 80

Allott, Gordon 145

ALP. *See* American Labor Party

Alterman, Eric 393

America Coming Together 56, 231

American Association of Retired Persons (AARP) **7**

American Conservative Union (ACU) 276

American Federation of Labor (AFL) 199, 390, 431

American Federation of Labor–Congress of Industrial Organizations (AFL-CIO), COPE of **74–75,** 199, 274, 279

American Independent Party (AIP) **7–8,** 294, 360, 469

American Labor Party (ALP) **8,** 198